הַהִתְגַּלּוּת

-סוֹף-

הַהִתְגַּלּוּת

בַּחוּץ יִהְיוּ הַכְּלָבִים וְהַמְכַשְּׁפִים, הַזּוֹנִים וְהַמְרַצְּחִים
bachutz yihyu hakkelavim vehamchashefim, hazzonim vehamratzechim
Without are the dogs, and the sorcerers, and the fornicators, and the murderers,

עוֹבְדֵי אֱלִילִים וְכָל אוֹהֵב שֶׁקֶר וְעוֹשֵׂהוּ
ovedei elilim vechol ohev sheker ve'osehu
and the idolaters, and every one that loveth and maketh a lie.

אֲנִי יֵשׁוּעַ שָׁלַחְתִּי אֶת מַלְאָכִי לְהָעִיד לָכֶם אֶת הַדְּבָרִים הָאֵלֶּה בַּקְּהִלּוֹת
ani yeshua shalachti et mal'achi leha'id lachem et haddevarim ha'elleh bakkehillot
I Jesus have sent mine angel to testify unto you these things for the churches.

אָנֹכִי שֹׁרֶשׁ דָּוִד וְצֶאֱצָאוֹ, כּוֹכַב נֹגַהּ הַשָּׁחַר
anochi shoresh david vetze'etza'o, kochav nogah hashachar
I am the root and the offspring of David, the bright, the morning star.

הָרוּחַ וְהַכַּלָּה אוֹמְרִים: בּוֹא!, וְהַשּׁוֹמֵעַ יֹאמַר נָא בֹא
haruach vehakkallah omerim: bo!, vehashomea yomar na bo
And the Spirit and the bride say, Come. And he that heareth, let him say, Come.

הַצָּמֵא יָבוֹא נָא, וְהֶחָפֵץ יִקַּח נָא מַיִם חַיִּים חִנָּם
hatzamei yavo na, vehechafetz yikkach na mayim chayim chinnam
And he that is athirst, let him come: he that will, let him take the water of life freely.

אָנֹכִי מֵעִיד בְּכָל מִי שֶׁשּׁוֹמֵעַ אֶת דִּבְרֵי נְבוּאַת הַסֵּפֶר הַזֶּה:
anochi me'id bechol mi sheshomea et divrei nevu'at hassefer hazzeh
I testify unto every man that heareth the words of the prophecy of this book,

אִישׁ אִם יוֹסִיף עֲלֵיהֶם, יוֹסִיף עָלָיו אֱלֹהִים אֶת הַמַּכּוֹת הַכְּתוּבוֹת בַּסֵּפֶר הַזֶּה
ish im yosif aleihem, yosif alav elohim et hammakkot hakketuvot bassefer hazzeh
If any man shall add unto them, God shall add unto him the plagues which are written in this book:

וְאִישׁ אִם יִגְרַע מִדִּבְרֵי סֵפֶר הַנְּבוּאָה הַזֹּאת
ve'ish im yigra middivrei sefer hannevu'ah hazzot
and if any man shall take away from the words of the book of this prophecy,

יִגְרַע הָאֱלֹהִים אֶת חֶלְקוֹ מֵעֵץ הַחַיִּים וּמֵעִיר הַקֹּדֶשׁ, מִן הַדְּבָרִים הַכְּתוּבִים בַּסֵּפֶר הַזֶּה
yigra ha'elohim et chelko me'etz hachayim ume'ir hakkodesh, min haddevarim hakketuvim bassefer hazzeh
God shall take away his part from the tree of life, and out of the holy city, which are written in this book.

הַמֵּעִיד אֶת הַדְּבָרִים הָאֵלֶּה אֹמֵר: אָכֵן, אֲנִי בָּא מַהֵר. אָמֵן. בּוֹא נָא הָאָדוֹן יֵשׁוּעַ
hamme'id et haddevarim ha'elleh omer: achen, ani ba maher. amen. bo na ha'adon yeshua'
He who testifieth these things saith, Yea: I come quickly. Amen: come, Lord Jesus.

חֶסֶד הָאָדוֹן יֵשׁוּעַ עִם כָּל הַקְּדוֹשִׁים. אָמֵן
chesed ha'adon yeshua im kol hakkedoshim. amen
The grace of the Lord Jesus be with the saints. Amen.

הַהִתְגַּלּוּת

הִנְנִי בָּא מַהֵר. אַשְׁרֵי הַשּׁוֹמֵר אֶת דִּבְרֵי הַנְּבוּאָה שֶׁל הַסֵּפֶר הַזֶּה
hineni ba maher. ashrei hashomer et divrei hannevu'ah shel hassefer hazzeh
And behold, I come quickly. Blessed is he that keepeth the words of the prophecy of this book.

וַאֲנִי, יוֹחָנָן, הָרוֹאֶה וְשׁוֹמֵעַ אֶת אֵלֶּה
va'ani, yochanan, haro'eh veshomea et elleh
And I John am he that heard and saw these things.

וְכַאֲשֶׁר שָׁמַעְתִּי וְרָאִיתִי, נָפַלְתִּי לְהִשְׁתַּחֲווֹת לְרַגְלֵי הַמַּלְאָךְ אֲשֶׁר הִרְאַנִי אֶת אֵלֶּה
vecha'asher shama'ti vera'iti, nafalti lehishtachavot leraglei hammal'ach asher hir'ani et elleh
And when I heard and saw, I fell down to worship before the feet of the angel that showed me these things.

אָמַר אֵלַי: רְאֵה, אַל-נָא; עֶבֶד-חָבֵר אֲנִי לְךָ וּלְאַחֶיךָ הַנְּבִיאִים
amar elai: re'eh, al-na; eved-chaver ani lecha ule'acheicha hannevi'im
And he saith unto me, See thou do it not: I am a fellow-servant with thee and with thy brethren the prophets,

וְלַשּׁוֹמְרִים אֶת דִּבְרֵי הַסֵּפֶר הַזֶּה. לֵאלֹהִים תִּשְׁתַּחֲוֶה
velashomerim et divrei hassefer hazzeh. le'elohim tishtachaveh
and with them that keep the words of this book: worship God.

עוֹד אָמַר אֵלַי: אַל תַּחְתֹּם אֶת דִּבְרֵי הַנְּבוּאָה שֶׁל הַסֵּפֶר הַזֶּה, כִּי קָרוֹב הַמּוֹעֵד
od amar elai: al tachtom et divrei hannevu'ah shel hassefer hazzeh, ki karov hammo'ed
And he saith unto me, Seal not up the words of the prophecy of this book; for the time is at hand.

הַמְעַוֵּל - שֶׁיּוֹסִיף לַעֲשׂוֹת עָוֶל; הַטָּמֵא - שֶׁיִּטָּמֵא עוֹד
ham'avvel - sheyosif la'asot avel; hattamei - sheyittamei od
He that is unrighteous, let him do unrighteousness still: and he that is filthy, let him be made filthy still:

הַצַּדִּיק - שֶׁיִּצְדַּק עוֹד; הַקָּדוֹשׁ - שֶׁיִּתְקַדֵּשׁ עוֹד
hatzaddik - sheyitzadek od; hakkadosh - sheyitkaddesh od
and he that is righteous, let him do righteousness still: and he that is holy, let him be made holy still.

הִנְנִי בָּא מַהֵר וְאִתִּי הַשָּׂכָר לְשַׁלֵּם לְכָל אִישׁ כְּמַעֲשֵׂהוּ
hineni ba maher ve'itti hassochar leshallem lechol ish kema'asehu
Behold, I come quickly; and my reward is with me, to render to each man according as his work is.

אֲנִי הָאָלֶף אַף אֲנִי הַתָּו, הָרִאשׁוֹן אַף הָאַחֲרוֹן, הָרֵאשִׁית וְהַתַּכְלִית
ani ha'alef af ani hattav, harishon af ha'acharon, hareshit vehattachlit
I am the Alpha and the Omega, the first and the last, the beginning and the end.

אַשְׁרֵי הַמְכַבְּסִים אֶת גְּלִימוֹתֵיהֶם, לְמַעַן תִּהְיֶה לָהֶם זְכוּת עַל עֵץ הַחַיִּים
ashrei hamchabbesim et glimoteihem, lema'an tihyeh lahem zechut al etz hachayim
Blessed are they that wash their robes, that they may have the right to come to the tree of life,

וְיִכָּנְסוּ הָעִירָה דֶּרֶךְ הַשְּׁעָרִים
veyikkanesu ha'irah derech hashe'arim
and may enter in by the gates into the city.

הַהִתְגַּלּוּת

כב

הוּא הֶרְאָה לִי נְהַר מַיִם חַיִּים, מַבְהִיק כִּבְדֹלַח, יוֹצֵא מִכִּסֵּא הָאֱלֹהִים וְהַשֶּׂה
hu her'ah li nehar mayim chayim, mavhik kivdolach, yotzei mikkissei ha'elohim vehasseh
And he showed me a river of water of life, bright as crystal, proceeding out of the throne of God and of the Lamb,

בְּאֶמְצַע רְחוֹב הָעִיר וְעַל שְׂפַת הַנָּהָר מִזֶּה וּמִזֶּה - עֵץ חַיִּים
be'emtza rechov ha'ir ve'al sefat hannahar mizzeh umizzeh - etz chayim
in the midst of the street thereof. And on this side of the river and on that was the tree of life,

עוֹשֶׂה פֵרוֹת שְׁתֵּים־עֶשְׂרֵה פְּעָמִים, בְּתִתּוֹ בְּכָל חֹדֶשׁ וְחֹדֶשׁ אֶת פִּרְיוֹ
oseh perot sheteim-'esreh pe'amim, betitto bechol chodesh vechodesh et piryo
bearing twelve manner of fruits, yielding its fruit every month:

וַעֲלֵה הָעֵץ לְמַרְפֵּא הַגּוֹיִם
va'aleh ha'etz lemarpei haggoyim
and the leaves of the tree were for the healing of the nations.

שׁוּם קְלָלָה לֹא תִּהְיֶה עוֹד
shum kelalah lo tihyeh od
And there shall be no curse any more:

כִּסֵּא אֱלֹהִים וְהַשֶּׂה יִהְיֶה בָּהּ וַעֲבָדָיו יְשָׁרְתוּהוּ
kissei elohim vehasseh yihyeh bah va'avadav yesharetuhu
and the throne of God and of the Lamb shall be therein: and his servants shall serve him;

הֵם יִרְאוּ אֶת פָּנָיו, וּשְׁמוֹ עַל מִצְחוֹתָם
hem yir'u et panav, ushemo al mitzchotam
and they shall see his face; and his name shall be on their foreheads.

וְלַיְלָה לֹא יִהְיֶה עוֹד וְלֹא יִצְטָרְכוּ לְאוֹר מְנוֹרָה
velaylah lo yihyeh od velo yitztarechu le'or menorah
And there shall be night no more; and they need no light of lamp,

וּלְאוֹר שֶׁמֶשׁ, כִּי יהוה אֱלֹהִים יָאִיר עֲלֵיהֶם וְיִמְלְכוּ לְעוֹלְמֵי עוֹלָמִים
ule'or shemesh, ki hashem elohim ya'ir aleihem veyimlechu le'olemei olamim
neither light of sun; for the Lord God shall give them light: and they shall reign for ever and ever.

עוֹד אָמַר אֵלַי: הַדְּבָרִים הָאֵלֶּה נֶאֱמָנִים וַאֲמִתִּיִּים וַיהוה אֱלֹהֵי רוּחוֹת הַנְּבִיאִים
od amar elai: haddevarim ha'elleh ne'emanim va'amittiyim vahashem elohei ruchot hannevi'im
And he said unto me, These words are faithful and true: and the Lord, the God of the spirits of the prophets,

שָׁלַח אֶת מַלְאָכוֹ לְהַרְאוֹת לַעֲבָדָיו אֶת אֲשֶׁר צָרִיךְ לִהְיוֹת בִּמְהֵרָה
shalach et mal'acho lehar'ot la'avadav et asher tzarich lihyot bimherah
sent his angel to show unto his servants the things which must shortly come to pass.

הַהִתְגַּלּוּת

הַחֲמִישִׁי יַהֲלֹם, הַשִּׁשִּׁי אֹדֶם, הַשְּׁבִיעִי תַּרְשִׁישׁ, הַשְּׁמִינִי שֹׁהַם
hachamishi yahalom, hashishi odem, hashevi'i tarshish, hashmini shoham
the fifth, sardonyx; the sixth, sardius; the seventh, chrysolite; the eighth, beryl;

הַתְּשִׁיעִי פִּטְדָה, הָעֲשִׂירִי נֹפֶךְ, הָאַחַד־עָשָׂר לֶשֶׁם, הַשְּׁנֵים־עָשָׂר אַחְלָמָה
hatteshi'i pitdah, ha'asiri nofech, ha'achad-'asar leshem, hasheneim-'asar achlamah
the ninth, topaz; the tenth, chrysoprase; the eleventh, jacinth; the twelfth, amethyst.

וּשְׁנֵים־עָשָׂר הַשְּׁעָרִים - שְׁתֵּים־עֶשְׂרֵה מַרְגָּלִיוֹת; כָּל שַׁעַר וְשַׁעַר הָיָה מִמַּרְגָּלִית אַחַת
usheneim-'asar hashe'arim - sheteim-'esreh margaliyot; kol sha'ar vesha'ar hayah mimmargalit achat
And the twelve gates were twelve pearls; each one of the several gates was of one pearl:

וּרְחוֹב הָעִיר זָהָב טָהוֹר כִּזְכוּכִית זַכָּה
urechov ha'ir zahav tahor kizchuchit zakkah
and the street of the city was pure gold, as it were transparent glass.

הֵיכָל לֹא רָאִיתִי בָהּ, כִּי הֵיכָלָהּ הוּא יהוה אֱלֹהִים צְבָאוֹת וְהַשֶּׂה
heichal lo ra'iti bah, ki heichalah hu hashem elohim tzeva'ot vehasseh
And I saw no temple therein: for the Lord God the Almighty, and the Lamb, are the temple thereof.

וְהָעִיר אֵינֶנָּה צְרִיכָה לַשֶּׁמֶשׁ וְלַיָּרֵחַ שֶׁיָּאִירוּ בָהּ
veha'ir einennah tzerichah lashemesh velayareach sheya'iru bah
And the city hath no need of the sun, neither of the moon, to shine upon it:

כִּי כְבוֹד אֱלֹהִים הֵאִיר אוֹתָהּ וְהַשֶּׂה הוּא מְנוֹרָתָהּ
ki kevod elohim he'ir otah vehasseh hu menoratah
for the glory of God did lighten it, and the lamp thereof is the Lamb.

הַגּוֹיִם יֵלְכוּ לְאוֹרָהּ וּמַלְכֵי הָאָרֶץ מְבִיאִים אֶת כְּבוֹדָם אֵלֶיהָ
haggoyim yelechu le'orah umalchei ha'aretz mevi'im et kevodam eleiha
And the nations shall walk amidst the light thereof: and the kings of the earth bring their glory into it.

שְׁעָרֶיהָ לֹא יִסָּגְרוּ בַיּוֹם; וַהֲרֵי לַיְלָה לֹא יִהְיֶה שָׁם
she'areiha lo yissageru bayom; vaharei laylah lo yihyeh sham
And the gates thereof shall in no wise be shut by day (for there shall be no night there):

אֶת כְּבוֹד הַגּוֹיִם וִיקָרָם יָבִיאוּ אֵלֶיהָ
et kevod haggoyim viykaram yavi'u eleiha
and they shall bring the glory and the honor of the nations into it:

וְלֹא יִכָּנֵס אֵלֶיהָ כָּל טָמֵא וְעוֹשֵׂה תוֹעֵבָה וָשֶׁקֶר
velo yikkanes eleiha kol tamei ve'oseh to'evah vasheker
and there shall in no wise enter into it anything unclean, or he that maketh an abomination and a lie:

כִּי אִם הַכְּתוּבִים בְּסֵפֶר הַחַיִּים שֶׁל הַשֶּׂה
ki im hakketuvim besefer hachayim shel hasseh
but only they that are written in the Lamb's book of life.

הַהִתְגַּלּוּת

מִמִּזְרָח שְׁלוֹשָׁה שְׁעָרִים, מִצָּפוֹן שְׁלוֹשָׁה שְׁעָרִים
mimmizrach sheloshah she'arim, mitzafon sheloshah she'arim,
on the east were three gates; and on the north three gates;

מִדָּרוֹם שְׁלוֹשָׁה שְׁעָרִים, מִמַּעֲרָב שְׁלוֹשָׁה שְׁעָרִים
middarom sheloshah she'arim, mimma'arav sheloshah she'arim
and on the south three gates; and on the west three gates.

וּלְחוֹמַת הָעִיר שְׁנֵים־עָשָׂר יְסוֹדוֹת וַעֲלֵיהֶם שְׁנֵים־עָשָׂר שֵׁמוֹת שֶׁל שְׁנֵים־עָשָׂר שְׁלִיחֵי הַשֶּׂה
ulechomat ha'ir sheneim-'asar yesodot va'aleihem sheneim-'asar shemot shel sheneim-'asar shelichei hasseh
And the wall of the city had twelve foundations, and on them twelve names of the twelve apostles of the Lamb.

הַמְדַבֵּר אֵלַי הֶחֱזִיק קְנֵה־מִדָּה מִזָּהָב כְּדֵי לִמְדֹד אֶת הָעִיר
hamdabber elai hechezik keneh-middah mizzahav kedei limdod et ha'ir
And he that spake with me had for a measure a golden reed to measure the city,

וְאֶת שְׁעָרֶיהָ וְאֶת חוֹמָתָהּ
ve'et she'areiha ve'et chomatah
and the gates thereof, and the wall thereof.

וְהָעִיר מְרֻבַּעַת, אָרְכָּהּ כְּרָחְבָּהּ. הוּא מָדַד אֶת הָעִיר בְּקָנֶה
veha'ir merubba'at, orkah kerachebah. hu madad et ha'ir bekaneh
And the city lieth foursquare, and the length thereof is as great as the breadth: and he measured the city with the reed,

אַלְפַּיִם וּשְׁלֹשׁ מֵאוֹת קִילוֹמֶטֶר; אָרְכָּהּ וְרָחְבָּהּ וְקוֹמָתָהּ שָׁוִים
alpayim usheloshme'ot kilometer; orkah verachebah vekomatah shavim
twelve thousand furlongs: the length and the breadth and the height thereof are equal.

גַּם אֶת חוֹמָתָהּ מָדַד, וְהַמִּדָּה מֵאָה וְאַרְבָּעִים וְאַרְבַּע אַמּוֹת
gam et chomatah madad, vehammiddah me'ah ve'arba'im ve'arba ammot
And he measured the wall thereof, a hundred and forty and four cubits,

לְפִי מִדָּה אֱנוֹשִׁית אֲשֶׁר הִיא מִדָּה שֶׁל מַלְאָךְ
lefi middah enoshit asher hi middah shel mal'ach
according to the measure of a man, that is, of an angel.

הַחוֹמָה בִּנְיָנָהּ אֶבֶן יָשְׁפֵה, וְהָעִיר זָהָב טָהוֹר כִּזְכוּכִית טְהוֹרָה
hachomah binyanah even yashfeh, veha'ir zahav tahor kizchuchit tehorah
And the building of the wall thereof was jasper: and the city was pure gold, like unto pure glass.

יְסוֹדוֹת חוֹמַת הָעִיר מְקֻשָּׁטִים בְּכָל אֶבֶן יְקָרָה
yesodot chomat ha'ir mekushatim bechol even yekarah
The foundations of the wall of the city were adorned with all manner of precious stones.

הַיְסוֹד הָרִאשׁוֹן יָשְׁפֵה, הַשֵּׁנִי סַפִּיר, הַשְּׁלִישִׁי שְׁבוֹ, הָרְבִיעִי בָּרֶקֶת
haysod harishon yashfeh, hasheni sappir, hashelishi shevo, harevi'i bareket
The first foundation was jasper; the second, sapphire; the third, chalcedony; the fourth, emerald;

הַהִתְגַּלּוּת

אֲנִי אֶתֵּן לַצָּמֵא מִמַּעְיַן הַמַּיִם שֶׁל הַחַיִּים - חִנָּם
ani etten latzamei mimma'yan hammayim shel hachayim - chinnam
I will give unto him that is athirst of the fountain of the water of life freely.

הַמְנַצֵּחַ יִירַשׁ אֶת אֵלֶּה וַאֲנִי אֶהְיֶה לּוֹ לֵאלֹהִים וְהוּא יִהְיֶה לִי לְבֵן
hamnatzeach yirash et elleh va'ani ehyeh lo le'elohim vehu yihyeh li leven
He that overcometh shall inherit these things; and I will be his God, and he shall be my son.

אֲבָל מוּגֵי הַלֵּב וְהַבִּלְתִּי מַאֲמִינִים, הַמְתֹעָבִים וְהַמְרַצְּחִים, הַזּוֹנִים
aval mugei hallev vehabbilti ma'aminim, hamto'avim vehamratzechim, hazzonim
But for the fearful, and unbelieving, and abominable, and murderers, and fornicators,

וְהַמְכַשְּׁפִים, עוֹבְדֵי הָאֱלִילִים וְכָל הַמְשַׁקְּרִים
vehamchashefim, ovedei ha'elilim vechol hamshakkerim
and sorcerers, and idolaters, and all liars,

חֶלְקָם בָּאֲגַם הַבּוֹעֵר בָּאֵשׁ וְגָפְרִית אֲשֶׁר הוּא הַמָּוֶת הַשֵּׁנִי
chelkam ba'agam habbo'er be'esh vegofrit asher hu hammavet hasheni
their part shall be in the lake that burneth with fire and brimstone; which is the second death.

אֶחָד מִשִּׁבְעַת הַמַּלְאָכִים, אֲשֶׁר לָהֶם שֶׁבַע הַקְּעָרוֹת הַמְּלֵאוֹת בְּשֶׁבַע הַמַּכּוֹת הָאַחֲרוֹנוֹת, בָּא
echad mishiv'at hammal'achim, asher lahem sheva hakke'arot hammele'ot besheva hammakkot ha'acharonot, ba
And there came one of the seven angels who had the seven bowls, who were laden with the seven last plagues;

וְדִבֶּר אִתִּי. בּוֹא אַרְאֶה לְךָ אֶת הַכַּלָּה אֵשֶׁת הַשֶּׂה, אָמַר
vedibber itti. bo ar'eh lecha et hakkallah eshet hasseh, amar
and he spake with me, saying, Come hither, I will show thee the bride, the wife of the Lamb.

הוּא נָשָׂא אוֹתִי, בָּרוּחַ, אֶל הַר גָּדוֹל וְגָבוֹהַּ
hu nasa oti, baruach, el har gadol vegavoah
And he carried me away in the Spirit to a mountain great and high,

וְהֶרְאָה לִי אֶת עִיר הַקֹּדֶשׁ, יְרוּשָׁלַיִם, יוֹרֶדֶת מִן הַשָּׁמַיִם מֵאֵת אֱלֹהִים
veher'ah li et ir hakkodesh, yerushalayim, yoredet min hashamayim me'et elohim
and showed me the holy city Jerusalem, coming down out of heaven from God,

וּכְבוֹד אֱלֹהִים לָהּ. אוֹר נֹגַהּ כְּאֶבֶן יְקָרָה מְאֹד, כְּאֶבֶן יָשְׁפֵה זַכָּה כִּבְדֹלַח
uchevod elohim lah. or noghah ke'even yekarah me'od, ke'even yashefeh zakkah kivdolach
having the glory of God: her light was like unto a stone most precious, as it were a jasper stone, clear as crystal:

וְיֵשׁ לָהּ חוֹמָה גְּדוֹלָה וּגְבוֹהָה עִם שְׁנֵים־עָשָׂר שְׁעָרִים, וְעַל הַשְּׁעָרִים שְׁנֵים־עָשָׂר מַלְאָכִים
veyesh lah chomah gdolah ugvohah im sheneim-'asar she'arim, ve'al hashe'arim sheneim-'asar mal'achim
having a wall great and high; having twelve gates, and at the gates twelve angels;

וְשֵׁמוֹת כְּתוּבִים עֲלֵיהֶם - שְׁנֵים־עָשָׂר שִׁבְטֵי בְּנֵי יִשְׂרָאֵל
veshemot ketuvim aleihem - sheneim-'asar shivtei benei yisra'el
and names written thereon, which are the names of the twelve tribes of the children of Israel:

ההתגלות

כא

רָאִיתִי שָׁמַיִם חֲדָשִׁים וְאֶרֶץ חֲדָשָׁה, כִּי הַשָּׁמַיִם הָרִאשׁוֹנִים וְהָאָרֶץ הָרִאשׁוֹנָה עָבְרוּ
ra'iti shamayim chadashim ve'eretz chadashah, ki hashamayim harishonim veha'aretz harishonah avru
And I saw a new heaven and a new earth: for the first heaven and the first earth are passed away;

וְהַיָּם אֵינֶנּוּ עוֹד
vehayam einennu od
and the sea is no more.

רָאִיתִי אֶת עִיר הַקֹּדֶשׁ, יְרוּשָׁלַיִם הַחֲדָשָׁה
ra'iti et ir hakkodesh, yerushalayim hachadashah
And I saw the holy city, new Jerusalem,

יוֹרֶדֶת מִן הַשָּׁמַיִם מֵאֵת הָאֱלֹהִים, מוּכָנָה כְּכַלָּה מְקֻשֶּׁטֶת לְבַעְלָהּ
yoredet min hashamayim me'et ha'elohim, muchanah kechallah mekushetet leva'alah
coming down out of heaven from God, made ready as a bride adorned for her husband.

וְשָׁמַעְתִּי קוֹל גָּדוֹל מִן הַכִּסֵּא - אוֹמֵר: הִנֵּה מִשְׁכַּן הָאֱלֹהִים עִם בְּנֵי אָדָם
veshama'ti kol gadol min hakkissei – omer: hinneh mishkan ha'elohim im benei adam
And I heard a great voice out of the throne saying, Behold, the tabernacle of God is with men,

וְיִשְׁכֹּן עִמָּהֶם; הֵמָּה יִהְיוּ לוֹ לְעַם וְהוּא הָאֱלֹהִים יִהְיֶה עִמָּהֶם
veyishkon immahem; hemmah yihyu lo le'am vehu ha'elohim yihyeh immahem
and he shall dwell with them, and they shall be his peoples, and God himself shall be with them, and be their God:

וְיִמְחֶה כָּל דִּמְעָה מֵעֵינֵיהֶם וְהַמָּוֶת לֹא יִהְיֶה עוֹד; גַּם אֵבֶל
veyimcheh kol dim'ah me'eineihem vehammavet lo yihyeh od
and he shall wipe away every tear from their eyes; and death shall be no more;

וּזְעָקָה וּכְאֵב לֹא יִהְיוּ עוֹד, כִּי הָרִאשֹׁנוֹת עָבְרוּ
gam evel uze'akah uche'ev lo yihyu od, ki harishonot avru
neither shall there be mourning, nor crying, nor pain, any more: the first things are passed away.

אָמַר הַיּוֹשֵׁב עַל הַכִּסֵּא: הִנְנִי עוֹשֶׂה הַכֹּל חָדָשׁ.
amar hayoshev al hakkisse: hineni oseh hakkol chadash
And he that sitteth on the throne said, Behold, I make all things new.

אָמַר אֵלַי: כְּתֹב, כִּי הַדְּבָרִים הָאֵלֶּה נֶאֱמָנִים וַאֲמִתִּיִּים הֵם
amar elai: ktov, ki haddevarim ha'elleh ne'emanim va'amittiyim hem
And he saith, Write: for these words are faithful and true.

הוֹסִיף וְאָמַר אֵלַי: הָיֹה נִהְיָה. אֲנִי הָאָלֶף וְהַתָּו, הָרֵאשִׁית וְהַתַּכְלִית
hosif ve'amar elai: hayoh nihyah. ani ha'alef vehattav, hareshit vehattachlit
And he said unto me, They are come to pass. I am the Alpha and the Omega, the beginning and the end.

הַהִתְגַּלּוּת

וְהַשָּׂטָן אֲשֶׁר הִדִּיחָם הֻשְׁלַךְ אֶל אֲגַם הָאֵשׁ וְהַגָּפְרִית
vehassatan asher hiddicham hushlach el agam ha'esh vehaggofrit
And the devil that deceived them was cast into the lake of fire and brimstone,

אֲשֶׁר שָׁם גַּם הַחַיָּה וּנְבִיא הַשֶּׁקֶר, וִיעֻנּוּ יוֹמָם וָלַיְלָה לְעוֹלְמֵי עוֹלָמִים
asher sham gam hachayah unevi hasheker, vi'unnu yomam valaylah le'olemei olamim
where are also the beast and the false prophet; and they shall be tormented day and night for ever and ever.

רָאִיתִי כִּסֵּא לָבָן גָּדוֹל וְאֶת הַיּוֹשֵׁב עָלָיו
ra'iti kissei lavan gadol ve'et hayoshev alav
And I saw a great white throne, and him that sat upon it,

אֲשֶׁר נָסוּ מִפָּנָיו הָאָרֶץ וְהַשָּׁמַיִם, וּמָקוֹם לֹא נִמְצָא לָהֶם
asher nasu mippanav ha'aretz vehashamayim, umakom lo nimtza lahem
from whose face the earth and the heaven fled away; and there was found no place for them.

וְרָאִיתִי אֶת הַמֵּתִים, הַקְּטַנִּים וְהַגְּדוֹלִים, עוֹמְדִים לִפְנֵי הַכִּסֵּא וּסְפָרִים נִפְתָּחוּ
vera'iti et hammetim, hakketannim vehaggdolim, omedim lifnei hakkissei usfarim niftechu
And I saw the dead, the great and the small, standing before the throne; and books were opened:

גַּם סֵפֶר אַחֵר נִפְתַּח, סֵפֶר הַחַיִּים
gam sefer acher niftach, sefer hachayim
and another book was opened, which is the book of life:

וְהַמֵּתִים נִשְׁפְּטוּ מִתּוֹךְ הַדְּבָרִים הַכְּתוּבִים בַּסְּפָרִים, לְפִי מַעֲשֵׂיהֶם
vehammetim nishpetu mittoch haddevarim hakketuvim bassfarim, lefi ma'aseihem
and the dead were judged out of the things which were written in the books, according to their works.

הַיָּם נָתַן אֶת הַמֵּתִים אֲשֶׁר בּוֹ, מָוֶת וּשְׁאוֹל נָתְנוּ אֶת מֵתֵיהֶם
hayam natan et hammetim asher bo, mavet ushe'ol natenu et meteihem
And the sea gave up the dead that were in it; and death and Hades gave up the dead that were in them:

וְאִישׁ אִישׁ נִשְׁפְּטוּ לְפִי מַעֲשֵׂיהֶם
ve'ish ish nishpetu lefi ma'aseihem
and they were judged every man according to their works.

הַמָּוֶת וְהַשְּׁאוֹל הֻשְׁלְכוּ אֶל אֲגַם הָאֵשׁ. זֶהוּ הַמָּוֶת הַשֵּׁנִי - אֲגַם הָאֵשׁ
hammavet vehashe'ol hushlechu el agam ha'esh. zehu hammavet hasheni - agam ha'esh
And death and Hades were cast into the lake of fire. This is the second death, even the lake of fire.

וּמִי שֶׁלֹּא נִמְצָא כָּתוּב בְּסֵפֶר הַחַיִּים, הֻשְׁלַךְ אֶל אֲגַם הָאֵשׁ
umi shello nimtza katuv besefer hachayim, hushlach el agam ha'esh
And if any was not found written in the book of life, he was cast into the lake of fire.

הַהִתְגַּלּוּת

וְנַפְשׁוֹת הַנֶּעֱרָפִים עַל עֵדוּת יֵשׁוּעַ וְעַל דְּבַר אֱלֹהִים
venafshot hanne'erafim al edut yeshua ve'al devar elohim
and I saw the souls of them that had been beheaded for the testimony of Jesus, and for the word of God,

וְאֵלֶּה אֲשֶׁר לֹא הִשְׁתַּחֲווּ לַחַיָּה וּלְצַלְמָהּ
ve'elleh asher lo hishtachavu lachayah uletzalmah
and such as worshipped not the beast, neither his image,

וְלֹא קִבְּלוּ אֶת הַתָּו עַל מִצְחָם וְעַל יָדָם -
velo kibblu et hattav al mitzcham ve'al yadam
and received not the mark upon their forehead and upon their hand;

חָיוּ וּמָלְכוּ עִם הַמָּשִׁיחַ אֶלֶף שָׁנִים
chayu umalchu im hammashiach elef shanim
and they lived, and reigned with Christ a thousand years.

שְׁאָר הַמֵּתִים לֹא חָיוּ עַד תֹּם אֶלֶף הַשָּׁנִים. זֹאת הַתְּחִיָּה הָרִאשׁוֹנָה
she'ar hammetim lo chayu ad tom elef hashanim. zot hattechiyah harishonah
The rest of the dead lived not until the thousand years should be finished. This is the first resurrection.

מְאֻשָּׁר וְקָדוֹשׁ מִי שֶׁחֶלְקוֹ בַּתְּחִיָּה הָרִאשׁוֹנָה; עַל אֵלֶּה אֵין לַמָּוֶת הַשֵּׁנִי שִׁלְטוֹן
me'ushar vekadosh mi shechelko battechiyah harishonah; al elleh ein lammavet hasheni shilton
Blessed and holy is he that hath part in the first resurrection: over these the second death hath no power;

כִּי יִהְיוּ כֹּהֲנִים לֵאלֹהִים וְלַמָּשִׁיחַ וְיִמְלְכוּ אִתּוֹ אֶלֶף שָׁנִים
ki yihyu kohanim lelohim velammashiach veyimlechu itto elef shanim
but they shall be priests of God and of Christ, and shall reign with him a thousand years.

אַחֲרֵי כְּלוֹת אֶלֶף הַשָּׁנִים יֻתַּר הַשָּׂטָן מִכִּלְאוֹ
acharei kelot elef hashanim yuttar hassatan mikkil'o
And when the thousand years are finished, Satan shall be loosed out of his prison,

וְיֵצֵא לְהַתְעוֹת אֶת הַגּוֹיִם בְּאַרְבַּע קְצוֹת הָאָרֶץ
veyetzei lehat'ot et haggoyim be'arba ketzot ha'aretz
and shall come forth to deceive the nations which are in the four corners of the earth,

אֶת גּוֹג וּמָגוֹג, לֶאֱסֹף אוֹתָם לַמִּלְחָמָה; וּמִסְפָּרָם כְּחוֹל הַיָּם
et gog umagog, le'esof otam lammilchamah; umisparam kechol hayam
Gog and Magog, to gather them together to the war: the number of whom is as the sand of the sea.

הֵם עָלוּ עַל מֶרְחַב הָאָרֶץ וְהִקִּיפוּ אֶת מַחֲנֵה הַקְּדוֹשִׁים וְאֶת הָעִיר הָאֲהוּבָה
hem alu al merchav ha'aretz vehikkifu et machaneh hakkedoshim ve'et ha'ir ha'ahuvah
And they went up over the breadth of the earth, and compassed the camp of the saints about, and the beloved city:

יָרְדָה אֵשׁ מִן הַשָּׁמַיִם מֵאֵת אֱלֹהִים וְאָכְלָה אוֹתָם
yaredah esh min hashamayim me'et elohim ve'achelah otam
and fire came down out of heaven, and devoured them.

הַהִתְגַּלּוּת

הַחַיָּה נִתְפְּסָה וְאִתָּהּ נְבִיא הַשֶּׁקֶר שֶׁעָשָׂה אֶת הָאוֹתוֹת לְפָנֶיהָ
hachayah nitpesah ve'ittah nevi hasheker she'asah et ha'otot lefaneiha
And the beast was taken, and with him the false prophet that wrought the signs in his sight,

וְהִתְעָה בְּאֶמְצָעוּתָם אֶת מְקַבְּלֵי תָּו הַחַיָּה וְאֶת הַמִּשְׁתַּחֲוִים לְצַלְמָהּ
vehit'ah be'emtza'utam et mekabbelei tav hachayah ve'et hammishtachavim letzalmah
wherewith he deceived them that had received the mark of the beast and them that worshipped his image:

הַשְּׁנַיִם הֻשְׁלְכוּ חַיִּים אֶל אֲגַם הָאֵשׁ הַבּוֹעֵר בְּגָפְרִית
hashenayim hushlechu chayim el agam ha'esh habbo'er begofrit
they two were cast alive into the lake of fire that burneth with brimstone:

וְהַנִּשְׁאָרִים נֶהֶרְגוּ בַּחֶרֶב
vehannish'arim nehergu bacherev
and the rest were killed with the sword of him that sat upon the horse,

הַיּוֹצֵאת מִפִּי הַיּוֹשֵׁב עַל הַסּוּס
hayotzet mippi hayoshev al hassus
even the sword which came forth out of his mouth:

וְכָל בַּעֲלֵי הַכָּנָף שָׂבְעוּ מִבְּשָׂרָם
vechol ba'alei hakkanaf save'u mibbesaram
and all the birds were filled with their flesh.

כ

רָאִיתִי מַלְאָךְ יוֹרֵד מִן הַשָּׁמַיִם וּבְיָדוֹ מַפְתֵּחַ הַתְּהוֹם וְשַׁרְשֶׁרֶת גְּדוֹלָה
ra'iti mal'ach yored min hashamayim uveyado mafteach hattehom vesharsheret gedolah
And I saw an angel coming down out of heaven, having the key of the abyss and a great chain in his hand.

הוּא תָּפַשׂ אֶת הַתַּנִּין, הַנָּחָשׁ הַקַּדְמוֹנִי אֲשֶׁר הוּא הַמַּלְשִׁין וְהַשָּׂטָן, וְקָשַׁר אוֹתוֹ לְאֶלֶף שָׁנִים
hu tafas et hattannin, hannachash hakkadmoni asher hu hammalshin vehassatan, vekashar oto le'elef shanim
And he laid hold on the dragon, the old serpent, which is the Devil and Satan, and bound him for a thousand years,

הִשְׁלִיךְ אוֹתוֹ אֶל הַתְּהוֹם וְסָגַר וְחָתַם עָלָיו כְּדֵי שֶׁלֹּא יַתְעֶה עוֹד אֶת הַגּוֹיִם
hishlich oto el hattehom vesagar vechatam alav kedei shello yat'eh od et haggoyim
and cast him into the abyss, and shut it, and sealed it over him, that he should deceive the nations no more,

עַד תֹּם אֶלֶף הַשָּׁנִים; אַחֲרֵי כֵן צָרִיךְ שֶׁיֻּתַּר לִזְמַן מְעָט
ad tom elef hashanim; acharei chen tzarich sheyuttar lizman me'at
until the thousand years should be finished: after this he must be loosed for a little time.

רָאִיתִי כִּסְאוֹת; הִתְיַשְׁבוּ עֲלֵיהֶם וּמִשְׁפָּט נִתַּן בְּיָדָם
ra'iti kis'ot; hityashevu aleihem umishpat nittan beyadam
And I saw thrones, and they sat upon them, and judgment was given unto them:

הַהִתְגַּלּוּת

צִבְאוֹת הַשָּׁמַיִם יוֹצְאִים אַחֲרָיו, רְכוּבִים עַל סוּסִים לְבָנִים וּלְבוּשִׁים בּוּץ לָבָן וְטָהוֹר
tziv'ot hashamayim yotz'im acharav, rechuvim al susim levanim ulevushim butz lavan vetahor
And the armies which are in heaven followed him upon white horses, clothed in fine linen, white and pure.

מִפִּיו יוֹצֵאת חֶרֶב חַדָּה לְהַכּוֹת בָּהּ אֶת הַגּוֹיִם
mippiv yotzet cherev chaddah lehakkot bah et haggoyim
And out of his mouth proceedeth a sharp sword, that with it he should smite the nations:

וְהוּא יִרְעֵם בְּשֵׁבֶט בַּרְזֶל. הוּא דּוֹרֵךְ אֶת גַּת הַיַּיִן שֶׁל חֲרוֹן אַף אֱלֹהֵי צְבָאוֹת
vehu yir'em beshevet barzel. hu dorech et gat hayayin shel charon af elohei tzeva'ot
and he shall rule them with a rod of iron: and he treadeth the winepress of the fierceness of the wrath of God, the Almighty.

וְעַל בִּגְדוֹ וְעַל יְרֵכוֹ כָּתוּב שֵׁם: מֶלֶךְ הַמְּלָכִים וַאֲדוֹן הָאֲדוֹנִים
ve'al bigdo ve'al yerecho katuv shem: melech hammelachim va'adon ha'adonim
And he hath on his garment and on his thigh a name written, KING OF KINGS, AND LORD OF LORDS.

רָאִיתִי מַלְאָךְ אֶחָד עוֹמֵד בַּשֶּׁמֶשׁ וְקוֹרֵא בְּקוֹל גָּדוֹל:
ra'iti mal'ach echad omed bashemesh vekorei bekol gadol
And I saw an angel standing in the sun; and he cried with a loud voice,

בְּאָמְרוֹ לְכָל בַּעֲלֵי כָנָף הַמְעוֹפְפִים בְּאֶמְצַע הַשָּׁמַיִם
be'omro lechol ba'alei kanaf ham'ofefim be'emtza hashamayim
saying to all the birds that fly in mid heaven,

בּוֹאוּ, הֵאָסְפוּ אֶל הַסְּעוּדָה הַגְּדוֹלָה אֲשֶׁר לֵאלֹהִים
bo'u, he'asefu el hasse'udah haggedolah asher le'elohim
Come and be gathered together unto the great supper of God;

לְמַעַן תֹּאכְלוּ בְּשַׂר מְלָכִים וּבְשַׂר שָׂרֵי אֲלָפִים, בְּשַׂר גִּבּוֹרִים
lema'an tochelu besar melachim uvesar sarei alafim, besar gibborim
that ye may eat the flesh of kings, and the flesh of captains, and the flesh of mighty men,

וּבְשַׂר סוּסִים וְרוֹכְבֵיהֶם, וּבְשַׂר הַכֹּל: גַּם חָפְשִׁים וַעֲבָדִים, גַּם קְטַנִּים וְגַם גְּדוֹלִים
uvesar susim verocheveihem uvesar hakkol. gam chofshim va'avadim, gam ktannim vegam gdolim
and the flesh of horses and of them that sit thereon, and the flesh of all men, both free and bond, and small and great.

וְרָאִיתִי אֶת הַחַיָּה וְאֶת מַלְכֵי הָאָרֶץ וְצִבְאוֹתֵיהֶם
vera'iti et hachayah ve'et malchei ha'aretz vetziv'oteihem
And I saw the beast, and the kings of the earth, and their armies,

נֶאֱסָפִים לַעֲשׂוֹת מִלְחָמָה בַּיּוֹשֵׁב עַל הַסּוּס וּבִצְבָאוֹ
ne'esafim la'asot milchamah bayoshev al hassus uvitzva'o
gathered together to make war against him that sat upon the horse, and against his army.

הַהִתְגַּלּוּת

וְנִתַּן לָהּ לִלְבֹּשׁ בּוּץ טָהוֹר וְצַח
venittan lah lilbosh butz tahor vetzach
And it was given unto her that she should array herself in fine linen, bright and pure:

כִּי הַבּוּץ הוּא צִדְקוֹת הַקְּדוֹשִׁים
ki habbutz hu tzidkot hakkedoshim
for the fine linen is the righteous acts of the saints.

אָמַר אֵלַי: כְּתֹב: אַשְׁרֵי הַקְּרוּאִים אֶל מִשְׁתֵּה חֲתֻנַּת הַשֶּׂה
amar elai: ketov. ashrei hakkeru'im el mishteh chatunnat hasseh
And he saith unto me, Write, Blessed are they that are bidden to the marriage supper of the Lamb.

הוֹסִיף וְאָמַר לִי: אֵלֶּה הֵם דִּבְרֵי אֱמֶת שֶׁל אֱלֹהִים
hosif ve'amar li: elleh hem divrei emet shel elohim
And he saith unto me, These are true words of God.

נָפַלְתִּי לְרַגְלָיו לְהִשְׁתַּחֲוֹת לוֹ, אַךְ הוּא אָמַר אֵלַי: רְאֵה, אַל נָא
nafalti leraglav lehishtachavot lo, ach hu amar elai: re'eh, al na.
And I fell down before his feet to worship him. And he saith unto me, See thou do it not:

עֶבֶד-חָבֵר אֲנִי לְךָ וּלְאַחֶיךָ אֲשֶׁר יֵשׁ לָהֶם עֵדוּת יֵשׁוּעַ
eved-chaver ani lecha ule'acheicha asher yesh lahem edut yeshua
I am a fellow-servant with thee and with thy brethren that hold the testimony of Jesus:

לֵאלֹהִים תִּשְׁתַּחֲוֶה! הֵן עֵדוּת יֵשׁוּעַ הִיא רוּחַ הַנְּבוּאָה
le'elohim tishtachaveh! hen edut yeshua hi ruach hannevu'ah
worship God: for the testimony of Jesus is the spirit of prophecy.

רָאִיתִי אֶת הַשָּׁמַיִם פְּתוּחִים וְהִנֵּה סוּס לָבָן
ra'iti et hashamayim petuchim vehinneh sus lavan
And I saw the heaven opened; and behold, a white horse,

וְהַיּוֹשֵׁב עָלָיו נִקְרָא נֶאֱמָן וַאֲמִתִּי; בְּצֶדֶק הוּא שׁוֹפֵט וְלוֹחֵם
vehayoshev alav nikra ne'eman va'amitti; betzedek hu shofet velochem
and he that sat thereon called Faithful and True; and in righteousness he doth judge and make war.

עֵינָיו שַׁלְהֶבֶת אֵשׁ, עַל רֹאשׁוֹ עֲטָרוֹת רַבּוֹת
einav shalhevet esh, al rosho atarot rabbot
And his eyes are a flame of fire, and upon his head are many diadems;

וְיֵשׁ לוֹ שֵׁם כָּתוּב אֲשֶׁר אֵין אִישׁ יוֹדֵעַ אוֹתוֹ מִלְּבַדּוֹ
veyesh lo shem katuv asher ein ish yodea oto millevaddo
and he hath a name written which no one knoweth but he himself.

הוּא לָבוּשׁ בֶּגֶד טָבוּל בְּדָם וּשְׁמוֹ נִקְרָא דְּבַר הָאֱלֹהִים
hu lavush beged tavul bedam ushemo nikra devar ha'elohim
And he is arrayed in a garment sprinkled with blood: and his name is called The Word of God.

הַהִתְגַּלּוּת

כִּי אֱמֶת וְצֶדֶק מִשְׁפָּטָיו; כִּי שָׁפַט אֶת הַזּוֹנָה הַגְּדוֹלָה
ki emet vetzedek mishpatav; ki shafat et hazzonah haggedolah
for true and righteous are his judgments; for he hath judged the great harlot,

אֲשֶׁר הִשְׁחִיתָה אֶת הָאָרֶץ בְּתַזְנוּתָהּ
asher hishchitah et ha'aretz betaznutah
her that corrupted the earth with her fornication,

וְנָקַם אֶת דַּם עֲבָדָיו מִיָּדָהּ
venakam et dam avadav miyadah
and he hath avenged the blood of his servants at her hand.

וְשֵׁנִית אָמְרוּ: הַלְלוּיָהּ! עֲשָׁנָהּ עוֹלֶה לְעוֹלְמֵי עוֹלָמִים
veshenit ameru: haleluyah! ashanah oleh le'olemei olamim
And a second time they say, Hallelujah. And her smoke goeth up for ever and ever.

וְעֶשְׂרִים וְאַרְבָּעָה הַזְּקֵנִים וְאַרְבַּע הַחַיּוֹת נָפְלוּ וְהִשְׁתַּחֲווּ לֵאלֹהִים הַיּוֹשֵׁב עַל הַכִּסֵּא
ve'esrim ve'arba'ah hazzekenim ve'arba hachayot naflu vehishtachavu lelohim hayoshev al hakkissei
And the four and twenty elders and the four living creatures fell down and worshipped God that sitteth on the throne,

בְּאָמְרָם: אָמֵן, הַלְלוּיָהּ
be'omram: amen, haleluyah
saying, Amen; Hallelujah.

יָצָא קוֹל מִן הַכִּסֵּא - אוֹמֵר
yatza kol min hakkissei - omer
And a voice came forth from the throne, saying,

הַלְלוּ אֶת אֱלֹהֵינוּ כָּל עֲבָדָיו - הַיְרֵאִים אוֹתוֹ, הַקְּטַנִּים וְהַגְּדוֹלִים
halelu et eloheinu kol avadav - hayre'im oto, hakktannim vehaggedolim
Give praise to our God, all ye his servants, ye that fear him, the small and the great.

וְשָׁמַעְתִּי קוֹל כְּקוֹל הָמוֹן רַב וּכְקוֹל מַיִם רַבִּים
veshama'ti kol kekol hamon rav uchekol mayim rabbim
And I heard as it were the voice of a great multitude, and as the voice of many waters,

וּכְקוֹל רְעָמִים חֲזָקִים - אוֹמֵר: הַלְלוּיָהּ כִּי מָלַךְ יהוה אֱלֹהֵינוּ, אֱלֹהֵי צְבָאוֹת
uchekol re'amim chazakim – omer: haleluyah ki malach hashem eloheinu, elohei tzeva'ot
and as the voice of mighty thunders, saying, Hallelujah: for the Lord our God, the Almighty, reigneth.

נָגִילָה וְנִשְׂמְחָה וְנִתֵּן לוֹ כָּבוֹד
nagilah venismechah venitten lo kavod
Let us rejoice and be exceeding glad, and let us give the glory unto him:

כִּי בָּאָה חֲתֻנַּת הַשֶּׂה וְאִשְׁתּוֹ הֵכִינָה עַצְמָהּ
ki ba'ah chatunnat hashoh ve'ishto hechinah atzmah
for the marriage of the Lamb is come, and his wife hath made herself ready.

הַהִתְגַּלּוּת

וּמַלְאָךְ חָזָק אֶחָד הֵרִים אֶבֶן, כְּאֶבֶן רֵיחַיִם גְּדוֹלָה, וְהִשְׁלִיךְ אוֹתָהּ לַיָּם בְּאָמְרוֹ
umal'ach chazak echad herim even, ke'even reichayim gedolah, vehishlich otah layam be'omro
And a strong angel took up a stone as it were a great millstone and cast it into the sea, saying,

כָּכָה תֻּשְׁלַךְ בְּשֶׁצֶף בָּבֶל הָעִיר הַגְּדוֹלָה וְלֹא תִּמָּצֵא עוֹד
kachah tushlach beshetzef bavel ha'ir haggedolah velo timmatzei od
Thus with a mighty fall shall Babylon, the great city, be cast down, and shall be found no more at all.

צְלִילֵי פּוֹרְטֵי נֶבֶל, צְלִילֵי נוֹגְנִים וּמְחַלְלֵי חֲלִילִים, וּצְלִילֵי תּוֹקְעִים בַּחֲצוֹצְרוֹת - לֹא יִשָּׁמְעוּ בָּךְ עוֹד
tzelilei poretei nevel, tzelilei nogenim umechallelei chalilim, utzelilei toke'im bachatzotzerot - lo yishame'u bach od
And the voice of harpers and minstrels and flute-players and trumpeters shall be heard no more at all in thee;

וְכָל אֻמָּן מִכָּל אֻמָּנוּת לֹא יִמָּצֵא בָּךְ עוֹד
vechol umman mikkol ummanut lo yimmatzei bach od
and no craftsman, of whatsoever craft, shall be found any more at all in thee;

וְלֹא יִשָּׁמַע עוֹד בְּקִרְבֵּךְ קוֹל רֵיחַיִם
velo yishama od bekirbech kol reichayim
and the voice of a mill shall be heard no more at all in thee;

אוֹר מְנוֹרָה לֹא יָאִיר בָּךְ עוֹד
or menorah lo ya'ir bach od
and the light of a lamp shall shine no more at all in thee;

וְקוֹל חָתָן וְכַלָּה לֹא יִשָּׁמַע בָּךְ עוֹד
vekol chatan vechallah lo yishama bach od
and the voice of the bridegroom and of the bride shall be heard no more at all in thee:

כִּי סוֹחֲרַיִךְ הָיוּ נִכְבְּדֵי הָאָרֶץ וּבִכְשׁוּפַיִךְ הֻתְעוּ כָּל הַגּוֹיִם
ki socharayich hayu nichbedei ha'aretz uvechishufayich hut'u kol haggoyim
for thy merchants were the princes of the earth; for with thy sorcery were all the nations deceived.

בָּהּ נִמְצָא דַם נְבִיאִים וּקְדוֹשִׁים וְדַם כָּל אֲשֶׁר נִטְבְּחוּ עֲלֵי אָרֶץ
bah nimtza dam nevi'im ukdoshim vedam kol asher nitbechu alei aretz
And in her was found the blood of prophets and of saints, and of all that have been slain upon the earth.

יט

אַחֲרֵי כֵן שָׁמַעְתִּי קוֹל גָּדוֹל כְּקוֹל הָמוֹן רַב בַּשָּׁמַיִם אוֹמֵר
acharei chen shama'ti kol gadol kekol hamon rav bashamayim omer
After these things I heard as it were a great voice of a great multitude in heaven, saying,

הַלְלוּיָהּ! הַיְשׁוּעָה וְהַכָּבוֹד וְהַגְּבוּרָה לֵאלֹהֵינוּ
haleluyah! hayshu'ah vehakkavod vehaggevurah le'eloheinu
Hallelujah; Salvation, and glory, and power, belong to our God:

ההתגלות

סוֹחֲרֵי הַדְּבָרִים הָאֵלֶּה, אֲשֶׁר הִתְעַשְּׁרוּ מִמֶּנָּה
socharei haddevarim ha'elleh, asher hit'asheru mimmennah
The merchants of these things, who were made rich by her,

יַעַמְדוּ מֵרָחוֹק מִפְּנֵי אֵימַת עִנּוּיָהּ, בּוֹכִים וּמִתְאַבְּלִים
ya'amdu merachok mippenei eimat innuyah, bochim umit'abbelim
shall stand afar off for the fear of her torment, weeping and mourning;

וְאוֹמְרִים: אוֹי, אוֹי, הָעִיר הַגְּדוֹלָה
ve'omerim: oy, oy, ha'ir haggedolah
saying, Woe, woe, the great city,

הַלְּבוּשָׁה שֵׁשׁ וְאַרְגָּמָן וְשָׁנִי וּמְקֻשֶּׁטֶת בְּזָהָב וְאֶבֶן יְקָרָה וּפְנִינִים
hallevushah shesh ve'argaman veshani umekushetet bezahav ve'even yekarah ufeninim
she that was arrayed in fine linen and purple and scarlet, and decked with gold and precious stone and pearl!

כִּי בְּשָׁעָה אַחַת הָחֳרַב עֹשֶׁר גָּדוֹל כָּזֶה! וְכָל רַב־חוֹבֵל וְכָל הַנּוֹסֵעַ לִמְחוֹז חֶפְצוֹ
ki besha'ah achat hochorav osher gadol kazeh! vechol rav-chovel vechol hannosea limchoz cheftzo
for in one hour so great riches is made desolate. And every shipmaster, and every one that saileth any whither,

גַּם מַלָּחִים וְכָל אֲשֶׁר מְלַאכְתָּם בַּיָּם, עָמְדוּ מֵרָחוֹק
gam mallachim vechol asher melachtam bayam, amdu merachok
and mariners, and as many as gain their living by sea, stood afar off,

וְצָעֲקוּ בִּרְאוֹתָם אֶת עֲשַׁן שְׂרֵפָתָהּ. מִי בֶעָרִים כָּעִיר הַגְּדוֹלָה? אָמְרוּ
vetza'aku bir'otam et ashan serefatah. mi be'arim ka'ir haggedolah? ameru
and cried out as they looked upon the smoke of her burning, saying, What city is like the great city?

הֵם זָרְקוּ עָפָר עַל רָאשֵׁיהֶם וְצָעֲקוּ בִּבְכִי וְיָגוֹן: אוֹי, אוֹי, הָעִיר הַגְּדוֹלָה
hem zarku afar al rasheihem vetza'aku bivchi veyagon: oy, oy, ha'ir haggedolah
And they cast dust on their heads, and cried, weeping and mourning, saying, Woe, woe, the great city,

אֲשֶׁר עָשְׁרוּ בָהּ מֵהוֹנָהּ כָּל בַּעֲלֵי הָאֳנִיּוֹת בַּיָּם,
asher asheru bah mehonah kol ba'alei ho'oniyot bayam
wherein all that had their ships in the sea were made rich by reason of her costliness!

כִּי בְּשָׁעָה אַחַת הָחְרְבָה
ki besha'ah achat hochrevah
for in one hour is she made desolate.

גִּילוּ עָלֶיהָ שָׁמַיִם, גַּם קְדוֹשִׁים וּשְׁלִיחִים וּנְבִיאִים
gilu aleiha shamayim, gam kedoshim ushelichim unevi'im
Rejoice over her, thou heaven, and ye saints, and ye apostles, and ye prophets;

כִּי שָׁפַט אֱלֹהִים אֶת מִשְׁפַּטְכֶם מִמֶּנָּה
ki shafat elohim et mishpatchem mimmennah
for God hath judged your judgment on her.

הַהִתְגַּלּוּת

וּמַלְכֵי הָאָרֶץ אֲשֶׁר זָנוּ וְהִתְעַנְּגוּ אִתָּהּ
umalchei ha'aretz asher zanu vehit'annegu ittah
And the kings of the earth, who committed fornication and lived wantonly with her,

יִבְכּוּ וְיִסְפְּדוּ עָלֶיהָ כִּרְאוֹתָם אֶת עֲשַׁן שְׂרֵפָתָהּ
yivku veyispedu aleiha kir'otam et ashan serefatah
shall weep and wail over her, when they look upon the smoke of her burning,

מֵרָחוֹק יַעַמְדוּ מִפְּנֵי אֵימַת עִנּוּיָהּ וְיֹאמְרוּ
merachok ya'amdu mippenei eimat innuyah veyomeru
standing afar off for the fear of her torment, saying,

אוֹי, אוֹי, בָּבֶל הָעִיר הַגְּדוֹלָה, הָעִיר הַחֲזָקָה, כִּי בְשָׁעָה אַחַת בָּא מִשְׁפָּטֵךְ
oy, oy, bavel ha'ir haggedolah, ha'ir hachazakah, ki besha'ah achat ba mishpatech
Woe, woe, the great city, Babylon, the strong city! for in one hour is thy judgment come.

גַּם סוֹחֲרֵי הָאָרֶץ בּוֹכִים וּמִתְאַבְּלִים עָלֶיהָ, כִּי אֵין קוֹנֶה עוֹד אֶת מִטְעַן סְחוֹרָתָם
gam socharei ha'aretz bochim umit'abblim aleiha, ki ein koneh od et mit'an schoratam
And the merchants of the earth weep and mourn over her, for no man buyeth their merchandise any more;

מִטְעַן שֶׁל זָהָב וְכֶסֶף וְאֶבֶן יְקָרָה וּפְנִינִים וּבוּץ וְאַרְגָּמָן וּמֶשִׁי וְשָׁנִי
mit'an shel zahav vechesef ve'even yekarah ufeninim uvutz ve'argaman umeshi veshani
merchandise of gold, and silver, and precious stone, and pearls, and fine linen, and purple, and silk, and scarlet;

כָּל עֵץ בֹּשֶׂם וְכָל כְּלִי שֶׁנְהָב, כָּל כְּלִי מֵעֵץ יָקָר
kol etz bosem vechol kli shenhav, kol kli me'etz yakar
and all thyine wood, and every vessel of ivory, and every vessel made of most precious wood,

וּמִנְּחֹשֶׁת, מִבַּרְזֶל וּמְשַׁיִשׁ
uminnechoshet, mibbarzel umishayish
and of brass, and iron, and marble;

קִנָּמוֹן וַאֲמוֹמוֹן, קְטֹרֶת סַמִּים, מֹר וּלְבוֹנָה, יַיִן וְשֶׁמֶן, סֹלֶת וְחִטָּה
kinnamon va'amomon, ktoret sammim, mor ulevonah, yayin veshemen, solet vechittah
and cinnamon, and spice, and incense, and ointment, and frankincense, and wine, and oil, and fine flour, and wheat,

בָּקָר וְצֹאן, סוּסִים וּמֶרְכָּבוֹת, עֲבָדִים וְנֶפֶשׁ אָדָם
bakar vetzon, susim umerkavot, avadim venefesh adam
and cattle, and sheep; and merchandise of horses and chariots and slaves; and souls of men.

סָר מִמֵּךְ הַפְּרִי חֶמְדַּת נַפְשֵׁךְ
sar mimmech happeri chemdat nafshech
And the fruits which thy soul lusted after are gone from thee,

כָּל הַמּוֹתָרוֹת וְכָל נוֹצֵץ אָבְדוּ מִמֵּךְ; לֹא יִמְצָאוּם עוֹד
kol hammotarot vechol notzetz avedu mimmech; lo yimtze'um od
and all things that were dainty and sumptuous are perished from thee, and men shall find them no more at all.

הַהִתְגַּלּוּת

כִּי מִיֵּין חֲרוֹן תַּזְנוּתָהּ שָׁתוּ כָּל הַגּוֹיִם

ki miyein charon taznutah shatu kol haggoyim
For by the wine of the wrath of her fornication all the nations are fallen;

וּמַלְכֵי הָאָרֶץ זָנוּ עִמָּהּ

umalchei ha'aretz zanu immah
and the kings of the earth committed fornication with her,

וְסוֹחֲרֵי הָאָרֶץ הִתְעַשְּׁרוּ מֵעֹצֶם מוֹתְרוֹתֶיהָ

vesocharei ha'aretz hit'asheru me'otzem moteroteiha
and the merchants of the earth waxed rich by the power of her wantonness.

שָׁמַעְתִּי קוֹל אַחֵר מִן הַשָּׁמַיִם אֹמֵר

shama'ti kol acher min hashamayim omer
And I heard another voice from heaven, saying,

צְאוּ מִמֶּנָּה, עַמִּי, פֶּן תִּשְׁתַּתְּפוּ בְחַטֹּאתֶיהָ וּפֶן תְּקַבְּלוּ מִמַּכּוֹתֶיהָ

tze'u mimmennah, ammi, pen tishtattefu bechattoteiha ufen tekabbelu mimmakkoteiha
Come forth, my people, out of her, that ye have no fellowship with her sins, and that ye receive not of her plagues:

כִּי הִגִּיעוּ חַטֹּאתֶיהָ עַד הַשָּׁמַיִם וְזָכַר אֱלֹהִים אֶת פְּשָׁעֶיהָ

ki higgi'u chattoteiha ad hashamayim uzechor elohim et pesha'eiha
for her sins have reached even unto heaven, and God hath remembered her iniquities.

שַׁלְּמוּ לָהּ כַּגְּמוּל שֶׁשִּׁלְּמָה גַּם הִיא וְכִפְלוּ לָהּ כִּפְלַיִם כְּמַעֲלָלֶיהָ

shallemu lah kaggemul sheshillemah gam hi vechiflu lah kiflayim kema'alaleiha
Render unto her even as she rendered, and double unto her the double according to her works:

בַּכּוֹס אֲשֶׁר מָסָכָה מִסְכוּ לָהּ כִּפְלַיִם

bakkos asher maschah mischu lah kiflayim
in the cup which she mingled, mingle unto her double.

בַּמִּדָּה שֶׁרוֹמְמָה עַצְמָהּ וְהִתְעַנְּגָה כֵּן תְּנוּ לָהּ מַכְאוֹב וָאֵבֶל

bammiddah sheromemah atzmah vehit'annegah ken tenu lah mach'ov va'evel
How much soever she glorified herself, and waxed wanton, so much give her of torment and mourning:

כִּי אָמְרָה בִּלְבָבָהּ: יוֹשֶׁבֶת אֲנִי, מַלְכָּה; אֵינֶנִּי אַלְמָנָה וְאֵבֶל לֹא אֶרְאֶה

ki amerah bilvavah: yoshevet ani, malkah; einenni almanah ve'evel lo er'eh
for she saith in her heart, I sit a queen, and am no widow, and shall in no wise see mourning.

עַל כֵּן בְּיוֹם אֶחָד תָּבֹאנָה מַכּוֹתֶיהָ: מָוֶת, אֵבֶל וְרָעָב,

al ken beyom echad tavonah makkoteiha: mavet, evel vera'av
Therefore in one day shall her plagues come, death, and mourning, and famine;

וּבָאֵשׁ תִּשָּׂרֵף; כִּי חָזָק יהוה אֱלֹהִים הַשֹּׁפֵט אֹתָהּ

uva'esh tissaref; ki chazak hashem elohim hashofet otah
and she shall be utterly burned with fire; for strong is the Lord God who judged her.

הַהִתְגַּלּוּת

עַמִּים וַהֲמוֹנִים הֵם, וְאֻמּוֹת וּלְשׁוֹנוֹת
ammim vahamonim hem, ve'ummot uleshonot
are peoples, and multitudes, and nations, and tongues.

עֶשֶׂר הַקְּרָנַיִם אֲשֶׁר רָאִיתָ וְהַחַיָּה - הַלָּלוּ יִשְׂנְאוּ אֶת הַזּוֹנָה
eser hakkarnayim asher ra'ita vehachayah - hallalu yisn'u et hazzonah
And the ten horns which thou sawest, and the beast, these shall hate the harlot,

וְיַעֲשׂוּהָ שׁוֹמֵמָה וַעֲרֻמָּה; גַּם יֹאכְלוּ אֶת בְּשָׂרָהּ וְאוֹתָהּ יִשְׂרְפוּ בָּאֵשׁ
veya'asuha shomemah va'arummah; gam yochelu et besarah ve'otah yisrefu ba'esh
and shall make her desolate and naked, and shall eat her flesh, and shall burn her utterly with fire.

כִּי אֱלֹהִים נָתַן בְּלִבָּם לְהוֹצִיא לַפֹּעַל אֶת כַּוָּנָתוֹ, וְלִהְיוֹת עֵצָה אַחַת
ki elohim natan belibbam lehotzi lappo'al et kavvanato, velihyot etzah achat
For God did put in their hearts to do his mind, and to come to one mind,

וְלָתֵת אֶת מַלְכוּתָם לַחַיָּה, עַד אֲשֶׁר יִתְמַלְאוּ דִּבְרֵי אֱלֹהִים
velatet et malchutam lachayah, ad asher yitmall'u divrei elohim
and to give their kingdom unto the beast, until the words of God should be accomplished.

וְהָאִשָּׁה אֲשֶׁר רָאִיתָ הִיא הָעִיר הַגְּדוֹלָה הַמּוֹלֶכֶת עַל מַלְכֵי הָאָרֶץ
veha'ishah asher ra'ita hi ha'ir haggedolah hammolechet al malchei ha'aretz
And the woman whom thou sawest is the great city, which reigneth over the kings of the earth.

יח

אַחֲרֵי כֵן רָאִיתִי מַלְאָךְ אַחֵר יוֹרֵד מִן הַשָּׁמַיִם
acharei chen ra'iti mal'ach acher yored min hashamayim
After these things I saw another angel coming down out of heaven,

רַבָּה הָיְתָה סַמְכוּתוֹ וְהָאָרֶץ הֵאִירָה מִכְּבוֹדוֹ
rabbah hayetah samchuto veha'aretz he'irah mikkvodo
having great authority; and the earth was lightened with his glory.

הוּא קָרָא בְּקוֹל חָזָק וְאָמַר
hu kara bekol chazak ve'amar
And he cried with a mighty voice, saying,

נָפְלָה נָפְלָה בָּבֶל הַגְּדוֹלָה וְהָיְתָה לִמְעוֹן שֵׁדִים
nafelah nafelah bavel haggedolah vehayetah lim'on shedim
Fallen, fallen is Babylon the great, and is become a habitation of demons,

וּלְבֵית כֶּלֶא לְכָל רוּחַ טְמֵאָה וּבֵית כֶּלֶא לְכָל עוֹף טָמֵא וּמָאוּס
uleveit kelei lechol ruach teme'ah uveit kelei lechol of tamei uma'us
and a hold of every unclean spirit, and a hold of every unclean and hateful bird.

הַהִתְגַּלּוּת

וְיוֹשְׁבֵי הָאָרֶץ אֲשֶׁר שְׁמָם לֹא נִכְתַּב בְּסֵפֶר הַחַיִּים
veyoshevei ha'aretz asher shmam lo nichtav besefer hachayim
And they that dwell on the earth shall wonder, they whose name hath not been written in the book of life

מֵעֵת הִוָּסֵד תֵּבֵל יִשְׁתּוֹמְמוּ כִּרְאוֹתָם אֶת הַחַיָּה שֶׁהָיְתָה וְאֵינֶנָּה וַעֲתִידָה לָבוֹא
me'et hivvased tevel yishtomemu kir'otam et hachayah shehayetah ve'einennah va'atidah lavo
from the foundation of the world, when they behold the beast, how that he was, and is not, and shall come.

כָּאן הַתְּבוּנָה שֶׁיֵּשׁ עִמָּהּ חָכְמָה! שִׁבְעַת הָרָאשִׁים הֵם שִׁבְעָה הָרִים אֲשֶׁר הָאִשָּׁה יוֹשֶׁבֶת עֲלֵיהֶם
kan hattevunah sheyesh immah chochmah! shiv'at harashim hem shiv'ah harim asher ha'ishah yoshevet aleihem
Here is the mind that hath wisdom. The seven heads are seven mountains, on which the woman sitteth:

גַּם שִׁבְעָה מְלָכִים הֵם: הַחֲמִשָּׁה נָפְלוּ; הָאֶחָד יֶשְׁנוֹ;
gam shiv'ah melachim hem: hachamishah nafelu; ha'echad yeshno
and they are seven kings; the five are fallen, the one is,

הָאַחֵר עוֹד לֹא בָא, וְכַאֲשֶׁר יָבוֹא הוּא צָרִיךְ לְהִשָּׁאֵר זְמַן מְעַט
ha'acher od lo ba, vecha'asher yavo hu tzarich lehisha'er zman me'at
the other is not yet come; and when he cometh, he must continue a little while.

הַחַיָּה אֲשֶׁר הָיְתָה וְאֵינֶנָּה הוּא הַשְּׁמִינִי; מִן הַשִּׁבְעָה הוּא וְלָאֲבַדּוֹן יֵלֵךְ
hachayah asher hayetah ve'einennah hu hashmini; min hashiv'ah hu vela'avaddon yelech
And the beast that was, and is not, is himself also an eighth, and is of the seven; and he goeth into perdition.

עֶשֶׂר הַקְּרָנַיִם אֲשֶׁר רָאִיתָ הֵם עֲשָׂרָה מְלָכִים אֲשֶׁר עֲדַיִן לֹא קִבְּלוּ מַלְכוּת
eser hakkarnayim asher ra'ita hem asarah melachim asher adayin lo kibbelu malchut
And the ten horns that thou sawest are ten kings, who have received no kingdom as yet;

אַךְ יְקַבְּלוּ סַמְכוּת כִּמְלָכִים לְשָׁעָה אַחַת יַחַד עִם הַחַיָּה
ach yekabbelu samchut kimlachim lesha'ah achat yachad im hachayah
but they receive authority as kings, with the beast, for one hour.

הַלָּלוּ כַּוָּנָה אַחַת לָהֶם וְיִתְּנוּ אֶת כֹּחָם וְסַמְכוּתָם לַחַיָּה
hallalu kavvanah achat lahem veyittenu et kocham vesamchutam lachayah
These have one mind, and they give their power and authority unto the beast.

הֵם יִלָּחֲמוּ בַּשֶּׂה וְהַשֶּׂה יְנַצֵּחַ אוֹתָם מִפְּנֵי שֶׁהוּא אֲדוֹן הָאֲדוֹנִים וּמֶלֶךְ הַמְּלָכִים
hem yillachamu basseh vehasseh yenatzeach otam mippenei shehu adon ha'adonim umelech hammelachim
These shall war against the Lamb, and the Lamb shall overcome them, for he is Lord of lords, and King of kings;

וְאִתּוֹ גַּם הַקְּרוּאִים וְנִבְחָרִים וְנֶאֱמָנִים
ve'itto gam hakkeru'im venivcharim vene'emanim
and they also shall overcome that are with him, called and chosen and faithful.

עוֹד אָמַר אֵלַי: הַמַּיִם אֲשֶׁר רָאִיתָ, אֲשֶׁר שָׁם הַזּוֹנָה יוֹשֶׁבֶת
od amar elai. hammayim asher ra'ita, asher sham hazzonah yoshevet
And he saith unto me, The waters which thou sawest, where the harlot sitteth,

הַהִתְגַּלּוּת

וְרָאִיתִי אִשָּׁה יוֹשֶׁבֶת עַל חַיָּה אֲדֻמָּה כְּשָׁנִי
vera'iti ishah yoshevet al chayah adummah keshani
and I saw a woman sitting upon a scarlet-colored beast,

וְהַחַיָּה מְלֵאָה שְׁמוֹת גִּדּוּפִים וּבַעֲלַת שִׁבְעָה רָאשִׁים וְעֶשֶׂר קַרְנַיִם
vehachayah mele'ah shmot giddufim uva'alat shiv'ah rashim ve'eser karnayim
full of names of blasphemy, having seven heads and ten horns.

הָאִשָּׁה הָיְתָה לְבוּשָׁה אַרְגָּמָן וְשָׁנִי וּמְקֻשֶּׁטֶת בְּזָהָב וְאֶבֶן יְקָרָה וּפְנִינִים
ha'ishah hayetah levushah argaman veshani umekushetet bezahav ve'even yekarah ufeninim
And the woman was arrayed in purple and scarlet, and decked with gold and precious stone and pearls,

בְּיָדָהּ כּוֹס זָהָב מְלֵאָה תּוֹעֵבוֹת וְטֻמְאוֹת תַּזְנוּתָהּ
beyadah kos zahav mele'ah to'evot vetum'ot taznutah
having in her hand a golden cup full of abominations, even the unclean things of her fornication,

וְעַל מִצְחָהּ כָּתוּב שֵׁם
ve'al mitzchah katuv shem
and upon her forehead a name written,

סוֹד: בָּבֶל הַגְּדוֹלָה, אֵם לְזוֹנוֹת וּלְתוֹעֲבוֹת הָאָרֶץ
sod. bavel haggedolah, em lezonot uleto'avot ha'aretz
"mystery, babylon the great, the mother of the harlots and of the abominations of the earth."

רָאִיתִי אֶת הָאִשָּׁה שִׁכּוֹרָה מִדַּם הַקְּדוֹשִׁים וּמִדַּם עֵדֵי יֵשׁוּעַ
ra'iti et ha'ishah shikkorah middam hakkedoshim umiddam edei yeshua
And I saw the woman drunken with the blood of the saints, and with the blood of the martyrs of Jesus.

כִּרְאוֹתִי אוֹתָהּ הִשְׁתּוֹמַמְתִּי שַׁמָּה גְדוֹלָה
kir'oti otah hishtomamti shammah gedolah
And when I saw her, I wondered with a great wonder.

שָׁאַל אוֹתִי הַמַּלְאָךְ: מַדּוּעַ הִשְׁתּוֹמַמְתָּ
sha'al oti hammal'ach: maddua hishtomamta
And the angel said unto me, Wherefore didst thou wonder?

אֲנִי אַגִּיד לְךָ אֶת סוֹד הָאִשָּׁה וְהַחַיָּה הַנּוֹשֵׂאת אוֹתָהּ
ani aggid lecha et sod ha'ishah vehachayah hannoset otah
I will tell thee the mystery of the woman, and of the beast that carrieth her,

אֲשֶׁר לָהּ שִׁבְעַת הָרָאשִׁים וְעֶשֶׂר הַקַּרְנַיִם
asher lah shiv'at harashim ve'eser hakkarnayim
which hath the seven heads and the ten horns.

הַחַיָּה אֲשֶׁר רָאִיתָ - הָיְתָה וְאֵינֶנָּה, וְהִיא עֲתִידָה לַעֲלוֹת מִן הַתְּהוֹם וְלָלֶכֶת לָאֲבַדּוֹן
hachayah asher ra'ita - hayetah ve'einennah, vehi atidah la'alot min hattehom velalechet la'avaddon
The beast that thou sawest was, and is not; and is about to come up out of the abyss, and to go into perdition.

הַהִתְגַּלּוּת

הָעִיר הַגְּדוֹלָה נֶחְלְקָה לִשְׁלוֹשָׁה חֲלָקִים וְעָרֵי הַגּוֹיִם נָפְלוּ
ha'ir haggedolah nechlekah lishloshah chalakim ve'arei haggoyim nafelu
And the great city was divided into three parts, and the cities of the nations fell:

וְזִכְרוֹן בָּבֶל הַגְּדוֹלָה עָלָה לִפְנֵי הָאֱלֹהִים
vezichron bavel haggedolah alah lifnei ha'elohim
and Babylon the great was remembered in the sight of God,

לָתֵת לָהּ אֶת כּוֹס יֵין חֲרוֹן אַפּוֹ
latet lah et kos yein charon appo
to give unto her the cup of the wine of the fierceness of his wrath.

כָּל אִי נָסוֹג וְהָרִים לֹא נִמְצָאוּ
kol i nasog veharim lo nimtze'u
And every island fled away, and the mountains were not found.

בָּרָד גָּדוֹל וּמִשְׁקָלוֹ כְּאַרְבָּעִים קִילוֹגְרַם יָרַד מִן הַשָּׁמַיִם עַל בְּנֵי אָדָם
barad gadol umishkalo ke'arba'im kilogeram yarad min hashamayim al benei adam
And great hail, every stone about the weight of a talent, cometh down out of heaven upon men:

וּבְנֵי אָדָם גִּדְּפוּ אֶת אֱלֹהִים בִּגְלַל מַכַּת הַבָּרָד, כִּי גְּדוֹלָה מְאֹד מַכָּתוֹ
uvenei adam gidfu et elohim biglal makkat habbarad, ki gedolah me'od makkato
and men blasphemed God because of the plague of the hail; for the plague thereof is exceeding great.

יז

אֶחָד מִשִּׁבְעַת הַמַּלְאָכִים נוֹשְׂאֵי שֶׁבַע הַקְּעָרוֹת בָּא וְדִבֶּר אִתִּי
echad mishiv'at hammal'achim nose'ei sheva hakke'arot ba vedibber itti
And there came one of the seven angels that had the seven bowls, and spake with me,

בּוֹא!, הוּא אָמַר, אַרְאֶה לְךָ אֶת מִשְׁפַּט הַזּוֹנָה הַגְּדוֹלָה הַיּוֹשֶׁבֶת עַל מַיִם רַבִּים
bo!, hu amar, ar'eh lecha et mishpat hazzonah haggedolah hayoshevet al mayim rabbim
saying, Come hither, I will show thee the judgment of the great harlot that sitteth upon many waters;

אֲשֶׁר מַלְכֵי הָאָרֶץ זָנוּ עִמָּהּ
asher malchei ha'aretz zanu immah
with whom the kings of the earth committed fornication,

וְשׁוֹכְנֵי הָאָרֶץ הִשְׁתַּכְּרוּ מִיֵּין תַּזְנוּתָהּ
veshochenei ha'aretz hishtakkru miyein taznutah
and they that dwell in the earth were made drunken with the wine of her fornication.

הוּא נְשָׂאַנִי לַמִּדְבָּר, בָּרוּחַ
hu nesa'ani lemidbar, baruach
And he carried me away in the Spirit into a wilderness:

הַהִתְגַּלּוּת

רָאִיתִי מִפִּי הַתַּנִּין
ra'iti mippi hattannin
And I saw coming out of the mouth of the dragon,

וּמִפִּי הַחַיָּה וּמִפִּי נְבִיא הַשֶּׁקֶר שָׁלֹשׁ רוּחוֹת טְמֵאוֹת דּוֹמוֹת לִצְפַרְדְּעִים
umippi hachayah umippi nevi hasheker shalosh ruchot tme'ot domot litzfarde'im
and out of the mouth of the beast, and out of the mouth of the false prophet, three unclean spirits, as it were frogs:

כִּי הֵן רוּחוֹת שֶׁל שֵׁדִים עוֹשֵׂי אוֹתוֹת - וְהֵן יוֹצְאוֹת אֶל מַלְכֵי הָאָרֶץ כֻּלָּהּ
ki hen ruchot shel shedim osei otot - vehen yotze'ot el malchei ha'aretz kullah
for they are spirits of demons, working signs; which go forth unto the kings of the whole world,

לֶאֱסֹף אוֹתָם לְמִלְחֶמֶת הַיּוֹם הַגָּדוֹל אֲשֶׁר לֵאלֹהֵי צְבָאוֹת
le'esof otam lemilchemet hayom haggadol asher lelohei tzeva'ot
to gather them together unto the war of the great day of God, the Almighty.

הִנְנִי בָּא כְּגַנָּב
hineni ba kegannav
(Behold, I come as a thief.

אַשְׁרֵי הַשּׁוֹקֵד וְשׁוֹמֵר אֶת בְּגָדָיו, פֶּן יֵלֵךְ עָרוֹם וְיִרְאוּ אֶת עֶרְוָתוֹ
ashrei hashoked veshomer et begadav, pen yelech arom veyir'u et ervato
Blessed is he that watcheth, and keepeth his garments, lest he walk naked, and they see his shame.)

וְהוּא אָסַף אוֹתָם אֶל הַמָּקוֹם הַנִּקְרָא בְּעִבְרִית הַר מְגִדּוֹן
vehu asaf otam el hammakom hannikra be'ivrit har megiddon
And they gathered them together into the place which is called in Hebrew Har-Magedon.

הַשְּׁבִיעִי שָׁפַךְ אֶת קַעֲרָתוֹ אֶל הָאֲוִיר
hashevi'i shafach et ka'arato el ha'avir
And the seventh poured out his bowl upon the air;

וְקוֹל גָּדוֹל יָצָא מִן הַהֵיכָל מֵעִם הַכִּסֵּא - אוֹמֵר: הָיֹה נִהְיְתָה
vekol gadol yatza min haheichal me'im hakkissei - omer: hayoh nihyetah
and there came forth a great voice out of the temple, from the throne, saying, It is done:

בְּרָקִים וְקוֹלוֹת וּרְעָמִים הִתְחוֹלְלוּ
berakim vekolot ure'amim hitcholelu
and there were lightnings, and voices, and thunders;

וּרְעִידַת־אֲדָמָה גְּדוֹלָה אֲשֶׁר לֹא הָיְתָה כָּמוֹהָ מֵאָז הֱיוֹת אָדָם עַל הָאָרֶץ
ure'idat-'adamah gedolah asher lo hayetah kamoha me'az heyot adam al ha'aretz
and there was a great earthquake, such as was not since there were men upon the earth,

רְעִידַת־אֲדָמָה גְּדוֹלָה כָּל כָּךְ
re'idat-'adamah gdolah kol kach
so great an earthquake, so mighty.

ההתגלות

צַדִּיק אַתָּה הַהֹוֶה וְהָיָה, הַקָּדוֹשׁ - שֶׁכָּךְ שָׁפַטְתָּ
tzaddik attah hahoveh vehayah, hakkadosh - shekkach shafatta
Righteous art thou, who art and who wast, thou Holy One, because thou didst thus judge:

כִּי דַם קְדוֹשִׁים וּנְבִיאִים שָׁפְכוּ, וְדָם נָתַתָּ לָהֶם לִשְׁתּוֹת; רְאוּיִים הֵם
ki dam kedoshim unevi'im shafchu, vedam natata lahem lishtot; re'uyim hem
for they poured out the blood of saints and prophets, and blood hast thou given them to drink: they are worthy.

וְשָׁמַעְתִּי אֶת הַמִּזְבֵּחַ אוֹמֵר: כֵּן, יהוה אֱלֹהֵי צְבָאוֹת, אֱמֶת וְצֶדֶק מִשְׁפָּטֶיךָ
veshama'ti et hammizbeach omer: ken, hashem elohei tzeva'ot, emet vetzedek mishpateicha
And I heard the altar saying, Yea, O Lord God, the Almighty, true and righteous are thy judgments.

שָׁפַךְ הָרְבִיעִי אֶת קַעֲרָתוֹ עַל הַשֶּׁמֶשׁ וְנִתַּן לוֹ לִצְרֹב אֶת הָאֲנָשִׁים בָּאֵשׁ
shafach harevi'i et ka'arato al hashemesh venittan lo litzrov et ha'anashim ba'esh
And the fourth poured out his bowl upon the sun; and it was given unto it to scorch men with fire.

נִצְרְבוּ הָאֲנָשִׁים בְּחֹם גָּדוֹל
nitzrevu ha'anashim bechom gadol
And men were scorched with great heat:

וְגִדְּפוּ אֶת שֵׁם אֱלֹהִים אֲשֶׁר לוֹ הַשִּׁלְטוֹן עַל הַמַּכּוֹת הָאֵלֶּה
vegiddfu et shem elohim asher lo hashilton al hammakkot ha'elleh
and they blasphemed the name of God who hath the power over these plagues;

וְלֹא חָזְרוּ בִּתְשׁוּבָה לָתֵת לוֹ כָּבוֹד
velo chazeru bitshuvah latet lo kavod
and they repented not to give him glory.

הַחֲמִישִׁי שָׁפַךְ אֶת קַעֲרָתוֹ עַל כִּסֵּא הַחַיָּה וְחָשְׁכָה מַלְכוּתָהּ
hachamishi shafach et ka'arato al kissei hachayah vechashchah malchutah
And the fifth poured out his bowl upon the throne of the beast; and his kingdom was darkened;

הֵם נָשְׁכוּ אֶת לְשׁוֹנָם מִכְּאֵב
hem nashechu et leshonam mikke'ev
and they gnawed their tongues for pain,

וְגִדְּפוּ אֶת אֱלֹהֵי הַשָּׁמַיִם מִמַּכְאוֹבָם וּשְׁחִינָם, וְלֹא שָׁבוּ מִמַּעֲשֵׂיהֶם
vegiddfu et elohei hashamayim mimmach'ovam ushechinam, velo shavu mimma'aseihem
and they blasphemed the God of heaven because of their pains and their sores; and they repented not of their works.

הַשִּׁשִּׁי שָׁפַךְ אֶת קַעֲרָתוֹ עַל הַנָּהָר הַגָּדוֹל, נְהַר פְּרָת
hashishi shafach et ka'arato al hannahar haggadol, nehar perat
And the sixth poured out his bowl upon the great river, the river Euphrates;

וּמֵימָיו יָבְשׁוּ כְּדֵי לְהָכִין אֶת הַדֶּרֶךְ שֶׁל הַמְּלָכִים מִמִּזְרַח שֶׁמֶשׁ
umeimav yavshu kedei lehachin et hadderech shel hammelachim mimmizrach shemesh
and the water thereof was dried up, that the way might be made ready for the kings that come from the sunrising.

הַהִתְגַּלּוּת

וְהַהֵיכָל נִתְמַלֵּא עָשָׁן מִכְּבוֹד אֱלֹהִים וְעֻזּוֹ

vehaheichal nitmallei ashan mikkevod elohim ve'uzzo
And the temple was filled with smoke from the glory of God, and from his power;

וְלֹא יָכֹל אִישׁ לְהִכָּנֵס אֶל הַהֵיכָל עַד אֲשֶׁר יִגָּמְרוּ שֶׁבַע הַמַּכּוֹת שֶׁל שִׁבְעַת הַמַּלְאָכִים

velo yachol ish lehikkanes el haheichal ad asher yiggameru sheva hammakkot shel shiv'at hammal'achim
and none was able to enter into the temple, till the seven plagues of the seven angels should be finished.

טז

שָׁמַעְתִּי קוֹל גָּדוֹל מִן הַהֵיכָל אוֹמֵר לְשִׁבְעַת הַמַּלְאָכִים

shama'ti kol gadol min haheichal omer leshiv'at hammal'achim
And I heard a great voice out of the temple, saying to the seven angels,

לְכוּ וְשִׁפְכוּ עַל הָאָרֶץ אֶת שֶׁבַע קַעֲרוֹת זַעַם אֱלֹהִים

lechu veshifchu al ha'aretz et sheva ka'arot za'am elohim
Go ye, and pour out the seven bowls of the wrath of God into the earth.

הָלַךְ הָרִאשׁוֹן וְשָׁפַךְ אֶת קַעֲרָתוֹ עַל הָאָרֶץ

halach harishon veshafach et ka'arato al ha'aretz
And the first went, and poured out his bowl into the earth;

וְנִתְהַוָּה שְׁחִין רַע וּמַכְאִיב בָּאֲנָשִׁים

venit'havah shchin ra umach'iv ba'anashim
and it became a noisome and grievous sore upon the men

הַנּוֹשְׂאִים אֶת תָּו הַחַיָּה וּמִשְׁתַּחֲוִים לְצַלְמָהּ

hannose'im et tav hachayah umishtachavim letzalmah
that had the mark of the beast, and that worshipped his image.

שָׁפַךְ הַשֵּׁנִי אֶת קַעֲרָתוֹ עַל הַיָּם וְהַיָּם נֶהְפַּךְ לְדָם כְּדָמוֹ שֶׁל מֵת

shafach hasheni et ka'arato al hayam vehayam nehpach ledam kedamo shel met
And the second poured out his bowl into the sea; and it became blood as of a dead man;

וְכָל נֶפֶשׁ חַיָּה אֲשֶׁר בַּיָּם מֵתָה

vechol nefesh chayah asher bayam metah
and every living soul died, even the things that were in the sea.

שָׁפַךְ הַשְּׁלִישִׁי אֶת קַעֲרָתוֹ בַּנְּהָרוֹת וּבְמַעְיְנוֹת הַמַּיִם, וְנִהְיוּ לְדָם

shafach hashelishi et ka'arato banneharot uvema'aynot hammayim, venihyu ledam
And the third poured out his bowl into the rivers and the fountains of the waters; and it became blood.

שָׁמַעְתִּי אֶת מַלְאַךְ הַמַּיִם אוֹמֵר

shama'ti et mal'ach hammayim omer
And I heard the angel of the waters saying,

הַהִתְגַּלּוּת

רָאִיתִי כְּמוֹ יָם זְכוּכִית מְעֹרָב בָּאֵשׁ
ra'iti kemo yam zechuchit me'orav be'esh
And I saw as it were a sea of glass mingled with fire;

וְאֶת הַמִּתְגַּבְּרִים עַל הַחַיָּה וְעַל צַלְמָהּ
ve'et hammitgabberim al hachayah ve'al tzalmah
and them that come off victorious from the beast, and from his image,

וְעַל מִסְפַּר שְׁמָהּ עוֹמְדִים עַל יָם הַזְּכוּכִית; כִּנּוֹרוֹת אֱלֹהִים בְּיָדָם
ve'al mispar shmah omedim al yam hazzechuchit; kinnorot elohim beyadam
and from the number of his name, standing by the sea of glass, having harps of God.

וְהֵם שָׁרִים אֶת שִׁירַת מֹשֶׁה עֶבֶד אֱלֹהִים וְשִׁירַת הַשֶּׂה לֵאמֹר
vehem sharim et shirat mosheh eved elohim veshirat hasseh lemor
And they sing the song of Moses the servant of God, and the song of the Lamb, saying,

גְּדוֹלִים וְנִפְלָאִים מַעֲשֶׂיךָ, יהוה אֱלֹהֵי צְבָאוֹת; צֶדֶק וֶאֱמֶת דְּרָכֶיךָ, מֶלֶךְ הַגּוֹיִם
gdolim venifla'im ma'aseicha, hashem elohei tzeva'ot; tzedek ve'emet deracheicha, melech haggoyim
Great and marvellous are thy works, O Lord God, the Almighty; righteous and true are thy ways, thou King of the ages.

מִי לֹא יִירָאֲךָ, יהוה, וְלֹא יִתֵּן כָּבוֹד לְשִׁמְךָ? כִּי אַתָּה לְבַדְּךָ קָדוֹשׁ
mi lo yira'acha, hashem, velo yitten kavod leshimcha? ki attah levaddcha kadosh
Who shall not fear, O Lord, and glorify thy name? for thou only art holy;

הֵן כָּל הַגּוֹיִם יָבוֹאוּ וְיִשְׁתַּחֲווּ לְפָנֶיךָ; כִּי נִגְלוּ מִשְׁפְּטֵי צִדְקֶךָ
hen kol haggoyim yavo'u veyishtachavu lefaneicha; ki niglu mishpetei tzidkecha
for all the nations shall come and worship before thee; for thy righteous acts have been made manifest.

אַחֲרֵי כֵן רָאִיתִי כִּי נִפְתַּח הֵיכַל מִשְׁכַּן הָעֵדוּת בַּשָּׁמַיִם
acharei chen ra'iti ki niftach heichal mishkan ha'edut bashamayim
And after these things I saw, and the temple of the tabernacle of the testimony in heaven was opened:

וּמִן הַהֵיכָל יָצְאוּ שִׁבְעַת הַמַּלְאָכִים נוֹשְׂאֵי שֶׁבַע הַמַּכּוֹת
umin haheichal yatze'u shiv'at hammal'achim nose'ei sheva hammakkot
and there came out from the temple the seven angels that had the seven plagues,

לְבוּשִׁים בַּד טָהוֹר וְצַח וַחֲגוּרִים חֲגוֹרוֹת זָהָב עַל חֲזוֹתֵיהֶם
levushim bad tahor vetzach vachagurim chagorot zahav al chazoteihem
arrayed with precious stone, pure and bright, and girt about their breasts with golden girdles.

אַחַת מֵאַרְבַּע הַחַיּוֹת נָתְנָה לְשִׁבְעַת הַמַּלְאָכִים שֶׁבַע קְעָרוֹת זָהָב מְלֵאוֹת זַעַם הָאֱלֹהִים
achat me'arba hachayot natnah leshiv'at hammal'achim sheva ka'arot zahav mele'ot za'am ha'elohim
And one of the four living creatures gave unto the seven angels seven golden bowls full of the wrath of God,

הַחַי לְעוֹלְמֵי עוֹלָמִים
hachai le'olemei olamim
who liveth for ever and ever.

הַהִתְגַּלּוּת

הֵטִיל הַיּוֹשֵׁב עַל הֶעָנָן אֶת מַגָּלוֹ עַל הָאָרֶץ וְהָאָרֶץ נִקְצְרָה
hetil hayoshev al he'anan et maggalo al ha'aretz veha'aretz niktzerah
And he that sat on the cloud cast his sickle upon the earth; and the earth was reaped.

וּמַלְאָךְ אַחֵר יָצָא מִן הַהֵיכָל אֲשֶׁר בַּשָּׁמַיִם וְגַם לוֹ מַגָּל חַד
umal'ach acher yatza min haheichal asher bashamayim vegam lo maggal chad
And another angel came out from the temple which is in heaven, he also having a sharp sickle.

מַלְאָךְ אַחֵר, אֲשֶׁר לוֹ הַשִּׁלְטוֹן עַל הָאֵשׁ, יָצָא מִן הַמִּזְבֵּחַ
mal'ach acher, asher lo hashilton al ha'esh yatza min hammizbeach
And another angel came out from the altar, he that hath power over fire;

וּבְקוֹל גָּדוֹל קָרָא אֶל הָאוֹחֵז אֶת הַמַּגָּל הַחַד וְאָמַר
uvekol gadol kara el ha'ochez et hammaggal hachad ve'amar
and he called with a great voice to him that had the sharp sickle, saying,

שְׁלַח אֶת מַגָּלְךָ הַחַד וּבְצֹר אֶת אֶשְׁכְּלוֹת גֶּפֶן הָאָרֶץ, כִּי בָשְׁלוּ עֲנָבֶיהָ
shelach et maggalcha hachad uvetzor et eshkelot gefen ha'aretz, ki bashelu anaveiha
Send forth thy sharp sickle, and gather the clusters of the vine of the earth; for her grapes are fully ripe.

הֵטִיל הַמַּלְאָךְ אֶת מַגָּלוֹ אֶל הָאָרֶץ, בָּצַר אֶת גֶּפֶן הָאָרֶץ
hetil hammal'ach et maggalo el ha'aretz, batzar et gefen ha'aretz
And the angel cast his sickle into the earth, and gathered the vintage of the earth,

וְהִשְׁלִיךְ אֶל הַגַּת הַגְּדוֹלָה שֶׁל חֲרוֹן הָאֱלֹהִים
vehishlich el haggat haggedolah shel charon ha'elohim
and cast it into the winepress, the great winepress, of the wrath of God.

הַגַּת נִדְרְכָה מִחוּץ לָעִיר וְהַדָּם יָצָא מִן הַגַּת
haggat nidrechah michutz la'ir vehaddam yatza min haggat
And the winepress was trodden without the city, and there came out blood from the winepress,

עַד רִסְנֵי הַסּוּסִים לְמֶרְחָק שֶׁל שְׁלֹשׁ מֵאוֹת קִילוֹמֶטֶר
ad risnei hassusim lemerchak shel shelosh me'ot kilometer
even unto the bridles of the horses, as far as a thousand and six hundred furlongs.

טו

רָאִיתִי אוֹת אַחֵר בַּשָּׁמַיִם, גָּדוֹל וּמַפְלִיא
ra'iti ot acher bashamayim, gadol umafli
And I saw another sign in heaven, great and marvellous,

שִׁבְעָה מַלְאָכִים נוֹשְׂאִים אֶת שֶׁבַע הַמַּכּוֹת הָאַחֲרוֹנוֹת, כִּי בָּהֶן נִשְׁלַם זַעַם אֱלֹהִים
shiv'ah mal'achim nos'im et sheva hammakkot ha'acharonot, ki bahen nishlam za'am elohim
seven angels having seven plagues, which are the last, for in them is finished the wrath of God.

הַהִתְגַּלּוּת

כָּל הַמִּשְׁתַּחֲוֶה לַחַיָּה וּלְצַלְמָהּ וּמְקַבֵּל תָּו עַל מִצְחוֹ אוֹ עַל יָדוֹ
kol hammishtachaveh lachayah uletzalmah umekabbel tav al mitzcho o al yado
If any man worshippeth the beast and his image, and receiveth a mark on his forehead, or upon his hand,

גַּם הוּא יִשְׁתֶּה מִיֵּין חֲרוֹן אֱלֹהִים הַמָּזוּג בְּכוֹס זַעְמוֹ וְאֵינֶנּוּ מָהוּל
gam hu yishteh miyein charon elohim hammazug bechos za'mo ve'einennu mahul
he also shall drink of the wine of the wrath of God, which is prepared unmixed in the cup of his anger;

וִיעֻנֶּה בָּאֵשׁ וְגָפְרִית לִפְנֵי הַמַּלְאָכִים הַקְּדוֹשִׁים וְלִפְנֵי הַשֶּׂה
vi'unneh be'esh vegofrit lifnei hammal'achim hakkedoshim velifnei hasseh
and he shall be tormented with fire and brimstone in the presence of the holy angels, and in the presence of the Lamb:

עֲשַׁן עִנּוּיָם יַעֲלֶה לְעוֹלְמֵי עוֹלָמִים וְלֹא תִהְיֶה לָהֶם מְנוּחָה יוֹמָם וָלַיְלָה
ashan innuyam ya'aleh le'olemei olamim velo tihyeh lahem menuchah yomam valaylah
and the smoke of their torment goeth up for ever and ever; and they have no rest day and night,

לַמִּשְׁתַּחֲוִים לַחַיָּה וּלְצַלְמָהּ וּלְמִי שֶׁמְּקַבֵּל אֶת תָּו שְׁמָהּ
lammishtachavim lachayah uletzalmah ulemi shemmekabbel et tav shemah
they that worship the beast and his image, and whoso receiveth the mark of his name.

בָּזֶה סַבְלָנוּתָם שֶׁל הַקְּדוֹשִׁים הַשּׁוֹמְרִים אֶת מִצְווֹת אֱלֹהִים וֶאֱמוּנַת יֵשׁוּעַ
bazeh savlanutam shel hakkedoshim hashomerim et mitzvot elohim ve'emunat yeshua
Here is the patience of the saints, they that keep the commandments of God, and the faith of Jesus.

שָׁמַעְתִּי קוֹל מִן הַשָּׁמַיִם אוֹמֵר: כְּתֹב: אַשְׁרֵי הַמֵּתִים אֲשֶׁר מֵתִים בָּאָדוֹן מֵעַתָּה
shama'ti kol min hashamayim omer: ketov: ashrei hammetim asher metim ba'adon me'attah
And I heard a voice from heaven saying, Write, Blessed are the dead who die in the Lord from henceforth:

כֵּן!, אוֹמֶרֶת הָרוּחַ, שֶׁיָּנוּחוּ מֵעֲמָלָם, כִּי מַעֲשֵׂיהֶם הוֹלְכִים אַחֲרֵיהֶם
ken!, omeret haruach, sheyanuchu me'amalam, ki ma'aseihem holechim achareihem
yea, saith the Spirit, that they may rest from their labors; for their works follow with them.

רָאִיתִי וְהִנֵּה עָנָן לָבָן וְעַל הֶעָנָן יוֹשֵׁב כִּדְמוּת בֶּן אָדָם;
ra'iti vehinneh anan lavan ve'al he'anan yoshev kidmut ben adam
And I saw, and behold, a white cloud; and on the cloud I saw one sitting like unto a son of man,

עֲטֶרֶת זָהָב עַל רֹאשׁוֹ וּמַגָּל חַד בְּיָדוֹ
ateret zahav al rosho umaggal chad beyado
having on his head a golden crown, and in his hand a sharp sickle.

וּמַלְאָךְ אַחֵר יָצָא מִן הַהֵיכָל, קוֹרֵא בְּקוֹל גָּדוֹל אֶל הַיּוֹשֵׁב עַל הֶעָנָן
umal'ach acher yatza min haheichal, korei bekol gadol el hayoshev al he'anan
And another angel came out from the temple, crying with a great voice to him that sat on the cloud,

שְׁלַח אֶת מַגָּלְךָ וּקְצֹר, כִּי בָּאָה הַשָּׁעָה לִקְצֹר, כִּי יָבֵשׁ קְצִיר הָאָרֶץ
shlach et maggalecha uketzor, ki ba'ah hasha'ah liktzor, ki yavesh ketzir ha'aretz
Send forth thy sickle, and reap: for the hour to reap is come; for the harvest of the earth is ripe.

הַהִתְגַּלּוּת

אֵלֶּה הֵם אֲשֶׁר לֹא נִטְמְאוּ בְנָשִׁים, כִּי בְתוּלִים הֵם
elleh hem asher lo nitme'u benashim, ki betulim hem
These are they that were not defiled with women; for they are virgins.

אֵלֶּה הֵם הַהוֹלְכִים אַחֲרֵי הַשֶּׂה לְכָל אֲשֶׁר יֵלֵךְ
elleh hem haholechim acharei hasseh lechol asher yelech
These are they that follow the Lamb whithersoever he goeth.

אֵלֶּה נִפְדּוּ מִבְּנֵי אָדָם בִּכּוּרִים לֵאלֹהִים וְלַשֶּׂה
elleh nifdu mibbenei adam bikkurim lelohim velasseh
These were purchased from among men, to be the firstfruits unto God and unto the Lamb.

מִרְמָה לֹא נִמְצְאָה בְּפִיהֶם, נְקִיִּים הֵם מִדֹּפִי
mirmah lo nimtze'ah befihem, nekiyim hem middofi
And in their mouth was found no lie: they are without blemish.

רָאִיתִי מַלְאָךְ אַחֵר מְעוֹפֵף בְּאֶמְצַע הַשָּׁמַיִם
ra'iti mal'ach acher me'ofef be'emtza hashamayim
And I saw another angel flying in mid heaven,

אֲשֶׁר לוֹ בְּשׂוֹרַת עוֹלָם לְבַשֵּׂר לְיוֹשְׁבֵי הָאָרֶץ
asher lo besorat olam levasser leyoshevei ha'aretz
having eternal good tidings to proclaim unto them that dwell on the earth,

וּלְכָל אֻמָּה וְשֵׁבֶט וְלָשׁוֹן וְעַם
ulechol ummah veshevet velashon ve'am
and unto every nation and tribe and tongue and people;

וְהוּא קוֹרֵא בְּקוֹל גָּדוֹל: יְראוּ אֶת אֱלֹהִים וּתְנוּ לוֹ כָבוֹד, כִּי בָּאָה עֵת מִשְׁפָּטוֹ
vehu korei bekol gadol: yir'u et elohim utenu lo kavod, ki ba'ah et mishpato
and he saith with a great voice, Fear God, and give him glory; for the hour of his judgment is come:

הִשְׁתַּחֲווּ לְעוֹשֵׂה הַשָּׁמַיִם וְהָאָרֶץ וְהַיָּם וּמַעְיְנוֹת הַמָּיִם
hishtachavu le'oseh hashamayim veha'aretz vehayam uma'aynot hammayim
and worship him that made the heaven and the earth and sea and fountains of waters.

וּמַלְאָךְ אַחֵר, שֵׁנִי, בָּא אַחֲרָיו וְאָמַר
umal'ach acher, sheni, ba acharav ve'amar
And another, a second angel, followed, saying,

נָפְלָה נָפְלָה בָּבֶל הַגְּדוֹלָה אֲשֶׁר הִשְׁקְתָה אֶת כָּל הַגּוֹיִם מִיֵּין חֲרוֹן תַּזְנוּתָהּ
nafelah nafelah bavel haggedolah asher hishketah et kol haggoyim miyein charon taznutah
Fallen, fallen is Babylon the great, that hath made all the nations to drink of the wine of the wrath of her fornication.

מַלְאָךְ אַחֵר, שְׁלִישִׁי, בָּא אַחֲרֵיהֶם וְקָרָא בְּקוֹל גָּדוֹל:
mal'ach acher, shelishi, ba achareihem vekara bekol gadol
And another angel, a third, followed them, saying with a great voice,

הַהִתְגַּלּוּת

כְּדֵי שֶׁלֹּא יוּכַל אִישׁ לִקְנוֹת אוֹ לִמְכֹּר

kedei shello yuchal ish liknot o limkor

and that no man should be able to buy or to sell,

אֶלָּא מִי שֶׁיֵּשׁ לוֹ הַתָּו, שֵׁם הַחַיָּה אוֹ מִסְפַּר שְׁמָהּ

ella mi sheyesh lo hattav, shem hachayah o mispar shemah

save he that hath the mark, even the name of the beast or the number of his name.

בָּזֹאת הַחָכְמָה. מִי שֶׁבִּינָה לוֹ, יְחַשֵּׁב נָא אֶת מִסְפַּר הַחַיָּה, כִּי מִסְפַּר אָדָם הוּא

bazot hachachemah. mi shebbinah lo, yechashev na et mispar hachayah, ki mispar adam hu

Here is wisdom. He that hath understanding, let him count the number of the beast; for it is the number of a man:

וּמִסְפָּרוֹ שֵׁשׁ מֵאוֹת וְשִׁשִּׁים וָשֵׁשׁ

umisparo shesh me'ot veshishim vashesh

and his number is Six hundred and sixty and six.

יד

רָאִיתִי וְהִנֵּה הַשֶּׂה עוֹמֵד עַל הַר צִיּוֹן וְאִתּוֹ מֵאָה וְאַרְבָּעִים וְאַרְבָּעָה אֶלֶף

ra'iti vehinneh hasseh omed al har tziyon ve'itto me'ah ve'arba'im ve'arba'ah elef

And I saw, and behold, the Lamb standing on the mount Zion, and with him a hundred and forty and four thousand,

אֲשֶׁר שְׁמוֹ וְשֵׁם אָבִיו כְּתוּבִים עַל מִצְחוֹתֵיהֶם

asher shmo veshem aviv ketuvim al mitzchoteihem

having his name, and the name of his Father, written on their foreheads.

שָׁמַעְתִּי קוֹל מִן הַשָּׁמַיִם כְּקוֹל מַיִם רַבִּים וּכְקוֹל רַעַם גָּדוֹל

shama'ti kol min hashamayim kekol mayim rabbim uchekol ra'am gadol

And I heard a voice from heaven, as the voice of many waters, and as the voice of a great thunder:

וְהַקּוֹל אֲשֶׁר שָׁמַעְתִּי הוּא כְּקוֹל מְנַגְּנֵי־נֶבֶל הַפּוֹרְטִים עַל נִבְלֵיהֶם

vehakkol asher shama'ti hu kekol menaggenei-nevel happoretim al nivleihem

and the voice which I heard was as the voice of harpers harping with their harps:

הֵם שָׁרוּ שִׁיר חָדָשׁ לִפְנֵי הַכִּסֵּא וְלִפְנֵי אַרְבַּע הַחַיּוֹת וְהַזְּקֵנִים

hem sharu shir chadash lifnei hakkissei velifnei arba hachayot vehazzekenim

and they sing as it were a new song before the throne, and before the four living creatures and the elders:

וְאֵין אִישׁ יָכוֹל לִלְמֹד אֶת הַשִּׁיר

ve'ein ish yachol lilmod et hashir

and no man could learn the song

זוּלָתִי מֵאָה וְאַרְבָּעִים וְאַרְבָּעָה אֶלֶף הַפְּדוּיִים מִן הָאָרֶץ

zulati me'ah ve'arba'im ve'arba'ah elef happeduyim min ha'aretz

save the hundred and forty and four thousand, even they that had been purchased out of the earth.

הַהִתְגַּלּוּת

הִיא עוֹשָׂה אוֹתוֹת גְּדוֹלִים
hi osah otot gedolim
And he doeth great signs,

אֲפִלּוּ עַד כְּדֵי הוֹרָדַת אֵשׁ מִן הַשָּׁמַיִם אַרְצָה לְעֵינֵי בְּנֵי אָדָם
afillu ad kedei horadat esh min hashamayim artzah le'einei benei adam
that he should even make fire to come down out of heaven upon the earth in the sight of men.

וּמַתְעָה אֶת יוֹשְׁבֵי הָאָרֶץ
umat'ah et yoshevei ha'aretz
And he deceiveth them that dwell on the earth

עַל־יְדֵי הָאוֹתוֹת אֲשֶׁר נִתַּן לָהּ לַעֲשׂוֹת לְנֹכַח הַחַיָּה
al-yedei ha'otot asher nittan lah la'asot lenochach hachayah
by reason of the signs which it was given him to do in the sight of the beast;

בְּאָמְרָהּ לְיוֹשְׁבֵי הָאָרֶץ
be'omrah leyoshevei ha'aretz
saying to them that dwell on the earth,

לַעֲשׂוֹת צֶלֶם לַחַיָּה אֲשֶׁר הֻכְּתָה מַכַּת חֶרֶב וְחָיְתָה
la'asot tzelem lachayah asher hukketah makkat cherev vechayetah
that they should make an image to the beast who hath the stroke of the sword and lived.

גַּם נִתַּן לָהּ לָתֵת רוּחַ לְצֶלֶם הַחַיָּה
gam nittan lah latet ruach letzelem hachayah
And it was given unto him to give breath to it, even to the image of the beast,

בְּאֹפֶן שֶׁצֶּלֶם הַחַיָּה גַּם יְדַבֵּר
be'ofen shetzelem hachayah gam yedabber
that the image of the beast should both speak,

וְאַף יִגְרֹם לְכָךְ שֶׁיּוּמְתוּ כָּל אֲשֶׁר אֵינָם מִשְׁתַּחֲוִים לְצֶלֶם הַחַיָּה
ve'af yigrom lechach sheyumtu kol asher einam mishtachavim letzelem hachayah
and cause that as many as should not worship the image of the beast should be killed.

וְהִיא גּוֹרֶמֶת לְכָךְ שֶׁהַכֹּל, הַקְּטַנִּים וְהַגְּדוֹלִים, הָעֲשִׁירִים וְהָעֲנִיִּים, הַחָפְשִׁיִּים וְהָעֲבָדִים
vehi goremet lechach shehakkol, hakketannim vehaggedolim, ha'ashirim veha'aniyim, hachofeshiyim veha'avadim
And he causeth all, the small and the great, and the rich and the poor, and the free and the bond,

יָשִׂימוּ לָהֶם תָּו עַל יַד יְמִינָם אוֹ עַל מִצְחָם
yasimu lahem tav al yad yeminam o al mitzcham
that there be given them a mark on their right hand, or upon their forehead;

הַהִתְגַּלּוּת

הִיא פָּתְחָה אֶת פִּיהָ בְּנֶאָצוֹת כְּלַפֵּי הָאֱלֹהִים
hi patchah et piha bin'atzot kelappei ha'elohim
And he opened his mouth for blasphemies against God,

לְנָאֵץ אֶת שְׁמוֹ וְאֶת מִשְׁכָּנוֹ, אֶת הַשּׁוֹכְנִים בַּשָּׁמַיִם
lena'etz et shemo ve'et mishkano, et hashochenim bashamayim
to blaspheme his name, and his tabernacle, even them that dwell in the heaven.

נִתַּן לָהּ לַעֲשׂוֹת מִלְחָמָה עִם הַקְּדוֹשִׁים וּלְנַצְּחָם
nittan lah la'asot milchamah im hakkedoshim ulenatzecham
And it was given unto him to make war with the saints, and to overcome them:

וְנִתַּן לָהּ שִׁלְטוֹן עַל כָּל שֵׁבֶט וְעַם וְלָשׁוֹן וְאֻמָּה
venittan lah shilton al kol shevet ve'am velashon ve'ummah
and there was given to him authority over every tribe and people and tongue and nation.

וְיִשְׁתַּחֲווּ לָהּ כָּל יוֹשְׁבֵי הָאָרֶץ
veyishtachavu lah kol yoshevei ha'aretz
And all that dwell on the earth shall worship him,

אֲשֶׁר לֹא נִכְתְּבוּ שְׁמוֹתֵיהֶם בְּסֵפֶר הַחַיִּים שֶׁל הַשֶּׂה הַטָּבוּחַ מֵהִוָּסֵד תֵּבֵל
asher lo nichtevu shemoteihem besefer hachayim shel hasseh hattavuach mehivvased tevel
every one whose name hath not been written from the foundation of the world in the book of life of the Lamb that hath been slain.

מִי שֶׁאֹזֶן לוֹ, יִשְׁמַע נָא
mi she'ozen lo, yishma na
If any man hath an ear, let him hear.

הַמְיֻעָד לַשְּׁבִי יֵלֵךְ בַּשְּׁבִי
hamyu'ad lashevi yelech bashevi
If any man is for captivity, into captivity he goeth:

וְהַמְיֻעָד לְהָרֵג בַּחֶרֶב יֵהָרֵג בַּחֶרֶב. בָּזֶה סַבְלָנוּת הַקְּדוֹשִׁים וֶאֱמוּנָתָם
vehamyu'ad lehareg bacherev yehareg bacherev. bazeh savlanut hakkdoshim ve'emunatam
if any man shall kill with the sword, with the sword must he be killed. Here is the patience and the faith of the saints.

רָאִיתִי חַיָּה אַחֶרֶת עוֹלָה מִן הָאָרֶץ. הָיוּ לָהּ שְׁתֵּי קַרְנַיִם דּוֹמוֹת לְקַרְנֵי שֶׂה וְהִיא דִּבְּרָה כְּתַנִּין
ra'iti chayah acheret olah min ha'aretz. hayu lah shetei karnayim domot lekarnei seh vehi dibberah ketannin
And I saw another beast coming up out of the earth; and he had two horns like unto a lamb, and he spake as a dragon.

אֶת סַמְכוּת הַחַיָּה הָרִאשׁוֹנָה הִיא מוֹצִיאָה אֶל הַפֹּעַל לְפָנֶיהָ
et samchut hachayah harishonah hi motzi'ah el happo'al lefaneiha
And he exerciseth all the authority of the first beast in his sight.

וּמְאַלֶּצֶת אֶת הָאָרֶץ וְיוֹשְׁבֶיהָ לְהִשְׁתַּחֲווֹת לַחַיָּה הָרִאשׁוֹנָה אֲשֶׁר מַכַּת הַמָּוֶת שֶׁלָּהּ נִרְפְּאָה
ume'alletzet et ha'aretz veyoshveiha lehishtachavot lachayah harishonah asher makkat hammavet shellah nirpe'ah
And he maketh the earth and them that dwell therein to worship the first beast, whose death-stroke was healed.

הַהִתְגַּלּוּת

הַשּׁוֹמְרִים אֶת מִצְוֺות אֱלֹהִים וְלָהֶם עֵדוּת יֵשׁוּעַ
hashomerim et mitzvot elohim velahem edut yeshua
that keep the commandments of God, and hold the testimony of Jesus:

יג

וְהוּא עָמַד עַל חוֹל הַיָּם. רָאִיתִי חַיָּה עוֹלָה מִן הַיָּם
vehu amad al chol hayam. ra'iti chayah olah min hayam
and he stood upon the sand of the sea. And I saw a beast coming up out of the sea,

עֶשֶׂר קַרְנַיִם לָהּ וְשִׁבְעָה רָאשִׁים; עַל קַרְנֶיהָ עֲשָׂרָה כְּתָרִים וְעַל רָאשֶׁיהָ שְׁמוֹת גִּדּוּפִים
eser karnayim lah veshiv'ah rashim; al karneiha asarah ketarim ve'al rasheiha shemot giddufim
having ten horns and seven heads, and on his horns ten diadems, and upon his heads names of blasphemy.

וְהַחַיָּה אֲשֶׁר רָאִיתִי הָיְתָה דּוֹמָה לְנָמֵר, רַגְלֶיהָ כְּרַגְלֵי דֹּב
vehachayah asher ra'iti hayetah domah lenamer, ragleiha keraglei dov
And the beast which I saw was like unto a leopard, and his feet were as the feet of a bear,

וּפִיהָ כְּפִי אַרְיֵה. וְהַתַּנִּין נָתַן לָהּ אֶת כֹּחוֹ וְאֶת כִּסְאוֹ וְסַמְכוּת רַבָּה
ufiha kefi aryeh. vehattannin natan lah et kocho ve'et kis'o vesamchut rabbah
and his mouth as the mouth of a lion: and the dragon gave him his power, and his throne, and great authority.

אֶחָד מֵרָאשֶׁיהָ הָיָה כְּטָבוּחַ לַמָּוֶת, אַךְ מַכַּת הַמָּוֶת אֲשֶׁר לָהּ נִרְפְּאָה
echad merasheiha hayah ketavuach lammavet, ach makkat hammavet asher lah nirpe'ah
And I saw one of his heads as though it had been smitten unto death; and his death-stroke was healed:

וְכָל הָאָרֶץ הִשְׁתּוֹמְמָה עַל הַחַיָּה
vechol ha'aretz hishtomemah al hachayah
and the whole earth wondered after the beast;

הֵם הִשְׁתַּחֲווּ לַתַּנִּין מִפְּנֵי שֶׁנָּתַן אֶת הַשִּׁלְטוֹן לַחַיָּה,
hem hishtachavu lattannin mippenei shennatan et hashilton lachayah
and they worshipped the dragon, because he gave his authority unto the beast;

וְהִשְׁתַּחֲווּ לַחַיָּה בְּאָמְרָם: מִי כָּמוֹ הַחַיָּה? וּמִי יָכוֹל לְהִלָּחֵם עִמָּהּ
vehishtachavu lachayah be'ameram: mi kemo hachayah? umi yachol lehillachem immah
and they worshipped the beast, saying, Who is like unto the beast? and who is able to war with him?

נִתַּן לָהּ פֶּה מְדַבֵּר גְּדוֹלוֹת וּנְאָצוֹת
nittan lah peh medabber gedolot une'atzot
and there was given to him a mouth speaking great things and blasphemies;

וְנִתְּנָה לָהּ סַמְכוּת לִפְעֹל אַרְבָּעִים וּשְׁנַיִם חֳדָשִׁים
venittenah lah samchut lif'ol arba'im ushenayim chodashim
and there was given to him authority to continue forty and two months.

הַהִתְגַּלּוּת

עַל זֹאת שִׂמְחוּ שָׁמַיִם וְשֹׁכְנֵיהֶם. אוֹי לָאָרֶץ וְלַיָּם
al zot simchu shamayim veshocheneihem. oy la'aretz velayam
Therefore rejoice, O heavens, and ye that dwell in them. Woe for the earth and for the sea:

כִּי יָרַד אֲלֵיכֶם הַשָּׂטָן בְּחֵמָה גְדוֹלָה, בְּיָדְעוֹ כִּי קְצָרָה עִתּוֹ
ki yarad aleichem hassatan bechemah gedolah, beyod'o ki ketzarah itto
because the devil is gone down unto you, having great wrath, knowing that he hath but a short time.

כַּאֲשֶׁר רָאָה הַתַּנִּין כִּי הֻשְׁלַךְ אַרְצָה
ka'asher ra'ah hattannin ki hushlach artzah
And when the dragon saw that he was cast down to the earth,

רָדַף אֶת הָאִשָּׁה אֲשֶׁר יָלְדָה אֶת הַזָּכָר
radaf et ha'ishah asher yaldah et hazzachar
he persecuted the woman that brought forth the man child.

אָז נִתְּנוּ לָאִשָּׁה שְׁתֵּי כַּנְפֵי הַנֶּשֶׁר הַגָּדוֹל
az nittenu la'ishah shetei kanfei hannesher haggadol
And there were given to the woman the two wings of the great eagle,

כְּדֵי לָעוּף לַמִּדְבָּר אֶל מְקוֹמָהּ
kedei la'uf lammidbar el mekomah
that she might fly into the wilderness unto her place,

אֲשֶׁר תְּכֻלְכַּל שָׁם מוֹעֵד מוֹעֲדִים וַחֲצִי מוֹעֵד מִפְּנֵי הַנָּחָשׁ
asher techulkal sham mo'ed mo'adim vachatzi mo'ed mippenei hannachash
where she is nourished for a time, and times, and half a time, from the face of the serpent.

הֵטִיל הַנָּחָשׁ מִפִּיו נְהַר מַיִם אַחֲרֵי הָאִשָּׁה
hetil hannachash mippiv nehar mayim acharei ha'ishah
And the serpent cast out of his mouth after the woman water as a river,

לְשָׁטְפָהּ בַּנָּהָר
leshotfah bannahar
that he might cause her to be carried away by the stream.

אַךְ הָאָרֶץ עָזְרָה לָאִשָּׁה
ach ha'aretz azerah la'ishah
And the earth helped the woman,

פָּתְחָה הָאָרֶץ אֶת פִּיהָ וּבָלְעָה אֶת הַנָּהָר שֶׁהֵטִיל הַתַּנִּין מִפִּיו
patechah ha'aretz et piha uvale'ah et hannahar shehetil hattannin mippiv
and the earth opened her mouth and swallowed up the river which the dragon cast out of his mouth.

קָצַף הַתַּנִּין עַל הָאִשָּׁה וְהָלַךְ לַעֲשׂוֹת מִלְחָמָה עִם שְׁאָר זַרְעָהּ
katzaf hattannin al ha'ishah vehalach la'asot milchamah im she'ar zar'ah
And the dragon waxed wroth with the woman, and went away to make war with the rest of her seed,

הַהִתְגַּלּוּת

כְּדֵי שֶׁיְכַלְכְּלוּהָ שָׁם אֶלֶף וּמָאתַיִם וְשִׁשִּׁים יוֹם
kedei sheyechalkeluha sham elef umatayim veshishim yom
that there they may nourish her a thousand two hundred and threescore days.

וּמִלְחָמָה הִתְחוֹלְלָה בַּשָּׁמַיִם
umilchamah hitcholelah bashamayim
And there was war in heaven:

מִיכָאֵל וּמַלְאָכָיו נִלְחָמִים בַּתַּנִּין וְהַתַּנִּין נִלְחָם וּמַלְאָכָיו
micha'el umal'achav nilchamim battannin vehattannin nilcham umal'achav
Michael and his angels going forth to war with the dragon; and the dragon warred and his angels;

הֵם לֹא הִתְגַּבְּרוּ וְגַם מְקוֹמָם לֹא נִמְצָא עוֹד בַּשָּׁמַיִם
hem lo hitgabbru vegam mekomam lo nimtza od bashamayim
and they prevailed not, neither was their place found any more in heaven.

אָז הֻשְׁלַךְ הַתַּנִּין הַגָּדוֹל, הַנָּחָשׁ הַקַּדְמוֹנִי
az hushlach hattannin haggadol, hannachash hakkadmoni
And the great dragon was cast down, the old serpent,

הַנִּקְרָא מַלְשִׁין וְשָׂטָן, הַמַּתְעֶה אֶת כָּל תֵּבֵל
hannikra malshin vesatan, hammat'eh et kol tevel
he that is called the Devil and Satan, the deceiver of the whole world;

הוּא הֻשְׁלַךְ אַרְצָה וּמַלְאָכָיו הֻשְׁלְכוּ אִתּוֹ
hu hushlach artzah umal'achav hushlechu itto
he was cast down to the earth, and his angels were cast down with him.

וְשָׁמַעְתִּי קוֹל גָּדוֹל בַּשָּׁמַיִם אוֹמֵר
veshama'ti kol gadol bashamayim omer
And I heard a great voice in heaven, saying,

עַתָּה בָּאָה יְשׁוּעַת אֱלֹהֵינוּ, גְּבוּרָתוֹ וּמַלְכוּתוֹ וּמֶמְשֶׁלֶת מְשִׁיחוֹ
attah ba'ah yeshu'at eloheinu, gvurato umalchuto umemshelet meshicho
Now is come the salvation, and the power, and the kingdom of our God, and the authority of his Christ:

כִּי הֻשְׁלַךְ שׂוֹטֵן אַחֵינוּ הַמְקַטְרֵג עֲלֵיהֶם לִפְנֵי אֱלֹהֵינוּ יוֹמָם וָלַיְלָה
ki hushlach soten acheinu hamekatreg aleihem lifnei eloheinu yomam valaylah
for the accuser of our brethren is cast down, who accuseth them before our God day and night.

וְהֵם נִצְּחוּהוּ בְּדַם הַשֶּׂה
vehem nitzechuhu bedam basseh
And they overcame him because of the blood of the Lamb,

וּבִדְבַר עֵדוּתָם, וְלֹא אָהֲבוּ אֶת נַפְשָׁם עַד מָוֶת
uvidvar edutam, velo ahavu et nafsham ad mavet
and because of the word of their testimony; and they loved not their life even unto death.

ההתגלות

יב

אוֹת גָּדוֹל נִרְאָה בַּשָּׁמַיִם
ot gadol nir'ah bashamayim
And a great sign was seen in heaven:

אִשָּׁה אֲשֶׁר הַשֶּׁמֶשׁ לְבוּשָׁה, הַיָּרֵחַ תַּחַת רַגְלֶיהָ, וְעַל רֹאשָׁהּ עֲטֶרֶת שֶׁל שְׁנֵים־עָשָׂר כּוֹכָבִים
ishah asher hashemesh levushah, hayareach tachat ragleiha, ve'al roshah ateret shel sheneim-'asar kochavim
a woman arrayed with the sun, and the moon under her feet, and upon her head a crown of twelve stars;

הָרָה הִיא וְזוֹעֶקֶת מִכְּאֵבִים וְצִירֵי לֵדָה
harah hi vezo'eket mikke'evim vetzirei ledah
and she was with child; and she crieth out, travailing in birth, and in pain to be delivered.

גַּם אוֹת אַחֵר נִרְאָה בַּשָּׁמַיִם
gam ot acher nir'ah bashamayim
And there was seen another sign in heaven:

וְהִנֵּה תַּנִּין גָּדוֹל, אָדֹם כָּאֵשׁ, שִׁבְעָה רָאשִׁים לוֹ וְעֶשֶׂר קַרְנַיִם; עַל רָאשָׁיו שִׁבְעָה כְּתָרִים
vehinneh tannin gadol, adom ka'esh, shiv'ah rashim lo ve'eser karnayim; al rashav shiv'ah ketarim
and behold, a great red dragon, having seven heads and ten horns, and upon his heads seven diadems.

וּזְנָבוֹ סָחַב שְׁלִישׁ מִכּוֹכְבֵי הַשָּׁמַיִם וְהִשְׁלִיכָם אַרְצָה
uzenavo sachav shelish mikkochevei hashamayim vehishlicham artzah
And his tail draweth the third part of the stars of heaven, and did cast them to the earth:

וְהַתַּנִּין עָמַד לִפְנֵי הָאִשָּׁה הַקְּרוֹבָה לָלֶדֶת
vehattannin amad lifnei ha'ishah hakkerovah laledet
and the dragon standeth before the woman that is about to be delivered,

כְּדֵי לִבְלֹעַ אֶת בְּנָהּ בְּעֵת הַלֵּדָה
kedei livloa et benah be'et halledah
that when she is delivered he may devour her child.

לְאַחַר שֶׁיָּלְדָה בֵּן זָכָר, אֲשֶׁר עָתִיד לִרְעוֹת אֶת כָּל הַגּוֹיִם בְּשֵׁבֶט בַּרְזֶל
le'achar sheyaledah ben zachar, asher atid lir'ot et kol haggoyim beshevet barzel
And she was delivered of a son, a man child, who is to rule all the nations with a rod of iron:

נֶחְטַף בְּנָהּ אֶל הָאֱלֹהִים וְאֶל כִּסְאוֹ
nechtaf benah el ha'elohim ve'el kis'o
and her child was caught up unto God, and unto his throne.

וְהָאִשָּׁה בָּרְחָה לַמִּדְבָּר, אֲשֶׁר שָׁם הוּכַן לָהּ מָקוֹם מֵאֵת הָאֱלֹהִים
veha'ishah barechah lammidbar, asher sham huchan lah makom me'et ha'elohim
And the woman fled into the wilderness, where she hath a place prepared of God,

הַהִתְגַּלּוּת

וְהַנִּשְׁאָרִים נֶחֱרְדוּ וְנָתְנוּ כָבוֹד לֵאלֹהֵי הַשָּׁמָיִם

vehannish'arim necherdu venatenu kavod lelohei hashamayim
and the rest were affrighted, and gave glory to the God of heaven.

אוֹי שֵׁנִי חָלַף; הִנֵּה אוֹי שְׁלִישִׁי בָּא מַהֵר

oy sheni chalaf; hinneh oy shelishi ba maher
The second Woe is past: behold, the third Woe cometh quickly.

הַמַּלְאָךְ הַשְּׁבִיעִי תָּקַע בַּשּׁוֹפָר וְקוֹלוֹת גְּדוֹלוֹת נִשְׁמְעוּ בַּשָּׁמַיִם - אוֹמְרִים

hammal'ach hashevi'i taka bashofar vekolot gedolim nishme'u bashamayim - omrim
And the seventh angel sounded; and there followed great voices in heaven, and they said,

הָיְתָה מַמְלֶכֶת תֵּבֵל לְמַמְלַכְתּוֹ שֶׁל אֲדוֹנֵנוּ וְשֶׁל מְשִׁיחוֹ וְהוּא יִמְלֹךְ לְעוֹלְמֵי עוֹלָמִים

hayetah mamlechet tevel lemamlachto shel adonenu veshel meshicho vehu yimloch le'olemei olamim
The kingdom of the world is become the kingdom of our Lord, and of his Christ: and he shall reign for ever and ever.

עֶשְׂרִים וְאַרְבָּעָה הַזְּקֵנִים, הַיּוֹשְׁבִים עַל כִּסְאוֹתֵיהֶם לִפְנֵי הָאֱלֹהִים, נָפְלוּ עַל פְּנֵיהֶם וְהִשְׁתַּחֲווּ לֵאלֹהִים

esrim ve'arba'ah hazzekenim, hayoshevim al kis'oteihem lifnei ha'elohim, nafelu al peneihem vehishtachavu le'elohim
And the four and twenty elders, who sit before God on their thrones, fell upon their faces and worshipped God,

בְּאָמְרָם: מוֹדִים אֲנַחְנוּ לְךָ, יהוה צְבָאוֹת אֲשֶׁר

be'omram: modim anachnu lecha, hashem tzeva'ot
saying, We give thee thanks, O Lord God, the Almighty,

הֹוֶה וְהָיָה, כִּי לָבַשְׁתָּ עֻזְּךָ הַגָּדוֹל וַתִּמְלֹךְ

asher hoveh vehayah, ki lavashta uzzecha haggadol vattimloch
who art and who wast; because thou hast taken thy great power, and didst reign.

הַגּוֹיִם קָצְפוּ; וּבָא קִצְפְּךָ וְעֵת לִשְׁפֹּט הַמֵּתִים

haggoyim katzefu; uva kitzpecha ve'et lishpot hammetim
And the nations were wroth, and thy wrath came, and the time of the dead to be judged,

וְלָתֵת שָׂכָר לַעֲבָדֶיךָ הַנְּבִיאִים וְלַקְּדוֹשִׁים

velatet sachar la'avadeicha hannevi'im velakkedoshim
and the time to give their reward to thy servants the prophets, and to the saints,

וּלְיִרְאֵי שְׁמֶךָ, לַקְּטַנִּים וְלַגְּדוֹלִים, וּלְהַשְׁחִית אֶת מַשְׁחִיתֵי הָאָרֶץ

uleyir'ei shimcha, lakketannim velaggedolim, ulehashchit et mashchitei ha'aretz
and to them that fear thy name, the small and the great; and to destroy them that destroy the earth.

אָז נִפְתַּח הֵיכַל אֱלֹהִים בַּשָּׁמַיִם וַאֲרוֹן בְּרִיתוֹ נִרְאָה בְּהֵיכָלוֹ

az niftach heichal elohim bashamayim va'aron brito nir'ah beheichalo
And there was opened the temple of God that is in heaven; and there was seen in his temple the ark of his covenant;

בְּרָקִים וְקוֹלוֹת וּרְעָמִים הִתְחוֹלְלוּ, וּרְעִידַת אֲדָמָה וּבָרָד כָּבֵד

brakim vekolot ure'amim hitcholelu, ure'idat adamah uvarad kaved
and there followed lightnings, and voices, and thunders, and an earthquake, and great hail.

הַהִתְגַּלּוּת

גְּוִיּוֹתֵיהֶם תִּהְיֶינָה בִּרְחוֹב הָעִיר הַגְּדוֹלָה
geviyoteihem tihyeinah birchov ha'ir haggedolah
And their dead bodies lie in the street of the great city,

הַנִּקְרֵאת בְּאֹפֶן רוּחָנִי סְדוֹם וּמִצְרַיִם, אֲשֶׁר שָׁם גַּם נִצְלַב אֲדוֹנָם
hannikret be'ofen ruchani sedom umitzrayim, asher sham gam nitzlav adonam
which spiritually is called Sodom and Egypt, where also their Lord was crucified.

וּמִן הָעַמִּים וְהַשְּׁבָטִים וְהַלְּשׁוֹנוֹת וְהָאֻמּוֹת
umin ha'ammim vehashevatim vehalleshonot veha'ummot
And from among the peoples and tribes and tongues and nations

יִרְאוּ אֶת גְּוִיּוֹתֵיהֶם בְּמֶשֶׁךְ שְׁלוֹשָׁה יָמִים וָחֵצִי, וְלֹא יַרְשׁוּ לְהַנִּיחַ אֶת גְּוִיּוֹתֵיהֶם בְּקֶבֶר
yir'u et geviyoteihem bemeshech sheloshah yamim vachetzi, velo yarshu lehanniach et geviyoteihem bekever
do men look upon their dead bodies three days and a half, and suffer not their dead bodies to be laid in a tomb.

יוֹשְׁבֵי הָאָרֶץ יִשְׂמְחוּ עֲלֵיהֶם וְיַעַלְזוּ, וְיִשְׁלְחוּ מָנוֹת אִישׁ לְרֵעֵהוּ
yoshevei ha'aretz yismechu aleihem veya'alzu, veyishlechu manot ish lere'ehu
And they that dwell on the earth rejoice over them, and make merry; and they shall send gifts one to another;

שֶׁכֵּן שְׁנֵי הַנְּבִיאִים הָאֵלֶּה הִכְאִיבוּ לְיוֹשְׁבֵי הָאָרֶץ
shekken shenei hannevi'im ha'elleh hich'ivu leyoshevei ha'aretz
because these two prophets tormented them that dwell on the earth.

אַחֲרֵי שְׁלוֹשָׁה יָמִים וָחֵצִי בָּאָה בָּהֶם רוּחַ חַיִּים מֵאֵת הָאֱלֹהִים
acharei sheloshah yamim vachetzi ba'ah bahem ruach chayim me'et ha'elohim
And after the three days and a half the breath of life from God entered into them,

הֵם קָמוּ עַל רַגְלֵיהֶם וּפַחַד גָּדוֹל נָפַל עַל רוֹאֵיהֶם
hem kamu al ragleihem ufachad gadol nafal al ro'eihem
and they stood upon their feet; and great fear fell upon them that beheld them.

אָז שָׁמְעוּ קוֹל גָּדוֹל מִן הַשָּׁמַיִם אוֹמֵר לָהֶם: עֲלוּ הֵנָּה
az shame'u kol gadol min hashamayim omer lahem: alu hennah
And they heard a great voice from heaven saying unto them, Come up hither.

וְהֵם עָלוּ בֶּעָנָן הַשָּׁמַיְמָה לְעֵינֵי אוֹיְבֵיהֶם
vehem alu be'anan hashamaymah le'einei oyeveihem
And they went up into heaven in the cloud; and their enemies beheld them.

אוֹתָהּ שָׁעָה הִתְחוֹלְלָה רְעִידַת אֲדָמָה גְּדוֹלָה; עֲשִׂירִית הָעִיר נָפְלָה
otah sha'ah hitcholelah re'idat adamah gedolah; asirit ha'ir naflah
And in that hour there was a great earthquake, and the tenth part of the city fell;

וְשִׁבְעַת אֲלָפִים אֲנָשִׁים, לִשְׁמוֹתֵיהֶם, נֶהֶרְגוּ בִּרְעִידַת הָאֲדָמָה
veshiv'at alafim anashim, lishmoteihem, nehergu bir'idat ha'adamah
and there were killed in the earthquake seven thousand persons:

הַהִתְגַּלּוּת

אֲבָל אֶת הֶחָצֵר אֲשֶׁר מִחוּץ לַהֵיכָל הַשְׁאֵר בַּחוּץ וְאַל תִּמְדֹּד אוֹתָהּ, כִּי נִתְּנָה לַגּוֹיִם

aval et hechatzer asher michutz laheichal hash'er bachutz ve'al timdod otah, ki nittenah laggoyim
And the court which is without the temple leave without, and measure it not; for it hath been given unto the nations:

וְיִרְמְסוּ אֶת עִיר הַקֹּדֶשׁ אַרְבָּעִים וּשְׁנַיִם חֳדָשִׁים

veyirmesu et ir hakkodesh arba'im ushenayim chodashim
and the holy city shall they tread under foot forty and two months.

וְאֶתֵּן לִשְׁנֵי עֵדַי

ve'etten lishnei edai
And I will give unto my two witnesses,

וְיִנָּבְּאוּ אֶלֶף וּמָאתַיִם וְשִׁשִּׁים יָמִים כְּשֶׁהֵם לְבוּשֵׁי שַׂקִּים

vinabb'u elef umatayim veshishim yamim keshehem levushei sakkim
and they shall prophesy a thousand two hundred and threescore days, clothed in sackcloth.

אֵלֶּה הֵם שְׁנֵי הַזֵּיתִים וּשְׁתֵּי הַמְּנוֹרוֹת הָעוֹמְדִים לִפְנֵי אֲדוֹן הָאָרֶץ

elleh hem shenei hazzeitim ushetei hammenorot ha'omedim lifnei adon ha'aretz
These are the two olive trees and the two candlesticks, standing before the Lord of the earth.

וְאִישׁ אִם יִרְצֶה לְהָרַע לָהֶם, תֵּצֵא אֵשׁ מִפִּיהֶם וְתֹאכַל אֶת אוֹיְבֵיהֶם

ve'ish im yirtzeh lehara lahem, tetzei esh mippihem vetochal et oyeveihem
And if any man desireth to hurt them, fire proceedeth out of their mouth and devoureth their enemies;

מִי שֶׁיִּרְצֶה לְהָרַע לָהֶם, בְּדֶרֶךְ זֹאת מוֹת יוּמַת

mi sheyirtzeh lehara lahem, bederech zot mot yumat
and if any man shall desire to hurt them, in this manner must he be killed.

יֵשׁ לָהֶם הַסַּמְכוּת לַעֲצֹר אֶת הַשָּׁמַיִם כְּדֵי שֶׁלֹּא יֵרֵד גֶּשֶׁם בִּימֵי נְבוּאָתָם

yesh lahem hassamchut la'atzor et hashamayim kedei shello yered geshem biymei nevu'atam
These have the power to shut the heaven, that it rain not during the days of their prophecy:

וְסַמְכוּת לָהֶם עַל הַמַּיִם לַהֲפֹךְ אוֹתָם לְדָם

vesamchut lahem al hammayim lahafoch otam ledam
and they have power over the waters to turn them into blood,

וּלְהַכּוֹת אֶת הָאָרֶץ בְּכָל מַכָּה שֶׁיִּרְצוּ

ulehakkot et ha'aretz bechol makkah sheyirtzu
and to smite the earth with every plague, as often as they shall desire.

כַּאֲשֶׁר יִגְמְרוּ אֶת עֵדוּתָם

ka'asher yigmeru et edutam
And when they shall have finished their testimony,

הַחַיָּה הָעוֹלָה מִן הַתְּהוֹם תַּעֲשֶׂה עִמָּהֶם מִלְחָמָה, תְּנַצֵּחַ אוֹתָם וְתַהַרְגֵם

hachayah ha'olah min hattehom ta'aseh immahem milchamah, tenatzeach otam vetahargem
the beast that cometh up out of the abyss shall make war with them, and overcome them, and kill them.

הַהִתְגַּלּוּת

כְּמוֹ שֶׁבִּשֵּׂר לַעֲבָדָיו הַנְּבִיאִים
kemo shebisser la'avadav hannevi'im
according to the good tidings which he declared to his servants the prophets.

וְהַקּוֹל אֲשֶׁר שָׁמַעְתִּי מִן הַשָּׁמַיִם דִּבֶּר אֵלַי שׁוּב וְאָמַר
vehakkol asher shama'ti min hashamayim dibber elai shuv ve'amar
And the voice which I heard from heaven, I heard it again speaking with me, and saying,

לֵךְ קַח אֶת הַסֵּפֶר הַפָּתוּחַ שֶׁבְּיַד הַמַּלְאָךְ הָעוֹמֵד עַל הַיָּם וְעַל הָאָרֶץ
lech kach et hassefer happatuach shebbeyad hammal'ach ha'omed al hayam ve'al ha'aretz
Go, take the book which is open in the hand of the angel that standeth upon the sea and upon the earth.

הָלַכְתִּי אֶל הַמַּלְאָךְ וְאָמַרְתִּי לוֹ שֶׁיִּתֵּן לִי אֶת הַסֵּפֶר הַקָּטָן
halachti el hammal'ach ve'amarti lo sheyitten li et hassefer hakkatan
And I went unto the angel, saying unto him that he should give me the little book.

אָמַר אֵלַי: קַח וֶאֱכֹל אוֹתוֹ, הוּא יֵמַר בְּבִטְנְךָ
amar elai: kach ve'echol oto, hu yemar bevitnecha
And he saith unto me, Take it, and eat it up; and it shall make thy belly bitter,

אַךְ בְּפִיךָ יִהְיֶה מָתוֹק כִּדְבַשׁ
ach beficha yihyeh matok kidvash
but in thy mouth it shall be sweet as honey.

לָקַחְתִּי אֶת הַסֵּפֶר הַקָּטָן מִיָּדוֹ שֶׁל הַמַּלְאָךְ וַאֲכַלְתִּיו; בְּפִי הָיָה מָתוֹק כִּדְבַשׁ
lakachti et hassefer hakkatan miyado shel hammal'ach va'achaltiv; befi hayah matok kidvash
And I took the little book out of the angel's hand, and ate it up; and it was in my mouth sweet as honey:

אֲבָל אַחֲרֵי אָכְלִי אוֹתוֹ הֵמַר לְבִטְנִי
aval acharei ochli oto hemar levitni
and when I had eaten it, my belly was made bitter.

אָז אָמְרוּ לִי: עָלֶיךָ עוֹד לְהִנָּבֵא עַל עַמִּים וְאֻמּוֹת וּלְשׁוֹנוֹת וּמְלָכִים רַבִּים
az ameru li: aleicha od lehinnavei al ammim ve'ummot uleshonot umelachim rabbim
And they say unto me, Thou must prophesy again over many peoples and nations and tongues and kings.

יא

נִתַּן לִי קָנֶה דּוֹמֶה לְמַטֶּה, וְנֶאֱמַר לִי
nittan li kaneh domeh lematteh, vene'emar li
And there was given me a reed like unto a rod: and one said,

קוּם וּמְדֹד אֶת הֵיכַל אֱלֹהִים וְאֶת הַמִּזְבֵּחַ וְאֶת הַמִּשְׁתַּחֲוִים בּוֹ
kum umdod et heichal elohim ve'et hammizbeach ve'et hammishtachavim bo
Rise, and measure the temple of God, and the altar, and them that worship therein.

ההתגלות

I

רָאִיתִי מַלְאָךְ אַחֵר רַב־כֹּחַ יוֹרֵד מִן הַשָּׁמַיִם וְהוּא לָבוּשׁ עָנָן
ra'iti mal'ach acher rav-koach yored min hashamayim vehu lavush anan
And I saw another strong angel coming down out of heaven, arrayed with a cloud;

קֶשֶׁת עַל רֹאשׁוֹ, פָּנָיו כַּשֶּׁמֶשׁ וְרַגְלָיו כְּעַמּוּדֵי אֵשׁ
keshet al rosho, panav kashemesh veraglav ke'ammudei esh
and the rainbow was upon his head, and his face was as the sun, and his feet as pillars of fire;

וּבְיָדוֹ סֵפֶר קָטָן פָּתוּחַ. הוּא שָׂם אֶת רַגְלוֹ הַיְמָנִית עַל הַיָּם וְאֶת הַשְּׂמָאלִית עַל הָאָרֶץ
uveyado sefer katan patuach. hu sam et raglo haymanit al hayam ve'et hasmalit al ha'aretz
and he had in his hand a little book open: and he set his right foot upon the sea, and his left upon the earth;

וְקָרָא בְּקוֹל גָּדוֹל כְּאַרְיֵה שׁוֹאֵג. כַּאֲשֶׁר קָרָא דִּבְּרוּ שִׁבְעַת הָרְעָמִים בְּקוֹלוֹתֵיהֶם
vekara bekol gadol ke'aryeh sho'eg. ka'asher kara dibbru shiv'at hare'amim bekoloteihem
and he cried with a great voice, as a lion roareth: and when he cried, the seven thunders uttered their voices.

וּכְשֶׁדִּבְּרוּ שִׁבְעַת הָרְעָמִים הִתְכַּוַּנְתִּי לִכְתֹּב, אַךְ שָׁמַעְתִּי קוֹל מִן הַשָּׁמַיִם אוֹמֵר
uchesheddibbru shiv'at hare'amim hitkavvanti lichtov, ach shama'ti kol min hashamayim omer
And when the seven thunders uttered their voices, I was about to write: and I heard a voice from heaven saying,

חֲתֹם אֶת אֲשֶׁר דִּבְּרוּ שִׁבְעַת הָרְעָמִים וְאַל תִּכְתֹּב זֹאת
chatom et asher dibberu shiv'at hare'amim ve'al tichtov zot
Seal up the things which the seven thunders uttered, and write them not.

וְהַמַּלְאָךְ שֶׁרְאִיתִיו עוֹמֵד עַל הַיָּם וְעַל הָאָרֶץ הֵרִים אֶת יַד יְמִינוֹ הַשָּׁמַיְמָה
vehammal'ach sher'itiv omed al hayam ve'al ha'aretz herim et yad yemino hashamaymah
And the angel that I saw standing upon the sea and upon the earth lifted up his right hand to heaven,

וְנִשְׁבַּע בַּחַי לְעוֹלְמֵי עוֹלָמִים, אֲשֶׁר בָּרָא אֶת הַשָּׁמַיִם וְאֶת אֲשֶׁר בָּם
venishba bachai le'olemei olamim, asher bara et hashamayim ve'et asher bam
and sware by him that liveth for ever and ever, who created the heaven and the things that are therein,

וְאֶת הָאָרֶץ וְאֶת אֲשֶׁר בָּהּ וְאֶת הַיָּם וְאֶת אֲשֶׁר בּוֹ
ve'et ha'aretz ve'et asher bah ve'et hayam ve'et asher bo
and the earth and the things that are therein, and the sea and the things that are therein,

שֶׁלֹּא תִּהְיֶה עוֹד שָׁהוּת
shello tihyeh od shahut
that there shall be delay no longer:

אוּלָם בִּימֵי קוֹל הַמַּלְאָךְ הַשְּׁבִיעִי, בְּעָמְדוֹ לִתְקֹעַ בַּשּׁוֹפָר, גַּם יֻשְׁלַם סוֹד הָאֱלֹהִים
ulam biymei kol hammal'ach hashevi'i, be'omdo litkoa bashofar, gam yushlam sod ha'elohim
but in the days of the voice of the seventh angel, when he is about to sound, then is finished the mystery of God,

הַהִתְגַּלּוּת

כָּךְ רָאִיתִי אֶת הַסּוּסִים בֶּחָזוֹן: לְרוֹכְבֵיהֶם
kach ra'iti et hassusim bechazon. lerocheveihem
And thus I saw the horses in the vision, and them that sat on them,

יֵשׁ שִׁרְיוֹנוֹת שֶׁל אֵשׁ וְלֶשֶׁם וְגָפְרִית; וְרָאשֵׁי הַסּוּסִים כְּרָאשֵׁי אֲרָיוֹת
yesh shiryonot shel esh veleshem vegofrit; verashei hassusim kerashei arayot
having breastplates as of fire and of hyacinth and of brimstone: and the heads of the horses are as the heads of lions;

וּמִפִּיהֶם יוֹצְאִים אֵשׁ וְעָשָׁן וְגָפְרִית
umippihem yotze'im esh ve'ashan vegofrit
and out of their mouths proceedeth fire and smoke and brimstone.

שְׁלִישׁ בְּנֵי הָאָדָם מֵתוּ בְּשָׁלֹשׁ הַמַּכּוֹת הָאֵלֶּה
shelish benei ha'adam metu beshalosh hammakkot ha'elleh
By these three plagues was the third part of men killed,

בָּאֵשׁ וּבֶעָשָׁן וּבַגָּפְרִית הַיּוֹצְאִים מִפִּיהֶם
ba'esh uve'ashan uvaggofrit hayotze'im mippihem
by the fire and the smoke and the brimstone, which proceeded out of their mouths.

שֶׁכֵּן כֹּחָם שֶׁל הַסּוּסִים הוּא בְּפִיּוֹתֵיהֶם וְגַם בְּזַנְבוֹתֵיהֶם,
shekken kocham shel hassusim hu befiyoteihem vegam bezanvoteihem
For the power of the horses is in their mouth, and in their tails:

כִּי זַנְבוֹתֵיהֶם דּוֹמִים לִנְחָשִׁים בִּהְיוֹת לָהֶם רָאשִׁים, וּבָהֶם יַזִּיקוּ
ki zanvoteihem domim linchashim bihyot lahem rashim, uvahem yazziku
for their tails are like unto serpents, and have heads; and with them they hurt.

שְׁאָר הָאֲנָשִׁים אֲשֶׁר לֹא נֶהֶרְגוּ בַּמַּכּוֹת הָאֵלֶּה, בְּכָל זֹאת לֹא שָׁבוּ מִמַּעֲשֵׂי יְדֵיהֶם
she'ar ha'anashim asher lo nehergu bammakkot ha'elleh, bechol zot lo shavu mimma'asei yedeihem
And the rest of mankind, who were not killed with these plagues, repented not of the works of their hands,

וְלֹא נִמְנְעוּ מֵהִשְׁתַּחֲווֹת לַשֵּׁדִים וְלֶאֱלִילֵי זָהָב וָכֶסֶף
velo nimne'u mehishtachavot lashedim vele'elilei zahav vechesef
that they should not worship demons, and the idols of gold, and of silver,

וּנְחֹשֶׁת וְאֶבֶן וְעֵץ אֲשֶׁר אֵינָם יְכוֹלִים לִרְאוֹת, אַף לֹא לִשְׁמֹעַ וּלְהַלֵּךְ
unechoshet ve'even ve'etz asher einam yecholim lir'ot, af lo lishmoa ulehallech
and of brass, and of stone, and of wood; which can neither see, nor hear, nor walk:

וְלֹא שָׁבוּ מֵרְצִיחוֹתֵיהֶם, אַף לֹא מִכִּשּׁוּפֵיהֶם, מִתַּזְנוּתָם וּמִגְּנֵבוֹתֵיהֶם
velo shavu meretzichoteihem, af lo mikkishufeihem, mittaznutam umiggenevoteihem
and they repented not of their murders, nor of their sorceries, nor of their fornication, nor of their thefts.

הַהִתְגַּלּוּת

וְקוֹל כַּנְפֵיהֶם כְּקוֹל מַרְכְּבוֹת סוּסִים רַבִּים הָרָצִים לַמִּלְחָמָה
vekol kanfeihem kekol markevot susim rabbim haratzim lammilchamah
and the sound of their wings was as the sound of chariots, of many horses rushing to war.

זְנָבוֹת לָהֶם כְּזַנְבוֹת עַקְרַבִּים, עִם עֳקָצִים, וּבְזַנְבוֹתֵיהֶם כֹּחַ לָהֶם לְהַזִּיק לִבְנֵי אָדָם חֲמִשָּׁה חֳדָשִׁים
zenavot lahem kezanvot akrabbim, im okatzim, uvezanvoteihem koach lahem lehazzik livnei adam chamishah chodashim
And they have tails like unto scorpions, and stings; and in their tails is their power to hurt men five months.

וְיֵשׁ לָהֶם מֶלֶךְ עֲלֵיהֶם, מַלְאַךְ הַתְּהוֹם
veyesh lahem melech aleihem, mal'ach hattehom
They have over them as king the angel of the abyss:

אֲשֶׁר שְׁמוֹ בְּעִבְרִית אֲבַדּוֹן וּבִיוָנִית שְׁמוֹ אַפּוֹלְיוֹן
asher shemo be'ivrit avaddon vivanit shemo appolyon
his name in Hebrew is Abaddon, and in the Greek tongue he hath the name Apollyon.

אוֹי אֶחָד חָלַף; הִנֵּה עוֹד אוֹי וְעוֹד אוֹי בָּאִים אַחֲרֵי כֵן
oy echad chalaf; hinneh od oy ve'od oy ba'im acharei chen
The first Woe is past: behold, there come yet two Woes hereafter.

הַמַּלְאָךְ הַשִּׁשִּׁי תָּקַע בַּשּׁוֹפָר וְשָׁמַעְתִּי קוֹל אֶחָד מֵאֵת אַרְבַּע קַרְנוֹת מִזְבַּח הַזָּהָב אֲשֶׁר לִפְנֵי הָאֱלֹהִים
hammal'ach hashishi taka bashofar veshama'ti kol echad me'et arba karnot mizbach hazzahav asher lifnei ha'elohim
And the sixth angel sounded, and I heard a voice from the horns of the golden altar which is before God,

אוֹמֵר לַמַּלְאָךְ הַשִּׁשִּׁי הַמַּחֲזִיק בַּשּׁוֹפָר
omer lammal'ach hashishi hammachazik bashofar
one saying to the sixth angel that had the trumpet,

הַתֵּר אֶת אַרְבַּעַת הַמַּלְאָכִים הָאֲסוּרִים עַל הַנָּהָר הַגָּדוֹל נְהַר פְּרָת
hatter et arba'at hammal'achim ha'asurim al hannahar haggadol nehar perat
Loose the four angels that are bound at the great river Euphrates.

אָז הֻתְּרוּ אַרְבַּעַת הַמַּלְאָכִים
az huttru arba'at hammal'achim
And the four angels were loosed,

הַמּוּכָנִים לַשָּׁעָה וְלַיּוֹם וְלַחֹדֶשׁ וְלַשָּׁנָה, כְּדֵי שֶׁיַּהַרְגוּ שְׁלִישׁ מִבְּנֵי הָאָדָם
hammuchanim lasha'ah velayom velachodesh velashanah, kedei sheyahargu shelish mibbenei ha'adam
that had been prepared for the hour and day and month and year, that they should kill the third part of men.

וּמִסְפַּר צִבְאוֹת הַפָּרָשִׁים עֶשְׂרִים אֶלֶף רְבָבוֹת
umispar tziv'ot happarashim esrim elef revavot
And the number of the armies of the horsemen was twice ten thousand times ten thousand:

שָׁמַעְתִּי אֶת מִסְפָּרָם
shama'ti et misparam
I heard the number of them.

הַהִתְגַּלּוּת

מִן הֶעָשָׁן יָצָא אַרְבֶּה עַל הָאָרֶץ
min he'ashan yatza arbeh al ha'aretz
And out of the smoke came forth locusts upon the earth;

וְנִתַּן לָהֶם כֹּחַ כַּכֹּחַ אֲשֶׁר לְעַקְרַבֵּי הָאָרֶץ
venittan lahem koach kakkoach asher le'akrabbei ha'aretz
and power was given them, as the scorpions of the earth have power.

נֶאֱמַר לָהֶם שֶׁלֹּא לְהַזִּיק לְעֵשֶׂב הָאָרֶץ, אַף לֹא לְכָל יֶרֶק וְכָל עֵץ
ne'emar lahem shello lehazzik le'esev ha'aretz, af lo lechol yerek vechol etz
And it was said unto them that they should not hurt the grass of the earth, neither any green thing, neither any tree,

אֶלָּא לָאֲנָשִׁים אֲשֶׁר אֵין לָהֶם חוֹתַם אֱלֹהִים עַל מִצְחוֹתֵיהֶם
ella la'anashim asher ein lahem chotam elohim al mitzchoteihem
but only such men as have not the seal of God on their foreheads.

לֹא נִתַּן לָהֶם לַהֲרֹג אוֹתָם, אֶלָּא לְעַנּוֹתָם חֲמִשָּׁה חֳדָשִׁים
lo nittan lahem laharog otam, ella le'annotam chamishah chodashim
And it was given them that they should not kill them, but that they should be tormented five months:

וְעִנּוּיָם הוּא כָּעִנּוּי שֶׁגּוֹרֵם עַקְרָב בְּעָקְצוֹ אָדָם
ve'innuyam hu ka'innui sheggorem akrav be'aketzo adam
and their torment was as the torment of a scorpion, when it striketh a man.

בַּיָּמִים הָהֵם יְחַפְּשׂוּ בְּנֵי הָאָדָם אֶת הַמָּוֶת וְלֹא יִמְצְאוּ אוֹתוֹ
bayamim hahem yechappesu benei ha'adam et hammavet velo yimtze'u oto
And in those days men shall seek death, and shall in no wise find it;

וְיִתְאַוּוּ לָמוּת וְהַמָּוֶת יִבְרַח מֵהֶם
veyit'avvu lamut vehammavet yivrach mehem
and they shall desire to die, and death fleeth from them.

בְּצוּרָתָם דּוֹמִים חַגְבֵי הָאַרְבֶּה לְסוּסִים עֲרוּכִים לְמִלְחָמָה
betzuratam domim chagvei ha'arbeh lesusim aruchim lemilchamah
And the shapes of the locusts were like unto horses prepared for war;

עַל רָאשֵׁיהֶם כַּעֲטָרוֹת דּוֹמוֹת לְזָהָב וּפְנֵיהֶם כִּפְנֵי בְּנֵי אָדָם
al rosheihem ka'atarot domot lezahav ufeneihem kifnei benei adam
and upon their heads as it were crowns like unto gold, and their faces were as men's faces.

שֵׂעָר לָהֶם כִּשְׂעַר נָשִׁים וְשִׁנֵּיהֶם כְּשִׁנֵּי אַרְיֵה
se'ar lahem kis'ar nashim veshinneihem keshinnei aryeh
And they had hair as the hair of women, and their teeth were as the teeth of lions.

שִׁרְיוֹנִים לָהֶם כְּשִׁרְיוֹנֵי בַּרְזֶל
shiryonim lahem keshiryonei barzel
And they had breastplates, as it were breastplates of iron;

הההתגלות

שֵׁם הַכּוֹכָב נִקְרָא לַעֲנָה - וּשְׁלִישׁ הַמַּיִם נֶהְפַּךְ לְלַעֲנָה
shem hakkochav nikra la'anah - ushelish hammayim nehpach lela'anah
and the name of the star is called Wormwood: and the third part of the waters became wormwood;

וְרַבִּים מִבְּנֵי אָדָם מֵתוּ מִן הַמַּיִם שֶׁנִּהְיוּ מָרִים
verabbim mibbenei adam metu min hammayim shennihyu marim
and many men died of the waters, because they were made bitter.

הַמַּלְאָךְ הָרְבִיעִי תָּקַע בַּשּׁוֹפָר וּשְׁלִישִׁית הַשֶּׁמֶשׁ לָקְתָה וְגַם שְׁלִישׁ הַיָּרֵחַ
hammal'ach harevi'i taka bashofar ushelishit hashemesh laketah vegam shelish hayareach
And the fourth angel sounded, and the third part of the sun was smitten, and the third part of the moon,

וּשְׁלִישׁ הַכּוֹכָבִים, כְּדֵי שֶׁיֶּחְשַׁךְ שְׁלִישׁ מֵהֶם
ushelish hakkochavim kedei sheyechshach shelish mehem
and the third part of the stars; that the third part of them should be darkened,

וְהַיּוֹם לֹא יָאִיר שְׁלִישִׁיתוֹ וְכֵן גַּם הַלַּיְלָה
vehayom lo ya'ir shelishito vechen gam hallaylah
and the day should not shine for the third part of it, and the night in like manner.

רָאִיתִי וְשָׁמַעְתִּי נֶשֶׁר אֶחָד מְעוֹפֵף בְּאֶמְצַע הַשָּׁמַיִם וְהוּא אוֹמֵר בְּקוֹל גָּדוֹל: אוֹי, אוֹי, אוֹי
ra'iti veshama'ti nesher echad me'ofef be'emtza hashamayim vehu omer bekol gadol: oy, oy, oy
And I saw, and I heard an eagle, flying in mid heaven, saying with a great voice, Woe, woe, woe,

לְיוֹשְׁבֵי הָאָרֶץ מִיֶּתֶר קוֹלוֹת הַשּׁוֹפָר אֲשֶׁר שְׁלֹשֶׁת הַמַּלְאָכִים עֲתִידִים לִתְקֹעַ
leyoshevei ha'aretz miyeter kolot hashofar asher sheloshet hammal'achim atidim litkoa
for them that dwell on the earth, by reason of the other voices of the trumpet of the three angels, who are yet to sound.

ט

הַמַּלְאָךְ הַחֲמִישִׁי תָּקַע בַּשּׁוֹפָר וְרָאִיתִי כּוֹכָב נוֹפֵל מִן הַשָּׁמַיִם אַרְצָה
hammal'ach hachamishi taka bashofar vera'iti kochav nofel min hashamayim artzah
And the fifth angel sounded, and I saw a star from heaven fallen unto the earth:

וְנִתַּן לוֹ מַפְתֵּחַ בּוֹר הַתְּהוֹם
venittan lo mafteach bor hattehom
and there was given to him the key of the pit of the abyss.

הוּא פָּתַח אֶת בּוֹר הַתְּהוֹם וְעָשָׁן עָלָה מִן הַבּוֹר, כַּעֲשַׁן כִּבְשָׁן גָּדוֹל
hu patach et bor hattehom ve'ashan alah min habbor, ka'ashan kivshan gadol
And he opened the pit of the abyss; and there went up a smoke out of the pit, as the smoke of a great furnace;

וְהַשֶּׁמֶשׁ וְהָאֲוִיר חָשְׁכוּ מֵעֲשַׁן הַבּוֹר
vehashemesh veha'avir chashchu me'ashan habbor
and the sun and the air were darkened by reason of the smoke of the pit.

הַהִתְגַּלּוּת

לָקַח הַמַּלְאָךְ אֶת הַמַּחְתָּה, מִלֵּא אוֹתָהּ אֵשׁ מִן הַמִּזְבֵּחַ וְהִשְׁלִיךְ עַל הָאָרֶץ
lakach hammal'ach et hammachtah, millei otah esh min hammizbeach vehishlich al ha'aretz
And the angel taketh the censer; and he filled it with the fire of the altar, and cast it upon the earth:

אָז הִתְחוֹלְלוּ רְעָמִים וְקוֹלוֹת וּבְרָקִים וּרְעִידוֹת אֲדָמָה
az hitcholelu re'amim vekolot uverakim ure'idot adamah
and there followed thunders, and voices, and lightnings, and an earthquake.

שִׁבְעַת הַמַּלְאָכִים אֲשֶׁר בְּיָדָם שִׁבְעַת הַשׁוֹפָרוֹת הִתְכּוֹנְנוּ לִתְקֹעַ
shiv'at hammal'achim asher beyadam shiv'at hashofarot hitkonenu litkoa
And the seven angels that had the seven trumpets prepared themselves to sound.

הָרִאשׁוֹן תָּקַע בַּשּׁוֹפָר וְהִנֵּה הִתְהַוּוּ בָּרָד וָאֵשׁ מְעֹרָבִים בְּדָם וְהֻשְׁלְכוּ אַרְצָה
harishon taka bashofar vehinneh hit'havvu barad ve'esh me'oravim bedam vehushlechu artzah
And the first sounded, and there followed hail and fire, mingled with blood, and they were cast upon the earth:

שְׁלִישׁ הָאָרֶץ נִשְׂרַף, שְׁלִישׁ הָעֵצִים נִשְׂרַף
shelish ha'aretz nisraf, shelish ha'etzim nisraf
and the third part of the earth was burnt up, and the third part of the trees was burnt up,

וְכָל יֶרֶק עֵשֶׂב נִשְׂרַף
vechol yerek esev nisraf
and all green grass was burnt up.

הַמַּלְאָךְ הַשֵּׁנִי תָּקַע בַּשּׁוֹפָר וּכְמוֹ הַר גָּדוֹל בּוֹעֵר בָּאֵשׁ הֻשְׁלַךְ אֶל הַיָּם
hammal'ach hasheni taka bashofar uchmo har gadol bo'er ba'esh hushlach el hayam
And the second angel sounded, and as it were a great mountain burning with fire was cast into the sea:

שְׁלִישׁ הַיָּם נִהְיָה לְדָם
shelish hayam nihyah ledam
and the third part of the sea became blood;

שְׁלִישׁ הַיְצוּרִים בַּיָּם - אֲשֶׁר נֶפֶשׁ לָהֶם - מֵתוּ
shelish haytzurim bayam - asher nefesh lahem - metu
and there died the third part of the creatures which were in the sea, even they that had life;

וּשְׁלִישׁ הָאֳנִיּוֹת נִשְׁמְדוּ
ushelish ho'oniyot nishmedu
and the third part of the ships was destroyed.

הַמַּלְאָךְ הַשְּׁלִישִׁי תָּקַע בַּשּׁוֹפָר וּמִן הַשָּׁמַיִם נָפַל כּוֹכָב גָּדוֹל בּוֹעֵר כַּלַּפִּיד
hammal'ach hashelishi taka bashofar umin hashamayim nafal kochav gadol bo'er kelappid
And the third angel sounded, and there fell from heaven a great star, burning as a torch,

הוּא נָפַל עַל שְׁלִישׁ הַנְּהָרוֹת וְעַל מַעְיְנוֹת הַמַּיִם
hu nafal al shelish hanneharot ve'al ma'aynot hammayim
and it fell upon the third part of the rivers, and upon the fountains of the waters;

הַהִתְגַּלּוּת

לָכֵן הֵם נִמְצָאִים לִפְנֵי כִּסֵּא אֱלֹהִים
lachen hem nimtza'im lifnei kissei elohim
Therefore are they before the throne of God;

וְעוֹבְדִים אוֹתוֹ יוֹמָם וָלַיְלָה בְּהֵיכָלוֹ, וְהַיּוֹשֵׁב עַל הַכִּסֵּא יִפְרֹשׂ מִשְׁכָּנוֹ עֲלֵיהֶם
ve'ovedim oto yomam valaylah beheichalo, vehayoshev al hakkissei yifros mishkano aleihem
and they serve him day and night in his temple: and he that sitteth on the throne shall spread his tabernacle over them.

לֹא יִרְעֲבוּ עוֹד וְלֹא יִצְמָאוּ, אַף לֹא תַכֶּה עֲלֵיהֶם הַשֶּׁמֶשׁ וְכָל שָׁרָב
lo yir'avu od velo yitzme'u, af lo takkeh aleihem hashemesh vechol sharav
They shall hunger no more, neither thirst any more; neither shall the sun strike upon them, nor any heat:

כִּי הַשֶּׂה אֲשֶׁר בְּאֶמְצַע הַכִּסֵּא יִרְעֶה אוֹתָם
ki hasseh asher be'emtza hakkissei yir'eh otam
for the Lamb that is in the midst of the throne shall be their shepherd,

וְיַנְהִיגֵם אֶל מַבּוּעֵי מַיִם חַיִּים
veyanhigem el mabbu'ei mayim chayim
and shall guide them unto fountains of waters of life:

וֵאלֹהִים יִמְחֶה כָּל דִּמְעָה מֵעֵינֵיהֶם
ve'elohim yimcheh kol dim'ah me'eineihem
and God shall wipe away every tear from their eyes.

ח

כַּאֲשֶׁר פָּתַח אֶת הַחוֹתָם הַשְּׁבִיעִי הָיְתָה דְּמָמָה בַּשָּׁמַיִם כַּחֲצִי שָׁעָה
ka'asher patach et hachotam hashevi'i hayetah demamah bashamayim kachatzi sha'ah
And when he opened the seventh seal, there followed a silence in heaven about the space of half an hour.

רָאִיתִי אֶת שִׁבְעַת הַמַּלְאָכִים הָעוֹמְדִים לִפְנֵי הָאֱלֹהִים; שִׁבְעָה שׁוֹפָרוֹת נִתְּנוּ לָהֶם
ra'iti et shiv'at hammal'achim ha'omedim lifnei ha'elohim; shiv'ah shofarot nittnu lahem
And I saw the seven angels that stand before God; and there were given unto them seven trumpets.

וּמַלְאָךְ אַחֵר בָּא וְעָמַד אֵצֶל הַמִּזְבֵּחַ; בְּיָדוֹ מַחְתַּת זָהָב, וּקְטֹרֶת רַבָּה נִתְּנָה לוֹ
umal'ach acher ba ve'amad etzel hammizbeach; beyado machtat zahav, uketoret rabbah nittenah lo
And another angel came and stood over the altar, having a golden censer; and there was given unto him much incense,

כְּדֵי לָשִׂים אוֹתָהּ בִּתְפִלּוֹת כָּל הַקְּדוֹשִׁים עַל מִזְבַּח הַזָּהָב אֲשֶׁר לִפְנֵי הַכִּסֵּא
kedei lasim otah bitfillot kol hakkedoshim al mizbach hazzahav asher lifnei hakkisse
that he should add it unto the prayers of all the saints upon the golden altar which was before the throne.

וַעֲשַׁן הַקְּטֹרֶת עָלָה בִּתְפִלּוֹת הַקְּדוֹשִׁים מִיָּדוֹ שֶׁל הַמַּלְאָךְ לִפְנֵי הָאֱלֹהִים
va'ashan hakketoret alah bitfillot hakkedoshim miyado shel hammal'ach lifnei ha'elohim
And the smoke of the incense, with the prayers of the saints, went up before God out of the angel's hand.

הַהִתְגַּלּוּת

אַחֲרֵי כֵן רָאִיתִי וְהִנֵּה הָמוֹן רַב, אֲשֶׁר לֹא יָכוֹל אִישׁ לִמְנוֹתוֹ
acharei chen ra'iti vehinneh hamon rav, asher lo yachol ish limnoto
After these things I saw, and behold, a great multitude, which no man could number,

מִכָּל הָאֻמּוֹת וְהַשְּׁבָטִים וְהָעַמִּים וְהַלְּשׁוֹנוֹת - עוֹמְדִים לִפְנֵי הַכִּסֵּא וְלִפְנֵי הַשֶּׂה
mikkol ha'ummot vehashvatim veha'ammim vehalleshonot - omdim lifnei hakkissei velifnei hasseh
out of every nation and of all tribes and peoples and tongues, standing before the throne and before the Lamb,

כְּשֶׁהֵם לְבוּשִׁים גְּלִימוֹת לְבָנוֹת וְכַפּוֹת תְּמָרִים בִּידֵיהֶם
kshehem levushim gelimot levanot vechappot temarim biydeihem
arrayed in white robes, and palms in their hands;

וְקוֹרְאִים בְּקוֹל גָּדוֹל: הַיְשׁוּעָה לֵאלֹהֵינוּ הַיּוֹשֵׁב עַל הַכִּסֵּא וְלַשֶּׂה
vekore'im bekol gadol. hayshu'ah leloheinu hayoshev al hakkissei velasseh
and they cry with a great voice, saying, Salvation unto our God who sitteth on the throne, and unto the Lamb.

כָּל הַמַּלְאָכִים עָמְדוּ סָבִיב לַכִּסֵּא
kol hammal'achim amedu saviv lakkissei
And all the angels were standing round about the throne,

וְלַזְּקֵנִים וּלְאַרְבַּע הַחַיּוֹת. הֵם נָפְלוּ עַל פְּנֵיהֶם לִפְנֵי הַכִּסֵּא וְהִשְׁתַּחֲווּ לֵאלֹהִים
velazzekenim ule'arba hachayot. hem naflu al peneihem lifnei hakkissei vehishtachavu le'elohim
and about the elders and the four living creatures; and they fell before the throne on their faces, and worshipped God,

בְּאָמְרָם: אָמֵן. הַבְּרָכָה וְהַכָּבוֹד, הַחָכְמָה וְהַתּוֹדָה, הַיְקָר
be'ameram: amen. habberachah vehakkavod, hachachemah vehattodah, haykar
saying, Amen: Blessing, and glory, and wisdom, and thanksgiving, and honor,

וְהַגְּבוּרָה וְהָעֹז לֵאלֹהֵינוּ לְעוֹלְמֵי עוֹלָמִים. אָמֵן
vehaggevurah veha'oz le'eloheinu le'olemei olamim. amen
and power, and might, be unto our God for ever and ever. Amen.

דִּבֶּר אַחַד הַזְּקֵנִים וְאָמַר אֵלַי
dibber achad hazzekenim ve'amar elai
And one of the elders answered, saying unto me,

אֵלֶּה הַלְּבוּשִׁים גְּלִימוֹת לְבָנוֹת מִי הֵם וּמֵאַיִן בָּאוּ
elleh hallevushim gelimot levanot mi hem ume'ayin ba'u
These that are arrayed in the white robes, who are they, and whence came they?

הֱשִׁבֹתִי לוֹ: אֲדוֹנִי, אַתָּה יוֹדֵעַ. אָמַר אֵלַי: אֵלֶּה הֵם הַבָּאִים מִן הַצָּרָה הַגְּדוֹלָה
heshavti lo: adoni, attah yodea. amar elai: elleh hem habba'im min hatzarah haggedolah
And I say unto him, My lord, thou knowest. And he said to me, These are they that come out of the great tribulation,

הֵם כִּבְּסוּ אֶת גְּלִימוֹתֵיהֶם וְהִלְבִּינוּ אוֹתָן בְּדַם הַשֶּׂה
hem kibbsu et gelimoteihem vehilbinu otan bedam hasseh
and they washed their robes, and made them white in the blood of the Lamb.

ההתגלות

הוּא קָרָא בְּקוֹל גָּדוֹל אֶל אַרְבַּעַת הַמַּלְאָכִים אֲשֶׁר נִתַּן לָהֶם לְחַבֵּל בָּאָרֶץ וּבַיָּם
hu kara bekol gadol el arba'at hammal'achim asher nittan lahem lechabbel ba'aretz uvayam
and he cried with a great voice to the four angels to whom it was given to hurt the earth and the sea,

בְּאָמְרוֹ: אַל תְּחַבְּלוּ בָּאָרֶץ וּבַיָּם וּבָעֵצִים
be'amero: al techabbelu ba'aretz uvayam uva'etzim
saying, Hurt not the earth, neither the sea, nor the trees,

עַד אֲשֶׁר נַחְתֹּם אֶת עַבְדֵי אֱלֹהֵינוּ עַל מִצְחוֹתֵיהֶם
ad asher nachtom et avdei eloheinu al mitzchoteihem
till we shall have sealed the servants of our God on their foreheads.

וְשָׁמַעְתִּי אֶת מִסְפַּר הַחֲתוּמִים
veshama'ti et mispar hachatumim
And I heard the number of them that were sealed,

מֵאָה וְאַרְבָּעִים וְאַרְבָּעָה אֶלֶף חֲתוּמִים מִכָּל שִׁבְטֵי בְּנֵי יִשְׂרָאֵל
me'ah ve'arba'im ve'arba'ah elef chatumim mikkol shivtei benei yisra'el
a hundred and forty and four thousand, sealed out of every tribe of the children of Israel:

מִשֵּׁבֶט יְהוּדָה שְׁנֵים־עָשָׂר אֶלֶף חֲתוּמִים
mishevet yehudah sheneim-'asar elef chatumim
Of the tribe of Judah were sealed twelve thousand;

מִשֵּׁבֶט רְאוּבֵן שְׁנֵים־עָשָׂר אֶלֶף, מִשֵּׁבֶט גָּד שְׁנֵים־עָשָׂר אֶלֶף
mishevet re'uven sheneim-'asar elef, mishevet gad sheneim-'asar elef
Of the tribe of Reuben twelve thousand; Of the tribe of Gad twelve thousand;

מִשֵּׁבֶט אָשֵׁר שְׁנֵים־עָשָׂר אֶלֶף
mishevet asher sheneim-'asar elef
Of the tribe of Asher twelve thousand;

מִשֵּׁבֶט נַפְתָּלִי שְׁנֵים־עָשָׂר אֶלֶף, מִשֵּׁבֶט מְנַשֶּׁה שְׁנֵים־עָשָׂר אֶלֶף
mishevet naftali sheneim-'asar elef, mishevet menasheh sheneim-'asar elef
Of the tribe of Naphtali twelve thousand; Of the tribe of Manasseh twelve thousand;

מִשֵּׁבֶט שִׁמְעוֹן שְׁנֵים־עָשָׂר אֶלֶף, מִשֵּׁבֶט לֵוִי שְׁנֵים־עָשָׂר אֶלֶף, מִשֵּׁבֶט יִשָּׂשכָר שְׁנֵים־עָשָׂר אֶלֶף
mishevet shim'on sheneim-'asar elef, mishevet levi sheneim-'asar elef, mishevet yishoschar sheneim-'asar elef
Of the tribe of Simeon twelve thousand; Of the tribe of Levi twelve thousand; Of the tribe of Issachar twelve thousand;

מִשֵּׁבֶט זְבוּלוּן שְׁנֵים־עָשָׂר אֶלֶף
mishevet zevulun sheneim-'asar elef
Of the tribe of Zebulun twelve thousand;

מִשֵּׁבֶט יוֹסֵף שְׁנֵים־עָשָׂר אֶלֶף, מִשֵּׁבֶט בִּנְיָמִין שְׁנֵים־עָשָׂר אֶלֶף חֲתוּמִים
mishevet yosef sheneim-'asar elef, mishevet binyamin sheneim-'asar elef chatumim
Of the tribe of Joseph twelve thousand; Of the tribe of Benjamin were sealed twelve thousand.

הַהִתְגַּלּוּת

כּוֹכְבֵי הַשָּׁמַיִם נָפְלוּ אַרְצָה, כִּתְאֵנָה הַמַּשְׁלִיכָה אֶת פַּגֶּיהָ כַּאֲשֶׁר הִיא מְטֻלְטֶלֶת בְּרוּחַ חֲזָקָה
kochevei hashamayim nafelu artzah, kit'enah hammashlichah et paggeiha ka'asher hi mittaltelet beruach chazakah
and the stars of the heaven fell unto the earth, as a fig tree casteth her unripe figs when she is shaken of a great wind.

הַשָּׁמַיִם נָסוֹגוּ כִּמְגִלָּה נִגְלֶלֶת
hashamayim nasogu kimgillah niglelet
And the heaven was removed as a scroll when it is rolled up;

כָּל הַר וָאִי נֶעְתְּקוּ מִמְּקוֹמָם
kol har ve'i ne'etku mimmekomam
and every mountain and island were moved out of their places.

וּמַלְכֵי הָאָרֶץ וְהַנִּכְבָּדִים, שָׂרֵי הָאֲלָפִים וְהָעֲשִׁירִים
umalchei ha'aretz vehannichbadim, sarei ha'alafim veha'ashirim
And the kings of the earth, and the princes, and the chief captains, and the rich,

וּבַעֲלֵי הָעָצְמָה, כָּל עֶבֶד וְכָל בֶּן־חוֹרִין, הִתְחַבְּאוּ בַּמְּעָרוֹת וּבְסַלְעֵי הֶהָרִים
uva'alei ha'otzmah, kol eved vechol ben-chorin, hitchabbe'u bamme'arot uvesal'ei heharim
and the strong, and every bondman and freeman, hid themselves in the caves and in the rocks of the mountains;

וְאָמְרוּ לֶהָרִים וְלַסְּלָעִים
ve'ameru leharim velassela'im
and they say to the mountains and to the rocks,

נִפְלוּ עָלֵינוּ וְהַסְתִּירוּ אוֹתָנוּ מִפְּנֵי הַיּוֹשֵׁב עַל הַכִּסֵּא וּמִזַּעַם הַשֶּׂה
niflu aleinu vehastiru otanu mippenei hayoshev al hakkissei umizza'am hasseh
Fall on us, and hide us from the face of him that sitteth on the throne, and from the wrath of the Lamb:

כִּי בָא הַיּוֹם הַגָּדוֹל, יוֹם חֲרוֹנָם, וּמִי יָכוֹל לַעֲמֹד
ki ba hayom haggadol, yom charonam, umi yachol la'amod
for the great day of their wrath is come; and who is able to stand?

ז

אַחֲרֵי כֵן רָאִיתִי אַרְבָּעָה מַלְאָכִים עוֹמְדִים בְּאַרְבַּע פִּנּוֹת הָאָרֶץ, אוֹחֲזִים אֶת אַרְבַּע רוּחוֹת הָאָרֶץ
acharei chen ra'iti arba'ah mal'achim omedim be'arba pinnot ha'aretz, ochazim et arba ruchot ha'aretz
After this I saw four angels standing at the four corners of the earth, holding the four winds of the earth,

כְּדֵי שֶׁלֹּא תִּשֹּׁב רוּחַ לֹא עַל הָאָרֶץ וְלֹא עַל הַיָּם וְלֹא עַל כָּל עֵץ
kedei shello tishov ruach lo al ha'aretz velo al hayam velo al kol etz
that no wind should blow on the earth, or on the sea, or upon any tree.

רָאִיתִי מַלְאָךְ אַחֵר עוֹלֶה מִמִּזְרַח שֶׁמֶשׁ וּבִרְשׁוּתוֹ חוֹתַם אֱלֹהִים חַיִּים
ra'iti mal'ach acher oleh mimmizrach shemesh uvirshuto chotam elohim chayim
And I saw another angel ascend from the sunrising, having the seal of the living God:

הַהִתְגַּלּוּת

וְנִתְּנָה לָהֶם סַמְכוּת עַל רֶבַע הָאָרֶץ
venittnah lahem samchut al reva ha'aretz
And there was given unto them authority over the fourth part of the earth,

לַהֲרֹג בַּחֶרֶב וּבָרָעָב וּבַמָּוֶת וְעַל־יְדֵי חַיּוֹת הָאָרֶץ
laharog bacherev uvara'av uvammavet ve'al-yedei chayot ha'aretz
to kill with sword, and with famine, and with death, and by the wild beasts of the earth.

כַּאֲשֶׁר פָּתַח אֶת הַחוֹתָם הַחֲמִישִׁי
ka'asher patach et hachotam hachamishi
And when he opened the fifth seal,

רָאִיתִי מִתַּחַת לַמִּזְבֵּחַ אֶת נַפְשׁוֹת הַטְּבוּחִים עַל דְּבַר הָאֱלֹהִים
ra'iti mittachat lammizbeach et nafshot hattevuchim al devar ha'elohim
I saw underneath the altar the souls of them that had been slain for the word of God,

וְעַל הָעֵדוּת שֶׁהֶחֱזִיקוּ בָהּ
ve'al ha'edut shehecheziku bah
and for the testimony which they held:

וְהֵם צָעֲקוּ בְּקוֹל גָּדוֹל
vehem tza'aku bekol gadol
and they cried with a great voice, saying,

עַד מָתַי, אֲדֹנָי הַקָּדוֹשׁ וַאֲמִתִּי, לֹא תִשְׁפֹּט וְתִנְקֹם אֶת דָּמֵינוּ מִיּוֹשְׁבֵי הָאָרֶץ
ad matai, adonai hakkadosh va'amitti, lo tishpot vetinkom et dameinu miyoshevei ha'aretz
How long, O Master, the holy and true, dost thou not judge and avenge our blood on them that dwell on the earth?

לְכָל אֶחָד מֵהֶם נִתְּנָה גְּלִימָה לְבָנָה וְנֶאֱמַר לָהֶם לָנוּחַ עוֹד זְמַן מְעַט
lechol echad mehem nittenah glimah levanah vene'emar lahem lanuach od zeman me'at
And there was given them to each one a white robe; and it was said unto them, that they should rest yet for a little time,

עַד שֶׁיִּמָּלֵא גַּם מִסְפַּר חַבְרֵיהֶם הָעֲבָדִים וַאֲחֵיהֶם הָעֲתִידִים לֵהָרֵג כְּמוֹהֶם
ad sheyimmalei gam mispar chavreihem ha'avadim va'acheihem ha'atidim lehareg kemohem
until their fellow-servants also and their brethren, who should be killed even as they were, should have fulfilled their course.

רָאִיתִי כְּשֶׁפָּתַח אֶת הַחוֹתָם הַשִּׁשִּׁי הִתְחוֹלְלָה רְעִידַת אֲדָמָה גְּדוֹלָה
ra'iti kesheppatach et hachotam hashishi hitcholelah re'idat adamah gedolah
And I saw when he opened the sixth seal, and there was a great earthquake;

הַשֶּׁמֶשׁ הִשְׁחִירָה כְּשַׂק שֵׂעָר וְהַיָּרֵחַ כֻּלּוֹ הָיָה כְּדָם
hashemesh hishchirah kesak se'ar vehayareach kullo hayah kedam
and the sun became black as sackcloth of hair, and the whole moon became as blood;

הַהִתְגַּלּוּת

וְשָׁמַעְתִּי אַחַת מֵאַרְבַּע הַחַיּוֹת אוֹמֶרֶת כְּמוֹ בְּקוֹל רַעַם: בּוֹא
veshama'ti achat me'arba hachayot omeret kemo bekol ra'am: bo
and I heard one of the four living creatures saying as with a voice of thunder, Come.

רָאִיתִי וְהִנֵּה סוּס לָבָן וְהַיּוֹשֵׁב עָלָיו נוֹשֵׂא קֶשֶׁת
ra'iti vehinneh sus lavan vehayoshev alav nosei keshet
And I saw, and behold, a white horse, and he that sat thereon had a bow;

עֲטֶרֶת נִתְּנָה לוֹ וְהוּא יָצָא מְנַצֵּחַ וּלְמַעַן יְנַצֵּחַ
ateret nittenah lo vehu yatza menatzeach ulema'an yenatzeach
and there was given unto him a crown: and he came forth conquering, and to conquer.

כַּאֲשֶׁר פָּתַח אֶת הַחוֹתָם הַשֵּׁנִי שָׁמַעְתִּי אֶת הַחַיָּה הַשְּׁנִיָּה אוֹמֶרֶת: בּוֹא
ka'asher patach et hachotam hasheni shama'ti et hachayah hasheniyah omeret: bo
And when he opened the second seal, I heard the second living creature saying, Come.

סוּס אַחֵר יָצָא, אָדֹם כָּאֵשׁ. לַיּוֹשֵׁב עָלָיו נִתַּן לְהָסִיר אֶת הַשָּׁלוֹם מִן הָאָרֶץ
sus acher yatza, adom ka'esh. layoshev alav nittan lehasir et hashalom min ha'aretz
And another horse came forth, a red horse: and to him that sat thereon it was given to take peace from the earth,

כְּדֵי שֶׁיַּהַרְגוּ זֶה אֶת זֶה; וְחֶרֶב גְּדוֹלָה נִתְּנָה לוֹ
kedei sheyahargu zeh et zeh; vecherev gedolah nittnah lo
and that they should slay one another: and there was given unto him a great sword.

כַּאֲשֶׁר פָּתַח אֶת הַחוֹתָם הַשְּׁלִישִׁי שָׁמַעְתִּי אֶת הַחַיָּה הַשְּׁלִישִׁית אוֹמֶרֶת: בּוֹא
ka'asher patach et hachotam hashelishi shama'ti et hachayah hashelishit omeret: bo
And when he opened the third seal, I heard the third living creature saying, Come.

רָאִיתִי וְהִנֵּה סוּס שָׁחוֹר וְהַיּוֹשֵׁב עָלָיו מַחֲזִיק מֹאזְנַיִם בְּיָדוֹ
ra'iti vehinneh sus shachor vehayoshev alav machazik moznayim beyado
And I saw, and behold, a black horse; and he that sat thereon had a balance in his hand.

וְשָׁמַעְתִּי כְּמוֹ קוֹל בֵּין אַרְבַּע הַחַיּוֹת אוֹמֵר
veshama'ti kemo kol bein arba hachayot omer
And I heard as it were a voice in the midst of the four living creatures saying,

לִיטֶר חִטִּים בְּדִינָר וּשְׁלוֹשָׁה לִיטְרִים שְׂעוֹרִים בְּדִינָר, וְלַשֶּׁמֶן וְלַיַּיִן אַל תַּזִּיק
liter chittim bedinar usheloshah literim se'orim bedinar, velashemen velayayin al tazzik
A measure of wheat for a shilling, and three measures of barley for a shilling; and the oil and the wine hurt thou not.

כַּאֲשֶׁר פָּתַח אֶת הַחוֹתָם הָרְבִיעִי שָׁמַעְתִּי אֶת קוֹל הַחַיָּה הָרְבִיעִית אוֹמֵר: בּוֹא
ka'asher patach et hachotam harevi'i shama'ti et kol hachayah harevi'it omer: bo
And when he opened the fourth seal, I heard the voice of the fourth living creature saying, Come.

רָאִיתִי וְהִנֵּה סוּס יְרַקְרַק וְהַיּוֹשֵׁב עָלָיו שְׁמוֹ מָוֶת, וּשְׁאוֹל הָלְכָה אַחֲרָיו
ra'iti vehinneh sus yerakrak vehayoshev alav shemo mavet, ushe'ol halechah acharav
And I saw, and behold, a pale horse: and he that sat upon him, his name was Death; and Hades followed with him.

הַהִתְגַּלּוּת

וְעָשִׂיתָ אוֹתָם מַמְלֶכֶת כֹּהֲנִים לֵאלֹהֵינוּ, וְיִמְלְכוּ עַל הָאָרֶץ
ve'asita otam mamlechet kohanim le'eloheinu, veyimlechu al ha'aretz
and madest them to be unto our God a kingdom and priests; and they reign upon the earth.

רָאִיתִי וְשָׁמַעְתִּי קוֹל מַלְאָכִים רַבִּים סָבִיב לַכִּסֵּא וְלַחַיּוֹת וְלַזְּקֵנִים
ra'iti veshama'ti kol mal'achim rabbim saviv lakkissei velachayot velazkenim
And I saw, and I heard a voice of many angels round about the throne and the living creatures and the elders;

מִסְפָּרָם רִבְבוֹת רְבָבוֹת וְאַלְפֵי אֲלָפִים
misparam rivevot revavot ve'alfei alafim
and the number of them was ten thousand times ten thousand, and thousands of thousands;

וְהֵם אוֹמְרִים בְּקוֹל גָּדוֹל: רָאוּי הַשֶּׂה שֶׁנִּזְבַּח לְקַבֵּל גְּבוּרָה, עֹשֶׁר
vehem omerim bekol gadol: ra'ui hasheh shennizbach lekabbel gevurah, osher
saying with a great voice, Worthy is the Lamb that hath been slain to receive the power, and riches,

וְחָכְמָה וְכֹחַ וִיקָר וְכָבוֹד וּבְרָכָה
vechachemah vechoach vikar vechavod uverachah
and wisdom, and might, and honor, and glory, and blessing.

וְכָל בְּרִיָּה אֲשֶׁר בַּשָּׁמַיִם וּבָאָרֶץ
vechol beriyah asher bashamayim uva'eretz
And every created thing which is in the heaven, and on the earth,

וּמִתַּחַת לָאָרֶץ וְעַל הַיָּם וְכֹל אֲשֶׁר בָּהֶם
umittachat la'aretz ve'al hayam vechol asher bahem
and under the earth, and on the sea, and all things that are in them,

שָׁמַעְתִּי אוֹמְרִים: לַיּוֹשֵׁב עַל הַכִּסֵּא וְלַשֶּׂה
shama'ti omerim: layoshev al hakkissei velasseh
heard I saying, Unto him that sitteth on the throne, and unto the Lamb,

הַבְּרָכָה וְהַיְקָר וְהַכָּבוֹד וְהָעֹז לְעוֹלְמֵי עוֹלָמִים
habbrachah vehaykar vehakkavod veha'oz le'olemei olamim
be the blessing, and the honor, and the glory, and the dominion, for ever and ever.

וְאַרְבַּע הַחַיּוֹת אָמְרוּ: אָמֵן! וְהַזְּקֵנִים נָפְלוּ וְהִשְׁתַּחֲווּ
ve'arba hachayot ameru: amen! vehazzkenim nafelu vehishtachavu
And the four living creatures said, Amen. And the elders fell down and worshipped.

|

רָאִיתִי כַּאֲשֶׁר פָּתַח הַשֶּׂה אֶת אֶחָד מִשִּׁבְעַת הַחוֹתָמוֹת
ra'iti ka'asher patach hasseh et echad mishiv'at hachotamot
And I saw when the Lamb opened one of the seven seals,

הַהִתְגַּלּוּת

וְלֹא יָכוֹל אִישׁ לֹא בַּשָּׁמַיִם וְלֹא בָּאָרֶץ וְלֹא מִתַּחַת לָאָרֶץ לִפְתֹּחַ אֶת הַסֵּפֶר, אַף לֹא לְהַבִּיט בּוֹ
velo yachol ish lo bashamayim velo ba'aretz velo mittachat la'aretz liftoach et hassefer, af lo lehabbit bo
And no one in the heaven, or on the earth, or under the earth, was able to open the book, or to look thereon.

וַאֲנִי בָּכִיתִי הַרְבֵּה, כִּי אִישׁ לֹא נִמְצָא רָאוּי לִפְתֹּחַ אֶת הַסֵּפֶר, אַף לֹא לְהַבִּיט בּוֹ
va'ani bachiti harbeh, ki ish lo nimtza ra'ui liftoach et hassefer, af lo lehabbit bo
And I wept much, because no one was found worthy to open the book, or to look thereon:

אָמַר אֵלַי אַחַד הַזְּקֵנִים: אַל תִּבְכֶּה. הִנֵּה נִצַּח הָאַרְיֵה מִשֵּׁבֶט יְהוּדָה
amar elai achad hazzkenim: al tivkeh. hinneh nitzach ha'aryeh mishevet yehudah
and one of the elders saith unto me, Weep not; behold, the Lion that is of the tribe of Judah,

שֹׁרֶשׁ דָּוִד, לִפְתֹּחַ אֶת הַסֵּפֶר וְאֶת שִׁבְעַת חוֹתָמָיו
shoresh david, liftoach et hassefer ve'et shiv'at chotamav
the Root of David, hath overcome to open the book and the seven seals thereof.

וְרָאִיתִי בֵּין הַכִּסֵּא וְאַרְבַּע הַחַיּוֹת וּבֵין הַזְּקֵנִים עוֹמֵד שֶׂה
vera'iti bein hakkissei ve'arba hachayot uvein hazzekenim omed seh
And I saw in the midst of the throne and of the four living creatures, and in the midst of the elders, a Lamb standing,

כְּמוֹ טָבוּחַ; שֶׁבַע קַרְנַיִם לוֹ, וְשֶׁבַע עֵינַיִם
kemo tavuach; sheva karnayim lo, vesheva einayim
as though it had been slain, having seven horns, and seven eyes,

אֲשֶׁר הֵן שֶׁבַע רוּחוֹת הָאֱלֹהִים הַשְּׁלוּחוֹת אֶל כָּל הָאָרֶץ
asher hen sheva ruchot ha'elohim hashluchot el kol ha'aretz
which are the seven Spirits of God, sent forth into all the earth.

הוּא בָּא וְלָקַח אֶת הַסֵּפֶר מִימִין הַיּוֹשֵׁב עַל הַכִּסֵּא
hu ba velakach et hassefer miymin hayoshev al hakkissei
And he came, and he taketh it out of the right hand of him that sat on the throne.

וְכַאֲשֶׁר לָקַח אוֹתוֹ נָפְלוּ אַרְבַּע הַחַיּוֹת וְעֶשְׂרִים וְאַרְבָּעָה הַזְּקֵנִים לִפְנֵי הַשֶּׂה
vecha'asher lakach oto nafelu arba hachayot ve'esrim ve'arba'ah hazkenim lifnei hasseh
And when he had taken the book, the four living creatures and the four and twenty elders fell down before the Lamb,

וּלְכָל אֶחָד נֶבֶל וְקַעֲרוֹת זָהָב מְלֵאוֹת קְטֹרֶת אֲשֶׁר הִיא תְּפִלּוֹת הַקְּדוֹשִׁים
ulechal echad nevel veka'arot zahav mele'ot ketoret asher hi tefillot hakkedoshim
having each one a harp, and golden bowls full of incense, which are the prayers of the saints.

וְשָׁרוּ שִׁיר חָדָשׁ: רָאוּי אַתָּה לָקַחַת אֶת הַסֵּפֶר וְלִפְתֹּחַ אֶת חוֹתָמָיו, כִּי אַתָּה נִשְׁחַטְתָּ
vesharu shir chadash. ra'ui attah lakachat et hassefer veliftoach et chotamav, ki attah nishchatta
And they sing a new song, saying, Worthy art thou to take the book, and to open the seals thereof: for thou wast slain,

וּבְדָמְךָ קָנִיתָ לֵאלֹהִים מִבְּנֵי כָּל שֵׁבֶט וְלָשׁוֹן, מִכָּל עַם וְאֻמָּה
uvedamecha kanita lelohim mibbenei kol shevet velashon, mikkol am ve'ummah
and didst purchase unto God with thy blood men of every tribe, and tongue, and people, and nation,

הַהִתְגַּלּוּת

וְיוֹמָם וָלַיְלָה אֵינָן חֲדֵלוֹת לוֹמַר
veyomam valaylah einan chadelot lomar
and they have no rest day and night, saying,

קָדוֹשׁ, קָדוֹשׁ, קָדוֹשׁ, יהוה אֱלֹהִים צְבָאוֹת אֲשֶׁר הָיָה וְהֹוֶה וְיָבוֹא
kadosh, kadosh, kadosh, hashem elohim tzeva'ot asher hayah vehoveh veyavo
Holy, holy, holy, is the Lord God, the Almighty, who was and who is and who is to come.

וּבְכָל עֵת שֶׁתִּתֵּנָּה הַחַיּוֹת כָּבוֹד וִיקָר וְתוֹדָה לַיּוֹשֵׁב עַל הַכִּסֵּא
uvechol et shettittennah hachayot kavod viykar vetodah layoshev al hakkisse
And when the living creatures shall give glory and honor and thanks to him that sitteth on the throne,

הַחַי לְעוֹלְמֵי עוֹלָמִים
hachai le'olemei olamim
to him that liveth for ever and ever,

יִפְּלוּ עֶשְׂרִים וְאַרְבָּעָה הַזְּקֵנִים לִפְנֵי הַיּוֹשֵׁב עַל הַכִּסֵּא
yippelu esrim ve'arba'ah hazzekenim lifnei hayoshev al hakkissei
the four and twenty elders shall fall down before him that sitteth on the throne,

וְיִשְׁתַּחֲווּ לַחַי לְעוֹלְמֵי עוֹלָמִים, וְיַנִּיחוּ אֶת עַטְרוֹתֵיהֶם לִפְנֵי הַכִּסֵּא בְּאָמְרָם
veyishtachavu lachai le'olemei olamim veyannichu et atroteihem lifnei hakkissei be'omram
and shall worship him that liveth for ever and ever, and shall cast their crowns before the throne, saying,

לְךָ יָאֶה, אֲדוֹנֵנוּ וֵאלֹהֵינוּ, לְקַבֵּל אֶת הַכָּבוֹד וְהַיְקָר וְהַגְּבוּרָה
lecha ya'eh, adonenu veloheinu, lekabbel et hakkavod vehaykar vehaggevurah
Worthy art thou, our Lord and our God, to receive the glory and the honor and the power:

כִּי אַתָּה בָּרָאתָ הַכֹּל וּבִרְצוֹנְךָ הָיוּ וְנִבְרָאוּ
ki attah barata hakkol uvirtzonecha hayu venivre'u
for thou didst create all things, and because of thy will they were, and were created.

ה

רָאִיתִי לִימִין הַיּוֹשֵׁב עַל הַכִּסֵּא
ra'iti limin hayoshev al hakkissei
And I saw in the right hand of him that sat on the throne

סֵפֶר כָּתוּב מִפָּנִים וּמֵאָחוֹר, חָתוּם בְּשִׁבְעָה חוֹתָמוֹת
sefer katuv mippanim ume'achor, chatum beshiv'ah chotamot
a book written within and on the back, close sealed with seven seals.

וְרָאִיתִי מַלְאָךְ רַב־כֹּחַ קוֹרֵא בְּקוֹל גָּדוֹל: מִי רָאוּי לִפְתֹּחַ אֶת הַסֵּפֶר וּלְהַתִּיר אֶת חוֹתָמָיו
vera'iti mal'ach rav-koach korei bekol gadol: mi ra'ui liftoach et hassefer ulehattir et chotamav
And I saw a strong angel proclaiming with a great voice, Who is worthy to open the book, and to loose the seals thereof?

הַהִתְגַּלּוּת

מִיָּד הָיִיתִי בְּהַשְׁרָאַת הָרוּחַ וְהִנֵּה כִּסֵּא מֻצָּב בַּשָּׁמַיִם וְעַל הַכִּסֵּא יוֹשֵׁב
miyad hayiti behashra'at haruach vehinneh kissei mutzav bashamayim ve'al hakkissei yoshev
Straightway I was in the Spirit: and behold, there was a throne set in heaven, and one sitting upon the throne;

וְהַיּוֹשֵׁב דּוֹמֶה בְּמַרְאֶה לְאֶבֶן יָשְׁפֵה וְאֹדֶם
vehayoshev domeh bemar'eh le'even yashfeh ve'odem
and he that sat was to look upon like a jasper stone and a sardius:

וְקֶשֶׁת סָבִיב לַכִּסֵּא דּוֹמָה בְּמַרְאֶה לְבָרֶקֶת
vekeshet saviv lakkissei domah bemar'eh levareket
and there was a rainbow round about the throne, like an emerald to look upon.

סָבִיב לַכִּסֵּא עֶשְׂרִים וְאַרְבָּעָה כִּסְאוֹת, וְעַל הַכִּסְאוֹת יוֹשְׁבִים עֶשְׂרִים וְאַרְבָּעָה זְקֵנִים
saviv lakkissei esrim ve'arba'ah kis'ot, ve'al hakkis'ot yoshevim esrim ve'arba'ah zkenim
And round about the throne were four and twenty thrones: and upon the thrones I saw four and twenty elders sitting,

לְבוּשִׁים בְּגָדִים לְבָנִים וְעַטְרוֹת זָהָב עַל רָאשֵׁיהֶם
levushim begadim levanim ve'atrot zahav al rasheihem
arrayed in white garments; and on their heads crowns of gold.

וּמִן הַכִּסֵּא יוֹצְאִים בְּרָקִים, קוֹלוֹת וּרְעָמִים
umin hakkissei yotze'im berakim, kolot ure'amim
And out of the throne proceed lightnings and voices and thunders.

וְשִׁבְעָה לַפִּידֵי אֵשׁ בּוֹעֲרִים לִפְנֵי הַכִּסֵּא, אֲשֶׁר הֵם שֶׁבַע רוּחוֹת הָאֱלֹהִים
veshiv'ah lappidei esh bo'arim lifnei hakkisse, asher hem sheva ruchot ha'elohim
And there were seven lamps of fire burning before the throne, which are the seven Spirits of God;

לִפְנֵי הַכִּסֵּא כְּיָם זְכוּכִית דּוֹמֶה לִבְדֹלַח
lifnei hakkissei keyam zchuchit domeh livdolach
and before the throne, as it were a sea of glass like unto crystal;

וּבְאֶמְצַע הַכִּסֵּא וְסָבִיב לַכִּסֵּא אַרְבַּע חַיּוֹת מְלֵאוֹת עֵינַיִם מִלְּפָנִים וּמֵאָחוֹר
uve'emtza hakkissei vesaviv lakkissei arba chayot mele'ot einayim millefanim ume'achor
and in the midst of the throne, and round about the throne, four living creatures full of eyes before and behind.

הַחַיָּה הָרִאשׁוֹנָה דּוֹמָה לְאַרְיֵה; הַחַיָּה הַשְּׁנִיָּה דּוֹמָה לְעֵגֶל
hachayah harishonah domah le'aryeh; hachayah hasheniyah domah le'egel
And the first creature was like a lion, and the second creature like a calf,

הַחַיָּה הַשְּׁלִישִׁית פָּנִים לָהּ כִּפְנֵי אָדָם; וְהַחַיָּה הָרְבִיעִית דּוֹמָה לְנֶשֶׁר מְעוֹפֵף
hachayah hashelishit panim lah kifnei adam; vehachayah harvi'it domah lenesher me'ofef
and the third creature had a face as of a man, and the fourth creature was like a flying eagle.

וְאַרְבַּע הַחַיּוֹת לְכָל אַחַת מֵהֶן שֵׁשׁ כְּנָפַיִם. מִסָּבִיב וּמִבִּפְנִים הֵן מְלֵאוֹת עֵינַיִם,
ve'arba hachayot lechol achat mehen shesh kenafayim. missaviv umibbifnim hen mele'ot einayim
And the four living creatures, having each one of them six wings, are full of eyes round about and within:

הַהִתְגַּלּוּת

וּבְגָדִים לְבָנִים לְמַעַן תִּתְלַבֵּשׁ וְלֹא תֵּרָאֶה בֹּשֶׁת עֶרְוָתְךָ

uvegadim levanim lema'an titlabbesh velo tera'eh boshet ervatcha

and white garments, that thou mayest clothe thyself, and that the shame of thy nakedness be not made manifest;

וְקִילוּרִית לִמְשֹׁחַ אֶת עֵינֶיךָ לְמַעַן תִּרְאֶה

vekilurit limshoach et eineicha lema'an tir'eh

and eyesalve to anoint thine eyes, that thou mayest see.

אֲנִי אֶת אֲשֶׁר אֹהַב אוֹכִיחַ וַאֲיַסֵּר. לָכֵן הֱיֵה נִמְרָץ וַחֲזֹר בִּתְשׁוּבָה

ani et asher ohav ochiach va'ayasser. lachen heyeh nimratz vachazor bitshuvah

As many as I love, I reprove and chasten: be zealous therefore, and repent.

הִנְנִי עוֹמֵד לְיַד הַדֶּלֶת וְדוֹפֵק.

hineni omed leyad haddelet vedofek

Behold, I stand at the door and knock:

אִישׁ כִּי יִשְׁמַע אֶת קוֹלִי וְיִפְתַּח אֶת הַדֶּלֶת, אֶכָּנֵס אֵלָיו וְאֶסְעַד אִתּוֹ וְהוּא אִתִּי

ish ki yishma et koli veyiftach et haddelet, ekkanes elav ve'es'ad itto vehu itti

if any man hear my voice and open the door, I will come in to him, and will sup with him, and he with me.

הַמְנַצֵּחַ, אֲנִי אֶתֵּן לוֹ לָשֶׁבֶת אִתִּי עַל כִּסְאִי

hamnatzeach, ani etten lo lashevet itti al kis'i

He that overcometh, I will give to him to sit down with me in my throne,

כְּמוֹ שֶׁגַּם אֲנִי נִצַּחְתִּי וְיָשַׁבְתִּי עִם אָבִי עַל כִּסְאוֹ

kemo sheggam ani nitzachti veyashavti im avi al kis'o

as I also overcame, and sat down with my Father in his throne.

מִי שֶׁאֹזֶן לוֹ, יִשְׁמַע נָא מַה שֶׁהָרוּחַ אוֹמֶרֶת לַקְּהִלּוֹת

mi she'ozen lo, yishma na mah sheharuach omeret lakkehillot

He that hath an ear, let him hear what the Spirit saith to the churches.

ד

אַחַר הַדְּבָרִים הָאֵלֶּה רָאִיתִי וְהִנֵּה דֶּלֶת פְּתוּחָה בַּשָּׁמַיִם

achar haddevarim ha'elleh ra'iti vehinneh delet ptuchah bashamayim

After these things I saw, and behold, a door opened in heaven,

וְהַקּוֹל הָרִאשׁוֹן - אֲשֶׁר שָׁמַעְתִּי כְּקוֹל שׁוֹפָר מְדַבֵּר אֵלַי - אוֹמֵר

vehakkol harishon - asher shama'ti kekol shofar medabber elai - omer

and the first voice that I heard, a voice as of a trumpet speaking with me, one saying,

עֲלֵה הֵנָּה וְאַרְאֶה לְךָ אֵת אֲשֶׁר צָרִיךְ לִהְיוֹת אַחֲרֵי כֵן

aleh hennah ve'ar'eh lecha et asher tzarich lihyot acharei chen

Come up hither, and I will show thee the things which must come to pass hereafter.

הַהִתְגַּלּוּת

אֲנִי בָּא מַהֵר. הַחֲזֵק בְּמָה שֶׁיֵּשׁ לָךְ, כְּדֵי שֶׁאִישׁ לֹא יִקַּח אֶת הָעֲטֶרֶת שֶׁלְּךָ
ani ba maher. hachazek bemah sheyesh lecha, kedei she'ish lo yikkach et ha'ateret shellecha
I come quickly: hold fast that which thou hast, that no one take thy crown.

הַמְנַצֵּחַ, אֲנִי אֶעֱשֵׂהוּ עַמּוּד בְּהֵיכַל אֱלֹהַי וְלֹא יֵצֵא עוֹד הַחוּצָה
hamnatzeach, ani e'esehu ammud beheichal elohai velo yetzei od hachutzah
He that overcometh, I will make him a pillar in the temple of my God, and he shall go out thence no more:

וְאֶכְתֹּב עָלָיו אֶת שֵׁם אֱלֹהַי וְאֶת שֵׁם עִיר אֱלֹהַי, יְרוּשָׁלַיִם הַחֲדָשָׁה
ve'echtov alav et shem elohai ve'et shem ir elohai, yerushalayim hachadashah
and I will write upon him the name of my God, and the name of the city of my God, the new Jerusalem,

הַיּוֹרֶדֶת מִשָּׁמַיִם מֵאֵת אֱלֹהַי, וְאֶת שְׁמִי הֶחָדָשׁ
hayoredet mishamayim me'et elohai, ve'et shemi hechadash
which cometh down out of heaven from my God, and mine own new name.

מִי שֶׁאֹזֶן לוֹ, יִשְׁמַע נָא מַה שֶׁהָרוּחַ אוֹמֶרֶת לַקְּהִלּוֹת
mi she'ozen lo, yishma na mah sheharuach omeret lakkehillot
He that hath an ear, let him hear what the Spirit saith to the churches.

אֶל מַלְאַךְ קְהִלַּת לָאוֹדִיקֵאָה כְּתֹב אֶת אֵלֶּה הַדְּבָרִים אֹמֵר
el mal'ach kehillat la'odike'ah ktov et elleh haddevarim omer
And to the angel of the church in Laodicea write: These things saith

הָאָמֵן, הָעֵד הַנֶּאֱמָן וְהָאֲמִתִּי, הָרֵאשִׁית שֶׁל בְּרִיאַת אֱלֹהִים
ha'amen, ha'ed hanne'eman veha'amitti, hareshit shel bri'at elohim
the Amen, the faithful and true witness, the beginning of the creation of God:

אֲנִי יוֹדֵעַ אֶת מַעֲשֶׂיךָ, שֶׁלֹּא קַר אַתָּה וְלֹא חַם. מִי יִתֵּן וְהָיִיתָ קַר אוֹ חַם
ani yodea et ma'aseicha, shello kar attah velo cham. mi yitten vehayita kar o cham
I know thy works, that thou art neither cold nor hot: I would thou wert cold or hot.

וּבְכֵן, מִפְּנֵי שֶׁאַתָּה פּוֹשֵׁר וְלֹא חַם וְלֹא קַר, אֲנִי עָתִיד לְהָקִיא אוֹתְךָ מִפִּי
uvchen, mippenei she'attah posher velo cham velo kar, ani atid lehaki otecha mippi
So because thou art lukewarm, and neither hot nor cold, I will spew thee out of my mouth.

מִכֵּיוָן שֶׁאַתָּה אוֹמֵר עָשִׁיר אֲנִי; עָשַׁרְתִּי וְלֹא חָסֵר לִי כְּלוּם
mikkeivan she'attah omer ashir ani; asharti velo chaser li klum
Because thou sayest, I am rich, and have gotten riches, and have need of nothing;

וְאֵינְךָ יוֹדֵעַ שֶׁאַתָּה הָאֻמְלָל וְהַמִּסְכֵּן, עָנִי וְעִוֵּר וְעָרוֹם
ve'eincha yodea she'attah ha'umlal vehammisken, ani ve'ivver ve'arom
and knowest not that thou art the wretched one and miserable and poor and blind and naked:

אָנֹכִי מַצִּיעַ לְךָ לִקְנוֹת מִמֶּנִּי זָהָב צָרוּף בָּאֵשׁ לְמַעַן תַּעֲשִׁיר,
anochi matzia lecha liknot mimmenni zahav tzaruf ba'esh lema'an ta'ashir
I counsel thee to buy of me gold refined by fire, that thou mayest become rich;

הַהִתְגַּלּוּת

הֵמָּה יֵלְכוּ אִתִּי בִּבְגָדִים לְבָנִים, כִּי רְאוּיִים הֵם
hemmah yelechu itti bivgadim levanim, ki re'uyim hem
and they shall walk with me in white; for they are worthy.

הַמְנַצֵּחַ יִלְבַּשׁ בְּגָדִים לְבָנִים וְלֹא אֶמְחֶה אֶת שְׁמוֹ מִסֵּפֶר הַחַיִּים
hamnatzeach yilbash begadim levanim velo emcheh et shemo missefer hachayim
He that overcometh shall thus be arrayed in white garments; and I will in no wise blot his name out of the book of life,

וְאוֹדֶה אֶת שְׁמוֹ לִפְנֵי אָבִי וְלִפְנֵי מַלְאָכָיו
ve'odeh et shemo lifnei avi velifnei mal'achav
and I will confess his name before my Father, and before his angels.

מִי שֶׁאֹזֶן לוֹ, יִשְׁמַע נָא מַה שֶׁהָרוּחַ אוֹמֶרֶת לַקְּהִלּוֹת
mi she'ozen lo, yishma na mah sheharuach omeret lakkehillot
He that hath an ear, let him hear what the Spirit saith to the churches.

אֶל מַלְאַךְ קְהִלַּת פִילָדֶלְפִיָּה כְּתֹב: אֶת אֵלֶּה הַדְּבָרִים אוֹמֵר הַקָּדוֹשׁ, הָאֲמִתִּי
el mal'ach kehillat filadelfiyah ktov: et elleh haddvarim omer hakkadosh, ha'amitti
And to the angel of the church in Philadelphia write: These things saith he that is holy, he that is true,

אֲשֶׁר לוֹ מַפְתֵּחַ דָּוִד, הַפּוֹתֵחַ וְאֵין סוֹגֵר וְסוֹגֵר וְאֵין פּוֹתֵחַ
asher lo mafteach david, happoteach ve'ein soger vesoger ve'ein poteach
he that hath the key of David, he that openeth and none shall shut, and that shutteth and none openeth:

אֲנִי יוֹדֵעַ אֶת מַעֲשֶׂיךָ. הִנֵּה נָתַתִּי לְפָנֶיךָ דֶּלֶת פְּתוּחָה אֲשֶׁר אֵין אִישׁ יָכוֹל לְסָגְרָהּ
ani yodea et ma'aseicha. hinneh natatti lefaneicha delet petuchah asher ein ish yachol lesagerah
I know thy works (behold, I have set before thee a door opened, which none can shut),

כִּי מְעַט כֹּחַ לְךָ וְשָׁמַרְתָּ אֶת דְּבָרַי וְלֹא הִתְכַּחַשְׁתָּ לִשְׁמִי
ki me'at koach lecha veshamarta et devarai velo hitkachashta lishmi
that thou hast a little power, and didst keep my word, and didst not deny my name.

הִנְנִי נוֹתֵן אֲנָשִׁים מִכְּנֶסֶת הַשָּׂטָן, הָאוֹמְרִים יְהוּדִים אֲנַחְנוּ וְאֵינָם; אֵין הֵם אֶלָּא מְשַׁקְּרִים
hineni noten anashim mikkeneset hassatan, ha'omerim yehudim anachnu ve'einam; ein hem ella meshakkerim
Behold, I give of the synagogue of Satan, of them that say they are Jews, and they are not, but do lie;

רְאֵה, אֲנִי אֶעֱשֶׂה שֶׁהֵם יָבוֹאוּ וְיִשְׁתַּחֲווּ לְרַגְלֶיךָ וְיֵדְעוּ שֶׁאֲנִי אֲהַבְתִּיךָ
re'eh, ani e'eseh shehem yavo'u veyishtachavu leragleicha veyed'u she'ani ahavticha
behold, I will make them to come and worship before thy feet, and to know that I have loved thee.

מִפְּנֵי שֶׁשָּׁמַרְתָּ אֶת מִצְוָתִי לַעֲמִידָה בְּסַבְלָנוּת, גַּם אֲנִי אֶשְׁמֹר אוֹתְךָ מִשְּׁעַת הַנִּסָּיוֹן
mippenei sheshamarta et mitzvati la'amidah besavlanut, gam ani eshmor otcha mishe'at hannissayon
Because thou didst keep the word of my patience, I also will keep thee from the hour of trial,

הָעֲתִידָה לָבוֹא עַל כָּל תֵּבֵל, לְנַסּוֹת אֶת יוֹשְׁבֵי הָאָרֶץ
ha'atidah lavo al kol tevel, lenassot et yoshevei ha'aretz
that hour which is to come upon the whole world, to try them that dwell upon the earth.

הַהִתְגַּלּוּת

כְּשֵׁם שֶׁגַּם אֲנִי קִבַּלְתִּי סַמְכוּת מֵאֵת אָבִי

keshem sheggam ani kibbalti samchut me'et avi
as I also have received of my Father:

וְאֶתֵּן לוֹ אֶת כּוֹכַב הַשַּׁחַר

ve'etten lo et kochav hashachar
and I will give him the morning star.

מִי שֶׁאֹזֶן לוֹ, יִשְׁמַע נָא מַה שֶׁהָרוּחַ אוֹמֶרֶת לַקְּהִלּוֹת

mi she'ozen lo, yishma na mah sheharuach omeret lakkehillot
He that hath an ear, let him hear what the Spirit saith to the churches.

ג

אֶל מַלְאַךְ קְהִלַּת סַרְדִּיס כְּתֹב

el mal'ach kehillat sardis ketov
And to the angel of the church in Sardis write:

אֶת אֵלֶּה הַדְּבָרִים אוֹמֵר זֶה אֲשֶׁר לוֹ שֶׁבַע רוּחוֹת הָאֱלֹהִים וְשִׁבְעַת הַכּוֹכָבִים

'et elleh haddevarim omer zeh asher lo sheva ruchot ha'elohim veshiv'at hakkochavim
These things saith he that hath the seven Spirits of God, and the seven stars:

אֲנִי יוֹדֵעַ אֶת מַעֲשֶׂיךָ; יֵשׁ לְךָ שֵׁם שֶׁאַתָּה חַי, וְאַתָּה מֵת

ani yodea et ma'aseicha; yesh lecha shem she'attah chai, ve'attah met
I know thy works, that thou hast a name that thou livest, and thou art dead.

שְׁקֹד וְחַזֵּק אֶת הַשְּׁאֵרִית שֶׁנָּטְתָה לָמוּת

shkod vechazzek et hashe'erit shennatetah lamut
Be thou watchful, and establish the things that remain, which were ready to die:

כִּי לֹא מָצָאתִי אֶת מַעֲשֶׂיךָ מֻשְׁלָמִים לִפְנֵי אֱלֹהָי

ki lo matzati et ma'aseicha mushlamim lifnei elohai
for I have found no works of thine perfected before my God.

לָכֵן זְכֹר כֵּיצַד קִבַּלְתָּ וְשָׁמַעְתָּ, וּשְׁמֹר וַחֲזֹר בִּתְשׁוּבָה

lachen zechor keitzad kibbalta veshama'ta, ushmor vachazor bitshuvah
Remember therefore how thou hast received and didst hear; and keep it, and repent.

אִם לֹא תִּשְׁקֹד אָבוֹא כְּגַנָּב וְלֹא תֵּדַע בְּאֵיזוֹ שָׁעָה אָבוֹא עָלֶיךָ

im lo tishkod avo kegannav velo teda be'eizo sha'ah avo aleicha
If therefore thou shalt not watch, I will come as a thief, and thou shalt not know what hour I will come upon thee.

וְאוּלָם יֵשׁ אֶצְלְךָ שֵׁמוֹת מְעַטִּים בְּסַרְדִּיס אֲשֶׁר לֹא הִכְתִּימוּ אֶת בִּגְדֵיהֶם

ve'ulam yesh etzlecha shemot me'attim besardis asher lo hichtimu et bigdeihem
But thou hast a few names in Sardis that did not defile their garments:

הַהִתְגַּלּוּת

אַךְ יֵשׁ לִי טַעֲנָה נֶגְדְּךָ, כִּי אַתָּה מַנִּיחַ לָאִשָּׁה אִיזֶבֶל הַקּוֹרֵאת לְעַצְמָהּ נְבִיאָה

ach yesh li ta'anah negdecha, ki attah manniach la'ishah izevel hakkoret le'atzmah nevi'ah
But I have this against thee, that thou sufferest the woman Jezebel, who calleth herself a prophetess;

וּמְלַמֶּדֶת וּמַדִּיחָה אֶת עֲבָדַי לִזְנוֹת וְלֶאֱכֹל זִבְחֵי אֱלִילִים

umelammedet umaddichah et avadai liznot vele'echol zivchei elilim
and she teacheth and seduceth my servants to commit fornication, and to eat things sacrificed to idols.

נָתַתִּי לָהּ זְמַן לַחֲזֹר בִּתְשׁוּבָה וְהִיא אֵינָהּ רוֹצָה לָשׁוּב מִתַּזְנוּתָהּ

natatti lah zeman lachazor bitshuvah vehi einah rotzah lashuv mittaznutah
And I gave her time that she should repent; and she willeth not to repent of her fornication.

הִנְנִי מַשְׁלִיךְ אוֹתָהּ לְמִטָּה, וְאֶת הַמְנָאֲפִים עִמָּהּ אַשְׁלִיךְ לְצָרָה גְדוֹלָה

hineni mashlich otah lemittah, ve'et hamna'afim immah ashlich letzarah gedolah
Behold, I cast her into a bed, and them that commit adultery with her into great tribulation,

אִם לֹא יָשׁוּבוּ מִמַּעֲשֵׂיהֶם

im lo yashuvu mimma'aseihem
except they repent of her works.

אֶהֱרֹג בַּמָּוֶת אֶת בָּנֶיהָ וְיֵדְעוּ כָּל הַקְּהִלּוֹת

eherog bammavet et baneiha veyede'u kol hakkehillot
And I will kill her children with death; and all the churches shall know

שֶׁאֲנִי הוּא הַחוֹקֵר כְּלָיוֹת וָלֵב, וְאֶתֵּן לָכֶם אִישׁ אִישׁ כְּמַעֲשָׂיו

she'ani hu hachoker kelayot valev, ve'etten lachem ish ish kema'aseichem
that I am he that searcheth the reins and hearts: and I will give unto each one of you according to your works.

אֲבָל אוֹמֵר אֲנִי לָכֶם, לִשְׁאָר הַנִּמְצָאִים בְּתִיאָטִירָה, כֹּל אֲשֶׁר אֵין לָהֶם הַתּוֹרָה הַזֹּאת

aval omer ani lachem, lish'ar hannimtza'im beti'atirah, kol asher ein lahem hattorah hazzot
But to you I say, to the rest that are in Thyatira, as many as have not this teaching,

וַאֲשֶׁר לֹא יָדְעוּ אֶת עֲמֻקּוֹת הַשָּׂטָן, כְּמוֹ שֶׁנּוֹהֲגִים לוֹמַר - לֹא אָטִיל עֲלֵיכֶם מַשָּׂא אַחֵר

va'asher lo yade'u et amukkot hassatan, kemo shennohagim lomar - lo attil aleichem masho acher
who know not the deep things of Satan, as they are wont to say; I cast upon you none other burden.

בְּרַם הַחֲזִיקוּ בַּמֶּה שֶׁיֵּשׁ לָכֶם עַד אֲשֶׁר אָבוֹא

bram hachaziku bemah sheyesh lachem ad asher avo
Nevertheless that which ye have, hold fast till I come.

הַמְנַצֵּחַ וְשׁוֹמֵר אֶת מַעֲשַׂי עַד קֵץ, אֲנִי אֶתֵּן לוֹ סַמְכוּת עַל הַגּוֹיִם

hamnatzeach veshomer et ma'asai ad ketz, ani etten lo samchut al haggoyim
And he that overcometh, and he that keepeth my works unto the end, to him will I give authority over the nations:

וְיִרְעֶה אוֹתָם בְּשֵׁבֶט בַּרְזֶל, כִּכְלִי חֶרֶס יְנֻפָּצוּ

veyir'eh otam beshevet barzel, kichli cheres yenuppetzu
and he shall rule them with a rod of iron, as the vessels of the potter are broken to shivers;

הַהִתְגַּלּוּת

אֲשֶׁר לִמֵּד אֶת בָּלָק לָשִׂים מִכְשׁוֹל לִפְנֵי בְּנֵי יִשְׂרָאֵל
asher limmed et balak lasim michshol lifnei benei yisra'el
who taught Balak to cast a stumblingblock before the children of Israel,

כְּדֵי שֶׁיֹּאכְלוּ מִזִּבְחֵי אֱלִילִים וְיִזְנוּ
kedei sheyochelu mizzivchei elilim veyiznu
to eat things sacrificed to idols, and to commit fornication.

כֵּן גַּם נִמְצָאִים אֶצְלְךָ אֲנָשִׁים הַמַּחֲזִיקִים בְּתוֹרַת הַנִּיקוֹלָסִים בְּאֹפֶן דּוֹמֶה
ken gam nimtza'im etzlecha anashim hammachazikim betorat hannikolasim be'ofen domeh
So hast thou also some that hold the teaching of the Nicolaitans in like manner.

לָכֵן חֲזֹר בִּתְשׁוּבָה; שֶׁאִם לֹא כֵן, אָבוֹא אֵלֶיךָ מַהֵר וְאֶלָּחֵם בָּהֶם בְּחֶרֶב פִּי
lachen chazor bitshuvah; she'im lo chen, avo eleicha maher ve'ellachem bahem becherev pi
Repent therefore; or else I come to thee quickly, and I will make war against them with the sword of my mouth.

מִי שֶׁאֹזֶן לוֹ, יִשְׁמַע נָא מַה שֶׁהָרוּחַ אוֹמֶרֶת לַקְּהִלּוֹת
mi she'ozen lo, yishma na mah sheharuach omeret lakkehillot
He that hath an ear, let him hear what the Spirit saith to the churches.

הַמְנַצֵּחַ, אֲנִי אֶתֵּן לוֹ מִן הַמָּן הַגָּנוּז
hamnatzeach, ani etten lo min hamman hagganuz
To him that overcometh, to him will I give of the hidden manna,

וְאֶתֵּן לוֹ אֶבֶן לְבָנָה וְעַל הָאֶבֶן כָּתוּב שֵׁם חָדָשׁ
ve'etten lo even levanah ve'al ha'even katuv shem chadash
and I will give him a white stone, and upon the stone a new name written,

אֲשֶׁר לֹא יְדָעֶנּוּ אִישׁ זוּלָתִי הַמְקַבֵּל
asher lo yeda'ennu ish zulati hamkabbel
which no one knoweth but he that receiveth it.

אֶל מַלְאַךְ קְהִלַּת תִּיאָטִירָה כְּתֹב
el mal'ach kehillat ti'atirah ktov
And to the angel of the church in Thyatira write:

אֶת אֵלֶּה הַדְּבָרִים אוֹמֵר בֶּן־הָאֱלֹהִים אֲשֶׁר עֵינָיו כְּשַׁלְהֶבֶת אֵשׁ וְרַגְלָיו כְּמוֹ נְחֹשֶׁת נוֹצֶצֶת
et elleh haddevarim omer ben-ha'elohim asher einav keshalhevet esh veraglav kemo nechoshet notzetzet
These things saith the Son of God, who hath his eyes like a flame of fire, and his feet are like unto burnished brass:

אֲנִי יוֹדֵעַ אֶת מַעֲשֶׂיךָ וְאֶת אַהֲבָתְךָ, אֶת אֱמוּנָתְךָ, אֶת שֵׁרוּתְךָ וְסַבְלָנוּתְךָ
ani yodea et ma'aseicha ve'et ahavatecha, et emunatcha, et sherutech vesavlanutecha
I know thy works, and thy love and faith and ministry and patience,

וּמַעֲשֶׂיךָ הָאַחֲרוֹנִים רַבִּים מִן הָרִאשׁוֹנִים
uma'aseicha ha'acharonim rabbim min harishonim
and that thy last works are more than the first.

הַהִתְגַּלּוּת

אֶל מַלְאַךְ קְהִלַּת זְמִירְנָה כְּתֹב: אֶת אֵלֶּה הַדְּבָרִים אוֹמֵר הָרִאשׁוֹן וְהָאַחֲרוֹן, אֲשֶׁר מֵת וַיֶּחִי
el mal'ach kehillat zmirnah ktov. 'et elleh haddevarim omer harishon veha'acharon, asher met vayechi
And to the angel of the church in Smyrna write: These things saith the first and the last, who was dead, and lived again:

אֲנִי יוֹדֵעַ אֶת צָרָתְךָ וְאֶת עָנְיְךָ - אֶלָּא שֶׁעָשִׁיר אַתָּה
ani yodea et tzaratcha ve'et onyecha - ella she'ashir attah
I know thy tribulation, and thy poverty (but thou art rich),

וְאֶת גִּדּוּפָם שֶׁל הָאוֹמְרִים 'יְהוּדִים אֲנַחְנוּ' וְאֵינָם אֶלָּא כְּנֶסֶת הַשָּׂטָן
ve'et giddufam shel ha'omerim 'yehudim anachnu' ve'einam ella keneset hassatan
and the blasphemy of them that say they are Jews, and they are not, but are a synagogue of Satan.

אַל תִּירָא מִפְּנֵי מַה שֶּׁאַתָּה עָתִיד לִסְבֹּל
al tira mippenei mah she'attah atid lisbol
Fear not the things which thou art about to suffer:

הִנֵּה עָתִיד הַשָּׂטָן לְהַשְׁלִיךְ אֲנָשִׁים מִכֶּם לַכֶּלֶא כְּדֵי שֶׁתְּנֻסּוּ, וְתִהְיֶה לָכֶם צָרָה עֲשֶׂרֶת יָמִים
hinneh atid hassatan lehashlich anashim mikkem lakkelei kedei shettenussu, vetihyeh lachem tzarah aseret yamim
behold, the devil is about to cast some of you into prison, that ye may be tried; and ye shall have tribulation ten days.

הֱיֵה נֶאֱמָן עַד מָוֶת וְאֶתֵּן לְךָ עֲטֶרֶת הַחַיִּים
heyeh ne'eman ad mavet ve'etten lecha ateret hachayim
Be thou faithful unto death, and I will give thee the crown of life.

מִי שֶׁאֹזֶן לוֹ, יִשְׁמַע נָא מַה שֶׁהָרוּחַ אוֹמֶרֶת לַקְּהִלּוֹת
mi she'ozen lo, yishma na mah sheharuach omeret lakkehillot
He that hath an ear, let him hear what the Spirit saith to the churches.

הַמְנַצֵּחַ לֹא יִנָּזֵק בַּמָּוֶת הַשֵּׁנִי
hamnatzeach lo yinnazek bammavet hasheni
He that overcometh shall not be hurt of the second death.

אֶל מַלְאַךְ קְהִלַּת פֶּרְגָמוֹס כְּתֹב אֶת אֵלֶּה הַדְּבָרִים אוֹמֵר זֶה אֲשֶׁר לוֹ חֶרֶב הַפִּיפִיּוֹת הַחַדָּה
el mal'ach kehillat pergamos ketov et elleh haddevarim omer zeh asher lo cherev happifiyot hachaddah
And to the angel of the church in Pergamum write: These things saith he that hath the sharp two-edged sword:

אֲנִי יוֹדֵעַ אֶת מְקוֹם שִׁבְתְּךָ, אֲשֶׁר שָׁם כִּסֵּא הַשָּׂטָן. אַתָּה מַחֲזִיק בִּשְׁמִי וְלֹא הִתְכַּחַשְׁתָּ לֶאֱמוּנָתִי
ani yodea et mekom shivtecha, asher sham kissei hassatan. attah machazik bishmi velo hitkachashta le'emunati
I know where thou dwellest, even where Satan's throne is; and thou holdest fast my name, and didst not deny my faith,

אֲפִלּוּ בִּימֵי אַנְטִיפָּס עֵדִי הַנֶּאֱמָן אֲשֶׁר נֶהֱרַג אֶצְלְכֶם בִּמְקוֹם מוֹשָׁבוֹ שֶׁל הַשָּׂטָן
afillu biymei antipas edi hanne'eman asher neherag etzlechem bimkom moshavo shel hassatan
even in the days of Antipas my witness, my faithful one, who was killed among you, where Satan dwelleth.

אַךְ יֵשׁ לִי נֶגְדְּךָ דְּבָרִים מְעַטִּים: יֵשׁ לְךָ שָׁם אֲנָשִׁים הַמַּחֲזִיקִים בְּתוֹרַת בִּלְעָם
ach yesh li negdecha devarim me'attim. yesh lecha sham anashim hammachazikim betorat bil'am
But I have a few things against thee, because thou hast there some that hold the teaching of Balaam,

ההתגלות

ב

אֶל מַלְאַךְ קְהִלַּת אֶפֶסוֹס כְּתֹב: אֶת אֵלֶּה הַדְּבָרִים אוֹמֵר הָאוֹחֵז בִּימִינוֹ אֶת שִׁבְעַת הַכּוֹכָבִים
el mal'ach kehillat efesos ketov: et elleh haddevarim omer ha'ochez bimino et shiv'at hakkochavim
To the angel of the church in Ephesus write: These things saith he that holdeth the seven stars in his right hand,

הַמִּתְהַלֵּךְ בֵּין שֶׁבַע מְנוֹרוֹת הַזָּהָב
hammit'hallech bein sheva menorot hazzahav
he that walketh in the midst of the seven golden candlesticks:

אֲנִי יוֹדֵעַ אֶת מַעֲשֶׂיךָ וְאֶת עֲמָלְךָ וְאֶת סַבְלָנוּתְךָ וְשֶׁאֵינְךָ יָכוֹל לָשֵׂאת אַנְשֵׁי רֶשַׁע
ani yodea et ma'aseicha ve'et amalcha ve'et savlanutecha veshe'einecha yachol laset anshei resha
I know thy works, and thy toil and patience, and that thou canst not bear evil men,

בָּחַנְתָּ אֶת הַמְכַנִּים עַצְמָם שְׁלִיחִים וְאֵינָם, וּמָצָאתָ אוֹתָם כּוֹזְבִים
bachanta et hamchannim atzmam shelichim ve'einam, umatzata otam kozevim
and didst try them that call themselves apostles, and they are not, and didst find them false;

יֵשׁ לְךָ סַבְלָנוּת וְסָבַלְתָּ בִּגְלַל שְׁמִי וְלֹא עָיַפְתָּ
yesh lecha savlanut vesavalta biglal shemi velo ayafta
and thou hast patience and didst bear for my name's sake, and hast not grown weary.

אֲבָל יֵשׁ לִי טַעֲנָה נֶגְדְּךָ, כִּי עָזַבְתָּ אֶת אַהֲבָתְךָ הָרִאשׁוֹנָה
aval yesh li ta'anah negdecha, ki azavta et ahavatcha harishonah
But I have this against thee, that thou didst leave thy first love.

לָכֵן זְכֹר מִנַּיִן נָפַלְתָּ וַחֲזֹר בִּתְשׁוּבָה וַעֲשֵׂה אֶת הַמַּעֲשִׂים הָרִאשׁוֹנִים
lachen zechor minnayin nafalta vachazor bitshuvah va'aseh et hamma'asim harishonim
Remember therefore whence thou art fallen, and repent and do the first works;

שֶׁאִם לֹא כֵן, אָבוֹא אֵלֶיךָ וְאָסִיר אֶת מְנוֹרָתְךָ מִמְּקוֹמָהּ - אִם לֹא תַּחֲזֹר בִּתְשׁוּבָה
she'im lo chen, avo eleicha ve'asir et menoratcha mimmekomah - im lo tachazor bitshuvah
or else I come to thee, and will move thy candlestick out of its place, except thou repent.

אַךְ זֹאת לִזְכוּתְךָ: אַתָּה שׂוֹנֵא אֶת מַעֲשֵׂי הַנִּיקוֹלְסִים אֲשֶׁר גַּם אֲנִי שׂוֹנֵא
ach zot lizchutecha: attah sonei et ma'asei hannikolasim asher gam ani sonei
But this thou hast, that thou hatest the works of the Nicolaitans, which I also hate.

מִי שֶׁאֹזֶן לוֹ, יִשְׁמַע נָא מַה שֶׁהָרוּחַ אוֹמֶרֶת לַקְּהִלּוֹת.
mi she'ozen lo, yishma na mah sheharuach omeret lakkehillot
He that hath an ear, let him hear what the Spirit saith to the churches.

הַמְנַצֵּחַ, אֲנִי אֶתֵּן לוֹ לֶאֱכֹל מֵעֵץ הַחַיִּים אֲשֶׁר בְּגַן אֱלֹהִים
hamnatzeach, ani etten lo le'echol me'etz hachayim asher began elohim
To him that overcometh, to him will I give to eat of the tree of life, which is in the Paradise of God.

הַהִתְגַּלּוּת

רֹאשׁוֹ וּשְׂעָרוֹ לְבָנִים כְּצֶמֶר לָבָן כַּשֶּׁלֶג, וְעֵינָיו כְּשַׁלְהֶבֶת אֵשׁ
rosho use'aro levanim ketzemer lavan kasheleg, ve'einav keshalhevet esh
And his head and his hair were white as white wool, white as snow; and his eyes were as a flame of fire;

רַגְלָיו כְּמוֹ נְחֹשֶׁת נוֹצֶצֶת שֶׁנִּצְרְפָה בַּכּוּר, וְקוֹלוֹ כְּקוֹל מַיִם רַבִּים
raglav kemo nechoshet notzetzet shennitzrefah bakkur, vekolo kekol mayim rabbim
and his feet like unto burnished brass, as if it had been refined in a furnace; and his voice as the voice of many waters.

בְּיַד יְמִינוֹ שִׁבְעָה כּוֹכָבִים; מִפִּיו יוֹצֵאת חֶרֶב פִּיפִיּוֹת חַדָּה
beyad yemino shiv'ah kochavim; mippiv yotzet cherev pifiyot chaddah
And he had in his right hand seven stars: and out of his mouth proceeded a sharp two-edged sword:

וּפָנָיו כַּשֶּׁמֶשׁ הַמְּאִירָה בִּגְבוּרָתָהּ
ufanav kashemesh hamme'irah bigvuratah
and his countenance was as the sun shineth in his strength.

כַּאֲשֶׁר רְאִיתִיו נָפַלְתִּי לְרַגְלָיו כַּמֵּת, וְהוּא שָׂם אֶת יַד יְמִינוֹ עָלַי וְאָמַר
ka'asher re'itiv nafalti leraglav kammet, vehu sam et yad yemino alai ve'amar
And when I saw him, I fell at his feet as one dead. And he laid his right hand upon me, saying,

אַל תִּירָא. אֲנִי הָרִאשׁוֹן וְהָאַחֲרוֹן וְהַחַי
al tira. ani harishon veha'acharon vehachai
Fear not; I am the first and the last,

הָיִיתִי מֵת וְהִנֵּה חַי אֲנִי לְעוֹלְמֵי עוֹלָמִים, וְלִי מַפְתְּחוֹת שְׁאוֹל וָמָוֶת
hayiti met vehinneh chai ani le'olemei olamim, veli maftechot she'ol vamavet
and the Living one; and I was dead, and behold, I am alive for evermore, and I have the keys of death and of Hades.

כְּתֹב אֵת אֲשֶׁר רָאִיתָ וְאֵת אֲשֶׁר הֹוֶה
ketov et asher ra'ita ve'et asher hoveh
Write therefore the things which thou sawest, and the things which are,

וְאֵת אֲשֶׁר עָתִיד לִהְיוֹת אַחֲרֵי כֵן
ve'et asher atid lihyot acharei chen
and the things which shall come to pass hereafter;

אֶת סוֹד שִׁבְעַת הַכּוֹכָבִים אֲשֶׁר רָאִיתָ בִּימִינִי וְשֶׁבַע מְנוֹרוֹת הַזָּהָב
et sod shiv'at hakkochavim asher ra'ita biymini vesheva menorot hazzahav
the mystery of the seven stars which thou sawest in my right hand, and the seven golden candlesticks.

שִׁבְעַת הַכּוֹכָבִים הֵם מַלְאֲכֵי שֶׁבַע הַקְּהִלּוֹת, וְשֶׁבַע הַמְּנוֹרוֹת הֵן שֶׁבַע קְהִלּוֹת
shiv'at hakkochavim hem mal'achei sheva hakkehillot, vesheva hammenorot hen sheva kehillot
The seven stars are the angels of the seven churches: and the seven candlesticks are seven churches.

הַהִתְגַּלּוּת

לוֹ הַכָּבוֹד וְהַגְּבוּרָה לְעוֹלְמֵי עוֹלָמִים. אָמֵן
lo hakkavod vehaggevurah le'olemei olamim. amen
to him be the glory and the dominion for ever and ever. Amen.

הִנֵּה הוּא בָּא עִם הָעֲנָנִים. כָּל עַיִן תִּרְאֶה אוֹתוֹ, גַּם אֵלֶּה שֶׁדְּקָרוּהוּ
hinneh hu ba im ha'ananim. kol ayin tir'eh oto, gam elleh sheddekaruhu
Behold, he cometh with the clouds; and every eye shall see him, and they that pierced him;

וְיִסְפְּדוּ עָלָיו כָּל מִשְׁפְּחוֹת הָאָרֶץ. כֵּן; אָמֵן
veyispedu alav kol mishpechot ha'aretz. ken; amen
and all the tribes of the earth shall mourn over him. Even so, Amen.

אֲנִי הָאָלֶף אַף אֲנִי הַתָּו, נְאֻם יהוה אֱלֹהִים, הַהֹוֶה וְהָיָה וְיָבוֹא, אֱלֹהֵי צְבָאוֹת
ani ha'alef af ani hattav, ne'um hashem elohim, hahoveh vehayah veyavo, elohei tzeva'ot
I am the Alpha and the Omega, saith the Lord God, who is and who was and who is to come, the Almighty.

אֲנִי יוֹחָנָן אֲחִיכֶם וְשֻׁתָּף בַּצָּרָה וּבַמַּלְכוּת וּבַסַּבְלָנוּת בְּיֵשׁוּעַ
ani yochanan achichem veshuttaf batzarah uvammalchut uvassavlanut beyeshua
I John, your brother and partaker with you in the tribulation and kingdom and patience which are in Jesus,

הָיִיתִי בָּאִי הַקָּרוּי פַּטְמוֹס בַּעֲבוּר דְּבַר אֱלֹהִים וְעֵדוּת יֵשׁוּעַ
hayiti ba'i hakkarui patmos ba'avur devar elohim ve'edut yeshua
was in the isle that is called Patmos, for the word of God and the testimony of Jesus.

הָיִיתִי בְּהַשְׁרָאַת הָרוּחַ בְּיוֹם הָאָדוֹן וְשָׁמַעְתִּי מֵאַחֲרַי קוֹל גָּדוֹל כְּקוֹל שׁוֹפָר
hayiti behashra'at haruach beyom ha'adon veshama'ti me'acharai kol gadol kekol shofar
I was in the Spirit on the Lord's day, and I heard behind me a great voice, as of a trumpet

אוֹמֵר: אֶת אֲשֶׁר אַתָּה רוֹאֶה כְּתֹב בְּסֵפֶר וּשְׁלַח אֶל שֶׁבַע הַקְּהִלּוֹת: אֶל אֶפֶסוֹס, אֶל זְמִירְנָה
Omer: et asher attah ro'eh ketov besefer ushelach el sheva hakkehillot: el efesos, el zemirenah
saying, What thou seest, write in a book and send it to the seven churches: unto Ephesus, and unto Smyrna,

אֶל פֶּרְגָמוֹס, אֶל תִּיאָטִירָה, אֶל סַרְדִּיס, אֶל פִילַדֶלְפִיָּה וְאֶל לָאוֹדִיקֵאָה
el pergamos, el ti'atirah, el sardis, el filadelfiyah ve'el la'odike'ah
and unto Pergamum, and unto Thyatira, and unto Sardis, and unto Philadelphia, and unto Laodicea.

פָּנִיתִי לִרְאוֹת אֶת הַקּוֹל הַמְדַבֵּר אֵלַי, וּכְשֶׁפָּנִיתִי רָאִיתִי שֶׁבַע מְנוֹרוֹת זָהָב
paniti lir'ot et hakkol hamedabber elai, ucheshepaniti ra'iti sheva menorot zahav
And I turned to see the voice that spake with me. And having turned I saw seven golden candlesticks;

וּבֵין שֶׁבַע הַמְּנוֹרוֹת כְּמַרְאֵה בֶּן־אָדָם
uvein sheva hammenorot kemar'eh ben-'adam
and in the midst of the candlesticks one like unto a son of man,

עוֹטֶה מְעִיל עַד מַרְגְּלוֹתָיו וְחָגוּר חֲגוֹרַת זָהָב עַל חָזֵהוּ
oteh me'il ad margelotav vechagur chagorat zahav al chazehu
clothed with a garment down to the foot, and girt about at the breasts with a golden girdle.

הַהִתְגַּלּוּת

הִתְגַּלּוּת יֵשׁוּעַ הַמָּשִׁיחַ שֶׁנָּתַן לוֹ הָאֱלֹהִים כְּדֵי לְהַרְאוֹת לַעֲבָדָיו
hitgallut yeshua hammashiach shennatan lo ha'elohim kedei lehar'ot la'avadav
The Revelation of Jesus Christ, which God gave him to show unto his servants,

אֵת אֲשֶׁר צָרִיךְ לִהְיוֹת בִּמְהֵרָה. וְהוּא שָׁלַח בְּיַד מַלְאָכוֹ וְהוֹדִיעַ לְעַבְדּוֹ יוֹחָנָן
et asher tzarich lihyot bimherah. vehu shalach beyad mal'acho vehodia le'avdo yochanan
even the things which must shortly come to pass: and he sent and signified it by his angel unto his servant John;

שֶׁהֵעִיד אֶת דְּבַר אֱלֹהִים וְאֶת עֵדוּת יֵשׁוּעַ הַמָּשִׁיחַ, אֵת כָּל אֲשֶׁר רָאָה
shehe'id et devar elohim ve'et edut yeshua hammashiach, et kol asher ra'ah
who bare witness of the word of God, and of the testimony of Jesus Christ, even of all things that he saw.

אַשְׁרֵי הַקּוֹרֵא וְאַשְׁרֵי הַשּׁוֹמְעִים אֶת דִּבְרֵי הַנְּבוּאָה
ashrei hakkorei ve'ashrei hashome'im et divrei hannevu'ah
Blessed is he that readeth, and they that hear the words of the prophecy,

וְשׁוֹמְרִים אֶת הַכָּתוּב בָּהּ, כִּי קְרוֹבָה הָעֵת
veshomerim et hakkatuv bah, ki kerovah ha'et
and keep the things that are written therein: for the time is at hand.

יוֹחָנָן אֶל שֶׁבַע הַקְּהִלּוֹת אֲשֶׁר בְּאַסְיָה
yochanan el sheva hakkehillot asher be'asyah
John to the seven churches that are in Asia:

חֶסֶד וְשָׁלוֹם לָכֶם מֵאֵת הַהֹוֶה וְהָיָה וְיָבוֹא
chesed veshalom lachem me'et hahoveh vehayah veyavo
Grace to you and peace, from him who is and who was and who is to come;

וּמֵאֵת שֶׁבַע הָרוּחוֹת אֲשֶׁר לִפְנֵי כִסְאוֹ
ume'et sheva haruchot asher lifnei kis'o
and from the seven Spirits that are before his throne;

וּמֵאֵת יֵשׁוּעַ הַמָּשִׁיחַ הָעֵד הַנֶּאֱמָן, בְּכוֹר הַמֵּתִים וְעֶלְיוֹן לְמַלְכֵי הָאָרֶץ
ume'et yeshua hammashiach ha'ed hanne'eman, bechor hammetim ve'elyon lemalchei ha'aretz
and from Jesus Christ, who is the faithful witness, the firstborn of the dead, and the ruler of the kings of the earth.

לָאוֹהֵב אוֹתָנוּ אֲשֶׁר בְּדָמוֹ שִׁחְרֵר אוֹתָנוּ מֵחֲטָאֵינוּ
la'ohev otanu asher bedamo shichrer otanu mechata'einu
Unto him that loveth us, and loosed us from our sins by his blood;

וְעָשָׂה אוֹתָנוּ מַמְלֶכֶת כֹּהֲנִים לֵאלֹהִים אָבִיו
ve'asah otanu mamlechet kohanim le'elohim aviv
and he made us to be a kingdom, to be priests unto his God and Father;

יְהוּדָה

לוֹ הַכָּבוֹד וְהַגְּדֻלָּה וְהָעֹז וְהַשִּׁלְטוֹן לִפְנֵי כָל עוֹלָם, גַּם עַתָּה גַּם לְכָל הָעוֹלָמִים. אָמֵן
lo hakkavod vehaggdullah veha'oz vehashilton lifnei kol olam, gam attah gam lechol ha'olamim. amen
be glory, majesty, dominion and power, before all time, and now, and for evermore. Amen.

יְהוּדָה

נוֹהֲגִים בְּמַשֹוֹא פָנִים לְמַעַן רֶוַח

nohagim bemasso panim lema'an revach
showing respect of persons for the sake of advantage.

אֲבָל אַתֶּם, אֲהוּבַי, זִכְרוּ אֶת הַדְּבָרִים שֶׁנֶּאֶמְרוּ קֹדֶם בְּיַד שְׁלִיחֵי אֲדוֹנֵנוּ יֵשׁוּעַ הַמָּשִׁיחַ

aval attem, ahuvai, zichru et haddevarim shenne'emru kodem beyad shelichei adonenu yeshua hammashiach
But ye, beloved, remember ye the words which have been spoken before by the apostles of our Lord Jesus Christ;

הֲרֵי אָמְרוּ לָכֶם כִּי, בְּאַחֲרִית הַיָּמִים יָבוֹאוּ לֵצִים הַהוֹלְכִים אַחַר תַּאֲווֹתֵיהֶם הַמְרֻשָּׁעוֹת

harei ameru lachem ki, be'acharit hayamim yavo'u leitzim haholechim achar ta'avoteihem hamrusha'ot
that they said to you, In the last time there shall be mockers, walking after their own ungodly lusts.

אֵלֶּה הֵם הַגּוֹרְמִים פִּלּוּגִים; מְשֻׁעְבָּדִים הֵם לַנֶּפֶשׁ, וְרוּחַ אֵין לָהֶם

elleh hem haggoremim pillugim; meshu'badim hem lannefesh, veruach ein lahem
These are they who make separations, sensual, having not the Spirit.

וְאַתֶּם, אֲהוּבַי, הִבָּנוּ בֶּאֱמוּנַתְכֶם הַנַּעֲלָה מְאֹד בִּקְדֻשָּׁתָהּ וְהִתְפַּלְלוּ בְּרוּחַ הַקֹּדֶשׁ

ve'attem, ahuvai, hibbanu be'emunatchem hanna'alah me'od bikdushatah vehitpallelu beruach hakkodesh
But ye, beloved, building up yourselves on your most holy faith, praying in the Holy Spirit,

שִׁמְרוּ אֶת עַצְמְכֶם בְּאַהֲבַת הָאֱלֹהִים וְחַכּוּ לְרַחֲמֵי אֲדוֹנֵנוּ יֵשׁוּעַ הַמָּשִׁיחַ לְשֵׁם חַיֵּי עוֹלָם

shimru et atzmechem be'ahavat ha'elohim vechakku lerachamei adonenu yeshua hammashiach leshem chayei olam
keep yourselves in the love of God, looking for the mercy of our Lord Jesus Christ unto eternal life.

יֵשׁ הַמְהַסְּסִים, הִתְנַהֲגוּ עִמָּהֶם בְּרַחֲמִים

yesh hamhassesim, hitnahagu immahem berachamim
And on some have mercy, who are in doubt;

חִטְפוּ אוֹתָם מִן הָאֵשׁ וְהוֹשִׁיעוּ אוֹתָם. עַל אֲחֵרִים רַחֲמוּ בְּיִרְאָה

chitfu otam min ha'esh vehoshi'u otam. al acherim rachamu beyir'ah
and some save, snatching them out of the fire; and on some have mercy with fear;

וְעִם זֹאת שִׂנְאוּ אֶת הַלְּבוּשׁ הַמְגֹאָל בְּטֻמְאַת הַבָּשָׂר

ve'im zot sin'u et hallevush hamgo'al betum'at habbasar
hating even the garment spotted by the flesh.

וְהוּא אֲשֶׁר יָכוֹל לִשְׁמֹר אֶתְכֶם מִמִּכְשׁוֹל

vehu asher yachol lishmor etchem mimmichshol
Now unto him that is able to guard you from stumbling,

וּלְהַעֲמִיד אֶתְכֶם לִפְנֵי כְּבוֹדוֹ נְקִיִּים מִדֹּפִי וּמְלֵאֵי גִיל

uleha'amid etchem lifnei kevodo nekiyim middofi umele'ei gil
and to set you before the presence of his glory without blemish in exceeding joy,

הָאֱלֹהִים הַיָּחִיד, מוֹשִׁיעֵנוּ עַל־יְדֵי יֵשׁוּעַ הַמָּשִׁיחַ אֲדוֹנֵנוּ

ha'elohim hayachid, moshi'enu al-yedei yeshua hammashich adonenu
to the only God our Saviour, through Jesus Christ our Lord,

יְהוּדָה

וּבַעֲבוּר שָׂכָר הִתְמַסְּרוּ לְטָעוּת בִּלְעָם, וְאָבְדוּ בְּמֶרֶד קֹרַח
uva'avur sachar hitmasseru leta'ut bil'am, ve'avedu bemered korach
and ran riotously in the error of Balaam for hire, and perished in the gainsaying of Korah.

אַבְנֵי נֶגֶף הֵם בִּסְעוּדוֹת הָאַחֲוָה שֶׁלָּכֶם
avnei negef hem bis'udot ha'achavah shellachem
These are they who are hidden rocks in your love-feasts when they feast with you,

סוֹעֲדִים עִמָּכֶם לְלֹא יִרְאָה וְדוֹאֲגִים רַק לְעַצְמָם; עֲנָנִים חַסְרֵי מַיִם הַנִּדָּפִים בָּרוּחַ
so'adim immachem lelo yir'ah vedo'agim rak le'atzmam; ananim chasrei mayim hanniddafim baruach
shepherds that without fear feed themselves; clouds without water, carried along by winds;

עֵצִים בְּשַׁלֶּכֶת בְּלֹא פְּרִי, אֲשֶׁר מֵתוּ פַּעֲמַיִם וְנֶעֶקְרוּ
etzim beshallechet belo peri, asher metu pa'amayim vene'ekru
autumn trees without fruit, twice dead, plucked up by the roots;

גַּלֵּי יָם עַזִּים הַמַּעֲלִים כְּקֶצֶף אֶת חֶרְפָּתָם
gallei yam azzim hamma'alim keketzef et cherpatam
wild waves of the sea, foaming out their own shame;

כּוֹכָבִים תּוֹעִים אֲשֶׁר חֶשְׁכַת אֹפֶל שְׁמוּרָה לָהֶם לְעוֹלָם
kochavim to'im asher cheshchat ofel shemurah lahem le'olam
wandering stars, for whom the blackness of darkness hath been reserved for ever.

גַּם חֲנוֹךְ, הַשְּׁבִיעִי לְאָדָם, נִבָּא עֲלֵיהֶם לֵאמֹר
gam chanoch, hashevi'i le'adam, nibba aleihem le'emor
And to these also Enoch, the seventh from Adam, prophesied, saying,

הִנֵּה יהוה בָּא בְּרִבְבוֹת קְדוֹשָׁיו
hinneh hashem ba berivevot kedoshav
Behold, the Lord came with ten thousands of his holy ones,

לַעֲשׂוֹת מִשְׁפָּט בַּכֹּל
la'asot mishpat bakkol
to execute judgment upon all,

וּלְהוֹכִיחַ אֶת כָּל הָרְשָׁעִים עַל כָּל מַעֲשֵׂי רִשְׁעָתָם
ulehochiach et kol haresha'im al kol ma'asei rish'atam
and to convict all the ungodly of all their works of ungodlinesswhich they have ungodly wrought,

וְעַל כָּל הַקָּשׁוֹת אֲשֶׁר דִּבְּרוּ עָלָיו חוֹטְאִים רְשָׁעִים
ve'al kol hakkashot asher dibbru alav chote'im resha'im
and of all the hard things which ungodly sinners have spoken against him.

הַלָּלוּ רוֹגְנִים הֵם, מִתְלוֹנְנִים, הוֹלְכִים אַחַר תַּאֲוֺתֵיהֶם וּפִיהֶם מְדַבֵּר גְּבוֹהָה
hallalu rogenim hem, mitlonenim, holechim achar ta'avoteihem ufihem medabber gevohah
These are murmurers, complainers, walking after their lusts (and their mouth speaketh great swelling words),

יְהוּדָה

וְאֶת הַמַּלְאָכִים, אֲשֶׁר לֹא שָׁמְרוּ אֶת מַעֲמָדָם הָרָם כִּי אִם עָזְבוּ אֶת מְעוֹנָם,
ve'et hammal'achim, asher lo shameru et ma'amadam haram ki im azvu et me'onam
And angels that kept not their own principality, but left their proper habitation,

שָׁמַר בְּכַבְלֵי עוֹלָם וּבַאֲפֵלָה לְמִשְׁפַּט הַיּוֹם הַגָּדוֹל
shamar bechavlei olam uva'afelah lemishpat hayom haggadol
he hath kept in everlasting bonds under darkness unto the judgment of the great day.

כְּשֵׁם שֶׁסְּדוֹם וַעֲמֹרָה וְהֶעָרִים הַקְּרוֹבוֹת
keshem shessedom va'amorah vehe'arim hakkrovot
Even as Sodom and Gomorrah, and the cities about them,

אֲשֶׁר בְּדֶרֶךְ דּוֹמָה לָהֶם הִתְמַכְּרוּ לִזְנוּת וְהָלְכוּ אַחַר יְצוּרִים אֲחֵרִים
asher bederech domah lahem hitmakkeru liznut vehalechu achar yetzurim acherim
having in like manner with these given themselves over to fornication and gone after strange flesh,

מֻצָּגוֹת לְדֻגְמָה בְּסָבְלָן דִּין אֵשׁ עוֹלָם
mutzagot ledugmah besovlan din esh olam
are set forth as an example, suffering the punishment of eternal fire.

כְּמוֹ כֵן גַּם בַּעֲלֵי־הַחֲלוֹמוֹת הָאֵלֶּה מְטַמְּאִים אֶת הַגּוּף
kemo chen gam ba'alei-hachalomot ha'elleh metamme'im et hagguf
Yet in like manner these also in their dreamings defile the flesh,

דּוֹחִים אֶת הַסַּמְכוּת הָעֶלְיוֹנָה וּמְגַדְּפִים אֶת נוֹשְׂאֵי הַמִּשְׂרוֹת הַנִּכְבָּדוֹת
dochim et hassamchut ha'elyonah umegaddefim et nose'ei hammisrot hannichbadot
and set at nought dominion, and rail at dignities.

אַךְ מִיכָאֵל, שַׂר הַמַּלְאָכִים, כַּאֲשֶׁר רָב עִם הַשָּׂטָן וְהִתְוַכֵּחַ עַל גְּוִיַּת מֹשֶׁה
ach micha'el, sar hammal'achim, ka'asher rav im hassatan vehitvakkeach al geviyat mosheh
But Michael the archangel, when contending with the devil he disputed about the body of Moses,

לֹא הֵעֵז לַחֲרֹץ מִשְׁפַּט גִּדּוּף, כִּי אִם אָמַר, יִגְעַר יהוה בְּךָ
lo he'ez lacharotz mishpat gidduf, ki im amar, yig'ar hashem becha
durst not bring against him a railing judgment, but said, The Lord rebuke thee.

אֵלֶּה, לְעֻמַּת זֹאת, מְגַדְּפִים אֵת אֲשֶׁר אֵינָם יוֹדְעִים; וּבִדְבָרִים אֲשֶׁר הֵם מְבִינִים בְּאֹפֶן טִבְעִי
elleh, le'ummat zot, megaddfim et asher einam yod'im; uvidvarim asher hem mevinim be'ofen tiv'i
But these rail at whatsoever things they know not: and what they understand naturally,

כַּחַיּוֹת חַסְרוֹת דַּעַת, בָּהֶם הֵם נִשְׁחָתִים
kechayot chasrot da'at, bahem hem nishchatim
like the creatures without reason, in these things are they destroyed.

אוֹי לָהֶם, כִּי בְּדֶרֶךְ קַיִן הָלְכוּ
oy lahem, ki bederech kayin halechu
Woe unto them! for they went in the way of Cain,

יְהוּדָה

מֵאֵת יְהוּדָה, עֶבֶד יֵשׁוּעַ הַמָּשִׁיחַ וְאָחִיו שֶׁל יַעֲקֹב
me'et yehudah, eved yeshua hammashiach ve'achiv shel ya'akov
Jude, a servant of Jesus Christ, and brother of James,

אֶל הַקְּרוּאִים, הָאֲהוּבִים עַל אֱלֹהִים הָאָב וּשְׁמוּרִים לְיֵשׁוּעַ הַמָּשִׁיחַ
el hakkeru'im, ha'ahuvim al elohim ha'av ushmurim leyeshua hammashiach
to them that are called, beloved in God the Father, and kept for Jesus Christ:

רַחֲמִים וְשָׁלוֹם וְאַהֲבָה יִשָּׁפְעוּ עֲלֵיכֶם לְמַכְבִּיר
rachamim veshalom ve'ahavah yishpe'u aleichem lemachbir
Mercy unto you and peace and love be multiplied.

אֲהוּבַי, כַּאֲשֶׁר שָׁקַדְתִּי בְּכָל מְאֹדִי לִכְתֹּב לָכֶם עַל־דְּבַר יְשׁוּעָתֵנוּ הַמְשֻׁתֶּפֶת
ahuvai, ka'asher shakadti bechol me'odi lichtov lachem al-devar yeshu'atenu hamshuttefet
Beloved, while I was giving all diligence to write unto you of our common salvation,

נֵעוֹר בִּי הַצֹּרֶךְ לִכְתֹּב אֲלֵיכֶם וְלַהֲאִיצְכֶם לְהִלָּחֵם לְמַעַן הָאֱמוּנָה
ne'or bi hatzorech lichtov aleichem velaha'itzechem lehillachem lema'an ha'emunah
I was constrained to write unto you exhorting you to contend earnestly for the faith

שֶׁנִּמְסְרָה אַחַת וּלְתָמִיד לַקְּדוֹשִׁים
shennimserah achat uletamid lakkdoshim
which was once for all delivered unto the saints.

כִּי הִתְגַּנְּבוּ אֲנָשִׁים אֲשֶׁר הַמִּשְׁפָּט הַזֶּה נֶחֱרַץ עֲלֵיהֶם מִקֶּדֶם
ki hitgannevu anashim asher hammishpat hazzeh necheratz aleihem mikkedem
For there are certain men crept in privily, even they who were of old written of beforehand unto this condemnation,

אַנְשֵׁי רֶשַׁע הַהוֹפְכִים אֶת חֶסֶד אֱלֹהֵינוּ לְזִמָּה
anshei resha hahofechim et chesed eloheinu lezimmah
ungodly men, turning the grace of our God into lasciviousness,

וְכוֹפְרִים בְּרִבּוֹנֵנוּ וַאֲדוֹנֵנוּ הַיָּחִיד יֵשׁוּעַ הַמָּשִׁיחַ
vechoferim beribbonenu va'adonenu hayachid yeshua hammashiach
and denying our only Master and Lord, Jesus Christ.

בִּרְצוֹנִי לְהַזְכִּיר לָכֶם דְּבָרִים שֶׁפַּעַם יְדַעְתֶּם הֵיטֵב
birtzoni lehazkir lachem devarim sheppa'am yeda'tem heitev
Now I desire to put you in remembrance, though ye know all things once for all,

שֶׁיהוה, אַחֲרֵי הוֹשִׁיעוֹ אֶת הָעָם מֵאֶרֶץ מִצְרַיִם, הִשְׁמִיד אֶת אֲשֶׁר לֹא הֶאֱמִינוּ
shehashem, acharei hoshi'o et ha'am me'eretz mitzrayim, hishmid et asher lo he'eminu
that the Lord, having saved a people out of the land of Egypt, afterward destroyed them that believed not.

יוֹחָנָן הַשְּׁלִישִׁית

וְאֶת הָרוֹצִים לְקַבְּלָם הוּא מוֹנֵעַ וּמְגָרֵשׁ מִן הַקְּהִלָּה
ve'et harotzim lekabbelam hu monea umegaresh min hakkehillah
and them that would he forbiddeth and casteth them out of the church.

חֲבִיבִי, אַל תֵּלֵךְ בְּעִקְּבוֹת הָרַע, כִּי אִם בְּעִקְּבוֹת הַטּוֹב
chavivi, al telech be'ikkevot hara, ki im be'ikkevot hattov
Beloved, imitate not that which is evil, but that which is good.

הָעוֹשֶׂה טוֹב מֵאֱלֹהִים הוּא, וְהָעוֹשֶׂה רַע לֹא רָאָה אֶת אֱלֹהִים
ha'oseh tov me'elohim hu, veha'oseh ra lo ra'ah et elohim
He that doeth good is of God: he that doeth evil hath not seen God.

עַל דְּמֶטְרִיּוֹס הֵעִידוּ הַכֹּל, גַּם הָאֱמֶת עַצְמָהּ
al demitriyos he'idu hakkol, gam ha'emet atzmah
Demetrius hath the witness of all men, and of the truth itself:

וְגַם אֲנַחְנוּ מְעִידִים, וְיוֹדֵעַ אַתָּה כִּי עֵדוּתֵנוּ אֱמֶת
vegam anachnu me'idim, veyodea attah ki edutenu emet
yea, we also bear witness; and thou knowest that our witness is true.

הַרְבֵּה יֵשׁ לִי לִכְתֹּב אֵלֶיךָ, אַךְ אֵינֶנִּי רוֹצֶה לִכְתֹּב אֵלֶיךָ בִּדְיוֹ וָעֵט
harbeh yesh li lichtov eleicha, ach einenni rotzeh lichtov eleicha bidyo ve'et
I had many things to write unto thee, but I am unwilling to write them to thee with ink and pen:

אֲנִי מְקַוֶּה לִרְאוֹתְךָ בִּמְהֵרָה וְאָז פֶּה אֶל פֶּה נְדַבֵּר
ani mekavveh lir'otecha bimherah ve'az peh el peh nedabber
but I hope shortly to see thee, and we shall speak face to face.

שָׁלוֹם לְךָ. הַיְדִידִים דּוֹרְשִׁים בִּשְׁלוֹמְךָ. דְּרֹשׁ בִּשְׁלוֹם הַיְדִידִים אִישׁ אִישׁ בִּשְׁמוֹ
shalom lecha. haydidim doreshim bishlomecha. derosh bishlom haydidim ish ish bishmo
Peace be unto thee. The friends salute thee. Salute the friends by name.

יוֹחָנָן הַשְּׁלִישִׁית

מֵאֵת הַזָּקֵן אֶל גָּיוֹס הָאָהוּב אֲשֶׁר אֲנִי אוֹהֲבוֹ בֶּאֱמֶת
me'et hazzaken el gayos ha'ahuv asher ani ohavo be'emet
The elder unto Gaius the beloved, whom I love in truth.

חֲבִיבִי, אֲנִי מִתְפַּלֵּל שֶׁיִּהְיֶה לְךָ טוֹב בַּכֹּל וְתִהְיֶה בָּרִיא, כְּשֵׁם שֶׁטּוֹב לְנַפְשְׁךָ
chavivi, ani mitpallel sheyihyeh lecha tov bakkol vetihyeh bari, keshem shettov lenafshecha
Beloved, I pray that in all things thou mayest prosper and be in health, even as thy soul prospereth.

שָׂמַחְתִּי מְאֹד כַּאֲשֶׁר בָּאוּ אַחִים וְהֵעִידוּ עַל הָאֱמֶת אֲשֶׁר בָּךְ, וְאָמְנָם כָּךְ אַתָּה מִתְהַלֵּךְ בֶּאֱמֶת
samachti me'od ka'asher ba'u achim vehe'idu al ha'emet asher becha, ve'amenam kach attah mit'hallech ba'emet
For I rejoiced greatly, when brethren came and bare witness unto thy truth, even as thou walkest in truth.

אֵין לִי שִׂמְחָה גְּדוֹלָה מִלִּשְׁמֹעַ שֶׁיְּלָדַי מִתְהַלְּכִים בֶּאֱמֶת
ein li simchah gedolah millishmoa sheyeladai mit'hallechim ba'emet
Greater joy have I none than this, to hear of my children walking in the truth.

חֲבִיבִי, אַתָּה נוֹהֵג בְּנֶאֱמָנוּת בְּכָל מַה שֶּׁאַתָּה עוֹשֶׂה לְמַעַן הָאַחִים אֲפִלּוּ כְּשֶׁהֵם זָרִים
chavivi, attah noheg bene'emanut bechol mah she'attah oseh lema'an ha'achim afillu kshehem zarim
Beloved, thou doest a faithful work in whatsoever thou doest toward them that are brethren and strangers withal;

הַלָּלוּ הֵעִידוּ עַל אַהֲבָתְךָ לִפְנֵי הַקְּהִלָּה, וְיָפֶה תַּעֲשֶׂה אִם תְּשַׁלַּח אוֹתָם כַּיָּאֶה לִפְנֵי הָאֱלֹהִים
hallalu he'idu al ahavatecha lifnei hakkehillah, veyafeh ta'aseh im teshalleach otam kaya'eh lifnei ha'elohim
who bare witness to thy love before the church: whom thou wilt do well to set forward on their journey worthily of God:

כִּי לְמַעַן הַשֵּׁם יָצְאוּ לַדֶּרֶךְ, וְלֹא לָקְחוּ דָּבָר מִן הַגּוֹיִם
ki lema'an hashem yatze'u ladderech, velo lakchu davar min haggoyim
because that for the sake of the Name they went forth, taking nothing of the Gentiles.

עַל כֵּן חוֹבָה עָלֵינוּ לִתְמֹךְ בַּאֲנָשִׁים כָּאֵלֶּה, כְּדֵי שֶׁנִּהְיֶה שֻׁתָּפִים לַעֲבוֹדָה בְּשֵׁרוּת הָאֱמֶת
al ken chovah aleinu litmoch ba'anashim ka'elleh, kdei shennihyeh shuttafim la'avodah besherut ha'emet
We therefore ought to welcome such, that we may be fellow-workers for the truth.

כָּתַבְתִּי אֶל הַקְּהִלָּה, אֲבָל דִּיּוֹטְרֶפֶס הַמִּתְאַוֶּה לִהְיוֹת לָהֶם לְרֹאשׁ אֵינֶנּוּ מְקַבֵּל אוֹתָנוּ
katavti el hakkehillah, aval diyoterefes hammit'avveh lihyot lahem lerosh einennu mekabbel otanu
I wrote somewhat unto the church: but Diotrephes, who loveth to have the preeminence among them, receiveth us not.

לָכֵן בְּבוֹאִי אַזְכִּיר אֶת הַמַּעֲשִׂים שֶׁהוּא עוֹשֶׂה. הוּא מַשְׁמִיץ אוֹתָנוּ בְּדִבְרֵי רֶשַׁע
lachen bevo'i azkir et hamma'asim shehu oseh. hu mashmitz otanu bedivrei resha
Therefore, if I come, I will bring to remembrance his works which he doeth, prating against us with wicked words:

וְאֵינוֹ מִסְתַּפֵּק בָּזֶה; גַּם אֵינֶנּוּ מְקַבֵּל אֶת הָאַחִים
ve'eino mistappek bazeh; gam einennu mekabbel et ha'achim
and not content therewith, neither doth he himself receive the brethren,

יוֹחָנָן הַשְּׁנִיָּה

הֵן מַתְעִים רַבִּים בָּאוּ לָעוֹלָם, אֲשֶׁר אֵינָם מוֹדִים בְּיֵשׁוּעַ הַמָּשִׁיחַ הַבָּא בִּלְבוּשׁ בָּשָׂר
hen mat'im rabbim ba'u la'olam, asher einam modim beyeshua hammashiach habba bilvush basar
For many deceivers are gone forth into the world, even they that confess not that Jesus Christ cometh in the flesh.

זֶהוּ הַמַּתְעֶה וְצוֹרֵר הַמָּשִׁיחַ
zehu hammat'eh vetzorer hammashiach
This is the deceiver and the anti-christ.

הִזָּהֲרוּ, כְּדֵי שֶׁלֹּא תְּאַבְּדוּ אֶת פְּרִי פָּעֳלְכֶם אֶלָּא שֶׁתְּקַבְּלוּ שָׂכָר מָלֵא
hizzaharu, kedei shello te'abbedu et peri po'alechem ella shettekabbelu sachar male
Look to yourselves, that ye lose not the things which we have wrought, but that ye receive a full reward.

כָּל הַמַּרְחִיק לֶכֶת וְאֵינוֹ עוֹמֵד בְּתוֹרַת הַמָּשִׁיחַ, אֵין לוֹ אֱלֹהִים
kol hammarchik lechet ve'eino omed betorat hammashiach, ein lo elohim
Whosoever goeth onward and abideth not in the teaching of Christ, hath not God:

הָעוֹמֵד בְּתוֹרַת הַמָּשִׁיחַ יֵשׁ לוֹ גַּם הָאָב וְגַם הַבֵּן
ha'omed betorat hammashiach yesh lo gam ha'av vegam habben
he that abideth in the teaching, the same hath both the Father and the Son.

אִישׁ אִם יָבוֹא אֲלֵיכֶם וְלֹא יָבִיא אֶת הַתּוֹרָה הַזֹּאת, אַל תְּקַבְּלוּ אוֹתוֹ הַבַּיְתָה וְאַל תֹּאמְרוּ לוֹ שָׁלוֹם
ish im yavo aleichem velo yavi et hattorah hazzot, al tekabbelu oto habbaytah ve'al tomeru lo shalom
If any one cometh unto you, and bringeth not this teaching, receive him not into your house, and give him no greeting:

כִּי הַמְבָרֵךְ אוֹתוֹ בְּבִרְכַּת שָׁלוֹם מִשְׁתַּתֵּף בְּמַעֲשָׂיו הָרָעִים
ki hamvarech oto bevirkat shalom mishtattef bema'asav hara'im
for he that giveth him greeting partaketh in his evil works.

הַרְבֵּה יֵשׁ לִי לִכְתֹּב אֲלֵיכֶם, אַךְ לֹא רָצִיתִי בִּנְיָר וּבִדְיוֹ
harbeh yesh li lichtov aleichem, ach lo ratziti binyar uvidyo
Having many things to write unto you, I would not write them with paper and ink:

אֲנִי מְקַוֶּה לָבוֹא אֲלֵיכֶם וּלְדַבֵּר פֶּה אֶל פֶּה כְּדֵי שֶׁתִּהְיֶה שִׂמְחָתֵנוּ שְׁלֵמָה
ani mekavveh lavo aleichem uledabber peh el peh kedei shettihyeh simchatenu shlemah
but I hope to come unto you, and to speak face to face, that your joy may be made full.

יַלְדֵי אֲחוֹתֵךְ הַבְּחִירָה דּוֹרְשִׁים בִּשְׁלוֹמֵךְ
yaldei achotech habbechirah doreshim bishlomech
The children of thine elect sister salute thee.

יוֹחָנָן הַשְּׁנִיָּה

מֵאֵת הַזָּקֵן אֶל הַגְּבִירָה הַבְּחִירָה וְאֶל יְלָדֶיהָ אֲשֶׁר אֲנִי אוֹהֵב בֶּאֱמֶת,
me'et hazzaken el haggvirah habbechirah ve'el yeladeiha asher ani ohev be'emet,
The elder unto the elect lady and her children, whom I love in truth;

וְלֹא רַק אֲנִי אֶלָּא גַּם כָּל יוֹדְעֵי הָאֱמֶת
velo rak ani ella gam kol yode'ei ha'emet
and not I only, but also all they that know the truth;

וְזֹאת הוֹדוֹת לָאֱמֶת הָעוֹמֶדֶת בְּקִרְבֵּנוּ וַאֲשֶׁר תִּהְיֶה עִמָּנוּ לְעוֹלָם
vezot hodot la'emet ha'omedet bekirbenu va'asher tihyeh immanu le'olam
for the truth's sake which abideth in us, and it shall be with us for ever:

חֶסֶד וְרַחֲמִים וְשָׁלוֹם יִהְיוּ עִמָּנוּ מֵאֵת הָאֱלֹהִים הָאָב
chesed verachamim veshalom yihyu immanu me'et ha'elohim ha'av
Grace, mercy, peace shall be with us, from God the Father,

וּמֵאֵת הָאָדוֹן יֵשׁוּעַ הַמָּשִׁיחַ בֶּן הָאָב, בֶּאֱמֶת וּבְאַהֲבָה
ume'et ha'adon yeshua hammashiach ben ha'av, be'emet uve'ahavah
and from Jesus Christ, the Son of the Father, in truth and love.

שָׂמַחְתִּי מְאֹד כִּי מָצָאתִי מִקֶּרֶב יְלָדַיִךְ מִתְהַלְּכִים בֶּאֱמֶת
samachti me'od ki matzati mikkerev yeladayich mit'hallechim ba'emet,
I rejoice greatly that I have found certain of thy children walking in truth,

כַּמִּצְוָה אֲשֶׁר קִבַּלְנוּ מֵאֵת הָאָב
kammitzvah asher kibbalnu me'et ha'av
even as we received commandment from the Father.

וְעַכְשָׁו מְבַקֵּשׁ אֲנִי מִמֵּךְ, הַגְּבִירָה, לֹא כְּכוֹתֵב אֵלַיִךְ מִצְוָה חֲדָשָׁה
ve'achshav mevakkesh ani mimmech, haggvirah, lo kechotev elayich mitzvah chadashah
And now I beseech thee, lady, not as though I wrote to thee a new commandment,

כִּי אִם מִצְוָה שֶׁהָיְתָה לָנוּ מֵרֵאשִׁית - שֶׁנֹּאהַב אִישׁ אֶת רֵעֵהוּ
ki im mitzvah shehayetah lanu mereshit - shennohav ish et re'ehu
but that which we had from the beginning, that we love one another.

וְזֹאת הִיא הָאַהֲבָה: שֶׁנִּתְהַלֵּךְ עַל־פִּי מִצְוֹותָיו
vezot hi ha'ahavah: shennit'hallech al-pi mitzvotav
And this is love, that we should walk after his commandments.

זֹאת הִיא הַמִּצְוָה כְּפִי שֶׁשְּׁמַעְתֶּם מֵרֵאשִׁית וַעֲלֵיכֶם לְהִתְהַלֵּךְ בָּהּ
zot hi hammitzvah kefi sheshema'tem mereshit va'aleichem lehit'hallech bah
This is the commandment, even as ye heard from the beginning, that ye should walk in it.

יוֹחָנָן הָרִאשׁוֹנָה

וַאֲנַחְנוּ בָּאֲמִתִּי, בִּבְנוֹ יֵשׁוּעַ הַמָּשִׁיחַ. הוּא הָאֵל הָאֲמִתִּי וְחַיֵּי הָעוֹלָמִים
va'anachnu ba'amitti, bivno yeshua hammashiach. hu ha'el ha'amitti vechayei ha'olamim
and we are in him that is true, even in his Son Jesus Christ. This is the true God, and eternal life.

יְלָדַי, הִשָּׁמְרוּ לָכֶם מִן הָאֱלִילִים
yeladai, hishamru lachem min ha'elilim
My little children, guard yourselves from idols.

יוֹחָנָן הָרִאשׁוֹנָה

הַמַּאֲמִינִים בְּשֵׁם בֶּן־הָאֱלֹהִים, לְמַעַן תֵּדְעוּ שֶׁיֵּשׁ לָכֶם חַיֵּי עוֹלָם

hamma'aminim beshem ben-ha'elohim, lema'an tede'u sheyesh lachem chayei olam
that ye may know that ye have eternal life, even unto you that believe on the name of the Son of God.

וּבְטָחוֹנֵנוּ בּוֹ שֶׁאִם נְבַקֵּשׁ דָּבָר כִּרְצוֹנוֹ יִשְׁמַע אוֹתָנוּ

uvitchonenu bo she'im nevakkesh davar kirtzono yishma otanu
And this is the boldness which we have toward him, that, if we ask anything according to his will, he heareth us:

וְאִם יוֹדְעִים אָנוּ שֶׁהוּא שׁוֹמֵעַ אוֹתָנוּ בְּכָל אֲשֶׁר נְבַקֵּשׁ

ve'im yod'im anu shehu shomea otanu bechol asher nevakkesh
and if we know that he heareth us whatsoever we ask,

יוֹדְעִים אָנוּ כִּי הַמִּשְׁאָלוֹת שֶׁבִּקַּשְׁנוּ מִמֶּנּוּ נִתָּנוֹת לָנוּ

yod'im anu ki hammish'alot shebbikkashnu mimmennu nittanot lanu
we know that we have the petitions which we have asked of him.

אִישׁ אִם יִרְאֶה אֶת אָחִיו חוֹטֵא חֵטְא שֶׁאֵינֶנּוּ חֵטְא־מָוֶת. יִתְפַּלֵּל

ish im yir'eh et achiv chotei chet she'einennu chet-mavet. yitpallel
If any man see his brother sinning a sin not unto death, he shall ask,

וְהוּא יִתֵּן לוֹ חַיִּים, לְאוֹתָם שֶׁלֹּא חָטְאוּ חֵטְא־מָוֶת.

vehu yitten lo chayim, le'otam shello chate'u chet-mavet
and God will give him life for them that sin not unto death.

יֵשׁ חֵטְא־מָוֶת; עַל זֶה אֵינֶנִּי אוֹמֵר שֶׁיִּתְפַּלֵּל

yesh chet-mavet; al zeh einenni omer sheyitpallel
There is a sin unto death: not concerning this do I say that he should make request.

כָּל עַוְלָה חֵטְא הִיא, אַךְ יֵשׁ חֵטְא שֶׁאֵינוֹ חֵטְא־מָוֶת

kol avlah chet hi, ach yesh chet she'eino chet-mavet
All unrighteousness is sin: and there is a sin not unto death.

יוֹדְעִים אָנוּ כִּי כָּל מִי שֶׁנּוֹלַד מֵאֱלֹהִים אֵינֶנּוּ חוֹטֵא

yode'im anu ki kol mi shennolad me'elohim einennu chote
We know that whosoever is begotten of God sinneth not;

הוּא אֲשֶׁר נוֹלַד מֵאֱלֹהִים שׁוֹמֵר אוֹתוֹ וְהָרַע אֵינוֹ נוֹגֵעַ בּוֹ

hu asher nolad me'elohim shomer oto vehara eino nogea bo
but he that was begotten of God keepeth himself, and the evil one toucheth him not.

יוֹדְעִים אָנוּ כִּי מֵאֱלֹהִים אֲנַחְנוּ וְכִי הָעוֹלָם כֻּלּוֹ שָׁרוּי בָּרָע

yode'im anu ki me'elohim anachnu vechi ha'olam kullo sharui bara
We know that we are of God, and the whole world lieth in the evil one.

וְיוֹדְעִים אָנוּ שֶׁבֶּן־הָאֱלֹהִים בָּא וְנָתַן לָנוּ בִּינָה לָדַעַת אֶת הָאֲמִתִּי

veyode'im anu shebben-ha'elohim ba venatan lanu binah lada'at et ha'amitti
And we know that the Son of God is come, and hath given us an understanding, that we know him that is true,

יוֹחָנָן הָרִאשׁוֹנָה

מִי הַמְנַצֵּחַ אֶת הָעוֹלָם בִּלְתִּי אִם הַמַּאֲמִין כִּי יֵשׁוּעַ הוּא בֶּן־הָאֱלֹהִים

mi hamnatzeach et ha'olam bilti im hamma'amin ki yeshua hu ben-ha'elohim
And who is he that overcometh the world, but he that believeth that Jesus is the Son of God?

זֶה הוּא אֲשֶׁר בָּא בְּמַיִם וּבְדָם - יֵשׁוּעַ הַמָּשִׁיחַ

zeh hu asher ba bemayim uvedam - yeshua hammashiach
This is he that came by water and blood, even Jesus Christ;

לֹא בַמַּיִם בִּלְבַד, כִּי אִם בַּמַּיִם וּבַדָּם

lo bammayim bilvad, ki im bammayim uvaddam
not with the water only, but with the water and with the blood.

וְהָרוּחַ הִיא הַמְּעִידָה, שֶׁהֲרֵי הָרוּחַ הִיא הָאֱמֶת

veharuach hi hamme'idah, sheharei haruach hi ha'emet
And it is the Spirit that beareth witness, because the Spirit is the truth.

הֵן שְׁלוֹשָׁה הֵם הַמְּעִידִים הָרוּחַ וְהַמַּיִם וְהַדָּם וּשְׁלָשְׁתָּם לְשֵׁם הָאֶחָד הֵם

hen sheloshah hem hamme'idim haruach vehammayim vehaddam usheloshtam leshem ha'echad hem
For there are three who bear witness, the Spirit, and the water, and the blood: and the three agree in one.

אִם מְקַבְּלִים אָנוּ עֵדוּת בְּנֵי אָדָם, עֵדוּת אֱלֹהִים גְּדוֹלָה מִמֶּנָּה

im mekabbelim anu edut benei adam, edut elohim gedolah mimmennah
If we receive the witness of men, the witness of God is greater:

שֶׁכֵּן זֹאת עֵדוּת אֱלֹהִים אֲשֶׁר הוּא הֵעִיד עַל בְּנוֹ

shekken zot edut elohim asher hu he'id al beno
for the witness of God is this, that he hath borne witness concerning his Son.

הַמַּאֲמִין בְּבֶן־הָאֱלֹהִים הָעֵדוּת נִמְצֵאת בְּקִרְבּוֹ. מִי שֶׁאֵינוֹ מַאֲמִין לֵאלֹהִים שָׂם אוֹתוֹ לְכוֹזֵב,

hamma'amin beven-ha'elohim ha'edut nimtzet bekirbo. mi she'eino ma'amin le'elohim sam oto lechozev
He that believeth on the Son of God hath the witness in him: he that believeth not God hath made him a liar;

מִפְּנֵי שֶׁלֹּא הֶאֱמִין בָּעֵדוּת אֲשֶׁר הֵעִיד אֱלֹהִים עַל בְּנוֹ

mippenei shello he'emin ba'edut asher he'id elohim al beno
because he hath not believed in the witness that God hath borne concerning his Son.

וְזֹאת הִיא הָעֵדוּת: אֱלֹהִים נָתַן לָנוּ חַיֵּי עוֹלָם, וְהַחַיִּים הָאֵלֶּה בִּבְנוֹ הֵם

vezot hi ha'edut: elohim natan lanu chayei olam, vehachayim ha'elleh bivno hem
And the witness is this, that God gave unto us eternal life, and this life is in his Son.

מִי שֶׁיֵּשׁ לוֹ הַבֵּן יֵשׁ לוֹ הַחַיִּים. מִי שֶׁאֵין לוֹ הַבֵּן אֵין לוֹ הַחַיִּים

mi sheyesh lo habben yesh lo hachayim. mi she'ein lo habben ein lo hachayim
He that hath the Son hath the life; he that hath not the Son of God hath not the life.

זֹאת כָּתַבְתִּי אֲלֵיכֶם

zot katavti aleichem
These things have I written unto you,

יוֹחָנָן הָרִאשׁוֹנָה

הֵן הַפַּחַד כָּרוּךְ בְּעֹנֶשׁ, וְהַמְפַחֵד אֵינֶנּוּ שָׁלֵם בָּאַהֲבָה
hen happachad karuch be'onesh, vehamfached einennu shalem ba'ahavah
because fear hath punishment; and he that feareth is not made perfect in love.

אֲנַחְנוּ אוֹהֲבִים מִפְּנֵי שֶׁהוּא אָהַב אוֹתָנוּ תְּחִלָּה
anachnu ohavim mippenei shehu ahav otanu techillah
We love, because he first loved us.

אִישׁ אִם יֹאמַר אֹהֵב אֲנִי אֶת אֱלֹהִים וְהוּא שׂוֹנֵא אֶת אָחִיו, שַׁקְרָן הוּא;
ish im yomar ohev ani et elohim vehu sonei et achiv, shakran hu
If a man say, I love God, and hateth his brother, he is a liar:

כִּי מִי שֶׁאֵינֶנּוּ אוֹהֵב אֶת אָחִיו אֲשֶׁר הוּא רוֹאֶה אוֹתוֹ לֹא יוּכַל לֶאֱהֹב אֶת הָאֱלֹהִים אֲשֶׁר הוּא אֵינֶנּוּ רוֹאֶה אוֹתוֹ
ki mi she'einennu ohev et achiv asher hu ro'eh oto lo yuchal le'ehov et ha'elohim asher hu einennu ro'eh oto
for he that loveth not his brother whom he hath seen, cannot love God whom he hath not seen.

מִצְוָה זֹאת קִבַּלְנוּ מִמֶּנּוּ, שֶׁהָאוֹהֵב אֶת אֱלֹהִים יֹאהַב גַּם אֶת אָחִיו
mitzvah zot kibbalnu mimmennu, sheha'ohev et elohim yohav gam et achiv
And this commandment have we from him, that he who loveth God love his brother also.

ה

כָּל הַמַּאֲמִין כִּי יֵשׁוּעַ הוּא הַמָּשִׁיחַ, נוֹלַד מֵאֱלֹהִים
kol hamma'amin ki yeshua hu hammashiach, nolad me'elohim
Whosoever believeth that Jesus is the Christ is begotten of God:

וְכָל הָאוֹהֵב אֶת הַמּוֹלִיד אוֹהֵב גַּם אֶת מִי שֶׁנּוֹלַד מִמֶּנּוּ
vechol ha'ohev et hammolid ohev gam et mi shennolad mimmennu
and whosoever loveth him that begat loveth him also that is begotten of him.

בָּזֹאת נֵדַע כִּי אוֹהֲבִים אָנוּ אֶת יַלְדֵי אֱלֹהִים: בִּהְיוֹתֵנוּ אוֹהֲבִים אֶת אֱלֹהִים וּמְקַיְּמִים אֶת מִצְווֹתָיו
bazot neda ki ohavim anu et yaldei Elohim: bihyotenu ohavim et elohim umekayemim et mitzvotav
Hereby we know that we love the children of God, when we love God and do his commandments.

הֵן זֹאת הִיא אַהֲבַת אֱלֹהִים, שֶׁנִּשְׁמֹר אֶת מִצְווֹתָיו. וּמִצְווֹתָיו אֵינָן קָשׁוֹת
hen zot hi ahavat elohim, shennishmor et mitzvotav. umitzvotav einan kashot
For this is the love of God, that we keep his commandments: and his commandments are not grievous.

שֶׁכֵּן כָּל הַנּוֹלָד מֵאֵת אֱלֹהִים מְנַצֵּחַ אֶת הָעוֹלָם
shekken kol hannolad me'et elohim menatzeach et ha'olam
For whatsoever is begotten of God overcometh the world:

וְזֶהוּ הַנִּצָּחוֹן הַמְנַצֵּחַ אֶת הָעוֹלָם - אֱמוּנָתֵנוּ
vezehu hannitzachon hamnatzeach et ha'olam - emunatenu
and this is the victory that hath overcome the world, even our faith.

יוֹחָנָן הָרִאשׁוֹנָה

וְשָׁלַח אֶת בְּנוֹ לִהְיוֹת כַּפָּרָה עַל חֲטָאֵינוּ
veshalach et bno lihyot kapparah al chata'einu
and sent his Son to be the propitiation for our sins.

אֲהוּבַי, אִם כָּכָה אָהַב אוֹתָנוּ הָאֱלֹהִים, גַּם אֲנַחְנוּ חַיָּבִים לֶאֱהֹב אִישׁ אֶת רֵעֵהוּ
ahuvai, im kachah ahav otanu ha'elohim, gam anachnu chayavim le'ehov ish et re'ehu
Beloved, if God so loved us, we also ought to love one another.

אֶת הָאֱלֹהִים לֹא רָאָה אִישׁ מֵעוֹלָם. אִם אֲנַחְנוּ אוֹהֲבִים זֶה אֶת זֶה
et ha'elohim lo ra'ah ish me'olam. im anachnu ohavim zeh et zeh
No man hath beheld God at any time: if we love one another,

הָאֱלֹהִים שׁוֹכֵן בְּקִרְבֵּנוּ וְאַהֲבָתוֹ נִשְׁלְמָה בָּנוּ
ha'elohim shochen bekirbenu ve'ahavato nishlemah banu
God abideth in us, and his love is perfected in us:

בָּזֹאת יוֹדְעִים אָנוּ שֶׁעוֹמְדִים אָנוּ בּוֹ וְהוּא בָּנוּ, כִּי נָתַן לָנוּ מֵרוּחוֹ
bazot yode'im anu she'omedim anu bo vehu banu, ki natan lanu merucho
hereby we know that we abide in him and he in us, because he hath given us of his Spirit.

וַאֲנַחְנוּ הִתְבּוֹנַנּוּ וַהֲרֵינוּ מְעִידִים כִּי הָאָב שָׁלַח אֶת הַבֵּן מוֹשִׁיעַ הָעוֹלָם
va'anachnu hitbonannu vahareinu me'idim ki ha'av shalach et habben moshia ha'olam
And we have beheld and bear witness that the Father hath sent the Son to be the Saviour of the world.

כָּל הַמּוֹדֶה כִּי יֵשׁוּעַ הוּא בֶּן־הָאֱלֹהִים, אֱלֹהִים שׁוֹכֵן בּוֹ וְהוּא בֵּאלֹהִים
kol hammodeh ki yeshua hu ben-ha'elohim, elohim shochen bo vehu belohim
Whosoever shall confess that Jesus is the Son of God, God abideth in him, and he in God.

וַאֲנַחְנוּ הִכַּרְנוּ אֶת הָאַהֲבָה שֶׁאֱלֹהִים מְקַיֵּם בָּנוּ וְהֶאֱמַנּוּ בָּהּ
va'anachnu hikkarnu et ha'ahavah she'elohim mekayem banu vehe'emannu bah
And we know and have believed the love which God hath in us.

הָאֱלֹהִים הוּא אַהֲבָה; הָעוֹמֵד בָּאַהֲבָה עוֹמֵד בֵּאלֹהִים וֵאלֹהִים עוֹמֵד בּוֹ
ha'elohim hu ahavah; ha'omed ba'ahavah omed be'elohim ve'elohim omed bo
God is love; and he that abideth in love abideth in God, and God abideth in him.

בָּזֶה נִשְׁלְמָה הָאַהֲבָה אֶצְלֵנוּ בְּאֹפֶן שֶׁיִּהְיֶה לָנוּ בִּטָּחוֹן בְּיוֹם הַדִּין
bazeh nishlemah ha'ahavah etzlenu be'ofen sheyihyeh lanu bittachon beyom haddin
Herein is love made perfect with us, that we may have boldness in the day of judgment;

שֶׁכֵּן כְּדֶרֶךְ שֶׁהָאֶחָד הַהוּא כֵּן גַּם אֲנַחְנוּ בָּעוֹלָם הַזֶּה
shekken kederech sheha'echad hahu ken gam anachnu ba'olam hazzeh
because as he is, even so are we in this world.

אֵין פַּחַד בָּאַהֲבָה. אַדְּרַבָּא, הָאַהֲבָה הַשְּׁלֵמָה מְגָרֶשֶׁת אֶת הַפַּחַד
ein pachad ba'ahavah. adderabba, ha'ahavah hashelemah megareshet et happachad
There is no fear in love: but perfect love casteth out fear,

יוֹחָנָן הָרִאשׁוֹנָה

וְכָל רוּחַ אֲשֶׁר אֵינֶנָּה מוֹדָה בְּיֵשׁוּעַ לֹא מֵאֱלֹהִים הִיא. זֹהִי רוּחַ צוֹרֵר הַמָּשִׁיחַ
vechol ruach asher einennah modah beyeshua lo me'elohim hi. zohi ruach tzorer hammashiach
and every spirit that confesseth not Jesus is not of God: and this is the spirit of the antichrist,

אֲשֶׁר שְׁמַעְתֶּם כִּי תָּבוֹא, וּכְבָר כָּעֵת הִיא בָּעוֹלָם
asher shema'tem ki tavo, uchevar ka'et hi ba'olam
whereof ye have heard that it cometh; and now it is in the world already.

אַתֶּם, יְלָדַי, מֵאֱלֹהִים אַתֶּם, וְנִצַּחְתֶּם אוֹתָם
attem, yeladai, me'elohim attem, venitzachtem otam
Ye are of God, my little children, and have overcome them:

שֶׁכֵּן הוּא אֲשֶׁר בָּכֶם גָּדוֹל מִזֶּה אֲשֶׁר בָּעוֹלָם
shekken hu asher bachem gadol mizzeh asher ba'olam
because greater is he that is in you than he that is in the world.

הֵם מִן הָעוֹלָם; לָכֵן הֵם מְדַבְּרִים דְּבָרִים הַנּוֹבְעִים מִן הָעוֹלָם וְהָעוֹלָם שׁוֹמֵעַ לָהֶם
hem min ha'olam; lachen hem medabberim devarim hannove'im min ha'olam veha'olam shomea lahem
They are of the world: therefore speak they as of the world, and the world heareth them.

אֲנַחְנוּ מֵאֱלֹהִים. הַיּוֹדֵעַ אֶת אֱלֹהִים שׁוֹמֵעַ לָנוּ; מִי שֶׁאֵינוֹ מֵאֱלֹהִים אֵינֶנּוּ שׁוֹמֵעַ לָנוּ
anachnu me'elohim. hayodea et elohim shomea lanu; mi she'eino me'elohim einennu shomea lanu
We are of God: he that knoweth God heareth us; he who is not of God heareth us not.

מִתּוֹךְ כָּךְ מַכִּירִים אָנוּ אֶת רוּחַ הָאֱמֶת וְאֶת רוּחַ הַתָּעוּת
mittoch kach makkirim anu et ruach ha'emet ve'et ruach hatta'ut
By this we know the spirit of truth, and the spirit of error.

אֲהוּבַי, נֹאהַב נָא אִישׁ אֶת רֵעֵהוּ, כִּי הָאַהֲבָה מֵאֱלֹהִים הִיא; וְכָל מִי שֶׁאוֹהֵב נוֹלַד מֵאֱלֹהִים וְיוֹדֵעַ אֶת אֱלֹהִים
ahuvai, nohav na ish et re'ehu, ki ha'ahavah me'elohim hi; vechol mi she'ohev nolad me'elohim veyodea et elohim
Beloved, let us love one another: for love is of God; and every one that loveth is begotten of God, and knoweth God.

מִי שֶׁאֵינוֹ אוֹהֵב אֵינוֹ יוֹדֵעַ אֶת אֱלֹהִים, שֶׁכֵּן הָאֱלֹהִים הוּא אַהֲבָה
mi she'eino ohev eino yodea et elohim, shekken ha'elohim hu ahavah
He that loveth not knoweth not God; for God is love.

בָּזֹאת נִגְלְתָה אַהֲבַת הָאֱלֹהִים בָּנוּ
bazot nigletah ahavat ha'elohim banu
Herein was the love of God manifested in us,

בָּעֻבְדָּה שֶׁאֱלֹהִים שָׁלַח אֶת בְּנוֹ יְחִידוֹ לָעוֹלָם לְמַעַן נִחְיֶה בִּזְכוּתוֹ
ba'uvdah she'elohim shalach et beno yechido la'olam lema'an nichyeh bizchuto
that God hath sent his only begotten Son into the world that we might live through him.

בָּזֹאת הִיא הָאַהֲבָה, לֹא שֶׁאֲנַחְנוּ אֲהַבְנוּ אֶת אֱלֹהִים, אֶלָּא שֶׁהוּא אָהַב אוֹתָנוּ
bazot hi ha'ahavah, lo she'anachnu ahavnu et elohim, ella shehu ahav otanu
Herein is love, not that we loved God, but that he loved us,

יוֹחָנָן הָרִאשׁוֹנָה

שֶׁכֵּן אִם לִבֵּנוּ יַרְשִׁיעַ אוֹתָנוּ, הָאֱלֹהִים גָּדוֹל מִלִּבֵּנוּ וְהוּא יוֹדֵעַ הַכֹּל

shekken im libbenu yarshia otanu, ha'elohim gadol millibbenu vehu yodea hakkol
because if our heart condemn us, God is greater than our heart, and knoweth all things.

אֲהוּבַי, אִם לִבֵּנוּ אֵינוֹ מַרְשִׁיעַ אוֹתָנוּ, עֹז לָנוּ לִפְנֵי אֱלֹהִים

ahuvai, im libbenu eino marshia otanu, oz lanu lifnei elohim
Beloved, if our heart condemn us not, we have boldness toward God;

וְכָל אֲשֶׁר נְבַקֵּשׁ נְקַבֵּל מִמֶּנּוּ

vechol asher nevakkesh nekabbel mimmennu
and whatsoever we ask we receive of him,

מִפְּנֵי שֶׁשּׁוֹמְרִים אָנוּ אֶת מִצְוֺתָיו וְעוֹשִׂים אֶת הַטּוֹב בְּעֵינָיו

mippenei sheshomerim anu et mitzvotav ve'osim et hattov be'einav
because we keep his commandments and do the things that are pleasing in his sight.

זֹאת מִצְוָתוֹ: לְהַאֲמִין בְּשֵׁם בְּנוֹ יֵשׁוּעַ הַמָּשִׁיחַ

zot mitzvato: leha'amin beshem beno yeshua hammashiach
And this is his commandment, that we should believe in the name of his Son Jesus Christ,

וְלֶאֱהֹב זֶה אֶת זֶה כְּפִי שֶׁצִּוָּנוּ

vele'ehov zeh et zeh kefi shetzivvanu
and love one another, even as he gave us commandment.

הַשּׁוֹמֵר אֶת מִצְוֺת אֱלֹהִים שׁוֹכֵן בֵּאלֹהִים וֵאלֹהִים בּוֹ.

hashomer et mitzvot elohim shochen be'elohim ve'elohim bo
And he that keepeth his commandments abideth in him, and he in him.

וּבְזֹאת נֵדַע שֶׁהוּא שׁוֹכֵן בָּנוּ: בָּרוּחַ אֲשֶׁר נָתַן לָנוּ

uvazot neda shehu shochen banu: baruach asher natan lanu
And hereby we know that he abideth in us, by the Spirit which he gave us.

ד

אֲהוּבַי, אַל תַּאֲמִינוּ לְכָל רוּחַ, כִּי אִם בַּחֲנוּ אֶת הָרוּחוֹת אִם מֵאֱלֹהִים הֵן

ahuvai, al ta'aminu lechol ruach, ki im bachanu et haruchot im me'elohim hen
Beloved, believe not every spirit, but prove the spirits, whether they are of God;

כִּי נְבִיאֵי שֶׁקֶר רַבִּים יָצְאוּ לָעוֹלָם

ki nevi'ei sheker rabbim yatz'u la'olam
because many false prophets are gone out into the world.

בָּזֶה תַּכִּירוּ אֶת רוּחַ אֱלֹהִים: כָּל רוּחַ הַמּוֹדָה כִּי יֵשׁוּעַ הַמָּשִׁיחַ בָּא בִּלְבוּשׁ בָּשָׂר, מֵאֱלֹהִים הִיא

bazeh takkiru et ruach Elohim: kol ruach hammodah ki yeshua hammashiach ba bilvush basar, me'elohim hi
Hereby know ye the Spirit of God: every spirit that confesseth that Jesus Christ is come in the flesh is of God:

יוֹחָנָן הָרִאשׁוֹנָה

לֹא כְּקַיִן אֲשֶׁר הָיָה מִן הָרַע וְהָרַג אֶת אָחִיו
lo kekayin asher hayah min hara veharag et achiv
not as Cain was of the evil one, and slew his brother.

וּמַדּוּעַ הֲרָגוֹ? מִפְּנֵי שֶׁמַּעֲשָׂיו הָיוּ רָעִים, אַךְ מַעֲשֵׂי אָחִיו מַעֲשֵׂי צֶדֶק
umaddua harago? mippnei shemma'asav hayu ra'im, ach ma'asei achiv ma'asei tzedek
And wherefore slew he him? Because his works were evil, and his brother's righteous.

אַחַי, אַל תִּתְמְהוּ אִם הָעוֹלָם שׂוֹנֵא אֶתְכֶם
achai, al titmehu im ha'olam sonei etchem
Marvel not, brethren, if the world hateth you.

אֲנַחְנוּ יוֹדְעִים כִּי עָבַרְנוּ מִן הַמָּוֶת אֶל הַחַיִּים, שֶׁכֵּן אוֹהֲבִים אֲנַחְנוּ אֶת אַחֵינוּ
anachnu yod'im ki avarnu min hammavet el hachayim, shekken ohavim anachnu et acheinu
We know that we have passed out of death into life, because we love the brethren.

אִישׁ אֲשֶׁר אֵינוֹ אוֹהֵב נִשְׁאַר בַּמָּוֶת
ish asher eino ohev nish'ar bammavet
He that loveth not abideth in death.

כָּל הַשּׂוֹנֵא אֶת אָחִיו רוֹצֵחַ הוּא. וְיוֹדְעִים אַתֶּם שֶׁכָּל רוֹצֵחַ אֵין חַיֵּי עוֹלָם מִתְקַיְּמִים בּוֹ
kol hassonei et achiv rotzeach hu. veyode'im attem shekkol rotzeach ein chayei olam mitkaymim bo
Whosoever hateth his brother is a murderer: and ye know that no murderer hath eternal life abiding in him.

בָּזֹאת הִכַּרְנוּ מַה הִיא אַהֲבָה, בָּעֻבְדָּה שֶׁהוּא מָסַר אֶת נַפְשׁוֹ בַּעֲדֵנוּ
bazot hikkarnu mah hi ahavah, ba'uvdah shehu masar et nafsho ba'adenu
Hereby know we love, because he laid down his life for us:

גַּם אֲנַחְנוּ חַיָּבִים לִמְסֹר אֶת נַפְשֵׁנוּ בְּעַד אַחֵינוּ
gam anachnu chayavim limsor et nafshenu be'ad acheinu
and we ought to lay down our lives for the brethren.

מִי שֶׁיֵּשׁ לוֹ נִכְסֵי הָעוֹלָם וְהוּא רוֹאֶה אֶת אָחִיו בְּמַחְסוֹר
mi sheyesh lo nichsei ha'olam vehu ro'eh et achiv bemachsor
But whoso hath the world's goods, and beholdeth his brother in need,

וּמוֹנֵעַ אֶת רַחֲמָיו מִמֶּנּוּ, אֵיךְ תַּעֲמֹד בּוֹ אַהֲבַת אֱלֹהִים
umonea et rachamav mimmennu, eich ta'amod bo ahavat elohim
and shutteth up his compassion from him, how doth the love of God abide in him?

יְלָדַי, אַל נָא נֹאהַב בְּמִלִּים וּבְדִבּוּר, כִּי אִם בְּפֹעַל וּבֶאֱמֶת
yeladai, al na nohav bemillim uvedibbur, ki im befo'al uve'emet
My little children, let us not love in word, neither with the tongue; but in deed and truth.

בָּזֶה נֵדַע כִּי מִן הָאֱמֶת אֲנַחְנוּ וְנַשְׁקִיט אֶת לְבָבֵנוּ לְפָנָיו
bazeh neda ki min ha'emet anachnu venashkit et levavenu lefanav
Hereby shall we know that we are of the truth, and shall assure our heart before him:

יוֹחָנָן הָרִאשׁוֹנָה

וְכָל מִי שֶׁנִּסְמָךְ עָלָיו בַּתִּקְוָה הַזֹּאת, מְטַהֵר אֶת עַצְמוֹ כְּפִי שֶׁטָּהוֹר הָאֶחָד הַהוּא
vechol mi shennismach alav battikvah hazzot, metaher et atzmo kefi shetahor ha'echad hahu
And every one that hath this hope set on him purifieth himself, even as he is pure.

כָּל מִי שֶׁחוֹטֵא גַּם עוֹבֵר עַל הַתּוֹרָה; הַחֵטְא הוּא עֲבֵרָה עַל הַתּוֹרָה
kol mi shechotei gam over al hattorah; hachet hu averah al hattorah
Every one that doeth sin doeth also lawlessness; and sin is lawlessness.

אַתֶּם יוֹדְעִים שֶׁהוּא נִגְלָה כְּדֵי לָשֵׂאת אֶת חֲטָאֵינוּ, וּבוֹ אֵין חֵטְא
attem yode'im shehu niglah kedei laset et chata'einu, uvo ein chet
And ye know that he was manifested to take away sins; and in him is no sin.

כָּל הָעוֹמֵד בּוֹ לֹא יֶחֱטָא; כָּל הַחוֹטֵא לֹא רָאָהוּ אַף לֹא יְדָעוֹ
kol ha'omed bo lo yecheta; kol hachotei lo ra'ahu af lo yeda'o
Whosoever abideth in him sinneth not: whosoever sinneth hath not seen him, neither knoweth him.

יְלָדַי, אַל יַתְעֶה אֶתְכֶם אִישׁ: הָעוֹשֶׂה צְדָקָה צַדִּיק, כְּשֵׁם שֶׁהַהוּא צַדִּיק
yeladai, al yat'eh etchem ish. ha'oseh tzedakah tzaddik, keshem shehahu tzaddik
My little children, let no man lead you astray: he that doeth righteousness is righteous, even as he is righteous:

הָעוֹשֶׂה חֵטְא מִן הַשָּׂטָן הוּא, כִּי הַשָּׂטָן חוֹטֵא מֵרֵאשִׁית
ha'oseh chet min hassatan hu, ki hassatan chotei mereshit
he that doeth sin is of the devil; for the devil sinneth from the beginning.

לָזֹאת נִגְלָה בֶּן־הָאֱלֹהִים, לְהָפֵר אֶת פְּעֻלּוֹת הַשָּׂטָן
lazot niglah ben-ha'elohim, lehafer et pe'ullot hassatan
To this end was the Son of God manifested, that he might destroy the works of the devil.

כָּל הַנּוֹלָד מֵאֱלֹהִים אֵינֶנּוּ חוֹטֵא, כִּי זַרְעוֹ נִשְׁאַר בּוֹ
kol hannolad me'elohim einennu chote, ki zar'o nish'ar bo
Whosoever is begotten of God doeth no sin, because his seed abideth in him:

וְאֵין הוּא יָכוֹל לַחֲטֹא, כִּי מֵאֱלֹהִים נוֹלַד
ve'ein hu yachol lachato, ki me'elohim nolad
and he cannot sin, because he is begotten of God.

בָּזֶה יִוָּדְעוּ יַלְדֵי הָאֱלֹהִים וְיַלְדֵי הַשָּׂטָן
bazeh yivvade'u yaldei ha'elohim veyaldei hassatan
In this the children of God are manifest, and the children of the devil:

כָּל מִי שֶׁאֵינוֹ עוֹשֶׂה צְדָקָה אֵינֶנּוּ מֵאֱלֹהִים, וְכֵן מִי שֶׁאֵינוֹ אוֹהֵב אֶת אָחִיו
kol mi she'eino oseh tzedakah einennu me'elohim, vechen mi she'eino ohev et achiv
whosoever doeth not righteousness is not of God, neither he that loveth not his brother.

הֵן זֶהוּ דְּבַר הַבְּשׂוֹרָה אֲשֶׁר שְׁמַעְתֶּם מֵרֵאשִׁית, שֶׁנֹּאהַב אִישׁ אֶת רֵעֵהוּ
hen zehu devar habbsorah asher shema'tem mereshit, shennohav ish et re'ehu
For this is the message which ye heard from the beginning, that we should love one another:

יוֹחָנָן הָרִאשׁוֹנָה

וְאֵינְכֶם צְרִיכִים לְמִישֶׁהוּ שֶׁיְּלַמֵּד אֶתְכֶם

ve'einchem tzerichim lemishehu sheyelammed etchem

and ye need not that any one teach you;

אֶלָּא כְּמוֹ שֶׁמְּשִׁיחָתוֹ מְלַמֶּדֶת אֶתְכֶם עַל־אֹדוֹת הַכֹּל - וְהִיא אֱמֶת וְאֵינֶנָּה כָּזָב

ella kemo shemmeshichato melammedet etchem al-'odot hakkol - vehi emet ve'einennah kazav

but as his anointing teacheth you concerning all things, and is true, and is no lie,

לְפִי מַה שֶּׁלִּמְּדָה אֶתְכֶם עִמְדוּ בּוֹ

lefi mah shellimmdah etchem imdu bo

and even as it taught you, ye abide in him.

וְעַתָּה, יְלָדַי, עִמְדוּ בּוֹ

ve'attah, yeladai, imdu bo

And now, my little children, abide in him;

כְּדֵי שֶׁיִּהְיֶה לָנוּ עֹז כַּאֲשֶׁר יִתְגַּלֶּה וְלֹא נֵבוֹשׁ מִפָּנָיו בְּבוֹאוֹ

kedei sheyihyeh lanu oz ka'asher yitgalleh velo nevosh mippanav bevo'o

that, if he shall be manifested, we may have boldness, and not be ashamed before him at his coming.

אִם יוֹדְעִים אַתֶּם שֶׁהוּא צַדִּיק, יוֹדְעִים אַתֶּם שֶׁגַּם כָּל עוֹשֵׂה צְדָקָה נוֹלַד מִמֶּנּוּ

im yode'im attem shehu tzaddik, yode'im attem sheggam kol oseh tzedakah nolad mimmennu

If ye know that he is righteous, ye know that every one also that doeth righteousness is begotten of him.

ג

רְאוּ אֵיזוֹ אַהֲבָה נָתַן לָנוּ הָאָב לְהִקָּרֵא יַלְדֵי אֱלֹהִים

re'u eizo ahavah natan lanu ha'av lehikkarei yaldei elohim

Behold what manner of love the Father hath bestowed upon us, that we should be called children of God;

וְאָכֵן כָּךְ אֲנַחְנוּ

ve'achen kach anachnu

and such we are.

מִשּׁוּם כָּךְ הָעוֹלָם אֵינוֹ מַכִּיר אוֹתָנוּ, מִשּׁוּם שֶׁלֹּא הִכִּיר אוֹתוֹ

mishum kach ha'olam eino makkir otanu, mishum shello hikkir oto

For this cause the world knoweth us not, because it knew him not.

אֲהוּבַי, עַכְשָׁו יַלְדֵי אֱלֹהִים אֲנַחְנוּ, וְעוֹד לֹא נִגְלָה מַה נִּהְיֶה

ahuvai, achshav yaldei elohim anachnu, ve'od lo niglah mah nihyeh

Beloved, now are we children of God, and it is not yet made manifest what we shall be.

יוֹדְעִים אָנוּ שֶׁבְּהִגָּלוֹתוֹ נִהְיֶה כָּמוֹהוּ, כִּי נִרְאֵהוּ כְּמוֹ שֶׁהוּא

yode'im anu shebbehiggaloto nihyeh kamohu, ki nir'ehu kemo shehu

We know that, if he shall be manifested, we shall be like him; for we shall see him even as he is.

יוֹחָנָן הָרִאשׁוֹנָה

אַךְ הֵם יָצְאוּ לְמַעַן יִוָּדַע שֶׁכֻּלָּם אֵינָם מִשֶּׁלָּנוּ
ach hem yatze'u lema'an yivvada shekkullam einam mishellanu
but they went out, that they might be made manifest that they all are not of us.

וְאַתֶּם יֵשׁ לָכֶם הַמְשִׁיחָה מֵאֵת הַקָּדוֹשׁ, וְכֻלְּכֶם יוֹדְעִים
ve'attem yesh lachem hamshichah me'et hakkadosh, vechullechem yode'im
And ye have an anointing from the Holy One, and ye know all things.

כָּתַבְתִּי אֲלֵיכֶם לֹא מִפְּנֵי שֶׁאֵינְכֶם יוֹדְעִים אֶת הָאֱמֶת
katavti aleichem lo mippenei she'einchem yode'im et ha'emet,
I have not written unto you because ye know not the truth,

אֶלָּא מִפְּנֵי שֶׁאַתֶּם יוֹדְעִים אוֹתָהּ וְיוֹדְעִים שֶׁכָּל שֶׁקֶר אֵינֶנּוּ מִן הָאֱמֶת
ella mippenei she'attem yod'im otah veyod'im shekkol sheker einennu min ha'emet
but because ye know it, and because no lie is of the truth.

מִי הוּא דּוֹבֵר שֶׁקֶר בִּלְתִּי אִם הַכּוֹפֵר בְּכָךְ שֶׁיֵּשׁוּעַ הוּא הַמָּשִׁיחַ
mi hu dover sheker bilti im hakkofer bechach sheyeshua hu hammashiach
Who is the liar but he that denieth that Jesus is the Christ?

זֶה הוּא צוֹרֵר הַמָּשִׁיחַ, הַכּוֹפֵר בָּאָב וּבַבֵּן
zeh hu tzorer hammashiach, hakkofer ba'av uvabben
This is the antichrist, even he that denieth the Father and the Son.

כָּל הַכּוֹפֵר בַּבֵּן גַּם הָאָב אֵין לוֹ; הַמּוֹדֶה בַּבֵּן יֵשׁ לוֹ גַּם הָאָב
kol hakkofer babben gam ha'av ein lo; hammodeh babben yesh lo gam ha'av
Whosoever denieth the Son, the same hath not the Father: he that confesseth the Son hath the Father also.

אַתֶּם, מַה שֶּׁשְּׁמַעְתֶּם מֵרֵאשִׁית יִשָּׁאֶר נָא בְּקִרְבְּכֶם
attem, mah sheshema'tem mereshit yisha'er na bekirbechem
As for you, let that abide in you which ye heard from the beginning.

אִם יִשָּׁאֵר בְּקִרְבְּכֶם מַה שֶּׁשְּׁמַעְתֶּם מֵרֵאשִׁית, אֲזַי גַּם אַתֶּם תִּשָּׁאֲרוּ בַּבֵּן וּבָאָב
im yisha'er bekirbechem mah sheshema'tem mereshit, azai gam attem tisha'aru babben uva'av
If that which ye heard from the beginning abide in you, ye also shall abide in the Son, and in the Father.

וְזוֹהִי הַהַבְטָחָה שֶׁהוּא הִבְטִיחַ לָנוּ - חַיֵּי עוֹלָם
vezohi hahavtachah shehu hivtiach lanu - chayei olam
And this is the promise which he promised us, even the life eternal.

אֶת הַדְּבָרִים הָאֵלֶּה כָּתַבְתִּי לָכֶם עַל־אוֹדוֹת הַמַּתְעִים אֶתְכֶם
et haddevarim ha'elleh katavti lachem al-'odot hammat'im etchem
These things have I written unto you concerning them that would lead you astray.

וְהַמְשִׁיחָה שֶׁאַתֶּם קִבַּלְתֶּם מֵאִתּוֹ נִשְׁאֶרֶת בְּקִרְבְּכֶם
vehamshichah she'attem kibbaltem me'itto nish'eret bekirbechem
And as for you, the anointing which ye received of him abideth in you,

יוֹחָנָן הָרִאשׁוֹנָה

כָּתַבְתִּי לָכֶם, יְלָדִים, מִפְּנֵי שֶׁהִכַּרְתֶּם אֶת הָאָב
katavti lachem, yeladim, mippenei shehikkartem et ha'av
I have written unto you, little children, because ye know the Father.

כָּתַבְתִּי לָכֶם, אָבוֹת, מִפְּנֵי שֶׁהִכַּרְתֶּם אוֹתוֹ אֲשֶׁר הוּא מֵרֵאשִׁית
katavti lachem, avot, mippenei shehikkartem oto asher hu mereshit
I have written unto you, fathers, because ye know him who is from the beginning.

כָּתַבְתִּי לָכֶם, בַּחוּרִים, מִפְּנֵי שֶׁאַתֶּם חֲזָקִים
katavti lachem, bachurim, mippenei she'attem chazakim
I have written unto you, young men, because ye are strong,

וּדְבַר אֱלֹהִים קַיָּם בְּקִרְבְּכֶם וְנִצַּחְתֶּם אֶת הָרַע
udevar elohim kayam bekirbechem venitzachtem et hara
and the word of God abideth in you, and ye have overcome the evil one.

אַל תֶּאֱהֲבוּ אֶת הָעוֹלָם, אַף לֹא אֶת מַה שֶּׁבָּעוֹלָם
al tohavu et ha'olam, af lo et mah shebba'olam.
Love not the world, neither the things that are in the world.

אִישׁ אִם יֹאהַב אֶת הָעוֹלָם אֵין בּוֹ אַהֲבַת הָאָב
ish im yohav et ha'olam ein bo ahavat ha'av
If any man love the world, the love of the Father is not in him.

כִּי כָּל אֲשֶׁר בָּעוֹלָם - תַּאֲוַת בְּשָׂרִים, תַּאֲוַת הָעֵינַיִם
ki kol asher ba'olam - ta'avat besarim, ta'avat ha'einayim
For all that is in the world, the lust of the flesh and the lust of the eyes

וְגַאֲוַת הַנְּכָסִים - לֹא מִן הָאָב הוּא כִּי אִם מִן הָעוֹלָם
vega'avat hannechasim - lo min ha'av hu ki im min ha'olam
and the vainglory of life, is not of the Father, but is of the world.

וְהָעוֹלָם עוֹבֵר עִם תַּאֲוֺתָיו, אַךְ הָעוֹשֶׂה אֶת רְצוֹן אֱלֹהִים עוֹמֵד לָעַד
veha'olam over im ta'avotav, ach ha'oseh et retzon elohim omed la'ad
And the world passeth away, and the lust thereof: but he that doeth the will of God abideth for ever.

יְלָדַי, זֹאת הַשָּׁעָה הָאַחֲרוֹנָה. וּכְמוֹ שֶׁשְּׁמַעְתֶּם כִּי יָבוֹא צוֹרֵר הַמָּשִׁיחַ
yeladai, zot hasha'ah ha'achronah. uchemo sheshema'tem ki yavo tzorer hammashiach
Little children, it is the last hour: and as ye heard that antichrist cometh,

גַּם עַכְשָׁו קָמוּ צוֹרְרֵי מָשִׁיחַ רַבִּים; מִכָּאן יוֹדְעִים אָנוּ שֶׁזּוֹהִי הַשָּׁעָה הָאַחֲרוֹנָה
gam achshav kamu tzorerei mashiach rabbim; mikkan yode'im anu shezzohi hasha'ah ha'achronah
even now have there arisen many antichrists; whereby we know that it is the last hour.

הַלָּלוּ מִקִּרְבֵּנוּ יָצְאוּ, אֲבָל לֹא מִשֶּׁלָּנוּ הָיוּ; כִּי אִלּוּ הָיוּ מִשֶּׁלָּנוּ, הָיוּ נִשְׁאָרִים אִתָּנוּ,
hallalu mikkirbenu yatze'u, aval lo mishellanu hayu; ki illu hayu mishellanu, hayu nish'arim ittanu
They went out from us, but they were not of us; for if they had been of us, they would have continued with us:

יוֹחָנָן הָרִאשׁוֹנָה

הָאוֹמֵר שֶׁהוּא עוֹמֵד בְּיֵשׁוּעַ, כַּדֶּרֶךְ שֶׁהִתְהַלֵּךְ יֵשׁוּעַ כֵּן גַּם עָלָיו לְהִתְהַלֵּךְ
ha'omer shehu omed beyeshua', kederech shehit'hallech yeshua ken gam alav lehit'hallech
he that saith he abideth in him ought himself also to walk even as he walked.

אֲהוּבַי, לֹא מִצְוָה חֲדָשָׁה כּוֹתֵב אֲנִי לָכֶם, כִּי אִם מִצְוָה יְשָׁנָה אֲשֶׁר הָיְתָה לָכֶם מֵרֵאשִׁית
ahuvai, lo mitzvah chadashah kotev ani lachem, ki im mitzvah yeshanah asher haytah lachem mereshit
Beloved, no new commandment write I unto you, but an old commandment which ye had from the beginning:

הַמִּצְוָה הַיְשָׁנָה הִיא הַדָּבָר אֲשֶׁר שְׁמַעְתֶּם
hammitzvah hayshanah hi haddavar asher shema'tem
the old commandment is the word which ye heard.

וּבְכָל זֹאת מִצְוָה חֲדָשָׁה כּוֹתֵב אֲנִי לָכֶם, דָּבָר שֶׁנָּכוֹן גַּם בּוֹ וְגַם בָּכֶם
uvechol zot mitzvah chadashah kotev ani lachem, davar shennachon gam bo vegam bachem
Again, a new commandment write I unto you, which thing is true in him and in you;

שֶׁהֲרֵי הַחֹשֶׁךְ עוֹבֵר וְהָאוֹר הָאֲמִתִּי כְּבָר זוֹרֵחַ
sheharei hachoshech over veha'or ha'amitti kvar zoreach
because the darkness is passing away, and the true light already shineth.

הָאוֹמֵר כִּי בָּאוֹר הוּא וְעִם זֹאת שׂוֹנֵא אֶת אָחִיו, עוֹדֶנּוּ בַּחֹשֶׁךְ
ha'omer ki ba'or hu ve'im zot sonei et achiv, odennu bachoshech
He that saith he is in the light and hateth his brother, is in the darkness even until now.

הָאוֹהֵב אֶת אָחִיו עוֹמֵד בָּאוֹר וּמִכְשׁוֹל אֵין בּוֹ
ha'ohev et achiv omed ba'or umichshol ein bo
He that loveth his brother abideth in the light, and there is no occasion of stumbling in him.

אֲבָל הַשּׂוֹנֵא אֶת אָחִיו בַּחֹשֶׁךְ הוּא; בַּחֹשֶׁךְ הוּא מִתְהַלֵּךְ ן
aval hassonei et achiv bachoshech hu; bachoshech hu mit'hallech
But he that hateth his brother is in the darkness, and walketh in the darkness,

וְאֵינוֹ יוֹדֵעַ לְאָן הוּא הוֹלֵךְ, כִּי הַחֹשֶׁךְ עִוֵּר אֶת עֵינָיו
ve'eino yodea le'an hu holech, ki hachoshech ivver et einav
and knoweth not whither he goeth, because the darkness hath blinded his eyes.

כּוֹתֵב אֲנִי לָכֶם, יְלָדַי, מִפְּנֵי שֶׁנִּסְלְחוּ לָכֶם חֲטָאֵיכֶם בַּעֲבוּר שְׁמוֹ
kotev ani lachem, yeladai, mippenei shennislechu lachem chata'eichem ba'avur shemo
I write unto you, my little children, because your sins are forgiven you for his name's sake.

כּוֹתֵב אֲנִי לָכֶם, אָבוֹת, מִפְּנֵי שֶׁהִכַּרְתֶּם אוֹתוֹ אֲשֶׁר הוּא מֵרֵאשִׁית
kotev ani lachem, avot, mippenei shehikkartem oto asher hu mereshit
I write unto you, fathers, because ye know him who is from the beginning.

כּוֹתֵב אֲנִי לָכֶם, בַּחוּרִים, מִפְּנֵי שֶׁנִּצַּחְתֶּם אֶת הָרַע
kotev ani lachem, bachurim, mippenei shennitzachtem et hara
I write unto you, young men, because ye have overcome the evil one.

יוֹחָנָן הָרִאשׁוֹנָה

אֲבָל אִם נִתְהַלֵּךְ בָּאוֹר, כְּמוֹ שֶׁהוּא בָּאוֹר, כִּי אָז הִתְחַבַּרְנוּ זֶה עִם זֶה
aval im nit'hallech ba'or, kemo shehu ba'or, ki az hitchabbarnu zeh im zeh
but if we walk in the light, as he is in the light, we have fellowship one with another,

וְדַם יֵשׁוּעַ הַמָּשִׁיחַ בְּנוֹ מְטַהֵר אוֹתָנוּ מִכָּל חֵטְא
vedam yeshua hammashiach bno metaher otanu mikkol chet
and the blood of Jesus his Son cleanseth us from all sin.

אִם נֹאמַר שֶׁאֵין בָּנוּ חֵטְא, מַתְעִים אָנוּ אֶת עַצְמֵנוּ וְהָאֱמֶת אֵינֶנָּה בָּנוּ
im nomar she'ein banu chet, mat'im anu et atzmenu veha'emet einennah banu
If we say that we have no sin, we deceive ourselves, and the truth is not in us.

אִם נִתְוַדֶּה עַל חֲטָאֵינוּ, נֶאֱמָן הוּא וְצַדִּיק לִסְלֹחַ לָנוּ עַל חֲטָאֵינוּ וּלְטַהֵר אוֹתָנוּ מִכָּל עַוְלָה
im nitvaddeh al chata'einu, ne'eman hu vetzaddik lisloach lanu al chata'einu uletaher otanu mikkol avlah
If we confess our sins, he is faithful and righteous to forgive us our sins, and to cleanse us from all unrighteousness.

אִם נֹאמַר שֶׁלֹּא חָטָאנוּ, לְכוֹזֵב שַׂמְנוּ אוֹתוֹ וּדְבָרוֹ אֵינוֹ בָּנוּ
im nomar shello chatanu, lechozev samnu oto udevaro eino banu
If we say that we have not sinned, we make him a liar, and his word is not in us.

ב

יְלָדַי, כּוֹתֵב אֲנִי לָכֶם אֶת הַדְּבָרִים הָאֵלֶּה לְמַעַן לֹא תֶּחֶטְאוּ
yeladai, kotev ani lachem et haddevarim ha'elleh lema'an lo techteu
My little children, these things write I unto you that ye may not sin.

וְאִם יֶחֱטָא אִישׁ יֵשׁ לָנוּ מֵלִיץ לִפְנֵי הָאָב - יֵשׁוּעַ הַמָּשִׁיחַ, הַצַּדִּיק
ve'im yecheta ish yesh lanu melitz lifnei ha'av - yeshua hammashiach, hatzaddik
And if any man sin, we have an Advocate with the Father, Jesus Christ the righteous:

וְהוּא כַּפָּרָה עַל חֲטָאֵינוּ, וְלֹא עַל חֲטָאֵינוּ בִּלְבַד, אֶלָּא גַּם עַל חֲטָאֵי כָּל הָעוֹלָם
vehu kapparah al chata'einu, velo al chata'einu bilvad, ella gam al chata'ei kol ha'olam
and he is the propitiation for our sins; and not for ours only, but also for the whole world.

וּבָזֶה נֵדַע שֶׁהִכַּרְנוּ אוֹתוֹ - אִם נִשְׁמֹר אֶת מִצְווֹתָיו
uvazeh neda shehikkarnu oto - im nishmor et mitzvotav
And hereby we know that we know him, if we keep his commandments.

הָאוֹמֵר אֲנִי מַכִּיר אוֹתוֹ וְאֵינוֹ שׁוֹמֵר אֶת מִצְווֹתָיו, דּוֹבֵר שֶׁקֶר הוּא וְהָאֱמֶת אֵינֶנָּה בּוֹ
ha'omer ani makkir oto ve'eino shomer et mitzvotav, dover sheker hu veha'emet einennah bo
He that saith, I know him, and keepeth not his commandments, is a liar, and the truth is not in him;

אַךְ הַשּׁוֹמֵר אֶת דְּבָרוֹ, בְּאוֹתוֹ הָאִישׁ נִשְׁלְמָה בֶּאֱמֶת אַהֲבַת אֱלֹהִים. בָּזֶה נֵדַע כִּי בוֹ אֲנַחְנוּ
ach hashomer et devaro, be'oto ha'ish nishlemah be'emet ahavat elohim. bazeh neda ki bo anachnu
but whoso keepeth his word, in him verily hath the love of God been perfected. Hereby we know that we are in him:

יוֹחָנָן הָרִאשׁוֹנָה

אֵת אֲשֶׁר הָיָה מֵרֵאשִׁית, אֵת אֲשֶׁר שָׁמַעְנוּ
et asher hayah mereshit, et asher shama'nu
That which was from the beginning, that which we have heard,

אֵת אֲשֶׁר רָאִינוּ בְּעֵינֵינוּ, אֲשֶׁר הִבַּטְנוּ בּוֹ וְיָדֵינוּ מִשְׁשׁוּ אוֹתוֹ, עַל־אוֹדוֹת דְּבַר הַחַיִּים
et asher ra'inu be'eineinu, asher hibbatnu bo veyadeinu misheshu oto, al-odot devar hachayim
that which we have seen with our eyes, that which we beheld, and our hands handled, concerning the Word of life

וְהַחַיִּים נִגְלוּ וַאֲנַחְנוּ רָאִינוּ, וַהֲרֵינוּ מְעִידִים
vehachayim niglu va'anachnu ra'inu, vahareinu me'idim
(and the life was manifested, and we have seen, and bear witness,

וּמוֹדִיעִים לָכֶם אֶת חַיֵּי הָעוֹלָמִים אֲשֶׁר הָיוּ אֵצֶל הָאָב וְנִגְלוּ לָנוּ
umodi'im lachem et chayei ha'olamim asher hayu etzel ha'av veniglu lanu
and declare unto you the life, the eternal life, which was with the Father, and was manifested unto us);

אֵת אֲשֶׁר רָאִינוּ וְשָׁמַעְנוּ מוֹדִיעִים אָנוּ גַּם לָכֶם, לְמַעַן תִּתְחַבְּרוּ עִמָּנוּ גַּם אַתֶּם
et asher ra'inu veshama'nu modi'im anu gam lachem, lema'an titchabberu immanu gam attem
that which we have seen and heard declare we unto you also, that ye also may have fellowship with us:

וְאָכֵן הִתְחַבְּרוּתֵנוּ הִיא עִם הָאָב וְעִם בְּנוֹ יֵשׁוּעַ הַמָּשִׁיחַ
ve'achen hitchabberutenu hi im ha'av ve'im bno yeshua hammashiach
yea, and our fellowship is with the Father, and with his Son Jesus Christ:

זֹאת אֲנַחְנוּ כּוֹתְבִים לְמַעַן תִּהְיֶה שִׂמְחָתֵנוּ שְׁלֵמָה
zot anachnu kotevim lema'an tihyeh simchatenu shlemah
and these things we write, that our joy may be made full.

וְזֶה דְּבַר הַבְּשׂוֹרָה אֲשֶׁר שָׁמַעְנוּ מִמֶּנּוּ וַאֲנַחְנוּ מַשְׁמִיעִים לָכֶם
vezeh devar habbesorah asher shama'nu mimmennu va'anachnu mashmi'im lachem
And this is the message which we have heard from him and announce unto you,

שֶׁהָאֱלֹהִים אוֹר הוּא וְכָל חֹשֶׁךְ אֵין בּוֹ
sheha'elohim or hu vechol choshech ein bo
that God is light, and in him is no darkness at all.

אִם נֹאמַר שֶׁהִתְחַבְּרוּת לָנוּ אִתּוֹ וְנִתְהַלֵּךְ בַּחֹשֶׁךְ,
im nomar shehitchabberut lanu itto venit'hallech bachoshech,
If we say that we have fellowship with him and walk in the darkness,

דּוֹבְרֵי שֶׁקֶר אֲנַחְנוּ וְאֵינֶנּוּ מְקַיְּמִים אֶת הָאֱמֶת
doverei sheker anachnu ve'einennu mekayemim et ha'emet
we lie, and do not the truth:

פֶּטְרוֹס הַשְּׁנִיָּה

יוֹם שֶׁבִּגְלָלוֹ הַשָּׁמַיִם יִתְפָּרְקוּ בָּאֵשׁ וְהַיְסוֹדוֹת יִבְעֲרוּ וְיִמַּסּוּ
yom shebbiglalo hashamayim yitpareku ba'esh vehaysodot yiv'aru veyimmassu
by reason of which the heavens being on fire shall be dissolved, and the elements shall melt with fervent heat?

וַאֲנַחְנוּ מְחַכִּים, עַל־פִּי הַבְטָחָתוֹ, לְשָׁמַיִם חֲדָשִׁים וּלְאֶרֶץ חֲדָשָׁה אֲשֶׁר צֶדֶק יִשְׁכֹּן בָּם
va'anachnu mechakkim, al-pi havtachato, leshamayim chadashim ule'eretz chadashah asher tzedek yishkon bam
But, according to his promise, we look for new heavens and a new earth, wherein dwelleth righteousness.

עַל כֵּן, אֲהוּבַי, בְּחַכּוֹתְכֶם לַדְּבָרִים הָאֵלֶּה
al ken, ahuvai, bechakkotechem laddevarim ha'elleh
Wherefore, beloved, seeing that ye look for these things,

שִׁקְדוּ לְהִמָּצֵא לְפָנָיו בְּשָׁלוֹם, נְקִיִּים וּבְלֹא דֹפִי
shikdu lehimmatzei lefanav beshalom, nekiyim uvelo dofi
give diligence that ye may be found in peace, without spot and blameless in his sight.

וְאֶת אֹרֶךְ־רוּחַ אֲדוֹנֵנוּ חִשְׁבוּ לִתְשׁוּעָה
ve'et orech-ruach adonenu chishvu litshu'ah
And account that the longsuffering of our Lord is salvation;

כְּמוֹ שֶׁגַּם אָחִינוּ הָאָהוּב שָׁאוּל כָּתַב לָכֶם לְפִי הַחָכְמָה הַנְּתוּנָה לוֹ
kemo sheggam achinu ha'ahuv sha'ul katav lachem lefi hachachemah hannetunah lo
even as our beloved brother Paul also, according to the wisdom given to him, wrote unto you;

וּכְמוֹ שֶׁכָּתוּב בְּכָל אִגְּרוֹתָיו, בְּדַבְּרוֹ עַל הַדְּבָרִים הָאֵלֶּה. יֵשׁ בָּהֶן דְּבָרִים קָשִׁים לַהֲבָנָה
uchemo shekkatuv bechol iggerotav, bedabbero al haddevarim ha'elleh. yesh bahen devarim kashim lahavanah
as also in all his epistles, speaking in them of these things; wherein are some things hard to be understood,

אֲשֶׁר הַנִּבְעָרִים וְהַבִּלְתִּי יַצִּיבִים מְעַוְּתִים אוֹתָם - כְּמוֹ שֶׁהֵם עוֹשִׂים בְּיֶתֶר הַכְּתוּבִים - לְאָבְדָנָם הֵם
asher hanniv'arim vehabbilti yatzivim me'avvetim otam - kemo shehem osim beyeter hakketuvim - le'avedanam hem
which the ignorant and unstedfast wrest, as they do also the other scriptures, unto their own destruction.

וְאַתֶּם, אֲהוּבַי, כֵּיוָן שֶׁאַתֶּם יוֹדְעִים זֹאת מֵרֹאשׁ
ve'attem, ahuvai, keivan she'attem yode'im zot merosh
Ye therefore, beloved, knowing these things beforehand,

הִשָּׁמְרוּ פֶּן תִּמָּשְׁכוּ בִּתְעוּתָם שֶׁל אַנְשֵׁי בְּלִיַּעַל וְתִפְּלוּ מִיַּצִּיבוּתְכֶם
hishameru pen timmashechu beta'utam shel anshei beliya'al vetipplu miyatzivutechem
beware lest, being carried away with the error of the wicked, ye fall from your own stedfastness.

גִּדְלוּ בְּחֶסֶד וּבְדַעַת אֲדוֹנֵנוּ וּמוֹשִׁיעֵנוּ יֵשׁוּעַ הַמָּשִׁיחַ. לוֹ הַכָּבוֹד גַּם עַכְשָׁו גַּם לְיוֹם עוֹלָם. אָמֵן
gidlu bechesed uveda'at adonenu umoshi'enu yeshua hammashiach. lo hakkavod gam achshav gam leyom olam. amen
But grow in the grace and knowledge of our Lord and Saviour Jesus Christ. To him be the glory both now and for ever. Amen.

פֶּטְרוֹס הַשְּׁנִיָּה

וְעַל־יְדֵי אֵלֶּה נֶהֱרַס הָעוֹלָם שֶׁהָיָה אָז, בְּהִשָּׁפְטוֹ בַּמַּיִם
ve'al-yedei elleh neheras ha'olam shehayah az, behishafto bammayim
by which means the world that then was, being overflowed with water, perished:

וְאוּלָם הַשָּׁמַיִם וְהָאָרֶץ הַנּוֹכְחִיִּים אֲצוּרִים עַל־יְדֵי אוֹתוֹ הַדָּבָר לָאֵשׁ
ve'ulam hashamayim veha'aretz hannochechiyim atzurim al-yedei oto haddavar la'esh
but the heavens that now are, and the earth, by the same word have been stored up for fire,

שְׁמוּרִים לְיוֹם הַדִּין, לְאָבְדַן אַנְשֵׁי הָרֶשַׁע
shemurim leyom haddin, le'ovdan anshei haresha
being reserved against the day of judgment and destruction of ungodly men.

אַךְ אַל יֵעָלֵם מִכֶּם הַדָּבָר הַזֶּה, אֲהוּבַי: יוֹם אֶחָד כְּאֶלֶף שָׁנִים בְּעֵינֵי יהוה
ach al ye'alem mikkem haddavar hazzeh, ahuvai. yom echad ke'elef shanim be'einei hashem
But forget not this one thing, beloved, that one day is with the Lord as a thousand years,

וְאֶלֶף שָׁנִים כְּיוֹם אֶחָד
ve'elef shanim keyom echad
and a thousand years as one day.

אֵין יהוה מְאַחֵר בַּדָּבָר אֲשֶׁר הִבְטִיחַ, כְּמוֹ שֶׁיֵּשׁ הַחוֹשְׁבִים זֹאת לְאִחוּר
ein hashem me'acher baddavar asher hivtiach, kemo sheyesh hachoshevim zot le'ichur
The Lord is not slack concerning his promise, as some count slackness;

אֶלָּא שֶׁהוּא מַאֲרִיךְ אַפּוֹ לָנוּ; אֵין הוּא רוֹצֶה שֶׁיֹּאבַד אִישׁ, אֶלָּא שֶׁהַכֹּל יָבוֹאוּ לִידֵי תְּשׁוּבָה
ella shehu ma'arich appo lanu; ein hu rotzeh sheyovad ish, ella shehakkol yavo'u liyedei teshuvah
but is longsuffering to you-ward, not wishing that any should perish, but that all should come to repentance.

יוֹם יהוה כְּגַנָּב יָבוֹא. אָז הַשָּׁמַיִם בְּשָׁאוֹן יַחְלֵפוּ
yom hashem kegannav yavo. az hashamayim besha'on yachlefu
But the day of the Lord will come as a thief; in the which the heavens shall pass away with a great noise,

וְהַיְסוֹדוֹת יִבְעֲרוּ וְיִתְפָּרְקוּ, וְהָאָרֶץ וְהַמַּעֲשִׂים אֲשֶׁר עָלֶיהָ
vehaysodot yiv'aru veyitpareku, veha'aretz vehamma'asim asher aleiha
and the elements shall be dissolved with fervent heat, and the earth and the works that are therein shall be burned up.

וְכֵיוָן שֶׁכָּל אֵלֶּה יִתְפָּרְקוּ
vecheivan shekkol elleh yitpareku,
Seeing that these things are thus all to be dissolved,

עַד כַּמָּה עֲלֵיכֶם לִחְיוֹת בִּקְדֻשָּׁה וּבַחֲסִידוּת
ad kammah aleichem lichyot bikdushah uvachasidut
what manner of persons ought ye to be in all holy living and godliness,

לְחַכּוֹת לְבוֹא יוֹם הָאֱלֹהִים וּלְהָחִישׁ אוֹתוֹ
lechakkot levo yom ha'elohim ulehachish oto
looking for and earnestly desiring the coming of the day of God,

פֶּטְרוֹס הַשְּׁנִיָּה

הִתְמַמֵּשׁ בָּהֶם הַמָּשָׁל הָאֲמִתִּי
hitmammesh bahem hammashal ha'amitti
It has happened unto them according to the true proverb,

הַכֶּלֶב שָׁב עַל־קֵאוֹ, וְגַם הַחֲזִיר עוֹלֶה מִן הָרַחְצָה לְהִתְגּוֹלֵל בָּרֶפֶשׁ
hakkelev shav al-ke'o, vegam hachazir oleh min harachatzah lehitgolel barefesh
The dog turning to his own vomit again, and the sow that had washed to wallowing in the mire.

ג

אֲהוּבַי, זֹאת כְּבָר הָאִגֶּרֶת הַשְּׁנִיָּה שֶׁאֲנִי כּוֹתֵב לָכֶם,
ahuvai, zot kevar ha'iggeret hasheniyah she'ani kotev lachem
This is now, beloved, the second epistle that I write unto you;

וּבִשְׁתֵּיהֶן אֲנִי מַזְכִּיר אֶתְכֶם וּמְעוֹרֵר אֶת מַחֲשַׁבְתְּכֶם הַתַּמָּה
uvishteihen ani mazkir etchem ume'orer et machashavtechem hattammah
and in both of them I stir up your sincere mind by putting you in remembrance;

לְמַעַן תִּזְכְּרוּ אֶת הַדְּבָרִים שֶׁנֶּאֶמְרוּ מִקֶּדֶם בְּיַד הַנְּבִיאִים הַקְּדוֹשִׁים
lema'an tizkeru et haddevarim shenne'emru mikkedem beyad hannevi'im hakkedoshim
that ye should remember the words which were spoken before by the holy prophets,

וְאֶת מִצְוַת שְׁלִיחֵיכֶם מִטַּעַם הָאָדוֹן וְהַמּוֹשִׁיעַ
ve'et mitzvat shelicheichem mitta'am ha'adon vehammoshia
and the commandment of the Lord and Saviour through your apostles:

וְקֹדֶם כֹּל דְּעוּ זֹאת, שֶׁבְּאַחֲרִית הַיָּמִים יָבוֹאוּ לֵצִים הַמִּתְהַלְּכִים לְפִי מַאֲוַיֵּיהֶם הָאִישִׁיִּים וְיִתְלוֹצְצוּ
vekodem kol de'u zot, shebbe'acharit hayamim yavo'u letzim hammit'halchim lefi ma'avayeihem ha'ishiyim veyitlotzetzu
knowing this first, that in the last days mockers shall come with mockery, walking after their own lusts,

לֵאמֹר אֵיפֹה בּוֹאוֹ הַמֻּבְטָח? הֲרֵי מֵאָז שָׁמְּטוּ הָאָבוֹת
lemor eifoh bo'o hammuvtach? harei me'az shemmetu ha'avot
and saying, Where is the promise of his coming? for, from the day that the fathers fell asleep,

הַכֹּל מַמְשִׁיךְ כְּמוֹ שֶׁהָיָה מֵרֵאשִׁית הַבְּרִיאָה
hakkol mamshich kemo shehayah mereshit habberi'ah
all things continue as they were from the beginning of the creation.

מֵרָצוֹן שׁוֹכְחִים הֵם אֶת הַדָּבָר הַזֶּה, שֶׁהַשָּׁמַיִם הָיוּ מִקֶּדֶם
meratzon shochechim hem et haddavar hazzeh, shehashamayim hayu mikkedem
For this they wilfully forget, that there were heavens from of old,

וְכִי הָאָרֶץ נִתְהַוְּתָה מִן הַמַּיִם וְעַל־יְדֵי הַמַּיִם בִּדְבַר אֱלֹהִים
vechi ha'aretz nit'havvetah min hammayim ve'al-yedei hammayim bidvar elohim
and an earth compacted out of water and amidst water, by the word of God;

פֶּטְרוֹס הַשְּׁנִיָּה

וְהָלְכוּ בְּדֶרֶךְ בִּלְעָם בֶּן בְּעוֹר אֲשֶׁר אָהַב אֶת שְׂכַר הָרֶשַׁע
vehalechu bederech bil'am ben be'or asher ahav et schar haresha
having followed the way of Balaam the son of Beor, who loved the hire of wrong-doing;

וְהוּכַח עַל עַוְלָתוֹ
vehuchach al avlato
but he was rebuked for his own transgression:

אָתוֹן אִלֶּמֶת דִּבְּרָה בְּקוֹל אָדָם וְעָצְרָה אֶת אִוֶּלֶת הַנָּבִיא
aton illemet dibberah bekol adam ve'atzerah et ivvelet hannavi
a dumb ass spake with man's voice and stayed the madness of the prophet.

בְּאֵרוֹת בְּלִי מַיִם הֵם, עֲנָנִים נִדָּפִים בִּסְעָרָה, אֲשֶׁר אֲפֵלַת חֹשֶׁךְ שְׁמוּרָה לָהֶם
be'erot beli mayim hem, ananim niddafim bis'arah, asher afelat choshech shmurah lahem
These are springs without water, and mists driven by a storm; for whom the blackness of darkness hath been reserved.

בְּדַבְּרָם גְּדוֹלוֹת, דְּבָרִים שֶׁאֵינָם אֶלָּא הֶבֶל, הֵם לוֹכְדִים בְּתַאֲווֹת בְּשָׂרִים
bedabberam gedolot, devarim she'einam ella hevel, hem lochedim beta'avot besarim
For, uttering great swelling words of vanity, they entice in the lusts of the flesh,

וּבְמַעֲשֵׂי זִמָּה אֶת אֵלֶּה אֲשֶׁר אַךְ נִמְלְטוּ מִידֵי הַהוֹלְכִים בְּדֶרֶךְ הַתָּעוּת
uvema'asei zimmah et elleh asher ach nimletu miydei haholechim bederech hatta'ut
by lasciviousness, those who are just escaping from them that live in error;

הֵם מַבְטִיחִים לָהֶם חֹפֶשׁ בְּשָׁעָה שֶׁהֵם עַצְמָם עֲבָדִים לְכָל אֲשֶׁר מַשְׁחִית
hem mavtichim lahem chofesh besha'ah shehem atzmam avadim lechol asher mashchit
promising them liberty, while they themselves are bondservants of corruption;

הֲרֵי לְמַה שֶּׁאָדָם נִכְנָע, לָזֶה הוּא מִשְׁתַּעְבֵּד
harei lemah she'adam nichna, lazeh hu mishta'bed
for of whom a man is overcome, of the same is he also brought into bondage.

הֲלֹא אִם אַחֲרֵי שֶׁנִּמְלְטוּ מִטֻּמְאוֹת הָעוֹלָם בִּידִיעָתָם אֶת אֲדוֹנֵנוּ וּמוֹשִׁיעֵנוּ יֵשׁוּעַ הַמָּשִׁיחַ
halo im acharei shennimletu mittum'ot ha'olam biyedi'atam et adonenu umoshi'enu yeshua hammashiach
For if, after they have escaped the defilements of the world through the knowledge of the Lord and Saviour Jesus Christ,

שׁוּב נִסְתַּבְּכוּ בָּהֶן וְנֻצְּחוּ - כִּי אָז מַצָּבָם הָאַחֲרוֹן גָּרוּעַ מִן הָרִאשׁוֹן
shuv nistabbechu bahen venutzechu - ki az matzavam ha'acharon garua min harishon
they are again entangled therein and overcome, the last state is become worse with them than the first.

מוּטָב הָיָה לָהֶם שֶׁלֹּא לָדַעַת אֶת דֶּרֶךְ הַצְּדָקָה
mutav hayah lahem shello lada'at et derech hatzedakah
For it were better for them not to have known the way of righteousness,

מֵאֲשֶׁר לָדַעַת אוֹתָהּ וְלָסוּר מִן הַמִּצְוָה הַקְּדוֹשָׁה הַמְּסוּרָה לָהֶם
me'asher lada'at otah velasur min hammitzvah hakkedoshah hammesurah lahem
than, after knowing it, to turn back from the holy commandment delivered unto them.

פֶּטְרוֹס הַשְּׁנִיָּה

אָכֵן יוֹדֵעַ יהוה לְהַצִּיל אֶת חֲסִידָיו מִנִּסָּיוֹן
achen yodea hashem lehatzil et chasidav minnissayon
the Lord knoweth how to deliver the godly out of temptation,

וְעִם זֹאת לַחֲשֹׂךְ אֶת הָרְשָׁעִים לְיוֹם הַדִּין כְּדֵי לְהַעֲנִישָׁם
ve'im zot lachasoch et haresha'im leyom haddin kedei leha'anisham
and to keep the unrighteous under punishment unto the day of judgment;

בְּיִחוּד אֶת הַהוֹלְכִים אַחַר הַבְּשָׂרִיּוּת בְּתַאֲוַת טֻמְאָה וּבוֹזִים אֶת הַסַּמְכוּת הָעֶלְיוֹנָה
beyichud et haholechim achar habbesariyut beta'avat tum'ah uvozim et hassamchut ha'elyonah
but chiefly them that walk after the flesh in the lust of defilement, and despise dominion.

חֲצוּפִים הֵם, הוֹלְכִים בִּשְׁרִירוּת לִבָּם וְאֵינָם נִרְתָּעִים מִלְּחָרֵף אֶת נוֹשְׂאֵי הַמִּשְׂרוֹת הַנִּכְבָּדוֹת
chatzufim hem, holechim bishrirut libbam ve'einam nirta'im millecharef et nose'ei hammisrot hannichbadot
Daring, self-willed, they tremble not to rail at dignities:

אֲשֶׁר אַף הַמַּלְאָכִים, הַגְּדוֹלִים מֵהֶם בְּעָצְמָה וְכֹחַ
asher af hammal'achim, haggedolim mehem be'otzmah vechoach
whereas angels, though greater in might and power,

אֵינָם מְבִיאִים עֲלֵיהֶם קִטְרוּג שֶׁל גִּדּוּף לִפְנֵי יהוה
einam mevi'im aleihem kitrug shel gidduf lifnei hashem
bring not a railing judgment against them before the Lord.

אַךְ הַלָּלוּ דּוֹמִים לְחַיּוֹת חֲסֵרוֹת תְּבוּנָה שֶׁבְּדֶרֶךְ הַטֶּבַע נוֹלָדוֹת כְּדֵי לְהִלָּכֵד וּלְהִשָּׁמֵד
ach hallalu domim lechayot chasrot tvunah shebbederech hatteva noladot kedei lehillached ulehishamed
But these, as creatures without reason, born mere animals to be taken and destroyed,

הֵם מְחָרְפִים מַה שֶּׁאֵינָם יוֹדְעִים, וּכְמוֹ שֶׁהֵן נִשְׁמָדוֹת גַּם הֵם יִשָּׁמֵדוּ
hem mecharefim mah she'einam yode'im, uchmo shehen nishmadot gam hem yishamedu
railing in matters whereof they are ignorant, shall in their destroying surely be destroyed,

וּבָזֶה יִסְבְּלוּ אֶת גְּמוּל עַוְלָתָם. אֶת הַהוֹלֵלוּת בַּיּוֹם חוֹשְׁבִים הֵם לְתַעֲנוּג
uvazeh yisbelu et gmul avlatam. et haholelut bayom choshevim hem leta'anug
suffering wrong as the hire of wrong-doing; men that count it pleasure to revel in the day-time,

כִּתְמֵי טֻמְאָה וּמוּמִים הֵם, הַסּוֹעֲדִים עִמָּכֶם וּמוֹצְאִים הֲנָאָה בְּתַרְמִיתָם
kitmei tum'ah umumim hem, hasso'adim immachem umotze'im hana'ah betarmitam
spots and blemishes, revelling in their deceivings while they feast with you;

עֵינַיִם לָהֶם מְלֵאוֹת נִאוּפִים וְאֵינָן מַרְפּוֹת מִן הַחֵטְא. הֵם לוֹכְדִים נְפָשׁוֹת בִּלְתִּי יַצִּיבוֹת
einayim lahem mele'ot ni'ufim ve'einan marpot min hachet. hem lochedim nefashot bilti yatzivot
having eyes full of adultery, and that cannot cease from sin; enticing unstedfast souls;

לִבָּם מֻרְגָּל בְּחַמְדָנוּת; אָכֵן בָּנִים אֲרוּרִים בְּעָזְבָם אֶת דֶּרֶךְ הַיָּשָׁר תָּעוּ
libbam murgal bechamdanut; achen banim arurim be'azevam et derech hayashar ta'u
having a heart exercised in covetousness; children of cursing; forsaking the right way, they went astray,

פֶּטְרוֹס הַשְּׁנִיָּה

וְיָבִיאוּ עַל עַצְמָם אָבְדָן פִּתְאֹם
veyavi'u al atzmam avedan pit'om
bringing upon themselves swift destruction.

רַבִּים יֵלְכוּ אַחֲרֵי תוֹעֲבוֹתֵיהֶם, וּבִגְלָלָם תְּגֻדַּף דֶּרֶךְ הָאֱמֶת
rabbim yelechu acharei to'avoteihem, uviglalam teguddaf derech ha'emet
And many shall follow their lascivious doings; by reason of whom the way of the truth shall be evil spoken of.

וּבְתַאֲוָתָם לַבֶּצַע יְדַבְּרוּ כָזָב וְיִסְחֲרוּ בָּכֶם
uveta'avatam labbetza yedabbru kazav veyischaru bachem
And in covetousness shall they with feigned words make merchandise of you:

וְאָמְנָם לֹא יִתְעַכֵּב מִשְׁפָּטָם שֶׁנֶּחֱרַץ מִקֶּדֶם, וְאָבְדָנָם לֹא יָנוּם
ve'omnam lo yit'akkev mishpatam shennecheratz mikkedem, ve'ovdanam lo yanum
whose sentence now from of old lingereth not, and their destruction slumbereth not.

הֵן אֱלֹהִים לֹא חָס עַל הַמַּלְאָכִים הַחוֹטְאִים, אֶלָּא הוֹרִידָם אֶל תַּחְתִּיּוֹת אֶרֶץ
hen elohim lo chas al hammal'achim hachote'im, ella horidam el tachtiyot eretz
For if God spared not angels when they sinned, but cast them down to hell,

וּנְתָנָם בְּכַבְלֵי אֹפֶל לְשָׁמְרָם לְמִשְׁפָּט וְגַם עַל הָעוֹלָם הַקָּדוּם לֹא חָס
unetanam bechavlei ofel leshomram lemishpat vegam al ha'olam hakkadum lo chas
and committed them to pits of darkness, to be reserved unto judgment; and spared not the ancient world,

אֲבָל בַּהֲבִיאוֹ מַבּוּל עַל עוֹלָם שֶׁל רְשָׁעִים שָׁמַר אֶת נֹחַ, מַטִּיף הַצֶּדֶק, וְהַשִּׁבְעָה אֲשֶׁר עִמּוֹ
aval bahavi'o mabbul al olam shel resha'im shamar et noach, mattif hatzedek, vehashiv'ah asher immo
but preserved Noah with seven others, a preacher of righteousness, when he brought a flood upon the world of the ungodly;

אֶת הֶעָרִים סְדוֹם וַעֲמֹרָה שָׂרַף לְאֵפֶר לְאַחַר שֶׁדָּן אוֹתָן לְמַהְפֵּכָה
et he'arim sedom va'amorah saraf le'efer le'achar sheddan otan lemahpechah
and turning the cities of Sodom and Gomorrah into ashes condemned them with an overthrow,

בְּשִׂימוֹ אוֹתָן לְדֻגְמָה לַעֲתִידִים לַעֲשׂוֹת רִשְׁעָה
besimo otan ledugmah la'atidim la'asot rish'ah
having made them an example unto those that should live ungodly;

וְהִצִּיל אֶת לוֹט הַצַּדִּיק, אֲשֶׁר נִדְכְּאָה נַפְשׁוֹ בִּגְלַל הִתְנַהֲגוּת הָרְשָׁעִים שְׁטוּפֵי זִמָּה
vehitzil et lot hatzaddik, asher nidke'ah nafsho biglal hitnahagut haresha'im shetufei zimmah
and delivered righteous Lot, sore distressed by the lascivious life of the wicked

כִּי הַצַּדִּיק הַזֶּה, אֲשֶׁר בְּשִׁבְתּוֹ בְּקִרְבָּם רָאָה וְשָׁמַע אֶת הַנַּעֲשֶׂה
ki hatzaddik hazzeh, asher beshivto bekirbam ra'ah veshama et hanna'aseh
(for that righteous man dwelling among them, in seeing and hearing,

יוֹם יוֹם הִתְעַנָּה בְּנַפְשׁוֹ הַיְשָׁרָה עַל מַעֲשֵׂי רִשְׁעָתָם
yom yom hit'annah benafsho hayesharah al ma'asei rish'atam
vexed his righteous soul from day to day with their lawless deeds):

פֶּטְרוֹס הַשְׁנִיָּה

לֹא אַחֲרֵי אַגָּדוֹת מְחֻכָּמוֹת הָלַכְנוּ
lo acharei aggadot mechukkamot halachnu
For we did not follow cunningly devised fables,

כַּאֲשֶׁר הוֹדַעְנוּ לָכֶם אֶת גְּבוּרַת אֲדוֹנֵנוּ יֵשׁוּעַ הַמָּשִׁיחַ וְאֶת בּוֹאוֹ
ka'asher hoda'nu lachem et gvurat adonenu yeshua hammashiach ve'et bo'o
when we made known unto you the power and coming of our Lord Jesus Christ,

אֶלָּא בְּמוֹ עֵינֵינוּ רָאִינוּ אֶת גְּדֻלָּתוֹ. שֶׁכֵּן קִבֵּל יְקָר וְכָבוֹד מֵאֵת אֱלֹהִים הָאָב
ella bemo eineinu ra'inu et gedullato. shekken kibbel yekar vechavod me'et elohim ha'av
but we were eyewitnesses of his majesty. For he received from God the Father honor and glory,

כַּאֲשֶׁר נִשָּׂא אֵלָיו הַקּוֹל הַזֶּה מֵהֲדָרַת הַכָּבוֹד: זֶה בְּנִי אֲהוּבִי אֲשֶׁר בּוֹ חָפַצְתִּי
ka'asher nissa elav hakkol hazzeh mehadrat hakkavod. zeh beni ahuvi asher bo chafatzti
when there was borne such a voice to him by the Majestic Glory, This is my beloved Son, in whom I am well pleased:

וְאֶת הַקּוֹל הַזֶּה שָׁמַעְנוּ בָּא מִן הַשָּׁמַיִם בִּהְיוֹתֵנוּ עִמּוֹ בְּהַר הַקֹּדֶשׁ
ve'et hakkol hazzeh shama'nu ba min hashamayim bihyotenu immo behar hakkodesh
and this voice we ourselves heard borne out of heaven, when we were with him in the holy mount.

אָכֵן נִתְאַשֵּׁר לָנוּ בְּיֶתֶר תֹּקֶף דְּבַר הַנְּבוּאָה, וְתֵיטִיבוּ לַעֲשׂוֹת בְּשִׂימְכֶם לֵב אֵלָיו
achen nit'asher lanu beyeter tokef devar hannevu'ah, veteitivu la'asot besimechem lev elav
And we have the word of prophecy made more sure; whereunto ye do well that ye take heed,

כְּאֵל נֵר מֵאִיר בִּמְקוֹם אֹפֶל, עַד כִּי יִבָּקַע אוֹר הַיּוֹם וְיִזְרַח כּוֹכַב הַנֹּגַהּ בִּלְבַבְכֶם
ke'el ner me'ir bimkom ofel, ad ki yivka or hayom veyizrach kochav hannogah bilvavchem
as unto a lamp shining in a dark place, until the day dawn, and the day-star arise in your hearts:

וְזֹאת דְּעוּ רִאשׁוֹנָה, שֶׁכָּל נְבוּאַת הַמִּקְרָא אֵינָהּ עִנְיָן שֶׁל פֵּרוּשׁ אִישִׁי
vezot de'u rishonah, shekkol nevu'at hammikra einah inyan shel perush ishi
knowing this first, that no prophecy of scripture is of private interpretation.

כִּי מֵעוֹלָם לֹא יָצְאָה נְבוּאָה עַל־פִּי רְצוֹן הָאָדָם, אֶלָּא רוּחַ הַקֹּדֶשׁ הֵנִיעָה בְּנֵי אָדָם לְדַבֵּר מִטַּעַם אֱלֹהִים
ki me'olam lo yatz'ah nevu'ah al-pi retzon ha'adam, ella ruach hakkodesh heni'ah benei adam ledabber mitta'am elohim
For no prophecy ever came by the will of man: but men spake from God, being moved by the Holy Spirit.

ב

אֲבָל גַּם נְבִיאֵי שֶׁקֶר הָיוּ בָּעָם, כְּשֵׁם שֶׁגַּם בֵּינֵיכֶם יִהְיוּ מוֹרֵי שֶׁקֶר
aval gam nevi'ei sheker hayu ba'am, keshem sheggam beineichem yihyu morei sheker
But there arose false prophets also among the people, as among you also there shall be false teachers,

הַלָּלוּ יַכְנִיסוּ בַּחֲשַׁאי תּוֹרוֹת הַרְסָנִיּוֹת וְיִכְפְּרוּ בָּאָדוֹן אֲשֶׁר קָנָה אוֹתָם
hallalu yachnisu bachasha torot harsaniyot veyichperu ba'adon asher kanah otam
who shall privily bring in destructive heresies, denying even the Master that bought them,

פֶּטְרוֹס הַשְּׁנִיָּה

וְעַל הַחֲסִידוּת אֶת הָאַחֲוָה, וְעַל הָאַחֲוָה אֶת הָאַהֲבָה
ve'al hachasidut et ha'achavah, ve'al ha'achavah et ha'ahavah
and in your godliness brotherly kindness; and in your brotherly kindness love.

שֶׁהֲרֵי אִם אֵלֶּה יִהְיוּ בָּכֶם וְיִרְבּוּ
sheharei im elleh yihyu bachem veyirbu
For if these things are yours and abound,

לֹא יַנִּיחַ לָכֶם לִהְיוֹת בְּטֵלִים וּבִלְתִּי פוֹרִיִּים בְּמַה שֶּׁנּוֹגֵעַ לִידִיעַת אֲדוֹנֵנוּ יֵשׁוּעַ הַמָּשִׁיחַ
lo yannich lachem lihyot betelim uvilti poriyim bemah shennogea lidi'at adonenu yeshua hammashiach
they make you to be not idle nor unfruitful unto the knowledge of our Lord Jesus Christ.

מִי שֶׁאֵין לוֹ הַדְּבָרִים הַלָּלוּ, עִוֵּר הוּא, קְצַר רְאוּת; הוּא שָׁכַח כִּי טֹהַר מֵחֲטָאָיו הָרִאשׁוֹנִים
mi she'ein lo haddevarim hallalu, ivver hu, ketzar re'ut; hu shachach ki tohar mechata'av harishonim
For he that lacketh these things is blind, seeing only what is near, having forgotten the cleansing from his old sins.

לָכֵן, אַחַי, שִׁקְדוּ בְּיֶתֶר שְׂאֵת לְחַזֵּק אֶת הַקְּרִיאָה וְהַבְּחִירָה שֶׁהֵן מְנָת חֶלְקְכֶם
lachen, achai, shikdu beyeter se'et lechazzek et hakkeri'ah vehabbechirah shehen menat chelkechem
Wherefore, brethren, give the more diligence to make your calling and election sure:

שֶׁהֲרֵי אִם כָּךְ תַּעֲשׂוּ לֹא תִּכָּשְׁלוּ אַף פַּעַם
sheharei im kach ta'asu lo tikkashelu af pa'am
for if ye do these things, ye shall never stumble:

וּבְדֶרֶךְ זֹאת יִפָּתַח לָכֶם לִרְוָחָה הַמָּבוֹא אֶל מַלְכוּת עוֹלָמִים שֶׁל אֲדוֹנֵנוּ וּמוֹשִׁיעֵנוּ יֵשׁוּעַ הַמָּשִׁיחַ
uvederech zot yippatach lachem lirvachah hammavo el malchut olamim shel adonenu umoshi'enu yeshua hammashiach
for thus shall be richly supplied unto you the entrance into the eternal kingdom of our Lord and Saviour Jesus Christ.

עַל כֵּן לֹא אֶחְדַּל לְהַזְכִּירְכֶם בְּכָל עֵת אֶת הַדְּבָרִים הַלָּלוּ
al ken lo echdal lehazkirechem bechol et et haddevarim hallalu
Wherefore I shall be ready always to put you in remembrance of these things,

אַף עַל פִּי שֶׁאַתֶּם יוֹדְעִים אוֹתָם וְהִנְּכֶם יַצִּיבִים בָּאֱמֶת הַזֹּאת
af al pi she'attem yode'im otam vehinnechem yatzivim ba'emet hazzot
though ye know them, and are established in the truth which is with you.

וְרוֹאֶה אֲנִי לְנָכוֹן לְהַזְכִּיר וּלְעוֹרֵר אֶתְכֶם כָּל עוֹד אֲנִי נִמְצָא בַּמִּשְׁכָּן הַזֶּה
vero'eh ani lenachon lehazkir ule'orer etchem kol od ani nimtza bammishkan hazzeh
And I think it right, as long as I am in this tabernacle, to stir you up by putting you in remembrance;

כִּי יָדוּעַ לִי שֶׁבְּקָרוֹב יוּסַר מִשְׁכָּנִי, כְּפִי שֶׁגִּלָּה לִי אֲדוֹנֵנוּ יֵשׁוּעַ הַמָּשִׁיחַ
ki yadua li shebbekarov yusar mishkani, kefi sheggillah li adonenu yeshua hammashiach
knowing that the putting off of my tabernacle cometh swiftly, even as our Lord Jesus Christ signified unto me.

אַךְ אֶשְׁתַּדֵּל שֶׁגַּם לְאַחַר פְּטִירָתִי יִהְיֶה לָכֶם תָּמִיד זִכְרוֹן הַדְּבָרִים הָאֵלֶּה
ach eshtaddel sheggam le'achar petirati yihyeh lachem tamid zichron haddevarim ha'elleh
Yea, I will give diligence that at every time ye may be able after my decease to call these things to remembrance.

פֶּטְרוֹס הַשְּׁנִיָּה

מֵאֵת שִׁמְעוֹן פֶּטְרוֹס, עֶבֶד יֵשׁוּעַ הַמָּשִׁיחַ וּשְׁלִיחוֹ
me'et shim'on petros, eved yeshua hammashiach ushelicho
Simon Peter, a servant and apostle of Jesus Christ,

לְאֵלֶּה אֲשֶׁר בְּצִדְקַת אֱלֹהֵינוּ וּמוֹשִׁיעֵנוּ יֵשׁוּעַ הַמָּשִׁיחַ קִבְּלוּ אֱמוּנָה יְקָרָה כְּשֶׁלָּנוּ
le'elleh asher betzidkat eloheinu umoshi'enu yeshua hammashiach kibblu emunah yekarah keshellanu
to them that have obtained a like precious faith with us in the righteousness of our God and the Saviour Jesus Christ:

חֶסֶד וְשָׁלוֹם יִשָּׁפְעוּ עֲלֵיכֶם לְמַכְבִּיר בִּידִיעַתְכֶם אֶת אֱלֹהִים וְיֵשׁוּעַ אֲדוֹנֵנוּ
chesed veshalom yishpe'u aleichem lemachbir biydi'atchem et elohim veyeshua adonenu
Grace to you and peace be multiplied in the knowledge of God and of Jesus our Lord;

הֵן גְּבוּרָתוֹ הָאֱלֹהִית נָתְנָה לָנוּ אֶת כָּל צְרָכֵינוּ לְחַיִּים וְלַחֲסִידוּת
hen gevurato ha'elohit natnah lanu et kol tzeracheinu lechayim velachasidut
seeing that his divine power hath granted unto us all things that pertain unto life and godliness,

עַל־יְדֵי יְדִיעָתֵנוּ אֶת הַקּוֹרֵא אוֹתָנוּ אֶל כְּבוֹדוֹ וְהוֹדוֹ
al-yedei yedi'atenu et hakkorei otanu el kvodo vehodo
through the knowledge of him that called us by his own glory and virtue;

בְּדֶרֶךְ זֹאת נָתַן לָנוּ הַבְטָחוֹת גְּדוֹלוֹת מְאֹד וִיקָרוֹת
bederech zot natan lanu havtachot gedolot me'od viykarot
whereby he hath granted unto us his precious and exceeding great promises;

לְמַעַן תִּהְיוּ שֻׁתָּפִים עַל־יָדָן בַּטֶּבַע הָאֱלֹהִי
lema'an tihyu shuttafim al-yadan batteva ha'elohi
that through these ye may become partakers of the divine nature,

בְּהִמָּלֶטְכֶם מֵהַכִּלָּיוֹן הַשּׁוֹרֵר בָּעוֹלָם בְּשֶׁל הַתַּאֲוָה
behimmaletchem mehakkillayon hassorer ba'olam beshel hatta'avah
having escaped from the corruption that is in the world by lust.

מִשּׁוּם כָּךְ שִׁקְדוּ בְּכָל מְאֹדְכֶם לְהוֹסִיף עַל אֱמוּנַתְכֶם אֶת הַמַּעֲלָה הַמּוּסָרִית
mishum kach shikdu bechol me'odechem lehosif al emunatchem et hamma'alah hammusarit
Yea, and for this very cause adding on your part all diligence, in your faith supply virtue;

וְעַל הַמַּעֲלָה הַמּוּסָרִית אֶת הַדַּעַת
ve'al hamma'alah hammusarit et hadda'at
and in your virtue knowledge;

וְעַל הַדַּעַת אֶת כִּבּוּשׁ הַיֵּצֶר, וְעַל כִּבּוּשׁ הַיֵּצֶר אֶת הַסַּבְלָנוּת, וְעַל הַסַּבְלָנוּת אֶת הַחֲסִידוּת
ve'al hadda'at et kibbush hayetzer, ve'al kibbush hayetzer et hassavlanut, ve'al hassavlanut et hachasidut
and in your knowledge self-control; and in your self-control patience; and in your patience godliness;

פֶּטְרוֹס הָרִאשׁוֹנָה

וֵאלֹהֵי כָּל חֶסֶד אֲשֶׁר קָרָא אֶתְכֶם אֶל כְּבוֹדוֹ לְעוֹלָמִים בַּמָּשִׁיחַ יֵשׁוּעַ
ve'elohei kol chesed asher kara etchem el kevodo le'olamim bammashiach yeshua
And the God of all grace, who called you unto his eternal glory in Christ,

אַחֲרֵי סִבְלְכֶם הַמְעַט הוּא יַשְׁלִים אֶתְכֶם וְגַם יְיַצֵּב וִיחַזֵּק וִיכוֹנֵן אֶתְכֶם
acharei sivlechem hamme'at hu yashlim etchem vegam yeyatzev vichazzek vichonen etchem
after that ye have suffered a little while, shall himself perfect, establish, strengthen you.

לוֹ הַכָּבוֹד וְהַגְּבוּרָה לְעוֹלְמֵי עוֹלָמִים. אָמֵן
lo hakkavod vehaggevurah le'olemei olamim. amen
To him be the dominion for ever and ever. Amen.

בְּיַד הָאָח סִילְוָנוֹס שֶׁאֲנִי חוֹשְׁבוֹ לְנֶאֱמָן, כָּתַבְתִּי לָכֶם דְּבָרִים מְעַטִּים לְעוֹרֵר
beyad ha'ach silvanos she'ani choshvo lene'eman, katavti lachem dvarim me'attim le'orer
By Silvanus, our faithful brother, as I account him, I have written unto you briefly, exhorting,

וּלְהָעִיד כִּי זֶהוּ חֶסֶד הָאֱלֹהִים, הַחֶסֶד הָאֲמִתִּי; עִמְדוּ בּוֹ
uleha'id ki zehu chesed ha'elohim, hachesed ha'amitti; imdu bo
and testifying that this is the true grace of God: stand ye fast therein.

הַקְּהִלָּה אֲשֶׁר בְּבָבֶל, שֶׁנִּבְחֲרָה אִתְּכֶם, דּוֹרֶשֶׁת בִּשְׁלוֹמְכֶם; וְכֵן גַּם מַרְקוֹס בְּנִי
hakkehillah asher bevavel, shennivcherah ittechem, doreshet bishlomechem; vechen gam markos beni
She that is in Babylon, elect together with you, saluteth you; and so doth Mark my son.

דִּרְשׁוּ אִישׁ בִּשְׁלוֹם רֵעֵהוּ בִּנְשִׁיקַת אַהֲבָה. שָׁלוֹם לְכֻלְּכֶם אֲשֶׁר בַּמָּשִׁיחַ יֵשׁוּעַ
dirshu ish bishlom re'ehu binshikat ahavah. shalom lechullechem asher bammashiach yeshua
Salute one another with a kiss of love. Peace be unto you all that are in Christ.

פֶּטְרוֹס הָרִאשׁוֹנָה

וְגַם שֻׁתָּף לַכָּבוֹד הֶעָתִיד לְהִתְגַּלּוֹת
vegam shuttaf lakkavod he'atid lehitgallot
who am also a partaker of the glory that shall be revealed:

רְעוּ אֶת עֵדֶר אֱלֹהִים הַנִּמְצָא עִמָּכֶם וְהַשְׁגִּיחוּ עָלָיו לֹא מִתּוֹךְ כְּפִיָּה כִּי אִם בְּרָצוֹן,
re'u et eder elohim hannimtza immachem vehashgichu alav lo mittoch kefiyah ki im beratzon
Tend the flock of God which is among you, exercising the oversight, not of constraint, but willingly,

כָּרָצוּי לֵאלֹהִים; לֹא בְחֶמְדַּת בֶּצַע כִּי אִם בְּנֶפֶשׁ חֲפֵצָה
keratzui le'elohim; lo bechemdat betza ki im benefesh chafetzah
according to the will of God; nor yet for filthy lucre, but of a ready mind;

לֹא כְרוֹדָנִים עַל מַה שֶּׁהֻפְקַד בְּיֶדְכֶם, אֶלָּא בִּהְיוֹתְכֶם מוֹפֵת לַצֹּאן
lo kerodanim al mah shehufkad beyedchem, ella bihyotechem mofet latzon
neither as lording it over the charge allotted to you, but making yourselves ensamples to the flock.

וּבְהוֹפָעַת שַׂר הָרוֹעִים תְּקַבְּלוּ עֲטֶרֶת כָּבוֹד אֲשֶׁר לֹא תִבֹּל
uvehofa'at sar haro'im tekabbelu ateret kavod asher lo tibbol
And when the chief Shepherd shall be manifested, ye shall receive the crown of glory that fadeth not away.

כְּמוֹ כֵן, הַצְּעִירִים, הִכָּנְעוּ לִפְנֵי הַזְּקֵנִים. וְאוּלָם חִגְרוּ כֻלְּכֶם נְמִיכוּת רוּחַ אִישׁ כְּלַפֵּי רֵעֵהוּ
kemo chen, hatze'irim, hikkane'u lifnei hazzekenim. ve'ulam chigru kullechem nemichut ruach ish kelappei re'ehu
Likewise, ye younger, be subject unto the elder. Yea, all of you gird yourselves with humility, to serve one another:

כִּי אֱלֹהִים לַלֵּצִים הוּא־יָלִיץ וְלַעֲנָוִים יִתֶּן־חֵן
ki elohim lalletzim hu-yalitz vela'anavim yitten-chen
for God resisteth the proud, but giveth grace to the humble.

הַשְׁפִּילוּ עַצְמְכֶם תַּחַת יַד אֱלֹהִים הַחֲזָקָה, לְמַעַן יְרוֹמֵם אֶתְכֶם בְּעִתּוֹ
hashpilu atzmechem tachat yad elohim hachazakah, lema'an yeromem etchem be'itto
Humble yourselves therefore under the mighty hand of God, that he may exalt you in due time;

הַשְׁלִיכוּ עָלָיו כָּל יְהָבְכֶם, כִּי הוּא דּוֹאֵג לָכֶם
hashlichu alav kol yehavchem, ki hu do'eg lachem
casting all your anxiety upon him, because he careth for you.

הֱיוּ עֵרִים וְעִמְדוּ עַל הַמִּשְׁמָר. אוֹיִבְכֶם הַשָּׂטָן מְשׁוֹטֵט כְּאַרְיֵה שׁוֹאֵג וּמְחַפֵּשׂ לוֹ לִטְרֹף מִישֶׁהוּ
heyu erim ve'imdu al hammishmar. oyivchem hassatan meshotet ke'aryeh sho'eg umechappes lo litrof mishehu
Be sober, be watchful: your adversary the devil, as a roaring lion, walketh about, seeking whom he may devour:

עִמְדוּ נֶגְדּוֹ יַצִּיבִים בָּאֱמוּנָה
imdu negdo yatzivim ba'emunah
whom withstand stedfast in your faith,

בִּידִיעָה שֶׁאוֹתָן הַצָּרוֹת עוֹבְרוֹת עַל אֲחֵיכֶם אֲשֶׁר בָּעוֹלָם
biydi'ah she'otan hatzarot overot al acheichem asher ba'olam
knowing that the same sufferings are accomplished in your brethren who are in the world.

פֶּטְרוֹס הָרִאשׁוֹנָה

אֶלָּא שִׂמְחוּ כְּכָל שֶׁחֵלֶק לָכֶם בְּסִבְלוֹת הַמָּשִׁיחַ
ella simchu kechal shechelek lachem besivlot hammashiach
but insomuch as ye are partakers of Christ's sufferings, rejoice;

לְמַעַן תִּשְׂמְחוּ וְתַעַלְצוּ גַּם בְּהִגָּלוֹת כְּבוֹדוֹ
lema'an tismechu veta'altzu gam behiggalot kvodo
that at the revelation of his glory also ye may rejoice with exceeding joy.

אַשְׁרֵיכֶם אִם יְחָרְפוּ אֶתְכֶם בַּעֲבוּר שֵׁם הַמָּשִׁיחַ
ashreichem im yecharefu etchem ba'avur shem hammashiach,
If ye are reproached for the name of Christ, blessed are ye;

כִּי אָז רוּחַ הַכָּבוֹד, רוּחַ אֱלֹהִים, נָחָה עֲלֵיכֶם
ki az ruach hakkavod, ruach elohim, nachah aleichem
because the Spirit of glory and the Spirit of God resteth upon you.

רַק אַל יִסְבֹּל אִישׁ מִכֶּם כְּרוֹצֵחַ אוֹ כְּגַנָּב אוֹ כְּעוֹשֵׂה רָעָה אוֹ כְּמִתְעָרֵב בְּעִנְיָנֵי אֲחֵרִים
rak al yisbol ish mikkem kerotzeach o kegannav o ke'oseh ra'ah o kemit'arev be'inyenei acherim
For let none of you suffer as a murderer, or a thief, or an evil-doer, or as a meddler in other men's matters:

וְאִם יִסְבֹּל כְּמָשִׁיחִי, אַל יֵבוֹשׁ כִּי אִם יְכַבֵּד אֶת אֱלֹהִים בַּשֵּׁם הַזֶּה
ve'im yisbol kimshichi, al yevosh ki im yechabbed et elohim bashem hazzeh
but if a man suffer as a Christian, let him not be ashamed; but let him glorify God in this name.

שֶׁהֲרֵי עֵת לְהַתְחִיל הַמִּשְׁפָּט מִבֵּית אֱלֹהִים
sheharei et lehatchil hammishpat mibbeit elohim
For the time is come for judgment to begin at the house of God:

וְאִם מֵאִתָּנוּ יַתְחִיל, מַה תִּהְיֶה אַחֲרִית הָאֲנָשִׁים שֶׁאֵינָם נִשְׁמָעִים לִבְשׂוֹרַת אֱלֹהִים
ve'im me'ittanu yatchil, mah tihyeh acharit ha'anashim she'einam nishma'im livsorat elohim
and if it begin first at us, what shall be the end of them that obey not the gospel of God?

אִם צַדִּיק בְּקֹשִׁי נוֹשָׁע, חוֹטֵא וְרָשָׁע מַה יִּהְיֶה עָלָיו
im tzaddik bekoshi nosha', chotei verasha mah yihyeh alav
And if the righteous is scarcely saved, where shall the ungodly and sinner appear?

לָכֵן גַּם הַסּוֹבְלִים כִּרְצוֹן אֱלֹהִים יַפְקִידוּ נָא אֶת נַפְשׁוֹתֵיהֶם בְּיַד הַבּוֹרֵא הַנֶּאֱמָן, בַּעֲשִׂיַּת הַטּוֹב
lachen gam hassovelim kirtzon elohim yafkidu na et nafshoteihem beyad habborei hanne'eman, ba'asiyat hattov
Wherefore let them also that suffer according to the will of God commit their souls in well-doing unto a faithful Creator.

ה

מִן הַזְּקֵנִים אֲשֶׁר בְּקִרְבְּכֶם אֲבַקֵּשׁ, אֲנִי הַזָּקֵן עֲמִיתָם וְעֵד סִבְלוֹת הַמָּשִׁיחַ
min hazzekenim asher bekirbechem avakkesh, ani hazzaken amitam ve'ed sivlot hammashiach
The elders therefore among you I exhort, who am a fellow-elder, and a witness of the sufferings of Christ,

פֶּטְרוֹס הָרִאשׁוֹנָה

כְּדֵי שֶׁיִּשָּׁפְטוּ כְּדֶרֶךְ בְּנֵי אָדָם בַּבָּשָׂר, אַךְ יִחְיוּ כְּדֶרֶךְ אֱלֹהִים בָּרוּחַ
kedei sheyishafetu kederech benei adam babbasar, ach yichyu kederech elohim baruach
that they might be judged indeed according to men in the flesh, but live according to God in the spirit.

הִנֵּה קֵץ הַכֹּל קָרֵב. עַל כֵּן הֱיוּ מְפֻכָּחִים, וֶהֱיוּ עֵרִים לְהִתְפַּלֵּל
hinneh ketz hakkol karev. al ken heyu mefukkachim, veheyu erim lehitpallel
But the end of all things is at hand: be ye therefore of sound mind, and be sober unto prayer:

בְּרֹאשׁ וּבָרִאשׁוֹנָה אֶהֱבוּ אִישׁ אֶת רֵעֵהוּ אַהֲבָה עַזָּה, כִּי עַל רֹב פְּשָׁעִים תְּכַסֶּה אַהֲבָה
berosh uvarishonah ehevu ish et re'ehu ahavah azzah, ki al rov pesha'im techasseh ahavah
above all things being fervent in your love among yourselves; for love covereth a multitude of sins:

הֱיוּ מְאָרְחִים זֶה אֶת זֶה בְּלִי לְהִתְלוֹנֵן
heyu me'arechim zeh et zeh beli lehitlonen
using hospitality one to another without murmuring:

אִישׁ אִישׁ כְּפִי הַמַּתָּנָה אֲשֶׁר קִבֵּל יְשָׁרֵת בָּהּ בְּקִרְבְּכֶם
ish ish kefi hammattanah asher kibbel yesharet bah bekirbechem
according as each hath received a gift, ministering it among yourselves,

כְּסוֹכְנִים טוֹבִים עַל חַסְדּוֹ רַב-הַפָּנִים שֶׁל אֱלֹהִים
kesochenim tovim al chasdo rav-happanim shel elohim
as good stewards of the manifold grace of God;

אִישׁ כִּי יְדַבֵּר, אִמְרֵי אֱלֹהִים יְדַבֵּר
ish ki yedabber, imrei elohim yedabber
if any man speaketh, speaking as it were oracles of God;

אִישׁ כִּי יְשָׁרֵת, יַעֲשֶׂה זֹאת מִתּוֹךְ הַכֹּחַ שֶׁנָּתַן לוֹ אֱלֹהִים
ish ki yesharet, ya'aseh zot mittoch hakoach shennatan lo elohim
if any man ministereth, ministering as of the strength which God supplieth:

וְזֹאת לְמַעַן יְכֻבַּד הָאֱלֹהִים בַּכֹּל דֶּרֶךְ יֵשׁוּעַ הַמָּשִׁיחַ
vezot lema'an yechubbad ha'elohim bakkol derech yeshua hammashiach
that in all things God may be glorified through Jesus Christ,

אֲשֶׁר לוֹ הַכָּבוֹד וְהַגְּבוּרָה לְעוֹלְמֵי עוֹלָמִים. אָמֵן
asher lo hakkavod vehaggevurah le'olemei olamim. amen
whose is the glory and the dominion for ever and ever. Amen.

אֲהוּבַי, בְּבוֹא עֲלֵיכֶם צְרִיפַת אֵשׁ
ahuvai, bevo aleichem tzerifat esh
Beloved, think it not strange concerning the fiery trial among you,

כְּדֵי לִבְחֹן אֶתְכֶם, אַל תִּתְמְהוּ כְּאִלּוּ מִקְרֶה מוּזָר קָרָה לָכֶם
kedei livchon etchem, al titmehu ke'illu mikreh muzar karah lachem
which cometh upon you to prove you, as though a strange thing happened unto you:

פֶּטְרוֹס הָרִאשׁוֹנָה

אֶלָּא הִתְחַיְּבוּת שֶׁל מַצְפּוּן טָהוֹר כְּלַפֵּי אֱלֹהִים - בִּתְחִיַּת יֵשׁוּעַ הַמָּשִׁיחַ
ella hitchayevut shel matzpun tahor klappei elohim - bitchiyat yeshua hammashiach
but the interrogation of a good conscience toward God, through the resurrection of Jesus Christ;

אֲשֶׁר עָלָה הַשָּׁמַיְמָה וְהוּא לִימִין אֱלֹהִים
asher alah hashamaymah vehu liymin elohim
who is on the right hand of God, having gone into heaven;

וּלְפָנָיו הֻכְנְעוּ מַלְאָכִים וְרָשֻׁיּוֹת וּגְבוּרוֹת
ulefanav huchne'u mal'achim verashyot ugevurot
angels and authorities and powers being made subject unto him.

ד

כֵּיוָן שֶׁהַמָּשִׁיחַ סָבַל בַּעֲדֵנוּ בְּגוּפוֹ, גַּם אַתֶּם הִתְאַזְּרוּ בְּאוֹתוֹ הֲלָךְ־הָרוּחַ
keivan shehammashiach saval ba'adenu begufo, gam attem hit'azzeru be'oto halach-haruach
Forasmuch then as Christ suffered in the flesh, arm ye yourselves also with the same mind;

שֶׁכֵּן הַסּוֹבֵל בְּגוּפוֹ חָדַל לַחֲטֹא
shekken hassovel begufo chadel lachato
for he that hath suffered in the flesh hath ceased from sin;

לְמַעַן לֹא יִחְיֶה עוֹד לְפִי תַּאֲווֹת בְּנֵי אָדָם בַּזְּמַן שֶׁנּוֹתַר לוֹ לִחְיוֹת בְּגוּפוֹ, אֶלָּא לְפִי רְצוֹן אֱלֹהִים
lema'an lo yichyeh od lefi ta'avot benei adam bazzman shennotar lo lichyot begufo, ella lefi retzon elohim
that ye no longer should live the rest of your time in the flesh to the lusts of men, but to the will of God.

הֵן דַּי הָיָה הַזְּמַן שֶׁעָבַר עֲלֵיכֶם בַּעֲשִׂיַּת חֵפֶץ הַגּוֹיִם, כַּאֲשֶׁר הִתְהַלַּכְתֶּם בְּדַרְכֵי זִמָּה
hen dai hayah hazzman she'avar aleichem ba'asiyat chefetz haggoyim, ka'asher hit'hallachtem bedarchei zimmah
For the time past may suffice to have wrought the desire of the Gentiles, and to have walked in lasciviousness,

וְתַאֲווֹת, שִׁכְרוּת וְהוֹלְלוּת, נִשְׁפֵּי שְׁתִיָּה וַעֲבוֹדַת אֱלִילִים אֲסוּרָה
veta'avot, shichrut veholelut, nishfei shetiyah va'avodat elilim asurah
lusts, winebibbings, revellings, carousings, and abominable idolatries:

וְכֵיוָן שֶׁאֵינְכֶם רָצִים עִמָּהֶם לְשֶׁטֶף זִמָּתָם, תְּמֵהִים הֵם עַל כָּךְ וּמְגַדְּפִים
vecheivan she'einechem ratzim immahem leshetef zimmatam, temehim hem al kach umegaddfim
wherein they think it strange that ye run not with them into the same excess of riot, speaking evil of you:

הַלָּלוּ יִתְּנוּ דִּין וְחֶשְׁבּוֹן לִפְנֵי מִי שֶׁעָתִיד לִשְׁפֹּט אֶת הַחַיִּים וְאֶת הַמֵּתִים
hallalu yittenu din vecheshbon lifnei mi she'atid lishpot et hachayim ve'et hammetim
who shall give account to him that is ready to judge the living and the dead.

לָכֵן הִתְבַּשְּׂרוּ גַּם הַמֵּתִים
lachen hitbassru gam hammetim
For unto this end was the gospel preached even to the dead,

פֶּטְרוֹס הָרִאשׁוֹנָה

וְתָמִיד הֱיוּ מוּכָנִים לְהָשִׁיב בַּעֲנָוָה וְיִרְאָה לְכָל מִישֶׁמְּבַקֵּשׁ מִכֶּם דִּין וְחֶשְׁבּוֹן בִּדְבַר הַתִּקְוָה שֶׁבְּלִבְּכֶם
vetamid heyu muchanim lehashiv ba'anavah veyir'ah lechol mishemmevakkesh mikkem din vecheshbon bidvar hattikvah shebbelibbechem
being ready always to give answer to every man that asketh you a reason concerning the hope that is in you, yet with meekness and fear:

יְהֵא מַצְפּוּנְכֶם טָהוֹר
yehei matzpunechem tahor
having a good conscience;

כְּדֵי שֶׁיֵּבוֹשׁוּ הַמַּשְׁמִיצִים מֵאוֹתָם דְּבָרִים שֶׁבִּגְלָלָם הֵם מְגַנִּים אֶת הִתְנַהֲגוּתְכֶם הַטּוֹבָה
kedei sheyevoshu hammashmitzim me'otam devarim shebbiglalam hem megannim et hitnahagutechem hattovah
that, wherein ye are spoken against, they may be put to shame who revile your good manner of life

בַּמָּשִׁיחַ
bammashiach
in Christ.

מוּטָב שֶׁתִּסְבְּלוּ, אִם זֶהוּ רְצוֹן אֱלֹהִים, בַּעֲשׂוֹתְכֶם אֶת הַטּוֹב מִשֶּׁתִּסְבְּלוּ בַּעֲשׂוֹתְכֶם רַע
mutav shettisbelu, im zehu retzon elohim, ba'asotechem et hattov mishettisbelu ba'asotechem ra
For it is better, if the will of God should so will, that ye suffer for well-doing than for evil-doing.

הֵן גַּם הַמָּשִׁיחַ מֵת לְכַפָּרַת חֲטָאִים, אַחַת וּלְתָמִיד, הַצַּדִּיק בְּעַד הָרְשָׁעִים
hen gam hammashiach met lechapparat chata'im, achat uletamid, hatzaddik be'ad haresha'im
Because Christ also suffered for sins once, the righteous for the unrighteous,

כְּדֵי לְקָרֵב אוֹתָנוּ אֶל הָאֱלֹהִים. הוּא הוּמַת בִּבְשָׂרוֹ, אַךְ הָחֳיָה בָּרוּחַ
kedei lekarev otanu el ha'elohim. hu humat bivsaro, ach hochoyah baruach
that he might bring us to God; being put to death in the flesh, but made alive in the spirit;

וּבָהּ גַּם הָלַךְ וּבִשֵּׂר לָרוּחוֹת הַכְּלוּאוֹת בַּמַּאֲסָר
uvah gam halach uvisser laruchot hakkelu'ot bamma'asar
in which also he went and preached unto the spirits in prison,

לְאֵלֶּה שֶׁלֹּא צִיְּתוּ כַּאֲשֶׁר חִכָּה אֱלֹהִים בְּאֹרֶךְ אַפּוֹ בִּימֵי נֹחַ
le'elleh shello tziyetu ka'asher chikkah elohim be'orech appo biymei noach
that aforetime were disobedient, when the longsuffering of God waited in the days of Noah,

בְּאוֹתָם יָמִים נִבְנְתָה הַתֵּבָה אֲשֶׁר מְעַטִּים בְּתוֹכָהּ - שְׁמוֹנָה נְפָשׁוֹת - נוֹשְׁעוּ בַּמַּיִם
be'otam yamim nivnetah hattevah asher me'attim betochah - shemoneh nefashot - nosh'u bammayim
while the ark was a preparing, wherein few, that is, eight souls, were saved through water:

וְזֶה מְסַמֵּל אֶת הַטְּבִילָה הַמּוֹשִׁיעָה כָּעֵת גַּם אֶתְכֶם - אֵין הִיא הֲסָרַת זֻהֲמַת הַגּוּף,
vezeh mesammel et hattevilah hammoshi'ah ka'et gam etchem - ein hi hasarat zuhamat hagguf
which also after a true likeness doth now save you, even baptism, not the putting away of the filth of the flesh,

פֶּטְרוֹס הָרִאשׁוֹנָה

כְּשֶׁתָּפוֹת בְּנַחֲלַת חֶסֶד הַחַיִּים, לְמַעַן לֹא תֵעָכַבְנָה תְּפִלּוֹתֵיכֶם
keshuttafot benachalat chesed hachayim, lema'an lo te'ukkavnah tefilloteichem
as being also joint-heirs of the grace of life; to the end that your prayers be not hindered.

סוֹף דָּבָר, הֱיוּ כֻלְּכֶם לֵב אֶחָד, שֻׁתָּפִים לְצַעַר הַזּוּלַת, אוֹהֲבֵי הָאַחִים, רַחֲמָנִים וַעֲנָוִים
sof davar, heyu kullechem lev echad, shuttafim letza'ar hazzulat, ohavei ha'achim, rachamanim va'anavim
Finally, be ye all likeminded, compassionate, loving as brethren, tenderhearted, humbleminded:

אַל תְּשַׁלְּמוּ רָעָה תַּחַת רָעָה וְלֹא חֵרוּף תַּחַת חֵרוּף; אַדְּרַבָּא - תְּבָרְכוּ
al teshallemu ra'ah tachatra'ah velo cheruf tachat cheruf; addrabba - tevarechu
not rendering evil for evil, or reviling for reviling; but contrariwise blessing;

שֶׁהֲרֵי לְכָךְ נִקְרֵאתֶם, לְמַעַן תִּירְשׁוּ אֶת הַבְּרָכָה
shehareilechach nikretem, lema'an tireshu et habberachah
for hereunto were ye called, that ye should inherit a blessing.

כִּי הָאִישׁ הֶחָפֵץ חַיִּים אֹהֵב יָמִים לִרְאוֹת טוֹב,
kiha'ish hechafetz chayim ohev yamim lir'ot tov
For, He that would love life, And see good days,

יִנְצֹר לְשׁוֹנוֹ מֵרָע, וּשְׂפָתָיו מִדַּבֵּר מִרְמָה
yintzor leshono mera, usfatav middabber mirmah
Let him refrain his tongue from evil, And his lips that they speak no guile:

סוּר מֵרָע וַעֲשֵׂה־טוֹב, בַּקֵּשׁ שָׁלוֹם וְרָדְפֵהוּ
yasur mera veya'aseh-tov, yevakkesh shalom veyirdefehu
And let him turn away from evil, and do good; Let him seek peace, and pursue it.

כִּי עֵינֵי יהוה אֶל־צַדִּיקִים, וְאָזְנָיו אֶל־שַׁוְעָתָם
ki einei hashem el-tzaddikim, ve'azenav el-shav'atam
For the eyes of the Lord are upon the righteous, And his ears unto their supplication:

וּפְנֵי יהוה בְּעֹשֵׂי רָע
ufnei hashem be'osei ra
But the face of the Lord is upon them that do evil.

וּמִי יָרֵעַ לָכֶם אִם תִּהְיוּ קַנָּאִים לַטּוֹב
umi yarea lachem im tihyu kanna'im lattov
And who is he that will harm you, if ye be zealous of that which is good?

אַךְ גַּם אִם תִּסְבְּלוּ לְמַעַן הַצְּדָקָה - אַשְׁרֵיכֶם. אַל תִּפְחֲדוּ מֵאֵימָתָם וְאַל תִּבָּהֵלוּ
ach gam imtisbelu lema'an hatzedakah - ashreichem. al tifchadu me'eimatamv'al tibbahalu
But even if ye should suffer for righteousness' sake, blessed are ye: and fear not their fear, neither be troubled;

אֶת הָאָדוֹן הַמָּשִׁיחַ הַקְדִּישׁוּ בִּלְבַבְכֶם
et ha'adon hammashiach hakdishu bilvavchem
but sanctify in your hearts Christ as Lord:

פֶּטְרוֹס הָרִאשׁוֹנָה

וְכָךְ, אִם יֵשׁ שֶׁאֵינָם מְצַיְּתִים לַדָּבָר, יִקָּנֶה לִבָּם לֹא עַל־יְדֵי דִּבּוּר אֶלָּא עַל־יְדֵי הִתְנַהֲגוּת הַנָּשִׁים
vechach, im yesh she'einam metzayetim laddavar, yikkaneh libbam lo al-yedei dibbur ella al-yedei hitnahagut hannashim
that, even if any obey not the word, they may without the word be gained by the behavior of their wives;

בִּרְאוֹתָם אֶת הִתְנַהֲגוּתְכֶן הַטְּהוֹרָה הַמְלֻוָּה בְּיִרְאָה
bir'otam et hitnahagutechen hattehorah hamluvvah beyir'ah
beholding your chaste behavior coupled with fear.

וּפְאֵרְכֶן אַל יְהֵא פְּאֵר חִיצוֹנִי שֶׁל מַחְלְפוֹת שֵׂעָר
ufe'erechen al yehei pe'er chitzoni shel machlefot se'ar
Whose adorning let it not be the outward adorning of braiding the hair,

וַעֲדִי זָהָב וּבְגָדִים
va'adi zahav uvegadim
and of wearing jewels of gold, or of putting on apparel;

אֶלָּא הָאָדָם אֲשֶׁר בְּסֵתֶר הַלֵּב, הַפְּאֵר הַבִּלְתִּי נִשְׁחָת שֶׁל רוּחַ עֲנָוָה וּשְׁקֵטָה
ella ha'adam asher beseter hallev, happe'er habbilti nishchat shel ruach anavah usheketah
but let it be the hidden man of the heart, in the incorruptible apparel of a meek and quiet spirit,

אֲשֶׁר יְקָרָה הִיא מְאֹד בְּעֵינֵי אֱלֹהִים
asher yekarah hi me'od be'einei elohim
which is in the sight of God of great price.

כָּךְ הִתְקַשְּׁטוּ בֶּעָבָר גַּם הַנָּשִׁים הַקְּדוֹשׁוֹת
kach hitkashetu be'avar gam hannashim hakkedoshot
For after this manner aforetime the holy women also,

וְהַמְיַחֲלוֹת לֵאלֹהִים, בְּהִכָּנְעָן לְבַעֲלֵיהֶן
vehamyachalot lelohim, behikkane'an leva'aleihen
who hoped in God, adorned themselves, being in subjection to their own husbands:

כְּשָׂרָה אֲשֶׁר שָׁמְעָה בְּקוֹל אַבְרָהָם וְקָרְאָה לוֹ אָדוֹן
kesarah asher shame'ah bekol avraham vekare'ah lo adon
as Sarah obeyed Abraham, calling him lord:

וְאַתֶּן נִהְיֵיתֶן בָּנוֹת לָהּ, אִם אַתֶּן עֹשׂוֹת אֶת הַטּוֹב וְאֵינְכֶן פּוֹחֲדוֹת פַּחַד
ve'atten nihyeiten banot lah, im atten osot et hattov ve'einechen pochadot pachad
whose children ye now are, if ye do well, and are not put in fear by any terror.

וְכֵן אַתֶּם, הַבְּעָלִים, חֲיוּ יַחַד עִמָּהֶן
vechen attem, habbe'alim, chayu yachad immahen
Ye husbands, in like manner, dwell with your wives

בִּידִיעָה שֶׁהָאִשָּׁה הִיא כְּלִי חַלָּשׁ יוֹתֵר, וּתְנוּ לָהֶן כָּבוֹד
biydi'ah sheha'ishah hi keli challash yoter, utnu lahen kavod
according to knowledge, giving honor unto the woman, as unto the weaker vessel,

פֶּטְרוֹס הָרִאשׁוֹנָה

שֶׁהֲרֵי מַה תְּהִלָּה בְּכָךְ אִם תַּעַמְדוּ בְּסֵבֶל שֶׁל מַכּוֹת עַל חֲטָאֵיכֶם

sheharei mah tehillah bechach im ta'amdu besevel shel makkot al chata'eichem
For what glory is it, if, when ye sin, and are buffeted for it, ye shall take it patiently?

אֲבָל אִם בַּעֲשׂוֹתְכֶם אֶת הַטּוֹב תִּסְבְּלוּ וְתַעַמְדוּ בַּסֵּבֶל, בִּרְכַּת חֶסֶד הִיא מִלִּפְנֵי אֱלֹהִים

aval im ba'asotechem et hattov tisbelu veta'amdu bassevel, birkat chesed hi millifnei elohim
but if, when ye do well, and suffer for it, ye shall take it patiently, this is acceptable with God.

אָכֵן לְזֹאת נִקְרֵאתֶם, כִּי גַם הַמָּשִׁיחַ סָבַל בַּעַדְכֶם

achen lazot nikretem, ki gam hammashiach saval ba'adchem
For hereunto were ye called: because Christ also suffered for you,

וְהִשְׁאִיר לָכֶם מוֹפֵת כְּדֵי שֶׁתֵּלְכוּ בְּעִקְּבוֹתָיו

vehish'ir lachem mofet kedei shettelechu be'ikkevotav
leaving you an example, that ye should follow his steps:

הוּא אֲשֶׁר חֵטְא לֹא עָשָׂה וְלֹא נִמְצְאָה מִרְמָה בְּפִיו

hu asher chet lo asah velo nimtze'ah mirmah befiv
who did no sin, neither was guile found in his mouth:

אֲשֶׁר חֵרְפוּהוּ וְלֹא הֵשִׁיב חֵרוּף, סָבַל וְלֹא אִיֵּם

asher cherefuhu velo heshiv cheruf, saval velo iyem
who, when he was reviled, reviled not again; when he suffered, threatened not;

כִּי אִם מָסַר דִּינוֹ לְשׁוֹפֵט הַצֶּדֶק

ki im masar dino leshofet hatzedek
but committed himself to him that judgeth righteously:

הוּא אֲשֶׁר אֶת חֲטָאֵינוּ נָשָׂא בְּגוּפוֹ עַל הָעֵץ

hu asher et chata'einu nasa begufo al ha'etz
who his own self bare our sins in his body upon the tree,

כְּדֵי שֶׁנָּמוּת לְגַבֵּי הַחֵטְא וְנִחְיֶה לַצְּדָקָה; אֲשֶׁר בְּחַבּוּרָתוֹ נִרְפָּא לָכֶם

kedei shennamut legabbei hachet venichyeh latzedakah; asher bechabburato nirpa lachem
that we, having died unto sins, might live unto righteousness; by whose stripes ye were healed.

כִּי הֱיִיתֶם כְּצֹאן אוֹבְדוֹת, אַךְ עַתָּה שַׁבְתֶּם אֶל הָרוֹעֶה הַשּׁוֹמֵר אֶת נַפְשׁוֹתֵיכֶם

ki heyitem ketzon ovedot, ach attah shavtem el haro'eh hashomer et nafshoteichem
For ye were going astray like sheep; but are now returned unto the Shepherd and Bishop of your souls.

ג

כֵּן גַּם אַתֶּן, הַנָּשִׁים, הִכָּנַעְנָה לְבַעֲלֵיכֶן

ken gam atten, hannashim, hikkana'nah leva'aleichen
In like manner, ye wives, be in subjection to your own husbands;

פֶּטְרוֹס הָרִאשׁוֹנָה

הַנִּלְחָמוֹת נֶגֶד הַנֶּפֶשׁ
hannilchamot neged hannefesh
which war against the soul;

הֵיטִיבוּ אֶת דַּרְכֵיכֶם בַּגּוֹיִם
heitivu et darcheichem baggoyim
having your behavior seemly among the Gentiles;

כְּדֵי שֶׁיִּתְבּוֹנְנוּ בְּמַעֲשֵׂיכֶם הַטּוֹבִים וִיהַלְלוּ אֶת אֱלֹהִים בְּיוֹם פְּקֻדָּה עַל אוֹתָם הַדְּבָרִים שֶׁבִּגְלָלָם הִשְׁמִיצוּ אֶתְכֶם כְּעוֹשֵׂי רָעָה
kedei sheyitbonenu bema'aseichem hattovim vihallelu et elohim beyom pekuddah al otam haddevarim shebbiglalam hishmitzu etchem ke'osei ra'ah
that, wherein they speak against you as evil-doers, they may by your good works, which they behold, glorify God in the day of visitation.

הִכָּנְעוּ לְכָל מוֹסָד אֱנוֹשִׁי לְמַעַן הָאָדוֹן: אִם לַמֶּלֶךְ, בִּהְיוֹתוֹ הָרֹאשׁ
hikkane'u lechol mosad enoshi lema'an ha'adon. im lammelech, bihyoto harosh
Be subject to every ordinance of man for the Lord's sake: whether to the king, as supreme;

אִם לַמּוֹשְׁלִים, בִּהְיוֹתָם שְׁלוּחִים מִטַּעֲמוֹ לִנְקָמָה בְּעוֹשֵׂי הָרַע, אַךְ לְמַתָּן שֶׁבַח לְעוֹשֵׂי הַטּוֹב
im lammoshelim, bihyotam sheluchim mitta'mo linkamah be'osei hara', ach lemattan shevach le'osei hattov
or unto governors, as sent by him for vengeance on evil-doers and for praise to them that do well.

הֵן זֶהוּ רְצוֹן אֱלֹהִים, שֶׁתַּעֲשׂוּ הַטּוֹב וְכָךְ תָּשִׂימוּ מַחְסוֹם לְאִוֶּלֶת הָאֲנָשִׁים אֲשֶׁר אֵין בָּהֶם דַּעַת
hen zehu retzon elohim, shetta'asu hattov vechach tasimu machsom le'ivvelet ha'anashim asher ein bahem da'at
For so is the will of God, that by well-doing ye should put to silence the ignorance of foolish men:

הִתְנַהֲגוּ כַּאֲנָשִׁים חָפְשִׁיִּים, לֹא כַּאֲנָשִׁים הַמַּחֲזִיקִים בַּחֹפֶשׁ כִּכְסוּת לָרֶשַׁע, אֶלָּא כְּעַבְדֵי אֱלֹהִים
hitnahagu ka'anashim chofshiyim, lo ka'anashim hammachazikim bachofesh kichsut laresha, ella ke'avdei elohim
as free, and not using your freedom for a cloak of wickedness, but as bondservants of God.

נַהֲגוּ כָּבוֹד בְּכָל אָדָם; אֶהֱבוּ אֶת הָאַחִים; יְראוּ אֶת אֱלֹהִים; כַּבְּדוּ אֶת הַמֶּלֶךְ
nahagu kavod bechol adam; ehevu et ha'achim; yir'u et elohim; kabbedu et hammelech
Honor all men. Love the brotherhood. Fear God. Honor the king.

הָעֲבָדִים, הִכָּנְעוּ לִפְנֵי אֲדוֹנֵיכֶם בְּכָל יִרְאָה, לֹא רַק לִפְנֵי הַטּוֹבִים וְהַנּוֹחִים לַבְּרִיּוֹת
ha'avadim, hikkane'u lifnei adoneichem bechol yir'ah, lo rak lifnei hattovim vehannochim labberiyot
Servants, be in subjection to your masters with all fear; not only to the good and gentle,

אֶלָּא גַּם לִפְנֵי הָעִקְּשִׁים
ella gam lifnei ha'ikshim
but also to the froward.

הֵן בִּרְכַּת חֶסֶד בְּכָךְ אִם בִּגְלַל הַכָּרָתוֹ בֵּאלֹהִים יִשָּׂא אָדָם מַכְאוֹב וְיִסְבֹּל שֶׁלֹּא בְּצֶדֶק
hen birkat chesed bechach im biglal hakkarato be'elohim yissa adam mach'ov veyisbol shello betzedek
For this is acceptable, if for conscience toward God a man endureth griefs, suffering wrongfully.

פֶּטְרוֹס הָרִאשׁוֹנָה

לִכְהֻנַּת קֹדֶשׁ, כְּדֵי לְהַעֲלוֹת זִבְחֵי רוּחַ רְצוּיִים לֵאלֹהִים בִּזְכוּת יֵשׁוּעַ הַמָּשִׁיחַ
lichhunnat kodesh, kedei leha'alot zivchei ruach retzuyim le'elohim bizchut yeshua hammashiach
to be a holy priesthood, to offer up spiritual sacrifices, acceptable to God through Jesus Christ.

מִשּׁוּם כָּךְ אוֹמֵר הַכָּתוּב: הִנְנִי יִסַּד בְּצִיּוֹן אֶבֶן פִּנָּה נִבְחָרָה וִיקָרָה,
mishum kach omer hakkatuv: hineni yissad betziyon even pinnah nivcharah viykarah
Because it is contained in scripture, Behold, I lay in Zion a chief corner stone, elect, precious:

וְהַמַּאֲמִין בָּהּ לֹא יֵבוֹשׁ
vehamma'amin bah lo yevosh
And he that believeth on him shall not be put to shame.

עַל כֵּן לָכֶם הַמַּאֲמִינִים הִיא אֶבֶן הַיְקָר
al ken lachem hamma'aminim hi even hayekar
For you therefore that believe is the preciousness:

אֲבָל לַסּוֹרְרִים - אֶבֶן מָאֲסוּ הַבּוֹנִים הָיְתָה לְרֹאשׁ פִּנָּה
aval lassorerim - even ma'asu habbonim hayetah lerosh pinnah
but for such as disbelieve, The stone which the builders rejected, The same was made the head of the corner;

וְגַם אֶבֶן נֶגֶף וְצוּר מִכְשׁוֹל. וְאָמְנָם הֵם נִכְשָׁלִים בַּדָּבָר
vegam even negef vetzur michshol. ve'omnam hem nichshalim baddavar
and, A stone of stumbling, and a rock of offence; for they stumble at the word,

בִּגְלַל סַרְבָנוּתָם, וּלְכָךְ גַּם נוֹעֲדוּ
biglal sarvanutam, ulechach gam no'adu
being disobedient: whereunto also they were appointed.

אֲבָל אַתֶּם עַם נִבְחָר, מַמְלֶכֶת כֹּהֲנִים וְגוֹי קָדוֹשׁ, עַם סְגֻלָּה,
aval attem am nivchar, mamlechet kohanim vegoy kadosh, am segullah
But ye are an elect race, a royal priesthood, a holy nation, a people for God's own possession,

לְמַעַן תְּסַפְּרוּ תְּהִלּוֹתָיו שֶׁל הַקּוֹרֵא אֶתְכֶם מֵחֹשֶׁךְ אֶל אוֹרוֹ הַנִּפְלָא
lema'an tesapperu tehillotav shel hakkorei etchem mechoshech el oro hannifla
that ye may show forth the excellencies of him who called you out of darkness into his marvellous light:

אַתֶּם אֲשֶׁר לְפָנִים לֹא עַם הֱיִיתֶם, אַךְ כָּעֵת עַם אֱלֹהִים אַתֶּם
attem asher lefanim lo am heyitem, ach ka'et am elohim attem
who in time past were no people, but now are the people of God:

אֲשֶׁר לְפָנִים לֹא רֻחָמוּ, אַךְ כָּעֵת מְרֻחָמִים
asher lefanim lo ruchamu, ach ka'et meruchamim
who had not obtained mercy, but now have obtained mercy.

אֲהוּבַי, שֶׁבִּבְחִינַת זָרִים וְגוֹלִים אַתֶּם, מַפְצִיר אֲנִי בָּכֶם לְהִנָּזֵר מִתַּאֲווֹת בְּשָׂרִים
ahuvai, shebbivchinat zarim vegolim attem, maftzir ani bachem lehinnazer mitta'avot besarim
Beloved, I beseech you as sojourners and pilgrims, to abstain from fleshly lusts,

פֶּטְרוֹס הָרִאשׁוֹנָה

וְכֵיוָן שֶׁטִּהַרְתֶּם אֶת נַפְשׁוֹתֵיכֶם בְּצַיֶּתְכֶם לָאֱמֶת
vecheivan shettihartem et nafshoteichem betzayetchem la'emet
Seeing ye have purified your souls in your obedience to the truth

וְהִגַּעְתֶּם אֱלֵי אַחֲוָה שֶׁאֵין בָּהּ חֲנֻפָּה, אֶהֱבוּ זֶה אֶת זֶה בְּכָל לְבַבְכֶם וּמְאֹדְכֶם
vehigga'tem elei achavah she'ein bah chanuppah, ehevu zeh et zeh bechol levavchem ume'odechem
unto unfeigned love of the brethren, love one another from the heart fervently:

שֶׁהֲרֵי נוֹלַדְתֶּם מֵחָדָשׁ לֹא מִזֶּרַע נִשְׁחָת כִּי אִם מִבִּלְתִּי נִשְׁחָת
sheharei noladtem mechadash lo mizzera nishchat ki im mibbilti nishchat,
having been begotten again, not of corruptible seed, but of incorruptible,

בִּדְבַר אֱלֹהִים הַחַי וְקַיָּם
bidvar elohim hachai vekayam
through the word of God, which liveth and abideth.

הֵן כָּל־הַבָּשָׂר חָצִיר וְכָל־חַסְדּוֹ כְּצִיץ הַשָּׂדֶה. יָבֵשׁ חָצִיר, נָבֵל צִיץ
hen kol-habbasar chatzir vechol-chasdo ketzitz hassadeh. yavesh chatzir, navel tzitz
For, All flesh is as grass, And all the glory thereof as the flower of grass. The grass withereth, and the flower falleth:

וּדְבַר־אֱלֹהֵינוּ יָקוּם לְעוֹלָם. וְהוּא הַדָּבָר אֲשֶׁר בִּשְׂרוּ לָכֶם
udevar-'eloheinu yakum le'olam. vehu haddavar asher bissru lachem
But the word of the Lord abideth for ever. And this is the word of good tidings which was preached unto you.

ב

וְעַתָּה הָסִירוּ מֵעֲלֵיכֶם כָּל רֶשַׁע וְכָל מִרְמָה, אֶת הַצְּבִיעוּת וְהַקִּנְאָה וְכָל לְשׁוֹן הָרָע
ve'attah hasiru me'aleichem kol resha vechol mirmah, et hatzevi'ut vehakkin'ah vechol lashon hara
Putting away therefore all wickedness, and all guile, and hypocrisies, and envies, and all evil speakings,

וּכְעוֹלָלִים אֲשֶׁר זֶה מִקָּרוֹב נוֹלְדוּ הִתְאַוּוּ לֶחָלָב הַזַּךְ שֶׁל הַדָּבָר, לְמַעַן תִּגְדְּלוּ בְּאֶמְצָעוּתוֹ לִישׁוּעָה
uche'olalim asher zeh mikkarov noledu hit'avvu lechalav hazzach shel haddavar, lema'an tigdelu be'emtza'uto liyshu'ah
as newborn babes, long for the spiritual milk which is without guile, that ye may grow thereby unto salvation;

אִם אָמְנָם טְעַמְתֶּם כִּי טוֹב הָאָדוֹן
im omnam te'amtem ki tov ha'adon
if ye have tasted that the Lord is gracious:

אֲשֶׁר אַתֶּם נִגָּשִׁים אֵלָיו - אֶבֶן חַיָּה שֶׁמְּאָסוּהָ בְּנֵי אָדָם, אַךְ נִבְחָרָה וִיקָרָה לֵאלֹהִים
asher attem niggashim elav - even chayah shemme'asuha benei adam, ach nivcharah vikarah le'elohim
unto whom coming, a living stone, rejected indeed of men, but with God elect, precious,

וְגַם אַתֶּם, כַּאֲבָנִים חַיּוֹת, נִבְנִים לְבַיִת רוּחָנִי
vegam attem, ka'avanim chayot, nivnim levayit ruchani
ye also, as living stones, are built up a spiritual house,

פֶּטְרוֹס הָרִאשׁוֹנָה

כְּבָנִים מְצַיְּתִים, אַל תִּתְנַהֲגוּ לְפִי הַתַּאֲווֹת שֶׁהָיוּ לָכֶם בֶּעָבַר כְּשֶׁהֱיִיתֶם חַסְרֵי דַעַת
kevanim metzayetim, al titnahagu lefi hatta'avot shehayu lachem be'avar ksheheyitem chasrei da'at
as children of obedience, not fashioning yourselves according to your former lusts in the time of your ignorance:

אֶלָּא הֱיוּ גַּם אַתֶּם קְדוֹשִׁים בְּכָל דַּרְכֵיכֶם כְּמוֹ שֶׁקָּדוֹשׁ הוּא אֲשֶׁר קָרָא אֶתְכֶם
ella heyu gam attem kedoshim bechol darcheichem kemo shekkadosh hu asher kara etchem
but like as he who called you is holy, be ye yourselves also holy in all manner of living;

שֶׁהֲרֵי כָּתוּב, קְדֹשִׁים תִּהְיוּ כִּי קָדוֹשׁ אָנִי
sheharei katuv, kedoshim tihyu ki kadosh ani
because it is written, Ye shall be holy; for I am holy.

וְאִם קוֹרְאִים אַתֶּם אֶל הָאָב,
ve'im kore'im attem el ha'av
And if ye call on him as Father,

הַשּׁוֹפֵט בְּלִי מַשּׂוֹא פָּנִים לְפִי מַעֲשֵׂי אִישׁ וָאִישׁ, אֲזַי הִתְהַלְּכוּ בְּיִרְאָה בִּימֵי מְגוּרֵיכֶם עֲלֵי אֲדָמוֹת
hashofet beli masso panim lefi ma'asei ish va'ish, azai hit'hallchu beyir'ah bimei megureichem alei adamot
who without respect of persons judgeth according to each man's work, pass the time of your sojourning in fear:

שֶׁהֲרֵי יוֹדְעִים אַתֶּם כִּי לֹא בְּדָבָר נִשְׁחָת, לֹא בְכֶסֶף וְלֹא בְזָהָב
sheharei yode'im attem ki lo bedavar nishchat, lo bechesef velo bezahav
knowing that ye were redeemed, not with corruptible things, with silver or gold,

נִפְדֵּיתֶם מִדַּרְכְּכֶם הַתְּפֵלָה שֶׁנְּחַלְתֶּם מֵאֲבוֹתֵיכֶם
nifdeitem middarkechem hattefelah shennechaltem me'avoteichem
from your vain manner of life handed down from your fathers;

כִּי אִם בְּדָם יָקָר שֶׁל שֶׂה תָּמִים שֶׁאֵין בּוֹ מוּם, בְּדָמוֹ שֶׁל הַמָּשִׁיחַ
ki im bedam yakar shel seh tamim she'ein bo mum, bedamo shel hammashiach
but with precious blood, as of a lamb without blemish and without spot, even the blood of Christ:

אֲשֶׁר נוֹדַע מִקֶּדֶם, לִפְנֵי הִוָּסֵד תֵּבֵל
asher noda mikkedem, lifnei hivvased tevel
who was foreknown indeed before the foundation of the world,

וְנִגְלָה בְּאַחֲרִית הַיָּמִים לְמַעַנְכֶם
veniglah be'acharit hayamim lema'anchem
but was manifested at the end of the times for your sake,

אַתֶּם אֲשֶׁר הוֹדוֹת לוֹ מַאֲמִינִים בֵּאלֹהִים שֶׁהֱקִימוֹ מִן הַמֵּתִים
attem asher hodot lo ma'aminim be'elohim shehekimo min hammetim
who through him are believers in God, that raised him from the dead,

וְנָתַן לוֹ כָּבוֹד לְמַעַן תִּהְיֶה אֱמוּנַתְכֶם וְתִקְוַתְכֶם בֵּאלֹהִים
venatan lo kavod lema'an tihyeh emunatchem vetikvatchem be'elohim
and gave him glory; so that your faith and hope might be in God.

פֶּטְרוֹס הָרִאשׁוֹנָה

הוּא אֲשֶׁר אַתֶּם אוֹהֲבִים אוֹתוֹ אַף כִּי לֹא רְאִיתֶם אוֹתוֹ, וַאֲשֶׁר כָּעֵת אֵינְכֶם רוֹאִים אוֹתוֹ וּבְכָל זֹאת מַאֲמִינִים אַתֶּם בּוֹ
hu asher attem ohavim oto af ki lo re'item oto, va'asher ka'et einchem ro'im oto uvechol zot ma'aminim attem bo
whom not having seen ye love; on whom, though now ye see him not, yet believing,

וְשָׂשִׂים בְּשִׂמְחָה מְפֹאָרָה וַעֲצוּמָה מִסַּפֵּר
vesasim besimchah mefo'arah va'atzumah missapper
ye rejoice greatly with joy unspeakable and full of glory:

בְּהַשִּׂיגְכֶם אֶת תַּכְלִית אֱמוּנַתְכֶם, אֶת יְשׁוּעַת נַפְשׁוֹתֵיכֶם
behassigechem et tachlit emunatchem, et yeshu'at nafshoteichem
receiving the end of your faith, even the salvation of your souls.

אֶת הַיְשׁוּעָה הַזֹּאת חָקְרוּ וְדָרְשׁוּ הַנְּבִיאִים
et hayshu'ah hazzot chakru vedareshu hannevi'im
Concerning which salvation the prophets sought and searched diligently,

שֶׁנִּבְּאוּ עַל הַחֶסֶד הַמְיֻעָד לָכֶם
shennibbe'u al hachesed hamyu'ad lachem
who prophesied of the grace that should come unto you:

הֵם חָקְרוּ מָה הָעֵת וְהַנְּסִבּוֹת שֶׁהוֹדִיעָה רוּחַ הַמָּשִׁיחַ אֲשֶׁר בְּקִרְבָּם
hem chakru mah ha'et vehannesibbot shehodi'ah ruach hammashiach asher bekirbam
searching what time or what manner of time the Spirit of Christ which was in them did point unto,

כְּשֶׁהֵעִידָה מֵרֹאשׁ עַל סִבְלוֹת הַמָּשִׁיחַ וְעַל הַכָּבוֹד וְהַתִּפְאֶרֶת שֶׁיָּבוֹאוּ אַחֲרֵיהֶן
keshehe'idah merosh al sivlot hammashiach ve'al hakkavod vehattif'eret sheyavo'u achareihen
when it testified beforehand the sufferings of Christ, and the glories that should follow them.

וְנִגְלָה לָהֶם כִּי לֹא לְמַעַן עַצְמָם אֶלָּא לְמַעַנְכֶם שֵׁרְתוּ בַּדְּבָרִים הָהֵם,
veniglah lahem ki lo lema'an atzmam ella lema'anchem sheretu baddevarim hahem
To whom it was revealed, that not unto themselves, but unto you, did they minister these things,

אֲשֶׁר כָּעֵת הֻשְׁמְעוּ לָכֶם מִפִּי הַמְבַשְּׂרִים אֶת הַבְּשׂוֹרָה
asher ka'et hushme'u lachem mippi hamvassrim et habbesorah
which now have been announced unto you through them that preached the gospel unto you

בְּרוּחַ הַקֹּדֶשׁ הַשְּׁלוּחָה מִן הַשָּׁמַיִם, דְּבָרִים אֲשֶׁר מַלְאָכִים נִכְסָפִים לְהַשְׁקִיף אֶל תּוֹכָם
beruach hakkodesh hasheluchah min hashamayim, devarim asher mal'achim nichsafim lehashkif el tocham
by the Holy Spirit sent forth from heaven; which things angels desire to look into.

לָכֵן חִגְרוּ מָתְנֵי שִׂכְלֵיכֶם
lachen chigru motnei sichleichem
Wherefore girding up the loins of your mind,

הֱיוּ עֵרָנִים וְקַוּוּ בְּכָל לְבַבְכֶם לַחֶסֶד הַבָּא עֲלֵיכֶם בְּהִתְגַּלּוֹת יֵשׁוּעַ הַמָּשִׁיחַ
heyu eranim vekavvu bechol levavchem lachesed habba aleichem behitgallot yeshua hammashiach
be sober and set your hope perfectly on the grace that is to be brought unto you at the revelation of Jesus Christ;

פֶּטְרוֹס הָרִאשׁוֹנָה

מֵאֵת פֶּטְרוֹס, שְׁלִיחַ יֵשׁוּעַ הַמָּשִׁיחַ
me'et petros, sheliach yeshua hammashiach
Peter, an apostle of Jesus Christ,

אֶל תּוֹשְׁבֵי תְּפוּצוֹת פּוֹנְטוֹס, גָּלַטְיָה, קַפָּדוֹקְיָה, אַסְיָה וּבִיתִינְיָה, הַנִּבְחָרִים
el toshavei tefutzot pontos, galatyah, kappadokeyah, asyah uvitineyah, hannivcharim
to the elect who are sojourners of the Dispersion in Pontus, Galatia, Cappadocia, Asia, and Bithynia,

עַל־פִּי יְדִיעָתוֹ מִקֶּדֶם שֶׁל אֱלֹהִים הָאָב, בְּקִדּוּשׁ הָרוּחַ
al-pi yedi'ato mikkedem shel elohim ha'av, bekiddush haruach
according to the foreknowledge of God the Father, in sanctification of the Spirit,

אֶל צִיּוּת יֵשׁוּעַ הַמָּשִׁיחַ וְהַזָּיַת דָּמוֹ: חֶסֶד וְשָׁלוֹם יִשְׁפְּעוּ עֲלֵיכֶם לְמַכְבִּיר
el tziyut yeshua hammashiach vehazzayat damo. chesed veshalom yishpe'u aleichem lemachbir
unto obedience and sprinkling of the blood of Jesus Christ: Grace to you and peace be multiplied.

בָּרוּךְ הָאֱלֹהִים אֲבִי אֲדוֹנֵנוּ יֵשׁוּעַ הַמָּשִׁיחַ
baruch ha'elohim avi adonenu yeshua hammashiach
Blessed be the God and Father of our Lord Jesus Christ,

אֲשֶׁר בְּרֹב רַחֲמָיו הוֹלִיד אוֹתָנוּ מְחַדָּשׁ לְתִקְוָה חַיָּה בִּתְחִיַּת יֵשׁוּעַ הַמָּשִׁיחַ מִן הַמֵּתִים
asher berov rachamav holid otanu mechadash letikvah chayah bitchiyat yeshua hammashiach min hammetim
who according to his great mercy begat us again unto a living hope by the resurrection of Jesus Christ from the dead,

לְנַחֲלָה אֲשֶׁר לֹא תִּשָּׁחֵת, לֹא תִּטָּמֵא וְלֹא תִּבֹּל, הַצְּפוּנָה לָכֶם בַּשָּׁמַיִם
lenachalah asher lo tishachet, lo tittamei velo tibbol, hatzfunah lachem bashamayim
unto an inheritance incorruptible, and undefiled, and that fadeth not away, reserved in heaven for you,

לָכֶם הַשְּׁמוּרִים בִּגְבוּרַת אֱלֹהִים, בִּזְכוּת אֱמוּנָה, אֱלֵי יְשׁוּעָה הָעֲתִידָה לְהִגָּלוֹת בְּעֵת קֵץ
lachem hashemurim bigvurat elohim, bizchut emunah, elei yeshu'ah ha'atidah lehiggalot be'et ketz
who by the power of God are guarded through faith unto a salvation ready to be revealed in the last time.

וּבָהּ שְׂמֵחִים אַתֶּם גַּם אִם מִן הַצֹּרֶךְ הוּא שֶׁתִּתְעַצְּבוּ זְמַן מָה בְּכָל מִינֵי מַסּוֹת
uvah semechim attem gam im min hatzorech hu shettit'atzevu zman mah bechol minei massot
Wherein ye greatly rejoice, though now for a little while, if need be, ye have been put to grief in manifold trials,

כְּדֵי שֶׁאֱמוּנַתְכֶם הַצְּרוּפָה וְהַיְקָרָה הַרְבֵּה יוֹתֵר מִזָּהָב, הַנִּשְׁחָת עַל אַף הִצָּרְפוֹ בָּאֵשׁ,
kedei she'emunatchem hatzerufah vehaykarah harbeh yoter mizzahav, hannishchat al af hitzarefo ba'esh
that the proof of your faith, being more precious than gold that perisheth though it is proved by fire,

תֵּצֵא לִתְהִלָּה וּלְכָבוֹד וּלְתִפְאֶרֶת בְּהִתְגַּלּוֹת יֵשׁוּעַ הַמָּשִׁיחַ
tetzei lit'hillah ulechavod uletif'eret behitgallot yeshua hammashiach
may be found unto praise and glory and honor at the revelation of Jesus Christ:

יַעֲקֹב

אִם יֵשׁ חוֹלֶה בֵּינֵיכֶם, יִקְרָא אֶת זִקְנֵי הַקְּהִלָּה

im yesh choleh beineichem, yikra et ziknei hakkehillah

Is any among you sick? let him call for the elders of the church;

וְיִתְפַּלְלוּ בַּעֲדוֹ בְּמָשְׁחָם אוֹתוֹ שֶׁמֶן בְּשֵׁם יהוה

veyitpallelu ba'ado bemoshcham oto shemen beshem hashem

and let them pray over him, anointing him with oil in the name of the Lord:

וּתְפִלַּת הָאֱמוּנָה תּוֹשִׁיעַ אֶת הַחוֹלֶה, וַיהוה יָקִים אוֹתוֹ

utefillat ha'emunah toshia et hacholeh, vahashem yakim oto

and the prayer of faith shall save him that is sick, and the Lord shall raise him up;

וְאִם חָטָא יִסָּלַח לוֹ

ve'im chata yissalach lo

and if he have committed sins, it shall be forgiven him.

הִתְוַדּוּ עַל חֲטָאֵיכֶם אִישׁ לִפְנֵי רֵעֵהוּ וְהִתְפַּלְלוּ אִישׁ בְּעַד רֵעֵהוּ, לְמַעַן תֵּרָפְאוּ

hitvaddu al chata'eichem ish lifnei re'ehu vehitpallelu ish be'ad re'ehu, lema'an terafu

Confess therefore your sins one to another, and pray one for another, that ye may be healed.

גָּדוֹל כֹּחָהּ שֶׁל תְּפִלַּת צַדִּיק בִּפְעֻלָּתָהּ

gadol kochah shel tefillat tzaddik bif'ullatah

The supplication of a righteous man availeth much in its working.

אֵלִיָּהוּ הָיָה אָדָם בַּעַל רְגָשׁוֹת כָּמוֹנוּ; הוּא הִתְפַּלֵּל בְּחָזְקָה שֶׁלֹּא יִהְיֶה מָטָר,

eliyahu hayah adam ba'al regashot kamonu; hu hitpallel bechazekah shello yihyeh matar

Elijah was a man of like passions with us, and he prayed fervently that it might not rain;

וְלֹא יָרַד מָטָר עַל הָאָרֶץ שָׁלוֹשׁ שָׁנִים וְשִׁשָּׁה חֳדָשִׁים

velo yarad matar al ha'aretz shalosh shanim veshishah chodashim

and it rained not on the earth for three years and six months.

הוּא הִתְפַּלֵּל שֵׁנִית, וְהַשָּׁמַיִם נָתְנוּ מָטָר וְהָאָרֶץ הִצְמִיחָה אֶת פִּרְיָהּ

hu hitpallel shenit, vehashamayim natenu matar veha'aretz hitzmichah et piryah

And he prayed again; and the heaven gave rain, and the earth brought forth her fruit.

אַחַי, אִם אִישׁ מִכֶּם סוֹטֶה מִן הָאֱמֶת וְאִישׁ אַחֵר מֵשִׁיב אוֹתוֹ

achai, im ish mikkem soteh min ha'emet ve'ish acher meshiv oto

My brethren, if any among you err from the truth, and one convert him;

דְּעוּ כִּי הַמֵּשִׁיב אֶת הַחוֹטֵא מִסְּטִיַּת דַּרְכּוֹ יוֹשִׁיעַ אֶת נַפְשׁוֹ מִמָּוֶת

de'u ki hammeshiv et hachotei missetiyat darko yoshia et nafsho mimmavet

let him know, that he who converteth a sinner from the error of his way shall save a soul from death,

וִיכַסֶּה עַל הֲמוֹן פְּשָׁעִים

vichasseh al hamon pesha'im

and shall cover a multitude of sins.

יַעֲקֹב

הִרְשַׁעְתֶּם וַהֲרַגְתֶּם אֶת הַצַּדִּיק וְהוּא אֵינוֹ קָם עֲלֵיכֶם
hirsha'tem vaharagtem et hatzaddik vehu eino kam aleichem
Ye have condemned, ye have killed the righteous one; he doth not resist you.

לָכֵן, אַחַי, הִתְאַזְּרוּ אֹרֶךְ רוּחַ עַד בּוֹא הָאָדוֹן
lachen, achai, hit'azzeru orech ruach ad bo ha'adon
Be patient therefore, brethren, until the coming of the Lord.

הִנֵּה הָאִכָּר מְחַכֶּה לִפְרִי הָאֲדָמָה הַיָּקָר
hinneh ha'ikkar mechakkeh lifri ha'adamah hayakar
Behold, the husbandman waiteth for the precious fruit of the earth,

וּמְיַחֵל לוֹ בְּסַבְלָנוּת עַד שֶׁיִּזְכֶּה לְיוֹרֶה וּמַלְקוֹשׁ
umeyachel lo besavlanut ad sheyizkeh leyoreh umalkosh
being patient over it, until it receive the early and latter rain.

גַּם אַתֶּם הִתְאַזְּרוּ אֹרֶךְ רוּחַ, כּוֹנְנוּ אֶת לְבַבְכֶם, כִּי קָרְבָה בִּיאַת הָאָדוֹן
gam attem hit'azzeru orech ruach, konenu et levavchem, ki karevah bi'at ha'adon
Be ye also patient; establish your hearts: for the coming of the Lord is at hand.

אַחַי, אַל תִּתְלוֹנְנוּ אִישׁ עַל רֵעֵהוּ, לְמַעַן לֹא תִּשָּׁפֵטוּ. הִנֵּה הַשּׁוֹפֵט עוֹמֵד בַּפֶּתַח
achai, al titlonenu ish al re'ehu, lema'an lo tishafetu. hinneh hashofet omed bappetach
Murmur not, brethren, one against another, that ye be not judged: behold, the judge standeth before the doors.

אַחַי, הַנְּבִיאִים אֲשֶׁר דִּבְּרוּ בְּשֵׁם יהוה יִהְיוּ לָכֶם לְדֻגְמָה שֶׁל סֵבֶל וְאֹרֶךְ רוּחַ
achai, hannevi'im asher dibberu beshem hashem yihyu lachem ledugmah shel sevel ve'orech ruach
Take, brethren, for an example of suffering and of patience, the prophets who spake in the name of the Lord.

הֵן חוֹשְׁבִים אָנוּ לִמְאֻשָּׁרִים אֶת הָעוֹמְדִים בַּסֵּבֶל. שְׁמַעְתֶּם עַל־אֹדוֹת עֲמִידָתוֹ שֶׁל אִיּוֹב בַּסֵּבֶל
hen choshevim anu lim'usharim et ha'omedim bassevel. shema'tem al-'odot amidato shel iyov bassevel
Behold, we call them blessed that endured: ye have heard of the patience of Job,

וּרְאִיתֶם אֶת תַּכְלִית יהוה - כִּי רַחוּם וְחַנּוּן יהוה
ure'item et tachlit hashem - ki rachum vechannun hashem
and have seen the end of the Lord, how that the Lord is full of pity, and merciful.

וְרֵאשִׁית כֹּל, אַחַי, אַל תִּשָּׁבְעוּ לֹא בַּשָּׁמַיִם וְלֹא בָּאָרֶץ וְלֹא כָּל שְׁבוּעָה אַחֶרֶת.
vereshit kol, achai, al tishave'u lo bashamayim velo ba'aretz velo kol shevu'ah acheret
But above all things, my brethren, swear not, neither by the heaven, nor by the earth, nor by any other oath:

יְהֵא הַכֵּן שֶׁלָּכֶם כֵּן, וְהַלֹא שֶׁלָּכֶם לֹא, פֶּן תִּפְּלוּ בִּידֵי הַדִּין
yehei hakken shellachem ken, vehalo shellachem lo, pen tippelu bidei haddin
but let your yea be yea, and your nay, nay; that ye fall not under judgment.

אִישׁ מִכֶּם אִם יִסְבֹּל, יִתְפַּלֵּל. אִם שִׂמְחָה בְּלִבּוֹ, יְזַמֵּר תְּהִלּוֹת
ish mikkem im yisbol, yitpallel. im simchah belibbo, yezammer tehillot
Is any among you suffering? let him pray. Is any cheerful? let him sing praise.

יַעֲקֹב

מַה הֵם חַיֵּיכֶם? הֲלֹא אֵד אַתֶּם, הַנִּרְאֶה לְרֶגַע וְאַחַר כָּךְ נֶעְלָם

mah hem chayeichem? halo ed attem, hannir'eh lerega ve'achar kach ne'elam
What is your life? For ye are a vapor that appeareth for a little time, and then vanisheth away.

רָאוּי הָיָה שֶׁתֹּאמְרוּ, אִם יִרְצֶה יהוה, נִחְיֶה וְנַעֲשֶׂה כָּזֹאת וְכָזֹאת

ra'ui hayah shettomeru, im yirtzeh hashem, nichyeh vena'aseh kazot vechazot
For that ye ought to say, If the Lord will, we shall both live, and do this or that.

אַךְ הִנֵּה אַתֶּם עוֹד מִתְגָּאִים בְּיָמְרוֹתֵיכֶם. כָּל גַּאֲוָה כָּזֹאת רָעָה הִיא

ach hinneh attem od mitga'im beyumroteichem. kol ga'avah kazot ra'ah hi
But now ye glory in your vauntings: all such glorying is evil.

לָכֵן הַיּוֹדֵעַ לַעֲשׂוֹת טוֹב וְאֵינֶנּוּ עוֹשֶׂה, לְחֵטְא יֵחָשֵׁב לוֹ

lachen hayodea la'asot tov ve'einennu oseh, lechet yechashev lo
To him therefore that knoweth to do good, and doeth it not, to him it is sin.

ה

הוֹי הָעֲשִׁירִים, בְּכוּ וְהֵילִילוּ עַל הַצָּרוֹת הַבָּאוֹת עֲלֵיכֶם

hoy ha'ashirim, bechu veheililu al hatzarot habba'ot aleichem
Come now, ye rich, weep and howl for your miseries that are coming upon you.

עָשְׁרְכֶם נִרְקַב, וּבִגְדֵיכֶם הָיוּ לְמַאֲכַל עָשׁ

oshrechem nirkav, uvigdeichem hayu lema'achal ash
Your riches are corrupted, and your garments are moth-eaten.

זְהַבְכֶם וְכַסְפְּכֶם נֶחְלְדוּ, וְחֶלְוּדָתָם תִּהְיֶה לְעֵדוּת נֶגְדְּכֶם וְתֹאכַל אֶת בְּשַׂרְכֶם כְּמוֹ אֵשׁ

zehavchem vechaspechem nechledu, vachaludatam tihyeh le'edut negdechem vetochal et besarchem kemo esh
Your gold and your silver are rusted; and their rust shall be for a testimony against you, and shall eat your flesh as fire.

אוֹצָר אֲצַרְתֶּם לְאַחֲרִית הַיָּמִים

otzar atzartem le'acharit hayamim
Ye have laid up your treasure in the last days.

הִנֵּה זֹעֵק שְׂכַר הַפּוֹעֲלִים קוֹצְרֵי שְׂדוֹתֵיכֶם אֲשֶׁר הֲלִינוֹתֶם אוֹתוֹ

hinneh zo'ek schar happo'alim kotzerei sedoteichem asher halinotem oto
Behold, the hire of the laborers who mowed your fields, which is of you kept back by fraud, crieth out:

וְצַעֲקַת הַקּוֹצְרִים בָּאָה בְּאָזְנֵי יהוה צְבָאוֹת

vetza'akat hakkotzerim ba'ah be'oznei hashem tzeva'ot
and the cries of them that reaped have entered into the ears of the Lord of Hosts.

חֲיִיתֶם בָּאָרֶץ חַיֵּי תַּעֲנוּגוֹת וְהוֹלֵלוּת; סְעַדְתֶּם אֶת לִבְּכֶם כְּמוֹ בְּיוֹם זֶבַח

chayitem ba'aretz chayei ta'anugot veholelut; se'adtem et libbchem kemo beyom zevach
Ye have lived delicately on the earth, and taken your pleasure; ye have nourished your hearts in a day of slaughter.

יַעֲקֹב

וְאוּלָם נוֹתֵן הוּא יֶתֶר חֵן. לָכֵן הַכָּתוּב אוֹמֵר אֱלֹהִים לַלֵּצִים הוּא־יָלִיץ וְלַעֲנָוִים יִתֶּן־חֵן
ve'ulam noten hu yeter chen. lachen hakkatuv omer elohim lalletzim hu-yalitz vela'anavim yitten-chen
But he giveth more grace. Wherefore the scripture saith, God resisteth the proud, but giveth grace to the humble.

עַל כֵּן הִכָּנְעוּ לִפְנֵי אֱלֹהִים. הִתְיַצְּבוּ נֶגֶד הַשָּׂטָן וְיִבְרַח מִפְּנֵיכֶם
al ken hikkane'u lifnei elohim. hityatzevu neged hashotan veyivrach mippeneichem
Be subject therefore unto God; but resist the devil, and he will flee from you.

קִרְבוּ לֵאלֹהִים וְיִקְרַב אֲלֵיכֶם
kirvu lelohim veyikrav aleichem
Draw nigh to God, and he will draw nigh to you.

הַחוֹטְאִים, רַחֲצוּ יְדֵיכֶם! טַהֲרוּ אֶת לְבַבְכֶם, הֲפַכְפַּכֵּי הַלֵּב
hachote'im, rachatzu yedeichem! taharu et levavchem, hafachpakkei hallev
Cleanse your hands, ye sinners; and purify your hearts, ye doubleminded.

הִתְעַנּוּ וְהִתְאַבְּלוּ וּבְכוּ; יֵהָפֵךְ נָא שְׂחוֹקְכֶם לְאֵבֶל וְשִׂמְחַתְכֶם לְיָגוֹן
hit'annu vehit'abbelu uvechu; yehafech na sechokechem le'evel vesimchatchem leyagon
Be afflicted, and mourn, and weep: let your laughter be turned to mourning, and your joy to heaviness.

הַשְׁפִּילוּ עַצְמְכֶם לִפְנֵי יהוה וְהוּא יְרוֹמֵם אֶתְכֶם. אַחַי, אַל תְּדַבְּרוּ רָעוֹת אִישׁ בְּרֵעֵהוּ
hashpilu atzmechem lifnei hashem vehu yeromem etchem. achai, al tedabberu ra'ot ish bere'ehu.
Humble yourselves in the sight of the Lord, and he shall exalt you. Speak not one against another, brethren.

הַמְדַבֵּר רָעָה בְּאָחִיו וְדָן אֶת אָחִיו, מְדַבֵּר רָעָה בַּתּוֹרָה
hamedabber ra'ah be'achiv vedan et achiv, medabber ra'ah battorah
He that speaketh against a brother, or judgeth his brother, speaketh against the law,

וְדָן אֶת הַתּוֹרָה. וְאִם תָּדִין אֶת הַתּוֹרָה, אֵינְךָ מְקַיֵּם הַתּוֹרָה כִּי אִם שׁוֹפֵט
vedan et hattorah. ve'im tadin et hattorah, eincha mekayem hattorah ki im shofet
and judgeth the law: but if thou judgest the law, thou art not a doer of the law, but a judge.

אֶחָד הוּא הַמְחוֹקֵק וְשׁוֹפֵט, הוּא אֲשֶׁר יָכוֹל לְהוֹשִׁיעַ וּלְאַבֵּד
echad hu hamchokek veshofet, hu asher yachol lehoshia ule'abbed
One only is the lawgiver and judge, even he who is able to save and to destroy:

וּמִי אַתָּה כִּי תִשְׁפֹּט אֶת עֲמִיתְךָ
umi attah ki tishpot et amitecha
but who art thou that judgest thy neighbor?

הוֹי הָאוֹמְרִים, הַיּוֹם אוֹ מָחָר נֵלֵךְ לְעִיר פְּלוֹנִית, נַעֲשֶׂה שָׁם שָׁנָה אַחַת, נִסְחַר וְנַעֲשֶׂה הוֹן
hoy ha'omerim, hayom o machar nelech le'ir plonit, na'aseh sham shanah achat, nischar vena'aseh hon
Come now, ye that say, To-day or to-morrow we will go into this city, and spend a year there, and trade, and get gain:

וְאֵינְכֶם יוֹדְעִים מַה יֵּלֶד יוֹם
ve'einechem yode'im mah yeled yom
whereas ye know not what shall be on the morrow.

יַעֲקֹב

נוֹחָה לְהִתְרַצּוֹת, מְלֵאָה רַחֲמִים וּפְרִי טוֹב, וְאֵין עִמָּהּ מַשּׂוֹא פָנִים וּצְבִיעוּת

nochah lehitratzot, mele'ah rachamim ufri tov, ve'ein immah masso panim utzevi'ut
easy to be entreated, full of mercy and good fruits, without variance, without hypocrisy.

וּלְעוֹשֵׂי שָׁלוֹם פְּרִי הַצֶּדֶק נִזְרָע בְּשָׁלוֹם

ule'osei shalom peri hatzedek nizra beshalom
And the fruit of righteousness is sown in peace for them that make peace.

ד

מֵאַיִן הַסִּכְסוּכִים וְהַמְּרִיבוֹת אֲשֶׁר בֵּינֵיכֶם

me'ayin hassichsuchim vehammerivot asher beineichem
Whence come wars and whence come fightings among you?

הַאִם לֹא מִתַּאֲוֺותֵיכֶם הַנִּלְחָמוֹת בְּתוֹךְ אֵיבְרֵיכֶם

ha'im lo mitta'avoteichem hannilchamot betoch eivereichem
come they not hence, even of your pleasures that war in your members?

אַתֶּם מִתְאַוִּים וְאֵין לָכֶם. אַתֶּם הוֹרְגִים וּמְקַנְּאִים וְאֵינְכֶם יְכוֹלִים לְהַשִּׂיג

attem mit'avvim ve'ein lachem. attem horegim umekanne'im ve'einechem yecholim lehassig
Ye lust, and have not: ye kill, and covet, and cannot obtain:

אַתֶּם רָבִים וְנִלְחָמִים וְאֵין לָכֶם מִפְּנֵי שֶׁאֵינְכֶם מְבַקְשִׁים

attem ravim venilchamim ve'ein lachem mippenei she'einechem mevakshim
ye fight and war; ye have not, because ye ask not.

אַתֶּם מְבַקְשִׁים וְאֵינְכֶם מְקַבְּלִים מִפְּנֵי שֶׁאַתֶּם מְבַקְשִׁים מִתּוֹךְ כַּוָּנָה רָעָה

attem mevakshim ve'einechem mekabbelim mippenei she'attem mevakshim mittoch kavvanah ra'ah
Ye ask, and receive not, because ye ask amiss,

כְּדֵי לְבַזְבֵּז בְּתַאֲווֹתֵיכֶם

kedei levazbez beta'avoteichem
that ye may spend it in your pleasures.

מְפִירֵי נֶאֱמָנוּת, הַאֵינְכֶם יוֹדְעִים כִּי יְדִידוּת עִם הָעוֹלָם הִיא אֵיבָה לֵאלֹהִים

mefirei ne'emanut, ha'einechem yode'im ki yedidut im ha'olam hi eivah le'elohim
Ye adulteresses, know ye not that the friendship of the world is enmity with God?

לְפִיכָךְ, מִי שֶׁרוֹצֶה לִהְיוֹת יָדִיד לָעוֹלָם הוֹפֵךְ לְאוֹיֵב אֱלֹהִים

lefichach, mi sherotzeh lihyot yadid la'olam hofech le'oyev elohim
Whosoever therefore would be a friend of the world maketh himself an enemy of God.

הַחוֹשְׁבִים אַתֶּם כִּי לַשָּׁוְא אוֹמֵר הַכָּתוּב: בְּקִנְאָה מִשְׁתּוֹקֵק אֱלֹהִים לָרוּחַ אֲשֶׁר הִשְׁכִּין בָּנוּ

hachoshevim attem ki lashav omer hakkatuv: bekin'ah mishtokek elohim laruach asher hishkin banu
Or think ye that the scripture speaketh in vain? Doth the spirit which he made to dwell in us long unto envying?

יַעֲקֹב

כָּל מִין בְּהֵמָה וְעוֹף וְרֶמֶשׂ וְחַיּוֹת הַיָּם, הַמִּין הָאֱנוֹשִׁי יָכוֹל לְהִשְׁתַּלֵּט עָלָיו, וְאָכֵן הִשְׁתַּלֵּט
kol min behemah ve'of veremes vechayot hayam, hammin ha'enoshi yachol lehishtallet alav, ve'achen hishtallet
For every kind of beasts and birds, of creeping things and things in the sea, is tamed, and hath been tamed by mankind:

אֲבָל הַלָּשׁוֹן אֵין אָדָם יָכוֹל לְהִשְׁתַּלֵּט עָלֶיהָ; רָעָה הִיא וַחֲסָרַת מַעְצוֹר, וּמְלֵאָה אֶרֶס מָוֶת
aval hallashon ein adam yachol lehishtallet aleiha; ra'ah hi vechasrat ma'tzor, umele'ah eres mavet
but the tongue can no man tame; it is a restless evil, it is full of deadly poison.

בָּהּ מְבָרְכִים אָנוּ אֶת הָאָדוֹן וְהָאָב, וּבָהּ מְקַלְּלִים אָנוּ אֲנָשִׁים שֶׁנַּעֲשׂוּ בְּצֶלֶם אֱלֹהִים
bah mevarechim anu et ha'adon veha'av, uvah mekallelim anu anashim shenna'asu betzelem elohim
Therewith bless we the Lord and Father; and therewith curse we men, who are made after the likeness of God:

מֵאוֹתוֹ הַפֶּה יוֹצֵאת בְּרָכָה וְגַם קְלָלָה. אַחַי, לֹא צָרִיךְ שֶׁיִּהְיֶה כַּדָּבָר הַזֶּה
me'oto happeh yotzet berachah vegam kelalah. achai, lo tzarich sheyihyeh kaddavar hazzeh
out of the same mouth cometh forth blessing and cursing. My brethren, these things ought not so to be.

הֲיַבִּיעַ הַמַּעְיָן מַיִם מְתוּקִים וּמַיִם מָרִים מִמּוֹצָא אֶחָד
hayabbia hamma'yan mayim metukim umayim marim mimmotza echad
Doth the fountain send forth from the same opening sweet water and bitter?

אַחַי, הֲיוּכַל עֵץ הַתְּאֵנָה לַעֲשׂוֹת זֵיתִים, אוֹ הֲתוּכַל הַגֶּפֶן לַעֲשׂוֹת תְּאֵנִים
achai, hayuchal etz hatte'enah la'asot zeitim, o hatuchal haggefen la'asot te'enim?
can a fig tree, my brethren, yield olives, or a vine figs?

כֵּן גַּם מְקוֹר מַיִם מְלוּחִים אֵינֶנּוּ מֵפִיק מַיִם מְתוּקִים
ken gam mekor mayim meluchim einennu mefik mayim metukim
neither can salt water yield sweet.

מִי בָכֶם חָכָם וְנָבוֹן? יַרְאֶה נָא מִתּוֹךְ הִתְנַהֲגוּתוֹ הַטּוֹבָה אֶת מַעֲשָׂיו הַנַּעֲשִׂים בַּעֲנָוָה וְחָכְמָה
mi bachem chacham venavon? yar'eh na mittoch hitnahaguto hattovah et ma'asav hanna'asim ba'anavah vechochmah
Who is wise and understanding among you? let him show by his good life his works in meekness of wisdom.

וְאִם קִנְאָה מָרָה וּמְרִיבָה בִּלְבַבְכֶם, אַל תִּתְגָּאוּ. אַל תְּשַׁקְּרוּ בָּאֱמֶת
ve'im kin'ah marah umerivah bilvavchem, al titga'u. al teshakkeru ba'emet
But if ye have bitter jealousy and faction in your heart, glory not and lie not against the truth.

אֵין זוֹ הַחָכְמָה הַיּוֹרֶדֶת מִמַּעַל, אֶלָּא זוֹ שֶׁהִיא אַרְצִית וְנוֹבַעַת מִן הַיֵּצֶר וְהַשֵּׁדִים
ein zo hachachemah hayoredet mimma'al, ella zo shehi artzit venova'at min hayetzer vehashedim
This wisdom is not a wisdom that cometh down from above, but is earthly, sensual, devilish.

הֵן בְּמָקוֹם שֶׁיֵּשׁ קִנְאָה וּמְרִיבָה, שָׁם מְהוּמָה וְכָל מַעֲשֶׂה רָע
hen bemakom sheyesh kin'ah umerivah, sham mehumah vechol ma'aseh ra
For where jealousy and faction are, there is confusion and every vile deed.

אֲבָל הַחָכְמָה אֲשֶׁר מִמַּעַל, רֵאשִׁית טְהוֹרָה הִיא; לְאַחַר זֹאת אוֹהֶבֶת שָׁלוֹם, סוֹבְלָנִית,
aval hachochmah asher mimma'al, reshit tehorah hi; le'achar zot ohevet shalom, sovlanit
But the wisdom that is from above is first pure, then peaceable, gentle,

יַעֲקֹב

כִּי כְּשֵׁם שֶׁהַגּוּף בְּלֹא הָרוּחַ מֵת הוּא, כֵּן גַּם הָאֱמוּנָה בְּלֹא מַעֲשִׂים מֵתָה הִיא
ki keshem shehagguf belo haruach met hu, ken gam ha'emunah belo ma'asim metah hi
For as the body apart from the spirit is dead, even so faith apart from works is dead.

ג

אַחַי, אַל יִהְיוּ רַבִּים מִכֶּם לְמוֹרִים, שֶׁהֲרֵי יְדַעְתֶּם כִּי עָלֵינוּ יִהְיֶה הַדִּין חָמוּר יוֹתֵר
achai, al yihyu rabbim mikkem lemorim, sheharei yeda'tem ki aleinu yihyeh haddin chamur yoter
Be not many of you teachers, my brethren, knowing that we shall receive heavier judgment.

וַהֲלֹא כֻּלָּנוּ מַרְבִּים לְהִכָּשֵׁל. מִי שֶׁאֵינוֹ נִכְשָׁל בְּדִבּוּר
vahalo kullanu marbim lehikkashel. mi she'eino nichshal bedibbur
For in many things we all stumble. If any stumbleth not in word,

אִישׁ מֻשְׁלָם הוּא וְיָכוֹל לָשִׂים רֶסֶן לְכָל גּוּפוֹ
ish mushlam hu veyachol lasim resen lechol gufo
the same is a perfect man, able to bridle the whole body also.

הִנֵּה בְּפִי הַסּוּסִים שָׂמִים אָנוּ רֶסֶן כְּדֵי שֶׁיִּשְׁמְעוּ לָנוּ, וְכָךְ מְנַהֲגִים אָנוּ אֶת כָּל גּוּפָם
hinneh befi hassusim samim anu resen kedei sheyishame'u lanu, vechach menahagim anu et kol gufam
Now if we put the horses' bridles into their mouths that they may obey us, we turn about their whole body also.

וְהִנֵּה גַּם הָאֳנִיּוֹת, אַף שֶׁגְּדוֹלוֹת הֵן וְנֶהְדָּפוֹת בְּרוּחַ עַזָּה
vehinneh gam ho'oniyot, af sheggedolot hen venehdafot beruach azzah
Behold, the ships also, though they are so great and are driven by rough winds,

הֶגֶה קָטָן יְנַהֵג אוֹתָן אֶל הַמָּקוֹם שֶׁיִּרְצֶה הַהַגַּאי
hegeh katan yenaheg otan el hammakom sheyirtzeh hahaggai
are yet turned about by a very small rudder, whither the impulse of the steersman willeth.

כֵּן גַּם הַלָּשׁוֹן אֵיבָר קָטָן הִיא, וּמְדַבֶּרֶת גְּדוֹלוֹת
ken gam hallashon eivar katan hi, umedabberet gedolot
So the tongue also is a little member, and boasteth great things.

רְאוּ אֵיזוֹ אֵשׁ קְטַנָּה מַבְעִירָה יַעַר גָּדוֹל
re'u eizo esh ketannah mav'irah ya'ar gadol
Behold, how much wood is kindled by how small a fire!

גַּם הַלָּשׁוֹן אֵשׁ הִיא, עוֹלָם שֶׁל עַוְלָה. הַלָּשׁוֹן נִצֶּבֶת בֵּין אֵיבָרֵינוּ
gam hallashon esh hi, olam shel avlah. hallashon nitzevet bein eivareinu
And the tongue is a fire: the world of iniquity among our members is the tongue,

וּמְטַמֵּאת אֶת כָּל הַגּוּף. הִיא מַצִּיתָה אֶת גַּלְגַּל הֲוָיָתֵנוּ וְנִצֶּתֶת בְּאֵשׁ גֵּיהִנֹּם
umetammet et kol hagguf. hi matzitah et galgal havayatenu venitzetet be'esh geihinnom
which defileth the whole body, and setteth on fire the wheel of nature, and is set on fire by hell.

יַעֲקֹב

כָּךְ גַּם הָאֱמוּנָה, אִם אֵין בָּהּ מַעֲשִׂים, מֵתָה הִיא כְּשֶׁלְעַצְמָהּ
kach gam ha'emunah, im ein bah ma'asim, metah hi keshelle'atzmah
Even so faith, if it have not works, is dead in itself.

וְאוּלָם מִישֶׁהוּ יֹאמַר, אַתָּה, יֵשׁ לְךָ אֱמוּנָה; וַאֲנִי, יֵשׁ לִי מַעֲשִׂים
ve'ulam mishehu yomar, attah, yesh lecha emunah; va'ani, yesh li ma'asim
Yea, a man will say, Thou hast faith, and I have works:

הַרְאֵנִי אֶת אֱמוּנָתְךָ בִּבְלִי הַמַּעֲשִׂים, וַאֲנִי אַרְאֶה לְךָ אֶת אֱמוּנָתִי מִתּוֹךְ מַעֲשַׂי
har'eni et emunatecha bivli hamma'asim, va'ani ar'eh lecha et emunati mittoch ma'asai
show me thy faith apart from thy works, and I by my works will show thee my faith.

אַתָּה מַאֲמִין שֶׁהָאֱלֹהִים אֶחָד הוּא. הֵיטַבְתָּ לַעֲשׂוֹת! גַּם הַשֵּׁדִים מַאֲמִינִים וְאַף רוֹעֲדִים
attah ma'amin sheha'elohim echad hu. heitavta la'asot! gam hashedim ma'aminim ve'af ro'adim
Thou believest that God is one; thou doest well: the demons also believe, and shudder.

אִישׁ בַּעַר, הַאִם רְצוֹנְךָ לְהִוָּכַח שֶׁאֱמוּנָה בְּלִי מַעֲשִׂים עֲקָרָה הִיא
ish ba'ar, ha'im retzonecha lehivvachach she'emunah beli ma'asim akarah hi
But wilt thou know, O vain man, that faith apart from works is barren?

אַבְרָהָם אָבִינוּ, הַאִם לֹא בְּמַעֲשָׂיו נִצְדַּק בְּהַעֲלוֹתוֹ אֶת יִצְחָק בְּנוֹ עַל הַמִּזְבֵּחַ
avraham avinu, ha'im lo bema'asav nitzdak beha'aloto et yitzchak bno al hammizbeach
Was not Abraham our father justified by works, in that he offered up Isaac his son upon the altar?

הִנְּךָ רוֹאֶה כִּי הָאֱמוּנָה עָזְרָה לְמַעֲשָׂיו וּמִתּוֹךְ הַמַּעֲשִׂים הֻשְׁלְמָה הָאֱמוּנָה
hinnecha ro'eh ki ha'emunah azerah lema'asav umittoch hamma'asim hushlemah ha'emunah
Thou seest that faith wrought with his works, and by works was faith made perfect;

וְהִתְקַיֵּם הַכָּתוּב הָאוֹמֵר, וְהֶאֱמִן אַבְרָהָם בַּיהוה
vehitkayem hakkatuv ha'omer, vehe'emin avraham bahashem
and the scripture was fulfilled which saith, And Abraham believed God,

וַיַּחְשְׁבֶהָ לוֹ צְדָקָה, וְגַם נִקְרָא אוֹהֵב אֱלֹהִים
vayachsheveha lo tzedakah, vegam nikra ohev elohim
and it was reckoned unto him for righteousness; and he was called the friend of God.

הִנְּכֶם רוֹאִים כִּי בְּמַעֲשִׂים יִצְדַּק אִישׁ וְלֹא בֶּאֱמוּנָה לְבַדָּהּ
hinnechem ro'im ki bema'asim yitzadek ish velo be'emunah levaddah
Ye see that by works a man is justified, and not only by faith.

וְכֵן גַּם רָחָב הַזּוֹנָה, הַאִם לֹא נִצְדְּקָה בְּמַעֲשִׂים
vechen gam rachav hazzonah, ha'im lo nitzdekah bema'asim
And in like manner was not also Rahab the harlot justified by works,

כַּאֲשֶׁר אָסְפָה אֶת שְׁלִיחֵי יְהוֹשֻׁעַ אֶל בֵּיתָהּ וְשִׁלְּחָה אוֹתָם בְּדֶרֶךְ אַחֶרֶת
ka'asher asefah et shelichei yehoshua el beitah veshillechah otam bederech acheret
in that she received the messengers, and sent them out another way?

יַעֲקֹב

הֲלֹא הֵם הַמְגַדְּפִים אֶת הַשֵּׁם הַטּוֹב הַנִּקְרָא עֲלֵיכֶם
halo hem hamgaddfim et hashem hattov hannikra aleichem
Do not they blaspheme the honorable name by which ye are called?

אִם בֶּאֱמֶת מְקַיְּמִים אַתֶּם אֶת תּוֹרַת הַמַּלְכוּת, כַּכָּתוּב, וְאָהַבְתָּ לְרֵעֲךָ כָּמוֹךָ, אֲזַי הֵיטַבְתֶּם לַעֲשׂוֹת
im be'emet mekayemim attem et torat hammalchut, kakkatuv, ve'ahavta lere'acha kamocha, azai heitavtem la'asot
Howbeit if ye fulfil the royal law, according to the scripture, Thou shalt love thy neighbor as thyself, ye do well:

אֲבָל אִם אַתֶּם נוֹהֲגִים בְּמַשּׂוֹא פָנִים, חוֹטְאִים אַתֶּם וְהַתּוֹרָה תַּאֲשִׁימְכֶם כְּעוֹבְרֵי עֲבֵרָה
aval im attem nohagim bemasso panim, chote'im attem vehattorah ta'ashimechem ke'overei averah
but if ye have respect of persons, ye commit sin, being convicted by the law as transgressors.

הֲרֵי מִי שֶׁמְּקַיֵּם אֶת כָּל הַתּוֹרָה וְנִכְשַׁל בְּדָבָר אֶחָד, אָשֵׁם הוּא בַּכֹּל
harei mi shemmekayem et kol hattorah venichshal bedavar echad, ashem hu bakkol
For whosoever shall keep the whole law, and yet stumble in one point, he is become guilty of all.

שֶׁכֵּן הָאוֹמֵר לֹא תִנְאָף אָמַר גַּם לֹא תִרְצָח
shekken ha'omer lo tin'af amar gam lo tirtzach
For he that said, Do not commit adultery, said also, Do not kill.

וְאִם אֵינְךָ נוֹאֵף אֲבָל רוֹצֵחַ, עוֹבֵר אַתָּה עַל מִצְווֹת הַתּוֹרָה
ve'im eincha no'ef aval rotzeach, over attah al mitzvot hattorah
Now if thou dost not commit adultery, but killest, thou art become a transgressor of the law.

דַּבְּרוּ וַעֲשׂוּ אֶת מַעֲשֵׂיכֶם כַּאֲנָשִׁים הָעֲתִידִים לְהִשָּׁפֵט עַל־פִּי תּוֹרָה שֶׁל חֵרוּת
dabbru va'asu et ma'aseichem ka'anashim ha'atidim lehishafet al-pi torah shel cherut
So speak ye, and so do, as men that are to be judged by a law of liberty.

אֵין רַחֲמִים בַּדִּין לְמִי שֶׁלֹּא נָהַג בְּרַחֲמִים; הָרַחֲמִים מִתְנַשְּׂאִים עַל הַדִּין
ein rachamim baddin lemi shello nahag berachamim; harachamim mitnass'im al haddin
For judgment is without mercy to him that hath showed no mercy: mercy glorieth against judgment.

אַחַי, מַה תּוֹעֶלֶת בַּדָּבָר אִם יֹאמַר אִישׁ, יֵשׁ לִי אֱמוּנָה, וְאֵין לוֹ מַעֲשִׂים? הֲתוּכַל הָאֱמוּנָה לְהוֹשִׁיעוֹ
achai, mah to'elet baddavar im yomar ish, yesh li emunah, ve'ein lo ma'asim? hatuchal ha'emunah lehoshi'o
What doth it profit, my brethren, if a man say he hath faith, but have not works? can that faith save him?

אָח אוֹ אָחוֹת אִם יִהְיוּ בְּעֵירֹם וְאֵין לָהֶם לֶחֶם חֻקָּם
ach o achot im yihyu be'eirom ve'ein lahem lechem chukkam
If a brother or sister be naked and in lack of daily food,

וְאִישׁ מִכֶּם יֹאמַר לָהֶם, לְכוּ לְשָׁלוֹם, הִתְחַמְּמוּ וְאִכְלוּ לָשֹׂבַע
ve'ish mikkem yomar lahem, lechu leshalom, hitchammemu ve'ichlu lassova
and one of you say unto them, Go in peace, be ye warmed and filled;

וְלֹא תִּתְּנוּ לָהֶם צָרְכֵי גוּפָם - מַה הוֹעַלְתֶּם
velo tittenu lahem tzarechei gufam - mah ho'altem
and yet ye give them not the things needful to the body; what doth it profit?

יַעֲקֹב

לִפְקֹד אֶת הַיְתוֹמִים וְהָאַלְמָנוֹת בְּצָרָתָם, וּלְהִשָּׁמֵר נָקִי מִטֻּמְאַת הָעוֹלָם
lifkod et hayetomim veha'almanot betzaratam, ulehishamer naki mittum'at ha'olam
to visit the fatherless and widows in their affliction, and to keep oneself unspotted from the world.

ב

אַחַי, אַל יְהֵא בָכֶם מַשּׂוֹא פָנִים בֶּאֱמוּנַת אֲדוֹנֵנוּ יֵשׁוּעַ הַמָּשִׁיחַ, אֲדוֹן הַכָּבוֹד
achai, al yehei bachem masso panim be'emunat adonenu yeshua hammashiach, adon hakkavod
My brethren, hold not the faith of our Lord Jesus Christ, the Lord of glory, with respect of persons.

אִם יָבוֹא אִישׁ לְבֵית הַכְּנֶסֶת שֶׁלָּכֶם וְטַבַּעַת זָהָב עַל יָדוֹ וּלְבוּשׁוֹ הָדוּר
im yavo ish leveit hakkneset shellachem vetabba'at zahav al yado ulevusho hadur
For if there come into your synagogue a man with a gold ring, in fine clothing,

וּבָא גַם אִישׁ עָנִי לָבוּשׁ בְּגָדִים בָּלִים
uva gam ish ani lavush begadim balim
and there come in also a poor man in vile clothing;

וְהִנֵּה פוֹנִים אַתֶּם אֶל הָאִישׁ אֲשֶׁר לְבוּשׁוֹ הָדוּר וְאוֹמְרִים: שֵׁב לְךָ פֹּה בְּטוֹב
vehinneh ponim attem el ha'ish asher levusho hadur ve'omerim: shev lecha poh betov
and ye have regard to him that weareth the fine clothing, and say, Sit thou here in a good place;

וְלֶעָנִי אַתֶּם אוֹמְרִים: עֲמֹד שָׁם אוֹ שֵׁב מִתַּחַת לַהֲדֹם רַגְלָי
vele'ani attem omerim: amod sham o shev mittachat lahadom raglai
and ye say to the poor man, Stand thou there, or sit under my footstool;

הַאִם אֵינְכֶם מַפְלִים בְּקִרְבְּכֶם בֵּין אִישׁ לְאִישׁ וְהוֹפְכִים לִהְיוֹת שׁוֹפְטִים בַּעֲלֵי מַחֲשָׁבוֹת רֶשַׁע
ha'im einechem maflim bekirbechem bein ish le'ish vehofechim lihyot shofetim ba'alei machashavot resha
do ye not make distinctions among yourselves, and become judges with evil thoughts?

שִׁמְעוּ, אַחַי אֲהוּבַי, הֲלֹא בַּעֲנִיֵּי הָעוֹלָם הַזֶּה בָּחַר אֱלֹהִים לִהְיוֹת עֲשִׁירֵי אֱמוּנָה
shim'u, achai ahuvai, halo ba'aniyei ha'olam hazzeh bachar elohim lihyot ashirei emunah
Hearken, my beloved brethren; did not God choose them that are poor as to the world to be rich in faith,

וְיוֹרְשֵׁי הַמַּלְכוּת אֲשֶׁר הִבְטִיחַ לְאוֹהֲבָיו
veyoreshei hammalchut asher hivtiach le'ohavav
and heirs of the kingdom which he promised to them that love him?

וְאַתֶּם בְּזִיתֶם אֶת הֶעָנִי
ve'attem bezitem et he'ani
But ye have dishonored the poor man.

הֲלֹא הָעֲשִׁירִים מְדַכְּאִים אֶתְכֶם וְסוֹחֲבִים אֶתְכֶם לְבָתֵּי מִשְׁפָּט
halo ha'ashirim medakke'im etchem vesochavim etchem levattei mishpat
Do not the rich oppress you, and themselves drag you before the judgment-seats?

יַעֲקֹב

עַל כֵּן, אַחַי אֲהוּבַי, יְהֵא כָּל אִישׁ מָהִיר לִשְׁמֹעַ, בִּלְתִּי נֶחְפָּז לְדַבֵּר וְקָשֶׁה לִכְעֹס

al ken, achai ahuvai, yehei kol ish mahir lishmoa', bilti nechpaz ledabber vekasheh lich'os
Ye know this, my beloved brethren. But let every man be swift to hear, slow to speak, slow to wrath:

שֶׁהֲרֵי כַּעַס אָדָם לֹא יִפְעַל צִדְקַת אֱלֹהִים

sheharei ka'as adam lo yif'al tzidkat elohim
for the wrath of man worketh not the righteousness of God.

לָכֵן הָסִירוּ מֵעֲלֵיכֶם כָּל טִנּוּף וְרֹב רֶשַׁע,

lachen hasiru me'aleichem kol tinnuf verov resha
Wherefore putting away all filthiness and overflowing of wickedness,

וְקַבְּלוּ בַּעֲנָוָה אֶת הַדָּבָר הַנָּטוּעַ אֲשֶׁר יָכוֹל לְהוֹשִׁיעַ אֶת נַפְשׁוֹתֵיכֶם

vekabbelu ba'anavah et haddavar hannatua asher yachol lehoshi et nafshoteichem
receive with meekness the implanted word, which is able to save your souls.

הֱיוּ עוֹשֵׂי הַדָּבָר וְלֹא רַק שׁוֹמְעִים, פֶּן תְּרַמּוּ אֶת עַצְמְכֶם

heyu osei haddavar velo rak shome'im, pen terammu et atzmechem
But be ye doers of the word, and not hearers only, deluding your own selves.

כִּי מִי שֶׁשּׁוֹמֵעַ אֶת הַדָּבָר וְאֵינוֹ עוֹשֶׂה, כָּמוֹהוּ כְּאִישׁ הַמַּבִּיט עַל תֹּאַר פָּנָיו בַּמַּרְאָה

ki mi sheshomea et haddavar ve'eino oseh, kamohu ke'ish hammabbit al to'ar panav bammar'ah
For if any one is a hearer of the word and not a doer, he is like unto a man beholding his natural face in a mirror:

הוּא הִתְבּוֹנֵן בְּעַצְמוֹ וְהָלַךְ לוֹ, וּמִיָּד שָׁכַח מַה צוּרָתוֹ

hu hitbonen be'atzmo vehalach lo, umiyad shachach mah tzurato
for he beholdeth himself, and goeth away, and straightway forgetteth what manner of man he was.

אֲבָל הַמַּשְׁקִיף בַּתּוֹרָה הַשְּׁלֵמָה, תּוֹרַת הַחֵרוּת, וְעוֹמֵד בָּהּ

aval hammashkif battorah hashelemah, torat hacherut, ve'omed bah
But he that looketh into the perfect law, the law of liberty, and so continueth,

מִבְּלִי לִהְיוֹת שׁוֹמֵעַ־וְשׁוֹכֵחַ, אֶלָּא עוֹשֶׂה בְּפֹעַל - אִישׁ זֶה מְבֹרָךְ יִהְיֶה בְּמַעֲשֵׂהוּ

mibbeli lihyot shomea'-veshochoeach, ella oseh befo'al - ish zeh mevorach yihyeh bema'asehu
being not a hearer that forgetteth but a doer that worketh, this man shall be blessed in his doing.

מִי שֶׁסָּבוּר שֶׁהוּא עוֹבֵד אֱלֹהִים

mi shessavur shehu oved elohim
If any man thinketh himself to be religious,

וְאֵינֶנּוּ שָׂם רֶסֶן לִלְשׁוֹנוֹ כִּי אִם מַתְעֶה אֶת לִבּוֹ, עֲבוֹדָתוֹ אֵינָהּ אֶלָּא הֶבֶל

ve'einennu sam resen lilshono ki im mat'eh et libbo, avodato einah ella hevel
while he bridleth not his tongue but deceiveth his heart, this man's religion is vain.

זֹאת הִיא עֲבוֹדַת אֱלֹהִים טְהוֹרָה וּתְמִימָה לִפְנֵי אֱלֹהִים אָבִינוּ

zot hi avodat elohim tehorah utemimah lifnei elohim avinu
Pure religion and undefiled before our God and Father is this,

יַעֲקֹב

הֵן בַּעֲלוֹת הַשֶּׁמֶשׁ הַלוֹהֶטֶת יִיבַשׁ הֶחָצִיר וְיִפֹּל צִיצוֹ וְיֹאבַד חֵן מַרְאֵהוּ
hen ba'alot hashemesh hallohetet yivash hechatzir veyippol tzitzo veyovad chen mar'ehu
For the sun ariseth with the scorching wind, and withereth the grass; and the flower thereof falleth,

כֵּן גַּם הֶעָשִׁיר יִבֹּל בַּהֲלִיכוֹתָיו
ken gam he'ashir yibbol bahalichotav
and the grace of the fashion of it perisheth: so also shall the rich man fade away in his goings.

אַשְׁרֵי הָאִישׁ הַמַּחֲזִיק מַעֲמָד בְּנִסָּיוֹן, כִּי לְאַחַר עָמְדוֹ בַּנִּסָּיוֹן
ashrei ha'ish hammachazik ma'amad benissayon, ki le'achar omdo bannissayon
Blessed is the man that endureth temptation; for when he hath been approved,

יְקַבֵּל אֶת עֲטֶרֶת הַחַיִּים אֲשֶׁר הִבְטִיחַ הָאָדוֹן לְאוֹהֲבָיו
yekabbel et ateret hachayim asher hivtiach ha'adon le'ohavav
he shall receive the crown of life, which the Lord promised to them that love him.

מִי שֶׁמִּתְנַסֶּה אַל יֹאמַר, אֱלֹהִים מְנַסֶּה אוֹתִי
mi shemmitnasseh al yomar, elohim menasseh oti
Let no man say when he is tempted, I am tempted of God;

שֶׁכֵּן אֱלֹהִים לֹא יְנֻסֶּה בָּרַע וְאֵין הוּא מְנַסֶּה אִישׁ
shekken elohim lo yenusseh bara ve'ein hu menasseh ish
for God cannot be tempted with evil, and he himself tempteth no man:

אֶלָּא שֶׁכָּל אִישׁ מִתְנַסֶּה כַּאֲשֶׁר הוּא נִמְשַׁךְ וּמִתְפַּתֶּה בְּתַאֲוָתוֹ שֶׁלּוֹ
ella shekkol ish mitnasseh ka'asher hu nimshach umitpatteh beta'avato shello
but each man is tempted, when he is drawn away by his own lust, and enticed.

אַחֲרֵי כֵן תַּהֲרֶה הַתַּאֲוָה וְתֵלֵד חֵטְא; וְהַחֵטְא כְּשֶׁיִּשְׁלַם יוֹלִיד מָוֶת
acharei chen tahareh hatta'avah veteled chet; vehachet kesheyishlam yolid mavet
Then the lust, when it hath conceived, beareth sin: and the sin, when it is fullgrown, bringeth forth death.

אַל נָא תִּטְעוּ, אַחַי אֲהוּבַי
al na tit'u, achai ahuvai
Be not deceived, my beloved brethren.

כָּל מַתָּנָה טוֹבָה וְכָל מַתָּנָה שְׁלֵמָה יוֹרֶדֶת מִמַּעַל מֵאֵת אֲבִי הָאוֹרוֹת
kol mattanah tovah vechol mattanah shlemah yoredet mimma'al me'et avi ha'orot
Every good gift and every perfect gift is from above, coming down from the Father of lights,

אֲשֶׁר כָּל שִׁנּוּי וְכָל צֵל חִלּוּף אֵין בּוֹ
asher kol shinnui vechol tzel chilluf ein bo
with whom can be no variation, neither shadow that is cast by turning.

הוּא כִּרְצוֹנוֹ הוֹלִיד אוֹתָנוּ בִּדְבַר הָאֱמֶת, לְמַעַן נִהְיֶה בִּכּוּרֵי יְצִירָיו
hu kirtzono holid otanu bidvar ha'emet, lema'an nihyeh bikkurei yetzirav
Of his own will he brought us forth by the word of truth, that we should be a kind of firstfruits of his creatures.

יַעֲקֹב

יַעֲקֹב

יַעֲקֹב, עֶבֶד אֱלֹהִים וַאֲדוֹנֵנוּ יֵשׁוּעַ הַמָּשִׁיחַ, דּוֹרֵשׁ בִּשְׁלוֹם שְׁנֵים־עָשָׂר הַשְּׁבָטִים שֶׁבַּגּוֹלָה
ya'akov, eved elohim va'adonenu yeshua hammashiach, doresh bishlom sheneim-'asar hashevatim shebbaggolah
James, a servant of God and of the Lord Jesus Christ, to the twelve tribes which are of the Dispersion, greeting.

לְשִׂמְחָה גְדוֹלָה חִשְׁבוּ זֹאת, אַחַי, כַּאֲשֶׁר אַתֶּם בָּאִים בְּכָל מִינֵי נִסְיוֹנוֹת
lesimchah gedolah chishvu zot, achai, ka'asher attem ba'im bechol minei nisyonot
Count it all joy, my brethren, when ye fall into manifold temptations;

שֶׁהֲרֵי יוֹדְעִים אַתֶּם כִּי בְחִינַת אֱמוּנַתְכֶם מְבִיאָה לִידֵי סַבְלָנוּת
sheharei yode'im attem ki bechinat emunatchem mevi'ah liydei savlanut
knowing that the proving of your faith worketh patience.

אֲבָל שֶׁתְּהֵא הַסַּבְלָנוּת שְׁלֵמָה בְּפָעֳלָהּ, לְמַעַן תִּהְיוּ שְׁלֵמִים וּבְלֹא דֹפִי וְלֹא יֶחְסַר לָכֶם דָּבָר
aval shettehei hassavlanut shelemah befo'olah, lema'an tihyu shelemim uvelo dofi velo yechsar lachem davar
And let patience have its perfect work, that ye may be perfect and entire, lacking in nothing.

אִישׁ מִכֶּם אִם יֶחְסַר חָכְמָה, יְבַקֵּשׁ מֵאֱלֹהִים
ish mikkem im yechsar chochmah, yevakkesh me'elohim
But if any of you lacketh wisdom, let him ask of God,

הַנּוֹתֵן לַכֹּל בִּנְדִיבוּת וּבְלֹא גְעָרָה, וְתִנָּתֵן לוֹ
hannoten lakkol bindivut uvelo ge'arah, vetinnaten lo
who giveth to all liberally and upbraideth not; and it shall be given him.

אַךְ יְבַקֵּשׁ בֶּאֱמוּנָה וּבְלִי סָפֵק, כִּי בַּעַל־סָפֵק דּוֹמֶה לְגַלֵּי הַיָּם הַנִּדְחָפִים וְסוֹעֲרִים מִפְּנֵי הָרוּחַ
ach yevakkesh be'emunah uvli safek, ki ba'al-safek domeh legallei hayam hannidchafim veso'arim mippenei haruach
But let him ask in faith, nothing doubting: for he that doubteth is like the surge of the sea driven by the wind and tossed.

אוֹתוֹ הָאִישׁ אַל יַחְשֹׁב כִּי יְקַבֵּל מַשֶּׁהוּ מֵאֵת יהוה
oto ha'ish al yachshov ki yekabbel mashehu me'et hashem
For let not that man think that he shall receive anything of the Lord;

בִּהְיוֹתוֹ אִישׁ הַפּוֹסֵחַ עַל שְׁתֵּי הַסְּעִפִּים הֲפַכְפַּךְ בְּכָל דְּרָכָיו
bihyoto ish happoseach al shetei hasse'ippim hafachpach bechol derachav
a doubleminded man, unstable in all his ways.

יִתְהַלֵּל הָאָח הַדַּל בְּרוֹמְמוּתוֹ
yit'hallel ha'ach haddal beromemuto
But let the brother of low degree glory in his high estate:

וְהֶעָשִׁיר שֶׁיִּתְהַלֵּל בְּשִׁפְלוֹ, כִּי כְּצִיץ חָצִיר הוּא יַחֲלֹף
vehe'ashir sheyit'hallel beshiflo, ki ketzitz chatzir hu yachalof
and the rich, in that he is made low: because as the flower of the grass he shall pass away.

הָעִבְרִים

וֵאלֹהֵי הַשָּׁלוֹם אֲשֶׁר בְּדַם בְּרִית עוֹלָם הֶעֱלָה מִן הַמֵּתִים אֶת רוֹעֵה הַצֹּאן הַגָּדוֹל, אֶת אֲדוֹנֵנוּ יֵשׁוּעַ
ve'elohei hashalom asher bedam berit olam he'elah min hammetim et ro'eh hatzon haggadol, et adonenu yeshua
Now the God of peace, who brought again from the dead the great shepherd of the sheep with the blood of an eternal covenant, even our Lord Jesus,

הוּא יַכְשִׁיר אֶתְכֶם לְכָל דָּבָר טוֹב כְּדֵי שֶׁתַּעֲשׂוּ אֶת רְצוֹנוֹ
hu yachshir etchem lechol davar tov kedei shetta'asu et retzono
make you perfect in every good thing to do his will,

בְּפָעֳלוֹ בָּכֶם אֶת הָרָצוּי לְפָנָיו בְּיַד יֵשׁוּעַ הַמָּשִׁיחַ
befo'olo bachem et haratzui lefanav beyad yeshua hammashiach
working in us that which is well-pleasing in his sight, through Jesus Christ;

אֲשֶׁר לוֹ הַכָּבוֹד לְעוֹלְמֵי עוֹלָמִים. אָמֵן
asher lo hakkavod le'olemei olamim. amen
to whom be the glory for ever and ever. Amen.

וַאֲנִי מְבַקֵּשׁ מִכֶּם, אַחַי, לְקַבֵּל בְּסַבְלָנוּת אֶת דְּבַר הַהַטָּפָה, שֶׁהֲרֵי בִּקְצָרָה כָּתַבְתִּי אֲלֵיכֶם
va'ani mevakkesh mikkem, achai, lekabbel besavlanut et devar hahattafah, sheharei biktzarah katavti aleichem
But I exhort you, brethren, bear with the word of exhortation: for I have written unto you in few words.

דְּעוּ כִּי טִימוֹתֵיאוֹס אָחִינוּ שֻׁלַּח לַחָפְשִׁי. אִם יַקְדִּים לָבוֹא, אָבוֹא יַחַד אִתּוֹ לִרְאוֹת אֶתְכֶם
de'u ki timotei'os achinu shullach lachofshi. im yakdim lavo, avo yachad itto lir'ot etchem
Know ye that our brother Timothy hath been set at liberty; with whom, if he come shortly, I will see you.

דִּרְשׁוּ בִּשְׁלוֹם כָּל מַנְהִיגֵיכֶם וְכָל הַקְּדוֹשִׁים. בְּנֵי אֶרֶץ אִיטַלְיָה דּוֹרְשִׁים בִּשְׁלוֹמְכֶם
dirshu bishlom kol manhigeichem vechol hakkedoshim. benei eretz italyah doreshim bishlomechem
Salute all them that have the rule over you, and all the saints. They of Italy salute you.

הַחֶסֶד עִם כֻּלְּכֶם. אָמֵן
hachesed im kullechem. amen
Grace be with you all. Amen.

הָעִבְרִים

לָכֵן גַּם יֵשׁוּעַ, כְּדֵי לְקַדֵּשׁ אֶת הָעָם בְּדָמוֹ, סָבַל מִחוּץ לַשַּׁעַר
lachen gam yeshua', kedei lekaddesh et ha'am bedamo, saval michutz lasha'ar
Wherefore Jesus also, that he might sanctify the people through his own blood, suffered without the gate.

עַל כֵּן נֵצֵא נָא אֵלָיו אֶל מִחוּץ לַמַּחֲנֶה וְנִשָּׂא אֶת חֶרְפָּתוֹ
al ken netzei na elav el michutz lammachaneh venissa et cherpato
Let us therefore go forth unto him without the camp, bearing his reproach.

כִּי אֵין לָנוּ פֹּה עִיר קֶבַע, אֶלָּא אֶת זוֹ שֶׁלֶּעָתִיד לָבוֹא מְבַקְשִׁים אָנוּ
ki ein lanu poh ir keva', ella et zo shelle'atid lavo mevakshim anu
For we have not here an abiding city, but we seek after the city which is to come.

לָכֵן בְּכָל עֵת נַקְרִיבָה בְּתִוּוּכוֹ זֶבַח תּוֹדָה לֵאלֹהִים
lachen bechol et nakrivah betivvucho zevach todah le'elohim
Through him then let us offer up a sacrifice of praise to God continually,

כְּלוֹמַר, פְּרִי שְׂפָתַיִם הַמּוֹדוֹת לִשְׁמוֹ
klomar, peri sfatayim hammodot lishmo
that is, the fruit of lips which make confession to his name.

וְאַל תִּשְׁכְּחוּ לִגְמֹל חֶסֶד וּלְשַׁתֵּף אֶת הַזּוּלַת בַּאֲשֶׁר לָכֶם, כִּי זְבָחִים כָּאֵלֶּה יֶעֶרְבוּ לֵאלֹהִים
ve'al tishkechu ligmol chesed uleshattef et hazzulat ba'asher lachem, ki zevachim ka'elleh ye'ervu lelohim
But to do good and to communicate forget not: for with such sacrifices God is well pleased.

שִׁמְעוּ בְּקוֹל מַנְהִיגֵיכֶם וְהִכָּנְעוּ לָהֶם
shim'u bekol manhigeichem vehikkan'u lahem
Obey them that have the rule over you, and submit to them:

כִּי מַשְׁגִּיחִים הֵם עַל נַפְשׁוֹתֵיכֶם כַּעֲתִידִים לָתֵת דִּין וְחֶשְׁבּוֹן; נַהֲגוּ כָּךְ,
ki mashgichim hem al nafshoteichem ka'atidim latet din vecheshbon; nahagu kach
for they watch in behalf of your souls, as they that shall give account;

לְמַעַן יַעֲשׂוּ זֹאת בְּשִׂמְחָה וְלֹא בַּאֲנָחָה
lema'an ya'asu zot besimchah velo ba'anachah
that they may do this with joy, and not with grief:

שֶׁאִם לֹא כֵן אֵין זֶה לְתוֹעֶלֶת לָכֶם
she'im lo chen ein zeh leto'elet lachem
for this were unprofitable for you.

הִתְפַּלְלוּ בַּעֲדֵנוּ. בְּטוּחִים אָנוּ כִּי שָׁלֵם מַצְפּוּנֵנוּ; רְצוֹנֵנוּ לְהִתְנַהֵג בְּיֹשֶׁר בְּכָל דָּבָר
hitpallelu ba'adenu. betuchim anu ki shalem matzpunenu; retzonenu lehitnaheg beyosher bechol davar
Pray for us: for we are persuaded that we have a good conscience, desiring to live honorably in all things.

מַפְצִיר אֲנִי בָּכֶם מְאֹד לַעֲשׂוֹת זֹאת, לְמַעַן יִנָּתֵן לִי לָשׁוּב אֲלֵיכֶם בִּמְהֵרָה
maftzir ani bachem me'od la'asot zot, lema'an yinnaten li lashuv aleichem bimherah
And I exhort you the more exceedingly to do this, that I may be restored to you the sooner.

הָעִבְרִים

חַיֵּי אִישׁוּת יְכֻבְּדוּ אֵצֶל הַכֹּל וִיצוּעֲכֶם אַל יְחֻלָּל. אֶת הַזּוֹנִים וְהַנּוֹאֲפִים יִשְׁפֹּט אֱלֹהִים
chayei ishut yechubbedu etzel hakkol viytzu'achem al yechullal. et hazzonim vehanno'afim yishpot elohim
Let marriage be had in honor among all, and let the bed be undefiled: for fornicators and adulterers God will judge.

רַחֲקוּ מֵאַהֲבַת כֶּסֶף וְשִׂמְחוּ בְחֶלְקְכֶם
rachaku me'ahavat kesef vesimchu bechelkechem
Be ye free from the love of money; content with such things as ye have:

כִּי הוּא אָמַר, לֹא אַרְפְּךָ וְלֹא אֶעֶזְבֶךָּ
ki hu amar, lo arpecha velo e'ezva
for himself hath said, I will in no wise fail thee, neither will I in any wise forsake thee.

עַל כֵּן נִבְטַח וְנֹאמַר, יְהוָה לִי בְּעֹזְרָי, לֹא אִירָא מַה-יַּעֲשֶׂה לִי אָדָם
al ken nivtach venomar, hashem li be'ozerai, lo ira mah-ya'aseh li adam
So that with good courage we say, The Lord is my helper; I will not fear: What shall man do unto me?

זִכְרוּ אֶת מַנְהִיגֵיכֶם אֲשֶׁר דִּבְּרוּ אֲלֵיכֶם אֶת דְּבַר אֱלֹהִים
zichru et manhigeichem asher dibberu aleichem et devar elohim
Remember them that had the rule over you, men that spake unto you the word of God;

הַבִּיטוּ אֶל אַחֲרִית דַּרְכָּם וּלְכוּ בְּעִקְּבוֹת אֱמוּנָתָם
habbitu el acharit darkam ulechu be'ikkevot emunatam
and considering the issue of their life, imitate their faith.

יֵשׁוּעַ הַמָּשִׁיחַ הוּא הוּא - אֶתְמוֹל, הַיּוֹם וּלְעוֹלָמִים
yeshua hammashiach hu hu - etmol, hayom ule'olamim
Jesus Christ is the same yesterday and to-day, yea and for ever.

אַל תִּסָּחֲפוּ עַל-יְדֵי תּוֹרוֹת שׁוֹנוֹת וְזָרוֹת; הֵן טוֹב לִסְעֹד אֶת הַלֵּב בְּחֶסֶד
al tissachafu al-yedei torot shonot vezarot; hen tov lis'od et hallev bechesed
Be not carried away by divers and strange teachings: for it is good that the heart be established by grace;

וְלֹא בְּדִבְרֵי מַאֲכָל אֲשֶׁר לֹא הוֹעִילוּ לְמִי שֶׁחַי עַל-פִּיהֶם
velo bedivrei ma'achal asher lo ho'ilu lemi shechai al-pihem
not by meats, wherein they that occupied themselves were not profited.

יֵשׁ לָנוּ מִזְבֵּחַ אֲשֶׁר אֵין רְשׁוּת לִמְשָׁרְתֵי הַמִּשְׁכָּן לֶאֱכֹל מֵעָלָיו
yesh lanu mizbeach asher ein reshut limsharetei hammishkan le'echol me'alav
We have an altar, whereof they have no right to eat that serve the tabernacle.

הַבְּהֵמוֹת אֲשֶׁר דָּמָן מוּבָא אֶל הַקֹּדֶשׁ
habbehemot asher daman muva el hakkodesh
For the bodies of those beasts whose blood is brought into the holy place

בְּיַד הַכֹּהֵן הַגָּדוֹל לְכַפָּרַת הַחֵטְא, גּוּפוֹתֵיהֶן נִשְׂרָפוֹת מִחוּץ לַמַּחֲנֶה
beyad hakkohen haggadol lechapparat hachet, gufoteihen nisrafot michutz lammachaneh
by the high priest as an offering for sin, are burned without the camp.

הָעִבְרִים

אֲשֶׁר קוֹלוֹ הִרְעִישׁ אָז אֶת הָאָרֶץ וְעַתָּה הִבְטִיחַ בְּאׇמְרוֹ
asher kolo hir'ish az et ha'aretz ve'attah hivtiach be'amero
whose voice then shook the earth: but now he hath promised, saying,

עוֹד אַחַת וַאֲנִי מַרְעִישׁ לֹא אֶת־הָאָרֶץ בִּלְבַד, אֶלָּא גַּם אֶת־הַשָּׁמַיִם
od achat va'ani mar'ish lo et-ha'aretz bilvad, ella gam et-hashamayim
Yet once more will I make to tremble not the earth only, but also the heaven.

עוֹד אַחַת מְצַיֵּן אֶת הֲסָרַת הַדְּבָרִים הַמִּתְמוֹטְטִים
od achat metzayen et hasarat haddevarim hammitmotetim
And this word, Yet once more, signifieth the removing of those things that are shaken,

כְּגוֹן דְּבָרִים שֶׁנַּעֲשׂוּ - לְמַעַן יִשָּׁאֲרוּ הַדְּבָרִים אֲשֶׁר לֹא יִמּוֹטוּ
kegon devarim shenna'asu - lema'an yisha'aru haddevarim asher lo yimmotu
as of things that have been made, that those things which are not shaken may remain.

וְכֵיוָן שֶׁאָנוּ מְקַבְּלִים מַלְכוּת אֲשֶׁר לֹא תִּמּוֹט, נִהְיֶה נָא מַכִּירֵי טוֹבָה
vecheivan she'anu mekabbelim malchut asher lo timmot, nihyeh na makkirei tovah
Wherefore, receiving a kingdom that cannot be shaken, let us have grace,

וּבְהַכָּרָה זֹאת נַעֲבֹד אֶת אֱלֹהִים כִּרְצוֹנוֹ, בַּחֲסִידוּת וּבְיִרְאָה
uvehakkarah zot na'avod et elohim kirtzono, bachasidut uveyir'ah
whereby we may offer service well-pleasing to God with reverence and awe:

כִּי אֱלֹהֵינוּ אֵשׁ אוֹכְלָה הוּא
ki eloheinu esh ochelah hu
for our God is a consuming fire.

יג

תְּהֵא אַהֲבַת אַחִים קַיֶּמֶת בֵּינֵיכֶם
tehei ahavat achim kayemet beineichem
Let love of the brethren continue.

הַכְנָסַת אוֹרְחִים אַל תִּשְׁכְּחוּ, כִּי יֵשׁ אֲשֶׁר הִכְנִיסוּ אֶל בֵּיתָם מַלְאָכִים מִבְּלִי לָדַעַת זֹאת
hachnasat orechim al tishkechu, ki yesh asher hichnisu el beitam mal'achim mibbeli lada'at zot
Forget not to show love unto strangers: for thereby some have entertained angels unawares.

זִכְרוּ אֶת הָאֲסוּרִים כְּאִלּוּ הֱיִיתֶם בַּמַּאֲסָר עִמָּהֶם
zichru et ha'asurim ke'illu heyitem bamma'asar immahem
Remember them that are in bonds, as bound with them;

זִכְרוּ אֶת הַמְעֻנִּים, כְּשֵׁם שֶׁגַּם אַתֶּם חַיִּים בַּגּוּף
zichru et ham'unnim, keshem sheggam attem chayim bagguf
them that are ill-treated, as being yourselves also in the body.

הָעִבְרִים

וְלֹא אֶל אֲפֵלָה וְחֹשֶׁךְ וּסְעָרָה
velo el afelah vechoshech use'arah
and unto blackness, and darkness, and tempest,

וְלֹא לְקוֹל שׁוֹפָר וּלְקוֹל דְּבָרִים
velo lekol shofar ulekol devarim
and the sound of a trumpet, and the voice of words;

אֲשֶׁר שֹׁמְעָיו בִּקְשׁוּ שֶׁלֹּא יוֹסִיף לְדַבֵּר עִמָּם
asher shome'av bikshu shello yosif ledabber immam
which voice they that heard entreated that no word more should be spoken unto them;

כִּי לֹא יָכְלוּ לָשֵׂאת אֶת מַה שֶּׁצֻוָּה, גַּם אִם בְּהֵמָה תִּגַּע בָּהָר סָקוֹל תִּסָּקֵל
ki lo yachlu laset et mah shetzuvvah, gam im behemah tigga bahar sakol tissakel
for they could not endure that which was enjoined, If even a beast touch the mountain, it shall be stoned;

וְהַמַּרְאֶה הָיָה נוֹרָא מְאֹד עַד כִּי מֹשֶׁה אָמַר, יָרֵא אֲנִי וְחָרֵד
vehammar'eh hayah nora me'od ad ki mosheh amar, yarei ani vechared
and so fearful was the appearance, that Moses said, I exceedingly fear and quake:

אַתֶּם בָּאתֶם אֶל הַר צִיּוֹן וְאֶל עִיר אֱלֹהִים חַיִּים
attem batem el har tziyon ve'el ir elohim chayim
but ye are come unto mount Zion, and unto the city of the living God,

אֶל יְרוּשָׁלַיִם הַשְּׁמֵימִית וְאֶל רִבְבוֹת הַמַּלְאָכִים, אֶל עֲצֶרֶת
el yerushalayim hashmeimit ve'el rivevot hammal'achim, el atzeret
the heavenly Jerusalem, and to innumerable hosts of angels,

אֶל קְהִלַּת הַבְּכוֹרִים הַכְּתוּבִים בַּשָּׁמַיִם
el kehillat habbechorim hakketuvim bashamayim
to the general assembly and church of the firstborn who are enrolled in heaven,

אֶל אֱלֹהִים שֹׁפֵט הַכֹּל, אֶל רוּחוֹת הַצַּדִּיקִים שֶׁנַּעֲשׂוּ מֻשְׁלָמִים
el elohim shofet hakkol, el ruchot hatzaddikim shenna'asu mushlamim
and to God the Judge of all, and to the spirits of just men made perfect,

אֶל יֵשׁוּעַ מְתַוֵּךְ הַבְּרִית הַחֲדָשָׁה וְאֶל דַּם הַהַזָּיָה הַמֵּיטִיב דַּבֵּר מִדַּם הֶבֶל
el yeshua metavvech habberit hachadashah ve'el dam hahazzayah hammeitiv dabber middam hevel
and to Jesus the mediator of a new covenant, and to the blood of sprinkling that speaketh better than that of Abel.

לָכֵן הִזָּהֲרוּ פֶּן תְּסָרְבוּ לַמְדַבֵּר, שֶׁכֵּן אִם לֹא נִמְלְטוּ אֵלֶּה שֶׁסֵּרְבוּ לַמְדַבֵּר עַל הָאָרֶץ
lachen hizzaharu pen tesarvu lamdabber, shekken im lo nimletu elleh shesserevu lamdabber al ha'aretz
See that ye refuse not him that speaketh. For if they escaped not when they refused him that warned them on earth,

עַל אַחַת כַּמָּה וְכַמָּה לֹא נִמָּלֵט אֲנַחְנוּ אִם נָסוּר מֵהַמְדַבֵּר מִן הַשָּׁמַיִם
al achat kammah vechammah lo nimmalet anachnu im nasur mehamedabber min hashamayim
much more shall not we escape who turn away from him that warneth from heaven:

הָעִבְרִים

אַךְ הוּא לְהוֹעִיל מְיַסֵּר אוֹתָנוּ, לְמַעַן יִהְיֶה לָנוּ חֵלֶק בִּקְדֻשָּׁתוֹ
ach hu leho'il meyasser otanu, lema'an yihyeh lanu chelek bikdushato
but he for our profit, that we may be partakers of his holiness.

כָּל מוּסָר בְּעֵת בּוֹאוֹ אֵינוֹ נֶחְשָׁב לְשִׂמְחָה כִּי אִם לְעֶצֶב,
kol musar be'et bo'o eino nechshav lesimchah ki im le'etzev
All chastening seemeth for the present to be not joyous but grievous;

אֲבָל אַחֲרֵי כֵן יִתֵּן פְּרִי שָׁלוֹם וּצְדָקָה לַמִּתְחַנְּכִים בּוֹ
aval acharei chen yitten peri shalom utzedakah lammitchannechim bo
yet afterward it yieldeth peaceable fruit unto them that have been exercised thereby, even the fruit of righteousness.

עַל כֵּן אַמְּצוּ יָדַיִם רָפוֹת וְחַזְּקוּ בִּרְכַּיִם כּוֹשְׁלוֹת
al ken ammetzu yadayim rafot vechazzeku birkayim koshelot
Wherefore lift up the hands that hang down, and the palsied knees;

וְכוֹנְנוּ נְתִיבוֹת יְשָׁרוֹת לְרַגְלֵיכֶם, לְמַעַן לֹא יִסְטֶה הַצּוֹלֵעַ כִּי אִם יֵרָפֵא
vechonenu netivot yesharot leragleichem, lema'an lo yisteh hatzolea ki im yerafe
and make straight paths for your feet, that that which is lame be not turned out of the way, but rather be healed.

רִדְפוּ שָׁלוֹם עִם כָּל אָדָם, וְגַם אֶת הַקְּדֻשָּׁה שֶׁבִּלְעָדֶיהָ לֹא יִרְאֶה אִישׁ אֶת הָאָדוֹן
ridfu shalom im kol adam, vegam et hakkedushah shebbil'adeiha lo yir'eh ish et ha'adon
Follow after peace with all men, and the sanctification without which no man shall see the Lord:

הִשָּׁמְרוּ פֶּן יִגָּרַע אִישׁ מֵחֶסֶד אֱלֹהִים
hishamru pen yiggara ish mechesed elohim
looking carefully lest there be any man that falleth short of the grace of God;

פֶּן יַפְרִיעַ אֶתְכֶם שֹׁרֶשׁ פֹּרֶה מְרִירוּת וְיִטַּמְּאוּ בוֹ רַבִּים
pen yafria etchem shoresh poreh merirut veyittame'u bo rabbim
lest any root of bitterness springing up trouble you, and thereby the many be defiled;

פֶּן יִהְיֶה אִישׁ זוֹנֶה אוֹ חֲסַר קְדֻשָּׁה כְּעֵשָׂו אֲשֶׁר בְּנָזִיד אֶחָד מָכַר אֶת בְּכוֹרָתוֹ
pen yihyeh ish zoneh o chasar kedushah ke'esav asher benazid echad machar et bechorato
lest there be any fornicator, or profane person, as Esau, who for one mess of meat sold his own birthright.

יוֹדְעִים אַתֶּם כִּי אַחֲרֵי כֵן, כַּאֲשֶׁר רָצָה לָרֶשֶׁת אֶת הַבְּרָכָה, נִדְחָה
yode'im attem ki acharei chen, ka'asher ratzah lareshet et habberachah, nidchah
For ye know that even when he afterward desired to inherit the blessing, he was rejected;

הוּא לֹא מָצָא מָקוֹם לַחֲזֹר בּוֹ, אַף כִּי בִּקֵּשׁ זֹאת בִּדְמָעוֹת
hu lo matza makom lachazor bo, af ki bikkesh zot bidma'ot
for he found no place for a change of mind in his father, though he sought it diligently with tears.

הֵן לֹא בָאתֶם אֶל הַר מוּחָשִׁי וּבוֹעֵר בָּאֵשׁ
hen lo batem el har muchashi uvo'er ba'esh
For ye are not come unto a mount that might be touched, and that burned with fire,

הָעִבְרִים

הִתְבּוֹנְנוּ אֶל הָאֶחָד שֶׁסָּבַל הִתְנַגְּדוּת כָּזֹאת מֵאֵת הַחוֹטְאִים

hitbonenu el ha'echad shessaval hitnaggedut kazot me'et hachote'im
For consider him that hath endured such gainsaying of sinners against himself,

כְּדֵי שֶׁלֹּא תִּתְעַיְּפוּ וְלֹא תִּרְפֶּה נַפְשְׁכֶם

kedei shello tit'ayefu velo tirpeh nafshechem
that ye wax not weary, fainting in your souls.

עֲדַיִן לֹא נִלְחַמְתֶּם עַד לַדָּם בְּמַאֲבַקְכֶם עִם הַחֵטְא

adayin lo nilchamtem ad laddam bema'avakchem im hachet
Ye have not yet resisted unto blood, striving against sin:

וּשְׁכַחְתֶּם אֶת מִלּוֹת הַנֹּחַם הַמְדַבְּרוֹת אֲלֵיכֶם כְּאֶל בָּנִים

ushechachtem et millot hannocham hamdabberot aleichem ke'el banim
and ye have forgotten the exhortation which reasoneth with you as with sons,

מוּסַר יהוה, בְּנִי, אַל־תִּמְאָס, וְאַל־תָּקֹץ בְּתוֹכַחְתּוֹ

musar hashem, bni, al-tim'as, ve'al-takotz betochachto
My son, regard not lightly the chastening of the Lord, Nor faint when thou art reproved of him;

כִּי אֶת אֲשֶׁר יֶאֱהַב יהוה יוֹכִיחַ, יַכְאִיב אֶת־בֵּן יִרְצֶה

ki et asher ye'ehav hashem yochiach, yach'iv et-ben yirtzeh
For whom the Lord loveth he chasteneth, And scourgeth every son whom he receiveth.

לְשֵׁם מוּסָר סוֹבְלִים אַתֶּם, וֵאלֹהִים נוֹהֵג עִמָּכֶם כְּעִם בָּנִים

leshem musar sovelim attem, ve'elohim noheg immachem ke'im banim;
It is for chastening that ye endure; God dealeth with you as with sons;

כִּי אֵיזֶהוּ הַבֵּן אֲשֶׁר אָבִיו אֵינוֹ מְיַסֵּר אוֹתוֹ

ki eizehu habben asher aviv eino meyasser oto
for what son is there whom his father chasteneth not?

אַךְ אִם אַתֶּם בְּלֹא מוּסָר, אֲשֶׁר הַכֹּל נוֹטְלִים בּוֹ חֶלְקָם, אֲזַי מַמְזֵרִים אַתֶּם וְלֹא בָנִים

ach im attem belo musar, asher hakkol notelim bo chelkam, azai mamzerim attem velo banim
But if ye are without chastening, whereof all have been made partakers, then are ye bastards, and not sons.

וְעוֹד, הָאָבוֹת שֶׁהוֹלִידוּ אֶת גּוּפֵנוּ יִסְּרוּ אוֹתָנוּ וְאָנוּ יְרֵאנוּ מֵהֶם

ve'od, ha'avot sheholidu et gufenu yisseru otanu ve'anu yarenu mehem
Furthermore, we had the fathers of our flesh to chasten us, and we gave them reverence:

הֲלֹא כָּל שֶׁכֵּן נִכָּנַע לִפְנֵי אֲבִי הָרוּחוֹת וְנִחְיֶה

halo kol shekken nikkana lifnei avi haruchot venichyeh
shall we not much rather be in subjection unto the Father of spirits, and live?

הֵם אָמְנָם יִסְּרוּנוּ יָמִים מְעַטִּים עַל־פִּי מַה שֶּׁהֵם רָאוּ לְנָכוֹן

hem omnam yisserunu yamim me'attim al-pi mah shehem ra'u lenachon
For they indeed for a few days chastened us as seemed good to them;

הָעִבְרִים

נִסְקְלוּ, נֻסּוּ בְּעִנּוּיִים, נֻסְּרוּ בְּמַשּׂוֹר, הוּמְתוּ בְּחֶרֶב
niskelu, nussu be'innuyim, nusseru bemassor, humetu becherev
they were stoned, they were sawn asunder, they were tempted, they were slain with the sword:

נָעוּ וְנָדוּ עֲטוּפֵי עוֹרוֹת כְּבָשִׂים וְעִזִּים, בְּסָבְלָם מַחְסוֹר, צָרוֹת וְהִתְעַלְּלוּת
na'u venadu atufei orot kevasim ve'izzim, besavelam machsor, tzarot vehit'allelut
they went about in sheepskins, in goatskins; being destitute, afflicted, ill-treated

אָכֵן הָעוֹלָם לֹא הָיָה רָאוּי לַאֲנָשִׁים אֲשֶׁר כָּאֵלֶּה - וְתוֹעִים הָיוּ בְּמִדְבָּרִיּוֹת, בֶּהָרִים, בִּמְעָרוֹת וּבְנִקִיקֵי הָאָרֶץ
achen ha'olam lo hayah ra'ui la'anashim asher ka'elleh - veto'im hayu bemidbariyot, beharim, bim'arot uvinkikei ha'aretz
(of whom the world was not worthy), wandering in deserts and mountains and caves, and the holes of the earth.

כָּל אֵלֶּה, אַף כִּי אֱמוּנָתָם הֵעִידָה עֲלֵיהֶם, לֹא רָאוּ בְּקִיּוּם הַהַבְטָחָה
kol elleh, af ki emunatam he'idah aleihem, lo ra'u bekiyum hahavtachah
And these all, having had witness borne to them through their faith, received not the promise,

וְאוּלָם אֱלֹהִים הֵכִין לָנוּ דָּבָר טוֹב יוֹתֵר, כְּדֵי שֶׁלֹּא יוּבְאוּ לִידֵי שְׁלֵמוּת בִּלְעָדֵינוּ
ve'ulam elohim hechin lanu davar tov yoter, kedei shello yuv'u lidei shelemut bil'adeinu
God having provided some better thing concerning us, that apart from us they should not be made perfect.

יב

לָכֵן גַּם אֲנַחְנוּ, אֲשֶׁר עֲנַן עֵדִים כָּזֶה אוֹפֵף אוֹתָנוּ
lachen gam anachnu, asher anan edim kazeh ofef otanu
Therefore let us also, seeing we are compassed about with so great a cloud of witnesses,

נָסִירָה נָא כָּל מַעֲמָסָה וְגַם אֶת הַחֵטְא הַלּוֹכֵד עַל נְקַלָּה
nasirah na kol ma'amasah vegam et hachet halloched al nekallah,
lay aside every weight, and the sin which doth so easily beset us,

וּבְסַבְלָנוּת נָרוּצָה אֶת הַמֵּרוֹץ הֶעָרוּךְ לְפָנֵינוּ
uvesavlanut narutzah et hammerotz he'aruch lefaneinu
and let us run with patience the race that is set before us,

בְּהַבִּיטֵנוּ אֶל יֵשׁוּעַ מְכוֹנֵן הָאֱמוּנָה וּמַשְׁלִימָהּ
behabbitenu el yeshua mechonen ha'emunah umashlimah
looking unto Jesus the author and perfecter of our faith,

אֲשֶׁר בְּעַד הַשִּׂמְחָה הָעֲרוּכָה לְפָנָיו סָבַל אֶת הַצְּלָב וּבָז לַחֶרְפָּה
asher be'ad hassimchah ha'aruchah lefanav saval et hatzelav uvaz lacherpah
who for the joy that was set before him endured the cross, despising shame,

וַיֵּשֶׁב לִימִין כִּסֵּא הָאֱלֹהִים
veyashav liymin kissei ha'elohim
and hath sat down at the right hand of the throne of God.

הָעִבְרִים

בֶּאֱמוּנָה עָבְרוּ בְיַם סוּף כְּמוֹ בַיַּבָּשָׁה, דָּבָר שֶׁנִּסּוּ הַמִּצְרִים וְטָבְעוּ
be'emunah averu beyam suf kemo bayabbashah, davar shennissu hammitzrim vetave'u
By faith they passed through the Red sea as by dry land: which the Egyptians assaying to do were swallowed up.

בִּגְלַל אֱמוּנָה נָפְלוּ חוֹמוֹת יְרִיחוֹ אַחֲרֵי שֶׁהִקִּיפוּ אוֹתָן שִׁבְעַת יָמִים
biglal emunah nafelu chomot yericho acharei shehikkifu otan shiv'at yamim
By faith the walls of Jericho fell down, after they had been compassed about for seven days.

בִּזְכוּת אֱמוּנָה לֹא נִסְפְּתָה רָחָב הַזּוֹנָה עִם הַסּוֹרְרִים, שֶׁכֵּן קִבְּלָה אֶת הַמְרַגְּלִים בְּשָׁלוֹם
bizchut emunah lo nispetah rachav hazzonah im hassorerim, shekken kibbelah et hamraggelim beshalom
By faith Rahab the harlot perished not with them that were disobedient, having received the spies with peace.

וּמָה עוֹד אֹמַר
umah od omar
And what shall I more say?

הֵן תִּקְצַר הָעֵת מִלְּסַפֵּר עַל גִּדְעוֹן וּבָרָק וְשִׁמְשׁוֹן וְיִפְתָּח וְדָוִד וּשְׁמוּאֵל וְהַנְּבִיאִים
hen tiktzar ha'et millesapper al gid'on uvarak veshimshon veyiftach vedavid ushemu'el vehannevi'im
for the time will fail me if I tell of Gideon, Barak, Samson, Jephthah; of David and Samuel and the prophets:

אֲשֶׁר עַל־יְדֵי אֱמוּנָה הִכְנִיעוּ מַמְלָכוֹת, פָּעֲלוּ צֶדֶק
asher al-yedei emunah hichni'u mamlachot, pa'alu tzedek
who through faith subdued kingdoms, wrought righteousness,

הִשִּׂיגוּ הַבְטָחוֹת, סָגְרוּ פִּי אֲרָיוֹת
hissigu havtachot, sageru pi arayot
obtained promises, stopped the mouths of lions,

כִּבּוּ לַהֲבוֹת אֵשׁ, נִמְלְטוּ מִפִּי חֶרֶב
kibbu lahavot esh, nimletu mippi cherev
quenched the power of fire, escaped the edge of the sword,

הִתְחַזְּקוּ מֵחֻלְשָׁה, עָשׂוּ חַיִל בַּמִּלְחָמָה וְהֵבִיסוּ צִבְאוֹת זָרִים
hitchazzeku mechulshah, asu chayil bammilchamah vehevisu tziv'ot zarim
from weakness were made strong, waxed mighty in war, turned to flight armies of aliens.

נָשִׁים קִבְּלוּ אֶת מֵתֵיהֶן שֶׁקָּמוּ לִתְחִיָּה
nashim kibblu et meteihen shekkamu litchiyah
Women received their dead by a resurrection:

אֲחֵרִים עֻנּוּ עַד מָוֶת וְלֹא הִסְכִּימוּ לְהִנָּצֵל, לְמַעַן יַשִּׂיגוּ תְּחִיָּה טוֹבָה יוֹתֵר
acherim unnu ad mavet velo hiskimu lehinnatzel, lema'an yassigu techiyah tovah yoter
and others were tortured, not accepting their deliverance; that they might obtain a better resurrection:

אֲחֵרִים הִתְנַסּוּ בְּחֶרְפַּת לַעַג וְהַלְקָאוֹת שׁוֹטִים וְגַם בְּכְבָלִים וְכֶלֶא
acherim hitnassu becherpat la'ag vehalka'ot shotim vegam bichvalim vechelei
and others had trial of mockings and scourgings, yea, moreover of bonds and imprisonment:

הָעִבְרִים

מִתּוֹךְ אֱמוּנָה בֵּרַךְ יַעֲקֹב לִפְנֵי מוֹתוֹ אֶת שְׁנֵי בְּנֵי יוֹסֵף, וְקַד מֵעַל רֹאשׁ הַמַּטֶּה
mittoch emunah berech ya'akov lifnei moto et shenei benei yosef, vekad me'al rosh hammatteh
By faith Jacob, when he was dying, blessed each of the sons of Joseph; and worshipped, leaning upon the top of his staff.

מִתּוֹךְ אֱמוּנָה הִזְכִּיר יוֹסֵף לִפְנֵי מוֹתוֹ אֶת יְצִיאַת בְּנֵי יִשְׂרָאֵל
mittoch emunah hizkir yosef lifnei moto et yetzi'at benei yisra'el
By faith Joseph, when his end was nigh, made mention of the departure of the children of Israel;

וְצִוָּה עַל־אֹדוֹת עַצְמוֹתָיו
vetzivvah al-'odot atzmotav
and gave commandment concerning his bones.

כְּשֶׁנּוֹלַד מֹשֶׁה, מִתּוֹךְ אֱמוּנָה הִסְתִּירוּהוּ הוֹרָיו בְּמֶשֶׁךְ שְׁלוֹשָׁה חֳדָשִׁים
keshennolad mosheh, mittoch emunah histiruhu horav bemeshech sheloshah chodashim
By faith Moses, when he was born, was hid three months by his parents,

כִּי רָאוּ שֶׁנָּאֶה הַיֶּלֶד, וְלֹא פָחֲדוּ מִגְּזֵרַת הַמֶּלֶךְ
ki ra'u shenna'eh hayeled, velo pachadu miggezerat hammelech
because they saw he was a goodly child; and they were not afraid of the king's commandment.

כַּאֲשֶׁר גָּדַל מֹשֶׁה, מִתּוֹךְ אֱמוּנָה סֵרֵב לְהִקָּרֵא בֶּן לְבַת פַּרְעֹה
ka'asher gadal mosheh, mittoch emunah serev lehikkarei ben levat par'oh
By faith Moses, when he was grown up, refused to be called the son of Pharaoh's daughter;

וּבָחַר לְהִתְעַנּוֹת עִם עַם אֱלֹהִים מִלְהִתְעַנֵּג לְשָׁעָה בְּתַעֲנוּגֵי הַחֵטְא
uvachar lehit'annot im am elohim millehit'anneg lesha'ah beta'anugei hachet
choosing rather to share ill treatment with the people of God, than to enjoy the pleasures of sin for a season;

הוּא חָשַׁב אֶת חֶרְפַּת הַמָּשִׁיחַ לְעֹשֶׁר גָּדוֹל מֵאוֹצְרוֹת מִצְרַיִם
hu chashav et cherpat hammashiach le'osher gadol me'otzerot mitzrayim
accounting the reproach of Christ greater riches than the treasures of Egypt:

כִּי נָשָׂא עֵינָיו אֶל הַגְּמוּל
ki nasa einav el haggemul
for he looked unto the recompense of reward.

בֶּאֱמוּנָה עָזַב אֶת מִצְרַיִם וְלֹא פָחַד מִזַּעַם הַמֶּלֶךְ, כִּי עָמַד בְּעֹז כְּרוֹאֶה אֶת מִי שֶׁאֵינֶנּוּ נִרְאֶה
be'emunah azav et mitzrayim velo pachad mizza'am hammelech, ki amad be'oz kero'eh et mi she'einennu nir'eh
By faith he forsook Egypt, not fearing the wrath of the king: for he endured, as seeing him who is invisible.

מִתּוֹךְ אֱמוּנָה עָשָׂה אֶת הַפֶּסַח וְאֶת נְתִינַת הַדָּם
mittoch emunah asah et happesach ve'et netinat haddam
By faith he kept the passover, and the sprinkling of the blood,

כְּדֵי שֶׁלֹּא יִגַּע בָּהֶם מַכֵּה הַבְּכוֹרִים
kedei shello yigga bahem makkeh habbechorim
that the destroyer of the firstborn should not touch them.

הָעִבְרִים

וְאוּלָם רָאוּ אוֹתָם מֵרָחוֹק
e'ulam ra'u otam merachok
but having seen them and greeted them from afar,

וְקִדְּמוּ אוֹתָם בִּבְרָכָה כְּשֶׁהֵם מוֹדִים כִּי זָרִים וְגוֹלִים הֵם בָּאָרֶץ
vekiddemu otam bivrachah keshehem modim ki zarim vegolim hem ba'aretz
and having confessed that they were strangers and pilgrims on the earth.

הֵן הַמְדַבְּרִים כָּךְ מַצְהִירִים שֶׁהֵם מְבַקְשִׁים לָהֶם אֶרֶץ מוֹשָׁב
hen hamdabberim kach matzhirim shehem mevakshim lahem eretz moshav
For they that say such things make it manifest that they are seeking after a country of their own.

וְאִלּוּ כִּוְּנוּ דַעְתָּם עַל הָאָרֶץ הַהִיא אֲשֶׁר יָצְאוּ מִמֶּנָּה
ve'illu kivvenu da'tam al ha'aretz hahi asher yatz'u mimmennah
And if indeed they had been mindful of that country from which they went out,

הָיָה לָהֶם זְמַן לָשׁוּב אֵלֶיהָ
hayah lahem zeman lashuv eleiha
they would have had opportunity to return.

אַךְ עַתָּה נִכְסָפִים הֵם לְטוֹבָה מִמֶּנָּה, לְאֶרֶץ מוֹשָׁב שְׁמֵימִית.
ach attah nichsafim hem letovah mimmennah, le'eretz moshav shmeimit
But now they desire a better country, that is, a heavenly:

לָכֵן לֹא בּוֹשׁ בָּהֶם הָאֱלֹהִים לְהִקָּרֵא אֱלֹהֵיהֶם, שֶׁהֲרֵי הֵכִין לָהֶם עִיר
lachen lo bosh bahem ha'elohim lehikkarei eloheihem, sheharei hechin lahem ir
wherefore God is not ashamed of them, to be called their God; for he hath prepared for them a city.

מִתּוֹךְ אֱמוּנָה הִקְרִיב אַבְרָהָם אֶת יִצְחָק בְּעֵת שֶׁנֻּסָּה
mittoch emunah hikriv avraham et yitzchak be'et shennussah
By faith Abraham, being tried, offered up Isaac:

הוּא שֶׁקִּבֵּל אֶת הַהַבְטָחוֹת הִקְרִיב אֶת יְחִידוֹ
hu shekkibbel et hahavtachot hikriv et yechido
yea, he that had gladly received the promises was offering up his only begotten son;

הוּא שֶׁנֶּאֱמַר לוֹ, כִּי בְיִצְחָק יִקָּרֵא לְךָ זָרַע
hu shenne'emar lo, ki veyitzchak yikkarei lecha zara
even he to whom it was said, In Isaac shall thy seed be called:

בְּחָשְׁבוֹ בְּלִבּוֹ כִּי הָאֱלֹהִים יָכוֹל לְהָקִים אֲפִלּוּ מֵעִם הַמֵּתִים; מִשָּׁם, בִּבְחִינַת מָשָׁל, אַף קִבֵּל אוֹתוֹ
bechoshvo belibbo ki ha'elohim yachol lehakim afillu me'im hammetim; misham, bivchinat mashal, af kibbel oto
accounting that God is able to raise up, even from the dead; from whence he did also in a figure receive him back.

מִתּוֹךְ אֱמוּנָה בֵּרַךְ יִצְחָק אֶת יַעֲקֹב וְאֶת עֵשָׂו בְּנוֹגֵעַ לִדְבָרִים עֲתִידִים לָבוֹא
mittoch emunah berech yitzchak et ya'akov ve'et esav benogea lidvarim atidim lavo
By faith Isaac blessed Jacob and Esau, even concerning things to come.

הָעִבְרִים

מִתּוֹךְ אֱמוּנָה בָּנָה נֹחַ תֵּבָה לְהַצָּלַת בֵּיתוֹ, בִּהְיוֹתוֹ יָרֵא אַחֲרֵי שֶׁהֻזְהַר עַל דְּבָרִים אֲשֶׁר עוֹד לֹא נִרְאוּ,
mittoch emunah banah noach tevah lehatzalat beito, bihyoto yarei acharei shehuzhar al devarim asher od lo nir'u
By faith Noah, being warned of God concerning things not seen as yet, moved with godly fear, prepared an ark to the saving of his house;

וּבֶאֱמוּנָתוֹ הִרְשִׁיעַ אֶת הָעוֹלָם וְהָיָה לְיוֹרֵשׁ הַצְּדָקָה הַמְיֻסֶּדֶת עַל אֱמוּנָה
uve'emunato hirshia et ha'olam vehayah leyoresh hatzedakah hamyussedet al emunah
through which he condemned the world, and became heir of the righteousness which is according to faith.

מִתּוֹךְ אֱמוּנָה צִיֵּת אַבְרָהָם בְּהִקָּרְאוֹ לָצֵאת אֶל מָקוֹם שֶׁהָיָה עָתִיד לְקַבֵּל לְנַחֲלָה,
mittoch emunah tziyet avraham behikkare'o latzet el makom shehayah atid lekabbel lenachalah
By faith Abraham, when he was called, obeyed to go out unto a place which he was to receive for an inheritance;

וְהוּא יָצָא מִבְּלִי לָדַעַת לְאָן יֵלֵךְ
vehu yatza mibbli lada'at le'an yelech
and he went out, not knowing whither he went.

מִתּוֹךְ אֱמוּנָה הִתְגּוֹרֵר בְּאֶרֶץ הַהַבְטָחָה כְּגֵר בְּאֶרֶץ זָרָה,
mittoch emunah hitgorer be'eretz hahavtachah keger be'eretz zarah
By faith he became a sojourner in the land of promise, as in a land not his own,

בְּשִׁבְתּוֹ בְּאֹהָלִים עִם יִצְחָק וְיַעֲקֹב אֲשֶׁר יָרְשׁוּ עִמּוֹ אֶת אוֹתָהּ הַהַבְטָחָה
beshivto be'ohalim im yitzchak veya'akov asher yareshu immo et otah hahavtachah
dwelling in tents, with Isaac and Jacob, the heirs with him of the same promise:

כִּי חִכָּה לָעִיר שֶׁיֵּשׁ לָהּ יְסוֹדוֹת, שֶׁאַדְרִיכָלָהּ וּמְקִימָהּ הוּא הָאֱלֹהִים
ki chikkah la'ir sheyesh lah yesodot, she'adrichalah umekimah hu ha'elohim
for he looked for the city which hath the foundations, whose builder and maker is God.

מִתּוֹךְ אֱמוּנָה קִבְּלָה גַּם שָׂרָה כֹּחַ לַהֲרוֹת אַף לְאַחַר שֶׁהִזְדַּקְּנָה
mittoch emunah kibbelah gam sarah koach laharot af le'achar shehizdakkenah
By faith even Sarah herself received power to conceive seed when she was past age,

שֶׁכֵּן חָשְׁבָה אֶת הַמַּבְטִיחַ לְנֶאֱמָן
shekken chashevah et hammavtiach lene'eman
since she counted him faithful who had promised:

עַל כֵּן גַּם מֵאֶחָד, שֶׁהָיָה בִּבְחִינַת מֵת
al ken gam me'echad, shehayah bivchinat met
wherefore also there sprang of one, and him as good as dead,

יָצְאוּ כְּכוֹכְבֵי הַשָּׁמַיִם לָרֹב וְכַחוֹל עַל שְׂפַת הַיָּם אֲשֶׁר לֹא יִסָּפֵר
yatze'u kechochevei hashamayim larov vechachol al sfat hayam asher lo yissafer
so many as the stars of heaven in multitude, and as the sand, which is by the sea-shore, innumerable.

בְּעוֹדָם מַחֲזִיקִים בֶּאֱמוּנָה מֵתוּ כָּל אֵלֶּה בְּלִי שֶׁהִשִּׂיגוּ אֶת הַדְּבָרִים הַמֻּבְטָחִים
be'odam machazikim be'emunah metu kol elleh beli shehissigu et haddevarim hammuvtachim, v
These all died in faith, not having received the promises,

הָעִבְרִים

יא

הָאֱמוּנָה הִיא בִּטָּחוֹן בְּמַמָּשׁוּת הַדְּבָרִים הַמְקֻוִּים, הוֹכָחַת דְּבָרִים שֶׁאֵינָם נִרְאִים
ha'emunah hi bittachon bemammashut haddevarim hamkuvvim, hochachat dvarim she'einam nir'im
Now faith is assurance of things hoped for, a conviction of things not seen.

בִּגְלָלָה הוּעַד עַל הַקַּדְמוֹנִים
biglalah hu'ad al hakkadmonim
For therein the elders had witness borne to them.

בֶּאֱמוּנָה נָבִין כִּי הָעוֹלָמִים הוּכְנוּ בִּדְבַר אֱלֹהִים
be'emunah navin ki ha'olamim huchnu bidvar elohim
By faith we understand that the worlds have been framed by the word of God,

בְּאֹפֶן שֶׁהַנִּרְאֶה נִתְהַוָּה מִן הַבִּלְתִּי נִרְאֶה
be'ofen shehannir'eh nit'havvah min habbilti nir'eh
so that what is seen hath not been made out of things which appear.

מִתּוֹךְ אֱמוּנָה הֵבִיא הֶבֶל לֵאלֹהִים קָרְבָּן טוֹב מִזֶּה שֶׁהֵבִיא קַיִן;
mittoch emunah hevi hevel lelohim korban tov mizzeh shehevi kayin
By faith Abel offered unto God a more excellent sacrifice than Cain,

בִּגְלָלָה הוּעַד עָלָיו כִּי צַדִּיק הוּא, שֶׁכֵּן אֱלֹהִים הֵעִיד עַל מַתְּנוֹתָיו
biglalah hu'ad alav ki tzaddik hu, shekken elohim he'id al mattnotav
through which he had witness borne to him that he was righteous, God bearing witness in respect of his gifts:

וּבִגְלָלָה הוּא מְדַבֵּר עֲדַיִן גַּם לְאַחַר שֶׁמֵּת
uviglalah hu medabber adayin gam le'achar shemmet
and through it he being dead yet speaketh.

בִּזְכוּת אֱמוּנָה לֻקַּח חֲנוֹךְ בְּלִי לִרְאוֹת מָוֶת, וְאֵינֶנּוּ, כִּי־לָקַח אֹתוֹ אֱלֹהִים
bizchut emunah lukkach chanoch bli lir'ot mavet, ve'einennu, ki-lakach oto elohim
By faith Enoch was translated that he should not see death; and he was not found, because God translated him:

וְהוּעַד עָלָיו לִפְנֵי הִלָּקְחוֹ כִּי אֶת הָאֱלֹהִים הִתְהַלֵּךְ
vehu'ad alav lifnei hillakecho ki et ha'elohim hit'hallech
for he hath had witness borne to him that before his translation he had been well-pleasing unto God:

וּבְלִי אֱמוּנָה אִי אֶפְשָׁר לִהְיוֹת רָצוּי לֵאלֹהִים
uveli emunah i efshar lihyot ratzui lelohim
And without faith it is impossible to be well-pleasing unto him;

כִּי כָּל הַקָּרֵב אֶל אֱלֹהִים צָרִיךְ לְהַאֲמִין שֶׁהוּא קַיָּם וְהוּא נוֹתֵן גְּמוּל לְדוֹרְשָׁיו
ki kol hakkarev el elohim tzarich leha'amin shehu kayam vehu noten gemul ledoreshav
for he that cometh to God must believe that he is, and that he is a rewarder of them that seek after him.

הָעִבְרִים

וְגַם יָדִין יהוה עַמּוֹ
vegam yadin hashem ammo
And again, The Lord shall judge his people.

אָכֵן נוֹרָא לִנְפֹּל בְּיַד אֱלֹהִים חַיִּים
achen nora linpol beyad elohim chayim
It is a fearful thing to fall into the hands of the living God.

זִכְרוּ אֶת הַיָּמִים הָרִאשׁוֹנִים, כַּאֲשֶׁר אֹרוּ עֵינֵיכֶם וַעֲמַדְתֶּם בְּמַאֲבָק קָשֶׁה וּבְצָרוֹת
zichru et hayamim harishonim, ka'asher oru eineichem va'amadtem bema'avak kasheh uvetzarot
But call to remembrance the former days, in which, after ye were enlightened, ye endured a great conflict of sufferings;

פְּעָמִים סְבַלְתֶּם חֲרָפוֹת וְצָרוֹת לְעֵינֵי כֹל
pe'amim sevaltem charafot vetzarot le'einei kol
partly, being made a gazingstock both by reproaches and afflictions;

וּפְעָמִים הִשְׁתַּתַּפְתֶּם עִם אֵלֶּה אֲשֶׁר סָבְלוּ כָּזֹאת
ufe'amim hishtattaftem im elleh asher savelu kazot
and partly, becoming partakers with them that were so used.

כִּי אָכֵן צַר הָיָה לָכֶם עַל הָאֲסִירִים, וְאֶת גְּזֵלַת רְכוּשְׁכֶם סְבַלְתֶּם בְּשִׂמְחָה,
ki achen tzar hayah lachem al ha'asirim, ve'et gezelat rechushechem sevaltem besimchah
For ye both had compassion on them that were in bonds, and took joyfully the spoiling of your possessions,

מִתּוֹךְ יְדִיעָה שֶׁיֵּשׁ לָכֶם בַּשָּׁמַיִם קִנְיָן טוֹב יוֹתֵר, יַצִּיב וְקַיָּם
mittoch yedi'ah sheyesh lachem bashamayim kinyan tov yoter, yatziv vekayam
knowing that ye have for yourselves a better possession and an abiding one.

לָכֵן אַל תַּשְׁלִיכוּ אֶת בִּטְחוֹנְכֶם אֲשֶׁר גָּדוֹל שְׂכָרוֹ
lachen al tashlichu et bitchonechem asher gadol secharo
Cast not away therefore your boldness, which hath great recompense of reward.

שֶׁהֲרֵי צְרִיכִים אַתֶּם לְסַבְלָנוּת כְּדֵי לְקַבֵּל אֶת הַמֻּבְטָח לְאַחַר שֶׁתַּעֲשׂוּ אֶת רְצוֹן אֱלֹהִים
sheharei tzerichim attem lesavlanut kedei lekabbel et hammuvtach le'achar shetta'asu et retzon elohim
For ye have need of patience, that, having done the will of God, ye may receive the promise.

כִּי עוֹד מְעַט קָט וְהַבָּא יָבוֹא, וְלֹא יְאַחֵר
ki'od me'at kat vehabba yavo, velo ye'acher
For yet a very little while, He that cometh shall come, and shall not tarry.

צַדִּיק בֶּאֱמוּנָתוֹ יִחְיֶה; וְאִם יִסּוֹג לֹא רָצְתָה נַפְשִׁי בּוֹ
tzaddik be'emunato yichyeh; ve'im yissog lo ratzetah nafshi bo
But my righteous one shall live by faith: And if he shrink back, my soul hath no pleasure in him.

אֲבָל אֲנַחְנוּ אֵינֶנּוּ מִן הַנְּסוֹגִים אֱלֵי אֲבַדּוֹן, כִּי אִם בְּנֵי הָאֱמוּנָה לְשֵׁם יְשׁוּעַת הַנֶּפֶשׁ
aval anachnu einennu min hannesogim elei avaddon, ki im bnei ha'emunah leshem yeshu'at hannefesh
But we are not of them that shrink back unto perdition; but of them that have faith unto the saving of the soul.

הָעִבְרִים

נַחֲזִיקָה נָא בַּתִּקְוָה שֶׁאָנוּ מַצְהִירִים עָלֶיהָ וְאַל נִמּוֹט, שֶׁכֵּן נֶאֱמָן הַמַּבְטִיחַ
nachazikah na battikvah she'anu matzhirim aleiha ve'al nimmot, shekken ne'eman hammavtiach
let us hold fast the confession of our hope that it waver not; for he is faithful that promised:

נָשִׂים לִבֵּנוּ אִישׁ אֶל רֵעֵהוּ, לְעוֹרֵר זֶה אֶת זֶה לְאַהֲבָה וּלְמַעֲשִׂים טוֹבִים
nasim libbenu ish el re'ehu, le'orer zeh et zeh le'ahavah ulema'asim tovim
and let us consider one another to provoke unto love and good works;

בַּל נַזְנִיחַ אֶת הִתְכַּנְּסוּתֵנוּ כְּמִנְהַג כַּמָּה אֲנָשִׁים
bal nazniach et hitkannesutenu keminhag kammah anashim
not forsaking our own assembling together, as the custom of some is,

כִּי אִם נְעוֹדֵד אִישׁ אֶת רֵעֵהוּ, וּבְיִחוּד בִּרְאוֹתְכֶם כִּי קָרֵב הַיּוֹם
ki im ne'oded ish et re'ehu, uveyichud bir'otechem ki karev hayom
but exhorting one another; and so much the more, as ye see the day drawing nigh.

הֵן אִם נֶחֱטָא בְּזָדוֹן לְאַחַר שֶׁקִּבַּלְנוּ אֶת יְדִיעַת הָאֱמֶת,
hen im necheta bezadon le'achar shekkibbalnu et yedi'at ha'emet,
For if we sin wilfully after that we have received the knowledge of the truth,

לֹא יִשָּׁאֵר עוֹד קָרְבָּן לְכַפֵּר עַל חֲטָאִים
lo yisha'er od korban lechapper al chata'im
there remaineth no more a sacrifice for sins,

אֶלָּא צִפִּיַּת חֲרָדָה לַדִּין, וְלַהַט אֵשׁ אֲשֶׁר תֹּאכַל אֶת הָאוֹיְבִים
ella tzippiyat charadah ledin, velahat esh asher tochal et ha'oyevim
but a certain fearful expectation of judgment, and a fierceness of fire which shall devour the adversaries.

הַמֵּפֵר אֶת תּוֹרַת מֹשֶׁה יוּמַת בְּלִי חֶמְלָה עַל־פִּי שְׁנֵי עֵדִים אוֹ עַל־פִּי שְׁלֹשָׁה־עֵדִים
hammefer et torat mosheh yumat beli chemlah al-pi shenei edim o al-pi sheloshah-'edim
A man that hath set at nought Moses' law dieth without compassion on the word of two or three witnesses:

כַּמָּה וְכַמָּה גָּדוֹל יוֹתֵר יִהְיֶה, לְפִי דַעְתְּכֶם, הָעֹנֶשׁ הָרָאוּי לְמִי שֶׁרוֹמֵס בְּרַגְלוֹ אֶת בֶּן־הָאֱלֹהִים
kammah vechammah gadol yoter yihyeh, lefi da'techem, ha'onesh hara'ui lemi sheromes beraglo et ben-ha'elohim
of how much sorer punishment, think ye, shall he be judged worthy, who hath trodden under foot the Son of God,

וּמְזַלְזֵל בְּדַם הַבְּרִית אֲשֶׁר הוּא מְקֻדָּשׁ בּוֹ
umezalzel bedam habbrit asher hu mekuddash bo
and hath counted the blood of the covenant wherewith he was sanctified an unholy thing,

וּמְחָרֵף אֶת רוּחַ הַחֶסֶד
umecharef et ruach hachesed
and hath done despite unto the Spirit of grace?

הֲרֵי מַכִּירִים אֲנַחְנוּ אֶת מִי שֶׁאָמַר, לִי נָקָם וְשִׁלֵּם
harei makkirim anachnu et mi she'amar, li nakam veshillem
For we know him that said, Vengeance belongeth unto me, I will recompense.

הָעִבְרִים

וּמֵאָז הוּא מְחַכֶּה עַד אֲשֶׁר יוּשְׁתוּ אוֹיְבָיו הֲדֹם לְרַגְלָיו
ume'az hu mechakkeh ad asher yushetu oyevav hadom leraglav
henceforth expecting till his enemies be made the footstool of his feet.

שֶׁכֵּן בְּקָרְבָּן אֶחָד הִשְׁלִים לְתָמִיד אֶת הַמְקֻדָּשִׁים
shekken bekorban echad hishlim letamid et hamkuddashim
For by one offering he hath perfected for ever them that are sanctified.

וְגַם רוּחַ הַקֹּדֶשׁ מְעִידָה לָנוּ עַל זֹאת, כִּי לְאַחַר שֶׁאָמַר
vegam ruach hakkodesh me'idah lanu al zot, ki le'achar she'amar
And the Holy Spirit also beareth witness to us; for after he hath said,

זֹאת הַבְּרִית אֲשֶׁר אֶכְרֹת אִתָּם אַחֲרֵי הַיָּמִים הָהֵם, נְאֻם־יְהוָה
zot habberit asher echrot ittam acharei hayamim hahem, ne'um-hashem
This is the covenant that I will make with them After those days, saith the Lord:

נָתַתִּי אֶת־תּוֹרָתִי בְּקִרְבָּם וְעַל־לִבָּם אֶכְתֳּבֶנָּה
natatti et-torati bekirbam ve'al-libbam echtovennah
I will put my laws on their heart, And upon their mind also will I write them; then saith he,

הוּא אוֹמֵר, וְלַעֲוֹנָם וּלְחַטֹּאתָם לֹא אֶזְכָּר־עוֹד
hu omer, vela'avonam ulechattatam lo ezkor-'od
And their sins and their iniquities will I remember no more.

וּבְמָקוֹם שֶׁהַלָּלוּ נִסְלָחִים אֵין עוֹד קָרְבָּן עַל חֲטָאִים
uvemakom shehallalu nislachim ein od korban al chata'im
Now where remission of these is, there is no more offering for sin.

לָכֵן, אַחַי, מִכֵּיוָן שֶׁיֵּשׁ לָנוּ בִּטָּחוֹן לְהִכָּנֵס אֶל הַקֹּדֶשׁ בְּדַם יֵשׁוּעַ
lachen, achai, mikkeivan sheyesh lanu bittachon lehikkanes el hakkodesh bedam yeshua
Having therefore, brethren, boldness to enter into the holy place by the blood of Jesus,

בְּדֶרֶךְ חֲדָשָׁה וְחַיָּה אֲשֶׁר הוּא חָנַךְ לָנוּ דֶּרֶךְ הַפָּרֹכֶת, שֶׁהִיא בְּשָׂרוֹ
bederech chadashah vechayah asher hu chanach lanu derech happarochet, shehi besaro
by the way which he dedicated for us, a new and living way, through the veil, that is to say, his flesh;

וּבִהְיוֹת לָנוּ כֹּהֵן גָּדוֹל עַל בֵּית אֱלֹהִים
uvihyot lanu kohen gadol al beit elohim
and having a great priest over the house of God;

נִתְקָרְבָה נָא בְּלֵבָב שָׁלֵם וּבִמְלוֹא וַדָּאוּת הָאֱמוּנָה, כְּשֶׁלִּבּוֹתֵינוּ מְטֹהָרִים מֵהַרְשָׁעַת מַצְפּוּן
nitkarevah na belevav shalem uvimlo vadda'ut ha'emunah, kshellibboteinu metoharim meharsha'at matzpun
let us draw near with a true heart in fulness of faith, having our hearts sprinkled from an evil conscience:

וְהַגּוּף רָחוּץ בְּמַיִם טְהוֹרִים
vehagguf rachutz bemayim tehorim
and having our body washed with pure water,

הָעִבְרִים

שֶׁכֵּן דַּם פָּרִים וּשְׂעִירִים אֵינוֹ יָכוֹל לְהָסִיר חֲטָאִים
shekken dam parim use'irim eino yachol lehasir chata'im
For it is impossible that the blood of bulls and goats should take away sins.

לָכֵן בְּהִכָּנְסוֹ אֶל הָעוֹלָם הוּא אוֹמֵר
lachen behikkaneso el ha'olam hu omer
Wherefore when he cometh into the world, he saith,

זֶבַח וּמִנְחָה לֹא־חָפַצְתָּ, גּוּף כּוֹנַנְתָּ לִי
zevach uminchah lo-chafatzta, guf konanta li
Sacrifice and offering thou wouldest not, But a body didst thou prepare for me;

עוֹלָה וַחֲטָאָה לֹא שָׁאַלְתָּ
olah vachata'ah lo sha'aleta
In whole burnt offerings and sacrifices for sin thou hadst no pleasure:

אָז אָמַרְתִּי: הִנֵּה־בָאתִי - בִּמְגִלַּת־סֵפֶר כָּתוּב עָלָי - לַעֲשׂוֹת־רְצוֹנְךָ, אֱלֹהָי
az amarti. hinneh-vati - bimgillat-sefer katuv alai - la'asot-retzonecha, elohai
Then said I, Lo, I am come (In the roll of the book it is written of me) To do thy will, O God.

בְּאָמְרוֹ לְעֵיל, זֶבַח וּמִנְחָה וְעוֹלָה וַחֲטָאָה לֹא חָפַצְתָּ
be'amero le'eil, zevach uminchah ve'olah vachata'ah lo chafatzta
Saying above, Sacrifices and offerings and whole burnt offerings and sacrifices for sin thou wouldest not,

אַף לֹא שָׁאַלְתָּ, אֲשֶׁר מַקְרִיבִים אוֹתָם עַל־פִּי הַתּוֹרָה
af lo sha'aleta, asher makrivim otam al-pi hattorah
neither hadst pleasure therein (the which are offered according to the law),

וּבְאָמְרוֹ אַחֲרֵי כֵן, הִנֵּה בָאתִי לַעֲשׂוֹת רְצוֹנְךָ, מֵסִיר הוּא אֶת הָרִאשׁוֹנָה כְּדֵי לְהָקִים אֶת הַשְּׁנִיָּה
uve'omro acharei chen, hinneh vati la'asot retzonecha, mesir hu et harishonah kedei lehakim et hashniyah
then hath he said, Lo, I am come to do thy will. He taketh away the first, that he may establish the second.

וּבְאוֹתוֹ הָרָצוֹן מְקֻדָּשִׁים אֲנַחְנוּ עַל־יְדֵי הַקְרָבַת גּוּפוֹ שֶׁל יֵשׁוּעַ הַמָּשִׁיחַ פַּעַם אַחַת וּלְתָמִיד
uve'oto haratzon mekuddashim anachnu al-yedei hakravat gufo shel yeshua hammashiach pa'am achat uletamid
By which will we have been sanctified through the offering of the body of Jesus Christ once for all.

כָּל כֹּהֵן עוֹמֵד יוֹם יוֹם לְשָׁרֵת בַּקֹּדֶשׁ וּמַקְרִיב פְּעָמִים רַבּוֹת אֶת אוֹתָם הַקָּרְבָּנוֹת
kol kohen omed yom yom lesharet bakkodesh umakriv pe'amim rabbot et otam hakkorbanot
And every priest indeed standeth day by day ministering and offering oftentimes the same sacrifices,

אֲשֶׁר אַף פַּעַם אֵינָם יְכוֹלִים לְהָסִיר חֲטָאִים
asher af pa'am einam yecholim lehasir chata'im
the which can never take away sins:

אֲבָל זֶה, לְאַחַר שֶׁהִקְרִיב קָרְבָּן אֶחָד עַל הַחֲטָאִים, יָשַׁב לִימִין הָאֱלֹהִים לְתָמִיד
aval zeh, le'achar shehikriv korban echad al hachata'im, yashav liymin ha'elohim letamid
but he, when he had offered one sacrifice for sins for ever, sat down on the right hand of God;

הָעִבְרִים

כַּכֹּהֵן הַגָּדוֹל הַנִּכְנָס שָׁנָה בְּשָׁנָה אֶל הַקֹּדֶשׁ בְּדָם אֲשֶׁר אֵינוֹ דָּמוֹ
kakkohen haggadol hannichnas shanah beshanah el hakkodesh bedam asher eino damo
as the high priest entereth into the holy place year by year with blood not his own;

שֶׁאִם כֵּן, הָיָה צָרִיךְ לִסְבֹּל פְּעָמִים רַבּוֹת מֵאָז הִוָּסֵד תֵּבֵל
she'im ken, hayah tzarich lisbol pe'amim rabbot me'az hivvased tevel
else must he often have suffered since the foundation of the world:

אֲבָל כָּעֵת נִגְלָה פַּעַם אַחַת, בְּקֵץ הָעוֹלָמִים, לְהָסִיר אֶת הַחֵטְא בְּקָרְבַּן עַצְמוֹ
aval ka'et niglah pa'am achat, beketz ha'olamim, lehasir et hachet bekorban atzmo
but now once at the end of the ages hath he been manifested to put away sin by the sacrifice of himself.

וּכְשֵׁם שֶׁנִּגְזַר עַל בְּנֵי אָדָם לָמוּת פַּעַם אַחַת וְאַחֲרֵי כֵן הַמִּשְׁפָּט
ucheshem shennigzar al benei adam lamut pa'am achat ve'acharei chen hammishpat
And inasmuch as it is appointed unto men once to die, and after this cometh judgment;

כָּךְ גַּם הַמָּשִׁיחַ, אַחֲרֵי שֶׁהֻקְרַב פַּעַם אַחַת לָשֵׂאת חֲטָאֵי רַבִּים, יוֹפִיעַ שֵׁנִית
kach gam hammashiach, acharei shehukrav pa'am achat laset chata'ei rabbim, yofia shenit
so Christ also, having been once offered to bear the sins of many, shall appear a second time,

־שֶׁלֹּא לְעִנְיָן הַחֵטְא - לַמְחַכִּים לוֹ לִישׁוּעָה
shello le'inyan hachet - lamchakkim lo liyshu'ah
apart from sin, to them that wait for him, unto salvation.

∎

הַתּוֹרָה, אֲשֶׁר צֵל הַטּוֹבוֹת הָעֲתִידוֹת בָּהּ וְלֹא עֶצֶם צֶלֶם הַדְּבָרִים
hattorah, asher tzel hattovot ha'atidot bah velo etzem tzelem haddevarim
For the law having a shadow of the good things to come, not the very image of the things,

אַף פַּעַם אֵינָהּ יְכוֹלָה לְהָבִיא לִידֵי שְׁלֵמוּת עַל־יְדֵי אוֹתָם הַקָּרְבָּנוֹת אֶת הַבָּאִים לְהַקְרִיבָם בְּהַתְמָדָה שָׁנָה בְּשָׁנָה
af pa'am einah yecholah lehavi liydei shelemut al-yedei otam hakkarebanot et habba'im lehakrivam behatmadah shanah beshanah
can never with the same sacrifices year by year, which they offer continually, make perfect them that draw nigh.

אִלּוּ יָכְלָה לַעֲשׂוֹת כֵּן, הָיְתָה מֻפְסֶקֶת הַקְרָבָתָם
illu yachelah la'asot ken, hayetah mufseket hakravatam
Else would they not have ceased to be offered?

כִּי לְאַחַר שֶׁהַמְשָׁרְתִים בַּקֹּדֶשׁ הָיוּ נִטְהָרִים פַּעַם אַחַת, לֹא הָיְתָה בָּהֶם עוֹד הַכָּרַת חֵטְא
ki le'achar shehamsharetim bakkodesh hayu nit'harim pa'am achat, lo hayetah bahem od hakkarat chet
because the worshippers, having been once cleansed, would have had no more consciousness of sins.

אֲבָל יֵשׁ בַּקָּרְבָּנוֹת הַלָּלוּ זִכְרוֹן חֲטָאִים מִדֵּי שָׁנָה בְּשָׁנָה
aval yesh bakkarebanot hallalu zichron chata'im middei shanah beshanah
But in those sacrifices there is a remembrance made of sins year by year.

הָעִבְרִים

כִּי כְּכַלּוֹת מֹשֶׁה לוֹמַר לְכָל הָעָם כָּל מִצְוָה לְפִי הַתּוֹרָה,
ki kechallot mosheh lomar lechol ha'am kol mitzvah lefi hattorah
For when every commandment had been spoken by Moses unto all the people according to the law,

לָקַח אֶת דַּם הָעֲגָלִים וְהַשְּׂעִירִים עִם מַיִם וְתוֹלַעַת שָׁנִי וְאֵזוֹב
lakach et dam ha'agalim vehasse'irim im mayim vetola'at shani ve'ezov
he took the blood of the calves and the goats, with water and scarlet wool and hyssop,

וְזָרַק אוֹתָם עַל הַסֵּפֶר וְעַל כָּל הָעָם
vezarak otam al hassefer ve'al kol ha'am
and sprinkled both the book itself and all the people,

בְּאָמְרוֹ, הִנֵּה דַם־הַבְּרִית אֲשֶׁר צִוָּה אֶתְכֶם אֱלֹהִים
be'omro, hinneh dam-habberit asher tzivvah etchem elohim
saying, This is the blood of the covenant which God commanded to you-ward.

וְכֵן גַּם עַל הַמִּשְׁכָּן וְעַל כָּל כְּלֵי הַשָּׁרֵת הִזָּה אֶת הַדָּם
vechen gam al hammishkan ve'al kol klei hasharet hizzah et haddam
Moreover the tabernacle and all the vessels of the ministry he sprinkled in like manner with the blood.

אָכֵן עַל־פִּי הַתּוֹרָה כִּמְעַט הַכֹּל מְטֹהָר בְּדָם
achen al-pi hattorah kim'at hakkol metohar bedam
And according to the law, I may almost say, all things are cleansed with blood,

וּבְלֹא שְׁפִיכַת דָּם אֵין מְחִילָה
uvelo shefichat dam ein mechilah
and apart from shedding of blood there is no remission.

לָכֵן הָיָה צָרִיךְ לְטַהֵר עַל־יְדֵי אֵלֶּה אֶת הַדְּבָרִים אֲשֶׁר הֵם תַּבְנִית הַדְּבָרִים הַנִּמְצָאִים בַּשָּׁמַיִם
lachen hayah tzarich letaher al-yedei elleh et haddevarim asher hem tavnit haddevarim hannimtza'im bashamayim
It was necessary therefore that the copies of the things in the heavens should be cleansed with these;

אֲבָל הַדְּבָרִים הַשְּׁמֵימִיִּים עַצְמָם דּוֹרְשִׁים זְבָחִים טוֹבִים מֵאֵלֶּה
aval haddevarim hashmeimiyim atzmam doreshim zevachim tovim me'elleh
but the heavenly things themselves with better sacrifices than these.

הֲרֵי הַמָּשִׁיחַ לֹא נִכְנַס אֶל מִקְדָּשׁ אֲשֶׁר נַעֲשָׂה בִּידֵי אָדָם וַאֲשֶׁר הוּא בָּבוּאָה שֶׁל הָאֲמִתִּי
harei hammashiach lo nichnas el mikdash asher na'asah biydei adam va'asher hu bavu'ah shel ha'amitti
For Christ entered not into a holy place made with hands, like in pattern to the true;

כִּי אִם בָּא אֶל עֶצֶם הַשָּׁמַיִם לְהֵרָאוֹת עַתָּה בַּעֲדֵנוּ לִפְנֵי הָאֱלֹהִים
ki im ba el etzem hashamayim lehera'ot attah ba'adenu lifnei ha'elohim
but into heaven itself, now to appear before the face of God for us:

אַף לֹא בָא לְהַקְרִיב אֶת עַצְמוֹ פְּעָמִים רַבּוֹת
af lo ba lehakriv et atzmo pe'amim rabbot
nor yet that he should offer himself often,

הָעִבְרִים

וּבְדָמוֹ הוּא, וְלֹא בְדַם שְׂעִירִים וַעֲגָלִים
uvedamo hu, velo bedam se'irim va'agalim
nor yet through the blood of goats and calves, but through his own blood,

נִכְנַס אַחַת וּלְתָמִיד אֶל הַקֹּדֶשׁ וְהִשִּׂיג פְּדוּת עוֹלָמִים
nichnas achat uletamid el hakkodesh vehissig pedut olamim
entered in once for all into the holy place, having obtained eternal redemption.

שֶׁכֵּן אִם דַּם פָּרִים וּשְׂעִירִים וְאֵפֶר הַפָּרָה, בְּהִזָּרְקָם עַל הַטְּמֵאִים
shekken im dam parim use'irim ve'efer happarah, behizzarekam al hattme'im
For if the blood of goats and bulls, and the ashes of a heifer sprinkling them that have been defiled,

יְקַדְּשׁוּ עַד כְּדֵי לְטַהֵר אֶת הַגּוּף
yekaddeshu ad kedei letaher et hagguf
sanctify unto the cleanness of the flesh:

עַל אַחַת כַּמָּה וְכַמָּה דָּמוֹ שֶׁל הַמָּשִׁיחַ אֲשֶׁר הִקְרִיב עַצְמוֹ לֵאלֹהִים בְּרוּחַ עוֹלָמִים וּבְלֹא מוּם
al achat kammah vechammah damo shel hammashiach asher hikriv atzmo le'elohim beruach olamim uvelo mum
how much more shall the blood of Christ, who through the eternal Spirit offered himself without blemish unto God,

יְטַהֵר אֶת מַצְפּוּנֵנוּ מִמַּעֲשֵׂי מָוֶת כְּדֵי שֶׁנַּעֲבֹד אֶת אֱלֹהִים חַיִּים
yetaher et matzpunenu mimma'asei mavet kedei shenna'avod et elohim chayim
cleanse your conscience from dead works to serve the living God?

לָכֵן הוּא מְתַוֵּךְ לִבְרִית חֲדָשָׁה
lachen hu metavvech livrit chadashah
And for this cause he is the mediator of a new covenant,

וְעַל־יְדֵי כָּךְ - מֵאַחַר שֶׁמֵּת לִפְדוֹת מִן הַפְּשָׁעִים אֲשֶׁר נַעֲשׂוּ בִּימֵי הַבְּרִית הָרִאשׁוֹנָה
ve'al-yedei kach - me'achar shemmet lifdot min happesha'im asher na'asu bimei habbrit harishonah
that a death having taken place for the redemption of the transgressions that were under the first covenant,

יְקַבְּלוּ הַמְקֹרָאִים אֶת נַחֲלַת עוֹלָם הַמֻּבְטַחַת
yekabbelu hamkora'im et nachalat olam hammuvtachat
they that have been called may receive the promise of the eternal inheritance.

הֵן בְּהִמָּצֵא צַוָּאָה צָרִיךְ שֶׁיְּאֻשַּׁר דְּבַר מוֹתוֹ שֶׁל בַּעַל הַצַּוָּאָה
hen behimmatzei tzavva'ah tzarich sheye'ushar devar moto shel ba'al hatzavva'ah
For where a testament is, there must of necessity be the death of him that made it.

כִּי רַק בְּמוֹת הַמֵּת תִּכֹּן הַצַּוָּאָה, וְאֵין לָהּ תֹּקֶף כָּל עוֹד חַי בַּעַל הַצַּוָּאָה
ki rak bemot hammet tikkon hatzavva'ah, ve'ein lah tokef kol od chai ba'al hatzavva'ah
For a testament is of force where there hath been death: for it doth never avail while he that made it liveth.

לָכֵן גַּם חֲנֻכַּת הַבְּרִית הָרִאשׁוֹנָה לֹא הָיְתָה בְּלִי דָם
lachen gam chanukkat habberit harishonah lo hayetah beli dam
Wherefore even the first covenant hath not been dedicated without blood.

הָעִבְרִים

בִּהְיוֹת כָּל אֵלֶּה עֲרוּכִים כָּךְ
bihyot kol elleh aruchim kach
Now these things having been thus prepared,

נִכְנָסִים הַכֹּהֲנִים בִּקְבִיעוּת אֶל הַמִּשְׁכָּן הַחִיצוֹן לְמַלֵּא אֶת שֵׁרוּתָם
nichnasim hakkohanim bikvi'ut el hammishkan hachitzon lemallei et sherutam
the priests go in continually into the first tabernacle, accomplishing the services;

אֲבָל אֶל הַמִּשְׁכָּן הַפְּנִימִי נִכְנָס הַכֹּהֵן הַגָּדוֹל לְבַדּוֹ פַּעַם אַחַת בְּשָׁנָה
aval el hammishkan happenimi nichnas hakkohen haggadol levaddo pa'am achat beshanah
but into the second the high priest alone, once in the year,

לֹא בְּלִי דָּם אֲשֶׁר הוּא מַקְרִיב בְּעַד עַצְמוֹ וּבְעַד שִׁגְגוֹת הָעָם
lo bli dam asher hu makriv be'ad atzmo uve'ad shigegot ha'am
not without blood, which he offereth for himself, and for the errors of the people:

בָּזֹאת רוּחַ הַקֹּדֶשׁ מוֹדִיעָה שֶׁהַדֶּרֶךְ אֶל הַקֹּדֶשׁ אֵינָהּ נִגְלֵית
bazot ruach hakkodesh modi'ah shehadderech el hakkodesh einah nigleit
the Holy Spirit this signifying, that the way into the holy place hath not yet been made manifest,

כָּל עוֹד הַמִּשְׁכָּן הַחִיצוֹן עוֹמֵד עַל מְכוֹנוֹ
kol od hammishkan hachitzon omed al mechono
while the first tabernacle is yet standing;

וְזֶה מָשָׁל לַזְּמַן הַזֶּה, כַּאֲשֶׁר מַקְרִיבִים מְנָחוֹת וּזְבָחִים
vezeh mashal lazzeman hazzeh, ka'asher makrivim menachot uzevachim
which is a figure for the time present; according to which are offered both gifts and sacrifices

שֶׁאֵינָם יְכוֹלִים לְהָבִיא אֶת מְשָׁרֵת הַקֹּדֶשׁ לִידֵי שְׁלֵמוּת בְּמַצְפּוּנוֹ
she'einam yecholim lehavi et mesharet hakkodesh liydei shelemut bematzpuno
that cannot, as touching the conscience, make the worshipper perfect,

וְשֶׁאֵינָם אֶלָּא כְרוּכִים בְּמַאֲכָל וּבְמַשְׁקֶה וּבְמִינֵי טְבִילוֹת
veshe'einam ella keruchim bema'achal uvemashkeh uveminei tevilot
being only (with meats and drinks and divers washings)

פִּקּוּדֵי־תוֹרָה חִיצוֹנִיִּים אֲשֶׁר נִתְּנוּ עַד עֵת תִּקּוּן
pikkudei-torah chitzoniyim asher nittenu ad et tikkun
carnal ordinances, imposed until a time of reformation.

אֲבָל הַמָּשִׁיחַ, בְּבוֹאוֹ לִהְיוֹת כֹּהֵן גָּדוֹל לַטּוֹבוֹת הָעֲתִידוֹת, עָבַר בְּמִשְׁכָּן גָּדוֹל וּמֻשְׁלָם יוֹתֵר
aval hammashiach, bevo'o lihyot kohen gadol lattovot ha'atidot, avar bemishkan gadol umushlam yoter
But Christ having come a high priest of the good things to come, through the greater and more perfect tabernacle,

שֶׁאֵינוֹ מַעֲשֵׂה יָדַיִם - כְּלוֹמַר, שֶׁאֵינוֹ שַׁיָּךְ לַבְּרִיאָה הַזֹּאת
she'eino ma'aseh yadayim - klomar, she'eino shayach labberi'ah hazzot
not made with hands, that is to say, not of this creation,

הָעִבְרִים

כִּי כוּלָּם יֵדְעוּ אוֹתִי לְמִקְּטַנָּם וְעַד־גְּדוֹלָם
ki chullam yede'u oti lemikketannam ve'ad-gedolam
For all shall know me, From the least to the greatest of them.

כִּי אֶסְלַח לַעֲוֹנָם, וּלְחַטָּאתָם לֹא אֶזְכָּר־עוֹד
ki eslach la'avonam, ulechattatam lo ezkor-'od
For I will be merciful to their iniquities, And their sins will I remember no more.

הִנֵּה בְּאָמְרוֹ בְּרִית חֲדָשָׁה יִשֵּׁן אֶת הָרִאשׁוֹנָה
hinneh be'amero brit chadashah yishen et harishonah
In that he saith, A new covenant, he hath made the first old.

וּמַה שֶּׁנּוֹשָׁן וּמַזְקִין קָרוֹב לַחֲלֹף
umah shenoshan umazkin karov lachalof
But that which is becoming old and waxeth aged is nigh unto vanishing away.

ט

וּבְכֵן לַבְּרִית הָרִאשׁוֹנָה הָיוּ גַם דִּינֵי עֲבוֹדָה וְגַם מִקְדָּשׁ גַּשְׁמִי בָּאָרֶץ
uvechen labberit harishonah hayu gam dinei avodah vegam mikdash gashmi ba'aretz
Now even the first covenant had ordinances of divine service, and its sanctuary, a sanctuary of this world.

כִּי הוּקַם מִשְׁכָּן חִיצוֹן אֲשֶׁר בּוֹ הַמְּנוֹרָה
ki hukam mishkan chitzon asher bo hammenorah
For there was a tabernacle prepared, the first, wherein were the candlestick,

וְהַשֻּׁלְחָן וְלֶחֶם הַפָּנִים, וְהוּא נִקְרָא קֹדֶשׁ
vehashulchan velechem happanim, vehu nikra kodesh
and the table, and the showbread; which is called the Holy place.

וּמִבֵּית לַפָּרֹכֶת הַשְּׁנִיָּה מִשְׁכָּן הַנִּקְרָא קֹדֶשׁ הַקֳּדָשִׁים
umibbeit lapparochet hasheniyah mishkan hannikra kodesh hakkodashim
And after the second veil, the tabernacle which is called the Holy of holies;

וּבוֹ מִזְבַּח זָהָב לִקְטֹרֶת וַאֲרוֹן הַבְּרִית הַמְצֻפֶּה זָהָב סָבִיב
uvo mizbach zahav liktoret va'aron habbrit hamtzuppeh zahav saviv
having a golden altar of incense, and the ark of the covenant overlaid round about with gold,

וּבָאָרוֹן צִנְצֶנֶת זָהָב אֲשֶׁר הַמָּן בְּתוֹכָהּ, מַטֵּה אַהֲרֹן אֲשֶׁר פָּרַח, וְלוּחוֹת הַבְּרִית
uva'aron tzintzenet zahav asher hamman betochah, matteh aharon asher parach, veluchot habberit
wherein was a golden pot holding the manna, and Aaron's rod that budded, and the tables of the covenant;

וּמִמַּעַל לוֹ כְּרוּבֵי הַכָּבוֹד הַסּוֹכְכִים עַל הַכַּפֹּרֶת. לֹא נְדַבֵּר כָּעֵת עַל כָּל אֶחָד וְאֶחָד מֵהֶם
umimma'al lo keruvei hakkavod hassochechim al hakkapporet. lo nedabber ka'et al kol echad ve'echad mehem
and above it cherubim of glory overshadowing the mercy-seat; of which things we cannot now speak severally.

הָעִבְרִים

בְּאוֹתָהּ מִדָּה שֶׁהוּא מְתַוֵּךְ שֶׁל בְּרִית מְעֻלָּה יוֹתֵר אֲשֶׁר נוֹסְדָה עַל הַבְטָחוֹת טוֹבוֹת יוֹתֵר
be'otah middah shehu metavvech shel berit me'ullah yoter asher nosedah al havtachot tovot yoter
by so much as he is also the mediator of a better covenant, which hath been enacted upon better promises.

אִלּוּ הָיְתָה הַבְּרִית הָרִאשׁוֹנָה בְּלִי חִסָּרוֹן, לֹא הָיָה נִדְרָשׁ מָקוֹם לַשְּׁנִיָּה
illu hayetah habberit harishonah beli chissaron, lo hayah nidrash makom lashniyah
For if that first covenant had been faultless, then would no place have been sought for a second.

הֲלֹא בְּהוֹכִיחוֹ אוֹתָם הוּא אוֹמֵר
halo behochicho otam hu omer
For finding fault with them, he saith,

הִנֵּה יָמִים בָּאִים, נְאֻם־יהוה,
hinneh yamim ba'im, ne'um-hashem,
Behold, the days come, saith the Lord,

וְכָרַתִּי אֶת־בֵּית יִשְׂרָאֵל וְאֶת־בֵּית יְהוּדָה בְּרִית חֲדָשָׁה
vecharatti et-beit yisra'el ve'et-beit yehudah brit chadashah
That I will make a new covenant with the house of Israel and with the house of Judah;

לֹא כַבְּרִית אֲשֶׁר כָּרַתִּי אֶת־אֲבוֹתָם
lo chabberit asher karatti et-'avotam
Not according to the covenant that I made with their fathers

בְּיוֹם הֶחֱזִיקִי בְיָדָם לְהוֹצִיאָם מֵאֶרֶץ מִצְרָיִם
beyom hecheziki veyadam lehotzi'am me'eretz mitzrayim
In the day that I took them by the hand to lead them forth out of the land of Egypt;

אֲשֶׁר־הֵמָּה הֵפֵרוּ אֶת־בְּרִיתִי וְאָנֹכִי בָּחַלְתִּי בָם, נְאֻם־יהוה
asher-hemmah heferu et-briti ve'anochi bachalti vam, ne'um-hashem
For they continued not in my covenant, And I regarded them not, saith the Lord.

כִּי זֹאת הַבְּרִית אֲשֶׁר אֶכְרֹת אֶת־בֵּית יִשְׂרָאֵל אַחֲרֵי הַיָּמִים הָהֵם, נְאֻם־יהוה
ki zot habberit asher echrot et-beit yisra'el acharei hayamim hahem, ne'um-hashem
For this is the covenant that I will make with the house of Israel After those days, saith the Lord;

נָתַתִּי אֶת־תּוֹרָתִי בְּקִרְבָּם וְעַל־לִבָּם אֶכְתֳּבֶנָּה
natatti et-torati bekirbam ve'al-libbam echtovennah
I will put my laws into their mind, And on their heart also will I write them:

וְהָיִיתִי לָהֶם לֵאלֹהִים וְהֵמָּה יִהְיוּ־לִי לְעָם
vehayiti lahem le'elohim vehemmah yihyu-li le'am
And I will be to them a God, And they shall be to me a people:

וְלֹא יְלַמְּדוּ עוֹד אִישׁ אֶת־רֵעֵהוּ וְאִישׁ אֶת־אָחִיו לֵאמֹר, דְּעוּ אֶת יהוה
velo yelammdu od ish et-re'ehu ve'ish et-'achiyu le'emor, de'u et hashem
And they shall not teach every man his fellow-citizen, And every man his brother, saying, Know the Lord:

הָעִבְרִים

אַךְ דְּבַר הַשְּׁבוּעָה שֶׁנֶּאֱמַר לְאַחַר הַתּוֹרָה הֶעֱמִיד אֶת הַבֵּן אֲשֶׁר הֻשְׁלַם לְעוֹלָם
ach devar hashevu'ah shenne'emar le'achar hattorah he'emid et habben asher hushlam le'olam
but the word of the oath, which was after the law, appointeth a Son, perfected for evermore.

ח

עִקַּר הַדְּבָרִים שֶׁנֶּאֶמְרוּ הוּא
ikkar haddevarim shenne'emru hu
Now in the things which we are saying the chief point is this:

יֵשׁ לָנוּ כֹּהֵן גָּדוֹל הַיּוֹשֵׁב לִימִין כִּסֵּא הַגְּדֻלָּה בַּשָּׁמַיִם
yesh lanu kohen gadol hayoshev liymin kissei haggedullah bashamayim
We have such a high priest, who sat down on the right hand of the throne of the Majesty in the heavens,

וְהוּא מְשָׁרֵת בַּקֹּדֶשׁ וּבַמִּשְׁכָּן הָאֲמִתִּי אֲשֶׁר כּוֹנֵן יהוה וְלֹא אָדָם
vehu mesharet bakkodesh uvammishkan ha'amitti asher konen hashem velo adam
a minister of the sanctuary, and of the true tabernacle, which the Lord pitched, not man.

כָּל כֹּהֵן גָּדוֹל תַּפְקִידוֹ לְהַקְרִיב מְנָחוֹת וּזְבָחִים
kol kohen gadol tafkido lehakriv menachot uzvachim
For every high priest is appointed to offer both gifts and sacrifices:

לָכֵן צָרִיךְ שֶׁגַּם זֶה יִהְיֶה לוֹ מַה לְהַקְרִיב
lachen tzarich sheggam zeh yihyeh lo mah lehakriv
wherefore it is necessary that this high priest also have somewhat to offer.

אִלּוּ הָיָה בָּאָרֶץ לֹא הָיָה כֹהֵן, כִּי יֵשׁ פֹּה כֹּהֲנִים הַמַּקְרִיבִים מְנָחוֹת לְפִי הַתּוֹרָה
illu hayah ba'aretz lo hayah kohen, ki yesh poh kohanim hammakrivim menachot lefi hattorah
Now if he were on earth, he would not be a priest at all, seeing there are those who offer the gifts according to the law;

וּמְשָׁרְתִים בַּקֹּדֶשׁ לְפִי תַּבְנִית וְצֵל שֶׁל הַדְּבָרִים הַשְּׁמֵימִיִּים,
umesharetim bakkodesh lefi tavnit vetzel shel haddevarim hashemeimiyim
who serve that which is a copy and shadow of the heavenly things,

כְּפִי שֶׁצֻּוָּה מֹשֶׁה בְּבוֹאוֹ לְהָקִים אֶת הַמִּשְׁכָּן
kefi shetzuvvah mosheh bevo'o lehakim et hammishkan
even as Moses is warned of God when he is about to make the tabernacle:

הֵן אָמַר אֵלָיו, רְאֵה וַעֲשֵׂה הַכֹּל כְּתַבְנִית אֲשֶׁר־אַתָּה מָרְאֶה בָּהָר
hen amar elav, re'eh va'aseh hakkol ketavnit asher-'attah mare'eh bahar
for, See, saith he, that thou make all things according to the pattern that was showed thee in the mount.

וְהִנֵּה יֵשׁוּעַ הִשִּׂיג כְּהֻנָּה נַעֲלָה יוֹתֵר
vehinneh yeshua hissig kehunnah na'alah yoter
But now hath he obtained a ministry the more excellent,

הָעִבְרִים

אָמְנָם הַלָּלוּ הָיוּ לְכֹהֲנִים בְּלִי שְׁבוּעָה, אַךְ הוּא בִּשְׁבוּעָה, עַל־יְדֵי הָאוֹמֵר לוֹ
omnam hallalu hayu lechohanim beli shevu'ah, ach hu bishvu'ah, al-yedei ha'omer lo
(for they indeed have been made priests without an oath; but he with an oath by him that saith of him,

נִשְׁבַּע יהוה וְלֹא יִנָּחֵם, אַתָּה־כֹהֵן לְעוֹלָם עַל־דִּבְרָתִי מַלְכִּי־צֶדֶק
nishba hashem velo yinnachem, attah-chohen le'olam al-divrati malki-tzedek
The Lord sware and will not repent himself, Thou art a priest for ever);

כָּךְ גַּם טוֹבָה יוֹתֵר הַבְּרִית אֲשֶׁר יֵשׁוּעַ נִהְיָה עָרֵב לָהּ
kach gam tovah yoter habberit asher yeshua nihyah arev lah
by so much also hath Jesus become the surety of a better covenant.

וְרַבִּים הָיוּ לְכֹהֲנִים, כִּי הַמָּוֶת מְנָעָם מִלְהַמְשִׁיךְ בַּכְּהֻנָּה
verabbim hayu lechohanim, ki hammavet mena'am millehamshich bakkehunah
And they indeed have been made priests many in number, because that by death they are hindered from continuing:

אֲבָל זֶה, מִכֵּיוָן שֶׁהוּא נִשְׁאָר לְעוֹלָם, יֵשׁ לוֹ כְּהֻנָּה שֶׁאֵינֶנָּה עוֹבֶרֶת
aval zeh, mikkeivan shehu nish'ar le'olam, yesh lo kehunnah she'einennah overet
but he, because he abideth for ever, hath his priesthood unchangeable.

לָכֵן הוּא גַם יָכוֹל לְהוֹשִׁיעַ לָנֶצַח אֶת הַבָּאִים לֵאלֹהִים דַּרְכּוֹ
lachen hu gam yachol lehoshia lanetzach et habba'im lelohim darko
Wherefore also he is able to save to the uttermost them that draw near unto God through him,

כִּי חַי הוּא תָּמִיד כְּדֵי לְהַפְגִּיעַ בַּעֲדָם
ki chai hu tamid kedei lehafgia ba'adam
seeing he ever liveth to make intercession for them.

אָכֵן כֹּהֵן גָּדוֹל כָּזֶה יָאֶה לָנוּ - קָדוֹשׁ, תָּמִים, טָהוֹר, נִבְדָּל מֵחוֹטְאִים וְנִשָּׂא מֵעַל הַשָּׁמַיִם
achen kohen gadol kazeh ya'eh lanu - kadosh, tamim, tahor, nivdal mechote'im venisho me'al hashamayim
For such a high priest became us, holy, guileless, undefiled, separated from sinners, and made higher than the heavens;

אֲשֶׁר אֵינוֹ צָרִיךְ יוֹם יוֹם, כַּכֹּהֲנִים הַגְּדוֹלִים, תְּחִלָּה לְהַקְרִיב קָרְבָּנוֹת
asher eino tzarich yom yom, kakkohanim haggedolim, techillah lehakriv korbanot
who needeth not daily, like those high priests, to offer up sacrifices,

עַל חֲטָאָיו וְאַחֲרֵי כֵן עַל חֲטָאֵי הָעָם
al chata'av ve'acharei chen al chata'ei ha'am
first for his own sins, and then for the sins of the people:

כִּי זֹאת עָשָׂה אַחַת וּלְתָמִיד בְּהַקְרִיבוֹ אֶת עַצְמוֹ
ki zot asah achat uletamid behakrivo et atzmo
for this he did once for all, when he offered up himself.

הֵן הַתּוֹרָה מְמַנָּה בְּנֵי אָדָם חֲלָשִׁים לְתַפְקִיד שֶׁל כֹּהֲנִים גְּדוֹלִים
hen hattorah minnetah benei adam chalashim letafkid shel kohanim gedolim
For the law appointeth men high priests, having infirmity;

הָעִבְרִים

לָכֵן אִלּוּ הֻשְׂגָּה שְׁלֵמוּת עַל־יְדֵי כְּהֻנַּת לֵוִי, שֶׁבִּזְמַנָּהּ קִבֵּל הָעָם אֶת הַתּוֹרָה
lachen illu hussgah shelemut al-yedei kehunnat levi, shebbizmannah kibbel ha'am et hattorah
Now if there was perfection through the Levitical priesthood (for under it hath the people received the law),

מַה צֹּרֶךְ עוֹד שֶׁיָּקוּם כֹּהֵן אַחֵר עַל־דִּבְרָתִי מַלְכִּי־צֶדֶק
mah tzorech od sheyakum kohen acher al-divrati malki-tzedek
what further need was there that another priest should arise after the order of Melchizedek,

וְלֹא יִקָּרֵא עַל־דִּבְרָתִי אַהֲרֹן
velo yikkarei al-divrati aharon
and not be reckoned after the order of Aaron?

אָכֵן כַּאֲשֶׁר מִשְׁתַּנֵּית הַכְּהֻנָּה, מִן הַהֶכְרֵחַ שֶׁתִּשְׁתַּנֶּה גַּם הַתּוֹרָה
achen ka'asher mishtanneit hakkehunnah, min hahechreach shettishtanneh gam hattorah
For the priesthood being changed, there is made of necessity a change also of the law.

וּמִי שֶׁנֶּאֱמַר עָלָיו הַדָּבָר הַזֶּה שַׁיָּךְ לְשֵׁבֶט אַחֵר אֲשֶׁר אִישׁ מִבָּנָיו לֹא שֵׁרֵת בַּמִּזְבֵּחַ
umi shenne'emar alav haddavar hazzeh shayach leshevet acher asher ish mibbanav lo sheret bammizbeach
For he of whom these things are said belongeth to another tribe, from which no man hath given attendance at the altar.

הֵן גָּלוּי וְיָדוּעַ שֶׁאֲדוֹנֵנוּ צָמַח מִיהוּדָה, שֵׁבֶט אֲשֶׁר מֹשֶׁה לֹא דִּבֶּר עָלָיו דָּבָר בְּעִנְיַן כְּהֻנָּה
hen galui veyadua she'adonenu tzamach miyehudah, shevet asher mosheh lo dibber alav davar be'inyan kehunnah
For it is evident that our Lord hath sprung out of Judah; as to which tribe Moses spake nothing concerning priests.

וְזֶה בָּרוּר עוֹד יוֹתֵר כַּאֲשֶׁר, בְּדוֹמֶה לְמַלְכִּי־צֶדֶק, קָם כֹּהֵן אַחֵר
vezeh barur od yoter ka'asher, bedomeh lemalki-tzedek, kam kohen acher
And what we say is yet more abundantly evident, if after the likeness of Melchizedek there ariseth another priest,

שֶׁהָיָה לְכֹהֵן לֹא עַל־פִּי תּוֹרַת חֻקִּים הַתְּלוּיָה בְּבָשָׂר וָדָם, אֶלָּא מִתֹּקֶף כֹּחַ הַחַיִּים שֶׁאֵין לָהֶם הֶפְסֵק
shehayah lechohen lo al-pi torat chukkim hatteluyah bevasar vadam, ella mittokef koach hachayim she'ein lahem hefsek
who hath been made, not after the law of a carnal commandment, but after the power of an endless life:

הֵן הֵעִיד עָלָיו, אַתָּה־כֹהֵן לְעוֹלָם עַל־דִּבְרָתִי מַלְכִּי־צֶדֶק
hen he'id alav, attah-chohen le'olam al-divrati malki-tzedek
for it is witnessed of him, Thou art a priest for ever After the order of Melchizedek.

וְאָכֵן הַמִּצְוָה שֶׁנִּתְּנָה בֶּעָבָר מִתְבַּטֶּלֶת בִּגְלַל חֻלְשָׁתָהּ וְאִי יְכָלְתָּהּ לְהוֹעִיל
ve'achen hammitzvah shennittenah be'avar mitbattelet biglal chulshatah ve'i yechaletah leho'il
For there is a disannulling of a foregoing commandment because of its weakness and unprofitableness

שֶׁכֵּן הַתּוֹרָה לֹא הִשְׁלִימָה דָּבָר; לְעֻמַּת זֹאת בָּאָה תִּקְוָה טוֹבָה יוֹתֵר וְעַל־יָדֶיהָ אֲנַחְנוּ מִתְקָרְבִים לֵאלֹהִים
shekken hattorah lo hishlimah davar; le'ummat zot ba'ah tikvah tovah yoter ve'al-yadeiha anachnu mitkarevim le'elohim
(for the law made nothing perfect), and a bringing in thereupon of a better hope, through which we draw nigh unto God.

וּכְשֵׁם שֶׁזֶּה לֹא הָיָה בְּלִי שְׁבוּעָה
ucheshem shezzeh lo hayah beli shevu'ah
And inasmuch as it is not without the taking of an oath

הָעִבְרִים

בְּלֹא אָב, בְּלֹא אֵם, בְּלֹא צִיּוּן יוּחֲסִין
belo av, belo em, belo tziyun yuchasin
without father, without mother, without genealogy,

אֵין תְּחִלָּה לְיָמָיו וְגַם לֹא סוֹף לְחַיָּיו, וּבִהְיוֹתוֹ דּוֹמֶה לְבֶן־הָאֱלֹהִים הוּא נִשְׁאַר כֹּהֵן לְתָמִיד
ein techillah leyamav vegam lo sof lechayav, uvihyoto domeh leven-ha'elohim hu nish'ar kohen letamid
having neither beginning of days nor end of life, but made like unto the Son of God), abideth a priest continually.

רְאוּ מַה גָּדוֹל הוּא זֶה אֲשֶׁר אַבְרָהָם אָבִינוּ נָתַן לוֹ מַעֲשֵׂר מִמֵּיטַב הַשָּׁלָל
re'u mah gadol hu zeh asher avraham avinu natan lo ma'aser mimmeitav hashalal
Now consider how great this man was, unto whom Abraham, the patriarch, gave a tenth out of the chief spoils.

הֲלֹא בְּנֵי לֵוִי, הַיּוֹרְשִׁים אֶת הַכְּהֻנָּה, צֻוּוּ עַל־פִּי הַתּוֹרָה
halo benei levi, hayoreshim et hakkehunnah, tzivvu al-pi hattorah
And they indeed of the sons of Levi that receive the priest's office have commandment

לָקַחַת מַעֲשֵׂר מִן הָעָם, כְּלוֹמַר מֵאֲחֵיהֶם
lakachat ma'aser min ha'am, klomar me'acheihem
to take tithes of the people according to the law, that is, of their brethren,

הֲגַם שֶׁהַלָּלוּ יוֹצְאֵי יֶרֶךְ אַבְרָהָם
hagam shehallalu yotze'ei yerech avraham
though these have come out of the loins of Abraham:

אֲבָל הוּא אֲשֶׁר לֹא הִתְיַחֵשׂ עַל מִשְׁפַּחְתָּם לָקַח מַעֲשֵׂר מֵאַבְרָהָם
aval hu asher lo hityaches al mishpachtam lakach ma'aser me'avraham
but he whose genealogy is not counted from them hath taken tithes of Abraham,

וּבֵרַךְ אֶת זֶה שֶׁהָיוּ לוֹ הַהַבְטָחוֹת
uverech et zeh shehayu lo hahavtachot
and hath blessed him that hath the promises.

אֵין עוֹרְרִים עַל כָּךְ שֶׁהַקָּטֹן יְבֹרַךְ מִפִּי הַגָּדוֹל מִמֶּנּוּ
ein orerim al kach shehakkaton yevorach mippi haggadol mimmennu
But without any dispute the less is blessed of the better.

וְהִנֵּה כָּאן לוֹקְחִים אֶת הַמַּעֲשֵׂר בְּנֵי אָדָם שֶׁסּוֹפָם לָמוּת, אַךְ שָׁם - מִי שֶׁהוּעַד עָלָיו שֶׁהוּא חַי
vehineh kan lokechim et hamma'aser benei adam shessofam lamut, ach sham - mi shehu'ad alav shehu chai
And here men that die receive tithes; but there one, of whom it is witnessed that he liveth.

וְאֶפְשָׁר לוֹמַר שֶׁגַּם לֵוִי, מְקַבֵּל הַמַּעַשְׂרוֹת, נָתַן מַעֲשֵׂר עַל־יְדֵי אַבְרָהָם
ve'efshar lomar sheggam levi, mekabbel hamma'serot, natan ma'aser al-yedei avraham
And, so to say, through Abraham even Levi, who receiveth tithes, hath paid tithes;

כִּי הָיָה בְּחַלְצֵי אָבִיו אַבְרָהָם בְּצֵאת מַלְכִּי־צֶדֶק לִקְרָאתוֹ
ki hayah bechaltzei aviv avraham betzet malki-tzedek likrato
for he was yet in the loins of his father, when Melchizedek met him.

הָעִבְרִים

וְכַאֲשֶׁר רָצָה אֱלֹהִים לְהַרְאוֹת בְּיֶתֶר תֹּקֶף לְיוֹרְשֵׁי הַהַבְטָחָה

vecha'asher ratzah elohim lehar'ot beyeter tokef leyoreshei hahavtachah
Wherein God, being minded to show more abundantly unto the heirs of the promise

כִּי כַּוָּנָתוֹ אֵינָהּ נִתֶּנֶת לְשִׁנּוּי, הִתְחַיֵּב בִּשְׁבוּעָה

ki kavvanato einah nittenet leshinnui, hitchayev bishvu'ah
the immutability of his counsel, interposed with an oath;

בְּאֹפֶן זֶה, עַל־סְמַךְ שְׁנֵי דְבָרִים בִּלְתִּי מִשְׁתַּנִּים שֶׁחָלִילָה לֵאלֹהִים לְשַׁקֵּר בָּהֶם

be'ofen zeh, al-smach shenei devarim bilti mishtannim shechalilah le'elohim leshakker bahem
that by two immutable things, in which it is impossible for God to lie,

אֲנַחְנוּ הַנִּמְלָטִים נִתְעוֹדֵד מְאֹד לֶאֱחֹז בַּתִּקְוָה הַמֻּנַּחַת לְפָנֵינוּ

anachnu hannimlatim nit'oded me'od le'echoz battikvah hammunnachat lefaneinu
we may have a strong encouragement, who have fled for refuge to lay hold of the hope set before us:

תִּקְוָה שֶׁהִיא כְּעֹגֶן בָּטוּחַ וְיַצִּיב לְנַפְשֵׁנוּ וּמַגִּיעָה אֶל מִבֵּית לַפָּרֹכֶת

tikvah shehi ke'ogen batuach veyatziv lenafshenu umaggi'ah el mibbeit lapparochet
which we have as an anchor of the soul, a hope both sure and stedfast and entering into that which is within the veil;

אֶל הַמָּקוֹם אֲשֶׁר יֵשׁוּעַ, הֶחָלוּץ הָעוֹבֵר לְפָנֵינוּ, נִכְנַס בַּעֲדֵנוּ

el hammakom asher yeshua', hechalutz ha'over lefaneinu, nichnas ba'adenu
whither as a forerunner Jesus entered for us,

וְהָיָה לְכֹהֵן גָּדוֹל לְעוֹלָם עַל־דִּבְרָתִי מַלְכִּי־צֶדֶק

vehayah lechohen gadol le'olam al-divrati malki-tzedek
having become a high priest for ever after the order of Melchizedek.

ז

מַלְכִּי־צֶדֶק זֶה, מֶלֶךְ שָׁלֵם, כֹּהֵן לְאֵל עֶלְיוֹן

malki-tzedek zeh, melech shalem, kohen le'el elyon
For this Melchizedek, king of Salem, priest of God Most High,

אֲשֶׁר יָצָא לִקְרַאת אַבְרָהָם בְּשׁוּב אַבְרָהָם מֵהַכּוֹת אֶת הַמְּלָכִים וּבֵרַךְ אוֹתוֹ

asher yatza likrat avraham beshuv avraham mehakkot et hammelachim uverech oto
who met Abraham returning from the slaughter of the kings and blessed him,

וַאֲשֶׁר אַבְרָהָם חָלַק לוֹ מַעֲשֵׂר מִכֹּל

va'asher avraham chalak lo ma'aser mikkol
to whom also Abraham divided a tenth part of all

פֵּרוּשׁ שְׁמוֹ בָּרִאשׁוֹנָה מֶלֶךְ צֶדֶק; וְהוּא גַם מֶלֶךְ שָׁלֵם, שֶׁפֵּרוּשׁוֹ מֶלֶךְ הַשָּׁלוֹם

perush shemo barishonah melech tzedek; vehu gam melech shalem, shepperusho melech hashalom
(being first, by interpretation, King of righteousness, and then also King of Salem, which is, King of peace;

הָעִבְרִים

וּמוֹצִיאָה עֵשֶׂב טוֹב לְעוֹבְדִים אוֹתָהּ, נוֹשֵׂאת בְּרָכָה מֵאֵת אֱלֹהִים
umotzi'ah esev tov la'ovedim otah, noset berachah me'et elohim
and bringeth forth herbs meet for them for whose sake it is also tilled, receiveth blessing from God:

אֲבָל אִם תַּצְמִיחַ קוֹצִים וְדַרְדָּרִים, פְּסוּלָה הִיא וּקְרוֹבָה לִקְלָלָה וְסוֹפָהּ לְהִשָּׂרֵף
aval im tatzmiach kotzim vedardarim, pesulah hi ukerovah liklalah vesofah lehissaref
but if it beareth thorns and thistles, it is rejected and nigh unto a curse; whose end is to be burned.

גַּם בְּדַבְּרֵנוּ כָּךְ בְּטוּחִים אָנוּ בָּכֶם, אֲהוּבַי, בְּנוֹגֵעַ לַדְּבָרִים הַטּוֹבִים יוֹתֵר הַטְּמוּנִים בְּחֻבָּם יְשׁוּעָה
gam bedabberenu kach betuchim anu bachem, ahuvai, benogea laddevarim hattovim yoter hattomenim bechubbam yeshu'ah
But, beloved, we are persuaded better things of you, and things that accompany salvation, though we thus speak:

שֶׁכֵּן אֱלֹהִים לֹא יְעַוֵּת צֶדֶק וְלֹא יִשְׁכַּח אֶת פָּעֳלְכֶם וְאֶת הָאַהֲבָה שֶׁהֶרְאֵיתֶם לְמַעַן שְׁמוֹ
shekken elohim lo ye'avvet tzedek velo yishkach et pa'alechem ve'et ha'ahavah sher'eitem lema'an shmo
for God is not unrighteous to forget your work and the love which ye showed toward his name,

בְּכָךְ שֶׁשֵּׁרַתֶּם אֶת הַקְּדוֹשִׁים וְעוֹדְכֶם מְשָׁרְתִים אוֹתָם
bechach shesherattem et hakkedoshim ve'odechem meshartim otam
in that ye ministered unto the saints, and still do minister.

חֲפֵצִים אָנוּ שֶׁכָּל אֶחָד מִכֶּם יַרְאֶה אֶת אוֹתָהּ שְׁקִידָה בְּעָמְדוֹ בְּבִטְחוֹן הַתִּקְוָה עַד הַסּוֹף
chafetzim anu shekkol echad mikkem yar'eh et otah shekidah be'amedo bevitchon hattikvah ad hassof
And we desire that each one of you may show the same diligence unto the fulness of hope even to the end:

כְּדֵי שֶׁלֹּא תִּהְיוּ לְנִרְפִּים, אֶלָּא תֵּלְכוּ בְּעִקְּבוֹתָם שֶׁל הַיּוֹרְשִׁים אֶת הַהַבְטָחוֹת עַל־יְדֵי אֱמוּנָה וְאֹרֶךְ רוּחַ
kedei shello tihyu lenirpim, ella telechu be'ikkevotam shel hayoreshim et hahavtachot al-yedei emunah ve'orech ruach
that ye be not sluggish, but imitators of them who through faith and patience inherit the promises.

כַּאֲשֶׁר אֱלֹהִים הִבְטִיחַ אֶת הַבְטָחָתוֹ לְאַבְרָהָם
ka'asher elohim hivtiach et havtachato le'avraham
For when God made promise to Abraham,

הוּא נִשְׁבַּע בְּנַפְשׁוֹ, מִפְּנֵי שֶׁאֵין גָּדוֹל מִמֶּנּוּ אֲשֶׁר בּוֹ הוּא יָכוֹל לְהִשָּׁבַע
hu nishba benafsho, mippenei she'ein gadol mimmennu asher bo hu yachol lehishava
since he could swear by none greater, he sware by himself,

הוּא אָמַר, כִּי־בָרֵךְ אֲבָרֶכְךָ וְהַרְבָּה אַרְבֶּה אוֹתָךְ
hu amar, ki-varech avarechcha veharbah arbeh otach
saying, Surely blessing I will bless thee, and multiplying I will multiply thee.

וְכָךְ, בְּעָמְדוֹ בְּאֹרֶךְ רוּחַ, הִשִּׂיג אַבְרָהָם אֶת אֲשֶׁר הֻבְטַח
vechach, be'amedo be'orech ruach, hishg avraham et asher huvtach
And thus, having patiently endured, he obtained the promise.

בְּנֵי אָדָם נִשְׁבָּעִים בַּגָּדוֹל מֵהֶם, וְהַשְּׁבוּעָה הִיא לָהֶם חוֹתָם שֶׁל אֱמֶת הַשָּׂם קֵץ לְכָל דִּין וּדְבָרִים
bnei adam nishba'im baggadol mehem, vehashevu'ah hi lahem chotam shel emet hashom ketz lechol din udevarim
For men swear by the greater: and in every dispute of theirs the oath is final for confirmation.

הָעִבְרִים

אֵלֶּה אֲשֶׁר חוּשֵׁיהֶם הֻרְגְּלוּ עַל־יְדֵי הַנִּסָּיוֹן הַמַּעֲשִׂי לְהַבְחִין בֵּין טוֹב לְרַע
elleh asher chusheihem hurgelu al-yedei hannissayon hamma'asi lehavchin bein tov lera
even those who by reason of use have their senses exercised to discern good and evil.

I

לָכֵן, לְאַחַר שֶׁעֲזַבְנוּ אֶת הַשָּׁלָב הָרִאשׁוֹן שֶׁל דְּבַר הַמָּשִׁיחַ, נִתְקַדֵּם נָא אֶל הַבַּגְרוּת
lachen, le'achar she'azavnu et hashlav harishon shel devar hammashiach, nitkaddem na el habbagrut
Wherefore leaving the doctrine of the first principles of Christ, let us press on unto perfection;

וְאַל נָשׁוּב לְהַנִּיחַ יְסוֹדוֹת שֶׁל חֲזָרָה בִּתְשׁוּבָה מִמַּעֲשִׂים מֵתִים, אֱמוּנָה בֵּאלֹהִים
ve'al nashuv lehanniach yesodot shel chazarah bitshuvah mimma'asim metim, emunah be'elohim
not laying again a foundation of repentance from dead works, and of faith toward God,

תּוֹרַת הַטְּבִילוֹת, סְמִיכַת יָדַיִם, תְּחִיַּת הַמֵּתִים, וּמִשְׁפַּט עוֹלָם
torat hattevilot, semichat yadayim, techiyat hammetim, umishpat olam
of the teaching of baptisms, and of laying on of hands, and of resurrection of the dead, and of eternal judgment.

וְזֹאת נַעֲשֶׂה אִם יִרְצֶה אֱלֹהִים
vezot na'aseh im yirtzeh elohim
And this will we do, if God permit.

הֵן אֵלֶּה שֶׁכְּבָר הוּאֲרוּ עֵינֵיהֶם וְטָעֲמוּ מִמַּתְּנַת הַשָּׁמַיִם
hen elleh shekkevar hu'aru eineihem veta'amu mimmattnat hashamayim
For as touching those who were once enlightened and tasted of the heavenly gift,

וְנִתַּן לָהֶם חֶלְקָם בְּרוּחַ הַקֹּדֶשׁ
venittan lahem chelkam beruach hakkodesh
and were made partakers of the Holy Spirit,

וְטָעֲמוּ אֶת דְּבַר אֱלֹהִים הַטּוֹב וְכֹחוֹת הָעוֹלָם הַבָּא
veta'amu et devar elohim hattov vechochot ha'olam habba
and tasted the good word of God, and the powers of the age to come,

וְנָסוֹגוּ - אִי אֶפְשָׁר לְחַדֵּשׁ אוֹתָם עוֹד לִתְשׁוּבָה
venasogu - i efshar lechaddesh otam od litshuvah
and then fell away, it is impossible to renew them again unto repentance;

בִּהְיוֹתָם צוֹלְבִים לָהֶם מֵחָדָשׁ אֶת בֶּן־הָאֱלֹהִים וְשָׂמִים אוֹתוֹ לְחֶרְפָּה
bihyotam tzolevim lahem mechadash et ben-ha'elohim vesamim oto lecherpah
seeing they crucify to themselves the Son of God afresh, and put him to an open shame.

הֲרֵי אֲדָמָה הַשּׁוֹתָה אֶת הַגֶּשֶׁם הַיּוֹרֵד עָלֶיהָ פְּעָמִים רַבּוֹת
harei adamah hashotah et haggeshem hayored aleiha pe'amim rabbot
For the land which hath drunk the rain that cometh oft upon it,

הָעִבְרִים

כְּמוֹ שֶׁגַּם בְּמָקוֹם אַחֵר הוּא אוֹמֵר, אַתָּה־כֹהֵן לְעוֹלָם עַל־דִּבְרָתִי מַלְכִּי־צֶדֶק
kemo sheggam bemakom acher hu omer, attah-chohen le'olam al-divrati malki-tzedek
as he saith also in another place, Thou art a priest for ever After the order of Melchizedek.

וּבִימֵי הֱיוֹתוֹ בְּגוּף בָּשָׂר וָדָם, הִקְרִיב תְּפִלּוֹת וְתַחֲנוּנִים בִּצְעָקָה גְדוֹלָה וּבִדְמָעוֹת
uvimei heyoto beguf basar vadam, hikriv tfillot vetachanunim bitz'akah gedolah uvidma'ot
Who in the days of his flesh, having offered up prayers and supplications with strong crying and tears

אֶל הַיָּכוֹל לְהוֹשִׁיעוֹ מִמָּוֶת, וְאָמְנָם נִשְׁמַע בִּגְלַל יִרְאַת הָאֱלֹהִים שֶׁבּוֹ
el hayachol lehoshi'o mimmavet, ve'omnam nishma biglal yir'at ha'elohim shebbo
unto him that was able to save him from death, and having been heard for his godly fear,

וְאַף כִּי הָיָה הַבֵּן, מִסִּבְלוֹתָיו לָמַד לְצַיֵּת
ve'af ki hayah habben, missivlotav lamad letzayet
though he was a Son, yet learned obedience by the things which he suffered;

וְכַאֲשֶׁר הֻשְׁלַם הָיָה לְמָקוֹר שֶׁל יְשׁוּעַת עוֹלָמִים לְכָל הַמְצַיְּתִים לוֹ
vecha'asher hushlam hayah lemakor shel yeshu'at olamim lechol hamtzayetim lo
and having been made perfect, he became unto all them that obey him the author of eternal salvation;

וֵאלֹהִים קָרָא לוֹ, כֹּהֵן גָּדוֹל עַל־דִּבְרָתִי מַלְכִּי־צֶדֶק
velohim kara lo, kohen gadol al-divrati malki-tzedek
named of God a high priest after the order of Melchizedek.

עַל זֹאת יֵשׁ לָנוּ לוֹמַר דְּבָרִים רַבִּים, אַךְ קָשֶׁה לְהַסְבִּירָם מִפְּנֵי שֶׁכָּבְדוּ אָזְנֵיכֶם
al zot yesh lanu lomar devarim rabbim, ach kasheh lehasbiram mippenei shekkavedu azeneichem
Of whom we have many things to say, and hard of interpretation, seeing ye are become dull of hearing.

הִנֵּה בִּזְמַן שֶׁעֲלֵיכֶם לִהְיוֹת כְּבָר מוֹרִים
hinneh bizman she'aleichem lihyot kevar morim
For when by reason of the time ye ought to be teachers,

שׁוּב צְרִיכִים אַתֶּם לְמִישֶׁהוּ שֶׁיְּלַמֵּד אֶתְכֶם אֶת רֵאשִׁית יְסוֹדוֹת דִּבְרֵי אֱלֹהִים
shuv tzerichim attem lemishehu sheyelammed etchem et reshit yesodot divrei elohim
ye have need again that some one teach you the rudiments of the first principles of the oracles of God;

וְנִהְיֵיתֶם זְקוּקִים לְחָלָב וְלֹא לְמָזוֹן מוּצָק
venihyeitem zekukim lechalav velo lemazon mutzak
and are become such as have need of milk, and not of solid food.

הֵן כָּל מִי שֶׁמַּאֲכָלוֹ חָלָב אֵינֶנּוּ מֵבִין בְּדִבְרֵי צֶדֶק, כִּי עוֹדֶנּוּ תִּינוֹק
hen kol mi shemma'achalo chalav einennu mevin bedivrei tzedek, ki odennu tinok
For every one that partaketh of milk is without experience of the word of righteousness; for he is a babe.

אַךְ הַמַּאֲכָל הַמּוּצָק הוּא לַמְבֻגָּרִים
ach hamma'achal hammutzak hu lamevuggarim
But solid food is for fullgrown men,

הָעִבְרִים

כִּי אֵין לָנוּ כֹּהֵן גָּדוֹל שֶׁאֵינוֹ יָכוֹל לָחוּשׁ עִמָּנוּ אֶת חֻלְשׁוֹתֵינוּ
ki ein lanu kohen gadol she'eino yachol lachush immanu et chulshoteinu
For we have not a high priest that cannot be touched with the feeling of our infirmities;

אֶלָּא אֶחָד שֶׁהִתְנַסָּה בַּכֹּל כָּמוֹנוּ מִבְּלִי חֵטְא
ella echad shehitnassah bakkol kamonu mibbli chet
but one that hath been in all points tempted like as we are, yet without sin.

עַל כֵּן נִקְרְבָה בְּבִטָּחוֹן אֶל כֵּס הַחֶסֶד
al ken nikrevah bevittachon el kes hachesed
Let us therefore draw near with boldness unto the throne of grace,

לְקַבֵּל רַחֲמִים וְלִמְצֹא חֶסֶד לְעֶזְרָה בְּעִתָּהּ
lekabbel rachamim velimtzo chesed le'ezrah be'ittah
that we may receive mercy, and may find grace to help us in time of need.

ה

כָּל כֹּהֵן גָּדוֹל הַלָּקוּחַ מִקֶּרֶב בְּנֵי אָדָם, מְמֻנֶּה לְמַעַן בְּנֵי אָדָם עַל עִנְיְנֵי אֱלֹהִים
kol kohen gadol hallakuach mikkerev benei adam, memunneh lema'an benei adam al inyenei elohim
For every high priest, being taken from among men, is appointed for men in things pertaining to God,

כְּדֵי לְהַקְרִיב מְנָחוֹת וּזְבָחִים עַל חֲטָאִים
kedei lehakriv menachot uzevachim al chata'im
that he may offer both gifts and sacrifices for sins:

הוּא יָכוֹל לַחֲמֹל עַל הַשּׁוֹגְגִים וְהַתּוֹעִים, מִשּׁוּם שֶׁגַּם הוּא מֻקָּף חֻלְשָׁה
hu yachol lachamol al hashogegim vehatto'im, mishum sheggam hu mukkaf chulshah
who can bear gently with the ignorant and erring, for that he himself also is compassed with infirmity;

מִסִּבָּה זֹאת הוּא חַיָּב לְהַקְרִיב עַל חֲטָאִים גַּם בְּעַד הָעָם וְגַם בְּעַד עַצְמוֹ
missibbah zot hu chayav lehakriv al chata'im gam be'ad ha'am vegam be'ad atzmo
and by reason thereof is bound, as for the people, so also for himself, to offer for sins.

וְאֵין אִישׁ לוֹקֵחַ לְעַצְמוֹ אֶת הַכָּבוֹד זוּלָתִי הַנִּקְרָא מִטַּעַם אֱלֹהִים, כְּאַהֲרֹן
ve'ein ish lokeach le'atzmo et hakkavod zulati hannikra mitta'am elohim, ke'aharon
And no man taketh the honor unto himself, but when he is called of God, even as was Aaron.

כֵּן גַּם הַמָּשִׁיחַ לֹא נָטַל לְעַצְמוֹ אֶת הַכָּבוֹד לִהְיוֹת כֹּהֵן גָּדוֹל,
ken gam hammashiach lo natal le'atzmo et hakkavod lihyot kohen gadol
So Christ also glorified not himself to be made a high priest,

אֶלָּא קִבֵּל זֹאת מֵאֵת הָאוֹמֵר אֵלָיו, בְּנִי אַתָּה, אֲנִי הַיּוֹם יְלִדְתִּיךָ
ella kibbel zot me'et ha'omer elav, beni attah, ani hayom yelidticha
but he that spake unto him, Thou art my Son, This day have I begotten thee:

הָעִבְרִים

הַיּוֹם אִם־בְּקֹלוֹ תִשְׁמָעוּ, אַל־תַּקְשׁוּ לְבַבְכֶם
hayom im-bekolo tishma'u, al-takshu levavchem
To-day if ye shall hear his voice, Harden not your hearts.

אִלּוּ הֱבִיאָם יְהוֹשֻׁעַ אֶל הַמְּנוּחָה, לֹא הָיָה מְדַבֵּר אַחֲרֵי כֵן עַל יוֹם אַחֵר
illu hevi'am yehoshua el hammenuchah, lo hayah medabber acharei chen al yom acher
For if Joshua had given them rest, he would not have spoken afterward of another day.

לְפִיכָךְ נוֹתְרָה מְנוּחַת שַׁבָּת לְעַם אֱלֹהִים
lefichach notrah menuchat shabbat le'am elohim
There remaineth therefore a sabbath rest for the people of God.

הֵן הַנִּכְנָס אֶל מְנוּחָתוֹ גַּם הוּא שָׁבַת מִמְּלַאכְתּוֹ, כְּמוֹ הָאֱלֹהִים מִשֶּׁלּוֹ
hen hannichnas el menuchato gam hu shavat mimmelachto, kemo ha'elohim mishello
For he that is entered into his rest hath himself also rested from his works, as God did from his.

לָכֵן נַחְתֹּר נָא לְהִכָּנֵס אֶל הַמְּנוּחָה הַהִיא, פֶּן יִכָּשֵׁל אִישׁ וְיִהְיֶה לְמַמְרֵה כְּמוֹהֶם
lachen nachtor na lehikkanes el hammenuchah hahi, pen yikkashel ish veyihyeh lemamreh kemohem
Let us therefore give diligence to enter into that rest, that no man fall after the same example of disobedience.

שֶׁהֲרֵי דְּבַר הָאֱלֹהִים חַי וּפוֹעֵל, וְחַד הוּא מֵחֶרֶב פִּיפִיּוֹת
sheharei devar ha'elohim chai ufo'el, vechad hu mecherev pifiyot
For the word of God is living, and active, and sharper than any two-edged sword,

וְחוֹדֵר עַד לְהַבְדִּיל בֵּין נֶפֶשׁ לְרוּחַ וּבֵין פְּרָקִים לְמֹחַ הָעֲצָמוֹת
vechoder ad lehavdil bein nefesh leruach uvein prakim lemoach ha'atzamot
and piercing even to the dividing of soul and spirit, of both joints and marrow,

וּבוֹחֵן מַחְשְׁבוֹת הַלֵּב וְכַוָּנוֹתָיו
uvochen machshevot hallev vechavvanotav
and quick to discern the thoughts and intents of the heart.

אֵין שׁוּם נִבְרָא נִסְתָּר מֵעֵינָיו
ein shum nivra nistar me'einav
And there is no creature that is not manifest in his sight:

הַכֹּל חָשׂוּף וְגָלוּי לְעֵינֵי מִי שֶׁלְּפָנָיו עָלֵינוּ לָתֵת דִּין וְחֶשְׁבּוֹן
hakkol chasuf vegalui le'einei mi shellefanav aleinu latet din vecheshbon
but all things are naked and laid open before the eyes of him with whom we have to do.

וְכֵיוָן שֶׁיֵּשׁ לָנוּ כֹּהֵן גָּדוֹל עֶלְיוֹן אֲשֶׁר עָבַר דֶּרֶךְ הַשָּׁמַיִם, הֲלֹא הוּא יֵשׁוּעַ בֶּן־הָאֱלֹהִים
vecheivan sheyesh lanu kohen gadol elyon asher avar derech hashamayim, halo hu yeshua ben-ha'elohim
Having then a great high priest, who hath passed through the heavens, Jesus the Son of God,

נַחֲזִיקָה בְּהַכְרָזַת אֱמוּנָתֵנוּ
nachazikah behachrazat emunatenu
let us hold fast our confession.

הָעִבְרִים

ד

לָכֵן, בְּעוֹד עוֹמֶדֶת הַהַבְטָחָה לְהִכָּנֵס אֶל מְנוּחָתוֹ, רָאוּי לָנוּ לַחֲשֹׁשׁ שֶׁמָּא יִמָּצֵא אִישׁ מִכֶּם מְאַחֵר לְהִכָּנֵס
lachen, be'od omedet hahavtachah lehikkanes el menuchato, ra'ui lanu lachashosh shemma yimmatzei ish mikkem me'acher lehikkanes
Let us fear therefore, lest haply, a promise being left of entering into his rest, any one of you should seem to have come short of it.

הֲרֵי גַּם אֲנַחְנוּ הִתְבַּשַּׂרְנוּ כְּמוֹהֶם
harei gam anachnu hitbashorenu kemohem
For indeed we have had good tidings preached unto us, even as also they:

אַךְ הַדָּבָר שֶׁנִּשְׁמַע לֹא הוֹעִיל לָהֶם מִשּׁוּם שֶׁלֹּא הִתְמַזֵּג עִם אֱמוּנָה בְּקֶרֶב הַשּׁוֹמְעִים
ach haddavar shennishma lo ho'il lahem mishum shello hitmazzeg im emunah bekerev hashome'im
but the word of hearing did not profit them, because it was not united by faith with them that heard.

אֲנַחְנוּ הַמַּאֲמִינִים נִכְנָסִים לַמְּנוּחָה
anachnu hamma'aminim nichnasim lammenuchah
For we who have believed do enter into that rest;

כְּשֵׁם שֶׁאָמַר, אֲשֶׁר־נִשְׁבַּעְתִּי בְאַפִּי אִם־יְבֹאוּן אֶל־מְנוּחָתִי
keshem she'amar, asher-nishba'ti ve'appi im-yevo'un el-menuchati
even as he hath said, As I sware in my wrath, They shall not enter into my rest:

אַף כִּי מֵהִוָּסֵד תֵּבֵל הֻשְׁלְמוּ הַמַּעֲשִׂים
af ki mehivvased tevel hushlemu hamma'asim
although the works were finished from the foundation of the world.

שֶׁכֵּן בְּמָקוֹם אֶחָד הוּא אוֹמֵר עַל הַיּוֹם הַשְּׁבִיעִי, וַיִּשְׁבֹּת אֱלֹהִים בַּיּוֹם הַשְּׁבִיעִי מִכָּל־מְלַאכְתּוֹ
shekken bemakom echad hu omer al hayom hashvi'i, vayishbot elohim bayom hashvi'i mikkol-melachto
For he hath said somewhere of the seventh day on this wise, And God rested on the seventh day from all his works;

וְכָאן שׁוּב, אִם־יְבֹאוּן אֶל־מְנוּחָתִי
vechan shuv, im-yevo'un el-menuchati
and in this place again, They shall not enter into my rest.

וּמֵאַחַר שֶׁיֵּשׁ אֲשֶׁר נוֹתָר לָהֶם לְהִכָּנֵס אֵלֶיהָ
ume'achar sheyesh asher notar lahem lehikkanes eleiha
Seeing therefore it remaineth that some should enter thereinto,

וְאֵלֶּה שֶׁהִתְבַּשְּׂרוּ בָּרִאשׁוֹנָה לֹא נִכְנְסוּ בִּגְלַל הַמֶּרִי
ve'elleh shehitbassru barishonah lo nichnesu biglal hammeri
and they to whom the good tidings were before preached failed to enter in because of disobedience,

שׁוּב יָעַד יוֹם מְסֻיָּם - הַיּוֹם - בְּאָמְרוֹ בְּפִי דָוִד כַּנֶּאֱמַר לְעֵיל, וְזֹאת לְאַחַר זְמַן רַב
shuv ya'ad yom mesuyam - hayom - be'amero befi david kanne'emar le'eil, vezot le'achar zman rav
he again defineth a certain day, To-day, saying in David so long a time afterward (even as hath been said before),

הָעִבְרִים

אֲשֶׁר־נִשְׁבַּעְתִּי בְאַפִּי אִם יְבֹאוּן אֶל־מְנוּחָתִי
asher-nishba'ti ve'appi im yevo'un el-menuchati
As I sware in my wrath, They shall not enter into my rest.

הִשָּׁמְרוּ, אַחַי, שֶׁלֹּא יִהְיֶה בְּאִישׁ מִכֶּם לֵב מְרֻשָּׁע וַחֲסַר אֱמוּנָה
hishameru, achai, shello yihyeh be'ish mikkem lev merusha vachasar emunah
Take heed, brethren, lest haply there shall be in any one of you an evil heart of unbelief,

הַסּוֹטֶה מֵאֱלֹהִים חַיִּים
hassoteh me'elohim chayim
in falling away from the living God:

עוֹדְדוּ אִישׁ אֶת רֵעֵהוּ יוֹם יוֹם, כָּל עוֹד הַזְּמַן מְכֻנֶּה הַיּוֹם
odedu ish et re'ehu yom yom, kol od hazzman mechunneh hayom
but exhort one another day by day, so long as it is called to-day;

לְמַעַן לֹא יִקְשֶׁה לֵב אִישׁ מִכֶּם בְּנִכְלֵי הַחֵטְא
lema'an lo yiksheh lev ish mikkem benichlei hachet
lest any one of you be hardened by the deceitfulness of sin:

הֵן נִהְיֵינוּ שֻׁתָּפִים לַמָּשִׁיחַ אִם נַחֲזִיק לְלֹא הֶרֶף, עַד הַסּוֹף, בַּבִּטָּחוֹן אֲשֶׁר הִתְחַלְנוּ בּוֹ
hen nihyeinu shuttafim lammashiach im nachazik lelo heref, ad hassof, babbittachon asher hitchalnu bo
for we are become partakers of Christ, if we hold fast the beginning of our confidence firm unto the end:

בְּעוֹד שֶׁנֶּאֱמַר הַיּוֹם אִם־בְּקֹלוֹ תִשְׁמָעוּ, אַל־תַּקְשׁוּ לְבַבְכֶם כִּמְרִיבָה
be'od shenne'emar hayom im-bekolo tishma'u, al-takshu levavchem kimrivah
while it is said, To-day if ye shall hear his voice, Harden not your hearts, as in the provocation.

כִּי מִי הַשּׁוֹמְעִים אֲשֶׁר רָבוּ אִם לֹא כָּל יוֹצְאֵי מִצְרַיִם בְּיַד מֹשֶׁה
ki mi hashom'im asher ravu im lo kol yotze'ei mitzrayim beyad mosheh
For who, when they heard, did provoke? nay, did not all they that came out of Egypt by Moses?

וּבְמִי נָקְטָה נַפְשׁוֹ אַרְבָּעִים שָׁנָה? הֲלֹא בַּחוֹטְאִים אֲשֶׁר נָפְלוּ פְגָרִים בַּמִּדְבָּר
uvemi naketah nafsho arba'im shanah? halo bachote'im asher nafelu pegarim bammidbar
And with whom was he displeased forty years? was it not with them that sinned, whose bodies fell in the wilderness?

וּלְמִי נִשְׁבַּע שֶׁלֹּא יָבוֹאוּ אֶל מְנוּחָתוֹ אִם לֹא לַסּוֹרְרִים
ulemi nishba shello yavo'u el menuchato im lo lassorerim
And to whom sware he that they should not enter into his rest, but to them that were disobedient?

אֲנַחְנוּ רוֹאִים כִּי לֹא יָכְלוּ לָבוֹא מִשּׁוּם שֶׁלֹּא הֶאֱמִינוּ
anachnu ro'im ki lo yachlu lavo mishum shello he'eminu
And we see that they were not able to enter in because of unbelief.

הָעִבְרִים

וַהֲרֵי הוּא נִמְצָא רָאוּי לְכָבוֹד רַב יוֹתֵר מִשֶּׁזָּכָה לוֹ מֹשֶׁה,
vaharei hu nimtza ra'ui lechavod rav yoter mishezzachah lo mosheh
For he hath been counted worthy of more glory than Moses,

בְּאוֹתָהּ מִדָּה שֶׁבּוֹנֶה הַבַּיִת נִכְבָּד יוֹתֵר מִן הַבַּיִת
be'otah middah shebboneh habbayit nichbad yoter min habbayit
by so much as he that built the house hath more honor than the house.

הֵן כָּל בַּיִת יֵשׁ לוֹ בּוֹנֶה, אַךְ בּוֹנֶה הַכֹּל הוּא הָאֱלֹהִים
hen kol bayit yesh lo boneh, ach boneh hakkol hu ha'elohim
For every house is builded by some one; but he that built all things is God.

מֹשֶׁה אָמְנָם הָיָה נֶאֱמָן בְּכָל בֵּיתוֹ, כְּעֶבֶד
mosheh omnam hayah ne'eman bechol beito, ke'eved
And Moses indeed was faithful in all his house as a servant,

לְשֵׁם עֵדוּת עַל הַדְּבָרִים אֲשֶׁר הָיוּ עֲתִידִים לְהֵאָמֵר
leshem edut al haddevarim asher hayu atidim lehe'amer
for a testimony of those things which were afterward to be spoken;

אֲבָל הַמָּשִׁיחַ הוּא כְּבֵן עַל בֵּיתוֹ; וַאֲנַחְנוּ בֵּיתוֹ
aval hammashiach hu keven al beito; va'anachnu beito
but Christ as a son, over his house; whose house are we,

אִם נַחֲזִיק עַד קֵץ בַּבִּטָּחוֹן וּבַתִּקְוָה שֶׁאָנוּ מִתְהַלְּלִים בָּהּ
im nachazik ad ketz babbittachon uvattikvah she'anu mit'hallelim bah
if we hold fast our boldness and the glorying of our hope firm unto the end.

עַל כֵּן, כְּמַאֲמַר רוּחַ הַקֹּדֶשׁ, הַיּוֹם אִם־בְּקֹלוֹ תִשְׁמָעוּ
al ken, kema'amar ruach hakkodesh, hayom im-bekolo tishma'u
Wherefore, even as the Holy Spirit saith, To-day if ye shall hear his voice,

אַל־תַּקְשׁוּ לְבַבְכֶם כִּמְרִיבָה, כְּיוֹם מַסָּה בַּמִּדְבָּר
al-takshu levavchem kimrivah, keyom massah bammidbar
Harden not your hearts, as in the provocation, Like as in the day of the trial in the wilderness,

אֲשֶׁר נִסּוּנִי אֲבוֹתֵיכֶם, בְּחָנוּנִי גַּם־רָאוּ פָעֳלִי אַרְבָּעִים שָׁנָה
asher nissuni avoteichem, bechanuni gam-ra'u fo'oli arba'im shanah
Where your fathers tried me by proving me, and saw my works forty years.

לָכֵן אָקוּט בְּדוֹר וָאֹמַר
lachen akut bedor va'omar
Wherefore I was displeased with this generation, And said,

עַם תֹּעֵי לֵבָב הֵם, וְהֵם לֹא־יָדְעוּ דְרָכָי
am to'ei levav hem, vehem lo-yade'u derachai
They do always err in their heart: But they did not know my ways;

הָעִבְרִים

וְכֵיוָן שֶׁלַּיְלָדִים הָיְתָה שֻׁתָּפוּת שֶׁל בָּשָׂר וָדָם, כְּמוֹ כֵן גַּם הוּא שִׁתֵּף עַצְמוֹ בְּבָשָׂר וָדָם
vecheivan shellayladim hayetah shuttafut shel basar vadam, kemo chen gam hu shittef atzmo bevasar vadam
Since then the children are sharers in flesh and blood, he also himself in like manner partook of the same;

כְּדֵי שֶׁיַּשְׁבִּית עַל־יְדֵי מוֹתוֹ אֶת זֶה שֶׁבְּיָדוֹ מֶמְשֶׁלֶת הַמָּוֶת - הוּא הַשָּׂטָן
kedei sheyashbit al-yedei moto et zeh shebbeyado memshelet hammavet - hu hassatan
that through death he might bring to nought him that had the power of death, that is, the devil;

וִישַׁחְרֵר אֶת אֵלֶּה שֶׁבִּגְלַל אֵימַת הַמָּוֶת הָיוּ נְתוּנִים לְעַבְדוּת כָּל יְמֵי חַיֵּיהֶם
vishachrer et elleh shebbiglal eimat hammavet hayu netunim le'avdut kol yemei chayeihem
and might deliver all them who through fear of death were all their lifetime subject to bondage.

הֵן לֹא בְמַלְאָכִים הוּא תּוֹמֵךְ, אֶלָּא בְּזֶרַע אַבְרָהָם
hen lo bemal'achim hu tomech, ella bezera avraham
For verily not to angels doth he give help, but he giveth help to the seed of Abraham.

לְפִיכָךְ הָיָה עָלָיו לְהִדַּמּוֹת לְאֶחָיו בְּכָל דָּבָר
lefichach hayah alav lehiddamot le'echav bechol davar
Wherefore it behooved him in all things to be made like unto his brethren,

לְמַעַן יִהְיֶה כֹּהֵן גָּדוֹל רַחֲמָן וְנֶאֱמָן בְּעִנְיְנֵי אֱלֹהִים
lema'an yihyeh kohen gadol rachaman vene'eman be'inyenei elohim
that he might become a merciful and faithful high priest in things pertaining to God,

לְכַפֵּר עַל חֲטָאֵי הָעָם
lechapper al chata'ei ha'am
to make propitiation for the sins of the people.

כִּי מֵאַחַר שֶׁהוּא עַצְמוֹ סָבַל כַּאֲשֶׁר הִתְנַסָּה, הוּא יָכוֹל לַעֲזֹר לְאֵלֶּה אֲשֶׁר נְתוּנִים בְּנִסָּיוֹן
ki me'achar shehu atzmo saval ka'asher hitnassah, hu yachol la'azor le'elleh asher netunim benissayon
For in that he himself hath suffered being tempted, he is able to succor them that are tempted.

ג

לָכֵן, אַחַי הַקְּדוֹשִׁים, אֲשֶׁר חֶלְקְכֶם בִּקְרִיאָה שְׁמֵימִית
lachen, achai hakkedoshim, asher chelkechem bikri'ah shemeimit
Wherefore, holy brethren, partakers of a heavenly calling,

הִתְבּוֹנְנוּ אֶל הַשָּׁלִיחַ וְהַכֹּהֵן הַגָּדוֹל שֶׁל הַכְרָזַת אֱמוּנָתֵנוּ, יֵשׁוּעַ
hitbonenu el hashaliach vehakkohen haggadol shel hachrazat emunatenu, yeshua
consider the Apostle and High Priest of our confession, even Jesus;

הַנֶּאֱמָן לַמְכוֹנֵן אוֹתוֹ, כְּמוֹ שֶׁהָיָה גַּם מֹשֶׁה בְּכָל בֵּיתוֹ
hanne'eman lamchonen oto, kemo shehayah gam mosheh bechol beito
who was faithful to him that appointed him, as also was Moses in all his house.

הָעִבְרִים

וְכָבוֹד וְהָדָר תְּעַטְּרֵהוּ, וַתַּמְשִׁילֵהוּ בְּמַעֲשֵׂי יָדֶיךָ
vechavod vehadar te'atterehu, vattamshilehu bema'asei yadeicha
Thou crownedst him with glory and honor, And didst set him over the works of thy hands:

כֹּל שַׁתָּה תַּחַת רַגְלָיו
kol shattah tachat raglav
Thou didst put all things in subjection under his feet.

הִנֵּה בַּהֲשִׁיתוֹ הַכֹּל תַּחְתָּיו לֹא הִשְׁאִיר דָּבָר שֶׁלֹּא הוּשַׁת תַּחְתָּיו
hinneh bahashito hakkol tachtav lo hish'ir davar shello hushat tachtav
For in that he subjected all things unto him, he left nothing that is not subject to him.

אַךְ כָּעֵת עֲדַיִן אֵין אָנוּ רֹאִים כִּי הַכֹּל הוּשַׁת תַּחְתָּיו
ach ka'et adayin ein anu ro'im ki hakkol hushat tachtav
But now we see not yet all things subjected to him.

אֲבָל רֹאִים אָנוּ אֶת יֵשׁוּעַ מְעֻטָּר בְּכָבוֹד וְהָדָר מִשּׁוּם שֶׁסָּבַל מָוֶת, הוּא אֲשֶׁר חֻסַּר מְעַט מִמַּלְאָכִים,
aval ro'im anu et yeshua me'uttar bechavod vehadar mishum shessaval mavet, hu asher chussar me'at mimmal'achim
But we behold him who hath been made a little lower than the angels, even Jesus, because of the suffering of death crowned with glory and honor,

כְּדֵי שֶׁבְּחֶסֶד אֱלֹהִים יִטְעַם מָוֶת בְּעַד הַכֹּל
kedei shebbechesed elohim yit'am mavet be'ad hakkol
that by the grace of God he should taste of death for every man.

אָכֵן הוּא אֲשֶׁר הַכֹּל לְמַעֲנוֹ וְהַכֹּל עַל־יָדָיו יָאֶה הָיָה לוֹ,
achen hu asher hakkol lema'ano vehakkol al-yadav ya'eh hayah lo
For it became him, for whom are all things, and through whom are all things,

בַּהֲבִיאוֹ בָּנִים רַבִּים לְכָבוֹד, לְהַשְׁלִים עַל־יְדֵי סֵבֶל אֶת מְכוֹנֵן יְשׁוּעָתָם
bahavi'o banim rabbim lechavod, lehashlim al-yedei sevel et mechonen yeshu'atam
in bringing many sons unto glory, to make the author of their salvation perfect through sufferings.

הֵן גַּם הַמְקַדֵּשׁ גַּם הַמְקֻדָּשִׁים כֻּלָּם מֵאֶחָד הֵמָּה
hen gam hamkaddesh gam hamkuddashim kullam me'echad hemmah
For both he that sanctifieth and they that are sanctified are all of one:

וְלָכֵן אֵינוֹ בּוֹשׁ מִקְּרֹא לָהֶם אַחִים
velachen eino bosh mikkero lahem achim
for which cause he is not ashamed to call them brethren,

בְּאָמְרוֹ, אֲסַפְּרָה שִׁמְךָ לְאֶחָי בְּתוֹךְ קָהָל אֲהַלְלֶךָּ
be'omro, asapperah shimcha le'echai betoch kahal ahalela
saying, I will declare thy name unto my brethren, In the midst of the congregation will I sing thy praise.

וְעוֹד, וְקִוִּיתִי־לוֹ, וְעוֹד, הִנֵּה אָנֹכִי וְהַיְלָדִים אֲשֶׁר נָתַן לִי יְהוָה
ve'od, vekivveti-lo, ve'od, hinneh anochi vehayladim asher natan li hashem
And again, I will put my trust in him. And again, Behold, I and the children whom God hath given me.

הָעִבְרִים

ב

עַל כֵּן חַיָּבִים אָנוּ לָשִׂים לִבֵּנוּ בְּיֶתֶר שְׂאֵת אֶל הַדְּבָרִים שֶׁשָּׁמַעְנוּ, פֶּן נָסוּר מִן הַדֶּרֶךְ
al ken chayavim anu lasim libbenu beyeter se'et el haddevarim sheshama'nu, pen nasur min hadderech
Therefore we ought to give the more earnest heed to the things that were heard, lest haply we drift away from them.

הֲרֵי אִם הַדָּבָר אֲשֶׁר נֶאֱמַר בְּפִי מַלְאָכִים קִבֵּל תֹּקֶף
harei im haddavar asher ne'emar befi mal'achim kibbel tokef
For if the word spoken through angels proved stedfast,

וְעַל כָּל עֲבֵרָה וּמְרִי נִתַּן גְּמוּל צוֹדֵק
ve'al kol averah umeri nittan gemul tzodek
and every transgression and disobedience received a just recompense of reward;

אֵיךְ נִמָּלֵט אֲנַחְנוּ אִם לֹא נָשִׂים לֵב לִישׁוּעָה גְּדוֹלָה כָּזֹאת אֲשֶׁר בַּתְּחִלָּה נֶאֶמְרָה בְּפִי הָאָדוֹן
eich nimmalet anachnu im lo nasim lev liyshu'ah gedolah kazot asher battechillah ne'emrah befi ha'adon
how shall we escape, if we neglect so great a salvation? which having at the first been spoken through the Lord,

וְאֻשְּׁרָה לָנוּ עַל־יְדֵי שׁוֹמְעָיו
ve'usherah lanu al-yedei shom'av
was confirmed unto us by them that heard;

וְגַם אֱלֹהִים הֵעִיד עָלֶיהָ בְּאוֹתוֹת וּבְמוֹפְתִים וּבְכָל מִינֵי גְּבוּרוֹת
vegam elohim he'id aleiha be'otot uvemofetim uvechol minei gevurot
God also bearing witness with them, both by signs and wonders, and by manifold powers,

וּבְמַתְּנוֹת רוּחַ הַקֹּדֶשׁ אֲשֶׁר חִלֵּק כִּרְצוֹנוֹ
uvemattenot ruach hakkodesh asher chillek kirtzono
and by gifts of the Holy Spirit, according to his own will.

הֵן לֹא תַּחַת יַד הַמַּלְאָכִים שָׁת אֶת הָעוֹלָם הַבָּא אֲשֶׁר אָנוּ מְדַבְּרִים עָלָיו
hen lo tachat yad hammal'achim shat et ha'olam habba asher anu medabberim alav
For not unto angels did he subject the world to come, whereof we speak.

אֲבָל בְּמָקוֹם אֶחָד הֵעִיד מִישֶׁהוּ לֵאמֹר
aval bemakom echad he'id mishehu lemor
But one hath somewhere testified, saying,

מָה־אֱנוֹשׁ כִּי־תִזְכְּרֶנּוּ וּבֶן־אָדָם כִּי תִפְקְדֶנּוּ
mah-'enosh ki-tizkerennu uven-'adam ki tifkedennu
What is man, that thou art mindful of him? Or the son of man, that thou visitest him?

וַתְּחַסְּרֵהוּ מְּעַט מֵאֱלֹהִים
vattechasserehu me'at me'elohim
Thou madest him a little lower than the angels;

הָעִבְרִים

אַךְ עַל הַבֵּן הוּא אוֹמֵר
ach al habben hu omer
but of the Son he saith,

כִּסְאֲךָ אֱלֹהִים, עוֹלָם וָעֶד, שֵׁבֶט מִישֹׁר שֵׁבֶט מַלְכוּתֶךָ
kis'acha elohim, olam va'ed, shevet mishor shevet malchutecha
Thy throne, O God, is for ever and ever; And the sceptre of uprightness is the sceptre of thy kingdom.

אָהַבְתָּ צֶּדֶק וַתִּשְׂנָא רֶשַׁע
ahavta tzedek vattisna resha
Thou hast loved righteousness, and hated iniquity;

עַל־כֵּן מְשָׁחֲךָ אֱלֹהִים, אֱלֹהֶיךָ, שֶׁמֶן שָׂשׂוֹן מֵחֲבֵרֶיךָ
al-ken meshachacha elohim, eloheicha, shemen sason mechavereicha
Therefore God, thy God, hath anointed thee With the oil of gladness above thy fellows.

וְעוֹד, אַתָּה אֲדֹנָי לְפָנִים הָאָרֶץ יָסַדְתָּ, וּמַעֲשֵׂה יָדֶיךָ שָׁמַיִם
ve'od, attah adonai lefanim ha'aretz yasadta, uma'aseh yadeicha shamayim
And, Thou, Lord, in the beginning didst lay the foundation of the earth, And the heavens are the works of thy hands:

הֵמָּה יֹאבֵדוּ וְאַתָּה תַעֲמֹד, וְכֻלָּם כַּבֶּגֶד יִבְלוּ
hemmah yovedu ve'attah ta'amod, vechullam kabbeged yivlu
They shall perish; but thou continuest: And they all shall wax old as doth a garment;

כַּלְּבוּשׁ תַּחֲלִיפֵם וְיַחֲלֹפוּ
kallevush tachalifem veyachalofu
And as a mantle shalt thou roll them up, As a garment, and they shall be changed:

וְאַתָּה הוּא וּשְׁנוֹתֶיךָ לֹא יִתַּמּוּ
ve'attah hu ushenoteicha lo yittamu
But thou art the same, And thy years shall not fail.

וְאֶל מִי מִן הַמַּלְאָכִים אָמַר מֵעוֹלָם
ve'el mi min hammal'achim amar me'olam
But of which of the angels hath he said at any time,

שֵׁב לִימִינִי עַד אָשִׁית אֹיְבֶיךָ הֲדֹם לְרַגְלֶיךָ
shev liymini ad ashit oyeveicha hadom leragleicha
Sit thou on my right hand, Till I make thine enemies the footstool of thy feet?

הַאֵין כֻּלָּם רוּחוֹת־שָׁרֵת, שְׁלוּחִים לְשֵׁרוּת לְמַעַן הָעֲתִידִים לָרֶשֶׁת יְשׁוּעָה
ha'ein kullam ruchot-sharet, shluchim lesherut lema'an ha'atidim lareshet yeshu'ah
Are they not all ministering spirits, sent forth to do service for the sake of them that shall inherit salvation?

הָעִבְרִים

הָאֱלֹהִים אֲשֶׁר דִּבֶּר מִקֶּדֶם פְּעָמִים רַבּוֹת וּבִדְרָכִים רַבּוֹת אֶל הָאָבוֹת בְּיַד הַנְּבִיאִים
ha'elohim asher dibber mikkedem pe'amim rabbot uvidrachim rabbot el ha'avot beyad hannevi'im
God, having of old time spoken unto the fathers in the prophets by divers portions and in divers manners,

דִּבֶּר אֵלֵינוּ בְּאַחֲרִית הַיָּמִים הָאֵלֶּה בְּיַד הַבֵּן אֲשֶׁר שָׂם לְיוֹרֵשׁ כֹּל
dibber eleinu be'acharit hayamim ha'elleh beyad habben asher sam leyoresh kol
hath at the end of these days spoken unto us in his Son, whom he appointed heir of all things,

וּבְיָדוֹ גַּם עָשָׂה שָׁמַיִם וָאָרֶץ
uveyado gam asah shamayim va'aretz
through whom also he made the worlds;

הוּא זֹהַר כְּבוֹדוֹ וְצֶלֶם עַצְמוּתוֹ
hu zohar kevodo vetzelem atzmuto
who being the effulgence of his glory, and the very image of his substance,

וְנוֹשֵׂא כֹל בִּדְבָרוֹ רַב־הַגְּבוּרָה
venosei kol bidvaro rav-haggevurah
and upholding all things by the word of his power,

וּלְאַחַר שֶׁעָשָׂה טִהוּר חֲטָאִים יָשַׁב לִימִין הַגְּדֻלָּה בַּמְּרוֹמִים
ule'achar she'asah tihur chata'im yashav limin haggedullah bamromim
when he had made purification of sins, sat down on the right hand of the Majesty on high;

וְהָיָה לְגָדוֹל בִּמְאֹד מִן הַמַּלְאָכִים, כִּהְיוֹת הַשֵּׁם שֶׁיָּרַשׁ נַעֲלֶה מִשֶּׁלָּהֶם
vehayah legadol bim'od min hammal'achim, kihyot hashem sheyarash na'aleh mishellahem
having become by so much better than the angels, as he hath inherited a more excellent name than they.

כִּי אֶל מִי מֵהַמַּלְאָכִים אָמַר מֵעוֹלָם
ki el mi mehammal'achim amar me'olam
For unto which of the angels said he at any time,

בְּנִי אַתָּה אֲנִי הַיּוֹם יְלִדְתִּיךָ וְעוֹד, אֲנִי אֶהְיֶה־לּוֹ לְאָב וְהוּא יִהְיֶה־לִּי לְבֵן
bni attah ani hayom yelidticha? ve'od, ani ehyeh-lo le'av vehu yihyeh-li leven
Thou art my Son, This day have I begotten thee? and again, I will be to him a Father, And he shall be to me a Son?

וְעוֹד, כַּאֲשֶׁר הוּא מֵבִיא אֶת הַבְּכוֹר אֶל הָעוֹלָם, הוּא אוֹמֵר, וְהִשְׁתַּחֲווּ לוֹ כָּל אֱלֹהִים
ve'od, ka'asher hu mevi et habbechor el ha'olam, hu omer, vehishtachavu lo kol elohim
And when he again bringeth in the firstborn into the world he saith, And let all the angels of God worship him.

וְעַל הַמַּלְאָכִים הוּא אוֹמֵר, עֹשֶׂה מַלְאָכָיו רוּחוֹת, מְשָׁרְתָיו אֵשׁ לֹהֵט
ve'al hammal'achim hu omer, oseh mal'achav ruchot, meshartav esh lohet
And of the angels he saith, Who maketh his angels winds, And his ministers a flame of fire:

פִּילִימוֹן

כֵּיוָן שֶׁבָּטַחְתִּי בְּהֵעָנוּתְךָ כָּתַבְתִּי לְךָ, וְיוֹדֵעַ אֲנִי כִּי תַּעֲשֶׂה גַּם יוֹתֵר מִמַּה שֶּׁאָמַרְתִּי
keivan shebbatachti behe'anutecha katavti lecha, veyodea ani ki ta'aseh gam yoter mimmah she'amarti
Having confidence in thine obedience I write unto thee, knowing that thou wilt do even beyond what I say.

נוֹסָף עַל כָּךְ, הָכֵן לִי מְקוֹם לִינָה, כִּי אֲנִי מְקַוֶּה שֶׁהוֹדוֹת לִתְפִלּוֹתֵיכֶם אֲשֻׁחְרַר וְאֶנָּתֵן לָכֶם
nosaf al kach, hachen li mekom linah, ki ani mekavveh shehodot litfilloteichem ashuchrar ve'ennaten lachem
But withal prepare me also a lodging: for I hope that through your prayers I shall be granted unto you.

דְּרִישַׁת שָׁלוֹם מֵאֶפָּפְרַס, חֲבֵרִי לַמַּאֲסָר לְמַעַן הַמָּשִׁיחַ יֵשׁוּעַ
derishat shalom me'eppaferas, chaveri lamma'asar lema'an hammashiach yeshua
Epaphras, my fellow-prisoner in Christ Jesus, saluteth thee;

גַּם מַרְקוֹס, אֲרִיסְטַרְכוֹס, דִּימַס וְלוּקַס, חֲבֵרַי לָעֲבוֹדָה, דּוֹרְשִׁים בִּשְׁלוֹמְךָ
gam markos, arisetarchos, dimas velukas, chaverai la'avodah, doreshim bishlomcha
and so do Mark, Aristarchus, Demas, Luke, my fellow-workers.

חֶסֶד הָאָדוֹן יֵשׁוּעַ הַמָּשִׁיחַ עִם רוּחֲכֶם
chesed ha'adon yeshua hammashiach im ruchachem
The grace of our Lord Jesus Christ be with your spirit. Amen.

פילימון

וַאֲנִי מֵשִׁיב אוֹתוֹ אֵלֶיךָ, אֶת אוֹנִיסִימוֹס אֲשֶׁר לִבִּי הוּא
va'ani meshiv oto eleicha, et onisimos asher libbi hu
whom I have sent back to thee in his own person, that is, my very heart:

חָפַצְתִּי לְהַחֲזִיקוֹ אֶצְלִי כְּדֵי שֶׁיְשָׁרֵת אוֹתִי בִּמְקוֹמְךָ בַּמַּאֲסָר שֶׁאֲנִי נָתוּן בּוֹ בִּגְלַל הַבְּשׂוֹרָה
chafatzti lehachaziko etzli kedei sheyesharet oti bimkomecha bamma'asar she'ani natun bo biglal habbesorah
whom I would fain have kept with me, that in thy behalf he might minister unto me in the bonds of the gospel:

אֲבָל לֹא רָצִיתִי לַעֲשׂוֹת דָּבָר בְּלֹא הַסְכָּמָתְךָ, וְזֹאת כְּדֵי שֶׁלֹּא יִהְיֶה פֹּעַל טוּבְךָ מִתּוֹךְ הֶכְרֵחַ
aval lo ratziti la'asot davar belo haskamatecha, vezot kedei shello yihyeh po'al tuvecha mittoch hechreach
but without thy mind I would do nothing; that thy goodness should not be as of necessity,

כִּי אִם מֵרָצוֹן
ki im meratzon
but of free will.

וּבִכְלָל, אוּלַי נִפְרַד מִמְּךָ לְשָׁעָה לְמַעַן יִהְיֶה לְךָ לְעוֹלָם
uvichlal, ulai nifrad mimmcha lesha'ah lema'an yihyeh lecha le'olam
For perhaps he was therefore parted from thee for a season, that thou shouldest have him for ever;

וְלֹא עוֹד כְּעֶבֶד אֶלָּא לְמַעְלָה מֵעֶבֶד, כְּאָח אָהוּב
velo od ke'eved ella lema'lah me'eved, ke'ach ahuv
no longer as a servant, but more than a servant, a brother beloved,

בִּמְיֻחָד לִי, וְעַל אַחַת כַּמָּה וְכַמָּה לְךָ, הֵן כְּאָדָם וְהֵן כְּאָח בָּאָדוֹן
bimyuchad li, ve'al achat kammah vechammah lecha, hen ke'adam vehen ke'ach ba'adon
specially to me, but how much rather to thee, both in the flesh and in the Lord.

לְפִיכָךְ, אִם אַתָּה חוֹשֵׁב אוֹתִי לְחָבֵר לָאֱמוּנָה, קַבֵּל אוֹתוֹ כְּמוֹ שֶׁהָיִיתָ מְקַבֵּל אוֹתִי
lefichach, im attah choshev oti lechaver la'emunah, kabbel oto kemo shehayita mekabbel oti
If then thou countest me a partner, receive him as myself.

וְאִם עָשָׂה לְךָ רָעָה אוֹ חַיָּב הוּא לְךָ דָּבָר, חֲשֹׁב זֹאת לְחוֹבָתִי
ve'im asah lecha ra'ah o chayav hu lecha davar, chashov zot lechovati
But if he hath wronged thee at all, or oweth thee aught, put that to mine account;

אֲנִי, שָׁאוּל, כּוֹתֵב זֹאת בְּמוֹ יָדִי - אֲנִי אֲשַׁלֵּם.
ani, sha'ul, kotev zot bemo yadi - ani ashallem.
I Paul write it with mine own hand, I will repay it:

וְאֵינֶנִּי צָרִיךְ לוֹמַר לְךָ שֶׁאַתָּה חַיָּב לִי גַּם אֶת נַפְשְׁךָ
ve'einenni tzarich lomar lecha she'attah chayav li gam et nafshecha
that I say not unto thee that thou owest to me even thine own self besides.

כֵּן, אָחִי, הֱיֵה נָא לִי לְמוֹעִיל בָּאָדוֹן; שׁוֹבֵב אֶת נַפְשִׁי בַּמָּשִׁיחַ
ken, achi, heyeh na li lemo'il ba'adon; shovev et nafshi bammashiach
Yea, brother, let me have joy of thee in the Lord: refresh my heart in Christ.

פילימון

מֵאֵת שָׁאוּל, אֲסִיר הַמָּשִׁיחַ יֵשׁוּעַ, וּמֵאֵת טִימוֹתֵיאוֹס אָחִינוּ, אֶל פִילִימוֹן הָאָהוּב חֲבֵרֵנוּ לָעֲבוֹדָה
me'et sha'ul, asir hammashiach yeshua, ume'et timotei'os achinu, el filimon ha'ahuv chaverenu la'avodah
Paul, a prisoner of Christ Jesus, and Timothy our brother, to Philemon our beloved and fellow-worker,

אֶל אַפִּיָה אֲחוֹתֵנוּ, אֶל אַרְכִיפּוֹס שֻׁתָּפֵנוּ לַמַּעֲרָכָה, וְאֶל הַקְּהִלָּה אֲשֶׁר בְּבֵיתְךָ
el appiyah achotenu, el archipos shuttafenu lamma'arachah, ve'el hakkehillah asher beveitecha
and to Apphia our sister, and to Archippus our fellow-soldier, and to the church in thy house:

חֶסֶד וְשָׁלוֹם לָכֶם מֵאֵת הָאֱלֹהִים אָבִינוּ וְהָאָדוֹן יֵשׁוּעַ הַמָּשִׁיחַ
chesed veshalom lachem me'et ha'elohim avinu veha'adon yeshua hammashiach
Grace to you and peace from God our Father and the Lord Jesus Christ.

אֲנִי מוֹדֶה לֵאלֹהַי בְּכָל עֵת שֶׁאֲנִי מַזְכִּיר אוֹתְךָ בִּתְפִלּוֹתַי
ani modeh le'elohai bechol et she'ani mazkir otcha bitfillotai
I thank my God always, making mention of thee in my prayers,

לְאַחַר שֶׁשָּׁמַעְתִּי עַל הָאַהֲבָה וְהָאֱמוּנָה אֲשֶׁר אַתָּה רוֹחֵשׁ לָאָדוֹן יֵשׁוּעַ וּלְכָל הַקְּדוֹשִׁים
le'achar sheshama'ti al ha'ahavah veha'emunah asher attah rochesh la'adon yeshua ulechal hakkedoshim
hearing of thy love, and of the faith which thou hast toward the Lord Jesus, and toward all the saints;

תְּפִלָּתִי הִיא שֶׁהָאֱמוּנָה אֲשֶׁר אַתָּה שֻׁתָּף לָהּ תִּפְעַל בְּךָ בְּהַכִּירְךָ אֶת כָּל הַטּוֹב הַטָּמוּן בָּנוּ לְתוֹעֶלֶת הַמָּשִׁיחַ
tefillati hi sheha'emunah asher attah shuttaf lah tif'al becha behakkirecha et kol hattov hattamun banu leto'elet hammashiach
that the fellowship of thy faith may become effectual, in the knowledge of every good thing which is in you, unto Christ.

אָחִי, הִנֵּה אַהֲבָתְךָ גָּרְמָה לִי שִׂמְחָה גְּדוֹלָה וְנֶחָמָה, מִשּׁוּם שֶׁהָיִיתָ לְמֵשִׁיב נֶפֶשׁ לַקְּדוֹשִׁים
achi, hinneh ahavatcha garemah li simchah gedolah venechamah, mishum shehayita lemeshiv nefesh lakkedoshim
For I had much joy and comfort in thy love, because the hearts of the saints have been refreshed through thee, brother.

לָכֵן, אַף שֶׁיֵּשׁ לִי הָעֹז בַּמָּשִׁיחַ לְצַוֹּתְךָ לַעֲשׂוֹת אֶת מַה שֶּׁנָּחוּץ
lachen, af sheyesh li ha'oz bammashiach letzavvotecha la'asot et mah shennachutz
Wherefore, though I have all boldness in Christ to enjoin thee that which is befitting,

הֲרֵי בִּגְלַל הָאַהֲבָה אֲנִי מַעֲדִיף לְבַקֵּשׁ, אֲנִי שָׁאוּל הַזָּקֵן וְעַכְשָׁו גַּם אֲסִיר הַמָּשִׁיחַ יֵשׁוּעַ
harei biglal ha'ahavah ani ma'dif levakkesh, ani sha'ul hazzaken ve'achshav gam asir hammashiach yeshua
yet for love's sake I rather beseech, being such a one as Paul the aged, and now a prisoner also of Christ Jesus:

אֲנִי מְבַקֵּשׁ מִמְּךָ עַל בְּנִי אוֹנִיסִימוֹס, אֲשֶׁר הוֹלַדְתִּי אוֹתוֹ לָאֱמוּנָה בִּהְיוֹתִי בַּמַּאֲסָר
ani mevakkesh mimmcha al bni onisimos, asher holadti oto la'emunah bihyoti bamma'asar
I beseech thee for my child, whom I have begotten in my bonds, Onesimus,

בֶּעָבָר הוּא לֹא הוֹעִיל לְךָ, אַךְ כָּעֵת יֵשׁ בּוֹ לְהוֹעִיל גַּם לְךָ וְגַם לִי
be'avar hu lo ho'il lecha, ach ka'et yesh bo leho'il gam lecha vegam li
who once was unprofitable to thee, but now is profitable to thee and to me:

טִיטוֹס

דְּבָרִים אֵלֶּה טוֹבִים וּמוֹעִילִים לִבְנֵי אָדָם
devarim elleh tovim umo'ilim livnei adam
These things are good and profitable unto men:

אֲבָל הִמָּנַע מֵחִקְרֵי שְׁאֵלוֹת תְּפֵלוֹת, מֶחְקְרֵי תּוֹלְדוֹת הַדּוֹרוֹת, מִמְּרִיבוֹת, וּמֵהִתְנַצְּחֻיוֹת עַל הַתּוֹרָה
aval himmana mechikrei she'elot tefelot, mechikrei toledot haddorot, mimmerivot, umehitnatzechyot al hattorah
but shun foolish questionings, and genealogies, and strifes, and fightings about the law;

כִּי אֵין בָּהֶם מוֹעִיל וְהֵמָּה הֶבֶל
ki ein bahem mo'il vehemmah hevel
for they are unprofitable and vain.

וְאִישׁ הַגּוֹרֵם לִפְלוּגִים, לְאַחַר שֶׁהוּכַח פַּעַם אַחַת וּפַעַם שְׁנִיָּה, אַל יְהֵא לְךָ דָּבָר עִמּוֹ
ve'ish haggorem lefillugim, le'achar shehuchach pa'am achat ufa'am sheniyah, al yehei lecha davar immo
A factious man after a first and second admonition refuse;

דַּע לְךָ כִּי אִישׁ כָּזֶה סוֹטֶה מִן הַדֶּרֶךְ וְהוּא חוֹטֵא הַמַּרְשִׁיעַ אֶת עַצְמוֹ
da lecha ki ish kazeh soteh min hadderech vehu chotei hammarshia et atzmo
knowing that such a one is perverted, and sinneth, being self-condemned.

כַּאֲשֶׁר אֶשְׁלַח אֵלֶיךָ אֶת אַרְטֵמַס אוֹ אֶת טִיכִיקוֹס, תְּמַהֵר לָבוֹא אֵלַי לְנִיקוֹפּוֹלִיס
ka'asher eshlach eleicha et artemas o et tichikos, temaher lavo elai lenikoppolis,
When I shall send Artemas unto thee, or Tychicus, give diligence to come unto me to Nicopolis:

כִּי הֶחְלַטְתִּי לִשְׁהוֹת שָׁם בַּחֹרֶף
ki hechlatti lishhot sham bachoref
for there I have determined to winter.

הִזְדָּרֵז לִשְׁלֹחַ אֶת זִינַס הַמְלֻמָּד בַּתּוֹרָה וְאֶת אַפּוֹלוֹס, וּדְאַג שֶׁלֹּא יַחְסְרוּ דָּבָר
hizdarez lishloach et zinas hamlummad battorah ve'et appolos, ude'ag shello yachseru davar
Set forward Zenas the lawyer and Apollos on their journey diligently, that nothing be wanting unto them.

וְיִלְמְדוּ גַּם אַנְשֵׁי קְהִלָּתֵנוּ לַעֲסֹק בְּמַעֲשִׂים טוֹבִים לְמִלּוּי צְרָכִים חִיּוּנִיִּים, כְּדֵי שֶׁלֹּא יִהְיוּ חַסְרֵי פְּרִי
veyilmedu gam anshei kehillatenu la'asok bema'asim tovim lemillui tzerachim chiyuniyim, kedei shello yihyu chasrei peri
And let our people also learn to maintain good works for necessary uses, that they be not unfruitful.

כָּל הַנִּמְצָאִים אִתִּי דּוֹרְשִׁים בִּשְׁלוֹמְךָ. דְּרִישַׁת שָׁלוֹם לְאוֹהֲבֵינוּ הַשֻּׁתָּפִים בָּאֱמוּנָה
kol hannimtza'im itti doreshim bishlomecha. derishat shalom le'ohaveinu hashuttafim ba'emunah.
All that are with me salute thee. Salute them that love us in faith.

הַחֶסֶד עִם כֻּלְּכֶם
hachesed im kullechem
Grace be with you all.

טִיטוֹס

ג

הַזְכֵּר לָהֶם לְהִכָּנַע לְשַׁלִּיטִים וּלְבַעֲלֵי סַמְכֻיּוֹת, לְצַיֵּת, לִהְיוֹת נְכוֹנִים לְכָל מַעֲשֶׂה טוֹב
hazker lahem lehikkana leshallitim uleva'alei samchyot, letzayet, lihyot nechonim lechol ma'aseh tov
Put them in mind to be in subjection to rulers, to authorities, to be obedient, to be ready unto every good work,

שֶׁלֹּא לְגַדֵּף אִישׁ, לַחְדֹּל מִמְּרִיבוֹת, לִהְיוֹת נוֹחִים לַבְּרִיּוֹת וּלְהִתְנַהֵג בַּעֲנָוָה עִם כָּל אָדָם
shello legaddef ish, lachdol mimmerivot, lihyot nochim labbriyot ulehitnaheg ba'anavah im kol adam
to speak evil of no man, not to be contentious, to be gentle, showing all meekness toward all men.

הֲרֵי לְפָנִים גַּם אֲנַחְנוּ הָיִינוּ חַסְרֵי דַעַת, סוֹרְרִים, תּוֹעִים, עֲבָדִים לְכָל מִינֵי תַּאֲווֹת וּתְשׁוּקוֹת
harei lefanim gam anachnu hayinu chasrei da'at, sorerim, to'im, avadim lechol minei ta'avot uteshukot
For we also once were foolish, disobedient, deceived, serving divers lusts and pleasures,

מְבַלִּים זְמַנֵּנוּ בְּרִשְׁעָה וְקִנְאָה, שְׂנוּאִים, וְשׂוֹנְאִים אִישׁ אֶת אָחִיו
mevallim zemannenu berish'ah vekin'ah, senu'im, vesone'im ish et achiv
living in malice and envy, hateful, hating one another.

אוּלָם כְּשֶׁנִּגְלָה טוּבוֹ שֶׁל הָאֱלֹהִים מוֹשִׁיעֵנוּ וְאַהֲבָתוֹ אֶת הָאָדָם
ulam keshenniglah tuvo shel ha'elohim moshi'enu ve'ahavato et ha'adam
But when the kindness of God our Saviour, and his love toward man, appeared,

אֲזַי לֹא בִּגְלַל מַעֲשֵׂי צְדָקָה שֶׁעָשִׂינוּ הוּא הוֹשִׁיעַ אוֹתָנוּ, כִּי אִם בְּרַחֲמָיו
azai lo biglal ma'asei tzedakah she'asinu hu hoshia otanu, ki im berachamav
not by works done in righteousness, which we did ourselves, but according to his mercy he saved us,

עַל־יְדֵי רְחִיצַת הַלֵּדָה הַחֲדָשָׁה וְהַהִתְחַדְּשׁוּת בְּרוּחַ הַקֹּדֶשׁ
al-yedei rechitzat halledah hachadashah vehahitchaddeshut beruach hakkodesh
through the washing of regeneration and renewing of the Holy Spirit,

אֲשֶׁר שָׁפַךְ עָלֵינוּ לְמַכְבִּיר עַל־יְדֵי יֵשׁוּעַ הַמָּשִׁיחַ מוֹשִׁיעֵנוּ
asher shafach aleinu lemachbir al-yedei yeshua hammashiach moshi'enu
which he poured out upon us richly, through Jesus Christ our Saviour;

לְמַעַן נִצְדַּק בְּחַסְדּוֹ וְנִהְיֶה לְיוֹרְשֵׁי חַיֵּי עוֹלָם בְּהֶתְאֵם לַתִּקְוָה
lema'an nutzdak bechasdo venihyeh leyoreshei chayei olam behet'em lattikvah
that, being justified by his grace, we might be made heirs according to the hope of eternal life.

מְהֵימָן הַדָּבָר, וּרְצוֹנִי שֶׁתַּעֲמֹד עַל כָּךְ בְּתֹקֶף
meheiman haddavar, uretzoni shetta'amod al kach betokef
Faithful is the saying, and concerning these things I desire that thou affirm confidently,

כְּדֵי שֶׁהַמַּאֲמִינִים בֵּאלֹהִים יָשִׁיתוּ לִבָּם לַעֲסֹק בְּמַעֲשִׂים טוֹבִים
kedei shehamma'aminim be'elohim yashitu libbam la'asok bema'asim tovim
to the end that they who have believed God may be careful to maintain good works.

טִיטוֹס

הַרְאֵה עַצְמְךָ מוֹפֵת לְמַעֲשִׂים טוֹבִים; תְּהֵא הוֹרָאָתְךָ טְהוֹרָה וּמְכֻבֶּדֶת
har'eh atzmecha mofet lema'asim tovim; tehei hora'atecha tehorah umechubbedet
in all things showing thyself an ensample of good works; in thy doctrine showing uncorruptness, gravity,

יִהְיוּ דְּבָרֶיךָ בְּרִיאִים וּבְלִי דֹּפִי
yihyu dvareicha beri'im uveli dofi
sound speech, that cannot be condemned;

לְמַעַן יֵבוֹשׁ הַמִּתְנַגֵּד בְּאֵין לוֹ שׁוּם דָּבָר רַע לוֹמַר עָלֵינוּ
lema'an yevosh hammitnagged be'ein lo shum davar ra lomar aleinu
that he that is of the contrary part may be ashamed, having no evil thing to say of us.

עַל הָעֲבָדִים לְהִכָּנַע לַאֲדוֹנֵיהֶם בַּכֹּל, לְהַשְׂבִּיעַ אֶת רְצוֹנָם וְלֹא לְהִתְוַכֵּחַ
al ha'avadim lehikkana la'adoneihem bakkol, lehasbia et retzonam velo lehitvakkeach
Exhort servants to be in subjection to their own masters, and to be well-pleasing to them in all things; not gainsaying;

אַל יִמְעֲלוּ, אֶלָּא יַרְאוּ נֶאֱמָנוּת מְלֵאָה כְּדֵי שֶׁבְּכָל דָּבָר יַרְבּוּ פְּאֵר לְתוֹרַת הָאֱלֹהִים מוֹשִׁיעֵנוּ
al yim'alu, ella yar'u ne'emanut mele'ah kedei shebbechal davar yarbu pe'er letorat ha'elohim moshi'enu
not purloining, but showing all good fidelity; that they may adorn the doctrine of God our Saviour in all things.

הֵן חֶסֶד הָאֱלֹהִים הוֹפִיעַ לִישׁוּעַת כָּל בְּנֵי אָדָם
hen chesed ha'elohim hofia lishu'at kol benei adam
For the grace of God hath appeared, bringing salvation to all men,

לְהַדְרִיכֵנוּ לְהִבָּדֵל מֵרֶשַׁע וְתַאֲווֹת הָעוֹלָם
lehadrichenu lehibbadel meresha veta'avot ha'olam
instructing us, to the intent that, denying ungodliness and worldly lusts,

כְּדֵי שֶׁנִּחְיֶה בָּעוֹלָם הַזֶּה בִּצְנִיעוּת וּבְצֶדֶק וּבַחֲסִידוּת
kedei shennichyeh ba'olam hazzeh bitzni'ut uvetzedek uvachasidut
we should live soberly and righteously and godly in this present world;

בְּצִפִּיָּה לְמִמּוּשׁ הַתִּקְוָה הַמְבֹרֶכֶת וּלְהוֹפָעַת הֲדַר אֱלֹהֵינוּ הַגָּדוֹל וּמוֹשִׁיעֵנוּ יֵשׁוּעַ הַמָּשִׁיחַ
betzippiyah lemimmush hattikvah hamvorachah ulehofa'at hadar eloheinu haggadol umoshi'enu yeshua hammashiach
looking for the blessed hope and appearing of the glory of the great God and our Saviour Jesus Christ;

אֲשֶׁר נָתַן אֶת עַצְמוֹ בַּעֲדֵנוּ כְּדֵי לִפְדּוֹת אוֹתָנוּ מִכָּל עָוֶל
asher natan et atzmo ba'adenu kedei lifdot otanu mikkol avel
who gave himself for us, that he might redeem us from all iniquity,

וּלְטַהֵר לוֹ עַם סְגֻלָּה שׁוֹקֵד עַל מַעֲשִׂים טוֹבִים
uletaher lo am segullah shoked al ma'asim tovim
and purify unto himself a people for his own possession, zealous of good works.

אֶת הַדְּבָרִים הָאֵלֶּה תְּדַבֵּר; הָעֵץ וְהוֹכֵחַ בִּמְלוֹא הַסַּמְכוּת. אִישׁ אַל יָבוּז לְךָ
et haddevarim ha'elleh tedabber; ha'etz vehocheach bimlo hassamchut. ish al yavuz lecha
These things speak and exhort and reprove with all authority. Let no man despise thee.

טיטוס

כִּי גַּם שִׂכְלָם וְגַם מַצְפּוּנָם טְמֵאִים
ki gam sichlam vegam matzpunam teme'im
but both their mind and their conscience are defiled.

הֵם מַצְהִירִים שֶׁהֵם יוֹדְעִים אֶת אֱלֹהִים, אַךְ בְּמַעֲשֵׂיהֶם כּוֹפְרִים בּוֹ
hem matzhirim shehem yode'im et elohim, ach bema'aseiheim koferim bo
They profess that they know God; but by their works they deny him,

נִתְעָבִים הֵם וְסָרְבָנִים, וְלֹא יִצְלְחוּ לְשׁוּם מַעֲשֶׂה טוֹב
nit'avim hem vesarevanim, velo yitzlechu leshum ma'aseh tov
being abominable, and disobedient, and unto every good work reprobate.

ב

וְאַתָּה דַּבֵּר אֶת אֲשֶׁר יָאֶה לְתוֹרָתֵנוּ הַבְּרִיאָה
ve'attah dabber et asher ya'eh letoratenu habberi'ah
But speak thou the things which befit the sound doctrine:

שֶׁיִּהְיוּ הַזְּקֵנִים מְפֻכָּחִים, רְצִינִיִּים, מְאֻפָּקִים, בְּרִיאִים בָּאֱמוּנָה, בָּאַהֲבָה וּבְסַבְלָנוּת
sheyihyu hazzekenim mefukkachim, retziniyim, me'uppakim, beri'im ba'emunah, be'ahavah uvesavlanut
that aged men be temperate, grave, sober-minded, sound in faith, in love, in patience:

וְכֵן גַּם הַזְּקֵנוֹת שֶׁתִּתְנַהֵגְנָה בִּקְדֻשָּׁה
vechen gam hazzekenot shettitnahegenah bikdushah
that aged women likewise be reverent in demeanor,

שֶׁלֹּא תִהְיֶינָה הוֹלְכוֹת רָכִיל וְלֹא תִתְמַכֵּרְנָה לְיַיִן, כִּי אִם תִּהְיֶינָה מְלַמְּדוֹת אֶת הַטּוֹב
shello tihyeinah holechot rachil velo titmakkerenah leyayin, ki im tihyeinah melammedot et hattov
not slanderers nor enslaved to much wine, teachers of that which is good;

כְּדֵי שֶׁתְּחַנֵּכְנָה אֶת הַנָּשִׁים הַצְּעִירוֹת לֶאֱהֹב אֶת בַּעֲלֵיהֶן וְיַלְדֵיהֶן
kedei shettechannechenah et hannashim hatze'irot le'ehov et ba'aleihen veyaldeihen
that they may train the young women to love their husbands, to love their children,

וְלִהְיוֹת צְנוּעוֹת, טְהוֹרוֹת, מַשְׁגִּיחוֹת עַל בֵּיתָן, טוֹבוֹת
velihyot tzenu'ot, tehorot, mashgichot al beitan, tovot
to be sober-minded, chaste, workers at home, kind,

נִשְׁמָעוֹת לְבַעֲלֵיהֶן; זֹאת לְמַעַן לֹא יְנֹאַץ דְּבַר הָאֱלֹהִים
nishma'ot leva'aleihen; zot lema'an lo yeno'atz devar ha'elohim
being in subjection to their own husbands, that the word of God be not blasphemed:

כְּמוֹ כֵן הָאֵץ בַּצְּעִירִים שֶׁיִּהְיוּ מְאֻפָּקִים בַּכֹּל
kemo chen ha'etz batze'irim sheyihyu me'uppakim bakkol
the younger men likewise exhort to be sober-minded:

טִיטוֹס

אִישׁ שֶׁאֵין בּוֹ דֹפִי, לֹא עִקֵּשׁ, לֹא רַגְזָן, לֹא מִתְמַכֵּר לְיַיִן, לֹא בַּעַל אֶגְרוֹף, לֹא רוֹדֵף בֶּצַע
ish she'ein bo dofi, lo ikkesh, lo ragzan, lo mitmakker leyayin, lo ba'al egrof, lo rodef betza
not self-willed, not soon angry, no brawler, no striker, not greedy of filthy lucre;

אֶלָּא מַכְנִיס אוֹרְחִים, אוֹהֵב אֶת הַטּוֹב, מְיֻשָּׁב בְּדַעְתּוֹ, צַדִּיק, קָדוֹשׁ, כּוֹבֵשׁ אֶת יִצְרוֹ
ella machnis orechim, ohev et hattov, meyushav beda'to, tzaddik, kadosh, kovesh et yitzro
but given to hospitality, a lover of good, sober-minded, just, holy, self-controlled;

וּמַחֲזִיק בַּדָּבָר הַמְהֵימָן אֲשֶׁר עַל־פִּי תּוֹרָתֵנוּ
umachazik baddavar hamheiman asher al-pi toratenu
holding to the faithful word which is according to the teaching,

לְמַעַן יוּכַל גַּם לְעוֹדֵד בְּהוֹרָאַת הַלֶּקַח הַבָּרִיא וְגַם לְהוֹכִיחַ אֶת הַמִּתְנַגְּדִים
lema'an yuchal gam le'oded behora'at hallekach habbari vegam lehochiach et hammitnaggedim
that he may be able both to exhort in the sound doctrine, and to convict the gainsayers.

כִּי יֵשׁ רַבִּים הַמְסָרְבִים לְהִשָּׁמַע, דּוֹבְרֵי הֶבֶל וּמַתְעִים, בִּפְרָט מִבֵּין הַנִּמּוֹלִים
ki yesh rabbim hamsarevim lehishama', doverei hevel umat'im, bifrat mibbein hannimmolim
For there are many unruly men, vain talkers and deceivers, specially they of the circumcision,

אֲשֶׁר מִן הַדִּין שֶׁיִּסָּכֵר פִּיהֶם; מַשְׁחִיתִים הֵם מִשְׁפָּחוֹת שְׁלֵמוֹת
asher min haddin sheyissacher pihem; mashchitim hem mishpachot shelemot
whose mouths must be stopped; men who overthrow whole houses,

בְּלַמְּדָם דְּבָרִים פְּסוּלִים, וְזֹאת לְמַעַן רֶוַח שָׁפָל
belammedam devarim pesulim, vezot lema'an revach shafel
teaching things which they ought not, for filthy lucre's sake.

וּכְבָר אָמַר אֶחָד מֵהֶם, שֶׁהוּא נָבִיא מִקִּרְבָּם.
ukevar amar echad mehem, shehu navi mikkirbam.
One of themselves, a prophet of their own, said,

הַכְּרֵתִיִּים מְשַׁקְּרִים תָּמִיד, חַיּוֹת רָעוֹת הֵם וּכְרֵשִׂים עֲצֵלִים
hakkeretiyim meshakkerim tamid, chayot ra'ot hem ucheresim atzelim.
Cretans are always liars, evil beasts, idle gluttons.

הָעֵדוּת הַזֹּאת אֱמֶת הִיא. עַל כֵּן הוֹכֵחַ אוֹתָם תּוֹכֵחָה קָשָׁה, לְמַעַן יִהְיוּ בְּרִיאִים בָּאֱמוּנָה
ha'edut hazzot emet hi. al ken hocheach otam tochechah kashah, lema'an yihyu beri'im ba'emunah
This testimony is true. For which cause reprove them sharply, that they may be sound in the faith,

וְלֹא יָשִׁיתוּ לִבָּם לְאַגָּדוֹת יְהוּדִיּוֹת וּלְמִצְווֹת בְּנֵי אָדָם הַסּוֹטִים מִן הָאֱמֶת
velo yashitu libbam le'aggadot yehudiyot ulemitzvot benei adam hasotim min ha'emet
not giving heed to Jewish fables, and commandments of men who turn away from the truth.

הַכֹּל טָהוֹר לַטְּהוֹרִים, אֲבָל לַטְּמֵאִים וּלְשֶׁאֵינָם מַאֲמִינִים שׁוּם דָּבָר אֵינוֹ טָהוֹר,
hakkol tahor lattehorim, aval latteme'im uleshe'einam ma'aminim shum davar eino tahor
To the pure all things are pure: but to them that are defiled and unbelieving nothing is pure;

טִיטוֹס

מֵאֵת שָׁאוּל, עֶבֶד אֱלֹהִים וּשְׁלִיחַ יֵשׁוּעַ הַמָּשִׁיחַ לְמַעַן אֱמוּנָתָם שֶׁל בְּחִירֵי אֱלֹהִים
me'et sha'ul, eved elohim ushliach yeshua hammashiach lema'an emunatam shel bchirei elohim
Paul, a servant of God, and an apostle of Jesus Christ, according to the faith of God's elect,

וְהַכָּרָתָם אֶת הָאֱמֶת אֲשֶׁר הִיא בְהֶתְאֵם לְיִרְאַת שָׁמַיִם
vehakkaratam et ha'emet asher hi behet'em leyir'at shamayim
and the knowledge of the truth which is according to godliness,

בְּתִקְוָה לְחַיֵּי עוֹלָם אֲשֶׁר הָאֱלֹהִים - אֲשֶׁר אֵינוֹ מְכַזֵּב - הִבְטִיחַ לִפְנֵי עִתּוֹת עוֹלָם
betikvah lechayei olam asher ha'elohim - asher eino mechazzev - hivtiach lifnei ittot olam
in hope of eternal life, which God, who cannot lie, promised before times eternal;

וּבְעִתּוֹתָיו גִּלָּה אֶת דְּבָרוֹ בְּהַכְרָזָה
uve'ittotav gillah et devaro behachrazah
but in his own seasons manifested his word in the message,

שֶׁהֻפְקְדָה בְּיָדִי עַל־פִּי מִצְוַת הָאֱלֹהִים מוֹשִׁיעֵנוּ
shehufkedah beyadi al-pi mitzvat ha'elohim moshi'enu
wherewith I was intrusted according to the commandment of God our Saviour;

אֶל טִיטוֹס בְּנִי הָאֲמִתִּי בָּאֱמוּנָה הַמְשֻׁתֶּפֶת
el titos beni ha'amitti ba'emunah hameshuttefet
to Titus, my true child after a common faith:

חֶסֶד וְשָׁלוֹם מֵאֵת הָאֱלֹהִים אָבִינוּ וְהַמָּשִׁיחַ יֵשׁוּעַ מוֹשִׁיעֵנוּ
chesed veshalom me'et ha'elohim avinu vehammashiach yeshua moshi'enu
Grace and peace from God the Father and Christ Jesus our Saviour.

הִשְׁאַרְתִּיךָ בִּכְרֵיתִים כְּדֵי שֶׁתְּסַדֵּר מַה שֶּׁיֵּשׁ עוֹד לְסַדֵּר
hish'articha bichreitim kedei shettesadder mah sheyesh od lesadder
For this cause left I thee in Crete, that thou shouldest set in order the things that were wanting,

וּתְמַנֶּה זְקֵנִים בְּכָל עִיר כְּפִי שֶׁצִּוִּיתִיךָ, כְּלוֹמַר
utemanneh zekenim bechol ir kefi shetzivviticha, klomar
and appoint elders in every city, as I gave thee charge;

אֶת מִי שֶׁאֵין בּוֹ דֹּפִי וְהוּא בַּעַל אִשָּׁה אַחַת וְיֵשׁ לוֹ בָּנִים מַאֲמִינִים אֲשֶׁר אֵין עֲלֵיהֶם טַעֲנַת הוֹלֵלוּת אוֹ סוֹרְרוּת
et mi she'ein bo dofi vehu ba'al ishah achat veyesh lo banim ma'aminim asher ein aleihem ta'anat holelut o sorerut
if any man is blameless, the husband of one wife, having children that believe, who are not accused of riot or unruly.

הֲלֹא בְּתוֹר סוֹכֵן עַל בֵּית אֱלֹהִים צָרִיךְ הַמַּנְהִיג לִהְיוֹת
halo betor sochen al beit elohim tzarich hammanhig lihyot
For the bishop must be blameless, as God's steward;

טִימוֹתֵיאוֹס ב

אֶת טִיכִיקוֹס שָׁלַחְתִּי לְאֶפֶסוֹס
et tichikos shalachti le'efesos
But Tychicus I sent to Ephesus.

כַּאֲשֶׁר תָּבוֹא, הָבֵא אֶת הַמְּעִיל שֶׁהִשְׁאַרְתִּי בִּטְרוֹאַס אֵצֶל קַרְפּוֹס, כֵּן גַּם אֶת הַמְּגִלּוֹת וּבְיִחוּד אֶת יְרִיעוֹת הַקְּלָף
ka'asher tavo, havei et hamme'il shehish'arti bitro'as etzel karpos, ken gam et hammegillot uveyichud et yeri'ot hakkelaf
The cloak that I left at Troas with Carpus, bring when thou comest, and the books, especially the parchments.

אֲלֶכְּסַנְדֵּר חָרָשׁ הַנְּחֹשֶׁת עָשָׂה לִי רָעוֹת רַבּוֹת, יִגְמֹל לוֹ יהוה כְּמַעֲשָׂיו
alekkesander charash hannechoshet asah li ra'ot rabbot, yigmol lo hashem kema'asav
Alexander the coppersmith did me much evil: the Lord will render to him according to his works:

גַּם אַתָּה הִשָּׁמֶר מִמֶּנּוּ, כִּי הִתְנַגֵּד בְּחָזְקָה לִדְבָרֵינוּ
gam attah hishamer mimmennu, ki hitnagged bechazekah lidvareinu
of whom do thou also beware; for he greatly withstood our words.

כְּשֶׁקַּמְתִּי לַהֲגַנָּתִי בַּפַּעַם הָרִאשׁוֹנָה, אִישׁ לֹא עָמַד לְצִדִּי, כִּי כֻּלָּם עֲזָבוּנִי; אַל יֵחָשֵׁב לָהֶם לְעָוֹן
keshekkamti lahagannati bappa'am harishonah, ish lo amad letziddi, ki kullam azavuni; al yechashev lahem le'avon
At my first defence no one took my part, but all forsook me: may it not be laid to their account.

אֲבָל הָאָדוֹן עָמַד אִתִּי וְחִזְּקַנִי, כְּדֵי שֶׁתֻּכְרַז עַל-יָדִי הַבְּשׂוֹרָה בִּמְלוֹאָהּ
aval ha'adon amad itti vechizzekani, kedei shettuchraz al-yadi habbesorah bimlo'ah
But the Lord stood by me, and strengthened me; that through me the message might be fully proclaimed,

וְיִשְׁמְעוּ כָּל הַגּוֹיִם, וְאָכֵן נִצַּלְתִּי מִפִּי הָאַרְיֵה
veyishme'u kol haggoyim, ve'achen nitzalti mippi ha'aryeh
and that all the Gentiles might hear: and I was delivered out of the mouth of the lion.

הָאָדוֹן יַצִּילֵנִי מִכָּל מַעֲשֵׂה רַע וְיוֹשִׁיעֵנִי אֶל מַלְכוּתוֹ שֶׁבַּשָּׁמַיִם
ha'adon yatzileni mikkol ma'aseh ra veyoshi'eni el malchuto shebbashamayim
The Lord will deliver me from every evil work, and will save me unto his heavenly kingdom:

לוֹ הַכָּבוֹד לְעוֹלְמֵי עוֹלָמִים. אָמֵן. דְּרֹשׁ בְּשָׁלוֹם פְּרִיסְקָה וַעֲקִילַס וּבֵית אוֹנִיסִיפוֹרוּס
lo hakkavod le'olemei olamim. amen. derosh bishlom perisekah va'aklas uveit onisiforus
to whom be the glory for ever and ever. Amen. Salute Prisca and Aquila, and the house of Onesiphorus.

אֶרַסְטוֹס נִשְׁאַר בְּקוֹרִינְתּוֹס. אֶת טְרוֹפִימוֹס הִשְׁאַרְתִּי בְּמִילֵטוֹס כְּשֶׁהוּא חוֹלֶה
erastos nish'ar bekorinetos. et terofimos hish'arti bemiletos keshehu choleh
Erastus remained at Corinth: but Trophimus I left at Miletus sick.

חוּשָׁה לָבוֹא לִפְנֵי הַחֹרֶף. אֶבּוּלוֹס דּוֹרֵשׁ בִּשְׁלוֹמְךָ, כֵּן גַּם פּוּדִיס, לִינוֹס, קְלוֹדְיָה, וְכָל הָאַחִים
chushah lavo lifnei hachoref. ebbulos doresh bishlomecha, ken gam pudis, linos, kelodeyah, vechol ha'achim
Give diligence to come before winter. Eubulus saluteth thee, and Pudens, and Linus, and Claudia, and all the brethren.

הָאָדוֹן עִם רוּחֲךָ. הַחֶסֶד עִמָּכֶם
ha'adon im ruchacha. hachesed immachem
The Lord be with thy spirit. Grace be with you.

טִימוֹתֵיאוֹס ב

הֵן יָבוֹא הַזְּמַן שֶׁלֹּא יִסְבְּלוּ אֶת הַלֶּקַח הַבָּרִיא
hen yavo hazzeman shello yisbelu et hallekach habbari
For the time will come when they will not endure the sound doctrine;

אֶלָּא יַאַסְפוּ לָהֶם מוֹרִים לְפִי מַאֲוַיֵּיהֶם לְשֵׁם שַׁעֲשׁוּעֵי אָזְנַיִם
ella ya'asfu lahem morim lefi ma'avayeihem leshem sha'ashu'ei oznayim
but, having itching ears, will heap to themselves teachers after their own lusts;

וּמִן הָאֱמֶת יַטּוּ אָזְנֵיהֶם לִפְנוֹת אֶל הָאַגָּדוֹת
umin ha'emet yattu azeneihem lifnot el ha'aggadot
and will turn away their ears from the truth, and turn aside unto fables.

אֲבָל אַתָּה עֲמֹד עַל הַמִּשְׁמָר בְּכָל דָּבָר, סְבֹל הָרָעוֹת, עֲשֵׂה אֶת מְלֶאכֶת הַמְבַשֵּׂר, וּמַלֵּא אֶת שֵׁרוּתְךָ
aval attah amod alhammishmar bechol davar, sevol hara'ot, aseh et melechet hamvasser, umallei et sherutecha
But be thou sober in all things, suffer hardship, do the work of an evangelist, fulfil thy ministry.

אֲנִי עַצְמִי כְּבָר מֻסָּךְ כְּנֶסֶךְ וְעֵת פְּטִירָתִי הִגִּיעָה
'ani atzmi kevar mussach kenesech ve'et petirati higgi'ah
For I am already being offered, and the time of my departure is come.

אֶת הַמִּלְחָמָה הַטּוֹבָה נִלְחַמְתִּי, אֶת הַמֵּרוֹץ הִשְׁלַמְתִּי, אֶת הָאֱמוּנָה שָׁמַרְתִּי
et hammilchamah hattovah nilchamti, et hammerotz hishlamti, et ha'emunah shamarti
I have fought the good fight, I have finished the course, I have kept the faith:

מֵעַתָּה שְׁמוּרָה לִי עֲטֶרֶת הַצְּדָקָה
me'attah shemurah li ateret hatzedakah
henceforth there is laid up for me the crown of righteousness,

אֲשֶׁר הָאָדוֹן, הַשּׁוֹפֵט הַצַּדִּיק, יִתֵּן לִי בַּיּוֹם הַהוּא
asher ha'adon, hashofet hatzaddik, yitten li bayom hahu
which the Lord, the righteous judge, shall give to me at that day;

וְלֹא רַק לִי בִּלְבַד, אֶלָּא גַם לְכָל אוֹהֲבֵי הוֹפָעָתוֹ. חוּשָׁה לָבוֹא אֵלַי עַד מְהֵרָה
velo rak li bilvad, ella gam lechol ohavei hofa'ato. chushah lavo elai ad meherah
and not to me only, but also to all them that have loved his appearing. Give diligence to come shortly unto me:

כִּי דִּימַס עֲזָבַנִי בִּגְלַל אַהֲבָתוֹ אֶת הָעוֹלָם הַזֶּה וְהָלַךְ לוֹ לְתֶסַּלוֹנִיקִי
ki dimas azavani biglal ahavato et ha'olam hazzeh vehalach lo letessaloniki
for Demas forsook me, having loved this present world, and went to Thessalonica;

קְרִיסְקִיס הָלַךְ לְגָלַטְיָה וְטִיטוֹס לְדַלְמַטְיָה
kerisikis halach legalatyah vetitos ledalmatyah
Crescens to Galatia, Titus to Dalmatia.

רַק לוּקָס לְבַדּוֹ אִתִּי. קַח אֶת מַרְקוֹס וַהֲבִיאֵהוּ אִתְּךָ, כִּי הוּא מוֹעִיל לִי לַשֵּׁרוּת
rak lukas levaddo itti. kach et markos vahavi'ehu ittcha, ki hu mo'il li lasherut
Only Luke is with me. Take Mark, and bring him with thee; for he is useful to me for ministering.

טִימוֹתִיאוֹס ב

אַךְ אֲנָשִׁים רָעִים וּמַדִּיחִים יַגְבִּירוּ רָעָתָם, יַתְעוּ וְיֻתְעוּ
ach anashim ra'im umaddichim yagbiru ra'atam, yat'u veyut'u
But evil men and impostors shall wax worse and worse, deceiving and being deceived.

אֲבָל אַתָּה עֲמֹד בַּדְּבָרִים אֲשֶׁר לָמַדְתָּ וַאֲשֶׁר מְצָאתָם נְכוֹנִים
aval attah amod baddevarim asher lamadta va'asher metzatam nechonim
But abide thou in the things which thou hast learned and hast been assured of,

שֶׁהֲרֵי יוֹדֵעַ אַתָּה מִמִּי לָמַדְתָּ וּמִנְּעוּרֶיךָ אַתָּה יוֹדֵעַ אֶת כִּתְבֵי הַקֹּדֶשׁ
sheharei yodea attah mimmi lamadta uminne'ureicha attah yodea et kitvei hakkodesh
knowing of whom thou hast learned them; and that from a babe thou hast known the sacred writings

הַיְכוֹלִים לְהַחְכִּימְךָ לִישׁוּעָה עַל־יְדֵי הָאֱמוּנָה בַּמָּשִׁיחַ יֵשׁוּעַ
haycholim lehachkimecha liyshu'ah al-yedei ha'emunah bammashiach yeshua
which are able to make thee wise unto salvation through faith which is in Christ Jesus.

כָּל הַכָּתוּב נִכְתַּב בְּרוּחַ אֱלֹהִים
kol hakkatuv nichtav beruach elohim
Every scripture inspired of God

וּמוֹעִיל הוּא לְהוֹרָאָה, לְתוֹכֵחָה, לְתִקּוּן, לְחִנּוּךְ בְּמַעְגְּלֵי צֶדֶק
umo'il hu lehora'ah, letochechah, letikkun, lechinnuch bema'gelei tzedek
is also profitable for teaching, for reproof, for correction, for instruction which is in righteousness:

לְמַעַן יִהְיֶה אִישׁ הָאֱלֹהִים מֻשְׁלָם, וּמֻכְשָׁר לְכָל מַעֲשֶׂה טוֹב
lema'an yihyeh ish ha'elohim mushlam, umuchshar lechol ma'aseh tov
that the man of God may be complete, furnished completely unto every good work.

ד

אֲנִי מֵעִיד בְּךָ לִפְנֵי אֱלֹהִים וְלִפְנֵי הַמָּשִׁיחַ יֵשׁוּעַ
ani me'id becha lifnei elohim velifnei hammashiach yeshua
I charge thee in the sight of God, and of Christ Jesus,

הֶעָתִיד לִשְׁפֹּט אֶת הַחַיִּים וְאֶת הַמֵּתִים בְּהוֹפָעָתוֹ וּבְמַלְכוּתוֹ
he'atid lishpot et hachayim ve'et hammetim behofa'ato uvemalchuto
who shall judge the living and the dead, and by his appearing and his kingdom:

הַכְרֵז אֶת הַדָּבָר, הַתְמֵד בְּעִתּוֹ וְשֶׁלֹּא בְּעִתּוֹ,
hachrez et haddavar, hatmed be'itto veshello be'itto
preach the word; be urgent in season, out of season;

הוֹכֵחַ, גְּעַר, הַפְצֵר, וְזֹאת בְּכָל אֹרֶךְ רוּחַ וְעַל־יְדֵי הַהוֹרָאָה
hocheach, ge'ar, haftzer, vezot bechol orech ruach ve'al-yedei hahora'ah
reprove, rebuke, exhort, with all longsuffering and teaching.

טִימוֹתִיאוֹס ב

לִכְאוֹרָה בַּעֲלֵי יִרְאַת שָׁמַיִם, אַךְ כּוֹפְרִים בְּתָקְפָּהּ. הִתְרַחֵק מֵאֵלֶּה
lich'orah ba'alei yir'at shamayim, ach koferim betakepah. hitrachek me'elleh
holding a form of godliness, but having denied the power thereof: from these also turn away.

הֵן מִקִּרְבָּם בָּאִים הָאֲנָשִׁים אֲשֶׁר מִתְגַּנְּבִים לְבָתִּים
hen mikkirbam ba'im ha'anashim asher mitgannevim levattim
For of these are they that creep into houses,

וְלוֹכְדִים נָשִׁים כְּסִילוֹת, עֲמוּסוֹת חֲטָאִים וְנִתָּעוֹת בְּכָל מִינֵי תַּאֲווֹת
velochedim nashim kesilot, amusot chata'im venit'ot bechol minei ta'avot
and take captive silly women laden with sins, led away by divers lusts,

הַלּוֹמְדוֹת תָּמִיד וְאַף פַּעַם אֵינָן יְכוֹלוֹת לְהַגִּיעַ לִכְלַל יְדִיעַת הָאֱמֶת
hallomedot tamid ve'af pa'am einan yecholot lehaggia lichlal yedi'at ha'emet
ever learning, and never able to come to the knowledge of the truth.

וּכְדֶרֶךְ שֶׁיּוֹחָנָה וּמַמְרֵא הִתְנַגְּדוּ לְמֹשֶׁה, כֵּן גַּם אֵלֶּה מִתְנַגְּדִים לָאֱמֶת
uchederech sheyochanah umamrei hitnaggedu lemosheh, ken gam elleh mitnaggedim la'emet
And even as Jannes and Jambres withstood Moses, so do these also withstand the truth;

אֲנָשִׁים אֲשֶׁר שִׂכְלָם מְעֻוָּת וְהֵם מַכְזִיבִים בָּאֱמוּנָה
anashim asher sichlam me'uvvat vehem machzivim ba'emunah
men corrupted in mind, reprobate concerning the faith.

אֲבָל לֹא יַצְלִיחוּ עוֹד, כִּי אִוַּלְתָּם תִּגָּלֶה לַכֹּל, כְּמוֹ שֶׁאֵרַע גַּם לָאֲנָשִׁים הָהֵם
aval lo yatzlichu od, ki ivvaltam tiggaleh lakkol, kemo she'era gam la'anashim hahem
But they shall proceed no further: for their folly shall be evident unto all men, as theirs also came to be.

אַךְ אַתָּה הָלַכְתָּ בְּעִקְּבוֹתַי בַּהוֹרָאָה, בַּהִתְנַהֲגוּת, בַּתַּכְלִית, בָּאֱמוּנָה
ach attah halachta be'ikkevotai bahora'ah, bahitnahagut, battachlit, ba'emunah
But thou didst follow my teaching, conduct, purpose, faith,

בְּאֹרֶךְ הָרוּחַ, בָּאַהֲבָה, בַּסַּבְלָנוּת
be'orech haruach, ba'ahavah, bassavlanut
longsuffering, love, patience,

בָּרְדִיפוֹת וּבַסֵּבֶל שֶׁבָּאוּ עָלַי בְּאַנְטִיוֹכְיָה, בְּאִיקוֹנְיוֹן וּבְלִיסְטְרָה, וְאֵילוּ רְדִיפוֹת סָבַלְתִּי
baredifot uvassevel shebba'u alai be'antiyocheyah, be'ikoneyon uveliseterah, ve'eilu redifot savalti
persecutions, sufferings; what things befell me at Antioch, at Iconium, at Lystra; what persecutions I endured:

וּמִכֻּלָּן הִצִּילַנִי הָאָדוֹן
umikkullan hitzilani ha'adon
and out of them all the Lord delivered me.

וְאָמְנָם כָּל הָרוֹצִים לִחְיוֹת חַיֵּי חֲסִידוּת בַּמָּשִׁיחַ יֵשׁוּעַ, יֵרָדְפוּ
ve'amenam kol harotzim lichyot chayei chasidut bammashiach yeshua', yeradefu
Yea, and all that would live godly in Christ Jesus shall suffer persecution.

טִימוֹתִיאוֹס ב

עִם כָּל הַקּוֹרְאִים אֶל יהוה בְּלֵב טָהוֹר
im kol hakkore'im el hashem belev tahor
with them that call on the Lord out of a pure heart.

רְחַק מִשְּׁאֵלוֹת אֱוִילִיּוֹת וְנִבְעָרוֹת; אַתָּה יוֹדֵעַ שֶׁהֵן גּוֹרְמוֹת מְרִיבוֹת
rechak mishe'elot eviliyot veniv'arot; attah yodea shehen goremot merivot
But foolish and ignorant questionings refuse, knowing that they gender strifes.

וְעֶבֶד הָאָדוֹן מִן הַדִּין שֶׁלֹּא יָרִיב, אֶלָּא יְהֵא נוֹחַ לַכֹּל, מֻכְשָׁר לְלַמֵּד, סַבְלָן
ve'eved ha'adon min haddin shello yariv, ella yehei noach lakkol, muchshar lelammed, savlan
And the Lord's servant must not strive, but be gentle towards all, apt to teach, forbearing,

וּמוֹכִיחַ בַּעֲנָוָה אֶת הַמִּתְנַגְּדִים
umochiach ba'anavah et hammitnaggedim
in meekness correcting them that oppose themselves;

אוּלַי יִתֵּן לָהֶם הָאֱלֹהִים לַחֲזֹר בִּתְשׁוּבָה כְּדֵי שֶׁיַּכִּירוּ אֶת הָאֱמֶת
ulai yitten lahem ha'elohim lachazor bitshuvah kedei sheyakkiru et ha'emet
if peradventure God may give them repentance unto the knowledge of the truth,

וְיִתְפַּכְּחוּ וְיֵצְאוּ מִמַּלְכֹּדֶת הַשָּׂטָן אֲשֶׁר לְכָדָם כִּרְצוֹנוֹ
veyitpakkechu veyetze'u mimmalkodet hassatan asher lechadam kirtzono
and they may recover themselves out of the snare of the devil, having been taken captive by him unto his will.

ג

וְזֹאת דַּע לְךָ: בְּאַחֲרִית הַיָּמִים יָבוֹאוּ זְמַנִּים קָשִׁים
vezot da lecha. be'acharit hayamim yavo'u zemannim kashim
But know this, that in the last days grievous times shall come.

כִּי יִהְיוּ הָאֲנָשִׁים אוֹהֲבֵי עַצְמָם, אוֹהֲבֵי כֶסֶף, גַּאַוְתָנִים, שַׁחְצָנִים,
ki yihyu ha'anashim ohavei atzmam, ohavei kesef, ga'avtanim, shachtzanim,
For men shall be lovers of self, lovers of money, boastful, haughty,

מְגַדְּפִים, מַמְרִים אֶת פִּי הוֹרֵיהֶם, כְּפוּיֵי טוֹבָה, חַסְרֵי קְדֻשָּׁה
megaddefim, mamrim et pi horeihem, kfuyei tovah, chasrei kedushah
railers, disobedient to parents, unthankful, unholy,

קְשׁוּחֵי לֵב, בִּלְתִּי מִתְרַצִּים, מַלְשִׁינִים, הוֹלְלִים, אַכְזָרִים, שׂוֹנְאֵי טוֹב
keshuchei lev, bilti mitratzim, malshinim, holelim, achzarim, sone'ei tov
without natural affection, implacable, slanderers, without self-control, fierce, no lovers of good,

בּוֹגְדִים, פּוֹחֲזִים, יְהִירִים, אוֹהֲבִים תַּעֲנוּגוֹת יוֹתֵר מִשֶּׁהֵם אוֹהֲבִים אֶת אֱלֹהִים
bogedim, pochazim, yehirim, ohavim ta'anugot yoter mishehem ohavim et elohim
traitors, headstrong, puffed up, lovers of pleasure rather than lovers of God;

טִימוֹתִיאוֹס ב

הֱיֵה שָׁקוּד לְהִתְיַצֵּב נֶאֱמָן לִפְנֵי אֱלֹהִים
heyeh shakud lehityatzev ne'eman lifnei elohim
Give diligence to present thyself approved unto God,

פּוֹעֵל לֹא יֵבוֹשׁ, הַמְחַלֵּק נְכוֹנָה אֶת דְּבַר הָאֱמֶת
po'el lo yevosh, hamchallek nechonah et devar ha'emet
a workman that needeth not to be ashamed, handling aright the word of truth.

רְחַק מִדִּבּוּרִים תְּפֵלִים וְחַסְרֵי קְדֻשָּׁה, כִּי בַּעֲלֵיהֶם יוֹסִיפוּ רֶשַׁע עַל רֶשַׁע
rechak middibburim tefelim vechasrei kedushah, ki ba'aleihem yosifu resha al resha
But shun profane babblings: for they will proceed further in ungodliness,

וּדְבָרָם כְּרָקָב יֹאכַל; עִמָּהֶם נִמְנִים הִימֶנֵאוֹס וּפִילִיטוֹס
udevaram kerakav yochal; immahem nimnim himene'us ufilitos
and their word will eat as doth a gangrene: of whom is Hymenæus and Philetus;

אֲשֶׁר תָּעוּ מִן הָאֱמֶת, בְּאָמְרָם כִּי תְּחִיַּת הַמֵּתִים כְּבָר הָיְתָה, וְהֵם מְמוֹטְטִים אֱמוּנַת כַּמָּה אֲנָשִׁים
asher ta'u min ha'emet, be'ameram ki techiyat hammetim kevar hayetah, vehem memotetim emunat kammah anashim
men who concerning the truth have erred, saying that the resurrection is past already, and overthrow the faith of some.

אֲבָל הַיְסוֹד הֶחָזָק שֶׁהִנִּיחַ אֱלֹהִים עוֹמֵד אֵיתָן וְיֵשׁ לוֹ הַחוֹתָם הַזֶּה
aval haysod hechazak shehinniach elohim omed eitan veyesh lo hachotam hazzeh
Howbeit the firm foundation of God standeth, having this seal, The Lord knoweth them that are his:

וְיֹדַע יהוה אֶת אֲשֶׁר לוֹ, וְגַם יָסוּר מֵעָוֶל כָּל הַקּוֹרֵא בְּשֵׁם יהוה
veyoda hashem et asher lo, vegam yasur me'avel kol hakkorei beshem hashem
and, Let every one that nameth the name of the Lord depart from unrighteousness.

הִנֵּה בְּבַיִת גָּדוֹל לֹא רַק כְּלֵי זָהָב וְכֶסֶף
hinneh bevayit gadol lo rak kelei zahav vechesef
Now in a great house there are not only vessels of gold and of silver,

אֶלָּא גַם כְּלֵי עֵץ וְחֶרֶס, וּמֵהֶם כַּמָּה לְכָבוֹד וְכַמָּה לְקָלוֹן
ella gam kelei etz vecheres, umehem kammah lechavod vechammah lekalon
but also of wood and of earth; and some unto honor, and some unto dishonor.

לְפִיכָךְ אִם אִישׁ יְטַהֵר אֶת עַצְמוֹ מֵאֵלֶּה יִהְיֶה כְּלִי לְכָבוֹד
lefichach im ish yetaher et atzmo me'elleh yihyeh keli lechavod
If a man therefore purge himself from these, he shall be a vessel unto honor

מְקֻדָּשׁ וּמוֹעִיל לְבַעַל הַבַּיִת וּמוּכָן לְכָל מַעֲשֶׂה טוֹב
mekuddash umo'il leva'al habbayit umuchan lechol ma'aseh tov
sanctified, meet for the master's use, prepared unto every good work.

בְּרַח לְךָ מִתַּאֲווֹת הַנְּעוּרִים וּרְדֹף צֶדֶק, אֱמוּנָה, אַהֲבָה וְשָׁלוֹם
berach lecha mitta'avot hanne'urim uredof tzedek, emunah, ahavah veshalom,
But flee youthful lusts, and follow after righteousness, faith, love, peace,

טִימוֹתִיאוֹס ב

הָאִכָּר הֶעָמֵל, מִן הַדִּין שֶׁיִּהְיֶה רִאשׁוֹן לָקַחַת חֵלֶק מִן הַפְּרִי
ha'ikkar he'amel, min haddin sheyihyeh rishon lakachat chelek min happeri
The husbandman that laboreth must be the first to partake of the fruits.

שִׂים לִבְּךָ לְמַה שֶּׁאֲנִי אוֹמֵר, וְהָאָדוֹן יִתֵּן לְךָ בִּינָה בַּכֹּל
sim libbecha lemah she'ani omer, veha'adon yitten lecha binah bakkol
Consider what I say; for the Lord shall give thee understanding in all things.

זְכֹר אֶת יֵשׁוּעַ הַמָּשִׁיחַ שֶׁנֵּעוֹר מִן הַמֵּתִים, אֲשֶׁר הוּא מִזֶּרַע דָּוִד כִּדְבַר בְּשׂוֹרָתִי
zechor et yeshua hammashiach shenne'or min hammetim, asher hu mizzera david kidvar besorati
Remember Jesus Christ, risen from the dead, of the seed of David, according to my gospel:

הִיא הַבְּשׂוֹרָה שֶׁבַּעֲבוּרָהּ אֲנִי סוֹבֵל רָעוֹת עַד כְּדֵי שִׁבְתִּי בִּכְבָלִים כְּעוֹשֵׂה עָוֶל
hi habbesorah shebba'avurah ani sovel ra'ot ad kedei shivti bichvalim ke'oseh avel
wherein I suffer hardship unto bonds, as a malefactor;

אוּלָם דְּבַר הָאֱלֹהִים אֵינֶנּוּ בִּכְבָלִים
ulam devar ha'elohim einennu bichvalim
but the word of God is not bound.

עַל כֵּן אֲנִי סוֹבֵל הַכֹּל לְמַעַן הַנִּבְחָרִים
al ken ani sovel hakkol lema'an hannivcharim
Therefore I endure all things for the elect's sake,

כְּדֵי שֶׁגַּם הֵם יַשִּׂיגוּ תְּשׁוּעָה בַּמָּשִׁיחַ יֵשׁוּעַ עִם כְּבוֹד עוֹלָמִים
kedei sheggam hem yassigu teshu'ah bammashiach yeshua im kevod olamim
that they also may obtain the salvation which is in Christ Jesus with eternal glory.

מְהֵימָן הַדָּבָר: אִם מַתְנוּ אִתּוֹ, גַּם נִחְיֶה אִתּוֹ
meheiman haddavar. im matnu itto, gam nichyeh itto
Faithful is the saying: For if we died with him, we shall also live with him:

אִם נַחֲזִיק מַעֲמָד, גַּם נִמְלֹךְ אִתּוֹ; אִם נִתְכַּחֵשׁ, גַּם הוּא יִתְכַּחֵשׁ לָנוּ
im nachazik ma'amad, gam nimloch itto; im nitkachesh, gam hu yitkachesh lanu
if we endure, we shall also reign with him: if we shall deny him, he also will deny us:

אִם אֵינֶנּוּ נֶאֱמָנִים, הוּא נִשְׁאָר נֶאֱמָן, כִּי לֹא יוּכַל לְהִתְכַּחֵשׁ לְעַצְמוֹ.
im einennu ne'emanim, hu nish'ar ne'eman, ki lo yuchal lehitkachesh le'atzmo.
if we are faithless, he abideth faithful; for he cannot deny himself.

הַזְכֵּר לָהֶם אֶת הַדְּבָרִים הָאֵלֶּה וְהַזְהֵר אוֹתָם לִפְנֵי הָאֱלֹהִים
hazker lahem et haddevarim ha'elleh vehazher otam lifnei ha'elohim
Of these things put them in remembrance, charging them in the sight of the Lord,

שֶׁלֹּא יִתְוַכְּחוּ עַל דְּבָרִים שֶׁאֵין בָּהֶם מוֹעִיל וְאֵינָם אֶלָּא הוֹרְסִים אֶת הַשּׁוֹמְעִים
shello yitvakkechu al devarim she'ein bahem mo'il ve'einam ella horesim et hashome'im
that they strive not about words, to no profit, to the subverting of them that hear.

טימותיאוס ב

זֹאת אַתָּה יוֹדֵעַ, שֶׁעֲזָבוּ אוֹתִי כָּל אֵלֶּה אֲשֶׁר בְּאַסְיָה וּבִכְלָלָם פִּיגְלוֹס וְהֶרְמוֹגֶנִיס
zot attah yodea', she'azevu oti kol elleh asher be'asyah uvichlalam figelos vehermogenis
This thou knowest, that all that are in Asia turned away from me; of whom are Phygelus and Hermogenes.

יַשְׁפִּיעַ הָאָדוֹן רַחֲמִים עַל בֵּית אוֹנִיסִיפוֹרוֹס, כִּי פְּעָמִים רַבּוֹת עוֹדֵד אֶת נַפְשִׁי וְלֹא בוֹשׁ בִּכְבָלַי
yashpia ha'adon rachamim al beit onisiforus, ki pe'amim rabbot oded et nafshi velo bosh bichvalai
The Lord grant mercy unto the house of Onesiphorus: for he oft refreshed me, and was not ashamed of my chain;

אַדְּרַבָּא, בִּהְיוֹתוֹ בְּרוֹמָא שָׁקַד לְחַפְּשֵׂנִי עַד כִּי מְצָאַנִי
adderabba, bihyoto beroma shakad lechappeseni ad ki metza'ani
but, when he was in Rome, he sought me diligently, and found me

יִתֵּן לוֹ הָאָדוֹן לִמְצֹא רַחֲמִים מִלִּפְנֵי יהוה בַּיּוֹם הַהוּא
yitten lo ha'adon limtzo rachamim millifnei hashem bayom hahu
(the Lord grant unto him to find mercy of the Lord in that day);

אַתָּה יוֹדֵעַ הֵיטֵב עַד כַּמָּה הִרְבָּה לְשָׁרֵת בְּאֶפֶסוֹס
Attah yodea heitev ad kammah hirbah lesharet be'efesos
and in how many things he ministered at Ephesus, thou knowest very well.

ב

וְאַתָּה, בְּנִי, הִתְחַזֵּק בַּחֶסֶד אֲשֶׁר בַּמָּשִׁיחַ יֵשׁוּעַ
ve'attah, beni, hitchazzek bachesed asher bammashiach yeshua
Thou therefore, my child, be strengthened in the grace that is in Christ Jesus.

וְהַדְּבָרִים שֶׁשָּׁמַעְתָּ מִמֶּנִּי בְּמַעֲמַד עֵדִים רַבִּים
vehaddevarim sheshama'ta mimmenni bema'amad edim rabbim
And the things which thou hast heard from me among many witnesses,

הַפְקֵד אוֹתָם בִּידֵי אֲנָשִׁים נֶאֱמָנִים הַמֻּכְשָׁרִים לְלַמֵּד גַּם אֲנָשִׁים אֲחֵרִים
hafked otam biydei anashim ne'emanim hammuchsharim lelammed gam anashim acherim
the same commit thou to faithful men, who shall be able to teach others also.

הִשְׁתַּתֵּף בַּסֵּבֶל כְּחַיָּל טוֹב שֶׁל הַמָּשִׁיחַ יֵשׁוּעַ
hishtattef bassevel kechayal tov shel hammashiach yeshua
Suffer hardship with me, as a good soldier of Christ Jesus.

אִישׁ הַמְשָׁרֵת בַּצָּבָא לֹא יִתְעָרֵב בְּעִסְקֵי הַחַיִּים, וְזֹאת כְּדֵי לְהַשְׂבִּיעַ אֶת רְצוֹן מְפַקְּדוֹ
ish hamsharet batzava lo yit'arev be'iskei hachayim, vezot kedei lehasbia et retzon mefakkedo
No soldier on service entangleth himself in the affairs of this life; that he may please him who enrolled him as a soldier.

וְגַם הַמִּשְׁתַּתֵּף בְּתַחֲרוּת לֹא יֻכְתָּר אִם לֹא יִתְחָרֶה לְפִי הַכְּלָלִים
vegam hammishtattef betacharut lo yuchtar im lo yitchareh lefi hakkelalim
And if also a man contend in the games, he is not crowned, except he have contended lawfully.

טִימוֹתֵיאוֹס ב

לָכֵן אַל תֵּבוֹשׁ לֹא בְּעֵדוּת אֲדוֹנֵנוּ וְלֹא בִּי, אֲסִירוֹ
lachen al tevosh lo be'edut adonenu velo bi, asiro
Be not ashamed therefore of the testimony of our Lord, nor of me his prisoner:

אֶלָּא סְבֹל אִתִּי אֶת חֶבְלֵי הַבְּשׂוֹרָה כְּפִי כֹּחַ הָאֱלֹהִים
ella sevol itti et chevlei habbesorah kefi koach ha'elohim
but suffer hardship with the gospel according to the power of God;

הַמּוֹשִׁיעַ אוֹתָנוּ וְקוֹרֵא אוֹתָנוּ בִּקְרִיאָה קְדוֹשָׁה, לֹא לְפִי מַעֲשֵׂינוּ
hammoshia otanu vekorei otanu bikri'ah kedoshah, lo lefi ma'aseinu
who saved us, and called us with a holy calling, not according to our works,

כִּי אִם לְפִי תָּכְנִיתוֹ וּלְפִי חַסְדּוֹ הַנָּתוּן לָנוּ בַּמָּשִׁיחַ יֵשׁוּעַ מִלִּפְנֵי עִתּוֹת עוֹלָם
ki im lefi tochnito ulefi chasdo hannatun lanu bammashiach yeshua millifnei ittot olam
but according to his own purpose and grace, which was given us in Christ Jesus before times eternal,

אֲבָל כָּעֵת נִגְלָה חַסְדּוֹ בְּהוֹפָעַת מוֹשִׁיעֵנוּ הַמָּשִׁיחַ יֵשׁוּעַ
aval ka'et niglah chasdo behofa'at moshi'enu hammashiach yeshua
but hath now been manifested by the appearing of our Saviour Christ Jesus,

הַמְבַטֵּל אֶת הַמָּוֶת וּמוֹצִיא לָאוֹר אֶת הַחַיִּים וְהָאַל-כִּלָּיוֹן עַל-יְדֵי הַבְּשׂוֹרָה
hamvattel et hammavet umotzi la'or et hachayim veha'al-killayon al-yedei habbesorah
who abolished death, and brought life and immortality to light through the gospel,

בְּשׂוֹרָה זֹאת - אֲנִי נִתְמַנֵּיתִי לָהּ לְכָרוֹז וְשָׁלִיחַ וּמוֹרֶה
besorah zot - ani nitmanneiti lah lecharoz veshaliach umoreh
whereunto I was appointed a preacher, and an apostle, and a teacher.

וּבַעֲבוּרָהּ אֲנִי סוֹבֵל גַּם אֶת הַדְּבָרִים הָאֵלֶּה. אַךְ אֵינֶנִּי בּוֹשׁ, כִּי יוֹדֵעַ אֲנִי בְּמִי הֶאֱמַנְתִּי
uva'avurah ani sovel gam et haddevarim ha'elleh. Ach einenni bosh, ki yodea ani bemi he'emanti
For which cause I suffer also these things: yet I am not ashamed; for I know him whom I have believed,

וּבָטוּחַ אֲנִי שֶׁהוּא יָכוֹל לִשְׁמֹר אֶת פִּקְדוֹנִי לַיּוֹם הַהוּא
uvatuach ani shehu yachol lishmor et pikdoni layom hahu
and I am persuaded that he is able to guard that which I have committed unto him against that day.

הַחֲזֵק בְּמַתְכֹּנֶת הַדְּבָרִים הַבְּרִיאִים אֲשֶׁר שָׁמַעְתָּ מִמֶּנִּי
hachazek bematkonet haddevarim habberi'im asher shama'ta mimmenni
Hold the pattern of sound words which thou hast heard from me,

בֶּאֱמוּנָה וּבְאַהֲבָה אֲשֶׁר בַּמָּשִׁיחַ יֵשׁוּעַ
ba'emunah uva'ahavah asher bammashiach yeshua
in faith and love which is in Christ Jesus.

שְׁמֹר אֶת הַפִּקָּדוֹן הַטּוֹב בְּעֶזְרַת רוּחַ הַקֹּדֶשׁ הַשּׁוֹכֶנֶת בָּנוּ
shemor et happikkadon hattov be'ezrat ruach hakkodesh hashochenet banu
That good thing which was committed unto thee guard through the Holy Spirit which dwelleth in us.

טִימוֹתִיאוֹס ב

מֵאֵת שָׁאוּל, שְׁלִיחַ הַמָּשִׁיחַ יֵשׁוּעַ בִּרְצוֹן אֱלֹהִים וּבְהֶתְאֵם לְהַבְטָחַת הַחַיִּים
Me'et sha'ul, sheliach hammashiach yeshua bertzon elohim uvehet'em lehavtachat hachayim
Paul, an apostle of Christ Jesus through the will of God, according to the promise of the life

אֲשֶׁר בַּמָּשִׁיחַ יֵשׁוּעַ
asher bammashiach yeshua
which is in Christ Jesus,

אֶל טִימוֹתֵיאוֹס בְּנִי הָאָהוּב: חֶסֶד וְרַחֲמִים וְשָׁלוֹם מֵאֵת אֱלֹהִים הָאָב וְהַמָּשִׁיחַ יֵשׁוּעַ אֲדוֹנֵנוּ
el timotei'os beni ha'ahuv: Chesed verachamim veshalom me'et elohim ha'av vehammashiach yeshua adonenu
to Timothy, my beloved child: Grace, mercy, peace, from God the Father and Christ Jesus our Lord.

אֲנִי מוֹדֶה לֵאלֹהִים אֲשֶׁר בְּעִקְּבוֹת אֲבוֹתַי אֲנִי עוֹבֵד אוֹתוֹ בְּמַצְפּוּן טָהוֹר
ani modeh le'elohim asher be'ikkvot avotai ani oved oto bematzpun tahor
I thank God, whom I serve from my forefathers in a pure conscience,

וְאֵינֶנִּי חָדֵל לִזְכֹּר אוֹתְךָ בִּתְפִלּוֹתַי יוֹמָם וָלַיְלָה
ve'einenni chadel lizkor otecha bitfillotai yomam valaylah
how unceasing is my remembrance of thee in my supplications, night and day

זְכוּרוֹת לִי דִמְעוֹתֶיךָ וַאֲנִי נִכְסָף לִרְאוֹתְךָ לְמַעַן אֶמָּלֵא שִׂמְחָה
zechurot li dim'oteicha va'ani nichsaf lir'otcha lema'an emmalei simchah
longing to see thee, remembering thy tears, that I may be filled with joy;

זוֹכֵר אֲנִי אֶת אֱמוּנָתְךָ הַכֵּנָה
zocher ani et emunatecha hakkenah
having been reminded of the unfeigned faith that is in thee;

אֱמוּנָה שֶׁשָּׁכְנָה תְּחִלָּה בְּלוֹאִיס סָבָתְךָ וּבְאֶבְנִיקָה אִמְּךָ, וּבְטוּחַנִי שֶׁהִיא שׁוֹכֶנֶת גַּם בְּךָ
emunah sheshachenah techillah belo'is savatecha uve'evnikah immcha, uvetuchani shehi shochenet gam becha
which dwelt first in thy grandmother Lois, and thy mother Eunice; and, I am persuaded, in thee also.

עַל כֵּן אֲנִי מַזְכִּירְךָ לְעוֹרֵר אֶת מַתְּנַת אֱלֹהִים
al ken ani mazkirecha le'orer et mattnat elohim
For which cause I put thee in remembrance that thou stir up the gift of God,

אֲשֶׁר הָעֳנְקָה לְךָ בִּסְמִיכַת יָדַי
asher ha'anekah lecha bismichat yadi
which is in thee through the laying on of my hands.

הֵן הָאֱלֹהִים לֹא נָתַן לָנוּ רוּחַ שֶׁל פַּחַד, אֶלָּא רוּחַ שֶׁל גְּבוּרָה וְאַהֲבָה וְיִשּׁוּב הַדַּעַת
hen ha'elohim lo natan lanu ruach shel pachad, ella ruach shel gevurah ve'ahavah veyishuv hadda'at
For God gave us not a spirit of fearfulness; but of power and love and discipline.

טִימוֹתִיאוֹס א

לִשְׁמֹר אֶת הַמִּצְוָה בְּטֹהַר וּבְלֹא דֹפִי עַד הוֹפָעַת אֲדוֹנֵנוּ יֵשׁוּעַ הַמָּשִׁיחַ
lishmor et hammitzvah betohar uvelo dofi ad hofa'at adonenu yeshua hammashiach
that thou keep the commandment, without spot, without reproach, until the appearing of our Lord Jesus Christ:

אֲשֶׁר בְּעִתּוֹתָיו יַרְאֶה אוֹתָהּ הַמְבֹרָךְ, הָרִבּוֹן הַיָּחִיד, מֶלֶךְ הַמְּלָכִים וַאֲדוֹן הָאֲדוֹנִים
asher be'ittotav yar'eh otah hamvorach, haribbon hayachid, melech hammelachim va'adon ha'adonim
which in its own times he shall show, who is the blessed and only Potentate, the King of kings, and Lord of lords;

לוֹ לְבַדּוֹ הָאַלְמָוֶת וְהוּא שׁוֹכֵן אוֹר נִשְׂגָּב מִקְּרֹב אֵלָיו; אָדָם לֹא רָאָהוּ וְאַף אֵינוֹ יָכוֹל לִרְאוֹתוֹ
lo levaddo ha'almavet vehu shochen or nisgav mikkerov elav; adam lo ra'ahu ve'af eino yachol lir'oto
who only hath immortality, dwelling in light unapproachable; whom no man hath seen, nor can see:

לוֹ הַכָּבוֹד וְהַגְּבוּרָה לְעוֹלָמִים. אָמֵן
lo hakkavod vehaggevurah le'olamim. amen
to whom be honor and power eternal. Amen.

אֶת עֲשִׁירֵי הָעוֹלָם הַזֶּה צַוֵּה שֶׁלֹּא יָרוּם לְבָבָם
et ashirei ha'olam hazzeh tzavveh shello yarum levavam
Charge them that are rich in this present world, that they be not highminded,

וְלֹא יִבְטְחוּ בָּעֹשֶׁר שֶׁאֵין בּוֹ בִּטָּחוֹן, אֶלָּא בֵּאלֹהִים הַמַּעֲנִיק לָנוּ אֶת הַכֹּל בְּשֶׁפַע לַהֲנָאָתֵנוּ
velo yivtechu ba'osher she'ein bo bittachon, ella belohim hamma'anik lanu et hakkol beshefa lahana'atenu
nor have their hope set on the uncertainty of riches, but on God, who giveth us richly all things to enjoy;

אֱמֹר לָהֶם לַעֲשׂוֹת אֶת הַטּוֹב, לְהַעֲשִׁיר בְּמַעֲשִׂים טוֹבִים, לִהְיוֹת נְכוֹנִים לָתֵת, לִהְיוֹת נְדִיבִים
emor lahem la'asot et hattov, leha'ashir bema'asim tovim, lihyot nechonim latet, lihyot nedivim
that they do good, that they be rich in good works, that they be ready to distribute, willing to communicate;

לֶאֱצֹר לְעַצְמָם אוֹצָר טוֹב לֶעָתִיד
le'etzor le'atzmam otzar tov le'atid
laying up in store for themselves a good foundation against the time to come,

כְּדֵי שֶׁיַּשִּׂיגוּ אֶת הַחַיִּים הָאֲמִתִּיִּים טִימוֹתִיאוֹס, שְׁמֹר אֶת הַפִּקָּדוֹן
kedei sheyassigu et hachayim ha'amittiyim. timotei'os, shmor et happikkadon
that they may lay hold on the life which is life indeed. O Timothy, guard that which is committed unto thee,

סוּר מִדִּבּוּרִים תְּפֵלִים וְחַסְרֵי קְדֻשָּׁה, וּמִטְּעָנוֹת וּפִרְכוֹת שֶׁל מַה שֶּׁבְּכָזָב מְכֻנֶּה דַעַת
sur middibburim tefelim vechasrei kedushah, umitte'anot ufirchot shel mah shebbechazav mechunneh da'at
turning away from the profane babblings and oppositions of the knowledge which is falsely so called;

יֵשׁ שֶׁהִתְיַמְּרוּ בָּהּ וְסָטוּ מִן הָאֱמוּנָה. הַחֶסֶד עִמָּכֶם. אָמֵן
yesh shehityammeru bah vesatu min ha'emunah. hachesed immachem. amen
which some professing have erred concerning the faith. Grace be with you.

טִימוֹתֵיאוֹס א

וְאָמְנָם חַיֵּי חֲסִידוּת הַמְלֻוִּים הִסְתַּפְּקוּת עַצְמִית רֶוַח גָּדוֹל הֵם
ve'omnam chayei chasidut hamluvvim histappekut atzmit revach gadol hem
But godliness with contentment is great gain:

שֶׁהֲרֵי מְאוּמָה לֹא הֲבֵאנוּ עִמָּנוּ לָעוֹלָם וְיָדוּעַ שֶׁלֹּא נוּכַל לְהוֹצִיא מִמֶּנּוּ מְאוּמָה
sheharei me'umah lo hevenu immanu la'olam veyadua shello nuchal lehotzi mimmennu me'umah
for we brought nothing into the world, for neither can we carry anything out;

וְכַאֲשֶׁר יֵשׁ לָנוּ מָזוֹן וּבְגָדִים, נִסְתַּפֵּק נָא בָּהֶם
vecha'asher yesh lanu mazon uvegadim, nistappek na bahem
but having food and covering we shall be therewith content.

אֲבָל הַשּׁוֹאֲפִים לְהִתְעַשֵּׁר נִלְכָּדִים בְּנִסָּיוֹן וּבְמַלְכֹּדֶת וּבְרֹב תַּאֲווֹת אֱוִילִיּוֹת וּמַזִּיקוֹת
aval hasho'afim lehit'asher nilkadim benissayon uvemalkodet uverov ta'avot eviliyot umazzikot
But they that are minded to be rich fall into a temptation and a snare and many foolish and hurtful lusts,

הַמּוֹרִידוֹת אֶת הָאָדָם אֱלֵי הֶרֶס וַאֲבַדּוֹן
hammoridot et ha'adam elei heres va'avaddon
such as drown men in destruction and perdition.

הֲלֹא שֹׁרֶשׁ כָּל הָרָעוֹת הוּא אַהֲבַת הַכֶּסֶף, וְיֵשׁ לְהוּטִים אַחֲרָיו שֶׁסָּטוּ מִן הָאֱמוּנָה
halo shoresh kol hara'ot hu ahavat hakkesef, veyesh lehutim acharav shessatu min ha'emunah
For the love of money is a root of all kinds of evil: which some reaching after have been led astray from the faith,

וְגָרְמוּ לְעַצְמָם מַכְאוֹבִים רַבִּים
vegarmu le'atzmam mach'ovim rabbim
and have pierced themselves through with many sorrows.

אֲבָל אַתָּה, אִישׁ הָאֱלֹהִים, בְּרַח לְךָ מֵאֵלֶּה. רְדֹף צֶדֶק, חֲסִידוּת, אֱמוּנָה, אַהֲבָה, סַבְלָנוּת וַעֲנָוָה
aval attah, ish ha'elohim, berach lecha me'elleh. redof tzedek, chasidut, emunah, ahavah, savlanut va'anavah
But thou, O man of God, flee these things; and follow after righteousness, godliness, faith, love, patience, meekness.

הֵאָבֵק הַמַּאֲבָק הַטּוֹב לְמַעַן הָאֱמוּנָה. אֱחֹז בְּחַיֵּי עוֹלָם אֲשֶׁר נִקְרֵאתָ אֲלֵיהֶם
he'avek hamma'avak hattov lema'an ha'emunah, echoz bechayei olam asher nikreta aleihem
Fight the good fight of the faith, lay hold on the life eternal, whereunto thou wast called,

וַאֲשֶׁר הִצְהַרְתָּ עֲלֵיהֶם אֶת הַהוֹדָאָה הַיָּפָה בְּמַעֲמַד עֵדִים רַבִּים
va'asher hitzharta aleihem et hahoda'ah hayafah bema'amad edim rabbim
and didst confess the good confession in the sight of many witnesses.

לְנֶגֶד עֵינֵי אֱלֹהִים הַמְחַיֶּה אֶת הַכֹּל וּלְנֶגֶד עֵינֵי הַמָּשִׁיחַ יֵשׁוּעַ, אֲשֶׁר הֵעִיד לִפְנֵי פּוֹנְטְיוּס פִּילָטוֹס בְּהוֹדָאָתוֹ הַיָּפָה, הִנְנִי מְצַוֶּה עָלֶיךָ
leneged einei elohim hamchayeh et hakkol uleneged einei hammashiach yeshua', asher he'id lifnei poneteyus pilatos behoda'ato hayafah, hineni metzavveh aleicha
I charge thee in the sight of God, who giveth life to all things, and of Christ Jesus, who before Pontius Pilate witnessed the good confession;

טִימוֹתִיאוֹס א

כָּךְ גְּלוּיִים גַּם הַמַּעֲשִׂים הַטּוֹבִים; וְאֵלֶה שֶׁאֵינָם גְּלוּיִים לֹא יוּכְלוּ לְהֵחָבֵא
kach geluyim gam hamma'asim hattovim; ve'elleh she'einam geluyim lo yuchelu lehechave
In like manner also there are good works that are evident; and such as are otherwise cannot be hid.

I

כָּל הַנִּמְצָאִים תַּחַת עֹל הָעַבְדוּת יַחְשְׁבוּ נָא אֶת אֲדוֹנֵיהֶם רְאוּיִם לִמְלֹא כָבוֹד
kol hannimtza'im tachat ol ha'avdut yachshevu na et adoneihem re'uyim limlo kavod
Let as many as are servants under the yoke count their own masters worthy of all honor,

לְמַעַן לֹא יְגֻדַּף שֵׁם אֱלֹהִים וְלֹא תְּגֻדַּף תּוֹרָתֵנוּ
lema'an lo yeguddaf shem elohim velo teguddaf toratenu
that the name of God and the doctrine be not blasphemed.

וְאֵלֶה אֲשֶׁר אֲדוֹנֵיהֶם מַאֲמִינִים, אַל יָקֵלוּ רֹאשׁ כְּנֶגְדָּם בְּשֶׁל הֱיוֹתָם אֲחֵיהֶם לָאֱמוּנָה
ve'elleh asher adoneihem ma'aminim, al yakellu rosh kenegdam beshel heyotam acheihem la'emunah;
And they that have believing masters, let them not despise them, because they are brethren;

אַדְּרַבָּא, יַעַבְדוּ נָא אוֹתָם מִשּׁוּם שֶׁהַנֶּהֱנִים מִשֵּׁרוּתָם הַטּוֹב מַאֲמִינִים הֵם וַאֲהוּבִים
adderabba, ya'avdu na otam mishum shehannehenim misherutam hattov ma'aminim hem va'ahuvim
but let them serve them the rather, because they that partake of the benefit are believing and beloved. These things teach and exhort.

אִישׁ הַמּוֹרֶה תּוֹרָה אַחֶרֶת וְאֵינוֹ מַסְכִּים לְדִבְרָיו הַבְּרִיאִים
ish hammoreh torah acheret ve'eino maskim lidvarav habberi'im
If any man teacheth a different doctrine, and consenteth not to sound words,

שֶׁל אֲדוֹנֵנוּ יֵשׁוּעַ הַמָּשִׁיחַ וְלַתּוֹרָה אֲשֶׁר בְּהֶתְאֵם לַחֲסִידוּת
shel adonenu yeshua hammashiach velattorah asher behet'em lachasidut
even the words of our Lord Jesus Christ, and to the doctrine which is according to godliness;

אֲזַי הַגַּאֲוָה הֶעֱבִירָה אוֹתוֹ עַל דַּעְתּוֹ וְאֵינוֹ מֵבִין דָּבָר, וְהוּא בַּעַל נְטִיָּה חוֹלָנִית לַחֲקִירוֹת וְוִכּוּחִים
azai hagga'avah he'evirah oto al da'to ve'eino mevin davar, vehu ba'al netiyah cholanit lachakirot uvikkuchim
he is puffed up, knowing nothing, but doting about questionings and disputes of words,

הַמְּבִיאִים לִידֵי קִנְאָה, רִיב, גִּדּוּפִים, חֲשָׁדוֹת מְרֻשָּׁעִים
hamvi'im liydei kin'ah, riv, giddufim, chashadot merusha'im
whereof cometh envy, strife, railings, evil surmisings,

וְלִידֵי הִתְנַצְּחֻיּוֹת שֶׁל אֲנָשִׁים אֲשֶׁר שִׂכְלָם הִתְנַוֵּן וְהָאֱמֶת נֶעֱדֶרֶת מֵהֶם
velidei hitnatzechyot shel anashim asher sichlam hitnavven veha'emet ne'deret mehem
wranglings of men corrupted in mind and bereft of the truth,

שֶׁבְּעֵינֵיהֶם חַיֵּי חֲסִידוּת פֵּרוּשָׁם לְהַרְוִיחַ רֶוַח
shebbe'eineihem chayei chasidut perusham leharviach revach
supposing that godliness is a way of gain.

טִימוֹתֵיאוֹס א

אִם לְמַאֲמִין אוֹ לְמַאֲמִינָה יֵשׁ אַלְמָנוֹת בְּמִשְׁפַּחְתָּם, יַעַזְרוּ לָהֶן; אַל תִּהְיֶינָה לְמַשָּׂא עַל הַקְּהִלָּה
im lema'amin o lema'aminah yesh almanot bemishpachtam, ya'azru lahen; al tihyeinah lemasho al hakkehillah
If any woman that believeth hath widows, let her relieve them, and let not the church be burdened;

כָּךְ תּוּכַל הַקְּהִלָּה לַעֲזֹר לָאַלְמָנוֹת הָרְשׁוּמוֹת
kach tuchal hakkehillah la'azor la'almanot hareshumot
that it may relieve them that are widows indeed.

הַזְּקֵנִים הַמֵּיטִיבִים לְנַהֵל רְאוּיִים לְמִשְׁנֵה כָּבוֹד, בְּעִקָּר הָעֲמֵלִים בְּהַטָּפַת הַדָּבָר וּבַהוֹרָאָה
hazzekenim hammeitivim lenahel re'uyim lemishneh kavod, be'ikkar ha'amelim behattafat haddavar uvahora'ah
Let the elders that rule well be counted worthy of double honor, especially those who labor in the word and in teaching.

הֵן הַכָּתוּב אוֹמֵר: לֹא תַחְסֹם שׁוֹר בְּדִישׁוֹ
hen hakkatuv omer: lo tachsom shor bedisho,
For the scripture saith, Thou shalt not muzzle the ox when he treadeth out the corn.

וְגַם הַפּוֹעֵל רָאוּי לִשְׂכָרוֹ
vegam happo'el ra'ui lischaro
And, The laborer is worthy of his hire.

אַל תְּקַבֵּל דְּבַר קִטְרוּג עַל זָקֵן, בִּלְתִּי אִם עַל־פִּי שְׁנַיִם אוֹ שְׁלוֹשָׁה עֵדִים
al tekabbel devar kitrug al zaken, bilti im al-pi shenayim o sheloshah edim
Against an elder receive not an accusation, except at the mouth of two or three witnesses.

אֶת הַחוֹטְאִים תּוֹכִיחַ לְעֵינֵי כֹל, לְמַעַן תִּהְיֶה יִרְאָה גַּם בְּלֵב הָאֲחֵרִים
et hachote'im tochiach le'einei kol, lema'an tihyeh yir'ah gam belev ha'acherim
Them that sin reprove in the sight of all, that the rest also may be in fear.

הִנְנִי מֵעִיד בְּךָ לִפְנֵי אֱלֹהִים וְהַמָּשִׁיחַ יֵשׁוּעַ וְלִפְנֵי הַמַּלְאָכִים הַבְּחִירִים
hineni me'id becha lifnei elohim vehammashiach yeshua velifnei hammal'achim habbechirim
I charge thee in the sight of God, and Christ Jesus, and the elect angels,

שֶׁתַּקְפִּיד לְקַיֵּם אֶת הַדְּבָרִים הָאֵלֶּה בְּלִי לַחֲרֹץ מִשְׁפָּט מֵרֹאשׁ, וְאַל תַּעֲשֶׂה דָּבָר בְּמַשּׂוֹא פָּנִים
shettakpid lekayem et haddevarim ha'elleh beli lacharotz mishpat merosh, ve'al ta'aseh davar bemasso panim
that thou observe these things without prejudice, doing nothing by partiality.

אַל תְּמַהֵר לִסְמֹךְ יָדַיִם עַל אִישׁ, וְאַל תְּהֵא שֻׁתָּף לַחֲטָאֵי אֲחֵרִים. הִשָּׁמֵר לִהְיוֹת טָהוֹר
al temaher lismoch yadayim al ish, ve'al tehei shuttaf lachata'ei acherim. hishamer lihyot tahor
Lay hands hastily on no man, neither be partaker of other men's sins: keep thyself pure.

אַל תּוֹסִיף לִשְׁתּוֹת רַק מַיִם, כִּי אִם שְׁתֵה קְצָת יַיִן בִּגְלַל קֵבָתְךָ וּמַחֲלוֹתֶיךָ הַתְּכוּפוֹת
al tosif lishtot rak mayim, ki im sheteh ketzat yayin biglal kevatecha umachaloteicha hattechufot
Be no longer a drinker of water, but use a little wine for thy stomach's sake and thine often infirmities.

יֵשׁ בְּנֵי אָדָם שֶׁחֲטָאֵיהֶם גְּלוּיִים עוֹד לִפְנֵי הַמִּשְׁפָּט, אַךְ יֵשׁ שֶׁחֲטָאֵיהֶם מִתְבָּרְרִים אַחֲרֵי כֵן
yesh benei adam shechata'eihem geluyim od lifnei hammishpat, ach yesh shechata'eihem mitbarerim acharei chen
Some men's sins are evident, going before unto judgment; and some men also they follow after.

טִימוֹתִיאוֹס א

וּמִי שֶׁאֵינוֹ דוֹאֵג לִקְרוֹבָיו, בְּיִחוּד לִבְנֵי בֵּיתוֹ
umi she'eino do'eg likrovav, beyichud livnei beito
But if any provideth not for his own, and specially his own household,

כָּפַר בָּאֱמוּנָה וְהוּא גָּרוּעַ מִמִּי שֶׁאֵינוֹ מַאֲמִין
kafar ba'emunah vehu garua mimmi she'eino ma'amin
he hath denied the faith, and is worse than an unbeliever.

אַלְמָנָה לֹא תֵּרָשֵׁם אֶלָּא אִם מָלְאוּ לָהּ שִׁשִּׁים שָׁנָה וְהָיְתָה נְשׂוּאָה לְאִישׁ אֶחָד
almanah lo terashem ella im male'u lah shishim shanah vehayetah nesu'ah le'ish echad
Let none be enrolled as a widow under threescore years old, having been the wife of one man,

וְלִזְכוּתָהּ עֵדוּת עַל מַעֲשִׂים טוֹבִים - שֶׁגִּדְּלָה בָּנִים, הִכְנִיסָה אוֹרְחִים
velizchutah edut al ma'asim tovim - sheggiddelah banim, hichnisah orechim
well reported of for good works; if she hath brought up children, if she hath used hospitality to strangers,

רָחֲצָה אֶת רַגְלֵי הַקְּדוֹשִׁים, הָיְתָה לְסַעַד לַסּוֹבְלִים וְהִתְמַסְּרָה לְכָל מַעֲשֶׂה טוֹב
rachatzah et raglei hakkedoshim, hayetah lesa'ad lassovelim vehitmasserah lechol ma'aseh tov
if she hath washed the saints' feet, if she hath relieved the afflicted, if she hath diligently followed every good work.

אַל תְּקַבֵּל אַלְמָנוֹת צְעִירוֹת, כִּי כַּאֲשֶׁר הַיֵּצֶר שֶׁלָּהֶן נוֹטֶה מֵעִם הַמָּשִׁיחַ הֵן רוֹצוֹת לְהִנָּשֵׂא
al tekabbel almanot tze'irot, ki ka'asher hayetzer shellahen noteh me'im hammashiach hen rotzot lehinnasei
But younger widows refuse: for when they have waxed wanton against Christ, they desire to marry;

וְנֶחֱרָץ עֲלֵיהֶן מִשְׁפָּט מִפְּנֵי שֶׁהֵפֵרוּ אֶת הַבְטָחָתָן הָרִאשׁוֹנָה
venecheratz aleihen mishpat mippenei sheheferu et havtachatan harishonah
having condemnation, because they have rejected their first pledge.

נוֹסָף עַל כָּךְ הֵן מְשׁוֹטְטוֹת מִבַּיִת לְבַיִת וּמִתְרַגְּלוֹת לִהְיוֹת בַּטְלָנִיּוֹת
nosaf al kach hen meshotetot mibbayit levayit umitraggelot lihyot batlaniyot
And withal they learn also to be idle, going about from house to house;

וְלֹא בַּטְלָנִיּוֹת בִּלְבַד, אֶלָּא גַּם רַכְלָנִיּוֹת וּמִתְעָרְבוֹת בְּעִנְיָנִים לֹא לָהֶן
velo batlaniyot bilvad, ella gam rachlaniyot umit'arevot be'inyanim lo lahen
and not only idle, but tattlers also and busybodies,

וּמְדַבְּרוֹת דְּבָרִים שֶׁאֵין צֹרֶךְ לְהַשְׁמִיעָם
umedabberot devarim she'ein tzorech lehashmi'am
speaking things which they ought not.

לָכֵן רְצוֹנִי שֶׁהָאַלְמָנוֹת הַצְּעִירוֹת תִּנָּשֶׂאנָה, תֵּלַדְנָה יְלָדִים, תְּנַהֵלְנָה אֶת הַבַּיִת
lachen retzoni sheha'almanot hatze'irot tinnasenah, teladnah yeladim, tenahelenah et habbayit
I desire therefore that the younger widows marry, bear children, rule the household,

וְלֹא תִּתֵּנָּה בְּיַד הַמִּתְנַגֵּד שׁוּם תּוֹאֲנָה לְקַטְרֵג. כִּי יֵשׁ מֵהֶן שֶׁכְּבָר סָרוּ אַחֲרֵי הַשָּׂטָן
velo tittennah beyad hammitnagged shum to'anah lekatreg: ki yesh mehen shekkevar saru acharei hassatan
give no occasion to the adversary for reviling: for already some are turned aside after Satan.

טימותֵיאוֹס א

הַתְמֵד בָּזֶה, כִּי בַּעֲשׂוֹתְךָ כֵּן תּוֹשִׁיעַ גַּם אֶת עַצְמְךָ וְגַם אֶת הַשּׁוֹמְעִים אֵלֶיךָ
hatmed bazeh, ki ba'asotecha ken toshia gam et atzmecha vegam et hashome'im eleicha
Continue in these things; for in doing this thou shalt save both thyself and them that hear thee.

ה

אַל תִּגְעַר בְּזָקֵן, כִּי אִם הַפְצֵר בּוֹ כְּבֵן הַפּוֹנֶה לְאָבִיו. פְּנֵה אֶל הַצְּעִירִים כְּאֶל אַחִים
al tig'ar bezaken, ki im haftzer bo keven happoneh le'aviv. peneh el hatze'irim ke'el achim
Rebuke not an elder, but exhort him as a father; the younger men as brethren:

אֶל הַזְּקֵנוֹת כְּאֶל אִמָּהוֹת, וְאֶל הַצְּעִירוֹת כְּאֶל אֲחָיוֹת - בִּמְלוֹא הַטֹּהַר
el hazzekenot ke'el immahot, ve'el hatze'irot ke'el achayot - bimlo hattohar
the elder women as mothers; the younger as sisters, in all purity.

כַּבֵּד אֶת הָאַלְמָנוֹת אֲשֶׁר הֵן אָכֵן אַלְמָנוֹת
kabbed et ha'almanot asher hen achen almanot
Honor widows that are widows indeed.

וְאִם לְאַלְמָנָה יֵשׁ בָּנִים אוֹ בְּנֵי בָנִים
ve'im le'almanah yesh banim o benei banim
But if any widow hath children or grandchildren,

עֲלֵיהֶם קֹדֶם כֹּל לִלְמֹד לַעֲשׂוֹת חֶסֶד עִם בֵּיתָם הֵם וּלְהָשִׁיב גְּמוּל לְהוֹרֵיהֶם
aleihem kodem kol lilmod la'asot chesed im beitam hem ulehashiv gmul lehoreihem
let them learn first to show piety towards their own family, and to requite their parents:

כִּי כֵן רָצוּי לִפְנֵי אֱלֹהִים
ki chen ratzui lifnei elohim
for this is acceptable in the sight of God.

הָאִשָּׁה שֶׁהִיא אָכֵן אַלְמָנָה וְנִשְׁאֲרָה לְבַדָּהּ, מְיַחֶלֶת לֵאלֹהִים
ha'ishah shehi achen almanah venish'arah levaddah, meyachelet le'elohim
Now she that is a widow indeed, and desolate, hath her hope set on God,

וּמַתְמִידָה בִּתְחִנּוֹת וּתְפִלּוֹת יוֹמָם וָלַיְלָה
umatmidah bitchinnot utefillot yomam valaylah
and continueth in supplications and prayers night and day.

אַךְ זוֹ שֶׁלִּבָּהּ לְתַעֲנוּגוֹת, הֲרֵיהִי בִּבְחִינַת מֵתָה בְּחַיֶּיהָ
ach zo shellibbah leta'anugot, hareihi bivchinat metah bechayeiha
But she that giveth herself to pleasure is dead while she liveth.

אֶת הַדְּבָרִים הָאֵלֶּה תְּצַוֶּה, כְּדֵי שֶׁלֹּא יִמָּצֵא בָּהֶן דֹּפִי
et haddevarim ha'elleh tetzavveh, kedei shello yimmatzei bahen dofi
These things also command, that they may be without reproach.

טימוֹתִיאוֹס א

שֶׁהֲרֵי הַהִתְאַמְּנוּת הַגּוּפָנִית מוֹעִילָה בְּמִדָּה מְעַטָּה, אֲבָל הַחֲסִידוּת מוֹעִילָה בַּכֹּל
sheharei hahit'ammenut haggufanit mo'ilah bemiddah me'attah, aval hachasidut mo'ilah bakkol
for bodily exercise is profitable for a little; but godliness is profitable for all things,

וּבָהּ הַבְטָחָה לַחַיִּים שֶׁבַּהֹוֶה וְלַחַיִּים שֶׁלֶּעָתִיד לָבוֹא
uvah havtachah lachayim shebahove velachayim shelle'atid lavo
having promise of the life which now is, and of that which is to come.

מְהֵימָן הַדָּבָר הַזֶּה וְרָאוּי לְהַסְכָּמָה מְלֵאָה
meheiman haddavar hazzeh vera'ui lehaskamah mele'ah
Faithful is the saying, and worthy of all acceptation.

וְאָמְנָם לְשֵׁם כָּךְ אֲנַחְנוּ עֲמֵלִים וְנֶאֱבָקִים - שֶׁתִּקְוָתֵנוּ הִיא בֵּאלֹהִים חַיִּים
ve'amenam leshem kach anachnu amelim vene'evakim - shettikvatenu hi belohim chayim
For to this end we labor and strive, because we have our hope set on the living God,

אֲשֶׁר הוּא הַמּוֹשִׁיעַ שֶׁל כָּל בְּנֵי אָדָם, בְּיִחוּד שֶׁל הַמַּאֲמִינִים
asher hu hammoshia shel kol benei adam, beyichud shel hamma'aminim
who is the Saviour of all men, specially of them that believe.

אֶת הַדְּבָרִים הָאֵלֶּה תְּצַוֶּה וּתְלַמֵּד
et haddevarim ha'elleh tetzavveh utelammed
These things command and teach.

אַל יָבוּז לְךָ אִישׁ בְּשֶׁל צְעִירוּתְךָ. וְאוּלָם הֱיֵה מוֹפֵת לַמַּאֲמִינִים
al yavuz lecha ish beshel tze'irutecha. ve'ulam heyeh mofet lamma'aminim
Let no man despise thy youth; but be thou an ensample to them that believe,

בְּדִבּוּר, בְּהִתְנַהֲגוּת, בְּאַהֲבָה, בֶּאֱמוּנָה וּבְטָהֳרָה
bedibbur, behitnahagut, be'ahavah, be'emunah uvetohorah
in word, in manner of life, in love, in faith, in purity.

שְׁקֹד עַל קְרִיאָה בְּצִבּוּר שֶׁל כִּתְבֵי הַקֹּדֶשׁ, עַל הַהַטָּפָה וְעַל הַהוֹרָאָה - עַד שֶׁאָבוֹא
shekod al keri'ah betzibbur shel kitvei hakkodesh, al hahattafah ve'al hahora'ah - ad she'avo
Till I come, give heed to reading, to exhortation, to teaching.

אַל תַּזְנִיחַ אֶת הַמַּתָּנָה אֲשֶׁר בְּךָ, שֶׁנִּתְּנָה לְךָ עַל-פִּי נְבוּאָה בִּסְמִיכַת יְדֵיהֶם שֶׁל זִקְנֵי הַקְּהִלָּה
al tazniach et hammattanah asher becha, shennittenah lecha al-pi nevu'ah bismichat yedeihem shel ziknei hakkehillah
Neglect not the gift that is in thee, which was given thee by prophecy, with the laying on of the hands of the presbytery.

שִׂים לִבְּךָ אֶל הַדְּבָרִים הָאֵלֶּה, הַתְמֵד בָּהֶם, לְמַעַן תֵּרָאֶה הִתְקַדְּמוּתְךָ לַכֹּל
sim libbcha el haddevarim ha'elleh, hatmed bahem, lema'an tera'eh hitkaddemutecha lakkol
Be diligent in these things; give thyself wholly to them; that thy progress may be manifest unto all.

הַשְׁגַּח עַל עַצְמְךָ וְשִׁית לִבְּךָ לַהוֹרָאָה
hashgach al atzmecha veshit libbecha lahora'ah
Take heed to thyself, and to thy teaching.

טִימוֹתֵיאוֹס א

נִרְאָה לַמַּלְאָכִים, הֻגַּד בַּגּוֹיִם, הָאֳמַן בָּעוֹלָם, הָעֲלָה לַמָּרוֹם בְּכָבוֹד
nir'ah lammal'achim, huggad baggoyim, ho'oman ba'olam, ho'olah lammarom bechavod
Seen of angels, Preached among the nations, Believed on in the world, Received up in glory.

ד

הָרוּחַ אוֹמֶרֶת בְּפֵרוּשׁ, שֶׁבְּרֻבּוֹת הַיָּמִים יָסֻטוּ אֲנָשִׁים מִן הָאֱמוּנָה
haruach omeret beferush, shebbirvot hayamim yistu anashim min ha'emunah
But the Spirit saith expressly, that in later times some shall fall away from the faith,

וְיִפְנוּ לְרוּחוֹת מַטְעוֹת וּלְתוֹרוֹת שֶׁל שֵׁדִים
veyifnu leruchot mat'ot uletorot shel shedim
giving heed to seducing spirits and doctrines of demons,

בְּאֶמְצָעוּת מַטִּיפֵי כָזָב מִתְחַסְּדִים אֲשֶׁר מַצְפּוּנָם שֶׁלָּהֶם קָהָה כְּחוּשִׁים שֶׁקָּהוּ בְּבַרְזֶל מְלֻבָּן
be'emtza'ut mattifei kazav mitchassdim asher matzpunam shellahem kahah kechushim shekkahu bevarzel melubban
through the hypocrisy of men that speak lies, branded in their own conscience as with a hot iron;

הַלָּלוּ יַאַסְרוּ לָשֵׂאת אִשָּׁה וְיַטִּילוּ אִסּוּר עַל מִינֵי מַאֲכָל
hallalu ya'asru laset ishah veyattilu issur al minei ma'achal
forbidding to marry, and commanding to abstain from meats,

אֲשֶׁר בְּרָאָם אֱלֹהִים לְמַעַן יֹאכְלוּם בְּתוֹדָה הַמַּאֲמִינִים וְיוֹדְעֵי הָאֱמֶת
asher bera'am elohim lema'an yochelum betodah hamma'aminim veyode'ei ha'emet
which God created to be received with thanksgiving by them that believe and know the truth.

הֵן כָּל מַה שֶּׁבָּרָא אֱלֹהִים טוֹב הוּא, וְאֵין לִפְסֹל דָּבָר אִם אוֹכְלִים אוֹתוֹ בִּבְרָכָה
hen kol mah shebbara elohim tov hu, ve'ein lifsol davar im ochelim oto bivrachah
For every creature of God is good, and nothing is to be rejected, if it be received with thanksgiving:

שֶׁכֵּן הוּא מְקֻדָּשׁ בִּדְבַר אֱלֹהִים וּבִתְפִלָּה
shekken hu mekuddash bidvar elohim uvitfillah
for it is sanctified through the word of God and prayer.

אִם תּוֹרֶה אֶת הַדְּבָרִים הָאֵלֶּה לָאַחִים, תִּהְיֶה מְשָׁרֵת טוֹב לַמָּשִׁיחַ יֵשׁוּעַ
im toreh et haddevarim ha'elleh la'achim, tihyeh mesharet tov lammashiach yeshua
If thou put the brethren in mind of these things, thou shalt be a good minister of Christ Jesus,

מְשָׁרֵת הַנִּזּוֹן מִדִּבְרֵי הָאֱמוּנָה וּמֵהַתּוֹרָה הַטּוֹבָה שֶׁדָּבַקְתָּ בָּהּ
mesharet hannizzon middivrei ha'emunah umehattorah hattovah sheddavakta bah
nourished in the words of the faith, and of the good doctrine which thou hast followed until now:

אוּלָם הִתְרַחֵק מֵאַגָּדוֹת טְפֵלוֹת וְנִפְסָדוֹת. אַמֵּן אֶת עַצְמְךָ לַחֲסִידוּת
ulam hitrachek me'aggadot tefelot venifsadot. ammen et atzmecha lachasidut
but refuse profane and old wives' fables. And exercise thyself unto godliness:

טִימוֹתֵיאוֹס א

לֹא מִתְמַכְּרִים לְיַיִן וְלֹא רוֹדְפֵי בֶּצַע
lo mitmakkerim leyayin velo rodefei betza
not given to much wine, not greedy of filthy lucre;

אֶלָּא אֲנָשִׁים הַמַּחֲזִיקִים אֶת סוֹד הָאֱמוּנָה בְּמַצְפּוּן טָהוֹר
ella anashim hammachazikim et sod ha'emunah bematzpun tahor
holding the mystery of the faith in a pure conscience.

הַלָּלוּ יִבָּחֲנוּ תְּחִלָּה; אַחֲרֵי שֶׁיִּמָּצֵא שֶׁאֵין בָּהֶם דֹּפִי יְשָׁרְתוּ כְּשַׁמָּשִׁים
hallalu yibbachanu techillah; acharei sheyimmatzei she'ein bahem dofi yesharetu keshammashim
And let these also first be proved; then let them serve as deacons, if they be blameless.

כְּמוֹ כֵן הַנָּשִׁים; עֲלֵיהֶן לִהְיוֹת רְצִינִיּוֹת, נִמְנָעוֹת מִלָּשׁוֹן הָרַע, מְפֻכָּחוֹת, נֶאֱמָנוֹת בְּכָל דָּבָר
kemo chen hannashim; aleihen lihyot retziniyot, nimna'ot millashon hara', mefukkachot, ne'emanot bechol davar
Women in like manner must be grave, not slanderers, temperate, faithful in all things.

הַשַּׁמָּשׁ יִהְיֶה בַּעַל אִשָּׁה אַחַת, אָדָם שֶׁמַּנְהִיג הֵיטֵב אֶת בָּנָיו וְאֶת בֵּיתוֹ
hashammash yihyeh ba'al ishah achat, adam shemmanhig heitev et banav ve'et beito
Let deacons be husbands of one wife, ruling their children and their own houses well.

הַמֵּיטִיבִים לְשָׁרֵת מַשִּׂיגִים לְעַצְמָם מַעֲמָד טוֹב
hammeitivim lesharet massigim le'atzmam ma'amad tov
For they that have served well as deacons gain to themselves a good standing,

וּבִטָּחוֹן רַב בָּאֱמוּנָה בַּמָּשִׁיחַ יֵשׁוּעַ
uvittachon rav ba'emunah bammashiach yeshua
and great boldness in the faith which is in Christ Jesus.

אֲנִי כּוֹתֵב לְךָ אֶת הַדְּבָרִים הָאֵלֶּה בְּתִקְוָה לָבוֹא אֵלֶיךָ בִּמְהֵרָה
ani kotev lecha et haddevarim ha'elleh betikvah lavo eleicha bimherah
These things write I unto thee, hoping to come unto thee shortly;

אֲבָל אִם אֶתְמַהְמַהּ, הִנֵּה תֵּדַע כֵּיצַד לְהִתְנַהֵג בְּבֵית אֱלֹהִים
aval im etmahmah, hinneh teda keitzad lehitnaheg beveit elohim
but if I tarry long, that thou mayest know how men ought to behave themselves in the house of God,

אֲשֶׁר הוּא קְהִלַּת אֱלֹהִים חַיִּים, עַמּוּד הָאֱמֶת וִיסוֹדָהּ
asher hu kehillat elohim chayim, ammud ha'emet viysodah
which is the church of the living God, the pillar and ground of the truth.

אָכֵן גָּדוֹל סוֹד הַחֲסִידוּת
'achen gadol sod hachasidut
And without controversy great is the mystery of godliness;

הִתְגַּלָּה בַּבָּשָׂר, נִצְדַּק בָּרוּחַ
hitgallah babbasar, nitzdak baruach
He who was manifested in the flesh, Justified in the spirit,

אָדָם לֹא נִפְתָּה, אֶלָּא הָאִשָּׁה שָׁמְעָה לְקוֹל הַמְפַתֶּה וּבָאָה לִידֵי עֲבֵרָה
adam lo niftah, ella ha'ishah shame'ah lekol hamfatteh uva'ah liydei averah
and Adam was not beguiled, but the woman being beguiled hath fallen into transgression:

אֲבָל הִיא תִּוָּשַׁע בְּלִדְתָּהּ יְלָדִים, אִם תַּעֲמֹד בָּאֱמוּנָה, בָּאַהֲבָה, בַּקְּדֻשָּׁה וּבַצְּנִיעוּת
aval hi tivvasha belidtah yeladim, im ta'amod ba'emunah, ba'ahavah, bakkedushah uvatzeni'ut
but she shall be saved through her child-bearing, if they continue in faith and love and sanctification with sobriety.

ג

מְהֵימָן הַדָּבָר: אִישׁ הַשּׁוֹאֵף לִהְיוֹת מַנְהִיג בַּקְּהִלָּה, הֲרֵיהוּ מִשְׁתּוֹקֵק לַעֲבוֹדָה נַעֲלָה
meheiman haddavar. ish hasho'ef lihyot manhig bik'hillah, hareihu mishtokek la'avodah na'alah
Faithful is the saying, If a man seeketh the office of a bishop, he desireth a good work.

לָכֵן הַמַּנְהִיג צָרִיךְ לִהְיוֹת אִישׁ שֶׁאֵין בּוֹ דֹּפִי, בַּעַל אִשָּׁה אַחַת
lachen hammanhig tzarich lihyot ish she'ein bo dofi, ba'al ishah achat
The bishop therefore must be without reproach, the husband of one wife,

אִישׁ מְפֻכָּח, מְאֻפָּק, מִתְנַהֵג בְּדֶרֶךְ אֶרֶץ, מַכְנִיס אוֹרְחִים, יוֹדֵעַ לְלַמֵּד
ish mefukkach, me'uppak, mitnaheg bederech eretz, machnis orechim, yodea lelammed
temperate, sober-minded, orderly, given to hospitality, apt to teach;

לֹא מִתְמַכֵּר לְיַיִן, לֹא בַּעַל אֶגְרוֹף אֶלָּא אָדָם הַנּוֹהֵג בְּסוֹבְלָנוּת, לֹא נִמְהָר לָרִיב וְלֹא רוֹדֵף כֶּסֶף
lo mitmakker leyayin, lo ba'al egrof ella adam hannoheg besovelanut, lo nimhar lariv velo rodef kesef
no brawler, no striker; but gentle, not contentious, no lover of money;

אָדָם שֶׁמַּנְהִיג הֵיטֵב אֶת בֵּיתוֹ שֶׁלּוֹ וּבָנָיו נִשְׁמָעִים לוֹ בִּמְלוֹא דֶּרֶךְ אֶרֶץ
adam shemmanhig heitev et beito shello uvanav nishma'im lo bimlo derech eretz
one that ruleth well his own house, having his children in subjection with all gravity;

הֲרֵי אִם לֹא יֵדַע אִישׁ לְנַהֵל אֶת בֵּיתוֹ שֶׁלּוֹ, כֵּיצַד יוּכַל לִדְאֹג לִקְהִלַּת אֱלֹהִים
harei im lo yeda ish lenahel et beito shello, keitzad yuchal lid'og lik'hillat elohim
(but if a man knoweth not how to rule his own house, how shall he take care of the church of God?)

וְאַל יְהֵא צָעִיר בָּאֱמוּנָה, פֶּן יִתְיַהֵר וְיִפֹּל בְּדִין הַשָּׂטָן
ve'al yehei tza'ir ba'emunah, pen yityaher veyippol bedin hassatan
not a novice, lest being puffed up he fall into the condemnation of the devil.

הוּא צָרִיךְ גַּם לְשֵׁם טוֹב בְּפִי אֵלֶּה שֶׁבַּחוּץ, כְּדֵי שֶׁלֹּא יִהְיֶה לְחֶרְפָּה וְלֹא יִפֹּל בְּפַח הַשָּׂטָן
hu tzarich gam leshem tov befi elleh shebbachutz, kedei shello yihyeh lecherpah velo yippol befach hassatan
Moreover he must have good testimony from them that are without; lest he fall into reproach and the snare of the devil.

כֵּן גַּם הַשַּׁמָּשִׁים צְרִיכִים לִהְיוֹת אֲנָשִׁים רְצִינִיִּים; לֹא הֲפַכְפְּכָנִים בְּדִבּוּרָם
ken gam hashammashim tzerichim lihyot anashim retziniyim; lo hafachpechanim bedibburam
Deacons in like manner must be grave, not double-tongued,

טִימוֹתֵיאוֹס א

הַחָפֵץ שֶׁכָּל בְּנֵי אָדָם יִוָּשְׁעוּ וְיַגִּיעוּ לְהַכָּרַת הָאֱמֶת
hechafetz shekkol benei adam yivvashe'u veyaggi'u lehakkarat ha'emet
who would have all men to be saved, and come to the knowledge of the truth.

הֵן אֶחָד הָאֱלֹהִים, וְאֶחָד הַמְתַוֵּךְ בֵּין אֱלֹהִים לִבְנֵי אָדָם - הָאָדָם הַמָּשִׁיחַ יֵשׁוּעַ
hen echad ha'elohim, ve'echad hamtavvech bein elohim livnei adam - ha'adam hammashiach yeshua
For there is one God, one mediator also between God and men, himself man, Christ Jesus,

אֲשֶׁר נָתַן אֶת עַצְמוֹ כֹּפֶר בְּעַד הַכֹּל. זֹאת הָעֵדוּת בְּעִתּוֹתֶיהָ
asher natan et atzmo kofer be'ad hakkol. zot ha'edut be'ittoteiha
who gave himself a ransom for all; the testimony to be borne in its own times;

אֲשֶׁר אֲנִי נִתְמַנֵּיתִי לָהּ לִכָרוֹז וּלְשָׁלִיחַ
asher ani nitmanneiti lah lecharoz uleshaliach
whereunto I was appointed a preacher and an apostle

אֱמֶת אֲנִי מְדַבֵּר, אֵינֶנִּי מְשַׁקֵּר - לְמוֹרֵה אֱמוּנָה וֶאֱמֶת לַגּוֹיִם
emet ani medabber, einenni meshakker - lemoreh emunah ve'emet laggoyim
(I speak the truth, I lie not), a teacher of the Gentiles in faith and truth.

רְצוֹנִי שֶׁהָאֲנָשִׁים יִתְפַּלְּלוּ בְּכָל מָקוֹם בִּנְשִׂיאַת יָדַיִם טְהוֹרוֹת, בְּלֹא כַּעַס וּבְלֹא מַחֲלֹקֶת
retzoni sheha'anashim yitpallelu bechol makom binsi'at yadayim tehorot, belo ka'as uvelo machaloket
I desire therefore that the men pray in every place, lifting up holy hands, without wrath and disputing.

כְּמוֹ כֵן תַּעֲטֶינָה הַנָּשִׁים תִּלְבֹּשֶׁת הוֹלֶמֶת
kemo chen ta'ateinah hannashim tilboshet holemet
In like manner, that women adorn themselves in modest apparel,

בִּצְנִיעוּת וּבְאִפּוּק; לֹא בְּהִתְגַּנְדְּרוּת שֵׂעָר, לֹא בְּזָהָב וּפְנִינִים, וְלֹא בְּמַלְבּוּשִׁים יְקָרִים
bitzni'ut uve'ippuk; lo behitganderut se'ar, lo bezahav ufeninim, velo bemalbushim yekarim
with shamefastness and sobriety; not with braided hair, and gold or pearls or costly raiment;

אֶלָּא בַּמֶּה שֶׁיָּאֶה לְנָשִׁים הַמַּצְהִירוֹת עַל יִרְאַת שָׁמַיִם - בְּמַעֲשִׂים טוֹבִים
ella bemah sheya'eh lenashim hammatzhirot al yir'at shamayim - bema'asim tovim
but (which becometh women professing godliness) through good works.

הָאִשָּׁה תִּלְמַד בְּדוּמִיָּה, בְּהִכָּנְעָה שְׁלֵמָה
ha'ishah tilmad bedumiyah, behachna'ah shelemah
Let a woman learn in quietness with all subjection.

אֵינֶנִּי מַרְשֶׁה לְאִשָּׁה לְלַמֵּד, אַף לֹא לְהִשְׂתָּרֵר עַל הָאִישׁ, אֶלָּא לְהִשָּׁאֵר בְּדוּמִיָּה
einenni marsheh la'ishah lelammed, af lo lehistarer al ha'ish, ella lehisha'er bedumiyah
But I permit not a woman to teach, nor to have dominion over a man, but to be in quietness.

כִּי אָדָם נוֹצַר רִאשׁוֹנָה וְאַחֲרֵי כֵן חַוָּה
ki adam notzar rishonah ve'acharei chen chavvah
For Adam was first formed, then Eve;

טִימוֹתֵיאוֹס א

וְאוּלָם מִשּׁוּם כָּךְ רֻחַמְתִּי, כְּדֵי שֶׁבִּי בָּרִאשׁוֹנָה יַרְאֶה יֵשׁוּעַ הַמָּשִׁיחַ אֶת כָּל אֹרֶךְ רוּחוֹ
ve'ulam mishum kach ruchamti, kedei shebbi barishonah yar'eh yeshua hammashiach et kol orech rucho
howbeit for this cause I obtained mercy, that in me as chief might Jesus Christ show forth all his longsuffering,

כְּמוֹפֵת לָעֲתִידִים לְהַאֲמִין בּוֹ לְשֵׁם חַיֵּי עוֹלָם
kemofet la'atidim leha'amin bo leshem chayei olam
for an ensample of them that should thereafter believe on him unto eternal life.

לְמֶלֶךְ הָעוֹלָמִים, הַקַּיָּם לְאֵין קֵץ וְהַבִּלְתִּי נִרְאֶה
lemelech ha'olamim, hakkayam le'ein ketz vehabbilti nir'eh
Now unto the King eternal, immortal, invisible,

אֲשֶׁר הוּא לְבַדּוֹ הָאֱלֹהִים, לוֹ הַכָּבוֹד וְהַתִּפְאֶרֶת לְעוֹלְמֵי עוֹלָמִים. אָמֵן
asher hu levaddo ha'elohim, lo hakkavod vehattif'eret le'olemei olamim. Amen
the only God, be honor and glory for ever and ever. Amen.

אֶת הַמִּצְוָה הַזֹּאת אֲנִי מוֹסֵר לְךָ, טִימוֹתֵיאוֹס בְּנִי
et hammitzvah hazzot ani moser lecha, timotei'os beni,
This charge I commit unto thee, my child Timothy,

עַל-פִּי נְבוּאוֹת מִן הֶעָבָר הַנּוֹגְעוֹת אֵלֶיךָ, כְּדֵי שֶׁתִּלָּחֵם בְּעֶזְרָתָן אֶת הַמִּלְחָמָה הַטּוֹבָה
al-pi nevu'ot min he'avar hannoge'ot eleicha, kedei shettillachem be'ezratan et hammilchamah hattovah
according to the prophecies which led the way to thee, that by them thou mayest war the good warfare;

מִתּוֹךְ אֱמוּנָה וּמַצְפּוּן יָשָׁר. יֵשׁ שֶׁהִשְׁלִיכוּ מֵעֲלֵיהֶם אֶת אֵלֶּה וְנִשְׁבְּרָה סְפִינַת אֱמוּנָתָם
mittoch emunah umatzpun yashar. yesh shehishlichu me'aleihem et elleh venishberah sfinat emunatam
holding faith and a good conscience; which some having thrust from them made shipwreck concerning the faith:

וּמֵהֶם הִימֶנְאוּס וַאֲלֶכְּסַנְדֵּר אֲשֶׁר מָסַרְתִּי אוֹתָם לַשָּׂטָן לְמַעַן יְחֻנְּכוּ שֶׁלֹּא לְגַדֵּף
umehem himene'us va'alekkesander asher masarti otam lassatan lema'an yechunnechu shello legaddef
of whom is Hymenæus and Alexander; whom I delivered unto Satan, that they might be taught not to blaspheme.

ב

קֹדֶם כֹּל אֲנִי מְבַקֵּשׁ מִכֶּם לָשֵׂאת תְּחִנּוֹת וּתְפִלּוֹת וּבַקָּשׁוֹת וְהוֹדָיוֹת בְּעַד כָּל בְּנֵי אָדָם
kodem kol ani mevakkesh mikkem laset techinnot utefillot uvakkashot vehodayot be'ad kol bnei adam
I exhort therefore, first of all, that supplications, prayers, intercessions, thanksgivings, be made for all men;

בְּעַד מְלָכִים וְכָל רָאשֵׁי הַשִּׁלְטוֹן, לְמַעַן נִחְיֶה חַיֵּי שַׁלְוָה וְהַשְׁקֵט בִּמְלוֹא חֲסִידוּת וְדֶרֶךְ אֶרֶץ
be'ad melachim vechol rashei hashilton, lema'an nichyeh chayei shalvah vehashket bimlo chasidut vederech eretz
for kings and all that are in high place; that we may lead a tranquil and quiet life in all godliness and gravity.

טוֹב הַדָּבָר הַזֶּה וְרָצוּי בְּעֵינֵי אֱלֹהִים מוֹשִׁיעֵנוּ
tov haddavar hazzeh veratzui be'einei elohim moshi'enu
This is good and acceptable in the sight of God our Saviour;

טִימוֹתִיאוֹס א

זֹאת יוֹדְעִים אָנוּ, שֶׁחֹק אֵינוֹ נִקְבַּע בִּשְׁבִיל אָדָם צַדִּיק,
zot yode'im anu, shechok eino nikba bishvil adam tzaddik,
as knowing this, that law is not made for a righteous man,

אֶלָּא מְכֻוָּן הוּא לְמֻפְקָרִים וּלְסוֹרְרִים, לִרְשָׁעִים וּלְחַטָּאִים
ella mechuvvan hu lemufkarim ulesorerim, lirsha'im ulechatta'im
but for the lawless and unruly, for the ungodly and sinners,

לִטְמֵאִים וְעוֹשֵׂי תּוֹעֵבָה, לְרוֹצְחֵי אָב וָאֵם וְלִמְרַצְּחִים
litme'im ve'osei to'evah, lerotzechei av va'em velimratzechim
for the unholy and profane, for murderers of fathers and murderers of mothers, for manslayers,

לְזוֹנִים וּלְשׁוֹכְבֵי זָכָר, לְחוֹטְפֵי אָדָם
lezonim uleshochevei zachar, lechotefei adam
for fornicators, for abusers of themselves with men, for menstealers,

וְשַׁקְרָנִים וְנִשְׁבָּעִים לַשֶּׁקֶר, לְכָל מַה שֶּׁנּוֹגֵד אֶת הַתּוֹרָה הַבְּרִיאָה
veshakranim venishba'im lasheker, lechol mah shennoged et hattorah habberi'ah
for liars, for false swearers, and if there be any other thing contrary to the sound doctrine;

אֲשֶׁר עַל־פִּי בְּשׂוֹרַת הַכָּבוֹד שֶׁל אֱלֹהִים הַמְבֹרָךְ, הִיא הַבְּשׂוֹרָה שֶׁהֻפְקְדָה בְּיָדִי
asher al-pi besorat hakkavod shel elohim hamevorach, hi habbesorah shehufkedah beyadi
according to the gospel of the glory of the blessed God, which was committed to my trust.

אֲנִי מַכִּיר טוֹבָה לַנּוֹתֵן בִּי כֹּחַ, לַמָּשִׁיחַ יֵשׁוּעַ אֲדוֹנֵנוּ, כִּי חֲשָׁבַנִי נֶאֱמָן וּמִנָּה אוֹתִי לְשֵׁרוּתוֹ
ani makkir tovah lannoten bi koach, lammashiach yeshua adonenu, ki chashavani ne'eman uminnah oti lesheruto
I thank him that enabled me, even Christ Jesus our Lord, for that he counted me faithful, appointing me to his service;

אַף שֶׁקֹּדֶם לָכֵן הָיִיתִי מְגַדֵּף, רוֹדֵף וּמְבַזֶּה
af shekkodem lachen hayiti megaddef, rodef umevazzeh
though I was before a blasphemer, and a persecutor, and injurious:

אֲבָל רֻחַמְתִּי מִפְּנֵי שֶׁבִּהְיוֹתִי חֲסַר אֱמוּנָה פָּעַלְתִּי בְּלִי דַעַת
aval ruchamti mippenei shebbihyoti chasar emunah pa'alti beli da'at
howbeit I obtained mercy, because I did it ignorantly in unbelief;

וְחֶסֶד אֲדוֹנֵנוּ שָׁפַע עָלַי יַחַד עִם אֱמוּנָה וְאַהֲבָה אֲשֶׁר בַּמָּשִׁיחַ יֵשׁוּעַ
vechesed adonenu shafa alai yachad im emunah ve'ahavah asher bammashiach yeshua
and the grace of our Lord abounded exceedingly with faith and love which is in Christ Jesus.

מְהֵימָן הַדָּבָר וְרָאוּי לְהַסְכָּמָה מְלֵאָה
meheiman haddavar vera'ui lehaskamah mele'ah
Faithful is the saying, and worthy of all acceptation,

שֶׁהַמָּשִׁיחַ יֵשׁוּעַ בָּא אֶל הָעוֹלָם לְהוֹשִׁיעַ חוֹטְאִים אֲשֶׁר אֲנִי הַגָּדוֹל בָּהֶם
shehammashiach yeshua ba el ha'olam lehoshia chote'im asher ani haggadol bahem
that Christ Jesus came into the world to save sinners; of whom I am chief:

טִימוֹתִיאוֹס א

טִימוֹתִיאוֹס א

מֵאֵת שָׁאוּל, שְׁלִיחַ הַמָּשִׁיחַ יֵשׁוּעַ עַל־פִּי מִצְוַת הָאֱלֹהִים מוֹשִׁיעֵנוּ וְהַמָּשִׁיחַ יֵשׁוּעַ תִּקְוָתֵנוּ
me'et sha'ul, sheliach hammashiach yeshua al-pi mitzvat ha'elohim moshi'enu vehammashiach yeshua tikvatenu
Paul, an apostle of Christ Jesus according to the commandment of God our Saviour, and Christ Jesus our hope;

אֶל טִימוֹתִיאוֹס בְּנִי הָאֲמִתִּי בָּאֱמוּנָה: חֶסֶד וְרַחֲמִים וְשָׁלוֹם
el timotei'os bni ha'amitti ba'emunah: chesed verachamim veshalom
unto Timothy, my true child in faith: Grace, mercy, peace,

מֵאֵת אֱלֹהִים אָבִינוּ וְהַמָּשִׁיחַ יֵשׁוּעַ אֲדוֹנֵנוּ
me'et elohim avinu vehammashiach yeshua adonenu
from God the Father and Christ Jesus our Lord.

כַּאֲשֶׁר הָלַכְתִּי לְמָקֵדוֹנְיָה בִּקַּשְׁתִּי מִמְּךָ
ka'asher halachti lemakedoneyah bikkashti mimmcha
As I exhorted thee to tarry at Ephesus, when I was going into Macedonia,

לְהִשָּׁאֵר בְּאֶפֶסוֹס וּלְצַוּוֹת עַל כַּמָּה אֲנָשִׁים שֶׁלֹּא יוֹרוּ תּוֹרָה אַחֶרֶת
lehisha'er be'efesos uletzavvot al kammah anashim shello yoru torah acheret
that thou mightest charge certain men not to teach a different doctrine,

וְלֹא יִתְּנוּ לִבָּם לְאַגָּדוֹת וּלְסִפּוּרִים אֵין קֵץ עַל תּוֹלְדוֹת הַדּוֹרוֹת
velo yittenu libbam le'aggadot ulesippurim ein ketz al toledot haddorot
neither to give heed to fables and endless genealogies,

דְּבָרִים הַנּוֹתְנִים מָקוֹם לְחִטּוּטִים וּוִכּוּחִים יוֹתֵר מֵאֲשֶׁר לְתָכְנִית אֱלֹהִים שֶׁיְּסוֹדָהּ בֶּאֱמוּנָה
dvarim hannotenim makom lechittutim uvikkuchim yoter me'asher letachenit elohim sheyesodah be'emunah
which minister questionings, rather than a dispensation of God which is in faith; so do I now.

תַּכְלִיתָהּ שֶׁל הַמִּצְוָה הַזֹּאת הִיא הָאַהֲבָה הַנּוֹבַעַת מִלֵּב טָהוֹר, מִמַּצְפּוּן יָשָׁר וּמֵאֱמוּנָה אֲמִתִּית
tachlitah shel hammitzvah hazzot hi ha'ahavah hannova'at millev tahor, mimmatzpun yashar ume'emunah amittit
But the end of the charge is love out of a pure heart and a good conscience and faith unfeigned:

יֵשׁ שֶׁסָּטוּ מִזֶּה וּפָנוּ לְדִבּוּרֵי הֶבֶל
yesh shessatu mizzeh ufanu ledibburei hevel
from which things some having swerved have turned aside unto vain talking;

רְצוֹנָם לִהְיוֹת מוֹרֵי תּוֹרָה, אַךְ אֵין הֵם מְבִינִים לֹא אֶת מַה שֶּׁהֵם אוֹמְרִים וְלֹא אֶת מַה שֶּׁהֵם טוֹעֲנִים בְּתֹקֶף
retzonam lihyot morei torah, ach ein hem mevinim lo et mah shehem omerim velo et mah shehem to'anim betokef
desiring to be teachers of the law, though they understand neither what they say, nor whereof they confidently affirm.

אֲנַחְנוּ יוֹדְעִים שֶׁהַתּוֹרָה טוֹבָה אִם חַיִּים בָּהּ לְפִי חֻקֶּיהָ
anachnu yode'im shehattorah tovah im chayim bah lefi chukkeiha
But we know that the law is good, if a man use it lawfully,

הַתֶּסָּלוֹנִיקִים ב

לֹא שֶׁאֵין לָנוּ זְכוּת לְכָךְ, אֶלָּא כְּדֵי שֶׁאֲנַחְנוּ נִהְיֶה לָכֶם לְמוֹפֵת וְתִתְנַהֲגוּ כָּמוֹנוּ
lo she'ein lanu zechut lechach, ella kedei she'anachnu nihyeh lachem lemofet vetitnahagu kamonu
not because we have not the right, but to make ourselves an ensample unto you, that ye should imitate us.

הֵן גַּם כַּאֲשֶׁר הָיִינוּ אֶצְלְכֶם, זֹאת צִוִּינוּ אֶתְכֶם: מִי שֶׁאֵינוֹ רוֹצֶה לַעֲבֹד, גַּם אַל יֹאכַל
hen gam ka'asher hayinu etzlechem, zot tzivvinu etchem: mi she'eino rotzeh la'avod, gam al yochal
For even when we were with you, this we commanded you, If any will not work, neither let him eat.

כִּי שָׁמַעְנוּ שֶׁיֵּשׁ הוֹלְכֵי בָּטֵל בֵּינֵיכֶם שֶׁאֵינָם עוֹבְדִים כְּלָל, אֶלָּא מִתְעַסְּקִים בַּהֲבָלִים
ki shama'nu sheyesh holechei batel beineichem she'einam ovedim kelal, ella mit'assekim bahavalim
For we hear of some that walk among you disorderly, that work not at all, but are busybodies.

אֲנַחְנוּ מְצַוִּים עַל אוֹתָם הָאֲנָשִׁים וְדוֹרְשִׁים מֵהֶם בְּשֵׁם הָאָדוֹן יֵשׁוּעַ הַמָּשִׁיחַ
anachnu metzavvim al otam ha'anashim vedoreshim mehem beshem ha'adon yeshua hammashiach,
Now them that are such we command and exhort in the Lord Jesus Christ,

שֶׁיַּעַבְדוּ בְּנַחַת וְיֹאכְלוּ אֶת לַחְמָם שֶׁלָּהֶם
sheya'avdu benachat veyochelu et lachmam shellahem
that with quietness they work, and eat their own bread.

וְאַתֶּם, אַחַי, אַל יִרְפּוּ יְדֵיכֶם בַּעֲשִׂיַּת הַטּוֹב
ve'attem, achai, al yirpu yedeichem ba'asiyat hattov
But ye, brethren, be not weary in well-doing.

אִם מִישֶׁהוּ לֹא יְצַיֵּת לַדְּבָרִים שֶׁכָּתַבְנוּ בָּאִגֶּרֶת, צַיְּנוּ לָכֶם אֶת הָאִישׁ הַזֶּה
im mishehu lo yetzayet laddvarim shekkatavnu ba'iggeret, tzayenu lachem et ha'ish hazze
And if any man obeyeth not our word by this epistle, note that man,

וְאַל תִּתְעָרְבוּ עִמּוֹ, לְמַעַן יֵבוֹשׁ
ve'al tit'arevu immo, lema'an yevosh
that ye have no company with him, to the end that he may be ashamed.

אֲבָל אַל תַּחְשְׁבוּהוּ לְאוֹיֵב, אֶלָּא הוֹכִיחוּ אוֹתוֹ כְּאָח
aval al tachshevuhu le'oyev, ella hochichu oto ke'ach
And yet count him not as an enemy, but admonish him as a brother.

וַאֲדוֹן הַשָּׁלוֹם יִתֵּן לָכֶם אֶת הַשָּׁלוֹם, תָּמִיד וּבְכָל מָקוֹם. הָאָדוֹן עִם כֻּלְּכֶם
va'adon hashalom yitten lachem et hashalom, tamid uvechol makom. ha'adon im kullechem
Now the Lord of peace himself give you peace at all times in all ways. The Lord be with you all.

פְּרִיסַת שָׁלוֹם בְּמוֹ כְּתַב יָדִי, אֲנִי שָׁאוּל. זֶהוּ הַסִּימָן בְּכָל אִגְּרוֹתַי; כָּךְ אֲנִי כּוֹתֵב
perisat shalom bemo ketav yadi, ani sha'ul. zehu hassiman bechol iggrotai; kach ani kotev
The salutation of me Paul with mine own hand, which is the token in every epistle: so I write.

חֶסֶד אֲדוֹנֵנוּ יֵשׁוּעַ הַמָּשִׁיחַ עִם כֻּלְּכֶם
chesed adonenu yeshua hammashiach im kullchem
The grace of our Lord Jesus Christ be with you all.

הַתֶּסָּלוֹנִיקִים ב

ג

סוֹף דָּבָר, אַחַי, הִתְפַּלְלוּ בַּעֲדֵנוּ שֶׁדְּבַר יהוה יוּפַץ מַהֵר וִיכֻבַּד, כְּמוֹ אֶצְלְכֶם
sof davar, achai, hitpallelu ba'adenu sheddevar hashem yufatz maher vichubbad, kemo etzlechem
Finally, brethren, pray for us, that the word of the Lord may run and be glorified, even as also it is with you;

וְשֶׁנִּנָּצֵל מֵאֲנָשִׁים רָעִים וּרְשָׁעִים, שֶׁהֲרֵי לֹא לְכָל בְּנֵי אָדָם הָאֱמוּנָה
veshenninnatzel me'anashim ra'im uresha'im, sheharei lo lechol benei adam ha'emunah
and that we may be delivered from unreasonable and evil men; for all have not faith.

אֲבָל נֶאֱמָן הָאָדוֹן וְהוּא יְחַזֵּק אֶתְכֶם וְיִשְׁמֹר אֶתְכֶם מִן הָרַע
aval ne'eman ha'adon vehu yechazzek etchem veyishmor etchem min hara
But the Lord is faithful, who shall establish you, and guard you from the evil one.

אֲנַחְנוּ בְּטוּחִים בָּאָדוֹן בְּנוֹגֵעַ אֲלֵיכֶם, שֶׁאַתֶּם עוֹשִׂים וְאַף תּוֹסִיפוּ לַעֲשׂוֹת אֶת מַה שֶׁצִוִּינוּ
anachnu betuchim ba'adon benogea aleichem, she'attem osim ve'af tosifu la'asot et mah shetzivvinu
And we have confidence in the Lord touching you, that ye both do and will do the things which we command.

יְכוֹנֵן הָאָדוֹן אֶת לְבַבְכֶם לְאַהֲבַת אֱלֹהִים וּלְסַבְלָנוּת הַמָּשִׁיחַ
yechonen ha'adon et levavchem le'ahavat elohim ulesavlanut hammashiach
And the Lord direct your hearts into the love of God, and into the patience of Christ.

אָנוּ מְצַוִּים אֶתְכֶם, אַחִים, בְּשֵׁם הָאָדוֹן יֵשׁוּעַ הַמָּשִׁיחַ,
anu metzavvim etchem, achim, beshem ha'adon yeshua hammashiach
Now we command you, brethren, in the name of our Lord Jesus Christ,

לְהִבָּדֵל מִכָּל אָח שֶׁהוֹלֵךְ בָּטֵל
lehibbadel mikkol ach sheholech batel
that ye withdraw yourselves from every brother that walketh disorderly,

וְאֵינֶנּוּ מִתְנַהֵג לְפִי הַמָּסֹרוֹת שֶׁקִּבַּלְתֶּם מֵאִתָּנוּ
ve'einennu mitnaheg lefi hammasorot shekkibbaltem me'ittanu
and not after the tradition which they received of us.

הֲרֵי אַתֶּם יוֹדְעִים שֶׁמִּן הָרָאוּי לְהִתְנַהֵג כָּמוֹנוּ, שֶׁכֵּן לֹא הוֹלְכֵי בָּטֵל הָיִינוּ בְּתוֹכְכֶם
harei attem yode'im shemmin hara'ui lehitnaheg kamonu, shekken lo holechei batel hayinu betochachem
For yourselves know how ye ought to imitate us: for we behaved not ourselves disorderly among you;

גַּם לֹא אָכַלְנוּ לֶחֶם חִנָּם מִידֵי אִישׁ, אֶלָּא בְּעָמָל וָיֶגַע
gam lo achalnu lechem chinnam miydei ish, ella be'amal vayega
neither did we eat bread for nought at any man's hand, but in labor and travail,

עָבַדְנוּ יוֹמָם וָלַיְלָה כְּדֵי שֶׁלֹּא נִהְיֶה לְמַשָּׂא עַל אִישׁ מִכֶּם
avadnu yomam valaylah kedei shello nihyeh lemasho al ish mikkem
working night and day, that we might not burden any of you:

הַתֶּסָּלוֹנִיקִים ב

וּבְכָל תַּרְמִית רֶשַׁע הַמְיֻעָדִים לִבְנֵי הָאֲבַדּוֹן
uvechol tarmit resha hamyu'adim livnei ha'avaddon
and with all deceit of unrighteousness for them that perish;

וְזֹאת מִפְּנֵי שֶׁלֹּא קִבְּלוּ אֶת אַהֲבַת הָאֱמֶת אֲשֶׁר יָכְלוּ לְהִוָּשַׁע בָּהּ
vezot mippenei shello kibbelu et ahavat ha'emet asher yachelu lehivvasha bah
because they received not the love of the truth, that they might be saved.

עַל כֵּן אֱלֹהִים שׁוֹלֵחַ לָהֶם מַדּוּחִים לְהַטְעוֹתָם לְהַאֲמִין לַשֶּׁקֶר
al ken elohim sholeach lahem madduchim lehat'otam leha'amin lasheker
And for this cause God sendeth them a working of error, that they should believe a lie:

לְמַעַן יִדּוֹנוּ כָּל אֲשֶׁר לֹא הֶאֱמִינוּ לָאֱמֶת אֶלָּא חָפְצוּ בָּעַוְלָה
lema'an yiddonu kol asher lo he'eminu la'emet ella chafetzu ba'avlah
that they all might be judged who believed not the truth, but had pleasure in unrighteousness.

חַיָּבִים אָנוּ לְהוֹדוֹת לֵאלֹהִים עֲלֵיכֶם בְּכָל עֵת, אַחַי אֲהוּבֵי הָאָדוֹן,
chayavim anu lehodot lelohim aleichem bechol et, achai ahuvei ha'adon
But we are bound to give thanks to God always for you, brethren beloved of the Lord,

כִּי מֵרֵאשִׁית בָּחַר בָּכֶם אֱלֹהִים לִישׁוּעָה בְּקִדּוּשׁ עַל־יְדֵי הָרוּחַ וּבֶאֱמוּנָה בָּאֱמֶת
ki mereshit bachar bachem elohim liyshu'ah bekiddush al-yedei haruach uve'emunah ba'emet
for that God chose you from the beginning unto salvation in sanctification of the Spirit and belief of the truth:

וּבְאֶמְצָעוּת בְּשׂוֹרָתֵנוּ אַף קָרָא אֶתְכֶם לְנַחֲלָה בְּתִפְאַרְתּוֹ שֶׁל אֲדוֹנֵנוּ יֵשׁוּעַ הַמָּשִׁיחַ
uve'emtza'ut besoratenu af kara etchem lenachalah betif'arto shel adonenu yeshua hammashiach
whereunto he called you through our gospel, to the obtaining of the glory of our Lord Jesus Christ.

לְפִיכָךְ, אַחַי, עִמְדוּ עֲמִידָה אֵיתָנָה וְהַחֲזִיקוּ בַּמָּסוֹרוֹת שֶׁלֻּמַּדְתֶּם
lefichach, achai, imdu amidah eitanah vehachaziku bammasorot shellummadtem
So then, brethren, stand fast, and hold the traditions which ye were taught,

הֵן עַל־יְדֵי דְבָרִים שֶׁאָמַרְנוּ וְהֵן עַל־יְדֵי אִגֶּרֶת שֶׁכָּתַבְנוּ וְהוּא, אֲדוֹנֵנוּ יֵשׁוּעַ הַמָּשִׁיחַ
hen al-yedei devarim she'amarnu vehen al-yedei iggeret shekkatavnu vehu, adonenu yeshua hammashiach
whether by word, or by epistle of ours. Now our Lord Jesus Christ himself,

וֵאלֹהִים אָבִינוּ, אֲשֶׁר אָהַב אוֹתָנוּ וּבְחַסְדּוֹ נָתַן לָנוּ נֶחָמַת עוֹלָם וְתִקְוָה טוֹבָה
ve'elohim avinu, asher ahav otanu uvechasdo natan lanu nechamat olam vetikvah tovah
and God our Father who loved us and gave us eternal comfort and good hope through grace,

הוּא יְנַחֵם אֶת לְבַבְכֶם וִיכוֹנֵן אֶתְכֶם בְּכָל דִּבּוּר אוֹ מַעֲשֶׂה טוֹב
hu yenachem et levavchem viychonen etchem bechol dibbur o ma'aseh tov
comfort your hearts and establish them in every good work and word.

הַתֶּסָלוֹנִיקִים ב

לֹא בִּגְלַל אֵיזֶה דִּבּוּר, וְלֹא בִּגְלַל אֵיזוֹ אִגֶּרֶת אֲשֶׁר כִּבְיָכוֹל נִשְׁלְחָה מֵאִתָּנוּ - כְּאִלּוּ הִגִּיעַ יוֹם יהוה ,
lo biglal eizeh dibbur, velo biglal eizo iggeret asher kivyachol nishlechah me'ittanu - ke'illu higgia yom hashem
or by word, or by epistle as from us, as that the day of the Lord is just at hand;

אַל יַטְעֶה אֶתְכֶם אִישׁ בְּאֵיזֶה אֹפֶן שֶׁהוּא, שֶׁכֵּן לֹא יַגִּיעַ אִם לֹא תִּהְיֶה בָרִאשׁוֹנָה הָעֲזִיבָה
al yat'eh etchem ish be'eizeh ofen shehu, shekken lo yaggia im lo tihyeh barishonah ha'azivah
let no man beguile you in any wise: for it will not be, except the falling away come first,

וְיִתְגַּלֶּה אִישׁ הָרֶשַׁע, בֶּן הָאֲבַדּוֹן
veyitgalleh ish haresha', ben ha'avaddon
and the man of sin be revealed, the son of perdition,

הַמִּתְקוֹמֵם וּמְרוֹמֵם עַצְמוֹ עַל כָּל הַנִּקְרָא אֱלוֹהַּ אוֹ קֹדֶשׁ
hammitkomem umeromem atzmo al kol hannikra eloah o kodesh,
he that opposeth and exalteth himself against all that is called God or that is worshipped;

עַד כִּי יֵשֵׁב בְּהֵיכַל הָאֱלֹהִים בְּהַצְהִירוֹ עַל עַצְמוֹ שֶׁהוּא אֱלֹהִים
ad ki yeshev beheichal ha'elohim behatzhiro al atzmo shehu elohim
so that he sitteth in the temple of God, setting himself forth as God.

הַאִם אֵינְכֶם זוֹכְרִים כִּי עוֹד בִּהְיוֹתִי אֶצְלְכֶם אָמַרְתִּי לָכֶם אֶת הַדְּבָרִים הָאֵלֶּה
ha'im einechem zochrim ki od bihyoti etzlechem amarti lachem et haddevarim ha'elleh
Remember ye not, that, when I was yet with you, I told you these things?

אַתֶּם יוֹדְעִים מַה מְעַכֵּב אוֹתוֹ כָּעֵת כְּדֵי שֶׁיִּתְגַּלֶּה בְּעִתּוֹ
attem yode'im mah me'akkev oto ka'et kedei sheyitgalleh be'itto
And now ye know that which restraineth, to the end that he may be revealed in his own season.

הֵן סוֹד הָרֶשַׁע כְּבָר פּוֹעֵל; רַק שֶׁכָּעֵת הַמְעַכֵּב נִמְצָא
hen sod haresha kevar po'el; rak shekka'et ham'akkev nimtza
For the mystery of lawlessness doth already work: only there is one that restraineth now,

עַד שֶׁיּוּצָא
ad sheyutza
until he be taken out of the way.

וְאָז יִתְגַּלֶּה הָרֶשַׁע אֲשֶׁר הָאָדוֹן יָמִית אוֹתוֹ בְּרוּחַ פִּיו
ve'az yitgalleh haresha asher ha'adon yamit oto beruach piv
And then shall be revealed the lawless one, whom the Lord Jesus shall slay with the breath of his mouth,

וִיכַלֵּהוּ בְּהוֹפָעַת בּוֹאוֹ
viychallehu behofa'at bo'o
and bring to nought by the manifestation of his coming;

אֶת הָרֶשַׁע אֲשֶׁר בִּיאָתוֹ הִיא בְּהֶתְאֵם לִפְעֻלַּת הַשָּׂטָן, מְלֻוָּה בְּכָל גְּבוּרָה, בְּאוֹתוֹת וּבְמוֹפְתֵי שֶׁקֶר
et haresha asher bi'ato hi behet'em lif'ullat hassatan, meluvvah bechol gevurah, be'otot uvemofetei sheker
even he, whose coming is according to the working of Satan with all power and signs and lying wonders,

הַתֶּסָּלוֹנִיקִים ב

בְּאֵשׁ לֶהָבָה, לְהָשִׁיב נָקָם לְאֵלֶּה שֶׁאֵינָם יוֹדְעִים אֶת הָאֱלֹהִים
be'esh lehavah, lehashiv nakam le'elleh she'einam yode'im et ha'elohim
rendering vengeance to them that know not God,

וּלְאֵלֶּה שֶׁאֵינָם נִשְׁמָעִים לִבְשׂוֹרַת אֲדוֹנֵנוּ יֵשׁוּעַ
ule'elleh she'einam nishma'im livsorat adonenu yeshua
and to them that obey not the gospel of our Lord Jesus:

הַלָּלוּ יֻטַּל עֲלֵיהֶם עֹנֶשׁ שֶׁל אֲבַדּוֹן עוֹלָם מִלִּפְנֵי הָאָדוֹן וּמֵהֲדַר עֻזּוֹ
hallalu yuttal aleihem onesh shel avaddon olam millifnei ha'adon umehadar uzzo
who shall suffer punishment, even eternal destruction from the face of the Lord and from the glory of his might,

כְּשֶׁיָּבוֹא בַּיּוֹם הַהוּא לְהִכָּבֵד בִּקְדוֹשָׁיו
kesheyavo bayom hahu lehikkaved bikdoshav
when he shall come to be glorified in his saints,

וְלִהְיוֹת נַעֲרָץ בֵּין כָּל הַמַּאֲמִינִים; וַהֲרֵי אַתֶּם הֶאֱמַנְתֶּם לְעֵדוּתֵנוּ
velihyot na'aratz bein kol hamma'aminim; vaharei attem he'emantem le'edutenu
and to be marvelled at in all them that believed (because our testimony unto you was believed) in that day.

לְכָךְ אָנוּ גַּם מִתְפַּלְּלִים בַּעַדְכֶם בְּכָל עֵת, שֶׁאֱלֹהֵינוּ יַעֲשֶׂה אֶתְכֶם רְאוּיִים לִקְרִיאָתוֹ
lechach anu gam mitpallelim ba'adchem bechol et, she'eloheinu ya'aseh etchem re'uyim likri'ato
To which end we also pray always for you, that our God may count you worthy of your calling,

וּבִגְבוּרָתוֹ יְמַלֵּא כָּל שְׁאִיפָה טוֹבָה וְיַשְׁלִים כָּל מַעֲשֵׂה אֱמוּנָה
uvigvurato yemallei kol she'ifah tovah veyashlim kol ma'aseh emunah
and fulfil every desire of goodness and every work of faith, with power;

לְמַעַן יְכֻבַּד שֵׁם אֲדוֹנֵנוּ יֵשׁוּעַ בָּכֶם וְאַתֶּם תְּכֻבְּדוּ בּוֹ
lema'an yechubbad shem adonenu yeshua bachem ve'attem techubbdu bo
that the name of our Lord Jesus may be glorified in you, and ye in him,

כְּפִי חֶסֶד אֱלֹהֵינוּ וְהָאָדוֹן יֵשׁוּעַ הַמָּשִׁיחַ
kefi chesed eloheinu veha'adon yeshua hammashiach
according to the grace of our God and the Lord Jesus Christ.

ב

אֲשֶׁר לְבוֹא אֲדוֹנֵנוּ יֵשׁוּעַ הַמָּשִׁיחַ וַאֲסִיפָתֵנוּ אֵלָיו, אָנוּ מְבַקְּשִׁים מִכֶּם, אַחַי
asher levo adonenu yeshua hammashiach va'asifatenu elav, anu mevakshim mikkem, achai
Now we beseech you, brethren, touching the coming of our Lord Jesus Christ, and our gathering together unto him;

אַל תְּמַהֲרוּ לְאַבֵּד אֶת עֶשְׁתּוֹנוֹתֵיכֶם וְאַל תִּבָּהֲלוּ, לֹא בִּגְלַל אֵיזוֹ הִתְבַּטְּאוּת שֶׁל רוּחַ
al temaharu le'abbed et eshtonoteichem ve'al tibbahalu, lo biglal eizo hitbatte'ut shel ruach
to the end that ye be not quickly shaken from your mind, nor yet be troubled, either by spirit,

הַתֶּסָּלוֹנִיקִים ב

הַתֶּסָּלוֹנִיקִים ב

מֵאֵת שָׁאוּל וְסִילְוָנוֹס וְטִימוֹתִיאוֹס, אֶל קְהִלַּת הַתֶּסָּלוֹנִיקִים אֲשֶׁר בֵּאלֹהִים אָבִינוּ וּבָאָדוֹן יֵשׁוּעַ הַמָּשִׁיחַ
me'et sha'ul vesilevanos vetimotei'os, el kehillat hattessalonikim asher belohim avinu uva'adon yeshua hammashiach
Paul, and Silvanus, and Timothy, unto the church of the Thessalonians in God our Father and the Lord Jesus Christ;

חֶסֶד וְשָׁלוֹם לָכֶם מֵאֵת הָאֱלֹהִים אָבִינוּ וְהָאָדוֹן יֵשׁוּעַ הַמָּשִׁיחַ
chesed veshalom lachem me'et ha'elohim avinu veha'adon yeshua hammashiach
Grace to you and peace from God the Father and the Lord Jesus Christ.

אַחַי, חַיָּבִים אֲנַחְנוּ לְהוֹדוֹת עֲלֵיכֶם לֵאלֹהִים בְּכָל עֵת; וְרָאוּי הַדָּבָר
achai, chayavim anachnu lehodot aleichem le'elohim bechol et; vera'ui haddavar
We are bound to give thanks to God always for you, brethren, even as it is meet,

מִשּׁוּם שֶׁאֱמוּנַתְכֶם גְּדֵלָה בְּיֶתֶר שְׂאֵת וְאַהֲבַת אִישׁ אֶת רֵעֵהוּ מִתְגַּבֶּרֶת אֵצֶל כֻּלְּכֶם
mishum she'emunatchem gedelah beyeter se'et ve'ahavat ish et re'ehu mitgabberet etzel kullchem
for that your faith groweth exceedingly, and the love of each one of you all toward one another aboundeth;

לְפִיכָךְ אֲנַחְנוּ עַצְמֵנוּ מִתְגָּאִים בָּכֶם בִּקְהִלּוֹת אֱלֹהִים עַל אֱמוּנַתְכֶם וְסַבְלָנוּתְכֶם
lefichach anachnu atzmenu mitga'im bachem bik'hillot elohim al emunatchem vesavlanutechem
so that we ourselves glory in you in the churches of God for your patience and faith

בְּכָל הָרְדִיפוֹת וְהַצָּרוֹת הָעוֹבְרוֹת עֲלֵיכֶם
bechol haredifot vehatzarot ha'overot aleichem
in all your persecutions and in the afflictions which ye endure;

אֲשֶׁר אוֹת הֵן לְמִשְׁפָּטוֹ הַצּוֹדֵק שֶׁל אֱלֹהִים
asher ot hen lemishpato hatzodek shel elohim
which is a manifest token of the righteous judgment of God;

שֶׁתִּמָּצְאוּ רְאוּיִים לְמַלְכוּת הָאֱלֹהִים אֲשֶׁר בַּעֲבוּרָהּ אַתֶּם גַּם סוֹבְלִים
shettimmatze'u re'uyim lemalchut ha'elohim asher ba'avurah attem gam sovelim
to the end that ye may be counted worthy of the kingdom of God, for which ye also suffer:

הֲלֹא מִן הַצֶּדֶק הוּא בְּעֵינֵי אֱלֹהִים לִגְמֹל צָרָה לְרוֹדְפֵיכֶם
halo min hatzedek hu be'einei elohim ligmol tzarah lerodfeichem
if so be that it is a righteous thing with God to recompense affliction to them that afflict you,

וְלָתֵת לָכֶם, הַנִּרְדָּפִים, רְוָחָה יַחַד עִמָּנוּ
velatet lachem, hannirdafim, revachah yachad immanu
and to you that are afflicted rest with us,

כַּאֲשֶׁר יִתְגַּלֶּה הָאָדוֹן יֵשׁוּעַ מִן הַשָּׁמַיִם עִם מַלְאֲכֵי עֻזּוֹ
ka'asher yitgalleh ha'adon yeshua min hashamayim im mal'achei uzzo
at the revelation of the Lord Jesus from heaven with the angels of his power in flaming fire,

הַתֶּסָּלוֹנִיקִים א

בַּחֲנוּ כָּל דָּבָר וְהַחֲזִיקוּ בַּטּוֹב
bachanu kol davar vehachaziku battov
prove all things; hold fast that which is good;

הִתְרַחֲקוּ מִן הָרַע עַל כָּל צוּרוֹתָיו
hitrachaku min hara al kol tzurotav
abstain from every form of evil.

יְקַדֵּשׁ אֶתְכֶם אֱלֹהֵי הַשָּׁלוֹם קְדֻשָּׁה שְׁלֵמָה
yekaddesh etchem elohei hashalom kedushah shlemah
And the God of peace himself sanctify you wholly;

וְתִשָּׁמֵר שְׁלֵמוּת רוּחֲכֶם וְנַפְשְׁכֶם וְגוּפְכֶם, לִהְיוֹת בְּלִי דֹּפִי בְּבוֹא אֲדוֹנֵנוּ יֵשׁוּעַ הַמָּשִׁיחַ
vetishamer shelemut ruchachem venafshechem vegufechem, lihyot bli dofi bevo adonenu yeshua hammashiach
and may your spirit and soul and body be preserved entire, without blame at the coming of our Lord Jesus Christ.

נֶאֱמָן הוּא הַקּוֹרֵא אֶתְכֶם, אֲשֶׁר גַּם יַעֲשֶׂה זֹאת
ne'eman hu hakkorei etchem, asher gam ya'aseh zot
Faithful is he that calleth you, who will also do it.

אַחַי, הִתְפַּלְּלוּ בַּעֲדֵנוּ
achai, hitpallelu ba'adenu
Brethren, pray for us.

דִּרְשׁוּ בִּשְׁלוֹם כָּל הָאַחִים בִּנְשִׁיקָה קְדוֹשָׁה
dirshu bishlom kol ha'achim binshikah kedoshah
Salute all the brethren with a holy kiss.

אֲנִי מַשְׁבִּיעַ אֶתְכֶם בָּאָדוֹן, שֶׁתִּקָּרֵא הָאִגֶּרֶת הַזֹּאת בְּאָזְנֵי כָּל הָאַחִים
ani mashbia etchem ba'adon, shettikkarei ha'iggeret hazzot be'oznei kol ha'achim
I adjure you by the Lord that this epistle be read unto all the brethren.

חֶסֶד אֲדוֹנֵנוּ יֵשׁוּעַ הַמָּשִׁיחַ עִמָּכֶם
chesed adonenu yeshua hammashiach immachem
The grace of our Lord Jesus Christ be with you.

הַתֶּסָּלוֹנִיקִים א

אָנוּ מְבַקְשִׁים מִכֶּם, אַחַי, לְהַכִּיר בָּאֲנָשִׁים הָעֲמֵלִים בְּקִרְבְּכֶם
anu mevakshim mikkem, achai, lehakkir ba'anashim ha'amelim bekirbechem
But we beseech you, brethren, to know them that labor among you,

הַמַּנְהִיגִים אֶתְכֶם בָּאָדוֹן וּמוֹכִיחִים אֶתְכֶם
hammanhigim etchem ba'adon umochichim etchem
and are over you in the Lord, and admonish you;

הוֹקִירוּ אוֹתָם בְּרֹב אַהֲבָה בַּעֲבוּר עֲבוֹדָתָם. הֱיוּ בְּשָׁלוֹם אִישׁ עִם רֵעֵהוּ
hokiru otam berov ahavah ba'avur avodatam. heyu beshalom ish im re'ehu
and to esteem them exceeding highly in love for their work's sake. Be at peace among yourselves.

אַחַי, אָנוּ מְבַקְשִׁים מִכֶּם: הוֹכִיחוּ אֶת הַהוֹלְכִים בָּטֵל;
achai, anu mevakshim mikkem: hochichu et haholchim batel
And we exhort you, brethren, admonish the disorderly,

עוֹדְדוּ אֶת הַנִּכְאִים; תִּמְכוּ בַּחַלָּשִׁים; הֱיוּ סַבְלָנִיִּים כְּלַפֵּי כָּל אָדָם
odedu et hanneche'im; timchu bachallashim; heyu savlaniyim kelappei kol adam
encourage the fainthearted, support the weak, be longsuffering toward all.

הִזָּהֲרוּ שֶׁלֹּא יִגְמֹל אִישׁ לְאִישׁ רָעָה תַּחַת רָעָה;
hizzaharu shello yigmol ish le'ish ra'ah tachat ra'ah
See that none render unto any one evil for evil;

בְּכָל עֵת חִתְרוּ לְהֵיטִיב אִישׁ עִם רֵעֵהוּ וְגַם עִם כָּל אָדָם
bechol et chitru leheitiv ish im re'ehu vegam im kol adam
but always follow after that which is good, one toward another, and toward all.

שִׂמְחוּ תָּמִיד
simchu tamid
Rejoice always;

הַתְמִידוּ לְהִתְפַּלֵּל
hatmidu lehitpallel
pray without ceasing;

הוֹדוּ עַל כָּל דָּבָר; כִּי זֶהוּ רְצוֹן אֱלֹהִים לְגַבֵּיכֶם בַּמָּשִׁיחַ יֵשׁוּעַ
hodu al kol davar; ki zehu retzon elohim legabbeichem bammashiach yeshua
in everything give thanks: for this is the will of God in Christ Jesus to you-ward.

אַל תְּכַבּוּ אֶת הָרוּחַ
al techabbu et haruach
Quench not the Spirit;

אַל תְּזַלְזְלוּ בַּנְּבוּאוֹת
al tezalzelu bannevu'ot
despise not prophesyings;

הַתֶּסָּלוֹנִיקִים א

הֲרֵי אַתֶּם יוֹדְעִים הֵיטֵב שֶׁיּוֹם יהוה יָבוֹא כְּגַנָּב בַּלַּיְלָה
harei attem yode'im heitev sheyom hashem yavo kegannav ballaylah
For yourselves know perfectly that the day of the Lord so cometh as a thief in the night.

כַּאֲשֶׁר יֹאמְרוּ הַבְּרִיּוֹת: שָׁלוֹם וּבִטָּחוֹן!, אָז יָבוֹא עֲלֵיהֶם שֶׁבֶר פִּתְאֹם
ka'asher yomeru habberiyot. shalom uvittachon!, az yavo aleihem shever pit'om
When they are saying, Peace and safety, then sudden destruction cometh upon them,

כְּצִירֵי לֵדָה עַל אִשָּׁה הָרָה, וְלֹא יוּכְלוּ לְהִמָּלֵט
ketzirei ledah al ishah harah, velo yuchelu lehimmalet
as travail upon a woman with child; and they shall in no wise escape.

אֲבָל אַתֶּם, אַחַי, אֵינְכֶם בַּחֹשֶׁךְ בְּאֹפֶן שֶׁיַּפְתִּיעַ אֶתְכֶם הַיּוֹם כְּגַנָּב
aval attem, achai, einchem bachoshech be'ofen sheyaftia etchem hayom kegannav
But ye, brethren, are not in darkness, that that day should overtake you as a thief:

אַתֶּם כֻּלְּכֶם בְּנֵי הָאוֹר וּבְנֵי הַיּוֹם. לֹא בְּנֵי הַלַּיְלָה אֲנַחְנוּ וְלֹא בְּנֵי הַחֹשֶׁךְ
attem kullechem benei ha'or uvenei hayom. lo benei hallaylah anachnu velo benei hachoshech
for ye are all sons of light, and sons of the day: we are not of the night, nor of darkness;

לָכֵן אַל נָא נִישַׁן כָּאֲחֵרִים, אֶלָּא נִהְיֶה עֵרִים וּמְפֻכָּחִים
lachen al na nishan ka'acherim, ella nihyeh erim umefukkachim
so then let us not sleep, as do the rest, but let us watch and be sober.

הֵן הַיְשֵׁנִים יְשֵׁנִים בַּלַּיְלָה, וְהַמִּשְׁתַּכְּרִים מִשְׁתַּכְּרִים בַּלַּיְלָה
hen hayshenim yeshenim ballaylah, vehammishtakkerim mishtakkerim ballaylah
For they that sleep sleep in the night; and they that are drunken are drunken in the night.

אֲבָל אָנוּ, אֲשֶׁר בְּנֵי הַיּוֹם אֲנַחְנוּ, נִהְיֶה נָא מְפֻכָּחִים
aval anu, asher benei hayom anachnu, nihyeh na mefukkachim
But let us, since we are of the day, be sober,

נִלְבַּשׁ אֶת שִׁרְיוֹן הָאֱמוּנָה וְהָאַהֲבָה וְנַחֲבֹשׁ כַּכּוֹבַע אֶת תִּקְוַת הַיְשׁוּעָה
nilbash et shiryon ha'emunah veha'ahavah venachavosh kakkova et tikvat hayshu'ah
putting on the breastplate of faith and love; and for a helmet, the hope of salvation.

כִּי אֱלֹהִים לֹא יְעָדָנוּ לְזַעַם, אֶלָּא לִנְחֹל יְשׁוּעָה עַל-יְדֵי אֲדוֹנֵנוּ יֵשׁוּעַ הַמָּשִׁיחַ
ki elohim lo ye'adanu leza'am, ella linchol yeshu'ah al-yedei adonenu yeshua hammashiach
For God appointed us not unto wrath, but unto the obtaining of salvation through our Lord Jesus Christ,

אֲשֶׁר מֵת בַּעֲדֵנוּ לְמַעַן נִחְיֶה יַחַד אִתּוֹ, בֵּין שֶׁאָנוּ עֵרִים בֵּין שֶׁאָנוּ יְשֵׁנִים
asher met ba'adenu lema'an nichyeh yachad itto, bein she'anu erim bein she'anu yeshenim
who died for us, that, whether we wake or sleep, we should live together with him.

עַל כֵּן עוֹדְדוּ זֶה אֶת זֶה וּבְנוּ אִישׁ אֶת אָחִיו, כְּפִי שֶׁאַתֶּם גַּם עוֹשִׂים
al ken odedu zeh et zeh uvenu ish et achiv, kefi she'attem gam osim
Wherefore exhort one another, and build each other up, even as also ye do.

הַתֶּסָּלוֹנִיקִים א

כְּדֵי שֶׁלֹּא תִּתְעַצְּבוּ כָּאֲחֵרִים אֲשֶׁר אֵין לָהֶם הַתִּקְוָה
kedei shello tit'atzevu ka'acherim asher ein lahem hattikvah
that ye sorrow not, even as the rest, who have no hope.

אִם אָמְנָם מַאֲמִינִים אָנוּ שֶׁיֵּשׁוּעַ מֵת וְקָם לִתְחִיָּה
im omnam ma'aminim anu sheyeshua met vekam litchiyah
For if we believe that Jesus died and rose again,

כָּךְ גַּם אֶת הַיְשֵׁנִים, בְּאֶמְצָעוּת יֵשׁוּעַ, אֱלֹהִים יָבִיא יַחַד אִתּוֹ
kach gam et hayshenim, be'emtza'ut yeshua', elohim yavi yachad itto
even so them also that are fallen asleep in Jesus will God bring with him.

הִנֵּה זֹאת אָנוּ אוֹמְרִים לָכֶם עַל־פִּי דְּבַר הָאָדוֹן: אֲנַחְנוּ הַחַיִּים
hinneh zot anu omerim lachem al-pi devar ha'adon. anachnu hachayim
For this we say unto you by the word of the Lord, that we that are alive,

אֲשֶׁר נִשָּׁאֵר עַד בּוֹא הָאָדוֹן לֹא נַקְדִּים אֶת הַמֵּתִים
asher nisha'er ad bo ha'adon lo nakdim et hammetim
that are left unto the coming of the Lord, shall in no wise precede them that are fallen asleep.

שֶׁכֵּן הָאָדוֹן עַצְמוֹ יֵרֵד מִן הַשָּׁמַיִם בִּקְרִיאָה שֶׁל פְּקֻדָּה, בְּקוֹל שַׂר הַמַּלְאָכִים
shekken ha'adon atzmo yered min hashamayim bikri'ah shel pekuddah, bekol sar hammal'achim
For the Lord himself shall descend from heaven, with a shout, with the voice of the archangel,

וּבְשׁוֹפַר אֱלֹהִים, וְהַמֵּתִים הַשַּׁיָּכִים לַמָּשִׁיחַ יָקוּמוּ רִאשׁוֹנָה
uveshofar elohim, vehammetim hashayachim lammashiach yakumu rishonah
and with the trump of God: and the dead in Christ shall rise first;

אַחֲרֵי כֵן אֲנַחְנוּ הַנִּשְׁאָרִים בַּחַיִּים נִלָּקַח יַחַד אִתָּם בָּעֲנָנִים לִפְגֹּשׁ אֶת הָאָדוֹן בָּאֲוִיר
acharei chen anachnu hannish'arim bachayim nillakach yachad ittam ba'ananim lifgosh et ha'adon ba'avir
then we that are alive, that are left, shall together with them be caught up in the clouds, to meet the Lord in the air:

וְכָךְ נִהְיֶה תָּמִיד עִם הָאָדוֹן
vechach nihyeh tamid im ha'adon
and so shall we ever be with the Lord.

עַל כֵּן עוֹדְדוּ זֶה אֶת זֶה בַּדְּבָרִים הָאֵלֶּה
al ken odedu zeh et zeh baddevarim ha'elleh
Wherefore comfort one another with these words.

ה

וְעַל־דְּבַר הָעִתִּים וְהַזְּמַנִּים, אַחַי, אֵין צֹרֶךְ לִכְתֹּב לָכֶם
ve'al-devar ha'ittim vehazzemannim, achai, ein tzorech lichtov lachem
But concerning the times and the seasons, brethren, ye have no need that aught be written unto you.

הַתֶּסָּלוֹנִיקִים א

לֹא בְּתַאֲוֺת זִמָּה כְּדֶרֶךְ הַגּוֹיִם אֲשֶׁר אֵינָם יוֹדְעִים אֶת אֱלֹהִים
lo beta'avat zimmah kederech haggoyim asher einam yode'im et elohim
not in the passion of lust, even as the Gentiles who know not God;

וְאִישׁ אַל יֶחֱטָא וְאַל יַעֲשֶׂה עָוֶל לְאָחִיו בָּעִנְיָן הַזֶּה
ve'ish al yecheta ve'al ya'aseh avel le'achiv ba'inyan hazzeh
that no man transgress, and wrong his brother in the matter:

כִּי נֹקֵם יהוה עַל כָּל זֹאת, כְּפִי שֶׁכְּבָר אָמַרְנוּ לָכֶם וְהִזְהַרְנוּ אֶתְכֶם
ki nokem hashem al kol zot, kefi shekkevar amarnu lachem vehizharnu etchem
because the Lord is an avenger in all these things, as also we forewarned you and testified.

הֵן אֱלֹהִים לֹא קָרָא אוֹתָנוּ לְטֻמְאָה, כִּי אִם לִקְדֻשָּׁה
hen elohim lo kara otanu letum'ah, ki im likdushah
For God called us not for uncleanness, but in sanctification.

עַל כֵּן הַדּוֹחֶה זֹאת, לֹא אָדָם הוּא דּוֹחֶה, אֶלָּא אֶת אֱלֹהִים הַנּוֹתֵן לָכֶם אֶת רוּחַ קָדְשׁוֹ
al ken haddocheh zot, lo adam hu docheh, ella et elohim hannoten lachem et ruach kodsho
Therefore he that rejecteth, rejecteth not man, but God, who giveth his Holy Spirit unto you.

עַל־דְּבַר אַהֲבַת אַחִים אֵין צֹרֶךְ לִכְתֹּב לָכֶם
al-devar ahavat achim ein tzorech lichtov lachem
But concerning love of the brethren ye have no need that one write unto you:

שֶׁכֵּן אַתֶּם בְּעַצְמְכֶם לִמּוּדֵי אֱלֹהִים וְיוֹדְעִים שֶׁעֲלֵיכֶם לֶאֱהֹב אִישׁ אֶת רֵעֵהוּ
shekken attem be'atzmechem lemudei elohim veyode'im she'aleichem le'ehov ish et re'ehu
for ye yourselves are taught of God to love one another;

וְאָמְנָם אַתֶּם נוֹהֲגִים כָּךְ כְּלַפֵּי כָּל הָאַחִים אֲשֶׁר בְּכָל מָקֵדוֹנְיָה
ve'amenam attem nohagim kach kelappei kol ha'achim asher bechol makedoneyah
for indeed ye do it toward all the brethren that are in all Macedonia.

אֲבָל מְבַקְשִׁים אָנוּ מִכֶּם, אַחַי, שֶׁתִּשְׁפְּעוּ עוֹד יוֹתֵר
aval mevakshim anu mikkem, achai, shettishpe'u od yoter
But we exhort you, brethren, that ye abound more and more;

הִשְׁתַּדְּלוּ לִחְיוֹת בְּהַשְׁקֵט, לַעֲסֹק בָּעִנְיָנִים שֶׁלָּכֶם וְלַעֲבֹד בִּידֵיכֶם אַתֶּם, כְּפִי שֶׁצִּוִּינוּ אֶתְכֶם
hishtaddelu lichyot behashket, la'asok ba'inyanim shellachem vela'avod bideichem attem, kefi shetzivvinu etchem
and that ye study to be quiet, and to do your own business, and to work with your hands, even as we charged you;

לְמַעַן תִּתְנַהֲגוּ כַּיָּאוּת עִם אֵלֶּה אֲשֶׁר בַּחוּץ וּלְמַעַן לֹא יֶחְסַר לָכֶם דָּבָר
lema'an titnahagu kaya'ut im elleh asher bachutz ulema'an lo yechsar lachem davar
that ye may walk becomingly toward them that are without, and may have need of nothing.

אַחַי, אֵין אָנוּ רוֹצִים שֶׁיֵּעָלֵם מִכֶּם מַה שֶׁנּוֹגֵעַ לִישֵׁנֵי עָפָר
achai, ein anu rotzim sheye'alem mikkem mah shennogea liyshenei afar
But we would not have you ignorant, brethren, concerning them that fall asleep;

הַתֶּסָּלוֹנִיקִים א

יְכַוֵּן אֱלֹהִים אָבִינוּ וַאֲדוֹנֵנוּ יֵשׁוּעַ אֶת דַּרְכֵּנוּ אֲלֵיכֶם
yechavven elohim avinu va'adonenu yeshua et darkenu aleichem
Now may our God and Father himself, and our Lord Jesus, direct our way unto you:

וְהָאָדוֹן יַרְבֶּה וְיַשְׂגֶּה אֶת הָאַהֲבָה בְּקִרְבְּכֶם, לֶאֱהֹב אִישׁ אֶת רֵעֵהוּ וְאֶת כָּל אָדָם
veha'adon yarbeh veyasgeh et ha'ahavah bekirbechem, le'ehov ish et re'ehu ve'et kol adam
and the Lord make you to increase and abound in love one toward another, and toward all men,

כְּשֵׁם שֶׁגַּם אֲנַחְנוּ אוֹהֲבִים אֶתְכֶם
keshem sheggam anachnu ohavim etchem
even as we also do toward you;

וְכָךְ יְכוֹנֵן אֶת לְבַבְכֶם לִהְיוֹת תָּמִים בִּקְדֻשָּׁה לִפְנֵי הָאֱלֹהִים אָבִינוּ
vechach yechonen et levavchem lihyot tamim bikdushah lifnei ha'elohim avinu
to the end he may establish your hearts unblameable in holiness before our God and Father,

בְּבוֹא אֲדוֹנֵנוּ יֵשׁוּעַ עִם כָּל קְדוֹשָׁיו
bevo adonenu yeshua im kol kedoshav
at the coming of our Lord Jesus with all his saints.

ד

לְבַסּוֹף, אַחַי, אָנוּ מְבַקְשִׁים מִכֶּם בָּאָדוֹן יֵשׁוּעַ וּמַפְצִירִים בָּכֶם
levassof, achai, anu mevakshim mikkem ba'adon yeshua umaftzirim bachem
Finally then, brethren, we beseech and exhort you in the Lord Jesus,

קִבַּלְתֶּם מֵאִתָּנוּ אֵיךְ עֲלֵיכֶם לְהִתְנַהֵג וְלִמְצֹא חֵן בְּעֵינֵי אֱלֹהִים
kibbaltem me'ittanu eich aleichem lehitnaheg velimtzo chen be'einei elohim
that, as ye received of us how ye ought to walk and to please God,

וְאָמְנָם כָּךְ אַתֶּם מִתְנַהֲגִים; אָנָּא, הִתְקַדְּמוּ עוֹד יוֹתֵר
ve'omnam kach attem mitnahagim; anna, hitkaddemu od yoter
even as ye do walk,—that ye abound more and more.

אַתֶּם יוֹדְעִים אֵילוּ מִצְווֹת נָתַנּוּ לָכֶם מִטַּעַם הָאָדוֹן יֵשׁוּעַ
attem yode'im eilu mitzvot natannu lachem mitta'am ha'adon yeshua
For ye know what charge we gave you through the Lord Jesus.

וְזֶהוּ רְצוֹן הָאֱלֹהִים: שֶׁתִּתְקַדְּשׁוּ, שֶׁתִּתְרַחֲקוּ מִן הַזְּנוּת
vezehu retzon ha'elohim: shettitkaddeshu, shettitrachaku min hazzenut
For this is the will of God, even your sanctification, that ye abstain from fornication;

שֶׁכָּל אֶחָד מִכֶּם יֵדַע לָקַחַת אִשָּׁה בִּקְדֻשָּׁה וּבְכָבוֹד
shekkol echad mikkem yeda lakachat ishah bikdushah uvechavod
that each one of you know how to possess himself of his own vessel in sanctification and honor,

הַתֶּסָּלוֹנִיקִים א

הֵן גַּם כַּאֲשֶׁר הָיִינוּ אֶצְלְכֶם אָמַרְנוּ לָכֶם מֵרֹאשׁ שֶׁעֲתִידִים אֲנַחְנוּ לִסְבֹּל
hen gam ka'asher hayinu etzlechem amarnu lachem merosh she'atidim anachnu lisbol
For verily, when we were with you, we told you beforehand that we are to suffer affliction;

מַה שֶּׁאָכֵן קָרָה וְגַם יָדוּעַ לָכֶם
mah she'achen karah vegam yadua lachem
even as it came to pass, and ye know.

לָכֵן כַּאֲשֶׁר לֹא יָכֹלְתִּי עוֹד לָשֵׂאת זֹאת, שָׁלַחְתִּי לְהִוָּדַע מַה מַּצָּב אֱמוּנַתְכֶם
lachen ka'asher lo yacholeti od laset zot, shalachti lehivvada mah matzav emunatchem
For this cause I also, when I could no longer forbear, sent that I might know your faith,

מֵחֲשָׁשׁ שֶׁמָּא נִסָּה אֶתְכֶם הַמְנַסֶּה וַעֲמָלֵנוּ הָיָה לָרִיק
mechashash shemma nissah etchem hamnasseh va'amalenu hayah larik
lest by any means the tempter had tempted you, and our labor should be in vain.

אֲבָל כָּעֵת טִימוֹתֵיאוֹס בָּא אֵלֵינוּ מִכֶּם וּבִשֵּׂר לָנוּ טֹבוֹת עַל אֱמוּנַתְכֶם וְאַהֲבַתְכֶם
aval ka'et timotei'os ba eleinu mikkem uvisher lanu tovot al emunatchem ve'ahavatchem
But when Timothy came even now unto us from you, and brought us glad tidings of your faith and love,

וְסִפֵּר שֶׁאַתֶּם זוֹכְרִים אוֹתָנוּ לְטוֹבָה בְּכָל עֵת
vesipper she'attem zocherim otanu letovah bechol et
and that ye have good remembrance of us always,

וְנִכְסָפִים לִרְאוֹתֵנוּ, כְּשֵׁם שֶׁגַּם אָנוּ נִכְסָפִים לִרְאוֹת אֶתְכֶם
venichsafim lir'otenu, keshem sheggam anu nichsafim lir'ot etchem
longing to see us, even as we also to see you;

עַל כֵּן, אַחַי, בְּכָל מְצוּקָתֵנוּ וְצָרָתֵנוּ הִתְעוֹדַדְנוּ בָּכֶם בִּגְלַל אֱמוּנַתְכֶם
al ken, achai, bechol metzukatenu vetzaratenu hit'odadnu bachem biglal emunatchem
for this cause, brethren, we were comforted over you in all our distress and affliction through your faith:

וְאָמְנָם עַכְשָׁו חַיִּים אֲנַחְנוּ, אִם אַתֶּם מַחֲזִיקִים מַעֲמָד בָּאָדוֹן
ve'omnam achshav chayim anachnu, im attem machazikim ma'amad ba'adon
for now we live, if ye stand fast in the Lord.

וְאֵילוּ תּוֹדוֹת יְכוֹלִים אָנוּ לְשַׁלֵּם לֵאלֹהִים בַּעַדְכֶם
ve'eilu todot yecholim anu leshallem le'elohim ba'adchem
For what thanksgiving can we render again unto God for you,

עַל כָּל הַשִּׂמְחָה שֶׁאָנוּ שְׂמֵחִים בִּגְלַלְכֶם לִפְנֵי אֱלֹהֵינוּ
al kol hassimchah she'anu semechim biglalchem lifnei eloheinu
for all the joy wherewith we joy for your sakes before our God;

יוֹמָם וָלַיְלָה מַרְבִּים אָנוּ לְהִתְפַּלֵּל שֶׁנִּרְאֶה אֶת פְּנֵיכֶם וְנַשְׁלִים אֶת הֶחָסֵר לֶאֱמוּנַתְכֶם
yomam valaylah marbim anu lehitpallel shennir'eh et peneichem venashlim et hechaser le'emunatchem
night and day praying exceedingly that we may see your face, and may perfect that which is lacking in your faith?

הַתֶּסָּלוֹנִיקִים א

בְּזֹאת הֵם מְמַלְּאִים אֶת סְאַת חַטֹּאתֵיהֶם בְּכָל עֵת
bazot hem memalle'im et se'at chattoteihem bechol et
to fill up their sins always:

וּבָא עֲלֵיהֶם הֶחָרוֹן עַד תֹּם
uva aleihem hecharon ad tom
but the wrath is come upon them to the uttermost.

אֲבָל אֲנַחְנוּ, אַחַי, לְאַחַר זְמַן קָצָר שֶׁהָיִינוּ מְרֻחָקִים מִכֶּם - מְרֻחָקִים בְּמַרְאֵה פָּנִים, אַךְ לֹא בַּלֵּב
aval anachnu, achai, le'achar zman katzar shehayinu meruchakim mikkem - meruchakim bemar'eh panim, ach lo ballev
But we, brethren, being bereaved of you for a short season, in presence not in heart,

נִכְסַפְנוּ עַד מְאֹד לִרְאוֹת אֶת פְּנֵיכֶם
nichsafnu ad me'od lir'ot et peneichem
endeavored the more exceedingly to see your face with great desire:

לְפִיכָךְ חָפַצְנוּ לָבוֹא אֲלֵיכֶם - אֲנִי שָׁאוּל רָצִיתִי בָּזֶה יוֹתֵר מִפַּעַם אַחַת, אֶלָּא שֶׁהַשָּׂטָן מָנַע בַּעֲדֵנוּ
lefichach chafatznu lavo aleichem - ani sha'ul ratziti bazeh yoter mippa'am achat, ella shehassatan mana ba'adenu
because we would fain have come unto you, I Paul once and again; and Satan hindered us.

כִּי מִי תִּקְוָתֵנוּ וְשִׂמְחָתֵנוּ וַעֲטֶרֶת תְּהִלָּתֵנוּ לְנֹכַח אֲדוֹנֵנוּ יֵשׁוּעַ בְּבוֹאוֹ, מִי אִם לֹא אַתֶּם
ki mi tikvatenu vesimchatenu va'ateret tehillatenu lenochach adonenu yeshua bevo'o, mi im lo attem
For what is our hope, or joy, or crown of glorying? Are not even ye, before our Lord Jesus at his coming?

הֲרֵי אַתֶּם תִּפְאַרְתֵּנוּ וְשִׂמְחָתֵנוּ
harei attem tif'artenu vesimchatenu
For ye are our glory and our joy.

ג

וּמֵאַחַר שֶׁלֹּא יָכֹלְנוּ עוֹד לִסְבֹּל זֹאת, הֶחְלַטְנוּ לְהִשָּׁאֵר לְבַדֵּנוּ בְּאַתּוּנָה
ume'achar shello yacholenu od lisbol zot, hechlatnu lehisha'er levaddenu be'attunah
Wherefore when we could no longer forbear, we thought it good to be left behind at Athens alone;

וְשָׁלַחְנוּ אֶת טִימוֹתֵיאוֹס אָחִינוּ וַעֲמִיתֵנוּ הַמְשָׁרֵת אֶת אֱלֹהִים בִּבְשׂוֹרַת הַמָּשִׁיחַ
veshalachnu et timotei'os achinu va'amitenu hamsharet et elohim bivesorat hammashiach
and sent Timothy, our brother and God's minister in the gospel of Christ,

שְׁלַחְנוּ אוֹתוֹ לְחַזֵּק וּלְעוֹדֵד אֶתְכֶם בֶּאֱמוּנַתְכֶם
shalachnu oto lechazzek ule'oded etchem be'emunatchem
to establish you, and to comfort you concerning your faith;

כְּדֵי שֶׁאִישׁ מִכֶּם לֹא יִמּוֹט בַּצָּרוֹת הָאֵלֶּה; הֲלֹא יוֹדְעִים אַתֶּם שֶׁלְּזֹאת יֻעַדְנוּ
kedei she'ish mikkem lo yimmot batzarot ha'elleh; halo yode'im attem shellazot yu'adnu
that no man be moved by these afflictions; for yourselves know that hereunto we are appointed.

הַתֶּסָּלוֹנִיקִים א

נָהַגְנוּ עִמָּכֶם הַמַּאֲמִינִים
nahagnu immachem hamma'aminim
we behaved ourselves toward you that believe:

וְיוֹדְעִים אַתֶּם כִּי כְּאָב אֶל בָּנָיו דִּבַּרְנוּ
veyode'im attem ki ke'av el banav dibbarnu
as ye know how we dealt with each one of you, as a father with his own children,

דִּבְרֵי מוּסָר וְעִדּוּד אֶל כָּל אֶחָד וְאֶחָד מִכֶּם
divrei musar ve'iddud el kol echad ve'echad mikkem
exhorting you, and encouraging you, and testifying,

וְהַעִידוֹנוּ בָּכֶם לְהִתְהַלֵּךְ כָּרָאוּי לִפְנֵי אֱלֹהִים הַקּוֹרֵא אֶתְכֶם לְמַלְכוּתוֹ וּכְבוֹדוֹ
veha'idonu bachem lehit'hallech kara'ui lifnei elohim hakkorei etchem lemalchuto uchevodo
to the end that ye should walk worthily of God, who calleth you into his own kingdom and glory.

גַּם מִסִּבָּה נוֹסֶפֶת מַתְמִידִים אָנוּ לְהוֹדוֹת לֵאלֹהִים
gam missibbah nosefet matmidim anu lehodot le'elohim
And for this cause we also thank God without ceasing,

כַּאֲשֶׁר קִבַּלְתֶּם אֶת דְּבַר אֱלֹהִים שֶׁשְּׁמַעְתֶּם מֵאִתָּנוּ, קִבַּלְתֶּם אוֹתוֹ לֹא כִּדְבַר בְּנֵי אָדָם
Ka'asher kibbaltem et devar elohim sheshema'tem me'ittanu, kibbaltem oto lo kidvar benei adam
that, when ye received from us the word of the message, even the word of God, ye accepted it not as the word of men,

אֶלָּא כְּפִי שֶׁהוּא בֶּאֱמֶת - דְּבַר אֱלֹהִים, הַדָּבָר אֲשֶׁר פּוֹעֵל גַּם בָּכֶם הַמַּאֲמִינִים
ella kefi shehu be'emet - devar elohim, haddavar asher po'el gam bachem hamma'aminim
but, as it is in truth, the word of God, which also worketh in you that believe.

הֲלֹא אַתֶּם, אַחַי, הֲלַכְתֶּם בְּעִקְּבוֹת קְהִלּוֹת אֱלֹהִים שֶׁבִּיהוּדָה הַשַּׁיָּכוֹת לַמָּשִׁיחַ יֵשׁוּעַ
halo attem, achai, halachtem be'ikkevot kehillot elohim shebbiyehudah hashayachot lammashiach yeshua
For ye, brethren, became imitators of the churches of God which are in Judæa in Christ Jesus:

כִּי גַּם אַתֶּם סְבַלְתֶּם מִידֵי בְּנֵי עַמְּכֶם כְּמוֹ שֶׁגַּם הֵם סָבְלוּ מִידֵי תוֹשְׁבֵי יְהוּדָה
ki gam attem sevaltem midei benei ammchem kemo sheggam hem savelu midei toshevei yehudah
for ye also suffered the same things of your own countrymen, even as they did of the Jews;

אֵלֶּה אֲשֶׁר הֵמִיתוּ גַּם אֶת הָאָדוֹן יֵשׁוּעַ וְגַם אֶת הַנְּבִיאִים, וְאוֹתָנוּ רָדְפוּ
eleh asher hemitu gam et ha'adon yeshua vegam et hannevi'im, ve'otanu radefu
who both killed the Lord Jesus and the prophets, and drove out us,

אֵין הֵם מַשְׂבִּיעִים אֶת רְצוֹן אֱלֹהִים וּמִתְנַגְּדִים לְכָל בְּנֵי אָדָם
ein hem masbi'im et retzon elohim umitnaggedim lechol benei adam
and please not God, and are contrary to all men;

בְּנַסּוֹתָם לִמְנֹעַ אוֹתָנוּ מֵהַגִּיד לַגּוֹיִם אֶת הַדֶּרֶךְ לִישׁוּעָה
benassotam limnoa otanu mehaggid laggoyim et hadderech liyshu'ah
forbidding us to speak to the Gentiles that they may be saved;

הַתֶּסָּלוֹנִיקִים א

בְּהֶתְאֵם לְכָךְ אֲנַחְנוּ מְדַבְּרִים
behet'em lechach anachnu medabberim,
so we speak;

לֹא כְּמַשְׂבִּיעִים אֶת רְצוֹן בְּנֵי אָדָם, אֶלָּא אֶת רְצוֹן אֱלֹהִים הַבּוֹחֵן אֶת לְבָבֵנוּ
lo kemasbi'im et retzon benei adam, ella et retzon elohim habbochen et levavenu
not as pleasing men, but God who proveth our hearts.

הֵן יוֹדְעִים אַתֶּם שֶׁמֵּעוֹלָם לֹא בָּאנוּ בְּמִלּוֹת חֲנֻפָּה, וְלֹא בְּתֵרוּצִים הַמְכַסִּים עַל שְׁאִיפָה לְבֶצַע
hen yode'im attem shemme'olam lo banu bemillot chanuppah, velo beterutzim hamchassim al she'ifah levetza
For neither at any time were we found using words of flattery, as ye know, nor a cloak of covetousness,

עֵד הָאֱלֹהִים
ed ha'elohim
God is witness;

אַף לֹא בִּקַּשְׁנוּ לָנוּ כָּבוֹד מִבְּנֵי אָדָם, לֹא מִכֶּם וְלֹא מֵאֲחֵרִים
af lo bikkashnu lanu kavod mibbenei adam, lo mikkem velo me'acherim
nor seeking glory of men, neither from you nor from others,

הֲגַם שֶׁבְּתוֹר שְׁלִיחֵי הַמָּשִׁיחַ הָיִינוּ רַשָּׁאִים לְהִתְכַּבֵּד
hagam shebbetor shelichei hammashiach hayinu rasha'im lehitkabbed
when we might have claimed authority as apostles of Christ.

אֲבָל נָהַגְנוּ בַּעֲדִינוּת כְּשֶׁהָיִינוּ אִתְּכֶם, כְּאִשָּׁה הַמְטַפֶּלֶת בִּילָדֶיהָ
aval nahagnu ba'adinut keshehayinu ittechem, ke'ishah hamtappelet biyeladeiha
But we were gentle in the midst of you, as when a nurse cherisheth her own children:

חִבַּבְנוּ אֶתְכֶם כָּל כָּךְ, שֶׁבְּחֵפֶץ לֵב שַׂשְׂנוּ לָתֵת לָכֶם
chibbavnu etchem kol kach, shebbechefetz lev sasnu latet lachem
even so, being affectionately desirous of you, we were well pleased to impart unto you,

לֹא רַק אֶת בְּשׂוֹרַת אֱלֹהִים אֶלָּא גַּם אֶת נַפְשֵׁנוּ, שֶׁכֵּן נִהְיֵיתֶם אֲהוּבִים עָלֵינוּ
lo rak et besorat elohim ella gam et nafshenu, shekken nihyeitem ahuvim aleinu
not the gospel of God only, but also our own souls, because ye were become very dear to us.

אַתֶּם זוֹכְרִים, אַחַי, אֶת עֲמָלֵנוּ וִיגִיעָתֵנוּ
attem zocherim, achai, et amalenu viygi'atenu
For ye remember, brethren, our labor and travail:

עָבַדְנוּ יוֹמָם וָלַיְלָה כְּדֵי שֶׁלֹּא לִהְיוֹת לְמַשָּׂא עַל אִישׁ מִכֶּם בְּעֵת שֶׁבִּשַּׂרְנוּ לָכֶם אֶת בְּשׂוֹרַת אֱלֹהִים
avadnu yomam valaylah kedei shello lihyot lemassa al ish mikkem be'et shebbissarnu lachem et besorat elohim
working night and day, that we might not burden any of you, we preached unto you the gospel of God.

עֵדִים אַתֶּם וְעֵד אֱלֹהִים כִּי בִּקְדֻשָּׁה וּבְצֶדֶק וּבְלֹא דֹּפִי
edim attem ve'ed elohim ki bikdushah uvetzedek uvelo dofi
Ye are witnesses, and God also, how holily and righteously and unblamably

הַתֶּסָּלוֹנִיקִים א

הֵן מִכֶּם יָצָא שֵׁמַע דְּבַר יהוה לֹא רַק בְּמֵקֵדוֹנְיָה וְאֲכַיָה בִּלְבַד
hen mikkem yatza shema devar hashem lo rak bemakedoneyah ve'achayah bilvad
For from you hath sounded forth the word of the Lord, not only in Macedonia and Achaia,

אֶלָּא בְּכָל מָקוֹם נִתְפַּרְסְמָה אֱמוּנַתְכֶם בֵּאלֹהִים עַד כִּי אֵין לָנוּ צֹרֶךְ לְהַגִּיד דָּבָר
ella bechol makom nitparsemah emunatchem be'elohim ad ki ein lanu tzorech lehaggid davar
but in every place your faith to God-ward is gone forth; so that we need not to speak anything.

שֶׁכֵּן הֵם בְּעַצְמָם מְסַפְּרִים כֵּיצַד קִבַּלְתֶּם אוֹתָנוּ
shekken hem be'atzmam mesapperim keitzad kibbaltem otanu
For they themselves report concerning us what manner of entering in we had unto you;

וְכֵיצַד פְּנִיתֶם מִן הָאֱלִילִים לֵאלֹהִים כְּדֵי לַעֲבֹד אֵל חַי וַאֲמִתִּי
vecheitzad penitem min ha'elilim le'elohim kedei la'avod el chai va'amitti
and how ye turned unto God from idols, to serve a living and true God,

וּלְחַכּוֹת לִבְנוֹ מִן הַשָּׁמַיִם, אֲשֶׁר הוּא הֱקִימוֹ מִן הַמֵּתִים
ulechakkot livno min hashamayim, asher hu hekimo min hammetim,
and to wait for his Son from heaven, whom he raised from the dead,

לְיֵשׁוּעַ הַמַּצִּיל אוֹתָנוּ מִן הַזַּעַם הַבָּא
leyeshua hammatzil otanu min hazza'am habba
even Jesus, who delivereth us from the wrath to come.

ב

אַחַי, הֲרֵי אַתֶּם יוֹדְעִים שֶׁבּוֹאֵנוּ אֲלֵיכֶם לֹא הָיָה לַשָּׁוְא
achai, harei attem yode'im shebbo'enu aleichem lo hayah lashav
For yourselves, brethren, know our entering in unto you, that it hath not been found vain:

אָמְנָם קֹדֶם לָכֵן סָבַלְנוּ וְהָיִינוּ לְבוּז בְּפִילִיפִּי, דָּבָר שֶׁיָּדוּעַ לָכֶם
omnam kodem lachen savalnu vehayinu levuz befilipi, davar sheyadua lachem
but having suffered before and been shamefully treated, as ye know, at Philippi,

אַךְ הִתְחַזַּקְנוּ בֵּאלֹהֵינוּ לְהַגִּיד לָכֶם אֶת בְּשׂוֹרַת אֱלֹהִים בִּנְסִבּוֹת שֶׁל מַאֲבָקִים רַבִּים
ach hitchazzaknu be'eloheinu lehaggid lachem et besorat elohim binsibbot shel ma'avakim rabbim
we waxed bold in our God to speak unto you the gospel of God in much conflict.

קְרִיאָתֵנוּ אֲלֵיכֶם אֵינָהּ נוֹבַעַת מִתּוֹךְ טָעוּת וְלֹא מִתּוֹךְ מְנִיעִים בִּלְתִּי טְהוֹרִים, אַף אֵינֶנָּה בְּרְמִיָּה
keri'atenu aleichem einah nova'at mittoch ta'ut velo mittoch meni'im bilti tehorim, af einennah birmiyah
For our exhortation is not of error, nor of uncleanness, nor in guile:

אֶלָּא כְּפִי שֶׁנִּמְצֵאנוּ נֶאֱמָנִים בְּעֵינֵי אֱלֹהִים לִהְיוֹת מֻפְקָדִים עַל הַבְּשׂוֹרָה,
ella kefi shennimtzenu ne'emanim be'einei elohim lihyot mufkadim al habbesorah,
but even as we have been approved of God to be intrusted with the gospel,

הַתֶּסָּלוֹנִיקִים א

מֵאֵת שָׁאוּל וְסִילְוָנוֹס וְטִימוֹתִיאוֹס, אֶל קְהִלַת הַתֶּסָּלוֹנִיקִים
Me'et sha'ul vesilevanos vetimotei'os, el kehillat hattessalonikim
Paul, and Silvanus, and Timothy, unto the church of the Thessalonians

אֲשֶׁר בֵּאלֹהִים הָאָב וּבָאָדוֹן יֵשׁוּעַ הַמָּשִׁיחַ: חֶסֶד וְשָׁלוֹם לָכֶם מֵאֵת הָאֱלֹהִים אָבִינוּ וְהָאָדוֹן יֵשׁוּעַ הַמָּשִׁיחַ
asher be'elohim ha'av uva'adon yeshua hammashiach. Chesed veshalom lachem me'et ha'elohim avinu veha'adon yeshua hammashiach
in God the Father and the Lord Jesus Christ: Grace to you and peace.

אָנוּ מַתְמִידִים לְהוֹדוֹת לֵאלֹהִים עַל כֻּלְּכֶם וּמַזְכִּירִים אֶתְכֶם בִּתְפִלּוֹתֵינוּ
anu matmidim lehodot le'elohim al kullechem umazkirim etchem bitfilloteinu
We give thanks to God always for you all, making mention of you in our prayers;

בְּזָכְרֵנוּ תָּמִיד לִפְנֵי אֱלֹהִים אָבִינוּ אֶת פֹּעַל אֱמוּנַתְכֶם, אֶת הֶעָמָל שֶׁעֲמַלְתֶּם
bezacherenu tamid lifnei elohim avinu et po'al emunatchem, et he'amal she'amaltem be'ahavah
remembering without ceasing your work of faith and labor of love

בְּאַהֲבָה, וְאֶת הִתְמַדַתְכֶם בַּתִּקְוָה לְבוֹא אֲדוֹנֵנוּ יֵשׁוּעַ הַמָּשִׁיחַ
ve'et hatmadatchem battikvah levo adonenu yeshua hammashiach
and patience of hope in our Lord Jesus Christ, before our God and Father;

אַחִים אֲהוּבֵי אֱלֹהִים, אָנוּ יוֹדְעִים שֶׁנִּבְחַרְתֶּם
achim ahuvei elohim, anu yode'im shennivchartem
knowing, brethren beloved of God, your election,

שֶׁהֲרֵי בְּשׂוֹרָתֵנוּ לֹא בָּאָה אֲלֵיכֶם רַק בְּמִלִּים, אֶלָּא גַּם בִּגְבוּרָה וּבְרוּחַ הַקֹּדֶשׁ וּבְבִטָּחוֹן רַב
sheharei bsoratenu lo ba'ah aleichem rak bemillim, ella gam bigvurah uveruach hakkodesh uvevittachon rav
how that our gospel came not unto you in word only, but also in power, and in the Holy Spirit, and in much assurance;

דָּבָר שֶׁאַתֶּם יוֹדְעִים מִשֶּׁנּוֹכַחְתֶּם כֵּיצַד הִתְנַהַגְנוּ לְמַעַנְכֶם כַּאֲשֶׁר הָיִינוּ בֵּינֵיכֶם
davar she'attem yode'im mishennochachtem keitzad hitnahagnu lema'anchem ka'asher hayinu beineichem
even as ye know what manner of men we showed ourselves toward you for your sake.

וְאַתֶּם הֲלַכְתֶּם בְּעִקְבוֹתֵינוּ וּבְעִקְבוֹת אֲדוֹנֵנוּ
ve'attem halachtem be'ikkevoteinu uve'ikkevot adonenu
And ye became imitators of us, and of the Lord,

וְקִבַּלְתֶּם אֶת דְּבַר הַבְּשׂוֹרָה בְּתוֹךְ סֵבֶל רַב, בְּשִׂמְחַת רוּחַ הַקֹּדֶשׁ
vekibbaltem et devar habbesorah betoch sevel rav, besimchat ruach hakkodesh
having received the word in much affliction, with joy of the Holy Spirit;

בְּכָךְ הֱיִיתֶם לְמוֹפֵת לְכָל הַמַּאֲמִינִים אֲשֶׁר בְּמַקֶּדוֹנְיָה וְאָכַיָה
bechach heyitem lemofet lechol hamma'aminim asher bemakedoneyah ve'achayah
so that ye became an ensample to all that believe in Macedonia and in Achaia.

הַקּוֹלוֹסִים

וְכֵן גַּם יֵשׁוּעַ הַמְכֻנֶּה יוּסְטוֹס. מִבֵּין הַנִּמּוֹלִים
vechen gam yeshua hamchunneh yusetos. mibbein hannimmolim
and Jesus that is called Justus, who are of the circumcision:

רַק הֵם חֲבֵרַי לַעֲבוֹדָה לְמַעַן מַלְכוּת אֱלֹהִים, וְאָכֵן הָיוּ לִי לְנֶחָמָה
rak hem chaverai la'avodah lema'an malchut elohim, ve'achen hayu li lenechamah
these only are my fellow-workers unto the kingdom of God, men that have been a comfort unto me.

;דְּרִישַׁת שָׁלוֹם מֵאֶפַּפְרַס, עֶבֶד הַמָּשִׁיחַ יֵשׁוּעַ וְאֶחָד מִכֶּם
derishat shalom me'eppafras, eved hammashiach yeshua ve'echad mikkem
Epaphras, who is one of you, a servant of Christ Jesus, saluteth you,

בְּכָל עֵת הוּא נֶאֱבָק לְמַעַנְכֶם בִּתְפִלּוֹת, לְמַעַן תַּעַמְדוּ מֻשְׁלָמִים וּמְלֵאֵי בִּטָּחוֹן בְּכָל אֲשֶׁר לִרְצוֹן אֱלֹהִים
bechol et hu ne'evak lema'anchem bitfillot, lema'an ta'amdu mushlamim umle'ei bittachon bechol asher lirtzon elohim
always striving for you in his prayers, that ye may stand perfect and fully assured in all the will of God.

מֵעִיד אֲנִי עָלָיו כִּי הוּא עָמֵל הַרְבֵּה לְמַעַנְכֶם וּלְמַעַן אַנְשֵׁי לָאוֹדִיקֵאָה וְאַנְשֵׁי הִירַפּוֹלִיס
me'id ani alav ki hu amel harbeh lema'anchem ulema'an anshei la'odike'ah ve'anshei hirappolis
For I bear him witness, that he hath much labor for you, and for them in Laodicea, and for them in Hierapolis.

לוּקָס, הָרוֹפֵא הָאָהוּב, וְדִימָס דּוֹרְשִׁים בִּשְׁלוֹמְכֶם
lukas, harofei ha'ahuv, vedimas doreshim bishlomechem
Luke, the beloved physician, and Demas salute you.

דִּרְשׁוּ בִּשְׁלוֹם הָאַחִים אֲשֶׁר בְּלָאוֹדִיקֵאָה, וּבִשְׁלוֹם נִימְפַס וְהַקְּהִלָּה הַמִּתְאַסֶּפֶת בְּבֵיתוֹ
dirshu bishlom ha'achim asher bela'odike'ah, uvishlom nimefas vehakkehillah hammit'assefet beveito
Salute the brethren that are in Laodicea, and Nymphas, and the church that is in their house.

אַחֲרֵי שֶׁתִּקָּרֵא אִגַּרְתִּי אֶצְלְכֶם, דַּאֲגוּ לְכָךְ שֶׁתִּקָּרֵא גַּם בִּקְהִלַּת לָאוֹדִיקֵאָה
acharei shettikkarei iggarti etzlechem, da'agu lechach shettikkarei gam bik'hillat la'odike'ah
And when this epistle hath been read among you, cause that it be read also in the church of the Laodiceans;

וְאֶת אִגַּרְתִּי אֲשֶׁר מִלָּאוֹדִיקֵאָה קִרְאוּ גַּם אַתֶּם
ve'et iggarti asher milla'odike'ah kir'u gam attem
and that ye also read the epistle from Laodicea.

אִמְרוּ לְאַרְכִיפּוֹס: שִׂים לִבְּךָ לְמַלֵּא אֶת הַשֵּׁרוּת שֶׁקִּבַּלְתָּ לְמַעַן הָאָדוֹן
imru le'archipos: sim libbecha lemallei et hasherut shekkibbalta lema'an ha'adon
And say to Archippus, Take heed to the ministry which thou hast received in the Lord, that thou fulfil it.

דְּרִישַׁת שָׁלוֹם בִּכְתַב יָדִי אֲנִי - שָׁאוּל. זִכְרוּ שִׁבְתִּי בַּמַּאֲסָר. הַחֶסֶד עִמָּכֶם
derishat shalom bichtav yadi ani - sha'ul. zichru shivti bamma'asar. hachesed immachem
The salutation of me Paul with mine own hand. Remember my bonds. Grace be with you.

הַקּוֹלוֹסִים

הַתְמִידוּ בִּתְפִלָּה וְשִׁקְדוּ בָּהּ בְּהוֹדָיָה
hatmidu bitfillah veshikdu bah behodayah
Continue stedfastly in prayer, watching therein with thanksgiving;

הִתְפַּלְלוּ גַּם בַּעֲדֵנוּ, כְּדֵי שֶׁאֱלֹהִים יִפְתַּח לָנוּ אֶת שַׁעַר הַדִּבּוּר לְהַגִּיד אֶת סוֹד הַמָּשִׁיחַ
hitpallelu gam ba'adenu, kedei she'elohim yiftach lanu et sha'ar haddibbur lehaggid et sod hammashiach
withal praying for us also, that God may open unto us a door for the word, to speak the mystery of Christ,

שֶׁבִּגְלָלוֹ אַף אָסִיר אָנֹכִי וּכְדֵי שֶׁאֲגַלֶּה אוֹתוֹ כְּפִי שֶׁעָלַי לְדַבֵּר
shebbiglalo af asir anochi uchedei she'agalleh oto kefi she'alai ledabber
for which I am also in bonds; that I may make it manifest, as I ought to speak.

הִתְנַהֲגוּ בְּחָכְמָה עִם אֵלֶּה אֲשֶׁר בַּחוּץ, וְנַצְּלוּ אֶת הַהִזְדַּמְּנוּת
hitnahagu bechochmah im elleh asher bachutz, venatzelu et hahizdammenut
Walk in wisdom toward them that are without, redeeming the time.

יִהְיוּ נָא דִבְרֵיכֶם מְלֵוִים תָּמִיד בְּחֵן וּמְתֻבָּלִים בְּמֶלַח, בְּאֹפֶן שֶׁתֵּדְעוּ אֵיךְ לְהָשִׁיב לְכָל שׁוֹאֵל
yihyu na divreichem meluvvim tamid bechen umetubbalim bemelach, be'ofen shettede'u eich lehashiv lechol sho'el
Let your speech be always with grace, seasoned with salt, that ye may know how ye ought to answer each one.

אֶת כָּל הַפְּרָטִים עַל־אוֹדוֹת מַצָּבִי יַגִּיד לָכֶם טִיכִיקוֹס,
et kol happeratim al-odot matzavi yaggid lachem tichikos
All my affairs shall Tychicus make known unto you,

הָאָח הָאָהוּב וְהַמְשָׁרֵת הַנֶּאֱמָן, חֲבֵרִי לָעֲבוֹדָה בָּאָדוֹן
ha'ach ha'ahuv vehamsharet hanne'eman, chaveri la'avodah ba'adon
the beloved brother and faithful minister and fellow-servant in the Lord:

לְשֵׁם כָּךְ שְׁלַחְתִּיו אֲלֵיכֶם, לְמַעַן יוֹדִיעַ לָכֶם מַה מַּצָּבֵנוּ וִיעוֹדֵד אֶתְכֶם
leshem kach shelachtiv aleichem, lema'an yodia lachem mah matzavenu vi'oded etchem
whom I have sent unto you for this very purpose, that ye may know our state, and that he may comfort your hearts;

וְיַחַד אִתּוֹ אוֹנִיסִימוֹס, הָאָח הַנֶּאֱמָן וְהָאָהוּב שֶׁהוּא אֶחָד מִכֶּם
veyachad itto onisimos, ha'ach hanne'eman veha'ahuv shehu echad mikkem
together with Onesimus, the faithful and beloved brother, who is one of you.

הֵם יוֹדִיעוּ לָכֶם אֶת כָּל הַנַּעֲשֶׂה כָּאן
hem yodi'u lachem et kol hanna'aseh kan
They shall make known unto you all things that are done here.

אֲרִיסְטַרְכוֹס, חֲבֵרִי לַמַּאֲסָר, דּוֹרֵשׁ בִּשְׁלוֹמְכֶם; כֵּן גַּם מַרְקוֹס
arisetarchos, chaveri lamma'asar, doresh bishlomechem; ken gam markos
Aristarchus my fellow-prisoner saluteth you, and Mark,

בֶּן אֲחוֹת בַּר־נַבָּא, אֲשֶׁר קִבַּלְתֶּם הוֹרָאוֹת בְּנוֹגֵעַ אֵלָיו - שֶׁאִם יָבוֹא אֲלֵיכֶם תְּקַבְּלוּהוּ
ben achot bar-nabba, asher kibbaltem hora'ot benogea elav - she'im yavo aleichem tekabbeluhu
the cousin of Barnabas (touching whom ye received commandments; if he come unto you, receive him),

הַקּוֹלוֹסִים

וְהוֹדוּ לֵאלֹהִים אָבִינוּ בְּאֶמְצָעוּתוֹ
vehodu le'elohim avinu be'emtza'uto
giving thanks to God the Father through him.

הַנָּשִׁים, הִכָּנַעְנָה לְבַעֲלֵיכֶן, כְּמוֹ שֶׁיָּאֶה לְנֹכַח הָאָדוֹן
hannashim, hikkana'nah leva'aleichen, kemo sheya'eh lenochach ha'adon
Wives, be in subjection to your husbands, as is fitting in the Lord.

הָאֲנָשִׁים, אֶהֱבוּ אֶת נְשֵׁיכֶם וְאַל תְּהֵא בִּלְבַבְכֶם מְרִירוּת נֶגְדָּן
ha'anashim, ehevu et nesheichem ve'al tehei bilvavchem merirut negdan
Husbands, love your wives, and be not bitter against them.

הַבָּנִים, שִׁמְעוּ בְּקוֹל הַהוֹרִים בְּכָל דָּבָר, כִּי זֶה לְרָצוֹן בְּעֵינֵי יהוה
habbanim, shim'u bekol hahorim bechol davar, ki zeh leratzon be'einei hashem
Children, obey your parents in all things, for this is well-pleasing in the Lord.

הָאָבוֹת, אַל תַּרְגִּיזוּ אֶת יַלְדֵיכֶם, פֶּן תִּפֹּל רוּחָם
ha'avot, al targizu et yaldeichem, pen tippol rucham
Fathers, provoke not your children, that they be not discouraged.

הָעֲבָדִים, הִשָּׁמְעוּ בְּכָל דָּבָר לַאֲדוֹנֵיכֶם אֲשֶׁר בָּעוֹלָם הַזֶּה
ha'avadim, hisham'u bechol davar la'adoneichem asher ba'olam hazzeh
Servants, obey in all things them that are your masters according to the flesh;

לֹא לְמַרְאִית עַיִן, כְּמִתְרַצִּים אֶל בְּנֵי אָדָם, אֶלָּא בְּתֹם לֵב וּבְיִרְאַת יהוה
lo lemar'it ayin, kemitratzim el benei adam, ella betom lev uveyir'at hashem
not with eye-service, as men-pleasers, but in singleness of heart, fearing the Lord:

כָּל מַה שֶּׁאַתֶּם עוֹשִׂים, עֲשׂוּ בְּכָל נַפְשְׁכֶם, כְּעוֹשִׂים לְמַעַן יהוה וְלֹא לְמַעַן בְּנֵי אָדָם
kol mah she'attem osim, asu bechol nafshechem, ke'osim lema'an hashem velo lema'an bnei adam
whatsoever ye do, work heartily, as unto the Lord, and not unto men;

שֶׁכֵּן יוֹדְעִים אַתֶּם כִּי תְּקַבְּלוּ מֵאֵת יהוה אֶת שְׂכַר הַנַּחֲלָה. אֶת הָאָדוֹן הַמָּשִׁיחַ אַתֶּם עוֹבְדִים
shekken yode'im attem ki tekabbelu me'et hashem et schar hannachalah. et ha'adon hammashiach attem ovedim
knowing that from the Lord ye shall receive the recompense of the inheritance: ye serve the Lord Christ.

אַךְ הָעוֹשֶׂה עָוֶל יְקַבֵּל אֶת גְּמוּל עַוְלָתוֹ, וְאֵין מַשּׂוֹא פָנִים
ach ha'oseh avel yekabbel et gemul avlato, ve'ein masso panim
For he that doeth wrong shall receive again for the wrong that he hath done: and there is no respect of persons.

ד

הָאֲדוֹנִים, הִתְנַהֲגוּ עִם עַבְדֵיכֶם בְּצֶדֶק וּבְיֹשֶׁר, שֶׁהֲרֵי יוֹדְעִים אַתֶּם כִּי גַּם לָכֶם אָדוֹן בַּשָּׁמַיִם
ha'adonim, hitnahagu im avdeichem betzedek uveyosher, sheharei yode'im attem ki gam lachem adon bashamayim
Masters, render unto your servants that which is just and equal; knowing that ye also have a Master in heaven.

הַקּוֹלוֹסִים

אַל תְּשַׁקְּרוּ אִישׁ לְרֵעֵהוּ, שֶׁכֵּן פְּשַׁטְתֶּם אֶת הָאָדָם הַיָּשָׁן עִם מַעֲשָׂיו
al teshakkru ish lere'ehu, shekken peshattem et ha'adam hayashan im ma'asav
lie not one to another; seeing that ye have put off the old man with his doings,

וּלְבַשְׁתֶּם אֶת הָאָדָם הֶחָדָשׁ, הַהוֹלֵךְ וּמִתְחַדֵּשׁ בְּדַעַת לְפִי צֶלֶם בּוֹרְאוֹ
ulevashtem et ha'adam hechadash, haholech umitchaddesh beda'at lefi tzelem bor'o
and have put on the new man, that is being renewed unto knowledge after the image of him that created him:

בַּמַּצָּב הַזֶּה אֵין יְוָנִי וִיהוּדִי, אֵין מִילָה וְעָרְלָה
bammatzav hazzeh ein yevani viyehudi, ein milah ve'orelah
where there cannot be Greek and Jew, circumcision and uncircumcision,

אֵין לוֹעֵז וּסְקִיתִי וְאֵין עֶבֶד וּבֶן חוֹרִין, אֶלָּא הַמָּשִׁיחַ הוּא הַכֹּל וּבַכֹּל
ein lo'ez usekiti ve'ein eved uven chorin, ella hammashiach hu hakkol uvakkol
barbarian, Scythian, bondman, freeman; but Christ is all, and in all.

לָכֵן אַתֶּם, כִּבְחִירֵי אֱלֹהִים קְדוֹשִׁים וַאֲהוּבִים, לִבְשׁוּ חֶמְלָה וְרַחֲמִים וּנְדִיבוּת לֵב
lachen attem, kivchirei elohim kedoshim va'ahuvim, livshu chemlah verachamim unedivut lev
Put on therefore, as God's elect, holy and beloved, a heart of compassion, kindness,

נְמִיכוּת רוּחַ וַעֲנָוָה וְאֶרֶךְ אַפַּיִם נַהֲגוּ בְּסַבְלָנוּת אִישׁ עִם רֵעֵהוּ, וְסִלְחוּ זֶה לָזֶה
nemichut ruach va'anavah ve'orech appayim nahagu besavlanut ish im re'ehu, vesilchu zeh lazeh
lowliness, meekness, longsuffering; forbearing one another, and forgiving each other,

כַּאֲשֶׁר לְמִישֶׁהוּ טַעֲנָה עַל רֵעֵהוּ. כְּשֵׁם שֶׁהָאָדוֹן סָלַח לָכֶם, כֵּן סִלְחוּ גַּם אַתֶּם
ka'asher lemishehu ta'anah al re'ehu. keshem sheha'adon salach lachem, ken silchu gam attem
if any man have a complaint against any; even as the Lord forgave you, so also do ye:

מֵעַל לְכָל אֵלֶּה תִּשְׂרֹר הָאַהֲבָה, שֶׁהִיא קֶשֶׁר הַשְּׁלֵמוּת
me'al lechol elleh tisror ha'ahavah, shehi kesher hashlemut
and above all these things put on love, which is the bond of perfectness.

וְיִשְׁלֹט נָא בִּלְבַבְכֶם שְׁלוֹם הַמָּשִׁיחַ, שֶׁהֲרֵי לָזֶה נִקְרֵאתֶם בְּגוּף אֶחָד, וֶהֱיוּ מַכִּירֵי טוֹבָה
veyishlot na bilvavchem shelom hammashiach, sheharei lezeh nikretem beguf echad, veheyu makkirei tovah
And let the peace of Christ rule in your hearts, to the which also ye were called in one body; and be ye thankful.

דְּבַר הַמָּשִׁיחַ יִשְׁכֹּן נָא בְּקִרְבְּכֶם בְּשֶׁפַע לַמְּדוּ וְהוֹכִיחוּ זֶה אֶת זֶה בִּמְלוֹא חָכְמָה
devar hammashiach yishkon na bekirbechem beshefa; lammdu vehochichu zeh et zeh bimlo chochmah
Let the word of Christ dwell in you richly; in all wisdom teaching and admonishing one another

שִׁירוּ לֵאלֹהִים בְּתוֹדָה וְנֹעַם בִּלְבַבְכֶם, בְּמִזְמוֹרִים וְתִשְׁבָּחוֹת וְשִׁירִים רוּחָנִיִּים
shiru le'elohim betodah veno'am bilvavchem, bemizmorim vetishbachot veshirim ruchaniyim
with psalms and hymns and spiritual songs, singing with grace in your hearts unto God.

וְכָל מַה שֶּׁתַּעֲשׂוּ, הֵן בְּאֹמֶר הֵן בְּמַעֲשֶׂה, עֲשׂוּ הַכֹּל בְּשֵׁם הָאָדוֹן יֵשׁוּעַ
vechol mah shetta'asu, hen be'omer hen bema'aseh, asu hakkol beshem ha'adon yeshua
And whatsoever ye do, in word or in deed, do all in the name of the Lord Jesus,

הַקוֹלוֹסִים

אַךְ אֵין זֶה מוֹעִיל נֶגֶד מַאֲוַיֵּי הַבָּשָׂר
ach ein zeh mo'il neged ma'avayei habbasar
but are not of any value against the indulgence of the flesh.

ג

לָכֵן אִם הוּקַמְתֶּם עִם הַמָּשִׁיחַ, שַׁאֲפוּ לַדְּבָרִים אֲשֶׁר לְמַעְלָה
lachen im hukamtem im hammashiach, sha'afu laddevarim asher lema'lah
If then ye were raised together with Christ, seek the things that are above,

אֲשֶׁר שָׁם הַמָּשִׁיחַ יוֹשֵׁב לִימִין אֱלֹהִים
asher sham hammashiach yoshev liyemin elohim
where Christ is, seated on the right hand of God.

בַּדְּבָרִים אֲשֶׁר לְמַעְלָה יֶהְגֶּה לְבַבְכֶם, לֹא בַּדְּבָרִים אֲשֶׁר בָּאָרֶץ
baddevarim asher lema'lah yehgeh levavchem, lo baddevarim asher ba'aretz
Set your mind on the things that are above, not on the things that are upon the earth.

כִּי מַתֶּם וְחַיֵּיכֶם צְפוּנִים עִם הַמָּשִׁיחַ בֵּאלֹהִים
ki mattem vechayeichem tzefunim im hammashiach be'elohim
For ye died, and your life is hid with Christ in God.

כַּאֲשֶׁר יִתְגַּלֶּה הַמָּשִׁיחַ, אֲשֶׁר הוּא חַיֵּינוּ, אָז גַּם אַתֶּם תִּגָּלוּ עִמּוֹ בַּהֲדַר כָּבוֹד
ka'asher yitgaleh hammashiach, asher hu chayeinu, az gam attem tiggalu immo bahadar kavod
When Christ, who is our life, shall be manifested, then shall ye also with him be manifested in glory.

עַל כֵּן מוֹתְתוּ אֶת הָאֵיבָרִים הַשַּׁיָּכִים לָאָרֶץ
al ken motetu et ha'eivarim hashayachim la'aretz
Put to death therefore your members which are upon the earth:

אֶת הַזְּנוּת וְהַטֻּמְאָה וְהַזִּמָּה וְהַתַּאֲוָה הָרָעָה, וְאֶת הַחַמְדָּנוּת שֶׁאֵינָהּ אֶלָּא עֲבוֹדַת אֱלִילִים
et hazznut vehattum'ah vehazzimmah vehatta'avah hara'ah, ve'et hachamdanut she'einah ella avodat elilim
fornication, uncleanness, passion, evil desire, and covetousness, which is idolatry;

כִּי בִּגְלַל אֵלֶּה בָּא חֲרוֹן אֱלֹהִים [עַל בְּנֵי הַמֶּרִי]
ki biglal elleh ba charon elohim ['al benei hammeri]
for which things' sake cometh the wrath of God upon the sons of disobedience:

בַּדְּבָרִים הַלָּלוּ גַּם אַתֶּם הִתְהַלַּכְתֶּם בֶּעָבָר, כַּאֲשֶׁר חֲיִיתֶם בָּהֶם
baddevarim hallalu gam attem hit'hallachtem be'avar, ka'asher chayitem bahem
wherein ye also once walked, when ye lived in these things;

אֲבָל כָּעֵת הָסִירוּ גַּם אַתֶּם אֶת כָּל אֵלֶּה: אֶת הָרֹגֶז וְהַכַּעַס וְאֶת הָרֶשַׁע וְהַגִּדּוּף וְאֶת נִבּוּל הַפֶּה
aval ka'et hasiru gam attem et kol elleh: et harogez vehakka'as ve'et haresha vehaggidduf ve'et nibbul happeh
but now do ye also put them all away: anger, wrath, malice, railing, shameful speaking out of your mouth:

הַקוֹלוֹסִים

לָכֵן אִישׁ אַל יַחֲרֹץ עֲלֵיכֶם מִשְׁפָּט עַל־דְּבַר מַאֲכָל וּמַשְׁקֶה אוֹ עַל־דְּבַר מוֹעֵד, רֹאשׁ חֹדֶשׁ אוֹ שַׁבָּת
lachen ish al yacharotz aleichem mishpat al-devar ma'achal umashkeh o al-devar mo'ed, rosh chodesh o shabbat
Let no man therefore judge you in meat, or in drink, or in respect of a feast day or a new moon or a sabbath day:

אֲשֶׁר הֵם צֵל הַדְּבָרִים הָעֲתִידִים לָבוֹא, אֲבָל הַגּוּף הוּא שֶׁל הַמָּשִׁיחַ
asher hem tzel haddevarim ha'atidim lavo, aval hagguf hu shel hammashiach
which are a shadow of the things to come; but the body is Christ's.

אִישׁ אַל יְבַטֵּל אֶתְכֶם כְּשֶׁהוּא מִתְגַּדֵּר בִּנְמִיכוּת רוּחַ וּבְפֻלְחָן לְמַלְאָכִים
ish al yevattel etchem kshehu mitgadder binmichut ruach uvefulchan lemal'achim
Let no man rob you of your prize by a voluntary humility and worshipping of the angels,

כְּשֶׁהוּא נֶאֱחָז בַּמֶּה שֶׁרָאָה וּבְלִבּוֹ גַּאֲוָה רֵיקָה הַנּוֹבַעַת מִשִּׂכְלוֹ הַבִּלְתִּי רוּחָנִי
kshehu ne'echaz bemah shera'ah uvelibbo ga'avah reikah hannova'at missichlo habbilti ruchani
dwelling in the things which he hath seen, vainly puffed up by his fleshly mind,

וְאֵין הוּא נִצְמָד לָרֹאשׁ אֲשֶׁר מִמֶּנּוּ כָּל הַגּוּף
ve'ein hu nitzmad larosh asher mimmennu kol hagguf
and not holding fast the Head, from whom all the body,

הַנִּזּוֹן וּמִתְחַבֵּר עַל־יְדֵי פְּרָקִים וְגִידִים - גָּדֵל גִּדּוּל כְּיַד הָאֱלֹהִים
hannizzon umitchabber al-yedei perakim vegidim - gadel giddul keyad ha'elohim
being supplied and knit together through the joints and bands, increaseth with the increase of God.

אִם מַתֶּם עִם הַמָּשִׁיחַ לְגַבֵּי עִקְרֵי הָעוֹלָם
im mattem im hammashiach legabbei ikkerei ha'olam
If ye died with Christ from the rudiments of the world,

לָמָּה אַתֶּם נוֹהֲגִים כְּמוֹ אֲנָשִׁים הַחַיִּים בָּעוֹלָם וְנִכְנָעִים לַחֻקִּים
lammah attem nohagim kemo anashim hachayim ba'olam venichna'im lachukkim
why, as though living in the world, do ye subject yourselves to ordinances,

אַל תֹּאחַז, אַל תִּטְעַם, אַל תִּגַּע
al tochaz, al tit'am, al tigga
Handle not, nor taste, nor touch

וְכֻלָּם דְּבָרִים שֶׁנּוֹעֲדוּ לְכִלָּיוֹן בְּשִׁמּוּשָׁם וְהֵם לְפִי מִצְווֹת וְהוֹרָאוֹת שֶׁל בְּנֵי אָדָם
vechullam devarim shenno'adu lechillayon beshimmusham vehem lefi mitzvot vehora'ot shel benei adam
(all which things are to perish with the using), after the precepts and doctrines of men?

דְּבָרִים שֶׁאָמְנָם יֵשׁ לָהֶם חֲזוּת שֶׁל חָכְמָה
devarim she'amenam yesh lahem chazut shel chochmah
Which things have indeed a show of wisdom

וְהֵם מִתְבַּטְּאִים בְּדָת שֶׁהִיא פְּרִי רְצוֹנָם וּבִנְמִיכוּת רוּחַ וְסִגּוּף הַגּוּף
vehem mitbatte'im bedat shehi peri retzonam uvinmichut ruach vesigguf hagguf
in will-worship, and humility, and severity to the body;

הַקוֹלוֹסִים

עַל־פִּי מָסוֹרוֹת שֶׁל בְּנֵי אָדָם, עַל־פִּי עִקְּרֵי הָעוֹלָם וְלֹא עַל־פִּי הַמָּשִׁיחַ
al-pi masorot shel benei adam, al-pi ikkerei ha'olam velo al-pi hammashiach
after the tradition of men, after the rudiments of the world, and not after Christ:

הֵן בַּמָּשִׁיחַ, בְּגוּפוֹ, שׁוֹכֵן כָּל מְלוֹא הָאֱלֹהוּת
hen bammashiach, begufo, shochen kol melo ha'elohut
for in him dwelleth all the fulness of the Godhead bodily,

וְאַתֶּם נִמְלֵאתֶם בּוֹ, אֲשֶׁר הוּא רֹאשׁ כָּל רָשׁוּת וְשִׁלְטוֹן
ve'attem nimletem bo, asher hu rosh kol rashut veshilton
and in him ye are made full, who is the head of all principality and power:

בּוֹ גַּם נִמַּלְתֶּם מִילָה שֶׁאֵינָהּ מַעֲשֵׂה יָדַיִם
bo gam nimmaltem milah she'einah ma'aseh yadayim
in whom ye were also circumcised with a circumcision not made with hands,

וְזֹאת בְּהַפְשָׁטַת הַגּוּף הַבְּשָׂרִי, בְּמִילַת הַמָּשִׁיחַ
vezot behafshatat hagguf habbesari, bemilat hammashiach
in the putting off of the body of the flesh, in the circumcision of Christ;

נִקְבַּרְתֶּם אִתּוֹ בַּטְּבִילָה, וְאִתּוֹ גַּם הוּקַמְתֶּם לִתְחִיָּה עַל־יְדֵי אֱמוּנַתְכֶם
nikbartem itto battevilah, ve'itto gam hukamtem litchiyah al-yedei emunatchem
having been buried with him in baptism, wherein ye were also raised with him through faith

בְּכֹחַ אֱלֹהִים אֲשֶׁר הֱקִימוֹ מִן הַמֵּתִים
bechoach elohim asher hekimo min hammetim
in the working of God, who raised him from the dead.

וּבִהְיוֹתְכֶם מֵתִים בְּפִשְׁעֵיכֶם וּבְעָרְלַת בְּשַׂרְכֶם
uvihyotechem metim befish'eichem uve'orlat besarchem
And you, being dead through your trespasses and the uncircumcision of your flesh,

הֶחֱיָה אֶתְכֶם עִמּוֹ. הוּא סָלַח לָנוּ עַל כָּל פְּשָׁעֵינוּ
hecheyah etchem immo. hu salach lanu al kol pesha'einu
you, I say, did he make alive together with him, having forgiven us all our trespasses;

בִּטֵּל אֶת שְׁטַר הַחוֹב אֲשֶׁר הָיָה נֶגְדֵּנוּ עַד תֻּמּוֹ
bittel et shetar hachov asher hayah negdenu ad tummo
having blotted out the bond written in ordinances that was against us, which was contrary to us:

וַהֲסִירוֹ בְּתָקְעוֹ אוֹתוֹ בַּצְּלָב
vehesiro betake'o oto batzlav
and he hath taken it out of the way, nailing it to the cross;

וּבְהַפְשִׁיטוֹ אֶת עָצְמַת הָרָשֻׁיּוֹת וְהַשְּׂרָרוֹת, הִצִּיגָן לְרַאֲוָה בְּתַהֲלוּכַת נִצְחוֹנוֹ, נִצָּחוֹן שֶׁהִשִּׂיג בּוֹ
uvehafshito et atzemat harashyot vehashorarot, hitzigan lera'avah betahaluchat nitzchono, nitzachon shehessig bo
having despoiled the principalities and the powers, he made a show of them openly, triumphing over them in it.

הַקּוֹלוֹסִים

ב

רְצוֹנִי שֶׁתֵּדְעוּ מַה גָּדוֹל הַמַּאֲבָק שֶׁאָנֹכִי נֶאֱבָק בַּעַדְכֶם וּבְעַד אַנְשֵׁי לָאוֹדִיקֵאָה
retzoni shetted'u mah gadol hamma'avak she'anochi ne'evak ba'adchem uve'ad anshei la'odike'ah
For I would have you know how greatly I strive for you, and for them at Laodicea,

וּבְעַד אֵלֶּה שֶׁלֹּא רָאוּ אוֹתִי פָּנִים אֶל פָּנִים
uv'ad elleh shello ra'u oti panim el panim
and for as many as have not seen my face in the flesh;

לְמַעַן יְנֻחַם לְבָבָם וְיִתְקַשְּׁרוּ יַחְדָּיו בְּאַהֲבָה
lema'an yenucham levavam veyitkasheru yachdav be'ahavah
that their hearts may be comforted, they being knit together in love,

וְיַגִּיעוּ אֶל כָּל הָעֹשֶׁר אֲשֶׁר בַּהֲבָנָה הַשְּׁלֵמָה, אֶל יְדִיעַת סוֹד הָאֱלֹהִים, הַמָּשִׁיחַ
veyaggi'u el kol ha'osher asher bahavanah hashelemah, el yedi'at sod ha'elohim, hammashiach
and unto all riches of the full assurance of understanding, that they may know the mystery of God, even Christ,

אֲשֶׁר צְפוּנִים בּוֹ כָּל אוֹצְרוֹת הַחָכְמָה וְהַדַּעַת
asher tzefunim bo kol otzerot hachachemah vehadda'at
in whom are all the treasures of wisdom and knowledge hidden.

זֹאת אֲנִי אוֹמֵר כְּדֵי שֶׁלֹּא יַטְעֶה אֶתְכֶם אִישׁ בְּדִבּוּרִים מְחֻכָּמִים
zot ani omer kedei shello yat'eh etchem ish bedibburim mechukkamim
This I say, that no one may delude you with persuasiveness of speech.

גַּם אִם נֶעְדָּר אֲנִי מִבֵּינֵיכֶם בְּגוּפִי, הֲרֵי בְּרוּחִי אֲנִי נִמְצָא בֵּינֵיכֶם
gam im ne'dar ani mibbeineichem begufi, harei beruchi ani nimtza beineichem
For though I am absent in the flesh, yet am I with you in the spirit,

וְשָׂמֵחַ אֲנִי בִּרְאוֹתִי אֶת הַסֵּדֶר אֲשֶׁר בְּקִרְבְּכֶם וְאֶת אֵיתָנוּת אֱמוּנַתְכֶם בַּמָּשִׁיחַ
vesameach ani bir'oti et hasseder asher bekirbechem ve'et eitanut emunatchem bammashiach
joying and beholding your order, and the stedfastness of your faith in Christ.

לָכֵן כְּשֵׁם שֶׁקִּבַּלְתֶּם אֶת הַמָּשִׁיחַ יֵשׁוּעַ, הָאָדוֹן, כֵּן הִתְהַלְּכוּ בּוֹ
lachen keshem shekkibbaltem et hammashiach yeshua', ha'adon, ken hit'hallechu bo
As therefore ye received Christ Jesus the Lord, so walk in him,

כְּשֶׁאַתֶּם מֻשְׁרָשִׁים וְנִבְנִים בּוֹ, מְבֻסָּסִים בָּאֱמוּנָה לְפִי מַה שֶּׁלֻּמַּדְתֶּם, וְשׁוֹפְעִים בְּהוֹדָיָה
keshe'attem mushrashim venivnim bo, mevussasim ba'emunah lefi mah shellummadtem, veshofe'im behodayah
rooted and builded up in him, and established in your faith, even as ye were taught, abounding in thanksgiving.

הִזָּהֲרוּ שֶׁאִישׁ לֹא יוֹלִיךְ אֶתְכֶם שׁוֹלָל בְּפִילוֹסוֹפְיָה וּבְתַעְתּוּעֵי הֶבֶל
hizzaharu she'ish lo yolich etchem sholal befilosofeyah uveta'tu'ei hevel
Take heed lest there shall be any one that maketh spoil of you through his philosophy and vain deceit,

הַקּוֹלוֹסִים

הִיא הַבְּשׂוֹרָה שֶׁהֻכְרְזָה לְכָל הַבְּרִיאָה מִתַּחַת לַשָּׁמַיִם, וַאֲנִי, שָׁאוּל, הָיִיתִי לָהּ לִמְשָׁרֵת
hi habbesorah shehuchrezah lechol habberi'ah mittachat lashamayim, va'ani, sha'ul, hayiti lah limsharet
which was preached in all creation under heaven; whereof I Paul was made a minister.

כָּעֵת אֲנִי שָׂמֵחַ בַּסֵּבֶל שֶׁאֲנִי סוֹבֵל לְמַעַנְכֶם
ka'et ani sameach bassevel she'ani sovel lema'anchem
Now I rejoice in my sufferings for your sake,

וַאֲנִי מְמַלֵּא בִּבְשָׂרִי אֶת סִבְלוֹת הַמָּשִׁיחַ שֶׁיֵּשׁ עוֹד לִסְבֹּל בְּעַד גּוּפוֹ - הַקְּהִלָּה
va'ani memallei bivsari et sivlot hammashiach sheyesh od lisbol be'ad gufo - hakkehillah
and fill up on my part that which is lacking of the afflictions of Christ in my flesh for his body's sake, which is the church;

נִהְיֵיתִי לָהּ לִמְשָׁרֵת בְּהֶתְאֵם לַתַּפְקִיד שֶׁאֱלֹהִים נָתַן לִי לְמַעַנְכֶם
nihyeiti lah limsharet behet'em lattafkid she'elohim natan li lema'anchem
whereof I was made a minister, according to the dispensation of God which was given me to you-ward,

לְהַשְׁלִים אֶת דְּבַר אֱלֹהִים
lehashlim et devar elohim
to fulfil the word of God,

בִּמְסִירַת הַסּוֹד שֶׁהָיָה צָפוּן מֵעוֹלָמִים וּמִדּוֹרוֹת וְעַתָּה נִגְלָה לִקְדוֹשָׁיו
bimsirat hassod shehayah tzafun me'olamim umiddorot ve'attah niglah likdoshav
even the mystery which hath been hid for ages and generations: but now hath it been manifested to his saints,

אָכֵן לָכֶם רָצָה אֱלֹהִים לְהוֹדִיעַ מַהוּ עֹשֶׁר תִּפְאֶרֶת הַסּוֹד הַזֶּה בְּקֶרֶב הַגּוֹיִם
achen lachem ratzah elohim lehodia mahu osher tif'eret hassod hazzeh bekerev haggoyim
to whom God was pleased to make known what is the riches of the glory of this mystery among the Gentiles,

וְהוּא: הַמָּשִׁיחַ בְּקִרְבְּכֶם, הַתִּקְוָה אֶל הַכָּבוֹד
vehu: hammashiach bekirbechem, hattikvah el hakkavod
which is Christ in you, the hope of glory:

עָלָיו אָנוּ מַכְרִיזִים וּבוֹ בַּזְּמַן מַזְהִירִים כָּל אָדָם וּמְלַמְּדִים כָּל אָדָם בְּכָל חָכְמָה
alav anu machrizim uvo bazzeman mazhirim kol adam umelammedim kol adam bechol chochmah
whom we proclaim, admonishing every man and teaching every man in all wisdom,

לְמַעַן נוּכַל לְהַצִּיג כָּל אָדָם כְּשֶׁהוּא מֻשְׁלָם בַּמָּשִׁיחַ
lema'an nuchal lehatzig kol adam keshehu mushlam bammashiach
that we may present every man perfect in Christ;

לְמַטָּרָה זֹאת אֲנִי גַּם עָמֵל וְנֶאֱבָק, כְּמִדַּת פְּעֻלָּתוֹ שֶׁל הַפּוֹעֵל בִּי בִּגְבוּרָה
lemattarah zot ani gam amel vene'evak, kemiddat pe'ullato shel happo'el bi bigvurah
whereunto I labor also, striving according to his working, which worketh in me mightily.

הַקּוֹלוֹסִים

וְהוּא קוֹדֵם לַכֹּל וְהַכֹּל קַיָּם בּוֹ
vehu kodem lakkol vehakkol kayam bo
and he is before all things, and in him all things consist.

הוּא הָרֹאשׁ שֶׁל הַגּוּף, כְּלוֹמַר, שֶׁל הַקְּהִלָּה. הוּא הָרֵאשִׁית
hu harosh shel hagguf, kelomar, shel hakkehillah. hu hareshit
And he is the head of the body, the church: who is the beginning,

בְּכוֹר מִבֵּין הַמֵּתִים, לְמַעַן יִהְיֶה רִאשׁוֹן בַּכֹּל
bechor mibbein hammetim, lema'an yihyeh rishon bakkol
the firstborn from the dead; that in all things he might have the preeminence.

כִּי כֵן הָיָה רָצוֹן לְשַׁכֵּן בּוֹ אֶת כָּל הַמְּלוֹא
ki chen hayah ratzon leshakken bo et kol hammelo
For it was the good pleasure of the Father that in him should all the fulness dwell;

וּבְאֶמְצָעוּתוֹ לְרַצּוֹת אֶל עַצְמוֹ אֶת הַכֹּל
uve'emtza'uto leratzot el atzmo et hakkol
and through him to reconcile all things unto himself,

הֵן מַה שֶּׁבַּשָּׁמַיִם וְהֵן מַה שֶׁבָּאָרֶץ, בְּאֶמְצָעוּתוֹ, בַּעֲשִׂיַּת שָׁלוֹם בְּדָמוֹ עַל הַצְּלָב
hen mah shebbashamayim vehen mah shebba'aretz, be'emtza'uto, ba'asiyat shalom bedamo al hatzelav
having made peace through the blood of his cross; through him, I say, whether things upon the earth, or things in the heavens.

אַתֶּם לְפָנִים הֱיִיתֶם נָכְרִים וְאוֹיְבִים בְּמַחְשְׁבוֹתֵיכֶם וּבְמַעֲשֵׂיכֶם הָרָעִים
attem lefanim heyitem nocherim ve'oyevim bemachshevoteichem uvema'aseichem hara'im
And you, being in time past alienated and enemies in your mind in your evil works,

אֲבָל כָּעֵת עָשָׂה רִצּוּי בְּגוּף בְּשָׂרוֹ עַל־יְדֵי מוֹתוֹ
aval ka'et asah ritzui beguf besaro al-yedei moto
yet now hath he reconciled in the body of his flesh through death,

כְּדֵי לְהַצִּיגְכֶם לְפָנָיו קְדוֹשִׁים, בְּלִי מוּם וּבְלִי דֹּפִי
kedei lehatzigechem lefanav kedoshim, beli mum uveli dofi
to present you holy and without blemish and unreproveable before him:

אִם אָמְנָם עוֹמְדִים אַתֶּם מְבֻסָּסִים וְיַצִּיבִים בָּאֱמוּנָה
im amenam omedim attem mevussasim veyatzivim ba'emunah
if so be that ye continue in the faith, grounded and stedfast,

וְאֵינְכֶם מַרְפִּים מֵהַתִּקְוָה הַכְּלוּלָה בַּבְּשׂוֹרָה שֶׁשְּׁמַעְתֶּם
ve'einechem marpim mehattikvah hakkelulah babbesorah sheshema'tem
and not moved away from the hope of the gospel which ye heard,

הַקּוֹלוֹסִים

אֲשֶׁר גַּם סִפֵּר לָנוּ עַל אַהֲבַתְכֶם שֶׁבָּרוּחַ
asher gam sipper lanu al ahavatchem shebbaruach
who also declared unto us your love in the Spirit.

מִשּׁוּם כָּךְ גַּם אָנוּ, מִיּוֹם שֶׁשָּׁמַעְנוּ אֶת זֹאת, אֵינֶנּוּ חֲדֵלִים לְהִתְפַּלֵּל בַּעַדְכֶם וּלְבַקֵּשׁ
mishum kach gam anu, miyom sheshama'nu et zot, einennu chadelim lehitpallel ba'adchem ulevakkesh
For this cause we also, since the day we heard it, do not cease to pray and make request for you,

שֶׁתִּמָּלְאוּ דַּעַת רְצוֹנוֹ, בְּלִוְיַת כָּל חָכְמָה וּתְבוּנָה רוּחָנִית
shettimmale'u da'at retzono, belivyat kol chochmah utevunah ruchanit
that ye may be filled with the knowledge of his will in all spiritual wisdom and understanding,

לְמַעַן תִּתְהַלְּכוּ כַּיָּאוּת לִפְנֵי הָאָדוֹן, כְּכָל חֶפְצוֹ, וּלְמַעַן תָּנִיבוּ פְּרִי בְּכָל מַעֲשֶׂה טוֹב
lema'an tit'hallechu kaya'ut lifnei ha'adon, kechal cheftzo, ulema'an tanivu peri bechol ma'aseh tov
to walk worthily of the Lord unto all pleasing, bearing fruit in every good work,

וְתִגְדְּלוּ בְּדַעַת אֱלֹהִים
vetigdelu beda'at elohim
and increasing in the knowledge of God;

וְתִתְחַזְּקוּ בְּכָל כֹּחַ כְּפִי עֹצֶם כְּבוֹדוֹ, וְתִהְיֶה לָכֶם סַבְלָנוּת וְאֹרֶךְ רוּחַ בַּכֹּל, וּבְשִׂמְחָה
vetitchazzeku bechol koach kefi otzem kvodo, vetihyeh lachem savlanut ve'orech ruach bakkol, uvsimchah
strengthened with all power, according to the might of his glory, unto all patience and longsuffering with joy;

תִּתְּנוּ תּוֹדָה לְאָבִינוּ שֶׁהִכְשִׁיר אֶתְכֶם לְהִשְׁתַּתֵּף בְּנַחֲלַת הַקְּדוֹשִׁים בָּאוֹר
tittenu todah le'avinu shehichshir etchem lehishtattef benachalat hakkedoshim ba'or
giving thanks unto the Father, who made us meet to be partakers of the inheritance of the saints in light;

הֵן הָאָב הִצִּילָנוּ מִשִּׁלְטוֹן הַחֹשֶׁךְ וְהֶעֱבִירָנוּ אֶל מַלְכוּת בְּנוֹ אֲהוּבוֹ
hen ha'av hitzilanu mishilton hachoshech vehe'eviranu el malchut beno ahuvo
who delivered us out of the power of darkness, and translated us into the kingdom of the Son of his love;

אֲשֶׁר בּוֹ לָנוּ הַפְּדוּת, סְלִיחַת הַחֲטָאִים
asher bo lanu happedut, selichat hachata'im
in whom we have our redemption, the forgiveness of our sins:

וְהוּא צֶלֶם שֶׁל הָאֱלֹהִים הַבִּלְתִּי נִרְאֶה, בְּכוֹר כָּל בְּרִיאָה
vehu tzelem shel ha'elohim habbilti nir'eh, bechor kol beri'ah
who is the image of the invisible God, the firstborn of all creation;

כִּי בוֹ נִבְרָא כָּל אֲשֶׁר בַּשָּׁמַיִם וַאֲשֶׁר בָּאָרֶץ, מַה שֶּׁנִּרְאֶה וּמַה שֶּׁבִּלְתִּי נִרְאֶה
ki bo nivra kol asher bashamayim va'asher ba'aretz, mah shenir'eh umah shebbilti nir'eh
for in him were all things created, in the heavens and upon the earth, things visible and things invisible,

גַּם כִּסְאוֹת וְרָשֻׁיּוֹת וְגַם מֶמְשָׁלוֹת וְשִׁלְטוֹנוֹת. הַכֹּל נִבְרָא בְּאֶמְצָעוּתוֹ וּלְמַעֲנוֹ
gam kis'ot verashuyot vegam memshalot veshiltonot. hakkol nivra be'emtza'uto ulema'ano
whether thrones or dominions or principalities or powers; all things have been created through him, and unto him;

הַקוֹלוֹסִים

מֵאֵת שָׁאוּל, שְׁלִיחַ הַמָּשִׁיחַ יֵשׁוּעַ בִּרְצוֹן אֱלֹהִים, וּמֵאֵת טִימוֹתֵיאוֹס אָחִינוּ
me'et sha'ul, shliach hammashiach yeshua birtzon elohim, ume'et timotei'os achinu
Paul, an apostle of Christ Jesus through the will of God, and Timothy our brother,

אֶל הַקְּדוֹשִׁים אֲשֶׁר בְּקוֹלוֹסָה, הָאַחִים הַנֶּאֱמָנִים בַּמָּשִׁיחַ
el hakkedoshim asher bekolosah, ha'achim hanne'emanim bammashiach
To the saints and faithful brethren in Christ that are at Colossæ:

חֶסֶד וְשָׁלוֹם לָכֶם מֵאֵת הָאֱלֹהִים אָבִינוּ וְהָאָדוֹן יֵשׁוּעַ הַמָּשִׁיחַ
chesed veshalom lachem me'et ha'elohim avinu veha'adon yeshua hammashiach
Grace to you and peace from God our Father.

מוֹדִים אֲנַחְנוּ לֵאלֹהִים אֲבִי אֲדוֹנֵנוּ יֵשׁוּעַ הַמָּשִׁיחַ וּמִתְפַּלְלִים בַּעַדְכֶם תָּמִיד
modim anachnu lelohim avi adonenu yeshua hammashiach umitpallelim ba'adchem tamid
We give thanks to God the Father of our Lord Jesus Christ, praying always for you,

כִּי שָׁמַעְנוּ עַל אֱמוּנַתְכֶם בַּמָּשִׁיחַ יֵשׁוּעַ וְעַל אַהֲבַתְכֶם לְכָל הַקְּדוֹשִׁים
ki shama'nu al emunatchem bammashiach yeshua ve'al ahavatchem lechol hakkedoshim
having heard of your faith in Christ Jesus, and of the love which ye have toward all the saints,

לְנֹכַח הַתִּקְוָה הַשְּׁמוּרָה לָכֶם בַּשָּׁמַיִם
lenochach hattikvah hashemurah lachem bashamayim
because of the hope which is laid up for you in the heavens

תִּקְוָה אֲשֶׁר שְׁמַעְתֶּם עָלֶיהָ קֹדֶם לָכֵן בִּדְבַר הָאֱמֶת שֶׁל הַבְּשׂוֹרָה
tikvah asher shema'tem aleiha kodem lachen bidvar ha'emet shel habbesorah
whereof ye heard before in the word of the truth of the gospel,

שֶׁהִגִּיעָה אֲלֵיכֶם. וּכְשֵׁם שֶׁהַבְּשׂוֹרָה עוֹשָׂה פְּרִי וּמִשְׂגְשֶׂגֶת בְּכָל הָעוֹלָם
shehiggi'ah aleichem. ucheshem shehabbesorah osah peri umesagseget bechol ha'olam
which is come unto you; even as it is also in all the world bearing fruit and increasing,

כֵּן גַּם בְּקִרְבְּכֶם לְמִן הַיּוֹם שֶׁשְּׁמַעְתֶּם וְהִכַּרְתֶּם בֶּאֱמֶת אֶת חֶסֶד אֱלֹהִים
ken gam bekirbechem lemin hayom sheshema'tem vehikkartem be'emet et chesed elohim
as it doth in you also, since the day ye heard and knew the grace of God in truth;

כַּדֶּרֶךְ שֶׁלְּמַדְתֶּם מֵאֵת אֶפַּפְרַס הָאָהוּב, חֲבֵרֵנוּ לַעֲבוֹדָה
kederech shellemadtem me'et eppafras ha'ahuv, chaverenu la'avodah
even as ye learned of Epaphras our beloved fellow-servant,

וּמְשָׁרֵת נֶאֱמָן שֶׁל הַמָּשִׁיחַ לְמַעַנְכֶם
umesharet ne'eman shel hammashiach lema'anchem
who is a faithful minister of Christ on our behalf,

הַפִילִיפִּים

עִם זֹאת טוֹב עֲשִׂיתֶם שֶׁהִשְׁתַּתַּפְתֶּם בְּצָרָתִי
im zot tov asitem shehishtattaftem betzarati
Howbeit ye did well that ye had fellowship with my affliction.

אַתֶּם הַפִילִיפִּים גַּם יוֹדְעִים שֶׁכַּאֲשֶׁר יָצָאתִי מִמַּקְדּוֹנְיָה בְּרֵאשִׁית יְמֵי הַבְּשׂוֹרָה
attem hafilipim gam yode'im shekka'asher yatzati mimmakedoneyah bereshit yemei habbesorah
And ye yourselves also know, ye Philippians, that in the beginning of the gospel, when I departed from Macedonia,

שׁוּם קְהִלָּה מִלְּבַדְּכֶם לֹא חָבְרָה אֵלַי בְּעִנְיַן מַתַּן עֶזְרָה אוֹ קַבָּלַת עֶזְרָה
shum kehillah millevaddchem lo chaverah elai be'inyan mattan ezrah o kabbalat ezrah
no church had fellowship with me in the matter of giving and receiving but ye only;

הֵן גַּם בִּהְיוֹתִי בְּתֶסַּלוֹנִיקִי שְׁלַחְתֶּם אֵלַי כַּמָּה פְּעָמִים לְסַפֵּק אֶת צְרָכַי
hen gam bihyoti betessaloniki shelachtem elai kammah pe'amim lesappek et tzerachai
for even in Thessalonica ye sent once and again unto my need.

לֹא שֶׁאֲנִי שׁוֹאֵף לְמַתָּנוֹת; שׁוֹאֵף אֲנִי לִפְרִי שֶׁיִּרְבֶּה לִזְכוּתְכֶם
lo she'ani sho'ef lemattanot; sho'ef ani lifri sheyirbeh lizchutechem
Not that I seek for the gift; but I seek for the fruit that increaseth to your account.

יֵשׁ לִי הַכֹּל בְּשֶׁפַע; מָלֵאתִי לְאַחַר שֶׁקִּבַּלְתִּי מִידֵי אֶפַּפְרוֹדִיטוֹס אֶת הַדְּבָרִים אֲשֶׁר שְׁלַחְתֶּם
yesh li hakkol beshefa'; maleti le'achar shekkibbalti midei eppafroditos et haddevarim asher shelachtem
But I have all things, and abound: I am filled, having received from Epaphroditus the things that came from you,

רֵיחַ נִיחוֹחַ הֵם, מִנְחָה עֲרֵבָה רְצוּיָה לֵאלֹהִים
reiach nichoach hem, minchah arevah retzuyah lelohim
an odor of a sweet smell, a sacrifice acceptable, well-pleasing to God.

וֵאלֹהַי יְמַלֵּא אֶת כָּל צָרְכְּכֶם כְּפִי עֹשֶׁר כְּבוֹדוֹ בַּמָּשִׁיחַ יֵשׁוּעַ
velohai yemallei et kol tzarekechem kefi osher kevodo bammashiach yeshua
And my God shall supply every need of yours according to his riches in glory in Christ Jesus.

לֵאלֹהִים אָבִינוּ הַכָּבוֹד לְעוֹלְמֵי עוֹלָמִים. אָמֵן
Le'elohim avinu hakkavod le'olemei olamim. amen
Now unto our God and Father be the glory for ever and ever. Amen.

דִּרְשׁוּ בִּשְׁלוֹם כָּל קָדוֹשׁ בַּמָּשִׁיחַ יֵשׁוּעַ. הָאַחִים אֲשֶׁר עִמִּי דּוֹרְשִׁים בִּשְׁלוֹמְכֶם
dirshu bishlom kol kadosh bammashiach yeshua. ha'achim asher immi doreshim bishlomechem
Salute every saint in Christ Jesus. The brethren that are with me salute you.

כָּל הַקְּדוֹשִׁים דּוֹרְשִׁים בִּשְׁלוֹמְכֶם, בְּעִקָּר אֵלֶּה אֲשֶׁר מִבֵּית הַקֵּיסָר
kol hakkedoshim doreshim bishlomechem, be'ikkar elleh asher mibbeit hakkeisar
All the saints salute you, especially they that are of Cæsar's household.

חֶסֶד הָאָדוֹן יֵשׁוּעַ הַמָּשִׁיחַ עִם רוּחֲכֶם
chesed ha'adon yeshua hammashiach im ruchachem
The grace of the Lord Jesus Christ be with your spirit.

הַפִילִיפִּים

סוֹף דָּבַר, אַחַי, כָּל אֲשֶׁר אֱמֶת, כָּל מַה שֶּׁנִּכְבָּד
sof davar, achai, kol asher emet, kol mah shennichbad
Finally, brethren, whatsoever things are true, whatsoever things are honorable,

כָּל דָּבָר יָשָׁר, טָהוֹר, מָלֵא נֹעַם
kol davar yashar, tahor, malei no'am
whatsoever things are just, whatsoever things are pure, whatsoever things are lovely,

כָּל אֲשֶׁר שָׁמְעוֹ טוֹב, כָּל מַעֲשֶׂה נַעֲלֶה, וְכָל דָּבָר הָרָאוּי לְשֶׁבַח - בְּאֵלֶּה יֶהְגֶּה לְבַבְכֶם
kol asher shim'o tov, kol ma'aseh na'aleh, vechol davar hara'ui leshevach - be'elleh yehgeh levavchem
whatsoever things are of good report; if there be any virtue, and if there be any praise, think on these things.

הַדְּבָרִים אֲשֶׁר לְמַדְתֶּם וְקִבַּלְתֶּם וּשְׁמַעְתֶּם מִמֶּנִּי, וַאֲשֶׁר רְאִיתֶם בִּי - אוֹתָם עֲשׂוּ
haddevarim asher lemadtem vekibbaltem ushema'tem mimmenni, va'asher re'item bi - otam asu
The things which ye both learned and received and heard and saw in me, these things do:

וֵאלֹהֵי הַשָּׁלוֹם יִהְיֶה עִמָּכֶם
ve'elohei hashalom yihyeh immachem
and the God of peace shall be with you.

אָכֵן שָׂמַחְתִּי מְאֹד בָּאָדוֹן שֶׁשּׁוּב עוֹרַרְתֶּם אֶת דַּאֲגַתְכֶם לִי
achen samachti me'od ba'adon sheshuv orartem et da'agatchem li
But I rejoice in the Lord greatly, that now at length ye have revived your thought for me;

אָמְנָם בֶּעָבַר דְּאַגְתֶּם לִי, אֶלָּא שֶׁלֹּא הָיְתָה לָכֶם הִזְדַּמְּנוּת לִפְעֹל
omnam be'avar de'agtem li, ella shello hayetah lachem hizdamnut lif'ol
wherein ye did indeed take thought, but ye lacked opportunity.

אֵינֶנִּי מְדַבֵּר מִתּוֹךְ מַחְסוֹר; לָמַדְתִּי לְהִסְתַּפֵּק בְּמַה שֶּׁיֵּשׁ לִי, בְּכָל מַצָּב
einenni medabber mittoch machsor; lamadti lehistappek bemah sheyesh li, bechol matzav
Not that I speak in respect of want: for I have learned, in whatsoever state I am, therein to be content.

יוֹדֵעַ אֲנִי לַעֲמֹד בְּעֹנִי, וְיוֹדֵעַ אֲנִי לַעֲמֹד בְּשֶׁפַע
yodea ani la'amod be'oni, veyodea ani la'amod beshefa
I know how to be abased, and I know also how to abound:

בְּכָל דָּבָר וּבְכָל הַנְּסִבּוֹת מֻרְגָּל אֲנִי גַּם לִשְׂבֹעַ וְגַם לִרְעֹב
bechol davar uvechol hannesibbot murgal ani gam lesva vegam lera'av,
in everything and in all things have I learned the secret both to be filled and to be hungry,

גַּם לְשֶׁפַע גַּם לְמַחְסוֹר
gam leshefa gam lemachsor
both to abound and to be in want.

הַכֹּל אֲנִי יָכוֹל בְּעֶזְרָתוֹ שֶׁל הַנּוֹתֵן בִּי כֹּחַ
hakkol ani yachol be'ezrato shel hannoten bi koach
I can do all things in him that strengtheneth me.

הַפִילִיפִּים

אֲשֶׁר יַחֲלִיף אֶת גּוּפֵנוּ הַנָּחוּת וְיַעֲשֵׂהוּ דּוֹמֶה לְגוּפוֹ הֶהָדוּר כָּבוֹד
asher yachalif et gufenu hannachut veya'asehu domeh legufo hehadur kavod
who shall fashion anew the body of our humiliation, that it may be conformed to the body of his glory,

כְּפִי כֹּחַ יְכָלְתּוֹ לְשַׁעְבֵּד אֵלָיו אֶת הַכֹּל
kefi koach yecholto lesha'bed elav et hakkol
according to the working whereby he is able even to subject all things unto himself.

ד

עַל כֵּן, אַחַי, הָאֲהוּבִים וְהַיְקָרִים, שִׂמְחָתִי וַעֲטֶרֶת רֹאשִׁי, בְּדֶרֶךְ זֹאת עִמְדוּ נָא בָּאָדוֹן, אֲהוּבַי
al ken, achai, ha'ahuvim vehaykarim, simchati va'ateret roshi, bederech zot imdu na ba'adon, ahuvai
Wherefore, my brethren beloved and longed for, my joy and crown, so stand fast in the Lord, my beloved.

הִנְנִי מַפְצִיר בְּאֶבְהוֹדְיָה וּבְסִינְטִיכִי לִהְיוֹת לֵב אֶחָד בָּאָדוֹן
hineni maftzir be'evhodeyah uvesinetichi lihyot lev echad ba'adon
I exhort Euodia, and I exhort Syntyche, to be of the same mind in the Lord.

וְאַתָּה, חֲבֵרִי הָאֲמִתִּי, הַנּוֹשֵׂא עִמִּי בָּעֹל, גַּם מִמְּךָ אֲנִי מְבַקֵּשׁ
ve'attah, chaveri ha'amitti, hannosei immi ba'ol, gam mimmecha ani mevakkesh
Yea, I beseech thee also, true yokefellow,

עֲזֹר נָא לָהֶן; הֵן הִשְׁתַּתְּפוּ עִמִּי בְּמַאֲבַק הַבְּשׂוֹרָה
azor na lahen; hen hishtattfu immi bema'avak habbesorah
help these women, for they labored with me in the gospel,

יַחַד עִם קְלֶמֶנְטוֹס וְעִם יֶתֶר שֻׁתָּפַי לָעֲבוֹדָה אֲשֶׁר שְׁמוֹתֵיהֶם בְּסֵפֶר הַחַיִּים
yachad im kelementos ve'im yeter shuttafai la'avodah asher shmoteihem besefer hachayim
with Clement also, and the rest of my fellow-workers, whose names are in the book of life.

שִׂמְחוּ בָּאָדוֹן בְּכָל עֵת; אֹמַר שׁוּב, שִׂמְחוּ
simchu ba'adon bechol et; omar shuv, simchu
Rejoice in the Lord always: again I will say, Rejoice.

נֹעַם הִתְנַהֲגוּתְכֶם יִוָּדַע נָא לְכָל אָדָם. הָאָדוֹן קָרוֹב. אַל תִּדְאֲגוּ לְשׁוּם דָּבָר
no'am hitnahagutechem yivvada na lechol adam. ha'adon karov. al tid'agu leshum davar
Let your forbearance be known unto all men. The Lord is at hand. In nothing be anxious;

כִּי אִם בְּכָל דָּבָר הַצִּיגוּ מִשְׁאֲלוֹתֵיכֶם לֵאלֹהִים בִּתְפִלָּה וּבְתַחֲנוּנִים וּבְהוֹדָיָה
ki im bechol davar hatzigu mish'aloteichem le'elohim bitfillah uvetachanunim uvehodayah
but in everything by prayer and supplication with thanksgiving let your requests be made known unto God.

וּשְׁלוֹם אֱלֹהִים הַנִּשְׂגָּב מִכָּל שֵׂכֶל יִנְצֹר אֶת לְבַבְכֶם וְאֶת מַחְשְׁבוֹתֵיכֶם בַּמָּשִׁיחַ יֵשׁוּעַ
ushelom elohim hannisgav mikkol sechel yintzor et levavchem ve'et machshevoteichem bammashiach yeshua
And the peace of God, which passeth all understanding, shall guard your hearts and your thoughts in Christ Jesus.

הַפִילִיפִּים

אַחַי, עֲדַיִן אֵינֶנִּי חוֹשֵׁב אֶת עַצְמִי לְמִי שֶׁהִשִּׂיג
achai, adayin einenni choshev et atzmi lemi shehisig
Brethren, I count not myself yet to have laid hold:

אֲבָל דָּבָר אֶחָד: אֲנִי שׁוֹכֵחַ אֶת אֲשֶׁר מֵאַחֲרַי וְנֶחֱלָץ קָדִימָה אֶל מַה שֶּׁלְּפָנַי
aval davar echad: ani shocheach et asher me'acharai venechelatz kadimah el mah shellefanai
but one thing I do, forgetting the things which are behind, and stretching forward to the things which are before,

אֲנִי רָץ אֶל הַמַּטָּרָה כְּדֵי לְהַשִּׂיג אֶת הַפְּרָס שֶׁבִּקְרִיאָה־שֶׁל־מַעְלָה, קְרִיאָתוֹ שֶׁל אֱלֹהִים בַּמָּשִׁיחַ יֵשׁוּעַ
ani ratz el hammattarah kedei lehashg et happeras shebbikri'ah-shel-ma'lah, keri'ato shel elohim bammashiach yeshua
I press on toward the goal unto the prize of the high calling of God in Christ Jesus.

לָכֵן כָּל בּוֹגֵר שֶׁבֵּינֵינוּ יַחְשֹׁב נָא כָּךְ
lachen kol boger shebbeineinu yachshov na kach
Let us therefore, as many as are perfect, be thus minded:

וְאִם בְּאֵיזֶה עִנְיָן חוֹשְׁבִים אַתֶּם אַחֶרֶת, גַּם אֶת זֹאת יְגַלֶּה לָכֶם אֱלֹהִים
ve'im be'eizeh inyan choshevim attem acheret, gam et zot yegalleh lachem elohim
and if in anything ye are otherwise minded, this also shall God reveal unto you:

אֲבָל מַה שֶׁהִגַּעְנוּ אֵלָיו, לְפִי זֶה עָלֵינוּ לְהִתְהַלֵּךְ
aval mah shehigga'nu elav, lefi zeh aleinu lehit'hallech
only, whereunto we have attained, by that same rule let us walk.

אַחַי, הִתְנַהֲגוּ כָּמוֹנִי. שִׂימוּ לְבַבְכֶם אֶל הָאֲנָשִׁים הַמִּתְהַלְּכִים עַל־פִּי הַדֻּגְמָה שֶׁיֵּשׁ לָכֶם בָּנוּ
achai, hitnahagu kamoni. simu levavchem el ha'anashim hammit'hallechim al-pi haddugmah sheyesh lachem banu
Brethren, be ye imitators together of me, and mark them that so walk even as ye have us for an ensample.

הֵן רַבִּים הַמִּתְהַלְּכִים אֲשֶׁר פְּעָמִים רַבּוֹת אָמַרְתִּי לָכֶם עֲלֵיהֶם ־וְעַתָּה גַּם בִּבְכִי אֲנִי אוֹמֵר
hen rabbim hammit'hallechim asher pe'amim rabbot amarti lachem aleihem -ve'attah gam bivchi ani omer
For many walk, of whom I told you often, and now tell you even weeping,

שֶׁהֵם אוֹיְבֵי צְלַב הַמָּשִׁיחַ. אֲנָשִׁים אֲשֶׁר סוֹפָם אֲבַדּוֹן, אֲשֶׁר הַכֶּרֶס הִיא אֱלֹהֵיהֶם
shehem oyevei tzlav hammashiach anashim asher sofam avaddon, asher hakkeres hi eloheihem
that they are the enemies of the cross of Christ: whose end is perdition, whose god is the belly,

תִּפְאַרְתָּם הִיא בְּמַעֲשֵׂיהֶם הַבְּזוּיִים וְהָאַרְצִיּוּת מְמַלֵּאת אֶת לִבָּם
tif'artam hi bema'aseihem habbezuyim veha'artziyut memallet et libbam
and whose glory is in their shame, who mind earthly things.

אֲשֶׁר לָנוּ, אֶזְרָחוּתֵנוּ בַּשָּׁמַיִם הִיא; מִשָּׁם גַּם יָבוֹא מוֹשִׁיעַ אֲשֶׁר מְחַכִּים אָנוּ לוֹ
asher lanu, ezrachutenu bashamayim hi; misham gam yavo moshia asher mechakkim anu lo
For our citizenship is in heaven; whence also we wait for a Saviour,

הָאָדוֹן יֵשׁוּעַ הַמָּשִׁיחַ
ha'adon yeshua hammashiach
the Lord Jesus Christ:

הַפִּילִיפִּים

עִבְרִי מִן הָעִבְרִים; אֲשֶׁר לַתּוֹרָה, מִכַּת הַפְּרוּשִׁים אֲנִי
ivri min ha'ivrim; asher lattorah, mikkat happerushim ani
a Hebrew of Hebrews; as touching the law, a Pharisee;

אֲשֶׁר לַקַּנָּאוּת, רוֹדֵף הַקְּהִלָּה אֲנִי; מִבְּחִינַת הַצְּדָקָה הַמֻּשְׁתֶּתֶת עַל הַתּוֹרָה, אֵין בִּי דֹּפִי
asher lakkanna'ut, rodef hakkehillah ani; mibbechinat hatzedakah hammushtetet al hattorah, ein bi dofi
as touching zeal, persecuting the church; as touching the righteousness which is in the law, found blameless.

אֲבָל הַדְּבָרִים שֶׁהָיוּ יִתְרוֹן בְּעֵינַי, אוֹתָם חָשַׁבְתִּי לְהֶפְסֵד בִּגְלַל הַמָּשִׁיחַ
aval haddevarim shehayu yitron be'einai, otam chashavti lehefsed biglal hammashiach
Howbeit what things were gain to me, these have I counted loss for Christ.

וְלֹא עוֹד אֶלָּא שֶׁאֲנִי חוֹשֵׁב אֶת הַכֹּל לְהֶפְסֵד בִּגְלַל הַיִּתְרוֹן לָדַעַת אֶת הַמָּשִׁיחַ יֵשׁוּעַ אֲדוֹנִי
velo od ella she'ani choshev et hakkol lehefsed biglal hayitron lada'at et hammashiach yeshua adoni
Yea verily, and I count all things to be loss for the excellency of the knowledge of Christ Jesus my Lord:

אֲשֶׁר לְמַעֲנוֹ הִפְסַדְתִּי אֶת כָּל הַדְּבָרִים; וַאֲנִי חוֹשְׁבָם לִפְסֹלֶת בִּשְׁאִיפָתִי לְהַרְוִיחַ אֶת הַמָּשִׁיחַ
asher lema'ano hifsadti et kol haddevarim; va'ani choshevam lifsolet bish'ifati leharviach et hammashiach
for whom I suffered the loss of all things, and do count them but refuse, that I may gain Christ,

וּלְהִמָּצֵא בוֹ - בְּאֹפֶן שֶׁצִּדְקָתִי לֹא תִּהְיֶה לִי מִן הַתּוֹרָה
ulehimmatzei bo - be'ofen shetzidkati lo tihyeh li min hattorah
and be found in him, not having a righteousness of mine own, even that which is of the law,

אֶלָּא תִּהְיֶה זוֹ הַצְּדָקָה אֲשֶׁר עַל־יְדֵי אֱמוּנַת הַמָּשִׁיחַ. צְדָקָה אֲשֶׁר מֵאֱלֹהִים הִיא וִיסוֹדָהּ בֶּאֱמוּנָה
ella tihyeh zo hatzedakah asher al-yedei emunat hammashiach. tzedakah asher me'elohim hi viysodah be'emunah
but that which is through faith in Christ, the righteousness which is from God by faith:

כְּדֵי לָדַעַת אוֹתוֹ
kedei lada'at oto ve'et koach techiyato
that I may know him, and the power of his resurrection,

וְאֶת כֹּחַ תְּחִיָּתוֹ וְאֶת הִשְׁתַּתְּפוּת בְּיִסּוּרָיו וּלְהִדַּמּוֹת לוֹ בְּמוֹתוֹ
ve'et hashuttafut beyissurav ulehiddammot lo bemoto
and the fellowship of his sufferings, becoming conformed unto his death;

בְּתִקְוָה שֶׁאַגִּיעַ לַתְּחִיָּה מִן הַמֵּתִים
betikvah she'aggia lattechiyah min hammetim
if by any means I may attain unto the resurrection from the dead.

לֹא שֶׁכְּבָר הִשַּׂגְתִּי אוֹ שֶׁכְּבָר הִגַּעְתִּי לִשְׁלֵמוּת
lo shekkevar hissagti o shekkevar higga'ti lishlemut
Not that I have already obtained, or am already made perfect:

אֲבָל רָץ אֲנִי בְּתִקְוָה לְהַשִּׂיג, כִּי מִשּׁוּם כָּךְ גַּם הִשִּׂיגַנִי הַמָּשִׁיחַ יֵשׁוּעַ
aval ratz ani betikvah lehashg, ki mishum kach gam hishgani hammashiach yeshua
but I press on, if so be that I may lay hold on that for which also I was laid hold on by Christ Jesus.

הַפִילִיפִּים

כְּדֵי שֶׁתִּשְׂמְחוּ בִּרְאוֹתְכֶם אוֹתוֹ שׁוּב, וְאָז יִמְעַט יְגוֹנִי
kedei shettismechu bir'otechem oto shuv, ve'az yim'at yegoni
that, when ye see him again, ye may rejoice, and that I may be the less sorrowful.

עַל כֵּן קַבְּלוּהוּ בָּאָדוֹן בִּמְלֹא שִׂמְחָה וְהוֹקִירוּ אֲנָשִׁים כָּאֵלֶּה
al ken kabbluhu ba'adon bimlo simchah vehokiru anashim ka'elleh
Receive him therefore in the Lord with all joy; and hold such in honor:

כִּי בִּגְלַל עֲבוֹדַת הַמָּשִׁיחַ הִגִּיעַ עַד סַף הַמָּוֶת
ki biglal avodat hammashiach higgia ad saf hammavet
because for the work of Christ he came nigh unto death,

בְּסַכְּנוֹ אֶת נַפְשׁוֹ כְּדֵי לְמַלֵּא אֶת מַה שֶׁנִּבְצַר מִכֶּם לַעֲשׂוֹת בְּשֵׁרוּתְכֶם לְמַעֲנִי
besakkeno et nafsho kedei lemallei et mah shennivtzar mikkem la'asot besherutechem lema'ani
hazarding his life to supply that which was lacking in your service toward me.

ג

וּבְכֵן, אַחַי, שִׂמְחוּ בָּאָדוֹן
uvechen, achai, simchu ba'adon
Finally, my brethren, rejoice in the Lord.

לִכְתֹּב לָכֶם שׁוּב אֶת אוֹתוֹ דָּבָר אֵינֶנּוּ לְטֹרַח עָלַי, אַךְ לָכֶם זֶה מוֹסִיף לְבִטָּחוֹן
lichtov lachem shuv et oto davar einennu letorach alai, ach lachem zeh mosif levittachon
To write the same things to you, to me indeed is not irksome, but for you it is safe.

הִזָּהֲרוּ מֵהַכְּלָבִים. הִזָּהֲרוּ מִפּוֹעֲלֵי הָרֶשַׁע. הִזָּהֲרוּ מִן הַחִתּוּךְ. הֲרֵי אֲנַחְנוּ בְּנֵי הַמִּילָה
hizzaharu mehakkelavim. hizzaharu mippo'alei haresha. hizzaharu min hachittuch. harei anachnu bnei hammilah
Beware of the dogs, beware of the evil workers, beware of the concision: for we are the circumcision,

הָעוֹבְדִים אֶת אֱלֹהִים בְּרוּחַ וּמִתְגָּאִים בַּמָּשִׁיחַ יֵשׁוּעַ בְּלִי לִבְטֹחַ בַּבָּשָׂר
ha'ovedim et elohim beruach umitga'im bammashiach yeshua beli livtoach babbasar
who worship by the Spirit of God, and glory in Christ Jesus, and have no confidence in the flesh:

אַף שֶׁאֲנִי עַצְמִי יָכוֹל לִבְטֹחַ גַּם בַּבָּשָׂר
af she'ani atzmi yachol livtoach gam babbasar
though I myself might have confidence even in the flesh:

אִם מִישֶׁהוּ סָבוּר שֶׁיּוּכַל לִבְטֹחַ בַּבָּשָׂר, אֲזַי אֲנִי יוֹתֵר
im mishehu savur sheyuchal livtoach babbasar, azai ani yoter
if any other man thinketh to have confidence in the flesh, I yet more:

נִמַּלְתִּי בִּהְיוֹתִי בֶּן שְׁמוֹנַת יָמִים; מִמּוֹצָא יִשְׂרָאֵל אָנֹכִי, מִשֵּׁבֶט בִּנְיָמִין
nimmalti bihyoti ben shemonat yamim; mimmotza yisra'el anochi, mishevet binyamin
circumcised the eighth day, of the stock of Israel, of the tribe of Benjamin,

הַפִּילִיפִּים

לְמַעַן אֶתְעוֹדֵד גַּם אֲנִי בְּהוֹדַע לִי מַה מַּצַּבְכֶם
lema'an et'oded gam ani behivvada li mah matzavchem
that I also may be of good comfort, when I know your state.

אֵין לִי אִישׁ תְּמִים דֵעִים עִמִּי כָּמוֹהוּ, אֲשֶׁר בְּלֵב שָׁלֵם יִדְאַג לְעִנְיְנֵיכֶם
ein li ish temim de'im immi kamohu, asher belev shalem yid'ag le'inyeneichem
For I have no man likeminded, who will care truly for your state.

הַכֹּל דּוֹאֲגִים לְעִנְיְנֵיהֶם, לֹא לַדְּבָרִים אֲשֶׁר לַמָּשִׁיחַ יֵשׁוּעַ
hakkol do'agim le'inyeneihem, lo laddevarim asher lammashiach yeshua
For they all seek their own, not the things of Jesus Christ.

אֲבָל יוֹדְעִים אַתֶּם אֶת אָפְיוֹ הַבָּחוּן; כְּמוֹ בֵן הָעוֹבֵד עִם אָבִיו הוּא שֵׁרֵת עִמִּי בַּעֲבוֹדַת הַבְּשׂוֹרָה
aval yode'im attem et afeyo habbachun; kemo ben ha'oved im aviv hu sheret immi ba'avodat habbesorah
But ye know the proof of him, that, as a child serveth a father, so he served with me in furtherance of the gospel.

לָכֵן אוֹתוֹ מְקַוֶּה אֲנִי לִשְׁלֹחַ מִיָּד לְאַחַר שֶׁאֶרְאֶה מַה יַּעֲשׂוּ בִּי
lachen oto mekavveh ani lishloach miyad le'achar she'er'eh mah ya'asu bi
Him therefore I hope to send forthwith, so soon as I shall see how it will go with me:

וּבוֹטֵחַ אֲנִי בָּאָדוֹן שֶׁגַּם אֲנִי אָבוֹא בִּמְהֵרָה
uvoteach ani ba'adon sheggam ani avo bimeherah
but I trust in the Lord that I myself also shall come shortly.

אֲבָל חָשַׁבְתִּי לְנָחוּץ לִשְׁלֹחַ אֲלֵיכֶם אֶת הָאָח אֶפַּפְרוֹדִיטוֹס, שֻׁתָּפִי לַעֲבוֹדָה וְלַמַּעֲרָכָה
aval chashavti lenachutz lishloach aleichem et ha'ach eppafroditos, shuttafi la'avodah velamma'arachah
But I counted it necessary to send to you Epaphroditus, my brother and fellow-worker and fellow-soldier,

וְגַם שְׁלִיחֲכֶם הַמְשָׁרֵת בְּמִלּוּי מַחְסוֹרִי
vegam shelichachem hamsharet bemillui machsori
and your messenger and minister to my need;

שֶׁכֵּן הִתְגַּעְגֵּעַ לְכֻלְּכֶם וְאַף נֶעֱצַב מְאֹד עַל שֶׁנּוֹדַע לָכֶם כִּי חָלָה
shekken hitga'gea lechullechem ve'af ne'etzav me'od al shennoda lachem ki chalah
since he longed after you all, and was sore troubled, because ye had heard that he was sick:

אָמְנָם חָלָה וְנָטָה לָמוּת, אַךְ אֱלֹהִים רִחֵם עָלָיו
amenam chalah venatah lamut, ach elohim richem alav
for indeed he was sick nigh unto death: but God had mercy on him;

וְלֹא רַק עָלָיו, אֶלָּא גַּם עָלַי, לְמַעַן לֹא יָבוֹא עָלַי יָגוֹן עַל יָגוֹן
velo rak alav, ella gam alai, lema'an lo yavo alai yagon al yagon
and not on him only, but on me also, that I might not have sorrow upon sorrow.

לָכֵן מִהַרְתִּי לְשָׁלְחוֹ אֲלֵיכֶם
lachen miharti leshalecho aleichem
I have sent him therefore the more diligently,

הַפִילִיפִּים

וְכָל לָשׁוֹן תּוֹדֶה כִּי יֵשׁוּעַ הַמָּשִׁיחַ הוּא הָאָדוֹן, לְתִפְאֶרֶת אֱלֹהִים הָאָב
vechol lashon todeh ki yeshua hammashiach hu ha'adon, letif'eret elohim ha'av
and that every tongue should confess that Jesus Christ is Lord, to the glory of God the Father.

לָכֵן אֲהוּבַי, כְּשֵׁם שֶׁצִּיַּתֶּם תָּמִיד, לֹא רַק כְּמוֹ בְּעֵת נוֹכְחוּתִי
lachen ahuvai, keshem shetziyattem tamid, lo rak kemo be'et nochechuti
So then, my beloved, even as ye have always obeyed, not as in my presence only,

אֶלָּא עַל אַחַת כַּמָּה וְכַמָּה כָּעֵת, בְּהֶעְדְּרִי - הִשָּׁמְעוּ עַתָּה, וּבְיִרְאָה וּבִרְתֵת פַּעֲלוּ לְמִמּוּשׁ תְּשׁוּעַתְכֶם
ella al achat kammah vechammah ka'et, behe'aderi - hisham'u attah, uveyir'ah uvirtet pa'alu lemimmush teshu'atchem
but now much more in my absence, work out your own salvation with fear and trembling;

וְאָמְנָם אֱלֹהִים הוּא הַפּוֹעֵל בָּכֶם גַּם שֶׁתִּרְצוּ וְגַם שֶׁתִּפְעֲלוּ כַּטּוֹב בְּעֵינָיו
ve'omnam elohim hu happo'el bachem gam shettirtzu vegam shettif'alu kattov be'einav
for it is God who worketh in you both to will and to work, for his good pleasure.

עֲשׂוּ כָּל דָּבָר בְּלִי לְהִתְלוֹנֵן וּבְלִי לְהִתְוַכֵּחַ
asu kol davar beli lehitlonen uveli lehitvakkeach
Do all things without murmurings and questionings:

לְמַעַן תִּהְיוּ נְקִיִּים מֵאָשָׁם וּטְהוֹרִים, בָּנִים לֵאלֹהִים אֵין דֹּפִי בָּהֶם
lema'an tihyu nekiyim me'asham utehorim, banim lelohim ein dofi bahem
that ye may become blameless and harmless, children of God without blemish

בְּתוֹךְ דּוֹר עִקֵּשׁ וּפְתַלְתֹּל אֲשֶׁר תּוֹפִיעוּ בּוֹ כִּמְאוֹרוֹת בָּעוֹלָם
betoch dor ikkesh ufetaltol asher tofi'u bo kim'orot ba'olam
in the midst of a crooked and perverse generation, among whom ye are seen as lights in the world,

בְּהַחֲזִיקְכֶם אֶת דְּבַר הַחַיִּים; זֹאת תִּהְיֶה לִי לִתְהִלָּה בְּיוֹם הַמָּשִׁיחַ
behachazikechem et devar hachayim; zot tihyeh li lit'hillah beyom hammashiach
holding forth the word of life; that I may have whereof to glory in the day of Christ,

שֶׁלֹּא לַשָּׁוְא רַצְתִּי וְלֹא לָרִיק עָמַלְתִּי
shello lashav ratzti velo larik amalti
that I did not run in vain neither labor in vain.

אֲבָל גַּם אִם אֶשָּׁפֵךְ כְּנֶסֶךְ עַל קָרְבַּן עֲבוֹדַת הַקֹּדֶשׁ שֶׁל אֱמוּנַתְכֶם, שָׂמֵחַ אֲנִי וְשָׂשׂ עִם כֻּלְּכֶם
aval gam im eshafech kenesech al korban avodat hakkodesh shel emunatchem, sameach ani vesas im kullchem
Yea, and if I am offered upon the sacrifice and service of your faith, I joy, and rejoice with you all:

כָּךְ שִׂמְחוּ גַּם אַתֶּם וְשִׂישׂוּ עִמִּי
kach simchu gam attem vesisu immi
and in the same manner do ye also joy, and rejoice with me.

תִּקְוָתִי בָּאָדוֹן יֵשׁוּעַ שֶׁאֶשְׁלַח אֲלֵיכֶם בִּמְהֵרָה אֶת טִימוֹתֵיאוֹס
tikvati ba'adon yeshua she'eshlach aleichem bimherah et timotei'os
But I hope in the Lord Jesus to send Timothy shortly unto you,

הַפִילִיפִּים

אֲזַי מַלְאוּ נָא אֶת שִׂמְחָתִי בָּזֶה שֶׁתִּהְיוּ תְּמִימֵי דֵעִים
azai malle'u na et simchati bazeh shettihyu temimei de'im
make full my joy, that ye be of the same mind,

חַדּוּרֵי אַהֲבָה אַחַת, בַּעֲלֵי כַּוָּנָה אַחַת וּמַחֲשָׁבָה אַחַת
chadurei ahavah achat, ba'alei kavvanah achat umachashavah achat
having the same love, being of one accord, of one mind;

וְאַל תַּעֲשׂוּ דָּבָר מִתּוֹךְ תַּחֲרוּת, אַף לֹא מִתּוֹךְ כְּבוֹד שָׁוְא
ve'al ta'asu davar mittoch tacharut, af lo mittoch kevod shav
doing nothing through faction or through vainglory,

אֶלָּא בִּנְמִיכוּת רוּחַ יַחְשֹׁב אִישׁ אִישׁ אֶת רֵעֵהוּ לְנִכְבָּד מִמֶּנּוּ
ella binmichut ruach yachshov ish ish et re'ehu lenichbad mimmennu
but in lowliness of mind each counting other better than himself;

כָּל אֶחָד אַל יִדְאַג רַק לְעִנְיָנָיו, אֶלָּא גַּם לְעִנְיָנָיו שֶׁל זוּלָתוֹ
kol echad al yid'ag rak le'inyanav, ella gam le'inyanav shel zulato
not looking each of you to his own things, but each of you also to the things of others.

יְהֵא בָּכֶם הֲלָךְ רוּחַ זֶה אֲשֶׁר הָיָה בַּמָּשִׁיחַ יֵשׁוּעַ
yehei bachem halach ruach zeh asher hayah bammashiach yeshua
Have this mind in you, which was also in Christ Jesus:

הוּא אֲשֶׁר הָיָה קַיָּם בִּדְמוּת אֱלֹהִים לֹא חָשַׁב לְשָׁלָל הֱיוֹת שָׁוֶה לֵאלֹהִים
hu asher hayah kayam bidmut elohim lo chashav leshalal heyot shaveh lelohim
who, existing in the form of God, counted not the being on an equality with God a thing to be grasped,

אֶלָּא הֵרִיק אֶת עַצְמוֹ, נָטַל דְּמוּת עֶבֶד וְנִהְיָה כִּבְנֵי אָדָם; וְכַאֲשֶׁר הָיָה בְּצוּרָתוֹ כְּאָדָם
ella herik et atzmo, natal demut eved venihyah kivnei adam; vecha'asher hayah betzurato ke'adam
but emptied himself, taking the form of a servant, being made in the likeness of men;

הִשְׁפִּיל עַצְמוֹ וְצַיֵּת עַד מָוֶת
hishpil atzmo vetziyet ad mavet
and being found in fashion as a man, he humbled himself, becoming obedient even unto death,

עַד מָוֶת בַּצְּלָב
ad mavet batzlav
yea, the death of the cross.

עַל כֵּן הִגְבִּיהוֹ אֱלֹהִים מְאֹד וְנָתַן לוֹ אֶת הַשֵּׁם הַנַּעֲלֶה עַל כָּל שֵׁם
al ken higbiho elohim me'od venatan lo et hashem hanna'aleh al kol shem
Wherefore also God highly exalted him, and gave unto him the name which is above every name;

לְמַעַן תִּכְרַע בְּשֵׁם יֵשׁוּעַ כָּל בֶּרֶךְ, בַּשָּׁמַיִם וּבָאָרֶץ וּמִתַּחַת לָאָרֶץ
lema'an tichra beshem yeshua kol berech, bashamayim uva'aretz umittachat la'aretz
that in the name of Jesus every knee should bow, of things in heaven and things on earth and things under the earth,

הַפִּילִיפִּים

לְמַעַן הִתְקַדְּמוּתְכֶם וְשִׂמְחַתְכֶם בָּאֱמוּנָה
lema'an hitkaddemutechem vesimchatchem ba'emunah
for your progress and joy in the faith;

וְאָז תַּרְבּוּ לְהִתְהַלֵּל בַּמָּשִׁיחַ יֵשׁוּעַ בִּגְלָלִי, בִּגְלַל נוֹכְחוּתִי שׁוּב עִמָּכֶם
ve'az tarbu lehit'hallel bammashiach yeshua biglali, biglal nochechuti shuv immachem
that your glorying may abound in Christ Jesus in me through my presence with you again.

רַק הִתְנַהֲגוּ כָּרָאוּי לִבְשׂוֹרַת הַמָּשִׁיחַ
rak hitnahagu kara'ui livsorat hammashiach
Only let your manner of life be worthy of the gospel of Christ:

לְמַעַן אֶשְׁמַע עֲלֵיכֶם - אִם בְּבוֹאִי לִרְאוֹתְכֶם, אִם בִּהְיוֹתִי רָחוֹק מִכֶּם - כִּי עוֹמְדִים אַתֶּם בְּרוּחַ אַחַת
lema'an eshma aleichem - im bevo'i lir'otechem, im bihyoti rachok mikkem - ki omedim attem beruach achat
that, whether I come and see you or be absent, I may hear of your state, that ye stand fast in one spirit,

וְנִלְחָמִים בְּלֵב אֶחָד בְּעַד אֱמוּנַת הַבְּשׂוֹרָה
venilchamim belev echad be'ad emunat habbesorah
with one soul striving for the faith of the gospel;

וְאֵינְכֶם פּוֹחֲדִים כְּלָל מִפְּנֵי הַמִּתְנַגְּדִים
ve'einechem pochadim kelal mippenei hammitnaggedim
and in nothing affrighted by the adversaries:

דָּבָר אֲשֶׁר לָהֶם הוּא אוֹת לַאֲבַדּוֹן וְלָכֶם אוֹת לִישׁוּעָה, וְזֹאת מֵאֵת הָאֱלֹהִים
davar asher lahem hu ot la'avaddon velachem ot liyshu'ah, vezot me'et ha'elohim
which is for them an evident token of perdition, but of your salvation, and that from God;

הֵן לָכֶם נִתַּן, לְמַעַן הַמָּשִׁיחַ, לֹא רַק לְהַאֲמִין בּוֹ, אֶלָּא גַּם לִסְבֹּל לְמַעֲנוֹ
hen lachem nittan, lema'an hammashiach, lo rak leha'amin bo, ella gam lisbol lema'ano
because to you it hath been granted in the behalf of Christ, not only to believe on him, but also to suffer in his behalf:

שֶׁהֲרֵי לָכֶם אוֹתוֹ הַמַּאֲבָק שֶׁבֶּעָבָר רְאִיתֶם אוֹתִי נֶאֱבָק בּוֹ וְכָעֵת אַתֶּם שׁוֹמְעִים כִּי אֲנִי נִמְצָא בּוֹ
sheharei lachem oto hamma'avak shebbe'avar re'item oti ne'evak bo vecha'et attem shome'im ki ani nimtza bo
having the same conflict which ye saw in me, and now hear to be in me.

ב

לָכֵן אִם יֵשׁ אֵיזֶה עִדּוּד בַּמָּשִׁיחַ
lachen im yesh eizeh iddud bammashiach
If there is therefore any exhortation in Christ,

אִם אֵיזוֹ נֶחָמָה שֶׁל אַהֲבָה, אִם אֵיזוֹ שֻׁתָּפוּת שֶׁל רוּחַ, אִם אֵילוּ רַחֲמִים וְחֶמְלָה
im eizo nechamah shel ahavah, im eizo shuttafut shel ruach, im eilu rachamim vechemlah
if any consolation of love, if any fellowship of the Spirit, if any tender mercies and compassions,

הַפִּילִיפִּים

וְאֵלֶּה מַכְרִיזִים אֶת הַמָּשִׁיחַ מִתּוֹךְ תַּחֲרוּת וְלֹא בְּלֵב טָהוֹר, וְכַוָּנָתָם לְהוֹסִיף צָרָה עַל כְּבָלַי
ve'elleh machrizim et hammashiach mittoch tacharut velo belev tahor, vechavvanatam lehosif tzarah al kevalai
but the other proclaim Christ of faction, not sincerely, thinking to raise up affliction for me in my bonds.

אָז מָה? הַתּוֹצָאָה הִיא שֶׁבֵּין כָּךְ וּבֵין כָּךְ, אִם בְּהַעֲמָדַת פָּנִים וְאִם מִתּוֹךְ כֵּנוּת, הַמָּשִׁיחַ מֻכְרָז
az mah? hattotza'ah hi shebbein kach uvein kach, im beha'amadat panim ve'im mittoch kenut, hammashiach muchraz
What then? only that in every way, whether in pretence or in truth, Christ is proclaimed;

וּבָזֹאת אֲנִי שָׂמֵחַ וְגַם אוֹסִיף לִשְׂמֹחַ
uvazot ani sameach vegam osif lismoach
and therein I rejoice, yea, and will rejoice.

כִּי יוֹדֵעַ אֲנִי שֶׁכָּל זֶה יָבִיא לִידֵי שִׁחְרוּרִי, בְּעֶזְרַת תְּפִלַּתְכֶם וּבִתְמִיכַת רוּחַ יֵשׁוּעַ הַמָּשִׁיחַ
ki yodea ani shekkol zeh yavi lidei shichruri, be'ezrat tefillatchem uvitmichat ruach yeshua hammashiach
For I know that this shall turn out to my salvation, through your supplication and the supply of the Spirit of Jesus Christ,

וְזֹאת בְּהֶתְאֵם לְצִפִּיָּתִי הָעֲמֻקָּה וְתִקְוָתִי
vezot behet'em letzippiyati ha'amukkah vetikvati
according to my earnest expectation and hope,

שֶׁלֹּא אֵבוֹשׁ בְּשׁוּם דָּבָר, אֶלָּא שֶׁבְּכָל עֹז, כְּתָמִיד
shello evosh beshum davar, ella shebbechal oz, ketamid
that in nothing shall I be put to shame, but that with all boldness, as always,

כֵּן גַּם עַתָּה, יְרוֹמַם וְיִתְגַּדֵּל הַמָּשִׁיחַ בְּגוּפִי, אִם עַל־יְדֵי חַיַּי וְאִם עַל־יְדֵי מוֹתִי
ken gam attah, yeromam veyitgaddel hammashiach begufi, im al-yedei chayai ve'im al-yedei moti
so now also Christ shall be magnified in my body, whether by life, or by death.

הֵן, לְגַבֵּי דִּידִי, לִחְיוֹת פֵּרוּשׁוֹ הַמָּשִׁיחַ, וְלָמוּת פֵּרוּשׁוֹ רֶוַח
hen, legabbei didi, lichyot perusho hammashiach, velamut perusho revach
For to me to live is Christ, and to die is gain.

אַךְ אִם לִחְיוֹת בַּגּוּף - הֲרֵי זֶה בִּשְׁבִילִי עֲבוֹדָה פּוֹרִיָּה וְאֵינֶנִּי יוֹדֵעַ בַּמֶּה לִבְחֹר
ach im lichyot bagguf - harei zeh bishvili avodah poriyah ve'einenni yodea bammeh livchor
But if to live in the flesh,—if this shall bring fruit from my work, then what I shall choose I know not.

אֲנִי לָחוּץ עַל־יְדֵי הַשְּׁנַיִם. אֲנִי מִשְׁתּוֹקֵק לְהִסְתַּלֵּק וְלִהְיוֹת עִם הַמָּשִׁיחַ, שֶׁכֵּן זֶה טוֹב הַרְבֵּה יוֹתֵר
ani lachutz al-yedei hashenayim. ani mishtokek lehistalek velihyot im hammashiach, shekken zeh tov harbeh yoter
But I am in a strait betwixt the two, having the desire to depart and be with Christ; for it is very far better:

אוּלָם הִשָּׁאֲרוּתִי בַּגּוּף נְחוּצָה יוֹתֵר לְמַעַנְכֶם
ulam hisha'aruti bagguf nechutzah yoter lema'anchem
yet to abide in the flesh is more needful for your sake.

וּבִהְיוֹתִי בָּטוּחַ בְּכָךְ אֲנִי יוֹדֵעַ שֶׁאֶשָּׁאֵר וְאַמְשִׁיךְ עִם כֻּלְּכֶם
uvihyoti batuach bechach ani yodea she'esha'er ve'amshich im kullechem
And having this confidence, I know that I shall abide, yea, and abide with you all,

הַפִּילִיפִּים

לְמַעַן תַּבְחִינוּ מַה הֵם הַדְּבָרִים הַמְצֻיָּנִים
lema'an tavchinu mah hem haddevarim hamtzuyanim
so that ye may approve the things that are excellent;

וְתִהְיוּ זַכִּים וּלְלֹא דֹּפִי לְיוֹם הַמָּשִׁיחַ
vetihyu zakkim ulelo dofi leyom hammashiach
that ye may be sincere and void of offence unto the day of Christ;

וּמְלֵאִים פְּרִי צְדָקָה שֶׁמֵּנִיב יֵשׁוּעַ הַמָּשִׁיחַ, לִכְבוֹדוֹ וּתְהִלָּתוֹ שֶׁל אֱלֹהִים
umele'im peri tzedakah shemmeniv yeshua hammashiach, lichvodo utehillato shel elohim
being filled with the fruits of righteousness, which are through Jesus Christ, unto the glory and praise of God.

אַחַי, רְצוֹנִי שֶׁתֵּדְעוּ
achai, retzoni shettede'u
Now I would have you know, brethren,

כִּי מַה שֶּׁקָּרָה לִי הָיָה דַּוְקָא לְטוֹבַת הַבְּשׂוֹרָה
ki mah shekkarah li hayah davka letovat habbesorah
that the things which happened unto me have fallen out rather unto the progress of the gospel;

הָעֻבְדָּה שֶׁאֲנִי חָבוּשׁ בְּמַאֲסָר לְמַעַן הַמָּשִׁיחַ נִתְפַּרְסְמָה
ha'uvdah she'ani chavush bema'asar lema'an hammashiach nitparsemah
so that my bonds became manifest in Christ

בֵּין כָּל אַנְשֵׁי מִשְׁמַר הַקֵּיסָר וְנוֹדְעָה לְכָל הַשְּׁאָר
bein kol anshei mishmar hakkeisar venode'ah lechol hashe'ar
throughout the whole prætorian guard, and to all the rest;

וְרֹב הָאַחִים בְּבִטְחָם בָּאָדוֹן
verov ha'achim bevatecham ba'adon
and that most of the brethren in the Lord,

הִתְחַזְּקוּ עוֹד יוֹתֵר בִּגְלַל מַאֲסָרִי וְהֵעֵזּוּ לְדַבֵּר בְּלִי פַּחַד אֶת דְּבַר הָאֱלֹהִים
hitchazzeku od yoter biglal ma'asari vehe'ezzu ledabber beli pachad et devar ha'elohim
being confident through my bonds, are more abundantly bold to speak the word of God without fear.

אָמְנָם יֵשׁ הַמַּכְרִיזִים אֶת הַמָּשִׁיחַ מִתּוֹךְ קִנְאָה וְתַחֲרוּת,
amenam yesh hammachrizim et hammashiach mittoch kin'ah vetacharut,
Some indeed preach Christ even of envy and strife;

אַךְ יֵשׁ הַמַּכְרִיזִים מִתּוֹךְ כַּוָּנָה טוֹבָה
ach yesh hammachrizim mittoch kavvanah tovah
and some also of good will:

אֵלֶּה עוֹשִׂים זֹאת מִתּוֹךְ אַהֲבָה, בְּיָדְעָם כִּי מֻפְקָד אֲנִי עַל הֲגַנַּת הַבְּשׂוֹרָה
elleh osim zot mittoch ahavah, beyade'am ki mufkad ani al hagannat habbesorah
the one do it of love, knowing that I am set for the defence of the gospel;

הַפִילִיפִים

מֵאֵת שָׁאוּל וְטִימוֹתֵיאוֹס, עַבְדֵי הַמָּשִׁיחַ יֵשׁוּעַ
me'et sha'ul vetimotei'os, avdei hammashiach yeshua
Paul and Timothy, servants of Christ Jesus,

אֶל כָּל הַקְּדוֹשִׁים בַּמָּשִׁיחַ יֵשׁוּעַ הַנִּמְצָאִים בְּפִילִיפִּי, וּמַנְהִיגֵי הַקְּהִלָּה וְהַשַּׁמָּשִׁים בִּכְלָל זֶה
el kol hakkedoshim bammashiach yeshua hannimtza'im befilipi, umanhigei hakkehillah vehashammashim bichlal zeh
to all the saints in Christ Jesus that are at Philippi, with the bishops and deacons:

חֶסֶד וְשָׁלוֹם לָכֶם מֵאֵת הָאֱלֹהִים אָבִינוּ וְהָאָדוֹן יֵשׁוּעַ הַמָּשִׁיחַ
chesed veshalom lachem me'et ha'elohim avinu veha'adon yeshua hammashiach
Grace to you and peace from God our Father and the Lord Jesus Christ.

מוֹדֶה אֲנִי לֵאלֹהִים מִדֵּי זָכְרִי אֶתְכֶם
modeh ani le'elohim middei zochri etchem
I thank my God upon all my remembrance of you,

וְתָמִיד, בְּכָל תְּפִלּוֹתַי בְּעַד כֻּלְּכֶם, מִתְפַּלֵּל אֲנִי מִתּוֹךְ שִׂמְחָה
vetamid, bechol tefillotai be'ad kullechem, mitpallel ani mittoch simchah
always in every supplication of mine on behalf of you all making my supplication with joy,

עַל הִשְׁתַּתְּפוּתְכֶם בַּבְּשׂוֹרָה לְמִן הַיּוֹם הָרִאשׁוֹן וְעַד עַתָּה
al hishtattefutechem babbesorah lemin hayom harishon ve'ad attah
for your fellowship in furtherance of the gospel from the first day until now;

בָּזֹאת בָּטוּחַ אֲנִי, שֶׁהַמַּתְחִיל בָּכֶם אֶת הַפְּעֻלָּה הַטּוֹבָה הַשְׁלֵם יַשְׁלִים אוֹתָהּ עַד יוֹם הַמָּשִׁיחַ יֵשׁוּעַ
bazot batuach ani, shehammatchil bachem et happe'ullah hattovah hashlem yashlim otah ad yom hammashiach yeshua
being confident of this very thing, that he who began a good work in you will perfect it until the day of Jesus Christ:

בְּצֶדֶק אֲנִי חוֹשֵׁב זֹאת עַל כֻּלְּכֶם, שֶׁכֵּן אֲנִי נוֹשֵׂא אֶתְכֶם בְּלִבִּי
betzedek ani choshev zot al kullechem, shekken ani nosei etchem belibbi
even as it is right for me to be thus minded on behalf of you all, because I have you in my heart,

בִּגְלַל הֱיוֹתְכֶם שֻׁתָּפִים לַחֶסֶד שֶׁהוּא מְנָת חֶלְקִי, הֵן בְּמַאֲסָרַי וְהֵן בִּפְעֻלָּתִי לַהֲגַנַּת הַבְּשׂוֹרָה וְחִזּוּקָהּ
biglal heyotechem shuttafim lachesed shehu menat chelki, hen bema'asari vehen bif'ullati lahagannat habbesorah vechizzukah
inasmuch as, both in my bonds and in the defence and confirmation of the gospel, ye all are partakers with me of grace.

הָאֱלֹהִים עֵד לִי, כַּמָּה נִכְסָף אֲנִי אֶל כֻּלְּכֶם בְּאַהֲבַת הַמָּשִׁיחַ יֵשׁוּעַ
ha'elohim ed li, kammah nichsaf ani el kullechem be'ahavat hammashiach yeshua
For God is my witness, how I long after you all in the tender mercies of Christ Jesus.

תְּפִלָּתִי הִיא שֶׁאַהֲבַתְכֶם תִּרְבֶּה יוֹתֵר וְיוֹתֵר וּתְלֻוֶּה בְּדַעַת וּבְכָל תְּבוּנָה
tefillati hi she'ahavatchem tirbeh yoter veyoter uteluvveh beda'at uvechol tevunah
And this I pray, that your love may abound yet more and more in knowledge and all discernment;

הָאֶפְסִים

וְגַם בַּעֲדִי, שֶׁתִּנָּתַנָּה לִי מִלִּים
vegam ba'adi, shettinnatannah li millim
and on my behalf, that utterance may be given unto me in opening my mouth,

וּבְאֹמֶץ לֵב אֶפְתַּח פִּי לְהוֹדִיעַ אֶת סוֹד הַבְּשׂוֹרָה
uve'ometz lev eftach pi lehodia et sod habbesorah
to make known with boldness the mystery of the gospel,

אֲשֶׁר בִּגְלָלָהּ אֲנִי שַׁגְרִיר אָסוּר בִּכְבָלִים, וַאֲדַבֵּר בְּבִטָּחוֹן כְּפִי שֶׁעָלַי לְדַבֵּר
asher biglalah ani shagrir asur bichvalim, va'adabber bevittachon kefi she'alai ledabber
for which I am an ambassador in chains; that in it I may speak boldly, as I ought to speak.

רְצוֹנִי שֶׁתֵּדְעוּ גַּם אַתֶּם מָה הַנְּסִבּוֹת שֶׁאֲנִי נָתוּן בָּהֶן וּמָה אֲנִי עוֹשֶׂה
retzoni shettede'u gam attem mah hannesibbot she'ani natun bahen umah ani oseh
But that ye also may know my affairs, how I do

לָכֵן טִיכִיקוֹס, הָאָח הֶחָבִיב וְהַמְשָׁרֵת הַנֶּאֱמָן בָּאָדוֹן יְסַפֵּר לָכֶם הַכֹּל
lachen tichikos, ha'ach hechaviv vehamsharet hanne'eman ba'adon yesapper lachem hakkol
Tychicus, the beloved brother and faithful minister in the Lord, shall make known to you all things:

שָׁלַחְתִּי אוֹתוֹ אֲלֵיכֶם לְמַטָּרָה זֹאת, כְּדֵי שֶׁתֵּדְעוּ מַה הַמַּצָּב אֶצְלֵנוּ וְהוּא יְעוֹדֵד אֶתְכֶם
shalachti oto aleichem lemattarah zot, kedei shettede'u mah hammatzav etzlenu vehu ye'oded etchem
whom I have sent unto you for this very purpose, that ye may know our state, and that he may comfort your hearts.

שָׁלוֹם לָאַחִים וְאַהֲבָה עִם אֱמוּנָה מֵאֵת אֱלֹהִים הָאָב וְהָאָדוֹן יֵשׁוּעַ הַמָּשִׁיחַ
shalom la'achim ve'ahavah im emunah me'et elohim ha'av veha'adon yeshua hammashiach
Peace be to the brethren, and love with faith, from God the Father and the Lord Jesus Christ.

חֶסֶד עִם כָּל הָאוֹהֲבִים אֶת אֲדוֹנֵנוּ יֵשׁוּעַ הַמָּשִׁיחַ בְּאַהֲבָה בִּלְתִּי דּוֹעֶכֶת
chesed im kol ha'ohavim et adonenu yeshua hammashiach be'ahavah bilti do'echet
Grace be with all them that love our Lord Jesus Christ with a love incorruptible.

הָאֶפְסִים

סוֹף דָּבָר, חִזְקוּ בַּיהוה וּבְכֹחַ גְּבוּרָתוֹ
sof davar, chizku baihvh uvechoach gevurato
Finally, be strong in the Lord, and in the strength of his might.

לִבְשׁוּ אֶת מְלוֹא נֶשֶׁק הָאֱלֹהִים לְמַעַן תּוּכְלוּ לַעֲמֹד נֶגֶד נִכְלֵי הַשָּׂטָן
livshu et melo neshek ha'elohim lema'an tuchelu la'amod neged nichlei hassatan
Put on the whole armor of God, that ye may be able to stand against the wiles of the devil.

כִּי לֹא עִם בָּשָׂר־וָדָם מִלְחָמָה לָנוּ, אֶלָּא עִם רָשֻׁיּוֹת וּשְׂרָרוֹת,
ki lo im basar-vadam milchamah lanu, ella im rashyot userarot
For our wrestling is not against flesh and blood, but against the principalities, against the powers,

עִם מוֹשְׁלֵי חֶשְׁכַת הָעוֹלָם הַזֶּה, עִם כֹּחוֹת רוּחָנִיִּים רָעִים בַּשָּׁמַיִם
im moshelei cheshchat ha'olam hazzeh, im kochot ruchaniyim ra'im bashamayim
against the world-rulers of this darkness, against the spiritual hosts of wickedness in the heavenly places.

עַל כֵּן קְחוּ אֶת מְלוֹא נֶשֶׁק הָאֱלֹהִים
al ken kechu et melo neshek ha'elohim
Wherefore take up the whole armor of God,

לְמַעַן תּוּכְלוּ לְהִתְנַגֵּד בַּיּוֹם הָרָע, וְלַעֲמֹד לְאַחַר עֲשׂוֹתְכֶם אֶת הַכֹּל
lema'an tuchelu lehitnagged bayom hara', vela'amod le'achar asotechem et hakkol
that ye may be able to withstand in the evil day, and, having done all, to stand.

עִמְדוּ כְּשֶׁהָאֱמֶת חֲגוּרָה עַל מָתְנֵיכֶם וְשִׁרְיוֹן הַצֶּדֶק לְבוּשְׁכֶם
imdu keshea'emet chagurah al motneichem veshiryon hatzedek levushchem
Stand therefore, having girded your loins with truth, and having put on the breastplate of righteousness,

וּכְשֶׁרַגְלֵיכֶם נְעוּלוֹת נְכוֹנוּת לִבְשׂוֹרַת הַשָּׁלוֹם
uchesheragleichem ne'ulot nechonut livsorat hashalom
and having shod your feet with the preparation of the gospel of peace;

עִם כָּל אֵלֶּה שְׂאוּ אֶת מָגֵן הָאֱמוּנָה אֲשֶׁר תּוּכְלוּ לְכַבּוֹת בּוֹ אֶת כָּל חִצָּיו הַבּוֹעֲרִים שֶׁל הָרַע
im kol elleh se'u et magen ha'emunah asher tuchelu lechabbot bo et kol chitzav habbo'arim shel hara
withal taking up the shield of faith, wherewith ye shall be able to quench all the fiery darts of the evil one.

וּקְחוּ אֶת כּוֹבַע הַיְשׁוּעָה וְאֶת חֶרֶב הָרוּחַ, שֶׁהִיא דְּבַר הָאֱלֹהִים
ukechu et kova hayshu'ah ve'et cherev haruach, shehi devar ha'elohim
And take the helmet of salvation, and the sword of the Spirit, which is the word of God:

בְּכָל תְּפִלָּה וּתְחִנָּה הִתְפַּלְּלוּ תָּמִיד בָּרוּחַ
bechol tefillah utechinnah hitpallelu tamid beruach
with all prayer and supplication praying at all seasons in the Spirit,

שִׁקְדוּ בִּתְפִלַּתְכֶם וְהַתְמִידוּ בִּתְחִנָּה בְּעַד כָּל הַקְּדוֹשִׁים
shikdu bitfillatchem vehatmidu bitchinnah be'ad kol hakkedoshim
and watching thereunto in all perseverance and supplication for all the saints,

הָאֶפְסִים

כַּבֵּד אֶת־אָבִיךָ וְאֶת־אִמֶּךָ, הִיא הַמִּצְוָה הָרִאשׁוֹנָה אֲשֶׁר הַבְטָחָה בְּצִדָּהּ
kabbed et-'avicha ve'et-'immecha, hi hammitzvah harishonah asher havtachah betziddah
Honor thy father and mother (which is the first commandment with promise),

לְמַעַן יַאֲרִיכֻן יָמֶיךָ וּלְמַעַן יִיטַב לָךְ עַל הָאֲדָמָה
lema'an ya'arichun yameicha ulema'an yitav lach al ha'adamah
that it may be well with thee, and thou mayest live long on the earth.

וְאַתֶּם הָאָבוֹת, אַל תַּכְעִיסוּ אֶת בְּנֵיכֶם, אֶלָּא גַּדְּלוּ אוֹתָם בְּמוּסַר יהוה וּבְתוֹכַחְתּוֹ
ve'attem ha'avot, al tach'isu et beneichem, ella gaddelu otam bemusar hashem uvetochachto
And, ye fathers, provoke not your children to wrath: but nurture them in the chastening and admonition of the Lord.

הָעֲבָדִים, הִשָּׁמְעוּ לַאֲדוֹנֵיכֶם שֶׁבָּעוֹלָם הַזֶּה
ha'avadim, hishame'u la'adoneichem shebba'olam hazzeh
Servants, be obedient unto them that according to the flesh are your masters,

בְּיִרְאָה וּבִרְתֵת וּבְתֹם לֵב, כְּמוֹ לַמָּשִׁיחַ
beyir'ah uvirtet uvetom lev, kemo lammashiach
with fear and trembling, in singleness of your heart, as unto Christ;

לֹא בְשֵׁרוּת לְמַרְאִית עַיִן, כִּמְבַקְשִׁים לִמְצֹא חֵן בְּעֵינֵי בְּנֵי אָדָם
lo besherut lemar'it ayin, kimvakshim limtzo chen be'einei benei adam
not in the way of eyeservice, as men-pleasers;

אֶלָּא כְּעַבְדֵי הַמָּשִׁיחַ הָעוֹשִׂים אֶת רְצוֹן אֱלֹהִים בְּכָל נַפְשָׁם
ella ke'avdei hammashiach ha'osim et retzon elohim bechol nafsham
but as servants of Christ, doing the will of God from the heart;

וּמְשָׁרְתִים בְּחֵפֶץ לֵב כַּעֲבָדִים לָאָדוֹן וְלֹא לִבְנֵי אָדָם
umesharetim bechefetz lev ka'avadim la'adon velo livnei adam
with good will doing service, as unto the Lord, and not unto men:

וְיוֹדְעִים שֶׁכָּל טוֹב אֲשֶׁר יַעֲשֶׂה אָדָם
veyode'im shekkol tov asher ya'aseh adam
knowing that whatsoever good thing each one doeth,

אֶת זֶה יְקַבֵּל מֵאֵת יהוה, אִם עֶבֶד הוּא וְאִם בֶּן חוֹרִין
et zeh yekabbel me'et hashem, im eved hu ve'im ben chorin
the same shall he receive again from the Lord, whether he be bond or free.

וְאַתֶּם הָאֲדוֹנִים, בְּאוֹתוֹ אֹפֶן הִתְנַהֲגוּ עִמָּהֶם. חִדְלוּ לְאַיֵּם עֲלֵיהֶם
ve'attem ha'adonim, be'oto ofen hitnahagu immahem. chidlu le'ayem aleihem
And, ye masters, do the same things unto them, and forbear threatening:

שֶׁכֵּן יוֹדְעִים אַתֶּם כִּי גַּם לָהֶם וְגַם לָכֶם הָאָדוֹן בַּשָּׁמַיִם, וְאֵין עִמּוֹ מַשּׂוֹא פָּנִים
shekken yode'im attem ki gam lahem vegam lachem ha'adon bashamayim, ve'ein immo masso panim
knowing that he who is both their Master and yours is in heaven, and there is no respect of persons with him.

הָאֶפְסִים

לְמַעַן יַעֲמִיד לְפָנָיו אֶת הַקְּהִלָּה כְּשֶׁהִיא מְפֹאֶרֶת בְּכָבוֹד
lema'an ya'amid lefanav et hakkehillah keshehi mefo'eret bechavod
that he might present the church to himself a glorious church,

לְלֹא כֶתֶם וְקֶמֶט וְכַדּוֹמֶה, לְמַעַן תִּהְיֶה קְדוֹשָׁה וּלְלֹא דֹפִי
lelo ketem vekemet vechaddomeh, lema'an tihyeh kedoshah ulelo dofi
not having spot or wrinkle or any such thing; but that it should be holy and without blemish.

כֵּן חַיָּבִים גַּם הָאֲנָשִׁים לֶאֱהֹב אֶת נְשֵׁיהֶם כְּאַהֲבָתָם אֶת גּוּפָם הֵם. הָאוֹהֵב אֶת אִשְׁתּוֹ אוֹהֵב אֶת עַצְמוֹ
ken chayavim gam ha'anashim le'ehov et nesheihem ke'ahavatam et gufam hem. ha'ohev et ishto ohev et atzmo
Even so ought husbands also to love their own wives as their own bodies. He that loveth his own wife loveth himself:

הֵן מֵעוֹלָם לֹא שָׂנֵא אִישׁ אֶת בְּשָׂרוֹ, אֶלָּא הוּא מְכַלְכֵּל וּמְטַפֵּחַ אוֹתוֹ כְּדֶרֶךְ
hen me'olam lo sanei ish et besaro, ella hu mechalkel umetappeach oto kederech
for no man ever hated his own flesh; but nourisheth and cherisheth it,

שֶׁגַּם הַמָּשִׁיחַ נוֹהֵג בַּקְּהִלָּה
sheggam hammashiach noheg bakkehillah
even as Christ also the church;

שֶׁהֲרֵי אֵיבְרֵי גוּפוֹ אֲנַחְנוּ
sheharei eiverei gufo anachnu
because we are members of his body.

עַל־כֵּן יַעֲזָב־אִישׁ אֶת־אָבִיו וְאֶת־אִמּוֹ וְדָבַק בְּאִשְׁתּוֹ, וְהָיוּ לְבָשָׂר אֶחָד
al-ken ya'azov-'ish et-'aviv ve'et-'immo vedavak be'ishto, vehayu levasar echad
For this cause shall a man leave his father and mother, and shall cleave to his wife; and the two shall become one flesh.

גָּדוֹל הַסּוֹד הַזֶּה, וַאֲנִי מִתְכַּוֵּן לַמָּשִׁיחַ וְלַקְּהִלָּה
gadol hassod hazzeh, va'ani mitkavven lammashiach velakkehillah
This mystery is great: but I speak in regard of Christ and of the church.

אֲבָל גַּם אַתֶּם, אִישׁ אִישׁ יֹאהַב אֶת אִשְׁתּוֹ כְּאַהֲבָתוֹ אֶת עַצְמוֹ
aval gam attem, ish ish yohav et ishto ke'ahavato et atzmo;
Nevertheless do ye also severally love each one his own wife even as himself;

וְהָאִשָּׁה תִּירָא אֶת בַּעֲלָהּ
veha'ishah tira et ba'alah
and let the wife see that she fear her husband.

I

הַבָּנִים, שִׁמְעוּ בְּקוֹל הוֹרֵיכֶם עַל־פִּי הָאָדוֹן, כִּי כָּךְ רָאוּי
habbanim, shim'u bekol horeichem al-pi ha'adon, ki kach ra'ui
Children, obey your parents in the Lord: for this is right.

הָאֶפְסִים

הַמְנַצְּלִים כָּל הִזְדַּמְּנוּת, שֶׁכֵּן הַיָּמִים רָעִים
hamnatzelim kol hizdammenut, shekken hayamim ra'im
redeeming the time, because the days are evil.

לָכֵן אַל תִּהְיוּ חַסְרֵי דַעַת, אֶלָּא הָבִינוּ לָדַעַת מַה רְצוֹנוֹ שֶׁל הָאָדוֹן
lachen al tihyu chasrei da'at, ella havinu lada'at mah retzono shel ha'adon
Wherefore be ye not foolish, but understand what the will of the Lord is.

אַל תִּשְׁתַּכְּרוּ מִיַּיִן, שֶׁכֵּן זֶה מֵבִיא לִידֵי פְּרִיצוּת, אֶלָּא הִמָּלְאוּ בְּרוּחַ
al tishtakkeru miyayin, shekken zeh mevi lidei peritzut, ella himmale'u beruach
And be not drunken with wine, wherein is riot, but be filled with the Spirit;

וְהַשְׁמִיעוּ בֵּינֵיכֶם תְּהִלּוֹת וְתִשְׁבָּחוֹת וְשִׁירוֹת רוּחָנִיּוֹת.
vehashmi'u beineichem tehillot vetishbachot veshirot ruchaniyot.
speaking one to another in psalms and hymns and spiritual songs,

שִׁירוּ וְזַמְּרוּ לַאדֹנָי בִּלְבַבְכֶם
shiru vezammeru la'adonai bilvavchem
singing and making melody with your heart to the Lord;

וּבְכָל עֵת הוֹדוּ עַל הַכֹּל לֵאלֹהִים אָבִינוּ בְּשֵׁם אֲדוֹנֵנוּ יֵשׁוּעַ הַמָּשִׁיחַ
uvechol et hodu al hakkol lelohim avinu beshem adonenu yeshua hammashiach
giving thanks always for all things in the name of our Lord Jesus Christ to God, even the Father;

הִכָּנְעוּ אִישׁ לְרֵעֵהוּ מִתּוֹךְ יִרְאַת הַמָּשִׁיחַ
hikkane'u ish lere'ehu mittoch yir'at hammashiach
subjecting yourselves one to another in the fear of Christ.

הַנָּשִׁים, הִכָּנַעְנָה לְבַעֲלֵיכֶן כְּמוֹ לַאֲדוֹנֵנוּ
hannashim, hikkana'nah leva'aleichen kemo la'adonenu
Wives, be in subjection unto your own husbands, as unto the Lord.

כִּי הָאִישׁ הוּא רֹאשׁ הָאִשָּׁה כְּפִי שֶׁהַמָּשִׁיחַ הוּא רֹאשׁ הַקְּהִלָּה - הַמּוֹשִׁיעַ שֶׁל הַגּוּף
ki ha'ish hu rosh ha'ishah kefi shehammashiach hu rosh hakkehillah - hammoshia shel hagguf
For the husband is the head of the wife, as Christ also is the head of the church, being himself the saviour of the body.

וּכְשֵׁם שֶׁהַקְּהִלָּה נִכְנַעַת לַמָּשִׁיחַ, כֵּן גַּם הַנָּשִׁים תִּכָּנַעְנָה לְבַעֲלֵיהֶן בְּכָל דָּבָר
uchshem shehakkehillah nichna'at lammashiach, ken gam hannashim tikkana'nah leva'aleihen bechol davar
But as the church is subject to Christ, so let the wives also be to their husbands in everything.

הָאֲנָשִׁים, אֶהֱבוּ אֶת נְשֵׁיכֶם כְּשֵׁם שֶׁגַּם הַמָּשִׁיחַ אָהַב אֶת הַקְּהִלָּה וּמָסַר אֶת עַצְמוֹ בַּעֲדָהּ
ha'anashim, ehevu et nesheichem keshem sheggam hammashiach ahav et hakkehillah umasar et atzmo ba'adah
Husbands, love your wives, even as Christ also loved the church, and gave himself up for it;

כְּדֵי לְקַדְּשָׁהּ וּלְטַהֲרָהּ עַל־יְדֵי רְחִיצַת מַיִם, בְּהַצְהָרָה
kedei lekaddeshah uletaharah al-yedei rechitzat mayim, behatzharah
that he might sanctify it, having cleansed it by the washing of water with the word,

הָאֶפְסִים

אֵין לוֹ נַחֲלָה בְּמַלְכוּת הַמָּשִׁיחַ וְהָאֱלֹהִים
ein lo nachalah bemalchut hammashiach veha'elohim
hath any inheritance in the kingdom of Christ and God.

אַל יַתְעֶה אֶתְכֶם אִישׁ בְּדִבּוּרֵי הֶבֶל
al yat'eh etchem ish bedibburei hevel
Let no man deceive you with empty words:

בִּגְלַל הַדְּבָרִים הַלָּלוּ בָּא זַעַם אֱלֹהִים עַל בְּנֵי הַמֶּרִי
biglal haddevarim hallalu ba za'am elohim al benei hammeri
for because of these things cometh the wrath of God upon the sons of disobedience.

עַל כֵּן אַל תִּהְיוּ שֻׁתָּפִים לָהֶם
al ken al tihyu shuttafim lahem
Be not ye therefore partakers with them;

בֶּעָבָר הֱיִיתֶם חֹשֶׁךְ, אַךְ עַכְשָׁו אוֹר אַתֶּם בָּאָדוֹן. הִתְנַהֲגוּ נָא כִּבְנֵי הָאוֹר
be'avar heyitem choshech, ach achshav or attem ba'adon. hitnahagu na kivnei ha'or
For ye were once darkness, but are now light in the Lord: walk as children of light

כִּי פְּרִי הָאוֹר הוּא כָּל טוּב וְכָל צְדָקָה וֶאֱמֶת
ki peri ha'or hu kol tuv vechol tzedakah ve'emet
(for the fruit of the light is in all goodness and righteousness and truth),

בַּחֲנוּ וְהִוָּכְחוּ מַה רָצוּי בְּעֵינֵי הָאָדוֹן
bachanu vehivvachechu mah ratzui be'einei ha'adon
proving what is well-pleasing unto the Lord;

אַל תִּשְׁתַּתְּפוּ בְּמַעֲשֵׂי הַחֹשֶׁךְ, אֲשֶׁר עֲקָרִים הֵם כֻּלָּם, אֶלָּא הוֹכֵחַ תּוֹכִיחוּ אֶת עוֹשֵׂיהֶם
al tishtattfu bema'asei hachoshech, asher akarim hem kullam, ella hocheach tochichu et oseihem
and have no fellowship with the unfruitful works of darkness, but rather even reprove them;

הֲרֵי מַה שֶּׁהֵם עוֹשִׂים בַּסֵּתֶר, חֶרְפָּה אֲפִלּוּ לְבַטֵּא בְּמִלִּים
harei mah shehem osim basseter, cherpah afillu levattei bemillim
for the things which are done by them in secret it is a shame even to speak of.

אֲבָל כָּל מַה שֶּׁמּוּכָח עַל־יְדֵי הָאוֹר נִרְאֶה בְּבֵרוּר, שֶׁהֲרֵי כָּל מַה שֶּׁנִּרְאֶה בְּבֵרוּר הוּא אוֹר
aval kol mah shemmuchach al-yedei ha'or nir'eh beverur, sheharei kol mah shennir'eh beverur hu or
But all things when they are reproved are made manifest by the light: for everything that is made manifest is light.

עַל כֵּן נֶאֱמַר: עוּרָה הַיָּשֵׁן וְקוּמָה מִן הַמֵּתִים, וְיָאִיר לְךָ הַמָּשִׁיחַ
al ken ne'emar. urah hayashen vekumah min hammetim, veya'ir lecha hammashiach
Wherefore he saith, Awake, thou that sleepest, and arise from the dead, and Christ shall shine upon thee.

וְעַתָּה שִׂימוּ לִבְּכֶם לְהִתְהַלֵּךְ בִּזְהִירוּת - לֹא כִּכְסִילִים, אֶלָּא כַּחֲכָמִים
ve'attah simu libbchem lehit'hallech bizhirut - lo kichsilim, ella kachachamim
Look therefore carefully how ye walk, not as unwise, but as wise;

הָאֶפֶסִים

אַל יֵצֵא מִפִּיכֶם כָּל דְּבַר נִבּוּל
al yetzei mippichem kol devar nibbul
Let no corrupt speech proceed out of your mouth,

אֶלָּא דָּבָר שֶׁהוּא טוֹב בְּעִתּוֹ וְיֵשׁ בּוֹ כְּדֵי לִבְנוֹת, לְמַעַן יַשְׁפִּיעַ נֹעַם עַל הַשּׁוֹמְעִים
ella davar shehu tov be'itto veyesh bo kedei livnot, lema'an yashpia no'am al hashome'im
but such as is good for edifying as the need may be, that it may give grace to them that hear.

וְאַל תַּעֲצִיבוּ אֶת רוּחַ הַקֹּדֶשׁ אֲשֶׁר נֶחְתַּמְתֶּם בָּהּ לְיוֹם הַגְּאֻלָּה
ve'al ta'atzivu et ruach hakkodesh asher nechtamtem bah leyom hagge'ullah
And grieve not the Holy Spirit of God, in whom ye were sealed unto the day of redemption.

הָסִירוּ מִכֶּם כָּל מְרִירוּת וְחֵמָה וְכַעַס וּצְעָקָה וְגִדּוּף וְכָל רִשְׁעָה
hasiru mikkem kol merirut vechemah vecha'as utze'akah vegidduf vechol rish'ah
Let all bitterness, and wrath, and anger, and clamor, and railing, be put away from you, with all malice:

הֱיוּ טוֹבִים אִישׁ לְרֵעֵהוּ; הֱיוּ מְלֵאֵי רַחֲמִים וְסִלְחוּ אִישׁ לְרֵעֵהוּ כְּשֵׁם שֶׁאֱלֹהִים סָלַח לָכֶם בַּמָּשִׁיחַ
heyu tovim ish lere'ehu; heyu mele'ei rachamim vesilchu ish lere'ehu keshem she'elohim salach lachem bammashiach
and be ye kind one to another, tenderhearted, forgiving each other, even as God also in Christ forgave you.

ה

וּבְכֵן לְכוּ בְּדַרְכֵי אֱלֹהִים כְּבָנִים אֲהוּבִים
uvechen lechu bedarchei elohim kevanim ahuvim
Be ye therefore imitators of God, as beloved children;

וְהִתְהַלְּכוּ בְּאַהֲבָה כְּשֵׁם שֶׁגַּם הַמָּשִׁיחַ אָהַב אוֹתָנוּ וּמָסַר אֶת עַצְמוֹ בַּעֲדֵנוּ
vehit'hallechu be'ahavah keshem sheggam hammashiach ahav otanu umasar et atzmo ba'adenu
and walk in love, even as Christ also loved you, and gave himself up for us,

כְּמִנְחָה וְקָרְבָּן לֵאלֹהִים, לְרֵיחַ נִיחוֹחַ
keminchah vekorban le'elohim, lereiach nichoach
an offering and a sacrifice to God for an odor of a sweet smell.

וְכָיָאֶה לַקְּדוֹשִׁים, אַף לֹא תַעֲלוּ עַל דַּל שִׂפְתֵיכֶם מַעֲשֵׂי זְנוּת וְכָל טֻמְאָה אוֹ תַּאַוְתָנוּת
vechaya'eh lakkedoshim, af lo ta'alu al dal sifteichem ma'asei znut vechol tum'ah o ta'avtanut
But fornication, and all uncleanness, or covetousness, let it not even be named among you, as becometh saints;

גַּם לֹא נִבּוּל פֶּה וְשִׂיחַת סְכָלוּת אוֹ הִתְלוֹצְצוּת, דְּבָרִים שֶׁאֵינָם יָאִים, אֶלָּא קוֹל תּוֹדָה
gam lo nibbul peh vesichat sichlut o hitlotzetzut, devarim she'einam ya'im, ella kol todah
nor filthiness, nor foolish talking, or jesting, which are not befitting: but rather giving of thanks.

זֹאת עֲלֵיכֶם לָדַעַת: כָּל זוֹנֶה אוֹ טָמֵא אוֹ בַּעַל תַּאֲווֹת, שֶׁאֵינוֹ אֶלָּא עוֹבֵד אֱלִילִים,
zot aleichem lada'at: kol zoneh o tamei o ba'al ta'avot, she'eino ella oved elilim
For this ye know of a surety, that no fornicator, nor unclean person, nor covetous man, who is an idolater,

הָאֶפְסִים

וְכֵיוָן שֶׁהִתְנַוְּנוּ הִתְמַכְּרוּ בְּתַאֲוָה לְזִמָּה וּלְכָל מַעֲשֵׂה טֻמְאָה
vecheivan shehitnavvenu hitmakkeru beta'avah lezimmah ulechal ma'aseh tum'ah
who being past feeling gave themselves up to lasciviousness, to work all uncleanness with greediness.

אֲבָל אַתֶּם לֹא בְדֶרֶךְ זֹאת לְמַדְתֶּם אֶת הַמָּשִׁיחַ
aval attem lo bederech zot lemadtem et hammashiach
But ye did not so learn Christ;

אִם אָמְנָם שְׁמַעְתֶּם אוֹתוֹ וְלֻמַּדְתֶּם בּוֹ אֶת הָאֱמֶת כְּפִי שֶׁהִיא בְּיֵשׁוּעַ
im omnam shema'tem oto velummadtem bo et ha'emet kefi shehi beyeshua
if so be that ye heard him, and were taught in him, even as truth is in Jesus:

שֶׁעֲלֵיכֶם לִפְשֹׁט אֶת הָאָדָם הַיָּשָׁן אֲשֶׁר הִתְנַהֲגוּתְכֶם הָרִאשׁוֹנָה כְּרוּכָה עִמּוֹ
she'aleichem lifshot et ha'adam hayashan asher hitnahagutechem harishonah keruchah immo
that ye put away, as concerning your former manner of life, the old man,

וְהוּא נִשְׁחָת בְּתַאֲווֹת מַתְעוֹת
vehu nishchat beta'avot mat'ot
that waxeth corrupt after the lusts of deceit;

וּלְהִתְחַדֵּשׁ הִתְחַדְּשׁוּת רוּחָנִית בְּשִׂכְלְכֶם
ulehitchaddesh hitchaddeshut ruchanit besichlechem
and that ye be renewed in the spirit of your mind,

וְלִלְבֹּשׁ אֶת הָאָדָם הֶחָדָשׁ הַנִּבְרָא כִּדְמוּת אֱלֹהִים בִּצְדָקָה וּקְדֻשָּׁה שֶׁל אֱמֶת
velilbosh et ha'adam hechadash hannivra kidmut elohim bitzdakah ukedushah shel emet
and put on the new man, that after God hath been created in righteousness and holiness of truth.

עַל כֵּן הָסִירוּ אֶת הַשֶּׁקֶר וְדַבְּרוּ אֱמֶת אִישׁ לְרֵעֵהוּ, כִּי אֵיבָרִים אֲנַחְנוּ אִישׁ לְרֵעֵהוּ
al ken hasiru et hasheker vedabberu emet ish lere'ehu, ki eivarim anachnu ish lere'ehu
Wherefore, putting away falsehood, speak ye truth each one with his neighbor: for we are members one of another.

רִגְזוּ וְאַל־תֶּחֱטָאוּ; אַל תִּשְׁקַע הַשֶּׁמֶשׁ עַל כַּעַסְכֶם
rigzu ve'al-techeta'u; al tishka hashemesh al ka'aschem
Be ye angry, and sin not: let not the sun go down upon your wrath:

וְאַל תִּתְּנוּ מָקוֹם לַשָּׂטָן
ve'al tittenu makom lassatan
neither give place to the devil.

הַגּוֹנֵב אַל יוֹסִיף לִגְנֹב, כִּי אִם יַעֲמֹל וּבְיָדָיו יַעֲשֶׂה אֶת הַטּוֹב
haggonev al yosif lignov, ki im ya'amol uveyadav ya'aseh et hattov
Let him that stole steal no more: but rather let him labor, working with his hands the thing that is good,

כְּדֵי שֶׁיּוּכַל לָתֵת לְמִי שֶׁשָּׁרוּי בְּמַחְסוֹר
kedei sheyuchal latet lemi shesharui bemachsor
that he may have whereof to give to him that hath need.

הָאֶפְסִים

כְּדֵי לְהַכְשִׁיר אֶת הַקְּדוֹשִׁים לַעֲבוֹדַת הַשָּׁרוּת, לִבְנִיַּת גּוּף הַמָּשִׁיחַ
kedei lehachshir et hakkedoshim la'avodat hasherut, livniyat guf hammashiach
for the perfecting of the saints, unto the work of ministering, unto the building up of the body of Christ:

עַד כִּי נַגִּיעַ כֻּלָּנוּ אֶל אַחְדוּת הָאֱמוּנָה וְאַחְדוּת יְדִיעַת בֶּן־הָאֱלֹהִים
ad ki naggia kullanu el achdut ha'emunah ve'achdut yedi'at ben-ha'elohim
till we all attain unto the unity of the faith, and of the knowledge of the Son of God,

אֶל הָאָדָם הַשָּׁלֵם, אֶל שִׁעוּר קוֹמָתוֹ הַמָּלֵא שֶׁל הַמָּשִׁיחַ
el ha'adam hashalem, el shi'ur komato hammalei shel hammashiach
unto a fullgrown man, unto the measure of the stature of the fulness of Christ:

וְכָךְ לֹא נִהְיֶה עוֹד יְלָדִים נִדָּפִים וּמְטֻלְטָלִים בְּרוּחַ שֶׁל כָּל תּוֹרָה הַמּוּפֶצֶת
vechach lo nihyeh od yeladim niddafim umittaltelim beruach shel kol torah hammufetzet
that we may be no longer children, tossed to and fro and carried about with every wind of doctrine,

עַל־יְדֵי בְּנֵי אָדָם בְּעָרְמָה וּבְתַרְמִית כְּדֵי לְהַטְעוֹת
al-yedei benei adam be'ormah uvetarmit kedei lehat'ot
by the sleight of men, in craftiness, after the wiles of error;

אֶלָּא נְדַבֵּר אֶת הָאֱמֶת בְּאַהֲבָה וְנִגְדַּל בְּכָל דָּבָר אֱלֵי הַמָּשִׁיחַ, אֲשֶׁר הוּא הָרֹאשׁ
ella nedabber et ha'emet be'ahavah venigdal bechol davar elei hammashiach, asher hu harosh
but speaking truth in love, may grow up in all things into him, who is the head, even Christ;

וְעַל־יָדָיו כָּל הַגּוּף מֻרְכָּב וּמִתְחַבֵּר בְּאֶמְצָעוּת כָּל קֶשֶׁר מְסַיֵּעַ
ve'al-yadav kol hagguf marekav umitchabber be'emtza'ut kol kesher mesayea
from whom all the body fitly framed and knit together through that which every joint supplieth,

בְּהֶתְאֵם לַפְּעֻלָּה הַמְיֻעֶדֶת לְכָל אֵיבָר וְאֵיבָר
behet'em lappe'ullah hamyu'edet lechol eivar ve'eivar
according to the working in due measure of each several part,

כְּדֵי שֶׁיִּגְדַּל הַגּוּף וְיִבָּנֶה בְּאַהֲבָה
kedei sheyigdal hagguf veyibbaneh be'ahavah
maketh the increase of the body unto the building up of itself in love.

הִנֵּה זֹאת אֲנִי אוֹמֵר וּמַכְרִיז מִטַּעַם הָאָדוֹן: אַל תֵּלְכוּ עוֹד כַּגּוֹיִם הַהוֹלְכִים בְּהַבְלֵי שִׂכְלָם
hinneh zot ani omer umachriz mitta'am ha'adon: al telechu od kaggoyim haholechim behavlei sichlam
This I say therefore, and testify in the Lord, that ye no longer walk as the Gentiles also walk, in the vanity of their mind,

חֲשׁוּכֵי דַעַת הֵם, זָרִים לְחַיֵּי אֱלֹהִים
chasuchei da'at hem, zarim lechayei elohim
being darkened in their understanding, alienated from the life of God,

בִּגְלַל בַּעֲרוּתָם וּקְשִׁי לִבָּם
biglal ba'arutam ukeshi libbam
because of the ignorance that is in them, because of the hardening of their heart;

הָאֶפְסִים

ד

לְפִיכָךְ אֲנִי, הָאָסִיר לְמַעַן הָאָדוֹן, מַפְצִיר בָּכֶם לְהִתְנַהֵג כַּיָּאֶה לַיִּעוּד שֶׁנִּקְרֵאתֶם אֵלָיו
lefichach ani, ha'asir lema'an ha'adon, maftzir bachem lehitnaheg kaya'eh layi'ud shennikretem elav
I therefore, the prisoner in the Lord, beseech you to walk worthily of the calling wherewith ye were called,

הִתְנַהֲגוּ בְּכָל עֲנָוָה וּנְמִיכוּת רוּחַ, וּבְאֶרֶךְ אַפַּיִם. סִבְלוּ אִישׁ אֶת רֵעֵהוּ בְּאַהֲבָה
hitnahagu bechol anavah unemichut ruach, uve'orech appayim. sivlu ish et re'ehu be'ahavah
with all lowliness and meekness, with longsuffering, forbearing one another in love;

שִׁקְדוּ לִשְׁמֹר אֶת אַחְדוּת הָרוּחַ בְּקֶשֶׁר שֶׁל שָׁלוֹם
shikdu lishmor et achdut haruach bekesher shel shalom
giving diligence to keep the unity of the Spirit in the bond of peace.

הִנֵּה: גּוּף אֶחָד וְרוּחַ אַחַת, כְּשֵׁם שֶׁגַּם אַתֶּם נִקְרֵאתֶם אֶל תִּקְוַת יִעוּדְכֶם הָאַחַת
Hinneh: guf echad veruach achat, keshem sheggam attem nikretem el tikvat yi'udechem ha'achat
There is one body, and one Spirit, even as also ye were called in one hope of your calling;

אָדוֹן אֶחָד, אֱמוּנָה אַחַת, טְבִילָה אַחַת
adon echad, emunah achat, tevilah achat
one Lord, one faith, one baptism,

אֵל וְאָב אֶחָד לַכֹּל, הוּא אֲשֶׁר מֵעַל כֹּל, פּוֹעֵל בַּכֹּל, וּבְתוֹךְ הַכֹּל
el ve'av echad lakkol, hu asher me'al kol, po'el bakkol, uvetoch hakkol
one God and Father of all, who is over all, and through all, and in all.

אֲבָל לְכָל אֶחָד וְאֶחָד מֵאִתָּנוּ הֻעֲנַק הַחֶסֶד כְּפִי הַמִּדָּה שֶׁהֶעֱנִיק לוֹ הַמָּשִׁיחַ
aval lechol echad ve'echad me'ittanu ho'onak chesed kefi hammiddah shehe'enik lo hammashiach
But unto each one of us was the grace given according to the measure of the gift of Christ.

לָכֵן נֶאֱמַר: עָלָה לַמָּרוֹם, שָׁבָה שֶׁבִי, וַיִּתֵּן מַתָּנוֹת לִבְנֵי אָדָם
lachen ne'emar: alah lammarom, shavah shevi, vayitten mattanot livnei adam
Wherefore he saith, When he ascended on high, he led captivity captive, And gave gifts unto men.

עָלָה מַה פֵּרוּשָׁהּ אִם לֹא שֶׁגַּם הִקְדִּים וְיָרַד אֶל תַּחְתִּיּוֹת אֶרֶץ
alah mah perushah im lo sheggam hikdim veyarad el tachtiyot aretz
(Now this, He ascended, what is it but that he also descended into the lower parts of the earth?

הַיּוֹרֵד הוּא אֲשֶׁר גַּם עָלָה אֶל מֵעַל כָּל הַשָּׁמַיִם, לְמַעַן יְמַלֵּא אֶת הַכֹּל
hayored hu asher gam alah el me'al kol hashamayim, lema'an yemallei et hakkol
He that descended is the same also that ascended far above all the heavens, that he might fill all things.)

וְהוּא נָתַן אֶת אֵלֶּה לִהְיוֹת שְׁלִיחִים, אֶת אֵלֶּה נְבִיאִים, אֶת אֵלֶּה מְבַשְּׂרִים, וְאֶת אֵלֶּה רוֹעִים וּמוֹרִים
vehu natan et elleh lihyot shelichim, et elleh nevi'im, et elleh mevassrim, ve'et elleh ro'im umorim
And he gave some to be apostles; and some, prophets; and some, evangelists; and some, pastors and teachers;

הָאֶפֶסִים

אֲשֶׁר בּוֹ לָנוּ עֹז וְגִישָׁה בְּטוּחָה עַל־יְדֵי אֱמוּנָתוֹ
asher bo lanu oz vegishah betuchah al-yedei emunato
in whom we have boldness and access in confidence through our faith in him.

לָכֵן אֲנִי מְבַקֵּשׁ שֶׁלֹּא תִּפֹּל רוּחֲכֶם בִּגְלַל צָרוֹתַי הַבָּאוֹת עָלַי לְמַעַנְכֶם, אֲשֶׁר לְכָבוֹד הֵן לָכֶם
lachen ani mevakkesh shello tippol ruchachem biglal tzarotai habba'ot alai lema'anchem, asher lechavod hen lachem
Wherefore I ask that ye may not faint at my tribulations for you, which are your glory.

מִשּׁוּם כָּךְ כּוֹרֵעַ אֲנִי עַל בִּרְכַּי לִפְנֵי הָאָב
mishum kach korea ani al birkai lifnei ha'av
For this cause I bow my knees unto the Father,

אֲשֶׁר קָרָא שֵׁם לְכָל מִשְׁפָּחָה בַּשָּׁמַיִם וּבָאָרֶץ
asher kara shem lechol mishpachah bashamayim uva'aretz
from whom every family in heaven and on earth is named,

שֶׁיִּתֵּן לָכֶם כֹּחַ, כְּפִי עֹשֶׁר כְּבוֹדוֹ
sheyitten lachem koach, kefi osher kevodo
that he would grant you, according to the riches of his glory,

לְהִתְחַזֵּק עַל־יְדֵי רוּחוֹ בָּאָדָם הַפְּנִימִי שֶׁלָּכֶם
lehitchazzek al-yedei rucho ba'adam happenimi shellachem
that ye may be strengthened with power through his Spirit in the inward man;

כְּדֵי שֶׁיִּשְׁכֹּן הַמָּשִׁיחַ בִּלְבַבְכֶם עַל־יְדֵי הָאֱמוּנָה וְתִהְיוּ מֻשְׁרָשִׁים וּמְיֻסָּדִים בְּאַהֲבָה
kedei sheyishkon hammashiach bilvavchem al-yedei ha'emunah vetihyu mushrashim umeyussadim be'ahavah
that Christ may dwell in your hearts through faith; to the end that ye, being rooted and grounded in love,

כָּךְ תּוּכְלוּ לְהָבִין יַחַד עִם כָּל הַקְּדוֹשִׁים מַה הָרֹחַב וְהָאֹרֶךְ וְהַגֹּבַהּ וְהָעֹמֶק
kach tuchelu lehavin yachad im kol hakkedoshim mah harochav veha'orech vehaggovah veha'omek
may be strong to apprehend with all the saints what is the breadth and length and height and depth,

וְלָדַעַת אֶת אַהֲבַת הַמָּשִׁיחַ הַנִּשְׂגָּבָה מִדַּעַת, לְמַעַן תִּמָּלְאוּ בְּכָל מְלוֹא הָאֱלֹהִים
velada'at et ahavat hammashiach hannisgavah midda'at, lema'an timmale'u bechol melo ha'elohim
and to know the love of Christ which passeth knowledge, that ye may be filled unto all the fulness of God.

וְלוֹ אֲשֶׁר יָכוֹל לַעֲשׂוֹת יוֹתֵר מִכָּל מַה שֶׁאָנוּ מְבַקְשִׁים אוֹ מִמַּה שֶׁעוֹלֶה עַל דַּעְתֵּנוּ
velo asher yachol la'asot yoter mikkol mah she'anu mevakshim o mimmah she'oleh al da'tenu
Now unto him that is able to do exceeding abundantly above all that we ask or think,

כְּפִי כֹּחוֹ הַפּוֹעֵל בָּנוּ
kefi kocho happo'el banu
according to the power that worketh in us,

לוֹ הַכָּבוֹד בַּקְּהִלָּה וּבַמָּשִׁיחַ יֵשׁוּעַ, בְּכָל הַדּוֹרוֹת לְעוֹלָם וָעֶד. אָמֵן
lo hakkavod bakkehillah uvammashiach yeshua, bechol haddorot le'olam va'ed. amen
unto him be the glory in the church and in Christ Jesus unto all generations for ever and ever. Amen.

הָאֶפֶסִים

הַסּוֹד אֲשֶׁר בַּדּוֹרוֹת הַקּוֹדְמִים לֹא נוֹדַע לִבְנֵי אָדָם
hassod asher baddorot hakkodemim lo noda livnei adam
which in other generations was not made known unto the sons of men,

כְּמוֹ שֶׁנִּגְלָה כָּעֵת לִשְׁלִיחָיו וְלִנְבִיאָיו הַקְּדוֹשִׁים, בְּדֶרֶךְ הָרוּחַ
kemo shenniglah ka'et lishlichav velinvi'av hakkedoshim, bederech haruach
as it hath now been revealed unto his holy apostles and prophets in the Spirit;

שֶׁיִּהְיוּ הַגּוֹיִם שֻׁתָּפֵי נַחֲלָה, שֻׁתָּפֵי גוּף
sheyihyu haggoyim shuttafei nachalah, shuttafei guf
to wit, that the Gentiles are fellow-heirs, and fellow-members of the body,

וְשֻׁתָּפֵי הַהַבְטָחָה בַּמָּשִׁיחַ יֵשׁוּעַ עַל־יְדֵי הַבְּשׂוֹרָה
veshuttafei hahavtachah bammashiach yeshua al-yedei habbesorah
and fellow-partakers of the promise in Christ Jesus through the gospel,

וְלַבְּשׂוֹרָה זֹאת הָיִיתִי לִמְשָׁרֵת
velivsorah zot hayiti limsharet
whereof I was made a minister,

מִתֹּקֶף מַתְּנַת הַחֶסֶד שֶׁאֱלֹהִים נָתַן לִי כְּפִי פְּעֻלַּת כֹּחוֹ
mittokef mattenat hachesed she'elohim natan li kefi pe'ullat kocho
according to the gift of that grace of God which was given me according to the working of his power.

לִי, הַקָּטָן מִכָּל הַקְּדוֹשִׁים
li, hakkatan mikkol hakkedoshim
Unto me, who am less than the least of all saints,

נִתַּן הַחֶסֶד הַזֶּה לְבַשֵּׂר לַגּוֹיִם אֶת עֹשֶׁר הַמָּשִׁיחַ, הֶעָצוּם לְאֵין חֵקֶר
natan hachesed hazzeh levashor laggoyim et osher hammashiach, he'atzum le'ein cheker
was this grace given, to preach unto the Gentiles the unsearchable riches of Christ;

וּלְהָאִיר עֵינֵי כֹל לָדַעַת מַהִי תָּכְנִית הַסּוֹד
uleha'ir einei kol lada'at mahi tachenit hassod
and to make all men see what is the dispensation of the mystery

אֲשֶׁר הָיָה צָפוּן מֵעוֹלָמִים בֵּאלֹהִים בּוֹרֵא הַכֹּל
asher hayah tzafun me'olamim be'elohim borei hakkol
which for ages hath been hid in God who created all things;

וְכָךְ בְּאֶמְצָעוּת הַקְּהִלָּה תִּוָּדַע עַתָּה לָרָשֻׁיּוֹת וְלַמֶּמְשָׁלוֹת שֶׁבַּשָּׁמַיִם חָכְמַת אֱלֹהִים הָעֲתִירָה
vechach be'emtza'ut hakkehillah tivvada attah larashyot velammemshalot shebbashamayim chachemat elohim ha'atirah
to the intent that now unto the principalities and the powers in the heavenly places might be made known through the church the manifold wisdom of God,

עַל־פִּי תָּכְנִית הָעוֹלָמִים שֶׁעָשָׂה בַּמָּשִׁיחַ יֵשׁוּעַ אֲדוֹנֵנוּ
al-pi tochnit ha'olamim she'asah bammashiach yeshua adonenu
according to the eternal purpose which he purposed in Christ Jesus our Lord:

הָאֶפֶסִים

וּכְדֵי שֶׁבְּגוּף אֶחָד יְרַצֶּה אֶת שְׁנֵיהֶם לֵאלֹהִים עַל־יְדֵי הַצְּלָב, בַּהֲמִיתוֹ בּוֹ אֶת הָאֵיבָה
uchedei shebbeguf echad yeratzeh et sheneihem lelohim al-yedei hatzelav, bahamito bo et ha'eivah
and might reconcile them both in one body unto God through the cross, having slain the enmity thereby:

הוּא בָּא וּבִשֵּׂר שָׁלוֹם, לָכֶם הָרְחוֹקִים וְגַם לַקְּרוֹבִים
hu ba uvisser shalom, lachem harechokim vegam lakkerovim
and he came and preached peace to you that were far off, and peace to them that were nigh:

דַּרְכּוֹ יֵשׁ לָכֶם וְלָנוּ גִּישָׁה בְּרוּחַ אַחַת אֶל הָאָב
darko yesh lachem velanu gishah beruach achat el ha'av
for through him we both have our access in one Spirit unto the Father.

לָכֵן אֵינְכֶם עוֹד זָרִים אוֹ תּוֹשָׁבִים נָכְרִים, אֶלָּא בְּנֵי עִירָם שֶׁל הַקְּדוֹשִׁים וּבְנֵי בֵּית אֱלֹהִים
lachen einechem od zarim o toshavim nochrim, ella benei iram shel hakkedoshim uvenei beit elohim
So then ye are no more strangers and sojourners, but ye are fellow-citizens with the saints, and of the household of God,

בְּנוּיִים עַל יְסוֹד הַשְּׁלִיחִים וְהַנְּבִיאִים, וְהַמָּשִׁיחַ יֵשׁוּעַ עַצְמוֹ הוּא אֶבֶן הַפִּנָּה
benuyim al yesod hashelichim vehannevi'im, vehammashiach yeshua atzmo hu even happinnah
being built upon the foundation of the apostles and prophets, Christ Jesus himself being the chief corner stone;

בּוֹ כָּל הַבִּנְיָן מְחֻבָּר יַחַד וְגָדֵל לִהְיוֹת הֵיכַל קֹדֶשׁ ליהוה
bo kol habbinyan mechubbar yachad vegadel lihyot heichal kodesh lashem
in whom each several building, fitly framed together, groweth into a holy temple in the Lord;

וּבוֹ גַּם אַתֶּם נִבְנִים יַחְדָּיו לִהְיוֹת מִשְׁכַּן אֱלֹהִים עַל־יְדֵי הָרוּחַ
uvo gam attem nivnim yachdav lihyot mishkan elohim al-yedei haruach
in whom ye also are builded together for a habitation of God in the Spirit.

ג

מִשּׁוּם כָּךְ אֲנִי, שָׁאוּל, אֲסִיר הַמָּשִׁיחַ יֵשׁוּעַ בַּעֲבוּרְכֶם הַגּוֹיִם
mishum kach ani, sha'ul, asir hammashiach yeshua ba'avurechem haggoyim
For this cause I Paul, the prisoner of Christ Jesus in behalf of you Gentiles,—

אִם אָמְנָם שְׁמַעְתֶּם עַל הַתַּפְקִיד הַנּוֹגֵעַ לְחֶסֶד אֱלֹהִים שֶׁנִּתַּן לִי לְמַעַנְכֶם
im amenam shema'tem al hattafkid hannogea lechesed elohim shennittan li lema'anchem
if so be that ye have heard of the dispensation of that grace of God which was given me to you-ward;

וְכֵיצַד בְּחָזוֹן נִגְלָה לִי הַסּוֹד, כְּפִי שֶׁכָּתַבְתִּי לְעֵיל בְּכַמָּה מִלִּים
vecheitzad bechazon niglah li hassod, kefi shekkatavti le'eil bechammah millim
how that by revelation was made known unto me the mystery, as I wrote before in few words,

כְּשֶׁתִּקְרְאוּ תּוּכְלוּ לִרְאוֹת אֶת הֲבָנָתִי בְּסוֹד הַמָּשִׁיחַ
keshettikre'u tuchlu lir'ot et havanati besod hammashiach
whereby, when ye read, ye can perceive my understanding in the mystery of Christ;

הָאֶפְסִים

הֵן בַּחֶסֶד נוֹשַׁעְתֶּם עַל־יְדֵי הָאֱמוּנָה; וְזֹאת לֹא מִיֶּדְכֶם, כִּי אִם מַתְּנַת אֱלֹהִים הִיא
hen bachesed nosha'tem al-yedei ha'emunah; vezot lo miyedchem, ki im mattnat elohim hi
for by grace have ye been saved through faith; and that not of yourselves, it is the gift of God;

אֵין זֶה נוֹבֵעַ מִמַּעֲשִׂים, כְּדֵי שֶׁלֹּא יִתְגָּאֶה אִישׁ
ein zeh novea mimma'asim, kedei shello yitga'eh ish
not of works, that no man should glory.

שֶׁהֲרֵי מַעֲשֵׂה יְדֵי אֱלֹהִים אֲנַחְנוּ, בְּרוּאִים בַּמָּשִׁיחַ יֵשׁוּעַ לְמַעֲשִׂים טוֹבִים
sheharei ma'aseh yedei elohim anachnu, beru'im bammashiach yeshua lema'asim tovim
For we are his workmanship, created in Christ Jesus for good works,

אֲשֶׁר אֱלֹהִים הֱכִינָם מִקֶּדֶם לְמַעַן נִחְיֶה בָהֶם
asher elohim hechinam mikkedem lema'an nichyeh bahem
which God afore prepared that we should walk in them.

עַל כֵּן זִכְרוּ אַתֶּם מֶה הָיָה בֶּעָבָר, אַתֶּם, הַגּוֹיִם מִבְּחִינָה גוּפָנִית
al ken zichru attem meh hayah be'avar, attem, haggoyim mibbechinah gufanit
Wherefore remember, that once ye, the Gentiles in the flesh,

הַנִּקְרָאִים עֲרֵלִים בְּפִי הַנִּקְרָאִים נִמּוֹלִים, אֲשֶׁר מִילָתָם בַּבָּשָׂר וּמַעֲשֵׂה יָדַיִם הִיא
hannikra'im arelim befi hannikra'im nimmolim, asher milatam babbasar uma'aseh yadayim hi
who are called Uncircumcision by that which is called Circumcision, in the flesh, made by hands;

בְּאוֹתָהּ עֵת הֱיִיתֶם בְּלִי מָשִׁיחַ, זָרִים לַעֲדַת יִשְׂרָאֵל
be'otah et heyitem beli mashiach, zarim la'adat yisra'el
that ye were at that time separate from Christ, alienated from the commonwealth of Israel,

וְנָכְרִים לִבְרִיתוֹת הַהַבְטָחָה, מְחֻסְּרֵי תִקְוָה וּלְלֹא אֱלֹהִים בָּעוֹלָם
venacherim livritot hahavtachah, mechusserei tikvah ulelo elohim ba'olam
and strangers from the covenants of the promise, having no hope and without God in the world.

אֲבָל כָּעֵת, בַּמָּשִׁיחַ יֵשׁוּעַ, אַתֶּם הָרְחוֹקִים בֶּעָבָר, נִהְיֵיתֶם קְרוֹבִים עַל־יְדֵי דַּם הַמָּשִׁיחַ
aval ka'et, bammashiach yeshua', attem harechokim be'avar, nihyeitem kerovim al-yedei dam hammashiach
But now in Christ Jesus ye that once were far off are made nigh in the blood of Christ.

הֵן הוּא שְׁלוֹמֵנוּ; הוּא עָשָׂה אֶת הַשְּׁנַיִם לְאֶחָד וְהָרַס בִּבְשָׂרוֹ אֶת מְחִצַּת הָאֵיבָה
hen hu shelomenu; hu asah et hashenayim le'echad veharas bivsaro et mechitzat ha'eivah
For he is our peace, who made both one, and brake down the middle wall of partition,

הוּא בִּטֵּל אֶת תּוֹרַת הַמִּצְווֹת שֶׁבַּחֻקִּים
hu bittel et torat hammitzvot shebbachukkim
having abolished in his flesh the enmity, even the law of commandments contained in ordinances;

כְּדֵי לִבְרֹא בּוֹ עַצְמוֹ אֶת הַשְּׁנַיִם לְאָדָם חָדָשׁ אֶחָד וּבְכָךְ לַעֲשׂוֹת שָׁלוֹם
kedei livro bo atzmo et hashnayim le'adam chadash echad uvechach la'asot shalom
that he might create in himself of the two one new man, so making peace;

הָאֶפֶסִים

וְאֶת הַכֹּל שָׁת תַּחַת רַגְלָיו וְנָתַן אוֹתוֹ לַקְּהִלָּה לְרֹאשׁ עַל כֹּל
ve'et hakkol shat tachat raglav venatan oto lakkehillah lerosh al kol
and he put all things in subjection under his feet, and gave him to be head over all things to the church,

וְהִיא גוּפוֹ, מְלוֹאוֹ שֶׁל הַמְמַלֵּא אֶת הַכֹּל בַּכֹּל
vehi gufo, melo'o shel hamemallei et hakkol bakkol
which is his body, the fulness of him that filleth all in all.

ב

גַּם אַתֶּם שֶׁהֱיִיתֶם מֵתִים בְּפִשְׁעֵיכֶם וַחֲטָאֵיכֶם
gam attem sheheyitem metim befish'eichem vachata'eichem
And you did he make alive, when ye were dead through your trespasses and sins,

בֶּעָבַר הִתְהַלַּכְתֶּם בָּהֶם לְפִי עִדָּן הָעוֹלָם הַזֶּה
be'avar hit'hallachtem bahem lefi iddan ha'olam hazzeh
wherein ye once walked according to the course of this world,

כִּרְצוֹן הַשַּׂר אֲשֶׁר לוֹ הַשִּׁלְטוֹן בִּסְפֵירַת הַבֵּינַיִם וְהוּא הָרוּחַ הַפּוֹעֶלֶת עַתָּה בִּבְנֵי הַמֶּרִי
kirtzon hasar asher lo hashilton bisfeirat habbeinayim vehu haruach happo'elet attah bivnei hammeri
according to the prince of the powers of the air, of the spirit that now worketh in the sons of disobedience;

וְגַם אֲנַחְנוּ כֻּלָּנוּ הָיִינוּ מְעֹרָבִים עִמָּהֶם בֶּעָבַר; עָסַקְנוּ בְּתַאֲוֹותֵינוּ הַבְּשָׂרִיּוֹת,
vegam anachnu kullanu hayinu me'oravim immahem be'avar; asaknu beta'avoteinu habbesariyot
among whom we also all once lived in the lusts of our flesh,

מִלֵּאנוּ אֶת תְּשׁוּקוֹת הַגּוּף וְאֶת דַּחַף הַמַּחֲשָׁבוֹת, וְהָיִינוּ מִטִּבְעֵנוּ בְּנֵי זַעַם כִּשְׁאָר בְּנֵי אָדָם
millenu et teshukot hagguf ve'et dachaf hammachashavot, vehayinu mittiv'enu benei za'am kish'ar benei adam
doing the desires of the flesh and of the mind, and were by nature children of wrath, even as the rest:—

אֲבָל אֱלֹהִים הַמָּלֵא רַחֲמִים אָהַב אוֹתָנוּ, וּבְאַהֲבָתוֹ הָרַבָּה
aval elohim hammalei rachamim ahav otanu, uve'ahavato harabbah
but God, being rich in mercy, for his great love wherewith he loved us,

אַף כִּי מֵתִים הָיִינוּ בִּפְשָׁעֵינוּ, הֶחֱיָנוּ עִם הַמָּשִׁיחַ - הֵן בַּחֶסֶד נוֹשַׁעְתֶּם
af ki metim hayinu bifsha'einu, hecheyanu im hammashiach - hen bachesed nosha'tem
even when we were dead through our trespasses, made us alive together with Christ (by grace have ye been saved),

וְהֵקִים אוֹתָנוּ עִמּוֹ וְהוֹשִׁיבָנוּ עִמּוֹ בַּשָּׁמַיִם, בַּמָּשִׁיחַ יֵשׁוּעַ
vehekim otanu immo vehoshivanu immo bashamayim, bammashiach yeshua
and raised us up with him, and made us to sit with him in the heavenly places, in Christ Jesus:

כְּדֵי לְהַרְאוֹת בָּעוֹלָמִים הַבָּאִים אֶת שֶׁפַע עֹשֶׁר חַסְדּוֹ בַּטּוֹבָה שֶׁגָּמַל עָלֵינוּ בַּמָּשִׁיחַ יֵשׁוּעַ
kedei lehar'ot ba'olamim habba'im et shefa osher chasdo battovah sheggamal aleinu bammashiach yeshua
that in the ages to come he might show the exceeding riches of his grace in kindness toward us in Christ Jesus:

הָאֶפֶסִים

וְעַל אַהֲבַתְכֶם לְכָל הַקְּדוֹשִׁים
ve'al ahavatchem lechol hakkedoshim
and the love which ye show toward all the saints,

אֵינֶנִּי חָדֵל לְהוֹדוֹת עֲלֵיכֶם וּלְהַזְכִּיר אֶתְכֶם בִּתְפִלּוֹתַי
einenni chadel lehodot aleichem ulehazkir etchem bitfillotai
cease not to give thanks for you, making mention of you in my prayers;

כְּדֵי שֶׁאֱלֹהֵי אֲדוֹנֵנוּ יֵשׁוּעַ הַמָּשִׁיחַ, אֲבִי הַכָּבוֹד
kedei she'elohei adonenu yeshua hammashiach, avi hakkavod
that the God of our Lord Jesus Christ, the Father of glory,

יִתֵּן לָכֶם רוּחַ שֶׁל חָכְמָה וְהִתְגַּלּוּת שֶׁתֵּיטִיבוּ לָדַעַת אוֹתוֹ
yitten lachem ruach shel chochmah vehitgallut shetteitivu lada'at oto
may give unto you a spirit of wisdom and revelation in the knowledge of him;

וְיָאִיר עֵינֵי לְבַבְכֶם לָדַעַת מַהִי הַתִּקְוָה הַצְּפוּנָה בִּקְרִיאָתוֹ
veya'ir einei levavchem lada'at mahi hattikvah hatzefunah bikri'ato
having the eyes of your heart enlightened, that ye may know what is the hope of his calling,

מָה עֲתִירַת כָּבוֹד נַחֲלָתוֹ בְּקֶרֶב הַקְּדוֹשִׁים
mah atirat kavod nachalato bekerev hakkdoshim
what the riches of the glory of his inheritance in the saints,

וּמַה נַּעֲלָה גְּדֻלַּת גְּבוּרָתוֹ הַשּׁוֹפַעַת עָלֵינוּ, הַמַּאֲמִינִים
umah na'alah gedullat gevurato hashofa'at aleinu, hamma'aminim
and what the exceeding greatness of his power to us-ward who believe,

כְּמִדַּת פֹּעַל כֹּחוֹ הֶעָצוּם
kemiddat po'al kocho he'atzum
according to that working of the strength of his might

אֲשֶׁר פָּעַל בַּמָּשִׁיחַ בַּהֲקִימוֹ אוֹתוֹ מִבֵּין הַמֵּתִים
asher pa'al bammashiach bahakimo oto mibbein hammetim
which he wrought in Christ, when he raised him from the dead,

וּבְהוֹשִׁיבוֹ אוֹתוֹ לִימִינוֹ בַּשָּׁמַיִם
uvehoshivo oto liyemino bashamayim
and made him to sit at his right hand in the heavenly places,

מֵעַל לְכָל מֶמְשָׁלָה וְשִׁלְטוֹן, גְּבוּרָה וּמִשְׂרָה, וְכָל שֵׁם נִקְרָא
me'al lechol memshalah veshilton, gevurah umisrah, vechol shem nikra
far above all rule, and authority, and power, and dominion, and every name that is named,

לֹא בָּעוֹלָם הַזֶּה בִּלְבַד, אֶלָּא גַּם בָּעוֹלָם הַבָּא
lo ba'olam hazzeh bilvad, ella gam ba'olam habba
not only in this world, but also in that which is to come:

הָאֶפֶסִים

כְּפִי עֹשֶׁר חֶסֶד הָאֱלֹהִים
kefi osher chesed ha'elohim
according to the riches of his grace,

אֶת הַחֶסֶד הַזֶּה הוּא הִשְׁפִּיעַ עָלֵינוּ בִּמְלוֹא חָכְמָה וּבִינָה
et hachesed hazzeh hu hishpia aleinu bimlo chochmah uvinah
which he made to abound toward us in all wisdom and prudence,

וְהוֹדִיעַ לָנוּ אֶת סוֹד רְצוֹנוֹ כְּפִי חֶפְצוֹ, אֶת הַתָּכְנִית שֶׁהִקְדִּים וְעָרַךְ בּוֹ
vehodia lanu et sod retzono kefi cheftzo, et hattochnit shehikdim ve'arach bo
making known unto us the mystery of his will, according to his good pleasure which he purposed in him

הַתָּכְנִית לְקַבֵּץ אֶת הַכֹּל בַּמָּשִׁיחַ בִּמְלֹאת הָעִתִּים
hattochnit lekabbetz et hakkol bammashiach bimlot ha'ittim
unto a dispensation of the fulness of the times, to sum up all things in Christ,

אֶת מַה שֶּׁבַּשָּׁמַיִם וְאֶת מַה שֶׁבָּאָרֶץ
et mah shebbashamayim ve'et mah shebba'aretz
the things in the heavens, and the things upon the earth; in him, I say,

וּבוֹ נוֹעֲדָה לָנוּ נַחֲלָה
uvo no'adah lanu nachalah
in whom also we were made a heritage,

כִּי נִבְחַרְנוּ מֵרֹאשׁ לְפִי תָּכְנִיתוֹ שֶׁל הַפּוֹעֵל בַּכֹּל בְּהֶתְאֵם לְמַחֲשֶׁבֶת רְצוֹנוֹ
ki nivcharnu merosh lefi tachenito shel happo'el bakkol behet'em lemachashevet retzono
having been foreordained according to the purpose of him who worketh all things after the counsel of his will;

כְּדֵי שֶׁנִּהְיֶה לִתְהִלַּת כְּבוֹדוֹ, אָנוּ הַמַּקְדִּימִים לְקַוּוֹת לַמָּשִׁיחַ
kedei shennihyeh lit'hillat kevodo, anu hammakdimim lekavvot lammashiach
to the end that we should be unto the praise of his glory, we who had before hoped in Christ:

וּבוֹ נַחֲלַתְכֶם גַּם אַתֶּם; שֶׁכֵּן בְּשָׁמְעֲכֶם אֶת דְּבַר הָאֱמֶת, אֶת בְּשׂוֹרַת יְשׁוּעַתְכֶם
uvo nachalatchem gam attem; shekken beshomechem et devar ha'emet, et besorat yeshu'atchem
in whom ye also, having heard the word of the truth, the gospel of your salvation,—

וּבְהַאֲמִינְכֶם בּוֹ, נֶחְתַּמְתֶּם גַּם אַתֶּם בְּרוּחַ הַהַבְטָחָה, רוּחַ הַקֹּדֶשׁ
uveha'aminechem bo, nechtamtem gam attem beruach hahavtachah, ruach hakkodesh
in whom, having also believed, ye were sealed with the Holy Spirit of promise,

אֲשֶׁר הִיא עֵרָבוֹן לְנַחֲלָתֵנוּ עַד לִפְדִיַּת הַקִּנְיָן, לִתְהִלַּת כְּבוֹדוֹ
asher hi eravon lenachalatenu ad lifdiyat hakkinyan, lit'hillat kevodo
which is an earnest of our inheritance, unto the redemption of God's own possession, unto the praise of his glory.

מִשּׁוּם כָּךְ גַּם אֲנִי, לְאַחַר שֶׁשָּׁמַעְתִּי עַל אֱמוּנַתְכֶם בָּאָדוֹן יֵשׁוּעַ
mishum kach gam ani, le'achar sheshama'ti al emunatchem ba'adon yeshua
For this cause I also, having heard of the faith in the Lord Jesus which is among you,

הָאֶפְסִים

מֵאֵת שָׁאוּל, שְׁלִיחַ הַמָּשִׁיחַ יֵשׁוּעַ בִּרְצוֹן אֱלֹהִים
me'et sha'ul, sheliach hammashiach yeshua birtzon elohim
Paul, an apostle of Christ Jesus through the will of God,

אֶל הַקְּדוֹשִׁים אֲשֶׁר [בְּאֶפְסוֹס], הַמַּאֲמִינִים בַּמָּשִׁיחַ יֵשׁוּעַ
el hakkedoshim asher [be'efesos], hamma'aminim bammashiach yeshua
to the saints that are at Ephesus, and the faithful in Christ Jesus:

חֶסֶד וְשָׁלוֹם לָכֶם מֵאֵת הָאֱלֹהִים אָבִינוּ וְהָאָדוֹן יֵשׁוּעַ הַמָּשִׁיחַ
chesed veshalom lachem me'et ha'elohim avinu veha'adon yeshua hammashiach
Grace to you and peace from God our Father and the Lord Jesus Christ.

בָּרוּךְ הָאֱלֹהִים אֲבִי אֲדוֹנֵנוּ יֵשׁוּעַ הַמָּשִׁיחַ
baruch ha'elohim avi adonenu yeshua hammashiach
Blessed be the God and Father of our Lord Jesus Christ,

אֲשֶׁר בֵּרַךְ אוֹתָנוּ בְּכָל בְּרָכָה רוּחָנִית בַּשָּׁמַיִם, בַּמָּשִׁיחַ
asher berech otanu bechol berachah ruchanit bashamayim, bammashiach
who hath blessed us with every spiritual blessing in the heavenly places in Christ:

כְּשֵׁם שֶׁבָּחַר אוֹתָנוּ בּוֹ בְּטֶרֶם הִוָּסֵד תֵּבֵל
keshem shebbachar otanu bo beterem hivvased tevel
even as he chose us in him before the foundation of the world,

לִהְיוֹת קְדוֹשִׁים וּבְלִי דֹפִי לְפָנָיו בְּאַהֲבָה
lihyot kedoshim uveli dofi lefanav be'ahavah
that we should be holy and without blemish before him in love:

הוּא יָעַד אוֹתָנוּ לִהְיוֹת לוֹ לְבָנִים עַל־יְדֵי יֵשׁוּעַ הַמָּשִׁיחַ
hu ya'ad otanu lihyot lo levanim al-yedei yeshua hammashiach
having foreordained us unto adoption as sons through Jesus Christ unto himself,

כַּחֵפֶץ רְצוֹנוֹ
kechefetz retzono
according to the good pleasure of his will,

לִתְהִלַּת כָּבוֹד עַל חַסְדוֹ אֲשֶׁר הֶעֱנִיק לָנוּ בַּאֲהוּבוֹ
lit'hillat kavod al chasdo asher he'enik lanu ba'ahuvo
to the praise of the glory of his grace, which he freely bestowed on us in the Beloved:

שֶׁבְּדָמוֹ יֵשׁ לָנוּ הַפְּדוּת, סְלִיחַת הַחֲטָאִים
shebbedamo yesh lanu happdut, selichat hachata'im
in whom we have our redemption through his blood, the forgiveness of our trespasses,

הַגָּלְטִים

שֶׁבָּאֶמְצָעוּתוֹ הָעוֹלָם צָלוּב לִי וַאֲנִי צָלוּב לְעוֹלָם
shebbe'emtza'uto ha'olam tzaluv li va'ani tzaluv la'olam
through which the world hath been crucified unto me, and I unto the world.

כִּי לֹא הַמִּילָה חֲשׁוּבָה אַף לֹא הָעָרְלָה, אֶלָּא בְּרִיאָה חֲדָשָׁה
ki lo hammilah chashuvah af lo ha'arelah, ella beri'ah chadashah
For neither is circumcision anything, nor uncircumcision, but a new creature.

כָּל הַנּוֹהֲגִים לְפִי כְּלָל זֶה, שָׁלוֹם וְרַחֲמִים עֲלֵיהֶם וְעַל יִשְׂרָאֵל הַשַּׁיָּכִים לֵאלֹהִים
kol hannohagim lefi kelal zeh, shalom verachamim aleihem ve'al yisra'el hashayachim le'elohim
And as many as shall walk by this rule, peace be upon them, and mercy, and upon the Israel of God.

מֵעַתָּה וְאֵילָךְ אַל נָא יוֹגִיעֵנִי אִישׁ, שֶׁכֵּן אֶת צַלֶּקוֹת יֵשׁוּעַ אֲנִי נוֹשֵׂא בְּגוּפִי
me'attah ve'eilach al na yogi'eni ish, shekken et tzallekot yeshua ani nosei begufi
Henceforth let no man trouble me; for I bear branded on my body the marks of Jesus.

אַחַי, חֶסֶד אֲדוֹנֵנוּ יֵשׁוּעַ הַמָּשִׁיחַ עִם רוּחֲכֶם. אָמֵן
achai, chesed adonenu yeshua hammashiach im ruchachem. amen
The grace of our Lord Jesus Christ be with your spirit, brethren. Amen.

הַגָּלָטִים

אַל תִּטְעוּ, בֵּאלֹהִים אֵין לְהָתֵל; כִּי מַה שֶּׁאָדָם זוֹרֵעַ, אֶת זֹאת גַּם יִקְצֹר
al tit'u, be'elohim ein lehatel; ki mah she'adam zorea', et zot gam yiktzor
Be not deceived; God is not mocked: for whatsoever a man soweth, that shall he also reap.

מִי שֶׁזּוֹרֵעַ בִּשְׂדֵה בְּשָׂרוֹ, מִן הַבָּשָׂר יִקְצֹר כִּלָּיוֹן
mi shezzorea bisdeh besaro, min habbasar yiktzor killayon
For he that soweth unto his own flesh shall of the flesh reap corruption;

אֲבָל הַזּוֹרֵעַ בִּשְׂדֵה הָרוּחַ, מִן הָרוּחַ יִקְצֹר חַיֵּי עוֹלָם
aval hazzorea bisdeh haruach, min haruach yiktzor chayei olam
but he that soweth unto the Spirit shall of the Spirit reap eternal life.

אַל נָא יִרְפּוּ יָדֵינוּ מֵעֲשׂוֹת טוֹב; בְּבוֹא הָעֵת נִקְצֹר, אִם לֹא נִרְפֶּה
al na yirpu yadeinu me'asot tov; bevo ha'et niktzor, im lo nirpeh
And let us not be weary in well-doing: for in due season we shall reap, if we faint not.

לָכֵן בְּעוֹד יֵשׁ לָנוּ הִזְדַּמְּנוּת, נִגְמֹל טוֹב לְכָל אָדָם
lachen be'od yesh lanu hizdammenut, nigmol tov lechol adam
So then, as we have opportunity, let us work that which is good toward all men,

וּבְיִחוּד לִבְנֵי אֱמוּנָתֵנוּ
uveyichud livnei emunatenu
and especially toward them that are of the household of the faith.

רְאוּ בְּאֵלּוּ אוֹתִיּוֹת גְּדוֹלוֹת כָּתַבְתִּי אֲלֵיכֶם בְּמוֹ יָדִי
re'u be'ellu otiyot gedolot katavti aleichem bemo yadi
See with how large letters I write unto you with mine own hand.

הָאֲנָשִׁים הַחֲפֵצִים לְהִתְהַדֵּר בַּבָּשָׂר מַכְרִיחִים אֶתְכֶם לְהִמּוֹל
ha'anashim hachafetzim lehit'hadder babbasar machrichim etchem lehimmol
As many as desire to make a fair show in the flesh, they compel you to be circumcised;

רַק כְּדֵי שֶׁלֹּא יֵרָדְפוּ עַל צְלַב הַמָּשִׁיחַ
rak kedei shello yeradefu al tzelav hammashiach
only that they may not be persecuted for the cross of Christ.

הֲרֵי אֲפִלּוּ הַנִּמּוֹלִים עַצְמָם אֵינָם שׁוֹמְרִים אֶת הַתּוֹרָה
harei afillu hannimmolim atzmam einam shomerim et hattorah
For not even they who receive circumcision do themselves keep the law;

אֲבָל רוֹצִים הֵם שֶׁתִּמּוֹלוּ לְמַעַן יִתְהַלְלוּ בִּבְשַׂרְכֶם
aval rotzim hem shettimmolu lema'an yit'hallelu bivsarchem
but they desire to have you circumcised, that they may glory in your flesh.

וַאֲנִי חָלִילָה לִי מֵהִתְהַלֵּל בִּלְתִּי אִם בִּצְלַב אֲדוֹנֵנוּ יֵשׁוּעַ הַמָּשִׁיחַ
va'ani chalilah li mehit'hallel bilti im bitzlav adonenu yeshua hammashiach
But far be it from me to glory, save in the cross of our Lord Jesus Christ,

הַגָּלָטִים

עֲנָוָה, רִסּוּן עַצְמִי - עַל מִדּוֹת כָּאֵלֶּה אֵין תּוֹרָה חָלָה

anavah, rissun atzmi - al middot ka'elleh ein torah chalah

meekness, self-control; against such there is no law.

הָאֲנָשִׁים הַשַּׁיָּכִים לַמָּשִׁיחַ צָלְבוּ אֶת בְּשָׂרָם עִם תְּשׁוּקוֹתָיו וְתַאֲווֹתָיו

ha'anashim hashayachim lammashiach tzalevu et bsaram im teshukotav veta'avotav

And they that are of Christ Jesus have crucified the flesh with the passions and the lusts thereof.

אִם חַיֵּינוּ מִן הָרוּחַ, הָבָה גַּם נִתְהַלֵּךְ עַל־פִּי הָרוּחַ

im chayeinu min haruach, havah gam nit'hallech al-pi haruach

If we live by the Spirit, by the Spirit let us also walk.

אַל נָא נִהְיֶה שׁוֹאֲפֵי כְּבוֹד שָׁוְא, הַמִּתְגָּרִים וּמְקַנְּאִים אִישׁ בְּרֵעֵהוּ

al na nihyeh sho'afei kevod shav, hammitgarim umekanne'im ish bere'ehu

Let us not become vainglorious, provoking one another, envying one another.

אַחַי, אִם יִכָּשֵׁל אִישׁ מִכֶּם בְּאֵיזוֹ עֲבֵרָה

achai, im yikkashel ish mikkem be'eizo averah

Brethren, even if a man be overtaken in any trespass,

אַתֶּם הָאֲנָשִׁים הָרוּחָנִיִּים תָּקִימוּ אוֹתוֹ בְּרוּחַ שֶׁל עֲנָוָה; וְהִזָּהֵר שֶׁלֹּא תָּבוֹא גַּם אַתָּה לִידֵי נִסָּיוֹן

attem ha'anashim haruchaniyim takimu oto beruach shel anavah; vehizzaher shello tavo gam attah lidei nissayon

ye who are spiritual, restore such a one in a spirit of gentleness; looking to thyself, lest thou also be tempted.

שְׂאוּ אִישׁ אֶת מַעֲמֶסֶת רֵעֵהוּ וְכָךְ תְּקַיְּמוּ אֶת תּוֹרַת הַמָּשִׁיחַ

se'u ish et ma'ameset re'ehu vechach tekayemu et torat hammashiach

Bear ye one another's burdens, and so fulfil the law of Christ.

אִם אָדָם חוֹשֵׁב אֶת עַצְמוֹ לְמַשֶּׁהוּ בְּעוֹד שֶׁאֵינוֹ כְּלוּם, הֲרֵיהוּ מַשְׁלֶה אֶת עַצְמוֹ

im adam choshev et atzmo lemashehu be'od she'eino kelum, hareihu mashleh et atzmo

For if a man thinketh himself to be something when he is nothing, he deceiveth himself.

יִבְחַן כָּל אֶחָד אֶת מַעֲשָׂיו וְאָז הַסִּבָּה לִתְהִלָּתוֹ תִּהְיֶה בּוֹ עַצְמוֹ בְּלִי תְּלוּת בַּזּוּלַת

yivchan kol echad et ma'asav ve'az hassibbah lit'hillato tihyeh bo atzmo bli telut bazulat

But let each man prove his own work, and then shall he have his glorying in regard of himself alone, and not of his neighbor.

שֶׁכֵּן כָּל אֶחָד יִשָּׂא אֶת הַנֵּטֶל שֶׁלּוֹ

shekken kol echad yisho et hannetel shello

For each man shall bear his own burden.

מִי שֶׁלּוֹמֵד אֶת דְּבַר אֱלֹהִים צָרִיךְ לְשַׁתֵּף בְּכָל הַדְּבָרִים הַטּוֹבִים אֶת מִי שֶׁמְּלַמֵּד אוֹתוֹ

mi shellomed et devar elohim tzarich leshattef bechol haddevarim hatovim et mi shemmelammed oto

But let him that is taught in the word communicate unto him that teacheth in all good things.

הַגָּלָטִים

הֲרֵי כָּל הַתּוֹרָה כְּלוּלָה בְּמַאֲמָר אֶחָד - וְאָהַבְתָּ לְרֵעֲךָ כָּמוֹךָ
harei kol hattorah kelulah bema'amar echad - ve'ahavta lere'acha kamocha
For the whole law is fulfilled in one word, even in this: Thou shalt love thy neighbor as thyself.

אַךְ אִם אַתֶּם נוֹשְׁכִים וְטוֹרְפִים זֶה אֶת זֶה, כִּי אָז תִּשָּׁמְדוּ אִישׁ בְּיַד רֵעֵהוּ
ach im attem noshechim vetorefim zeh et zeh, ki az tishamedu ish beyad re'ehu
But if ye bite and devour one another, take heed that ye be not consumed one of another.

אוֹמֵר אֲנִי לָכֶם; הִתְהַלְּכוּ בְּדֶרֶךְ הָרוּחַ וְלֹא תְמַלְּאוּ אֶת תַּאֲווֹת הַבָּשָׂר
omer ani lachem; hit'hallechu bederech haruach velo temalle'u et ta'avot habbasar
But I say, Walk by the Spirit, and ye shall not fulfil the lust of the flesh.

כִּי הַבָּשָׂר מִתְאַוֶּה לְמַה שֶׁבְּנִגּוּד לָרוּחַ, וְהָרוּחַ מִתְנַגֶּדֶת לַבָּשָׂר
ki habbasar mit'avveh lemah shebbeniggud laruach, veharuach mitnaggedet labbasar
For the flesh lusteth against the Spirit, and the Spirit against the flesh;

שְׁנֵיהֶם מִתְנַגְּדִים זֶה לָזֶה
sheneihem mitnaggedim zeh lazeh
for these are contrary the one to the other;

וְלָכֵן אֵינְכֶם יְכוֹלִים לַעֲשׂוֹת אֶת מַה שֶׁבִּרְצוֹנְכֶם
velachen einechem yecholim la'asot et mah shebbirtzonechem
that ye may not do the things that ye would.

אֲבָל אִם הָרוּחַ מַנְהִיגָה אֶתְכֶם, אֲזַי אֵינְכֶם כְּפוּפִים לַתּוֹרָה
aval im haruach manhigah etchem, azai einechem kefufim lattorah
But if ye are led by the Spirit, ye are not under the law.

מַעֲשֵׂי הַבָּשָׂר גְּלוּיִים וְאֵלֶּה הֵם: נִאוּף וּזְנוּת, טֻמְאָה, זִמָּה
ma'asei habbasar geluyim ve'elleh hem: ni'uf uzenut, tum'ah, zimmah
Now the works of the flesh are manifest, which are these: fornication, uncleanness, lasciviousness,

עֲבוֹדַת אֱלִילִים, כִּשּׁוּף, שִׂנְאָה, מָדוֹן, צָרוּת עַיִן, כַּעַס, מְרִיבָה, מַחֲלוֹקוֹת, כִּתּוֹת
avodat elilim, kishuf, sin'ah, madon, tzarut ayin, ka'as, merivah, machalokot, kittot
idolatry, sorcery, enmities, strife, jealousies, wraths, factions, divisions, parties,

קִנְאָה, שִׁכְרוּת, הוֹלְלוּת וְכַדּוֹמֶה. אוֹמֵר אֲנִי לָכֶם מֵרֹאשׁ מַה שֶׁכְּבָר אָמַרְתִּי
kin'ah, shichrut, holelut vechaddomeh. omer ani lachem merosh mah shekkevar amarti
envyings, drunkenness, revellings, and such like; of which I forewarn you, even as I did forewarn you,

עוֹשֵׂי מַעֲשִׂים כָּאֵלֶּה לֹא יִירְשׁוּ אֶת מַלְכוּת הָאֱלֹהִים
osei ma'asim ka'elleh lo yireshu et malchut ha'elohim
that they who practise such things shall not inherit the kingdom of God.

לְעֻמַּת זֹאת, פְּרִי הָרוּחַ הוּא אַהֲבָה, שִׂמְחָה, שָׁלוֹם, אֹרֶךְ רוּחַ, נְדִיבוּת, טוּב לֵב, נֶאֱמָנוּת
le'ummat zot, peri haruach hu ahavah, simchah, shalom, orech ruach, nedivut, tuv lev, ne'emanut
But the fruit of the Spirit is love, joy, peace, longsuffering, kindness, goodness, faithfulness,

הַגָּלְטִים

וַאֲנַחְנוּ, בְּרוּחַ, עַל־יְסוֹד אֱמוּנָה, מְיַחֲלִים לַתִּקְוָה, פְּרִי הַצִּדְקָתֵנוּ
va'anachnu, beruach, al-yesod emunah, meyachalim lattikvah, peri hatzdakatenu
For we through the Spirit by faith wait for the hope of righteousness.

שֶׁכֵּן בַּמָּשִׁיחַ יֵשׁוּעַ אֵין חֲשִׁיבוּת לֹא לַמִּילָה וְלֹא לְעָרְלָה, אֶלָּא לָאֱמוּנָה הַפּוֹעֶלֶת בְּדֶרֶךְ אַהֲבָה
shekken bammashiach yeshua ein chashivut lo lammilah velo la'arelah, ella la'emunah happo'elet bederech ahavah
For in Christ Jesus neither circumcision availeth anything, nor uncircumcision; but faith working through love.

מְרוּצַתְכֶם הָיְתָה טוֹבָה; מִי הֵנִיא אֶתְכֶם מִלְצַיֵּת לָאֱמֶת
merutzatchem hayetah tovah; mi heni etchem milletzayet la'emet
Ye were running well; who hindered you that ye should not obey the truth?

פִּתּוּי זֶה אֵינוֹ מֵאֵת הַקּוֹרֵא אֶתְכֶם
pittui zeh eino me'et hakkorei etchem
This persuasion came not of him that calleth you.

מְעַט שְׂאוֹר מַחֲמִיץ אֶת כָּל הַבָּצֵק
me'at se'or machamitz et kol habbatzek
A little leaven leaveneth the whole lump.

אֲנִי בּוֹטֵחַ בָּאָדוֹן בְּנוֹגֵעַ אֲלֵיכֶם שֶׁלֹּא תַּעֲלֶה עַל לִבְּכֶם שׁוּם מַחֲשָׁבָה זָרָה
ani boteach ba'adon benogea aleichem shello ta'aleh al libbechem shum machashavah zarah
I have confidence to you-ward in the Lord, that ye will be none otherwise minded:

וּמִי שֶׁעוֹכֵר אֶתְכֶם יִשָּׂא אֶת עֲווֹנוֹ, יִהְיֶה הָאִישׁ מִי שֶׁיִּהְיֶה
umi she'ocher etchem yissa et avono, yihyeh ha'ish mi sheyihyeh
but he that troubleth you shall bear his judgment, whosoever he be.

וַאֲנִי, אַחַי, אִם אֲנִי עֲדַיִן מַטִּיף בְּעַד הַמִּילָה, מַדּוּעַ זֶה מוֹסִיפִים לִרְדֹּף אוֹתִי
va'ani, achai, im ani adayin mattif be'ad hammilah, maddua zeh mosifim lirdof oti
But I, brethren, if I still preach circumcision, why am I still persecuted?

אִלּוּ הִטַּפְתִּי כָּךְ, הָיָה מִתְבַּטֵּל מִכְשׁוֹל הַצְּלָב
illu hittafti kach, hayah mitbattel michshol hatzelav
then hath the stumbling-block of the cross been done away.

מִי יִתֵּן וְיִכָּרְתוּ הַמַּתְעִים אֶתְכֶם
mi yitten veyikkaretu hammat'im etchem
I would that they that unsettle you would even go beyond circumcision.

אַחַי, לְחֵרוּת נִקְרֵאתֶם, רַק שֶׁלֹּא תְּהֵא הַחֵרוּת אֶמְצָעִי בִּידֵי הַבָּשָׂר
achai, lecherut nikretem, rak shello tehei hacherut emtza'i biydei habbasar
For ye, brethren, were called for freedom; only use not your freedom for an occasion to the flesh,

אֶלָּא שָׁרְתוּ אִישׁ אֶת רֵעֵהוּ בְּאַהֲבָה
ella sharetu ish et re'ehu be'ahavah
but through love be servants one to another.

הַגָּלָטִים

פִּצְחִי רִנָּה וְצַהֲלִי לֹא־חָלָה
pitzchi rinnah vetzahali lo-chalah
Break forth and cry, thou that travailest not:

כִּי־רַבִּים בְּנֵי־שׁוֹמֵמָה מִבְּנֵי בְעוּלָה
ki-rabbim benei-shomemah mibbenei ve'ulah
For more are the children of the desolate than of her that hath the husband.

וְאַתֶּם, אַחַי, אַתֶּם בְּנֵי הַהַבְטָחָה כְּיִצְחָק
ve'attem, achai, attem benei hahavtachah keyitzchak
Now we, brethren, as Isaac was, are children of promise.

וּכְשֵׁם שֶׁאָז רָדַף הַבֵּן שֶׁנּוֹלַד לְפִי הַבָּשָׂר אֶת הַבֵּן שֶׁנּוֹלַד לְפִי הָרוּחַ, כֵּן גַּם עַכְשָׁו
ucheshem she'az radaf habben shennolad lefi habbasar et habben shennolad lefi haruach, ken gam achshav
But as then he that was born after the flesh persecuted him that was born after the Spirit, so also it is now.

אֲבָל מָה אוֹמֵר הַכָּתוּב
aval mah omer hakkatuv
Howbeit what saith the scripture?

גָּרֵשׁ הָאָמָה וְאֶת־בְּנָהּ, כִּי לֹא יִירַשׁ בֶּן־הָאָמָה עִם־בֶּן הַחָפְשִׁיָּה
garesh ha'amah ve'et-benah, ki lo yirash ben-ha'amah im-ben hachofshiyah
Cast out the handmaid and her son: for the son of the handmaid shall not inherit with the son of the freewoman.

לְפִיכָךְ, אַחַי, אֵין אָנוּ בְּנֵי הָאָמָה, אֶלָּא בְּנֵי הַחָפְשִׁיָּה
lefichach, achai, ein anu benei ha'amah, ella benei hachofshiyah
Wherefore, brethren, we are not children of a handmaid, but of the freewoman.

ה

הַמָּשִׁיחַ שִׁחְרֵר אוֹתָנוּ אֱלֵי חֵרוּת, לָכֵן עִמְדוּ וְאַל תִּכָּנְעוּ שׁוּב לְעֹל הָעַבְדוּת
hammashiach shichrer otanu elei cherut, lachen imdu ve'al tikkan'u shuv le'ol ha'avdut
For freedom did Christ set us free: stand fast therefore, and be not entangled again in a yoke of bondage.

אֲנִי, שָׁאוּל, אוֹמֵר לָכֶם שֶׁאִם תִּמּוֹלוּ, לֹא יוֹעִיל לָכֶם הַמָּשִׁיחַ
ani, sha'ul, omer lachem she'im timmolu, lo yo'il lachem hammashiach
Behold, I Paul say unto you, that, if ye receive circumcision, Christ will profit you nothing.

אֲנִי חוֹזֵר וּמֵעִיד בְּכָל אִישׁ אֲשֶׁר יִמּוֹל, כִּי חוֹבָה עָלָיו לִשְׁמֹר אֶת כָּל הַתּוֹרָה
ani chozer ume'id bechol ish asher yimmol, ki chovah alav lishmor et kol hattorah
Yea, I testify again to every man that receiveth circumcision, that he is a debtor to do the whole law.

אַתֶּם הַמְבַקְשִׁים לְהִצָּדֵק בַּתּוֹרָה נִתַּקְתֶּם מִן הַמָּשִׁיחַ, נִשְׁמַטְתֶּם מִן הַחֶסֶד
attem hamvakshim lehitzadek battorah nuttaktem min hammashiach, nishmattem min hachesed
Ye are severed from Christ, ye who would be justified by the law; ye are fallen away from grace.

הַגַּלָטִים

טוֹב הַדָּבָר אִם תָּמִיד מְקַנְאִים לְטוֹבָה, וְלֹא רַק כְּשֶׁאֲנִי שׁוֹהֶה אֶצְלְכֶם
tov haddavar im tamid mekanne'im letovah, velo rak keshe'ani shoheh etzlechem
But it is good to be zealously sought in a good matter at all times, and not only when I am present with you.

יְלָדַי, שׁוּב נָתוּן אֲנִי בְּחֶבְלֵי לֵדָה עֲלֵיכֶם עַד אֲשֶׁר יִכּוֹן הַמָּשִׁיחַ בָּכֶם
yeladai, shuv natun ani bechevlei ledah aleichem ad asher yikkon hammashiach bachem
My little children, of whom I am again in travail until Christ be formed in you—

רְצוֹנִי לִהְיוֹת עִמָּכֶם עַכְשָׁו וּלְשַׁנּוֹת אֶת נִימַת קוֹלִי, שֶׁכֵּן אֲנִי נָבוֹךְ בְּנוֹגֵעַ אֲלֵיכֶם
retzoni lihyot immachem achshav uleshannot et nimat koli, shekken ani navoch benogea aleichem
but I could wish to be present with you now, and to change my tone; for I am perplexed about you.

אִמְרוּ לִי, אַתֶּם הָרוֹצִים לִהְיוֹת כְּפוּפִים לַתּוֹרָה, הַאֵינְכֶם שׁוֹמְעִים אֶת הַתּוֹרָה
imru li, attem harotzim lihyot kefufim lattorah, ha'einechem shome'im et hattorah
Tell me, ye that desire to be under the law, do ye not hear the law?

הֲלֹא כָּתוּב שֶׁלְּאַבְרָהָם הָיוּ שְׁנֵי בָנִים, הָאֶחָד מִן הָאָמָה וְהַשֵּׁנִי מֵהָאִשָּׁה הַחָפְשִׁיָּה
halo katuv shelle'avraham hayu shenei banim, ha'echad min ha'amah vehasheni meha'ishah hachofshiyah
For it is written, that Abraham had two sons, one by the handmaid, and one by the freewoman.

אַךְ בֶּן הָאָמָה נוֹלַד לְפִי הַבָּשָׂר, וְאִלּוּ בֶּן הַחָפְשִׁיָּה עַל־פִּי הַהַבְטָחָה
ach ben ha'amah nolad lefi habbasar, ve'ilu ben hachofshiyah al-pi hahavtachah
Howbeit the son by the handmaid is born after the flesh; but the son by the freewoman is born through promise.

הַדְּבָרִים הָאֵלֶּה הֵם מָשָׁל לִשְׁתֵּי הַבְּרִיתוֹת
haddevarim ha'elleh hem mashal lishtei habberitot
Which things contain an allegory: for these women are two covenants;

הָאַחַת מֵהַר סִינַי, הַיּוֹלֶדֶת לְעַבְדוּת, וְהִיא הָגָר
ha'achat mehar sinai, hayoledet le'avdut, vehi hagar
one from mount Sinai, bearing children unto bondage, which is Hagar.

הָגָר מְסַמֶּלֶת אֶת הַר סִינַי שֶׁבַּעֲרָב וּמַקְבִּילָה לִירוּשָׁלַיִם שֶׁל יָמֵינוּ
hagar mesammelet et har sinai shebba'arav umakbilah liyerushalayim shel yameinu
Now this Hagar is mount Sinai in Arabia and answereth to the Jerusalem that now is:

כִּי הִיא בְּעַבְדוּת עִם בָּנֶיהָ
ki hi be'avdut im baneiha
for she is in bondage with her children.

אֲבָל יְרוּשָׁלַיִם שֶׁל מַעְלָה בַּת חוֹרִין הִיא, וְהִיא אֵם לָנוּ
aval yerushalayim shel ma'lah bat chorin hi, vehi em lanu
But the Jerusalem that is above is free, which is our mother.

שֶׁהֲרֵי כָּתוּב: רָנִּי עֲקָרָה לֹא יָלָדָה
sheharei katuv: rani akarah lo yaladah
For it is written, Rejoice, thou barren that bearest not;

הַגָּלָטִים

אֲבָל כָּעֵת, כְּשֶׁאַתֶּם יוֹדְעִים אֶת אֱלֹהִים - אוֹ לְיֶתֶר דִּיּוּק, כְּשֶׁאֱלֹהִים יוֹדֵעַ אֶתְכֶם
aval ka'et, keshe'attem yode'im et elohim - o leyeter diyuk, keshe'elohim yodea etchem
but now that ye have come to know God, or rather to be known by God,

כֵּיצַד זֶה חוֹזְרִים אַתֶּם לַיְסוֹדוֹת הַחַלָּשִׁים וְהָעֲלוּבִים שֶׁבִּרְצוֹנְכֶם לְעָבְדָם מֵחָדָשׁ
keitzad zeh chozerim attem laysodot hachallashim veha'aluvim shebbirtzonechem le'avedam mechadash
how turn ye back again to the weak and beggarly rudiments, whereunto ye desire to be in bondage over again?

הִנֵּה אַתֶּם מְכַבְּדִים יָמִים וָחֳדָשִׁים; מוֹעֲדִים וְשָׁנִים
hinneh attem mechabbedim yamim vochodashim; mo'adim veshanim
Ye observe days, and months, and seasons, and years.

חוֹשְׁשַׁנִי כִּי לַשָּׁוְא עָמַלְתִּי בָּכֶם
chosheshani ki lashav amalti bachem
I am afraid of you, lest by any means I have bestowed labor upon you in vain.

הֱיוּ כָּמוֹנִי, כִּי גַּם אֲנִי נִהְיֵיתִי כְּמוֹכֶם, אַחַי! אֲנִי מְבַקֵּשׁ מִכֶּם! לֹא עֲשִׂיתֶם לִי שׁוּם רַע
heyu kamoni, ki gam ani nihyeiti kemochem, achai! ani mevakkesh mikkem! lo asitem li shum ra
I beseech you, brethren, become as I am, for I also am become as ye are. Ye did me no wrong:

אַתֶּם יוֹדְעִים שֶׁבִּנְסִבּוֹת שֶׁל חֻלְשַׁת הַגּוּף בִּשַּׂרְתִּי לָכֶם אֶת הַבְּשׂוֹרָה בַּתְּחִלָּה
attem yode'im shebbinsibbot shel chulshat hagguf bissarti lachem et habbesorah battechillah
but ye know that because of an infirmity of the flesh I preached the gospel unto you the first time:

וְלֹא בְּחַלְתֶּם בַּנִּסָּיוֹן שֶׁבָּא עֲלֵיכֶם בְּשֶׁל גּוּפִי, אַף לֹא הִגְבַּתֶּם בְּבוּז
velo bechaltem bannissayon shebba aleichem beshel gufi, af lo hegavtem bevuz
and that which was a temptation to you in my flesh ye despised not, nor rejected;

אֶלָּא קִבַּלְתֶּם אוֹתִי כְּמַלְאַךְ אֱלֹהִים, כַּמָּשִׁיחַ יֵשׁוּעַ
ella kibbaltem oti kemal'ach elohim, kammashiach yeshua
but ye received me as an angel of God, even as Christ Jesus.

אִם כֵּן אֵיפֹה חֶדְוַתְכֶם עַתָּה
im ken eifoh chedvatchem attah
Where then is that gratulation of yourselves?

הֲרֵינִי מֵעִיד עֲלֵיכֶם שֶׁאִלּוּ יְכָלְתֶּם הֱיִיתֶם עוֹקְרִים אֶת עֵינֵיכֶם כְּדֵי לְתִתָּן לִי
hareini me'id aleichem she'illu yechaltem heyitem okerim et eineichem kedei letittan li
for I bear you witness, that, if possible, ye would have plucked out your eyes and given them to me.

וְעַתָּה הַאִם הָפַכְתִּי לָכֶם לְאוֹיֵב בְּאָמְרִי לָכֶם אֶת הָאֱמֶת
ve'attah ha'im hafachti lachem le'oyev be'omri lachem et ha'emet
So then am I become your enemy, by telling you the truth?

הָאֲנָשִׁים הַלָּלוּ מְקַנְּאִים לָכֶם שֶׁלֹּא לְטוֹבָה; רְצוֹנָם לְהַרְחִיק אֶתְכֶם כְּדֵי שֶׁאַתֶּם תְּקַנְּאוּ לָהֶם
ha'anashim hallalu mekanne'im lachem shello letovah; retzonam leharchik etchem kedei she'attem tekanne'u lahem
They zealously seek you in no good way; nay, they desire to shut you out, that ye may seek them.

הַגָּלָטִים

אֵין יְהוּדִי אַף לֹא גּוֹי, אֵין עֶבֶד אַף לֹא בֶּן חוֹרִין
ein yehudi af lo goy, ein eved af lo ben chorin
There can be neither Jew nor Greek, there can be neither bond nor free,

לֹא זָכָר אַף לֹא נְקֵבָה, מִשּׁוּם שֶׁכֻּלְּכֶם אֶחָד בַּמָּשִׁיחַ יֵשׁוּעַ
lo zachar af lo nekevah, mishum shekkullechem echad bammashiach yeshua
there can be no male and female; for ye all are one man in Christ Jesus.

וְאִם אַתֶּם שַׁיָּכִים לַמָּשִׁיחַ, אֲזַי זֶרַע אַבְרָהָם אַתֶּם וְיוֹרְשִׁים עַל־פִּי הַהַבְטָחָה
ve'im attem shayachim lammashiach, azai zera avraham attem veyoreshim al-pi hahavtachah
And if ye are Christ's, then are ye Abraham's seed, heirs according to promise.

ד

הֲרֵינִי אוֹמֵר זֹאת: כָּל עוֹד הַיּוֹרֵשׁ קָטִין אֵין הוּא שׁוֹנֶה מֵעֶבֶד, אַף כִּי הוּא אֲדוֹן כָּל הַנַּחֲלָה
hareini omer zot: kol od hayoresh kattin ein hu shoneh me'eved, af ki hu adon kol hannachalah
But I say that so long as the heir is a child, he differeth nothing from a bondservant though he is lord of all;

וְאוּלָם הוּא נָתוּן לְמָרוּת שֶׁל אֶפִּטְרוֹפְּסִים וַאֲנָשִׁים הַמֻּפְקָדִים עַל הַבַּיִת עַד לַמּוֹעֵד שֶׁקָּבַע אָבִיו
ve'ulam hu natun lemarut shel eppitroppesim va'anashim hammufkadim al habbayit ad lammo'ed shekkava aviv
but is under guardians and stewards until the day appointed of the father.

כֵּן גַּם אֲנַחְנוּ, בְּעֵת הֱיוֹתֵנוּ קְטַנִּים - הָיִינוּ מְשֻׁעְבָּדִים לִיסוֹדוֹת הָעוֹלָם
ken gam anachnu, be'et heyotenu kattinim - hayinu meshu'badim liysodot ha'olam
So we also, when we were children, were held in bondage under the rudiments of the world:

אֲבָל כַּאֲשֶׁר מָלְאָה הָעֵת שָׁלַח אֱלֹהִים אֶת בְּנוֹ, יְלוּד אִשָּׁה וְכָפוּף לַתּוֹרָה
aval ka'asher male'ah ha'et shalach elohim et beno, yelud ishah vechafuf lattorah
but when the fulness of the time came, God sent forth his Son, born of a woman, born under the law,

לִפְדּוֹת אֶת הַכְּפוּפִים לַתּוֹרָה כְּדֵי שֶׁנְּקַבֵּל אֶת מַעֲמַד הַבָּנִים
lifdot et hakkefufim lattorah kedei shennekabbel et ma'amad habbanim
that he might redeem them that were under the law, that we might receive the adoption of sons.

וְכֵיוָן שֶׁאַתֶּם בָּנִים, אֱלֹהִים נָתַן בְּלִבַּבְכֶם אֶת רוּחַ בְּנוֹ הַקּוֹרֵאת אַבָּא, אָבִינוּ
vecheivan she'attem banim, elohim natan bilvavchem et ruach beno hakkoret abba, avinu
And because ye are sons, God sent forth the Spirit of his Son into our hearts, crying, Abba, Father.

לְפִיכָךְ אֵינְךָ עֶבֶד עוֹד, כִּי אִם בֵּן; וְאִם בֵּן, אֲזַי גַּם יוֹרֵשׁ מִטַּעַם אֱלֹהִים
lefichach eincha eved od, ki im ben; ve'im ben, azai gam yoresh mitta'am elohim
So that thou art no longer a bondservant, but a son; and if a son, then an heir through God.

בֶּעָבָר, בְּעֵת שֶׁלֹּא יְדַעְתֶּם אֶת אֱלֹהִים, עֲבַדְתֶּם אֶת מִי שֶׁבְּמַהוּתָם אֵינָם אֱלֹהִים
be'avar, be'et shello yeda'tem et elohim, avadtem et mi shebbemahutam einam elohim
Howbeit at that time, not knowing God, ye were in bondage to them that by nature are no gods:

הַגָּלָטִים

עַד כִּי יָבוֹא הַזֶּרַע אֲשֶׁר לוֹ מְכֻוֶּנֶת הַהַבְטָחָה
ad ki yavo hazzera asher lo mechuvvenet hahavtachah
till the seed should come to whom the promise hath been made;

הַתּוֹרָה נִמְסְרָה בְּאֶמְצָעוּת מַלְאָכִים בִּידֵי מְתַוֵּךְ
hattorah nimserah be'emtza'ut mal'achim biydei metavvech
and it was ordained through angels by the hand of a mediator.

הַמְתַוֵּךְ אֵינֶנּוּ שֶׁל אֶחָד וֵאלֹהִים הוּא אֶחָד
hamtavvech einennu shel echad ve'elohim hu echad
Now a mediator is not a mediator of one; but God is one.

הַאִם מִכָּאן שֶׁהַתּוֹרָה נוֹגֶדֶת אֶת הַבְטָחוֹת אֱלֹהִים? חָלִילָה
ha'im mikkan shehattorah nogedet et havtachot elohim? chalilah
Is the law then against the promises of God? God forbid:

שֶׁכֵּן אִלּוּ נִתְּנָה תוֹרָה שֶׁבְּיָכָלְתָּהּ לָתֵת חַיִּים, כִּי אָז בֶּאֱמֶת הָיָה אֶפְשָׁר לְהִצָּדֵק עַל־יְדֵי הַתּוֹרָה
shekken illu nittnah torah shebbichaletah latet chayim, ki az be'emet hayah efshar lehitzadek al-yedei hattorah
for if there had been a law given which could make alive, verily righteousness would have been of the law.

אֲבָל הַמִּקְרָא הִסְגִּיר אֶת הַכֹּל בְּיַד הַחֵטְא
aval hammikra hisgir et hakkol beyad hachet
But the scripture shut up all things under sin,

כְּדֵי שֶׁעַל סְמַךְ אֱמוּנַת יֵשׁוּעַ הַמָּשִׁיחַ תִּנָּתֵן הַהַבְטָחָה לַמַּאֲמִינִים
kedei she'al smach emunat yeshua hammashiach tinnaten hahavtachah lamma'aminim
that the promise by faith in Jesus Christ might be given to them that believe.

לִפְנֵי בּוֹא הָאֱמוּנָה נִשְׁמַרְנוּ תַּחַת יַד הַתּוֹרָה, כְּלוּאִים הָיִינוּ לִקְרַאת הָאֱמוּנָה הָעֲתִידָה לְהִגָּלוֹת
lifnei bo ha'emunah nishmarnu tachat yad hattorah, kelu'im hayinu likrat ha'emunah ha'atidah lehiggalot
But before faith came, we were kept in ward under the law, shut up unto the faith which should afterwards be revealed.

לְפִיכָךְ הָיְתָה הַתּוֹרָה אוֹמֶנֶת הַמַּדְרִיכָה אוֹתָנוּ אֶל הַמָּשִׁיחַ, לְמַעַן נֻצְדַּק עַל־יְדֵי אֱמוּנָה
lefichach hayetah hattorah omenet hammadrichah otanu el hammashiach, lema'an nutzdak al-yedei emunah
So that the law is become our tutor to bring us unto Christ, that we might be justified by faith.

אֲבָל לְאַחַר בּוֹא הָאֱמוּנָה אֵינֶנּוּ נְתוּנִים עוֹד לְמָרוּת הָאוֹמֶנֶת
aval le'achar bo ha'emunah einennu netunim od lemarut ha'omenet
But now that faith is come, we are no longer under a tutor.

כֻּלְּכֶם בָּנִים־לֵאלֹהִים עַל־יְדֵי הָאֱמוּנָה בַּמָּשִׁיחַ יֵשׁוּעַ
kulchem banim-lelohim al-yedei ha'emunah bammashiach yeshua
For ye are all sons of God, through faith, in Christ Jesus.

כִּי כֻּלְּכֶם אֲשֶׁר נִטְבַּלְתֶּם לַמָּשִׁיחַ לְבַשְׁתֶּם אֶת הַמָּשִׁיחַ
ki kullechem asher nitbaltem lammashiach levashtem et hammashiach
For as many of you as were baptized into Christ did put on Christ.

הַגָּלָטִים

שֶׁכֵּן הַכָּתוּב אוֹמֵר, קִלְלַת אֱלֹהִים תָּלוּי עַל־עֵץ
shekken hakkatuv omer, kilelat elohim talui al-'etz
for it is written, Cursed is every one that hangeth on a tree:

כְּדֵי שֶׁבְּיֵשׁוּעַ הַמָּשִׁיחַ תַּגִּיעַ בִּרְכַּת אַבְרָהָם אֶל הַגּוֹיִם
kedei shebbeyeshua hammashiach taggia birkat avraham el haggoyim
that upon the Gentiles might come the blessing of Abraham in Christ Jesus;

לְמַעַן נִנְחַל עַל־יְדֵי הָאֱמוּנָה אֶת הָרוּחַ הַמֻּבְטַחַת
lema'an ninchal al-yedei ha'emunah et haruach hammuvtachat
that we might receive the promise of the Spirit through faith.

אַחַי, אֲדַבֵּר מִנְּקֻדַּת רְאוּת אֱנוֹשִׁית
achai, adabber minnekuddat re'ut enoshit
Brethren, I speak after the manner of men:

אֲפִלּוּ צַוָּאָה שֶׁל אָדָם, לְאַחַר שֶׁקִּבְּלָה תֹּקֶף, אִישׁ אֵינוֹ יָכוֹל לְבַטְּלָהּ אוֹ לְהוֹסִיף עָלֶיהָ
afillu tzavva'ah shel adam, le'achar shekkibbelah tokef, ish eino yachol levattelah o lehosif aleiha
Though it be but a man's covenant, yet when it hath been confirmed, no one maketh it void, or addeth thereto.

וְהִנֵּה הַהַבְטָחוֹת נֶאֶמְרוּ לְאַבְרָהָם, וּלְזַרְעוֹ
vehinneh hahavtachot ne'emru le'avraham, ulezar'o
Now to Abraham were the promises spoken, and to his seed.

לֹא נֶאֱמַר לִזְרָעֶיךָ, כְּמוֹ עַל רַבִּים, אֶלָּא לְזַרְעֲךָ, כְּמוֹ עַל יָחִיד, וְהוּא הַמָּשִׁיחַ
lo ne'emar lizra'eicha, kemo al rabbim, ella lezar'acha, kemo al yachid, vehu hammashiach
He saith not, And to seeds, as of many; but as of one, And to thy seed, which is Christ.

הֲרֵינִי אוֹמֵר זֹאת: בְּרִית אֲשֶׁר אֱלֹהִים כָּרַת מִקֶּדֶם
hareini omer zot: berit asher elohim karat mikkedem
Now this I say: A covenant confirmed beforehand by God,

הַתּוֹרָה שֶׁנִּתְּנָה אַחֲרֵי אַרְבַּע מֵאוֹת וּשְׁלוֹשִׁים שָׁנָה לֹא תּוּכַל לְהָפֵר אוֹתָהּ וּלְבַטֵּל אֶת הַהַבְטָחָה
hattorah shennittenah acharei arba me'ot usheloshim shanah lo tuchal lehafer otah ulevattel et hahavtachah
the law, which came four hundred and thirty years after, doth not disannul, so as to make the promise of none effect.

שֶׁהֲרֵי אִם הַנַּחֲלָה הִיא מִן הַתּוֹרָה, אֲזַי אֵינֶנָּה מְבֻסֶּסֶת עוֹד עַל הַהַבְטָחָה
sheharei im hannachalah hi min hattorah, azai einennah mevusseset od al hahavtachah
For if the inheritance is of the law, it is no more of promise:

אֲבָל בְּהַבְטָחָה הֶעֱנִיק אֱלֹהִים לְאַבְרָהָם אֶת הַנַּחֲלָה
aval behavtachah he'enik elohim le'avraham et hannachalah
but God hath granted it to Abraham by promise.

אִם כֵּן לְשֵׁם מָה הַתּוֹרָה? הִיא נוֹסְפָה בִּגְלַל הָעֲבֵרוֹת
im ken leshem mah hattorah? hi nosefah biglal ha'averot
What then is the law? It was added because of transgressions,

הַגָּלָטִים

הַמַּאֲצִיל עֲלֵיכֶם אֶת הָרוּחַ וְעוֹשֶׂה בְּקִרְבְּכֶם נִפְלָאוֹת
hamma'atzil aleichem et haruach ve'oseh bekirbechem nifla'ot
He therefore that supplieth to you the Spirit, and worketh miracles among you,

הַאִם הוּא עוֹשֶׂה זֹאת בְּשֶׁל קִיּוּם מִצְוֹת הַתּוֹרָה, אוֹ בְּשֶׁל שְׁמִיעָה שֶׁבָּאֱמוּנָה
ha'im hu oseh zot beshel kiyum mitzvot hattorah, o beshel shemi'ah shebba'emunah
doeth he it by the works of the law, or by the hearing of faith?

כְּמוֹ שֶׁאַבְרָהָם הֶאֱמִין בֵּאלֹהִים וְנֶחְשְׁבָה לוֹ צְדָקָה
kemo she'avraham he'emin be'elohim venechshevah lo tzedakah
Even as Abraham believed God, and it was reckoned unto him for righteousness.

וּבְכֵן דְּעוּ כִּי בְּנֵי הָאֱמוּנָה הֵם בְּנֵי אַבְרָהָם
uvechen de'u ki benei ha'emunah hem benei avraham
Know therefore that they that are of faith, the same are sons of Abraham.

וְהַכָּתוּב, בְּיָדְעוֹ מֵרֹאשׁ שֶׁאֱלֹהִים יַצְדִּיק אֶת הַגּוֹיִם עַל־יְדֵי אֱמוּנָה
vehakkatuv, beyade'o merosh she'elohim yatzdik et haggoyim al-yedei emunah
And the scripture, foreseeing that God would justify the Gentiles by faith

הִקְדִּים לְבַשֵּׂר לְאַבְרָהָם: וְנִבְרְכוּ בְךָ כָּל הַגּוֹיִם
hikdim levasser le'avraham. venivrechu vecha kol haggoyim
preached the gospel beforehand unto Abraham, saying, In thee shall all the nations be blessed.

מִכָּאן שֶׁהַמַּחֲזִיקִים בָּאֱמוּנָה מְבֹרָכִים יַחַד עִם אַבְרָהָם הַמַּאֲמִין
mikkan shehammachazikim ba'emunah mevorachim yachad im avraham hamma'amin
So then they that are of faith are blessed with the faithful Abraham.

הַנִּשְׁעָנִים עַל קִיּוּם מִצְוֹת הַתּוֹרָה נְתוּנִים תַּחַת קְלָלָה,
hannish'anim al kiyum mitzvot hattorah netunim tachat kelalah
For as many as are of the works of the law are under a curse:

שֶׁהֲרֵי כָּתוּב, אָרוּר כָּל מִי שֶׁלֹּא יָקִים אֶת כָּל הַדְּבָרִים הַכְּתוּבִים בְּסֵפֶר הַתּוֹרָה לַעֲשׂוֹת אוֹתָם
sheharei katuv, arur kol mi shello yakim et kol haddevarim hakketuvim besefer hattorah la'asot otam
for it is written, Cursed is every one who continueth not in all things that are written in the book of the law, to do them.

דָּבָר בָּרוּר הוּא שֶׁאִישׁ לֹא יֻצְדַּק לִפְנֵי אֱלֹהִים עַל־יְדֵי הַתּוֹרָה, שֶׁכֵּן צַדִּיק בֶּאֱמוּנָתוֹ יִחְיֶה
davar barur hu she'ish lo yutzdak lifnei elohim al-yedei hattorah, shekken tzaddik be'emunato yichyeh
Now that no man is justified by the law before God, is evident: for, The righteous shall live by faith;

וְהַתּוֹרָה אֵינֶנָּה נִזְקֶקֶת לֶאֱמוּנָה, אֶלָּא שֶׁיַּעֲשֶׂה הָאָדָם אֶת דְּבָרֶיהָ וְחַי בָּהֶם
vehattorah einennah nizkeket le'emunah, ella sheya'aseh ha'adam et devareiha vachai bahem
and the law is not of faith; but, He that doeth them shall live in them.

הַמָּשִׁיחַ פָּדָה אוֹתָנוּ מִקִּלְלַת הַתּוֹרָה בְּכָךְ שֶׁהָיָה לִקְלָלָה בַּעֲדֵנוּ
hammashiach padah otanu mikkilelat hattorah bechach shehayah liklalah ba'adenu
Christ redeemed us from the curse of the law, having become a curse for us;

הַגָּלְטִים

שֶׁהֲרֵי אִם אֲנִי בּוֹנֶה שׁוּב אֶת מַה שֶׁהֲרַסְתִּי, בְּכָךְ אֲנִי מֵעִיד עַל עַצְמִי שֶׁאֲנִי עֲבַרְיָן
sheharei im ani boneh shuv et mah sheharasti, bechach ani me'id al atzmi she'ani avaryan
For if I build up again those things which I destroyed, I prove myself a transgressor.

אֲנִי מַתִּי לְגַבֵּי הַתּוֹרָה בִּגְלַל הַתּוֹרָה, כְּדֵי שֶׁאֶחְיֶה לֵאלֹהִים
ani matti legabbei hattorah biglal hattorah, kedei she'echyeh lelohim
For I through the law died unto the law, that I might live unto God.

עִם הַמָּשִׁיחַ נִצְלַבְתִּי וְלֹא עוֹד אֲנִי חַי, אֶלָּא הַמָּשִׁיחַ חַי בִּי.
im hammashiach nitzlavti velo od ani chai, ella hammashiach chai bi
I have been crucified with Christ; and it is no longer I that live, but Christ liveth in me:

הַחַיִּים שֶׁאֲנִי חַי עַכְשָׁו בַּבָּשָׂר, אֲנִי חַי אוֹתָם בֶּאֱמוּנַת בֶּן־הָאֱלֹהִים
hachayim she'ani chai achshav babbasar, ani chai otam be'emunat ben-ha'elohim
and that life which I now live in the flesh I live in faith, the faith which is in the Son of God,

אֲשֶׁר אֲהֵבַנִי וּמָסַר עַצְמוֹ בַּעֲדִי
asher ahevani umasar atzmo ba'adi
who loved me, and gave himself up for me.

אֵינֶנִּי מְבַטֵּל אֶת חֶסֶד אֱלֹהִים. הֲלֹא אִם אֶפְשָׁר לְהִצָּדֵק עַל־יְדֵי הַתּוֹרָה, הֲרֵי שֶׁהַמָּשִׁיחַ מֵת לַשָּׁוְא
einenni mevattel et chesed elohim. halo im efshar lehitzadek al-yedei hattorah, harei shehammashiach met lashav
I do not make void the grace of God: for if righteousness is through the law, then Christ died for nought.

ג

הוֹי גָּלְטִים כְּסִילִים! מִי אִחֵז אֶת עֵינֵיכֶם אַחֲרֵי שֶׁהוֹדִיעוּכֶם בְּפֵרוּשׁ שֶׁיֵּשׁוּעַ הַמָּשִׁיחַ נִצְלַב
hoy galatim kesilim! mi ichez et eineichem acharei shehodi'uchem beferush sheyeshua hammashiach nitzlav
O foolish Galatians, who did bewitch you, before whose eyes Jesus Christ was openly set forth crucified?

דָּבָר אֶחָד רוֹצֶה אֲנִי שֶׁתּוֹדִיעוּנִי
davar echad rotzeh ani shettodi'uni
This only would I learn from you,

הַאִם בְּשֶׁל קִיּוּם מִצְווֹת הַתּוֹרָה קִבַּלְתֶּם אֶת הָרוּחַ, אוֹ בְּשֶׁל שְׁמִיעָה שֶׁבָּאֱמוּנָה
ha'im beshel kiyum mitzvot hattorah kibbaltem et haruach, o beshel shemi'ah shebba'emunah
Received ye the Spirit by the works of the law, or by the hearing of faith?

הַאִם כְּסִילִים אַתֶּם כָּל כָּךְ? הַאִם לְאַחַר שֶׁהִתְחַלְתֶּם בָּרוּחַ תַּגִּיעוּ כָּעֵת לִשְׁלֵמוּת עַל־יְדֵי הַבָּשָׂר
ha'im kesilim attem kol kach? ha'im le'achar shehitchaltem baruach taggi'u ka'et lishlemut al-yedei habbasar
Are ye so foolish? having begun in the Spirit, are ye now perfected in the flesh?

הַאִם לַשָּׁוְא הִתְנַסֵּיתֶם בִּדְבָרִים רַבִּים כָּל כָּךְ? הַאֻמְנָם לַשָּׁוְא
ha'im lashav hitnasseitem bidvarim rabbim kol kach? ha'umnam lashav
Did ye suffer so many things in vain? if it be indeed in vain.

הַגָּלָטִים

וְיֶתֶר הָאַחִים הַיְהוּדִים כִּחֲשׁוּ כָּמוֹהוּ
veyeter ha'achim hayehudim kichashu kamohu
And the rest of the Jews dissembled likewise with him;

עַד שֶׁאֲפִלּוּ בַּר-נַבָּא נִגְרַר אַחֲרֵיהֶם בְּכַחֲשָׁם
ad she'afillu bar-nabba nigrar achareihem bechachasham
insomuch that even Barnabas was carried away with their dissimulation.

בִּרְאוֹתִי כִּי הֵם סוֹטִים מֵאֱמֶת הַבְּשׂוֹרָה
bir'oti ki hem sotim me'emet habbesorah
But when I saw that they walked not uprightly according to the truth of the gospel,

אָמַרְתִּי לְכֵיפָא לְעֵינֵי כָּל הַנּוֹכְחִים: אִם אַתָּה הַיְהוּדִי מִתְנַהֵג כְּגוֹי וְלֹא כִּיהוּדִי
amarti lecheifa le'einei kol hannochechim. im attah hayehudi mitnaheg kegoy velo kiyehudi
I said unto Cephas before them all, If thou, being a Jew, livest as do the Gentiles, and not as do the Jews,

מַדּוּעַ תְּאַלֵּץ אֶת הַגּוֹיִם לִחְיוֹת כִּיהוּדִים
maddua te'alletz et haggoyim lichyot kiyehudim
how compellest thou the Gentiles to live as do the Jews?

אָנוּ יְהוּדִים בְּנֵי יְהוּדִים, לֹא אֲנָשִׁים חַטָּאִים מִן הַגּוֹיִם
anu yehudim benei yehudim, lo anashim chatta'im min haggoyim
We being Jews by nature, and not sinners of the Gentiles,

וְכֵיוָן שֶׁיּוֹדְעִים אָנוּ כִּי הָאָדָם אֵינוֹ נִצְדָּק בְּקִיּוּם מִצְווֹת הַתּוֹרָה, אֶלָּא בֶּאֱמוּנַת הַמָּשִׁיחַ יֵשׁוּעַ
vecheivan sheyode'im anu ki ha'adam eino nitzdak bekiyum mitzvot hattorah, ella be'emunat hammashiach yeshua
yet knowing that a man is not justified by the works of the law but through faith in Jesus Christ,

הֶאֱמַנּוּ גַּם אֲנַחְנוּ בַּמָּשִׁיחַ יֵשׁוּעַ
he'emannu gam anachnu bammashiach yeshua
even we believed on Christ Jesus,

לְמַעַן נִצְדַּק מִתּוֹךְ אֱמוּנָה בַּמָּשִׁיחַ וְלֹא בְּקִיּוּם מִצְווֹת הַתּוֹרָה
lema'an nutzdak mittoch emunah bammashiach velo bekiyum mitzvot hattorah
that we might be justified by faith in Christ, and not by the works of the law:

שֶׁכֵּן בְּקִיּוּם מִצְווֹת הַתּוֹרָה לֹא יִצְדַּק כָּל בָּשָׂר
shekken bekiyum mitzvot hattorah lo yutzdak kol basar
because by the works of the law shall no flesh be justified.

אֲבָל אִם בְּשָׁעָה שֶׁאֲנַחְנוּ מְבַקְשִׁים לְהִצָּדֵק בַּמָּשִׁיחַ
aval im besha'ah she'anachnu mevakshim lehitzadek bammashiach
But if, while we sought to be justified in Christ,

יִמָּצֵא שֶׁגַּם אֲנַחְנוּ אֲנָשִׁים חוֹטְאִים, הַאִם נוֹבֵעַ מִזֶּה שֶׁהַמָּשִׁיחַ מְשָׁרֵת לַחֵטְא? חַס וְחָלִילָה
yimmatzei sheggam anachnu anashim chote'im, ha'im novea mizzeh shehammashiach mesharet lachet? chas vechalilah
we ourselves also were found sinners, is Christ a minister of sin? God forbid.

הַגָּלָטִים

בְּעֵינַי לֹא קוֹבֵעַ מֶה הָיָה מַעֲמָדָם אָז, שֶׁהֲרֵי אֱלֹהִים אֵינֶנּוּ נוֹשֵׂא פְּנֵי אִישׁ
be'einai lo kovea meh hayah ma'amadam az, sheharei elohim einennu nosei penei ish
(whatsoever they were, it maketh no matter to me: God accepteth not man's person)—

לֹא הוֹסִיפוּ לִי דָּבָר
lo hosifu li davar
they, I say, who were of repute imparted nothing to me:

אַדְּרַבָּא, הֵם הִכִּירוּ שֶׁבְּיָדַי הֻפְקְדָה הַבְּשׂוֹרָה אֲשֶׁר לָעֲרֵלִים
addrabba, hem hikkiru shebbeyadi hufkedah habbesorah asher la'arelim
but contrariwise, when they saw that I had been intrusted with the gospel of the uncircumcision,

כְּשֵׁם שֶׁבִּידֵי פֶּטְרוֹס הֻפְקְדָה הַבְּשׂוֹרָה אֲשֶׁר לַנִּמּוֹלִים
keshem shebbiyedei petros hufkedah habbesorah asher lannimmolim
even as Peter with the gospel of the circumcision

הֲרֵי מִי שֶׁעוֹרֵר אֶת פֶּטְרוֹס לִשְׁלִיחוּת אֶל הַנִּמּוֹלִים עוֹרֵר גַּם אוֹתִי אֶל הַגּוֹיִם
harei mi she'orer et petros lishlichut el hannimmolim orer gam oti el haggoyim
(for he that wrought for Peter unto the apostleship of the circumcision wrought for me also unto the Gentiles);

וְכַאֲשֶׁר יַעֲקֹב, כֵּיפָא וְיוֹחָנָן, הַנֶּחְשָׁבִים לְעַמּוּדֵי תָּוֶךְ, הִכִּירוּ בַּחֶסֶד שֶׁנִּתַּן לִי
vecha'asher ya'akov, keifa veyochanan, hannechshavim le'ammudei tavech, hikkiru bachesed shennittan li
and when they perceived the grace that was given unto me, James and Cephas and John, they who were reputed to be pillars,

הֵם הוֹשִׁיטוּ לִי וּלְבַר־נַבָּא אֶת יַד יְמִינָם לְאוֹת שִׁתּוּף
hem hoshitu li ulevar-nabba et yad yeminam le'ot shittuf
gave to me and Barnabas the right hands of fellowship,

שֶׁאָנוּ נֵלֵךְ לַגּוֹיִם וְהֵם לַנִּמּוֹלִים
she'anu nelech laggoyim vehem lannimmolim
that we should go unto the Gentiles, and they unto the circumcision;

וּבִלְבַד שֶׁנִּזְכֹּר אֶת הָעֲנִיִּים. וְאָכֵן אֶת זֹאת שָׁקַדְתִּי לַעֲשׂוֹת
uvilvad shennizkor et ha'aniyim. ve'achen et zot shakadti la'asot
only they would that we should remember the poor; which very thing I was also zealous to do.

כְּשֶׁבָּא כֵּיפָא לְאַנְטְיוֹכְיָה הִתְיַצַּבְתִּי נֶגְדּוֹ מִפְּנֵי שֶׁנִּמְצָא בּוֹ דְּבַר אַשְׁמָה
keshebba keifa le'antiyocheyah hityatzavti negdo mippenei shennimtza bo devar ashmah
But when Cephas came to Antioch, I resisted him to the face, because he stood condemned.

בְּטֶרֶם בָּאוּ כַּמָּה אֲנָשִׁים מֵאֵת יַעֲקֹב הוּא סָעַד יַחַד עִם הָאַחִים מִן הַגּוֹיִם
beterem ba'u kammah anashim me'et ya'akov hu sa'ad yachad im ha'achim min haggoyim
For before that certain came from James, he ate with the Gentiles;

אֲבָל כַּאֲשֶׁר בָּאוּ הַלָּלוּ נָסוֹג מֵהֶם בִּגְלַל פַּחְדּוֹ מִן הָאַחִים הַנִּמּוֹלִים
aval ka'asher ba'u hallalu nasog mehem biglal pachdo min ha'achim hannimmolim
but when they came, he drew back and separated himself, fearing them that were of the circumcision.

הַגָּלְטִים

ב

אַחֲרֵי אַרְבַּע־עֶשְׂרֵה שָׁנִים עָלִיתִי שׁוּב לִירוּשָׁלַיִם יַחַד עִם בַּר-נַבָּא, וְגַם אֶת טִיטוֹס לָקַחְתִּי אִתִּי
acharei arba'-'esreh shanim aliti shuv liyerushalayim yachad im bar-nabba, vegam et titos lakachti itti
Then after the space of fourteen years I went up again to Jerusalem with Barnabas, taking Titus also with me.

עָלִיתִי לְשָׁם עַל־פִּי הִתְגַּלּוּת שֶׁקִּבַּלְתִּי, וְהִצַּגְתִּי לִפְנֵיהֶם אֶת הַבְּשׂוֹרָה שֶׁאֲנִי מְבַשֵּׂר בַּגּוֹיִם
aliti lesham al-pi hitgallut shekkibbalti, vehitzagti lifneihem et habbesorah she'ani mevasser baggoyim
And I went up by revelation; and I laid before them the gospel which I preach among the Gentiles

הִצַּגְתִּיהָ לִפְנֵי הַחֲשׁוּבִים שֶׁבָּהֶם בִּפְגִישָׁה מְיֻחֶדֶת
hitzagtiha lifnei hachashuvim shebbahem bifgishah meyuchedet
but privately before them who were of repute,

כְּדֵי שֶׁלֹּא לַשָּׁוְא יִהְיֶה הַמֵּרוֹץ אֲשֶׁר רַצְתִּי וְעוֹדֶנִּי רָץ
kedei shello lashav yihyeh hammerotz asher ratzti ve'odenni ratz
lest by any means I should be running, or had run, in vain.

אֲפִלּוּ טִיטוֹס שֶׁהָיָה אִתִּי, עַל אַף הֱיוֹתוֹ יְוָנִי, לֹא הֻכְרַח לְהִמּוֹל
afillu titos shehayah itti, al af heyoto yevani, lo huchrach lehimmol
But not even Titus who was with me, being a Greek, was compelled to be circumcised:

בִּגְלַל אוֹתָם אֲחֵי שֶׁקֶר
biglal otam achei sheker
and that because of the false brethren privily brought in,

שֶׁהִסְתַּנְּנוּ בַּחֲשַׁאי כְּדֵי לִבְלֹשׁ אַחַר הַחֵרוּת שֶׁיֵּשׁ לָנוּ בַּמָּשִׁיחַ יֵשׁוּעַ
shehistannenu bachashai kedei livlosh achar hacherut sheyesh lanu bammashiach yeshua
who came in privily to spy out our liberty which we have in Christ Jesus,

כָּל כַּוָּנָתָם הָיְתָה לְשַׁעְבֵּד אוֹתָנוּ
kol kavvanatam hayetah lesha'bed otanu
that they might bring us into bondage:

אַךְ לֹא נִכְנַעְנוּ לָהֶם אַף לְרֶגַע, וְזֹאת
ach lo nichna'nu lahem af lerega, vezot
to whom we gave place in the way of subjection, no, not for an hour;

לְמַעַן תַּעֲמֹד בְּקִרְבְּכֶם אֱמֶת הַבְּשׂוֹרָה
lema'an ta'amod bekirbechem emet habbesorah
that the truth of the gospel might continue with you.

בְּרַם - הָאֲנָשִׁים הַנֶּחְשָׁבִים לַחֲשׁוּבִים
beram - ha'anashim hannechshavim lachashuvim
But from those who were reputed to be somewhat

הַגָּלָטִים

שֶׁהִקְדִּישַׁנִי מֵרֶחֶם אִמִּי וּקְרָאַנִי בְּחַסְדּוֹ
merechem immi ukera'ani bechasdo
even from my mother's womb, and called me through his grace,

רָצָה לְגַלּוֹת בִּי אֶת בְּנוֹ כְּדֵי שֶׁאֲבַשְּׂרֶנּוּ בַּגּוֹיִם, לֹא נוֹעַצְתִּי אָז עִם בָּשָׂר וָדָם
ratzah legallot bi et beno kedei she'avasserennu baggoyim, lo no'atzti az im basar vadam
to reveal his Son in me, that I might preach him among the Gentiles; straightway I conferred not with flesh and blood:

גַּם לֹא עָלִיתִי לִירוּשָׁלַיִם אֶל מִי שֶׁהָיוּ שְׁלִיחִים לְפָנַי
gam lo aliti liyerushalayim el mi shehayu shelichim lefanai
neither went I up to Jerusalem to them that were apostles before me:

אֶלָּא יָצָאתִי לָעֲרָב וְאַחַר כָּךְ חָזַרְתִּי לְדַמֶּשֶׂק
ella yatzati la'arav ve'achar kach chazarti ledammesek
but I went away into Arabia; and again I returned unto Damascus.

אַחֲרֵי שָׁלֹשׁ שָׁנִים עָלִיתִי לִירוּשָׁלַיִם לִרְאוֹת אֶת כֵּיפָא וְשָׁהִיתִי אֶצְלוֹ חֲמִשָּׁה־עָשָׂר יָמִים
acharei shalosh shanim aliti liyerushalayim lir'ot et keifa veshahiti etzlo chamishah-'asar yamim
Then after three years I went up to Jerusalem to visit Cephas, and tarried with him fifteen days.

שָׁלִיחַ אַחֵר לֹא רָאִיתִי, אֶלָּא אֶת יַעֲקֹב אֲחִי אֲדוֹנֵנוּ
shaliach acher lo ra'iti, ella et ya'akov achi adonenu
But other of the apostles saw I none, save James the Lord's brother.

וַאֲשֶׁר לַדְּבָרִים שֶׁאֲנִי כּוֹתֵב אֲלֵיכֶם, אֱלֹהִים עֵד שֶׁאֵינֶנִּי מְשַׁקֵּר
va'asher laddevarim she'ani kotev aleichem, elohim ed she'einenni meshakker
Now touching the things which I write unto you, behold, before God, I lie not.

אַחֲרֵי כֵן בָּאתִי אֶל גְּלִילוֹת סוּרְיָה וְקִילִיקְיָה
acharei chen bati el gelilot sureyah vekilikeyah
Then I came into the regions of Syria and Cilicia.

אֲבָל לֹא הָיִיתִי מֻכָּר בְּאֹפֶן אִישִׁי בִּקְהִלּוֹת הַמָּשִׁיחַ אֲשֶׁר בִּיהוּדָה
aval lo hayiti mukkar be'ofen ishi bik'hillot hammashiach asher biyehudah
And I was still unknown by face unto the churches of Judæa which were in Christ:

הֵם רַק שָׁמְעוּ כִּי הָאִישׁ אֲשֶׁר רָדַף אוֹתָנוּ בֶּעָבָר, מַטִּיף עַכְשָׁו אֶת הָאֱמוּנָה אֲשֶׁר בֶּעָבָר עָשָׂה בָּהּ שַׁמּוֹת
hem rak shame'u ki ha'ish asher radaf otanu be'avar, mattif achshav et ha'emunah asher be'avar asah bah shammot
but they only heard say, He that once persecuted us now preacheth the faith of which he once made havoc;

וְהִלְּלוּ אֶת אֱלֹהִים בַּעֲבוּרִי
vehillelu et elohim ba'avuri
and they glorified God in me.

הַגָּלָטִים

יְבַשֵּׂר לָכֶם בְּשׂוֹרָה שׁוֹנָה מִזּוֹ שֶׁבִּשַּׂרְנוּ לָכֶם, חֵרֶם יִהְיֶה
yevasser lachem bsorah shonah mizzo shebbissrenu lachem, cherem yihyeh
should preach unto you any gospel other than that which we preached unto you, let him be anathema.

אֲנִי חוֹזֵר וְאוֹמֵר מַה שֶּׁאָמַרְנוּ קֹדֶם לָכֵן
ani chozer ve'omer mah she'amarnu kodem lachen
As we have said before, so say I now again,

אִם מִישֶׁהוּ יַשְׁמִיעַ לָכֶם בְּשׂוֹרָה שׁוֹנָה מִזּוֹ שֶׁקִּבַּלְתֶּם, חֵרֶם יִהְיֶה
im mishehu yashmia lachem besorah shonah mizzo shekkibbaltem, cherem yihyeh
If any man preacheth unto you any gospel other than that which ye received, let him be anathema.

הַאִם אֶל בְּנֵי אָדָם אֲנִי מִתְרַצֶּה כָּעֵת, אוֹ אֶל אֱלֹהִים? הַאִם מִשְׁתַּדֵּל אֲנִי לִמְצֹא חֵן בְּעֵינֵי בְּנֵי אָדָם
ha'im el bnei adam ani mitratzeh ka'et, o el elohim? ha'im mishtaddel ani limtzo chen be'einei bnei adam
For am I now seeking the favor of men, or of God? or am I striving to please men?

אִלּוּ עֲדַיִן הִשְׁתַּדַּלְתִּי לִמְצֹא חֵן בְּעֵינֵי בְּנֵי אָדָם, לֹא הָיִיתִי עֶבֶד הַמָּשִׁיחַ
illu adayin hishtaddalti limtzo chen be'einei bnei adam, lo hayiti eved hammashiach
if I were still pleasing men, I should not be a servant of Christ.

הֲרֵינִי מוֹדִיעַ לָכֶם, אַחַי, כִּי הַבְּשׂוֹרָה שֶׁבִּשַּׂרְתִּי אֵינָהּ לְפִי מַחֲשֶׁבֶת אָדָם
hareini modia lachem, achai, ki habbsorah shebissarti einah lefi machashevet adam
For I make known to you, brethren, as touching the gospel which was preached by me, that it is not after man.

שֶׁכֵּן לֹא קִבַּלְתִּיהָ מֵאָדָם אַף לֹא לִמְּדוּנִי אוֹתָהּ, אֶלָּא קִבַּלְתִּיהָ בְּהִתְגַּלּוּת שֶׁל יֵשׁוּעַ הַמָּשִׁיחַ
shekken lo kibbaltiha me'adam af lo limmeduni otah, ella kibbaltiha behitgallut shel yeshua hammashiach
For neither did I receive it from man, nor was I taught it, but it came to me through revelation of Jesus Christ.

הֲרֵי שְׁמַעְתֶּם עַל הִתְנַהֲגוּתִי בֶּעָבָר בַּיַּהֲדוּת
harei shema'tem al hitnahaguti be'avar bayahadut
For ye have heard of my manner of life in time past in the Jews' religion,

שֶׁרָדַפְתִּי נִמְרָצוֹת אֶת קְהִלַּת אֱלֹהִים וְעָשִׂיתִי בָּהּ שַׁמּוֹת
sheradafti nimratzot et kehillat elohim ve'asiti bah shammot
how that beyond measure I persecuted the church of God, and made havoc of it:

וְהִתְעַלֵּיתִי בַּיַּהֲדוּת עַל רַבִּים מִבְּנֵי גִילִי אֲשֶׁר בְּעַמִּי
vehit'alleiti bayahadut al rabbim mibbenei gili asher be'ammi
and I advanced in the Jews' religion beyond many of mine own age

מִשּׁוּם קִנְאָתִי הַיְתֵרָה לְמָסוֹרוֹת אֲבוֹתַי
mishum kin'ati hayterah lemasorot avotai
among my countrymen, being more exceedingly zealous for the traditions of my fathers.

אֲבָל כַּאֲשֶׁר אֱלֹהִים
aval ka'asher elohim, shehikdishani
But when it was the good pleasure of God, who separated me,

הַגָּלְטִים

מֵאֵת שָׁאוּל - שָׁלִיחַ שֶׁאֵינוֹ מִטַּעַם בְּנֵי אָדָם אַף לֹא נִתְמַנָּה עַל־יְדֵי אָדָם, אֶלָּא עַל־יְדֵי יֵשׁוּעַ הַמָּשִׁיחַ
me'et sha'ul - shaliach she'eino mitta'am benei adam af lo nitmannah al-yedei adam, ella al-yedei yeshua hammashiach
Paul, an apostle (not from men, neither through man, but through Jesus Christ,

וֵאלֹהִים הָאָב שֶׁהֱקִימוֹ מִן הַמֵּתִים
ve'elohim ha'av shehekimo min hammetim
and God the Father, who raised him from the dead),

וּמֵאֵת כָּל הָאַחִים אֲשֶׁר אִתִּי, אֶל קְהִלּוֹת גַּלַטְיָה
ume'et kol ha'achim asher itti, el kehillot galatyah
and all the brethren that are with me, unto the churches of Galatia:

חֶסֶד וְשָׁלוֹם לָכֶם מֵאֵת הָאֱלֹהִים אָבִינוּ וּמֵאֵת אֲדוֹנֵנוּ יֵשׁוּעַ הַמָּשִׁיחַ
chesed veshalom lachem me'et ha'elohim avinu ume'et adonenu yeshua hammashiach
Grace to you and peace from God the Father, and our Lord Jesus Christ,

שֶׁנָּתַן אֶת עַצְמוֹ עַל חֲטָאֵינוּ כְּדֵי לְחַלְּצֵנוּ מִן הָעוֹלָם הָרָע הַזֶּה
shennatan et atzmo al chata'einu kedei lechalletzenu min ha'olam hara hazzeh
who gave himself for our sins, that he might deliver us out of this present evil world,

כִּרְצוֹן אֱלֹהִים אָבִינוּ
kirtzon elohim avinu
according to the will of our God and Father:

לֵאלֹהִים הַכָּבוֹד לְעוֹלְמֵי עוֹלָמִים. אָמֵן
lelohim hakkavod le'olemei olamim. amen
to whom be the glory for ever and ever. Amen.

מִתְפַּלֵּא אֲנִי שֶׁכֹּל כָּךְ מַהֵר אַתֶּם סָרִים מִמִּי שֶׁקָּרָא אֶתְכֶם
mitpallei ani shekkol kach maher attem sarim mimmi shekkara etchem
I marvel that ye are so quickly removing from him that called you

בְּחֶסֶד הַמָּשִׁיחַ וְעוֹבְרִים אֶל בְּשׂוֹרָה אַחֶרֶת
bechesed hammashiach ve'overim el besorah acheret
in the grace of Christ unto a different gospel;

וְאֵין אַחֶרֶת, אֶלָּא שֶׁיֵּשׁ כַּמָּה אֲנָשִׁים הַמְבַלְבְּלִים אֶתְכֶם וַחֲפֵצִים לְעַוֵּת אֶת בְּשׂוֹרַת הַמָּשִׁיחַ
ve'ein acheret, ella sheyesh kammah anashim hamvalbelim etchem vachafetzim le'avvet et bsorat hammashiach
which is not another gospel: only there are some that trouble you, and would pervert the gospel of Christ.

אַךְ אִם מִישֶׁהוּ, אֲפִלּוּ אֲנַחְנוּ אוֹ מַלְאָךְ מִן הַשָּׁמַיִם
ach im mishehu, afillu anachnu o mal'ach min hashamayim
But though we, or an angel from heaven,

אֶל הַקּוֹרִינְתִּים ב

אֲבָל מְקַוֶּה אֲנִי שֶׁתַּכִּירוּ כִּי אֲנַחְנוּ לֹא נִכְשַׁלְנוּ
aval mekavveh ani shettakkiru ki anachnu lo nichshalnu
But I hope that ye shall know that we are not reprobate.

וַאֲנַחְנוּ מִתְפַּלְלִים לֵאלֹהִים שֶׁלֹּא תַּעֲשׂוּ שׁוּם רַע
va'anachnu mitpallelim lelohim shello ta'asu shum ra
Now we pray to God that ye do no evil;

לֹא כְּדֵי שֶׁאֲנַחְנוּ נֵרָאֶה מְהֵימָנִים, אֶלָּא כְּדֵי שֶׁאַתֶּם תַּעֲשׂוּ אֶת הַטּוֹב וַאֲנַחְנוּ נִהְיֶה כְּבִלְתִּי מְהֵימָנִים
lo kedei she'anachnu nera'eh meheimanim, ella kedei she'attem ta'asu et hattov va'anachnu nihyeh kevilti meheimanim
not that we may appear approved, but that ye may do that which is honorable, though we be as reprobate.

הֲרֵי אֵין אָנוּ יְכוֹלִים לַעֲשׂוֹת מְאוּמָה נֶגֶד הָאֱמֶת, אֶלָּא בְּעַד הָאֱמֶת
harei ein anu yecholim la'asot me'umah neged ha'emet, ella be'ad ha'emet
For we can do nothing against the truth, but for the truth.

אָנוּ שְׂמֵחִים כַּאֲשֶׁר אֲנַחְנוּ חַלָּשִׁים וְאַתֶּם חֲזָקִים; וְזוֹהִי גַּם תְּפִלָּתֵנוּ - שֶׁתָּבוֹאוּ לִידֵי תִּקּוּן
anu smechim ka'asher anachnu challashim ve'attem chazakim; vezohi gam tefillatenu - shettavo'u lidei tikkun
For we rejoice, when we are weak, and ye are strong: this we also pray for, even your perfecting.

עַל כֵּן כָּתַבְתִּי אֶת הַדְּבָרִים הָאֵלֶּה בִּהְיוֹתִי רָחוֹק מִכֶּם,
al ken katavti et haddevarim ha'elleh bihyoti rachok mikkem
For this cause I write these things while absent,

כְּדֵי שֶׁבִּהְיוֹתִי אֶצְלְכֶם לֹא אֶצְטָרֵךְ לִנְהֹג בְּחֻמְרָה
kedei shebbihyoti etzlechem lo etztarech linhog bechumrah
that I may not when present deal sharply,

עַל-פִּי הַסַּמְכוּת שֶׁנָּתַן לִי הָאָדוֹן - לִבְנוֹת וְלֹא לַהֲרֹס. סוֹף דָּבָר, אַחַי, שִׂמְחוּ
al-pi hassamchut shennatan li ha'adon - livnot velo laharos. sof davar, achai, simchu
according to the authority which the Lord gave me for building up, and not for casting down. Finally, brethren, farewell.

תַּקְּנוּ אֶת עַצְמְכֶם וְהִתְעוֹדְדוּ. הֱיוּ לֵב אֶחָד, חֲיוּ בְּשָׁלוֹם, וֵאלֹהֵי הָאַהֲבָה וְהַשָּׁלוֹם יִהְיֶה עִמָּכֶם
takkenu et atzmechem vehit'odedu. heyu lev echad, chayu beshalom, velohei ha'ahavah vehashalom yihyeh immachem
Be perfected; be comforted; be of the same mind; live in peace: and the God of love and peace shall be with you.

בָּרְכוּ לְשָׁלוֹם אִישׁ אֶת רֵעֵהוּ בִּנְשִׁיקָה קְדוֹשָׁה
barchu leshalom ish et re'ehu binshikah kedoshah
Salute one another with a holy kiss.

כָּל הַקְּדוֹשִׁים דּוֹרְשִׁים בִּשְׁלוֹמְכֶם
kol hakkedoshim doreshim bishlomechem
All the saints salute you.

חֶסֶד הָאָדוֹן יֵשׁוּעַ הַמָּשִׁיחַ וְאַהֲבַת הָאֱלֹהִים וְהִתְחַבְּרוּת בְּרוּחַ הַקֹּדֶשׁ עִם כֻּלְּכֶם
chesed ha'adon yeshua hammashiach ve'ahavat ha'elohim vehitchabberut beruach hakkodesh im kullechem
The grace of the Lord Jesus Christ, and the love of God, and the communion of the Holy Spirit, be with you all.

אֶל הַקּוֹרִינְתִּים ב

יג

זוֹ הַפַּעַם הַשְּׁלִישִׁית אָבוֹא אֲלֵיכֶם. עַל־פִּי שְׁנֵי עֵדִים אוֹ עַל־פִּי שְׁלֹשָׁה־עֵדִים יָקוּם דָּבָר
zo happa'am hashelishit avo aleichem. al-pi shenei edim o al-pi sheloshah-'edim yakum davar
This is the third time I am coming to you. At the mouth of two witnesses or three shall every word be established.

בִּהְיוֹתִי אֶצְלְכֶם בַּפַּעַם הַשְּׁנִיָּה כְּבָר אָמַרְתִּי
bihyoti etzlechem bappa'am hasheniyah kevar amarti
I have said beforehand, and I do say beforehand, as when I was present the second time,

וְעַתָּה, כְּשֶׁאֵינֶנִּי עִמָּכֶם, אֲנִי מַקְדִּים וְאוֹמֵר לְאוֹתָם אֲנָשִׁים אֲשֶׁר חָטְאוּ בֶּעָבָר, וּלְכָל הַשְּׁאָר
ve'attah, keshe'einenni immachem, ani makdim ve'omer le'otam anashim asher chate'u be'avar, ulechal hashe'ar
so now, being absent, to them that have sinned heretofore, and to all the rest,

שֶׁאִם אָבוֹא שׁוּב, לֹא אָחוּס
she'im avo shuv, lo achus
that, if I come again, I will not spare;

שֶׁכֵּן מְבַקְשִׁים אַתֶּם לְהִוָּכַח אִם הַמָּשִׁיחַ מְדַבֵּר בִּי
shekken mevakshim attem lehivvachach im hammashiach medabber bi,
seeing that ye seek a proof of Christ that speaketh in me;

הַמָּשִׁיחַ אֲשֶׁר אֵינוֹ חַלָּשׁ לִפְנֵיכֶם כִּי אִם חָזָק בְּקִרְבְּכֶם
hammashiach asher eino challash lifneichem ki im chazak bekirbechem
who to you-ward is not weak, but is powerful in you:

וְאַף כִּי נִצְלַב כְּשֶׁהָיָה חַלָּשׁ, הוּא חַי בִּגְבוּרַת אֱלֹהִים
ve'af ki nitzlav kshehayah challash, hu chai bigvurat elohim
for he was crucified through weakness, yet he liveth through the power of God.

אָמְנָם גַּם אֲנַחְנוּ חַלָּשִׁים בּוֹ, אַךְ נִחְיֶה אִתּוֹ בִּגְבוּרַת אֱלֹהִים הַמְכֻוֶּנֶת אֲלֵיכֶם
omnam gam anachnu challashim bo, ach nichyeh itto bigvurat elohim hamchuvvenet aleichem
For we also are weak in him, but we shall live with him through the power of God toward you.

נַסּוּ אֶת עַצְמְכֶם אִם עוֹמְדִים אַתֶּם בָּאֱמוּנָה, בַּחֲנוּ אֶת עַצְמְכֶם
nassu et atzmechem im omedim attem ba'emunah, bachanu et atzmechem
Try your own selves, whether ye are in the faith; prove your own selves.

אוֹ שֶׁמָּא אַתֶּם עַצְמְכֶם אֵינְכֶם מַבְחִינִים שֶׁהָאָדוֹן יֵשׁוּעַ בְּקִרְבְּכֶם
o shemma attem atzmechem einechem mavchinim sheha'adon yeshua bekirbechem
Or know ye not as to your own selves, that Jesus Christ is in you?

אִם אָמְנָם לֹא נִכְשַׁלְתֶּם אַתֶּם בַּמִּבְחָן
im omnam lo nichshaltem attem bammivchan
unless indeed ye be reprobate.

אֶל הַקּוֹרִינְתִּים ב

הַגִּידוּ לִי, הַאִם הוֹנֵיתִי אֶתְכֶם עַל־יְדֵי אִישׁ מֵהָאֲנָשִׁים אֲשֶׁר שָׁלַחְתִּי אֲלֵיכֶם
haggidu li, ha'im honeiti etchem al-yedei ish meha'anashim asher shalachti aleichem
Did I take advantage of you by any one of them whom I have sent unto you?

בִּקַּשְׁתִּי מִטִּיטוֹס וְשָׁלַחְתִּי אִתּוֹ אֶת הָאָח
bikkashti mittitos veshalachti itto et ha'ach
I exhorted Titus, and I sent the brother with him.

הַאִם טִיטוֹס הוֹנָה אֶתְכֶם? הַאִם לֹא הִתְהַלַּכְנוּ לְפִי אוֹתָהּ רוּחַ? הַאִם לֹא בְּאוֹתָהּ דֶּרֶךְ
ha'im titos honah etchem? ha'im lo hit'hallachnu lefi otah ruach? ha'im lo be'otah derech
Did Titus take any advantage of you? walked we not in the same spirit? walked we not in the same steps?

זֶה מִכְּבָר סְבוּרִים אַתֶּם שֶׁאֲנַחְנוּ מְגִנִּים עַל עַצְמֵנוּ לִפְנֵיכֶם
zeh mikkvar sevurim attem she'anachnu meginnim al atzmenu lifneichem
Ye think all this time that we are excusing ourselves unto you.

וּבְכֵן לִפְנֵי אֱלֹהִים, בַּמָּשִׁיחַ, אֲנַחְנוּ מְדַבְּרִים; וְהַכֹּל, חֲבִיבַי, כְּדֵי שֶׁתִּבָּנוּ
uvechen lifnei elohim, bammashiach, anachnu medabberim; vehakkol, chavivai, kedei shettibbanu
In the sight of God speak we in Christ. But all things, beloved, are for your edifying.

חוֹשֵׁשׁ אֲנִי שֶׁבְּבוֹאִי
choshesh ani shebbevo'i
For I fear, lest by any means, when I come,

לֹא אֶמְצָא אֶתְכֶם כִּלְבָבִי, וְאַתֶּם לֹא תִּמְצָאוּנִי כִּלְבַבְכֶם
lo emtza etchem kilvavi, ve'attem lo timtze'uni kilvavchem
I should find you not such as I would, and should myself be found of you such as ye would not;

שֶׁמָּא אֶמְצָא מְרִיבָה, קִנְאָה, רֹגֶז, תַּחֲרוּת, דִּבָּה רָעָה, רְכִילוּת, יְהִירוּת וְאַנְדְּרָלָמוּסְיָה
shemma emtza merivah, kin'ah, rogez, tacharut, dibbah ra'ah, rechilut, yehirut ve'anderalamuseyah
lest by any means there should be strife, jealousy, wraths, factions, backbitings, whisperings, swellings, tumults;

וְשֶׁמָּא בְּשׁוּבִי אֲלֵיכֶם יַשְׁפִּילֵנִי אֱלֹהַי אֶצְלְכֶם
veshemma beshuvi aleichem yashpileni elohai etzlechem
lest again when I come my God should humble me before you,

וְאֶתְאַבֵּל עַל רַבִּים אֲשֶׁר חָטְאוּ כְּבָר
ve'et'abbel al rabbim asher chat'u kevar
and I should mourn for many of them that have sinned heretofore,

וְלֹא חָזְרוּ בִּתְשׁוּבָה עַל הַטֻּמְאָה וְהַזְּנוּת וְהַזִּמָּה שֶׁעָשׂוּ
velo chazeru bitshuvah al hattum'ah vehazznut vehazzimmah she'asu
and repented not of the uncleanness and fornication and lasciviousness which they committed.

אֶל הַקּוֹרִינְתִּים ב

כִּי כַּאֲשֶׁר אֲנִי חַלָּשׁ, דַּוְקָא אָז חָזָק אֲנִי
ki ka'asher ani challash, davka az chazak ani
for when I am weak, then am I strong.

כְּסִיל נִהְיֵיתִי! אַתֶּם אִלַּצְתֶּם אוֹתִי. הֵן מִן הָרָאוּי הָיָה שֶׁאֲקַבֵּל אֶת שְׁבָחַי מִכֶּם
ksil nihyeiti! attem illatztem oti. hen min hara'ui hayah she'akabbel et shivchai mikkem
I am become foolish: ye compelled me; for I ought to have been commended of you:

כִּי אֵינֶנִּי נוֹפֵל בְּשׁוּם דָּבָר מִן הַשְּׁלִיחִים הַמְעֻלִּים, אַף שֶׁכְּאַיִן וּכְאֶפֶס אָנֹכִי
ki einenni nofel beshum davar min hashelichim ham'ullim, af shekke'ayin uche'efes anochi
for in nothing was I behind the very chiefest apostles, though I am nothing.

הֲרֵי אוֹתוֹת הַהֶכֵּר שֶׁל הַשָּׁלִיחַ נַעֲשׂוּ בְּקִרְבְּכֶם בִּמְלוֹא סַבְלָנוּת, בְּאוֹתוֹת וּבְמוֹפְתִים וּבִגְבוּרוֹת
harei otot hahekker shel hashaliach na'asu bekirbechem bimlo savlanut, be'otot uvemofetim uvigvurot
Truly the signs of an apostle were wrought among you in all patience, by signs and wonders and mighty works.

וּבַמֶּה נִגְרַעְתֶּם לְעֻמַּת שְׁאָר הַקְּהִלּוֹת
uvemah nigra'tem le'ummat she'ar hakkehillot,
For what is there wherein ye were made inferior to the rest of the churches,

זוּלָתִי בָּזֶה שֶׁאֲנִי עַצְמִי לֹא הָיִיתִי לָכֶם לְמַעֲמָסָה? סִלְחוּ נָא לִי אֶת הָעָוֶל הַזֶּה
zulati bazeh she'ani atzmi lo hayiti lachem lema'amasah? silchu na li et ha'avel hazzeh
except it be that I myself was not a burden to you? forgive me this wrong.

הֲרֵינִי מוּכָן לָבוֹא אֲלֵיכֶם פַּעַם שְׁלִישִׁית; וְלֹא אֶהְיֶה לְטֹרַח עֲלֵיכֶם
hareini muchan lavo aleichem pa'am shelishit; velo ehyeh letorach aleichem
Behold, this is the third time I am ready to come to you; and I will not be a burden to you:

שֶׁכֵּן אֵינֶנִּי מְבַקֵּשׁ אֶת אֲשֶׁר לָכֶם, אֶלָּא אֶתְכֶם
shekken einenni mevakkesh et asher lachem, ella etchem
for I seek not yours, but you:

הֲלֹא הַבָּנִים אֵינָם חַיָּבִים לֶאֱצֹר אוֹצָרוֹת לְהוֹרֵיהֶם, אֶלָּא הַהוֹרִים לִבְנֵיהֶם
halo habbanim einam chayavim le'etzor otzarot lehoreihem, ella hahorim livneihem
for the children ought not to lay up for the parents, but the parents for the children.

וַאֲנִי בְּשִׂמְחָה אֶתֵּן גַּם אֶת מַה שֶּׁיֵּשׁ לִי וְגַם אֶת עַצְמִי לְמַעַן נַפְשׁוֹתֵיכֶם
va'ani besimchah etten gam et mah sheyesh li vegam et atzmi lema'an nafshoteichem
And I will most gladly spend and be spent for your souls.

אִם אֲנִי אוֹהֵב אֶתְכֶם בְּמִדָּה יְתֵרָה, הֲתֹאֲהָבוּ אוֹתִי בְּמִדָּה פְּחוּתָה
im ani ohev etchem bemiddah yeterah, hatohavu oti bemiddah pchutah
If I love you more abundantly, am I loved the less?

כֵּן, אֲנִי לֹא הָיִיתִי לְמַעֲמָסָה עֲלֵיכֶם, אַךְ הוֹאִיל וַאֲנִי אִישׁ עַרְמוּמִי לָכַדְתִּי אֶתְכֶם בְּעָרְמָה
ken, ani lo hayiti lema'amasah aleichem, ach ho'il va'ani ish armumi lachadti etchem be'ormah
But be it so, I did not myself burden you; but, being crafty, I caught you with guile.

אֶל הַקּוֹרִינְתִּים ב

אֲנִי מַכִּיר אִישׁ כָּזֶה - אֵינֶנִּי יוֹדֵעַ אִם בְּגוּפוֹ אוֹ מִחוּץ לְגוּפוֹ, הָאֱלֹהִים יוֹדֵעַ
ani makkir ish kazeh - einenni yodea im begufo o michutz legufo, ha'elohim yodea
And I know such a man (whether in the body, or apart from the body, I know not; God knoweth),

אֲשֶׁר נִלְקַח אֶל גַּן עֵדֶן וְשָׁמַע מִלִּים שֶׁאֵין לְבַטְּאָן, שֶׁאָסוּר לְאָדָם לְמַלְּלָן
asher nilkach el gan eden veshama millim she'ein levatte'an, she'asur le'adam lemallelan
how that he was caught up into Paradise, and heard unspeakable words, which it is not lawful for a man to utter.

בְּאִישׁ כָּזֶה אֶתְגָּאֶה, אַךְ בִּי עַצְמִי לֹא אֶתְגָּאֶה, זוּלָתִי בְּחֻלְשׁוֹתַי
be'ish kazeh etga'eh, ach bi atzmi lo etga'eh, zulati bechulshotai
On behalf of such a one will I glory: but on mine own behalf I will not glory, save in my weaknesses.

גַּם אִם אֶרְצֶה לְהִתְגָּאוֹת לֹא אֶהְיֶה בְּחֶזְקַת כְּסִיל, שֶׁכֵּן אֲדַבֵּר אֱמֶת
gam im ertzeh lehitga'ot lo ehyeh bechezkat kesil, shekken adabber emet
For if I should desire to glory, I shall not be foolish; for I shall speak the truth:

אֲבָל נִמְנָע אֲנִי, פֶּן יַחְשְׁבוּנִי לְיוֹתֵר מִמַּה שֶּׁרוֹאִים בִּי אוֹ שׁוֹמְעִים מִמֶּנִּי
aval nimna ani, pen yachshevuni leyoter mimmah shero'im bi o shome'im mimmenni
but I forbear, lest any man should account of me above that which he seeth me to be, or heareth from me.

וּכְדֵי שֶׁלֹּא אֶתְנַשֵּׂא בִּגְלַל הַהִתְגַּלֻּיּוֹת הַנַּעֲלוֹת, נִתַּן לִי קוֹץ בִּבְשָׂרִי - מַלְאָכוֹ שֶׁל הַשָּׂטָן - לְהַכּוֹתֵנִי כְּדֵי שֶׁלֹּא אֶתְנַשֵּׂא
uchedei shello etnasho biglal hahitgallyot hanna'alot, nittan li kotz bivsari - mal'acho shel hassatan - lehakkoteni kedei shello etnasho
And by reason of the exceeding greatness of the revelations, that I should not be exalted overmuch, there was given to me a thorn in the flesh, a messenger of Satan to buffet me, that I should not be exalted overmuch.

עַל זֹאת הִתְחַנַּנְתִּי שָׁלֹשׁ פְּעָמִים אֶל הָאָדוֹן לַהֲסִירוֹ מִמֶּנִּי
al zot hitchannanti shalosh pe'amim el ha'adon lahasiro mimmenni
Concerning this thing I besought the Lord thrice, that it might depart from me.

אַךְ הוּא אָמַר לִי: דַּי לְךָ חַסְדִּי, כִּי בַּחֻלְשָׁה תֻּשְׁלַם גְּבוּרָתִי
ach hu amar li: dai lecha chasdi, ki bachulshah tushlam gevurati
And he hath said unto me, My grace is sufficient for thee: for my power is made perfect in weakness.

עַל כֵּן בְּשִׂמְחָה רַבָּה אֶתְגָּאֶה בְּחֻלְשׁוֹתַי, כְּדֵי שֶׁתִּשְׁרֶה עָלַי גְּבוּרַת הַמָּשִׁיחַ
al ken besimchah rabbah etga'eh bechulshotai, kedei shettishreh alai gvurat hammashiach
Most gladly therefore will I rather glory in my weaknesses, that the power of Christ may rest upon me.

מִשּׁוּם כָּךְ מְרֻצֶּה אֲנִי בְּחֻלְשׁוֹת, בַּחֲרָפוֹת, בִּמְצוּקוֹת מַחְסוֹר, בִּרְדִיפוֹת וּבְצָרוֹת
mishum kach merutzeh ani bechulshot, bacharafot, bimtzukot machsor, birdifot uvetzarot
Wherefore I take pleasure in weaknesses, in injuries, in necessities, in persecutions, in distresses,

הַבָּאוֹת עָלַי לְמַעַן הַמָּשִׁיחַ
habba'ot alai lema'an hammashiach
for Christ's sake:

אֶל הַקּוֹרִינְתִּים ב

בְּסַכָּנוֹת בָּעִיר וּבַמִּדְבָּר וּבַיָּם, בְּסַכָּנוֹת בְּקֶרֶב אֲחֵי שֶׁקֶר

besakkanot ba'ir uvammidbar uvayam, besakkanot bekerev achei sheker
in perils in the city, in perils in the wilderness, in perils in the sea, in perils among false brethren;

בְּעָמָל וּבִתְלָאָה, בְּלֵילוֹת רַבִּים לְלֹא שֵׁנָה, בְּרָעָב וּבְצָמָא, בְּצוֹמוֹת הַרְבֵּה, בְּקֹר וּבְעֵירֹם

be'amal uvitla'ah, beleilot rabbim lelo shenah, bera'av uvetzama, betzomot harbeh, bekor uve'eirom
in labor and travail, in watchings often, in hunger and thirst, in fastings often, in cold and nakedness.

וּמִלְּבַד דְּבָרִים אֲחֵרִים, הַטֹּרַח הַבָּא עָלַי יוֹם יוֹם, הַדְּאָגָה לְכָל הַקְּהִלּוֹת

umillevad devarim acherim, hattorach habba alai yom yom, hadde'agah lechol hakkehillot
Besides those things that are without, there is that which presseth upon me daily, anxiety for all the churches.

מִי יֶחֱלַשׁ וַאֲנִי לֹא אֶחֱלַשׁ עִמּוֹ? מִי יִכָּשֵׁל וְלִבִּי אֵינוֹ בּוֹעֵר

mi yechelash va'ani lo echelash immo? mi yikkashel velibbi eino bo'er
Who is weak, and I am not weak? who is caused to stumble, and I burn not?

אִם מִן הָרָאוּי לְהִתְגָּאוֹת, אֶתְגָּאֶה בִּדְבָרִים הַנּוֹגְעִים לְחֻלְשָׁתִי

im min hara'ui lehitga'ot, etga'eh bidvarim hannoge'im lechulshati
If I must needs glory, I will glory of the things that concern my weakness.

הָאֱלֹהִים וַאֲבִי הָאָדוֹן יֵשׁוּעַ, הוּא הַמְבֹרָךְ לְעוֹלָמִים, יוֹדֵעַ שֶׁאֵינֶנִּי מְשַׁקֵּר

ha'elohim va'avi ha'adon yeshua', hu hamevorach le'olamim, yodea she'einenni meshakker
The God and Father of the Lord Jesus, he who is blessed for evermore knoweth that I lie not.

בְּדַמֶּשֶׂק הִצִּיב הַמּוֹשֵׁל מִטַּעַם הַמֶּלֶךְ אֲרֶטַס שְׁמִירָה עַל הָעִיר כְּדֵי לְתָפְשֵׂנִי

bedammesek hitziv hammoshel mitta'am hammelech aretas shemirah al ha'ir kedei letofseni
In Damascus the governor under Aretas the king guarded the city of the Damascenes in order to take me:

אֶלָּא שֶׁהוֹרִידוּנִי בְּסַל דֶּרֶךְ חַלּוֹן אֲשֶׁר בַּחוֹמָה וְנִמְלַטְתִּי מִיָּדָיו

'ella shehoriduni besal derech challon asher bachomah venimlatti miyadav
and through a window was I let down in a basket by the wall, and escaped his hands.

יב

אֲנִי נֶאֱלָץ לְהִתְגָּאוֹת; אָמְנָם אֵין בָּזֶה מוֹעִיל, אַךְ אֶפְנֶה לְחֶזְיוֹנוֹת וּלְהִתְגַּלֻּיּוֹת אֲשֶׁר מֵאֵת הָאָדוֹן

ani ne'elatz lehitga'ot; omnam ein bazeh mo'il, ach efneh lechezyonot ulehitgallyot asher me'et ha'adon
I must needs glory, though it is not expedient; but I will come to visions and revelations of the Lord.

אֲנִי מַכִּיר אִישׁ בַּמָּשִׁיחַ, אֲשֶׁר לִפְנֵי אַרְבַּע־עֶשְׂרֵה שָׁנִים

ani makkir ish bammashiach, asher lifnei arba'-'esreh shanim
I know a man in Christ, fourteen years ago

נִלְקַח אֶל הָרָקִיעַ הַשְּׁלִישִׁי; אֵינֶנִּי יוֹדֵעַ אִם בְּגוּפוֹ אוֹ מִחוּץ לְגוּפוֹ, הָאֱלֹהִים יוֹדֵעַ

nilkach el harakia hashelishi; einenni yodea im begufo o michutz legufo, ha'elohim yodea
(whether in the body, I know not; or whether out of the body, I know not; God knoweth), such a one caught up even to the third heaven.

אֶל הַקּוֹרִינְתִּים ב

אִם מִישֶׁהוּ מְשַׁעְבֵּד אֶתְכֶם, מְכַרְסֵם בָּכֶם, עוֹשֵׁק אֶתְכֶם, מִתְנַשֵּׂא עֲלֵיכֶם אוֹ סוֹטֵר לָכֶם עַל הַפָּנִים - אַתֶּם סוֹבְלִים זֹאת
im mishehu mesha'bed etchem, mecharsem bachem, oshek etchem, mitnasso aleichem o soter lachem al happanim - attem sovelim zot
For ye bear with a man, if he bringeth you into bondage, if he devoureth you, if he taketh you captive, if he exalteth himself, if he smiteth you on the face.

בִּתְחוּשַׁת בּוּשָׁה אֲנִי אוֹמֵר זֹאת, כְּאִלּוּ הָיִינוּ אֲנַחְנוּ חַלָּשִׁים
bitchushat bushah ani omer zot, ke'illu hayinu anachnu challashim
I speak by way of disparagement, as though we had been weak.

וְאוּלָם בְּכָל דָּבָר שֶׁיָּעֵז אִישׁ - וַאֲנִי מְדַבֵּר בֶּאֱוִילוּת - אַרְהִיב עֹז גַּם אֲנִי
ve'ulam bechol davar sheya'ez ish - va'ani medabber be'evilut - arhiv oz gam ani
Yet whereinsoever any is bold (I speak in foolishness), I am bold also.

עִבְרִים הֵם? כֵּן גַּם אֲנִי. יִשְׂרְאֵלִים הֵם? כֵּן גַּם אֲנִי. צֶאֱצָאֵי אַבְרָהָם? כֵּן גַּם אֲנִי
ivrim hem? ken gam ani. yisre'elim hem? ken gam ani. tze'etza'ei avraham? ken gam ani
Are they Hebrews? so am I. Are they Israelites? so am I. Are they the seed of Abraham? so am I.

מְשָׁרְתֵי הַמָּשִׁיחַ הֵם? - כְּאֱוִיל אֲדַבֵּר - אֲנִי עוֹד יוֹתֵר;
mesharetei hammashiach hem? - ke'evil adabber - ani od yoter
Are they ministers of Christ? (I speak as one beside himself) I more;

בְּעָמָל, אֲנִי יוֹתֵר מֵהֶם; בְּבָתֵּי כֶלֶא, אֲנִי יוֹתֵר; בְּמַלְקוֹת, אֲנִי הַרְבֵּה יוֹתֵר; בְּסַכָּנַת מָוֶת - פְּעָמִים רַבּוֹת
be'amal, ani yoter mehem; bevattei kele, ani yoter; bemalkot, ani harbeh yoter; besakkanat mavet - pe'amim rabbot
in labors more abundantly, in prisons more abundantly, in stripes above measure, in deaths oft.

חָמֵשׁ פְּעָמִים הִלְקוּנִי הַיְּהוּדִים אַרְבָּעִים חָסֵר אַחַת
chamesh pe'amim hilkuni hayehudim arba'im chaser achat
Of the Jews five times received I forty stripes save one.

שָׁלֹשׁ פְּעָמִים הֻלְקֵיתִי בְּשׁוֹטִים; פַּעַם אַחַת נִרְגַּמְתִּי בָּאֲבָנִים
shalosh pe'amim hulkeiti beshotim; pa'am achat nirgamti ba'avanim
Thrice was I beaten with rods, once was I stoned,

שָׁלֹשׁ פְּעָמִים נִטְרְפָה סְפִינָתִי, וּפַעַם שֶׁהָיִיתִי בַּמַּיִם בְּמֶשֶׁךְ יְמָמָה
shalosh pe'amim nitrefah sefinati, ufa'am shahiti bammayim bemeshech yemamah
thrice I suffered shipwreck, a night and a day have I been in the deep;

נִתְנַסֵּיתִי בְּמַסָּעוֹת רַבִּים, בְּסַכָּנוֹת עַל פְּנֵי נְהָרוֹת, בְּסַכָּנוֹת מִפְּנֵי שׁוֹדְדִים
nitnasseiti bemassa'ot rabbim, besakkanot al penei neharot, besakkanot mippenei shodedim
in journeyings often, in perils of rivers, in perils of robbers,

בְּסַכָּנוֹת מִבְּנֵי עַמִּי, בְּסַכָּנוֹת מִן הַגּוֹיִם
besakkanot mibbenei ammi, besakkanot min haggoyim
in perils from my countrymen, in perils from the Gentiles,

אֶל הַקּוֹרִינְתִּים ב

וּמַדּוּעַ? הַאִם מִשּׁוּם שֶׁאֵינֶנִּי אוֹהֵב אֶתְכֶם? הָאֱלֹהִים יוֹדֵעַ
umaddua'? ha'im mishum she'einenni ohev etchem? ha'elohim yodea
Wherefore? because I love you not? God knoweth.

אֲבָל אֶת אֲשֶׁר אֲנִי עוֹשֶׂה גַּם אוֹסִיף לַעֲשׂוֹת כְּדֵי לְהָסִיר עִלָּה מִידֵי הַמְבַקְשִׁים עִלָּה
aval et asher ani oseh gam osif la'asot kedei lehasir illah miyedei hamvakshim illah
But what I do, that I will do, that I may cut off occasion from them that desire an occasion;

לְהִשְׁתַּוּוֹת לָנוּ בַּדָּבָר שֶׁהֵם מִתְגָּאִים בּוֹ
lehishtavvot lanu baddavar shehem mitga'im bo
that wherein they glory, they may be found even as we.

הֲרֵי אֲנָשִׁים כָּאֵלֶּה שְׁלִיחֵי שֶׁקֶר הֵם, פּוֹעֲלֵי רְמִיָּה הַמִּתְחַפְּשִׂים לִשְׁלִיחֵי הַמָּשִׁיחַ
harei anashim ka'elleh shelichei sheker hem, po'alei remiyah hammitchappesim lishlichei hammashiach
For such men are false apostles, deceitful workers, fashioning themselves into apostles of Christ.

וְאֵין לִתְמֹהַּ עַל כָּךְ, שֶׁהֲרֵי הַשָּׂטָן עַצְמוֹ מִתְחַפֵּשׂ לְמַלְאַךְ אוֹר
ve'ein litmoah al kach, sheharei hassatan atzmo mitchappes lemalach or
And no marvel; for even Satan fashioneth himself into an angel of light.

עַל כֵּן אֵין רְבוּתָא בְּכָךְ שֶׁגַּם מְשָׁרְתָיו מִתְחַפְּשִׂים לִמְשָׁרְתֵי הַצֶּדֶק
al ken ein revuta bechach sheggam mesharetav mitchappesim limsharetei hatzedek
It is no great thing therefore if his ministers also fashion themselves as ministers of righteousness;

סוֹפָם יִהְיֶה כְּפִי מַעַלְלֵיהֶם
sofam yihyeh kefi ma'aleleihem
whose end shall be according to their works.

אֲנִי חוֹזֵר וְאוֹמֵר: אַל יַחְשְׁבֵנִי אִישׁ לִכְסִיל
ani chozer ve'omer: al yachsheveni ish lichsil
I say again, Let no man think me foolish;

אֲבָל אִם אָכֵן כָּזֶה אֲנִי בְּעֵינֵיכֶם, כִּכְסִיל קַבְּלוּ אוֹתִי, כְּדֵי שֶׁגַּם אֲנִי אֶתְגָּאֶה קִמְעָה
aval im achen kazeh ani be'eineichem, kichsil kabbelu oti, kedei sheggam ani etga'eh kim'ah
but if ye do, yet as foolish receive me, that I also may glory a little.

בְּדַבְּרִי כָּךְ לֹא כְּדֶרֶךְ הָאָדוֹן אֲנִי מְדַבֵּר, אֶלָּא כְּמוֹ בֶּאֱוִילוּת, בְּבִטְחוֹן הַגַּאֲוָה הַזֹּאת
bedabbri kach lo kederech ha'adon ani medabber, ella kemo be'evilut, bevitchon hagga'avah hazzot
That which I speak, I speak not after the Lord, but as in foolishness, in this confidence of glorying.

וּמֵאַחַר שֶׁרַבִּים מִתְגָּאִים כְּדֶרֶךְ בָּשָׂר וָדָם, אֶתְגָּאֶה גַּם אֲנִי
ume'achar sherabbim mitga'im kederech basar vadam, etga'eh gam ani
Seeing that many glory after the flesh, I will glory also.

שֶׁהֲרֵי בְּשִׂמְחָה אַתֶּם סוֹבְלִים אֶת הָאֱוִילִים, אַתֶּם הַחֲכָמִים
sheharei besimchah attem sovelim et ha'evilim, attem hachachamim
For ye bear with the foolish gladly, being wise yourselves.

אֶל הַקּוֹרִינְתִּים ב

שֶׁכֵּן אִם בָּא מִישֶׁהוּ וּמַכְרִיז לָכֶם עַל יֵשׁוּעַ אַחֵר אֲשֶׁר לֹא הִכְרַזְנוּ
shekken im ba mishehu umachriz lachem al yeshua acher asher lo hichraznu
For if he that cometh preacheth another Jesus, whom we did not preach,

אוֹ בְּקַבֶּלְכֶם רוּחַ שׁוֹנָה מִזּוֹ שֶׁנִּתְּנָה לָכֶם
o bekabbelchem ruach shonah mizzo shennittenah lachem
or if ye receive a different spirit, which ye did not receive,

אוֹ בְּשׂוֹרָה שׁוֹנָה מִזּוֹ שֶׁקִּבַּלְתֶּם, אֲזַי אַתֶּם סוֹבְלִים אוֹתוֹ הֵיטֵב
o besorah shonah mizzo shekkibbaltem, azai attem sovelim oto heitev
or a different gospel, which ye did not accept, ye do well to bear with him.

סְבוּרַנִי שֶׁאֵינֶנִּי נוֹפֵל בִּמְאוּמָה מֵאוֹתָם שְׁלִיחִים מְעֻלִּים
sevurani she'einenni nofel bim'umah me'otam shelichim me'ullim
For I reckon that I am not a whit behind the very chiefest apostles.

וְגַם אִם בַּעַר אֲנִי בְּדִבּוּר אֵינֶנִּי בַּעַר בְּדַעַת
vegam im ba'ar ani bedibbur einenni ba'ar beda'at
But though I be rude in speech, yet am I not in knowledge;

אֶלָּא בַּכֹּל, בְּכָל דָּבָר, הֶרְאֵינוּ לָכֶם אֶת זֹאת
ella bakkol, bechol davar, her'einu lachem et zot
nay, in every way have we made this manifest unto you in all things.

הִשְׁפַּלְתִּי אֶת עַצְמִי כְּדֵי לְרוֹמֵם אֶתְכֶם בְּבַשְּׂרִי לָכֶם אֶת בְּשׂוֹרַת אֱלֹהִים בְּחִנָּם; הַאִם חֵטְא עָשִׂיתִי בְּכָךְ
hishpalti et atzmi kedei leromem etchem bevassri lachem et besorat elohim bechinnam; ha'im chet asiti bechach
Or did I commit a sin in abasing myself that ye might be exalted, because I preached to you the gospel of God for nought?

מִקְּהִלּוֹת אֲחֵרוֹת נָטַלְתִּי, מֵהֶם לָקַחְתִּי שָׂכָר כְּדֵי לְשָׁרֵת אֶתְכֶם
mik'hillot acherot natalti, mehem lakachti sachar kedei lesharet etchem
I robbed other churches, taking wages of them that I might minister unto you;

וְכַאֲשֶׁר הָיִיתִי אֶצְלְכֶם וְחָסַר לִי דְּבַר מָה, לֹא הָיִיתִי לְמַעֲמָסָה עַל אִישׁ
vecha'asher hayiti etzlechem vechasar li devar mah, lo hayiti lema'amasah al ish
and when I was present with you and was in want, I was not a burden on any man;

כִּי הָאַחִים שֶׁבָּאוּ מִמַּקֶדוֹנְיָה נָתְנוּ לִי דֵּי צָרְכִּי
ki ha'achim shebba'u mimmakedoneyah natenu li dei tzorki
for the brethren, when they came from Macedonia, supplied the measure of my want;

וּבְכָל דָּבָר נִשְׁמַרְתִּי שֶׁלֹּא אֶהְיֶה לְמַשָּׂא עֲלֵיכֶם, וְכֵן אַמְשִׁיךְ וְאֶשָּׁמֵר
uvechol davar nishmarti shello ehyeh lemassa aleichem, vechen amshich ve'eshamer
and in everything I kept myself from being burdensome unto you, and so will I keep myself.

כְּשֵׁם שֶׁאֱמֶת הַמָּשִׁיחַ בִּי, כֵּן הַגַּאֲוָה הַזֹּאת לֹא תִּשָּׁלֵל מִמֶּנִּי בִּגְלִילוֹת אֲכַיָּה
keshem she'emet hammashiach bi, ken hagga'avah hazzot lo tishalel mimmenni biglilot achayah
As the truth of Christ is in me, no man shall stop me of this glorying in the regions of Achaia.

אֶל הַקּוֹרִינְתִּים ב

אֲבָל מְקַוִּים אָנוּ כִּי בִּגְדֹל אֱמוּנַתְכֶם

aval mekavvim anu ki bigdol emunatchem
but having hope that, as your faith groweth,

נִגְדַּל בְּקִרְבְּכֶם בִּמְלוֹא הַמִּדָּה הַנְּתוּנָה לָנוּ

nigdal bekirbechem bimlo hammiddah hannetunah lanu
we shall be magnified in you according to our province unto further abundance,

עַד כְּדֵי לְבַשֵּׂר אֶת הַבְּשׂוֹרָה בִּמְקוֹמוֹת אֲשֶׁר מֵעֵבֶר לְאֵזוֹרְכֶם

ad kedei levasser et habbesorah bimkomot asher me'ever le'ezorechem
so as to preach the gospel even unto the parts beyond you,

וְלֹא נִתְגָּאֶה בְּמַה שֶּׁכְּבָר נַעֲשָׂה בִּתְחוּמָם שֶׁל אֲחֵרִים

velo nitga'eh bemah shekkevar na'asah bitchumam shel acherim
and not to glory in another's province in regard of things ready to our hand.

הַמִּתְהַלֵּל יִתְהַלֵּל בַּיהוה

hammit'hallel yit'hallel bahashem
But he that glorieth, let him glory in the Lord.

כִּי לֹא הַמְשַׁבֵּחַ אֶת עַצְמוֹ מְהֵימָן, אֶלָּא מִי שֶׁיהוה מְשַׁבְּחוֹ

ki lo hamshabbeach et atzmo meheiman, ella mi shehashem meshabbcho
For not he that commendeth himself is approved, but whom the Lord commendeth.

יא

מִי יִתֵּן וְתִסְבְּלוּנִי עַל אִוֶּלֶת־מָה! וְאוּלָם אַתֶּם סוֹבְלִים אוֹתִי

mi yitten vetisbeluni al ivvelet-mah! ve'ulam attem sovelim oti
Would that ye could bear with me in a little foolishness: but indeed ye do bear with me.

מְקַנֵּא אֲנִי לָכֶם קִנְאַת אֱלֹהִים

mekannei ani lachem kin'at elohim
For I am jealous over you with a godly jealousy:

כִּי הֵאֵרַשְׂתִּי אֶתְכֶם לְאִישׁ אֶחָד, לַמָּשִׁיחַ, כְּדֵי לְהַצִּיגְכֶם בְּתוּלָה טְהוֹרָה לְפָנָיו

ki he'erasti etchem le'ish echad, lammashiach, kedei lehatzigechem betulah tehorah lefanav
for I espoused you to one husband, that I might present you as a pure virgin to Christ.

אַךְ חוֹשְׁשַׁנִי שֶׁמָּא

ach chosheshani shemma
But I fear, lest by any means,

תֻּדַּחְנָה מַחְשְׁבוֹתֵיכֶם מִן הַפַּשְׁטוּת שֶׁבַּמָּשִׁיחַ, כְּמוֹ שֶׁאֵרַע לְחַוָּה כַּאֲשֶׁר הִדִּיחַ אוֹתָהּ הַנָּחָשׁ בְּעָרְמָתוֹ

tuddachnah machshevoteichem min happashtut shebbammashiach, kemo she'era lechavvah ka'asher hiddiach otah hannachash be'aremato
as the serpent beguiled Eve in his craftiness, your minds should be corrupted from the simplicity and the purity that is toward Christ.

אֶל הַקּוֹרִינְתִים ב

הָאוֹמֵר כָּךְ יֵדַע נָא אֶת זֹאת
ha'omer kach yeda na et zot
Let such a one reckon this,

כְּדֶרֶךְ שֶׁאֲנַחְנוּ בְּאֹמֶר עַל־יְדֵי אִגְּרוֹת בְּעֵת הֵעָדְרֵנוּ, כֵּן אֲנַחְנוּ גַם בְּמַעֲשֶׂה בְּעֵת נוֹכְחוּתֵנוּ
kederech she'anachnu be'omer al-yedei iggerot be'et he'aderenu, ken anachnu gam bema'aseh be'et nochechutenu
that, what we are in word by letters when we are absent, such are we also in deed when we are present.

אֵין אָנוּ מְעִזִּים
ein anu me'izzim
For we are not bold

לִכְלֹל עַצְמֵנוּ עִם כַּמָּה מֵאוֹתָם אֲנָשִׁים הַמְשַׁבְּחִים אֶת עַצְמָם, גַּם לֹא נָעֵז לְהַשְׁווֹת עַצְמֵנוּ אֲלֵיהֶם
lichlol atzmenu im kammah me'otam anashim hamshabbechim et atzmam, gam lo na'ez lehashvot atzmenu aleihem
to number or compare ourselves with certain of them that commend themselves:

הַלָּלוּ מוֹדְדִים אֶת עַצְמָם כְּשֶׁהֵם מְשַׁמְּשִׁים קְנֵי מִדָּה לְעַצְמָם
hallalu modedim et atzmam keshehem meshammeshim kenei middah le'atzmam
but they themselves, measuring themselves by themselves,

וּמַשְׁוִים אֶת עַצְמָם לְעַצְמָם, וְאֵינָם אֶלָּא חַסְרֵי בִינָה
umashvim et atzmam le'atzmam, ve'einam ella chasrei binah
and comparing themselves with themselves, are without understanding.

אֲנַחְנוּ לֹא נִתְגָּאֶה יוֹתֵר מִן הַמִּדָּה
anachnu lo nitga'eh yoter min hammiddah
But we will not glory beyond our measure,

אֶלָּא בַּמִּדָּה הַהוֹלֶמֶת אֶת הַתְּחוּם שֶׁהִקְצָה לָנוּ אֱלֹהִים, תְּחוּם הַמַּגִּיעַ גַּם עֲדֵיכֶם
ella bammiddah haholemet et hattechum shehiktzah lanu elohim, techum hammaggia gam adeichem
but according to the measure of the province which God apportioned to us as a measure, to reach even unto you.

אֵין אָנוּ מַשִּׂיגִים גְּבוּל, כְּאִלּוּ לֹא הִגַּעְנוּ עֲדֵיכֶם
ein anu massigim gevul, ke'illu lo higga'nu adeichem
For we stretch not ourselves overmuch, as though we reached not unto you:

שֶׁהֲרֵי גַּם אֲלֵיכֶם הִגַּעְנוּ עִם בְּשׂוֹרַת הַמָּשִׁיחַ
sheharei gam aleichem higga'nu im besorat hammashiach
for we came even as far as unto you in the gospel of Christ:

אֵין גַּאֲוָתֵנוּ חוֹרֶגֶת מִן הַמִּדָּה בְּאֹפֶן שֶׁנִּתְגָּאֶה בַּעֲמָלָם שֶׁל אֲחֵרִים
ein ga'avatenu choreget min hammiddah be'ofen shennitga'eh ba'amalam shel acherim
not glorying beyond our measure, that is, in other men's labors;

אֶל הַקּוֹרִינְתִּים ב

אָמְנָם חַיִּים אָנוּ כְּבָשָׂר וָדָם, אַךְ אֵין אָנוּ נִלְחָמִים כְּדֶרֶךְ בָּשָׂר וָדָם
omnam chayim anu kevasar vadam, ach ein anu nilchamim kederech basar vadam
For though we walk in the flesh, we do not war according to the flesh

שֶׁכֵּן כְּלֵי מִלְחַמְתֵּנוּ עָצְמָתָם אֵינָהּ מִבָּשָׂר וָדָם, אֶלָּא עָצְמַת אֱלֹהִים בָּהֶם לַהֲרֹס מִבְצָרִים
shekken klei milchamtenu otzmatam einah mibbasar vadam, ella atzemat elohim bahem laharos mivtzarim
(for the weapons of our warfare are not of the flesh, but mighty before God to the casting down of strongholds);

אֲנַחְנוּ מְמוֹטְטִים תַּחְבּוּלוֹת וְכָל דָּבָר רָם שֶׁמִּתְנַשֵּׂא נֶגֶד דַּעַת אֱלֹהִים
anachnu memotetim tachbulot vechol davar ram shemmitnasse neged da'at elohim
casting down imaginations, and every high thing that is exalted against the knowledge of God,

וּמַכְנִיעִים כָּל מַחֲשָׁבָה לְשֵׁם צִיּוּת לַמָּשִׁיחַ
umachni'im kol machashavah leshem tziyut lammashiach
and bringing every thought into captivity to the obedience of Christ;

וּמוּכָנִים לְהַעֲנִישׁ עַל כָּל הֲפָרַת מִשְׁמַעַת, כַּאֲשֶׁר תֻּשְׁלַם מִשְׁמַעְתְּכֶם אַתֶּם
umuchanim leha'anish al kol hafarat mishma'at, ka'asher tushlam mishma'techem attem
and being in readiness to avenge all disobedience, when your obedience shall be made full.

לְפִי מַרְאֶה חִיצוֹנִי בּוֹחֲנִים אַתֶּם אֶת הַדְּבָרִים! אִם מִישֶׁהוּ בָּטוּחַ בְּעַצְמוֹ שֶׁהוּא שַׁיָּךְ לַמָּשִׁיחַ
lefi mar'eh chitzoni bochanim attem et haddevarim! im mishehu batuach be'atzmo shehu shayach lammashiach
Ye look at the things that are before your face. If any man trusteth in himself that he is Christ's,

יַחֲזֹר נָא וְיִתֵּן דַּעְתּוֹ עַל זֹאת: כְּשֵׁם שֶׁהוּא שַׁיָּךְ לַמָּשִׁיחַ, כֵּן גַּם אֲנַחְנוּ
yachazor na veyitten da'to al zot. keshem shehu shayach lammashiach, ken gam anachnu
let him consider this again with himself, that, even as he is Christ's, so also are we.

וְגַם אִם אֶתְגָּאֶה קְצָת יוֹתֵר מִדַּי בַּסַּמְכוּת
vegam im etga'eh ketzat yoter middai bassamchut
For though I should glory somewhat abundantly concerning our authority

אֲשֶׁר נָתַן לָנוּ הָאָדוֹן לִבְנוֹת וְלֹא לַהֲרֹס, לֹא אֵבוֹשׁ
asher natan lanu ha'adon livnot velo laharos, lo evosh
(which the Lord gave for building you up, and not for casting you down), I shall not be put to shame:

אֵין כַּוָּנָתִי לְהֵרָאוֹת כִּמְאַיֵּם עֲלֵיכֶם בָּאִגְּרוֹת
ein kavvanati lehera'ot kim'ayem aleichem be'iggerot
that I may not seem as if I would terrify you by my letters.

יֵשׁ אוֹמְרִים: אִגְּרוֹתָיו אָמְנָם מַרְשִׁימוֹת וְתַקִּיפוֹת
yesh omerim: iggerotav amenam marshimot vetakkifot
For, His letters, they say, are weighty and strong;

אַךְ בְּעָמְדוֹ לְפָנֵינוּ בְּגוּפוֹ הֲרֵיהוּ חַלָּשׁ וּדְבָרוֹ חֲסַר־עֵרֶךְ
ach be'omdo lefaneinu begufo hareihu challash udevaro chasar-'erech
but his bodily presence is weak, and his speech of no account.

אֶל הַקּוֹרִינְתִּים ב

בִּגְלַל הַשָּׁרוּת הַזֶּה שֶׁעָמַד בַּמִּבְחָן יְשַׁבְּחוּ אֶת אֱלֹהִים
biglal hasherut hazzeh she'amad bammivchan yeshabbechu et elohim
seeing that through the proving of you by this ministration they glorify God

עַל צִיּוּתְכֶם לִבְשׂוֹרַת הַמָּשִׁיחַ וְהוֹדָאַתְכֶם בָּהּ
al tziyutechem livsorat hammashiach vehoda'atchem bah
for the obedience of your confession unto the gospel of Christ,

וְעַל הִשְׁתַּתְּפוּתְכֶם הַנְּדִיבָה בְּעֶזְרָה לָהֶם וְלַכֹּל
ve'al hishtattefutechem hannedivah ba'ezrah lahem velakkol
and for the liberality of your contribution unto them and unto all;

וְהֵם מִתּוֹךְ כִּסּוּפִים אֲלֵיכֶם יִתְפַּלְּלוּ בַּעַדְכֶם
vehem mittoch kissufim aleichem yitpallelu ba'adchem
while they themselves also, with supplication on your behalf, long after you

הוֹדוֹת לְחֶסֶד אֱלֹהִים שֶׁשָּׁפַע בְּקִרְבְּכֶם
hodot lechesed elohim sheshafa bekirbechem
by reason of the exceeding grace of God in you.

לֵאלֹהִים הַתּוֹדָה עַל מַתְּנָתוֹ הָעֲצוּמָה מִסַּפֵּר
le'elohim hattodah al mattnato ha'atzumah missapper
Thanks be to God for his unspeakable gift.

∎

אֲנִי עַצְמִי, שָׁאוּל, מַפְצִיר בָּכֶם בְּנֹעַם הַמָּשִׁיחַ וּבְעַנְוְתוֹ
ani atzmi, sha'ul, maftzir bachem beno'am hammashiach uve'anvato
Now I Paul myself entreat you by the meekness and gentleness of Christ,

אֲנִי אֲשֶׁר בְּעָמְדִי לִפְנֵיכֶם חַלּוּשׁ אָנֹכִי, אַךְ בְּהֵעָדְרִי מִפְּנֵיכֶם נוֹעָז אֲנִי כְּלַפֵּיכֶם
ani asher be'omdi lifneichem chalush anochi, ach behe'adri mippeneichem no'az ani klappeichem
I who in your presence am lowly among you, but being absent am of good courage toward you:

מְבַקֵּשׁ אֲנִי שֶׁבִּהְיוֹתִי אֶצְלְכֶם לֹא אֶצְטָרֵךְ לִנְהֹג בְּעֹז
mevakkesh ani shebbihyoti etzlechem lo etztarech linhog be'oz
yea, I beseech you, that I may not when present show courage

בְּאוֹתוֹ בִּטָּחוֹן שֶׁאֲנִי מִתְכַּוֵּן לָצֵאת בּוֹ נֶגֶד כַּמָּה אֲנָשִׁים
be'oto bittachon she'ani mitkavven latzet bo neged kammah anashim
with the confidence wherewith I count to be bold against some,

הַחוֹשְׁבִים אוֹתָנוּ לְמִתְנַהֲגִים עַל־פִּי מַחֲשֶׁבֶת בָּשָׂר וָדָם
hachoshevim otanu lemitnahagim al-pi machashevet basar vadam
who count of us as if we walked according to the flesh.

אֶל הַקּוֹרִינְתִּים ב

הֵן הַזּוֹרֵעַ בְּצִמְצוּם יִקְצֹר בְּצִמְצוּם,
hen hazzorea betzimtzum yiktzor betzimtzum,
But this I say, He that soweth sparingly shall reap also sparingly;

וְהַזּוֹרֵעַ בִּנְדִיבוּת יִקְצֹר בְּשֶׁפַע
vehazzorea bindivut yiktzor beshefa
and he that soweth bountifully shall reap also bountifully.

כָּל אִישׁ כְּפִי שֶׁיִּדְּבֶנּוּ לִבּוֹ יִתֵּן
kol ish kefi sheyiddevennu libbo yitten
Let each man do according as he hath purposed in his heart:

לֹא מִתּוֹךְ צַעַר אוֹ הֶכְרֵחַ, שֶׁהֲרֵי אֶת הַנּוֹתֵן בְּשִׂמְחָה אוֹהֵב אֱלֹהִים
lo mittoch tza'ar o hechreach, sheharei et hannoten besimchah ohev elohim
not grudgingly, or of necessity: for God loveth a cheerful giver.

וֵאלֹהִים יָכוֹל לְהַשְׁפִּיעַ עֲלֵיכֶם כָּל חֶסֶד
ve'elohim yachol lehashpia aleichem kol chesed
And God is able to make all grace abound unto you;

כְּדֵי שֶׁיִּהְיֶה לָכֶם תָּמִיד דֵּי צָרְכְּכֶם בְּכָל דָּבָר, וְהוֹתֵר לְכָל מַעֲשֶׂה טוֹב
kedei sheyihyeh lachem tamid dei tzarekechem bechol davar, vehoter lechol ma'aseh tov
that ye, having always all sufficiency in everything, may abound unto every good work:

כַּכָּתוּב: פִּזַּר נָתַן לָאֶבְיוֹנִים, צִדְקָתוֹ עֹמֶדֶת לָעַד
kakkatuv: pizzar natan la'evyonim, tzidkato omedet la'ad
as it is written, He hath scattered abroad, he hath given to the poor; His righteousness abideth for ever.

וְהַנּוֹתֵן זֶרַע לַזּוֹרֵעַ וְלֶחֶם לָאֹכֵל
vehannoten zera lazzorea velechem la'ochel
And he that supplieth seed to the sower and bread for food,

יִתֵּן לָכֶם זֶרַע בְּשֶׁפַע וְיַרְבֶּה פְּרִי צִדְקַתְכֶם
yitten lachem zera beshefa veyarbeh peri tzidkatchem
shall supply and multiply your seed for sowing, and increase the fruits of your righteousness:

וְתַעֲשִׁירוּ בְּכָל דַּרְכֵי נְדִיבוּת שֶׁתָּבִיא לִידֵי הוֹדָיָה לֵאלֹהִים בִּגְלָלֵנוּ
veta'ashiru bechol darchei nedivut shettavi lidei hodayah lelohim biglalenu
ye being enriched in everything unto all liberality, which worketh through us thanksgiving to God.

שֶׁכֵּן עֲשִׂיַּת הַשֵּׁרוּת הַזֶּה לֹא רַק תְּמַלֵּא אֶת מַחְסוֹר הַקְּדוֹשִׁים
shekken asiyat hasherut hazzeh lo rak temallei et machsor hakkedoshim
For the ministration of this service not only filleth up the measure of the wants of the saints,

אֶלָּא גַּם תְּעוֹרֵר הוֹדָיָה רַבָּה לֵאלֹהִים
ella gam te'orer hodayah rabbah le'elohim
but aboundeth also through many thanksgivings unto God;

אֶל הַקּוֹרִינְתִּים ב

עַל כֵּן, לְעֵינֵי הַקְּהִלּוֹת, הַרְאוּ לָהֶם אֶת אַהֲבַתְכֶם וְהוֹכִיחוּ אֶת צִדְקַת גַּאֲוָתֵנוּ בָּכֶם
al ken, le'einei hakkehillot, har'u lahem et ahavatchem vehochichu et tzidkat ga'avatenu bachem
Show ye therefore unto them in the face of the churches the proof of your love, and of our glorying on your behalf.

ט

בְּנוֹגֵעַ לַשֵּׁרוּת לְמַעַן הַקְּדוֹשִׁים אֵינֶנִּי צָרִיךְ לִכְתֹּב אֲלֵיכֶם
benogea lasherut lema'an hakkedoshim einenni tzarich lichtov aleichem
For as touching the ministering to the saints, it is superfluous for me to write to you:

כִּי יוֹדֵעַ אֲנִי אֶת נְכוֹנוּתְכֶם, אֲשֶׁר בִּגְלָלָהּ אֲנִי מִתְגָּאֶה בָּכֶם לִפְנֵי אַנְשֵׁי מַקֵּדוֹנְיָה
ki yodea ani et nechonutechem, asher biglalah ani mitga'eh bachem lifnei anshei makedoneyah
for I know your readiness, of which I glory on your behalf to them of Macedonia,

בְּאָמְרִי שֶׁאֲכַיָּה הָיְתָה נְכוֹנָה כְּבָר לִפְנֵי שָׁנָה; וְאָמְנָם הַלַּהַט שֶׁלָּכֶם עוֹרֵר אֶת רֻבָּם
be'omri she'achayah hayetah nechonah kevar lifnei shanah; ve'omnam hallahat shellachem orer et rubbam
that Achaia hath been prepared for a year past; and your zeal hath stirred up very many of them.

אֲבָל שָׁלַחְתִּי אֶת הָאַחִים מִתּוֹךְ כַּוָּנָה שֶׁגַּאֲוָתֵנוּ בָּכֶם לֹא תִהְיֶה לָרִיק בָּעִנְיָן הַזֶּה
aval shalachti et ha'achim mittoch kavvanah shegga'avatenu bachem lo tihyeh larik ba'inyan hazzeh
But I have sent the brethren, that our glorying on your behalf may not be made void in this respect;

וּכְדֵי שֶׁתִּהְיוּ מוּכָנִים כְּפִי שֶׁאָמַרְתִּי
uchedei shettihyu muchanim kefi she'amarti
that, even as I said, ye may be prepared:

הֲלֹא אִם יָבוֹאוּ עִמִּי אֲנָשִׁים מִמַּקֵּדוֹנְיָה וְיִמְצְאוּ שֶׁאֵינְכֶם מוּכָנִים
halo im yavo'u immi anashim mimmakedoneyah veyimtze'u she'einechem muchanim
lest by any means, if there come with me any of Macedonia and find you unprepared,

אֲזַי אֲנַחְנוּ - שֶׁלֹּא לוֹמַר אַתֶּם - נֵבוֹשׁ בַּבִּטָּחוֹן הַזֶּה
azai anachnu - shello lomar attem - nevosh babbittachon hazzeh
we (that we say not, ye) should be put to shame in this confidence.

עַל כֵּן מָצָאתִי לְנָחוּץ לְבַקֵּשׁ מֵהָאַחִים כִּי יַקְדִּימוּ לָבוֹא אֲלֵיכֶם
al ken matzati lenachutz levakkesh meha'achim ki yakdimu lavo aleichem
I thought it necessary therefore to entreat the brethren, that they would go before unto you,

וִיסַדְּרוּ אֶת עִנְיַן הַתְּרוּמָה שֶׁהִבְטַחְתֶּם
viysadderu et inyan hatterumah shehivtachtem
and make up beforehand your aforepromised bounty,

לְמַעַן תִּהְיֶה מוּכָנָה מִתּוֹךְ נְדִיבוּת וְלֹא מִתּוֹךְ קַמְצָנוּת
lema'an tihyeh muchanah mittoch nedivut velo mittoch kamtzanut
that the same might be ready as a matter of bounty, and not of extortion.

אֶל הַקּוֹרִינְתִּים ב

כְּפִי שֶׁכָּתוּב: וְלֹא הֶעְדִּיף הַמַּרְבֶּה וְהַמַּמְעִיט לֹא הֶחְסִיר
kefi shekkatuv: velo he'dif hammarbeh vehammam'it lo hechsir
as it is written, He that gathered much had nothing over; and he that gathered little had no lack.

תּוֹדָה לֵאלֹהִים הַנּוֹתֵן בְּלֵב טִיטוֹס אֶת אוֹתָהּ חֲרִיצוּת לְמַעַנְכֶם
todah lelohim hannoten belev titos et otah charitzut lema'anchem
But thanks be to God, who putteth the same earnest care for you into the heart of Titus.

כִּי אָכֵן שָׁמַע לַבַּקָּשָׁה וּמִתּוֹךְ חֲרִיצוּתוֹ הַיְתֵרָה הָלַךְ אֲלֵיכֶם מֵרָצוֹן
ki achen shama labbakkashah umittoch charitzuto hayterah halach aleichem meratzon
For he accepted indeed our exhortation; but being himself very earnest, he went forth unto you of his own accord.

יַחַד אִתּוֹ שָׁלַחְנוּ אֶת הָאָח אֲשֶׁר שֵׁם טוֹב לוֹ בְּכָל הַקְּהִלּוֹת עַל חֶלְקוֹ בְּהַכְרָזַת הַבְּשׂוֹרָה
yachad itto shalachnu et ha'ach asher shem tov lo bechol hakkehillot al chelko behachrazat habbsorah
And we have sent together with him the brother whose praise in the gospel is spread through all the churches;

וְלֹא עוֹד אֶלָּא שֶׁהַקְּהִלּוֹת בָּחֲרוּ בּוֹ לִהְיוֹת חֲבֵרֵנוּ לַמַּסָּע בַּהֲבָאַת הַתְּרוּמָה הַזֹּאת
velo od ella shehakkehillot bacharu bo lihyot chaverenu lammassa bahava'at hatterumah hazzot
and not only so, but who was also appointed by the churches to travel with us in the matter of this grace,

שֵׁרוּת שֶׁאָנוּ עוֹשִׂים לִכְבוֹד הָאָדוֹן מִתּוֹךְ נְכוֹנוּתֵנוּ אָנוּ
sherut she'anu osim lichvod ha'adon mittoch nechonutenu anu
which is ministered by us to the glory of the Lord, and to show our readiness:

וַאֲנַחְנוּ נִשְׁמָרִים מִלָּתֵת לְאִישׁ פִּתְחוֹן פֶּה נֶגְדֵּנוּ עַל־דְּבַר הַתְּרוּמוֹת הָרַבּוֹת שֶׁאָנוּ מֻפְקָדִים עֲלֵיהֶן
va'anachnu nishmarim millatet le'ish pitchon peh negdenu al-devar hatterumot harabbot she'anu mufkadim aleihen
avoiding this, that any man should blame us in the matter of this bounty which is ministered by us:

שֶׁכֵּן נוֹתְנִים אָנוּ דַּעְתֵּנוּ לִנְהֹג בְּיֹשֶׁר לֹא רַק לִפְנֵי הָאָדוֹן, אֶלָּא גַּם לִפְנֵי בְּנֵי אָדָם
shekken notnim anu da'tenu linhog beyosher lo rak lifnei ha'adon, ella gam lifnei benei adam
for we take thought for things honorable, not only in the sight of the Lord, but also in the sight of men.

שָׁלַחְנוּ אִתָּם אֶת אָחִינוּ אֲשֶׁר פְּעָמִים רַבּוֹת וּבִדְבָרִים רַבִּים הוּכְחָה לָנוּ חֲרִיצוּתוֹ
shalachnu ittam et achinu asher pe'amim rabbot uvidvarim rabbim huchechah lanu charitzuto
And we have sent with them our brother, whom we have many times proved earnest in many things,

וְעַתָּה חֲרִיצוּתוֹ רַבָּה עוֹד יוֹתֵר בִּגְלַל הָאֵמוּן הָרַב שֶׁהוּא נוֹתֵן בָּכֶם
ve'attah charitzuto rabbah od yoter biglal ha'emun harav shehu noten bachem
but now much more earnest, by reason of the great confidence which he hath in you.

אֲשֶׁר לְטִיטוֹס, שֻׁתָּפִי הוּא וְעוֹבֵד אִתִּי לְמַעַנְכֶם
asher letitos, shuttafi hu ve'oved itti lema'anchem
Whether any inquire about Titus, he is my partner and my fellow-worker to you-ward;

אֲשֶׁר לְאַחֵינוּ, שְׁלִיחֵי הַקְּהִלּוֹת הֵם לְתִפְאֶרֶת הַמָּשִׁיחַ
asher le'acheinu, shlichei hakkehillot hem letif'eret hammashiach
or our brethren, they are the messengers of the churches, they are the glory of Christ.

אֶל הַקּוֹרִינְתִּים ב

אֵינֶנִּי מְדַבֵּר בְּדֶרֶךְ שֶׁל פְּקֻדָּה
einenni medabber bederech shel pekuddah,
I speak not by way of commandment,

אֶלָּא שֶׁעַל־יְדֵי חֲרִיצוּתָם שֶׁל אֲחֵרִים אֲנִי בּוֹחֵן גַּם אֶת אֲמִתּוּת אַהֲבַתְכֶם
ella she'al-yedei charitzutam shel acherim ani bochen gam et amittut ahavatchem
but as proving through the earnestness of others the sincerity also of your love.

הֵן יוֹדְעִים אַתֶּם אֶת מַעֲשֵׂה הַחֶסֶד שֶׁל אֲדוֹנֵנוּ יֵשׁוּעַ הַמָּשִׁיחַ
hen yode'im attem et ma'aseh hachesed shel adonenu yeshua hammashiach
For ye know the grace of our Lord Jesus Christ,

שֶׁבִּהְיוֹתוֹ עָשִׁיר נַעֲשָׂה עָנִי לְמַעַנְכֶם, כְּדֵי שֶׁתַּעֲשִׁירוּ אַתֶּם עַל־יְדֵי עֲנִיּוּתוֹ
shebbihyoto ashir na'asah ani lema'anchem, kedei shetta'ashiru attem al-yedei aniyuto
that, though he was rich, yet for your sakes he became poor, that ye through his poverty might become rich.

מְחַוֶּה אֲנִי אֶת דַּעְתִּי בְּעִנְיָן זֶה, שֶׁכֵּן הַדָּבָר יוֹעִיל לָכֶם, אַתֶּם אֲשֶׁר לִפְנֵי שָׁנָה הִקְדַּמְתֶּם וְהִתְחַלְתֶּם
mechavveh ani et da'ti be'inyan zeh, shekken haddavar yo'il lachem, attem asher lifnei shanah hikdamtem vehitchaltem
And herein I give my judgment: for this is expedient for you, who were the first to make a beginning a year ago,

לֹא רַק לַעֲשׂוֹת אֶלָּא גַּם לִרְצוֹת
lo rak la'asot ella gam lirtzot
not only to do, but also to will.

אֲבָל כָּעֵת הַשְׁלִימוּ גַּם אֶת הַמַּעֲשֶׂה
aval ka'et hashlimu gam et hamma'aseh
But now complete the doing also;

כְּדֵי שֶׁתִּהְיֶה הַשְׁלָמַת הַמַּעֲשֶׂה מִתּוֹךְ מַה שֶּׁמַּשֶּׂגֶת יֶדְכֶם, כְּפִי שֶׁהָיְתָה הַנְּכוֹנוּת לִרְצוֹת
kedei shettihyeh hashlamat hamma'aseh mittoch mah shemmasseget yedchem, kefi shehayetah hannechonut lirtzot
that as there was the readiness to will, so there may be the completion also out of your ability.

שֶׁהֲרֵי אִם קַיֶּמֶת הַנְּכוֹנוּת, רְצוּיָה הִיא לְפִי מַה שֶּׁיֵּשׁ בְּיַד אִישׁ, לֹא לְפִי מַה שֶׁאֵין בְּיָדוֹ
sheharei im kayemet hannechonut, retzuyah hi lefi mah sheyesh beyad ish, lo lefi mah she'ein beyado
For if the readiness is there, it is acceptable according as a man hath, not according as he hath not.

אֵין זֶה כְּדֵי שֶׁתִּהְיֶה לַאֲחֵרִים רְוָחָה וְלָכֶם מַחְסוֹר, אֶלָּא לְשֵׁם הַשִּׁוְיוֹן
ein zeh kedei shettihyeh la'acherim revachah velachem machsor, ella leshem hashivyon
For I say not this that others may be eased and ye distressed; but by equality:

כָּעֵת הַשֶּׁפַע שֶׁלָּכֶם יְמַלֵּא אֶת מַחְסוֹרָם
ka'et hashefa shellachem yemallei et machsoram
your abundance being a supply at this present time for their want,

כְּדֵי שֶׁבְּעֵת הַצֹּרֶךְ יְמַלֵּא הַשֶּׁפַע שֶׁלָּהֶם אֶת מַחְסוֹרְכֶם אַתֶּם, וְכָךְ יְקֻיַּם הַשִּׁוְיוֹן
kedei shebbe'et hatzorech yemallei hashefa shellahem et machsorechem attem, vechach yekuyam hashivyon
that their abundance also may become a supply for your want; that there may be equality:

אֶל הַקּוֹרִינְתִּים ב

ח

וְעַתָּה, אַחַי, נְסַפֵּר לָכֶם עַל חֶסֶד אֱלֹהִים שֶׁהָאֱצַל בִּקְהִלּוֹת מַקְדוֹנְיָה
ve'attah, achai, nesapper lachem al chesed elohim sheho'otzal bik'hillot makedoneyah
Moreover, brethren, we make known to you the grace of God which hath been given in the churches of Macedonia;

פְּעָמִים רַבּוֹת עָמְדוּ בְּמִבְחַן הַצָּרוֹת
pe'amim rabbot amdu bemivchan hatzarot
how that in much proof of affliction the abundance of their joy

וּמִתּוֹךְ שִׁפְעַת שִׂמְחָתָם וְעֹמֶק עֲנִיּוּתָם גָּאָה עֹשֶׁר נְדִיבוּתָם
umittoch shif'at simchatam ve'omek aniyutam ga'ah osher nedivutam
and their deep poverty abounded unto the riches of their liberality.

הֲרֵינִי מֵעִיד כִּי נָדְבוּ כְּפִי יְכָלְתָּם, וְיוֹתֵר מִכְּפִי יְכָלְתָּם
hareini me'id ki niddvu kefi yecholtam, veyoter mikkefi yecholtam
For according to their power, I bear witness, yea and beyond their power, they gave of their own accord,

וּבְהַפְצָרוֹת רַבּוֹת בִּקְשׁוּ מֵאִתָּנוּ אֶת הַזְּכוּת לְהִשְׁתַּתֵּף בָּעֶזְרָה לַקְּדוֹשִׁים
uvehaftzarot rabbot bikshu me'ittanu et hazzchut lehishtattef ba'ezrah lakkedoshim
beseeching us with much entreaty in regard of this grace and the fellowship in the ministering to the saints:

וְלֹא כְּפִי שֶׁצִּפִּינוּ, אֶלָּא קֹדֶם הִקְדִּישׁוּ אֶת עַצְמָם לָאָדוֹן וְאַחַר כָּךְ לָנוּ, כִּרְצוֹן אֱלֹהִים
velo kefi shetzippinu, ella kodem hikdishu et atzmam la'adon ve'achar kach lanu, kirtzon elohim
and this, not as we had hoped, but first they gave their own selves to the Lord, and to us through the will of God.

עַל כֵּן בִּקַּשְׁנוּ מִטִּיטוֹס
al ken bikkashnu mittitos
Insomuch that we exhorted Titus,

כִּי כְּשֵׁם שֶׁהִקְדִּים וְהִתְחִיל, כֵּן גַּם יַשְׁלִים בְּקִרְבְּכֶם אֶת מַעֲשֵׂה הַחֶסֶד הַזֶּה
ki keshem shehikdim vehitchil, ken gam yashlim bekirbechem et ma'aseh hachesed hazzeh
that as he had made a beginning before, so he would also complete in you this grace also.

וּכְשֵׁם שֶׁאַתֶּם שׁוֹפְעִים בַּכֹּל - בֶּאֱמוּנָה, בַּהַטָּפָה, בְּדַעַת
ucheshem she'attem shofe'im bakkol - be'emunah, behattafah, beda'at
But as ye abound in everything, in faith, and utterance, and knowledge,

בְּכָל שְׁקִידָה, וּבָאַהֲבָה אֲשֶׁר עוֹרַרְנוּ בָּכֶם
bechol shekidah, uva'ahavah asher orarnu bachem
and in all earnestness, and in your love to us,

שִׁפְעוּ גַּם בַּחֶסֶד הַזֶּה
shif'u gam bachesed hazzeh
see that ye abound in this grace also.

אֶל הַקּוֹרִינְתִּים ב

הִתְנַצְּלוּת, הִתְלַהֲטוּת, יִרְאָה
hitnatzelut, hitlahatut, yir'ah
yea what clearing of yourselves, yea what indignation, yea what fear,

כִּסּוּפִים, קִנְאָה, נְכוֹנוּת לַעֲשִׂיַּת דִּין
kissufim, kin'ah, nechonut la'asiyat din
yea what longing, yea what zeal, yea what avenging!

מִכָּל הַבְּחִינוֹת הוֹכַחְתֶּם שֶׁאֵין בָּכֶם דֹּפִי בָּעִנְיָן הַהוּא
mikkol habbechinot hochachtem she'ein bachem dofi ba'inyan hahu
In everything ye approved yourselves to be pure in the matter.

וּבְכֵן, גַּם כְּשֶׁכָּתַבְתִּי אֲלֵיכֶם, לֹא כָתַבְתִּי לְמַעַן זֶה שֶׁעָשָׂה אֶת הָרָעָה וְלֹא לְמַעַן זֶה שֶׁסָּבַל אֶת הָרָעָה
uvechen, gam keshekkatavti aleichem, lo katavti lema'an zeh she'asah et hara'ah velo lema'an zeh shessaval et hara'ah
So although I wrote unto you, I wrote not for his cause that did the wrong, nor for his cause that suffered the wrong,

אֶלָּא לְמַעַן תִּוָּכְחוּ לָדַעַת לְנֹכַח הָאֱלֹהִים מַהִי מְסִירוּתְכֶם לָנוּ
ella lema'an tivvachechu lada'at lenochach ha'elohim mahi mesirutechem lanu
but that your earnest care for us might be made manifest unto you in the sight of God.

לָכֵן נֻחַמְנוּ. אֲבָל הַרְבֵּה יוֹתֵר מִשֶּׁנֻּחַמְנוּ שָׂמַחְנוּ בְּשִׂמְחַת טִיטוֹס
lachen nuchamnu. aval harbeh yoter mishennuchamnu samachnu besimchat titos
Therefore we have been comforted: and in our comfort we joyed the more exceedingly for the joy of Titus,

שֶׁכֵּן כֻּלְּכֶם גְּרַמְתֶּם לוֹ נַחַת רוּחַ
shekken kullechem geramtem lo nachat ruach
because his spirit hath been refreshed by you all.

אִם בְּמִדַּת מָה הִתְגָּאֵיתִי בָּכֶם לְפָנָיו, לֹא הִתְאַכְזַבְתִּי - אֶלָּא כְּשֵׁם שֶׁתָּמִיד דִּבַּרְנוּ אֲלֵיכֶם אֱמֶת
im bemiddat mah hitga'eiti bachem lefanav, lo hit'achzavti - ella keshem shettamid dibbarnu aleichem emet
For if in anything I have gloried to him on your behalf, I was not put to shame; but as we spake all things to you in truth,

כֵּן גַּם דִּבְרֵי הִתְגָּאוּתֵנוּ לִפְנֵי טִיטוֹס הוּכְחוּ כֶּאֱמֶת
ken gam divrei hitga'utenu lifnei titos huchechu ke'emet
so our glorying also which I made before Titus was found to be truth.

הוּא רוֹחֵשׁ לָכֶם אַהֲבָה רַבָּה עַד מְאֹד, כִּי זוֹכֵר הוּא אֶת הַצִּיּוּת שֶׁל כֻּלְּכֶם
hu rochesh lachem ahavah rabbah ad me'od, ki zocher hu et hatziyut shel kullchem
And his affection is more abundantly toward you, while he remembereth the obedience of you all,

כְּשֶׁקִּבַּלְתֶּם אוֹתוֹ בְּיִרְאָה וּבַחֲרָדָה
keshekkibbaltem oto beyir'ah uvacharadah
how with fear and trembling ye received him.

אֲנִי שָׂמֵחַ שֶׁבְּכָל דָּבָר אֲנִי בָּטוּחַ בָּכֶם
ani sameach shebbechol davar ani batuach bachem
I rejoice that in everything I am of good courage concerning you.

אֶל הַקּוֹרִינְתִּים ב

אֶלָּא צָרוֹת מִכָּל עֵבֶר, מַאֲבָקִים מִחוּץ וַחֲשָׁשׁוֹת מִבַּיִת
ella tzarot mikkol ever, ma'avakim michutz vachashashot mibbayit
but we were afflicted on every side; without were fightings, within were fears.

אֲבָל אֱלֹהִים, הַמְנַחֵם אֶת הַנִּדְכָּאִים, נִחֵם אוֹתָנוּ בְּבוֹאוֹ שֶׁל טִיטוֹס
aval elohim, hamnachem et hannidka'im, nichem otanu bevo'o shel titos
Nevertheless he that comforteth the lowly, even God, comforted us by the coming of Titus;

וְלֹא בְּבוֹאוֹ בִּלְבַד, אֶלָּא גַּם בַּנֶּחָמָה שֶׁהוּא נֻחַם בָּכֶם
velo bevo'o bilvad, ella gam bannechamah shehu nucham bachem
and not by his coming only, but also by the comfort wherewith he was comforted in you,

שֶׁכֵּן סִפֵּר לָנוּ עַל כִּסּוּפֵיכֶם, עַל רֹב צַעֲרְכֶם,
shekken sipper lanu al kissufeichem, al rov tza'archem,
while he told us your longing, your mourning,

עַל הַקִּנְאָה שֶׁאַתֶּם מְקַנְּאִים לִי, וְלָכֵן שָׂמַחְתִּי עוֹד יוֹתֵר
al hakkin'ah she'attem mekanne'im li, velachen samachti od yoter
your zeal for me; so that I rejoiced yet more.

הֵן גַּם אִם הֶעֱצַבְתִּי אֶתְכֶם בְּאִגַּרְתִּי, אֵינֶנִּי מִתְחָרֵט
hen gam im he'etzavti etchem be'iggarti, einenni mitcharet
For though I made you sorry with my epistle, I do not regret it:

גַּם אִם הִתְחָרַטְתִּי - אֲנִי רוֹאֶה שֶׁהָאִגֶּרֶת הַהִיא הֶעֱצִיבָה אֶתְכֶם, אַף כִּי רַק לִזְמַן מָה
gam im hitcharatti - ani ro'eh sheha'iggeret hahi he'etzivah etchem, af ki rak lizman mah
though I did regret it (for I see that that epistle made you sorry, though but for a season),

כָּעֵת אֲנִי שָׂמֵחַ לֹא עַל שֶׁנֶּעֱצַבְתֶּם, אֶלָּא עַל שֶׁהָעֶצֶב הַזֶּה הֵבִיא אֶתְכֶם לִידֵי תְּשׁוּבָה
ka'et ani sameach lo al shenne'etzavtem, ella al sheha'etzev hazzeh hevi etchem liydei teshuvah
I now rejoice, not that ye were made sorry, but that ye were made sorry unto repentance;

כִּי נֶעֱצַבְתֶּם כִּרְצוֹן אֱלֹהִים, בְּאֹפֶן שֶׁלֹּא נִגְרַם לָכֶם שׁוּם נֶזֶק עַל־יָדֵינוּ
ki ne'etzavtem kirtzon elohim, be'ofen shello nigram lachem shum nezek al-yadeinu
for ye were made sorry after a godly sort, that ye might suffer loss by us in nothing.

הֵן הָעֶצֶב שֶׁהוּא כִּרְצוֹן אֱלֹהִים מְעוֹרֵר לִתְשׁוּבָה אֲשֶׁר תּוֹצָאָתָהּ יְשׁוּעָה, וְעַל עֶצֶב כָּזֶה אֵין לְהִצְטַעֵר
hen ha'etzev shehu kirtzon elohim me'orer litshuvah asher totza'atah yeshu'ah, ve'al etzev kazeh ein lehitztaer
For godly sorrow worketh repentance unto salvation, a repentance which bringeth no regret:

אֲבָל הָעֶצֶב כְּדֶרֶךְ הָעוֹלָם גּוֹרֵם מָוֶת
aval ha'etzev kederech ha'olam gorem mavet
but the sorrow of the world worketh death.

רְאוּ מָה עוֹרֵר בָּכֶם הָעֶצֶב הַזֶּה אֲשֶׁר כִּרְצוֹן אֱלֹהִים! הוּא עוֹרֵר בָּכֶם חֲרִיצוּת
re'u mah orer bachem ha'etzev hazzeh asher kirtzon elohim! hu orer bachem charitzut
For behold, this selfsame thing, that ye were made sorry after a godly sort, what earnest care it wrought in you,

אֶל הַקּוֹרִינְתִּים ב

עַל כֵּן צְאוּ מִתּוֹכָם וְהִבָּרוּ, נְאֻם יהוה

al ken tze'u mittocham vehibbaru, ne'um hashem
Wherefore Come ye out from among them, and be ye separate, saith the Lord,

וְטָמֵא אַל־תִּגָּעוּ; וַאֲנִי אֲקַבֵּל אֶתְכֶם

vetamei al-tigga'u; va'ani akabbel etchem
And touch no unclean thing; And I will receive you,

וְהָיִיתִי לָכֶם לְאָב וְאַתֶּם תִּהְיוּ לִי לְבָנִים וּלְבָנוֹת, נְאֻם יהוה צְבָאוֹת

vehayiti lachem le'av ve'attem tihyu li levanim ulevanot, ne'um hashem tzeva'ot
And will be to you a Father, And ye shall be to me sons and daughters, saith the Lord Almighty.

ז

לָכֵן, חֲבִיבַי, בִּהְיוֹת לָנוּ הַהַבְטָחוֹת הָאֵלֶּה

lachen, chavivai, bihyot lanu hahavtachot ha'elleh
Having therefore these promises, beloved,

נְטַהֵר אֶת עַצְמֵנוּ מִכָּל טֻמְאַת גּוּף וְרוּחַ וְנַשְׁלִים קְדֻשָּׁתֵנוּ בְּיִרְאַת אֱלֹהִים

netaher et atzmenu mikkol tum'at guf veruach venashlim kedushatenu beyir'at elohim
let us cleanse ourselves from all defilement of flesh and spirit, perfecting holiness in the fear of God.

הַרְחִיבוּ לָנוּ לְבַבְכֶם; לֹא עָשִׂינוּ עָוֶל לְאִישׁ, לֹא גָּרַמְנוּ נֶזֶק לְאִישׁ, לֹא רִמִּינוּ אִישׁ

harchivu lanu levavchem; lo asinu avel le'ish, lo garamnu nezek le'ish, lo rimminu ish
Open your hearts to us: we wronged no man, we corrupted no man, we took advantage of no man.

אֵינֶנִּי מְדַבֵּר מִתּוֹךְ כַּוָּנָה לְהַרְשִׁיעַ, שֶׁהֲרֵי כְּבָר אָמַרְתִּי

einenni medabber mittoch kavvanah leharshia, sheharei kevar amarti
I say it not to condemn you: for I have said before,

שֶׁאַתֶּם בְּלִבֵּנוּ, גַּם לַחַיִּים גַּם לַמָּוֶת

she'attem belibbenu, gam lachayim gam lammavet
that ye are in our hearts to die together and live together.

רַב בִּטְחוֹנִי בָּכֶם. גְּדוֹלָה גַּאֲוָתִי בָּכֶם

rav bitchoni bachem. gdolah ga'avati bachem
Great is my boldness of speech toward you, great is my glorying on your behalf:

מָלֵאתִי נֶחָמָה וַאֲנִי שׁוֹפֵעַ שִׂמְחָה בְּכָל צָרָתֵנוּ

maleti nechamah va'ani shofea simchah bechol tzaratenu
I am filled with comfort, I overflow with joy in all our affliction.

הֵן גַּם כַּאֲשֶׁר בָּאנוּ לְמַקֵדוֹנְיָה לֹא הָיָה מָנוֹחַ לְגוּפֵנוּ

hen gam ka'asher banu lemakedoneyah lo hayah manoach legufenu
For even when we were come into Macedonia our flesh had no relief,

אֶל הַקּוֹרִינְתִּים ב

בְּדִבּוּר אֱמֶת, בִּגְבוּרַת אֱלֹהִים, בְּנֶשֶׁק הַצֶּדֶק שֶׁבִּימִינֵנוּ וּבִשְׂמֹאלֵנוּ
bedibbur emet, bigvurat elohim, beneshek hatzedek shebbeyeminenu uvismolenu
in the word of truth, in the power of God; by the armor of righteousness on the right hand and on the left,

בְּכָבוֹד וּבְקָלוֹן, בְּשֵׁם רַע וּבְשֵׁם טוֹב; כְּאִלּוּ מַתְעִים, אַךְ אָנוּ נֶאֱמָנִים
bechavod uvekalon, beshem ra uveshem tov; ke'illu mat'im, ach anu ne'emanim
by glory and dishonor, by evil report and good report; as deceivers, and yet true;

כְּאִלּוּ בִּלְתִּי מֻכָּרִים, אַךְ אָנוּ מֻכָּרִים; כְּמֵתִים וְהִנֵּה אָנוּ חַיִּים; כְּנֶעֱנָשִׁים וְלֹא מוּמָתִים
ke'illu bilti mukkarim, ach anu mukkarim; kemetim vehinneh anu chayim; kene'enashim velo mumatim
as unknown, and yet well known; as dying, and behold, we live; as chastened, and not killed;

כְּנֶעֱצָבִים, אַךְ שְׂמֵחִים תָּמִיד; כַּעֲנִיִּים, אַךְ מַעֲשִׁירִים אֶת הָרַבִּים; כַּחַסְרֵי כֹּל וְעִם זֹאת יֵשׁ לָנוּ הַכֹּל
kene'etzavim, ach semechim tamid; ka'aniyim, ach ma'ashirim et harabbim; kechasrei kol ve'im zot yesh lanu hakkol
as sorrowful, yet always rejoicing; as poor, yet making many rich; as having nothing, and yet possessing all things.

קוֹרִינְתִּים, דִּבַּרְנוּ אֲלֵיכֶם בִּכֵנוּת וְנָהַגְנוּ בְּרֹחַב לֵב
korintim, dibbarnu aleichem bechenut venahagnu berochav lev
Our mouth is open unto you, O Corinthians, our heart is enlarged.

לֹא צַר לָכֶם הַמָּקוֹם בִּלְבָבֵנוּ; בִּלְבַבְכֶם צַר הַמָּקוֹם
lo tzar lachem hammakom bilvavenu; bilvavchem tzar hammakom
Ye are not straitened in us, but ye are straitened in your own affections.

הָשִׁיבוּ אֶת אוֹתוֹ הַגְּמוּל - כְּאֶל בָּנַי אֲנִי מְדַבֵּר - וְהִתְנַהֲגוּ בְּרֹחַב לֵב גַּם אַתֶּם
hashivu et oto haggmul - ke'el banai ani medabber - vehitnahagu berochav lev gam attem
Now for a recompense in like kind (I speak as unto my children), be ye also enlarged.

אַל תֵּרָתְמוּ לְעֹל אֶחָד עִם הַבִּלְתִּי מַאֲמִינִים; כִּי אֵיזוֹ שֻׁתָּפוּת לִצְדָקָה עִם עַוְלָה
al teratmu le'ol echad im habbilti ma'aminim; ki eizo shuttafut litzdakah im avlah
Be not unequally yoked with unbelievers: for what fellowship have righteousness and iniquity?

וּמַה רֵעוּת יֵשׁ לָאוֹר עִם חֹשֶׁךְ
umah re'ut yesh le'or im choshech
or what communion hath light with darkness?

מַה הַסְכָּמָה יֵשׁ לַמָּשִׁיחַ עִם בְּלִיַּעַל? אוֹ מַה חֵלֶק לְמַאֲמִין עִם מִי שֶׁאֵינוֹ מַאֲמִין
mah haskamah yesh lammashiach im beliya'al? o mah chelek lema'amin im mi she'eino ma'amin
And what concord hath Christ with Belial? or what portion hath a believer with an unbeliever?

וּמַה קֶּשֶׁר יֵשׁ לְהֵיכַל אֱלֹהִים עִם אֱלִילִים? הֵן אֲנַחְנוּ הֵיכַל אֱלֹהִים חַיִּים, כְּפִי שֶׁאָמַר אֱלֹהִים:
umah kesher yesh leheichal elohim im elilim? hen anachnu heichal elohim chayim, kfi she'amar elohim
And what agreement hath a temple of God with idols? for we are a temple of the living God; even as God said,

וְשָׁכַנְתִּי בְּתוֹכָם; וְהִתְהַלַּכְתִּי בְּתוֹכֲכֶם וְהָיִיתִי לָהֶם לֵאלֹהִים וְהֵמָּה יִהְיוּ לִי לְעָם
veshachanti betocham; vehit'hallachti betochachem; vehayiti lahem le'elohim vehemah yihyu li le'am
I will dwell in them, and walk in them; and I will be their God, and they shall be my people.

אֶל הַקּוֹרִינְתִּים ב

לָכֵן שַׁגְרִירֵי הַמָּשִׁיחַ אָנוּ וֵאלֹהִים כְּמוֹ מַפְצִיר בְּאֶמְצָעוּתֵנוּ·
lachen shagrirei hammashiach anu ve'elohim kemo maftzir be'emtza'utenu
We are ambassadors therefore on behalf of Christ, as though God were entreating by us:

וּבְכֵן מַפְצִירִים אָנוּ בְּשֵׁם הַמָּשִׁיחַ: הִתְרַצּוּ נָא לֵאלֹהִים
uvechen maftzirim anu beshem hammashiach: hitratzu na le'elohim
we beseech you on behalf of Christ, be ye reconciled to God.

אֶת זֶה אֲשֶׁר לֹא יָדַע חַטָּאת עָשָׂה לְחַטָּאת בַּעֲדֵנוּ, כְּדֵי שֶׁאָנוּ נִלְבַּשׁ אֶת הַצְּדָקָה שֶׁל אֱלֹהִים בּוֹ
et zeh asher lo yada chattat asah lechattat ba'adenu, kedei she'anu nilbash et hatzdakah shel elohim bo
Him who knew no sin he made to be sin on our behalf; that we might become the righteousness of God in him.

I

כֵּיוָן שֶׁאֲנַחְנוּ שֻׁתָּפִים לְפָעֳלוֹ, אָנוּ גַּם מְבַקְשִׁים מִכֶּם: אַל נָא תְּקַבְּלוּ לָרִיק אֶת חֶסֶד אֱלֹהִים
keivan she'anachnu shuttafim lefo'alo, anu gam mevakshim mikkem. al na tekabbelu larik et chesed elohim
And working together with him we entreat also that ye receive not the grace of God in vain

הֵן הוּא אוֹמֵר: בְּעֵת רָצוֹן עֲנִיתִיךָ וּבְיוֹם יְשׁוּעָה עֲזַרְתִּיךָ
hen hu omer: be'et ratzon aniticha uveyom yeshu'ah azarticha
(for he saith, At an acceptable time I hearkened unto thee, And in a day of salvation did I succor thee:

הִנֵּה עַתָּה עֵת רָצוֹן, הִנֵּה עַתָּה יוֹם יְשׁוּעָה
hinneh attah et ratzon, hinneh attah yom yeshu'ah
behold, now is the acceptable time; behold, now is the day of salvation):

אֵין אָנוּ שָׂמִים מִכְשׁוֹל בְּשׁוּם דָּבָר, פֶּן יִהְיֶה שֵׁרוּתֵנוּ לְשִׁמְצָה
ein anu samim michshol beshum davar, pen yihyeh sherutenu leshimtzah
giving no occasion of stumbling in anything, that our ministration be not blamed;

אַדְּרַבָּא, בְּכָל דָּבָר אֲנַחְנוּ מַצִּיגִים אֶת עַצְמֵנוּ כִּמְשָׁרְתֵי אֱלֹהִים
addrabba, bechol davar anachnu matzigim et atzmenu kimshartei elohim
but in everything commending ourselves, as ministers of God,

בְּרֹב סַבְלָנוּת, בְּצָרוֹת, בְּמַחְסוֹר, בִּמְצוּקוֹת, בְּמַכּוֹת
berov savlanut, betzarot, bemachsor, bimtzukot, bemakkot
in much patience, in afflictions, in necessities, in distresses, in stripes,

בְּבָתֵּי כֶלֶא, בִּמְהוּמוֹת, בְּעָמָל, בְּלֵילוֹת לְלֹא שֵׁנָה, בְּצוֹמוֹת
bevattei kele, bimehumot, be'amal, beleilot lelo shenah, betzomot
in imprisonments, in tumults, in labors, in watchings, in fastings;

בְּטָהֳרָה, בְּדַעַת, בְּאֹרֶךְ רוּחַ, בִּנְדִיבוּת לֵב, בְּרוּחַ הַקֹּדֶשׁ, בְּאַהֲבָה אֲמִתִּית
betohorah, beda'at, be'orech ruach, bindivut lev, beruach hakkodesh, be'ahavah amittit
in pureness, in knowledge, in longsuffering, in kindness, in the Holy Spirit, in love unfeigned,

אֶל הַקּוֹרִינְתִּים ב

אֵין אָנוּ שׁוּב מְשַׁבְּחִים אֶת עַצְמֵנוּ לִפְנֵיכֶם, אֶלָּא נוֹתְנִים בְּיֶדְכֶם סִבָּה לְהִתְגָּאוֹת בָּנוּ
ein anu shuv meshabbechim et atzmenu lifneichem, ella notenim beyedchem sibbah lehitga'ot banu
We are not again commending ourselves unto you, but speak as giving you occasion of glorying on our behalf,

כְּדֵי שֶׁיִּהְיֶה לָכֶם מַה לְהַצִּיב נֶגֶד הָאֲנָשִׁים הַמִּתְגָּאִים בְּמַרְאֵה פָנִים וְלֹא בַּמֶּה שֶׁבַּלֵּב
kedei sheyihyeh lachem mah lehatziv neged ha'anashim hammitga'im bemar'eh panim velo bemah shebballev
that ye may have wherewith to answer them that glory in appearance, and not in heart.

וְאִם יָצָאנוּ מִדַּעְתֵּנוּ, הֲרֵי זֶה לְמַעַן אֱלֹהִים; וְאִם מְפֻקָּחִים אָנוּ, הֲרֵי זֶה לְמַעַנְכֶם
ve'im yatzanu midda'tenu, harei zeh lema'an elohim; ve'im mefukkachim anu, harei zeh lema'anchem
For whether we are beside ourselves, it is unto God; or whether we are of sober mind, it is unto you.

שֶׁכֵּן אַהֲבַת הַמָּשִׁיחַ דּוֹחֶקֶת בָּנוּ, בְּהַכִּירֵנוּ שֶׁאֶחָד מֵת בְּעַד הַכֹּל, לָכֵן הַכֹּל מֵתוּ
shekken ahavat hammashiach docheket banu, behakkirenu she'echad met be'ad hakkol, lachen hakkol metu
For the love of Christ constraineth us; because we thus judge, that one died for all, therefore all died;

וּבְעַד הַכֹּל הוּא מֵת, כְּדֵי שֶׁאֵלֶּה הַחַיִּים לֹא יִחְיוּ עוֹד לְמַעַן עַצְמָם
uve'ad hakkol hu met, kedei she'elleh hachayim lo yichyu od lema'an atzmam
and he died for all, that they that live should no longer live unto themselves,

אֶלָּא לְמַעַן זֶה אֲשֶׁר מֵת וְקָם בַּעֲדָם
ella lema'an zeh asher met vekam ba'adam
but unto him who for their sakes died and rose again.

עַל כֵּן מֵעַתָּה אֵין אָנוּ מַכִּירִים אִישׁ עַל־פִּי רְאוּת אֱנוֹשִׁית
al ken me'attah ein anu makkirim ish al-pi re'ut enoshit
Wherefore we henceforth know no man after the flesh:

וְגַם אִם הִכַּרְנוּ אֶת הַמָּשִׁיחַ עַל־פִּי רְאוּת אֱנוֹשִׁית, הֲרֵי כָּעֵת אֵינֶנּוּ מַכִּירִים אוֹתוֹ עוֹד בְּאֹפֶן כָּזֶה
vegam im hikkarnu et hammashiach al-pi re'ut enoshit, harei ka'et einennu makkirim oto od be'ofen kazeh
even though we have known Christ after the flesh, yet now we know him so no more.

עַל כֵּן מִי שֶׁנִּמְצָא בַּמָּשִׁיחַ הוּא בְּרִיאָה חֲדָשָׁה. הַיְשָׁנוֹת עָבְרוּ; הִנֵּה נִהְיוּ חֲדָשׁוֹת
al ken mi shennimtza bammashiach hu bri'ah chadashah. hayshanot averu; hinneh nihyu chadashot
Wherefore if any man is in Christ, he is a new creature: the old things are passed away; behold, they are become new.

וְהַכֹּל מֵאֵת הָאֱלֹהִים שֶׁרִצָּה אוֹתָנוּ אֵלָיו עַל־יְדֵי הַמָּשִׁיחַ, וּמָסַר לָנוּ אֶת שֵׁרוּת הָרִצּוּי
vehakkol me'et ha'elohim sheritzah otanu elav al-yedei hammashiach, umasar lanu et sherut haritzui
But all things are of God, who reconciled us to himself through Christ, and gave unto us the ministry of reconciliation;

כְּלוֹמַר: אֱלֹהִים הָיָה בַּמָּשִׁיחַ מְרַצֶּה אֶת הָעוֹלָם אֶל עַצְמוֹ
Klomar: elohim hayah bammashiach meratzeh et ha'olam el atzmo
to wit, that God was in Christ reconciling the world unto himself,

מִבְּלִי לַחְשֹׁב לָהֶם אֶת עֲווֹנוֹתֵיהֶם, וְהוּא שָׂם בָּנוּ אֶת דְּבַר הָרִצּוּי
mibbeli lachshov lahem et avonoteihem, vehu sam banu et devar haritzui
not reckoning unto them their trespasses, and having committed unto us the word of reconciliation.

אֶל הַקּוֹרִינְתִּים ב

שֶׁהֲרֵי אֵינֶנּוּ חֲפֵצִים לְהִתְפַּשֵּׁט, אֶלָּא לְהוֹסִיף לְבוּשׁ
sheharei einennu chafetzim lehitpashet, ella lehosif levush
not for that we would be unclothed, but that we would be clothed upon,

בְּאֹפֶן שֶׁהַכָּפוּף לַמָּוֶת יְבֻלַּע עַל־יְדֵי הַחַיִּים
be'ofen shehakkafuf lammavet yibbala al-yedei hachayim
that what is mortal may be swallowed up of life.

וֵאלֹהִים הוּא אֲשֶׁר הֵכִין אוֹתָנוּ לְכָךְ וְנָתַן לָנוּ אֶת עֶרְבוֹן הָרוּחַ
ve'elohim hu asher hechin otanu lechach venatan lanu et erevon haruach
Now he that wrought us for this very thing is God, who gave unto us the earnest of the Spirit.

עַל כֵּן מְלֵאֵי בִּטָּחוֹן אָנוּ בְּכָל עֵת
al ken mele'ei bittachon anu bechol et
Being therefore always of good courage,

וְיוֹדְעִים כִּי בְּהִמָּצְאֵנוּ בַּגּוּף רְחוֹקִים אָנוּ מִן הָאָדוֹן
veyode'im ki behimmatze'enu bagguf rechokim anu min ha'adon
and knowing that, whilst we are at home in the body, we are absent from the Lord

שֶׁכֵּן עַל־פִּי אֱמוּנָה אֲנַחְנוּ מִתְהַלְּכִים וְלֹא עַל־פִּי מַרְאֵה עֵינַיִם
shekken al-pi emunah anachnu mit'hallechim velo al-pi mar'eh einayim
(for we walk by faith, not by sight);

וְאוּלָם מְלֵאֵי בִּטָּחוֹן אָנוּ וּמַעְדִּיפִים לָצֵאת מִמִּשְׁכַּן הַגּוּף וְלָבוֹא הַבַּיְתָה אֶל הָאָדוֹן
ve'ulam mele'ei bittachon anu uma'difim latzet mimmishkan hagguf velavo habbaytah el ha'adon
we are of good courage, I say, and are willing rather to be absent from the body, and to be at home with the Lord.

לָכֵן גַּם שׁוֹאֲפִים אָנוּ לִהְיוֹת רְצוּיִים לְפָנָיו, בֵּין שֶׁאָנוּ בְּמִשְׁכָּנֵנוּ בֵּין שֶׁאָנוּ מִחוּצָה לוֹ
lachen gam sho'afim anu lihyot retzuyim lefanav, bein she'anu bemishkanenu bein she'anu michutzah lo
Wherefore also we make it our aim, whether at home or absent, to be well-pleasing unto him.

כִּי כֻּלָּנוּ חַיָּבִים לְהֵרָאוֹת לִפְנֵי כֵּס הַמִּשְׁפָּט שֶׁל הַמָּשִׁיחַ
ki kullanu chayavim lehera'ot lifnei kes hammishpat shel hammashiach
For we must all be made manifest before the judgment-seat of Christ;

לְמַעַן יְקַבֵּל כָּל אֶחָד כְּפִי הַמַּעֲשִׂים שֶׁעָשָׂה בְּעֵת הֱיוֹתוֹ בַּגּוּף, אִם טוֹב וְאִם רַע
lema'an yekabbel kol echad kefi hamma'asim she'asah be'et heyoto bagguf, im tov ve'im ra
that each one may receive the things done in the body, according to what he hath done, whether it be good or bad.

מִתּוֹךְ הַכָּרַת יִרְאַת אֲדֹנָי אֲנַחְנוּ מְדַבְּרִים עַל לֵב בְּנֵי אָדָם כְּדֵי לְשַׁכְנְעָם. גְּלוּיִים אָנוּ לֵאלֹהִים
mittoch hakkarat yir'at adonai anachnu medabberim al lev benei adam kedei leshachne'am. geluyim anu lelohim
Knowing therefore the fear of the Lord, we persuade men, but we are made manifest unto God;

וַאֲנִי מְקַוֶּה שֶׁאֲנַחְנוּ גְּלוּיִים גַּם לְעֵינֵי מַצְפּוּנְכֶם
va'ani mekavveh she'anachnu geluyim gam le'einei matzpunechem
and I hope that we are made manifest also in your consciences.

אֶל הַקּוֹרִינְתִּים ב

וְכָךְ בְּשֶׁל הַחֶסֶד שֶׁשָּׁפַע בִּגְלַל הָרַבִּים תִּרְבֶּה הַהוֹדָיָה לִכְבוֹד אֱלֹהִים
vechach beshel hachesed sheshafa biglal harabbim tirbeh hahodayah lichvod elohim
that the grace, being multiplied through the many, may cause the thanksgiving to abound unto the glory of God.

לָכֵן אֵין אָנוּ מִתְיָאֲשִׁים, וְאַף עַל פִּי שֶׁהָאָדָם הַחִיצוֹנִי שֶׁלָּנוּ הוֹלֵךְ וּבָלֶה
lachen ein anu mitya'ashim, ve'af al pi sheha'adam hachitzoni shellanu holech uvaleh
Wherefore we faint not; but though our outward man is decaying,

הָאָדָם הַפְּנִימִי שֶׁלָּנוּ מִתְחַדֵּשׁ יוֹם יוֹם
ha'adam happenimi shellanu mitchaddesh yom yom
yet our inward man is renewed day by day.

הֵן צָרָתֵנוּ הַקַּלָּה שֶׁל הָרֶגַע מְכִינָה לָנוּ כְּבוֹד עוֹלָמִים גָּדוֹל וְרַב עַד מְאֹד
hen tzaratenu hakkallah shel harega mechinah lanu kevod olamim gadol verav ad me'od
For our light affliction, which is for the moment, worketh for us more and more exceedingly an eternal weight of glory;

וְאֵין אָנוּ צוֹפִים אֶל הַדְּבָרִים הַנִּרְאִים, אֶלָּא אֶל אֲשֶׁר אֵינָם נִרְאִים
ve'ein anu tzofim el haddvarim hannir'im, ella el asher einam nir'im
while we look not at the things which are seen, but at the things which are not seen:

כִּי הַדְּבָרִים הַנִּרְאִים לְשָׁעָה הֵם, אֲבָל הַבִּלְתִּי נִרְאִים - לְעוֹלָמִים
ki haddevarim hannir'im lesha'ah hem, aval habbilti nir'im - le'olamim
for the things which are seen are temporal; but the things which are not seen are eternal.

ה

אָנוּ יוֹדְעִים שֶׁאִם יֵהָרֵס בֵּית מִשְׁכָּנֵנוּ הָאַרְצִי
anu yode'im she'im yehares beit mishkanenu ha'artzi
For we know that if the earthly house of our tabernacle be dissolved,

יֵשׁ לָנוּ בִּנְיָן מֵאֵת אֱלֹהִים, בַּיִת שֶׁאֵינוֹ מַעֲשֵׂה יָדַיִם וְהוּא בַּשָּׁמַיִם לְעוֹלָמִים
yesh lanu binyan me'et elohim, bayit she'eino ma'aseh yadayim vehu bashamayim le'olamim
we have a building from God, a house not made with hands, eternal, in the heavens.

הֵן בָּזֶה, בְּמִשְׁכָּנֵנוּ הָאַרְצִי, נֶאֱנָחִים אָנוּ וְעַזִּים כִּסּוּפֵינוּ לִלְבּוֹשׁ גַּם אֶת בֵּיתֵנוּ אֲשֶׁר מִן הַשָּׁמַיִם
hen bazeh, bemishkanenu ha'artzi, ne'enachim anu ve'azzim kissufeinu lilbosh gam et beitenu asher min hashamayim
For verily in this we groan, longing to be clothed upon with our habitation which is from heaven:

אִם אָמְנָם נִמָּצֵא עוֹד לְבוּשִׁים וְלֹא עֲרֻמִּים
im omenam nimmatzei od levushim velo arummim
if so be that being clothed we shall not be found naked.

כִּי גַּם בִּהְיוֹתֵנוּ בְּמִשְׁכָּנֵנוּ כָּעֵת, נֶאֱנָחִים אָנוּ מִכֹּבֶד הַמַּשָּׂא
ki gam bihyotenu bemishkanenu ka'et, ne'enachim anu mikkoved hammassa
For indeed we that are in this tabernacle do groan, being burdened;

אֶל הַקּוֹרִינְתִּים ב

בְּרַם הָאוֹצָר הַזֶּה נָתוּן לָנוּ בִּכְלֵי חֶרֶס
beram ha'otzar hazzeh natun lanu bichlei cheres
But we have this treasure in earthen vessels,

כְּדֵי שֶׁיִּהְיֶה הַכֹּחַ הַנִּשְׂגָּב מֵאֵת אֱלֹהִים וְלֹא מִיָּדֵינוּ אָנוּ
kedei sheyihyeh hakkoach hannisgav me'et elohim velo miyadeinu anu
that the exceeding greatness of the power may be of God, and not from ourselves;

נִלְחָצִים אֲנַחְנוּ מִכָּל עֵבֶר, אַךְ אֵינֶנּוּ רְצוּצִים; נְבוֹכִים, אַךְ לֹא נוֹאָשִׁים
nilchatzim anachnu mikkol ever, ach einennu retzutzim; nevochim, ach lo no'ashim
we are pressed on every side, yet not straitened; perplexed, yet not unto despair;

נִרְדָּפִים, אַךְ לֹא נְטוּשִׁים; מֻשְׁלָכִים אַרְצָה, אַךְ לֹא נִשְׁמָדִים
nirdafim, ach lo netushim; mushlachim artzah, ach lo nishmadim
pursued, yet not forsaken; smitten down, yet not destroyed;

וְתָמִיד נוֹשְׂאִים אָנוּ בַּגּוּף אֶת מוֹת יֵשׁוּעַ, כְּדֵי שֶׁגַּם חַיֵּי יֵשׁוּעַ יִתְגַּלּוּ בְּגוּפֵנוּ
vetamid nose'im anu bagguf et mot yeshua', kedei sheggam chayei yeshua yitgallu begufenu
always bearing about in the body the dying of Jesus, that the life also of Jesus may be manifested in our body.

כִּי אֲנַחְנוּ הַחַיִּים נִמְסָרִים תָּמִיד לַמָּוֶת בַּעֲבוּר יֵשׁוּעַ
ki anachnu hachayim nimsarim tamid lammavet ba'avur yeshua
For we who live are always delivered unto death for Jesus' sake,

כְּדֵי שֶׁגַּם חַיֵּי יֵשׁוּעַ יִתְגַּלּוּ בִּבְשָׂרֵנוּ בֶּן־הַתְּמוּתָה
kdei sheggam chayei yeshua yitgallu bivsarenu ben-hattemutah
that the life also of Jesus may be manifested in our mortal flesh.

לְפִיכָךְ בָּנוּ פּוֹעֵל הַמָּוֶת, וּבָכֶם - הַחַיִּים
lefichach banu po'el hammavet, uvachem - hachayim
So then death worketh in us, but life in you.

אֲבָל יֵשׁ לָנוּ אוֹתָהּ רוּחַ שֶׁל אֱמוּנָה, כַּכָּתוּב
aval yesh lanu otah ruach shel emunah, kakkatuv
But having the same spirit of faith, according to that which is written,

הֶאֱמַנְתִּי כִּי אֲדַבֵּר, וְאָמְנָם אֲנַחְנוּ מַאֲמִינִים וְלָכֵן גַּם מְדַבְּרִים
he'emanti ki adabber, ve'omnam anachnu ma'aminim velachen gam medabberim
I believed, and therefore did I speak; we also believe, and therefore also we speak;

בְּיָדְעֵנוּ כִּי הוּא אֲשֶׁר הֵקִים לִתְחִיָּה אֶת הָאָדוֹן יֵשׁוּעַ, יָקִים גַּם אוֹתָנוּ עִם יֵשׁוּעַ וְיַצִּיגֵנוּ עִמָּכֶם
beyade'enu ki hu asher hekim litchiyah et ha'adon yeshua, yakim gam otanu im yeshua veyatzigenu immachem
knowing that he that raised up the Lord Jesus shall raise up us also with Jesus, and shall present us with you.

אָכֵן הַכֹּל לְמַעַנְכֶם
achen hakkol lema'anchem
For all things are for your sakes,

אֶל הַקּוֹרִינְתִּים ב

ד

הַשֵּׁרוּת הַזֶּה הֻפְקַד בְּיָדֵינוּ כְּפִי שֶׁגַּם רֻחַמְנוּ. לָכֵן אֵין אָנוּ מִתְיָאֲשִׁים
hasherut hazzeh hufkad beyadeinu kefi sheggam ruchamnu. lachen ein anu mitya'ashim
Therefore seeing we have this ministry, even as we obtained mercy, we faint not:

סִלַּקְנוּ יָדֵינוּ מִמַּעֲשֵׂי הַסֵּתֶר הַמְּבִישִׁים
sillaknu yadeinu mimma'asei hasseter hammevishim
but we have renounced the hidden things of shame,

אֵין אָנוּ הוֹלְכִים בְּדַרְכֵי מִרְמָה וְאֵינֶנּוּ מְסַלְּפִים אֶת דְּבַר אֱלֹהִים
ein anu holechim bedarchei mirmah ve'einennu mesallefim et devar elohim
not walking in craftiness, nor handling the word of God deceitfully;

אֶלָּא מְגַלִּים אָנוּ אֶת הָאֱמֶת וּבְכָךְ אָנוּ מַמְלִיצִים עַל עַצְמֵנוּ לִפְנֵי מַצְפּוּנוֹ שֶׁל כָּל אָדָם לְנֶגֶד עֵינֵי אֱלֹהִים
ella megallim anu et ha'emet uvechach anu mamlitzim al atzmenu lifnei matzpuno shel kol adam leneged einei elohim
but by the manifestation of the truth commending ourselves to every man's conscience in the sight of God.

אַךְ אִם נִסְתֶּרֶת בְּשׂוֹרָתֵנוּ, נִסְתֶּרֶת הִיא לָאוֹבְדִים
ach im nisteret besoratenu, nisteret hi la'ovedim
And even if our gospel is veiled, it is veiled in them that perish:

אֵל הָעוֹלָם הַזֶּה עִוֵּר אֶת שִׂכְלָם שֶׁל הַבִּלְתִּי מַאֲמִינִים
el ha'olam hazzeh ivver et sichlam shel habbilti ma'aminim
in whom the god of this world hath blinded the minds of the unbelieving,

לְבַל יִזְרַח עֲלֵיהֶם אוֹר הַבְּשׂוֹרָה שֶׁל כְּבוֹד הַמָּשִׁיחַ אֲשֶׁר הוּא צֶלֶם הָאֱלֹהִים
leval yizrach aleihem or habbesorah shel kevod hammashiach asher hu tzelem ha'elohim
that the light of the gospel of the glory of Christ, who is the image of God, should not dawn upon them.

הֲרֵי לֹא עַל עַצְמֵנוּ אָנוּ מַכְרִיזִים, אֶלָּא עַל הַמָּשִׁיחַ יֵשׁוּעַ כְּאָדוֹן
harei lo al atzmenu anu machrizim, ella al hammashiach yeshua ke'adon
For we preach not ourselves, but Christ Jesus as Lord,

וְאִלּוּ עַל עַצְמֵנוּ כְּעַל עַבְדֵיכֶם לְמַעַן יֵשׁוּעַ
ve'illu al atzmenu ke'al avdeichem lema'an yeshua
and ourselves as your servants for Jesus' sake.

הָאֱלֹהִים הָאוֹמֵר יוֹפַע אוֹר מֵחֹשֶׁךְ
ha'elohim ha'omer yofa or mechoshech
Seeing it is God, that said, Light shall shine out of darkness,

הוּא הִגִּיהַּ אוֹר בְּלִבֵּנוּ לְהָאִיר דַּעַת עַל־אוֹדוֹת כְּבוֹד אֱלֹהִים אֲשֶׁר בְּפָנָיו שֶׁל הַמָּשִׁיחַ
hu higgiah or belibbenu leha'ir da'at al-'odot kvod elohim asher befanav shel hammashiach
who shined in our hearts, to give the light of the knowledge of the glory of God in the face of Jesus Christ.

אֶל הַקּוֹרִינְתִּים ב

וְאִם מַה שֶּׁבָּטֵל לָבַשׁ כָּבוֹד, הַבִּלְתִּי חוֹלֵף נִכְבָּד עַל אַחַת כַּמָּה וְכַמָּה
ve'im mah shebbatel lavash kavod, habbilti cholef nichbad al achat kammah vechammah
For if that which passeth away was with glory, much more that which remaineth is in glory.

לָכֵן בִּהְיוֹת לָנוּ תִּקְוָה כָּזֹאת, יֶתֶר עֹז לָנוּ
lachen bihyot lanu tikvah kazot, yeter oz lanu
Having therefore such a hope, we use great boldness of speech,

וְאֵין אָנוּ כְּמֹשֶׁה שֶׂשָּׂם מַסְוֶה עַל פָּנָיו
ve'ein anu kemosheh shesam masveh al panav
and are not as Moses, who put a veil upon his face,

כְּדֵי שֶׁבְּנֵי יִשְׂרָאֵל לֹא יִתְבּוֹנְנוּ אֶל קֵץ הַדָּבָר הַמִּתְבַּטֵּל
kedei shebbenei yisra'el lo yitbonenu el ketz haddavar hammitbattel
that the children of Israel should not look stedfastly on the end of that which was passing away:

בְּרַם לִבּוֹתֵיהֶם קָהוּ, כִּי עַד הַיּוֹם הַזֶּה בְּקָרְאָם בַּבְּרִית הַיְשָׁנָה נִשְׁאַר אוֹתוֹ הַמַּסְוֶה בִּלְתִּי מְסֻלָּק
bram libboteihem kahu, ki ad hayom hazzeh bekare'am babbrit hayshanah nish'ar oto hammasveh bilti mesullak
but their minds were hardened: for until this very day at the reading of the old covenant the same veil remaineth,

שֶׁכֵּן בַּמָּשִׁיחַ הוּא מִתְבַּטֵּל
shekken bammashiach hu mitbattel
it not being revealed to them that it is done away in Christ.

עַד הַיּוֹם הַזֶּה, כַּאֲשֶׁר הֵם קוֹרְאִים אֶת דִּבְרֵי מֹשֶׁה, הַמַּסְוֶה מֻנָּח עַל לִבָּם
ad hayom hazzeh, ka'asher hem kore'im et divrei mosheh, hammasveh munnach al libbam
But unto this day, whensoever Moses is read, a veil lieth upon their heart.

אַךְ כַּאֲשֶׁר יִפְנֶה לִבָּם אֶל יהוה יוּסַר הַמַּסְוֶה
ach ka'asher yifneh libbam el hashem yusar hammasveh
But whensoever it shall turn to the Lord, the veil is taken away.

יהוה הוּא הָרוּחַ וּבַאֲשֶׁר רוּחַ יהוה שָׁם הַחֵרוּת
hashem hu haruach uva'asher ruach hashem sham hacherut
Now the Lord is the Spirit: and where the Spirit of the Lord is, there is liberty.

אֲבָל אֲנַחְנוּ כֻּלָּנוּ בְּפָנִים מְגֻלִּים רוֹאִים בְּמַרְאָה אֶת כְּבוֹד יהוה
aval anachnu kullanu befanim megullim ro'im bemar'ah et kevod hashem
But we all, with unveiled face beholding as in a mirror the glory of the Lord,

וְנֶהְפָּכִים לְאוֹתוֹ צֶלֶם, מִכָּבוֹד אֶל כָּבוֹד, כְּמוֹ מִיַּד יהוה - הָרוּחַ
venehpachim le'oto tzelem, mikkavod el kavod, kemo miyad hashem - haruach
are transformed into the same image from glory to glory, even as from the Lord the Spirit.

אֶל הַקוֹרִינְתִּים ב

וּבִגְלַל הַמָּשִׁיחַ יֵשׁ לָנוּ בִּטָּחוֹן כָּזֶה בֵּאלֹהִים
uviglal hammashiach yesh lanu bittachon kazeh be'elohim
And such confidence have we through Christ to God-ward:

לֹא שֶׁאֲנַחְנוּ בְּעַצְמֵנוּ מֻכְשָׁרִים בְּאֹפֶן שֶׁנַּחְשֹׁב כְּאִלּוּ מַשֶּׁהוּ נוֹבֵעַ מֵעַצְמֵנוּ
lo she'anachnu be'atzmenu muchsharim be'ofen shennachshov ke'illu mashehu novea me'atzmenu
not that we are sufficient of ourselves, to account anything as from ourselves;

אֶלָּא שֶׁכּוֹשְׁרֵנוּ בָּא מֵאֵת אֱלֹהִים
ella shekkosherenu ba me'et elohim
but our sufficiency is from God;

הוּא הִכְשִׁיר אוֹתָנוּ לִהְיוֹת מְשָׁרְתִים שֶׁל בְּרִית חֲדָשָׁה, לֹא שֶׁל אוֹת כְּתוּבָה, אֶלָּא שֶׁל הָרוּחַ
hu hichshir otanu lihyot meshartim shel brit chadashah, lo shel ot ketuvah, ella shel haruach
who also made us sufficient as ministers of a new covenant; not of the letter, but of the spirit:

שֶׁכֵּן הָאוֹת מְמִיתָה, אֲבָל הָרוּחַ מְחַיָּה
shekken ha'ot memitah, aval haruach mechayah
for the letter killeth, but the spirit giveth life.

וְאִם שֵׁרוּת שֶׁל מִשְׁטָר הַמָּוֶת, הֶחָקוּק אוֹתִיּוֹת בְּאֶבֶן, נִמְלָא כָּבוֹד
ve'im sherut shel mishtar hammavet, hechakuk otiyot be'even, nimla kavod
But if the ministration of death, written, and engraven on stones, came with glory,

עַד כְּדֵי כָּךְ שֶׁבְּנֵי יִשְׂרָאֵל לֹא יָכְלוּ לְהַבִּיט אֶל פְּנֵי מֹשֶׁה בִּגְלַל זִיו פָּנָיו
ad kedei kach shebbnei yisra'el lo yachelu lehabbit el penei mosheh biglal ziv panav
so that the children of Israel could not look stedfastly upon the face of Moses for the glory of his face;

הַחוֹלֵף
hacholef
which glory was passing away:

הַאִם שֵׁרוּת שֶׁל מִשְׁטָר הָרוּחַ לֹא יִמָּלֵא כָּבוֹד עַל אַחַת כַּמָּה וְכַמָּה
ha'im sherut shel mishtar haruach lo yimmalei kavod al achat kammah vechammah
how shall not rather the ministration of the spirit be with glory?

הֲרֵי אִם שֵׁרוּת הַהַרְשָׁעָה לוֹבֵשׁ כָּבוֹד, כָּל שֶׁכֵּן מַרְבֶּה לְהִתְעַלּוֹת בְּכָבוֹד שֵׁרוּת הַהַצְדָּקָה
harei im sherut haharsha'ah lovesh kavod, kol shekken marbeh lehit'allot bechavod sherut hahatzdakah
For if the ministration of condemnation hath glory, much rather doth the ministration of righteousness exceed in glory.

הֵן אֲפִלּוּ מַה שֶּׁלָּבַשׁ כָּבוֹד, כְּבוֹדוֹ הָיָה לְאַיִן
hen afillu mah shellavash kavod, kevodo hayah le'ayin
For verily that which hath been made glorious hath not been made glorious in this respect,

בִּגְלַל הַכָּבוֹד הַנַּעֲלֶה יוֹתֵר
biglal hakkavod hanna'aleh yoter
by reason of the glory that surpasseth.

אֶל הַקּוֹרִינְתִּים ב

אֲבָל תּוֹדָה לֵאלֹהִים הַמּוֹבִיל אוֹתָנוּ בְּמַסָּע נִצָּחוֹן בַּמָּשִׁיחַ

aval todah le'elohim hammovil otanu bemassa nitzachon bammashiach

But thanks be unto God, who always leadeth us in triumph in Christ,

וּמֵפִיץ עַל־יָדֵינוּ אֶת נִיחוֹחַ דַּעַת אֱלֹהִים בְּכָל מָקוֹם

umefitz al-yadeinu et nichoach da'at elohim bechol makom

and maketh manifest through us the savor of his knowledge in every place.

הֲלֹא נִיחוֹחַ הַמָּשִׁיחַ אֲנַחְנוּ לֵאלֹהִים, בְּקֶרֶב הַנּוֹשָׁעִים וּבְקֶרֶב הָאוֹבְדִים

halo nichoach hammashiach anachnu le'elohim, bekerev hannosha'im uvekerev ha'ovedim

For we are a sweet savor of Christ unto God, in them that are saved, and in them that perish;

לָאַחֲרוֹנִים רֵיחַ שֶׁל מָוֶת אֱלֵי מָוֶת, לָרִאשׁוֹנִים רֵיחַ שֶׁל חַיִּים אֱלֵי חַיִּים. וּמִי הָרָאוּי לְכָךְ

la'acharonim reiach shel mavet elei mavet, larishonim reiach shel chayim elei chayim. umi hara'ui lechach

to the one a savor from death unto death; to the other a savor from life unto life. And who is sufficient for these things?

הֲרֵי אֵין אָנוּ כְּמוֹ הָרַבִּים הָעוֹשִׂים מִסְחָר בִּדְבַר אֱלֹהִים, אֶלָּא לְנֶגֶד עֵינֵי אֱלֹהִים

harei ein anu kemo harabbim ha'osim mischar bidvar elohim, ella leneged einei elohim

For we are not as the many, corrupting the word of God:

בְּיֹשֶׁר לֵב וּמִטַּעַם אֱלֹהִים, בַּמָּשִׁיחַ אָנוּ מְדַבְּרִים

beyosher lev umitta'am elohim, bammashiach anu medabberim

but as of sincerity, but as of God, in the sight of God, speak we in Christ.

ג

הַאִם נַתְחִיל שׁוּב לְשַׁבֵּחַ אֶת עַצְמֵנוּ? אוֹ שֶׁמָּא זְקוּקִים אָנוּ, כָּאֲחֵרִים, לְאִגְּרוֹת שֶׁבַח אֲלֵיכֶם אוֹ מִכֶּם

ha'im natchil shuv leshabbeach et atzmenu? o shemma zekukim anu, ka'acherim, le'iggrot shevach aleichem o mikkem

Are we beginning again to commend ourselves? or need we, as do some, epistles of commendation to you or from you?

הֲרֵי אַתֶּם אִגַּרְתֵּנוּ הַכְּתוּבָה בְּלִבֵּנוּ, וְכָל אָדָם מַכִּיר אוֹתָהּ וְקוֹרֵא אוֹתָהּ

harei attem iggartenu hakketuvah belibbenu, vechol adam makkir otah vekorei otah

Ye are our epistle, written in our hearts, known and read of all men;

רוֹאִים בְּבֵרוּר שֶׁאַתֶּם אִגֶּרֶת הַמָּשִׁיחַ הַנֶּעֱזֶרֶת עַל־יָדֵינוּ

ro'im beverur she'attem iggeret hammashiach hanne'ezeret al-yadeinu

being made manifest that ye are an epistle of Christ, ministered by us,

כְּתוּבָה לֹא בִּדְיוֹ, אֶלָּא בְּרוּחַ אֱלֹהִים חַיִּים

ketuvah lo bidyo, ella beruach elohim chayim

written not with ink, but with the Spirit of the living God;

לֹא עַל לוּחוֹת אֶבֶן, אֶלָּא עַל לוּחוֹת שֶׁל לֵב בָּשָׂר

lo al luchot even, ella al luchot shel lev basar

not in tables of stone, but in tables that are hearts of flesh.

אֶל הַקּוֹרִינְתִּים ב

וְאִם מִישֶׁהוּ גָּרַם צַעַר, הֲרֵי לֹא אוֹתִי צִעֵר, אֶלָּא אֶת כֻּלְּכֶם - לְפָחוֹת בְּמִדַּת מָה, כְּדֵי שֶׁלֹּא לְהַגְזִים
ve'im mishehu garam tza'ar, harei lo oti tzi'er, ella et kullchem - lefachot bemiddat mah, kedei shello lehagzim
But if any hath caused sorrow, he hath caused sorrow, not to me, but in part (that I press not too heavily) to you all.

דַּי לוֹ לְאִישׁ כָּזֶה הַתּוֹכֵחָה הַזֹּאת מֵאֵת הָרַבִּים
dai lo le'ish kazeh hattochechah hazzot me'et harabbim
Sufficient to such a one is this punishment which was inflicted by the many;

וּבְכֵן, לְהֶפֶךְ, עָדִיף שֶׁתִּסְלְחוּ לוֹ וּתְנַחֲמוּהוּ
uvechen, lehefech, adif shettislechu lo utenachamuhu
so that contrariwise ye should rather forgive him and comfort him,

לְמַעַן לֹא יִתְמוֹטֵט הָאִישׁ מֵרֹב צַעַר
lema'an lo yitmotet ha'ish merov tza'ar
lest by any means such a one should be swallowed up with his overmuch sorrow.

עַל כֵּן אֲנִי מְבַקֵּשׁ מִכֶּם שֶׁתּוֹכִיחוּ לוֹ אֶת אַהֲבַתְכֶם
al ken ani mevakkesh mikkem shettochichu lo et ahavatchem
Wherefore I beseech you to confirm your love toward him.

לְשֵׁם כָּךְ גַּם כָּתַבְתִּי, לְהִוָּכַח אִם מְצַיְּתִים אַתֶּם בְּכָל הַדְּבָרִים
leshem kach gam katavti, lehivvachach im metzayetim attem bechol haddevarim
For to this end also did I write, that I might know the proof of you, whether ye are obedient in all things.

וְאִישׁ אֲשֶׁר תִּסְלְחוּ לוֹ עַל אֵיזֶה דָּבָר, גַּם אֲנִי אֶסְלַח לוֹ; כִּי גַּם מַה שֶּׁאֲנִי סָלַחְתִּי, אִם סָלַחְתִּי עַל דְּבַר מָה
ve'ish asher tislechu lo al eizeh davar, gam ani eslach lo; ki gam mah she'ani salachti, im salachti al devar mah
But to whom ye forgive anything, I forgive also: for what I also have forgiven, if I have forgiven anything,

הֲרֵי סָלַחְתִּי לְמַעַנְכֶם לְנֹכַח הַמָּשִׁיחַ
harei salachti lema'anchem lenochach hammashiach
for your sakes have I forgiven it in the presence of Christ;

כְּדֵי שֶׁלֹּא יַעֲרִים עָלֵינוּ הַשָּׂטָן, שֶׁכֵּן מְזִמּוֹתָיו לֹא נֶעֶלְמוּ מֵאִתָּנוּ
kedei shello ya'arim aleinu hassatan, shekken mezimmotav lo ne'elmu me'ittanu
that no advantage may be gained over us by Satan: for we are not ignorant of his devices.

כַּאֲשֶׁר בָּאתִי לִטְרוֹאַס לְבַשֵּׂר אֶת בְּשׂוֹרַת הַמָּשִׁיחַ גַּם נִפְתַּח לִי פֶּתַח מִטַּעַם הָאָדוֹן
ka'asher bati litro'as levasser et besorat hammashiach gam niftach li petach mitta'am ha'adon
Now when I came to Troas for the gospel of Christ, and when a door was opened unto me in the Lord,

אַךְ לֹא הָיָה מָנוֹחַ לְרוּחִי מִפְּנֵי שֶׁלֹּא מָצָאתִי אֶת טִיטוֹס אָחִי
ach lo hayah manoach leruchi mippenei shello matzati et titos achi
I had no relief for my spirit, because I found not Titus my brother:

אָז נִפְרַדְתִּי מֵהֶם וְיָצָאתִי אֶל מָקֵדוֹנְיָה
az nifradti mehem veyatzati el makedoneyah
but taking my leave of them, I went forth into Macedonia.

אֶל הַקּוֹרִינְתִּים ב

לָכֵן הָאָמֵן שֶׁאָנוּ נוֹתְנִים בּוֹ כָּבוֹד לֵאלֹהִים גַּם הוּא בְּאֶמְצָעוּתוֹ
lachen ha'amen she'anu notenim bo kavod lelohim gam hu be'emtza'uto
wherefore also through him is the Amen, unto the glory of God through us.

וֵאלֹהִים הוּא הַמְכוֹנֵן אוֹתָנוּ עִמָּכֶם בַּמָּשִׁיחַ. הוּא מָשַׁח אוֹתָנוּ
Ve'elohim hu hamchonen otanu immachem bammashiach. hu mashach otanu
Now he that establisheth us with you in Christ, and anointed us, is God;

וְהוּא אֲשֶׁר גַּם חָתַם אוֹתָנוּ בְּחוֹתָמוֹ וְשָׂם בְּלִבֵּנוּ אֶת הָעֵרָבוֹן שֶׁל הָרוּחַ
vehu asher gam chatam otanu bechotamo vesam belibbenu et ha'eravon shel haruach
who also sealed us, and gave us the earnest of the Spirit in our hearts.

אֲנִי קוֹרֵא לֵאלֹהִים לְהָעִיד עָלַי, שֶׁחַסְתִּי עֲלֵיכֶם וְלָכֵן לֹא בָּאתִי עוֹד פַּעַם לְקוֹרִינְתּוֹס
ani korei lelohim leha'id alai, shechasti aleichem velachen lo bati od pa'am lekorinetos
But I call God for a witness upon my soul, that to spare you I forbare to come unto Corinth.

לֹא שֶׁאֲדוֹנִים אָנוּ עַל אֱמוּנַתְכֶם, אֶלָּא פּוֹעֲלִים אָנוּ אִתְּכֶם לְמַעַן שִׂמְחַתְכֶם, שֶׁכֵּן בָּאֱמוּנָה אַתֶּם יַצִּיבִים
lo she'adonim anu al emunatchem, ella po'alim anu ittchem lema'an simchatchem, shekken ba'emunah attem yatzivim
Not that we have lordship over your faith, but are helpers of your joy: for in faith ye stand fast.

ב

גָּמַרְתִּי אֹמֶר בְּלִבִּי שֶׁלֹּא אָבוֹא עוֹד לְצַעֵר אֶתְכֶם
gamarti omer belibbi shello avo od letza'er etchem
But I determined this for myself, that I would not come again to you with sorrow.

שֶׁהֲרֵי אִם אֲצַעֵר אֶתְכֶם, מִי יְשַׂמַּח אוֹתִי מִלְּבַד מִי שֶׁגָּרַמְתִּי לוֹ צַעַר
sheharei im atza'er etchem, mi yesammach oti millevad mi sheggaramti lo tza'ar
For if I make you sorry, who then is he that maketh me glad but he that is made sorry by me?

כָּתַבְתִּי אֶת הַדָּבָר הַזֶּה כְּדֵי שֶׁבְּבוֹאִי לֹא יְצַעֲרוּנִי אֵלֶּה אֲשֶׁר צָרִיךְ הָיִיתִי לִשְׂמֹחַ בָּהֶם
katavti et haddavar hazzeh kedei shebbevo'i lo yetza'aruni elleh asher tzarich hayiti lismoach bahem
And I wrote this very thing, lest, when I came, I should have sorrow from them of whom I ought to rejoice;

וּבוֹטֵחַ אֲנִי בְּכֻלְּכֶם שֶׁשִּׂמְחָתִי הִיא שִׂמְחַת כֻּלְּכֶם
uvoteach ani bechullchem shessimchati hi simchat kullchem
having confidence in you all, that my joy is the joy of you all.

כָּתַבְתִּי לָכֶם מִתּוֹךְ מְצוּקָה רַבָּה וְעָגְמַת לֵב וּבְדְמָעוֹת רַבּוֹת
katavti lachem mittoch metzukah rabbah ve'ougmat lev uvidma'ot rabbot
For out of much affliction and anguish of heart I wrote unto you with many tears;

לֹא כְּדֵי לְצַעֵר אֶתְכֶם, אֶלָּא כְּדֵי שֶׁתֵּדְעוּ מָה רַבָּה אַהֲבָתִי אֲלֵיכֶם
lo kedei letza'er etchem, ella kedei shettede'u mah rabbah ahavati aleichem
not that ye should be made sorry, but that ye might know the love which I have more abundantly unto you.

אֶל הַקּוֹרִינְתִּים ב

וַאֲנִי מְקַוֶּה שֶׁתַּכִּירוּ בָּנוּ לַחֲלוּטִין
va'ani mekavveh shettakkiru banu lachalutin
and I hope ye will acknowledge unto the end:

כְּמוֹ שֶׁגַּם הִכַּרְתֶּם בְּאֹפֶן חֶלְקִי, שֶׁאֲנַחְנוּ תְּהִלַּתְכֶם
kemo sheggam hikkartem be'ofen chelki, she'anachnu tehillatchem
as also ye did acknowledge us in part, that we are your glorying,

כְּשֵׁם שֶׁגַּם אַתֶּם תְּהִלָּתֵנוּ בְּיוֹם אֲדוֹנֵנוּ יֵשׁוּעַ
keshem sheggam attem tehillatenu beyom adonenu yeshua
even as ye also are ours, in the day of our Lord Jesus.

מִתּוֹךְ בִּטָּחוֹן זֶה רָצִיתִי לָבוֹא קֹדֶם כֹּל אֲלֵיכֶם, לְמַעַן תִּהְיֶה עֲלֵיכֶם בִּרְכַּת חֶסֶד פַּעַם שְׁנִיָּה
mittoch bittachon zeh ratziti lavo kodem kol aleichem, lema'an tihyeh aleichem birkat chesed pa'am sheniyah
And in this confidence I was minded to come first unto you, that ye might have a second benefit;

וּמִכֶּם לְהַמְשִׁיךְ אֶת דַּרְכִּי אֶל מָקֵדוֹנְיָה, וּמִמָּקֵדוֹנְיָה לַחֲזֹר אֲלֵיכֶם
umikkem lehamshich et darki el makedoneyah, umimmakedoneyah lachazor aleichem
and by you to pass into Macedonia, and again from Macedonia to come unto you,

וְאַחֲרֵי כֵן שֶׁתְּשַׁלְּחוּנִי לְאֶרֶץ יְהוּדָה
ve'acharei chen shetteshallechuni le'eretz yehudah
and of you to be set forward on my journey unto Judæa.

כְּשֶׁהֶחְלַטְתִּי כָּךְ, כְּלוּם נָהַגְתִּי בְּקַלּוּת דַּעַת? וּמַה שֶּׁאֲנִי מַחְלִיט
keshehechlatti kach, klum nahagti bekallut da'at? umah she'ani machlit
When I therefore was thus minded, did I show fickleness? or the things that I purpose,

הַאִם עַל־פִּי מַחֲשֶׁבֶת בָּשָׂר־וָדָם אֲנִי מַחְלִיט, בְּאֹפֶן שֶׁאוּכַל לְהַחֲזִיק בְּכֵן כֵּן וְלֹא לֹא, בְּבַת אַחַת
ha'im al-pi machashevet basar-vadam ani machlit, be'ofen she'uchal lehachazik beken ken velo lo, bevat achat
do I purpose according to the flesh, that with me there should be the yea yea and the nay nay?

נֶאֱמָן הָאֱלֹהִים שֶׁדְּבָרֵנוּ אֲלֵיכֶם אֵינֶנּוּ כֵּן וְלֹא
ne'eman ha'elohim sheddvarenu aleichem einennu ken velo
But as God is faithful, our word toward you is not yea and nay.

שֶׁהֲרֵי בֶּן־הָאֱלֹהִים הַמָּשִׁיחַ יֵשׁוּעַ, שֶׁאֲנִי וְסִילְוָנוֹס וְטִימוֹתִיאוֹס הִכְרַזְנוּ עָלָיו בְּקִרְבְּכֶם
sheharei ben-ha'elohim hammashiach yeshua, she'ani vesilevanos vetimotei'os hichraznu alav bekirbechem
For the Son of God, Jesus Christ, who was preached among you by us, even by me and Silvanus and Timothy,

לֹא הָיָה כֵּן וְלֹא, אֶלָּא כֵּן הָיָה בּוֹ
lo hayah ken velo, ella ken hayah bo
was not yea and nay, but in him is yea.

כִּי כָּל הַבְטָחוֹת אֱלֹהִים כֵּן הֵן בּוֹ
ki kol havtachot elohim ken hen bo
For how many soever be the promises of God, in him is the yea:

אֶל הַקּוֹרִינְתִּים ב

וְתִקְוָתֵנוּ עַל־אוֹדוֹתֵיכֶם אֵיתָנָה הִיא
vetikvatenu al-'odoteichem eitanah hi
and our hope for you is stedfast;

בְּיָדְעֵנוּ כִּי כְּשֵׁם שֶׁאַתֶּם שֻׁתָּפִים לַצָּרוֹת, כֵּן גַּם שֻׁתָּפִים אַתֶּם לַנֶּחָמָה
beyade'enu ki keshem she'attem shuttafim latzarot, ken gam shuttafim attem lannechamah
knowing that, as ye are partakers of the sufferings, so also are ye of the comfort.

אַחִים, אֵינֶנּוּ רוֹצִים שֶׁיֵּעָלֵם מִכֶּם דְּבַר הַצָּרָה שֶׁעָבְרָה עָלֵינוּ בְּאַסְיָה
achim, einennu rotzim sheye'alem mikkem devar hatzarah she'averah aleinu be'asyah
For we would not have you ignorant, brethren, concerning our affliction which befell us in Asia,

נִלְחַצְנוּ לְלֹא נְשׂא, עַד כְּדֵי כָּךְ שֶׁנּוֹאַשְׁנוּ אֲפִלּוּ מֵחַיֵּינוּ
nilchatznu lelo neso, ad kedei kach shenno'ashnu afillu mechayeinu
that we were weighed down exceedingly, beyond our power, insomuch that we despaired even of life:

פְּסַק דִּין מָוֶת קִנֵּן בְּתוֹכֵנוּ,
psak din mavet kinnen betochenu
yea, we ourselves have had the sentence of death within ourselves,

וְזֹאת כְּדֵי שֶׁלֹּא נִבְטַח בְּעַצְמֵנוּ, אֶלָּא בֵּאלֹהִים הַמְחַיֶּה אֶת הַמֵּתִים
vezot kdei shello nivtach be'atzmenu, ella be'elohim hamchayeh et hammetim
that we should not trust in ourselves, but in God who raiseth the dead:

הוּא הִצִּילָנוּ מִמָּוֶת חָמוּר כָּל כָּךְ וְעוֹד יָשׁוּב וְיַצִּילֵנוּ; בּוֹ אָנוּ תוֹלִים תִּקְוָתֵנוּ כִּי יוֹסִיף לְהַצִּילֵנוּ
hu hitzilanu mimmavet chamur kol kach ve'od yashuv veyatzilenu; bo anu tolim tikvatenu ki yosif lehatzilenu
who delivered us out of so great a death, and will deliver: on whom we have set our hope that he will also still deliver us;

גַּם אַתֶּם הִשְׁתַּתַּפְתּוּ בַּתְּפִלָּה בַּעֲדֵנוּ
gam attem hishtattefu battefillah ba'adenu
ye also helping together on our behalf by your supplication;

כְּדֵי שֶׁרַבִּים יוֹדוּ בִּגְלָלֵנוּ עַל מַתְּנַת הַחֶסֶד שֶׁנִּתְּנָה לָנוּ בִּזְכוּת רַבִּים
kdei sherabbim yodu biglalenu al mattnat hachesed shennittenah lanu bizchut rabbim
that, for the gift bestowed upon us by means of many, thanks may be given by many persons on our behalf.

זֹאת הִיא גַּאֲוָתֵנוּ: עֵדוּת מַצְפּוּנֵנוּ כִּי הִתְנַהַגְנוּ בָּעוֹלָם, וּבְעִקָּר כְּלַפֵּיכֶם, בִּקְדֻשָּׁה וּבְיֹשֶׁר אֱלֹהִים - לֹא בְּחָכְמַת בָּשָׂר־וָדָם, אֶלָּא בְּחֶסֶד אֱלֹהִים
zot hi ga'avatenu. edut matzpunenu ki hitnahagnu ba'olam, uve'ikkar kelappeichem, bikdushah uveyosher elohim - lo bechachemat basar-vadam, ella bechesed elohim
For our glorying is this, the testimony of our conscience, that in holiness and sincerity of God, not in fleshly wisdom but in the grace of God, we behaved ourselves in the world, and more abundantly to you-ward.

אֵינֶנּוּ כּוֹתְבִים לָכֶם דְּבָרִים שׁוֹנִים מִמַּה שֶּׁאַתֶּם קוֹרְאִים וְגַם מַכִּירִים
einennu kotevim lachem devarim shonim mimmah she'attem kore'im vegam makkirim
For we write no other things unto you, than what ye read or even acknowledge,

אֶל הַקּוֹרִינְתִּים ב

אִגֶּרֶת הַשְׁנִיָּה אֶל הַקּוֹרִינְתִּים

מֵאֵת שָׁאוּל, שְׁלִיחַ הַמָּשִׁיחַ יֵשׁוּעַ עַל־פִּי רְצוֹן אֱלֹהִים, וּמֵאֵת הָאָח טִימוֹתֵיאוֹס
me'et sha'ul, shliach hammashiach yeshua al-pi retzon elohim, ume'et ha'ach timotei'os
Paul, an apostle of Christ Jesus through the will of God, and Timothy our brother,

אֶל קְהִלַּת אֱלֹהִים אֲשֶׁר בְּקוֹרִינְתּוֹס
el kehillat elohim asher bekorinetos
unto the church of God which is at Corinth,

וּלְכָל הַקְּדוֹשִׁים אֲשֶׁר בַּאֲכַיָּה
ulechol hakkedoshim asher be'achayah
with all the saints that are in the whole of Achaia:

חֶסֶד וְשָׁלוֹם לָכֶם מֵאֵת הָאֱלֹהִים אָבִינוּ וְהָאָדוֹן יֵשׁוּעַ הַמָּשִׁיחַ
chesed veshalom lachem me'et ha'elohim avinu veha'adon yeshua hammashiach
Grace to you and peace from God our Father and the Lord Jesus Christ.

בָּרוּךְ הָאֱלֹהִים אֲבִי אֲדוֹנֵנוּ יֵשׁוּעַ הַמָּשִׁיחַ, אַב הָרַחֲמִים וֵאלֹהֵי כָּל נֶחָמָה
baruch ha'elohim avi adonenu yeshua hammashiach, av harachamim ve'elohei kol nechamah
Blessed be the God and Father of our Lord Jesus Christ, the Father of mercies and God of all comfort;

הַמְנַחֵם אוֹתָנוּ בְּכָל צָרוֹתֵינוּ בְּאֹפֶן שֶׁנּוּכַל לְנַחֵם אֶת הַלְּחוּצִים בְּכָל צָרָה שֶׁהִיא
hamenachem otanu bechol tzaroteinu be'ofen shennuchal lenachem et hallechutzim bechol tzarah shehi
who comforteth us in all our affliction, that we may be able to comfort them that are in any affliction,

בַּנֶּחָמָה שֶׁנֻּחַמְנוּ אָנוּ מֵאֵת אֱלֹהִים
bannechamah shennuchamnu anu me'et elohim
through the comfort wherewith we ourselves are comforted of God.

כִּי כְּשֵׁם שֶׁשּׁוֹפְעִים בָּנוּ סִבְלוֹת הַמָּשִׁיחַ, כֵּן גַּם שׁוֹפַעַת נֶחָמָתֵנוּ עַל־יְדֵי הַמָּשִׁיחַ
ki keshem sheshof'im banu sivlot hammashiach, ken gam shofa'at nechamatenu al-yedei hammashiach
For as the sufferings of Christ abound unto us, even so our comfort also aboundeth through Christ.

וְאִם אֲנַחְנוּ סוֹבְלִים, הֲרֵי זֶה לְמַעַן נֶחָמַתְכֶם וִישׁוּעַתְכֶם
ve'im anachnu sovelim, harei zeh lema'an nechamatchem viyshu'atchem
But whether we are afflicted, it is for your comfort and salvation;

אִם אֲנַחְנוּ מְנֻחָמִים, הֲרֵי זֶה לְמַעַן נֶחָמַתְכֶם
im anachnu menuchamim, harei zeh lema'an nechamatchem
or whether we are comforted, it is for your comfort,

כְּדֵי שֶׁתּוּכְלוּ לְהַחֲזִיק מַעֲמָד בְּאוֹתָן הַצָּרוֹת שֶׁגַּם אֲנַחְנוּ סוֹבְלִים
kdei shettuchelu lehachazik ma'amad be'otan hatzarot sheggam anachnu sovlim
which worketh in the patient enduring of the same sufferings which we also suffer:

אֶל הַקּוֹרִינְתִּים א

חֶסֶד הָאָדוֹן יֵשׁוּעַ עִמָּכֶם
chesed ha'adon yeshua immachem
The grace of the Lord Jesus Christ be with you.

אַהֲבָתִי אֶל כֻּלְּכֶם בַּמָּשִׁיחַ יֵשׁוּעַ
ahavati el kullchem bammashiach yeshua
My love be with you all in Christ Jesus. Amen.

אֶל הַקּוֹרִינְתִּים א

וַאֲנִי מְבַקֵּשׁ מִכֶּם, אַחַי
va'ani mevakkesh mikkem, achai
Now I beseech you, brethren

אַתֶּם מַכִּירִים אֶת מִשְׁפַּחַת סְטֶפָנַס; הֲרֵי הֵם רִאשׁוֹנֵי הַמַּאֲמִינִים בְּאַכַיָה
attem makkirim et mishpachat setefanas; harei hem rishonei hamma'aminim be'achayah
(ye know the house of Stephanas that it is the firstfruits of Achaia,

וְאַף קִבְּלוּ עַל עַצְמָם לְשָׁרֵת אֶת הַקְּדוֹשִׁים
ve'af kibbelu al atzmam lesharet et hakkedoshim
and that they have set themselves to minister unto the saints),

לָכֵן גַּם אַתֶּם הִשָּׁמְעוּ לַאֲנָשִׁים כָּאֵלֶּה וּלְכָל מִי שֶׁעוֹבֵד וְעָמֵל עִמָּהֶם
lachen gam attem hisham'u la'anashim ka'elleh ulechol mi she'oved ve'amel immahem
that ye also be in subjection unto such, and to every one that helpeth in the work and laboreth.

שָׂמֵחַ אֲנִי עַל בּוֹאָם שֶׁל סְטֶפָנַס וּפוֹרְטוּנָטוֹס וַאֲכַיְקוֹס
sameach ani al bo'am shel setefanas uforetunatos va'achaykos
And I rejoice at the coming of Stephanas and Fortunatus and Achaicus:

כִּי הֵם הָיוּ לִי לְפִצּוּי עַל חֶסְרוֹנְכֶם
ki hem hayu li lefitzui al chesronechem
for that which was lacking on your part they supplied.

וְהִרְגִּיעוּ אֶת רוּחִי וְאֶת רוּחֲכֶם. לָכֵן הֱיוּ מוֹקִירִים אֲנָשִׁים כָּאֵלֶּה
vehirgi'u et ruchi ve'et ruchachem. lachen heyu mokirim anashim ka'elleh
For they refreshed my spirit and yours: acknowledge ye therefore them that are such.

הַקְּהִלּוֹת אֲשֶׁר בְּאַסְיָה דּוֹרְשׁוֹת בִּשְׁלוֹמְכֶם
hakkehillot asher be'asyah doreshot bishlomechem
The churches of Asia salute you.

עֲקִילַס וּפְרִיסְקִילָה עִם הַקְּהִלָּה אֲשֶׁר בְּבֵיתָם מוֹסְרִים לָכֶם בִּרְכַּת שָׁלוֹם רַב בָּאָדוֹן
akilas uferisekilah im hakkehillah asher beveitam mosrim lachem birkat shalom rav ba'adon
Aquila and Prisca salute you much in the Lord, with the church that is in their house.

הָאַחִים כֻּלָּם דּוֹרְשִׁים בִּשְׁלוֹמְכֶם. בָּרְכוּ לְשָׁלוֹם אִישׁ אֶת רֵעֵהוּ בִּנְשִׁיקָה קְדוֹשָׁה
ha'achim kullam doreshim bishlomechem. barechu leshalom ish et re'ehu binshikah kedoshah
All the brethren salute you. Salute one another with a holy kiss.

אֲנִי שָׁאוּל שׁוֹלֵחַ לָכֶם בִּרְכַּת שָׁלוֹם בִּכְתָב יָדִי
ani sha'ul sholeach lachem birkat shalom bichtav yadi
The salutation of me Paul with mine own hand.

מִי שֶׁאֵינֶנּוּ אוֹהֵב אֶת הָאָדוֹן, חֵרֶם יִהְיֶה! מָרָנָא תָא
mi she'einennu ohev et ha'adon, cherem yihyeh! marana ta
If any man loveth not the Lord, let him be anathema. Maranatha.

אֶל הַקּוֹרִינְתִּים א

אוּלַי אֶשְׁהֶה אֶצְלְכֶם, אוּלַי אֲפִלּוּ בְּמֶשֶׁךְ כָּל הַחֹרֶף, וּלְאַחַר מִכֵּן תְּשַׁלְּחוּנִי לְהֵיכָן שֶׁעָלַי לָלֶכֶת
ulai eshheh etzlechem, ulai afillu bemeshech kol hachoref, ule'achar mikken teshallchuni leheichan she'alai lalechet
but with you it may be that I shall abide, or even winter, that ye may set me forward on my journey whithersoever I go.

אֵינֶנִּי חָפֵץ לִרְאוֹת אֶתְכֶם כָּעֵת כְּעוֹבֵר אֹרַח; אֲנִי מְקַוֶּה לִהְיוֹת זְמַן מָה אֶצְלְכֶם, אִם יִרְצֶה יהוה
einenni chafetz lir'ot etchem ka'et ke'over orach; ani mekavveh lihyot zeman mah etzlechem, im yirtzeh hashem
For I do not wish to see you now by the way; for I hope to tarry a while with you, if the Lord permit.

אֲבָל אֶתְעַכֵּב בְּאֶפֶסוֹס עַד חַג הַשָּׁבוּעוֹת
aval et'akkev be'efesos ad chag hashavu'ot
But I will tarry at Ephesus until Pentecost;

כִּי נִפְתַּח לִי פֶּתַח רָחָב לִפְעֻלָּה פּוֹרִיָּה, וְרַבִּים הַמִּתְנַגְּדִים
ki niftach li petach rachav lif'ullah poriyah, verabbim hammitnaggedim
for a great door and effectual is opened unto me, and there are many adversaries.

אִם טִימוֹתֵיאוֹס יָבוֹא, דַּאֲגוּ לְכָךְ שֶׁיֵּשֵׁב עִמָּכֶם בְּלֹא חֲשָׁשׁוֹת
im timotei'os yavo, da'agu lechach sheyeshev immachem belo chashashot
Now if Timothy come, see that he be with you without fear;

שֶׁכֵּן הוּא עָסוּק בַּעֲבוֹדָתוֹ שֶׁל הָאָדוֹן כָּמוֹנִי
shekken hu asuk ba'avodato shel ha'adon kamoni
for he worketh the work of the Lord, as I also do:

אִישׁ אַל יָקֵל רֹאשׁ כְּנֶגְדּוֹ
ish al yakel rosh kenegdo
let no man therefore despise him.

אֶלָּא שַׁלְּחוּ אוֹתוֹ בְּשָׁלוֹם לָבוֹא אֵלַי, כִּי אֲנִי מְחַכֶּה לוֹ וְלָאַחִים אֲשֶׁר אִתּוֹ
ella shallechu oto beshalom lavo elai, ki ani mechakkeh lo vela'achim asher itto
But set him forward on his journey in peace, that he may come unto me: for I expect him with the brethren.

בְּנוֹגֵעַ לְאָחִינוּ אַפּוֹלוֹס, הִפְצַרְתִּי בּוֹ הַרְבֵּה שֶׁיָּבוֹא אֲלֵיכֶם עִם הָאַחִים
benogea le'achinu appolos, hiftzarti bo harbeh sheyavo aleichem im ha'achim
But as touching Apollos the brother, I besought him much to come unto you with the brethren:

אַךְ בְּשׁוּם פָּנִים לֹא רָצָה לָבוֹא עַתָּה. הוּא יָבוֹא כַּאֲשֶׁר תִּהְיֶה לוֹ הִזְדַּמְּנוּת
ach beshum panim lo ratzah lavo attah. hu yavo ka'asher tihyeh lo hizdammenut
and it was not at all his will to come now; but he will come when he shall have opportunity.

שִׁקְדוּ, עִמְדוּ בָּאֱמוּנָה, חִזְקוּ וְאִמְצוּ
shikdu, imdu ba'emunah, chizku ve'imtzu
Watch ye, stand fast in the faith, quit you like men, be strong.

אֶת כָּל מַעֲשֵׂיכֶם עֲשׂוּ בְּאַהֲבָה
et kol ma'aseichem asu be'ahavah
Let all that ye do be done in love.

אֶל הַקּוֹרִינְתִּים א

אַיֵּה עָקְצְךָ מָוֶת? אַיֵּה נִצְחוֹנְךָ מָוֶת
ayeh aketzecha mavet? ayeh nitzchoncha mavet
O death, where is thy victory? O death, where is thy sting?

עֹקֶץ הַמָּוֶת הוּא הַחֵטְא, וְהַחֵטְא תָּקְפּוֹ בָּא מִן הַתּוֹרָה
oketz hammavet hu hachet, vehachet tokpo ba min hattorah
The sting of death is sin; and the power of sin is the law:

אֲבָל תּוֹדָה לֵאלֹהִים הַנּוֹתֵן לָנוּ אֶת הַנִּצָּחוֹן עַל־יְדֵי אֲדוֹנֵנוּ יֵשׁוּעַ הַמָּשִׁיחַ
aval todah lelohim hannoten lanu et hannitzachon al-yedei adonenu yeshua hammashiach
but thanks be to God, who giveth us the victory through our Lord Jesus Christ.

עַל כֵּן, אַחַי הָאֲהוּבִים, עִמְדוּ הֵיטֵב וִהְיוּ יַצִּיבִים; הֱיוּ תָּמִיד עֲתִירֵי פֹּעַל בַּעֲבוֹדָתוֹ שֶׁל הָאָדוֹן
al ken, achai ha'ahuvim, imdu heitev vihyu yatzivim; heyu tamid atirei po'al ba'avodato shel ha'adon
Wherefore, my beloved brethren, be ye stedfast, unmoveable, always abounding in the work of the Lord,

בִּידִיעָה שֶׁעֲמַלְכֶם אֵינֶנּוּ לָרִיק בָּאָדוֹן
biydi'ah she'amalchem einennu larik ba'adon
forasmuch as ye know that your labor is not vain in the Lord.

טז

בְּעִנְיַן אִסּוּף הַתְּרוּמוֹת לְעֶזְרַת הַקְּדוֹשִׁים, כְּפִי שֶׁהוֹרֵיתִי לַקְּהִלּוֹת בְּגָלַטְיָה כֵּן עֲשׂוּ גַּם אַתֶּם
be'inyan issuf hattrumot le'ezrat hakkedoshim, kefi shehoreiti lakkehillot begalatyah ken asu gam attem
Now concerning the collection for the saints, as I gave order to the churches of Galatia, so also do ye.

מִדֵּי רִאשׁוֹן בַּשָּׁבוּעַ יַנִּיחַ כָּל אֶחָד מִכֶּם תְּרוּמָה כְּפִי שֶׁיָּדוֹ מַשֶּׂגֶת וְיִשְׁמְרֶהָ אֶצְלוֹ
middei rishon bashavua yanniach kol echad mikkem trumah kefi sheyado masseget veyishmereha etzlo
Upon the first day of the week let each one of you lay by him in store, as he may prosper,

כְּדֵי שֶׁלֹּא יַתְחִילוּ בְּאִסּוּף הַתְּרוּמוֹת בְּעֵת בּוֹאִי
kedei shello yatchilu be'issuf hattrumot be'et bo'i
that no collections be made when I come.

וְכַאֲשֶׁר אָבוֹא אֶשְׁלַח אֶת הָאֲנָשִׁים הַטּוֹבִים בְּעֵינֵיכֶם עִם אִגְּרוֹת בְּיָדָם לְהָבִיא אֶת תְּרוּמַתְכֶם לִירוּשָׁלַיִם
vecha'asher avo eshlach et ha'anashim hattovim be'eineichem im iggerot beyadam lehavi et trumatchem liyerushalayim
And when I arrive, whomsoever ye shall approve, them will I send with letters to carry your bounty unto Jerusalem:

אִם יִמָּצֵא לְנָכוֹן שֶׁגַּם אֲנִי אֵלֵךְ, יֵלְכוּ אִתִּי
im yimmatzei lenachon sheggam ani elech, yelechu itti
and if it be meet for me to go also, they shall go with me.

אָבוֹא אֲלֵיכֶם אַחֲרֵי שֶׁאֶעֱבֹר בְּמַקֵדוֹנְיָה, כִּי אֲנִי עוֹבֵר דֶּרֶךְ מַקֵדוֹנְיָה
avo aleichem acharei she'e'evor bemakedoneyah, ki ani over derech makedoneyah
But I will come unto you, when I shall have passed through Macedonia; for I pass through Macedonia;

אֶל הַקּוֹרִנְתִּים א

לֹא הָרוּחָנִי הוּא הָרִאשׁוֹן, אֶלָּא הַנַּפְשִׁי, וְאַחֲרֵי כֵן הָרוּחָנִי
lo haruchani hu harishon, ella hannafshi, ve'acharei chen haruchani
Howbeit that is not first which is spiritual, but that which is natural; then that which is spiritual.

הָאָדָם הָרִאשׁוֹן הוּא עָפָר מִן הָאֲדָמָה; הָאָדָם הַשֵּׁנִי מִן הַשָּׁמַיִם הוּא
ha'adam harishon hu afar min ha'adamah; ha'adam hasheni min hashamayim hu
The first man is of the earth, earthy: the second man is of heaven.

כְּאֶחָד שֶׁהוּא עָפָר כֵּן גַּם אֵלֶּה אֲשֶׁר עָפָר הֵם; כְּאֶחָד שֶׁהוּא שְׁמֵימִי כֵּן גַּם אֵלֶּה אֲשֶׁר שְׁמֵימִיִּים הֵם
ka'echad shehu afar ken gam elleh asher afar hem; ka'echad shehu shemeimi ken gam elleh asher shemeimiyim hem
As is the earthy, such are they also that are earthy: and as is the heavenly, such are they also that are heavenly.

וּכְמוֹ שֶׁלָּבַשְׁנוּ אֶת צַלְמוֹ שֶׁל הָאַרְצִי נִלְבַּשׁ גַּם אֶת צֶלֶם הַשְּׁמֵימִי
uchemo shellavashnu et tzalmo shel ha'artzi nilbash gam et tzelem hashemeimi
And as we have borne the image of the earthy, we shall also bear the image of the heavenly.

אֹמַר זֹאת, אַחַי: בָּשָׂר וָדָם אֵינוֹ יָכוֹל לָרֶשֶׁת אֶת מַלְכוּת הָאֱלֹהִים
omar zot, achai: basar vadam eino yachol lareshet et malchut ha'elohim
Now this I say, brethren, that flesh and blood cannot inherit the kingdom of God;

גַּם אֵין הַכִּלָּיוֹן יוֹרֵשׁ אַל־כִּלָּיוֹן
gam ein hakkillayon yoresh al-killayon
neither doth corruption inherit incorruption.

הִנֵּה סוֹד אַגִּיד לָכֶם: לֹא כֻּלָּנוּ נָמוּת, אֲבָל כֻּלָּנוּ נִשְׁתַּנֶּה
hinneh sod aggid lachem: lo kullanu namut, aval kullanu nishtanneh
Behold, I tell you a mystery: We all shall not sleep, but we shall all be changed,

בֶּן רֶגַע וּכְהֶרֶף עַיִן בַּשּׁוֹפָר הָאַחֲרוֹן
bin rega ucheheref ayin bashofar ha'acharon
in a moment, in the twinkling of an eye, at the last trump:

שֶׁכֵּן יִתָּקַע בְּשׁוֹפָר וְהַמֵּתִים יָקוּמוּ בְּלִי כִּלָּיוֹן וַאֲנַחְנוּ נִשְׁתַּנֶּה
shekken yittaka beshofar vehammetim yakumu beli killayon va'anachnu nishtanneh
for the trumpet shall sound, and the dead shall be raised incorruptible, and we shall be changed.

כִּי מִן הָרָאוּי שֶׁזֶּה הַכָּפוּף לְכִלָּיוֹן יִלְבַּשׁ אַל־כִּלָּיוֹן וְזֶה הַכָּפוּף לַמָּוֶת יִלְבַּשׁ אַלְמָוֶת
ki min hara'ui shezzeh hakkafuf lechillayon yilbash al-killayon vezeh hakkafuf lammavet yilbash almavet
For this corruptible must put on incorruption, and this mortal must put on immortality.

וְכַאֲשֶׁר הַכָּפוּף לְכִלָּיוֹן יִלְבַּשׁ אַל־כִּלָּיוֹן וְהַכָּפוּף לַמָּוֶת יִלְבַּשׁ אַלְמָוֶת
vecha'asher hakkafuf lechillayon yilbash al-killayon vehakkafuf lammavet yilbash almavet
But when this corruptible shall have put on incorruption, and this mortal shall have put on immortality,

אָז יִתְקַיֵּם דְּבַר הַכָּתוּב: בֻּלַּע הַמָּוֶת לָנֶצַח
az yitkayem devar hakkatuv: bulla hammavet lanetzach
then shall come to pass the saying that is written, Death is swallowed up in victory.

אֶל הַקּוֹרִינְתִים א

אֶלָּא גַּרְגִּיר עָרוֹם שֶׁל חִטָּה, אוֹ זֶרַע אַחֵר
ella gargir arom shel chittah, o zera acher
but a bare grain, it may chance of wheat, or of some other kind;

וֵאלֹהִים נוֹתֵן לוֹ גּוּף כִּרְצוֹן אֱלֹהִים, וּלְכָל זֶרַע אֶת גּוּפוֹ הוּא
Ve'elohim noten lo guf kirtzon elohim, ulechal zera et gufo hu
but God giveth it a body even as it pleased him, and to each seed a body of its own.

לֹא כָּל בָּשָׂר הוּא אוֹתוֹ הַבָּשָׂר; לָאָדָם בָּשָׂר מִשֶּׁלּוֹ, לַחַיּוֹת בָּשָׂר אַחֵר
lo kol basar hu oto habbasar; la'adam basar mishelo, lachayot basar acher
All flesh is not the same flesh: but there is one flesh of men, and another flesh of beasts,

לָעוֹפוֹת בָּשָׂר אַחֵר וְלַדָּגִים אַחֵר
la'ofot basar acher veladdagim acher
and another flesh of birds, and another of fishes.

יֵשׁ גּוּפִים שְׁמֵימִיִּים וְגוּפִים אַרְצִיִּים
yesh gufim shemeimiyim vegufim artziyim
There are also celestial bodies, and bodies terrestrial:

אַךְ שׁוֹנֶה הוּא הֲדַר הַגּוּפִים הַשְּׁמֵימִיִּים מֵהֲדַר הַגּוּפִים הָאַרְצִיִּים
ach shoneh hu hadar haggufim hashemeimiyim mehadar haggufim ha'artziyim
but the glory of the celestial is one, and the glory of the terrestrial is another.

לַשֶּׁמֶשׁ הֲדַר מִשֶּׁלָּהּ, אֲבָל אַחֵר הוּא הֲדַר הַיָּרֵחַ וְאַחֵר הוּא הֲדַר הַכּוֹכָבִים
lashemesh hadar mishellah, aval acher hu hadar hayareach ve'acher hu hadar hakkochavim
There is one glory of the sun, and another glory of the moon, and another glory of the stars;

שֶׁהֲרֵי כּוֹכָב מִכּוֹכָב שׁוֹנֶה בַּהֲדָרוֹ
sheharei kochav mikkochav shoneh bahadaro
for one star differeth from another star in glory.

כֵּן גַּם תְּחִיַּת הַמֵּתִים: מַה שֶּׁנִּזְרַע בְּמַצָּב שֶׁל כִּלָּיוֹן יָקוּם בְּאִי כִּלָּיוֹן
ken gam techiyat hammetim. mah shennizra bematzav shel killayon yakum be'i killayon
So also is the resurrection of the dead. It is sown in corruption; it is raised in incorruption:

נִזְרַע בְּקָלוֹן וְיָקוּם בְּכָבוֹד; נִזְרַע בְּחֻלְשָׁה וְיָקוּם בִּגְבוּרָה
nizra bekalon veyakum bechavod; nizra bechulshah veyakum bigvurah
it is sown in dishonor; it is raised in glory: it is sown in weakness; it is raised in power:

נִזְרַע גּוּף נַפְשִׁי וְיָקוּם גּוּף רוּחָנִי. אִם יֵשׁ גּוּף נַפְשִׁי יֵשׁ גַּם גּוּף רוּחָנִי
nizra guf nafshi veyakum guf ruchani. im yesh guf nafshi yesh gam guf ruchani
it is sown a natural body; it is raised a spiritual body. If there is a natural body, there is also a spiritual body.

וְכֵן כָּתוּב עַל אָדָם הָרִאשׁוֹן: וַיְהִי הָאָדָם לְנֶפֶשׁ חַיָּה, אֲבָל אָדָם הָאַחֲרוֹן - לְרוּחַ מְחַיָּה
vechen katuv al adam harishon: vayhi ha'adam lenefesh chayah, aval adam ha'acharon - leruach mechayah
So also it is written, The first man Adam became a living soul. The last Adam became a life-giving spirit.

אֶל הַקּוֹרִינְתִּים א

אִם לֹא כֵן, מַה יַּעֲשׂוּ הָאֲנָשִׁים שֶׁנִּטְבָּלִים בְּעַד הַמֵּתִים
im lo chen, mah ya'asu ha'anashim shennitbalim be'ad hammetim
Else what shall they do that are baptized for the dead?

אִם אָמְנָם אֵין הַמֵּתִים קָמִים לִתְחִיָּה, לָמָּה הֵם נִטְבָּלִים בַּעֲדָם
im omnam ein hammetim kamim litchiyah, lammah hem nitbalim ba'adam
If the dead are not raised at all, why then are they baptized for them?

וְלָמָּה אֲנַחְנוּ נְתוּנִים בְּסַכָּנָה שָׁעָה שָׁעָה
velammah anachnu netunim besakkanah sha'ah sha'ah
Why do we also stand in jeopardy every hour?

אַחַי, אֲנִי נִשְׁבָּע בַּגַּאֲוָה שֶׁיֵּשׁ לִי בָּכֶם בַּמָּשִׁיחַ יֵשׁוּעַ אֲדוֹנֵנוּ, כִּי יוֹם יוֹם אֲנִי מֵת
achai, ani nishba bagga'avah sheyesh li bachem bammashiach yeshua adonenu, ki yom yom ani met
I protest by that glorying in you, brethren, which I have in Christ Jesus our Lord, I die daily.

אִם כְּדֶרֶךְ בְּנֵי אָדָם נֶאֱבַקְתִּי בְּאֶפְסוֹס עִם חַיּוֹת רָעוֹת, מָה הַתּוֹעֶלֶת שֶׁתִּצְמַח לִי מִזֶּה?
im kederech benei adam ne'evakti be'efesos im chayot ra'ot, mah hatto'elet shettitzmach li mizzeh
If after the manner of men I fought with beasts at Ephesus, what doth it profit me?

אִם אֵין תְּקוּמַת מֵתִים, הָבָה נֹאכַל וְנִשְׁתֶּה, כִּי מָחָר נָמוּת
im ein tkumat metim, havah nochal venishteh, ki machar namut
If the dead are not raised, let us eat and drink, for to-morrow we die.

אַל תִּטְעוּ: חֶבְרַת אֲנָשִׁים רָעִים תַּשְׁחִית מִדּוֹת טוֹבוֹת
al tit'u: chevrat anashim ra'im tashchit middot tovot
Be not deceived: Evil companionships corrupt good morals.

הִתְפַּכְּחוּ לַצֶּדֶק וְאַל תֶּחֱטָאוּ,
hitpakkechu latzedek ve'al techet'u
Awake to soberness righteously, and sin not;

כִּי יֵשׁ כַּמָּה שֶׁאֵין בָּהֶם דַּעַת אֱלֹהִים; לְבָשְׁתְּכֶם אֲנִי אוֹמֵר זֹאת
ki yesh kammah she'ein bahem da'at elohim; levoshetchem ani omer zot
for some have no knowledge of God: I speak this to move you to shame.

אֲבָל אֵיךְ יָקוּמוּ הַמֵּתִים? יִשְׁאַל אֶחָד, בְּאֵיזֶה גוּף הֵם יָבוֹאוּ
aval eich yakumu hammetim? yish'al echad, be'eizeh guf hem yavo'u
But some one will say, How are the dead raised? and with what manner of body do they come?

אַתָּה הַסָּכָל, הֵן מַה שֶּׁתִּזְרַע לֹא יִחְיֶה אֶלָּא אִם יָמוּת
attah hassachal, hen mah shettizra lo yichyeh ella im yamut
Thou foolish one, that which thou thyself sowest is not quickened except it die:

כַּאֲשֶׁר אַתָּה זוֹרֵעַ אֵינְךָ זוֹרֵעַ אֶת הַגּוּף שֶׁיִּתְהַוֶּה
ka'asher attah zorea eincha zorea et hagguf sheyit'havveh
and that which thou sowest, thou sowest not the body that shall be,

אֶל הַקּוֹרִינְתִּים א

אֲבָל כָּעֵת הַמָּשִׁיחַ קָם מִן הַמֵּתִים, בִּכּוּרֵי כָּל יְשֵׁנֵי עָפָר
aval ka'et hammashiach kam min hammetim, bikkurei kol yeshenei afar
But now hath Christ been raised from the dead, the firstfruits of them that are asleep.

וּמֵאַחַר שֶׁהַמָּוֶת בָּא עַל־יְדֵי אָדָם, גַּם תְּחִיַּת הַמֵּתִים הִיא עַל־יְדֵי אָדָם
ume'achar shehammavet ba al-yedei adam, gam techiyat hammetim hi al-yedei adam
For since by man came death, by man came also the resurrection of the dead.

שֶׁכֵּן כְּמוֹ שֶׁבְּאָדָם הַכֹּל מֵתִים, כָּךְ גַּם בַּמָּשִׁיחַ הַכֹּל יְחִיוּ
shekken kemo shebbe'adam hakkol metim, kach gam bammashich hakkol yacheyu
For as in Adam all die, so also in Christ shall all be made alive.

אַךְ כָּל אֶחָד כְּסִדְרוֹ: הָרִאשׁוֹן הוּא הַמָּשִׁיחַ; אַחֲרֵי כֵן, בְּבוֹאוֹ, הַשַּׁיָּכִים לַמָּשִׁיחַ
ach kol echad kesidro. harishon hu hammashiach; acharei chen, bevo'o, hashayachim lammashiach
But each in his own order: Christ the firstfruits; then they that are Christ's, at his coming.

אַחֲרֵי כֵן הַקֵּץ, כַּאֲשֶׁר יִמְסֹר לֵאלֹהִים הָאָב אֶת הַמַּלְכוּת
acharei chen hakketz, ka'asher yimsor le'elohim ha'av et hammalchut
Then cometh the end, when he shall deliver up the kingdom to God, even the Father;

לְאַחַר שֶׁיְּבַטֵּל כָּל מִמְשָׁל וְכָל סַמְכוּת וְשִׁלְטוֹן
le'achar sheyevattel kol mimshal vechol samchut veshilton
when he shall have abolished all rule and all authority and power.

כִּי עָלָיו לִמְלֹךְ עַד כִּי יָשִׁית אֶת כָּל אוֹיְבָיו תַּחַת רַגְלָיו
ki alav limloch ad ki yashit et kol oyevav tachat raglav
For he must reign, till he hath put all his enemies under his feet.

הָאוֹיֵב הָאַחֲרוֹן שֶׁיְּמֻגַּר הוּא הַמָּוֶת
ha'oyev ha'acharon sheyemuggar hu hammavet
The last enemy that shall be abolished is death.

שֶׁכֵּן הָאֱלֹהִים שָׁת הַכֹּל תַּחַת רַגְלָיו. וּבְאָמְרוֹ שֶׁהַכֹּל הוּשַׁת תַּחְתָּיו
shekken ha'elohim shat hakkol tachat raglav. uve'omro shehakkol hushat tachtav
For, He put all things in subjection under his feet. But when he saith, All things are put in subjection,

בָּרוּר כִּי הַשָּׁת אֶת הַכֹּל תַּחְתָּיו אֵינֶנּוּ בַּכְּלָל הַזֶּה
barur ki hashat et hakkol tachtav einennu bakkelal hazzeh
it is evident that he is excepted who did subject all things unto him.

וְכַאֲשֶׁר הַכֹּל יוּשַׁת תַּחְתָּיו
vecha'asher hakkol yushat tachtav
And when all things have been subjected unto him,

אָז גַּם הַבֵּן עַצְמוֹ יִהְיֶה כָּפוּף לְמִי שֶׁשָּׁת תַּחְתָּיו אֶת הַכֹּל, לְמַעַן יִהְיֶה הָאֱלֹהִים הַכֹּל בַּכֹּל
az gam habben atzmo yihyeh kafuf lemi sheshat tachtav et hakkol, lema'an yihyeh ha'elohim hakkol bakkol
then shall the Son also himself be subjected to him that did subject all things unto him, that God may be all in all.

אֶל הַקּוֹרִינְתִים א

עַל כָּל פָּנִים, בֵּין שֶׁאֲנִי בֵּין שֶׁהֵם, כָּךְ אָנוּ מְבַשְׂרִים וְכָךְ הֶאֱמַנְתֶּם
al kol panim, bein she'ani bein shehem, kach anu mevassrim vechach he'emantem
Whether then it be I or they, so we preach, and so ye believed.

וּבְכֵן אִם מֻכְרָז כִּי הַמָּשִׁיחַ קָם מִן הַמֵּתִים
uvechen im muchraz ki hammashiach kam min hammetim
Now if Christ is preached that he hath been raised from the dead,

אֵיךְ אוֹמְרִים כַּמָּה מִכֶּם שֶׁאֵין תְּחִיַּת מֵתִים
eich omerim kammah mikkem she'ein techiyat metim
how say some among you that there is no resurrection of the dead?

אִם אֵין תְּחִיַּת מֵתִים, גַּם הַמָּשִׁיחַ לֹא קָם
im ein techiyat metim, gam hammashiach lo kam
But if there is no resurrection of the dead, neither hath Christ been raised:

וְאִם הַמָּשִׁיחַ לֹא קָם, הַכְרָזָתֵנוּ הֶבֶל וְגַם אֱמוּנַתְכֶם הֶבֶל
ve'im hammashiach lo kam, hachrazatenu hevel vegam emunatchem hevel
and if Christ hath not been raised, then is our preaching vain, your faith also is vain.

וְאָז גַּם נִמְצָא עֵדֵי שֶׁקֶר לֵאלֹהִים
ve'az gam nimmatzei edei sheker le'elohim
Yea, and we are found false witnesses of God;

שֶׁכֵּן הֵעִידוֹנוּ עַל אֱלֹהִים כִּי הֵקִים אֶת הַמָּשִׁיחַ לִתְחִיָּה -
shekken ha'idonu al elohim ki hekim et hammashiach litchiyah -
because we witnessed of God that he raised up Christ:

וְהוּא לֹא הֱקִימוֹ אִם אָמְנָם אֵין הַמֵּתִים קָמִים לִתְחִיָּה
vehu lo hekimo im omnam ein hammetim kamim litchiyah
whom he raised not up, if so be that the dead are not raised.

וְאִם אֵין הַמֵּתִים קָמִים לִתְחִיָּה, גַּם הַמָּשִׁיחַ לֹא קָם לִתְחִיָּה
ve'im ein hammetim kamim litchiyah, gam hammashiach lo kam litchiyah
For if the dead are not raised, neither hath Christ been raised:

וְאִם הַמָּשִׁיחַ לֹא קָם לִתְחִיָּה, לַשָּׁוְא אֱמוּנַתְכֶם וַעֲדַיִן שְׁרוּיִים אַתֶּם בַּחֲטָאֵיכֶם
ve'im hammashiach lo kam litchiyah, lashav emunatchem va'adayin sheruyim attem bachata'eichem
and if Christ hath not been raised, your faith is vain; ye are yet in your sins.

וְאָז גַּם הָאֲנָשִׁים אֲשֶׁר מֵתוּ בִּהְיוֹתָם שַׁיָּכִים לַמָּשִׁיחַ - אֲבוּדִים הֵם
ve'az gam ha'anashim asher metu bihyotam shayachim lammashiach - avudim hem
Then they also that are fallen asleep in Christ have perished.

אִם אֲנַחְנוּ תּוֹלִים תִּקְוָה בַּמָּשִׁיחַ אַךְ וְרַק לְמַעַן חַיִּים אֵלֶּה, אֲזַי אֻמְלָלִים אָנוּ מִכָּל אָדָם
im anachnu tolim tikvah bammashiach ach verak lema'an chayim elleh, azai umlalim anu mikkol adam
If we have only hoped in Christ in this life, we are of all men most pitiable.

אֶל הַקּוֹרִינְתִּים א

בְּאֶמְצָעוּתָהּ אַתֶּם גַּם נוֹשָׁעִים, אִם מַחֲזִיקִים אַתֶּם בַּדָּבָר שֶׁבִּשַּׂרְתִּי לָכֶם
be'emtza'utah attem gam nosha'im, im machazikim attem baddavar shebissarti lachem
by which also ye are saved, if ye hold fast the word which I preached unto you,

שֶׁאִם לֹא כֵן, לַשָּׁוְא הָיְתָה אֱמוּנַתְכֶם
she'im lo chen, lashav hayetah emunatchem
except ye believed in vain.

מָסַרְתִּי לָכֶם בָּרֹאשׁ וּבָרִאשׁוֹנָה מַה שֶּׁגַּם קִבַּלְתִּי, שֶׁהַמָּשִׁיחַ מֵת בְּעַד חֲטָאֵינוּ, לְפִי הַכְּתוּבִים
masarti lachem barosh uvarishonah mah sheggam kibbalti, shehammashiach met be'ad chata'einu, lefi hakktuvim
For I delivered unto you first of all that which also I received: that Christ died for our sins according to the scriptures;

נִקְבַּר וְקָם לִתְחִיָּה בַּיּוֹם הַשְּׁלִישִׁי, לְפִי הַכְּתוּבִים
nikbar vekam litchiyah bayom hashelishi, lefi hakktuvim
and that he was buried; and that he hath been raised on the third day according to the scriptures;

וְנִרְאָה אֶל כֵּיפָא וְאַחַר כָּךְ אֶל הַשְּׁנֵים־עָשָׂר
venir'ah el keifa ve'achar kach el hasheneim-'asar
and that he appeared to Cephas; then to the twelve;

אַחֲרֵי כֵן נִרְאָה בְּבַת אַחַת אֶל יוֹתֵר מֵחֲמֵשׁ מֵאוֹת אַחִים
acharei chen nir'ah bevat achat el yoter mechamesh me'ot achim
then he appeared to above five hundred brethren at once,

אֲשֶׁר רֻבָּם עוֹדָם בַּחַיִּים וּמִקְצָתָם מֵתִים
asher rubbam odam bachayim umiktzatam metim
of whom the greater part remain until now, but some are fallen asleep;

אַחַר כָּךְ נִרְאָה אֶל יַעֲקֹב וּלְאַחַר מִכֵּן אֶל כָּל הַשְּׁלִיחִים
achar kach nir'ah el ya'akov ule'achar mikken el kol hashelichim
then he appeared to James; then to all the apostles;

אַחֲרֵי כֻלָּם נִרְאָה גַּם אֵלַי, אֲנִי, הָאַחֲרוֹן, אֲשֶׁר כְּנֵפֶל אָנִי
acharei kullam nir'ah gam elai, ani, ha'acharon, asher kenefel ani
and last of all, as to the child untimely born, he appeared to me also.

שֶׁכֵּן אֲנִי הַפָּחוּת בַּשְּׁלִיחִים וְאֵינֶנִּי רָאוּי לְהִקָּרֵא שָׁלִיחַ מִשּׁוּם שֶׁרָדַפְתִּי אֶת קְהִלַּת אֱלֹהִים
shekken ani happachut bashelichim ve'einenni ra'ui lehikkarei shaliach mishum sheradafti et kehillat elohim
For I am the least of the apostles, that am not meet to be called an apostle, because I persecuted the church of God.

אֲבָל בְּחֶסֶד אֱלֹהִים הֲרֵינִי מַה שֶּׁאֲנִי וְחַסְדּוֹ עָלַי לֹא הָיָה לָרִיק
aval bechesed elohim hareini mah she'ani vechasdo alai lo hayah larik
But by the grace of God I am what I am: and his grace which was bestowed upon me was not found vain;

אַדְּרַבָּא, עָמַלְתִּי יוֹתֵר מִכֻּלָּם, אַךְ לֹא אֲנִי אֶלָּא חֶסֶד אֱלֹהִים אֲשֶׁר אִתִּי
addrabba, amalti yoter mikkullam, ach lo ani ella chesed elohim asher itti
but I labored more abundantly than they all: yet not I, but the grace of God which was with me.

אֶל הַקּוֹרִינְתִּים א

אֶלָּא תִּכָּנַעְנָה לְמָרוּת, כְּמוֹ שֶׁגַּם הַתּוֹרָה אוֹמֶרֶת
ella tikkana'nah lemarut, kemo sheggam hattorah omeret
but let them be in subjection, as also saith the law.

וְאִם רְצוֹנָן לִלְמֹד דָּבָר, תִּשְׁאַלְנָה אֶת בַּעֲלֵיהֶן בַּבַּיִת
ve'im retzonan lilmod davar, tish'alnah et ba'aleihen babbayit
And if they would learn anything, let them ask their own husbands at home:

כִּי לֹא יָאֶה שֶׁאִשָּׁה תְּדַבֵּר בַּקְּהִלָּה
ki lo ya'eh she'ishah tedabber bakkehillah
for it is shameful for a woman to speak in the church.

הַאִם מִכֶּם יָצָא דְּבַר אֱלֹהִים? וְכִי רַק אֲלֵיכֶם הִגִּיעַ
ha'im mikkem yatza devar elohim? vechi rak aleichem higgia
What? was it from you that the word of God went forth? or came it unto you alone?

כָּל הַחוֹשֵׁב שֶׁהוּא עַצְמוֹ נָבִיא אוֹ אִישׁ רוּחָנִי
kol hachoshev shehu atzmo navi o ish ruchani
If any man thinketh himself to be a prophet, or spiritual,

שֶׁיַּכִּיר כִּי הַדְּבָרִים אֲשֶׁר כָּתַבְתִּי אֲלֵיכֶם מִצְווֹת הָאָדוֹן הֵם
sheyakkir ki haddevarim asher katavti aleichem mitzvot ha'adon hem
let him take knowledge of the things which I write unto you, that they are the commandment of the Lord.

וְאִם מִישֶׁהוּ אֵינוֹ מַכִּיר, לֹא יֻכַּר בּוֹ
ve'im mishehu eino makkir, lo yukkar bo
But if any man is ignorant, let him be ignorant.

וּבְכֵן, אַחַי, הִשְׁתּוֹקְקוּ לְהִתְנַבֵּא וְאַל תִּמְנְעוּ דִּבּוּר בִּלְשׁוֹנוֹת
uvechen, achai, hishtokeku lehitnabbei ve'al timne'u dibbur bilshonot
Wherefore, my brethren, desire earnestly to prophesy, and forbid not to speak with tongues.

אֲבָל יֵעָשֶׂה נָא הַכֹּל בְּאֹפֶן רָאוּי וּבְסֵדֶר
aval ye'aseh na hakkol be'ofen ra'ui uveseder
But let all things be done decently and in order.

טו

אַחַי, אֲנִי מַזְכִּיר לָכֶם אֶת הַבְּשׂוֹרָה שֶׁהִשְׁמַעְתִּי לָכֶם
achai, ani mazkir lachem et habbsorah shehishma'ti lachem
Now I make known unto you brethren, the gospel which I preached unto you,

בְּשׂוֹרָה אֲשֶׁר גַּם קִבַּלְתֶּם אוֹתָהּ וְגַם עוֹמְדִים אַתֶּם בָּהּ
bsorah asher gam kibbaltem otah vegam omedim attem bah
which also ye received, wherein also ye stand,

אֶל הַקּוֹרִינְתִּים א

סִתְרֵי לִבּוֹ יִגָּלוּ וְהוּא יִפֹּל עַל פָּנָיו בְּהִשְׁתַּחֲוָיָה לֵאלֹהִים
sitrei libbo yiggalu vehu yippol al panav behishtachavayah le'elohim
the secrets of his heart are made manifest; and so he will fall down on his face and worship God,

וְיַכְרִיז כִּי אָכֵן יֵשׁ אֱלֹהִים בְּקִרְבְּכֶם
veyachriz ki achen yesh elohim bekirbechem
declaring that God is among you indeed.

וּבְכֵן מַה תַּעֲשׂוּ, אַחַי? כַּאֲשֶׁר אַתֶּם נִקְהָלִים יַחְדָּיו, לְאֶחָד יֵשׁ מִזְמוֹר
uvechen mah ta'asu, achai? ka'asher attem nik'halim yachdav, le'echad yesh mizmor
What is it then, brethren? When ye come together, each one hath a psalm,

לְאַחֵר יֵשׁ דְּבַר־הוֹרָאָה, לָזֶה הִתְגַּלּוּת, לָזֶה לָשׁוֹן וְלָזֶה פֵּרוּשׁ; יְהֵא נָא הַכֹּל לְמַעַן תִּבָּנוּ
le'acher yesh devar-hora'ah, lazeh hitgallut, lazeh lashon velazeh perush; yehei na hakkol lema'an tibbanu
hath a teaching, hath a revelation, hath a tongue, hath an interpretation. Let all things be done unto edifying.

אִם מְדַבְּרִים בְּלָשׁוֹן, יְדַבְּרוּ שְׁנַיִם אוֹ שְׁלוֹשָׁה, לֹא יוֹתֵר; זֶה אַחַר זֶה יְדַבְּרוּ וְאֶחָד יְפָרֵשׁ
im medabberim belashon, yedabberu shenayim o sheloshah, lo yoter; zeh achar zeh yedabberu ve'echad yefaresh
If any man speaketh in a tongue, let it be by two, or at the most three, and that in turn; and let one interpret:

אַךְ אִם אֵין מְפָרֵשׁ, יַחֲרִישׁוּ בַּקְּהִלָּה וִידַבְּרוּ לְעַצְמָם וְלֵאלֹהִים
ach im ein mefaresh, yacharishu bakkehillah vidabberu le'atzmam vele'elohim
but if there be no interpreter, let him keep silence in the church; and let him speak to himself, and to God.

אֲשֶׁר לַנְּבִיאִים, שְׁנַיִם אוֹ שְׁלוֹשָׁה יְדַבְּרוּ וְהַשְּׁאָר יִבְחֲנוּ אֶת דִּבְרֵיהֶם
asher lannevi'im, shenayim o sheloshah yedabberu vehashe'ar yivchanu et divreihem
And let the prophets speak by two or three, and let the others discern.

אִם יִגָּלֶה דָּבָר לְאַחַד הַיּוֹשְׁבִים שָׁם יַחֲרִישׁ הָרִאשׁוֹן
im yiggaleh davar le'achad hayoshevim sham yacharish harishon
But if a revelation be made to another sitting by, let the first keep silence.

כִּי כֻּלְּכֶם יְכוֹלִים לְהִתְנַבֵּא זֶה אַחַר זֶה בְּאֹפֶן שֶׁהַכֹּל יִלְמְדוּ וְהַכֹּל יִתְעוֹדְדוּ
ki kullechem yecholim lehitnabbei zeh achar zeh be'ofen shehakkol yilmedu vehakkol yit'odedu
For ye all can prophesy one by one, that all may learn, and all may be exhorted;

וְרוּחוֹת הַנְּבִיאִים כְּפוּפוֹת לַנְּבִיאִים
veruchot hannevi'im kefufot lannevi'im
and the spirits of the prophets are subject to the prophets;

שֶׁהֲרֵי אֱלֹהִים אֵינוֹ אֱלֹהֵי מְהוּמָה אֶלָּא אֱלֹהֵי הַשָּׁלוֹם. כַּנָּהוּג בְּכָל קְהִלּוֹת הַקְּדוֹשִׁים
sheharei elohim eino elohei mehumah ella elohei hashalom. kannahug bechol kehillot hakkedoshim
for God is not a God of confusion, but of peace. As in all the churches of the saints,

הַנָּשִׁים תֶּחֱשֶׁינָה בַּקְּהִלּוֹת; אֵין לָהֶן רְשׁוּת לְדַבֵּר
hannashim techesheinah bakkehillot; ein lahen reshut ledabber
let the women keep silence in the churches: for it is not permitted unto them to speak;

אֶל הַקּוֹרִינְתִּים א

בְּרַם בַּקְּהִלָּה אֲנִי מַעֲדִיף לוֹמַר חָמֵשׁ מִלִּים בְּעֶזְרַת שִׂכְלִי כְּדֵי לְלַמֵּד גַּם אֲחֵרִים-
beram bakkehillah ani ma'adif lomar chamesh millim be'ezrat sichli kedei lelammed gam acherim
howbeit in the church I had rather speak five words with my understanding, that I might instruct others also,

מֵאֲשֶׁר לְהַשְׁמִיעַ רִבְבוֹת מִלִּים בְּלָשׁוֹן
me'asher lehashmia rivevot millim belashon
than ten thousand words in a tongue.

אַחַי, אַל תִּהְיוּ יְלָדִים בַּהֲבָנַתְכֶם; בַּאֲשֶׁר לָרַע הֱיוּ יְלָדִים, אַךְ בַּהֲבָנַתְכֶם הֱיוּ מְבֻגָּרִים
achai, al tihyu yeladim bahavanatchem; ba'asher lara heyu yeladim, ach bahavanatchem heyu mevuggarim
Brethren, be not children in mind: yet in malice be ye babes, but in mind be men.

בַּתּוֹרָה כָּתוּב: כִּי בְלַעֲגֵי שָׂפָה וּבְלָשׁוֹן אַחֶרֶת יְדַבֵּר אֶל־הָעָם הַזֶּה
battorah katuv: ki bela'agei safah uvelashon acheret yedabber el-ha'am hazzeh
In the law it is written, By men of strange tongues and by the lips of strangers will I speak unto this people;

וְלֹא אָבוּא שְׁמוֹעַ
velo avu shemoa
and not even thus will they hear me, saith the Lord.

לְפִיכָךְ הַלְּשׁוֹנוֹת אֵינָן אוֹת לַמַּאֲמִינִים, אֶלָּא לְבִלְתִּי מַאֲמִינִים
lefichach halleshonot einan ot lamma'aminim, ella labbilti ma'aminim
Wherefore tongues are for a sign, not to them that believe, but to the unbelieving:

וְהַנְּבוּאָה אֵינֶנָּה לְבִלְתִּי מַאֲמִינִים, אֶלָּא לַמַּאֲמִינִים
vehannevu'ah einennah labbilti ma'aminim, ella lamma'aminim
but prophesying is for a sign, not to the unbelieving, but to them that believe.

וְהִנֵּה אִם תִּתְכַּנֵּס כָּל הַקְּהִלָּה וְכֻלָּם יְדַבְּרוּ בִּלְשׁוֹנוֹת
vehinneh im titkannes kol hakkehillah vechullam yedabberu bilshonot
If therefore the whole church be assembled together and all speak with tongues,

וְיִכָּנְסוּ אֲנָשִׁים שֶׁאֵין לָהֶם מֻשָּׂג בָּעִנְיָן, אוֹ אֲנָשִׁים בִּלְתִּי מַאֲמִינִים
veyikkanesu anashim she'ein lahem mussag ba'inyan, o anashim bilti ma'aminim
and there come in men unlearned or unbelieving,

כְּלוּם לֹא יֹאמְרוּ שֶׁאַתֶּם מְשֻׁגָּעִים
klum lo yomeru she'attem meshugga'im
will they not say that ye are mad?

אֲבָל אִם הַכֹּל מִתְנַבְּאִים וְיִכָּנֵס אִישׁ בִּלְתִּי מַאֲמִין, אוֹ מִי שֶׁאֵין לוֹ מֻשָּׂג בָּעִנְיָן
aval im hakkol mitnabbe'im veyikkanes ish bilti ma'amin, o mi she'ein lo mussag ba'inyan
But if all prophesy, and there come in one unbelieving or unlearned,

אֲזַי יוּכַח עַל־יְדֵי כֻּלָּם וְיִדּוֹן עַל־יְדֵי כֻּלָּם
azai yuchach al-yedei kullam veyiddon al-yedei kullam
he is reproved by all, he is judged by all;

אֶל הַקּוֹרִינְתִּים א

לְפִיכָךְ אִם אֵינֶנִּי מֵבִין אֶת הַתֹּכֶן שֶׁל הַקּוֹל, אֶהְיֶה לוֹעֵז בְּעֵינֵי הַמְדַבֵּר
lefichach im einenni mevin et hattochen shel hakkol, ehyeh lo'ez be'einei hamdabber
If then I know not the meaning of the voice, I shall be to him that speaketh a barbarian,

וְהַמְדַבֵּר יִהְיֶה לוֹעֵז בְּעֵינַי
vehamdabber yihyeh lo'ez be'einai
and he that speaketh will be a barbarian unto me.

כֵּן גַּם אַתֶּם, הֱיוֹת וְאַתֶּם לְהוּטִים אַחֲרֵי מַתָּנוֹת רוּחָנִיּוֹת
ken gam attem, heyot ve'attem lehutim acharei mattanot ruchaniyot
So also ye, since ye are zealous of spiritual gifts,

בַּקְּשׁוּ לְהַעֲשִׁיר בַּמֶּה שֶׁבּוֹנֶה אֶת הַקְּהִלָּה
bakkshu leha'ashir bemah shebboneh et hakkehillah
seek that ye may abound unto the edifying of the church.

לָכֵן הַמְדַבֵּר בְּלָשׁוֹן יִתְפַּלֵּל שֶׁיּוּכַל לְפָרֵשׁ אֶת דְּבָרָיו
lachen hamdabber belashon yitpallel sheyuchal lefaresh et devarav
Wherefore let him that speaketh in a tongue pray that he may interpret.

אִם אֲנִי מִתְפַּלֵּל בְּלָשׁוֹן רוּחִי מִתְפַּלֶּלֶת, אֲבָל שִׂכְלִי אֵינֶנּוּ עוֹשֶׂה פְּרִי
im ani mitpallel belashon ruchi mitpallelet, aval sichli einennu oseh pri
For if I pray in a tongue, my spirit prayeth, but my understanding is unfruitful.

אִם כֵּן מַה לַעֲשׂוֹת? אֶתְפַּלֵּל בְּאֶמְצָעוּת הָרוּחַ וְאֶתְפַּלֵּל גַּם בְּאֶמְצָעוּת הַשֵּׂכֶל
im ken mah la'asot? etpallel be'emtza'ut haruach ve'etpallel gam be'emtza'ut hassechel
What is it then? I will pray with the spirit, and I will pray with the understanding also:

אָשִׁיר בְּאֶמְצָעוּת הָרוּחַ וְאָשִׁיר גַּם בְּאֶמְצָעוּת הַשֵּׂכֶל
ashir be'emtza'ut haruach ve'ashir gam be'emtza'ut hassechel
I will sing with the spirit, and I will sing with the understanding also.

שֶׁכֵּן אִם תְּבָרֵךְ בָּרוּחַ, כֵּיצַד יֹאמַר אָמֵן עַל הוֹדָיָתְךָ מִי שֶׁנִּמְנֶה עִם הַבִּלְתִּי מְבִינִים
shekken im tevarech beruach, keitzad yomar amen al hodayatecha mi shennimneh im habbilti mevinim
Else if thou bless with the spirit, how shall he that filleth the place of the unlearned say the Amen at thy giving of thanks,

הֲרֵי אֵין הוּא יוֹדֵעַ מָה אַתָּה אוֹמֵר
harei ein hu yodea mah attah omer
seeing he knoweth not what thou sayest?

אַתָּה אָמְנָם מַשְׁמִיעַ תּוֹדָה כָּרָאוּי, אַךְ רֵעֲךָ אֵינֶנּוּ נִבְנֶה
attah omnam mashmia todah kara'ui, ach re'acha einennu nivneh
For thou verily givest thanks well, but the other is not edified.

אֲנִי מוֹדֶה לֵאלֹהִים שֶׁאֲנִי מְדַבֵּר בִּלְשׁוֹנוֹת יוֹתֵר מִכֻּלְּכֶם
ani modeh lelohim she'ani medabber bilshonot yoter mikkullechem
I thank God, I speak with tongues more than you all:

אֶל הַקּוֹרִינְתִּים א

הַמְדַבֵּר בְּלָשׁוֹן בּוֹנֶה אֶת עַצְמוֹ; הַמִּתְנַבֵּא בּוֹנֶה אֶת הַקְּהִלָּה
hamedabber belashon boneh et atzmo; hammitnabbei boneh et hakkehillah
He that speaketh in a tongue edifieth himself; but he that prophesieth edifieth the church.

רְצוֹנִי שֶׁכֻּלְּכֶם תְּדַבְּרוּ בִּלְשׁוֹנוֹת, אַךְ עָדִיף שֶׁתִּתְנַבְּאוּ
retzoni shekkullechem tedabberu bilshonot, ach adif shettitnabbe'u
Now I would have you all speak with tongues, but rather that ye should prophesy:

הַמִּתְנַבֵּא גָּדוֹל מִן הַמְדַבֵּר בִּלְשׁוֹנוֹת
hammitnabbei gadol min hamdabber bilshonot
and greater is he that prophesieth than he that speaketh with tongues,

זוּלָתִי אִם יְפָרֵשׁ הָאַחֲרוֹן אֶת דְּבָרָיו כְּדֵי שֶׁהַקְּהִלָּה תִּבָּנֶה
zulati im yefaresh ha'acharon et dvarav kedei shehakkehillah tibbaneh
except he interpret, that the church may receive edifying.

וְעַתָּה, אַחַי, אִם אָבוֹא אֲלֵיכֶם וַאֲדַבֵּר בִּלְשׁוֹנוֹת, מָה אוֹעִיל לָכֶם
ve'attah, achai, im avo aleichem va'adabber bilshonot, mah o'il lachem
But now, brethren, if I come unto you speaking with tongues, what shall I profit you,

אִם לֹא אַגִּיד לָכֶם דְּבַר הִתְגַּלּוּת אוֹ דְּבַר דַּעַת, דְּבַר נְבוּאָה אוֹ דְּבַר הוֹרָאָה
im lo aggid lachem devar hitgallut o devar da'at, devar nevu'ah o devar hora'ah
unless I speak to you either by way of revelation, or of knowledge, or of prophesying, or of teaching?

אֲפִלּוּ עֲצָמִים דּוֹמְמִים שֶׁנִּתַּן לְהָפִיק מֵהֶם קוֹל, כְּגוֹן חָלִיל אוֹ כִנּוֹר, אִם לֹא יַשְׁמִיעוּ שִׁנּוּיֵי צְלִילִים
afillu atzamim domemim shennittan lehafik mehem kol, kegon chalil o kinnor, im lo yashmi'u shinnuyei tzelilim
Even things without life, giving a voice, whether pipe or harp, if they give not a distinction in the sounds,

כֵּיצַד תֻּכַּר הַנְּעִימָה הַמְנֻגֶּנֶת בְּחָלִיל אוֹ בְּכִנּוֹר
keitzad tukkar hanne'imah hamnuggenet bechalil o bechinnor
how shall it be known what is piped or harped?

וְאִם הַחֲצוֹצְרָה תַּשְׁמִיעַ קוֹל בִּלְתִּי בָּרוּר, מִי יִתְכּוֹנֵן לַקְּרָב
ve'im hachatzotzerah tashmia kol bilti barur, mi yitkonen lakkrav
For if the trumpet give an uncertain voice, who shall prepare himself for war?

כֵּן גַּם אַתֶּם, אִם לֹא תַּשְׁמִיעוּ דְּבָרִים בְּרוּרִים בַּלָּשׁוֹן, כֵּיצַד יוּבַן מַה שֶּׁנֶּאֱמַר
ken gam attem, im lo tashmi'u devarim berurim ballashon, keitzad yuvan mah shenne'emar
So also ye, unless ye utter by the tongue speech easy to be understood, how shall it be known what is spoken?

הֲרֵי תִּהְיוּ מְדַבְּרִים אֶל הָאֲוִיר
harei tihyu medabbrim el ha'avir
for ye will be speaking into the air.

רַבִּים הֵם מִינֵי הַקּוֹלוֹת בָּעוֹלָם וְאֵין אֶחָד מֵהֶם שֶׁאֵינוֹ מַבִּיעַ מַשֶּׁהוּ
rabbim hem minei hakkolot ba'olam ve'ein echad mehem she'eino mabbia mashehu
There are, it may be, so many kinds of voices in the world, and no kind is without signification.

אֶל הַקּוֹרִינְתִּים א

כִּי חֶלְקִית הִיא יְדִיעָתֵנוּ וּבְאֹרַח חֶלְקִי מִתְנַבְּאִים אָנוּ
ki chelkit hi yedi'atenu uve'orach chelki mitnabb'im anu
For we know in part, and we prophesy in part;

אַךְ בְּבוֹא הַמְּשֻׁלָּם יְבֻטַּל הַחֶלְקִי
ach bevo hammushlam yevuttal hachelki
but when that which is perfect is come, that which is in part shall be done away.

בִּהְיוֹתִי יֶלֶד דִּבַּרְתִּי כְיֶלֶד, הֵבַנְתִּי כְיֶלֶד, חָשַׁבְתִּי כְיֶלֶד.
bihyoti yeled dibbarti keyeled, hevanti keyeled, chashavti keyeled
When I was a child, I spake as a child, I felt as a child, I thought as a child:

כְּשֶׁהָיִיתִי לְאִישׁ שַׂמְתִּי קֵץ לְדִבְרֵי הַיַּלְדוּת
keshehayiti le'ish samti ketz ledivrei hayaldut
now that I am become a man, I have put away childish things.

עַכְשָׁו רוֹאִים אָנוּ בְּמַרְאָה, בִּמְעֻרְפָּל, אֲבָל אָז - פָּנִים אֶל פָּנִים
achshav ro'im anu bemar'ah, bim'urpal, aval az - panim el panim
For now we see in a mirror, darkly; but then face to face:

עַכְשָׁו יְדִיעָתִי חֶלְקִית, אֲבָל אָז אַכִּיר כַּדֶּרֶךְ שֶׁגַּם אֲנִי מֻכָּר
achshav yedi'ati chelkit, aval az akkir kederech sheggam ani mukkar
now I know in part; but then shall I know fully even as also I was fully known.

אַךְ כָּעֵת עוֹמְדוֹת שָׁלֹשׁ אֵלֶּה: אֱמוּנָה, תִּקְוָה, אַהֲבָה; וְהַגְּדוֹלָה שֶׁבָּהֶן - אַהֲבָה
ach ka'et omedot shalosh elleh: emunah, tikvah, ahavah; vehaggedolah shebbahen - ahavah
But now abideth faith, hope, love, these three; and the greatest of these is love.

יד

רִדְפוּ אַהֲבָה וְהִשְׁתּוֹקְקוּ לְמַתָּנוֹת רוּחָנִיּוֹת, וּבָעִקָּר שֶׁתִּתְנַבְּאוּ
ridfu ahavah vehishtokeku lemattanot ruchaniyot, uve'ikkar shettitnabbe'u
Follow after love; yet desire earnestly spiritual gifts, but rather that ye may prophesy.

הַמְדַבֵּר בְּלָשׁוֹן אֵינוֹ מְדַבֵּר לַאֲנָשִׁים אֶלָּא לֵאלֹהִים
hamdabber belashon eino medabber la'anashim ella le'elohim
For he that speaketh in a tongue speaketh not unto men, but unto God;

אִישׁ אֵינֶנּוּ מֵבִין אוֹתוֹ, כִּי בָּרוּחַ הוּא מְבַטֵּא סוֹדוֹת
ish einennu mevin oto, ki beruach hu mevattei sodot
for no man understandeth; but in the spirit he speaketh mysteries.

אֲבָל הַמִּתְנַבֵּא מַשְׁמִיעַ לַאֲנָשִׁים דְּבָרִים שֶׁתַּכְלִיתָם לִבְנוֹת, לְעוֹדֵד וּלְנַחֵם
aval hammitnabbei mashmia la'anashim devarim shettachlitam livnot, le'oded ulenachem
But he that prophesieth speaketh unto men edification, and exhortation, and consolation.

אֶל הַקּוֹרִינְתִּים א

יג

אִם בִּלְשׁוֹנוֹת בְּנֵי אָדָם וּמַלְאָכִים אֲדַבֵּר וְאֵין בִּי אַהֲבָה, הֲרֵינִי כִּנְחֹשֶׁת הוֹמָה אוֹ כִּמְצִלְתַּיִם רוֹעֲשִׁים
im bilshonot bnei adam umal'achim adabber ve'ein bi ahavah, hareini kinchoshet homah o kimtziltayim ro'ashim
If I speak with the tongues of men and of angels, but have not love, I am become sounding brass, or a clanging cymbal.

אִם תִּהְיֶה לִי מַתַּת הַנְּבוּאָה וְאֵדַע כָּל הַסּוֹדוֹת וְאַשִּׂיג כָּל הַדַּעַת
im tihyeh li mattat hannevu'ah ve'eda kol hassodot ve'assig kol hadda'at
And if I have the gift of prophecy, and know all mysteries and all knowledge;

וְאִם תִּהְיֶה בִּי כָּל הָאֱמוּנָה עַד לְהַעְתִּיק הָרִים מִמְּקוֹמָם, וְאֵין בִּי אַהֲבָה, הֲרֵינִי כְּאַיִן וּכְאֶפֶס
ve'im tihyeh bi kol ha'emunah ad leha'tik harim mimmekomam, ve'ein bi ahavah, hareini ke'ayin uche'efes
and if I have all faith, so as to remove mountains, but have not love, I am nothing.

אִם אֲחַלֵּק אֶת כָּל רְכוּשִׁי לִצְדָקָה וְגַם אֶתֵּן אֶת גּוּפִי לִשְׂרֵפָה
im achallek et kol rechushi litzdakah vegam etten et gufi lisrefah
And if I bestow all my goods to feed the poor, and if I give my body to be burned,

וְאֵין בִּי אַהֲבָה - לֹא יוֹעִיל לִי דָּבָר
ve'ein bi ahavah - lo yo'il li davar
but have not love, it profiteth me nothing.

הָאַהֲבָה סַבְלָנִית וּנְדִיבָה; הָאַהֲבָה אֵינָהּ מְקַנֵּאת; הָאַהֲבָה לֹא תִּתְפָּאֵר וְלֹא תִּתְנַשֵּׂא
ha'ahavah savlanit unedivah; ha'ahavah einah mekannet; ha'ahavah lo titpa'er velo titnasse
Love suffereth long, and is kind; love envieth not; love vaunteth not itself, is not puffed up,

הִיא לֹא תִּנְהַג בְּגַסּוּת, לֹא תִּדְרֹשׁ טוֹבַת עַצְמָהּ, לֹא תִּרְגַּז וְלֹא תַּחְשֹׁב רָעָה
hi lo tinhag begassut, lo tidrosh tovat atzmah, lo tirgaz velo tachashov ra'ah
doth not behave itself unseemly, seeketh not its own, is not provoked, taketh not account of evil;

הָאַהֲבָה לֹא תִּשְׂמַח בְּעַוְלָה, כִּי בָּאֱמֶת שִׂמְחָתָהּ
ha'ahavah lo tismach ba'avlah, ki ba'emet simchatah
rejoiceth not in unrighteousness, but rejoiceth with the truth;

הִיא תְּכַסֶּה עַל הַכֹּל, תַּאֲמִין בַּכֹּל, תְּקַוֶּה לַכֹּל וְתִסְבֹּל אֶת הַכֹּל
hi techasseh al hakkol, ta'amin bakkol, tekavveh lakkol vetisbol et hakkol
beareth all things, believeth all things, hopeth all things, endureth all things.

הָאַהֲבָה לֹא תָּמוֹט לְעוֹלָם, אַךְ נְבוּאוֹת תִּבָּטַלְנָה
ha'ahavah lo timmot le'olam, ach nevu'ot tibbatalnah
Love never faileth: but whether there be prophecies, they shall be done away;

לְשׁוֹנוֹת תֶּחְדַּלְנָה, דַּעַת תִּבָּטֵל
leshonot techdalnah, da'at tibbatel
whether there be tongues, they shall cease; whether there be knowledge, it shall be done away.

אֶל הַקּוֹרִינְתִּים א

לְעֻמַּת זֹאת, אֵיבָרֵינוּ הַהֲגוּנִים אֵינָם זְקוּקִים לָזֶה
le'ummat zot, eivareinu hahagunim einam zekukim lazeh
whereas our comely parts have no need:

אֱלֹהִים הִרְכִּיב אֶת הַגּוּף בְּאֹפֶן שֶׁנָּתַן כָּבוֹד רַב יוֹתֵר לְאֵיבָרִים נְטוּלֵי כָּבוֹד
elohim hirkiv et hagguf be'ofen shennatan kavod rav yoter le'eivarim netulei kavod
but God tempered the body together, giving more abundant honor to that part which lacked;

לְמַעַן לֹא תִּהְיֶה מַחֲלֹקֶת בַּגּוּף אֶלָּא שֶׁיִּדְאֲגוּ הָאֵיבָרִים זֶה לָזֶה
lema'an lo tihyeh machaloket bagguf ella sheyid'agu ha'eivarim zeh lazeh
that there should be no schism in the body; but that the members should have the same care one for another.

וְאִם יִכְאַב אֵיבָר אֶחָד, כָּל הָאֵיבָרִים יִסְבְּלוּ אִתּוֹ
ve'im yich'av eivar echad, kol ha'eivarim yisbelu itto
And whether one member suffereth, all the members suffer with it;

וְאִם יְכֻבַּד אֵיבָר אֶחָד, כָּל הָאֵיבָרִים יִשְׂמְחוּ אִתּוֹ
ve'im yechubbad eivar echad, kol ha'eivarim yismechu itto
or one member is honored, all the members rejoice with it.

אַתֶּם גּוּף הַמָּשִׁיחַ וְאֵיבָרָיו, אִישׁ אִישׁ לְפִי חֶלְקוֹ
attem guf hammashiach ve'eivarav, ish ish lefi chelko
Now ye are the body of Christ, and severally members thereof.

וּמֵהֶם הֵקִים אֱלֹהִים בַּקְּהִלָּה - רֵאשִׁית שְׁלִיחִים
umehem hekim elohim bakkehillah - reshit shelichim
And God hath set some in the church, first apostles,

שֵׁנִית נְבִיאִים, שְׁלִישִׁית מוֹרִים, אַחֲרֵי כֵן עוֹשֵׂי נִסִּים
shenit nevi'im, shelishit morim, acharei chen osei nissim
secondly prophets, thirdly teachers, then miracles,

אַחֲרֵי כֵן מַתְּנוֹת הָרִפּוּי, עֶזְרָה לַזּוּלַת, הַנְהָגָה, וּמִינֵי לְשׁוֹנוֹת
acharei chen mattnot harippui, ezrah lazzulat, hanhagah, uminei leshonot
then gifts of healings, helps, governments, divers kinds of tongues.

הַאִם כֻּלָּם שְׁלִיחִים? הַאִם כֻּלָּם נְבִיאִים? כֻּלָּם מוֹרִים? כֻּלָּם עוֹשֵׂי נִסִּים
ha'im kullam shlichim? ha'im kullam nevi'im? kullam morim? kullam osei nissim
Are all apostles? are all prophets? are all teachers? are all workers of miracles?

הַאִם לְכֻלָּם מַתְּנוֹת הָרִפּוּי? הַאִם כֻּלָּם מְדַבְּרִים בִּלְשׁוֹנוֹת? כֻּלָּם מְבָאֲרֵי לְשׁוֹנוֹת
ha'im lechullam mattnot harippui? ha'im kullam medabbrim bilshonot? kullam meva'arei leshonot
have all gifts of healings? do all speak with tongues? do all interpret?

וּבְכֵן הִשְׁתּוֹקְקוּ לַמַּתָּנוֹת הַחֲשׁוּבוֹת יוֹתֵר; עִם זֹאת אַרְאֶה לָכֶם דֶּרֶךְ נַעֲלָה בְּיוֹתֵר
uvechen hishtokeku lammattanot hachashuvot yoter; im zot ar'eh lachem derech na'alah beyoter
But desire earnestly the greater gifts. And moreover a most excellent way show I unto you.

אֶל הַקּוֹרִינְתִּים א

וְכֻלָּנוּ הֻשְׁקֵינוּ רוּחַ אַחַת
vechullanu hushkeinu ruach achat
and were all made to drink of one Spirit.

וְאָכֵן אֵין הַגּוּף אֵיבָר אֶחָד אֶלָּא רַבִּים
ve'achen ein hagguf eivar echad ella rabbim
For the body is not one member, but many.

אִם תֹּאמַר הָרֶגֶל: אֵינֶנִּי יָד, לָכֵן אֵינֶנִּי שַׁיֶּכֶת לַגּוּף, הַאִם מִשּׁוּם כָּךְ אֵינָהּ שַׁיֶּכֶת לַגּוּף
im tomar haregel: einenni yad, lachen einenni shayechet lagguf, ha'im mishum kach einah shayechet lagguf
If the foot shall say, Because I am not the hand, I am not of the body; it is not therefore not of the body.

וְאִם תֹּאמַר הָאֹזֶן: אֵינֶנִּי עַיִן, לָכֵן אֵינֶנִּי שַׁיֶּכֶת לַגּוּף, הַאִם מִשּׁוּם כָּךְ אֵינָהּ שַׁיֶּכֶת לַגּוּף
ve'im tomar ha'ozen: einenni ayin, lachen einenni shayechet lagguf, ha'im mishum kach einah shayechet lagguf
And if the ear shall say, Because I am not the eye, I am not of the body; it is not therefore not of the body.

אִם הַגּוּף כֻּלּוֹ יִהְיֶה עַיִן, כֵּיצַד תִּהְיֶה שְׁמִיעָה? וְאִם כֻּלּוֹ יִהְיֶה אֵיבָר שְׁמִיעָה, כֵּיצַד יוּכַל לְהָרִיחַ
im hagguf kullo yihyeh ayin, keitzad tihyeh shmi'ah? ve'im kullo yihyeh eivar shmi'ah, keitzad yuchal lehariach
If the whole body were an eye, where were the hearing? If the whole were hearing, where were the smelling?

אֲבָל אֱלֹהִים שָׂם אֶת הָאֵיבָרִים בַּגּוּף, כָּל אֶחָד וְאֶחָד מֵהֶם עַל-פִּי רְצוֹן אֱלֹהִים
aval elohim sam et ha'eivarim bagguf, kol echad ve'echad mehem al-pi retzon elohim
But now hath God set the members each one of them in the body, even as it pleased him.

וְאִלּוּ הָיוּ כֻּלָּם אֵיבָר אֶחָד, אֵיפֹה הַגּוּף
ve'illu hayu kullam eivar echad, eifoh hagguf
And if they were all one member, where were the body?

וְהִנֵּה יֵשׁ אֵיבָרִים רַבִּים, אַךְ גּוּף אֶחָד
vehinneh yesh eivarim rabbim, ach guf echad
But now they are many members, but one body.

הָעַיִן לֹא תּוּכַל לוֹמַר אֶל הַיָּד: אֵין לִי צֹרֶךְ בָּךְ; גַּם הָרֹאשׁ לֹא יוּכַל לוֹמַר אֶל הָרַגְלַיִם: אֵין לִי צֹרֶךְ בָּכֶן
ha'ayin lo tuchal lomar el hayad: ein li tzorech bach; gam harosh lo yuchal lomar el haraglayim: ein li tzorech bachen
And the eye cannot say to the hand, I have no need of thee: or again the head to the feet, I have no need of you.

אַדְּרַבָּא, אֵיבְרֵי הַגּוּף שֶׁלִּכְאוֹרָה חַלָּשִׁים יוֹתֵר, הֵם הַנְּחוּצִים יוֹתֵר
addrabba, eiverei hagguf shellich'orah challashim yoter, hem hannechutzim yoter
Nay, much rather, those members of the body which seem to be more feeble are necessary:

אֵיבְרֵי הַגּוּף הַנִּרְאִים לָנוּ נְקַלִּים, אוֹתָם אָנוּ עוֹטְרִים בְּיֶתֶר כָּבוֹד
eiverei hagguf hannir'im lanu niklim, otam anu oterim beyeter kavod
and those parts of the body, which we think to be less honorable, upon these we bestow more abundant honor;

וְהָאֵיבָרִים שֶׁהֵם לְבֹשֶׁת לָנוּ זוֹכִים לְיֶתֶר כָּבוֹד
veha'eivarim shehem levoshet lanu zochim leyeter kavod
and our uncomely parts have more abundant comeliness;

אֶל הַקּוֹרִינְתִּים א

יֵשׁ תַּפְקִידִים שׁוֹנִים, אַךְ אוֹתוֹ אָדוֹן
yesh tafkidim shonim, ach oto adon
And there are diversities of ministrations, and the same Lord.

וְיֵשׁ פְּעֻלּוֹת שׁוֹנוֹת, אַךְ אוֹתוֹ אֱלֹהִים הוּא הַפּוֹעֵל הַכֹּל בַּכֹּל
veyesh pe'ullot shonot, ach oto elohim hu happo'el hakkol bakkol
And there are diversities of workings, but the same God, who worketh all things in all.

וּלְכָל אִישׁ נִתֶּנֶת הִתְגַּלּוּת הָרוּחַ כְּדֵי לְהוֹעִיל
ulechol ish nittenet hitgallut haruach kedei leho'il
But to each one is given the manifestation of the Spirit to profit withal.

לָזֶה נִתַּן עַל־יְדֵי הָרוּחַ דְּבַר חָכְמָה; לָזֶה נִתַּן דְּבַר דַּעַת
lazeh nittan al-yedei haruach devar chochmah; lazeh nittan devar da'at
For to one is given through the Spirit the word of wisdom; and to another the word of knowledge,

עַל־פִּי אוֹתָהּ רוּחַ
al-pi otah ruach
according to the same Spirit:

לָזֶה נִתֶּנֶת אֱמוּנָה עַל־יְדֵי אוֹתָהּ רוּחַ; לָזֶה מַתְּנוֹת הָרִפּוּי עַל־יְדֵי אוֹתָהּ רוּחַ
lazeh nittenet emunah al-yedei otah ruach; lazeh mattenot harippui al-yedei otah ruach
to another faith, in the same Spirit; and to another gifts of healings, in the one Spirit;

לָזֶה יְכֹלֶת לַעֲשׂוֹת נִסִּים, לָזֶה נְבוּאָה, לָזֶה הַבְחָנָה בֵּין הָרוּחוֹת
lazeh yecholet la'asot nissim, lazeh nevu'ah, lazeh havchanah bein haruchot
and to another workings of miracles; and to another prophecy; and to another discernings of spirits:

לָזֶה מִינֵי לְשׁוֹנוֹת וְלָזֶה פֵּרוּשׁ לְשׁוֹנוֹת
lazeh minei leshonot velazeh perush leshonot
to another divers kinds of tongues; and to another the interpretation of tongues:

וְאֶת כָּל הַדְּבָרִים הַלָּלוּ פּוֹעֶלֶת אוֹתָהּ רוּחַ אַחַת הַחוֹלֶקֶת כִּרְצוֹנָהּ לְכָל אִישׁ וָאִישׁ
ve'et kol haddevarim hallalu po'elet otah ruach achat hacholeket kirtzonah lechol ish va'ish
but all these worketh the one and the same Spirit, dividing to each one severally even as he will.

כְּשֵׁם שֶׁהַגּוּף הוּא אֶחָד וְאֵיבָרִים רַבִּים לוֹ
keshem shehagguf hu echad ve'eivarim rabbim lo
For as the body is one, and hath many members,

וְכָל אֵיבְרֵי הַגּוּף הֵם גּוּף אֶחָד אַף כִּי רַבִּים הֵם, כֵּן גַּם הַמָּשִׁיחַ
vechol eiverei hagguf hem guf echad af ki rabbim hem, ken gam hammashiach
and all the members of the body, being many, are one body; so also is Christ.

הֲרֵי בְּרוּחַ אַחַת הֻטְבַּלְנוּ כֻּלָּנוּ לְגוּף אֶחָד, יְהוּדִים כְּיְוָנִים, עֲבָדִים כִּבְנֵי חוֹרִין
harei beruach achat hutbalnu kullanu leguf echad, yehudim kiyevanim, avadim kivnei chorin
For in one Spirit were we all baptized into one body, whether Jews or Greeks, whether bond or free;

אֶל הַקּוֹרִינְתִּים א

מִסִּבָּה זֹאת רַבִּים מִכֶּם חַלָּשִׁים וְחוֹלִים וְיֵשׁ אֲשֶׁר מֵתוּ
missibbah zot rabbim mikkem challashim vecholim veyesh asher metu
For this cause many among you are weak and sickly, and not a few sleep.

אִם נִבְחַן אֶת עַצְמֵנוּ לֹא נִשָּׁפֵט
im nivchan et atzmenu lo nishafet
But if we discerned ourselves, we should not be judged.

אֲבָל כַּאֲשֶׁר הָאָדוֹן שׁוֹפֵט אוֹתָנוּ הוּא מְיַסֵּר אוֹתָנוּ כְּדֵי שֶׁלֹּא נֵרָשַׁע עִם הָעוֹלָם
aval ka'asher ha'adon shofet otanu hu meyasser otanu kedei shello nursha im ha'olam
But when we are judged, we are chastened of the Lord, that we may not be condemned with the world.

עַל כֵּן, אַחַי, הַמְתִּינוּ זֶה לָזֶה כְּשֶׁאַתֶּם נֶאֱסָפִים לֶאֱכֹל
al ken, achai, hamtinu zeh lazeh kshe'attem ne'esafim le'echol
Wherefore, my brethren, when ye come together to eat, wait one for another.

מִי שֶׁרָעֵב יֹאכַל בַּבַּיִת, לְמַעַן לֹא תֵּאָסְפוּ לְמִשְׁפָּט
mi shera'ev yochal babbayit, lema'an lo te'asefu lemishpat
If any man is hungry, let him eat at home; that your coming together be not unto judgment.

וְאֶת יֶתֶר הַדְּבָרִים אֲסַדֵּר בְּבוֹאִי
ve'et yeter haddvarim asadder bevo'i
And the rest will I set in order whensoever I come.

יב

בְּעִנְיַן הַמַּתָּנוֹת הָרוּחָנִיּוֹת, אַחַי, אֵינֶנִּי רוֹצֶה שֶׁיֵּעָלֵם מִכֶּם דָּבָר
be'inyan hammattanot haruchaniyot, achai, einenni rotzeh sheye'alem mikkem davar
Now concerning spiritual gifts, brethren, I would not have you ignorant.

אַתֶּם יוֹדְעִים כִּי בְּעֵת הֱיוֹתְכֶם עוֹבְדֵי אֱלִילִים נִדַּחְתֶּם וְנִמְשַׁכְתֶּם אֶל אֱלִילִים אִלְּמִים
attem yode'im ki be'et heyotechem ovdei elilim niddachtem venimshachtem el elilim illmim
Ye know that when ye were Gentiles ye were led away unto those dumb idols, howsoever ye might be led.

וּבְכֵן אֲנִי מוֹדִיעַ לָכֶם: אֵין אִישׁ מְדַבֵּר בְּהַשְׁרָאַת רוּחַ אֱלֹהִים וְאוֹמֵר יֵשׁוּעַ חֵרֶם הוּא
uvechen ani modia lachem: ein ish medabber behashra'at ruach elohim ve'omer yeshua cherem hu
Wherefore I make known unto you, that no man speaking in the Spirit of God saith, Jesus is anathema;

וְאֵין אִישׁ יָכוֹל לוֹמַר יֵשׁוּעַ הוּא הָאָדוֹן אֶלָּא בְּרוּחַ הַקֹּדֶשׁ
ve'ein ish yachol lomar yeshua hu ha'adon ella beruach hakkodesh
and no man can say, Jesus is Lord, but in the Holy Spirit.

אָמְנָם יֵשׁ מַתָּנוֹת שׁוֹנוֹת, אֲבָל הָרוּחַ הִיא אוֹתָהּ רוּחַ
omnam yesh mattanot shonot, aval haruach hi otah ruach
Now there are diversities of gifts, but the same Spirit.

אֶל הַקּוֹרִינְתִּים א

מַה אֹמַר לָכֶם? אֲשַׁבֵּחַ אֶתְכֶם? עַל זֹאת לֹא אֲשַׁבֵּחַ
mah omar lachem? ashabbeach etchem? al zot lo ashabbeach
What shall I say to you? shall I praise you? In this I praise you not.

אָכֵן אֲנִי קִבַּלְתִּי מֵאֵת הָאָדוֹן אֵת אֲשֶׁר גַּם מָסַרְתִּי לָכֶם
achen ani kibbalti me'et ha'adon et asher gam masarti lachem
For I received of the Lord that which also I delivered unto you,

שֶׁהָאָדוֹן יֵשׁוּעַ, בַּלַּיְלָה שֶׁהֻסְגַּר בּוֹ, לָקַח אֶת הַלֶּחֶם
sheha'adon yeshua, ballaylah shehusgar bo, lakach et hallechem
that the Lord Jesus in the night in which he was betrayed took bread;

בֵּרֵךְ, בָּצַע אוֹתוֹ וְאָמַר: זֶה גּוּפִי הַנִּבְצָע בַּעַדְכֶם, זֹאת עֲשׂוּ לְזִכְרִי
berech, batza oto ve'amar: zeh gufi hannivtza ba'adchem, zot asu lezichri
and when he had given thanks, he brake it, and said, This is my body, which is for you: this do in remembrance of me.

כֵּן גַּם לָקַח אֶת הַכּוֹס לְאַחַר הַסְּעוּדָה וְאָמַר
ken gam lakach et hakkos le'achar hasse'udah ve'amar
In like manner also the cup, after supper, saying,

הַכּוֹס הַזֹּאת הִיא הַבְּרִית הַחֲדָשָׁה בְּדָמִי, זֹאת עֲשׂוּ לְזִכְרִי בְּכָל עֵת שֶׁתִּשְׁתּוּ
hakkos hazzot hi habberit hachadashah bedami, zot asu lezichri bechol et shettishtu
This cup is the new covenant in my blood: this do, as often as ye drink it, in remembrance of me.

הֵן בְּכָל עֵת שֶׁאַתֶּם אוֹכְלִים אֶת הַלֶּחֶם הַזֶּה וְשׁוֹתִים מִן הַכּוֹס הַזֹּאת
hen bechol et she'attem ochlim et hallechem hazzeh veshotim min hakkos hazzot
For as often as ye eat this bread, and drink the cup,

אַתֶּם מַזְכִּירִים אֶת מוֹת אֲדוֹנֵנוּ, עַד שֶׁיָּבוֹא
attem mazkirim et mot adonenu, ad sheyavo
ye proclaim the Lord's death till he come.

לָכֵן מִי שֶׁאוֹכֵל מֵהַלֶּחֶם הַזֶּה אוֹ שׁוֹתֶה מִכּוֹס הָאָדוֹן שֶׁלֹּא כָּרָאוּי
lachen mi she'ochel mehallechem hazzeh o shoteh mikkos ha'adon shello kara'ui
Wherefore whosoever shall eat the bread or drink the cup of the Lord in an unworthy manner,

יִהְיֶה אָשֵׁם לְגַבֵּי גּוּף הָאָדוֹן וְדָמוֹ
yihyeh ashem legabbei guf ha'adon vedamo
shall be guilty of the body and the blood of the Lord.

יִבְחַן נָא אִישׁ אֶת עַצְמוֹ וְכָךְ יֹאכַל מִן הַלֶּחֶם וְיִשְׁתֶּה מִן הַכּוֹס
yivchan na ish et atzmo vechach yochal min hallechem veyishteh min hakkos
But let a man prove himself, and so let him eat of the bread, and drink of the cup.

כִּי הָאוֹכֵל וְהַשּׁוֹתֶה מִבְּלִי לִנְהֹג הַבְחָנָה בְּגוּף הָאָדוֹן, אוֹכֵל וְשׁוֹתֶה דִּין לְעַצְמוֹ
ki ha'ochel vehashoteh mibbli linhog havchanah beguf ha'adon, ochel veshoteh din le'atzmo
For he that eateth and drinketh, eateth and drinketh judgment unto himself, if he discern not the body.

אֶל הַקּוֹרִינְתִּים א

שִׁפְטוּ אַתֶּם בְּעַצְמְכֶם: הֲיָאֶה לְאִשָּׁה לְהִתְפַּלֵּל לֵאלֹהִים בְּגִלּוּי רֹאשׁ
shiftu attem be'atzmechem: haya'eh le'ishah lehitpallel lelohim begillui rosh
Judge ye in yourselves: is it seemly that a woman pray unto God unveiled?

כְּלוּם הַטֶּבַע עַצְמוֹ אֵינוֹ מְלַמֵּד אֶתְכֶם שֶׁאִם לָאִישׁ שֵׂעָר אָרֹךְ הֲרֵי זֶה לִבְזוּתוֹ
klum hatteva atzmo eino melammed etchem she'im la'ish se'ar aroch harei zeh livzuto
Doth not even nature itself teach you, that, if a man have long hair, it is a dishonor to him?

אֲבָל הָאִשָּׁה אִם יֵשׁ לָהּ שֵׂעָר אָרֹךְ הֲרֵי זֶה לְכָבוֹד לָהּ, כִּי נִתַּן לָהּ הַשֵּׂעָר לִכְסוּת
aval ha'ishah im yesh lah se'ar aroch harei zeh lechavod lah, ki nittan lah hasho'ar lichsut
But if a woman have long hair, it is a glory to her: for her hair is given her for a covering.

וְאִם מִישֶׁהוּ מִתְכַּוֵּן לְהִתְוַכֵּחַ, לָנוּ אֵין מִנְהָג כָּזֶה, אַף לֹא לִקְהִלּוֹת אֱלֹהִים
ve'im mishehu mitkavven lehitvakkeach, lanu ein minhag kazeh, af lo lik'hillot elohim
But if any man seemeth to be contentious, we have no such custom, neither the churches of God.

בְּמָסְרִי אֶת הַהוֹרָאוֹת הָאֵלֶּה אֵינֶנִּי מְשַׁבֵּחַ אֶתְכֶם, שֶׁכֵּן אֵינְכֶם נֶאֱסָפִים יַחַד לְטוֹבָה אֶלָּא לְרָעָה
bemosri et hahora'ot ha'elleh einenni meshabbeach etchem, shekken einechem ne'esafim yachad letovah ella lera'ah
But in giving you this charge, I praise you not, that ye come together not for the better but for the worse.

רֵאשִׁית כֹּל, שָׁמַעְתִּי כִּי בְּעֵת שֶׁאַתֶּם מִתְאַסְּפִים בִּקְהִלָּה מִתְגַּלְּעוֹת מַחֲלֹקוֹת בֵּינֵיכֶם
reshit kol, shama'ti ki be'et she'attem mit'assfim bik'hillah mitgalle'ot machalokot beineichem
For first of all, when ye come together in the church, I hear that divisions exist among you;

בְּמִדַּת מָה אֲנִי מַאֲמִין בָּזֶה
bemiddat mah ani ma'amin bazeh
and I partly believe it.

שֶׁכֵּן צָרִיךְ שֶׁיִּהְיוּ פִּלּוּגִים בֵּינֵיכֶם לְמַעַן יִוָּדַע מִי הֵם הַנֶּאֱמָנִים בֵּינֵיכֶם
shekken tzarich sheyihyu pillugim beineichem lema'an yivvada mi hem hanne'emanim beineichem
For there must be also factions among you, that they that are approved may be made manifest among you.

וְהִנֵּה כַּאֲשֶׁר אַתֶּם נֶאֱסָפִים יַחַד לְמָקוֹם אֶחָד, אֵין זֹאת כְּדֵי לֶאֱכֹל אֶת סְעוּדַת הָאָדוֹן
vehinneh ka'asher attem ne'esafim yachad lemakom echad, ein zot kdei le'echol et se'udat ha'adon
When therefore ye assemble yourselves together, it is not possible to eat the Lord's supper:

כִּי כָּל אֶחָד מַקְדִּים לֶאֱכֹל אֶת אֲרוּחָתוֹ, וְהַתּוֹצָאָה - זֶה רָעֵב וְזֶה שִׁכּוֹר
ki kol echad makdim le'echol et aruchato, vehattotza'ah - zeh ra'ev vezeh shikkor
for in your eating each one taketh before other his own supper; and one is hungry, and another is drunken.

הַאֻמְנָם אֵין לָכֶם בָּתִּים לֶאֱכֹל וְלִשְׁתּוֹת בָּהֶם
ha'omnam ein lachem battim le'echol velishtot bahem?
What, have ye not houses to eat and to drink in?

אוֹ שֶׁמָּא בָּזִים אַתֶּם לִקְהִלַּת אֱלֹהִים וּמְבַיְּשִׁים אֶת מִי שֶׁאֵין לוֹ
o shemma bazim attem lik'hillat elohim umevayeshim et mi she'ein lo
or despise ye the church of God, and put them to shame that have not?

אֶל הַקּוֹרִינְתִּים א

כָּל אִישׁ הַמִּתְפַּלֵּל אוֹ מִתְנַבֵּא וְרֹאשׁוֹ מְכֻסֶּה, מְבַזֶּה הוּא אֶת רֹאשׁוֹ
kol ish hamitpallel o mitnabbei verosho mechusseh, mevazzeh hu et rosho
Every man praying or prophesying, having his head covered, dishonoreth his head.

וְכָל אִשָּׁה הַמִּתְפַּלֶּלֶת אוֹ מִתְנַבֵּאת בְּגִלּוּי רֹאשׁ, מְבַזָּה אֶת רֹאשָׁהּ
vechol ishah hammitpallelet o mitnabbet begillui rosh, mevazzah et roshah
But every woman praying or prophesying with her head unveiled dishonoreth her head;

שֶׁכֵּן כָּמוֹהָ כְּמִי שֶׁגֻּלַּח שְׂעַר רֹאשָׁהּ
shekken kamoha kemi sheggullach se'ar roshah
for it is one and the same thing as if she were shaven.

אִם רֹאשׁ הָאִשָּׁה אֵינוֹ מְכֻסֶּה, אֲזַי גַּם רָאוּי שֶׁיִּגָּזֵז שְׂעַר רֹאשָׁהּ
im rosh ha'ishah eino mechusseh, azai gam ra'ui sheyiggazez se'ar roshah
For if a woman is not veiled, let her also be shorn:

אֲבָל אִם בּוּשָׁה הִיא לְאִשָּׁה לִגְזֹז אוֹ לְגַלֵּחַ אֶת שְׂעָרָהּ, שֶׁתִּתְכַּסֶּה
aval im bushah hi le'ishah ligzoz o legalleach et se'arah, shettitkasseh
but if it is a shame to a woman to be shorn or shaven, let her be veiled.

הָאִישׁ אָמְנָם אֵינוֹ חַיָּב לְכַסּוֹת אֶת רֹאשׁוֹ, מִהְיוֹתוֹ צֶלֶם אֱלֹהִים וּכְבוֹדוֹ
ha'ish omnam eino chayav lechassot et rosho, mihyoto tzelem elohim uchevodo
For a man indeed ought not to have his head veiled, forasmuch as he is the image and glory of God:

אַךְ הָאִשָּׁה הִיא כְּבוֹד הָאִישׁ
ach ha'ishah hi kevod ha'ish
but the woman is the glory of the man.

כִּי אֵין הָאִישׁ מִן הָאִשָּׁה, אֶלָּא הָאִשָּׁה מִן הָאִישׁ
ki ein ha'ish min ha'ishah, ella ha'ishah min ha'ish
For the man is not of the woman; but the woman of the man:

גַּם, הָאִישׁ לֹא נִבְרָא לְמַעַן הָאִשָּׁה, כִּי אִם הָאִשָּׁה לְמַעַן הָאִישׁ
gam, ha'ish lo nivra lema'an ha'ishah, ki im ha'ishah lema'an ha'ish
for neither was the man created for the woman; but the woman for the man:

מִשּׁוּם כָּךְ חוֹבָה שֶׁתִּהְיֶה מָרוּת עַל רֹאשׁ הָאִשָּׁה מִפְּנֵי הַמַּלְאָכִים
mishum kach chovah shettihyeh marut al rosh ha'ishah mippenei hammal'achim
for this cause ought the woman to have a sign of authority on her head, because of the angels.

וְאוּלָם בָּאָדוֹן אֵין הָאִשָּׁה בְּלִי תְּלוּת בָּאִישׁ וְאֵין הָאִישׁ בְּלִי תְּלוּת בָּאִשָּׁה
ve'ulam ba'adon ein ha'ishah beli tlut ba'ish ve'ein ha'ish beli tlut ba'ishah
Nevertheless, neither is the woman without the man, nor the man without the woman, in the Lord.

כִּי כְּשֵׁם שֶׁהָאִשָּׁה מִן הָאִישׁ כֵּן גַּם הָאִישׁ נוֹלַד מִן הָאִשָּׁה, וְהַכֹּל מֵאֱלֹהִים
ki keshem sheha'ishah min ha'ish ken gam ha'ish nolad min ha'ishah, vehakkol me'elohim
For as the woman is of the man, so is the man also by the woman; but all things are of God.

אֶל הַקּוֹרִינְתִּים א

מַצְפּוּן, אֲנִי אוֹמֵר - לֹא זֶה שֶׁלְּךָ אֶלָּא שֶׁל הָאַחֵר

matzpun, ani omer - lo zeh shellcha ella shel ha'acher,
conscience, I say, not thine own, but the other's;

שֶׁכֵּן לָמָּה שֶׁתִּשָּׁפֵט חֵרוּתִי עַל־יְדֵי מַצְפּוּנוֹ שֶׁל אַחֵר

shekken lammah shettishafet cheruti al-yedei matzpuno shel acher
for why is my liberty judged by another conscience?

אִם אֲנִי מְבָרֵךְ וְאוֹכֵל לָמָּה שֶׁיְּדֻבַּר בִּי רָעוֹת בִּגְלַל מַה שֶּׁאֲנִי מְבָרֵךְ עָלָיו

im ani mevarech ve'ochel lammah sheyedubbar bi ra'ot biglal mah she'ani mevarech alav
If I partake with thankfulness, why am I evil spoken of for that for which I give thanks?

וּבְכֵן אִם תֹּאכְלוּ אוֹ תִשְׁתּוּ, אוֹ כָּל מַה שֶּׁתַּעֲשׂוּ - עֲשׂוּ אֶת הַכֹּל לְמַעַן כְּבוֹד אֱלֹהִים

uvechen im tochelu o tishtu, o kol mah shetta'asu - asu et hakkol lema'an kvod elohim
Whether therefore ye eat, or drink, or whatsoever ye do, do all to the glory of God.

אַל תִּהְיוּ מִכְשׁוֹל לֹא לַיְּהוּדִים וְלֹא לַגּוֹיִם וְלֹא לִקְהִלַּת אֱלֹהִים

al tihyu michshol lo layehudim velo laggoyim velo lik'hillat elohim
Give no occasion of stumbling, either to Jews, or to Greeks, or to the church of God:

כְּדֶרֶךְ שֶׁגַּם אֲנִי מִשְׁתַּדֵּל לִהְיוֹת רָצוּי לְכֻלָּם בְּכָל דָּבָר וְאֵינֶנִּי מְבַקֵּשׁ אֶת טוֹבָתִי אֲנִי,

kederech sheggam ani mishtaddel lihyot ratzui lechullam bechol davar ve'einenni mevakkesh et tovati ani
even as I also please all men in all things, not seeking mine own profit,

אֶלָּא אֶת טוֹבַת הָרַבִּים לְמַעַן יִוָּשֵׁעוּ

ella et tovat harabbim lema'an yivvashe'u
but the profit of the many, that they may be saved.

יא

לְכוּ בְּעִקְּבוֹתַי, כְּשֵׁם שֶׁגַּם אֲנִי הוֹלֵךְ בְּעִקְּבוֹת הַמָּשִׁיחַ

lechu be'ikkvotai, keshem sheggam ani holech be'ikkvot hammashiach
Be ye imitators of me, even as I also am of Christ.

אַחַי, מְשַׁבֵּחַ אֲנִי אֶתְכֶם עַל שֶׁאַתֶּם זוֹכְרִים אוֹתִי בְּכָל דָּבָר וּמַחֲזִיקִים בַּמָּסֹרֶת שֶׁמָּסַרְתִּי לָכֶם

achai, meshabbeach ani etchem al she'attem zochrim oti bechol davar umachzikim bammasoret shemmasarti lachem
Now I praise you that ye remember me in all things, and hold fast the traditions, even as I delivered them to you.

רְצוֹנִי שֶׁתֵּדְעוּ כִּי רֹאשׁ כָּל אִישׁ הוּא הַמָּשִׁיחַ

retzoni shettede'u ki rosh kol ish hu hammashiach
But I would have you know, that the head of every man is Christ;

וְרֹאשׁ הָאִשָּׁה הוּא הָאִישׁ, וְרֹאשׁ הַמָּשִׁיחַ הוּא אֱלֹהִים

verosh ha'ishah hu ha'ish, verosh hammashiach hu elohim
and the head of the woman is the man; and the head of Christ is God.

אֶל הַקּוֹרִינְתִים א

וְאֵינֶנִּי רוֹצֶה שֶׁתִּהְיוּ שֻׁתָּפִים לַשֵּׁדִים
ve'einenni rotzeh shettihyu shuttafim lashedim
and I would not that ye should have communion with demons.

אֵינְכֶם יְכוֹלִים לִשְׁתּוֹת מִכּוֹס הָאָדוֹן וּמִכּוֹס הַשֵּׁדִים
einchem yecholim lishtot mikkos ha'adon umikkos hashedim
Ye cannot drink the cup of the Lord, and the cup of demons:

אֵינְכֶם יְכוֹלִים לְהִשְׁתַּתֵּף בְּשֻׁלְחַן הָאָדוֹן וּבְשֻׁלְחַן הַשֵּׁדִים
einchem yecholim lehishtattef beshulchan ha'adon uveshulchan hashedim
ye cannot partake of the table of the Lord, and of the table of demons.

הַאִם נָעֵז לְעוֹרֵר אֶת קִנְאַת הָאָדוֹן? כְּלוּם חֲזָקִים אֲנַחְנוּ מִמֶּנּוּ
ha'im na'ez le'orer et kin'at ha'adon? klum chazakim anachnu mimmennu
Or do we provoke the Lord to jealousy? are we stronger than he?

הַכֹּל מֻתָּר, אַךְ לֹא הַכֹּל מוֹעִיל; הַכֹּל מֻתָּר, אַךְ לֹא הַכֹּל בּוֹנֶה
hakkol muttar, ach lo hakkol mo'il; hakkol muttar, ach lo hakkol boneh
All things are lawful; but not all things are expedient. All things are lawful; but not all things edify.

אִישׁ אַל יְבַקֵּשׁ אֶת טוֹבַת עַצְמוֹ אֶלָּא אֶת טוֹבַת זוּלָתוֹ
ish al yevakkesh et tovat atzmo ella et tovat zulato
Let no man seek his own, but each his neighbor's good.

אִכְלוּ כָּל מַה שֶׁנִּמְכָּר בַּשּׁוּק וְאַל תִּשְׁאֲלוּ שׁוּם שְׁאֵלָה שֶׁל מַצְפּוּן
ichlu kol mah shennimkar bashuk ve'al tish'alu shum she'elah shel matzpun
Whatsoever is sold in the shambles, eat, asking no question for conscience' sake;

כִּי לַיהוה הָאָרֶץ וּמְלוֹאָהּ
ki lahashem ha'aretz umelo'ah
for the earth is the Lord's, and the fulness thereof.

אִם יַזְמִינְכֶם אִישׁ בִּלְתִּי מַאֲמִין וּרְצוֹנְכֶם לָלֶכֶת אֵלָיו
im yazminechem ish bilti ma'amin uretzonechem lalechet elav
If one of them that believe not biddeth you to a feast, and ye are disposed to go;

אִכְלוּ כָּל מַה שֶׁיֻּגַּשׁ לָכֶם וְאַל תִּשְׁאֲלוּ שׁוּם שְׁאֵלָה שֶׁל מַצְפּוּן
ichlu kol mah sheyuggash lachem ve'al tish'alu shum she'elah shel matzpun
whatsoever is set before you, eat, asking no question for conscience' sake.

אֲבָל אִם מִישֶׁהוּ יֹאמַר לָכֶם
aval im mishehu yomar lachem
But if any man say unto you,

זֶה נִזְבַּח לֶאֱלִיל, אַל תֹּאכְלוּ לְמַעַן הָאִישׁ שֶׁהוֹדִיעַ לָכֶם וּלְמַעַן הַמַּצְפּוּן
zeh nizbach le'elil, al tochlu lema'an ha'ish shehodia lachem ulema'an hammatzpun
This hath been offered in sacrifice, eat not, for his sake that showed it, and for conscience' sake:

אֶל הַקּוֹרִינְתִּים א

לָכֵן מִי שֶׁחוֹשֵׁב כִּי עֲמִידָתוֹ אֵיתָנָה, יִזָּהֵר פֶּן יִפֹּל
lachen mi shechoshev ki amidato eitanah, yizzaher pen yippol
Wherefore let him that thinketh he standeth take heed lest he fall.

שׁוּם נִסָּיוֹן לֹא בָּא עֲלֵיכֶם מִלְּבַד נִסָּיוֹן אֱנוֹשִׁי רָגִיל
shum nissayon lo ba aleichem millevad nissayon enoshi ragil
There hath no temptation taken you but such as man can bear:

נֶאֱמָן הוּא הָאֱלֹהִים וְלֹא יַנִּיחַ לָכֶם לְהִתְנַסּוֹת לְמַעְלָה מִיְּכָלְתְּכֶם
ne'eman hu ha'elohim velo yanniach lachem lehitnassot lema'lah miyacholtechem
but God is faithful, who will not suffer you to be tempted above that ye are able;

אֶלָּא עִם הַנִּסָּיוֹן יָכִין גַּם אֶת דֶּרֶךְ הַמּוֹצָא כְּדֵי שֶׁתּוּכְלוּ לַעֲמֹד בּוֹ
ella im hannissayon yachin gam et derech hammotza kedei shettuchlu la'amod bo
but will with the temptation make also the way of escape, that ye may be able to endure it.

עַל כֵּן, חֲבִיבַי, תִּבְרְחוּ מֵעֲבוֹדַת אֱלִילִים
al ken, chavivai, tivrechu me'avodat elilim
Wherefore, my beloved, flee from idolatry.

כְּאֶל אֲנָשִׁים נְבוֹנִים אֲנִי מְדַבֵּר; שִׁפְטוּ אַתֶּם מַה שֶּׁאֲנִי אוֹמֵר
ke'el anashim nevonim ani medabber; shiftu attem mah she'ani omer
I speak as to wise men; judge ye what I say.

כּוֹס הַבְּרָכָה שֶׁאָנוּ מְבָרְכִים עָלֶיהָ, הַאֵין הִיא הִתְחַבְּרוּת לְדַם הַמָּשִׁיחַ
kos habbrachah she'anu mevarechim aleiha, ha'ein hi hitchabberut ledam hammashiach
The cup of blessing which we bless, is it not a communion of the blood of Christ?

הַלֶּחֶם שֶׁאָנוּ בּוֹצְעִים, הַאֵין הוּא הִתְחַבְּרוּת לְגוּף הַמָּשִׁיחַ
hallechem she'anu botze'im, ha'ein hu hitchabberut leguf hammashiach
The bread which we break, is it not a communion of the body of Christ?

מִשּׁוּם שֶׁהַלֶּחֶם אֶחָד, אֲנַחְנוּ הָרַבִּים גּוּף אֶחָד; שֶׁכֵּן כֻּלָּנוּ מִשְׁתַּתְּפִים בַּלֶּחֶם הָאֶחָד
mishum shehallechem echad, anachnu harabbim guf echad; shekken kullanu mishtattfim ballechem ha'echad
seeing that we, who are many, are one bread, one body: for we all partake of the one bread.

רְאוּ נָא אֶת עַם יִשְׂרָאֵל. הַאִם אֵין הָאוֹכְלִים מִן הַקָּרְבָּנוֹת שֻׁתָּפִים בַּמִּזְבֵּחַ
re'u na et am yisra'el. ha'im ein ha'ochelim min hakkorbanot shuttafim bammizbeach
Behold Israel after the flesh: have not they that eat the sacrifices communion with the altar?

וּבְכֵן מַה אֲנִי אוֹמֵר - שֶׁיֵּשׁ מַמָּשׁ בְּזִבְחֵי אֱלִילִים? שֶׁיֵּשׁ מַמָּשׁ בָּאֱלִיל
uvechen mah ani omer - sheyesh mammash bezivchei elilim? sheyesh mammash ba'elil
What say I then? that a thing sacrificed to idols is anything, or that an idol is anything?

לֹא! אֶלָּא מַה שֶׁהַגּוֹיִם מַקְרִיבִים, לְשֵׁדִים הֵם מַקְרִיבִים וְלֹא לֵאלֹהִים
lo! ella mah shehaggoyim makrivim, leshedim hem makrivim velo le'elohim
But I say, that the things which the Gentiles sacrifice, they sacrifice to demons, and not to God:

אֶל הַקּוֹרִינְתִּים א

וְכֻלָּם נִטְבְּלוּ לְמֹשֶׁה בֶּעָנָן וּבַיָּם
vechullam nitbelu lemosheh be'anan uvayam
and were all baptized unto Moses in the cloud and in the sea;

כֻּלָּם אָכְלוּ אוֹתוֹ מַאֲכָל רוּחָנִי
kullam achlu oto ma'achal ruchani
and did all eat the same spiritual food;

וְכֻלָּם שָׁתוּ אוֹתוֹ מַשְׁקֶה רוּחָנִי, כִּי שָׁתוּ מִן הַצּוּר הָרוּחָנִי הַהוֹלֵךְ עִמָּהֶם וְהַצּוּר הוּא הַמָּשִׁיחַ
vechullam shatu oto mashkeh ruchani, ki shatu min hatzur haruchani haholech immahem vehatzur hu hammashiach
and did all drink the same spiritual drink: for they drank of a spiritual rock that followed them: and the rock was Christ.

אֲבָל בְּרֻבָּם לֹא רָצָה אֱלֹהִים וְהֵם הוּמְתוּ בַּמִּדְבָּר
aval berubbam lo ratzah elohim vehem humetu bammidbar
Howbeit with most of them God was not well pleased: for they were overthrown in the wilderness.

כָּל זֶה הָיָה דֻגְמָה לָנוּ, לְמַעַן לֹא נִתְאַוֶּה לִרְעוֹת כְּשֵׁם שֶׁהִתְאַוּוּ הֵם
kol zeh hayah dugmah lanu, lema'an lo nit'avveh lera'ot keshem shehit'avvu hem
Now these things were our examples, to the intent we should not lust after evil things, as they also lusted.

אַל תִּהְיוּ עוֹבְדֵי אֱלִילִים כְּשֵׁם שֶׁהָיוּ כַּמָּה מֵהֶם
al tihyu ovdei elilim keshem shehayu kammah mehem
Neither be ye idolaters, as were some of them;

כַּכָּתוּב: וַיֵּשֶׁב הָעָם לֶאֱכֹל וְשָׁתוֹ וַיָּקֻמוּ לְצַחֵק
kakkatuv: vayeshev ha'am le'echol veshato vayakumu letzachek
as it is written, The people sat down to eat and drink, and rose up to play.

גַּם אַל נִזְנֶה כְּשֵׁם שֶׁזָּנוּ כַּמָּה מֵהֶם וּבְיוֹם אֶחָד נָפְלוּ עֶשְׂרִים וּשְׁלוֹשָׁה אֶלֶף
gam al nizneh keshem shezzanu kammah mehem uveyom echad naflu esrim ushloshah elef
Neither let us commit fornication, as some of them committed, and fell in one day three and twenty thousand.

וְאַל נְנַסֶּה אֶת יהוה כְּשֵׁם שֶׁנִּסּוּהוּ אֲנָשִׁים מֵהֶם וְהוּמְתוּ עַל־יְדֵי הַנְּחָשִׁים
ve'al nenasseh et hashem keshem shennissuhu anashim mehem vehumetu al-yedei hannechashim
Neither let us make trial of the Lord, as some of them made trial, and perished by the serpents.

אַף אַל תִּתְלוֹנְנוּ כְּשֵׁם שֶׁהִתְלוֹנְנוּ כַּמָּה מֵהֶם וּמֵתוּ בִּידֵי הַמַּלְאָךְ הַמַּשְׁחִית
af al titlonenu keshem shehitlonenu kammah mehem umetu biyedei hammal'acha hammashchit
Neither murmur ye, as some of them murmured, and perished by the destroyer.

מַה שֶּׁקָּרָה לָהֶם הָיָה לֶקַח לְדֻגְמָה
mah shekkarah lahem hayah lekach ledugmah
Now these things happened unto them by way of example;

וְזֶה נִכְתַּב כְּדֵי לְהַזְהִיר אוֹתָנוּ, אֲנַחְנוּ אֲשֶׁר קִצֵּי הָעוֹלָמִים הִגִּיעוּ אֵלֵינוּ
vezeh nichtav kedei lehazhir otanu, anachnu asher kitzei ha'olamim higgi'u eleinu
and they were written for our admonition, upon whom the ends of the ages are come.

אֶל הַקּוֹרִינְתִּים א

לְמַעַן הַחַלָּשִׁים אֲנִי חַלָּשׁ כְּדֵי לְהַשִּׂיג אֶת הַחַלָּשִׁים
lema'an hachallashim ani challash kedei lehassig et hachallashim
To the weak I became weak, that I might gain the weak:

אֲנִי הַכֹּל לְמַעַן הַכֹּל כְּדֵי שֶׁאוֹשִׁיעַ לְפָחוֹת כַּמָּה מֵהֶם
ani hakkol lema'an hakkol kedei she'oshia lefachot kammah mehem
I am become all things to all men, that I may by all means save some.

אַךְ אֶת הַכֹּל אֲנִי עוֹשֶׂה בַּעֲבוּר הַבְּשׂוֹרָה כְּדֵי שֶׁיִּהְיֶה לִי חֵלֶק בָּהּ
ach et hakkol ani oseh ba'avur habbsorah kedei sheyihyeh li chelek bah
And I do all things for the gospel's sake, that I may be a joint partaker thereof.

הַאִם אֵינְכֶם יוֹדְעִים שֶׁהָרָצִים בְּאִצְטַדְיוֹן אָמְנָם רָצִים כֻּלָּם, אֲבָל אֶחָד מְקַבֵּל אֶת הַפְּרָס
ha'im einechem yode'im sheharatzim be'itztadyon omnam ratzim kullam, aval echad mekabbel et happeras?
Know ye not that they that run in a race run all, but one receiveth the prize?

בְּדוֹמֶה לְכָךְ, רוּצוּ לְמַעַן תַּשִּׂיגוּהוּ
bedomeh lechach, rutzu lema'an tashguhu
Even so run; that ye may attain.

כָּל מִתְחָרֶה נוֹהֵג לְהִנָּזֵר בְּכָל הַתְּחוּמִים
kol mitchareh noheg lehinnazer bechol hattechumim
And every man that striveth in the games exerciseth self-control in all things.

הַלָּלוּ - כְּדֵי לְהַשִּׂיג זֵר נוֹבֵל, אֲבָל אֲנַחְנוּ כְּדֵי לְהַשִּׂיג זֵר שֶׁלֹּא יִבֹּל
hallalu - kedei lehassig zer novel, aval anachnu kedei lehassig zer shello yibbol
Now they do it to receive a corruptible crown; but we an incorruptible.

לָכֵן אֲנִי רָץ לֹא כְּמִי שֶׁמְּגַשֵּׁשׁ בָּאֲפֵלָה, וַאֲנִי נֶאֱבָק לֹא כְּמִי שֶׁמַּכֶּה בָּאֲוִיר
lachen ani ratz lo kemi shemmegashesh ba'afelah, va'ani ne'evak lo kemi shemmakkeh ba'avir
I therefore so run, as not uncertainly; so fight I, as not beating the air:

אֶלָּא נוֹהֵג אֲנִי בִּקְשִׁיחוּת עִם גּוּפִי וּמְשַׁעְבְּדוֹ
ella noheg ani bikshichut im gufi umesha'bedo
but I buffet my body, and bring it into bondage:

שֶׁמָּא לְאַחַר שֶׁאַטִּיף לַאֲחֵרִים, אֲנִי עַצְמִי אֶמָּצֵא פָּסוּל
shemma le'achar she'attif la'acherim, ani atzmi emmatzei pasul
lest by any means, after that I have preached to others, I myself should be rejected.

▌

אַחַי, אֵינֶנִּי רוֹצֶה שֶׁיֵּעָלֵם מִכֶּם שֶׁאֲבוֹתֵינוּ כֻּלָּם הָיוּ תַּחַת הֶעָנָן, וְכֻלָּם עָבְרוּ בְּתוֹךְ הַיָּם
achai, einenni rotzeh sheye'alem mikkem she'avoteinu kullam hayu tachat he'anan, vechullam averu betoch hayam
For I would not, brethren, have you ignorant, that our fathers were all under the cloud, and all passed through the sea;

אֶל הַקּוֹרִינְתִים א

כִּי כַּאֲשֶׁר אֲנִי מְבַשֵּׂר אֶת הַבְּשׂוֹרָה אֵין לִי מַה לְהִתְהַלֵּל, שֶׁכֵּן חוֹבָה מֻטֶּלֶת עָלַי

ki ka'asher ani mevasser et habbesorah ein li mah lehit'hallel, shekken chovah muttelet alai
For if I preach the gospel, I have nothing to glory of; for necessity is laid upon me;

וְאוֹי לִי אִם לֹא אֲבַשֵּׂר

ve'oy li im lo avasser
for woe is unto me, if I preach not the gospel.

אִם מֵרְצוֹנִי אֲנִי עוֹשֶׂה זֹאת, מַגִּיעַ לִי שָׂכָר. אֲבָל אִם לֹא מֵרְצוֹנִי, הֲרֵי שֶׁתַּפְקִיד הֻפְקַד בְּיָדִי

im meretzoni ani oseh zot, maggia li sachar. aval im lo meretzoni, harei shettafkid hufkad beyadi
For if I do this of mine own will, I have a reward: but if not of mine own will, I have a stewardship intrusted to me.

מָה אֵפוֹא שְׂכָרִי

mah efo schari
What then is my reward?

בָּזֶה שֶׁאֲנִי מְבַשֵּׂר אֶת הַבְּשׂוֹרָה וּמַצִּיעַ אוֹתָהּ בְּלֹא מְחִיר מִבְּלִי לְנַצֵּל אֶת הַזְּכוּת שֶׁיֵּשׁ לִי בַּבְּשׂוֹרָה

bazeh she'ani mevasser et habbsorah umatzia otah belo mechir mibbeli lenatzel et hazzechut sheyesh li babbsorah
That, when I preach the gospel, I may make the gospel without charge, so as not to use to the full my right in the gospel.

אַף כִּי אֵינֶנִּי מְשֻׁעְבָּד לְאִישׁ שִׁעְבַּדְתִּי אֶת עַצְמִי לַכֹּל כְּדֵי לִרְכֹּשׁ אֶת הָרַבִּים

af ki einenni meshu'bad le'ish shi'badti et atzmi lakkol kedei lirkosh et harabbim
For though I was free from all men, I brought myself under bondage to all, that I might gain the more.

לְמַעַן הַיְהוּדִים אֲנִי כִּיהוּדִי כְּדֵי לְהַשִּׂיג יְהוּדִים; לְמַעַן הַכְּפוּפִים לַתּוֹרָה אֲנִי כְּמוֹ כָּפוּף לַתּוֹרָה

lema'an hayehudim ani kiyehudi kedei lehashg yehudim; lema'an hakkefufim lattorah ani kemo kafuf lattorah
And to the Jews I became as a Jew, that I might gain Jews; to them that are under the law, as under the law,

הֲגַם שֶׁאֵינֶנִּי כָּפוּף לַתּוֹרָה - כְּדֵי לְהַשִּׂיג אֶת הַכְּפוּפִים לַתּוֹרָה

hagam she'einenni kafuf lattorah - kedei lehassig et hakkefufim lattorah
not being myself under the law, that I might gain them that are under the law;

לְמַעַן אֵלֶּה שֶׁאֵין לָהֶם תּוֹרָה אֲנִי כְּמוֹ בְּלִי תּוֹרָה

lema'an elleh she'ein lahem torah ani kemo bli torah
to them that are without law, as without law,

אַף שֶׁאֵינֶנִּי עוֹמֵד בְּלֹא תּוֹרַת אֱלֹהִים בִּהְיוֹתִי כָּפוּף לְתוֹרַת הַמָּשִׁיחַ

af she'einenni omed belo torat elohim bihyoti kafuf letorat hammashiach
not being without law to God, but under law to Christ,

כְּדֵי לְהַשִּׂיג אֶת אֵלֶּה שֶׁאֵין לָהֶם תּוֹרָה

kedei lehasig et elleh she'ein lahem torah
that I might gain them that are without law.

אֶל הַקּוֹרִינְתִּים א

הֲרֵי בְּתוֹרַת מֹשֶׁה כָּתוּב
harei betorat mosheh katuv
For it is written in the law of Moses,

לֹא־תַחְסֹם שׁוֹר בְּדִישׁוֹ. הַאִם לַשְּׁוָרִים דּוֹאֵג אֱלֹהִים
lo-tachsom shor bedisho. ha'im lashvarim do'eg elohim
Thou shalt not muzzle the ox when he treadeth out the corn. Is it for the oxen that God careth,

אוֹ שֶׁבִּכְלָל לְמַעֲנֵנוּ הוּא אוֹמֵר זֹאת? אָכֵן לְמַעֲנֵנוּ זֶה נִכְתַּב
o shebbichlal lema'anenu hu omer zot? achen lema'anenu zeh nichtav
or saith he it assuredly for our sake? Yea, for our sake it was written:

כְּדֵי שֶׁהַחוֹרֵשׁ יַחֲרֹשׁ בְּתִקְוָה וְהַדָּשׁ יָדוּשׁ בְּתִקְוָה לְהִשְׁתַּתֵּף בַּיְבוּל
kedei shehachoresh yacharosh betikvah vehaddash yadush betikvah lehishtattef bayvul
because he that ploweth ought to plow in hope, and he that thresheth, to thresh in hope of partaking.

אִם זָרַעְנוּ לָכֶם דְּבָרִים רוּחָנִיִּים, מָה רְבוּתָא בְּכָךְ אִם נִקְצֹר דְּבָרִים חָמְרִיִּים מִכֶּם
im zara'nu lachem devarim ruchaniyim, mah revuta bechach im niktzor devarim chomeriyim mikkem
If we sowed unto you spiritual things, is it a great matter if we shall reap your carnal things?

וְאִם לַאֲחֵרִים יֵשׁ חֵלֶק בַּזְּכוּת עֲלֵיכֶם, הֲלֹא כָּל שֶׁכֵּן לָנוּ
ve'im la'acherim yesh chelek bazzechut aleichem, halo kol shekken lanu
If others partake of this right over you, do not we yet more?

אֲבָל לֹא נִצַּלְנוּ אֶת הַזְּכוּת הַזֹּאת, אֶלָּא סוֹבְלִים אָנוּ הַכֹּל לְמַעַן לֹא נָשִׂים שׁוּם מִכְשׁוֹל לִבְשׂוֹרַת הַמָּשִׁיחַ
aval lo nitzalnu et hazzechut hazzot, ella sovelim anu hakkol lema'an lo nasim shum michshol livsorat hammashiach
Nevertheless we did not use this right; but we bear all things, that we may cause no hindrance to the gospel of Christ.

הַאֵינְכֶם יוֹדְעִים כִּי הָעוֹבְדִים בַּקֹּדֶשׁ פַּרְנָסָתָם מִבֵּית הַמִּקְדָּשׁ
ha'einechem yode'im ki ha'ovedim bakkodesh parnasatam mibbeit hammikdash
Know ye not that they that minister about sacred things eat of the things of the temple,

וּמְשָׁרְתֵי הַמִּזְבֵּחַ נוֹטְלִים אֶת חֶלְקָם מִן הַמִּזְבֵּחַ
umesharetei hammizbeach notelim et chelkam min hammizbeach
and they that wait upon the altar have their portion with the altar?

כָּךְ גַּם תִּקֵּן הָאָדוֹן, שֶׁהַמַּכְרִיזִים אֶת הַבְּשׂוֹרָה יִחְיוּ מִן הַבְּשׂוֹרָה
kach gam tikken ha'adon, shehammachrizim et habbesorah yichyu min habbesorah
Even so did the Lord ordain that they that proclaim the gospel should live of the gospel.

בְּרַם אֲנִי לֹא נִצַּלְתִּי דָּבָר מִן הַדְּבָרִים הָאֵלֶּה, אַף לֹא כָּתַבְתִּי זֹאת כְּדֵי שֶׁלִּי יִהְיֶה כָּךְ
bram ani lo nitzalti davar min haddvarim ha'elleh, af lo katavti zot kedei shelli yihyeh kach
But I have used none of these things: and I write not these things that it may be so done in my case;

מוּטָב לִי לָמוּת וְשֶׁלֹּא יָשִׂים אִישׁ אֶת תְּהִלָּתִי זוֹ לָרִיק
mutav li lamut veshello yasim ish et tehillati zo larik
for it were good for me rather to die, than that any man should make my glorying void.

אֶל הַקּוֹרִינְתִּים א

לְמַעַן לֹא אַכְשִׁיל אֶת אָחִי
lema'an lo achshil et achi
that I cause not my brother to stumble.

ט

הַאִם אֵינֶנִּי חָפְשִׁי? הַאִם אֵינֶנִּי שָׁלִיחַ? הַאִם לֹא רָאִיתִי אֶת יֵשׁוּעַ אֲדוֹנֵנוּ? הַאִם אַתֶּם אֵינְכֶם פֹּעֲלֵי בָּאָדוֹן
ha'im einenni chofshi? ha'im einenni shaliach? ha'im lo ra'iti et yeshua adonenu? ha'im attem einchem po'ali ba'adon
Am I not free? am I not an apostle? have I not seen Jesus our Lord? are not ye my work in the Lord?

אִם לַאֲחֵרִים אֵינֶנִּי שָׁלִיחַ, לָכֶם בְּוַדַּאי שֶׁאֲנִי שָׁלִיחַ, שֶׁהֲרֵי חוֹתַם שְׁלִיחוּתִי אַתֶּם בָּאָדוֹן
im la'acherim einenni shaliach, lachem bevadda she'ani shaliach, sheharei chotam shlichuti attem ba'adon
If to others I am not an apostle, yet at least I am to you; for the seal of mine apostleship are ye in the Lord.

תְּשׁוּבָתִי לַמּוֹתְחִים עָלַי בִּקֹּרֶת הִיא זֹאת
tshuvati lammotechim alai bikkoret hi zot
My defence to them that examine me is this.

הַאֵין לָנוּ רְשׁוּת לֶאֱכֹל וְלִשְׁתּוֹת
ha'ein lanu reshut le'echol velishtot
Have we no right to eat and to drink?

הַאֵין לָנוּ רְשׁוּת לְהוֹבִיל אִתָּנוּ אִשָּׁה מַאֲמִינָה
ha'ein lanu reshut lehovil ittanu ishah ma'aminah
Have we no right to lead about a wife that is a believer,

כְּמוֹ לְיֶתֶר הַשְּׁלִיחִים, לַאֲחֵי הָאָדוֹן וּלְכֵיפָא
kemo leyeter hashelichim, la'achei ha'adon ulecheifa
even as the rest of the apostles, and the brethren of the Lord, and Cephas?

אוֹ רַק אֲנִי וּבַר־נַבָּא אֵין לָנוּ רְשׁוּת לִהְיוֹת פְּטוּרִים מֵעֲבוֹדָה
o rak ani uvar-nabba ein lanu reshut lihyot pturim me'avodah
Or I only and Barnabas, have we not a right to forbear working?

מִי מְשָׁרֵת בַּצָּבָא וּמְשַׁלֵּם אֶת כַּלְכָּלָתוֹ שֶׁלּוֹ? מִי נוֹטֵעַ כֶּרֶם וְאֵינוֹ אוֹכֵל מִפִּרְיוֹ
mi mesharet batzava umeshallem et kalkalato shello? mi notea kerem ve'eino ochel mippiryo
What soldier ever serveth at his own charges? who planteth a vineyard, and eateth not the fruit thereof?

מִי רוֹעֶה עֵדֶר וְאֵינוֹ שׁוֹתֶה מִן הֶחָלָב שֶׁל הָעֵדֶר
mi ro'eh eder ve'eino shoteh min hechalav shel ha'eder
or who feedeth a flock, and eateth not of the milk of the flock?

וְכִי אֲנִי אוֹמֵר אֶת הַדְּבָרִים הָאֵלֶּה עַל־פִּי בְּנֵי אָדָם? הַאֵין גַּם הַתּוֹרָה אוֹמֶרֶת זֹאת
vechi ani omer et haddvarim ha'elleh al-pi bnei adam? ha'ein gam hattorah omeret zot
Do I speak these things after the manner of men? or saith not the law also the same?

אֶל הַקּוֹרִינְתִּים א

הֲרֵי לָנוּ יֵשׁ אֱלֹהִים אֶחָד, הָאָב אֲשֶׁר הַכֹּל מִמֶּנּוּ וַאֲנַחְנוּ לְמַעֲנוֹ
harei lanu yesh elohim echad, ha'av asher hakkol mimmennu va'anachnu lema'ano
yet to us there is one God, the Father, of whom are all things, and we unto him;

וְאָדוֹן אֶחָד, יֵשׁוּעַ הַמָּשִׁיחַ, אֲשֶׁר הַכֹּל דַּרְכּוֹ וְדַרְכּוֹ אֲנַחְנוּ מִתְקַיְּמִים
ve'adon echad, yeshua hammashiach, asher hakkol darko vedarko anachnu mitkayemim
and one Lord, Jesus Christ, through whom are all things, and we through him.

אַךְ לֹא הַכֹּל יוֹדְעִים זֹאת
ach lo hakkol yod'im zot
Howbeit there is not in all men that knowledge:

יֵשׁ אֲנָשִׁים שֶׁעֲדַיִן רְגִילִים לֶאֱלִיל
yesh anashim she'adayin regilim le'elil
but some, being used until now to the idol,

וְאוֹכְלִים אֶת הַמַּאֲכָל כְּאִלּוּ הוּא זֶבַח לֶאֱלִיל, וּמֵאַחַר שֶׁמַּצְפּוּנָם חַלָּשׁ הֲרֵי שֶׁהוּא נִטְמָא
ve'ochelim et hamma'achal ke'illu hu zevach le'elil, ume'achar shemmatzpunam challash harei shehu nitma
eat as of a thing sacrificed to an idol; and their conscience being weak is defiled.

אוּלָם הַמַּאֲכָל לֹא יְקָרֵב אוֹתָנוּ לֵאלֹהִים. אִם לֹא נֹאכַל לֹא נַפְסִיד, וְאִם נֹאכַל לֹא נַשִּׂיג יִתְרוֹן
ulam hamma'achal lo yekarev otanu lelohim. im lo nochal lo nafsid, ve'im nochal lo nassig yitron
But food will not commend us to God: neither, if we eat not, are we the worse; nor, if we eat, are we the better.

אֲבָל הִזָּהֲרוּ שֶׁלֹּא תִּהְיֶה רְשׁוּתְכֶם זוֹ מִכְשׁוֹל לַחַלָּשִׁים
aval hizzaharu shello tihyeh reshutechem zo michshol lachallashim
But take heed lest by any means this liberty of yours become a stumblingblock to the weak.

שֶׁכֵּן אִם יִרְאוּ אוֹתְךָ, אַתָּה אֲשֶׁר לְךָ הַדַּעַת, מֵסֵב בְּבֵית אֱלִילִים
shekken im yir'u otecha, attah asher lecha hadda'at, mesev beveit elilim
For if a man see thee who hast knowledge sitting at meat in an idol's temple,

כְּלוּם לֹא יְעוֹדֵד הַדָּבָר אֶת בַּעַל הַמַּצְפּוּן הַחַלָּשׁ לֶאֱכֹל זִבְחֵי אֱלִילִים
klum lo ye'oded haddavar et ba'al hammatzpun hachallash le'echol zivchei elilim
will not his conscience, if he is weak, be emboldened to eat things sacrificed to idols?

וּבִגְלַל הַדַּעַת שֶׁלְּךָ יֵהָרֵס הָאָח הַחַלָּשׁ שֶׁלְּמַעֲנוֹ מֵת הַמָּשִׁיחַ
uviglal hadda'at shellcha yehares ha'ach hachallash shellema'ano met hammashiach
For through thy knowledge he that is weak perisheth, the brother for whose sake Christ died.

אִם כָּךְ תֶּחֶטְאוּ לַאֲחֵיכֶם וְתִפְגְּעוּ בְּמַצְפּוּנָם הַחַלָּשׁ - לַמָּשִׁיחַ אַתֶּם חוֹטְאִים
im kach techet'u la'acheichem vetifge'u bematzpunam hachallash - lammashiach attem chot'im
And thus, sinning against the brethren, and wounding their conscience when it is weak, ye sin against Christ.

לָכֵן אִם מַאֲכָל הוּא מִכְשׁוֹל לְאָחִי, לֹא אֹכַל בָּשָׂר לְעוֹלָם
lachen im ma'achal hu michshol le'achi, lo ochal basar le'olam
Wherefore, if meat causeth my brother to stumble, I will eat no flesh for evermore,

אֶל הַקּוֹרִינְתִּים א

וְזֶה שֶׁאֵינוֹ נוֹשֵׂא אוֹתָהּ יֵיטִיב עוֹד יוֹתֵר לַעֲשׂוֹת
vezeh she'eino nosei otah yeitiv od yoter la'asot
and he that giveth her not in marriage shall do better.

הָאִשָּׁה קְשׁוּרָה לְבַעְלָהּ כָּל זְמַן שֶׁהוּא חַי
ha'ishah kshurah leva'lah kol zeman shehu chai
A wife is bound for so long time as her husband liveth;

וְאִם יָמוּת הַבַּעַל, רַשָּׁאִית הִיא לְהִנָּשֵׂא לְמִי שֶׁתִּרְצֶה וּבִלְבַד שֶׁזֶּה יִהְיֶה בָּאָדוֹן
ve'im yamut habba'al, rasha'it hi lehinnasei lemi shettirtzeh uvilvad shezzeh yihyeh ba'adon
but if the husband be dead, she is free to be married to whom she will; only in the Lord.

וְאוּלָם הִיא תִּהְיֶה מְאֻשֶּׁרֶת יוֹתֵר אִם תִּשָּׁאֵר פְּנוּיָה; זוֹ דַּעְתִּי, וְחוֹשְׁבַנִי שֶׁגַּם בִּי רוּחַ אֱלֹהִים
ve'ulam hi tihyeh me'usheret yoter im tisha'er penuyah; zo da'ti, vechoshvani sheggam bi ruach elohim
But she is happier if she abide as she is, after my judgment: and I think that I also have the Spirit of God.

ח

בְּעִנְיַן זִבְחֵי אֱלִילִים
be'inyan zivchei elilim
Now concerning things sacrificed to idols:

אָנוּ יוֹדְעִים שֶׁלְּכֻלָּנוּ דַּעַת. דַּעַת מְבִיאָה לִידֵי גַּאֲוָה, אַךְ הָאַהֲבָה בּוֹנָה
anu yod'im shellechullanu da'at. da'at mevi'ah lidei ga'avah, ach ha'ahavah bonah
We know that we all have knowledge. Knowledge puffeth up, but love edifieth.

מִי שֶׁסָּבוּר כִּי הוּא יוֹדֵעַ דְּבַר מָה, עֲדַיִן אֵינוֹ יוֹדֵעַ כְּפִי שֶׁצָּרִיךְ לָדַעַת
mi shessavur ki hu yodea dvar mah, adayin eino yodea kefi shetzarich lada'at
If any man thinketh that he knoweth anything, he knoweth not yet as he ought to know;

אֲבָל מִי שֶׁאוֹהֵב אֶת אֱלֹהִים, הוּא יָדוּעַ לֵאלֹהִים
aval mi she'ohev et elohim, hu yadua le'elohim
but if any man loveth God, the same is known by him.

וּבְכֵן בְּנוֹגֵעַ לַאֲכִילַת זִבְחֵי אֱלִילִים
uvchen benogea la'achilat zivchei elilim
Concerning therefore the eating of things sacrificed to idols,

אֲנַחְנוּ יוֹדְעִים כִּי אֵין מַמָּשׁוּת לֶאֱלִיל בָּעוֹלָם וְכִי אֵין אֱלֹהִים אֶלָּא אֶחָד
anachnu yod'im ki ein mammashut le'elil ba'olam vechi ein elohim ella echad
we know that no idol is anything in the world, and that there is no God but one.

וְגַם אִם יֵשׁ הַקְּרוּיִים אֵלִים, אִם בַּשָּׁמַיִם וְאִם בָּאָרֶץ, - כְּשֵׁם שֶׁיֵּשׁ אֵלִים רַבִּים וַאֲדוֹנִים רַבִּים
vegam im yesh hakkeruyim elim, im bashamayim ve'im ba'aretz, - keshem sheyesh elim rabbim va'adonim rabbim
For though there be that are called gods, whether in heaven or on earth; as there are gods many, and lords many;

אֶל הַקּוֹרִינְתִּים א

אֲבָל מִי שֶׁנָּשׂוּי דּוֹאֵג לַדְּבָרִים הָאַרְצִיִּים, אֵיךְ יֵיטַב בְּעֵינֵי הָאִשָּׁה
aval mi shennasui do'eg laddevarim ha'artziyim, eich yitav be'einei ha'ishah
but he that is married is careful for the things of the world, how he may please his wife,

וּתְשׂוּמַת לִבּוֹ מְפֻלֶּגֶת. וְהָאִשָּׁה שֶׁאֵינָהּ נְשׂוּאָה, אוֹ הַבְּתוּלָה, דּוֹאֶגֶת לַדְּבָרִים אֲשֶׁר לָאָדוֹן
utesumat libbo mefulleget. veha'ishah she'einah nesu'ah, o habbetulah, do'eget laddevarim asher la'adon
and is divided. So also the woman that is unmarried and the virgin is careful for the things of the Lord,

כְּדֵי שֶׁתִּהְיֶה קְדוֹשָׁה הֵן בַּגּוּף וְהֵן בָּרוּחַ
kedei shettihyeh kedoshah hen bagguf vehen baruach
that she may be holy both in body and in spirit:

אֲבָל הַנְּשׂוּאָה דּוֹאֶגֶת לַדְּבָרִים הָאַרְצִיִּים, כֵּיצַד תֵּיטַב בְּעֵינֵי בַּעְלָהּ
aval hannesu'ah do'eget laddevarim ha'artziyim, keitzad titav be'einei ba'lah
but she that is married is careful for the things of the world, how she may please her husband.

זֹאת אֲנִי אוֹמֵר לְטוֹבַתְכֶם, לֹא כְּדֵי לְהַכְבִּיד עֲלֵיכֶם, אֶלָּא כְּדֵי שֶׁתִּתְנַהֲגוּ כַּיָּאוּת
zot ani omer letovatchem, lo kedei lehachbid aleichem, ella kedei shettitnahagu kaya'ut
And this I say for your own profit; not that I may cast a snare upon you, but for that which is seemly,

וְתִתְמַסְּרוּ לָאָדוֹן בְּאֵין מַפְרִיעַ
vetitmasseru la'adon be'ein mafria
and that ye may attend upon the Lord without distraction.

מִי שֶׁסָּבוּר כִּי אֵינוֹ נוֹהֵג כַּשּׁוּרָה בִּבְתוּלָתוֹ
mi shessavur ki eino noheg kashurah bivtulato
But if any man thinketh that he behaveth himself unseemly toward his virgin daughter,

אִם יַעַבְרוּ עָלֶיהָ יְמֵי נְעוּרֶיהָ
im ya'avru aleiha yemei ne'ureiha
if she be past the flower of her age,

וְשֶׁהַדָּבָר הוּא בִּלְתִּי נִמְנָע, יַעֲשֶׂה כִּרְצוֹנוֹ. שֶׁיִּתְחַתְּנוּ; אֵין הוּא חוֹטֵא
veshehaddavar hu bilti nimna, ya'aseh kirtzono. sheyitchattenu; ein hu chotei
and if need so requireth, let him do what he will; he sinneth not; let them marry.

אֲבָל אִישׁ אֵיתָן בְּדַעְתּוֹ, שֶׁאֵינוֹ שָׁרוּי בְּצֹרֶךְ וְהוּא שׁוֹלֵט עַל רְצוֹנוֹ
aval ish eitan beda'to, she'eino sharui betzorech vehu sholet al retzono
But he that standeth stedfast in his heart, having no necessity, but hath power as touching his own will,

אִם הֶחְלִיט בִּלְבָבוֹ לִשְׁמֹר אֶת בְּתוּלָתוֹ - טוֹב יַעֲשֶׂה
im hechlit bilvavo lishmor et betulato - tov ya'aseh
and hath determined this in his own heart, to keep his own virgin daughter, shall do well.

לְפִיכָךְ, הַנּוֹשֵׂא אֶת בְּתוּלָתוֹ טוֹב הוּא עוֹשֶׂה
lefichach, hannosei et betulato tov hu oseh
So then both he that giveth his own virgin daughter in marriage doeth well;

אֶל הַקּוֹרִינְתִּים א

אֲנִי סָבוּר שֶׁמִּפְּנֵי הַמְּצוּקָה הַנּוֹכְחִית
ani savur shemmippnei hammetzukah hannochechit
I think therefore that this is good by reason of the distress that is upon us, namely,

מוּטָב לְאִישׁ לְהִשָּׁאֵר כָּךְ
mutav le'ish lehisha'er kach
that it is good for a man to be as he is.

אִם אַתָּה קָשׁוּר לְאִשָּׁה, אַל תְּבַקֵּשׁ לְהַתִּיר אֶת הַקֶּשֶׁר; אִם אֵינְךָ קָשׁוּר לְאִשָּׁה, אַל תְּבַקֵּשׁ לְךָ אִשָּׁה
im attah kashur le'ishah, al tevakkesh lehattir et hakkesher; im eincha kashur le'ishah, al tevakkesh lecha ishah
Art thou bound unto a wife? seek not to be loosed. Art thou loosed from a wife? seek not a wife.

אַךְ אִם תִּקַּח לְךָ אִשָּׁה אֵינְךָ חוֹטֵא. וְהַבְּתוּלָה אִם תִּנָּשֵׂא אֵינֶנָּה חוֹטֵאת
ach im tikkach lecha ishah eincha chote. vehabbetulah im tinnasei einennah chotet
But shouldest thou marry, thou hast not sinned; and if a virgin marry, she hath not sinned.

אֶלָּא שֶׁיִּהְיוּ לָהֶם צָרוֹת בִּבְשָׂרָם וַאֲנִי חָס עֲלֵיכֶם
ella sheyihyu lahem tzarot bivsaram va'ani chas aleichem
Yet such shall have tribulation in the flesh: and I would spare you.

וְזֹאת אֹמַר לָכֶם, אַחַי: הַזְּמַן דּוֹחֵק
vezot omar lachem, achai: hazzman dochek.
But this I say, brethren, the time is shortened,

עַל כֵּן יִהְיוּ אֵלֶּה שֶׁיֵּשׁ לָהֶם נָשִׁים כְּאִלּוּ אֵין לָהֶם
al ken yihyu elleh sheyesh lahem nashim ke'illu ein lahem
that henceforth both those that have wives may be as though they had none;

יִהְיוּ הַבּוֹכִים כְּאִלּוּ אֵינָם בּוֹכִים; הַשְּׂמֵחִים כְּאִלּוּ אֵינָם שְׂמֵחִים
yihyu habbochim ke'illu einam bochim; hassmechim ke'illu einam smechim
and those that weep, as though they wept not; and those that rejoice, as though they rejoiced not;

הַקּוֹנִים כְּאִלּוּ אֵינָם בַּעֲלֵי קִנְיָן
hakkonim ke'illu einam ba'alei kinyan
and those that buy, as though they possessed not;

וְהַנֶּהֱנִים מִן הָעוֹלָם הַזֶּה כְּאִלּוּ אֵינָם נֶהֱנִים מִמֶּנּוּ, כִּי חָלוֹף תַּחֲלֹף צוּרַת הָעוֹלָם הַזֶּה
vehannehenim min ha'olam hazzeh ke'illu einam nehenim mimmennu, ki chalof tachalof tzurat ha'olam hazzeh
and those that use the world, as not using it to the full: for the fashion of this world passeth away.

רְצוֹנִי לִמְנֹעַ דְּאָגָה מִכֶּם
retzoni limnoa de'agah mikkem
But I would have you to be free from cares.

מִי שֶׁאֵינוֹ נָשׂוּי דּוֹאֵג לַדְּבָרִים אֲשֶׁר לָאָדוֹן, אֵיךְ יִיטַב בְּעֵינֵי הָאָדוֹן
mi she'eino nasui do'eg laddevarim asher la'adon, eich yitav be'einei ha'adon
He that is unmarried is careful for the things of the Lord, how he may please the Lord:

אֶל הַקּוֹרִינְתִּים א

כָּךְ אֲנִי מְצַוֶּה בְּכָל הַקְּהִלּוֹת
kach ani metzavveh bechol hakkehillot
And so ordain I in all the churches.

אִם נִקְרָא הָאִישׁ בְּעֵת הֱיוֹתוֹ נִמּוֹל, אַל יִמְשֹׁךְ לוֹ עָרְלָה
im nikra ha'ish be'et heyoto nimmol, al yimshoch lo orlah
Was any man called being circumcised? let him not become uncircumcised.

אִם נִקְרָא כְּשֶׁהוּא עָרֵל, אַל יִמּוֹל
im nikra keshehu arel, al yimmol
Hath any been called in uncircumcision? let him not be circumcised.

לֹא הַמִּילָה חֲשׁוּבָה, אַף לֹא הָעָרְלָה, אֶלָּא שְׁמִירַת מִצְווֹת הָאֱלֹהִים
lo hammilah chashuvah, af lo ha'orlah, ella shemirat mitzvot ha'elohim
Circumcision is nothing, and uncircumcision is nothing; but the keeping of the commandments of God.

יִשָּׁאֵר כָּל אִישׁ בַּמַּעֲמָד שֶׁבּוֹ נִקְרָא
yisha'er kol ish bamma'amad shebbo nikra
Let each man abide in that calling wherein he was called.

אִם נִקְרֵאתָ בְּעֵת הֱיוֹתְךָ עֶבֶד, אַל תִּדְאַג. אֲבָל אִם בִּיכָלְתְּךָ לָצֵאת לַחָפְשִׁי, אַדְּרַבָּא, נַצֵּל זֹאת
im nikreta be'et heyotecha eved, al tid'ag. aval im bichaletecha latzet lachofshi, adderabba, natzel zot
Wast thou called being a bondservant? care not for it: nay, even if thou canst become free, use it rather.

הֲרֵי עֶבֶד שֶׁנִּקְרָא מִטַּעַם הָאָדוֹן, בֶּן־חוֹרִין הוּא לָאָדוֹן
harei eved shennikra mitta'am ha'adon, ben-chorin hu la'adon
For he that was called in the Lord being a bondservant, is the Lord's freedman:

כֵּן מִי שֶׁנִּקְרָא בִּהְיוֹתוֹ בֶּן־חוֹרִין, עֶבֶד הוּא לַמָּשִׁיחַ
ken mi shennikra bihyoto ben-chorin, eved hu lammashiach
likewise he that was called being free, is Christ's bondservant.

בִּמְחִיר נִקְנֵיתֶם; אַל תִּשְׁתַּעְבְּדוּ לִבְנֵי אָדָם
bimchir nikneitem; al tishta'bedu livnei adam
Ye were bought with a price; become not bondservants of men.

אַחַי, אִישׁ אִישׁ בַּמַּעֲמָד שֶׁנִּקְרָא בּוֹ, בּוֹ יַעֲמֹד לִפְנֵי אֱלֹהִים
achai, ish ish bamma'amad shennikra bo, bo ya'amod lifnei elohim
Brethren, let each man, wherein he was called, therein abide with God.

עַל־אוֹדוֹת הַבְּתוּלוֹת אֵין לִי מִצְוָה מֵאֵת הָאָדוֹן
al-'odot habbetulot ein li mitzvah me'et ha'adon
Now concerning virgins I have no commandment of the Lord:

אֲבָל אֲחַוֶּה דַּעְתִּי בְּתוֹר מִי שֶׁזָּכָה, בְּרַחֲמֵי הָאָדוֹן, לִהְיוֹת נֶאֱמָן
aval achavveh da'ti betor mi shezzachah, berachmei ha'adon, lihyot ne'eman
but I give my judgment, as one that hath obtained mercy of the Lord to be trustworthy.

אֶל הַקּוֹרִינְתִּים א

וְאַל יַעֲזֹב אִישׁ אֶת אִשְׁתּוֹ
ve'al ya'azov ish et ishto
and that the husband leave not his wife.

אֶל הַשְּׁאָר אֲנִי אוֹמֵר, וְלֹא הָאָדוֹן: אִם לְאִישׁ מַאֲמִין יֵשׁ אִשָּׁה בִּלְתִּי מַאֲמִינָה
el hashe'ar ani omer, velo ha'adon: im le'ish ma'amin yesh ishah bilti ma'aminah
But to the rest say I, not the Lord: If any brother hath an unbelieving wife,

וְהִיא רוֹצָה לְהִשָּׁאֵר אִתּוֹ, אַל יַעֲזֹב אוֹתָהּ
vehi rotzah lehisha'er itto, al ya'azov otah
and she is content to dwell with him, let him not leave her.

וְאִשָּׁה שֶׁיֵּשׁ לָהּ בַּעַל בִּלְתִּי מַאֲמִין וְהוּא חָפֵץ לְהִשָּׁאֵר אִתָּהּ, אַל תַּעֲזֹב הִיא אוֹתוֹ
ve'ishah sheyesh lah ba'al bilti ma'amin vehu chafetz lehishaer ittah, al ta'azov hi oto
And the woman that hath an unbelieving husband, and he is content to dwell with her, let her not leave her husband.

כִּי הַבַּעַל שֶׁאֵינֶנּוּ מַאֲמִין מְקֻדָּשׁ בְּאִשְׁתּוֹ, וְהָאִשָּׁה שֶׁאֵינֶנָּה מַאֲמִינָה מְקֻדֶּשֶׁת בְּבַעְלָהּ
ki habba'al she'einennu ma'amin mekuddash be'ishto, veha'ishah she'einennah ma'aminah mekuddeshet beva'lah
For the unbelieving husband is sanctified in the wife, and the unbelieving wife is sanctified in the brother:

אִם לֹא כֵן, בְּנֵיכֶם טְמֵאִים, וְאִלּוּ עַתָּה קְדוֹשִׁים הֵם
im lo chen, beneichem tme'im, ve'illu attah kdoshim hem
else were your children unclean; but now are they holy.

אֲבָל אִם זֶה שֶׁאֵינֶנּוּ מַאֲמִין נִפְרָד, שֶׁיִּפָּרֵד לוֹ
aval im zeh she'einennu ma'amin nifrad, sheyippared lo
Yet if the unbelieving departeth, let him depart:

גַּם הַמַּאֲמִין גַּם הַמַּאֲמִינָה אֵינָם מְשֻׁעְבָּדִים בְּמִקְרִים כָּאֵלֶּה
gam hamma'amin gam hamma'aminah einam meshu'badim bemikrim ka'elleh
the brother or the sister is not under bondage in such cases:

הֲרֵי לְשָׁלוֹם קָרָא אוֹתָנוּ הָאֱלֹהִים
harei leshalom kara otanu ha'elohim
but God hath called us in peace.

כְּלוּם יוֹדַעַת אַתְּ, אִשָּׁה, אִם תּוֹשִׁיעִי אֶת בַּעְלֵךְ
kelum yoda'at at, ishah, im toshi'i et ba'lech
For how knowest thou, O wife, whether thou shalt save thy husband?

אוֹ כְּלוּם יוֹדֵעַ אַתָּה, הַבַּעַל, אִם תּוֹשִׁיעַ אֶת אִשְׁתְּךָ
o klum yodea attah, habba'al, im toshia et ishtecha
or how knowest thou, O husband, whether thou shalt save thy wife?

כָּל אִישׁ יִחְיֶה אֶת חַיָּיו לְפִי מַה שֶּׁחָלַק לוֹ הָאָדוֹן, לְפִי מַצָּבוֹ כַּאֲשֶׁר קָרָא לוֹ הָאֱלֹהִים
kol ish yichyeh et chayav lefi mah shechalak lo ha'adon, lefi matzavo ka'asher kara lo ha'elohim
Only, as the Lord hath distributed to each man, as God hath called each, so let him walk.

אֶל הַקּוֹרִינְתִּים א

הָאִישׁ יְקַיֵּם אֶת חוֹבָתוֹ לְאִשְׁתּוֹ, וְכֵן גַּם הָאִשָּׁה תְּקַיֵּם אֶת חוֹבָתָהּ לְבַעְלָהּ
ha'ish yekayem et chovato le'ishto, vechen gam ha'ishah tekayem et chovatah leva'lah
Let the husband render unto the wife her due: and likewise also the wife unto the husband.

הָאִשָּׁה אֵין גּוּפָהּ בִּרְשׁוּתָהּ אֶלָּא בִּרְשׁוּת בַּעְלָהּ
ha'ishah ein gufah birshutah ella birshut ba'lah
The wife hath not power over her own body, but the husband:

כֵּן גַּם הָאִישׁ, אֵין גּוּפוֹ בִּרְשׁוּתוֹ אֶלָּא בִּרְשׁוּת אִשְׁתּוֹ
ken gam ha'ish, ein gufo birshuto ella birshut ishto
and likewise also the husband hath not power over his own body, but the wife.

אַל תִּמְנְעוּ אֶת עַצְמְכֶם זֶה מִזֶּה בִּלְתִּי אִם מִתּוֹךְ הַסְכָּמָה לִזְמַן מְסֻיָּם כְּדֵי לְהִתְפַּנּוֹת לִתְפִלָּה
al timneu et atzmechem zeh mizzeh bilti im mittoch haskamah lizman mesuyam kedei lehitpannot litfillah
Defraud ye not one the other, except it be by consent for a season, that ye may give yourselves unto prayer,

אַחֲרֵי כֵן שׁוּבוּ וְהִתְאַחֲדוּ, פֶּן יְנַסֶּה אֶתְכֶם הַשָּׂטָן בִּגְלַל אִי יְכָלְתְּכֶם לִרְסֵן אֶת הַיֵּצֶר
acharei chen shuvu vehit'achadu, pen yenasseh etchem hashotan biglal i yechaletechem lerassen et hayetzer
and may be together again, that Satan tempt you not because of your incontinency.

זֹאת אֲנִי אוֹמֵר בְּדֶרֶךְ שֶׁל רְשׁוּת וְלֹא בְּדֶרֶךְ שֶׁל פְּקֻדָּה
zot ani omer bederech shel reshut velo bederech shel pekuddah
But this I say by way of concession, not of commandment.

מִי יִתֵּן וְכָל הָאֲנָשִׁים יִהְיוּ כָּמוֹנִי,
mi yitten vechol ha'anashim yihyu kamoni
Yet I would that all men were even as I myself.

אֶלָּא שֶׁלְּכָל אֶחָד מַתְּנָתוֹ שֶׁלּוֹ מֵאֵת הָאֱלֹהִים, זֶה בְּכֹה וְזֶה בְּכֹה
ella shellechal echad mattnato shello me'et ha'elohim, zeh bechoh vezeh bechoh
Howbeit each man hath his own gift from God, one after this manner, and another after that.

וְאֶל הַפְּנוּיִים וְהָאַלְמָנוֹת אֹמַר: כְּדַאי לָהֶם לְהִשָּׁאֵר כָּמוֹנִי
ve'el happenuyim veha'almanot omar: kedai lahem lehisha'er kamoni
But I say to the unmarried and to widows, It is good for them if they abide even as I.

אֲבָל אִם אֵינָם יְכוֹלִים לִכְבֹּשׁ אֶת יִצְרָם - שֶׁיִּתְחַתְּנוּ; מוּטָב לָשֵׂאת אִשָּׁה מִלִּבְעֹר בְּתַאֲוָה
aval im einam yecholim lichbosh et yitzram - sheyitchattenu; mutav laset ishah milliv'or beta'avah
But if they have not continency, let them marry: for it is better to marry than to burn.

וְעַל הַנְּשׂוּאִים אֲנִי מְצַוֶּה, וְלֹא אֲנִי כִּי אִם הָאָדוֹן, שֶׁלֹּא תִּפָּרֵד אִשָּׁה מִבַּעְלָהּ
ve'al hannesu'im ani metzavveh, velo ani ki im ha'adon, shello tippared ishah mibba'lah
But unto the married I give charge, yea not I, but the Lord, That the wife depart not from her husband

-אַךְ אִם נִפְרְדָה, שֶׁתִּשָּׁאֵר פְּנוּיָה אוֹ תִּתְפַּיֵּס עִם בַּעְלָהּ
ach im nifredah, shettisha'er penuyah o titpayes im ba'lah
(but should she depart, let her remain unmarried, or else be reconciled to her husband);

אֶל הַקוֹרִינְתִּים א

לְפִיכָךְ, הַאִם אֶקַח אֶת אֵיבְרֵי הַמָּשִׁיחַ וְאֶעֱשֶׂה אוֹתָם לְאֵיבְרֵי זוֹנָה? חַס וְחָלִילָה
lefichach, ha'im ekkach et eiverei hammashiach ve'e'eseh otam le'eiverei zonah? chas vechalilah
shall I then take away the members of Christ, and make them members of a harlot? God forbid.

הַאֵינְכֶם יוֹדְעִים כִּי הַדָּבֵק בְּזוֹנָה נִהְיֶה עִמָּהּ לְגוּף אֶחָד
ha'einchem yode'im ki haddavek bezonah nihyeh immah leguf echad?
Or know ye not that he that is joined to a harlot is one body?

שֶׁהֲרֵי נֶאֱמַר: וְהָיוּ שְׁנֵיהֶם לְבָשָׂר אֶחָד
sheharei ne'emar: vehayu sheneihem levasar echad
for, The twain, saith he, shall become one flesh.

אֲבָל הַדָּבֵק בָּאָדוֹן, רוּחַ אַחַת הוּא אִתּוֹ
aval haddavek ba'adon, ruach achat hu itto
But he that is joined unto the Lord is one spirit.

הִתְרַחֲקוּ מִן הַזְּנוּת. כָּל חֵטְא שֶׁאָדָם עוֹשֶׂה הוּא מִחוּץ לְגוּפוֹ
hitrachaku min hazzenut. kol chet she'adam oseh hu michutz legufo
Flee fornication. Every sin that a man doeth is without the body;

אֲבָל הַזּוֹנֶה חוֹטֵא לְגוּפוֹ שֶׁלּוֹ
aval hazzoneh chotei legufo shello
but he that committeth fornication sinneth against his own body.

הַאִם אֵינְכֶם יוֹדְעִים כִּי גוּפְכֶם הוּא הֵיכָל שֶׁל רוּחַ הַקֹּדֶשׁ הַשּׁוֹכֶנֶת בְּתוֹכְכֶם
ha'im einechem yode'im ki gufchem hu heichal shel ruach hakkodesh hashochenet betochechem
Or know ye not that your body is a temple of the Holy Spirit which is in you,

אֲשֶׁר קִבַּלְתֶּם אוֹתָהּ מֵאֵת אֱלֹהִים
asher kibbaltem otah me'et elohim
which ye have from God?

וְכִי אֵינְכֶם שַׁיָּכִים לְעַצְמְכֶם הֲלֹא בִּמְחִיר נִקְנֵיתֶם, לָכֵן כַּבְּדוּ אֶת אֱלֹהִים בְּגוּפְכֶם
vechi einechem shayachim le'atzmechem halo bimchir nikneitem, lachen kabbdu et elohim begufechem
and ye are not your own; for ye were bought with a price: glorify God therefore in your body.

ז

לְעִנְיַן מַה שֶּׁכְּתַבְתֶּם אֵלַי: טוֹב לוֹ לְאִישׁ לְהִמָּנַע מֵאִשָּׁה
le'inyan mah shekketavtem elai: tov lo le'ish lehimmana me'ishah
Now concerning the things whereof ye wrote: It is good for a man not to touch a woman.

אַךְ מִשּׁוּם הַזְּנוּת - כָּל אִישׁ יִשָּׂא לוֹ אִשָּׁה וְכָל אִשָּׁה יִהְיֶה לָהּ בַּעַל
ach mishum hazznut - kol ish yissa lo ishah vechol ishah yihyeh lah ba'al
But, because of fornications, let each man have his own wife, and let each woman have her own husband.

אֶל הַקּוֹרִינְתִּים א

וְאוּלָם אַתֶּם בְּעַצְמְכֶם עוֹשִׂים עָוֶל וְעוֹשְׁקִים, וְלַאֲחֵיכֶם אַתֶּם עוֹשִׂים זֹאת
ve'ulam attem be'atzmechem osim avel ve'oshekim, vela'acheichem attem osim zot
Nay, but ye yourselves do wrong, and defraud, and that your brethren.

אוֹ שֶׁמָּא אֵינְכֶם יוֹדְעִים כִּי עוֹשֵׂי עָוֶל לֹא יִירְשׁוּ אֶת מַלְכוּת הָאֱלֹהִים
o shemma einechem yode'im ki osei avel lo yireshu et malchut ha'elohim
Or know ye not that the unrighteous shall not inherit the kingdom of God?

אַל תִּטְעוּ; לֹא זוֹנִים וְלֹא עוֹבְדֵי אֱלִילִים, לֹא מְנָאֲפִים וְלֹא עוֹשֵׂי זִמָּה וְלֹא יוֹדְעֵי מִשְׁכַּב זָכָר
al tit'u; lo zonim velo ovedei elilim, lo mena'afim velo osei zimmah velo yode'ei mishkav zachar
Be not deceived: neither fornicators, nor idolaters, nor adulterers, nor effeminate, nor abusers of themselves with men,

לֹא גַנָּבִים וְלֹא חַמְדָנִים, לֹא סוֹבְאִים וְלֹא מְגַדְּפִים וְלֹא חוֹמְסִים יִירְשׁוּ אֶת מַלְכוּת הָאֱלֹהִים
lo gannavim velo chamdanim, lo sove'im velo megaddefim velo chomesim yireshu et malchut ha'elohim
nor thieves, nor covetous, nor drunkards, nor revilers, nor extortioners, shall inherit the kingdom of God.

וְכָאֵלֶּה הָיוּ כַּמָּה מִכֶּם, אֲבָל אַתֶּם רֻחַצְתֶּם, אַתֶּם קֻדַּשְׁתֶּם
vecha'elleh hayu kammah mikkem, aval attem ruchatztem, attem kuddashtem
And such were some of you: but ye were washed, but ye were sanctified,

אַתֶּם הֻצְדַּקְתֶּם בְּשֵׁם הָאָדוֹן יֵשׁוּעַ הַמָּשִׁיחַ וּבְרוּחַ אֱלֹהֵינוּ
attem hutzdaktem beshem ha'adon yeshua hammashiach uveruach eloheinu
but ye were justified in the name of the Lord Jesus Christ, and in the Spirit of our God.

הַכֹּל מֻתָּר לִי, אֲבָל לֹא הַכֹּל מוֹעִיל
hakkol muttar li, aval lo hakkol mo'il
All things are lawful for me; but not all things are expedient.

הַכֹּל מֻתָּר לִי, אַךְ לֹא אֶשְׁתַּעְבֵּד לְשׁוּם דָּבָר
hakkol muttar li, ach lo eshta'bed leshum davar
All things are lawful for me; but I will not be brought under the power of any.

הַמַּאֲכָל הוּא בִּשְׁבִיל הַכֶּרֶס וְהַכֶּרֶס בִּשְׁבִיל הַמַּאֲכָל, וֵאלֹהִים יְכַלֶּה גַּם אֶת זֶה וְגַם אֶת זֶה
hamma'achal hu bishvil hakkeres vehakkeres bishvil hamma'achal, ve'elohim yechalleh gam et zeh vegam et zeh
Meats for the belly, and the belly for meats: but God shall bring to nought both it and them.

אֲבָל הַגּוּף אֵינוֹ בִּשְׁבִיל הַזְּנוּת, אֶלָּא בִּשְׁבִיל הָאָדוֹן, וְהָאָדוֹן בִּשְׁבִיל הַגּוּף
aval hagguf eino bishvil hazznut, ella bishvil ha'adon, veha'adon bishvil hagguf
But the body is not for fornication, but for the Lord; and the Lord for the body:

וֵאלֹהִים הֵקִים לִתְחִיָּה אֶת אֲדוֹנֵנוּ וּבִגְבוּרָתוֹ יָקִים גַּם אוֹתָנוּ
Ve'elohim hekim litchiyah et adonenu uvigvurato yakim gam otanu
and God both raised the Lord, and will raise up us through his power.

הַאִם אֵינְכֶם יוֹדְעִים שֶׁגּוּפֵיכֶם הֵם אֵיבְרֵי הַמָּשִׁיחַ?
ha'im einechem yode'im sheggufeichem hem eiverei hammashiach
Know ye not that your bodies are members of Christ?

אֶל הַקּוֹרִינְתִּים א

I

הַאִם מֵעֵז אִישׁ מִכֶּם, שֶׁיֵּשׁ לוֹ דָּבָר נֶגֶד רֵעֵהוּ, לְהָבִיא אֶת מִשְׁפָּטוֹ לִפְנֵי הָרְשָׁעִים וְלֹא לִפְנֵי הַקְּדוֹשִׁים
ha'im me'ez ish mikkem, sheyesh lo davar neged re'ehu, lehavi et mishpato lifnei haresha'im velo lifnei hakkdoshim
Dare any of you, having a matter against his neighbor, go to law before the unrighteous, and not before the saints?

הַאִם אֵינְכֶם יוֹדְעִים שֶׁהַקְּדוֹשִׁים יִשְׁפְּטוּ אֶת הָעוֹלָם
ha'im einechem yode'im shehakkdoshim yishpetu et ha'olam
Or know ye not that the saints shall judge the world?

וְאִם אֶת הָעוֹלָם תִּשְׁפְּטוּ, כֵּיצַד אֵינְכֶם מְסֻגָּלִים לִשְׁפֹּט בָּעִנְיָנִים הַפְּעוּטִים בְּיוֹתֵר
ve'im et ha'olam tishpetu, keitzad einechem mesuggalim lishpot ba'inyanim happe'utim beyoter
and if the world is judged by you, are ye unworthy to judge the smallest matters?

הַאִם אֵינְכֶם יוֹדְעִים שֶׁאֲנַחְנוּ נִשְׁפֹּט מַלְאָכִים? כָּל שֶׁכֵּן דְּבָרִים הַשַּׁיָּכִים לְחַיֵּי יוֹם יוֹם
ha'im einechem yode'im she'anachnu nishpot mal'achim? kol shekken devarim hashayachim lechayei yom yom
Know ye not that we shall judge angels? how much more, things that pertain to this life?

וְהִנֵּה כְּשֶׁיֵּשׁ בֵּינֵיכֶם עִנְיָנִים שֶׁל חַיֵּי יוֹם יוֹם
vehinneh ksheyesh beineichem inyanim shel chayei yom yom
If then ye have to judge things pertaining to this life,

דַּוְקָא אֶת הַנִּקְלִים בְּעֵינֵי הַקְּהִלָּה אַתֶּם מוֹשִׁיבִים לְשׁוֹפְטִים
davka et hanniklim be'einei hakkehillah attem moshivim leshofetim
do ye set them to judge who are of no account in the church?

אֲנִי אוֹמֵר זֹאת לְבָשְׁתְּכֶם
ani omer zot levashtechem
I say this to move you to shame.

וְכִי אֵין בָּכֶם שׁוּם חָכָם שֶׁיָּכוֹל לִשְׁפֹּט בֵּין אִישׁ לְאָחִיו
vechi ein bachem shum chacham sheyachol lishpot bein ish le'achiv
What, cannot there be found among you one wise man who shall be able to decide between his brethren,

בִּמְקוֹם זֹאת אָח נִשְׁפָּט עִם אָחִיו, וְזֹאת לִפְנֵי בִּלְתִּי מַאֲמִינִים
bimkom zot ach nishpat im achiv, vezot lifnei bilti ma'aminim
but brother goeth to law with brother, and that before unbelievers?

בִּכְלָל, בְּעֶצֶם הָעֻבְדָּה שֶׁאַתֶּם תּוֹבְעִים זֶה אֶת זֶה לְמִשְׁפָּט, כְּבָר הִפְסַדְתֶּם
bichlal, be'etzem ha'uvdah she'attem tove'im zeh et zeh lemishpat, kevar hifsadtem
Nay, already it is altogether a defect in you, that ye have lawsuits one with another.

מַדּוּעַ לֹא תְּבַכְּרוּ לִהְיוֹת מְקֻפָּחִים? מַדּוּעַ לֹא תְּבַכְּרוּ לִהְיוֹת נֶעֱשָׁקִים
maddua lo tevakkeru lihyot mekuppachim? maddua lo tevakkeru lihyot ne'eshakim
Why not rather take wrong? why not rather be defrauded?

אֶל הַקּוֹרִנְתִּים א

הִתְפָּאֲרוּתְכֶם אֵינֶנָּה הוֹלֶמֶת. הַאִם אֵינְכֶם יוֹדְעִים שֶׁמְּעַט שְׂאוֹר מַחְמִיץ אֶת כָּל הָעִסָּה
hitpa'arutchem einennah holemet. ha'im einechem yode'im shemme'at se'or machmitz et kol ha'issah
Your glorying is not good. Know ye not that a little leaven leaveneth the whole lump?

בַּעֲרוּ אֶת הַשְּׂאוֹר הַיָּשָׁן לְמַעַן תִּהְיוּ עִסָּה חֲדָשָׁה. הֲלֹא אַתֶּם כְּמַצּוֹת
ba'aru et haso'or hayashan lema'an tihyu issah chadashah. halo attem kematzot
Purge out the old leaven, that ye may be a new lump, even as ye are unleavened.

שֶׁהֲרֵי נִזְבַּח שֶׂה הַפֶּסַח שֶׁלָּנוּ - הַמָּשִׁיחַ
sheharei nizbach seh happesach shellanu - hammashiach
For our passover also hath been sacrificed, even Christ:

לָכֵן נָחֹגָּה לֹא בִּשְׂאוֹר יָשָׁן וְלֹא בִּשְׂאוֹר הָרַע וְהָרֶשַׁע
lachen nachoggah lo bis'or yashan velo bis'or haroa veharesha
wherefore let us keep the feast, not with old leaven, neither with the leaven of malice and wickedness,

אֶלָּא בְּמַצּוֹת הַתֹּם וְהָאֱמֶת
ella bematzot hattom veha'emet
but with the unleavened bread of sincerity and truth.

כָּתַבְתִּי לָכֶם בָּאִגֶּרֶת שֶׁלֹּא לְהִתְעָרֵב עִם זוֹנִים
katavti lachem ba'iggeret shello lehit'arev im zonim
I wrote unto you in my epistle to have no company with fornicators;

אֵינֶנִּי מִתְכַּוֵּן לַזּוֹנִים בְּנֵי הָעוֹלָם הַזֶּה
einenni mitkavven lazzonim benei ha'olam hazzeh
not at all meaning with the fornicators of this world,

אוֹ לַחַמְדָנִים, לַחוֹמְסִים וְעוֹבְדֵי אֱלִילִים, שֶׁכֵּן אָז הֱיִיתֶם חַיָּבִים לָצֵאת מִן הָעוֹלָם
o lachamdanim, lachomesim ve'ovedei elilim, shekken az heyitem chayavim latzet min ha'olam
or with the covetous and extortioners, or with idolaters; for then must ye needs go out of the world:

אֲבָל כָּתַבְתִּי לָכֶם שֶׁלֹּא לְהִתְעָרֵב עִם מִי שֶׁנִּקְרָא אָח וְהוּא זוֹנֶה
aval katavti lachem shello lehit'arev im mi shennikra ach vehu zoneh
but as it is, I wrote unto you not to keep company, if any man that is named a brother be a fornicator,

אוֹ חוֹמֵד אֶת אֲשֶׁר לַזּוּלַת, אוֹ עוֹבֵד אֱלִילִים אוֹ מְגַדֵּף אוֹ סוֹבֵא אוֹ חוֹמֵס; אַף אַל תָּסֵבּוּ לֶאֱכֹל עִם אִישׁ כָּזֶה
o chomed et asher lazzulat, o oved elilim o megaddef o sovei o chomes; af al tasebbu le'echol im ish kazeh
or covetous, or an idolater, or a reviler, or a drunkard, or an extortioner; with such a one no, not to eat.

כִּי מַה לִּי לִשְׁפֹּט אֶת אֵלֶּה אֲשֶׁר בַּחוּץ? הַאִם אֵינְכֶם שׁוֹפְטִים אֶת אֵלֶּה שֶׁבְּקִרְבְּכֶם
ki mah li lishpot et elleh asher bachutz? ha'im einechem shofetim et elleh shebbekirbechem
For what have I to do with judging them that are without? Do not ye judge them that are within?

אֵלֶּה אֲשֶׁר בַּחוּץ אֱלֹהִים יִשְׁפְּטֵם. אַתֶּם בַּעֲרוּ אֶת הָרַע מִקִּרְבְּכֶם
elleh asher bachutz elohim yishpetem. attem ba'aru et hara mikkirbechem
But them that are without God judgeth. Put away the wicked man from among yourselves.

אֶל הַקּוֹרִינְתִּים א

אוּלָם אֲנִי אָבוֹא אֲלֵיכֶם בְּקָרוֹב, אִם יִרְצֶה הָאָדוֹן, וְאֶרְאֶה לֹא אֶת דִּבּוּרָם שֶׁל הַמִּתְנַשְּׂאִים, אֶלָּא אֶת כֹּחָם
ulam ani avo aleichem bekarov, im yirtzeh ha'adon, ve'er'eh lo et dibburam shel hammitnassim, ella et kocham
But I will come to you shortly, if the Lord will; and I will know, not the word of them that are puffed up, but the power.

שֶׁכֵּן מַלְכוּת הָאֱלֹהִים אֵינָהּ בְּדִבּוּר כִּי אִם בְּכֹחַ הַפֹּעַל
shekken malchut ha'elohim einah bedibbur ki im bechoach happo'al
For the kingdom of God is not in word, but in power.

מָה אַתֶּם רוֹצִים? שֶׁאָבוֹא אֲלֵיכֶם בְּשֵׁבֶט מוּסָר, אוֹ בְּאַהֲבָה וְעַנְוַת רוּחַ
mah attem rotzim? she'avo aleichem beshevet musar, o be'ahavah ve'anvat ruach
What will ye? shall I come unto you with a rod, or in love and a spirit of gentleness?

ה

בְּאָזְנַי כֹּל נִשְׁמַע שֶׁיֵּשׁ זְנוּת בְּקִרְבְּכֶם
be'azenei kol nishma sheyesh znut bekirbechem
It is actually reported that there is fornication among you,

וּזְנוּת אֲשֶׁר אֵין כָּמוֹהָ אֲפִלּוּ בֵּין הַגּוֹיִם: אִישׁ לָקַח לוֹ אֶת אֵשֶׁת אָבִיו
uznut asher ein kamoha afillu bein haggoyim. ish lakach lo et eshet aviv
and such fornication as is not even among the Gentiles, that one of you hath his father's wife.

וְאַתֶּם עוֹד מִתְגָּאִים בִּמְקוֹם לְהִתְאַבֵּל כְּדֵי שֶׁעוֹשֶׂה הַמַּעֲשֶׂה הַזֶּה יֻרְחַק מִקִּרְבְּכֶם
ve'attem od mitga'im bimkom lehit'abbel kedei she'oseh hamma'asheh hazzeh yurchak mikkirbechem
And ye are puffed up, and did not rather mourn, that he that had done this deed might be taken away from among you.

וַאֲנִי, אַף כִּי אֲנִי נֶעְדָּר מִבֵּינֵיכֶם בְּגוּפִי (אַךְ נוֹכֵחַ בְּרוּחִי)
va'ani, af ki ani ne'dar mibbeineichem begufi (ach nocheach beruchi)
For I verily, being absent in body but present in spirit,

כְּבָר שָׁפַטְתִּי אֶת עוֹשֵׂה הַמַּעֲשֶׂה הַזֶּה כְּאִלּוּ הָיִיתִי אִתְּכֶם
kvar shafatti et oseh hamma'aseh hazzeh ke'illu hayiti ittechem
have already as though I were present judged him that hath so wrought this thing,

בְּשֵׁם הָאָדוֹן יֵשׁוּעַ, כַּאֲשֶׁר תִּתְאַסְּפוּ וְרוּחִי בֵּינֵיכֶם עִם גְּבוּרַת אֲדוֹנֵנוּ יֵשׁוּעַ
beshem ha'adon yeshua, ka'asher titassfu veruchi beineichem im gvurat adonenu yeshua
in the name of our Lord Jesus, ye being gathered together, and my spirit, with the power of our Lord Jesus,

תִּמְסְרוּ אֶת הָאִישׁ הַהוּא לַשָּׂטָן לְאָבְדַן הַגּוּף
timseru et ha'ish hahu lassatan le'ovdan hagguf
to deliver such a one unto Satan for the destruction of the flesh,

כְּדֵי שֶׁרוּחוֹ תִּוָּשַׁע בְּיוֹם יהוה
kedei sherucho tivvasha beyom hashem
that the spirit may be saved in the day of the Lord Jesus.

אֶל הַקּוֹרִינְתִּים א

אֲנַחְנוּ חַלָּשִׁים, אַךְ אַתֶּם חֲזָקִים! אַתֶּם נִכְבָּדִים, אַךְ אֲנַחְנוּ נִקְלִים
anachnu challashim, ach attem chazakim! attem nichbadim, ach anachnu niklim
we are weak, but ye are strong; ye have glory, but we have dishonor.

עַד עֶצֶם הַשָּׁעָה הַזֹּאת אֲנַחְנוּ רְעֵבִים וּצְמֵאִים, עֲרֻמִּים
ad etzem hasha'ah hazzot anachnu re'evim utzeme'im, arummim
Even unto this present hour we both hunger, and thirst, and are naked,

וּמֻכִּים וְנָדִים מִמָּקוֹם לְמָקוֹם
umukkim venadim mimmakom lemakom
and are buffeted, and have no certain dwelling-place;

וִיגֵעִים בַּעֲמַל יָדֵינוּ. מְגַדְּפִים אוֹתָנוּ - אֲנַחְנוּ מְבָרְכִים; רוֹדְפִים אוֹתָנוּ - אֲנַחְנוּ נוֹשְׂאִים זֹאת
vige'im ba'amal yadeinu. megaddfim otanu - anachnu mevarechim; rodfim otanu - anachnu nose'im zot
and we toil, working with our own hands: being reviled, we bless; being persecuted, we endure;

מְחָרְפִים אוֹתָנוּ, אַךְ בְּפִינוּ מִלּוֹת עִדּוּד; כִּסְחִי הָעוֹלָם הָיִינוּ, מְאוּסִים לַכֹּל עַד הַיּוֹם הַזֶּה
mecharfim otanu, ach befinu millot iddud; kischi ha'olam hayinu, me'usim lakkol ad hayom hazzeh
being defamed, we entreat: we are made as the filth of the world, the offscouring of all things, even until now.

לֹא כְּדֵי לְבַיֵּשׁ אֶתְכֶם אֲנִי כּוֹתֵב אֶת הַדְּבָרִים הָאֵלֶּה, אֶלָּא לְהַזְהִיר אֶתְכֶם כִּילָדַי הָאֲהוּבִים
lo kedei levayesh etchem ani kotev et haddevarim ha'elleh, ella lehazhir etchem kiyeladai ha'ahuvim
I write not these things to shame you, but to admonish you as my beloved children.

הֲלֹא גַּם אִם יֵשׁ לָכֶם עֲשֶׂרֶת אֲלָפִים מְחַנְּכִים בַּמָּשִׁיחַ, אֵין לָכֶם אָבוֹת רַבִּים
halo gam im yesh lachem aseret alafim mechannchim bammashiach, ein lachem avot rabbim
For though ye have ten thousand tutors in Christ, yet have ye not many fathers;

כִּי אֲנִי, עַל-יְדֵי הַבְּשׂוֹרָה, הוֹלַדְתִּי אֶתְכֶם בַּמָּשִׁיחַ יֵשׁוּעַ
ki ani, al-yedei habbesorah, holadti etchem bammashiach yeshua
for in Christ Jesus I begat you through the gospel.

לָכֵן אֲנִי מְבַקֵּשׁ מִכֶּם לְהִתְנַהֵג כָּמוֹנִי
lachen ani mevakkesh mikkem lehitnaheg kamoni
I beseech you therefore, be ye imitators of me.

מִשּׁוּם כָּךְ שָׁלַחְתִּי אֲלֵיכֶם אֶת טִימוֹתֵיאוֹס בְּנִי הָאָהוּב וְהַנֶּאֱמָן בָּאָדוֹן
mishum kach shalachti aleichem et timotei'os beni ha'ahuv vehanne'eman ba'adon
For this cause have I sent unto you Timothy, who is my beloved and faithful child in the Lord,

הוּא יַזְכִּיר לָכֶם אֶת דְּרָכַי בַּמָּשִׁיחַ, כְּפִי שֶׁאֲנִי מְלַמֵּד בְּכָל קְהִלָּה וּקְהִלָּה בְּכָל מָקוֹם
hu yazkir lachem et drachai bammashiach, kfi she'ani melammed bechol kehillah ukehillah bechol makom
who shall put you in remembrance of my ways which are in Christ, even as I teach everywhere in every church.

יֵשׁ אֲשֶׁר הֵחֵלּוּ לְהִתְנַשֵּׂא וּלְהִתְנַהֵג כְּאִלּוּ לֹא אָבוֹא אֲלֵיכֶם
yesh asher hechellu lehitnasse ulehitnaheg ke'illu lo avo aleichem
Now some are puffed up, as though I were not coming to you.

אֶל הַקּוֹרִינְתִּים א

אֲשֶׁר גַּם יוֹצִיא לָאוֹר אֶת תַּעֲלוּמוֹת הַחֹשֶׁךְ
asher gam yotzi la'or et ta'alumot hachoshech
who will both bring to light the hidden things of darkness,

וְגַם יְגַלֶּה אֶת מַחְשְׁבוֹת הַלֵּב. אָז תִּנָּתֵן הַתְּהִלָּה לְכָל אִישׁ מֵאֵת הָאֱלֹהִים
vegam yegalleh et machshevot hallev. az tinnaten hattehillah lechol ish me'et ha'elohim
and make manifest the counsels of the hearts; and then shall each man have his praise from God.

אַחַי, הֲסִבּוֹתִי אֶת הַדְּבָרִים הָאֵלֶּה עַל עַצְמִי וְעַל אַפּוֹלוֹס בִּשְׁבִילְכֶם
achai, hasibboti et haddevarim ha'elleh al atzmi ve'al appolos bishvilechem
Now these things, brethren, I have in a figure transferred to myself and Apollos for your sakes;

לְמַעַן תִּלְמְדוּ מֵהַדֻּגְמָה הַנּוֹגַעַת לָנוּ שֶׁלֹּא לַחֲרֹג מִן הַכָּתוּב
lema'an tilmedu mehaddugmah hannoga'at lanu shello lacharog min hakkatuv
that in us ye might learn not to go beyond the things which are written;

כְּדֵי שֶׁלֹּא יִתְנַשֵּׂא אִישׁ עַל רֵעֵהוּ בִּשְׁמוֹ שֶׁל אַחֵר
kedei shello yitnasse ish al re'ehu bishmo shel acher
that no one of you be puffed up for the one against the other.

שֶׁכֵּן מִי מַקְנֶה לְךָ יִחוּד? וּמַה יֵּשׁ לְךָ שֶׁלֹּא קִבַּלְתָּ
shekken mi makneh lecha yichud? umah yesh lecha shello kibbalta
For who maketh thee to differ? and what hast thou that thou didst not receive?

וְאִם אָמְנָם קִבַּלְתָּ, מַדּוּעַ תִּתְגָּאֶה כְּאִלּוּ שֶׁלֹּא קִבַּלְתָּ
ve'im omnam kibbalta, maddua titga'eh ke'illu shello kibbalta
but if thou didst receive it, why dost thou glory as if thou hadst not received it?

אַתֶּם כְּבָר שְׂבֵעִים! אַתֶּם כְּבָר עֲשִׁירִים! בִּלְעָדֵינוּ אַתֶּם מוֹלְכִים
attem kevar seve'im! attem kevar ashirim! bil'adeinu attem molchim
Already are ye filled, already ye are become rich, ye have come to reign without us:

הַלְוַאי שֶׁמְּלַכְתֶּם בֶּאֱמֶת כְּדֵי שֶׁגַּם אֲנַחְנוּ נִמְלֹךְ אִתְּכֶם
halevai shemmelachtem be'emet kedei sheggam anachnu nimloch ittechem
yea and I would that ye did reign, that we also might reign with you.

אֲשֶׁר לָנוּ הַשְּׁלִיחִים, אֲנִי סָבוּר שֶׁאֱלֹהִים הִצִּיב אוֹתָנוּ אַחֲרוֹנִים, כְּנִדּוֹנִים לַמָּוֶת
asher lanu hashelichim, ani savur she'elohim hitziv otanu acharonim, keniddonim lemavet
For, I think, God hath set forth us the apostles last of all, as men doomed to death:

כִּי הָיִינוּ לְמַחֲזֶה לָעוֹלָם, הֵן לְמַלְאָכִים הֵן לִבְנֵי אָדָם
ki hayinu lemachazeh la'olam, hen lemal'achim hen livnei adam
for we are made a spectacle unto the world, both to angels and men.

אָנוּ כְּסִילִים בִּגְלַל הַמָּשִׁיחַ, אַךְ אַתֶּם חֲכָמִים בַּמָּשִׁיחַ!
anu kesilim biglal hammashiach, ach attem chachamim bammashiach
We are fools for Christ's sake, but ye are wise in Christ;

אֶל הַקּוֹרִינְתִים א

אִם מִישֶׁהוּ מִכֶּם סָבוּר שֶׁהוּא חָכָם בָּעוֹלָם הַזֶּה, יְהֵא נָא לִכְסִיל לְמַעַן יֶחְכַּם
im mishehu mikkem savur shehu chacham ba'olam hazzeh, yehei na lichsil lema'an yechkam
If any man thinketh that he is wise among you in this world, let him become a fool, that he may become wise.

כִּי חָכְמַת הָעוֹלָם הַזֶּה הִיא סִכְלוּת בְּעֵינֵי אֱלֹהִים, שֶׁהֲרֵי כָּתוּב: לֹכֵד חֲכָמִים בְּעָרְמָם
ki chochmat ha'olam hazzeh hi sichlut be'einei elohim, sheharei katuv: loched chachamim be'aremam
For the wisdom of this world is foolishness with God. For it is written, He that taketh the wise in their craftiness:

וְעוֹד: יהוה יֹדֵעַ מַחְשְׁבוֹת אָדָם, כִּי־הֵמָּה הָבֶל
ve'od: hashem yodea machshevot adam, ki-hemmah havel
and again, The Lord knoweth the reasonings of the wise, that they are vain.

עַל כֵּן, אַל יִתְהַלֵּל אִישׁ בִּבְנֵי אָדָם. הֲרֵי הַכֹּל שֶׁלָּכֶם
al ken, al yit'hallel ish bivnei adam. harei hakkol shellachem
Wherefore let no one glory in men. For all things are yours;

שָׁאוּל, אַפּוֹלוֹס, כֵּיפָא, הָעוֹלָם, הַחַיִּים, הַמָּוֶת, דְּבָרִים שֶׁבַּהֹוֶה, דְּבָרִים שֶׁבֶּעָתִיד - הַכֹּל שֶׁלָּכֶם
sha'ul, appolos, keifa, ha'olam, hachayim, hammavet, devarim shebbahoh, devarim shebbe'atid - hakkol shellachem
whether Paul, or Apollos, or Cephas, or the world, or life, or death, or things present, or things to come; all are yours;

וְאַתֶּם שֶׁל הַמָּשִׁיחַ, וְהַמָּשִׁיחַ הוּא שֶׁל אֱלֹהִים
ve'attem shel hammashiach, vehammashiach hu shel elohim
and ye are Christ's; and Christ is God's.

ד

וּבְכֵן צָרִיךְ שֶׁהַבְּרִיּוֹת יִרְאוּ אוֹתָנוּ כִּמְשָׁרְתֵי הַמָּשִׁיחַ וּכְמֻפְקָדִים עַל סוֹדוֹת אֱלֹהִים
uvchen tzarich shehabberiyot yir'u otanu kimsharetei hammashiach uchemufkadim al sodot elohim
Let a man so account of us, as of ministers of Christ, and stewards of the mysteries of God.

וְאוּלָם מִן הַמֻּפְקָדִים נִדְרָשׁ לְהִמָּצֵא נֶאֱמָנִים
ve'ulam min hammufkadim nidrash lehimmatzei ne'emanim
Here, moreover, it is required in stewards, that a man be found faithful.

לְגַבֵּי דִּידִי דָּבָר פָּחוּת עֵרֶךְ הוּא לְהִשָּׁפֵט עַל־יְדֵיכֶם אוֹ לְהִשָּׁפֵט בְּיוֹם דִּין אֱנוֹשִׁי. אֲנִי אַף לֹא דָּן אֶת עַצְמִי
legabbei didi davar pchut erech hu lehishafet al-yedeichem o lehishafet beyom din enoshi. ani af lo dan et atzmi
But with me it is a very small thing that I should be judged of you, or of man's judgment: yea, I judge not mine own self.

כִּי אֵינֶנִּי יוֹדֵעַ דָּבָר נֶגֶד עַצְמִי. אֲבָל לֹא בְּכָךְ אֲנִי יוֹצֵא זַכַּאי; הָאָדוֹן הוּא הַשּׁוֹפֵט אוֹתִי
ki einenni yodea davar neged atzmi. aval lo bechach ani yotzei zakkai; ha'adon hu hashofet oti
For I know nothing against myself; yet am I not hereby justified: but he that judgeth me is the Lord.

לָכֵן אַל תִּשְׁפְּטוּ דָּבָר בְּטֶרֶם עֵת, עַד כִּי יָבוֹא הָאָדוֹן
lachen al tishpetu davar beterem et, ad ki yavo ha'adon
Wherefore judge nothing before the time, until the Lord come,

אֶל הַקּוֹרִינְתִּים א

שֶׁכֵּן אֲנַחְנוּ עוֹבְדִים יַחַד עִם אֱלֹהִים וְאַתֶּם שְׂדֵה אֱלֹהִים, בִּנְיַן אֱלֹהִים
shekken anachnu ovedim yachad im elohim ve'attem sdeh elohim, binyan elohim
For we are God's fellow-workers: ye are God's husbandry, God's building.

כְּפִי חֶסֶד אֱלֹהִים שֶׁנִּתַּן לִי הִנַּחְתִּי יְסוֹד כְּבַנַּאי חָכָם
kefi chesed elohim shennittan li hinnachti yesod kevanna chacham
According to the grace of God which was given unto me, as a wise masterbuilder I laid a foundation;

וְאַחֵר בּוֹנֶה עָלָיו. אֲבָל יַשְׁגִּיחַ כָּל אֶחָד כֵּיצַד הוּא בוֹנֶה
ve'acher boneh alav. aval yashgiach kol echad keitzad hu boneh
and another buildeth thereon. But let each man take heed how he buildeth thereon.

כִּי אִישׁ לֹא יוּכַל לְהַנִּיחַ יְסוֹד אַחֵר זוּלָתִי הַיְסוֹד שֶׁהֻנַּח, וְהוּא יֵשׁוּעַ הַמָּשִׁיחַ
ki ish lo yuchal lehanniach yesod acher zulati haysod shehunnach, vehu yeshua hammashiach
For other foundation can no man lay than that which is laid, which is Jesus Christ.

וְכָל אִישׁ, אִם יִבְנֶה עַל הַיְסוֹד הַזֶּה זָהָב אוֹ כֶסֶף אוֹ אֲבָנִים יְקָרוֹת אוֹ עֵץ אוֹ חָצִיר אוֹ קַשׁ
vechol ish, im yivneh al haysod hazzeh zahav o kesef o avanim yekarot o etz o chatzir o kash
But if any man buildeth on the foundation gold, silver, costly stones, wood, hay, stubble;

מַעֲשֵׂהוּ יִתְבָּרֵר
ma'asehu yitbarer
each man's work shall be made manifest:

שֶׁכֵּן הַיּוֹם יוֹצִיאוֹ לָאוֹר, מִפְּנֵי שֶׁבָּאֵשׁ יִתְגַּלֶּה; וְהָאֵשׁ תִּבְחַן אֶת מַעֲשֵׂהוּ שֶׁל כָּל אִישׁ וָאִישׁ
shekken hayom yotzi'o la'or, mippenei shebba'esh yitgalleh; veha'esh tivchan et ma'asehu shel kol ish va'ish
for the day shall declare it, because it is revealed in fire; and the fire itself shall prove each man's work of what sort it is.

אִם יַעֲמֹד הַמַּעֲשֶׂה שֶׁבָּנָה, יְקַבֵּל הָאִישׁ אֶת שְׂכָרוֹ
im ya'amod hamma'aseh shebbanah, yekabbel ha'ish et scharo
If any man's work shall abide which he built thereon, he shall receive a reward.

אִם יִשָּׂרֵף מַעֲשֵׂהוּ - יַפְסִיד; הוּא עַצְמוֹ יִוָּשַׁע, אַךְ זֹאת כְּעוּד מֻצָּל מֵאֵשׁ
im yishoref ma'asehu - yafsid; hu atzmo yivvasha, ach zot ke'ud mutzal me'esh
If any man's work shall be burned, he shall suffer loss: but he himself shall be saved; yet so as through fire.

הַאִם אֵינְכֶם יוֹדְעִים כִּי הֵיכַל אֱלֹהִים אַתֶּם וְכִי רוּחַ אֱלֹהִים שׁוֹכֶנֶת בְּקִרְבְּכֶם
ha'im einchem yode'im ki heichal elohim attem vechi ruach elohim shochenet bekirbechem
Know ye not that ye are a temple of God, and that the Spirit of God dwelleth in you?

אִם יַשְׁחִית אִישׁ אֶת הֵיכַל אֱלֹהִים, אֱלֹהִים יַשְׁחִית אוֹתוֹ; כִּי הֵיכַל הָאֱלֹהִים קָדוֹשׁ, וְאַתֶּם הֵיכָלוֹ
im yashchit ish et heichal elohim, elohim yashchit oto; ki heichal ha'elohim kadosh, ve'attem heichalo
If any man destroyeth the temple of God, him shall God destroy; for the temple of God is holy, and such are ye.

אִישׁ אַל יַטְעֶה אֶת עַצְמוֹ
ish al yat'eh et atzmo
Let no man deceive himself.

אֶל הַקּוֹרִינְתִּים א

ג

וַאֲנִי, אַחַי, לֹא יָכֹלְתִּי לְדַבֵּר אֲלֵיכֶם כְּאֶל אֲנָשִׁים רוּחָנִיִּים
va'ani, achai, lo yacholeti ledabber aleichem ke'el anashim ruchaniyim
And I, brethren, could not speak unto you as unto spiritual,

אֶלָּא כְּאֶל בִּלְתִּי־רוּחָנִיִּים, כְּאֶל תִּינוֹקוֹת בַּמָּשִׁיחַ
ella ke'el bilti-ruchaniyim, ke'el tinokot bammashiach
but as unto carnal, as unto babes in Christ.

בְּחָלָב הֵזַנְתִּי אֶתְכֶם, לֹא בְמַאֲכָל, כִּי עוֹד לֹא יְכָלְתֶּם לֶאֱכֹל. אֲבָל גַּם כָּעֵת אֵינְכֶם יְכוֹלִים
bechalav hezanti etchem, lo bema'achal, ki od lo yecholtem le'echol. aval gam ka'et einchem yecholim
I fed you with milk, not with meat; for ye were not yet able to bear it: nay, not even now are ye able;

כִּי עוֹדְכֶם בִּלְתִּי־רוּחָנִיִּים. וּמֵאַחַר שֶׁיֵּשׁ בְּקִרְבְּכֶם קִנְאָה וּמְרִיבָה
ki odchem bilti-ruchaniyim. ume'achar sheyesh bekirbechem kin'ah umerivah
for ye are yet carnal: for whereas there is among you jealousy and strife,

הַאֵין אַתֶּם בִּלְתִּי־רוּחָנִיִּים וּמִתְנַהֲגִים כְּמוֹ הָאֲנָשִׁים
ha'ein attem bilti-ruchaniyim umitnahagim kemo ha'anashim
are ye not carnal, and do ye not walk after the manner of men?

הֲלֹא כַּאֲשֶׁר מִישֶׁהוּ אוֹמֵר אֲנִי שַׁיָּךְ לְשָׁאוּל וְאַחֵר אוֹמֵר אֲנִי לְאַפּוֹלוֹס, הַאֵין אַתֶּם כְּכָל הָאָדָם
halo ka'asher mishehu omer ani shayach lesha'ul ve'acher omer ani le'appolos, ha'ein attem kechol ha'adam
For when one saith, I am of Paul; and another, I am of Apollos; are ye not men?

מִי הוּא אֵפוֹא אַפּוֹלוֹס? וּמִי הוּא שָׁאוּל
mi hu efo appolos? umi hu sha'ul
What then is Apollos? and what is Paul?

מְשָׁרְתִים אֲשֶׁר בְּאֶמְצָעוּתָם בָּאתֶם לָאֱמוּנָה! וְאִישׁ אִישׁ כְּפִי שֶׁחָלַק לוֹ הָאָדוֹן
meshartim asher be'emtza'utam batem la'emunah! ve'ish ish kefi shechalak lo ha'adon
Ministers through whom ye believed; and each as the Lord gave to him.

אֲנִי נָטַעְתִּי, אַפּוֹלוֹס הִשְׁקָה, אֲבָל הָאֱלֹהִים הִצְמִיחַ
ani nata'ti, appolos hishkah, aval ha'elohim hitzmiach
I planted, Apollos watered; but God gave the increase.

לְפִיכָךְ לֹא הַנּוֹטֵעַ חָשׁוּב, אַף לֹא הַמַּשְׁקֶה, אֶלָּא הָאֱלֹהִים - הַמַּצְמִיחַ
lefichach lo hannotea chashuv, af lo hammashkeh, ella ha'elohim - hammatzmiach
So then neither is he that planteth anything, neither he that watereth; but God that giveth the increase.

הַנּוֹטֵעַ וְהַמַּשְׁקֶה הֵם הַיְנוּ הַךְ, וְכָל אֶחָד יְקַבֵּל אֶת שְׂכָרוֹ כְּפִי עֲמָלוֹ
hannotea vehammashkeh hem haynu hach, vechol echad yekabbel et scharo kefi amalo
Now he that planteth and he that watereth are one: but each shall receive his own reward according to his own labor.

אֶל הַקּוֹרִינְתִּים א

וְלֹא עָלָה עַל לֵב אִישׁ כֹּל אֲשֶׁר הֵכִין הָאֱלֹהִים לְאֹהֲבָיו
velo alah al lev ish kol asher hechin ha'elohim le'ohavav
And which entered not into the heart of man, Whatsoever things God prepared for them that love him.

אַךְ לָנוּ גִּלָּה אֱלֹהִים עַל־יְדֵי רוּחוֹ אֲפִלּוּ אֶת עֲמֻקּוֹת הָאֱלֹהִים, מִשּׁוּם שֶׁהָרוּחַ חוֹקֶרֶת הַכֹּל
ach lanu gillah elohim al-yedei rucho afillu et amukkot ha'elohim, mishum sheharuach chokeret hakkol
But unto us God revealed them through the Spirit: for the Spirit searcheth all things, yea, the deep things of God.

מִי מִבְּנֵי אָדָם יוֹדֵעַ אֶת אֲשֶׁר בָּאָדָם, זוּלָתִי רוּחַ הָאָדָם אֲשֶׁר בְּקִרְבּוֹ
mi mibbenei adam yodea et asher ba'adam, zulati ruach ha'adam asher bekirbo
For who among men knoweth the things of a man, save the spirit of the man, which is in him?

כֵּן גַּם אֶת אֲשֶׁר בֵּאלֹהִים אֵין יוֹדֵעַ זוּלָתִי רוּחַ הָאֱלֹהִים
ken gam et asher belohim ein yodea zulati ruach ha'elohim
even so the things of God none knoweth, save the Spirit of God.

וַאֲנַחְנוּ לֹא קִבַּלְנוּ אֶת רוּחַ הָעוֹלָם, אֶלָּא אֶת הָרוּחַ אֲשֶׁר מֵאֵת הָאֱלֹהִים,
va'anachnu lo kibbalnu et ruach ha'olam, ella et haruach asher me'et ha'elohim
But we received, not the spirit of the world, but the spirit which is from God;

כְּדֵי שֶׁנֵּדַע אֶת הַדְּבָרִים שֶׁאֱלֹהִים נוֹתֵן לָנוּ בְּחַסְדּוֹ
kedei shenneda et haddevarim she'elohim noten lanu bechasdo
that we might know the things that were freely given to us of God.

וְאוֹתָם אֲנַחְנוּ מַבִּיעִים לֹא בְּמִלִּים שֶׁחָכְמַת אֱנוֹשׁ מְלַמֶּדֶת, אֶלָּא בְּמִלִּים שֶׁהָרוּחַ מְלַמֶּדֶת
ve'otam anachnu mabbi'im lo bemillim shechochmat enosh melammedet, ella bemillim sheharuach melammedet
Which things also we speak, not in words which man's wisdom teacheth, but which the Spirit teacheth;

כְּשֶׁאָנוּ מְפָרְשִׁים דְּבָרִים רוּחָנִיִּים בְּהַגְדָּרוֹת רוּחָנִיּוֹת
keshe'anu mefareshim devarim ruchaniyim behagdarot ruchaniyot
combining spiritual things with spiritual words.

אַךְ הָאָדָם הַנַּפְשִׁי אֵינוֹ מְקַבֵּל אֶת דִּבְרֵי רוּחַ אֱלֹהִים,
ach ha'adam hannafshi eino mekabbel et divrei ruach elohim
Now the natural man receiveth not the things of the Spirit of God:

שֶׁכֵּן סִכְלוּת הֵם בְּעֵינָיו; גַּם אֵין הוּא יָכוֹל לָדַעַת אוֹתָם, מִשּׁוּם שֶׁהֵם נִבְחָנִים בְּאֹפֶן רוּחָנִי
shekken sichlut hem be'einav; gam ein hu yachol lada'at otam, mishum shehem nivchanim be'ofen ruchani
for they are foolishness unto him; and he cannot know them, because they are spiritually judged.

לְעֻמַּת זֹאת הָאָדָם הָרוּחָנִי בּוֹחֵן אֶת הַכֹּל וְאִישׁ לֹא יִבְחַן אוֹתוֹ
le'ummat zot ha'adam haruchani bochen et hakkol ve'ish lo yivchan oto
But he that is spiritual judgeth all things, and he himself is judged of no man.

כִּי מִי־תִכֵּן אֶת־רוּחַ יהוה וְאִישׁ עֲצָתוֹ יוֹדִיעֶנּוּ? אַךְ אֲנַחְנוּ יֵשׁ לָנוּ רוּחַ הַמָּשִׁיחַ
ki mi-tikken et-ruach hashem ve'ish atzato yodi'ennu? ach anachnu yesh lanu ruach hammashiach
For who hath known the mind of the Lord, that he should instruct him? But we have the mind of Christ.

אֶל הַקּוֹרִינְתִּים א

הֶחְלַטְתִּי אָז שֶׁלֹּא לָדַעַת דָּבָר בְּקִרְבְּכֶם זוּלַת יֵשׁוּעַ הַמָּשִׁיחַ וְהוּא - צָלוּב

hechlatti az shello lada'at davar bekirbechem zulat yeshua hammashiach vehu - tzaluv
For I determined not to know anything among you, save Jesus Christ, and him crucified.

וַאֲנִי בְּחֻלְשָׁה וּבְפַחַד וּבִרְעָדָה רַבָּה הָיִיתִי אֶצְלְכֶם

va'ani bechulshah uvefachad uvir'adah rabbah hayiti etzlechem
And I was with you in weakness, and in fear, and in much trembling.

דִּבּוּרִי וְהַטָּפָתִי לֹא לֻוּוּ בְּפִתּוּיֵי מִלִּים שֶׁל חָכְמָה אֱנוֹשִׁית,

dibburi vehattafati lo luvvu befittuyei millim shel chochmah enoshit
And my speech and my preaching were not in persuasive words of wisdom,

אֶלָּא בְּהוֹכָחָה שֶׁל רוּחַ וּגְבוּרָה

ella behochachah shel ruach ugevurah
but in demonstration of the Spirit and of power:

כְּדֵי שֶׁלֹּא תִּסָּמֵךְ אֱמוּנַתְכֶם עַל חָכְמַת בְּנֵי אָדָם אֶלָּא עַל גְּבוּרַת אֱלֹהִים

kedei shello tissamech emunatchem al chochmat benei adam ella al gevurat elohim
that your faith should not stand in the wisdom of men, but in the power of God.

אֲנַחְנוּ דּוֹבְרִים חָכְמָה בֵּין הַמְבֻגָּרִים

anachnu doverim chochmah bein hamvuggarim
We speak wisdom, however, among them that are fullgrown:

אַךְ לֹא חָכְמַת הָעוֹלָם הַזֶּה, גַּם לֹא חָכְמַת שַׁלִּיטֵי הָעוֹלָם הַזֶּה הַבָּאִים אֶל קִצָּם

ach lo chochmat ha'olam hazzeh, gam lo chachemat shallitei ha'olam hazzeh habba'im el kitzam
yet a wisdom not of this world, nor of the rulers of this world, who are coming to nought:

אֲנַחְנוּ דּוֹבְרִים אֶת חָכְמַת אֱלֹהִים הַנִּסְתֶּרֶת, הַחָכְמָה שֶׁהָיְתָה גְּנוּזָה

anachnu doverim et chochmat elohim hannisteret, hachochmah shehaytah genuzah
but we speak God's wisdom in a mystery, even the wisdom that hath been hidden,

וַאֲשֶׁר לִפְנֵי הָעוֹלָמִים יְעָדָהּ אֱלֹהִים לְתִפְאַרְתֵּנוּ

va'asher lifnei ha'olamim ye'adah elohim letif'artenu
which God foreordained before the worlds unto our glory:

וְאִישׁ מִשַּׁלִּיטֵי הָעוֹלָם הַזֶּה לֹא יְדָעָהּ

ve'ish mishallitei ha'olam hazzeh lo yeda'ah,
which none of the rulers of this world hath known:

שֶׁכֵּן אִלּוּ יְדָעוּהָ לֹא הָיוּ צוֹלְבִים אֶת אֲדוֹן הַכָּבוֹד

shekken illu yeda'uha lo hayu tzolvim et adon hakkavod
for had they known it, they would not have crucified the Lord of glory:

כְּמוֹ שֶׁכָּתוּב אֲשֶׁר עַיִן לֹא רָאַתָה וְאֹזֶן לֹא שָׁמְעָה

kemo shekkatuv asher ayin lo ra'atah ve'ozen lo shame'ah
but as it is written, Things which eye saw not, and ear heard not,

אֶל הַקּוֹרִינְתִּים א

לֹא רַבִּים חֲזָקִים וְלֹא רַבִּים רָמֵי יַחַשׂ
lo rabbim chazakim velo rabbim ramei yachas
not many mighty, not many noble, are called:

אֲבָל אֱלֹהִים בָּחַר בַּכְּסִילִים אֲשֶׁר בָּעוֹלָם כְּדֵי לְבַיֵּשׁ אֶת הַחֲכָמִים
aval elohim bachar bakksilim asher ba'olam kedei levayesh et hachachamim
but God chose the foolish things of the world, that he might put to shame them that are wise;

וּבַחַלָּשִׁים אֲשֶׁר בָּעוֹלָם כְּדֵי לְבַיֵּשׁ אֶת הַחֲזָקִים
uvachallashim asher ba'olam kedei levayesh et hachazakim
and God chose the weak things of the world, that he might put to shame the things that are strong;

בַּנְּחוּתִים אֲשֶׁר בָּעוֹלָם וּבַנֶּחְשָׁבִים לִפְחוּתֵי עֵרֶךְ בָּחַר אֱלֹהִים
bannechutim asher ba'olam uvannechshavim lifchutei erech bachar elohim
and the base things of the world, and the things that are despised, did God choose,

בַּדְּבָרִים שֶׁהֵם כְּאֶפֶס, כְּדֵי לְהַשְׁפִּיל עַד לְאֶפֶס אֶת הַדְּבָרִים הַקַּיָּמִים
baddvarim shehem ke'efes, kedei lehashpil ad le'efes et haddevarim hakkayamim
yea and the things that are not, that he might bring to nought the things that are:

לְמַעַן לֹא יִתְהַלֵּל אִישׁ לִפְנֵי הָאֱלֹהִים
lema'an lo yit'hallel ish lifnei ha'elohim
that no flesh should glory before God.

אֲבָל מִמֶּנּוּ קַיָּמִים אַתֶּם בַּמָּשִׁיחַ יֵשׁוּעַ אֲשֶׁר הָיָה לָנוּ לְחָכְמָה מֵאֵת אֱלֹהִים
aval mimmennu kayamim attem bammashiach yeshua asher hayah lanu lechochmah me'et elohim
But of him are ye in Christ Jesus, who was made unto us wisdom from God,

לִצְדָקָה, לִקְדֻשָּׁה וְלִפְדוּת
litzdakah, likdushah velifdut
and righteousness and sanctification, and redemption:

כְּדֵי שֶׁהַמִּתְהַלֵּל יִתְהַלֵּל בַּיהוה, כְּמוֹ שֶׁגַּם כָּתוּב
kedei shehammit'hallel yit'hallel bahashem, kemo sheggam katuv
that, according as it is written, He that glorieth, let him glory in the Lord.

ב

וַאֲנִי, אַחַי, כְּשֶׁבָּאתִי
va'ani, achai, kshebbati
And I, brethren, when I came unto you,

לְהוֹדִיעַ לָכֶם אֶת סוֹד אֱלֹהִים, לֹא בָּאתִי אֲלֵיכֶם בְּמִלִּים רָמוֹת אוֹ בְּרוֹמְמוּת חָכְמָה
lehodia lachem et sod elohim, lo bati aleichem bemillim ramot o beromemut chochmah
came not with excellency of speech or of wisdom, proclaiming to you the testimony of God.

אֶל הַקּוֹרִנְתִּים א

הֵן דְּבַר הַצְּלָב הוּא סִכְלוּת בְּעֵינֵי הָאוֹבְדִים, אַךְ לָנוּ הַנּוֹשָׁעִים הוּא גְּבוּרַת אֱלֹהִים
hen devar hatzlav hu sichlut be'einei ha'ovedim, ach lanu hannosha'im hu gevurat elohim
For the word of the cross is to them that perish foolishness; but unto us who are saved it is the power of God.

שֶׁהֲרֵי כָּתוּב: אֲאַבֵּד חָכְמַת חֲכָמִים וּבִינַת נְבוֹנִים אַסְתִּיר
sheharei katuv: a'abbed chochmat chachamim uvinat nevonim astir
For it is written, I will destroy the wisdom of the wise, And the discernment of the discerning will I bring to nought.

אַיֵּה הֶחָכָם? אַיֵּה הַבָּקִי בַּתּוֹרָה? אַיֵּה הַמִּתְפַּלְמֵס שֶׁל הָעוֹלָם הַזֶּה
ayeh hechacham? ayeh habbaki battorah? ayeh hammitpalmes shel ha'olam hazzeh
Where is the wise? where is the scribe? where is the disputer of this world?

הַאִם לֹא שָׂם הָאֱלֹהִים אֶת חָכְמַת הָעוֹלָם לְאִוֶּלֶת
ha'im lo sam ha'elohim et chochmat ha'olam le'ivvelet
hath not God made foolish the wisdom of the world?

וּמֵאַחַר שֶׁבְּחָכְמַת הָאֱלֹהִים לֹא הִשְׂכִּיל הָעוֹלָם לָדַעַת אֶת אֱלֹהִים בְּאֶמְצָעוּת חָכְמָה,
ume'achar shebbechochemat ha'elohim lo hiskil ha'olam lada'at et elohim be'emtza'ut chochmah
For seeing that in the wisdom of God the world through its wisdom knew not God,

רָאָה אֱלֹהִים לְנָכוֹן לְהוֹשִׁיעַ אֶת הַמַּאֲמִינִים עַל־יְדֵי הַכְרָזָה שֶׁנֶּחְשֶׁבֶת לְסִכְלוּת
ra'ah elohim lenachon lehoshia et hamma'aminim al-yedei hachrazah shennechshevet lesichlut
it was God's good pleasure through the foolishness of the preaching to save them that believe.

הִנֵּה הַיְּהוּדִים מְבַקְשִׁים אוֹתוֹת וְהַיְּוָנִים מְחַפְּשִׂים חָכְמָה
hinneh hayehudim mevakshim otot vehayevanim mechappsim chochmah
Seeing that Jews ask for signs, and Greeks seek after wisdom:

אֲבָל אֲנַחְנוּ מַכְרִיזִים מָשִׁיחַ צָלוּב, אֶבֶן נֶגֶף לַיְּהוּדִים וְסִכְלוּת בְּעֵינֵי הַיְּוָנִים
aval anachnu machrizim mashiach tzaluv, even negef layehudim vesichlut be'einei hayevanim
but we preach Christ crucified, unto Jews a stumblingblock, and unto Gentiles foolishness;

אוּלָם לַנִּקְרָאִים הֵן מִקֶּרֶב הַיְּהוּדִים הֵן מִקֶּרֶב הַיְּוָנִים -
ulam lannikra'im hen mikkerev hayehudim hen mikkerev hayevanim -
but unto them that are called, both Jews and Greeks,

מָשִׁיחַ שֶׁהוּא גְּבוּרַת אֱלֹהִים וְחָכְמַת אֱלֹהִים
mashiach shehu gevurat elohim vechochemat elohim
Christ the power of God, and the wisdom of God.

הֵן סִכְלוּת אֱלֹהִים חֲכָמָה מִבְּנֵי אָדָם, וְחֻלְשַׁת אֱלֹהִים חֲזָקָה מִבְּנֵי אָדָם
hen sichlut elohim chachamah mibbnei adam, vechulshat elohim chazakah mibbnei adam
Because the foolishness of God is wiser than men; and the weakness of God is stronger than men.

אַחַי, רְאוּ מִי אַתֶּם שֶׁנִּקְרֵאתֶם: לֹא רַבִּים מִכֶּם חֲכָמִים מִבְּחִינַת הָעוֹלָם הַזֶּה
achai, re'u mi attem shennikretem. lo rabbim mikkem chachamim mibbechinat ha'olam hazzeh
For behold your calling, brethren, that not many wise after the flesh,

אֶל הַקּוֹרִינְתִים א

וְשֶׁלֹּא יִהְיוּ פְּלוּגִים בֵּינֵיכֶם
veshello yihyu pillugim beineichem
and that there be no divisions among you;

אֶלָּא עִמְדוּ מְאֻחָדִים לְגַמְרֵי בְּאוֹתָהּ מַחֲשָׁבָה וּבְאוֹתָהּ דֵּעָה
ella imdu me'uchadim legamrei be'otah machashavah uve'otah de'ah
but that ye be perfected together in the same mind and in the same judgment.

אַחַי, נִמְסַר לִי מֵאֵת בְּנֵי מִשְׁפַּחַת כְּלוֹאָה
achai, nimsar li me'et benei mishpachat kelo'ah
For it hath been signified unto me concerning you, my brethren, by them that are of the household of Chloe,

שֶׁיֵּשׁ מְרִיבוֹת בֵּינֵיכֶם
sheyesh merivot beineichem
that there are contentions among you.

אֲנִי מִתְכַּוֵּן לְכָךְ שֶׁכָּל אֶחָד מִכֶּם אוֹמֵר
ani mitkavven lechach shekkol echad mikkem omer
Now this I mean, that each one of you saith,

אֲנִי שַׁיָּךְ לְשָׁאוּל, אוֹ אֲנִי לְאַפּוֹלוֹס, אֲנִי שֶׁל כֵּיפָא, וַאֲנִי שֶׁל הַמָּשִׁיחַ
ani shayach lesha'ul, o ani le'appolos, ani shel keifa, va'ani shel hammashiach
I am of Paul; and I of Apollos; and I of Cephas; and I of Christ.

וּבְכֵן, הַאִם הַמָּשִׁיחַ הִתְפַּלֵּג? הַאִם שָׁאוּל נִצְלַב בַּעַדְכֶם? אוֹ לְשֵׁם שָׁאוּל נִטְבַּלְתֶּם
uvechen, ha'im hammashiach hitpalleg? ha'im sha'ul nitzlav ba'adchem? o leshem sha'ul nitbaltem
Is Christ divided? was Paul crucified for you? or were ye baptized into the name of Paul?

תּוֹדָה לָאֵל שֶׁלֹּא הִטְבַּלְתִּי אִישׁ מִכֶּם זוּלַת קְרִיסְפּוֹס וְגָיוֹס
todah la'el shello hitbalti ish mikkem zulat krisepos vegayos
I thank God that I baptized none of you, save Crispus and Gaius;

פֶּן יֹאמַר מִישֶׁהוּ כִּי לִשְׁמִי נִטְבַּלְתֶּם
pen yomar mishehu ki lishmi nitbaltem
lest any man should say that ye were baptized into my name.

אָמְנָם הִטְבַּלְתִּי גַּם אֶת בְּנֵי בֵּיתוֹ שֶׁל סְטֶפָנַס. מִלְּבַד אֵלֶּה, אֵינֶנִּי יוֹדֵעַ אִם הִטְבַּלְתִּי אִישׁ
amenam hitbalti gam et benei beito shel setefanas. millevad elleh, einenni yodea im hitbalti ish
And I baptized also the household of Stephanas: besides, I know not whether I baptized any other.

כִּי הַמָּשִׁיחַ לֹא שְׁלָחַנִי לְהַטְבִּיל, אֶלָּא לְבַשֵּׂר אֶת הַבְּשׂוֹרָה
ki hammashiach lo shelachani lehatbil, ella levasser et habbesorah
For Christ sent me not to baptize, but to preach the gospel:

לֹא בְּחָכְמַת מִלִּים, פֶּן יִהְיֶה לָרִיק צְלָב הַמָּשִׁיחַ
lo bechochmat millim, pen yihyeh larik tzlav hammashiach
not in wisdom of words, lest the cross of Christ should be made void.

אֶל הַקּוֹרִינְתִּים א

אִגֶּרֶת הָרִאשׁוֹנָה אֶל הַקּוֹרִינְתִּים

מֵאֵת שָׁאוּל, שֶׁנִּקְרָא לִהְיוֹת שְׁלִיחַ הַמָּשִׁיחַ יֵשׁוּעַ בִּרְצוֹן אֱלֹהִים, וּמֵאֵת סוֹסְתֶּנִיס אָחִינוּ
me'et sha'ul, shennikra lihyot sheliach hammashiach yeshua birtzon elohim, ume'et sostenis achinu
Paul, called to be an apostle of Jesus Christ through the will of God, and Sosthenes our brother,

אֶל קְהִלַּת אֱלֹהִים שֶׁבְּקוֹרִינְתּוֹס, לְאֵלֶּה אֲשֶׁר קֻדְּשׁוּ בַּמָּשִׁיחַ יֵשׁוּעַ וְנִקְרְאוּ לִהְיוֹת קְדוֹשִׁים
el kehillat elohim shebbekorintos, le'elleh asher kuddeshu bammashiach yeshua venikre'u lihyot kedoshim
unto the church of God which is at Corinth, even them that are sanctified in Christ Jesus, called to be saints,

יַחַד עִם כָּל הַקּוֹרְאִים בְּכָל מָקוֹם וּמָקוֹם בְּשֵׁם אֲדוֹנֵנוּ יֵשׁוּעַ הַמָּשִׁיחַ - אֲדוֹנֵנוּ כַּאֲדוֹנָם
yachad im kol hakkore'im bechol makom umakom beshem adonenu yeshua hammashiach - adonenu ka'adonam
with all that call upon the name of our Lord Jesus Christ in every place, their Lord and ours:

חֶסֶד וְשָׁלוֹם לָכֶם מֵאֵת הָאֱלֹהִים אָבִינוּ וְהָאָדוֹן יֵשׁוּעַ הַמָּשִׁיחַ
chesed veshalom lachem me'et ha'elohim avinu veha'adon yeshua hammashiach
Grace to you and peace from God our Father and the Lord Jesus Christ.

אֲנִי מוֹדֶה לֵאלֹהַי בְּכָל עֵת בַּעֲבוּרְכֶם עַל חֶסֶד אֱלֹהִים שֶׁנִּתַּן לָכֶם בַּמָּשִׁיחַ יֵשׁוּעַ
ani modeh le'elohai bechol et ba'avurechem al chesed elohim shennittan lachem bammashiach yeshua
I thank my God always concerning you, for the grace of God which was given you in Christ Jesus;

כִּי בוֹ נַעֲשֵׂיתֶם עֲשִׁירִים בַּכֹּל, בְּכָל אֹמֶר וּבְכָל דַּעַת
ki bo na'aseitem ashirim bakkol, bechol omer uvechol da'at
that in everything ye were enriched in him, in all utterance and all knowledge;

וְעֵדוּת הַמָּשִׁיחַ קִבְּלָה תֹּקֶף בְּקִרְבְּכֶם
ve'edut hammashiach kibblah tokef bekirbechem
even as the testimony of Christ was confirmed in you:

בְּאֹפֶן שֶׁאֵינְכֶם חֲסֵרִים שׁוּם מַתָּנָה רוּחָנִית בְּצִפִּיָּתְכֶם לְהִתְגַּלּוּת אֲדוֹנֵנוּ יֵשׁוּעַ הַמָּשִׁיחַ
be'ofen she'einechem chaserim shum mattanah ruchanit betzippiyatchem lehitgallut adonenu yeshua hammashiach
so that ye come behind in no gift; waiting for the revelation of our Lord Jesus Christ;

אֲשֶׁר גַּם יְחַזֵּק אֶתְכֶם עַד קֵץ לְמַעַן תִּהְיוּ נְקִיִּים מִכָּל אַשְׁמָה בְּיוֹם אֲדוֹנֵנוּ יֵשׁוּעַ הַמָּשִׁיחַ
asher gam yechazzek etchem ad ketz lema'an tihyu nekiyim mikkol ashmah beyom adonenu yeshua hammashiach
who shall also confirm you unto the end, that ye be unreproveable in the day of our Lord Jesus Christ.

נֶאֱמָן הוּא הָאֱלֹהִים אֲשֶׁר קָרָא אֶתְכֶם לְחֶבְרַת בְּנוֹ יֵשׁוּעַ הַמָּשִׁיחַ אֲדוֹנֵנוּ
ne'eman hu ha'elohim asher kara etchem lechevrat beno yeshua hammashiach adonenu
God is faithful, through whom ye were called into the fellowship of his Son Jesus Christ our Lord.

אַחַי, אֲנִי מַפְצִיר בָּכֶם בְּשֵׁם אֲדוֹנֵנוּ יֵשׁוּעַ הַמָּשִׁיחַ שֶׁתִּהְיוּ כֻּלְּכֶם תְּמִימֵי דֵעִים בְּמוֹצָא פִיכֶם
achai, ani maftzir bachem beshem adonenu yeshua hammashiach shettihyu kullchem tmimei de'im bemotza pichem
Now I beseech you, brethren, through the name of our Lord Jesus Christ, that ye all speak the same thing,

הָרוֹמִים

אֶרַסְטוֹס גִּזְבַּר הָעִיר וּקוֹרְטוֹס אָחִינוּ דּוֹרְשִׁים בִּשְׁלוֹמְכֶם
erastos gizbar ha'ir ukvartos achinu doreshim bishlomechem
Erastus the treasurer of the city saluteth you, and Quartus the brother.

וְהוּא אֲשֶׁר יָכוֹל לְחַזֵּק אֶתְכֶם לְפִי בְּשׂוֹרָתִי וְהַכְרָזַת יֵשׁוּעַ הַמָּשִׁיחַ
vehu asher yachol lechazzek etchem lefi besorati vehachrazat yeshua hammashiach
Now to him that is able to establish you according to my gospel and the preaching of Jesus Christ,

לְפִי הִתְגַּלּוּת הַסּוֹד שֶׁהָיָה כָּמוּס בְּעִתּוֹת עוֹלָם
lefi hitgallut hassod shehayah kamus be'ittot olam
according to the revelation of the mystery which hath been kept in silence through times eternal,

אַךְ כָּעֵת, בִּפְקֻדַּת אֱלֹהֵי עוֹלָם, נִתְגַּלָּה עַל־יְדֵי כְּתוּבִים נְבוּאִיִּים
ach ka'et, bifkuddat elohei olam, nitgallah al-yedei ketuvim nevu'iyim
but now is manifested, and by the scriptures of the prophets,

וּפֻרְסַם לְכָל הַגּוֹיִם כְּדֵי לַהֲבִיאָם לִידֵי צִיּוּת שֶׁבָּאֱמוּנָה
ufursam lechol haggoyim kedei lahavi'am liydei tziyut shebba'emunah
according to the commandment of the eternal God, is made known unto all the nations unto obedience of faith:

הָאֱלֹהִים אֲשֶׁר לוֹ לְבַדּוֹ הַחָכְמָה, לוֹ הַכָּבוֹד בְּיֵשׁוּעַ הַמָּשִׁיחַ לְעוֹלְמֵי עוֹלָמִים. אָמֵן
ha'elohim asher lo levaddo hachochemah, lo hakkavod beyeshua hammashiach le'olemei olamim. amen
to the only wise God, through Jesus Christ, to whom be the glory for ever. Amen.

הָרוֹמִים

בָּרְכוּ לְשָׁלוֹם אִישׁ אֶת רֵעֵהוּ בִּנְשִׁיקָה קְדוֹשָׁה. כָּל קְהִלּוֹת הַמָּשִׁיחַ דּוֹרְשׁוֹת בִּשְׁלוֹמְכֶם
barechu leshalom ish et re'ehu binshikah kedoshah. kol kehillot hammashiach doreshot bishlomechem
Salute one another with a holy kiss. All the churches of Christ salute you.

וַאֲנִי מְבַקֵּשׁ מִכֶּם, אַחַי: הִשָּׁמְרוּ מִן הַמְעוֹרְרִים מַחֲלוֹקוֹת וּמִן הַמַּכְשִׁילִים,
va'ani mevakkesh mikkem, achai. hishameru min ham'orerim machalokot umin hammachshilim,
Now I beseech you, brethren, mark them that are causing the divisions and occasions of stumbling,

הַפּוֹעֲלִים בְּנִגּוּד לַלִּמּוּד שֶׁלְּמַדְתֶּם, וְהִתְרַחֲקוּ מֵהֶם
happo'alim beniggud lallimmud shellummadtem, vehitrachaku mehem
contrary to the doctrine which ye learned: and turn away from them.

אֲנָשִׁים כָּאֵלֶּה אֵינָם מְשָׁרְתִים אֶת אֲדוֹנֵנוּ הַמָּשִׁיחַ, אֶלָּא אֶת הַכֶּרֶס שֶׁלָּהֶם
anashim ka'elleh einam mesharetim et adonenu hammashiach, ella et hakkeres shellahem
For they that are such serve not our Lord Christ, but their own belly;

וּבְאִמְרֵי נֹעַם וּבְדִבּוּרִים יָפִים הֵם מוֹלִיכִים שׁוֹלָל אֶת לֵב הַתְּמִימִים
uve'imrei no'am uvedibburim yafim hem molichim sholal et lev hattemimim
and by their smooth and fair speech they beguile the hearts of the innocent.

שָׂמֵחַ אֲנִי עֲלֵיכֶם, כִּי צִיּוּתְכֶם נוֹדַע לַכֹּל
sameach ani aleichem, ki tziyutchem noda lakkol
I rejoice therefore over you: For your obedience is come abroad unto all men.

אֲבָל רְצוֹנִי שֶׁתִּהְיוּ חֲכָמִים לַטּוֹב וּתְמִימִים לְגַבֵּי הָרַע
aval retzoni shettihyu chachamim lattov utemimim legabbei hara
but I would have you wise unto that which is good, and simple unto that which is evil.

וֵאלֹהֵי הַשָּׁלוֹם יַכְרִיעַ בִּמְהֵרָה אֶת הַשָּׂטָן תַּחַת רַגְלֵיכֶם
Ve'elohei hashalom yachria bimeherah et hassatan tachat ragleichem.
And the God of peace shall bruise Satan under your feet shortly.

חֶסֶד אֲדוֹנֵנוּ יֵשׁוּעַ הַמָּשִׁיחַ עִמָּכֶם
chesed adonenu yeshua hammashiach immachem
The grace of our Lord Jesus Christ be with you.

טִימוֹתֵיאוֹס, חֲבֵרִי לַעֲבוֹדָה, וְגַם לוּקְיוֹס וְיָסוֹן וְסוֹסִיפַּטְרוֹס בְּנֵי־עַמִּי דּוֹרְשִׁים בִּשְׁלוֹמְכֶם
timotei'os, chaveri la'avodah, vegam lukeyos veyason vesosipatros benei-'ammi dorshim bishlomechem
Timothy my fellow-worker saluteth you; and Lucius and Jason and Sosipater, my kinsmen.

אֲנִי טֶרְטִיּוֹס, הַכּוֹתֵב אֶת הָאִגֶּרֶת הַזֹּאת, שׁוֹאֵל בִּשְׁלוֹמְכֶם בָּאָדוֹן
ani terteyos, hakkotev et ha'iggeret hazzot, sho'el bishlomechem ba'adon
I Tertius, who write the epistle, salute you in the Lord.

גָּיוֹס הַמְאָרֵחַ אוֹתִי וְאֶת כָּל הַקְּהִלָּה דּוֹרֵשׁ בִּשְׁלוֹמְכֶם
gayos ham'areach oti ve'et kol hakkehillah doresh bishlomechem
Gaius my host, and of the whole church, saluteth you.

הָרוֹמִים

דְּרְשׁוּ בְּשָׁלוֹם אֶפֵּינֶטוֹס יַקִּירִי, שֶׁהָיָה פְּרִי רִאשׁוֹן לַמָּשִׁיחַ בִּמְחוֹז אַסְיָה
dirshu bishlom eppeinetos yakkiri, shehayah pri rishon lammashiach bimchoz asyah
Salute Epænetus my beloved, who is the firstfruits of Asia unto Christ.

דְּרְשׁוּ בְּשָׁלוֹם מִרְיָם, שֶׁעָמְלָה רַבּוֹת בִּשְׁבִילְכֶם
dirshu bishlom miryam, she'amlah rabbot bishvilechem
Salute Mary, who bestowed much labor on you.

דְּרְשׁוּ בְּשָׁלוֹם אַנְדְּרוֹנִיקוֹס וְיוּנְיָס, בְּנֵי־עַמִּי שֶׁהָיוּ אִתִּי בַּמַּאֲסָר
dirshu bishlom anderonikos veyuneyas, benei-'ammi shehayu itti bamma'asar
Salute Andronicus and Junias, my kinsmen, and my fellow-prisoners,

נִכְבָּדִים הֵם בְּקֶרֶב הַשְּׁלִיחִים וְגַם הָיוּ בַּמָּשִׁיחַ לְפָנַי
nichbadim hem bekerev hashlichim vegam hayu bammashiach lefanai
who are of note among the apostles, who also have been in Christ before me.

דְּרִישַׁת שָׁלוֹם לְאַמְפְּלִיאָטוֹס יַקִּירִי בָּאָדוֹן
derishat shalom le'ampeli'atos yakkiri ba'adon
Salute Ampliatus my beloved in the Lord.

דְּרִישַׁת שָׁלוֹם לְאוּרְבָּנוֹס חֲבֵרֵנוּ לַעֲבוֹדָה בַּמָּשִׁיחַ, וּלְאִיסְטַכִיס יַקִּירִי
derishat shalom le'urebanos chaverenu la'avodah bammashiach, ule'isetachis yakkiri
Salute Urbanus our fellow-worker in Christ, and Stachys my beloved.

דְּרִישַׁת שָׁלוֹם לְאַפֵּלִיס הַבָּחוּן בַּמָּשִׁיחַ וְלִבְנֵי בֵּיתוֹ שֶׁל אֲרִיסְטוֹבּוּלוֹס
derishat shalom le'appellis habbachun bammashiach velivnei beito shel arisetobbulos
Salute Apelles the approved in Christ. Salute them that are of the household of Aristobulus.

דְּרִישַׁת שָׁלוֹם לְהוֹרוֹדְיוֹן בֶּן־עַמִּי וְלִבְנֵי בֵּיתוֹ שֶׁל נַרְקִיסוֹס אֲשֶׁר בָּאָדוֹן
derishat shalom lehorodeyon ben-'ammi velivnei beito shel narkisos asher ba'adon
Salute Herodion my kinsman. Salute them of the household of Narcissus, that are in the Lord.

דְּרִישַׁת שָׁלוֹם לִטְרִיפֵינָה וּטְרִיפוֹסָה הָעֲמֵלוֹת בָּאָדוֹן, וּלְפֶרְסִיס הַחֲבִיבָה שֶׁעָמְלָה רַבּוֹת בָּאָדוֹן
derishat shalom litrifeinah uterifosah ha'amelot ba'adon, ulepersis hachavivah she'amelah rabbot ba'adon
Salute Tryphæna and Tryphosa, who labor in the Lord. Salute Persis the beloved, who labored much in the Lord.

דְּרִישַׁת שָׁלוֹם לְרוּפוֹס הַנִּבְחָר בָּאָדוֹן, וּלְאִמּוֹ שֶׁהִיא כְּאֵם לִי
derishat shalom lerufos hannivchar ba'adon, ule'immo shehi ke'em li
Salute Rufus the chosen in the Lord, and his mother and mine.

דְּרִישַׁת שָׁלוֹם לַאֲסִינְקְרִיטוֹס, לִפְלִיגוֹן, לְהֶרְמֵס, לְפַטְרוֹבַּס וְהֶרְמַס וְלָאַחִים אֲשֶׁר אִתָּם
derishat shalom la'asinekeritos, lifleigon, lehermes, lepatrobbas vehermas vela'achim asher ittam
Salute Asyncritus, Phlegon, Hermes, Patrobas, Hermas, and the brethren that are with them.

דְּרִישַׁת שָׁלוֹם לְפִילוֹלוֹגוֹס וְיוּלְיָה, לְנֵרֵאַס וַאֲחוֹתוֹ, לְאוֹלִימְפַּס וְכָל הַקְּדוֹשִׁים אֲשֶׁר אִתָּם
derishat shalom lefilologos veyuleyah, lenire'as va'achoto, le'olimepas vechol hakkedoshim asher ittam
Salute Philologus and Julia, Nereus and his sister, and Olympas, and all the saints that are with them.

הָרוֹמִים

כְּדֵי שֶׁאֶנָּצֵל מִידֵי הַסּוֹרְרִים בְּאֶרֶץ יְהוּדָה

kedei she'ennatzel midei hassorerim be'eretz yehudah
that I may be delivered from them that are disobedient in Judæa,

וְשֵׁרוּתִי לְמַעַן יְרוּשָׁלַיִם יִהְיֶה לְרָצוֹן בְּעֵינֵי הַקְּדוֹשִׁים

vesheruti lema'an yerushalayim yihyeh leratzon be'einei hakkdoshim
and that my ministration which I have for Jerusalem may be acceptable to the saints;

וּכְדֵי שֶׁאָבוֹא אֲלֵיכֶם בְּשִׂמְחָה, כִּרְצוֹן אֱלֹהִים, וְאָנוּחַ בְּחֶבְרַתְכֶם

uchedei she'avo aleichem besimchah, kirtzon elohim, ve'anuach bechevratchem
that I may come unto you in joy through the will of God, and together with you find rest.

אֱלֹהֵי הַשָּׁלוֹם עִם כֻּלְּכֶם. אָמֵן.

elohei hashalom im kullchem. amen
Now the God of peace be with you all. Amen.

טז

אֲנִי מַמְלִיץ לִפְנֵיכֶם עַל אֲחוֹתֵנוּ פֶבִּי, שַׁמָּשִׁית הַקְּהִלָּה בְּקֶנְכְּרֶאָה

ani mamlitz lifneichem al achotenu febbi, shammashit hakkehillah bekenkere'ah
I commend unto you Phoebe our sister, who is a servant of the church that is at Cenchreæ:

קַבְּלוּ נָא אוֹתָהּ בָּאָדוֹן, כַּיָּאֶה לַקְּדוֹשִׁים

kabbelu na otah ba'adon, kaya'eh lakkedoshim
that ye receive her in the Lord, worthily of the saints,

וְעִזְרוּ לָהּ בְּכָל דָּבָר שֶׁתִּזְדַּקֵּק לָכֶם

ve'izru lah bechol davar shettizdakek lachem
and that ye assist her in whatsoever matter she may have need of you:

כִּי אָכֵן הָיְתָה עֵזֶר לְרַבִּים וְגַם לִי

ki achen hayetah ezer lerabbim vegam li
for she herself also hath been a helper of many, and of mine own self.

דִּרְשׁוּ בִּשְׁלוֹם פְּרִיסְקִילָה וַעֲקִילַס חֲבֵרַי לָעֲבוֹדָה בַּמָּשִׁיחַ יֵשׁוּעַ

dirshu bishlom perisekilah va'akilas chaverai la'avodah bammashiach yeshua
Salute Prisca and Aquila my fellow-workers in Christ Jesus,

אֲשֶׁר סִכְּנוּ אֶת רֹאשָׁם בְּעַד נַפְשִׁי, וְלֹא רַק אֲנִי מַכִּיר לָהֶם טוֹבָה, אֶלָּא גַּם כָּל קְהִלּוֹת הַגּוֹיִם

asher sikkenu et rosham be'ad nafshi, velo rak ani makkir lahem tovah, ella gam kol kehillot haggoyim
who for my life laid down their own necks; unto whom not only I give thanks, but also all the churches of the Gentiles:

וּדְרִישַׁת שָׁלוֹם לַקְּהִלָּה שֶׁבְּבֵיתָם

uderishat shalom lakkehillah shebbeveitam
and salute the church that is in their house.

הָרוֹמִים

וּלְאַחַר שֶׁאֶהֱנֶה קִמְעָה אֶצְלְכֶם תְּשַׁלְּחוּנִי לְהֶמְשֵׁךְ דַּרְכִּי
ule'achar she'ehaneh kim'ah etzlechem teshallechuni lehemshech darki
and to be brought on my way thitherward by you, if first in some measure I shall have been satisfied with your company)—

אוּלָם כָּעֵת אֲנִי עוֹלֶה לִירוּשָׁלַיִם לְעֶזְרַת הַקְּדוֹשִׁים
ulam ka'et ani oleh liyerushalayim le'ezrat hakkedoshim
but now, I say, I go unto Jerusalem, ministering unto the saints.

כִּי מְקֵדוֹנְיָה וְאָכַיָה רָאוּ לְנָכוֹן
ki makedoneyah ve'achayah ra'u lenachon
For it hath been the good pleasure of Macedonia and Achaia

לִתְרֹם תְּרוּמָה לַעֲנִיֵּי הַקְּדוֹשִׁים
litrom terumah la'aniyei hakkedoshim
to make a certain contribution for the poor among the saints that are at Jerusalem.

הֵם רָאוּ זֹאת לְנָכוֹן וְזוֹהִי חוֹבָתָם כְּלַפֵּיהֶם
hem ra'u zot lenachon vezohi chovatam klappeihem
Yea, it hath been their good pleasure; and their debtors they are.

שֶׁכֵּן אִם הַגּוֹיִם שֻׁתְּפוּ בַּדְּבָרִים הָרוּחָנִיִּים שֶׁלָּהֶם
shekken im haggoyim shuttfu baddevarim haruchaniyim shellahem
For if the Gentiles have been made partakers of their spiritual things,

עֲלֵיהֶם גַּם לְסַיֵּעַ לָהֶם בִּדְבָרִים חָמְרִיִּים
aleihem gam lesayea lahem bidvarim chomeriyim
they owe it to them also to minister unto them in carnal things.

לָכֵן לְאַחַר שֶׁאַשְׁלִים זֹאת וְאֶמְסֹר לָהֶם בַּחֲתִימָתִי אֶת הַתְּרוּמָה הַזֹּאת, אָסוּר אֲלֵיכֶם בְּדַרְכִּי לִסְפָרַד
lachen le'achar she'ashlim zot ve'emsor lahem bachatimati et hattrumah hazzot, asur aleichem bedarki lisfarad
When therefore I have accomplished this, and have sealed to them this fruit, I will go on by you unto Spain.

אֲנִי בָּטוּחַ כִּי כַּאֲשֶׁר אָבוֹא אֲלֵיכֶם, אָבוֹא בִּמְלוֹא בִּרְכַּת הַמָּשִׁיחַ
ani batuach ki ka'asher avo aleichem, avo bimlo birkat hammashiach
And I know that, when I come unto you, I shall come in the fulness of the blessing of Christ.

וַאֲנִי מְבַקֵּשׁ מִכֶּם, אַחַי, לְמַעַן אֲדוֹנֵנוּ יֵשׁוּעַ הַמָּשִׁיחַ וּלְמַעַן אַהֲבַת הָרוּחַ
va'ani mevakkesh mikkem, achai, lema'an adonenu yeshua hammashiach ulema'an ahavat haruach
Now I beseech you, brethren, by our Lord Jesus Christ, and by the love of the Spirit,

לְהֵאָבֵק יַחַד אִתִּי בִּתְפִלּוֹת לֵאלֹהִים בַּעֲדִי
lehe'avek yachad itti bitfillot lelohim ba'adi
that ye strive together with me in your prayers to God for me;

הָרוֹמִים

כְּדֵי שֶׁהַגּוֹיִם יִהְיוּ לְמִנְחָה רְצוּיָה, מְקֻדֶּשֶׁת בְּרוּחַ הַקֹּדֶשׁ
kedei shehaggoyim yihyu leminchah retzuyah, mekuddeshet beruach hakkodesh
that the offering up of the Gentiles might be made acceptable, being sanctified by the Holy Spirit.

לָכֵן, הוֹדוֹת לַמָּשִׁיחַ יֵשׁוּעַ יָכוֹל אֲנִי לְהִתְגָּאוֹת בַּדְּבָרִים הַשַּׁיָּכִים לֵאלֹהִים
lachen, hodot lammashiach yeshua yachol ani lehitga'ot bidvarim hashayachim le'elohim
I have therefore my glorying in Christ Jesus in things pertaining to God.

וְלֹא אָעֵז לְדַבֵּר בִּלְתִּי אִם עַל הַדְּבָרִים שֶׁהַמָּשִׁיחַ עָשָׂה דַּרְכִּי
velo a'ez ledabber bilti im al haddvarim shehammashiach asah darki
For I will not dare to speak of any things save those which Christ wrought through me,

כְּדֵי לְהָבִיא אֶת הַגּוֹיִם לִידֵי צִיּוּת, וְזֹאת עַל־יְדֵי דִּבּוּר וּמַעֲשֶׂה
kedei lehavi et haggoyim liydei tziyut, vezot al-yedei dibbur uma'aseh
for the obedience of the Gentiles, by word and deed,

בְּכֹחַ אוֹתוֹת וּמוֹפְתִים, וּבְכֹחַ רוּחַ הַקֹּדֶשׁ
bechoach otot umoftim, uvechoach ruach hakkodesh
in the power of signs and wonders, in the power of the Holy Spirit;

בְּאֹפֶן שֶׁהִסְפַּקְתִּי לְבַשֵּׂר אֶת בְּשׂוֹרַת הַמָּשִׁיחַ מִירוּשָׁלַיִם וּסְבִיבוֹתֶיהָ עַד אִלּוּרִיקוֹן
be'ofen shehispakti levashor et besorat hammashiach miyerushalayim usevivoteiha ad illurikon
so that from Jerusalem, and round about even unto Illyricum, I have fully preached the gospel of Christ;

וְאָמְנָם הִשְׁתַּדַּלְתִּי לְבַשֵּׂר בִּמְקוֹמוֹת שֶׁטֶּרֶם הִשְׁמִיעוּ בָּהֶם אֶת שֵׁם הַמָּשִׁיחַ
ve'omnam hishtaddalti levashor bimkomot shetterem hishmi'u bahem et shem hammashiach
yea, making it my aim so to preach the gospel, not where Christ was already named,

כְּדֵי שֶׁלֹּא אֶבְנֶה עַל יְסוֹד שֶׁל אֲחֵרִים
kedei shello evneh al yesod shel acherim
that I might not build upon another man's foundation;

אֶלָּא כַּכָּתוּב: אֲשֶׁר לֹא־סֻפַּר לָהֶם רָאוּ, וַאֲשֶׁר לֹא־שָׁמְעוּ הִתְבּוֹנָנוּ
'ella kakkatuv: asher lo-suppar lahem ra'u, va'asher lo-shame'u hitbonanu
but, as it is written, They shall see, to whom no tidings of him came, And they who have not heard shall understand.

לָכֵן גַּם פְּעָמִים רַבּוֹת נִמְנַע מִמֶּנִּי לָבוֹא אֲלֵיכֶם
lachen gam pe'amim rabbot nimna mimmenni lavo aleichem
Wherefore also I was hindered these many times from coming to you:

אֲבָל כָּעֵת, הוֹאִיל וְאֵין לִי עוֹד מָקוֹם לִפְעֻלָּה בָּאֲזוֹרִים הָאֵלֶּה, וְשָׁנִים רַבּוֹת מִשְׁתּוֹקֵק אֲנִי לָבוֹא אֲלֵיכֶם
aval ka'et, ho'il ve'ein li od makom lif'ullah ba'azorim ha'elleh, veshanim rabbot mishtokek ani lavo aleichem
but now, having no more any place in these regions, and having these many years a longing to come unto you,

אֲנִי מְקַוֶּה שֶׁבְּדַרְכִּי לִסְפָרַד אָסוּר לִרְאוֹתְכֶם
ani mekavveh shebbedarki lisfarad asur lir'otechem
whensoever I go unto Spain (for I hope to see you in my journey,

הָרוֹמִים

עַל־כֵּן אוֹדְךָ יהוה בַּגּוֹיִם וּלְשִׁמְךָ אֲזַמֵּר
al-ken odecha hashem baggoyim uleshimcha azammer
Therefore will I give praise unto thee among the Gentiles, And sing unto thy name.

וְעוֹד הוּא אוֹמֵר: הַרְנִינוּ גוֹיִם עַמּוֹ
ve'od hu omer: harninu goyim ammo
And again he saith, Rejoice, ye Gentiles, with his people.

וְעוֹד: הַלְלוּ־אֶת יהוה כָּל־גּוֹיִם, שַׁבְּחוּהוּ כָּל־הָאֻמִּים
ve'od: halelu-'et hashem kol-goyim, shabbechuhu kol-ha'ummim
And again, Praise the Lord, all ye Gentiles; And let all the peoples praise him.

וִישַׁעְיָהוּ אוֹמֵר: וְהָיָה שֹׁרֶשׁ יִשַׁי
viysha'yahu omer: vehayah shoresh yishai
And again, Isaiah saith, There shall be the root of Jesse,

אֲשֶׁר עֹמֵד לְנֵס עַמִּים, אֵלָיו גּוֹיִם יִדְרֹשׁוּ
asher omed lenes ammim, elav goyim yidroshu
And he that ariseth to rule over the Gentiles; On him shall the Gentiles hope.

וֵאלֹהֵי הַתִּקְוָה יְמַלֵּא אֶתְכֶם כָּל שִׂמְחָה וְשָׁלוֹם בֶּאֱמוּנַתְכֶם
Ve'elohei hattikvah yemallei etchem kol simchah veshalom be'emunatchem
Now the God of hope fill you with all joy and peace in believing,

כְּדֵי שֶׁתִּגְאֶה בָּכֶם הַתִּקְוָה בְּכֹחַ רוּחַ הַקֹּדֶשׁ
kedei shettig'eh bachem hattikvah bechoach ruach hakkodesh
that ye may abound in hope, in the power of the Holy Spirit.

אֲנִי בָּטוּחַ, אַחַי, שֶׁאַתֶּם שׁוֹפְעִים טוּב
ani batuach, achai, she'attem shofe'im tuv
And I myself also am persuaded of you, my brethren, that ye yourselves are full of goodness,

מְלֵאִים כָּל דַּעַת וְיוֹדְעִים גַּם לְהוֹכִיחַ אִישׁ אֶת רֵעֵהוּ
mele'im kol da'at veyode'im gam lehochiach ish et re'ehu
filled with all knowledge, able also to admonish one another.

בְּכָל זֹאת כָּתַבְתִּי לָכֶם פֹּה וָשָׁם בְּהֶעָזָה רַבָּה לְמַדַּי
bechol zot katavti lachem poh vasham behe'azah rabbah lemaddai
But I write the more boldly unto you in some measure,

כְּמִי שֶׁמְּעוֹרֵר אֶת זִכְרוֹנְכֶם, וְזֹאת עַל־סְמַךְ הַחֶסֶד הַנָּתוּן לִי מֵאֵת אֱלֹהִים
kemi shemme'orer et zichronechem, vezot al-smach hachesed hannatun li me'et elohim
as putting you again in remembrance, because of the grace that was given me of God,

לִהְיוֹת מְשָׁרֵת־קֹדֶשׁ שֶׁל הַמָּשִׁיחַ יֵשׁוּעַ בִּשְׁבִיל הַגּוֹיִם וּלְכַהֵן בִּבְשׂוֹרַת אֱלֹהִים
lihyot mesharet-kodesh shel hammashiach yeshua bishvil haggoyim ulechahen bivsorat elohim
that I should be a minister of Christ Jesus unto the Gentiles, ministering the gospel of God,

הָרוֹמִים

טו

אֲנַחְנוּ הַחֲזָקִים חַיָּבִים לָשֵׂאת אֶת חֻלְשׁוֹת הַחַלָּשִׁים וְלֹא לְבַקֵּשׁ הֲנָאָה לְעַצְמֵנוּ
anachnu hachazakim chayavim laset et chulshot hachallashim velo levakkesh hana'ah le'atzmenu
Now we that are strong ought to bear the infirmities of the weak, and not to please ourselves.

כָּל אֶחָד מֵאִתָּנוּ יִדְאַג לְטוֹבַת רֵעֵהוּ כְּדֵי שֶׁרֵעֵהוּ יִבָּנֶה
kol echad me'ittanu yid'ag letovat re'ehu kedei shere'ehu yibbaneh
Let each one of us please his neighbor for that which is good, unto edifying.

שֶׁכֵּן גַּם הַמָּשִׁיחַ לֹא בִּקֵּשׁ הֲנָאָה לְעַצְמוֹ, אֶלָּא כַּכָּתוּב: וְחֶרְפּוֹת חוֹרְפֶיךָ נָפְלוּ עָלַי
shekken gam hammashiach lo bikkesh hana'ah le'atzmo, ella kakkatuv: vecherpot chorfeicha nafelu alai
For Christ also pleased not himself; but, as it is written, The reproaches of them that reproached thee fell upon me.

וַהֲרֵי כָּל מַה שֶּׁנִּכְתַּב מִקֶּדֶם, נִכְתַּב לְהַדְרָכָתֵנוּ
vaharei kol mah shennichtav mikkedem, nichtav lehadrachatenu
For whatsoever things were written aforetime were written for our learning,

כְּדֵי שֶׁתִּהְיֶה לָנוּ תִּקְוָה מִתּוֹךְ הַסַּבְלָנוּת וְהַנֶּחָמָה שֶׁבַּכְּתוּבִים
kedei shettihyeh lanu tikvah mittoch hassavlanut vehannechamah shebbakketuvim
that through patience and through comfort of the scriptures we might have hope.

וֵאלֹהֵי הַסַּבְלָנוּת וְהַנֶּחָמָה יִתֵּן וְתִהְיוּ תְּמִימֵי דֵעִים זֶה עִם זֶה כִּרְצוֹן הַמָּשִׁיחַ יֵשׁוּעַ
velohei hassavlanut vehannechamah yitten vetihyu temimei de'im zeh im zeh kirtzon hammashiach yeshua
Now the God of patience and of comfort grant you to be of the same mind one with another according to Christ Jesus:

כְּדֵי שֶׁבְּלֵב אֶחָד וּבְפֶה אֶחָד תְּהַלְלוּ אֶת אֱלֹהִים, אֲבִי אֲדוֹנֵנוּ יֵשׁוּעַ הַמָּשִׁיחַ
kedei shebbelev echad uvefeh echad tehallelu et elohim, avi adonenu yeshua hammashiach
that with one accord ye may with one mouth glorify the God and Father of our Lord Jesus Christ.

עַל כֵּן קַבְּלוּ אִישׁ אֶת רֵעֵהוּ, כְּשֵׁם שֶׁגַּם הַמָּשִׁיחַ קִבֵּל אוֹתָנוּ לִכְבוֹד אֱלֹהִים
al ken kabblu ish et re'ehu, keshem sheggam hammashiach kibbel otanu lichvod elohim
Wherefore receive ye one another, even as Christ also received you, to the glory of God.

וַאֲנִי אוֹמֵר שֶׁהַמָּשִׁיחַ הָיָה לִמְשָׁרֵת הַנִּמּוֹלִים בִּגְלַל נֶאֱמָנוּת אֱלֹהִים
va'ani omer shehammashiach hayah limsharet hannimmolim biglal ne'emanut elohim
For I say that Christ hath been made a minister of the circumcision for the truth of God,

כְּדֵי לְקַיֵּם אֶת הַהַבְטָחוֹת שֶׁנִּתְּנוּ לָאָבוֹת
kedei lekayem et hahavtachot shennittenu la'avot
that he might confirm the promises given unto the fathers,

וּכְדֵי שֶׁהַגּוֹיִם יְהַלְלוּ אֶת אֱלֹהִים עַל רַחֲמָיו, כַּכָּתוּב
uchedei shehaggoyim yehallelu et elohim al rachamav, kakkatuv
and that the Gentiles might glorify God for his mercy; as it is written,

הָרוֹמִים

אִם בִּגְלַל הַמַּאֲכָל שֶׁלְּךָ נִגְרַם צַעַר לְאָחִיךָ, הֲרֵי שֶׁאֵינְךָ מִתְהַלֵּךְ עוֹד בְּדֶרֶךְ שֶׁל אַהֲבָה
im biglal hamma'achal shellecha nigram tza'ar le'achicha, harei she'einecha mit'hallech od bederech shel ahavah
For if because of meat thy brother is grieved, thou walkest no longer in love.

אַל נָא תַּהֲרֹס בְּמַאֲכָלְךָ אָדָם שֶׁהַמָּשִׁיחַ מֵת בַּעֲדוֹ
al na taharos bema'achalecha adam shehammashiach met ba'ado
Destroy not with thy meat him for whom Christ died.

וּבְכֵן, שֶׁלֹּא יֵצֵא שֵׁם רַע לְמַה שֶׁטּוֹב בְּעֵינֵיכֶם
uvechen, shello yetzei shem ra lemah shettov be'eineichem
Let not then your good be evil spoken of:

כִּי מַלְכוּת אֱלֹהִים אֵינָהּ אֲכִילָה וּשְׁתִיָּה, אֶלָּא צֶדֶק וְשָׁלוֹם וְשִׂמְחָה בְּרוּחַ הַקֹּדֶשׁ
ki malchut elohim einah achilah ushetiyah, ella tzedek veshalom vesimchah beruach hakkodesh
for the kingdom of God is not eating and drinking, but righteousness and peace and joy in the Holy Spirit.

מִי שֶׁמְּשָׁרֵת אֶת הַמָּשִׁיחַ בְּדֶרֶךְ זוֹ, רָצוּי הוּא לֵאלֹהִים וּמְקֻבָּל עַל הַבְּרִיּוֹת
mi shemmesharet et hammashiach bederech zo, ratzui hu le'elohim umekubbal al habberiyot
For he that herein serveth Christ is well-pleasing to God, and approved of men.

לָכֵן נַחְתֹּר נָא אֶל דְּבָרִים שֶׁמְּבִיאִים לִידֵי שָׁלוֹם, וְאֶל דְּבָרִים שֶׁבְּאֶמְצָעוּתָם יִבְנֶה אִישׁ אֶת רֵעֵהוּ
lachen nachtor na el devarim shemmevi'im liydei shalom, ve'el devarim shebbe'emtza'utam yivneh ish et re'ehu
So then let us follow after things which make for peace, and things whereby we may edify one another.

אַל תַּהֲרֹס אֶת מְלֶאכֶת אֱלֹהִים בִּגְלַל מַאֲכָל
al taharos et melechet elohim biglal ma'achal
Overthrow not for meat's sake the work of God.

אָמְנָם הַכֹּל טָהוֹר, אַךְ רַע הַמַּעֲשֶׂה כְּשֶׁאָדָם אוֹכֵל וְהָאֲכִילָה הִיא לְמִכְשׁוֹל
omnam hakkol tahor, ach ra hamma'aseh keshe'adam ochel veha'achilah hi lemichshol
All things indeed are clean; howbeit it is evil for that man who eateth with offence.

מוּטָב שֶׁלֹּא לֶאֱכֹל בָּשָׂר וְלֹא לִשְׁתּוֹת יַיִן וּלְהִמָּנַע מִכָּל מַה שֶׁיֵּשׁ בּוֹ כְּדֵי לְהַכְשִׁיל אֶת אָחִיךָ
mutav shello le'echol basar velo lishtot yayin ulehimmana mikkol mah sheyesh bo kedei lehachshil et achicha
It is good not to eat flesh, nor to drink wine, nor to do anything whereby thy brother stumbleth.

יֵשׁ לְךָ אֱמוּנָה, חֲיֵה בָּהּ בְּעַצְמְךָ לִפְנֵי אֱלֹהִים
yesh lecha emunah, chayeh bah be'atzmecha lifnei elohim
The faith which thou hast, have thou to thyself before God.

אַשְׁרֵי הָאָדָם שֶׁאֵינוֹ מַרְשִׁיעַ אֶת עַצְמוֹ בַּמֶּה שֶׁהוּא בּוֹרֵר לוֹ
ashrei ha'adam she'eino marshia et atzmo bemah shehu borer lo
Happy is he that judgeth not himself in that which he approveth.

אַךְ הָאוֹכֵל וּבְלִבּוֹ סָפֵק - אָשֵׁם, כִּי לֹא מִתּוֹךְ אֱמוּנָה פָּעַל. וְכָל מַה שֶׁאֵינוֹ מִתּוֹךְ אֱמוּנָה חֵטְא הוּא
ach ha'ochel uvelibbo safek - ashem, ki lo mittoch emunah pa'al. vechol mah she'eino mittoch emunah chet hu
But he that doubteth is condemned if he eat, because he eateth not of faith; and whatsoever is not of faith is sin.

הָרוֹמִים

אִישׁ מֵאִתָּנוּ אֵינוֹ חַי אֶת חַיָּיו לְשֵׁם עַצְמוֹ וְאִישׁ אֵינוֹ מֵת לְשֵׁם עַצְמוֹ
ish me'ittanu eino chai et chayav leshem atzmo ve'ish eino met leshem atzmo
For none of us liveth to himself, and none dieth to himself.

כְּשֶׁאָנוּ חַיִּים, לְשֵׁם הָאָדוֹן אָנוּ חַיִּים. כְּשֶׁאָנוּ מֵתִים, לְשֵׁם הָאָדוֹן אָנוּ מֵתִים
keshe'anu chayim, leshem ha'adon anu chayim. keshe'anu metim, leshem ha'adon anu metim
For whether we live, we live unto the Lord; or whether we die, we die unto the Lord:

לְפִיכָךְ, בֵּין שֶׁחַיִּים בֵּין שֶׁמֵּתִים, לָאָדוֹן אָנוּ שַׁיָּכִים
lefichach, bein shechayim bein shemmetim, la'adon anu shayachim
whether we live therefore, or die, we are the Lord's.

שֶׁהֲרֵי הַמָּשִׁיחַ מֵת וְקָם שׁוּב לְחַיִּים כְּדֵי שֶׁיִּהְיֶה אָדוֹן גַּם לַמֵּתִים גַּם לַחַיִּים
sheharei hammashiach met vekam shuv lechayim kedei sheyihyeh adon gam lammetim gam lachayim
For to this end Christ died and lived again, that he might be Lord of both the dead and the living.

וּמַדּוּעַ אַתָּה חוֹרֵץ מִשְׁפָּט עַל אָחִיךָ? מַדּוּעַ אַתָּה בָּז לְאָחִיךָ
umaddua attah choretz mishpat al achicha? maddua attah baz le'achicha
But thou, why dost thou judge thy brother? or thou again, why dost thou set at nought thy brother?

הֲרֵי כֻּלָּנוּ נַעֲמֹד לִפְנֵי כֵּס הַמִּשְׁפָּט שֶׁל אֱלֹהִים
harei kullanu na'amod lifnei kes hammishpat shel elohim
For we shall all stand before the judgment-seat of God.

הֲלֹא כָתוּב: חַי־אָנִי, נְאֻם־יהוה, כִּי־לִי תִּכְרַע כָּל־בֶּרֶךְ וְכָל־לָשׁוֹן תּוֹדֶה לֵאלֹהִים
halo katuv. chai-'ani, ne'um-hashem, ki-li tichra kol-berech vechol-lashon todeh lelohim
For it is written, As I live, saith the Lord, to me every knee shall bow, And every tongue shall confess to God.

וּבְכֵן כָּל אֶחָד מֵאִתָּנוּ יִתֵּן דִּין וְחֶשְׁבּוֹן עַל עַצְמוֹ לִפְנֵי אֱלֹהִים
uvechen kol echad me'ittanu yitten din vecheshbon al atzmo lifnei elohim
So then each one of us shall give account of himself to God.

לָכֵן אַל נִשְׁפֹּט עוֹד אִישׁ אֶת רֵעֵהוּ, אֶלָּא שֶׁזֶּה יִהְיֶה שִׁפּוּטְכֶם
lachen al nishpot od ish et re'ehu, ella shezzeh yihyeh shipputechem
Let us not therefore judge one another any more: but judge ye this rather,

שֶׁלֹּא יִתֵּן אִישׁ אֶבֶן נֶגֶף אוֹ מִכְשׁוֹל לִפְנֵי אָחִיו
shello yitten ish even negef o michshol lifnei achiv
that no man put a stumblingblock in his brother's way, or an occasion of falling.

יוֹדֵעַ אֲנִי, וְגַם בָּטוּחַ אֲנִי בָּאָדוֹן יֵשׁוּעַ, שֶׁשּׁוּם דָּבָר אֵינוֹ טָמֵא בִּפְנֵי עַצְמוֹ
yodea ani, vegam batuach ani ba'adon yeshua', sheshum davar eino tamei bifnei atzmo
I know, and am persuaded in the Lord Jesus, that nothing is unclean of itself:

אֶלָּא טָמֵא הוּא לְמִי שֶׁחוֹשֵׁב אוֹתוֹ לְטָמֵא
ella tamei hu lemi shechoshev oto letame
save that to him who accounteth anything to be unclean, to him it is unclean.

הָרוֹמִים

יד

קַבְּלוּ אֶת הַחַלָּשׁ בָּאֱמוּנָה, אַךְ לֹא לְשֵׁם וִכּוּחִים עַל דֵּעוֹת
kabbelu et hachallash ba'emunah, ach lo leshem vikkuchim al de'ot
But him that is weak in faith receive ye, yet not for decision of scruples.

אֶחָד מַאֲמִין שֶׁמֻּתָּר לֶאֱכֹל הַכֹּל; אַחֵר, שֶׁהוּא חַלָּשׁ, אוֹכֵל מַאֲכָלִים צִמְחִיִּים
echad ma'amin shemmuttar le'echol hakkol; acher, shehu challash, ochel ma'achalim tzimchiyim
One man hath faith to eat all things: but he that is weak eateth herbs.

אַל יָבוּז הָאוֹכֵל לְזֶה שֶׁאֵינוֹ אוֹכֵל
al yavuz ha'ochel lezeh she'eino ochel,
Let not him that eateth set at nought him that eateth not;

וְזֶה שֶׁאֵינוֹ אוֹכֵל אַל יַחֲרֹץ מִשְׁפָּט עַל הָאוֹכֵל, שֶׁכֵּן אֱלֹהִים קִבֵּל אוֹתוֹ בְּרָצוֹן
vezeh she'eino ochel al yacharotz mishpat al ha'ochel, shekken elohim kibbel oto beratzon
and let not him that eateth not judge him that eateth: for God hath received him.

מִי אַתָּה כִּי תִּשְׁפֹּט אֶת עַבְדּוֹ שֶׁל אַחֵר? הֲרֵי בְּעֵינֵי אֲדוֹנָיו הוּא עוֹמֵד אוֹ נוֹפֵל
mi attah ki tishpot et avdo shel acher? harei be'einei adonav hu omed o nofel
Who art thou that judgest the servant of another? to his own lord he standeth or falleth.

אַךְ הוּא יַעֲמֹד, כִּי הָאָדוֹן יָכוֹל לַעֲזֹר לוֹ לַעֲמֹד
ach hu ya'amod, ki ha'adon yachol la'azor lo la'amod
Yea, he shall be made to stand; for the Lord hath power to make him stand.

יֵשׁ אָדָם הַמַּחְשִׁיב יוֹם אֶחָד יוֹתֵר מִיּוֹם אַחֵר, וְיֵשׁ שֶׁמַּחְשִׁיב כָּל יוֹם וָיוֹם
yesh adam hammachshiv yom echad yoter miyom acher, veyesh shemmachshiv kol yom veyom
One man esteemeth one day above another: another esteemeth every day alike.

יְהֵא כָּל אָדָם בָּטוּחַ בְּדַעְתּוֹ
yehei kol adam batuach beda'to
Let each man be fully assured in his own mind.

מִי שֶׁמַּחְשִׁיב אֶת הַיּוֹם מַחְשִׁיב אוֹתוֹ לְשֵׁם יהוה.
mi shemmachshiv et hayom machshiv oto leshem hashem
He that regardeth the day, regardeth it unto the Lord:

הָאוֹכֵל אוֹכֵל לְשֵׁם יהוה, שֶׁכֵּן הוּא מוֹדֶה לֵאלֹהִים
ha'ochel ochel leshem hashem, shekken hu modeh le'elohim
and he that eateth, eateth unto the Lord, for he giveth God thanks;

וְזֶה שֶׁאֵינוֹ אוֹכֵל, לְשֵׁם יהוה אֵינוֹ אוֹכֵל וְגַם הוּא מוֹדֶה לֵאלֹהִים
vezeh she'eino ochel, leshem hashem eino ochel vegam hu modeh le'elohim
and he that eateth not, unto the Lord he eateth not, and giveth God thanks.

הָרוֹמִים

מֶכֶס לְמִי שֶׁעַל הַמֶּכֶס; יִרְאָה לְמִי שֶׁרָאוּי לִירֹא מִמֶּנּוּ; כָּבוֹד לְמִי שֶׁמַּגִּיעַ לוֹ כָּבוֹד
meches lemi she'al hammeches; yir'ah lemi shera'ui liro mimmennu; kavod lemi shemmaggia lo kavod
custom to whom custom; fear to whom fear; honor to whom honor.

אַל תִּהְיוּ חַיָּבִים דָּבָר לְאִישׁ מִלְּבַד אַהֲבַת הַזּוּלַת, כִּי הָאוֹהֵב אֶת הַזּוּלַת קִיֵּם אֶת הַתּוֹרָה
al tihyu chayavim davar le'ish millevad ahavat hazzulat, ki ha'ohev et hazzulat kiyem et hattorah
Owe no man anything, save to love one another: for he that loveth his neighbor hath fulfilled the law.

הֵן הַמִּצְווֹת לֹא תִנְאָף, לֹא תִרְצַח, לֹא תִגְנֹב, לֹא תַחְמֹד
hen hammitzvot lo tin'af, lo tirtzach, lo tignov, lo tachmod
For this, Thou shalt not commit adultery, Thou shalt not kill, Thou shalt not steal, Thou shalt not covet,

וְכָל מִצְוָה אַחֶרֶת, כְּלוּלוֹת בַּמַּאֲמָר וְאָהַבְתָּ לְרֵעֲךָ כָּמוֹךָ
vechol mitzvah acheret, kelulot bamma'amar ve'ahavta lere'acha kamocha
and if there be any other commandment, it is summed up in this word, namely, Thou shalt love thy neighbor as thyself.

הָאַהֲבָה אֵינָהּ גּוֹרֶמֶת רָעָה לַזּוּלַת, לָכֵן הָאַהֲבָה הִיא קִיּוּם הַתּוֹרָה בִּמְלוֹאָהּ
ha'ahavah einah goremet ra'ah lazzulat, lachen ha'ahavah hi kiyum hattorah bimlo'ah
Love worketh no ill to his neighbor: love therefore is the fulfilment of the law.

נוֹסָף עַל כָּךְ, יְדוּעִים לָכֶם הַזְּמַנִּים, הַיְנוּ שֶׁכָּעֵת הַשָּׁעָה לְהִתְעוֹרֵר מִן הַשֵּׁנָה
nosaf al kach, yedu'im lachem hazzemannim, haynu shekka'et hasha'ah lehit'orer min hashenah
And this, knowing the season, that already it is time for you to awake out of sleep:

כִּי יְשׁוּעָתֵנוּ קְרוֹבָה עַכְשָׁו יוֹתֵר מִשֶּׁהָיְתָה בַּיּוֹם שֶׁהִתְחַלְנוּ לְהַאֲמִין
ki yeshu'atenu kerovah achshav yoter mishehayetah bayom shehitchalnu leha'amin
for now is salvation nearer to us than when we first believed.

הַלַּיְלָה חוֹלֵף וְהַיּוֹם קָרֵב
hallaylah cholef vehayom karev
The night is far spent, and the day is at hand:

עַל כֵּן נָסִירָה מֵעָלֵינוּ אֶת מַעֲשֵׂי הַחֹשֶׁךְ וְנִלְבַּשׁ אֶת שִׁרְיוֹן הָאוֹר
al ken nasirah me'aleinu et ma'asei hachoshech venilbash et shiryon ha'or
let us therefore cast off the works of darkness, and let us put on the armor of light.

וּכְמוֹ בַּיּוֹם נִתְנַהֵג נָא כָּיָאוּת, לֹא בְּהוֹלְלוּת וּבְשִׁכְרוּת
uchemo bayom nitnaheg na kaya'ut, lo beholelut uveshichrut
Let us walk becomingly, as in the day; not in revelling and drunkenness,

לֹא בְּזִמָּה וּפְרִיצוּת, לֹא בְּרִיב וְקִנְאָה
lo bezimmah uferitzut, lo beriv vekin'ah
not in chambering and wantonness, not in strife and jealousy.

כִּי אִם לִבְשׁוּ אֶת הָאָדוֹן יֵשׁוּעַ הַמָּשִׁיחַ, וְאַל תִּדְאֲגוּ לַגּוּף בִּמְגַמָּה לְהַשְׂבִּיעַ אֶת הַתַּאֲווֹת
ki im livshu et ha'adon yeshua hammashiach, ve'al tid'agu lagguf bimgammah lehasbia et hatta'avot
But put ye on the Lord Jesus Christ, and make not provision for the flesh, to fulfil the lusts thereof.

הָרוֹמִים

יג

כָּל אָדָם יִכָּנַע לְרָשֻׁיּוֹת הַשִּׁלְטוֹן
kol adam yikkana lerashyot hashilton
Let every soul be in subjection to the higher powers:

שֶׁהֲרֵי אֵין שִׁלְטוֹן אֶלָּא מִטַּעַם אֱלֹהִים, וְהַשִּׁלְטוֹנוֹת הַנּוֹכְחִיִּים נִקְבְּעוּ מִטַּעַם אֱלֹהִים
sheharei ein shilton ella mitta'am elohim, vehashiltonot hannochechiyim nikbe'u mitta'am elohim
for there is no power but of God; and the powers that be are ordained of God.

לְפִיכָךְ כָּל הַמִּתְקוֹמֵם נֶגֶד הַשִּׁלְטוֹן מִתְנַגֵּד לְצַו אֱלֹהִים
lefichach kol hammitkomem neged hashilton mitnagged letzav elohim
Therefore he that resisteth the power, withstandeth the ordinance of God:

וְהַמִּתְנַגְּדִים יָבִיאוּ עַל עַצְמָם מִשְׁפָּט
vehammitnaggedim yavi'u al atzmam mishpat
and they that withstand shall receive to themselves judgment.

הֲרֵי אֵין פַּחַד הַשַּׁלִּיטִים עַל עוֹשֵׂה הַטּוֹב, אֶלָּא עַל עוֹשֵׂה הָרַע
harei ein pachad hashallitim al oseh hattov, ella al oseh hara
For rulers are not a terror to the good work, but to the evil.

הַאִם אַתָּה רוֹצֶה שֶׁלֹּא לִפְחֹד מִן הַשִּׁלְטוֹנוֹת? עֲשֵׂה אֶת הַטּוֹב וְתִזְכֶּה לְשֶׁבַח מֵהֶם
ha'im attah rotzeh shello lifchod min hashiltonot? aseh et hattov vetizkeh leshevach mehem
And wouldest thou have no fear of the power? do that which is good, and thou shalt have praise from the same:

הַשִּׁלְטוֹנוֹת הֵם מְשָׁרְתֵי אֱלֹהִים לְטוֹבָתְךָ. אַךְ אִם תַּעֲשֶׂה אֶת הָרַע, עָלֶיךָ לִפְחֹד;
hashiltonot hem mesharetei elohim letovatcha. ach im ta'aseh et hara', aleicha lifchod
for he is a minister of God to thee for good. But if thou do that which is evil, be afraid;

שֶׁהֲרֵי לֹא לְחִנָּם הֵם מַחֲזִיקִים בַּחֶרֶב, כִּי מְשָׁרְתֵי אֱלֹהִים הֵם לִנְקֹם וְלִשְׁפֹּךְ זַעַם עַל עוֹשֵׂי הָרַע
sheharei lo lechinnam hem machazikim bacherev, ki mesharetei elohim hem linkom velishpoch za'am al osei hara
for he beareth not the sword in vain: for he is a minister of God, an avenger for wrath to him that doeth evil.

לָכֵן עָלֶיךָ לְהִכָּנַע לֹא רַק בִּגְלַל הַזַּעַם, אֶלָּא גַּם בִּגְלַל הַמַּצְפּוּן
lachen aleicha lehikkana lo rak biglal hazza'am, ella gam biglal hammatzpun
Wherefore ye must needs be in subjection, not only because of the wrath, but also for conscience' sake.

וְלָכֵן אַתֶּם גַּם מְשַׁלְּמִים מִסִּים, כִּי מְשָׁרְתֵי אֱלֹהִים הֵם הַשּׁוֹקְדִים עַל מִלּוּי תַּפְקִידָם זֶה
velachen attem gam meshallemim missim, ki meshartei elohim hem hashokedim al millui tafkidam zeh
For for this cause ye pay tribute also; for they are ministers of God's service, attending continually upon this very thing.

תְּנוּ לְכָל אָדָם מַה שֶּׁמַּגִּיעַ לוֹ: מַס לְמִי שֶׁעַל הַמַּס
tnu lechol adam mah shemmaggia lo. mas lemi she'al hammas
Render to all their dues: tribute to whom tribute is due;

הָרוֹמִים

בָּרְכוּ אֶת רוֹדְפֵיכֶם, בָּרְכוּ וְאַל תְּקַלְּלוּ
barchu et rodefeichem, barchu ve'al tekallelu
Bless them that persecute you; bless, and curse not.

שִׂמְחוּ עִם הַשְּׂמֵחִים וּבְכוּ עִם הַבּוֹכִים
simchu im hashomechim uvechu im habbochim
Rejoice with them that rejoice; weep with them that weep.

הֱיוּ תְּמִימֵי דֵעִים זֶה עִם זֶה.
heyu temimei de'im zeh im zeh
Be of the same mind one toward another.

אַל תְּהַלְּכוּ בִּגְדוֹלוֹת וְאַל תִּבָּדְלוּ מֵאֲנָשִׁים פְּשׁוּטִים. אַל תִּהְיוּ חֲכָמִים בְּעֵינֵיכֶם
al tehallechu bigdolot ve'al tibbadelu me'anashim peshutim. al tihyu chachamim be'eineichem
Set not your mind on high things, but condescend to things that are lowly. Be not wise in your own conceits.

אַל תְּשַׁלְּמוּ לְאִישׁ רָעָה תַּחַת רָעָה. בַּקְּשׁוּ אֶת הַטּוֹב בְּעֵינֵי כָּל בְּנֵי אָדָם
al teshallemu le'ish ra'ah tachat ra'ah. bakkeshu et hattov be'einei kol benei adam
Render to no man evil for evil. Take thought for things honorable in the sight of all men.

עַד כַּמָּה שֶׁהַדָּבָר בְּיֶדְכֶם חֱיוּ בְּשָׁלוֹם עִם כָּל אָדָם
ad kammah shehaddavar beyedchem chayu beshalom im kol adam
If it be possible, as much as in you lieth, be at peace with all men.

יַקִּירַי, אַל תִּתְנַקְּמוּ אֶלָּא הַנִּיחוּ לַזַּעַם
yakkirai, al titnakkemu ella hannichu lazza'am
Avenge not yourselves, beloved, but give place unto the wrath of God:

כִּי כָתוּב לִי נָקָם וְשִׁלֵּם אָמַר יהוה
ki katuv li nakam veshillem amar hashem
for it is written, Vengeance belongeth unto me; I will recompense, saith the Lord.

אֲבָל אִם־רָעֵב שֹׂנַאֲךָ הַאֲכִילֵהוּ לָחֶם, וְאִם־צָמֵא הַשְׁקֵהוּ מָיִם
aval im-ra'ev sonacha ha'achilehu lachem, ve'im-tzamei hashkehu mayim
But if thine enemy hunger, feed him; if he thirst, give him to drink:

כִּי גֶחָלִים אַתָּה חֹתֶה עַל־רֹאשׁוֹ
ki gechalim attah choteh al-rosho
for in so doing thou shalt heap coals of fire upon his head.

אַל תַּנִּיחַ לָרַע לְהִתְגַּבֵּר עָלֶיךָ, אֶלָּא הִתְגַּבֵּר עַל הָרַע בַּטּוֹב
al tanniach lara lehitgabber aleicha, ella hitgabber al hara battov
Be not overcome of evil, but overcome evil with good.

הָרוֹמִים

כְּשֵׁם שֶׁבְּגוּף אֶחָד יֵשׁ לָנוּ אֵיבָרִים רַבִּים וְלֹא לְכָל הָאֵיבָרִים אוֹתוֹ תַּפְקִיד
keshem shebbeguf echad yesh lanu eivarim rabbim velo lechol ha'eivarim oto tafkid
For even as we have many members in one body, and all the members have not the same office:

כָּךְ אֲנַחְנוּ הָרַבִּים מְהַוִּים גּוּף אֶחָד בַּמָּשִׁיחַ וְכָל אֶחָד אֵיבָר לַחֲבֵרוֹ
kach anachnu harabbim mehavvim guf echad bammashiach vechol echad eivar lachavero
so we, who are many, are one body in Christ, and severally members one of another.

וְיֵשׁ לָנוּ מַתָּנוֹת שׁוֹנוֹת, לְפִי הַחֶסֶד הַנִּתָּן לָנוּ
veyesh lanu mattanot shonot, lefi hachesed hannittan lanu
And having gifts differing according to the grace that was given to us,

אִם נְבוּאָה הֲרֵיהִי כְּמִדַּת הָאֱמוּנָה
im nevu'ah hareihi kemiddat ha'emunah
whether prophecy, let us prophesy according to the proportion of our faith;

אִם לְאִישׁ שֵׁרוּת, יְשָׁרֵת; אִם הוּא מוֹרֶה, יְלַמֵּד
im le'ish sherut, yesharet; im hu moreh, yelammed
or ministry, let us give ourselves to our ministry; or he that teacheth, to his teaching;

מִי שֶׁמַּתְּנָתוֹ הָעִדּוּד, יְעוֹדֵד; הַנּוֹתֵן יִתֵּן בְּתוֹם לֵב
mi shemmattnato ha'iddud, ye'oded; hannoten yitten betom lev
or he that exhorteth, to his exhorting: he that giveth, let him do it with liberality;

הַמַּנְהִיג יְמַלֵּא אֶת תַּפְקִידוֹ בִּשְׁקִידָה; וְהַגּוֹמֵל חֶסֶד יַעֲשֶׂה זֹאת בִּמְאוֹר פָּנִים
hammanhig yemallei et tafkido bishkidah; vehaggomel chesed ya'aseh zot bim'or panim
he that ruleth, with diligence; he that showeth mercy, with cheerfulness.

תְּהֵא אַהֲבַתְכֶם לְלֹא הַעֲמָדַת פָּנִים. שִׂנְאוּ אֶת הָרַע וְדִבְקוּ בַּטּוֹב
tehei ahavatchem lelo ha'amadat panim. sin'u et hara vedivku battov
Let love be without hypocrisy. Abhor that which is evil; cleave to that which is good.

אֶהֱבוּ אִישׁ אֶת רֵעֵהוּ בְּאַהֲבַת אַחִים כֵּנָה. הַקְדִּימוּ לִנְהֹג כָּבוֹד אִישׁ בְּרֵעֵהוּ
ehevu ish et re'ehu be'ahavat achim kenah. hakdimu linhog kavod ish bere'ehu
In love of the brethren be tenderly affectioned one to another; in honor preferring one another;

שִׁקְדוּ וְאַל תִּתְעַצְּלוּ. הֱיוּ נִלְהֲבֵי רוּחַ וְשָׁרְתוּ אֶת הָאָדוֹן
shikdu ve'al tit'atzelu. heyu nilhavei ruach vesharetu et ha'adon
in diligence not slothful; fervent in spirit; serving the Lord;

גִּילוּ בַּתִּקְוָה. הֱיוּ סַבְלָנִים בְּצָרָה. הַתְמִידוּ בִּתְפִלָּה
gilu battikvah. heyu savlanim betsara. hatmidu bitfillah
rejoicing in hope; patient in tribulation; continuing stedfastly in prayer;

תְּנוּ אֶת חֶלְקְכֶם לְצָרְכֵי הַקְּדוֹשִׁים וְשַׁאֲפוּ לְהַכְנִיס אוֹרְחִים
tnu et chelkechem letzorchei hakkedoshim vesha'afu lehachnis orechim
communicating to the necessities of the saints; given to hospitality.

הָרוֹמִים

אֵין חֵקֶר לְמִשְׁפָּטָיו וְאֵין מַשִּׂיג אֶת דְּרָכָיו
ein cheker lemishpatav ve'ein massig et derachav
how unsearchable are his judgments, and his ways past tracing out!

כִּי מִי־תִכֵּן אֶת־רוּחַ יהוה וְאִישׁ עֲצָתוֹ יוֹדִיעֶנּוּ
ki mi-tikken et-ruach hashem ve'ish atzato yodi'ennu
For who hath known the mind of the Lord? or who hath been his counsellor?

וּמִי הִקְדִּים לָתֵת לוֹ דָּבָר וִישַׁלֶּם לוֹ
umi hikdim latet lo davar viyshullam lo
or who hath first given to him, and it shall be recompensed unto him again?

הֲרֵי הַכֹּל מִמֶּנּוּ, הַכֹּל דַּרְכּוֹ, וְהַכֹּל אֵלָיו. לוֹ הַכָּבוֹד לְעוֹלָמִים! אָמֵן
harei hakkol mimmennu, hakkol darko, vehakkol elav. lo hakkavod le'olamim! amen
For of him, and through him, and unto him, are all things. To him be the glory for ever. Amen.

יב

וּבְכֵן, אַחַי, בִּגְלַל רַחֲמֵי אֱלֹהִים אֲנִי מְבַקֵּשׁ מִכֶּם שֶׁתִּמְסְרוּ אֶת גּוּפְכֶם קָרְבָּן חַי
uvechen, achai, biglal rachamei elohim ani mevakkesh mikkem shettimseru et gufchem korban chai
I beseech you therefore, brethren, by the mercies of God, to present your bodies a living sacrifice,

קָדוֹשׁ וְרָצוּי לֵאלֹהִים; כָּךְ תַּעַבְדוּהוּ עֲבוֹדָה שֶׁבַּלֵּב
kadosh veratzui le'elohim; kach ta'avduhu avodah shebballev
holy, acceptable to God, which is your spiritual service.

וְאַל תִּדַּמּוּ לָעוֹלָם הַזֶּה, כִּי אִם הִשְׁתַּנּוּ עַל־יְדֵי הִתְחַדְּשׁוּת הַדַּעַת
ve'al tiddammu la'olam hazzeh, ki im hishtannu al-yedei hitchaddeshut hadda'at
And be not fashioned according to this world: but be ye transformed by the renewing of your mind,

כְּדֵי שֶׁתִּבְחִינוּ מַהוּ רְצוֹן אֱלֹהִים, מַהוּ הַטּוֹב וְהָרָצוּי וְהַמֻּשְׁלָם בְּעֵינָיו
kedei shettavchinu mahu retzon elohim, mahu hattov veharatzui vehammushlam be'einav
that ye may prove what is the good and acceptable and perfect will of God.

עַל־סְמַךְ הַחֶסֶד אֲשֶׁר נִתַּן לִי, הֲרֵינִי אוֹמֵר לְכָל אֶחָד מִכֶּם
al-smach hachesed asher nittan li, hareini omer lechol echad mikkem
For I say, through the grace that was given me, to every man that is among you,

אִישׁ אַל יַחְשֹׁב אֶת עַצְמוֹ לְיוֹתֵר מִשֶּׁרָאוּי לוֹ לַחְשֹׁב
ish al yachshov et atzmo leyoter mishera'ui lo lachshov
not to think of himself more highly than he ought to think;

אֶלָּא יְהֵא צָנוּעַ בְּהַעֲרָכָתוֹ, כְּמִדַּת הָאֱמוּנָה שֶׁהֶעֱנִיק לוֹ אֱלֹהִים
ella yehei tzanua beha'arachato, kemiddat ha'emunah shehe'enik lo elohim
but so to think as to think soberly, according as God hath dealt to each man a measure of faith.

הָרוֹמִים

הֵן, אַחַי, אֵינֶנִּי רוֹצֶה שֶׁיֵּעָלֵם מִכֶּם הַסּוֹד הַזֶּה, פֶּן תִּהְיוּ חֲכָמִים בְּעֵינֵיכֶם
hen, achai, einenni rotzeh sheye'alem mikkem hassod hazzeh, pen tihyu chachamim be'eineichem
For I would not, brethren, have you ignorant of this mystery, lest ye be wise in your own conceits,

קְהוּת לֵב אֲחָזָה בְּמִדַּת מָה אֶת יִשְׂרָאֵל, עַד אֲשֶׁר יִכָּנֵס מְלוֹא הַגּוֹיִם
kehut lev achazah bemiddat mah et yisra'el, ad asher yikkanes melo haggoyim
that a hardening in part hath befallen Israel, until the fulness of the Gentiles be come in;

וְכָךְ כָּל יִשְׂרָאֵל יִוָּשַׁע, כְּמוֹ שֶׁכָּתוּב
vechach kol yisra'el yivvasha, kemo shekkatuv
and so all Israel shall be saved: even as it is written,

וּבָא מִצִּיּוֹן גּוֹאֵל וְיָשִׁיב פֶּשַׁע בְּיַעֲקֹב נְאֻם יהוה
uva mitziyon go'el veyashiv pesha beya'akov ne'um hashem
There shall come out of Zion the Deliverer; He shall turn away ungodliness from Jacob:

וַאֲנִי זֹאת בְּרִיתִי אוֹתָם, כִּי אֶסְלַח לַעֲוֹנָם
va'ani zot beriti otam, ki eslach la'avonam
And this is my covenant unto them, When I shall take away their sins.

אָמְנָם בְּמַה שֶּׁנּוֹגֵעַ לַבְּשׂוֹרָה הֵם אוֹיְבִים בִּגְלַלְכֶם
omnam bemah shennogea labbesorah hem oyevim biglalchem
As touching the gospel, they are enemies for your sake:

אֲבָל בְּמַה שֶּׁנּוֹגֵעַ לַבְּחִירָה אֲהוּבִים הֵם בִּגְלַל הָאָבוֹת
aval bemah shennogea labbechirah ahuvim hem biglal ha'avot
but as touching the election, they are beloved for the fathers' sake.

שֶׁהֲרֵי אֵין הָאֱלֹהִים מִתְחָרֵט עַל מַתְּנוֹתָיו וְעַל בְּחִירָתוֹ
sheharei ein ha'elohim mitcharet al mattnotav ve'al bechirato
For the gifts and the calling of God are not repented of.

וּכְשֵׁם שֶׁאַתֶּם בֶּעָבָר לֹא צִיַּתֶּם לֵאלֹהִים, אַךְ כָּעֵת רֻחַמְתֶּם אַגַּב אִי־צִיּוּתָם
ucheshem she'attem be'avar lo tziyattem lelohim, ach ka'et ruchamtem aggav i-tziyutam
For as ye in time past were disobedient to God, but now have obtained mercy by their disobedience,

כֵּן גַּם אֵלֶּה לֹא צִיְּתוּ כָּעֵת, וְכָךְ בָּרַחֲמִים אֲשֶׁר הֻשְׁפְּעוּ עֲלֵיכֶם יְרֻחֲמוּ גַּם הֵם כָּעֵת
ken gam elleh lo tziyetu ka'et, vechach barachamim asher hushpe'u aleichem yeruchamu gam hem ka'et
even so have these also now been disobedient, that by the mercy shown to you they also may now obtain mercy.

כִּי אֱלֹהִים כָּלָא אֶת הַכֹּל בְּאִי־צִיּוּת כְּדֵי שֶׁיְּרַחֵם עַל הַכֹּל
ki elohim kala et hakkol be'i-tziyut kedei sheyerachem al hakkol
For God hath shut up all unto disobedience, that he might have mercy upon all.

מָה עֹמֶק עֹשֶׁר הָאֱלֹהִים, מָה עֹמֶק חָכְמָתוֹ וְדַעְתּוֹ
mah omek osher ha'elohim, mah omek chochmato veda'to
O the depth of the riches both of the wisdom and the knowledge of God!

הָרוֹמִים

וְאִם נִכְרְתוּ כַּמָּה עֲנָפִים מֵעֵץ הַזַּיִת, וְאַתָּה, זֵית־בָּר, הֻרְכַּבְתָּ בִּמְקוֹמָם
ve'im nichretu kammah anafim me'etz hazzayit, ve'attah, zeit-bar, hurkavta bimkomam
But if some of the branches were broken off, and thou, being a wild olive, wast grafted in among them,

וְשֻׁתַּפְתָּ בְּשֹׁרֶשׁ הָעֵץ וּבְלִשְׁדּוֹ
veshuttafta beshoresh ha'etz uvilshaddo
and didst become partaker with them of the root of the fatness of the olive tree;

אֲזַי אַל תִּתְנַשֵּׂא עַל הָעֲנָפִים. אִם תִּתְנַשֵּׂא, דַּע לְךָ שֶׁלֹּא אַתָּה נוֹשֵׂא אֶת הַשֹּׁרֶשׁ, אֶלָּא הַשֹּׁרֶשׁ נוֹשֵׂא אוֹתְךָ
azai al titnasse al ha'anafim. im titnasse, da lecha shello attah nosei et hashoresh, ella hashoresh nosei otcha
glory not over the branches: but if thou gloriest, it is not thou that bearest the root, but the root thee.

אַתָּה תֹּאמַר: הָעֲנָפִים נִכְרְתוּ כְּדֵי שֶׁאֻרְכַּב אֲנִי
attah tomar: ha'anafim nichretu kedei she'urkav ani
Thou wilt say then, Branches were broken off, that I might be grafted in.

יָפֶה! בִּגְלַל אִי־אֱמוּנָה נִכְרְתוּ, אַךְ אַתָּה עַל־יְדֵי אֱמוּנָה מַחֲזִיק מַעֲמָד. אַל תִּתְגָּאֶה אֶלָּא הִמָּלֵא יִרְאָה
yafeh! biglal i-'emunah nichretu, ach attah al-yedei emunah machazik ma'amad. al titga'eh ella himmalei yir'ah
Well; by their unbelief they were broken off, and thou standest by thy faith. Be not highminded, but fear:

שֶׁהֲרֵי אִם לֹא חָס אֱלֹהִים עַל הָעֲנָפִים הַמְּקוֹרִיִּים, גַּם עָלֶיךָ לֹא יָחוּס
sheharei im lo chas elohim al ha'anafim hammekoriyim, gam aleicha lo yachus
for if God spared not the natural branches, neither will he spare thee.

לָכֵן שִׂים לֵב לְטוּבוֹ שֶׁל אֱלֹהִים וּלְחֻמְרָתוֹ: מֵחַד גִּיסָא חֻמְרָה כְּלַפֵּי הַנִּכְשָׁלִים; מֵאִידָךְ גִּיסָא
lachen sim lev letuvo shel elohim ulechumrato. mechad gisa chumrah kelappei hannichshalim; me'idach gisa
Behold then the goodness and severity of God: toward them that fell, severity; but toward thee,

טוּבוֹ שֶׁל אֱלֹהִים עָלֶיךָ אִם תַּעֲמֹד בְּטוּבוֹ, וְלֹא - גַּם אַתָּה תִּכָּרֵת
tuvo shel elohim aleicha im ta'amod betuvo, valo - gam attah tikkaret
God's goodness, if thou continue in his goodness: otherwise thou also shalt be cut off.

וְאִם לֹא יַמְשִׁיכוּ בְּחֹסֶר אֱמוּנָתָם יֻרְכְּבוּ גַּם הֵם, שֶׁכֵּן אֱלֹהִים יָכוֹל לְהַחֲזִירָם וּלְהַרְכִּיבָם
ve'im lo yamshichu bechoser emunatam yurkevu gam hem, shekken elohim yachol lehachaziram uleharkivam
And they also, if they continue not in their unbelief, shall be grafted in: for God is able to graft them in again.

הֲרֵי אִם אַתָּה נִכְרַתָּ מֵעֵץ זַיִת בַּר מִטִּבְעוֹ
harei im attah nichrata me'etz zayit bar mittiv'o
For if thou wast cut out of that which is by nature a wild olive tree,

וּבְנִגּוּד לַטֶּבַע הֻרְכַּבְתָּ עַל עֵץ זַיִת טוֹב
uveniggud latteva hurkavta al etz zayit tov
and wast grafted contrary to nature into a good olive tree;

כָּל שֶׁכֵּן אֵלֶּה, הַמְּקוֹרִיִּים, יֻרְכְּבוּ עַל עֵץ הַזַּיִת שֶׁלָּהֶם
kol shekken elleh, hammekoriyim, yurkevu al etz hazzayit shellahem
how much more shall these, which are the natural branches, be grafted into their own olive tree?

הָרוֹמִים

כַּכָּתוּב
kakkatuv
according as it is written,

נָתַן לָהֶם הָאֱלֹהִים רוּחַ תַּרְדֵּמָה, עֵינַיִם לֹא לִרְאוֹת וְאָזְנַיִם לֹא לִשְׁמֹעַ עַד הַיּוֹם הַזֶּה
natan lahem ha'elohim ruach tardemah, einayim lo lir'ot ve'oznayim lo lishmoa ad hayom hazzeh
God gave them a spirit of stupor, eyes that they should not see, and ears that they should not hear, unto this very day.

וְדָוִד אוֹמֵר: יְהִי־שֻׁלְחָנָם לִפְנֵיהֶם לְפַח וּלְרֶשֶׁת וְלִשְׁלוּמִים לְמוֹקֵשׁ
vedavid omer: yehi-shulchanam lifneihem lefach ulereshet velishlomim lemokesh
And David saith, Let their table be made a snare, and a trap, And a stumblingblock, and a recompense unto them:

תֶּחְשַׁכְנָה עֵינֵיהֶם מֵרְאוֹת, וּמָתְנֵיהֶם תָּמִיד הַמְעַד
techshachnah eineihem mer'ot, umateneihem tamid ham'ad
Let their eyes be darkened, that they may not see, And bow thou down their back always.

עַל כֵּן שׁוֹאֵל אֲנִי, הַאִם מָעֲדוּ כְּדֵי שֶׁיִּפְּלוּ לְלֹא קוּם? חַס וְחָלִילָה
al ken sho'el ani, ha'im ma'adu kedei sheyippelu lelo kum? chas vechalilah
I say then, Did they stumble that they might fall? God forbid:

אֶלָּא שֶׁבְּמִעִידָתָם הַיְשׁוּעָה לַגּוֹיִם, לְהַקְנִיא אוֹתָם
ella shebbim'idatam hayshu'ah laggoyim, lehakni otam
but by their fall salvation is come unto the Gentiles, to provoke them to jealousy.

וְאִם מְעִידָתָם הִיא עֹשֶׁר לָעוֹלָם וְהֶפְסֵדָם הוּא עֹשֶׁר לַגּוֹיִם, שְׁלֵמוּתָם - עַל אַחַת כַּמָּה וְכַמָּה
ve'im me'idatam hi osher la'olam vehefsedam hu osher laggoyim, shelemutam - al achat kammah vechammah
Now if their fall is the riches of the world, and their loss the riches of the Gentiles; how much more their fulness?

אֲלֵיכֶם הַגּוֹיִם אֲנִי מְדַבֵּר; בִּהְיוֹתִי אֲנִי שָׁלִיחַ לַגּוֹיִם מְכַבֵּד אֲנִי אֶת שֵׁרוּתִי
aleichem haggoyim ani medabber; bihyoti ani shaliach laggoyim mechabbed ani et sheruti
But I speak to you that are Gentiles. Inasmuch then as I am an apostle of Gentiles, I glorify my ministry;

בְּתִקְוָה לְעוֹרֵר קִנְאָה בִּבְנֵי עַמִּי וּלְהוֹשִׁיעַ כַּמָּה מֵהֶם
betikvah le'orer kin'ah bivnei ammi ulehoshia kammah mehem
if by any means I may provoke to jealousy them that are my flesh, and may save some of them.

הֲרֵי אִם הַדְּחִיָּתָם הִיא רִצּוּי בִּשְׁבִיל הָעוֹלָם
harei im haddachatam hi ritzui bishvil ha'olam,
For if the casting away of them is the reconciling of the world,

מַה תִּהְיֶה הֲשָׁבָתָם אִם לֹא תְּקוּמָה מִמָּוֶת אֱלֵי חַיִּים
mah tihyeh hashavatam im lo tekumah mimmavet elei chayim
what shall the receiving of them be, but life from the dead?

אִם תְּרוּמַת הָעִסָּה קֹדֶשׁ, כֵּן גַּם כָּל הַבָּצֵק! וְאִם הַשֹּׁרֶשׁ קֹדֶשׁ, כֵּן גַּם הָעֲנָפִים
im trumat ha'issah kodesh, ken gam kol habbatzek! ve'im hashoresh kodesh, ken gam ha'anafim
And if the firstfruit is holy, so is the lump: and if the root is holy, so are the branches.

הָרוֹמִים

יא

אִם כֵּן, אֲנִי שׁוֹאֵל, הַאִם נָטַשׁ אֱלֹהִים אֶת עַמּוֹ? בְּשׁוּם פָּנִים לֹא! הֲרֵי גַּם אֲנִי בֶּן עַם יִשְׂרָאֵל
im ken, ani sho'el, ha'im natash elohim et ammo? beshum panim lo! harei gam ani ben am yisra'el
I say then, Did God cast off his people? God forbid. For I also am an Israelite,

מִזֶּרַע אַבְרָהָם וּמִשֵּׁבֶט בִּנְיָמִין
mizzera avraham umishevet binyamin
of the seed of Abraham, of the tribe of Benjamin.

אֱלֹהִים לֹא נָטַשׁ אֶת עַמּוֹ, הָעָם שֶׁהוּא יָדַע מִקֶּדֶם. וְכִי אֵינְכֶם יוֹדְעִים מָה אוֹמֵר הַכָּתוּב עַל אֵלִיָּהוּ
elohim lo natash et ammo, ha'am shehu yada mikkedem. vechi einechem yode'im mah omer hakkatuv al eliyahu
God did not cast off his people which he foreknew. Or know ye not what the scripture saith of Elijah?

כֵּיצַד הִתְלוֹנֵן עַל יִשְׂרָאֵל לִפְנֵי אֱלֹהִים
keitzad hitlonen al yisra'el lifnei elohim
how he pleadeth with God against Israel:

אֲדֹנָי, אֶת־נְבִיאֶיךָ הָרְגוּ וְאֶת־מִזְבְּחוֹתֶיךָ הָרָסוּ; וָאִוָּתֵר אֲנִי לְבַדִּי, וַיְבַקְשׁוּ אֶת־נַפְשִׁי לְקַחְתָּהּ
adonai, et-nevi'eicha haregu ve'et-mizbechoteicha harasu; va'ivvater ani levaddi, vayvakshu et-nafshi lekachtah
Lord, they have killed thy prophets, they have digged down thine altars; and I am left alone, and they seek my life.

אַךְ מָה אוֹמֵר לוֹ דְּבַר אֱלֹהִים
ach mah omer lo devar elohim
But what saith the answer of God unto him?

הִשְׁאַרְתִּי לִי בְיִשְׂרָאֵל שִׁבְעַת אֲלָפִים אֲשֶׁר לֹא־כָרְעוּ לַבַּעַל
hish'arti li veyisra'el shiv'at alafim asher lo-chare'u labba'al
I have left for myself seven thousand men, who have not bowed the knee to Baal.

כֵּן גַּם בְּיָמֵינוּ נִשְׁאֲרָה שְׁאֵרָה עַל־פִּי בְּחִירָה שֶׁל חֶסֶד
ken gam beyameinu nish'arah she'erit al-pi bchirah shel chesed
Even so then at this present time also there is a remnant according to the election of grace.

וְאִם בְּחֶסֶד, הֲרֵי שֶׁלֹּא עוֹד מִתּוֹךְ מַעֲשִׂים; אַחֶרֶת הַחֶסֶד חָדֵל לִהְיוֹת חֶסֶד
ve'im bechesed, harei shello od mittoch ma'asim; acheret hachesed chadel lihyot chesed
But if it is by grace, it is no more of works: otherwise grace is no more grace.

וּבְכֵן מָה? יִשְׂרָאֵל לֹא הִשִּׂיג אֶת מְבֻקָּשׁוֹ, אֲבָל הַנִּבְחָרִים הִשִּׂיגוּ
uvechen mah? yisra'el lo hissig et mevukkasho, aval hannivcharim hissigu
What then? That which Israel seeketh for, that he obtained not; but the election obtained it,

וְהַשְּׁאָר הִקְשׁוּ לְבָבָם
vehashe'ar hikshu levavam
and the rest were hardened:

הָרוֹמִים

וְכֵיצַד יַאֲמִינוּ בָּזֶה אֲשֶׁר לֹא שָׁמְעוּ אוֹתוֹ? וְכֵיצַד יִשְׁמְעוּ בְּאֵין מְבַשֵּׂר
vecheitzad ya'aminu bazeh asher lo shame'u oto? vecheitzad yishme'u be'ein mevasser
and how shall they believe in him whom they have not heard? and how shall they hear without a preacher?

כֵּיצַד יְבַשְּׂרוּ אִם לֹא יִשָּׁלְחוּ? הֵן כָּתוּב
keitzad yevashoru im lo yishalechu? hen katuv
and how shall they preach, except they be sent? even as it is written,

מַה־נָּאווּ רַגְלֵי מְבַשְּׂרֵי טוֹב
mah-navu raglei mevassrei tov
How beautiful are the feet of them that bring glad tidings of good things!

אֲבָל לֹא הַכֹּל צִיְּתוּ לַבְּשׂוֹרָה, שֶׁכֵּן יְשַׁעְיָהוּ אוֹמֵר: אֲדֹנָי, מִי הֶאֱמִין לִשְׁמֻעָתֵנוּ
aval lo hakkol tziyetu labbesorah, shekken yesha'yahu omer. adonai, mi he'emin lishmu'atenu
But they did not all hearken to the glad tidings. For Isaiah saith, Lord, who hath believed our report?

לְפִיכָךְ הָאֱמוּנָה בָּאָה בִּשְׁמִיעָה וְהַשְּׁמִיעָה - בְּהַכְרָזַת דְּבַר הַמָּשִׁיחַ
lefichach ha'emunah ba'ah bishmi'ah vehashemi'ah - behachrazat dvar hammashiach
So belief cometh of hearing, and hearing by the word of Christ.

שׁוֹאֵל אֲנִי, הַאִם לֹא שָׁמְעוּ? בְּוַדַּאי שֶׁכֵּן, הֲלֹא בְּכָל־הָאָרֶץ יָצָא קַוָּם
sho'el ani, ha'im lo shame'u? bevadda shekken, halo bechol-ha'aretz yatza kavvam
But I say, Did they not hear? Yea, verily, Their sound went out into all the earth,

וּבִקְצֵה תֵבֵל מִלֵּיהֶם
uviktzeh tevel milleihem
And their words unto the ends of the world.

וְעוֹד שׁוֹאֵל אֲנִי, הַאִם יִשְׂרָאֵל לֹא יָדַע? הֲרֵי מֹשֶׁה כְּבָר אָמַר: אֲנִי אַקְנִיאֲכֶם בְּלֹא עָם
ve'od sho'el ani, ha'im yisra'el lo yada'? harei mosheh kevar amar: ani akni'achem belo am
But I say, Did Israel not know? First Moses saith, I will provoke you to jealousy with that which is no nation,

בְּגוֹי נָבָל אַכְעִיסְכֶם
begoy naval ach'isechem
With a nation void of understanding will I anger you.

וִישַׁעְיָהוּ מֵעֵז לוֹמַר
viysha'yahu me'ez lomar
And Isaiah is very bold, and saith,

נִדְרַשְׁתִּי לְלוֹא שְׁאָלוּ נִמְצֵאתִי לְלֹא בִקְשֻׁנִי
nidrashti lelo sha'alu nimtzeti lelo vikshuni
I was found of them that sought me not; I became manifest unto them that asked not of me.

וְהוּא אוֹמֵר לְיִשְׂרָאֵל: פֵּרַשְׂתִּי יָדַי כָּל־הַיּוֹם אֶל־עַם סוֹרֵר וּמֹרֶה
vehu omer leyisra'el. perasti yadai kol-hayom el-'am sorer umoreh
But as to Israel he saith, All the day long did I spread out my hands unto a disobedient and gainsaying people.

הָרוֹמִים

מֹשֶׁה אָמְנָם כָּתַב עַל הַצְּדָקָה שֶׁמִּתּוֹךְ הַתּוֹרָה אֲשֶׁר יַעֲשֶׂה אֹתָם הָאָדָם וָחַי בָּהֶם
mosheh omnam katav al hatzedakah shemmittoch hattorah asher ya'aseh otam ha'adam vachai bahem
For Moses writeth that the man that doeth the righteousness which is of the law shall live thereby.

אַךְ כָּךְ אוֹמֶרֶת הַצְּדָקָה שֶׁמִּתּוֹךְ אֱמוּנָה
ach kach omeret hatzedakah shemmittoch emunah
But the righteousness which is of faith saith thus,

אַל־תֹּאמַר בִּלְבָבְךָ מִי יַעֲלֶה הַשָּׁמַיְמָה? זֹאת, כְּדֵי לְהוֹרִיד אֶת הַמָּשִׁיחַ
al-tomar bilvavecha mi ya'aleh hashamaymah? zot, kedei lehorid et hammashiach
Say not in thy heart, Who shall ascend into heaven? (that is, to bring Christ down:)

אוֹ מִי יֵרֵד לַתְּהוֹם? זֹאת, כְּדֵי לְהַעֲלוֹת אֶת הַמָּשִׁיחַ מִן הַמֵּתִים
o mi yered lattehom? zot, kedei leha'alot et hammashiach min hammetim
or, Who shall descend into the abyss? (that is, to bring Christ up from the dead.)

אֲבָל מַה הִיא אוֹמֶרֶת? כִּי־קָרוֹב אֵלֶיךָ הַדָּבָר, בְּפִיךָ וּבִלְבָבְךָ. זֶהוּ דְּבַר הָאֱמוּנָה שֶׁאָנוּ מְבַשְּׂרִים
aval mah hi omeret? ki-karov eleicha haddavar, beficha uvilvavecha. zehu devar ha'emunah she'anu mevassrim
But what saith it? The word is nigh thee, in thy mouth, and in thy heart: that is, the word of faith, which we preach:

וְאִם אַתָּה מוֹדֶה בְּפִיךָ שֶׁיֵּשׁוּעַ הוּא הָאָדוֹן
ve'im attah modeh beficha sheyeshua hu ha'adon
because if thou shalt confess with thy mouth Jesus as Lord,

וּמַאֲמִין בִּלְבָבְךָ שֶׁאֱלֹהִים הֵקִים אוֹתוֹ מִן הַמֵּתִים - תִּוָּשַׁע
uma'amin bilvavecha she'elohim hekim oto min hammetim - tivvasha
and shalt believe in thy heart that God raised him from the dead, thou shalt be saved:

הֲרֵי בְּלִבּוֹ מַאֲמִין אִישׁ וְיִצְדַּק, וּבְפִיו יוֹדֶה וְיִוָּשַׁע
harei belibbo ma'amin ish veyutzdak, uvefiv yodeh veyivvasha
for with the heart man believeth unto righteousness; and with the mouth confession is made unto salvation.

וְהַכָּתוּב אוֹמֵר: כָּל הַמַּאֲמִין בּוֹ לֹא יֵבוֹשׁ
vehakkatuv omer: kol hamma'amin bo lo yevosh
For the scripture saith, Whosoever believeth on him shall not be put to shame.

אֵין הֶבְדֵּל בָּזֶה בֵּין יְהוּדִי לְלֹא־יְהוּדִי, כִּי אָדוֹן אֶחָד לְכֻלָּם וְרַב חֶסֶד הוּא לְכָל הַקּוֹרְאִים אֵלָיו
ein hevdel bazeh bein yehudi lelo-yehudi, ki adon echad lechullam verav chesed hu lechol hakkore'im elav
For there is no distinction between Jew and Greek: for the same Lord is Lord of all, and is rich unto all that call upon him:

שֶׁכֵּן כֹּל אֲשֶׁר־יִקְרָא בְּשֵׁם יהוה יִמָּלֵט
shekken kol asher-yikra beshem hashem yimmalet
for, Whosoever shall call upon the name of the Lord shall be saved.

אַךְ כֵּיצַד יִקְרְאוּ אֶל מִי שֶׁלֹּא הֶאֱמִינוּ בּוֹ
ach keitzad yikre'u el mi shello he'eminu bo
How then shall they call on him in whom they have not believed?

הָרוֹמִים

אִם כֵּן מַה נֹּאמַר? גּוֹיִם שֶׁלֹּא רָדְפוּ צְדָקָה
im ken mah nomar? goyim shello radfu tzdakah
What shall we say then? That the Gentiles, who followed not after righteousness,

הִשִּׂיגוּ צְדָקָה, אֲבָל צְדָקָה שֶׁעַל־יְסוֹד אֱמוּנָה
hishgu tzdakah, aval tzdakah she'al-yesod emunah
attained to righteousness, even the righteousness which is of faith:

יִשְׂרָאֵל, לְעֻמַּת זֹאת, חָתְרוּ לְתוֹרָה שֶׁל צְדָקָה, אַךְ לְתוֹרָה זוֹ לֹא הִגִּיעוּ
yisra'el, le'ummat zot, chateru letorah shel tzdakah, ach letorah zo lo higgi'u
but Israel, following after a law of righteousness, did not arrive at that law.

מַדּוּעַ? מִפְּנֵי שֶׁלֹּא בִּקְשׁוּהָ מִתּוֹךְ אֱמוּנָה, אֶלָּא מִתּוֹךְ מַעֲשִׂים. הֵם נִכְשְׁלוּ בְּאֶבֶן הַנֶּגֶף
maddua'? mippenei shello bikshuha mittoch emunah, ella mittoch ma'asim. hem nichshelu be'even hannegef
Wherefore? Because they sought it not by faith, but as it were by works. They stumbled at the stone of stumbling;

כַּכָּתוּב: הִנְנִי יִסַּד בְּצִיּוֹן אֶבֶן נֶגֶף וְצוּר מִכְשׁוֹל
Kakkatuv: hineni yissad betziyon even negef vetzur michshol
even as it is written, Behold, I lay in Zion a stone of stumbling and a rock of offence:

וְהַמַּאֲמִין בּוֹ לֹא יֵבוֹשׁ
vehamma'amin bo lo yevosh
And he that believeth on him shall not be put to shame.

∎

אַחַי, מִשְׁאֶלֶת לִבִּי וּתְפִלָּתִי לֵאלֹהִים - שֶׁיִּוָּשֵׁעוּ
achai, mish'elet libbi utefillati le'elohim - sheyivvashe'u
Brethren, my heart's desire and my supplication to God is for them, that they may be saved.

אֲנִי מֵעִיד עֲלֵיהֶם שֶׁיֵּשׁ לָהֶם קִנְאָה לֵאלֹהִים, אֲבָל קִנְאָה שֶׁאֵין עִמָּהּ דַּעַת
ani me'id aleihem sheyesh lahem kin'ah lelohim, aval kin'ah she'ein immah da'at
For I bear them witness that they have a zeal for God, but not according to knowledge.

כִּי מֵאַחַר שֶׁלֹּא יָדְעוּ אֶת צִדְקַת הָאֱלֹהִים וְנִסּוּ לְהָקִים צְדָקָה מִשֶּׁלָּהֶם
ki me'achar shello yade'u et tzidkat ha'elohim venissu lehakim tzedakah mishellahem
For being ignorant of God's righteousness, and seeking to establish their own,

לֹא נִכְנְעוּ לַצְּדָקָה שֶׁל אֱלֹהִים
lo nichne'u latzdakah shel elohim
they did not subject themselves to the righteousness of God.

הֲרֵי הַמָּשִׁיחַ הוּא תַּכְלִית הַתּוֹרָה, כְּדֵי שֶׁיֻּצְדַּק כָּל מִי שֶׁמַּאֲמִין
harei hammashiach hu tachlit hattorah, kedei sheyutzdak kol mi shemma'amin
For Christ is the end of the law unto righteousness to every one that believeth.

הָרוֹמִים

וּמָה אִם אֱלֹהִים, אַף כִּי חָפֵץ לְהַרְאוֹת אֶת זַעֲמוֹ וּלְגַלּוֹת אֶת כֹּחוֹ
umah im elohim, af ki chafetz lehar'ot et za'mo ulegallot et kocho
What if God, willing to show his wrath, and to make his power known,

סָבַל בְּאֹרֶךְ רוּחַ רַב כְּלֵי זַעַם מוּכָנִים לְהֶרֶס
saval be'orech ruach rav kelei za'am muchanim leheres
endured with much longsuffering vessels of wrath fitted unto destruction:

כְּדֵי לְגַלּוֹת אֶת עֹשֶׁר כְּבוֹדוֹ בִּכְלֵי חֲנִינָה שֶׁמֵּרֹאשׁ הֵכִין אוֹתָם לְכָבוֹד
kedei legallot et osher kvodo bichlei chaninah shemmerosh hechin otam lechavod
and that he might make known the riches of his glory upon vessels of mercy, which he afore prepared unto glory,

כְּלוֹמַר, אוֹתָנוּ אֲשֶׁר גַּם קָרָא לֹא רַק מִקֶּרֶב הַיְּהוּדִים אֶלָּא גַּם מִקֶּרֶב הַגּוֹיִם
klomar, otanu asher gam kara lo rak mikkerev hayehudim ella gam mikkerev haggoyim
even us, whom he also called, not from the Jews only, but also from the Gentiles?

כְּמוֹ שֶׁהוּא אוֹמֵר גַּם בְּהוֹשֵׁעַ: אֶקְרָא לְלֹא־עַמִּי עַמִּי, וּלְלֹא־רֻחָמָה רֻחָמָה
kemo shehu omer gam behoshea: ekra lelo-'ammi ammi, ulelo-ruchamah ruchamah
As he saith also in Hosea, I will call that my people, which was not my people; And her beloved, that was not beloved.

וְהָיָה בִּמְקוֹם אֲשֶׁר־יֵאָמֵר לָהֶם
vehayah bimkom asher-ye'amer lahem
And it shall be, that in the place where it was said unto them,

לֹא־עַמִּי אַתֶּם, יֵאָמֵר לָהֶם בְּנֵי אֵל־חָי
lo-'ammi attem, ye'amer lahem benei el-chai
Ye are not my people, There shall they be called sons of the living God.

וִישַׁעְיָהוּ מַכְרִיז עַל יִשְׂרָאֵל
visha'yahu machriz al yisra'el
And Isaiah crieth concerning Israel,

כִּי אִם־יִהְיֶה מִסְפַּר בְּנֵי יִשְׂרָאֵל כְּחוֹל הַיָּם, שְׁאָר יָשׁוּב בּוֹ
ki im-yihyeh mispar benei yisra'el kechol hayam, she'ar yashuv bo
If the number of the children of Israel be as the sand of the sea, it is the remnant that shall be saved:

כִּי־כָלָה וְנֶחֱרָצָה אֲדֹנָי עֹשֶׂה בְּקֶרֶב הָאָרֶץ
ki-chalah venecheratzah adonai oseh bekerev ha'aretz
for the Lord will execute his word upon the earth, finishing it and cutting it short.

וְכֵן אָמַר יְשַׁעְיָהוּ קֹדֶם לָכֵן: לוּלֵי יְהוָה צְבָאוֹת הוֹתִיר לָנוּ שָׂרִיד
vechen amar yesha'yahu kodem lachen: lulei hashem tzeva'ot hotir lanu sarid
And, as Isaiah hath said before, Except the Lord of Sabaoth had left us a seed,

כִּמְעַט כִּסְדֹם הָיִינוּ לַעֲמֹרָה דָּמִינוּ
kim'at kisdom hayinu la'amorah daminu
We had become as Sodom, and had been made like unto Gomorrah.

הָרוֹמִים

כַּכָּתוּב: וָאֹהַב אֶת־יַעֲקֹב, וְאֶת־עֵשָׂו שָׂנֵאתִי
Kakkatuv: va'ohav et-ya'akov, ve'et-'esav saneti
Even as it is written, Jacob I loved, but Esau I hated.

אִם כֵּן מַה נֹּאמַר? הֲיֵשׁ אִי־צֶדֶק אֵצֶל אֱלֹהִים? חַס וְחָלִילָה
im ken mah nomar? hayesh i-tzedek etzel elohim? chas vechalilah
What shall we say then? Is there unrighteousness with God? God forbid.

הֲרֵי לְמֹשֶׁה הוּא אוֹמֵר: וְחַנֹּתִי אֶת־אֲשֶׁר אָחֹן, וְרִחַמְתִּי אֶת־אֲשֶׁר אֲרַחֵם
harei lemosheh hu omer: vechannoti et-'asher achon, verichamti et-'asher arachem
For he saith to Moses, I will have mercy on whom I have mercy, and I will have compassion on whom I have compassion.

לְפִיכָךְ אֵין זֶה בְּיָדָיו שֶׁל הָאָדָם הָרוֹצֶה אוֹ הַמִּתְאַמֵּץ, כִּי אִם בִּידֵי אֱלֹהִים הַמְרַחֵם
lefichach ein zeh beyadav shel ha'adam harotzeh o hammit'ammetz, ki im biydei elohim hamrachem
So then it is not of him that willeth, nor of him that runneth, but of God that hath mercy.

וְאָכֵן אוֹמֵר הַכָּתוּב לְפַרְעֹה: בַּעֲבוּר זֹאת הֶעֱמַדְתִּיךָ
ve'achen omer hakkatuv lefar'oh. ba'avur zot he'emadticha
For the scripture saith unto Pharaoh, For this very purpose did I raise thee up,

בַּעֲבוּר הַרְאֹתְךָ אֶת כֹּחִי, וּלְמַעַן סַפֵּר שְׁמִי בְּכָל־הָאָרֶץ
ba'avur har'otecha et kochi, ulema'an sapper shmi bechol-ha'aretz
that I might show in thee my power, and that my name might be published abroad in all the earth.

וּבְכֵן הוּא מְרַחֵם עַל מִי שֶׁהוּא רוֹצֶה, וּמַקְשֶׁה אֶת לֵב מִי שֶׁהוּא רוֹצֶה
uvechen hu merachem al mi shehu rotzeh, umaksheh et lev mi shehu rotzeh
So then he hath mercy on whom he will, and whom he will he hardeneth.

אֲזַי אַתָּה תֹּאמַר לִי: מַדּוּעַ הוּא עוֹד מַאֲשִׁים, שֶׁהֲרֵי מִי יַעֲמֹד נֶגֶד רְצוֹנוֹ
azai attah tomar li: maddua hu od ma'ashim, sheharei mi ya'amod neged retzono
Thou wilt say then unto me, Why doth he still find fault? For who withstandeth his will?

אַךְ מִי אַתָּה, בֶּן־אָדָם, כִּי תִּתְוַכַּח עִם אֱלֹהִים
ach mi attah, ben-'adam, ki titvakkeach im elohim
Nay but, O man, who art thou that repliest against God?

הַאִם יֹאמַר מַעֲשֶׂה לְעוֹשֵׂהוּ מַדּוּעַ כָּכָה עֲשִׂיתָנִי
ha'im yomar ma'aseh le'osehu maddua kachah asitani
Shall the thing formed say to him that formed it, Why didst thou make me thus?

הַאִם מֵאוֹתוֹ חֹמֶר אֵין יוֹצֵר רַשַּׁאי לִיצֹר כְּלִי אֶחָד לְכָבוֹד
ha'im me'oto chomer ein yotzer rasha litzor kli echad lechavod
Or hath not the potter a right over the clay, from the same lump to make one part a vessel unto honor,

וּכְלִי אַחֵר לְשִׁמּוּשׁ שֶׁאֵין בּוֹ כָּבוֹד
uchli acher leshimmush she'ein bo kavod
and another unto dishonor?

הָרוֹמִים

בְּנֵי יִשְׂרָאֵל; אֲשֶׁר לָהֶם מַעֲמַד הַבָּנִים, הַכָּבוֹד, הַבְּרִיתוֹת
benei yisra'el; asher lahem ma'amad habbanim, hakkavod, habberitot
who are Israelites; whose is the adoption, and the glory, and the covenants,

מַתַּן הַתּוֹרָה, עֲבוֹדַת הַקֹּדֶשׁ וְהַהַבְטָחוֹת
mattan hattorah, avodat hakkodesh vehahavtachot
and the giving of the law, and the service of God, and the promises;

לָהֶם הָאָבוֹת, וּמֵהֶם, מִצַּד יְחוּסוֹ הָאֱנוֹשִׁי, הַמָּשִׁיחַ שֶׁהוּא מֵעַל כֹּל, אֵל מְבֹרָךְ לְעוֹלָמִים. אָמֵן
lahem ha'avot, umehem, mitzad yichuso ha'enoshi, hammashiach shehu me'al kol, el mevorach le'olamim. amen
whose are the fathers, and of whom is Christ as concerning the flesh, who is over all, God blessed for ever. Amen.

לֹא כְּאִלּוּ דְּבַר אֱלֹהִים שָׁב רֵיקָם. הֲרֵי לֹא כָּל אֲשֶׁר מִיִּשְׂרָאֵל יִשְׂרָאֵל הֵם
lo ke'illu devar elohim shav reikam. harei lo kol asher miyisra'el yisra'el hem
But it is not as though the word of God hath come to nought. For they are not all Israel, that are of Israel:

גַּם לֹא מִשּׁוּם הֱיוֹתָם צֶאֱצָאֵי אַבְרָהָם הַכֹּל בָּנִים, אֶלָּא - בְּיִצְחָק יִקָּרֵא לְךָ זָרַע
gam lo mishum heyotam tze'etza'ei avraham hakkol banim, ella - beyitzchak yikkarei lecha zara
neither, because they are Abraham's seed, are they all children: but, In Isaac shall thy seed be called.

כְּלוֹמַר, לֹא בְּנֵי הַבָּשָׂר הֵם בָּנִים לֵאלֹהִים
klomar, lo benei habbasar hem banim lelohim
That is, it is not the children of the flesh that are children of God;

אֶלָּא בְּנֵי הַהַבְטָחָה נֶחְשָׁבִים לַזֶּרַע
ella benei hahavtachah nechshavim lazzera
but the children of the promise are reckoned for a seed.

הֵן זֶה דְּבַר הַהַבְטָחָה: לַמּוֹעֵד אָשׁוּב אֵלֶיךָ כָּעֵת חַיָּה וּלְשָׂרָה בֵן
hen zeh devar hahavtachah. lammo'ed ashuv eleicha ka'et chayah ulesarah ven
For this is a word of promise, According to this season will I come, and Sarah shall have a son.

וְלֹא זוֹ בִּלְבַד, אֶלָּא גַּם רִבְקָה בִּהְיוֹתָהּ הָרָה לְאִישׁ אֶחָד, לְיִצְחָק אָבִינוּ
velo zo bilvad, ella gam rivkah bihyotah harah le'ish echad, leyitzchak avinu
And not only so; but Rebecca also having conceived by one, even by our father Isaac—

בְּטֶרֶם נוֹלְדוּ בָּנֶיהָ וּבְטֶרֶם עָשׂוּ טוֹב אוֹ רַע
beterem noledu baneiha uveterem asu tov o ra
for the children being not yet born, neither having done anything good or bad,

נֶאֱמַר לָהּ וְרַב יַעֲבֹד צָעִיר, כְּדֵי שֶׁתִּכּוֹן תָּכְנִית אֱלֹהִים הַמֻּשְׁתֶּתֶת עַל בְּחִירָה, לֹא מִתּוֹךְ מַעֲשִׂים אֶלָּא לְפִי קְרִיאָתוֹ שֶׁל הַקּוֹרֵא
ne'emar lah verav ya'avod tza'ir, kedei shettikkon tachenit elohim hammushtetet al bechirah, lo mittoch ma'asim ella lefi keri'ato shel hakkorei
that the purpose of God according to election might stand, not of works, but of him that calleth, it was said unto her, The elder shall serve the younger.

הָרוֹמִים

הַאִם צָרָה אוֹ מְצוּקָה, רְדִיפוֹת אוֹ רָעָב, הַאִם עֵירֹם אוֹ סַכָּנָה אוֹ חֶרֶב
ha'im tzarah o metzukah, redifot o ra'av, ha'im eirom o sakkanah o cherev
shall tribulation, or anguish, or persecution, or famine, or nakedness, or peril, or sword?

כַּכָּתוּב: כִּי־עָלֶיךָ הֹרַגְנוּ כָל־הַיּוֹם, נֶחְשַׁבְנוּ כְּצֹאן טִבְחָה
Kakkatuv: ki-'aleicha horagnu chol-hayom, nechshavnu ketzon tivchah
Even as it is written, For thy sake we are killed all the day long; We were accounted as sheep for the slaughter.

בְּרַם בְּכָל אֵלֶּה, בְּעֶזְרַת הָאוֹהֵב אוֹתָנוּ, אֲנַחְנוּ יוֹתֵר מִמְּנַצְּחִים
bram bechol elleh, be'ezrat ha'ohev otanu, anachnu yoter mimmenatzechim
Nay, in all these things we are more than conquerors through him that loved us.

וַאֲנִי בָּטוּחַ כִּי לֹא הַמָּוֶת וְלֹא הַחַיִּים
va'ani batuach ki lo hammavet velo hachayim
For I am persuaded, that neither death, nor life,

לֹא מַלְאָכִים וְלֹא שַׁלִּיטִים, לֹא דְּבָרִים שֶׁבַּהֹוֶה וְלֹא דְּבָרִים שֶׁעֲתִידִים לָבוֹא, לֹא כֹּחוֹת
lo mal'achim velo shallitim, lo devarim shebbahoh velo devarim she'atidim lavo, lo kochot
nor angels, nor principalities, nor things present, nor things to come, nor powers,

לֹא גְבָהִים וְלֹא מַעֲמַקִּים וְלֹא שׁוּם יְצוּר אַחֵר
lo gevahim velo ma'amakkim velo shum yetzur acher
nor height, nor depth, nor any other creature,

לֹא יוּכְלוּ לְהַפְרִידֵנוּ מֵאַהֲבַת אֱלֹהִים שֶׁבַּמָּשִׁיחַ יֵשׁוּעַ אֲדוֹנֵנוּ
lo yuchelu lehafridenu me'ahavat elohim shebbammashiach yeshua adonenu
shall be able to separate us from the love of God, which is in Christ Jesus our Lord.

ט

אֱמֶת אֲנִי מְדַבֵּר, בַּמָּשִׁיחַ, אֵינֶנִּי מְשַׁקֵּר; מַצְפּוּנִי מֵעִיד עִמָּדִי בְּרוּחַ הַקֹּדֶשׁ
emet ani medabber, bammashiach, einenni meshakker; matzpuni me'id immadi beruach hakkodesh
I say the truth in Christ, I lie not, my conscience bearing witness with me in the Holy Spirit,

גָּדוֹל צַעֲרִי וְלִבִּי דּוֹאֵב תָּמִיד
gadol tza'ari velibbi do'ev tamid
that I have great sorrow and unceasing pain in my heart.

עַד כִּי הָיִיתִי מוּכָן לִהְיוֹת מְנֻדֶּה מִן הַמָּשִׁיחַ לְמַעַן אַחַי
ad ki hayiti muchan lihyot menuddeh min hammashiach lema'an achai
For I could wish that I myself were anathema from Christ for my brethren's sake,

שֶׁהֵם בְּנֵי עַמִּי, עַצְמִי וּבְשָׂרִי
shehem benei ammi, atzmi uvsari
my kinsmen according to the flesh:

הָרוֹמִים

אָנוּ יוֹדְעִים כִּי אֱלֹהִים גּוֹרֵם לְכָךְ שֶׁכָּל הַדְּבָרִים חוֹבְרִים יַחַד לְטוֹבַת אוֹהֲבָיו
anu yode'im ki elohim gorem lechach shekkol haddvarim choverim yachad letovat ohavav
And we know that to them that love God all things work together for good,

הַקְּרוּאִים עַל־פִּי תָּכְנִיתוֹ
hakkeru'im al-pi tochnito
even to them that are called according to his purpose.

שֶׁכֵּן אֶת אֵלֶּה שֶׁהִכִּיר מִקֶּדֶם, אוֹתָם גַּם יָעַד לְהִדַּמּוֹת לְצֶלֶם בְּנוֹ
shekken et elleh shehikkir mikkedem, otam gam ya'ad lehiddammot letzelem beno
For whom he foreknew, he also foreordained to be conformed to the image of his Son,

כְּדֵי שֶׁיִּהְיֶה הַבְּכוֹר בֵּין אַחִים רַבִּים
kedei sheyihyeh habbechor bein achim rabbim
that he might be the firstborn among many brethren:

וְאֶת אֵלֶּה שֶׁיָּעַד, לָהֶם גַּם קָרָא; וְאֶת הַקְּרוּאִים גַּם הִצְדִּיק
ve'et elleh sheya'ad, lahem gam kara; ve'et hakkru'im gam hitzdik
and whom he foreordained, them he also called: and whom he called, them he also justified:

וְאֶת הַמֻּצְדָּקִים אַף פֵּאֵר בִּכְבוֹדוֹ
ve'et hammutzdakim af pe'er bichvodo
and whom he justified, them he also glorified.

אִם כֵּן מַה נֹּאמַר עַל הַדְּבָרִים הָאֵלֶּה? אִם אֱלֹהִים אִתָּנוּ, מִי יַעֲמֹד נֶגְדֵּנוּ
im ken mah nomar al haddvarim ha'elleh? im elohim ittanu, mi ya'amod negdenu
What then shall we say to these things? If God is for us, who is against us?

הוּא אֲשֶׁר לֹא חָשַׂךְ אֶת בְּנוֹ שֶׁלּוֹ, אֶלָּא מָסַר אוֹתוֹ בְּעַד כֻּלָּנוּ, הַאִם לֹא יַעֲנִיק לָנוּ אִתּוֹ אֶת הַכֹּל
hu asher lo chasach et beno shello, ella masar oto be'ad kullanu, ha'im lo ya'anik lanu itto et hakkol
He that spared not his own Son, but delivered him up for us all, how shall he not also with him freely give us all things?

מִי יִטְעַן נֶגֶד בְּחִירֵי אֱלֹהִים? הֲרֵי אֱלֹהִים הוּא הַמַּצְדִּיק
mi yit'an neged bechirei elohim? harei elohim hu hammatzdik
Who shall lay anything to the charge of God's elect? It is God that justifieth;

מִי הַמַּרְשִׁיעַ? הַאִם הַמָּשִׁיחַ יֵשׁוּעַ אֲשֶׁר מֵת, וְלֹא זוֹ בִּלְבַד כִּי אִם קָם לִתְחִיָּה
mi hammarshia? ha'im hammashiach yeshua asher met, velo zo bilvad ki im kam litchiyah
who is he that condemneth? It is Christ Jesus that died, yea rather, that was raised from the dead,

וְהוּא נִמְצָא לִימִין אֱלֹהִים וּמַפְגִּיעַ בַּעֲדֵנוּ
vehu nimtza liymin elohim umafgia ba'adenu
who is at the right hand of God, who also maketh intercession for us.

מִי יַפְרִידֵנוּ מֵאַהֲבַת הַמָּשִׁיחַ
mi yafridenu me'ahavat hammashiach
Who shall separate us from the love of Christ?

הָרוֹמִים

שֶׁגַּם הַבְּרִיאָה עַצְמָהּ תְּשֻׁחְרַר מִשִּׁעְבּוּד הַכִּלָּיוֹן
sheggam habberi'ah atzmah teshuchrar mishi'bud hakkillayon
that the creation itself also shall be delivered from the bondage of corruption

אֶל הַחֵרוּת וְהַכָּבוֹד שֶׁל הַבָּנִים־לֵאלֹהִים
el hacherut vehakkavod shel habbanim-le'elohim
into the liberty of the glory of the children of God.

אָנוּ יוֹדְעִים שֶׁכָּל הַבְּרִיאָה נֶאֱנַחַת וְסוֹבֶלֶת כְּבִצְירֵי לֵדָה עַד הַיּוֹם הַזֶּה
anu yode'im shekkol habberi'ah ne'enachat vesovelet kivtzirei ledah ad hayom hazzeh
For we know that the whole creation groaneth and travaileth in pain together until now.

וְלֹא זֹאת בִּלְבַד, אֶלָּא גַּם אֲנַחְנוּ, שֶׁיֵּשׁ לָנוּ בִּכּוּרֵי הָרוּחַ,
velo zot bilvad, ella gam anachnu, sheyesh lanu bikkurei haruach
And not only so, but ourselves also, who have the first-fruits of the Spirit,

נֶאֱנָחִים בְּנַפְשֵׁנוּ וּמְצַפִּים לְמִמּוּשׁ אִמּוּצֵנוּ לְבָנִים - לִפְדוּת גּוּפֵנוּ
ne'enachim benafshenu umetzappim lemimmush immutzenu levanim - lifdut gufenu
even we ourselves groan within ourselves, waiting for our adoption, to wit, the redemption of our body.

שֶׁכֵּן בַּתִּקְוָה נוֹשַׁעְנוּ. אַךְ תִּקְוָה לְדָבָר שֶׁנִּרְאֶה לָעֵינַיִם אֵינָהּ תִּקְוָה
shekken battikvah nosha'nu. ach tikvah ledavar shennir'eh la'einayim einah tikvah
For in hope were we saved: but hope that is seen is not hope:

כִּי מַדּוּעַ יְקַוֶּה אָדָם לְמַה שֶּׁהוּא רוֹאֶה
ki maddua yekavveh adam lemah shehu ro'eh
for who hopeth for that which he seeth?

אֲבָל אִם אָנוּ מְקַוִּים לְדָבָר שֶׁאֵינֶנּוּ רוֹאִים, מְצַפִּים אָנוּ לוֹ בְּסַבְלָנוּת
aval im anu mekavvim ledavar she'einennu ro'im, metzappim anu lo besavlanut
But if we hope for that which we see not, then do we with patience wait for it.

וְכֵן גַּם הָרוּחַ עוֹזֶרֶת לָנוּ בְּחֻלְשׁוֹתֵינוּ, כִּי אֵין אָנוּ יוֹדְעִים לְהִתְפַּלֵּל כָּרָאוּי
vechen gam haruach ozeret lanu bechulshoteinu, ki ein anu yode'im lehitpallel kara'ui
And in like manner the Spirit also helpeth our infirmity: for we know not how to pray as we ought;

וְאוּלָם הָרוּחַ עַצְמָהּ מַפְגִּיעָה בַּעֲדֵנוּ בַּאֲנָחוֹת עֲמֻקּוֹת מִמִּלִּים
ve'ulam haruach atzmah mafgi'ah ba'adenu ba'anachot amukkot mimmillim
but the Spirit himself maketh intercession for us with groanings which cannot be uttered;

וְהַבּוֹחֵן לְבָבוֹת יוֹדֵעַ אֶת מַחְשְׁבוֹת הָרוּחַ
vehabbochen levavot yodea et machshevot haruach
and he that searcheth the hearts knoweth what is the mind of the Spirit,

מִפְּנֵי שֶׁהִיא מַפְגִּיעָה בְּעַד הַקְּדוֹשִׁים בְּהֶתְאֵם לִרְצוֹן אֱלֹהִים
mippenei shehi mafgi'ah be'ad hakkdoshim behet'em lirtzon elohim
because he maketh intercession for the saints according to the will of God.

הָרוֹמִים

לָכֵן, אַחַי, חַיָּבִים אֲנַחְנוּ, אַךְ לֹא לַבָּשָׂר חַיָּבִים אָנוּ שֶׁנִּחְיֶה עַל־פִּיו
lachen, achai, chayavim anachnu, ach lo labbasar chayavim anu shennichyeh al-piv
So then, brethren, we are debtors, not to the flesh, to live after the flesh:

אִם תִּחְיוּ לְפִי הַבָּשָׂר, תָּמוּתוּ. אַךְ אִם עַל־יְדֵי הָרוּחַ תָּמִיתוּ אֶת מַעַלְלֵי הַגּוּף, תִּחְיוּ
im tichyu lefi habbasar, tamutu. ach im al-yedei haruach tamitu et ma'alelei hagguf, tichyu
for if ye live after the flesh, ye must die; but if by the Spirit ye put to death the deeds of the body, ye shall live.

כָּל אֲשֶׁר רוּחַ אֱלֹהִים מַדְרִיכָה אוֹתָם, בָּנִים הֵם לֵאלֹהִים
kol asher ruach elohim madrichah otam, banim hem lelohim
For as many as are led by the Spirit of God, these are sons of God.

הֲרֵי לֹא קִבַּלְתֶּם רוּחַ שֶׁל עַבְדוּת לַחֲזֹר אֶל הַפַּחַד, אֶלָּא קִבַּלְתֶּם רוּחַ הַמַּקְנָה מַעֲמָד שֶׁל בָּנִים
harei lo kibbaltem ruach shel avdut lachazor el happachad, ella kibbaltem ruach hammaknah ma'amad shel banim
For ye received not the spirit of bondage again unto fear; but ye received the spirit of adoption,

וּבְרוּחַ זֹאת אָנוּ קוֹרְאִים אַבָּא, אָבִינוּ
uveruach zot anu kore'im abba, avinu
whereby we cry, Abba, Father.

הָרוּחַ עַצְמָהּ מְעִידָה יַחַד עִם רוּחֵנוּ שֶׁבָּנִים לֵאלֹהִים אָנוּ
haruach atzmah me'idah yachad im ruchenu shebbanim le'elohim anu
The Spirit himself beareth witness with our spirit, that we are children of God:

וְאִם בָּנִים, אֲזַי יוֹרְשִׁים: יוֹרְשֵׁי נַחֲלַת אֱלֹהִים וְגַם יוֹרְשִׁים הַשֻּׁתָּפִים לַמָּשִׁיחַ,
ve'im banim, azai yorshim. yorshei nachalat elohim vegam yoreshim hashuttafim lammashiach
and if children, then heirs; heirs of God, and joint-heirs with Christ;

שֶׁכֵּן סוֹבְלִים אָנוּ עִמּוֹ כְּדֵי שֶׁגַּם נִזְכֶּה לְכָבוֹד עִמּוֹ
shekken sovelim anu immo kedei sheggam nizkeh lechavod immo
if so be that we suffer with him, that we may be also glorified with him.

אֲנִי סָבוּר שֶׁסִּבְלוֹת הַזְּמַן הַזֶּה
ani savur shessivlot hazzman hazzeh
For I reckon that the sufferings of this present time

אֵינָם שְׁקוּלִים כְּנֶגֶד הַכָּבוֹד הֶעָתִיד לְהִגָּלוֹת בָּנוּ
einam shkulim keneged hakkavod he'atid lehiggalot banu
are not worthy to be compared with the glory which shall be revealed to us-ward.

כָּל הַבְּרִיאָה מְצַפָּה בְּכִסּוּפִים לְהִתְגַּלּוּת הַבָּנִים־לֵאלֹהִים
kol habberi'ah metzappah bechissufim lehitgallut habbanim-le'elohim
For the earnest expectation of the creation waiteth for the revealing of the sons of God.

הֵן הַבְּרִיאָה - לֹא מֵרְצוֹנָהּ אֶלָּא עַל־יְדֵי הַמַּכְנִיעַ אוֹתָהּ - הֻכְנְעָה לַהֶבֶל בְּתִקְוָה
hen habberi'ah - lo meretzonah ella al-yedei hammachnia otah - huchne'ah lahevel betikvah
For the creation was subjected to vanity, not of its own will, but by reason of him who subjected it, in hope

הָרוֹמִים

אַךְ אֲנָשִׁים שֶׁחַיִּים לְפִי הָרוּחַ הוֹגִים בְּמַה שֶּׁשַּׁיָּךְ לָרוּחַ
ach anashim shechayim lefi haruach hogim bemah sheshayach laruach
but they that are after the Spirit the things of the Spirit.

מַחְשְׁבוֹת הַבָּשָׂר מָוֶת הֵן, אֲבָל מַחְשְׁבוֹת הָרוּחַ הֵן חַיִּים וְשָׁלוֹם
machshevot habbasar mavet hen, aval machshevot haruach hen chayim veshalom
For the mind of the flesh is death; but the mind of the Spirit is life and peace:

שֶׁהֲרֵי מַחְשְׁבוֹת הַבָּשָׂר עוֹיְנוֹת אֶת אֱלֹהִים
sheharei machshevot habbasar oyenot et elohim
because the mind of the flesh is enmity against God;

מִפְּנֵי שֶׁאֵינָן נִכְנָעוֹת לְתוֹרַת אֱלֹהִים, אַף אֵינָן יְכוֹלוֹת לְהִכָּנַע
mippenei she'einan nichna'ot letorat elohim, af einan yecholot lehikkana
for it is not subject to the law of God, neither indeed can it be:

וְהַכְּפוּפִים לַבָּשָׂר אֵינָם יְכוֹלִים לִהְיוֹת רְצוּיִים לֵאלֹהִים
vehakkefufim labbasar einam yecholim lihyot retzuyim lelohim
and they that are in the flesh cannot please God.

אַךְ אַתֶּם אֵינְכֶם כְּפוּפִים לַבָּשָׂר, כִּי אִם לָרוּחַ, אִם אָמְנָם רוּחַ אֱלֹהִים שׁוֹכֶנֶת בָּכֶם
ach attem einchem kefufim labbasar, ki im laruach, im omnam ruach elohim shochenet bachem
But ye are not in the flesh but in the Spirit, if so be that the Spirit of God dwelleth in you.

וּמִי שֶׁאֵין לוֹ רוּחַ הַמָּשִׁיחַ אֵינוֹ שַׁיָּךְ לַמָּשִׁיחַ
umi she'ein lo ruach hammashiach eino shayach lammashiach
But if any man hath not the Spirit of Christ, he is none of his.

אֲבָל אִם הַמָּשִׁיחַ בְּקִרְבְּכֶם, אֲזַי הַגּוּף אָמְנָם מֵת עֵקֶב הַחֵטְא
aval im hammashiach bekirbechem, azai hagguf omnam met ekev hachet,
And if Christ is in you, the body is dead because of sin;

אַךְ הָרוּחַ הִיא חַיִּים מִפְּנֵי שֶׁהֻצְדַּקְתֶּם
ach haruach hi chayim mippenei shehutzdaktem
but the spirit is life because of righteousness.

וְאִם רוּחוֹ שֶׁל הַמֵּקִים אֶת יֵשׁוּעַ מִן הַמֵּתִים שׁוֹכֶנֶת בְּקִרְבְּכֶם
ve'im rucho shel hammekim et yeshua min hammetim shochenet bekirbechem
But if the Spirit of him that raised up Jesus from the dead dwelleth in you,

זֶה שֶׁהֵקִים אֶת הַמָּשִׁיחַ מִן הַמֵּתִים
zeh shehekim et hammashiach min hammetim
he that raised up Christ Jesus from the dead

יְחַיֶּה גַּם אֶת גּוּפְכֶם בֶּן הַתְּמוּתָה עַל־יְדֵי רוּחוֹ הַשּׁוֹכֶנֶת בְּקִרְבְּכֶם
yechayeh gam et gufchem ben hattemutah al-yedei rucho hashochenet bekirbechem
shall give life also to your mortal bodies through his Spirit that dwelleth in you.

הָרוֹמִים

וּמְשַׁעְבֵּד אוֹתִי לְחֹק הַחֵטְא הַשּׁוֹרֵר בְּאֵיבָרַי
umesha'bed oti lechok hachet hassorer be'eivarai
and bringing me into captivity under the law of sin which is in my members.

אוֹי לִי, אָדָם אֻמְלָל שֶׁכָּמוֹתִי, מִי יַצִּילֵנִי מִגּוּף זֶה שֶׁהַמָּוֶת בּוֹ
oy li, adam umlal shekkemoti, mi yatzileni migguf zeh shehammavet bo
Wretched man that I am! who shall deliver me out of the body of this death?

תּוֹדָה לֵאלֹהִים עַל יֵשׁוּעַ הַמָּשִׁיחַ אֲדוֹנֵנוּ
todah lelohim al yeshua hammashiach adonenu
I thank God through Jesus Christ our Lord.

וּבְכֵן, בְּשִׂכְלִי אֲנִי עֶבֶד לְתוֹרַת אֱלֹהִים, אַךְ בִּבְשָׂרִי אֲנִי מְשֻׁעְבָּד לְחֹק הַחֵטְא
uvechen, besichli ani eved letorat elohim, ach bivsari ani meshu'abad lechok hachet
So then I of myself with the mind, indeed, serve the law of God; but with the flesh the law of sin.

ח

לָכֵן אֵין עַכְשָׁו שׁוּם הַרְשָׁעָה עַל אֵלֶּה שֶׁנִּמְצָאִים בַּמָּשִׁיחַ יֵשׁוּעַ
lachen ein achshav shum harsha'ah al elleh shennimtza'im bammashiach yeshua
There is therefore now no condemnation to them that are in Christ Jesus.

כִּי חֹק רוּחַ הַחַיִּים שֶׁבַּמָּשִׁיחַ יֵשׁוּעַ שִׁחְרֵר אוֹתִי מֵחֹק הַחֵטְא וְהַמָּוֶת
ki chok ruach hachayim shebbammashiach yeshua shichrer oti mechok hachet vehammavet
For the law of the Spirit of life in Christ Jesus made me free from the law of sin and of death.

שֶׁכֵּן מַה שֶּׁלֹּא יָכְלָה הַתּוֹרָה לַעֲשׂוֹת, מִפְּנֵי שֶׁלֹּא יָכְלָה לְהִתְגַּבֵּר עַל הַבָּשָׂר
shekken mah shello yachlah hattorah la'asot, mippenei shello yachelah lehitgabber al habbasar
For what the law could not do, in that it was weak through the flesh,

זֹאת עָשָׂה אֱלֹהִים: הוּא שָׁלַח אֶת בְּנוֹ לָבוּשׁ בָּשָׂר בִּדְמוּת בְּשַׂר הַחֵטְא, לִהְיוֹת קָרְבָּן עַל חֵטְא
zot asah elohim: hu shalach et beno lavush basar bidmut bsar hachet, lihyot korban al chet
God, sending his own Son in the likeness of sinful flesh and for sin,

וְחָרַץ אֶת דִּינוֹ שֶׁל הַחֵטְא בַּבָּשָׂר
vecharatz et dino shel hachet babbasar
condemned sin in the flesh:

כְּדֵי שֶׁחֻקַּת הַתּוֹרָה תִּתְקַיֵּם בָּנוּ, הַמִּתְהַלְּכִים לֹא לְפִי הַבָּשָׂר אֶלָּא לְפִי הָרוּחַ
kedei shechukkat hattorah titkayem banu, hammit'hallechim lo lefi habbasar ella lefi haruach
that the ordinance of the law might be fulfilled in us, who walk not after the flesh, but after the Spirit.

אֲנָשִׁים שֶׁחַיִּים לְפִי הַבָּשָׂר הוֹגִים בְּמַה שֶּׁשַּׁיָּךְ לַבָּשָׂר
anashim shechayim lefi habbasar hogim bemah sheshayach labbasar
For they that are after the flesh mind the things of the flesh;

הָרוֹמִים

כְּדֵי שֶׁעַל־יְדֵי הַדִּבֵּר יֻבְלַט הַחֵטְא בִּמְלֹא חֻמְרָתוֹ
kedei she'al-yedei haddibber yuvlat hachet bimlo chumrato
that through the commandment sin might become exceeding sinful.

אָנוּ יוֹדְעִים שֶׁהַתּוֹרָה הִיא רוּחָנִית, אַךְ אֲנִי הִנְנִי בָּשָׂר וָדָם וּמָכוּר לַחֵטְא
anu yode'im shehattorah hi ruchanit, ach ani hineni basar vadam umachur lachet
For we know that the law is spiritual: but I am carnal, sold under sin.

אָכֵן אֵינֶנִּי מֵבִין אֶת מַעֲשַׂי, כִּי לֹא אֶת מַה שֶׁאֲנִי חָפֵץ אֲנִי עוֹשֶׂה, אֶלָּא דַּוְקָא אֶת מַה שֶׁשָּׂנוּא עָלַי אֲנִי עוֹשֶׂה
achen einenni mevin et ma'asai, ki lo et mah she'ani chafetz ani oseh, ella davka et mah␣shesanu alai ani oseh
For that which I do I know not: for not what I would, that do I practise; but what I hate, that I do.

וְאִם אֲנִי עוֹשֶׂה אֶת מַה שֶׁאֵינֶנִּי חָפֵץ לַעֲשׂוֹת, אֲנִי מוֹדֶה שֶׁהַתּוֹרָה טוֹבָה
ve'im ani oseh et mah she'einenni chafetz la'asot, ani modeh shehattorah tovah
But if what I would not, that I do, I consent unto the law that it is good.

מִכָּאן שֶׁלֹּא עוֹד אֲנִי עוֹשֶׂה אֶת הַמַּעֲשֶׂה, אֶלָּא הַחֵטְא הַשּׁוֹכֵן בִּי
mikkan shello od ani oseh et hamma'aseh, ella hachet hashochen bi
So now it is no more I that do it, but sin which dwelleth in me.

שֶׁהֲרֵי אֲנִי יוֹדֵעַ כִּי בִּי, כְּלוֹמַר בִּבְשָׂרִי, לֹא שׁוֹכֵן הַטּוֹב
sheharei ani yodea ki bi, klomar bivsari, lo shochen hattov
For I know that in me, that is, in my flesh, dwelleth no good thing:

אָמְנָם לִרְצוֹת אֲנִי יָכוֹל, אַךְ לַעֲשׂוֹת אֶת הַטּוֹב אֵינֶנִּי יָכוֹל
omnam lirtzot ani yachol, ach la'asot et hattov einenni yachol
for to will is present with me, but to do that which is good is not.

כִּי אֵינֶנִּי עוֹשֶׂה אֶת הַטּוֹב שֶׁאֲנִי חָפֵץ בּוֹ, אֶלָּא אֶת הָרַע שֶׁאֵינֶנִּי חָפֵץ בּוֹ - אוֹתוֹ אֲנִי עוֹשֶׂה
ki einenni oseh et hattov she'ani chafetz bo, ella et hara she'einenni chafetz bo - oto ani oseh
For the good which I would I do not: but the evil which I would not, that I practise.

וְאִם אֲנִי עוֹשֶׂה אֶת מַה שֶׁבְּנִגּוּד לִרְצוֹנִי, הֲרֵי שֶׁלֹּא עוֹד אֲנִי עוֹשֶׂה אוֹתוֹ, אֶלָּא הַחֵטְא הַשּׁוֹכֵן בִּי
ve'im ani oseh et mah shebbeniggud␣lirtzoni, harei shello od ani oseh oto, ella hachet hashochen bi
But if what I would not, that I do, it is no more I that do it, but sin which dwelleth in me.

לְפִיכָךְ אֲנִי מוֹצֵא אֶת הַחֹק הַזֶּה: רְצוֹנִי לַעֲשׂוֹת אֶת הַטּוֹב, אֶלָּא שֶׁהָרַע עוֹמֵד לְפָנַי
lefichach ani motzei et hachok hazzeh: retzoni la'asot et hattov, ella shehara omed lefanai
I find then the law, that, to me who would do good, evil is present.

בָּאָדָם הַפְּנִימִי שֶׁבִּי אֲנִי שָׂמֵחַ בְּתוֹרַת אֱלֹהִים
ba'adam happenimi shebbi ani sameach betorat elohim
For I delight in the law of God after the inward man:

אַךְ בְּאֵיבָרַי אֲנִי רוֹאֶה חֹק אַחֵר, וְהוּא נִלְחָם נֶגֶד הַחֹק שֶׁבְּשִׂכְלִי
ach be'eivarai ani ro'eh chok acher, vehu nilcham neged hachok shebbesichli
but I see a different law in my members, warring against the law of my mind,

הָרוֹמִים

אֲבָל כָּעֵת, לְאַחַר שֶׁמַּתְנוּ לְגַבֵּי מַה שֶׁקַּבַּל אוֹתָנוּ, שֻׁחְרַרְנוּ מִן הַתּוֹרָה
aval ka'et, le'achar shemmatnu legabbei mah shekkaval otanu, shuchrarnu min hattorah
But now we have been discharged from the law, having died to that wherein we were held;

כְּדֵי לַעֲבֹד אֶת אֱלֹהִים בְּחַדְשׁוּת הָרוּחַ וְלֹא בְּיֹשֶׁן שֶׁל אוֹת כְּתוּבָה
kedei la'avod et elohim bechadshut haruach velo beyoshen shel ot ktuvah
so that we serve in newness of the spirit, and not in oldness of the letter.

אִם כֵּן, מַה נֹּאמַר? הַאִם הַתּוֹרָה הִיא בְּחֶזְקַת חֵטְא? חַס וְחָלִילָה! אַךְ לֹא הָיִיתִי יוֹדֵעַ מַהוּ חֵטְא אִלּוּלֵי הַתּוֹרָה
im ken, mah nomar? ha'im hattorah hi bechezkat chet? chas vechalilah! ach lo hayiti yodea mahu chet illulei hattorah
What shall we say then? Is the law sin? God forbid. Howbeit, I had not known sin, except through the law:

הֲרֵי לֹא הָיִיתִי מַכִּיר אֶת הַתַּאֲוָה אִלּוּ לֹא אָמְרָה הַתּוֹרָה לֹא־תַחְמֹד
harei lo hayiti makkir et hatta'avah illu lo amerah hattorah lo-tachmod
for I had not known coveting, except the law had said, Thou shalt not covet:

הַחֵטְא נִצֵּל אֶת הָאִסּוּר שֶׁבַּדִּבֵּר כְּדֵי לְעוֹרֵר בְּקִרְבִּי כָּל מִינֵי תַּאֲווֹת
hachet nitzel et ha'issur shebbaddibber kedei le'orer bekirbi kol minei ta'avot,
but sin, finding occasion, wrought in me through the commandment all manner of coveting:

שֶׁכֵּן בְּלִי תּוֹרָה הַחֵטְא מֵת
shekken beli torah hachet met
for apart from the law sin is dead.

בֶּעָבָר אֲנִי הָיִיתִי חַי בְּלִי תּוֹרָה, אַךְ כְּשֶׁהוֹפִיעַ הַדִּבֵּר נֵעוֹר הַחֵטְא לְחַיִּים
be'avar ani hayiti chai beli torah, ach kshehofia haddibber ne'or hachet lechayim
And I was alive apart from the law once: but when the commandment came, sin revived, and I died;

וַאֲנִי מַתִּי. וּמָצָאתִי כִּי הַדִּבֵּר, שֶׁהָיָה דֶּרֶךְ לְחַיִּים, גּוֹרֵם מָוֶת
va'ani matti. umatzati ki haddibber, shehayah derech lechayim, gorem mavet
and the commandment, which was unto life, this I found to be unto death:

שֶׁכֵּן הַחֵטְא, בְּנַצְּלוֹ אֶת הַדִּבֵּר, הִתְעָה אוֹתִי וּבְאֶמְצָעוּתוֹ הֵמִית אוֹתִי
shekken hachet, benatzelo et haddibber, hit'ah oti uve'emtza'uto hemit oti
for sin, finding occasion, through the commandment beguiled me, and through it slew me.

וּבְכֵן הַתּוֹרָה קְדוֹשָׁה, וְהַדִּבֵּר הוּא קָדוֹשׁ וְיָשָׁר וְטוֹב
uvechen hattorah kedoshah, vehaddibber hu kadosh veyashar vetov
So that the law is holy, and the commandment holy, and righteous, and good.

הֲיִתָּכֵן, מִכָּאן, שֶׁדָּבָר טוֹב גָּרַם לִי מָוֶת? בְּשׁוּם פָּנִים לֹא! אוּלָם הַחֵטְא, לְמַעַן יֵרָאֶה שֶׁהוּא חֵטְא
hayittachen, mikkan, sheddavar tov garam li mavet? beshum panim lo! ulam hachet, lema'an yera'eh shehu chet
Did then that which is good become death unto me? God forbid. But sin, that it might be shown to be sin,

גָּרַם לִי מָוֶת בְּאֶמְצָעוּת מַשֶּׁהוּ טוֹב
garam li mavet be'emtza'ut mashehu tov
by working death to me through that which is good;—

הָרוֹמִים

ז

אַחַי, הַאִם אֵינְכֶם יוֹדְעִים - וַהֲרֵי אֲנִי מְדַבֵּר אֶל יוֹדְעֵי תּוֹרָה
achai, ha'im einechem yod'im - vaharei ani medabber el yod'ei torah
Or are ye ignorant, brethren (for I speak to men who know the law),

כִּי לַתּוֹרָה יֵשׁ מָרוּת עַל הָאָדָם כָּל זְמַן שֶׁהוּא חַי
ki lattorah yesh marut al ha'adam kol zeman shehu chai
that the law hath dominion over a man for so long time as he liveth?

הָאִשָּׁה הַנְּשׂוּאָה קְשׁוּרָה לְבַעֲלָהּ עַל־יְדֵי הַתּוֹרָה כָּל עוֹד הוּא חַי
ha'ishah hannesu'ah keshurah leva'alah al-yedei hattorah kol od hu chai
For the woman that hath a husband is bound by law to the husband while he liveth;

אַךְ אִם יָמוּת בַּעֲלָהּ פְּטוּרָה הִיא מֵחֹק הַתּוֹרָה הַקּוֹשֵׁר אוֹתָהּ לְבַעֲלָהּ
ach im yamut ba'alah pturah hi mechok hattorah hakkosher otah leva'alah
but if the husband die, she is discharged from the law of the husband.

לָכֵן אִם תִּנָּשֵׂא לְאִישׁ אַחֵר בְּעוֹד בַּעֲלָהּ חַי, הִיא תִּקָּרֵא נוֹאֶפֶת
lachen im tinnasei le'ish acher be'od ba'alah chai, hi tikkarei no'efet
So then if, while the husband liveth, she be joined to another man, she shall be called an adulteress:

אַךְ אִם יָמוּת בַּעֲלָהּ, פְּטוּרָה הִיא מֵאוֹתוֹ חֹק וּבְהִנָּשְׂאָהּ לְאִישׁ אַחֵר אֵין הִיא נוֹאֶפֶת
ach im yamut ba'alah, pturah hi me'oto chok uvehinnase'ah le'ish acher ein hi no'efet
but if the husband die, she is free from the law, so that she is no adulteress, though she be joined to another man.

כֵּן גַּם אַתֶּם, אַחַי, מֵתֶּם לְגַבֵּי הַתּוֹרָה בְּגוּפוֹ שֶׁל הַמָּשִׁיחַ,
ken gam attem, achai, mattem legabbei hattorah begufo shel hammashiach
Wherefore, my brethren, ye also were made dead to the law through the body of Christ;

בְּאֹפֶן שֶׁנַּעֲשִׂיתֶם שַׁיָּכִים לְאַחֵר, לָזֶה שֶׁהוּקַם מִן הַמֵּתִים,
be'ofen shenna'aseitem shayachim le'acher, lazeh shehukam min hammetim,
that ye should be joined to another, even to him who was raised from the dead,

כְּדֵי שֶׁנַּעֲשֶׂה פְּרִי לֵאלֹהִים
kedei shenna'aseh peri le'elohim
that we might bring forth fruit unto God.

הֲרֵי כַּאֲשֶׁר הָיִינוּ מְשֻׁעְבָּדִים לַבְּשָׂרִיּוּת, תַּאֲווֹת הַחֵטְא שֶׁנֵּעוֹרוּ עַל־יְדֵי הַתּוֹרָה
harei ka'asher hayinu meshu'badim labbesariyut, ta'avot hachet shenne'oru al-yedei hattorah
For when we were in the flesh, the sinful passions, which were through the law,

פָּעֲלוּ בְּאֵיבָרֵינוּ לַעֲשׂוֹת פְּרִי הַגּוֹרֵם לְמָוֶת
pa'alu be'eivareinu la'asot peri haggorem lemavet
wrought in our members to bring forth fruit unto death.

הָרוֹמִים

נִשְׁמַעְתֶּם בְּכָל לֵב לְדֶרֶךְ הַתּוֹרָה אֲשֶׁר חֻנַּכְתֶּם בָּהּ
nishma'tem bechol lev lederech hattorah asher chunnachtem bah
ye became obedient from the heart to that form of teaching whereunto ye were delivered;

וּלְאַחַר שֶׁשֻּׁחְרַרְתֶּם מִן הַחֵטְא נַעֲשֵׂיתֶם עֲבָדִים לַצְּדָקָה
ule'achar sheshuchrartem min hachet na'aseitem avadim latzedakah
and being made free from sin, ye became servants of righteousness.

אֲנִי מְדַבֵּר בְּדֻגְמָאוֹת אֱנוֹשִׁיּוֹת בִּגְלַל חֻלְשַׁתְכֶם, חֻלְשַׁת בָּשָׂר וָדָם
ani medabber bedugma'ot enoshiyot biglal chulshatchem, chulshat basar vadam
I speak after the manner of men because of the infirmity of your flesh:

כְּמוֹ שֶׁכַּעֲבָדִים לְטֻמְאָה וְרֶשַׁע מְסַרְתֶּם אֶת אֵיבְרֵיכֶם לְתַכְלִית שֶׁל רֶשַׁע,
kemo shekka'avadim letum'ah veresha mesartem et eivereichem letachlit shel resha
for as ye presented your members as servants to uncleanness and to iniquity unto iniquity,

כֵּן עַתָּה כַּעֲבָדִים לַצְּדָקָה מִסְרוּ אֶת אֵיבְרֵיכֶם לְתַכְלִית שֶׁל קְדֻשָּׁה
ken attah ka'avadim latzedakah misru et eivereichem letachlit shel kedushah
even so now present your members as servants to righteousness unto sanctification.

הֲרֵי בְּעֵת שֶׁהֱיִיתֶם עֲבָדִים לַחֵטְא חָפְשִׁים הֱיִיתֶם מִן הַצְּדָקָה
harei be'et sheheyitem avadim lachet chofshiim heyitem min hatzedakah
For when ye were servants of sin, ye were free in regard of righteousness.

וְאוּלָם אֵיזֶה פְּרִי הָיָה לָכֶם אָז מֵאוֹתָם דְּבָרִים שֶׁאַתֶּם מִתְבַּיְשִׁים בָּהֶם עַכְשָׁו
ve'ulam eizeh peri hayah lachem az me'otam dvarim she'attem mitbayeshim bahem achshav?
What fruit then had ye at that time in the things whereof ye are now ashamed?

הֲלֹא הַמָּוֶת הוּא תּוֹצָאָתָם
halo hammavet hu totza'atam
for the end of those things is death.

אֲבָל כָּעֵת, כְּשֶׁאַתֶּם מְשֻׁחְרָרִים מֵהַחֵטְא וּמְשֻׁעְבָּדִים לֵאלֹהִים
aval ka'et, keshe'attem meshuchrarim mehachet umeshu'badim le'elohim
But now being made free from sin and become servants to God,

יֵשׁ לָכֶם פְּרִי הַמֵּבִיא לִידֵי קְדֻשָּׁה, וְהַתּוֹצָאָה הִיא חַיֵּי עוֹלָם
yesh lachem peri hammevi lidei kdushah, vehattotza'ah hi chayei olam
ye have your fruit unto sanctification, and the end eternal life.

כִּי שְׂכַר הַחֵטְא הוּא מָוֶת, אֲבָל מַתְּנָתוֹ שֶׁל אֱלֹהִים הִיא חַיֵּי עוֹלָם בַּמָּשִׁיחַ יֵשׁוּעַ אֲדוֹנֵנוּ
ki schar hachet hu mavet, aval mattnato shel elohim hi chayei olam bammashiach yeshua adonenu
For the wages of sin is death; but the free gift of God is eternal life in Christ Jesus our Lord.

הָרוֹמִים

אֲנַחְנוּ יוֹדְעִים כִּי הַמָּשִׁיחַ, לְאַחַר שֶׁקָּם מִן הַמֵּתִים, לֹא יָמוּת עוֹד; הַמָּוֶת לֹא יוֹסִיף לִשְׁלֹט בּוֹ
anachnu yode'im ki hammashiach, le'achar shekkam min hammetim, lo yamut od; hammavet lo yosif lishlot bo
knowing that Christ being raised from the dead dieth no more; death no more hath dominion over him.

הֲרֵי בְּמוֹתוֹ מֵת אַחַת וּלְתָמִיד לְגַבֵּי הַחֵטְא, אַךְ בְּחִיּוּתוֹ הוּא חַי לֵאלֹהִים
harei bemoto met achat uletamid legabbei hachet, ach bichyoto hu chai le'elohim
For the death that he died, he died unto sin once: but the life that he liveth, he liveth unto God.

בְּדֶרֶךְ זֹאת גַּם אַתֶּם חִשְׁבוּ אֶת עַצְמְכֶם מֵתִים לְגַבֵּי הַחֵטְא, אַךְ חַיִּים לֵאלֹהִים בַּמָּשִׁיחַ יֵשׁוּעַ
bederech zot gam attem chishvu et atzmechem metim legabbei hachet, ach chayim le'elohim bammashiach yeshua'
Even so reckon ye also yourselves to be dead unto sin, but alive unto God in Christ Jesus.

לָכֵן, אַל יִמְשֹׁל הַחֵטְא בְּגוּפְכֶם בֶּן הַתְּמוּתָה וְאַל יַכְנִיעַ אֶתְכֶם לְתַאֲוֹתָיו
lachen, al yimshol hachet begufechem ben hattmutah ve'al yachnia etchem leta'avotav
Let not sin therefore reign in your mortal body, that ye should obey the lusts thereof:

וְאַל תִּמְסְרוּ אֶת אֵיבְרֵיכֶם לַחֵטְא כְּכֵלִים שֶׁל רֶשַׁע
ve'al timseru et eivereichem lachet kechelim shel resha
neither present your members unto sin as instruments of unrighteousness;

אֶלָּא מִסְרוּ אֶת עַצְמְכֶם לֵאלֹהִים כַּאֲנָשִׁים חַיִּים שֶׁהוּקְמוּ מִן הַמֵּתִים
ella misru et atzmechem lelohim ka'anashim chayim shehukemu min hammetim
but present yourselves unto God, as alive from the dead,

וְאֶת אֵיבְרֵיכֶם תִּמְסְרוּ לֵאלֹהִים כְּכֵלִים שֶׁל צֶדֶק
ve'et eivereichem timseru le'elohim kechelim shel tzedek
and your members as instruments of righteousness unto God.

הַחֵטְא לֹא יִשְׁלֹט בָּכֶם, כִּי אֵינְכֶם תַּחַת יַד הַתּוֹרָה אֶלָּא תַּחַת יַד הַחֶסֶד
hachet lo yishlot bachem, ki einchem tachat yad hattorah ella tachat yad hachesed
For sin shall not have dominion over you: for ye are not under law, but under grace.

וּבְכֵן מַה? הַאִם נֶחֱטָא מִפְּנֵי שֶׁאֵין אָנוּ תַּחַת יַד הַתּוֹרָה אֶלָּא תַּחַת יַד הַחֶסֶד? חַס וְחָלִילָה
uvechen mah? ha'im nechta mippenei she'ein anu tachat yad hattorah ella tachat yad hachesed? chas vechalilah
What then? shall we sin, because we are not under law, but under grace? God forbid.

הַאֵינְכֶם יוֹדְעִים שֶׁכַּאֲשֶׁר אַתֶּם מוֹסְרִים אֶת עַצְמְכֶם כַּעֲבָדִים לְמִישֶׁהוּ כְּדֵי לְצַיֵּת לוֹ
ha'einechem yode'im shekka'asher attem moserim et atzmechem ka'avadim lemishehu kedei letzayet lo
Know ye not, that to whom ye present yourselves as servants unto obedience,

עֲבָדִים אַתֶּם לְמִי שֶׁאַתֶּם מְצַיְּתִים - אוֹ לַחֵטְא הַמּוֹלִיךְ אֶל מָוֶת, אוֹ לְצִיּוּת הַמּוֹלִיךְ אֱלֵי צְדָקָה
avadim attem lemi she'attem metzayetim - o lachet hammolich el mavet, o latziyut hammolich elei tzedakah
his servants ye are whom ye obey; whether of sin unto death, or of obedience unto righteousness?

אַךְ תּוֹדָה לֵאלֹהִים עַל שֶׁאַתֶּם, אֲשֶׁר קֹדֶם לָכֵן הֱיִיתֶם עֲבָדִים לַחֵטְא
ach todah lelohim al she'attem, asher kodem lachen heyitem avadim lachet
But thanks be to God, that, whereas ye were servants of sin,

הָרוֹמִים

I

אִם כֵּן, מַה נֹּאמַר? הֲנַמְשִׁיךְ בַּחֵטְא כְּדֵי שֶׁיִּרְבֶּה הַחֶסֶד
im ken, mah nomar? hanamshich bachet kedei sheyirbeh hachesed
What shall we say then? Shall we continue in sin, that grace may abound?

חַס וְחָלִילָה! אָנוּ שֶׁמַּתְנוּ לְגַבֵּי הַחֵטְא, אֵיךְ נַמְשִׁיךְ וְנִחְיֶה בּוֹ
chas vechalilah! anu shemmatnu legabbei hachet, eich namshich venichyeh bo
God forbid. We who died to sin, how shall we any longer live therein?

הַאֵינְכֶם יוֹדְעִים כִּי כֻּלָּנוּ אֲשֶׁר נִטְבַּלְנוּ לַמָּשִׁיחַ יֵשׁוּעַ, לְמוֹתוֹ נִטְבַּלְנוּ
ha'einechem yode'im ki kullanu asher nitbalnu lammashiach yeshua, lemoto nitbalnu
Or are ye ignorant that all we who were baptized into Christ Jesus were baptized into his death?

נִקְבַּרְנוּ אִתּוֹ בַּטְּבִילָה לַמָּוֶת
nikbarnu itto battevilah lammavet
We were buried therefore with him through baptism into death:

כְּדֵי שֶׁנִּתְהַלֵּךְ גַּם אֲנַחְנוּ בְּחַיִּים חֲדָשִׁים, כְּשֵׁם שֶׁהַמָּשִׁיחַ הוּקַם מִן הַמֵּתִים עַל־יְדֵי כְּבוֹדוֹ שֶׁל הָאָב
kedei shennit'hallech gam anachnu bechayim chadashim, keshem shehammashiach hukam min hammetim al-yedei kevodo shel ha'av
that like as Christ was raised from the dead through the glory of the Father, so we also might walk in newness of life.

שֶׁכֵּן אִם הִתְאַחַדְנוּ אִתּוֹ בְּמָוֶת דּוֹמֶה לְמוֹתוֹ
shekken im hit'achadnu itto bemavet domeh lemoto
For if we have become united with him in the likeness of his death,

כָּךְ גַּם נִתְאַחֵד אִתּוֹ בִּתְחִיָּתוֹ
kach gam nit'ached itto bitchiyato
we shall be also in the likeness of his resurrection;

זֹאת אָנוּ יוֹדְעִים: הָאָדָם הַיָּשָׁן אֲשֶׁר בָּנוּ נִצְלַב אִתּוֹ
zot anu yode'im: ha'adam hayashan asher banu nitzlav itto
knowing this, that our old man was crucified with him,

כְּדֵי שֶׁיֵּהָרֵס גּוּף הַחֵטְא וְלֹא נִהְיֶה עוֹד עֲבָדִים לַחֵטְא
kedei sheyehares guf hachet velo nihyeh od avadim lachet
that the body of sin might be done away, that so we should no longer be in bondage to sin;

שֶׁהֲרֵי הַמֵּת מְשֻׁחְרָר מִן הַחֵטְא
sheharei hammet meshuchrar min hachet
for he that hath died is justified from sin.

אֲבָל אִם מַתְנוּ עִם הַמָּשִׁיחַ, מַאֲמִינִים אָנוּ כִּי גַּם נִחְיֶה עִמּוֹ
aval im matnu im hammashiach, ma'aminim anu ki gam nichyeh immo
But if we died with Christ, we believe that we shall also live with him;

הָרוֹמִים

שֶׁהֲרֵי אִם עַל־יְדֵי עֲבֵרָה שֶׁל אָדָם אֶחָד מָלַךְ הַמָּוֶת
sheharei im al-yedei averah shel adam echad malach hammavet
For if, by the trespass of the one, death reigned through the one;

כָּל שֶׁכֵּן הַמְקַבְּלִים אֶת שֶׁפַע הַחֶסֶד וְאֶת מַתְּנַת הַצְּדָקָה יִמְלְכוּ בַחַיִּים בִּגְלַל הָאֶחָד
kol shekken hamkabbelim et shefa hachesed ve'et mattenat hatzedakah yimlechu bachayim biglal ha'echad
much more shall they that receive the abundance of grace and of the gift of righteousness reign in life through the one,

יֵשׁוּעַ הַמָּשִׁיחַ
yeshua hammashiach
even Jesus Christ.

וּבְכֵן, כְּשֵׁם שֶׁעֲבֵרָה אַחַת הִיא הַרְשָׁעָה לְכָל בְּנֵי אָדָם
uvechen, keshem she'averah achat hi harsha'ah lechol benei adam
So then as through one trespass the judgment came unto all men to condemnation;

כֵּן גַּם מַעֲשֵׂה צְדָקָה אֶחָד הוּא זִכּוּי שֶׁל חַיִּים לְכָל בְּנֵי אָדָם
ken gam ma'aseh tzedakah echad hu zikkui shel chayim lechol benei adam
even so through one act of righteousness the free gift came unto all men to justification of life.

כִּי כְּשֵׁם שֶׁבִּגְלַל אִי־צִיּוּתוֹ שֶׁל אָדָם אֶחָד נַעֲשׂוּ הָרַבִּים לְחוֹטְאִים
ki keshem shebbiglal i-tziyuto shel adam echad na'asu harabbim lechote'im
For as through the one man's disobedience the many were made sinners,

כֵּן גַּם בִּגְלַל צִיּוּתוֹ שֶׁל הָאֶחָד יֵעָשׂוּ הָרַבִּים לְצַדִּיקִים
ken gam biglal tziyuto shel ha'echad ye'asu harabbim letzaddikim
even so through the obedience of the one shall the many be made righteous.

הַתּוֹרָה בָּאָה וּבְכָךְ רַבּוּ הָעֲבֵרוֹת. אֲבָל הֵיכָן שֶׁהִתְרַבָּה הַחֵטְא
hattorah ba'ah uvechach rabbu ha'averot. aval heichan shehitrabbah hachet
And the law came in besides, that the trespass might abound; but where sin abounded,

הַחֶסֶד שָׁפַע עוֹד יוֹתֵר
hachesed shafa od yoter
grace did abound more exceedingly:

וְכָךְ כְּשֵׁם שֶׁהַחֵטְא מָשַׁל בַּמָּוֶת
vechach keshem shehachet mashal bammavet,
that, as sin reigned in death,

כֵּן גַּם יִמְשֹׁל הַחֶסֶד בְּאֶמְצָעוּת צְדָקָה, וְהַתּוֹצָאָה - חַיֵּי עוֹלָם עַל־יְדֵי יֵשׁוּעַ הַמָּשִׁיחַ אֲדוֹנֵנוּ
ken gam yimshol hachesed be'emtza'ut tzedakah, vehattotza'ah - chayei olam al-yedei yeshua hammashiach adonenu
even so might grace reign through righteousness unto eternal life through Jesus Christ our Lord.

הָרוֹמִים

וְלֹא זֹאת בִּלְבַד, אֲנַחְנוּ גַּם מִתְהַלְּלִים בֵּאלֹהִים הוֹדוֹת לַאֲדוֹנֵנוּ יֵשׁוּעַ הַמָּשִׁיחַ
velo zot bilvad, anachnu gam mit'hallelim belohim hodot la'adonenu yeshua hammashiach
and not only so, but we also rejoice in God through our Lord Jesus Christ,

שֶׁבְּאֶמְצָעוּתוֹ קִבַּלְנוּ עַתָּה אֶת הָרִצּוּי
shebbe'emtza'uto kibbalnu attah et haritzui
through whom we have now received the reconciliation.

לְפִיכָךְ, כְּשֵׁם שֶׁעַל־יְדֵי אָדָם אֶחָד בָּא הַחֵטְא לָעוֹלָם, וְעֵקֶב הַחֵטְא בָּא הַמָּוֶת
lefichach, keshem she'al-yedei adam echad ba hachet la'olam, ve'ekev hachet ba hammavet
Therefore, as through one man sin entered into the world, and death through sin;

כָּךְ עָבַר הַמָּוֶת לְכָל בְּנֵי אָדָם מִשּׁוּם שֶׁכֻּלָּם חָטְאוּ
kach avar hammavet lechol benei adam mishum shekkullam chat'u
and so death passed unto all men, for that all sinned:—

הֲרֵי עוֹד לִפְנֵי הַתּוֹרָה הָיָה הַחֵטְא בָּעוֹלָם, אֶלָּא שֶׁאֵין הוּא נֶחְשָׁב בְּאֵין תּוֹרָה
harei od lifnei hattorah hayah hachet ba'olam, ella she'ein hu nechshav be'ein torah
for until the law sin was in the world; but sin is not imputed when there is no law.

בְּכָל זֹאת שָׁלַט הַמָּוֶת מֵאָדָם וְעַד מֹשֶׁה
bechol zot shalat hammavet me'adam ve'ad mosheh
Nevertheless death reigned from Adam until Moses,

גַּם עַל אֵלֶּה שֶׁלֹּא חָטְאוּ בַּעֲבֵרָה דּוֹמָה לַעֲבֵרָה שֶׁל אָדָם
gam al elleh shello chate'u ba'averah domah la'averah shel adam
even over them that had not sinned after the likeness of Adam's transgression,

אֲשֶׁר הוּא דְּמוּת מַקְבִּילָה לְאֶחָד שֶׁהָיָה עָתִיד לָבוֹא
asher hu demut makbilah la'echad shehayah atid lavo
who is a figure of him that was to come.

אוּלָם לֹא הֲרֵי הָעֲבֵרָה כַּהֲרֵי מַתְּנַת הַחֶסֶד; שֶׁכֵּן אִם בִּגְלַל הָעֲבֵרָה שֶׁל אֶחָד מֵתוּ הָרַבִּים
ulam lo harei ha'averah kaharei mattenat hachesed; shekken im biglal ha'averah shel echad metu harabbim,
But not as the trespass, so also is the free gift. For if by the trespass of the one the many died,

עַל אַחַת כַּמָּה וְכַמָּה, בְּחֶסֶד הָאָדָם הָאֶחָד יֵשׁוּעַ הַמָּשִׁיחַ, שָׁפְעוּ לָרַבִּים חֶסֶד אֱלֹהִים וּמַתְּנָתוֹ
al achat kammah vechammah, bechesed ha'adam ha'echad yeshua hammashiach, shafe'u larabbim chesed elohim umattnato
much more did the grace of God, and the gift by the grace of the one man, Jesus Christ, abound unto the many.

וְאֵין הַמַּתָּנָה כְּמַעֲשֵׂה הָאֶחָד שֶׁחָטָא; כִּי הַמִּשְׁפָּט עֵקֶב עֲבֵרָה אַחַת יָצָא לְהַרְשָׁעָה
ve'ein hammattanah kema'aseh ha'echad shechata; ki hammishpat ekev averah achat yatza leharsha'ah
And not as through one that sinned, so is the gift: for the judgment came of one unto condemnation,

אֲבָל לְאַחַר עֲבֵרוֹת רַבּוֹת מַתְּנַת הַחֶסֶד הִיא זִכּוּי
aval le'achar averot rabbot mattnat hachesed hi zikkui
but the free gift came of many trespasses unto justification.

הָרוֹמִים

דַּרְכּוֹ יֵשׁ לָנוּ גַּם גִּישָׁה, בְּאֶמְצָעוּת אֱמוּנָה, לַחֶסֶד הַזֶּה שֶׁאָנוּ עוֹמְדִים בּוֹ
darko yesh lanu gam gishah, be'emtza'ut emunah, lachesed hazzeh she'anu omedim bo
through whom also we have had our access by faith into this grace wherein we stand;

וְאָנוּ מִתְהַלְלִים בַּתִּקְוָה אֶל כְּבוֹד אֱלֹהִים
ve'anu mit'hallelim battikvah el kevod elohim
and we rejoice in hope of the glory of God.

אַךְ לֹא זֹאת בִּלְבַד; אֲנַחְנוּ מִתְהַלְלִים גַּם בַּצָּרוֹת, שֶׁכֵּן יוֹדְעִים אָנוּ כִּי הַצָּרָה מְבִיאָה לִידֵי סַבְלָנוּת
ach lo zot bilvad; anachnu mit'hallelim gam batzarot, shekken yode'im anu ki hatzarah mevi'ah liydei savlanut
And not only so, but we also rejoice in our tribulations: knowing that tribulation worketh stedfastness;

וְהַסַּבְלָנוּת לִידֵי עֲמִידָה בְּנִסָּיוֹן, וַעֲמִידָה בַּנִּסָּיוֹן לִידֵי תִּקְוָה
vehassavlanut liydei amidah benissayon, va'amidah bannissayon lidei tikvah
and stedfastness, approvedness; and approvedness, hope:

וְהַתִּקְוָה אֵינָהּ מַכְזִיבָה
vehattikvah einah machzivah
and hope putteth not to shame;

כִּי אַהֲבַת אֱלֹהִים הוּצְקָה לְתוֹךְ לִבֵּנוּ עַל-יְדֵי רוּחַ הַקֹּדֶשׁ שֶׁנִּתְּנָה לָנוּ
ki ahavat elohim hutzkah letoch libbenu al-yedei ruach hakkodesh shennittenah lanu
because the love of God hath been shed abroad in our hearts through the Holy Spirit which was given unto us.

הִנֵּה בְּעוֹד שֶׁהָיִינוּ חַסְרֵי אוֹנִים, בְּהַגִּיעַ הַשָּׁעָה מֵת הַמָּשִׁיחַ בְּעַד הָרְשָׁעִים
hinneh be'od shehayinu chasrei onim, behaggia hasha'ah met hammashiach be'ad haresha'im
For while we were yet weak, in due season Christ died for the ungodly.

וַהֲרֵי לֹא בִּמְהֵרָה יָמוּת מִישֶׁהוּ בְּעַד אָדָם צַדִּיק, אִם כִּי בְּעַד הָאִישׁ הַטּוֹב אוּלַי יָעֵז מִישֶׁהוּ לָמוּת
vaharei lo bimherah yamut mishehu be'ad adam tzaddik, im ki be'ad ha'ish hattov ulai ya'ez mishehu lamut
For scarcely for a righteous man will one die: for peradventure for the good man some one would even dare to die.

אוּלָם אֱלֹהִים מְגַלֶּה אֶת אַהֲבָתוֹ אֵלֵינוּ בְּכָךְ שֶׁהַמָּשִׁיחַ מֵת בַּעֲדֵנוּ כַּאֲשֶׁר עוֹד הָיִינוּ אֲנָשִׁים חוֹטְאִים
ulam elohim megalleh et ahavato eleinu bechach shehammashiach met ba'adenu ka'asher od hayinu anashim chote'im
But God commendeth his own love toward us, in that, while we were yet sinners, Christ died for us.

וְכָעֵת, לְאַחַר שֶׁכְּבָר הֻצְדַּקְנוּ בְּדָמוֹ, בְּוַדַּאי וּבְוַדַּאי שֶׁנִּוָּשַׁע עַל-יָדוֹ מִן הַזַּעַם
vecha'et, le'achar shekkevar hutzdaknu bedamo, bevadda uvevadda shennivvasha al-yado min hazza'am
Much more then, being now justified by his blood, shall we be saved from the wrath of God through him.

שֶׁכֵּן אִם בִּזְמַן שֶׁהָיִינוּ אוֹיְבִים נִרְצֵינוּ לֵאלֹהִים בְּמוֹת בְּנוֹ
shekken im bizman shehayinu oyevim nirtzeinu le'elohim bemot beno
For if, while we were enemies, we were reconciled to God through the death of his Son,

עַל אַחַת כַּמָּה וְכַמָּה נִוָּשַׁע בְּחַיֵּי בְּנוֹ לְאַחַר שֶׁכְּבָר נִרְצֵינוּ
al achat kammah vechammah nivvasha bechayei beno le'achar shekkevar nirtzeinu
much more, being reconciled, shall we be saved by his life;

הָרוֹמִים

אֱמוּנָתוֹ לֹא נִתְרוֹפְפָה

emunato lo nitrofefah
And without being weakened in faith

גַּם כַּאֲשֶׁר בִּהְיוֹתוֹ כְּבֶן מֵאָה שָׁנִים חָשַׁב עַל תְּשִׁישׁוּת גּוּפוֹ

gam ka'asher bihyoto keven me'ah shanim chashav al teshishut gufo
he considered his own body now as good as dead (he being about a hundred years old),

וְעַל עֲקָרוּת שָׂרָה

ve'al akarut sarah
and the deadness of Sarah's womb;

הוּא לֹא חָדַל מֵאֱמוּנָה וְלֹא פִּקְפֵּק בְּהַבְטָחַת אֱלֹהִים

hu lo chadal me'emunah velo pikpek behavtachat elohim
yet, looking unto the promise of God, he wavered not through unbelief,

אֶלָּא הִתְחַזֵּק בֶּאֱמוּנָתוֹ וְנָתַן כָּבוֹד לֵאלֹהִים

ella hitchazzek be'emunato venatan kavod lelohim
but waxed strong through faith, giving glory to God,

בִּהְיוֹתוֹ בָּטוּחַ לַחֲלוּטִין כִּי אֶת אֲשֶׁר הִבְטִיחַ יוּכַל גַּם לְקַיֵּם

bihyoto batuach lachalutin ki et asher hivtiach yuchal gam lekayem
and being fully assured that what he had promised, he was able also to perform.

לָכֵן נֶחְשְׁבָה לוֹ זֹאת לִצְדָקָה

lachen nechshevah lo zot litzdakah
Wherefore also it was reckoned unto him for righteousness.

וְלֹא לְמַעֲנוֹ בִּלְבַד נִכְתַּב שֶׁנֶּחְשְׁבָה לוֹ

velo lema'ano bilvad nichtav shennechshevah lo
Now it was not written for his sake alone, that it was reckoned unto him;

כִּי אִם גַּם לְמַעֲנֵנוּ; וְהִיא עֲתִידָה לְהֵחָשֵׁב לָנוּ ־הַמַּאֲמִינִים בְּמִי שֶׁהֵקִים אֶת יֵשׁוּעַ אֲדוֹנֵנוּ מִן הַמֵּתִים

ki im gam lema'anenu; vehi atidah lehechashev lanu -hamma'aminim bemi shehekim et yeshua adonenu min hammetim
but for our sake also, unto whom it shall be reckoned, who believe on him that raised Jesus our Lord from the dead,

הוּא אֲשֶׁר נִמְסַר לַמָּוֶת מִפְּנֵי חֲטָאֵינוּ וְהוּקַם לִתְחִיָּה מִפְּנֵי שֶׁהֻצְדַּקְנוּ׃

hu asher nimsar lammavet mippenei chata'einu vehukam litchiyah mippenei shehutzdaknu
who was delivered up for our trespasses, and was raised for our justification.

ה

עַל כֵּן לְאַחַר שֶׁהֻצְדַּקְנוּ עַל־סְמַךְ אֱמוּנָה יֵשׁ לָנוּ שָׁלוֹם עִם אֱלֹהִים הוֹדוֹת לַאֲדוֹנֵנוּ יֵשׁוּעַ הַמָּשִׁיחַ

al ken le'achar shehutzdaknu al-semach emunah yesh lanu shalom im elohim hodot la'adonenu yeshua hammashiach
Being therefore justified by faith, we have peace with God through our Lord Jesus Christ;

הָרוֹמִים

וְאָב לַנִּמּוֹלִים, לְאוֹתָם שֶׁאֵינָם נִמּוֹלִים בִּלְבַד
ve'av lannimmolim, le'otam she'einam nimmolim bilvad
and the father of circumcision to them who not only are of the circumcision,

אֶלָּא גַם הוֹלְכִים בְּעִקְּבוֹת הָאֱמוּנָה שֶׁהָיְתָה לְאַבְרָהָם אָבִינוּ בְּטֶרֶם נִמּוֹל
ella gam holechim be'ikkevot ha'emunah shehayetah le'avraham avinu beterem nimmol
but who also walk in the steps of that faith of our father Abraham which he had in uncircumcision.

הֲרֵי הַהַבְטָחָה כִּי יִירַשׁ אֶת הָעוֹלָם לֹא נִתְּנָה לְאַבְרָהָם אוֹ לְזַרְעוֹ עַל־סְמַךְ תּוֹרָה
harei hahavtachah ki yirash et ha'olam lo nittenah le'avraham o lezar'o al-semach torah
For not through the law was the promise to Abraham or to his seed that he should be heir of the world,

אֶלָּא עַל־סְמַךְ צְדָקָה שֶׁהִשִּׂיג בֶּאֱמוּנָה
ella al-semach tzedakah shehisig be'emunah
but through the righteousness of faith.

שֶׁכֵּן אִם מַחֲזִיקֵי הַתּוֹרָה הֵם הַיּוֹרְשִׁים, אֲזַי הָאֱמוּנָה הִיא לַשָּׁוְא וְהַהַבְטָחָה חֲסֵרַת תֹּקֶף
shekken im machazikei hattorah hem hayoreshim, azai ha'emunah hi lashav vehahavtachah chasrat tokef
For if they that are of the law are heirs, faith is made void, and the promise is made of none effect:

הַתּוֹרָה מְבִיאָה זַעַם, וּבְמָקוֹם שֶׁאֵין תּוֹרָה אֵין עֲבֵרָה עַל הַתּוֹרָה
hattorah mevi'ah za'am, uvemakom she'ein torah ein averah al hattorah
for the law worketh wrath; but where there is no law, neither is there transgression.

לָכֵן עַל־יְדֵי אֱמוּנָה, כְּדֵי שֶׁכָּל זֶה יִהְיֶה בְּחֶסֶד וְהַהַבְטָחָה תָּחוּל עַל כָּל הַצֶּאֱצָאִים,
lachen al-yedei emunah, kedei shekkol zeh yihyeh bechesed vehahavtachah tachul al kol hatze'etza'im
For this cause it is of faith, that it may be according to grace; to the end that the promise may be sure to all the seed;

לֹא רַק עַל בְּנֵי הַתּוֹרָה, אֶלָּא גַם עַל בְּנֵי אֱמוּנַת אַבְרָהָם, שֶׁהוּא אָב לְכֻלָּנוּ
lo rak al benei hattorah, ella gam al benei emunat avraham, shehu av lechullanu
not to that only which is of the law, but to that also which is of the faith of Abraham, who is the father of us all

כְּפִי שֶׁכָּתוּב: כִּי אַב־הֲמוֹן גּוֹיִם נְתַתִּיךָ - לְעֵינֵי אֱלֹהִים אֲשֶׁר בּוֹ הֶאֱמִין
kefi shekkatuv: ki av-hamon goyim netatticha - le'einei elohim asher bo he'emin
(as it is written, A father of many nations have I made thee) before him whom he believed,

הָאֱלֹהִים הַמְחַיֶּה אֶת הַמֵּתִים וְהַקּוֹרֵא בְּשֵׁם דְּבָרִים בְּעוֹד אֵינָם בְּנִמְצָא
ha'elohim hamchayeh et hammetim vehakkorei beshem devarim be'od einam benimtza
even God, who giveth life to the dead, and calleth the things that are not, as though they were.

וּבְאֵין סִבָּה לְתִקְוָה הוּא הֶאֱמִין וְקִוָּה כִּי יִהְיֶה לְאַב־הֲמוֹן גּוֹיִם
uve'ein sibbah letikvah hu he'emin vekivvah ki yihyeh le'av-hamon goyim
Who in hope believed against hope, to the end that he might become a father of many nations,

כְּפִי שֶׁנֶּאֱמַר: כֹּה יִהְיֶה זַרְעֶךָ
kefi shenne'emar: koh yihyeh zar'echa
according to that which had been spoken, So shall thy seed be.

הָרוֹמִים

אֲבָל זֶה שֶׁאֵינוֹ עוֹבֵד, אֶלָּא מַאֲמִין בַּמַּצְדִּיק אֶת הַחוֹטֵא, אֱמוּנָתוֹ נֶחְשֶׁבֶת לוֹ לִצְדָקָה
aval zeh she'eino oved, ella ma'amin bammatzdik et hachote, emunato nechshevet lo litzdakah
But to him that worketh not, but believeth on him that justifieth the ungodly, his faith is reckoned for righteousness.

כָּךְ גַּם דָּוִד מַבִּיעַ אֶת אָשְׁרוֹ שֶׁל הָאִישׁ אֲשֶׁר אֱלֹהִים יַחְשֹׁב לוֹ צְדָקָה בְּלִי תְּלוּת בְּמַעֲשִׂים
kach gam david mabbia et oshro shel ha'ish asher elohim yachshov lo tzedakah beli telut bema'asim
Even as David also pronounceth blessing upon the man, unto whom God reckoneth righteousness apart from works,

אַשְׁרֵי־נְשׂוּי פֶּשַׁע, כְּסוּי חֲטָאָה
ashrei-nesui pesha', kesui chata'ah
saying, Blessed are they whose iniquities are forgiven, And whose sins are covered.

אַשְׁרֵי־אָדָם לֹא יַחְשֹׁב יהוה לוֹ עָוֹן
ashrei-'adam lo yachsv hashem lo avon
Blessed is the man to whom the Lord will not reckon sin.

הַאִם הָאֹשֶׁר הַזֶּה רַק לַנִּמּוֹלִים, אוֹ גַּם לָעֲרֵלִים?
ha'im ha'osher hazzeh rak lannimmolim, o gam la'arelim
Is this blessing then pronounced upon the circumcision, or upon the uncircumcision also?

וַהֲרֵי אָנוּ אוֹמְרִים כִּי אֱמוּנָתוֹ שֶׁל אַבְרָהָם נֶחְשְׁבָה לוֹ צְדָקָה
vaharei anu omerim ki emunato shel avraham nechshevah lo tzedakah
for we say, To Abraham his faith was reckoned for righteousness.

מָתַי נֶחְשְׁבָה לוֹ? כַּאֲשֶׁר הָיָה נִמּוֹל אוֹ כְּשֶׁהָיָה עָרֵל
matai nechshevah lo? ka'asher hayah nimmol o kshehayah arel
How then was it reckoned? when he was in circumcision, or in uncircumcision?

לֹא בִּהְיוֹתוֹ נִמּוֹל, כִּי אִם בִּהְיוֹתוֹ עָרֵל
lo bihyoto nimmol, ki im bihyoto arel
Not in circumcision, but in uncircumcision:

הוּא קִבֵּל אֶת אוֹת הַמִּילָה
hu kibbel et ot hammilah
and he received the sign of circumcision,

כְּחוֹתָם לַצְּדָקָה שֶׁזָּכָה בָּהּ בִּגְלַל הָאֱמוּנָה בְּעוֹדֶנּוּ עָרֵל
kechotam latzdakah shezzachah bah biglal ha'emunah be'odennu arel
a seal of the righteousness of the faith which he had while he was in uncircumcision:

כְּדֵי שֶׁיִּהְיֶה אָב לְכָל הַמַּאֲמִינִים הַבִּלְתִּי נְמוֹלִים
kedei sheyihyeh av lechol hamma'aminim habbilti nimmolim
that he might be the father of all them that believe, though they be in uncircumcision,

לְמַעַן תֵּחָשֵׁב גַּם לָהֶם צְדָקָה
lema'an techashev gam lahem tzdakah
that righteousness might be reckoned unto them;

הָרוֹמִים

שֶׁהוּא צַדִּיק וּמַצְדִּיק אֶת בֶּן אֱמוּנַת יֵשׁוּעַ
shehu tzaddik umatzdik et ben emunat yeshua
that he might himself be just, and the justifier of him that hath faith in Jesus.

אִם כֵּן, הֲיֵשׁ מָקוֹם לְגַאֲוָה? לֹא, אֵין לָהּ מָקוֹם. הוֹדוֹת לְאֵיזוֹ תּוֹרָה? שֶׁל הַמַּעֲשִׂים?
im ken, hayesh makom lega'avah? lo, ein lah makom. hodot le'eizo torah? shel hamma'asim?
Where then is the glorying? It is excluded. By what manner of law? of works?

לֹא, הוֹדוֹת לְתוֹרָה שֶׁל אֱמוּנָה
lo, hodot letorah shel emunah
Nay: but by a law of faith.

וְאָמְנָם אָנוּ קוֹבְעִים שֶׁהָאָדָם מֻצְדָּק עַל־יְדֵי אֱמוּנָה לְלֹא תְּלוּת בְּמַעֲשֵׂי הַתּוֹרָה
ve'omnam anu kove'im sheha'adam mutzdak al-yedei emunah lelo tlut bema'asei hattorah
We reckon therefore that a man is justified by faith apart from the works of the law.

אוֹ שֶׁמָּא הוּא אֱלֹהֵי הַיְּהוּדִים בִּלְבַד? הַאֵין הוּא גַּם אֱלֹהֵי הַגּוֹיִם? כֵּן, גַּם אֱלֹהֵי הַגּוֹיִם הוּא
o shemma hu elohei hayehudim bilvad? ha'ein hu gam elohei haggoyim? ken, gam elohei haggoyim hu
Or is God the God of Jews only? is he not the God of Gentiles also? Yea, of Gentiles also:

שֶׁכֵּן אֱלֹהִים אֶחָד הוּא הַמַּצְדִּיק אֶת הַנִּמּוֹלִים עַל־יְסוֹד אֱמוּנָה, וְאֶת הָעֲרֵלִים עַל־יְדֵי הָאֱמוּנָה
shekken elohim echad hu hammatzdik et hannimmolim al-yesod emunah, ve'et ha'arelim al-yedei ha'emunah
if so be that God is one, and he shall justify the circumcision by faith, and the uncircumcision through faith.

הַאִם אָנוּ מְבַטְּלִים אֵפוֹא אֶת הַתּוֹרָה עַל־יְדֵי הָאֱמוּנָה? חַס וְחָלִילָה! אַדְּרַבָּא, אָנוּ נוֹתְנִים תֹּקֶף לַתּוֹרָה
ha'im anu mevattelim efo et hattorah al-yedei ha'emunah? chas vechalilah! addrabba, anu notenim tokef lattorah
Do we then make the law of none effect through faith? God forbid: nay, we establish the law.

ד

וּבְכֵן, מַה נֹּאמַר עַל אַבְרָהָם אָבִינוּ, מַה הִשִּׂיג בִּזְכוּת מַעֲשָׂיו הוּא
uvchen, mah nomar al avraham avinu, mah hisig bizchut ma'asav hu
What then shall we say that Abraham, our forefather, hath found according to the flesh?

אִם אָמְנָם הֻצְדַּק אַבְרָהָם בִּגְלַל מַעֲשִׂים, כִּי אָז יֵשׁ לוֹ בַּמֶּה לְהִתְפָּאֵר, אַךְ לֹא לִפְנֵי אֱלֹהִים
im amenam hutzdak avraham biglal ma'asim, ki az yesh lo bammeh lehitpa'er, ach lo lifnei elohim
For if Abraham was justified by works, he hath whereof to glory; but not toward God.

מָה אוֹמֵר הַכָּתוּב? וְהֶאֱמִן אַבְרָהָם בַּיהוה וַיַּחְשְׁבֶהָ לּוֹ צְדָקָה
mah omer hakkatuv? vehe'emin avraham ba'adonai vayachsheveha lo tzedakah
For what saith the scripture? And Abraham believed God, and it was reckoned unto him for righteousness.

וַהֲרֵי שְׂכָרוֹ שֶׁל עוֹבֵד אֵינוֹ נֶחְשָׁב לוֹ כְּחֶסֶד, אֶלָּא כְּחוֹב הַמַּגִּיעַ לוֹ
vaharei secharo shel oved eino nechshav lo kechesed, ella kechov hammaggia lo
Now to him that worketh, the reward is not reckoned as of grace, but as of debt.

הָרוֹמִים

אֵין־פַּחַד אֱלֹהִים לְנֶגֶד עֵינֵיהֶם
ein-pachad elohim leneged eineihem
There is no fear of God before their eyes.

אָנוּ יוֹדְעִים כִּי כָּל מַה שֶׁהַתּוֹרָה אוֹמֶרֶת, הִיא אוֹמֶרֶת לָאֲנָשִׁים הַכְּפוּפִים לַתּוֹרָה,
anu yode'im ki kol mah shehattorah omeret, hi omeret la'anashim hakkfufim lattorah
Now we know that what things soever the law saith, it speaketh to them that are under the law;

כְּדֵי שֶׁלֹּא יִהְיֶה פִּתְחוֹן פֶּה לְאִישׁ וְכָל הָעוֹלָם יִמָּצֵא אָשֵׁם לִפְנֵי אֱלֹהִים
kedei shello yihyeh pitchon peh le'ish vechol ha'olam yimmatzei ashem lifnei elohim
that every mouth may be stopped, and all the world may be brought under the judgment of God:

זֹאת מִפְּנֵי שֶׁבְּמַעֲשֵׂי הַתּוֹרָה לֹא יִצְדַּק לְפָנָיו כָּל בָּשָׂר, כִּי הַתּוֹרָה רַק מְבִיאָה לִידֵי הַכָּרַת חֵטְא
zot mippenei shebbema'asei hattorah lo yitzdak lefanav kol basar, ki hattorah rak mevi'ah liydei hakkarat chet
because by the works of the law shall no flesh be justified in his sight; for through the law cometh the knowledge of sin.

אַךְ כָּעֵת נִגְלְתָה צִדְקַת הָאֱלֹהִים בְּלִי תּוֹרָה, צְדָקָה שֶׁהַתּוֹרָה וְהַנְּבִיאִים מְעִידִים עָלֶיהָ
ach ka'et nigletah tzidkat ha'elohim beli torah, tzedakah shehattorah vehannevi'im me'idim aleiha
But now apart from the law a righteousness of God hath been manifested, being witnessed by the law and the prophets;

וְהִיא צְדָקָה שֶׁל הָאֱלֹהִים, בְּאֶמְצָעוּת אֱמוּנַת יֵשׁוּעַ הַמָּשִׁיחַ, אֶל כָּל וְעַל כָּל הַמַּאֲמִינִים
vehi tzedakah shel ha'elohim, be'emtza'ut emunat yeshua hammashiach, el kol ve'al kol hamma'aminim
even the righteousness of God through faith in Jesus Christ unto all them that believe;

שֶׁהֲרֵי אֵין הֶבְדֵּל
sheharei ein hevdel
for there is no distinction;

כִּי הַכֹּל חָטְאוּ וּמְחֻסְּרֵי כְּבוֹד אֱלֹהִים הֵמָּה
ki hakkol chate'u umechusserei kevod elohim hemmah
for all have sinned, and fall short of the glory of God;

אַךְ הֵם מֻצְדָּקִים בְּחַסְדּוֹ, בְּחִנָּם, הוֹדוֹת לַפְּדוּת שֶׁבַּמָּשִׁיחַ יֵשׁוּעַ
ach hem mutzdakim bechasdo, bechinnam, hodot lappdut shebbammashiach yeshua
being justified freely by his grace through the redemption that is in Christ Jesus:

אֲשֶׁר הָאֱלֹהִים שָׂם אוֹתוֹ לְכַפָּרָה בְּדָמוֹ, כַּפָּרָה עַל־יְסוֹד אֱמוּנָה
asher ha'elohim sam oto lechapparah bedamo, kapparah al-yesod emunah
whom God set forth to be a propitiation, through faith, in his blood,

כָּל זֶה כְּדֵי לְהַרְאוֹת אֶת הַצְּדָקָה שֶׁל אֱלֹהִים בְּכָךְ שֶׁבְּאֹרֶךְ רוּחוֹ פָּסַח עַל חֲטָאֵי הֶעָבָר
kol zeh kedei lehar'ot et hatzdakah shel elohim bechach shebbe'orech rucho pasach al chata'ei he'avar
to show his righteousness because of the passing over of the sins done aforetime, in the forbearance of God;

וּלְהַרְאוֹת אֶת צִדְקָתוֹ בַּזְּמַן הַזֶּה
ulehar'ot et tzidkato bazzman hazzeh
for the showing, I say, of his righteousness at this present season:

הָרוֹמִים

אָכֵן מִשְׁפַּט צֶדֶק נֶחֱרַץ עֲלֵיהֶם

achen mishpat tzedek necheratz aleihem
whose condemnation is just.

וּבְכֵן, הֲטוֹבִים אָנוּ מֵאֲחֵרִים? לֹא, כְּלָל וּכְלָל לֹא

uvechen, hatovim anu me'acherim? lo, kelal uchelal lo
What then? are we better than they? No, in no wise:

שֶׁהֲרֵי כְּבָר הוֹכַחְנוּ לְעֵיל כִּי הַיְהוּדִים וְהַגּוֹיִם כְּאֶחָד מְשֻׁעְבָּדִים כֻּלָּם לַחֵטְא

sheharei kvar hochachnu le'eil ki hayehudim vehaggoyim ke'echad meshu'badim kullam lachet
for we before laid to the charge both of Jews and Greeks, that they are all under sin;

כַּכָּתוּב: אֵין צַדִּיק, אֵין גַּם אֶחָד

Kakkatuv: ein tzaddik, ein gam echad
as it is written, There is none righteous, no, not one;

אֵין מַשְׂכִּיל, אֵין דֹּרֵשׁ אֶת־אֱלֹהִים

ein maskil, ein doresh et-'elohim
There is none that understandeth, There is none that seeketh after God;

הַכֹּל סָר, יַחְדָּו נֶאֱלָחוּ

hakkol sar, yachdav ne'elachu
They have all turned aside, they are together become unprofitable;

אֵין עֹשֵׂה־טוֹב, אֵין גַּם־אֶחָד

ein oseh-tov, ein gam-'echad
There is none that doeth good, no, not so much as one:

קֶבֶר־פָּתוּחַ גְּרֹנָם, לְשׁוֹנָם יַחֲלִיקוּן, חֲמַת עַכְשׁוּב תַּחַת שְׂפָתֵימוֹ

kever-patuach gronam, leshonam yachalikun, chamat achshuv tachat sfateimo
Their throat is an open sepulchre; With their tongues they have used deceit: The poison of asps is under their lips:

אֲשֶׁר אָלָה פִּיהֶם מָלֵא וּמְרֹרוֹת

asher alah pihem malei umrorot
Whose mouth is full of cursing and bitterness:

רַגְלֵיהֶם יְמַהֲרוּ לִשְׁפֹּךְ דָּם

ragleihem yemaharu lishpoch dam
Their feet are swift to shed blood;

שֹׁד וָשֶׁבֶר בִּמְסִלּוֹתָם

shod vashever bimsillotam
Destruction and misery are in their ways;

וְדֶרֶךְ שָׁלוֹם לֹא יָדָעוּ

vederech shalom lo yada'u
And the way of peace have they not known:

הָרוֹמִים

וּמִילָה הִיא זוֹ שֶׁבַּלֵּב, לְפִי הָרוּחַ וְלֹא לְפִי אוֹת כְּתוּבָה; שִׁבְחוֹ אֵינוֹ בָא מִבְּנֵי אָדָם, כִּי אִם מֵאֱלֹהִים
umilah hi zo shebballev, lefi haruach velo lefi ot ketuvah; shivcho eino ba mibbenei adam, ki im me'elohim
and circumcision is that of the heart, in the spirit not in the letter; whose praise is not of men, but of God.

ג

אִם כֵּן, מַהוּ יִתְרוֹנוֹ שֶׁל הַיְּהוּדִי אוֹ מַה הַתּוֹעֶלֶת אֲשֶׁר בַּמִּילָה
im ken, mahu yitrono shel hayehudi o mah hatto'elet asher bammilah
What advantage then hath the Jew? or what is the profit of circumcision?

הַרְבֵּה, עַל כָּל פָּנִים; רֵאשִׁית כֹּל, בִּידֵיהֶם הֻפְקְדוּ דִּבְרֵי אֱלֹהִים
harbeh, al kol panim; reshit kol, biydeihem hufkedu divrei elohim
Much every way: first of all, that they were intrusted with the oracles of God.

וְאִם יֵשׁ שֶׁלֹּא הֶאֱמִינוּ, אֲזַי מָה? הַאִם יְבַטֵּל חֹסֶר אֱמוּנָתָם אֶת נֶאֱמָנוּתוֹ שֶׁל אֱלֹהִים
ve'im yesh shello he'eminu, azai mah? ha'im yevattel choser emunatam et ne'emanuto shel elohim
For what if some were without faith? shall their want of faith make of none effect the faithfulness of God?

חֲלִילָה! צָרִיךְ שֶׁיֻּכַּר כִּי הָאֱלֹהִים נֶאֱמָן וְכָל אָדָם כּוֹזֵב, כַּכָּתוּב
chalilah! tzarich sheyukkar ki ha'elohim ne'eman vechol adam kozev, kakkatuv
God forbid: yea, let God be found true, but every man a liar; as it is written,

לְמַעַן תִּצְדַּק בְּדָבְרֶךָ, תִּזְכֶּה בְשָׁפְטֶךָ
lema'an titzdak bedovrecha, tizkeh veshoftecha
That thou mightest be justified in thy words, And mightest prevail when thou comest into judgment.

אֲבָל אִם רִשְׁעָתֵנוּ מַפְגִּינָה אֶת הַצֶּדֶק שֶׁל אֱלֹהִים, מַה נֹּאמַר?
aval im rish'atenu mafginah et hatzedek shel elohim, mah nomar
But if our unrighteousness commendeth the righteousness of God, what shall we say?

הַאִם יֵשׁ עָוֶל בֵּאלֹהִים הַשּׁוֹפֵךְ אֶת זַעֲמוֹ -וַאֲנִי מְדַבֵּר מִנְּקֻדַּת מַבָּטוֹ שֶׁל הָאָדָם
ha'im yesh avel belohim hashofech et za'amo -va'ani medabber minnekuddat mabbato shel ha'adam
Is God unrighteous who visiteth with wrath? (I speak after the manner of men.)

חַס וְחָלִילָה! שֶׁאִם כֵּן, אֵיךְ יִשְׁפֹּט אֱלֹהִים אֶת הָעוֹלָם
chas vechalilah! she'im ken, eich yishpot elohim et ha'olam
God forbid: for then how shall God judge the world?

אַךְ אִם בִּגְלַל מִרְמָתִי מַשְׂגֶּשֶׁת אֱמֶת הָאֱלֹהִים לִתְהִלָּתוֹ, מַדּוּעַ עוֹד אֶשָּׁפֵט כְּחוֹטֵא
ach im biglal mirmati mesagseget emet ha'elohim lit'hillato, maddua od eshafet kechote
But if the truth of God through my lie abounded unto his glory, why am I also still judged as a sinner?

וּמַדּוּעַ לֹא נַעֲשֶׂה אֶת הָרַע כְּדֵי שֶׁיֵּצֵא טוֹב, כְּפִי שֶׁמַּעֲלִילִים עָלֵינוּ וְטוֹעֲנִים כִּי כָּךְ אָנוּ אוֹמְרִים
umaddua lo na'aseh et hara kedei sheyetzei tov, kefi shemma'alilim aleinu veto'anim ki kach anu omerim
and why not (as we are slanderously reported, and as some affirm that we say), Let us do evil, that good may come?

הָרוֹמִים

אַתָּה הָאוֹמֵר לֹא תִּנְאַף, הֲתִנְאַף אַתָּה
attah ha'omer lo tin'af, hatin'af attah
thou that sayest a man should not commit adultery, dost thou commit adultery?

אַתָּה הַמְתַעֵב אֶת הָאֱלִילִים, הֲתִבְזֹז אֶת מִקְדְּשֵׁיהֶם
attah hamta'ev et ha'elilim, hativzoz et mikdesheihem
thou that abhorrest idols, dost thou rob temples?

אַתָּה הַמִּתְגָּאֶה בַּתּוֹרָה, הַתְחַלֵּל אֶת שֵׁם אֱלֹהִים בַּהֲפִירְךָ אֶת הַתּוֹרָה
attah hammitga'eh battorah, hatchallel et shem elohim bahafirecha et hattorah
thou who gloriest in the law, through thy transgression of the law dishonorest thou God?

הֲרֵי, כְּפִי שֶׁכָּתוּב, שֵׁם אֱלֹהִים מְחֻלָּל בַּגּוֹיִם בִּגְלַלְכֶם
harei, kefi shekkatuv, shem elohim mechullal baggoyim biglalchem
For the name of God is blasphemed among the Gentiles because of you, even as it is written.

אָמְנָם יֵשׁ עֵרֶךְ לַמִּילָה אִם אַתָּה מְקַיֵּם אֶת הַתּוֹרָה
omnam yesh erech lammilah im attah mekayem et hattorah
For circumcision indeed profiteth, if thou be a doer of the law:

אַךְ אִם אַתָּה מֵפֵר אֶת הַתּוֹרָה, מִילָתְךָ נִהְיֵית לְעָרְלָה
ach im attah mefer et hattorah, milatecha nihyeit le'arelah
but if thou be a transgressor of the law, thy circumcision is become uncircumcision.

לָכֵן אִם יִשְׁמֹר עָרֵל אֶת דִּינֵי הַתּוֹרָה
lachen im yishmor arel et dinei hattorah
If therefore the uncircumcision keep the ordinances of the law,

הַאִם לֹא תֵּחָשֵׁב לוֹ עָרְלָתוֹ לְמִילָה
ha'im lo techashev lo orlato lemilah
shall not his uncircumcision be reckoned for circumcision?

וְהֶעָרֵל מִבְּחִינָה גוּפָנִית, הַמְקַיֵּם אֶת הַתּוֹרָה, יַחֲרֹץ עָלֶיךָ מִשְׁפָּט
vehe'arel mibbechinah gufanit, hamkayem et hattorah, yacharotz aleicha mishpat
and shall not the uncircumcision which is by nature, if it fulfil the law, judge thee,

שֶׁהֲרֵי לְךָ הַכְּתוּבִים וְהַמִּילָה וְאַתָּה מֵפֵר אֶת הַתּוֹרָה
sheharei lecha hakketuvim vehammilah ve'attah mefer et hattorah
who with the letter and circumcision art a transgressor of the law?

הֵן לֹא עַל־פִּי מַרְאִית עַיִן יְהוּדִי הוּא יְהוּדִי, וְלֹא מַה שֶּׁרוֹאִים בַּגּוּף הוּא מִילָה
hen lo al-pi mar'it ayin yehudi hu yehudi, velo mah shero'im bagguf hu milah
For he is not a Jew who is one outwardly; neither is that circumcision which is outward in the flesh:

יְהוּדִי הוּא זֶה שֶׁבְּתוֹךְ תּוֹכוֹ הוּא יְהוּדִי
yehudi hu zeh shebbetoch tocho hu yehudi
but he is a Jew who is one inwardly;

הָרוֹמִים

גּוֹיִם שֶׁאֵין לָהֶם תּוֹרָה וְהֵם מְקַיְּמִים אֶת דִּבְרֵי הַתּוֹרָה כְּדָבָר מוּבָן מֵאֵלָיו
goyim she'ein lahem torah vehem mekayemim et divrei hattorah kedavar muvan me'elav
(for when Gentiles that have not the law do by nature the things of the law,

הֵם תּוֹרָה לְעַצְמָם אַף שֶׁאֵין לָהֶם תּוֹרָה
hem torah le'atzmam af she'ein lahem torah
these, not having the law, are the law unto themselves;

הֵם מַרְאִים שֶׁפֹּעַל הַתּוֹרָה כָּתוּב בְּלִבָּם, שֶׁכֵּן מַצְפּוּנָם מֵעִיד בָּהֶם
hem mar'im sheppo'al hattorah katuv belibbam, shekken matzpunam me'id bahem
in that they show the work of the law written in their hearts, their conscience bearing witness therewith,

וּמַחְשְׁבוֹתֵיהֶם מְחַיְּבוֹת אוֹ מְזַכּוֹת אוֹתָם
umachshevoteihem mechayevot o mezakkot otam
and their thoughts one with another accusing or else excusing them);

בַּיּוֹם שֶׁיִּשְׁפֹּט אֱלֹהִים אֶת תַּעֲלוּמוֹת בְּנֵי אָדָם עַל־יְדֵי יֵשׁוּעַ הַמָּשִׁיחַ, כִּדְבַר בְּשׂוֹרָתִי
bayom sheyishpot elohim et ta'alumot benei adam al-yedei yeshua hammashiach, kidvar besorati
in the day when God shall judge the secrets of men, according to my gospel, by Jesus Christ.

אֲבָל אִם אַתָּה נִקְרָא יְהוּדִי וְאַתָּה נִשְׁעָן עַל הַתּוֹרָה וּמִתְהַלֵּל בֵּאלֹהִים
aval im attah nikra yehudi ve'attah nish'an al hattorah umit'hallel belohim
But if thou bearest the name of a Jew, and restest upon the law, and gloriest in God,

וְאַתָּה יוֹדֵעַ אֶת רְצוֹנוֹ וּמַבְחִין בַּדְּבָרִים הַטּוֹבִים, מִהְיוֹתְךָ מְחֻנָּךְ בַּתּוֹרָה
ve'attah yodea et retzono umavchin baddevarim hattovim, mihyotecha mechunnach battorah
and knowest his will, and approvest the things that are excellent, being instructed out of the law,

וְאַתָּה סָמוּךְ וּבָטוּחַ כִּי אַתָּה מוֹרֶה דֶּרֶךְ לַעִוְרִים, אוֹר לַשְּׁרוּיִים בַּחֹשֶׁךְ
ve'attah samuch uvatuach ki attah moreh derech la'ivrim, or lasheruyim bachoshech
and art confident that thou thyself art a guide of the blind, a light of them that are in darkness,

מַדְרִיךְ לַפְּתָאִים וּמְלַמֵּד לְעוֹלָלִים, וּלְךָ בִּטּוּי הַדַּעַת וְהָאֱמֶת שֶׁבַּתּוֹרָה
madrich lappeta'im umelammed la'olalim, ulecha bittui hadda'at veha'emet shebbattorah
a corrector of the foolish, a teacher of babes, having in the law the form of knowledge and of the truth;

הַאִם לֹא תְלַמֵּד אֶת עַצְמְךָ, אַתָּה הַמְלַמֵּד אֲחֵרִים?
ha'im lo telammed et atzmecha, attah hamlammed acherim?
thou therefore that teachest another, teachest thou not thyself?

אַתָּה הַמַּכְרִיז לֹא תִגְנֹב, הֲתִגְנֹב אַתָּה
attah hammachriz lo tignov, hatignov attah
thou that preachest a man should not steal, dost thou steal?

הָרוֹמִים

וְאֵינְךָ מֵבִין כִּי טוּבוֹ זֶה שֶׁל אֱלֹהִים מַדְרִיךְ אוֹתְךָ לִתְשׁוּבָה
ve'eincha mevin ki tuvo zeh shel elohim madrich otecha litshuvah
not knowing that the goodness of God leadeth thee to repentance?

בְּעַקְשָׁנוּתְךָ וּבְסֵרוּב לְבָבְךָ לַחֲזֹר בִּתְשׁוּבָה אַתָּה צוֹבֵר לְךָ זַעַם
be'akshanutecha uvseruv levavecha lachazor bitshuvah attah tzover lecha za'am
but after thy hardness and impenitent heart treasurest up for thyself wrath

לְיוֹם זַעַם, בַּיּוֹם שֶׁיִּתְגַּלֶּה מִשְׁפַּט־הַצֶּדֶק שֶׁל אֱלֹהִים
leyom za'am, bayom sheyitgalleh mishpat-hatzedek shel elohim
in the day of wrath and revelation of the righteous judgment of God;

אֲשֶׁר יְשַׁלֵּם לְכָל אִישׁ כְּמַעֲשָׂיו
asher yeshallem lechol ish kema'asav
who will render to every man according to his works:

חַיֵּי עוֹלָם לָאֲנָשִׁים הַמַּתְמִידִים לַעֲשׂוֹת אֶת הַטּוֹב וּמְבַקְשִׁים אֶת הַתִּפְאֶרֶת וְהַכָּבוֹד וְהָאַלְמָוֶת
chayei olam la'anashim hammatmidim la'asot et hattov umevakshim et hattif'eret vehakkavod veha'almavet
to them that by patience in well-doing seek for glory and honor and incorruption, eternal life:

אַךְ חֵמָה וְזַעַם לַסּוֹרְרִים אֲשֶׁר אֵינָם נִשְׁמָעִים לָאֱמֶת אֶלָּא לָעַוְלָה
ach chemah veza'am lassorerim asher einam nishma'im la'emet ella la'avlah
but unto them that are factious, and obey not the truth, but obey unrighteousness, shall be wrath and indignation,

צָרָה וּמְצוּקָה עַל נֶפֶשׁ כָּל אָדָם הָעוֹשֶׂה רַע, עַל הַיְהוּדִי בָּרִאשׁוֹנָה וְגַם עַל הַלֹּא־יְהוּדִי
tzarah umetzukah al nefesh kol adam ha'oseh ra', al hayehudi barishonah vegam al hallo-yehudi
tribulation and anguish, upon every soul of man that worketh evil, of the Jew first, and also of the Greek;

אַךְ תִּפְאֶרֶת וְכָבוֹד וְשָׁלוֹם לְכָל הָעוֹשֶׂה אֶת הַטּוֹב, לַיְהוּדִי בָּרִאשׁוֹנָה וְגַם לְמִי שֶׁאֵינוֹ יְהוּדִי
ach tif'eret vechavod veshalom lechol ha'oseh et hattov, layehudi barishonah vegam lemi she'eino yehudi
but glory and honor and peace to every man that worketh good, to the Jew first, and also to the Greek:

כִּי אֵין מַשּׂוֹא פָנִים עִם הָאֱלֹהִים
ki ein masso panim im ha'elohim
for there is no respect of persons with God.

שֶׁכֵּן כָּל אֲשֶׁר חָטְאוּ בְּלִי תּוֹרָה גַּם יֹאבְדוּ בְּלִי תּוֹרָה
shekken kol asher chate'u beli torah gam yovedu beli torah
For as many as have sinned without the law shall also perish without the law:

וְכָל אֲשֶׁר חָטְאוּ וְיֵשׁ לָהֶם תּוֹרָה, עַל־פִּי הַתּוֹרָה יִשָּׁפְטוּ
vechol asher chate'u veyesh lahem torah, al-pi hattorah yishaftu
and as many as have sinned under the law shall be judged by the law;

הֲרֵי לֹא שׁוֹמְעֵי הַתּוֹרָה צַדִּיקִים לִפְנֵי אֱלֹהִים, אֶלָּא הַמְקַיְּמִים אֶת הַתּוֹרָה הֵם אֲשֶׁר יֻצְדְּקוּ
harei lo shome'ei hattorah tzaddikim lifnei elohim, ella hamkaymim et hattorah hem asher yutzdeku
for not the hearers of the law are just before God, but the doers of the law shall be justified;

הָרוֹמִים

חַמְדָּנוּת, רֹעַ; מְלֵאֵי קִנְאָה, רֶצַח, מְרִיבָה, מִרְמָה, מְזִמָּה

chamdanut, roa'; mele'ei kin'ah, retzach, merivah, mirmah, mezimmah
covetousness, maliciousness; full of envy, murder, strife, deceit, malignity; whisperers,

הוֹלְכֵי רָכִיל הֵם, מוֹצִיאֵי דִבָּה, שׂוֹנְאֵי אֱלֹהִים, חֲצוּפִים, גֵּאִים, רַבְרְבָנִים, חוֹרְשֵׁי רָעָה, מַמְרִים פִּי הוֹרִים

holechei rachil hem, motzi'ei dibbah, sone'ei elohim, chatzufim, ge'im, ravrevanim, choreshei ra'ah, mamrim pi horim
backbiters, hateful to God, insolent, haughty, boastful, inventors of evil things, disobedient to parents,

חַסְרֵי הֲבָנָה, בִּלְתִּי נֶאֱמָנִים, קְשׁוּחֵי לֵב, אַכְזָרִים

chasrei havanah, bilti ne'emanim, keshuchei lev, achzarim
without understanding, covenant-breakers, without natural affection, unmerciful:

הֵם יוֹדְעִים אֶת חֻקַּת אֱלֹהִים, אֲשֶׁר לְפִיהָ עוֹשֵׂי מַעֲשִׂים כָּאֵלֶּה רְאוּיִים לְמִיתָה

hem yode'im et chukkat elohim, asher lefiha osei ma'asim ka'elleh re'uyim lemitah
who, knowing the ordinance of God, that they that practise such things are worthy of death,

אַךְ לֹא זֹאת בִּלְבַד שֶׁהֵם עוֹשִׂים אוֹתָם, הֵם גַּם תּוֹמְכִים בְּעוֹשֵׂיהֶם

ach lo zot bilvad shehem osim otam, hem gam tomchim be'oseihem
not only do the same, but also consent with them that practise them.

ב

עַל כֵּן אַתָּה, בֶּן־אָדָם הַחוֹרֵץ מִשְׁפָּט, אֵין לְךָ בַּמֶּה לְהִצְטַדֵּק, וְתִהְיֶה מִי שֶׁתִּהְיֶה

al ken attah, ben-'adam hachoretz mishpat, ein lecha bammeh lehitztaddek, vetihyeh mi shettihyeh
Wherefore thou art without excuse, O man, whosoever thou art that judgest:

כִּי בְּשָׁפְטְךָ אֶת הַזּוּלַת אַתָּה מַרְשִׁיעַ אֶת עַצְמְךָ, שֶׁכֵּן אַתָּה הַחוֹרֵץ מִשְׁפָּט עוֹשֶׂה אוֹתָם דְּבָרִים

ki beshoftecha et hazzulat attah marshia et atzmecha, shekken attah hachoretz mishpat oseh otam devarim
for wherein thou judgest another, thou condemnest thyself; for thou that judgest dost practise the same things.

אֲנַחְנוּ יוֹדְעִים שֶׁאֱלֹהִים שׁוֹפֵט עַל־פִּי הָאֱמֶת אֶת הָעוֹשִׂים דְּבָרִים כָּאֵלֶּה

anachnu yode'im she'elohim shofet al-pi ha'emet et ha'osim dvarim ka'elleh
And we know that the judgment of God is according to truth against them that practise such things.

וְאַתָּה, בֶּן־אָדָם, הַחוֹרֵץ מִשְׁפָּט עַל הָעוֹשִׂים דְּבָרִים כָּאֵלֶּה

ve'attah, ben-'adam, hachoretz mishpat al ha'osim dvarim ka'elleh
And reckonest thou this, O man, who judgest them that practise such things,

וּבְעַצְמְךָ עוֹשֶׂה אוֹתָם, הַחוֹשֵׁב אַתָּה כִּי תִּמָּלֵט מִמִּשְׁפַּט אֱלֹהִים

uve'atzmecha oseh otam, hachoshev attah ki timmalet mimmishpat elohim
and doest the same, that thou shalt escape the judgment of God?

אוֹ שֶׁמָּא אַתָּה מְזַלְזֵל בְּשֶׁפַע טוּבוֹ וְאֹרֶךְ רוּחוֹ וְסַבְלָנוּתוֹ,

o shemma attah mezalzel beshefa tuvo ve'orech rucho vesavlanuto
Or despisest thou the riches of his goodness and forbearance and longsuffering,

הָרוֹמִים

וּבִדְמוּת צַלְמֵי עוֹפוֹת, חַיּוֹת וּרְמָשִׂים
uvidmut tzalmei ofot, chayot uremasim
and of birds, and four-footed beasts, and creeping things.

לָכֵן מְסָרָם אֱלֹהִים לְטֻמְאָה בִּידֵי תַּאֲווֹת לִבָּם
lachen mesaram elohim letum'ah biydei ta'avot libbam
Wherefore God gave them up in the lusts of their hearts unto uncleanness,

לְחַלֵּל אֶת גּוּפָם בֵּינָם לְבֵין עַצְמָם
lechallel et gufam beinam levein atzmam
that their bodies should be dishonored among themselves:

אֲנָשִׁים שֶׁהֱמִירוּ אֶת אֱמֶת הָאֱלֹהִים בַּשֶּׁקֶר
anashim shehemiru et emet ha'elohim basheker
for that they exchanged the truth of God for a lie,

וְכִבְּדוּ וְעָבְדוּ אֶת הַנִּבְרָא בִּמְקוֹם אֶת הַבּוֹרֵא הַמְבֹרָךְ לְעוֹלָמִים. אָמֵן
vechibbedu ve'avedu et hannivra bimkom et habborei hamevorach le'olamim. amen
and worshipped and served the creature rather than the Creator, who is blessed for ever. Amen.

מִשּׁוּם כָּךְ הִסְגִּירָם אֱלֹהִים לִתְשׁוּקוֹת בְּזוּיוֹת
mishum kach hisgiram elohim litshukot bzuyot
For this cause God gave them up unto vile passions:

עַד כִּי אֲפִלּוּ נְשֵׁיהֶם הֶחֱלִיפוּ יְחָסִים טִבְעִיִּים בְּבִלְתִּי טִבְעִיִּים
ad ki afillu nesheihem hechelifu yechasim tiv'iyim bevilti tiv'iyim
for their women changed the natural use into that which is against nature:

וְכֵן גַּם הַגְּבָרִים נָטְשׁוּ אֶת הַיְחָסִים הַטִּבְעִיִּים עִם הַנָּשִׁים וּבָעֲרוּ בְּתַאֲוָה זֶה אֶל זֶה
vechen gam haggevarim nateshu et haychasim hattiv'iyim im hannashim uva'aru beta'avah zeh el zeh
and likewise also the men, leaving the natural use of the woman, burned in their lust one toward another,

גְּבָרִים עָשׂוּ תּוֹעֵבָה בִּגְבָרִים וְקִבְּלוּ בְּגוּפָם הֵם אֶת הַגְּמוּל הָרָאוּי לִסְטִיָּה שֶׁלָּהֶם
gevarim asu to'evah bigvarim vekibbelu begufam hem et haggemul hara'ui lassetiyah shellahem
men with men working unseemliness, and receiving in themselves that recompense of their error which was due.

וְכֵיוָן שֶׁלֹּא חָשְׁבוּ לְנָכוֹן לְהַכִּיר בֵּאלֹהִים
vecheivan shello chashvu lenachon lehakkir belohim
And even as they refused to have God in their knowledge,

הִסְגִּירָם אֱלֹהִים לְהֲלָךְ־רוּחַ מְגֻנֶּה, לַעֲשׂוֹת אֶת הַדְּבָרִים שֶׁאֵינָם הֲגוּנִים
hisgiram elohim lahalach-ruach megunneh, la'asot et haddevarim she'einam hagunim
God gave them up unto a reprobate mind, to do those things which are not fitting;

אָכֵן מְלֵאִים הֵם בְּכָל עַוְלָה, רֶשַׁע,
achen mele'im hem bechol avlah, resha
being filled with all unrighteousness, wickedness,

הָרוֹמִים

שֶׁהֲרֵי הִיא כֹּחַ הָאֱלֹהִים לְהוֹשִׁיעַ אֶת כָּל מִי שֶׁמַּאֲמִין, אֶת הַיְהוּדִי בָּרִאשׁוֹנָה וְגַם אֶת הַלֹּא־יְהוּדִי
sheharei hi koach ha'elohim lehoshia et kol mi shemma'amin, et hayehudi barishonah vegam et hallo-yehudi
for it is the power of God unto salvation to every one that believeth; to the Jew first, and also to the Greek.

כִּי בָּהּ צִדְקַת הָאֱלֹהִים מִתְגַּלֵּית מִתּוֹךְ אֱמוּנָה לְתַכְלִית אֱמוּנָה, כַּכָּתוּב: וְצַדִּיק בֶּאֱמוּנָתוֹ יִחְיֶה
ki bah tzidkat ha'elohim mitgalleit mittoch emunah letachlit emunah, kakkatuv: vetzaddik be'emunato yichyeh
For therein is revealed a righteousness of God from faith unto faith: as it is written, But the righteous shall live by faith.

וְאָמְנָם זַעַם אֱלֹהִים נִגְלֶה מִן הַשָּׁמַיִם עַל כָּל עַוְלָתָם וְרִשְׁעָתָם שֶׁל בְּנֵי אָדָם
ve'omnam za'am elohim nigleh min hashamayim al kol avlatam verish'atam shel benei adam
For the wrath of God is revealed from heaven against all ungodliness and unrighteousness of men,

הַמְעַכְּבִים בְּרִשְׁעָתָם אֶת הָאֱמֶת
ham'akkevim berish'atam et ha'emet
who hinder the truth in unrighteousness;

כִּי מַה שֶּׁנּוֹדַע עַל אֱלֹהִים גָּלוּי בְּקִרְבָּם, שֶׁהֲרֵי אֱלֹהִים גִּלָּה לָהֶם
ki mah shennoda al elohim galui bekirbam, sheharei elohim gillah lahem
because that which is known of God is manifest in them; for God manifested it unto them.

הֲלֹא עַצְמוּתוֹ הַנֶּעְלֶמֶת, הִיא כֹּחוֹ הַנִּצְחִי וֶאֱלֹהוּתוֹ, נִרְאֵית בְּבֵרוּר מֵאָז בְּרִיאַת הָעוֹלָם
halo atzmuto hanne'lemet, hi kocho hannitzchi ve'elohuto, nir'eit beverur me'az beri'at ha'olam
For the invisible things of him since the creation of the world are clearly seen,

בִּהְיוֹתָהּ נִתְפֶּסֶת בַּשֵּׂכֶל בְּאֶמְצָעוּת הַדְּבָרִים שֶׁנִּבְרְאוּ
bihyotah nitpeset bashochel be'emtza'ut haddevarim shennivre'u
being perceived through the things that are made, even his everlasting power and divinity;

לָכֵן אֵין לָהֶם בַּמֶּה לְהִצְטַדֵּק
lachen ein lahem bammeh lehitztaddek
that they may be without excuse:

שֶׁהֲרֵי לַמְרוֹת שֶׁיּוֹדְעִים הֵם אֶת אֱלֹהִים לֹא כִּבְּדוּ אוֹתוֹ כָּרָאוּי לֵאלֹהִים, אַף לֹא הוֹדוּ לוֹ
sheharei lamrot sheyode'im hem et elohim lo kibbdu oto kara'ui lelohim, af lo hodu lo
because that, knowing God, they glorified him not as God, neither gave thanks;

אֶלָּא נִתְפְּסוּ לְמַחֲשֶׁבֶת הֶבֶל וְנִטַּמְטַם לִבָּם הָאֱוִילִי
ella nitpesu lemachashevet hevel venittamtem libbam ha'evili
but became vain in their reasonings, and their senseless heart was darkened.

הֵם הִתְיַמְּרוּ לִהְיוֹת חֲכָמִים, אַךְ נִהְיוּ לִכְסִילִים
hem hityammeru lihyot chachamim, ach nihyu lichsilim
Professing themselves to be wise, they became fools,

וְהֵמִירוּ אֶת כְּבוֹדוֹ שֶׁל אֱלֹהִים בִּלְתִּי חוֹלֵף בִּדְמוּת צַלְמוֹ שֶׁל אָדָם בֶּן־חֲלוֹף
vehemiru et kevodo shel elohim bilti cholef bidmut tzalmo shel adam ben-chalof
and changed the glory of the incorruptible God for the likeness of an image of corruptible man,

הָרוֹמִים

מִשּׁוּם שֶׁדֻּבַּר אֱמוּנַתְכֶם נִשְׁמָע בְּכָל הָעוֹלָם
mishum sheddvar emunatchem nishma bechol ha'olam
that your faith is proclaimed throughout the whole world.

וְהָאֱלֹהִים אֲשֶׁר אֲנִי עוֹבֵד אוֹתוֹ בְּרוּחִי בְּהַכְרִיזִי אֶת בְּשׂוֹרַת בְּנוֹ, הוּא
veha'elohim asher ani oved oto beruchi behachrizi et besorat beno, hu edi
For God is my witness, whom I serve in my spirit in the gospel of his Son,

עֵדִי לְכָךְ שֶׁאֲנִי מַזְכִּיר אֶתְכֶם לְלֹא הֶרֶף בִּתְפִלּוֹתַי
lechach she'ani mazkir etchem lelo heref bitfillotai
how unceasingly I make mention of you, always in my prayers

וּמְבַקֵּשׁ אֲנִי תָּמִיד כִּי אַצְלִיחַ פַּעַם בְּאֵיזֶה אֹפֶן שֶׁהוּא לָבוֹא אֲלֵיכֶם, אִם יִרְצֶה אֱלֹהִים
umevakkesh ani tamid ki atzliach pa'am be'eizeh ofen shehu lavo aleichem, im yirtzeh elohim
making request, if by any means now at length I may be prospered by the will of God to come unto you.

שֶׁכֵּן אֲנִי נִכְסָף לִרְאוֹתְכֶם כְּדֵי לַחֲלֹק עִמָּכֶם מַתָּנָה רוּחָנִית לְחִזּוּקְכֶם
shekken ani nichsaf lir'otchem kedei lachalok immachem mattanah ruchanit lechizzukechem
For I long to see you, that I may impart unto you some spiritual gift, to the end ye may be established;

כְּלוֹמַר, שֶׁנִּתְעוֹדֵד יַחְדָּיו בָּאֱמוּנָה הַמְשֻׁתֶּפֶת לָכֶם וְגַם לִי
klomar, shennit'oded yachdav ba'emunah hamshuttefet lachem vegam li
that is, that I with you may be comforted in you, each of us by the other's faith, both yours and mine.

אֵינֶנִּי רוֹצֶה שֶׁיֵּעָלֵם מִכֶּם, אַחַי, שֶׁפְּעָמִים רַבּוֹת הִתְכַּוַּנְתִּי לָבוֹא אֲלֵיכֶם
einenni rotzeh sheye'alem mikkem, achai, sheppe'amim rabbot hitkavvanti lavo aleichem
And I would not have you ignorant, brethren, that oftentimes I purposed to come unto you (and was hindered hitherto),

כְּדֵי שֶׁגַּם בְּקִרְבְּכֶם אוּכַל לַעֲשׂוֹת פְּרִי כְּבְקֶרֶב יֶתֶר הַגּוֹיִם
kedei sheggam bekirbechem uchal la'asot pri kivkerev yeter haggoyim,
that I might have some fruit in you also, even as in the rest of the Gentiles.

אַךְ עַד כֹּה נִמְנַע מִמֶּנִּי לָבוֹא
ach ad koh nimna mimmenni lavo
But up to now I have been prevented from coming.

חַיָּב אֲנִי לַיְּוָנִים וְגַם לִבְנֵי עַמִּים אֲחֵרִים, לִבְנֵי תַּרְבּוּת וְגַם לְחַסְרֵי תַּרְבּוּת
chayav ani layevanim vegam livnei ammim acherim, livnei tarbut vegam lechasrei tarbut
I am debtor both to Greeks and to Barbarians, both to the wise and to the foolish.

מִשּׁוּם כָּךְ בִּרְצוֹנִי לְבַשֵּׂר אֶת הַבְּשׂוֹרָה גַּם לָכֶם הַנִּמְצָאִים בְּרוֹמָא
mishum kach birtzoni levasser et habbesorah gam lachem hannimtza'im beroma
So, as much as in me is, I am ready to preach the gospel to you also that are in Rome.

אֵינֶנִּי בּוֹשׁ בִּבְשׂוֹרַת הַמָּשִׁיחַ,
einenni bosh bivsorat hammashiach
For I am not ashamed of the gospel:

הָרוֹמִים

מֵאֵת שָׁאוּל, עֶבֶד הַמָּשִׁיחַ יֵשׁוּעַ, אֲשֶׁר נִקְרָא לִהְיוֹת שָׁלִיחַ וְיֻחַד לִבְשׂוֹרַת אֱלֹהִים
me'et sha'ul, eved hammashiach yeshua, asher nikra lihyot shaliach veyuchad livsorat elohim
Paul, a servant of Jesus Christ, called to be an apostle, separated unto the gospel of God,

בְּשׂוֹרָה שֶׁאֱלֹהִים הִבְטִיחַ מִקֶּדֶם בְּפִי נְבִיאָיו בְּכִתְבֵי הַקֹּדֶשׁ
besorah she'elohim hivtiach mikkedem befi nevi'av bechitvei hakkodesh
which he promised afore through his prophets in the holy scriptures,

עַל־אֹדוֹת בְּנוֹ, יֵשׁוּעַ הַמָּשִׁיחַ אֲדוֹנֵנוּ, שֶׁלְּפִי הַבָּשָׂר מוֹצָאוֹ מִזֶּרַע דָּוִד
al-'odot beno, yeshua hammashiach adonenu, shellefi habbasar motza'o mizzera david
concerning his Son, who was born of the seed of David according to the flesh,

וּלְפִי רוּחַ הַקֹּדֶשׁ הֻפְגַן שֶׁהוּא בֶּן־אֱלֹהִים בִּגְבוּרָה
ulefi ruach hakkodesh hufgan shehu ben-'elohim bigvurah
who was declared to be the Son of God with power, according to the spirit of holiness,

בִּתְחִיָּתוֹ מִן הַמֵּתִים
bitchiyato min hammetim
by the resurrection from the dead; even Jesus Christ our Lord,

דַּרְכּוֹ קִבַּלְנוּ חֶסֶד וּשְׁלִיחוּת
darko kibbalnu chesed ushlichut
through whom we received grace and apostleship,

לְהָבִיא לִידֵי צִיּוּת שֶׁבָּאֱמוּנָה בְּכָל הָאֻמּוֹת לְמַעַן שְׁמוֹ
lehavi liydei tziyut shebba'emunah bechol ha'ummot lema'an shemo
unto obedience of faith among all the nations, for his name's sake;

בֵּינֵיהֶם גַּם אַתֶּם קְרוּאֵי יֵשׁוּעַ הַמָּשִׁיחַ
beineihem gam attem keru'ei yeshua hammashiach
among whom are ye also, called to be Jesus Christ's:

וּבְכֵן, אֶל כָּל אֲהוּבֵי אֱלֹהִים בְּרוֹמָא הַנִּקְרָאִים לִהְיוֹת קְדוֹשִׁים
uvechen, el kol ahuvei elohim beroma hannikra'im lihyot kedoshim
to all that are in Rome, beloved of God, called to be saints:

חֶסֶד וְשָׁלוֹם לָכֶם מֵאֵת הָאֱלֹהִים אָבִינוּ וְהָאָדוֹן יֵשׁוּעַ הַמָּשִׁיחַ
chesed veshalom lachem me'et ha'elohim avinu veha'adon yeshua hammashiach
Grace to you and peace from God our Father and the Lord Jesus Christ.

רֵאשִׁית, אֲנִי מוֹדֶה לֵאלֹהַי עַל כֻּלְּכֶם בְּאֶמְצָעוּת יֵשׁוּעַ הַמָּשִׁיחַ
reshit, ani modeh le'elohai al kullechem be'emtza'ut yeshua hammashiach
First, I thank my God through Jesus Christ for you all,

מַעֲשֵׂי הַשְּׁלִיחִים

הַשְׁמֵן לֵב־הָעָם הַזֶּה וְאָזְנָיו הַכְבֵּד וְעֵינָיו הָשַׁע
hashmen lev-ha'am hazzeh ve'azenav hachbed ve'einav hasha
For this people's heart is waxed gross, And their ears are dull of hearing, And their eyes they have closed;

פֶּן־יִרְאֶה בְעֵינָיו וּבְאָזְנָיו יִשְׁמָע וּלְבָבוֹ יָבִין
pen-yir'eh ve'einav uve'ozenav yishma ulevavo yavin
Lest haply they should perceive with their eyes, And hear with their ears, And understand with their heart,

וָשָׁב וְרָפָא לוֹ
vashav verafa lo
And should turn again, And I should heal them.

לָכֵן שֶׁיְהֵא יָדוּעַ לָכֶם כִּי אֶל הַגּוֹיִם נִשְׁלְחָה תְּשׁוּעַת אֱלֹהִים וְהֵם יִשְׁמָעוּ
lachen sheyehei yadua lachem ki el haggoyim nishlechah teshu'at elohim vehem yishme'u
Be it known therefore unto you, that this salvation of God is sent unto the Gentiles: they will also hear.

שָׁאוּל יָשַׁב שְׁנָתַיִם תְּמִימוֹת בְּדִירָה שֶׁשָּׂכַר לוֹ, וְקִבֵּל אֶת כָּל הַבָּאִים אֵלָיו
sha'ul yashav shenatayim temimot bedirah sheshochar lo, vekibbel et kol habba'im elav
And he abode two whole years in his own hired dwelling, and received all that went in unto him,

הוּא הִכְרִיז אֶת מַלְכוּת הָאֱלֹהִים
hu hichriz et malchut ha'elohim
preaching the kingdom of God,

וְלִמֵּד עַל־אֹדוֹת הָאָדוֹן יֵשׁוּעַ בְּלִי כָּל פַּחַד וּבְאֵין מַפְרִיעַ
velimmed al-'odot ha'adon yeshua beli kol pachad uve'ein mafria
and teaching the things concerning the Lord Jesus Christ with all boldness, none forbidding him.

מַעֲשֵׂי הַשְּׁלִיחִים

הֵשִׁיבוּ וְאָמְרוּ לוֹ: לֹא קִבַּלְנוּ אִגְּרוֹת עַל־אוֹדוֹתֶיךָ מֵאֶרֶץ יְהוּדָה,
heshivu ve'ameru lo: lo kibbalnu iggerot al-'odoteicha me'eretz yehudah
And they said unto him, We neither received letters from Judæa concerning thee,

אַף לֹא הִגִּיעַ אִישׁ מִן הָאַחִים וְהוֹדִיעַ אוֹ דִבֶּר מַשֶּׁהוּ רַע עָלֶיךָ
af lo higgia ish min ha'achim vehodia o dibber mashehu ra aleicha
nor did any of the brethren come hither and report or speak any harm of thee.

אֲבָל מִן הָרָאוּי שֶׁנִּשְׁמַע מִפִּיךָ מַה דֵּעוֹתֶיךָ
aval min hara'ui shennishma mippicha mah de'oteicha
But we desire to hear of thee what thou thinkest:

כִּי יָדוּעַ לָנוּ שֶׁבְּכָל מָקוֹם מִתְנַגְּדִים לַכַּת הַזֹּאת
ki yadua lanu shebbechal makom mitnaggedim lakkat hazzot
for as concerning this sect, it is known to us that everywhere it is spoken against.

הֵם קָבְעוּ אִתּוֹ מוֹעֵד וּבַיּוֹם שֶׁנִּקְבַּע בָּאוּ רַבִּים עוֹד יוֹתֵר אֶל מְקוֹם מְגוּרָיו
hem kave'u itto mo'ed uvayom shennikba ba'u rabbim od yoter el mekom megurav
And when they had appointed him a day, they came to him into his lodging in great number;

הוּא הֵעִיד מֵהַבֹּקֶר עַד הָעֶרֶב וְהִסְבִּיר לָהֶם אֶת מַלְכוּת הָאֱלֹהִים, וְהוֹכִיחַ לָהֶם עַל־אוֹדוֹת יֵשׁוּעַ מִתּוֹרַת מֹשֶׁה וּמִן הַנְּבִיאִים
hu he'id mehabboker ad ha'erev vehisbir lahem et malchut ha'elohim, vehochiach lahem al-'odot yeshua mittorat mosheh umin hannevi'im
to whom he expounded the matter, testifying the kingdom of God, and persuading them concerning Jesus, both from the law of Moses and from the prophets, from morning till evening.

יֵשׁ שֶׁהִשְׁתַּכְנְעוּ מִדְּבָרָיו וְיֵשׁ שֶׁלֹּא הֶאֱמִינוּ
yesh shehishtachne'u middevarav veyesh shello he'eminu
And some believed the things which were spoken, and some disbelieved.

הֵם לֹא הִסְכִּימוּ אִישׁ עִם רֵעֵהוּ וְהָלְכוּ לְדַרְכָּם לְאַחַר שֶׁשָּׁאוּל אָמַר לָהֶם
hem lo hiskimu ish im re'ehu vehalechu ledarkam le'achar shesha'ul amar lahem
And when they agreed not among themselves, they departed after that Paul had spoken one word,

הֵיטֵב דִּבְּרָה רוּחַ הַקֹּדֶשׁ לַאֲבוֹתֵיכֶם בְּפִי יְשַׁעְיָהוּ הַנָּבִיא לֵאמֹר
heitev dibberah ruach hakkodesh la'avoteichem befi yesha'yahu hannavi lemor
Well spake the Holy Spirit through Isaiah the prophet unto your fathers,

לֵךְ וְאָמַרְתָּ לָעָם הַזֶּה: שִׁמְעוּ שָׁמוֹעַ וְאַל־תָּבִינוּ
lech ve'amarta la'am hazzeh: shim'u shamoa ve'al-tavinu
saying, Go thou unto this people, and say, By hearing ye shall hear, and shall in no wise understand;

וּרְאוּ רָאוֹ וְאַל־תֵּדָעוּ
ure'u ra'o ve'al-teda'u
And seeing ye shall see, and shall in no wise perceive:

מַעֲשֵׂי הַשְּׁלִיחִים

מָצָאנוּ שָׁם אַחִים וְנִתְבַּקַּשְׁנוּ לְהִשָּׁאֵר אֶצְלָם שִׁבְעָה יָמִים. כָּךְ בָּאנוּ לְרוֹמָא
matzanu sham achim venitbakkashnu lehisha'er etzlam shiv'ah yamim. kach banu leroma
where we found brethren, and were entreated to tarry with them seven days: and so we came to Rome.

הָאַחִים אֲשֶׁר שָׁם שָׁמְעוּ עָלֵינוּ וְיָצְאוּ לִקְרָאתֵנוּ עַד לְכִכַּר אַפְּיוֹס
ha'achim asher sham shame'u aleinu veyatze'u likratenu ad lechikkar appiyos
And from thence the brethren, when they heard of us, came to meet us as far as The Market of Appius

וּשְׁלֹשֶׁת הַפֻּנְדָּקִים. כְּשֶׁרָאָה אוֹתָם שָׁאוּל, הוֹדָה לֵאלֹהִים וְהִתְעוֹדֵד
usheloshet happundakim. kesheera'ah otam sha'ul, hodah lelohim vehit'oded
and The Three Taverns; whom when Paul saw, he thanked God, and took courage.

בָּאנוּ לְרוֹמָא וְשָׁם הֻתַּר לְשָׁאוּל לְהִתְגּוֹרֵר לְבַדּוֹ עִם חַיָּל שֶׁשָּׁמַר עָלָיו
banu leroma vesham huttar lesha'ul lehitgorer levaddo im chayal sheshamar alaiv
And when we entered into Rome, Paul was suffered to abide by himself with the soldier that guarded him.

אַחֲרֵי שְׁלוֹשָׁה יָמִים הִזְמִין שָׁאוּל אֶת רָאשֵׁי הַיְּהוּדִים
acharei sheloshah yamim hizmin sha'ul et rashei hayehudim
And it came to pass, that after three days he called together those that were the chief of the Jews:

כַּאֲשֶׁר הִתְכַּנְּסוּ יַחַד אָמַר לָהֶם: אֲנָשִׁים אַחִים, אֲנִי לֹא עָשִׂיתִי דָּבָר נֶגֶד הָעָם
ka'asher hitkannesu yachad amar lahem: anashim achim, ani lo asiti davar neged ha'am
and when they were come together, he said unto them, I, brethren, though I had done nothing against the people,

אוֹ נֶגֶד מִנְהֲגֵי אֲבוֹתֵינוּ וּבְכָל זֹאת נִמְסַרְתִּי כְּאָסִיר מִירוּשָׁלַיִם לִידֵי הָרוֹמָאִים
o neged minhagei avoteinu uvchol zot nimsarti ke'asir miyerushalayim lidei haroma'im
or the customs of our fathers, yet was delivered prisoner from Jerusalem into the hands of the Romans:

הַלָּלוּ חָקְרוּ אוֹתִי וּכְשֶׁלֹּא מָצְאוּ בִּי שׁוּם אַשְׁמַת מָוֶת הִתְכַּוְּנוּ לְשַׁחְרְרֵנִי
hallalu chakeru oti ucheshello matz'u bi shum ashmat mavet hitkavvenu leshachrereni
who, when they had examined me, desired to set me at liberty, because there was no cause of death in me.

אֲבָל רָאשֵׁי הַיְּהוּדִים הִתְנַגְּדוּ וְלָכֵן נֶאֱלַצְתִּי לִפְנוֹת אֶל הַקֵּיסָר
aval rashei hayehudim hitnaggedu velachen ne'elatzti lifnot el hakkeisar
But when the Jews spake against it, I was constrained to appeal unto Cæsar;

לֹא שֶׁיֵּשׁ לִי אֵיזֶה דָּבָר לְהַאֲשִׁים בּוֹ אֶת עַמִּי
lo sheyesh li eizeh davar leha'ashim bo et ammi
not that I had aught whereof to accuse my nation.

מִשּׁוּם כָּךְ בִּקַּשְׁתִּי לִרְאוֹת אֶתְכֶם וּלְדַבֵּר עִמָּכֶם
mishum kach bikkashti lir'ot etchem uledabber immachem
For this cause therefore did I entreat you to see and to speak with me:

כִּי בִּגְלַל תִּקְוַת יִשְׂרָאֵל אֲנִי אָסוּר בַּכֶּבֶל הַזֶּה
ki biglal tikvat yisra'el ani asur bakkevel hazzeh
for because of the hope of Israel I am bound with this chain.

מַעֲשֵׂי הַשְּׁלִיחִים

שִׁנּוּ דַעְתָּם וְאָמְרוּ שֶׁהוּא אֵל
shinnu da'tam ve'ameru shehu el
they changed their minds, and said that he was a god.

סָמוּךְ לְאוֹתוֹ מָקוֹם הָיוּ שְׂדוֹתָיו שֶׁל רֹאשׁ הָאִי, פּוֹבְּלִיּוֹס שְׁמוֹ
samuch le'oto makom hayu sdotav shel rosh ha'i, pobbeliyos shemo
Now in the neighborhood of that place were lands belonging to the chief man of the island, named Publius;

הוּא קִבֵּל אוֹתָנוּ וְאֵרַח אוֹתָנוּ בִּידִידוּת שְׁלוֹשָׁה יָמִים
hu kibbel otanu ve'erach otanu biyedidut sheloshah yamim
who received us, and entertained us three days courteously.

אוֹתָהּ עֵת שָׁכַב אָבִיו שֶׁל פּוֹבְּלִיּוֹס כְּשֶׁהוּא סוֹבֵל מֵחֹם וְדִיזֶנְטֶרְיָה
otah et shachav aviv shel pobbeliyos kshehu sovel mechom vedizenteryah
And it was so, that the father of Publius lay sick of fever and dysentery:

שָׁאוּל נִכְנַס אֵלָיו, הִתְפַּלֵּל וְסָמַךְ יָדָיו עָלָיו וְרִפֵּא אוֹתוֹ
sha'ul nichnas elav, hitpallel vesamach yadav alav verippei oto
unto whom Paul entered in, and prayed, and laying his hands on him healed him.

אַחֲרֵי כֵן בָּאוּ גַם יֶתֶר הַחוֹלִים אֲשֶׁר בָּאִי וְנִרְפְּאוּ
acharei chen ba'u gam yeter hacholim asher ba'i venirpe'u
And when this was done, the rest also that had diseases in the island came, and were cured:

הֵם כִּבְּדוּ אוֹתָנוּ בִּמְחֶוֹות כָּבוֹד רַבּוֹת וּכְשֶׁעָמַדְנוּ לְהַפְלִיג נָתְנוּ לָנוּ אֶת הָאַסְפָּקָה הַנְּחוּצָה
hem kibbedu otanu bemechevot kavod rabbot uchshe'amadnu lehaflig natenu lanu et ha'aspakah hannechutzah
who also honored us with many honors; and when we sailed, they put on board such things as we needed.

אַחֲרֵי שְׁלוֹשָׁה חֳדָשִׁים
acharei sheloshah chodashim
And after three months

עָלִינוּ עַל אֳנִיָּה אֲלֶכְּסַנְדְּרִית נוֹשֵׂאת סֵמֶל הָאֵלִים הַתְּאוֹמִים, שֶׁהִמְתִּינָה כָּל הַחֹרֶף בָּאִי
alinu al oniyah alekkesanderit noset semel ha'elim hatte'omim, shehimtinah kol hachoref ba'i
we set sail in a ship of Alexandria which had wintered in the island, whose sign was The Twin Brothers.

יָרַדְנוּ בְּסִירָקוּז וְנִשְׁאַרְנוּ שָׁם שְׁלוֹשָׁה יָמִים
yaradnu besirakuz venish'arnu sham shloshah yamim
And touching at Syracuse, we tarried there three days.

מִשָּׁם שַׁטְנוּ הָלְאָה וְהִגַּעְנוּ לְרֶגְיוּם
misham shatnu hale'ah vehigga'nu leregyum
And from thence we made a circuit, and arrived at Rhegium:

יוֹם אֶחָד אַחֲרֵי כֵן נָשְׁבָה רוּחַ דְּרוֹמִית וּלְמָחֳרַת בָּאנוּ אֶל פּוֹטְיוֹלִי
yom echad acharei chen nashevah ruach deromit ulemacharat banu el poteyoli
and after one day a south wind sprang up, and on the second day we came to Puteoli;

מַעֲשֵׂי הַשְּׁלִיחִים

בְּדֶרֶךְ זֹאת נֶחְלְצוּ כֻלָּם אֶל הַיַּבָּשָׁה
bederech zot nechletzu kullam el hayabbashah
And so it came to pass, that they all escaped safe to the land.

כח

אַחֲרֵי שֶׁנִּצַּלְנוּ הִתְבָּרֵר לָנוּ כִּי שֵׁם הָאִי מַלְטָה
acharei shennitzalnu hitbarer lanu ki shem ha'i maltah
And when we were escaped, then we knew that the island was called Melita.

הַתּוֹשָׁבִים, שֶׁלֹּא הָיוּ יְוָנִים, נָהֲגוּ בָּנוּ בִּנְדִיבוּת בִּלְתִּי רְגִילָה
hattoshavim, shello hayu yevanim, nahagu banu bindivut bilti regilah
And the barbarians showed us no common kindness:

כִּי הִדְלִיקוּ אֵשׁ בִּגְלַל הַגֶּשֶׁם הַיּוֹרֵד וְהַקֹּר וְקִבְּלוּ אֶת כֻּלָּנוּ
ki hidliku esh biglal haggeshem hayored vehakkor vekibbelu et kullanu
for they kindled a fire, and received us all, because of the present rain, and because of the cold.

שָׁאוּל אָסַף מְלֹא יָדָיו שִׁבְרֵי עֲנָפִים וּכְשֶׁשָּׂם אוֹתָם עַל הָאֵשׁ
sha'ul asaf melo yadav shivrei anafim uchesheshom otam al ha'esh
But when Paul had gathered a bundle of sticks and laid them on the fire,

יָצָא מִתּוֹכָם צֶפַע, בִּגְלַל הַחֹם, וְנִצְמַד אֶל יָדוֹ
yatza mittocham tzefa', biglal hachom, venitzmad el yado
a viper came out by reason of the heat, and fastened on his hand.

רָאוּ הַתּוֹשָׁבִים אֶת הַחַיָּה תְּלוּיָה עַל יָדוֹ וְאָמְרוּ זֶה אֶל זֶה
ra'u hattoshavim et hachayah teluyah al yado ve'ameru zeh el zeh
And when the barbarians saw the venomous creature hanging from his hand, they said one to another,

אֵין סָפֵק שֶׁהָאִישׁ הַזֶּה רוֹצֵחַ. נִצַּל מִן הַיָּם, אַךְ הַצֶּדֶק לֹא הִנִּיחַ לוֹ לִחְיוֹת
ein safek sheha'ish hazzeh rotzeach. nitzal min hayam, ach hatzedek lo hinniach lo lichyot
No doubt this man is a murderer, whom, though he hath escaped from the sea, yet Justice hath not suffered to live.

אֲבָל שָׁאוּל נִעֵר אֶת הַחַיָּה אֶל תּוֹךְ הָאֵשׁ וְלֹא נִזַּק כְּלָל
aval sha'ul ni'er et hachayah el toch ha'esh velo nizzak kelal
Howbeit he shook off the creature into the fire, and took no harm.

הֵם צִפּוּ שֶׁגּוּפוֹ יִתְנַפֵּחַ אוֹ שֶׁיִּפֹּל מֵת פִּתְאוֹם
hem tzippu sheggufo yitnappeach o sheyippol met pit'om
But they expected that he would have swollen, or fallen down dead suddenly:

חִכּוּ שָׁעָה אֲרֻכָּה וְרָאוּ שֶׁלֹּא קָרָה לוֹ שׁוּם רַע
chikku sha'ah arukkah vera'u shello karah lo shum ra
but when they were long in expectation and beheld nothing amiss came to him,

מַעֲשֵׂי הַשְּׁלִיחִים

אַחֲרֵי שֶׁאָכְלוּ לָשֹׂבַע הֵקֵלּוּ מֵעַל הָאֳנִיָּה בַּהֲטִילָם אֶת הַחִטָּה לַיָּם
acharei she'achelu lasova hekkelu me'al ha'oniyah bahatilam et hachittah layam
And when they had eaten enough, they lightened the ship, throwing out the wheat into the sea.

כְּשֶׁהֵאִיר הַיּוֹם לֹא הִכִּירוּ אֶת הָאָרֶץ,
kshehe'ir hayom lo hikkiru et ha'aretz
And when it was day, they knew not the land:

אַךְ הִבְחִינוּ בְּמִפְרָץ עִם חוֹף חוֹלִי וְהֶחְלִיטוּ לְהַסִּיעַ אֶת הָאֳנִיָּה לְשָׁם, אִם אֶפְשָׁר
ach hivchinu bemifratz im chof choli vehechlitu lehassia et ho'oniyah lesham, im efshar
but they perceived a certain bay with a beach, and they took counsel whether they could drive the ship upon it.

הֵם נִתְּקוּ אֶת קִשְׁרֵי הָעֳגָנִים וְעָזְבוּ אוֹתָם בַּיָּם. יַחַד עִם זֹאת הִתִּירוּ אֶת הַחֲבָלִים שֶׁל הַהֶגָאִים
hem nittku et kishrei ho'oganim ve'azevu otam bayam. yachad im zot hittiru et hachavalim shel hahaga'im
And casting off the anchors, they left them in the sea, at the same time loosing the bands of the rudders;

פָּרְשׂוּ אֶת הַמִּפְרָשׂ הַקִּדְמִי אֶל הָרוּחַ וְכִוְּנוּ אֶת הָאֳנִיָּה אֶל הַחוֹף
paresu et hammifras hakkidmi el haruach vechivvenu et ho'oniyah el hachof
and hoisting up the foresail to the wind, they made for the beach.

אָז הִגִּיעוּ לְמָקוֹם בֵּין זְרָמִים וְהֶעֱלוּ אֶת הָאֳנִיָּה עַל שִׂרְטוֹן
az higgi'u lemakom bein zeramim vehe'elu et ho'oniyah al sirton
But lighting upon a place where two seas met, they ran the vessel aground;

הַחַרְטוֹם נִתְקַע וְנִשְׁאַר קָבוּעַ בִּמְקוֹמוֹ
hachartom nitka venish'ar kavua bimkomo
and the foreship struck and remained unmoveable,

אֲבָל הַיַּרְכָתַיִם נִשְׁבְּרוּ מֵעָצְמַת הַגַּלִּים
aval hayarchatayim nishberu me'otzemat haggallim
but the stern began to break up by the violence of the waves.

כַּוָּנַת הַחַיָּלִים הָיְתָה לַהֲרֹג אֶת הָאֲסִירִים, כְּדֵי שֶׁלֹּא יִשְׂחֶה אִישׁ מֵהֶם וְיִמָּלֵט
kavvanat hachayalim hayetah laharog et ha'asirim, kedei shello yischeh ish mehem veyimmalet
And the soldiers' counsel was to kill the prisoners, lest any of them should swim out, and escape.

אַךְ שַׂר הַמֵּאָה רָצָה לְהַצִּיל אֶת שָׁאוּל וְהֵנִיא אוֹתָם מִכַּוָּנָתָם
ach sar hamme'ah ratzah lehatzil et sha'ul veheni otam mikkavvanatam
But the centurion, desiring to save Paul, stayed them from their purpose;

הוּא צִוָּה שֶׁהַיּוֹדְעִים לִשְׂחוֹת יִקְפְּצוּ רִאשׁוֹנִים וְיַגִּיעוּ אֶל הַיַּבָּשָׁה
hu tzivvah shehayode'im lischot yikpetzu rishonim veyaggi'u el hayabbashah
and commanded that they who could swim should cast themselves overboard, and get first to the land;

וְהַיֶּתֶר, שֶׁיַּעֲשׂוּ זֹאת חֶלְקָם עַל קְרָשִׁים וְחֶלְקָם עַל חֲפָצִים מִן הָאֳנִיָּה.
vehayeter, sheya'asu zot chelkam al kerashim vechelkam al chafatzim min ho'oniyah
and the rest, some on planks, and some on other things from the ship.

מַעֲשֵׂי הַשְּׁלִיחִים

כְּשֶׁנִּסּוּ הַמַּלָּחִים לִבְרֹחַ מִן הָאֳנִיָּה וְהִתְחִילוּ לְהוֹרִיד אֶת הַסִּירָה אֶל הַיָּם
keshennissu hammallachim livroach min ho'oniyah vehitchilu lehorid et hassirah el hayam
And as the sailors were seeking to flee out of the ship, and had lowered the boat into the sea,

בַּאֲמַתְלָה שֶׁהֵם מִתְכַּוְּנִים לִמְשֹׁךְ עֳגָנִים מֵחַרְטֹם הָאֳנִיָּה
ba'amatlah shehem mitkavvenim limshoch oganim mechartom ho'oniyah
under color as though they would lay out anchors from the foreship,

אָמַר שָׁאוּל לְשַׂר הַמֵּאָה וְלַחַיָּלִים: אִם אֵלֶּה לֹא יִשָּׁאֲרוּ בָּאֳנִיָּה לֹא תּוּכְלוּ אַתֶּם לְהִנָּצֵל
amar sha'ul lesar hamme'ah velachayalim. im elleh lo yisha'aru bo'oniyah lo tuchelu attem lehinnatzel
Paul said to the centurion and to the soldiers, Except these abide in the ship, ye cannot be saved.

אָז חָתְכוּ הַחַיָּלִים אֶת חַבְלֵי הַסִּירָה וְהִנִּיחוּ לָהּ לִפֹּל
az chatechu hachayalim et chavlei hassirah vehinnichu lah lippol
Then the soldiers cut away the ropes of the boat, and let her fall off.

עוֹד לִפְנֵי אוֹר הַבֹּקֶר בִּקֵּשׁ שָׁאוּל מִכָּל הָאֲנָשִׁים שֶׁיֹּאכְלוּ, בְּאָמְרוֹ
od lifnei or habboker bikkesh sha'ul mikkol ha'anashim sheyochelu, be'amero
And while the day was coming on, Paul besought them all to take some food, saying,

הַיּוֹם כְּבָר הַיּוֹם הָאַרְבָּעָה־עָשָׂר שֶׁאַתֶּם מַמְשִׁיכִים וּמְחַכִּים בְּלֹא לֶאֱכֹל כְּלוּם
hayom kevar hayom ha'arba'ah-'asar she'attem mamshichim umechakkim belo le'echol klum
This day is the fourteenth day that ye wait and continue fasting, having taken nothing.

לָכֵן אֲנִי מְבַקֵּשׁ מִכֶּם לֶאֱכֹל, כִּי זֶה נָחוּץ לְהַצָּלַתְכֶם
lachen ani mevakkesh mikkem le'echol, ki zeh nachutz lehatzalatchem
Wherefore I beseech you to take some food: for this is for your safety:

שֶׁכֵּן לֹא תֹאבַד שַׂעֲרָה מֵרֹאשׁוֹ שֶׁל אִישׁ מִכֶּם
shekken lo tovad sa'arah merosho shel ish mikkem
for there shall not a hair perish from the head of any of you.

לְאַחַר שֶׁאָמַר זֹאת לָקַח לֶחֶם, הוֹדָה לֵאלֹהִים לְעֵינֵי כֻּלָּם
le'achar she'amar zot lakach lechem, hodah le'elohim le'einei kullam
And when he had said this, and had taken bread, he gave thanks to God in the presence of all;

בָּצַע וְהֵחֵל לֶאֱכֹל
batza vehechel le'echol
and he brake it, and began to eat.

הַכֹּל הִתְעוֹדְדוּ וְגַם הֵם אָכְלוּ
hakkol hit'odedu vegam hem achelu
Then were they all of good cheer, and themselves also took food.

בְּסַךְ הַכֹּל הָיִינוּ מָאתַיִם וְשִׁבְעִים וָשֵׁשׁ נְפָשׁוֹת בָּאֳנִיָּה
besach hakkol hayinu matayim veshiv'im vashesh nefashot ba'oniyah
And we were in all in the ship two hundred threescore and sixteen souls.

מַעֲשֵׂי הַשְּׁלִיחִים

וְעַכְשָׁו אֲנִי מַצִּיעַ לָכֶם לְהִתְעוֹדֵד, כִּי לֹא תֹאבַד שׁוּם נֶפֶשׁ מִכֶּם; רַק הָאֳנִיָּה תֹּאבַד
ve'achshav ani matzia lachem lehit'oded, ki lo toavad shum nefesh mikkem; rak ho'oniyah toavad
And now I exhort you to be of good cheer; for there shall be no loss of life among you, but only of the ship.

כִּי בַּלַּיְלָה נִצַּב עָלַי מַלְאָךְ שֶׁל אֱלֹהִים אֲשֶׁר לוֹ אֲנִי שַׁיָּךְ וְאוֹתוֹ אֲנִי עוֹבֵד
ki ballaylah nitzav alai mal'ach shel elohim asher lo ani shayach ve'oto ani oved
For there stood by me this night an angel of the God whose I am, whom also I serve,

וְאָמַר, אַל תִּפְחַד, שָׁאוּל, אַתָּה צָרִיךְ לַעֲמֹד לִפְנֵי הַקֵּיסָר
ve'amar, al tifchad, sha'ul, attah tzarich la'amod lifnei hakkeisar,
saying, Fear not, Paul; thou must stand before Cæsar:

וְהִנֵּה הָאֱלֹהִים בְּחַסְדּוֹ חָנַן לְךָ אֶת כָּל הַמַּפְלִיגִים אִתְּךָ
vehinneh ha'elohim bechasdo chanan lecha et kol hammafligim ittecha
and lo, God hath granted thee all them that sail with thee.

וּבְכֵן, חֲבֵרִים, הִתְעוֹדְדוּ! אֲנִי בּוֹטֵחַ בֵּאלֹהִים שֶׁכְּמוֹ שֶׁנֶּאֱמַר לִי כֵּן יִהְיֶה
uvchen, chaverim, hit'odedu! ani boteach belohim shekkemo shenne'emar li ken yihyeh
Wherefore, sirs, be of good cheer: for I believe God, that it shall be even so as it hath been spoken unto me.

אֲבָל עָלֵינוּ לְהִסָּחֵף אֶל אֵיזֶה אִי
aval aleinu lehissachef el eizeh i
But we must be cast upon a certain island.

בַּחֲצוֹת הַלַּיְלָה הָאַרְבָּעָה-עָשָׂר, כְּשֶׁנִּסְחַפְנוּ הֵנָּה וָהֵנָּה בַּיָּם הָאַדְרִיָּטִי
bachatzot hallaylah ha'arba'ah-'asar, keshennischafnu hennah vahennah bayam ha'adriyati
But when the fourteenth night was come, as we were driven to and fro in the sea of Adria,

סָבְרוּ הַמַּלָּחִים שֶׁאָנוּ מִתְקָרְבִים לְאֵיזוֹ אֶרֶץ
saveru hammallachim she'anu mitkarevim le'eizo eretz
about midnight the sailors surmised that they were drawing near to some country:

הֵם הוֹרִידוּ אֲנָךְ וּמָצְאוּ שֶׁהָעֹמֶק שְׁלוֹשִׁים וְשִׁבְעָה מֶטְרִים
hem horidu anach umatze'u sheha'omek shloshim veshiv'ah metrim
and they sounded, and found twenty fathoms;

אַחֲרֵי מֶרְחָק מְעַט מָדְדוּ שֵׁנִית וּמָצְאוּ עֶשְׂרִים וְשִׁבְעָה מֶטְרִים
acharei merchak me'at madedu shenit umatze'u esrim veshiv'ah metrim
and after a little space, they sounded again, and found fifteen fathoms.

הוֹאִיל וְחָשְׁשׁוּ שֶׁמָּא נִסָּחֵף אֶל אֲזוֹרֵי סְלָעִים
ho'il vechasheshu shemma nissachef el azorei sela'im
And fearing lest haply we should be cast ashore on rocky ground,

הֵטִילוּ אַרְבָּעָה עֹגָנִים מִן הַצַּד הָאֲחוֹרִי שֶׁל הָאֳנִיָּה וְהִתְפַּלְּלוּ שֶׁיָּאִיר הַיּוֹם
hetilu arba'ah oganim min hatzad ha'achori shel ho'oniyah vehitpallelu sheya'ir hayom
they let go four anchors from the stern, and wished for the day.

מַעֲשֵׂי הַשְּׁלִיחִים

לָכֵן הֵרִימוּ עֹגֶן וְשָׁטוּ סָמוּךְ לַיַּבָּשָׁה לְאֹרֶךְ חוֹף כְּרֵתִים
lachen herimu ogen veshatu samuch layabbashah le'orech chof keretim
they weighed anchor and sailed along Crete, close in shore.

לְאַחַר זְמַן קָצָר נָשְׁבָה מִן הָאִי רוּחַ סוּפָה צְפוֹנִית מִזְרָחִית הַנִּקְרֵאת אִירָקִילוֹן
le'achar zman katzar nashvah min ha'i ruach sufah tzefonit mizrachit hannikret eirakilon
But after no long time there beat down from it a tempestuous wind, which is called Euraquilo:

כֵּיוָן שֶׁהָאֳנִיָּה נִלְכְּדָה וְלֹא יָכְלָה לָשׁוּט נֶגֶד הָרוּחַ, נִכְנַעְנוּ וְנִסְחַפְנוּ
keivan sheho'oniyah nilkedah velo yachelah lashut neged haruach, nichna'nu venischafnu
and when the ship was caught, and could not face the wind, we gave way to it, and were driven.

כַּאֲשֶׁר עָבַרְנוּ עַל־יַד אִי אֶחָד, קוֹדָה שְׁמוֹ, הִצְלַחְנוּ בְּמַאֲמָץ רַב לְהִשְׁתַּלֵּט עַל הַסִּירָה הַנִּגְרֶרֶת
ka'asher avarnu al-yad i echad, kodah shemo, hitzlachnu bema'amatz rav lehishtallet al hassirah hannigreret
And running under the lee of a small island called Cauda, we were able, with difficulty, to secure the boat:

הֵם הֶעֱלוּ אוֹתָהּ לַסִּפּוּן וְהִשְׁתַּמְּשׁוּ בַּחֲבָלִים לַחֲגִירַת דָּפְנוֹת הָאֳנִיָּה
hem he'elu otah lassippun vehishtammeshu bachavalim lachagirat dafnot ho'oniyah
and when they had hoisted it up, they used helps, under-girding the ship;

וּמֵאַחַר שֶׁפָּחֲדוּ שֶׁמָּא יִסָּחֲפוּ אֶל חוֹלוֹת סִירְטִיס, הִנְמִיכוּ אֶת הַמִּפְרָשׂ וְנִסְחֲפוּ בְּאֹפֶן זֶה
ume'achar sheppachadu shemma yissachafu el cholot siretis, hinmichu et hammifras venischafu be'ofen zeh
and, fearing lest they should be cast upon the Syrtis, they lowered the gear, and so were driven.

לְמָחֳרָת, בִּהְיוֹתֵנוּ מְטֻלְטָלִים בְּחָזְקָה עַל־יְדֵי הַסְּעָרָה, הֵקֵלּוּ מִמַּשָּׂא הָאֳנִיָּה
lemachorat, bihyotenu metultalim bechazekah al-yedei hasse'arah, hekellu mimmasho ho'oniyah
And as we labored exceedingly with the storm, the next day they began to throw the freight overboard;

אַחֲרֵי יוֹם נוֹסָף הִשְׁלִיכוּ בְּמוֹ יְדֵיהֶם אֶת צִיּוּד הָאֳנִיָּה
acharei yom nosaf hishlichu bemo yedeihem et tziyud ho'oniyah
and the third day they cast out with their own hands the tackling of the ship.

הוֹאִיל וְיָמִים רַבִּים לֹא הוֹפִיעוּ הַשֶּׁמֶשׁ וְהַכּוֹכָבִים וְהִתְחוֹלְלָה סְעָרָה חֲזָקָה
ho'il veyamim rabbim lo hofi'u hashemesh vehakkochavim vehitcholelah se'arah chazakah
And when neither sun nor stars shone upon us for many days, and no small tempest lay on us,

אָפְסָה כָּל תִּקְוָה שֶׁנִּנָּצֵל
afesah kol tikvah shenninnatzel
all hope that we should be saved was now taken away.

אַחֲרֵי שֶׁנִּמְנְעוּ זְמַן רַב מֵאֹכֶל, עָמַד שָׁאוּל בֵּינֵיהֶם וְאָמַר: וּבְכֵן
acharei shennimne'u zeman rav me'ochel, amad sha'ul beineihem ve'amar: uvechen
And when they had been long without food, then Paul stood forth in the midst of them, and said,

חֲבֵרִים, הָיָה צָרִיךְ לִשְׁמֹעַ בְּקוֹלִי וְלֹא לְהַפְלִיג מִכְּרֵתִים וּלְהַגִּיעַ לִידֵי הַנֶּזֶק וְהָאֲבַדָּן הַזֶּה
chaverim, hayah tzarich lishmoa bekoli velo lehaflig mikkeretim ulehaggia liydei hannezek veha'ovedan hazzeh
Sirs, ye should have hearkened unto me, and not have set sail from Crete, and have gotten this injury and loss.

מַעֲשֵׂי הַשְּׁלִיחִים

שַׁטְנוּ סָמוּךְ לָאִי בְּקֹשִׁי רַב וְהִגַּעְנוּ לְמָקוֹם אֶחָד שֶׁנִּקְרָא הַמַּעֲגָנִים הַטּוֹבִים
shatnu samuch la'i bekoshi rav vehigga'nu lemakom echad shennikra hamma'aganim hattovim
and with difficulty coasting along it we came unto a certain place called Fair Havens;

קָרוֹב לָעִיר לָסַיָּה
karov la'ir lasayah
nigh whereunto was the city of Lasea.

מִכֵּיוָן שֶׁעָבַר זְמַן נִכָּר וְהַשַּׁיִט כְּבָר הָיָה מְסֻכָּן
mikkeivan she'avar zeman nikkar vehashayit kevar hayah mesukkan
And when much time was spent, and the voyage was now dangerous,

שֶׁכֵּן אֲפִלּוּ יוֹם הַכִּפּוּרִים כְּבָר עָבַר, הִזְהִיר אוֹתָם שָׁאוּל
shekken afillu yom hakkippurim kvar avar, hizhir otam sha'ul
because the Fast was now already gone by, Paul admonished them,

בְּאָמְרוֹ. אֲנָשִׁים, אֲנִי רוֹאֶה שֶׁלַּמַּסָּע צָפוּי נֶזֶק עִם אָבְדָן רַב
be'amero. anashim, ani ro'eh shellammassa tzafui nezek im ovdan rav
and said unto them, Sirs, I perceive that the voyage will be with injury and much loss,

לֹא רַק לַמִּטְעָן וְלָאֳנִיָּה, אֶלָּא גַּם לְחַיֵּינוּ
lo rak lammit'an velo'oniyah, ella gam lechayeinu
not only of the lading and the ship, but also of our lives.

אַךְ שַׂר הַמֵּאָה הֶאֱמִין יוֹתֵר לְרַב הַחוֹבֵל וּלְבַעַל הָאֳנִיָּה
ach sar hamme'ah he'emin yoter lerav hachovel uleva'al ho'oniyah
But the centurion gave more heed to the master and to the owner of the ship,

מֵאֲשֶׁר לְדִבְרֵי שָׁאוּל
me'asher ledivrei sha'ul
than to those things which were spoken by Paul.

הוֹאִיל וְהַנָּמֵל לֹא הִתְאִים לַעֲגִינַת חֹרֶף הִצִּיעַ הָרֹב לְהַפְלִיג מִשָּׁם
ho'il vehannamel lo hit'im la'aginat choref hitzia harov lehaflig misham
And because the haven was not commodious to winter in, the more part advised to put to sea from thence,

בְּתִקְוָה שֶׁיּוּכְלוּ לְהַגִּיעַ לְפֶנִיקֶס
betikvah sheyuchelu lehaggia lefenikes
if by any means they could reach Phoenix,

נְמֵל כְּרֵתִי הַפּוֹנֶה לִדְרוֹם מַעֲרָב וְלִצְפוֹן מַעֲרָב - וְלִשְׁהוֹת שָׁם בַּחֹרֶף
namel kereti happoneh lidrom ma'arav velitzfon ma'arav - velishhot sham bachoref
and winter there; which is a haven of Crete, looking north-east and south-east.

רוּחַ אִטִּית נָשְׁבָה מִן הַדָּרוֹם וְהֵם חָשְׁבוּ שֶׁיַּשִּׂיגוּ אֶת מַטְּרָתָם
ruach ittit nashevah min haddarom vehem chashevu sheyassigu et matteratam
And when the south wind blew softly, supposing that they had obtained their purpose,

מַעֲשֵׂי הַשְּׁלִיחִים

כז

כַּאֲשֶׁר הֻחְלַט שֶׁנַּפְלִיג לְאִיטַלְיָה
ka'asher huchlat shennaflig le'italyah
And when it was determined that we should sail for Italy,

מָסְרוּ אֶת שָׁאוּל עִם כַּמָּה אֲסִירִים אֲחֵרִים לִידֵי שַׂר מֵאָה מִן הַגְּדוּד הַקֵּיסָרִי, יוּלְיוֹס שְׁמוֹ
masru et sha'ul im kammah asirim acherim liydei sar me'ah min haggedud hakkeisari, yuleyos shemo
they delivered Paul and certain other prisoners to a centurion named Julius, of the Augustan band.

נִכְנַסְנוּ לָאֳנִיָּה אַדְרַמִיטִית, שֶׁעָמְדָה לִנְסֹעַ לִמְקוֹמוֹת אֲשֶׁר לְאֹרֶךְ חוֹף אַסְיָה וְהִפְלַגְנוּ.
nichnasnu lo'oniyah adramitit, she'amdah linsoa limkomot asher le'orech chof asyah vehiflagnu
And embarking in a ship of Adramyttium, which was about to sail unto the places on the coast of Asia, we put to sea,

אִתָּנוּ הָיָה אֲרִיסְטַרְכוֹס, מַקֵּדוֹנִי מִתֶּסָּלוֹנִיקִי
ittanu hayah arisetarchos, makedoni mittessaloniki
Aristarchus, a Macedonian of Thessalonica, being with us.

לְמָחֳרָת הִגַּעְנוּ לְצִידוֹן. יוּלְיוֹס נָהַג בִּנְדִיבוּת עִם שָׁאוּל
lemacharat higga'nu letzidon. yuleyos nahag bindivut im sha'ul
And the next day we touched at Sidon: and Julius treated Paul kindly,

וְהִרְשָׁה לוֹ לָלֶכֶת אֶל חֲבֵרָיו וְלֵהָנוֹת מֵעֶזְרָתָם
vehirshah lo lalechet el chaverav velehanot me'ezratam
and gave him leave to go unto his friends and refresh himself.

מִשָּׁם הִפְלַגְנוּ וְשַׁטְנוּ עַל־יַד קַפְרִיסִין בִּגְלַל הָרוּחוֹת הַנֶּגְדִּיּוֹת
misham hiflagnu veshatnu al-yad kafrisin biglal haruchot hannegdiyot
And putting to sea from thence, we sailed under the lee of Cyprus, because the winds were contrary.

עָבַרְנוּ בַּיָּם שֶׁמִּמּוּל לְקִילִיקְיָה וּפַמְפִילְיָה וּבָאנוּ אֶל מִירָה אֲשֶׁר בְּלִיקְיָה
avarnu bayam shemmimmul lekilikeyah vepamfileyah uvanu el mirah asher belikeyah
And when we had sailed across the sea which is off Cilicia and Pamphylia, we came to Myra, a city of Lycia.

שַׂר הַמֵּאָה מָצָא שָׁם אֳנִיָּה מֵאֲלֶכְּסַנְדֶּרְיָה שֶׁמְּגַמַּת פָּנֶיהָ לְאִיטַלְיָה וְהֶעֱבִיר אוֹתָנוּ אֵלֶיהָ
sar hamme'ah matza sham oniyah me'alekkesanderiyah shemmegammat paneiha le'italyah vehe'evir otanu eleiha
And there the centurion found a ship of Alexandria sailing for Italy; and he put us therein.

שַׁטְנוּ כַּמָּה יָמִים בְּאִטִּיּוּת וְהִגַּעְנוּ בְּקֹשִׁי רַב אֶל מוּל קְנִידוֹס
shatnu kammah yamim be'ittiyut vehigga'nu bekoshi rav el mul kenidos
And when we had sailed slowly many days, and were come with difficulty over against Cnidus,

מֵאַחַר שֶׁהָרוּחַ הַנּוֹשֶׁבֶת הִפְרִיעָה לָנוּ, שַׁטְנוּ עַל־יַד כְּרֵתִים וְעָבַרְנוּ עַל־פְּנֵי כֵּף סַלְמוֹנִי
me'achar sheharuach hannoshevet hifri'ah lanu, shatnu al-yad keretim ve'avarnu al-penei kef salmoni
the wind not further suffering us, we sailed under the lee of Crete, over against Salmone;

מַעֲשֵׂי הַשְּׁלִיחִים

אַתָּה מִשְׁתַּגֵּעַ, שָׁאוּל! הַלִּמּוּד הָרַב מֵבִיא אוֹתְךָ לִידֵי שִׁגָּעוֹן
attah mishtaggea', sha'ul! hallimmud harav mevi otcha lidei shigga'on
Paul, thou art mad; thy much learning is turning thee mad.

הֵשִׁיב שָׁאוּל: אֵינֶנִּי מִשְׁתַּגֵּעַ, הוֹד מַעֲלָתוֹ פֶסְטוֹס, אֶלָּא דְּבָרִים שֶׁל אֱמֶת וְשֶׁל טַעַם אֲנִי מַשְׁמִיעַ
heshiv sha'ul: einenni mishtaggea', hod ma'alato festos, ella devarim shel emet veshel ta'am ani mashmia
But Paul saith, I am not mad, most excellent Festus; but speak forth words of truth and soberness.

הֲרֵי הַמֶּלֶךְ יוֹדֵעַ אֶת הָעִנְיָנִים הָאֵלֶּה וַאֲנִי מְדַבֵּר אֵלָיו בְּבִטָּחוֹן
harei hammelech yodea et ha'inyanim ha'elleh va'ani medabber elav bevittachon
For the king knoweth of these things, unto whom also I speak freely:

שֶׁכֵּן אֲנִי בָּטוּחַ שֶׁלֹּא נֶעְלָם מִמֶּנּוּ דָּבָר מִן הַדְּבָרִים הָאֵלֶּה, כִּי לֹא בְּקֶרֶן זָוִית נֶעֶשְׂתָה זֹאת
shekken ani batuach shello ne'lam mimmennu davar min haddevarim ha'elleh, ki lo bekeren zavit ne'estah zot
for I am persuaded that none of these things is hidden from him; for this hath not been done in a corner.

הַמֶּלֶךְ אַגְרִיפַּס, הֲמַאֲמִין אַתָּה בַּנְּבִיאִים? אֲנִי יוֹדֵעַ שֶׁאַתָּה מַאֲמִין
hammelech agripas, hama'amin attah bannevi'im? ani yodea she'attah ma'amin
King Agrippa, believest thou the prophets? I know that thou believest.

עָנָה אַגְרִיפַּס לְשָׁאוּל: עוֹד מְעַט וְאַתָּה מְשַׁכְנֵעַ אוֹתִי לִהְיוֹת מְשִׁיחִי
anah agripas lesha'ul: od me'at ve'attah meshachnea oti lihyot meshichi
And Agrippa said unto Paul, With but little persuasion thou wouldest fain make me a Christian.

אָמַר שָׁאוּל: אִם עוֹד מְעַט וְאִם עוֹד הַרְבֵּה, תְּפִלָּתִי לֵאלֹהִים
amar sha'ul: im od me'at ve'im od harbeh, tefillati le'elohim
And Paul said, I would to God, that whether with little or with much,

שֶׁלֹּא רַק אַתָּה אֶלָּא גַּם כָּל הַשּׁוֹמְעִים אוֹתִי הַיּוֹם, יִהְיוּ כָּמוֹנִי - רַק בְּלִי הַכְּבָלִים הָאֵלֶּה
shello rak attah ella gam kol hashome'im oti hayom, yihyu kamoni - rak beli hakkevalim ha'elleh
not thou only, but also all that hear me this day, might become such as I am, except these bonds.

הַמֶּלֶךְ וְהַנָּצִיב קָמוּ וְכֵן גַּם בֶּרְנִיקָה וְהַיּוֹשְׁבִים אִתָּם
hammelech vehannatziv kamu vechen gam bernikah vehayoshevim ittam
And the king rose up, and the governor, and Bernice, and they that sat with them:

אַחֲרֵי צֵאתָם דִּבְּרוּ זֶה אֶל זֶה וְאָמְרוּ: הָאִישׁ הַזֶּה לֹא עָשָׂה שׁוּם דָּבָר הַמְחַיֵּב מָוֶת אוֹ מַאֲסָר
acharei tzetam dibberu zeh el zeh ve'ameru: ha'ish hazzeh lo asah shum davar hamchayev mavet o ma'asar
And when they had withdrawn, they spake one to another, saying, This man doeth nothing worthy of death or of bonds.

אָמַר אַגְרִיפַּס לְפֶסְטוֹס: הָאִישׁ הַזֶּה הָיָה יָכוֹל לְהִשְׁתַּחְרֵר לוּלֵא פָּנָה אֶל הַקֵּיסָר
amar agripas lefestos: ha'ish hazzeh hayah yachol lehishtachrer lulei panah el hakkeisa
And Agrippa said unto Festus, This man might have been set at liberty, if he had not appealed unto Cæsar.

מַעֲשֵׂי הַשְּׁלִיחִים

לִפְקֹחַ אֶת עֵינֵיהֶם, לְהָשִׁיב אוֹתָם מֵחֹשֶׁךְ לְאוֹר וּמִשִּׁלְטוֹן הַשָּׂטָן לֵאלֹהִים
lifkoach et eineihem, lehashiv otam mechoshech le'or umishilton hassatan le'elohim
to open their eyes, that they may turn from darkness to light and from the power of Satan unto God,

כְּדֵי שֶׁיְּקַבְּלוּ עַל־יְדֵי אֱמוּנָה בִּי סְלִיחַת חֲטָאִים וְנַחֲלָה בְּקֶרֶב הַמְקֻדָּשִׁים
kedei sheyekabbelu al-yedei emunah bi slichat chata'im venachalah bekerev hamkuddashim
that they may receive remission of sins and an inheritance among them that are sanctified by faith in me.

עַל כֵּן, הַמֶּלֶךְ אַגְרִיפַּס, לֹא הִתְנַגַּדְתִּי לְצַיֵּת לַמַּרְאֶה מִן הַשָּׁמַיִם
al ken, hammelech agripas, lo hitnaggadti letzayet lammar'eh min hashamayim
Wherefore, O king Agrippa, I was not disobedient unto the heavenly vision:

כִּי אִם הִגַּדְתִּי תְּחִלָּה לְאַנְשֵׁי דַמֶּשֶׂק, וְכֵן גַּם בִּירוּשָׁלַיִם-
ki im higgadti techillah le'anshei dammesek, vechen gam biyerushalayim
but declared both to them of Damascus first, and at Jerusalem,

וּבְכָל אֶרֶץ יְהוּדָה וְגַם לַגּוֹיִם
uvechol eretz yehudah vegam laggoyim
and throughout all the country of Judæa, and also to the Gentiles,

לַחֲזוֹר בִּתְשׁוּבָה וְלִפְנוֹת אֶל אֱלֹהִים בַּעֲשׂוֹתָם מַעֲשִׂים רְאוּיִים לִתְשׁוּבָה
lachazor bitshuvah velifnot el elohim ba'asotam ma'asim re'uyim litshuvah
that they should repent and turn to God, doing works worthy of repentance.

בִּגְלַל זֶה תְּפָסוּנִי יְהוּדִים בַּמִּקְדָּשׁ וְנִסּוּ לַהֲרֹג אוֹתִי
biglal zeh tefasuni yehudim bammikdash venissu laharog oti
For this cause the Jews seized me in the temple, and assayed to kill me.

וּבִהְיוֹת הָאֱלֹהִים בְּעֶזְרִי עַד הַיּוֹם הַזֶּה, הֲרֵינִי עוֹמֵד וּמֵעִיד לִפְנֵי קְטַנִּים וּגְדוֹלִים
uvihyot ha'elohim be'ezri ad hayom hazzeh, hareini omed ume'id lifnei ketannim ugedolim
Having therefore obtained the help that is from God, I stand unto this day testifying both to small and great,

וְאֵינֶנִּי אוֹמֵר דָּבָר מִלְּבַד הַדְּבָרִים שֶׁהַנְּבִיאִים וּמֹשֶׁה אָמְרוּ כִּי עֲתִידִים הֵם לִקְרוֹת
ve'einenni omer davar millevad haddevarim shehannevi'im umosheh ameru ki atidim hem likrot
saying nothing but what the prophets and Moses did say should come;

שֶׁהַמָּשִׁיחַ יִסְבֹּל
shehammashiach yisbol
how that the Christ must suffer,

יִהְיֶה רִאשׁוֹן לִתְחִיַּת הַמֵּתִים וִיבַשֵּׂר אוֹר לָעָם וְלַגּוֹיִם
yihyeh rishon litchiyat hammetim viyivasser or la'am velaggoyim
and how that he first by the resurrection of the dead should proclaim light both to the people and to the Gentiles.

כְּשֶׁאָמַר אֶת הַדְּבָרִים הָאֵלֶּה לַהֲגַנָּתוֹ, אָמַר פֶסְטוֹס בְּקוֹל רָם
keshe'amar et haddevarim ha'elleh lahagannato, amar festos bekol ram
And as he thus made his defence, Festus saith with a loud voice,

מַעֲשֵׂי הַשְּׁלִיחִים

פְּעָמִים רַבּוֹת, בְּכָל בָּתֵּי הַכְּנֶסֶת, הֶעֱנַשְׁתִּי אוֹתָם וְדָחַקְתִּי בָּהֶם לְגַדֵּף אֶת שְׁמוֹ,
pe'amim rabbot, bechol battei hakkeneset, he'enashti otam vedachakti bahem legaddef et shmo
And punishing them oftentimes in all the synagogues, I strove to make them blaspheme;

וּבְשֶׁצֶף זַעְמִי עֲלֵיהֶם רָדַפְתִּי אוֹתָם אֲפִלּוּ עַד עָרִים מִחוּץ לָאָרֶץ
uveshetzef za'mi aleihem radafti otam afillu ad arim michutz la'aretz
and being exceedingly mad against them, I persecuted them even unto foreign cities.

הָלַכְתִּי לְשֵׁם כָּךְ לְדַמֶּשֶׂק עִם סַמְכוּת וּרְשׁוּת מִטַּעַם רָאשֵׁי הַכֹּהֲנִים
halachti leshem kach ledammesek im samchut ureshut mitta'am rashei hakkohanim
Whereupon as I journeyed to Damascus with the authority and commission of the chief priests,

וְהִנֵּה, אֲדוֹנִי הַמֶּלֶךְ, בִּהְיוֹתִי בַּדֶּרֶךְ, בַּצָּהֳרַיִם, רָאִיתִי אוֹר מִן הַשָּׁמַיִם
vehinneh, adoni hammelech, bihyoti badderech, batzohorayim, ra'iti or min hashamayim
at midday, O king, I saw on the way a light from heaven,

מַבְרִיק יוֹתֵר מִזֹּהַר הַשֶּׁמֶשׁ
mavrik yoter mizzohar hashemesh
above the brightness of the sun,

נוֹגֵהַּ סָבִיב לִי וְלַהוֹלְכִים אִתִּי
nogeah saviv li velaholechim itti
shining round about me and them that journeyed with me.

כֻּלָּנוּ נָפַלְנוּ אַרְצָה וַאֲנִי שָׁמַעְתִּי קוֹל אוֹמֵר אֵלַי בַּלָּשׁוֹן הָעִבְרִית
kullanu nafalnu artzah va'ani shama'ti kol omer elai ballashon ha'ivrit
And when we were all fallen to the earth, I heard a voice saying unto me in the Hebrew language,

שָׁאוּל, שָׁאוּל, לָמָּה אַתָּה רוֹדֵף אוֹתִי? קָשֶׁה לְךָ לִבְעֹט בַּדָּרְבָנוֹת
sha'ul, sha'ul, lammah attah rodef oti? kasheh lecha liv'ot baddorvanot
Saul, Saul, why persecutest thou me? it is hard for thee to kick against the goad.

שָׁאַלְתִּי, מִי אַתָּה, אֲדוֹנִי? וְהָאָדוֹן הֵשִׁיב, אֲנִי יֵשׁוּעַ שֶׁאַתָּה רוֹדֵף
sha'alti, mi attah, adoni? veha'adon heshiv, ani yeshua she'attah rodef
And I said, Who art thou, Lord? And the Lord said, I am Jesus whom thou persecutest.

אֲבָל קוּם וַעֲמֹד עַל רַגְלֶיךָ, כִּי לְשֵׁם כָּךְ נִרְאֵיתִי אֵלֶיךָ - לְמַנּוֹת אוֹתְךָ לִמְשָׁרֵת
aval kum va'amod al ragleicha, ki leshem kach nir'eiti eleicha - lemannot otecha limsharet
But arise, and stand upon thy feet: for to this end have I appeared unto thee, to appoint thee a minister

וּלְעֵד עַל דָּבָר זֶה שֶׁרָאִיתָ אוֹתִי וְעַל הַדְּבָרִים שֶׁלִּשְׁמָם אֵרָאֶה אֵלֶיךָ
ule'ed al devar zeh shera'ita oti ve'al haddevarim shellishmam era'eh eleicha
and a witness both of the things wherein thou hast seen me, and of the things wherein I will appear unto thee;

בְּהַצִּילִי אוֹתְךָ מִן הָעָם וּמִן הַגּוֹיִם אֲשֶׁר אֲנִי שׁוֹלֵחַ אוֹתְךָ אֲלֵיהֶם
behatzili otecha min ha'am umin haggoyim asher ani sholeach otcha aleihem
delivering thee from the people, and from the Gentiles, unto whom I send thee,

מַעֲשֵׂי הַשְּׁלִיחִים

מֵרֵאשִׁית יְמֵי מְגוּרַי בְּקֶרֶב עַמִּי בִּירוּשָׁלַיִם

mereshit yemei megurai bekerev ammi biyerushalayim
which was from the beginning among mine own nation and at Jerusalem, know all the Jews;

הֵם הִכִּירוּנִי מִתְּחִלָּה - אִם יֵאוֹתוּ לְהָעִיד - וְיוֹדְעִים
hem hikkiruni mittechillah - im ye'otu leha'id - veyode'im
having knowledge of me from the first, if they be willing to testify,

שֶׁחָיִיתִי כְפָרוּשׁ עַל־פִּי הַכַּת הָאֲדוּקָה בְּיוֹתֵר שֶׁל דָּתֵנוּ
shechayiti kefarush al-pi hakkat ha'adukah beyoter shel datenu
that after the straitest sect of our religion I lived a Pharisee.

וְעַכְשָׁו אֲנִי עוֹמֵד לְמִשְׁפָּט עַל תִּקְוַת הַהַבְטָחָה שֶׁהִבְטִיחַ אֱלֹהִים לַאֲבוֹתֵינוּ
ve'achshav ani omed lemishpat al tikvat hahavtachah shehivtiach elohim la'avoteinu
And now I stand here to be judged for the hope of the promise made of God unto our fathers;

הַבְטָחָה אֲשֶׁר שְׁנֵים־עָשָׂר שְׁבָטֵינוּ.
havtachah asher shneim-'asar shvateinu
unto which promise our twelve tribes,

מְקַוִּים לְהַגִּיעַ לְהַגְשָׁמָתָהּ בְּעָבְדָם אֶת אֱלֹהִים בִּדְבֵקוּת יוֹמָם וָלַיְלָה
mekavvim lehaggia lehagshamatah be'avedam et elohim bidvekut yomam valaylah
earnestly serving God night and day, hope to attain.

עַל־דְּבַר הַתִּקְוָה הַזֹּאת, הַמֶּלֶךְ אַגְרִיפַּס, יֵשׁ יְהוּדִים הַמַּאֲשִׁימִים אוֹתִי
al-dvar hattikvah hazzot, hammelech agripas, yesh yehudim hamma'ashimim oti
And concerning this hope I am accused by the Jews, O king!

מַדּוּעַ תַּחְשְׁבוּ לְדָבָר לֹא יֵאָמֵן שֶׁאֱלֹהִים מְחַיֶּה מֵתִים
maddu'attachshevu ledavar lo ye'amen she'elohim mechayeh metim
Why is it judged incredible with you, if God doth raise the dead?

אָכֵן אֲנִי עַצְמִי חָשַׁבְתִּי כִּי מְחוֹבָתִי לַעֲשׂוֹת דְּבָרִים רַבִּים נֶגֶד שֵׁם יֵשׁוּעַ מִנַּצְרַת
achen ani atzmi chashavti ki mechovati la'asot devarim rabbim neged shem yeshua minnatzrat
I verily thought with myself that I ought to do many things contrary to the name of Jesus of Nazareth.

מַה שֶּׁגַּם עָשִׂיתִי בִּירוּשָׁלַיִם. קְדוֹשִׁים רַבִּים כָּלָאתִי בְּבָתֵּי כֶלֶא
mah sheggam asiti biyerushalayim. kedoshim rabbim kalati bevattei kele
And this I also did in Jerusalem: and I both shut up many of the saints in prisons,

עַל־פִּי הַסַּמְכוּת שֶׁקִּבַּלְתִּי מֵאֵת רָאשֵׁי הַכֹּהֲנִים, וְכַאֲשֶׁר הוּצְאוּ לַהוֹרֵג הִצְבַּעְתִּי עִם הַמְחַיְּבִים
al-pi hassamchut shekkibbalti me'et rashei hakkohanim, vecha'asher hutze'u lahoreg hitzba'ti im hamchayevim
having received authority from the chief priests, and when they were put to death I gave my vote against them.

מַעֲשֵׂי הַשְּׁלִיחִים

אַךְ מִכֵּיוָן שֶׁבִּקֵּשׁ לְהִשָּׁפֵט לִפְנֵי הַקֵּיסָר הֶחְלַטְתִּי לִשְׁלֹחַ אוֹתוֹ
ach mikkeivan shebbikkesh lehishafet lifnei hakkeisar hechlatti lishloach oto
and as he himself appealed to the emperor I determined to send him.

אֲבָל אֵין לִי שׁוּם דָּבָר בָּרוּר לִכְתֹּב עָלָיו לַאֲדוֹנֵנוּ. לָכֵן הֵבֵאתִי אוֹתוֹ לִפְנֵיכֶם
aval ein li shum davar barur lichtov alav la'adonenu. lachen heveti oto lifneichem
Of whom I have no certain thing to write unto my lord. Wherefore I have brought him forth before you,

וּבְיִחוּד לְפָנֶיךָ, הַמֶּלֶךְ אַגְרִיפַּס, כְּדֵי שֶׁיֵּחָקֵר וְיִהְיֶה לִי מַה לִּכְתֹּב
uveyichud lefaneicha, hammelech agripas, kedei sheyechaker veyihyeh li mah lichtov
and specially before thee, king Agrippa, that, after examination had, I may have somewhat to write.

שֶׁהֲרֵי לֹא מִתְקַבֵּל עַל דַּעְתִּי לִשְׁלֹחַ אָסִיר בְּלִי לְהוֹדִיעַ גַּם אֶת הָאַשְׁמוֹת הַמְיֻחָסוֹת לוֹ
sheharei lo mitkabbel al da'ti lishloach asir beli lehodia gam et ha'ashamot hamyuchasot lo
For it seemeth to me unreasonable, in sending a prisoner, not withal to signify the charges against him.

כו

אָמַר אַגְרִיפַּס אֶל שָׁאוּל: נִתָּן לְךָ לְלַמֵּד זְכוּת עַל עַצְמְךָ
amar agripas el sha'ul: nittan lecha lelammed zchut al atzmecha
And Agrippa said unto Paul, Thou art permitted to speak for thyself.

הוֹשִׁיט שָׁאוּל אֶת יָדוֹ וְהֵחֵל לְהָגֵן עַל עַצְמוֹ
hoshit sha'ul et yado vehechel lehagen al atzmo
Then Paul stretched forth his hand, and made his defence:

הַמֶּלֶךְ אַגְרִיפַּס, חוֹשֵׁב אֲנִי אֶת עַצְמִי לִמְאֻשָּׁר
hammelech agripas, choshev ani et atzmi lim'ushar
I think myself happy, king Agrippa,

עַל שֶׁאֲנִי מֵגֵן עַל עַצְמִי לְפָנֶיךָ הַיּוֹם בְּעִנְיָן כָּל מַה שֶׁיְּהוּדִים אֲחָדִים מַאֲשִׁימִים אוֹתִי
al she'ani megen al atzmi lefaneicha hayom be'inyan kol mah sheyehudim achadim ma'ashimim oti
that I am to make my defence before thee this day touching all the things whereof I am accused by the Jews:

בְּיִחוּד מִשּׁוּם שֶׁאַתָּה בָּקִי בְּכָל הַמִּנְהָגִים וְהַשְּׁאֵלוֹת שֶׁבְּקֶרֶב הַיְּהוּדִים
beyichud mishum she'attah baki bechol hamminhagim vehashe'elot shebbekerev hayehudim
especially because thou art expert in all customs and questions which are among the Jews:

לְפִיכָךְ מְבַקֵּשׁ אֲנִי מִמְּךָ לִשְׁמֹעַ אוֹתִי בְּאֹרֶךְ־רוּחַ
lefichach mevakkesh ani mimmecha lishmoa oti be'orech-ruach
wherefore I beseech thee to hear me patiently.

וּבְכֵן, כָּל הַיְּהוּדִים יוֹדְעִים אֶת דַּרְכֵי חַיַּי מִתְּקוּפַת נְעוּרַי
uvechen, kol hayehudim yode'im et drchei chayai mittekufat ne'urai
My manner of life then from my youth up,

מַעֲשֵׂי הַשְּׁלִיחִים

אֲנִי לֹא הִתְמַצֵּאתִי בַּחֲקִירַת הָעִנְיָנִים הָאֵלֶּה
ani lo hitmatzeti bachakirat ha'inyanim ha'elleh
And I, being perplexed how to inquire concerning these things,

וְשָׁאַלְתִּי אִם הוּא רוֹצֶה לַעֲלוֹת לִירוּשָׁלַיִם וּלְהִשָּׁפֵט שָׁם עַל הַדְּבָרִים הָאֵלֶּה
vesha'alti im hu rotzeh la'alot liyerushalayim ulehishafet sham al haddevarim ha'elleh
asked whether he would go to Jerusalem and there be judged of these matters.

אַךְ הוֹאִיל וְשָׁאוּל עִרְעֵר כְּדֵי שֶׁיִּשְׁמְרוּהוּ עַד לְהַחְלָטַת הַקֵּיסָר,
ach ho'il vesha'ul ir'er kedei sheyishmeruhu ad lehachlatat hakkeisar,
But when Paul had appealed to be kept for the decision of the emperor,

צִוִּיתִי לִשְׁמֹר אוֹתוֹ עַד אֲשֶׁר אֶשְׁלַח אוֹתוֹ אֶל הוֹד מַלְכוּתוֹ
tzivviti lishmor oto ad asher eshlach oto el hod malchuto
I commanded him to be kept till I should send him to Cæsar.

אָמַר אַגְרִיפַּס אֶל פֶסְטוֹס: גַּם אֲנִי חָפַצְתִּי לִשְׁמֹעַ אֶת הָאִישׁ. הֵשִׁיב פֶסְטוֹס: מָחָר תִּשְׁמַע אוֹתוֹ
amar agripas el festos: gam ani chafatzti lishmoa et ha'ish. heshiv festos: machar tishma oto
And Agrippa said unto Festus, I also could wish to hear the man myself. To-morrow, saith he, thou shalt hear him.

לְמָחֳרָת בָּאוּ אַגְרִיפַּס וּבֶרְנִיקָה בְּרֹב הָדָר
lemacharat ba'u agripas uvernikah berov hadar
So on the morrow, when Agrippa was come, and Bernice, with great pomp,

וְנִכְנְסוּ לָאוּלָם
venichnesu la'ulam
and they were entered into the place of hearing

עִם שָׂרֵי הָאֶלֶף וְנִכְבַּדֵּי הָעִיר, וּפֶסְטוֹס צִוָּה לְהָבִיא אֶת שָׁאוּל
im sarei ha'elef venichbaddei ha'ir, ufestos tzivvah lehavi et sha'ul
with the chief captains and the principal men of the city, at the command of Festus Paul was brought in.

אָמַר פֶסְטוֹס: אַגְרִיפַּס הַמֶּלֶךְ וְכָל הָאֲנָשִׁים הַנִּמְצָאִים אִתָּנוּ, אַתֶּם רוֹאִים אֶת הָאִישׁ הַזֶּה
amar festos: agripas hammelech vechol ha'anashim hannimtza'im ittanu, attem ro'im et ha'ish hazzeh
And Festus saith, King Agrippa, and all men who are here present with us, ye behold this man,

אֲשֶׁר בִּגְלָלוֹ פָּנוּ אֵלַי כָּל קְהַל הַיְּהוּדִים, גַּם בִּירוּשָׁלַיִם וְגַם פֹּה
asher biglalo panu elai kol kehal hayehudim, gam biyerushalayim vegam poh
about whom all the multitude of the Jews made suit to me, both at Jerusalem and here,

וְצָעֲקוּ שֶׁאֵינוֹ רָאוּי לִחְיוֹת עוֹד
vetza'aku she'eino ra'ui lichyot od
crying that he ought not to live any longer.

אֲנִי נוֹכַחְתִּי כִּי לֹא עָשָׂה שׁוּם דָּבָר הַמְחַיֵּב מָוֶת
ani nochachti ki lo asah shum davar hamchayev mavet
But I found that he had committed nothing worthy of death:

מַעֲשֵׂי הַשְּׁלִיחִים

כְּרְבוֹת יְמֵי שֶׁהָיָתָם שָׁם סִפֵּר פֶסְטוֹס לַמֶּלֶךְ עַל־אֹדוֹת שָׁאוּל וְאָמַר
kirvot yemei shehiyatam sham sipper festos lammelech al-'odot sha'ul ve'amar
And as they tarried there many days, Festus laid Paul's case before the king, saying,

יֵשׁ אִישׁ אֶחָד אֲשֶׁר פֶלִיקֶס הִשְׁאִיר אוֹתוֹ בַּמַּאֲסָר
yesh ish echad asher felikes hish'ir oto bamma'asar
There is a certain man left a prisoner by Felix;

כַּאֲשֶׁר הָיִיתִי בִּירוּשָׁלַיִם הוֹדִיעוּ לִי רָאשֵׁי הַכֹּהֲנִים וְזִקְנֵי הַיְהוּדִים עַל־אֹדוֹתָיו
ka'asher hayiti biyerushalayim hodi'u li rashei hakkohanim veziknei hayehudim al-'odotav
about whom, when I was at Jerusalem, the chief priests and the elders of the Jews informed me,

וּבִקְשׁוּ אֶת הַרְשָׁעָתוֹ
uvikshu et harsha'ato
asking for sentence against him.

אָמַרְתִּי לָהֶם שֶׁאֵין הָרוֹמִים נוֹהֲגִים לְהַסְגִּיר אָדָם נֶאֱשָׁם
amarti lahem she'ein haromim nohagim lehasgir adam ne'esham
To whom I answered, that it is not the custom of the Romans to give up any man,

בְּטֶרֶם יַעֲמֹד מוּל הַמַּאֲשִׁימִים
beterem ya'amod mul hamma'ashimim
before that the accused have the accusers face to face,

וְתִנָּתֵן לוֹ אֶפְשָׁרוּת לְהָגֵן עַל עַצְמוֹ מִפְּנֵי הָהַאֲשָׁמָה
vetinnaten lo efsharut lehagen al atzmo mippenei haha'ashamah
and have had opportunity to make his defence concerning the matter laid against him.

לָכֵן כְּשֶׁבָּאוּ יַחַד הֵנָּה לֹא הִתְמַהְמַהְתִּי,
lachen keshebba'u yachad hennah lo hitmahmahti
When therefore they were come together here, I made no delay,

וּלְמָחֳרָת יָשַׁבְתִּי עַל כֵּס הַמִּשְׁפָּט וְצִוִּיתִי לְהָבִיא אֶת הָאִישׁ
ulemochorat yashavti al kes hammishpat vetzivviti lehavi et ha'ish
but on the next day sat on the judgment-seat, and commanded the man to be brought.

אָז עָמְדוּ מַאֲשִׁימָיו וְלֹא הֵבִיאוּ נֶגְדּוֹ דָבָר מִן הַדְּבָרִים הָרָעִים שֶׁחָשַׁדְתִּי
az amdu ma'ashimav velo hevi'u negdo davar min haddevarim hara'im shachashadti
Concerning whom, when the accusers stood up, they brought no charge of such evil things as I supposed;

אַךְ הָיוּ לָהֶם כַּמָּה חִלּוּקֵי דֵעוֹת אִתּוֹ עַל הַדָּת שֶׁלָּהֶם וְעַל אֵיזֶה יֵשׁוּעַ
ach hayu lahem kammah chillukei de'ot itto al haddat shellahem ve'al eizeh yeshua
but had certain questions against him of their own religion, and of one Jesus,

שֶׁמֵּת, אֲשֶׁר שָׁאוּל טָעַן שֶׁהוּא חַי
shemmet, asher sha'ul ta'an shehu chai
who was dead, whom Paul affirmed to be alive.

מַעֲשֵׂי הַשְּׁלִיחִים

וְהֶאֱשִׁימוּ אוֹתוֹ בְּאַשְׁמוֹת רַבּוֹת וְקָשׁוֹת אֲשֶׁר לֹא יָכְלוּ לְהוֹכִיחַ אוֹתָן
vehe'eshimu oto ba'ashamot rabbot vekashot asher lo yachlu lehochiach otan
bringing against him many and grievous charges which they could not prove;

הֵגֵן שָׁאוּל עַל עַצְמוֹ וְאָמַר
hegen sha'ul al atzmo ve'amar
while Paul said in his defence,

לֹא חָטָאתִי בִּמְאוּמָה לְחֻקֵּי הַיְּהוּדִים, אַף לֹא לַמִּקְדָּשׁ וְלֹא לַקֵּיסָר
lo chatati bim'umah lechukkei hayehudim, af lo lammikdash velo lakkeisar
Neither against the law of the Jews, nor against the temple, nor against Cæsar, have I sinned at all.

אַךְ פֶּסְטוֹס, בְּחֶפְצוֹ לְהַרְאוֹת חֶסֶד לְרָאשֵׁי הַיְּהוּדִים, פָּנָה אֶל שָׁאוּל וְשָׁאַל
ach festos, becheftzo lehar'ot chesed lerashei hayehudim, panah el sha'ul vesha'al
But Festus, desiring to gain favor with the Jews, answered Paul and said,

הַאִם אַתָּה רוֹצֶה לַעֲלוֹת לִירוּשָׁלַיִם וּלְהִשָּׁפֵט שָׁם לְפָנַי עַל הַדְּבָרִים הָאֵלֶּה
ha'im attah rotzeh la'alot liyerushalayim ulehishafet sham lefanai al haddevarim ha'elleh
Wilt thou go up to Jerusalem, and there be judged of these things before me?

עָנָה שָׁאוּל: לִפְנֵי כֵּס הַמִּשְׁפָּט שֶׁל הַקֵּיסָר אֲנִי עוֹמֵד וְשָׁם עָלַי לְהִשָּׁפֵט
anah sha'ul: lifnei kes hammishpat shel hakkeisar ani omed vesham alai lehishafet
But Paul said, I am standing before Cæsar's judgment-seat, where I ought to be judged:

לֹא עָשִׂיתִי עָוֶל לְאַף יְהוּדִי, וְזֹאת גַּם אַתָּה יוֹדֵעַ הֵיטֵב
lo asiti avel le'af yehudi, vezot gam attah yodea heitev
to the Jews have I done no wrong, as thou also very well knowest.

אִם אָמְנָם גָּרַמְתִּי עָוֶל וְעָשִׂיתִי דָּבָר הַמְחַיֵּב מָוֶת הַמְחַיֵּב מָוֶת אֵינֶנִּי מְסָרֵב לָמוּת
im amenam garamti avel ve'asiti davar hamchayev mavet einenni mesarev lamut
If then I am a wrong-doer, and have committed anything worthy of death, I refuse not to die;

אֲבָל אִם אֵין מְאוּמָה בַּמֶּה שֶׁאֵלֶּה מַאֲשִׁימִים אוֹתִי, אִישׁ לֹא יוּכַל לְהַסְגִּירֵנִי בְּיָדָם. אֶל הַקֵּיסָר אֲנִי פוֹנֶה
aval im ein me'umah bemah she'elleh ma'ashimim oti, ish lo yuchal lehasgireni beyadam. el hakkeisar ani poneh
but if none of those things is true whereof these accuse me, no man can give me up unto them. I appeal unto Cæsar.

נוֹעַץ פֶּסְטוֹס עִם הַיּוֹעֲצִים וְהֵשִׁיב
no'atz festos im hayo'atzim veheshiv
Then Festus, when he had conferred with the council, answered,

פָּנִיתָ אֶל הַקֵּיסָר, אֶל הַקֵּיסָר תֵּלֵךְ
panita el hakkeisar, el hakkeisar telech
Thou hast appealed unto Cæsar: unto Cæsar shalt thou go.

יָמִים מִסְפָּר אַחֲרֵי כֵן בָּאוּ אַגְרִיפַּס הַמֶּלֶךְ וּבֶרְנִיקָה לְקֵיסַרְיָה לְבָרֵךְ אֶת פֶּסְטוֹס
yamim mispar acharei chen ba'u agripas hammelech uvernikah lekeisaryah levarech et festos
Now when certain days were passed, Agrippa the king and Bernice arrived at Cæsarea, and saluted Festus.

מַעֲשֵׂי הַשְּׁלִיחִים

כה

פֶסְטוֹס הִגִּיעַ לַמְּדִינָה וּלְאַחַר שְׁלוֹשָׁה יָמִים עָלָה מִקֵּיסָרְיָה לִירוּשָׁלַיִם
festos higgia lammedinah ule'achar shloshah yamim alah mikkeisaryah liyerushalayim
Festus therefore, having come into the province, after three days went up to Jerusalem from Cæsarea.

שָׁם הוֹדִיעוּ לוֹ רָאשֵׁי הַכֹּהֲנִים וְרָאשֵׁי הַיְּהוּדִים אֶת עִנְיָנָם נֶגֶד שָׁאוּל
sham hodi'u lo rashei hakkohanim verashei hayehudim et inyanam neged sha'ul
And the chief priests and the principal men of the Jews informed him against Paul; and they besought him,

הֵם הִפְצִירוּ בּוֹ וּבִקְשׁוּ מִמֶּנּוּ שֶׁיַּעֲשֶׂה עִמָּהֶם חֶסֶד וְיִשְׁלַח לַהֲבִיאוֹ לִירוּשָׁלַיִם
hem hiftziru bo uviksho mimmennu sheya'aseh immahem chesed veyishlach lahavi'o liyerushalayim
asking a favor against him, that he would send for him to Jerusalem;

שֶׁכֵּן הֵם הִתְנַכְּלוּ לוֹ לְהָרְגוֹ בַּדֶּרֶךְ
shekken hem hitnakkelu lo leharego badderech
laying a plot to kill him on the way.

הֵשִׁיב פֶסְטוֹס וְאָמַר
heshiv festos ve'amar
Howbeit Festus answered,

שָׁאוּל עָצוּר בְּקֵיסָרְיָה וַאֲנִי עוֹמֵד לָצֵאת לְשָׁם בְּקָרוֹב
sha'ul atzur bekeisaryah va'ani omed latzet lesham bekarov
that Paul was kept in charge at Cæsarea, and that he himself was about to depart thither shortly.

לָכֵן יֵרְדוּ נָא אִתִּי בַּעֲלֵי הַסַּמְכוּת שֶׁבָּכֶם
lachen yeredu na itti ba'alei hassamchut shebbachem
Let them therefore, saith he, that are of power among you go down with me,

וְאִם יֵשׁ עָווֹן בָּאִישׁ, שֶׁיִּטְעֲנוּ נֶגְדּוֹ
ve'im yesh avon ba'ish, sheyit'anu negdo
and if there is anything amiss in the man, let them accuse him.

הוּא שָׁהָה שָׁם לֹא יוֹתֵר מִשְּׁמוֹנָה אוֹ עֲשָׂרָה יָמִים. לְאַחַר מִכֵּן יָרַד לְקֵיסָרְיָה
hu shahah sham lo yoter mishemonah o asarah yamim. le'achar mikken yarad lekeisaryah
And when he had tarried among them not more than eight or ten days, he went down unto Cæsarea;

וּלְמָחֳרָת יָשַׁב עַל כֵּס הַמִּשְׁפָּט וְצִוָּה לְהָבִיא אֶת שָׁאוּל
ulemochorat yashav al kes hammishpat vetzivvah lehavi et sha'ul
and on the morrow he sat on the judgment-seat, and commanded Paul to be brought.

כַּאֲשֶׁר בָּא נִצְּבוּ סְבִיבוֹ הַיְּהוּדִים שֶׁיָּרְדוּ מִירוּשָׁלַיִם,
ka'asher ba nitzevu sevivo hayehudim sheyaredu miyerushalayim
And when he was come, the Jews that had come down from Jerusalem stood round about him,

מַעֲשֵׂי הַשְּׁלִיחִים

כַּאֲשֶׁר יֵרֵד אֵלַי לִיסִיאַס שַׂר הָאֶלֶף אַחְלִיט בְּנוֹגֵעַ לְעִנְיָנְכֶם
ka'asher yered elai lisi'as sar ha'elef achlit benogea le'inyanchem
When Lysias the chief captain shall come down, I will determine your matter.

הוּא צִוָּה עַל שַׂר הַמֵּאָה לָשִׂים עַל שָׁאוּל מִשְׁמָר, אַךְ לְהָקֵל עָלָיו
hu tzivvah al sar hamme'ah lasim al sha'ul mishmar, ach lehakel alav
And he gave order to the centurion that he should be kept in charge, and should have indulgence;

וְלֹא לִמְנֹעַ אִישׁ מֵאֲנָשָׁיו מִלְּשָׁרֵת אוֹתוֹ
velo limnoa ish me'anashav millesharet oto
and not to forbid any of his friends to minister unto him.

אַחֲרֵי כַּמָּה יָמִים בָּא פֶלִיקְס עִם דְּרוּסִילָה אִשְׁתּוֹ, שֶׁהָיְתָה יְהוּדִיָּה
acharei kammah yamim ba felikes im derusilah ishto, shehayetah yehudiyah
But after certain days, Felix came with Drusilla, his wife, who was a Jewess,

הוּא שָׁלַח לִקְרֹא לְשָׁאוּל וְשָׁמַע אוֹתוֹ עַל־דְּבַר הָאֱמוּנָה בַּמָּשִׁיחַ יֵשׁוּעַ
hu shalach likro lesha'ul veshama oto al-devar ha'emunah bammashiach yeshua
and sent for Paul, and heard him concerning the faith in Christ Jesus.

כְּשֶׁדִּבֵּר עַל הַצֶּדֶק וְעַל כִּבּוּשׁ הַיֵּצֶר וְעַל הַדִּין הֶעָתִיד לָבוֹא, פָּחַד פֶלִיקְס וְאָמַר:
kesheddibber al hatzedek ve'al kibbush hayetzer ve'al haddin he'atid lavo, pachad felikes ve'amar
And as he reasoned of righteousness, and self-control, and the judgment to come, Felix was terrified, and answered,

לֵךְ לְעֵת עַתָּה, אֲבָל כְּשֶׁאֶמְצָא לִי פְּנַאי אֶקְרָא לְךָ
lech le'et attah, aval keshe'emtza li pena ekra lecha
Go thy way for this time; and when I have a convenient season, I will call thee unto me.

בְּאָמְרוֹ זֹאת גַּם קִוָּה שֶׁשָּׁאוּל יִתֵּן לוֹ כֶּסֶף
be'amero zot gam kivvah shesha'ul yitten lo kesef
He hoped withal that money would be given him of Paul:

לָכֵן קָרָא לוֹ פְּעָמִים רַבּוֹת וְשׂוֹחֵחַ אִתּוֹ
lachen kara lo pe'amim rabbot vesochach itto
wherefore also he sent for him the oftener, and communed with him.

אַחֲרֵי שְׁנָתַיִם יָרַשׁ פּוֹרְקֵיוֹס פֶסְטוֹס אֶת מְקוֹמוֹ שֶׁל פֶלִיקְס
acharei shenatayim yarash porekeyos festos et mekomo shel felikes
But when two years were fulfilled, Felix was succeeded by Porcius Festus;

רָצָה פֶלִיקְס לְהַרְאוֹת חֶסֶד לְרָאשֵׁי הַיְּהוּדִים וְעָזַב אֶת שָׁאוּל בַּמַּאֲסָר
ratzah felikes lehar'ot chesed lerashei hayehudim ve'azav et sha'ul bamma'asar
and desiring to gain favor with the Jews, Felix left Paul in bonds.

מַעֲשֵׂי הַשְּׁלִיחִים

וּמַאֲמִין בְּכָל הַכָּתוּב בַּתּוֹרָה וּבַנְּבִיאִים
uma'amin bechol hakkatuv battorah uvannevi'im
believing all things which are according to the law, and which are written in the prophets;

וְיֵשׁ לִי תִּקְוָה בֵּאלֹהִים
veyesh li tikvah be'elohim
having hope toward God,

שֶׁתִּהְיֶה תְּחִיָּה הֵן שֶׁל הַצַּדִּיקִים וְהֵן שֶׁל הָרְשָׁעִים, דָּבָר שֶׁגַּם הֵם מְחַכִּים לוֹ
shettihyeh techiyah hen shel hatzaddikim vehen shel haresha'im, davar sheggam hem mechakkim lo
which these also themselves look for, that there shall be a resurrection both of the just and unjust.

לָכֵן אֲנִי גַּם מִתְאַמֵּץ שֶׁיִּהְיֶה לִי מַצְפּוּן נָקִי לִפְנֵי אֱלֹהִים וּבְנֵי אָדָם בְּכָל עֵת
lachen ani gam mit'ammetz sheyihyeh li matzpun naki lifnei elohim uvenei adam vechol et
Herein I also exercise myself to have a conscience void of offence toward God and men always.

וְהִנֵּה אַחֲרֵי שָׁנִים רַבּוֹת בָּאתִי לְהָבִיא נְדָבוֹת לְעַמִּי וְכֵן גַּם קָרְבָּנוֹת
vehinneh acharei shanim rabbot bati lehavi nedavot le'ammi vechen gam korbanot
Now after some years I came to bring alms to my nation, and offerings:

וּבַהֲבִיאִי אֶת אֵלֶּה מְצָאוּנִי בַּמִּקְדָּשׁ לְאַחַר שֶׁנִּטְהַרְתִּי; לֹא הָיִיתִי כָּרוּךְ לֹא בֶּהָמוֹן וְלֹא בִּמְהוּמָה
uvahavi'i et elleh metza'uni bammikdash le'achar shennit'harti; lo hayiti karuch lo behamon velo bimhumah
amidst which they found me purified in the temple, with no crowd, nor yet with tumult:

אֲבָל הָיוּ כַּמָּה יְהוּדִים מֵאַסְיָה
aval hayu kammah yehudim me'asyah
but there were certain Jews from Asia—

וְהַלָּלוּ הָיוּ צְרִיכִים לַעֲמֹד לְפָנֶיךָ וּלְהַאֲשִׁימֵנִי אִם יֵשׁ לָהֶם מַשֶּׁהוּ נֶגְדִּי
vehallalu hayu tzerichim la'amod lefaneicha uleha'ashimeni im yesh lahem mashehu negdi
who ought to have been here before thee, and to make accusation, if they had aught against me.

אוֹ שֶׁיַּגִּידוּ אֵלֶּה אֲשֶׁר כָּאן, אֵיזֶה עָוֶל מָצְאוּ בִּי כַּאֲשֶׁר עָמַדְתִּי לִפְנֵי הַסַּנְהֶדְרִין
o sheyaggidu elleh asher kan, eizeh avel matze'u bi ka'asher amadti lifnei hassanhedrin
Or else let these men themselves say what wrong-doing they found when I stood before the council,

מִלְּבַד הַהַכְרָזָה הָאַחַת הַזֹּאת שֶׁהִכְרַזְתִּי בְּעָמְדִי בֵּינֵיהֶם
millevad hahachrazah ha'achat hazzot shehichrazti be'omdi beineihem
except it be for this one voice, that I cried standing among them,

עַל תְּחִיַּת הַמֵּתִים אֲנִי נִשְׁפָּט הַיּוֹם לִפְנֵיכֶם
al techiyat hammetim ani nishpat hayom lifneichem
Touching the resurrection of the dead I am called in question before you this day.

פֶלִיקְס, שֶׁהָיְתָה לוֹ יְדִיעָה בְּרוּרָה עַל אוֹתָהּ דֶּרֶךְ, דָּחָה אֶת הַדִּיּוּן בְּעִנְיָנָם בְּאָמְרוֹ:
felikes, shehayetah lo yedi'ah berurah al otah derech, dachah et haddiyun be'inyanam be'omro
But Felix, having more exact knowledge concerning the Way, deferred them, saying,

מַעֲשֵׂי הַשְּׁלִיחִים

גַּם נִסָּה לְחַלֵּל אֶת הַמִּקְדָּשׁ, אַךְ תְּפַסְנוּ אוֹתוֹ
gam nissah lechallel et hammikdash, ach tafasnu oto
who moreover assayed to profane the temple: on whom also we laid hold:

אִם תַּחְקֹר אוֹתוֹ תּוּכַל לָדַעַת בְּעַצְמְךָ מַה כָּל הַדְּבָרִים שֶׁבָּהֶם אֲנַחְנוּ מַאֲשִׁימִים אוֹתוֹ
im tachakor oto tuchal lada'at be'atzmecha mah kol haddevarim shebbahem anachnu ma'ashimim oto
from whom thou wilt be able, by examining him thyself, to take knowledge of all these things whereof we accuse him.

גַּם הַיְהוּדִים הָעוֹמְדִים שָׁם הִסְכִּימוּ אִתּוֹ, בְּאָמְרָם שֶׁכָּךְ הֵם הַדְּבָרִים
gam hayehudim ha'omedim sham hiskimu itto, be'ameram shekkach hem haddevarim
And the Jews also joined in the charge, affirming that these things were so.

רָמַז הַנָּצִיב לְשָׁאוּל לְדַבֵּר וְשָׁאוּל הֵשִׁיב
ramaz hannatziv lesha'ul ledabber vesha'ul heshiv
And when the governor had beckoned unto him to speak, Paul answered,

אֲנִי יוֹדֵעַ כִּי שָׁנִים רַבּוֹת אַתָּה הַשּׁוֹפֵט שֶׁל הָאֻמָּה הַזֹּאת,
ani yodea ki shanim rabbot attah hashofet shel ha'ummah hazzot,
Forasmuch as I know that thou hast been of many years a judge unto this nation,

לָכֵן בְּבִטָּחוֹן אֲנִי מֵגֵן עַל עַצְמִי וְכָל מַה שֶּׁנּוֹגֵעַ לְעִנְיָנִי
lachen bevittachon ani megen al atzmi vechal mah shennogea le'inyani
I cheerfully make my defence:

יָכוֹל אַתָּה לְהִוָּכַח
yachol attah lehivvachach
seeing that thou canst take knowledge

שֶׁלֹּא עָבְרוּ יוֹתֵר מִשְּׁנֵים־עָשָׂר יוֹם מֵאָז שֶׁעָלִיתִי לִירוּשָׁלַיִם לְהִשְׁתַּחֲוֹת לַאדֹנָי
shello averu yoter misheneim-'asar yom me'az she'aliti liyerushalayim lehishtachavot la'adonai
that it is not more than twelve days since I went up to worship at Jerusalem:

וְלֹא בְּבֵית הַמִּקְדָּשׁ מְצָאוּנִי מִתְוַכֵּחַ עִם אִישׁ אוֹ גּוֹרֵם לְהִתְפָּרְעוּת הָמוֹן
velo beveit hammikdash metza'uni mitvakkeach im ish o gorem lehitpare'ut hamon
and neither in the temple did they find me disputing with any man or stirring up a crowd,

אַף לֹא בְּבָתֵּי כְּנֶסֶת וְלֹא בָּעִיר
af lo bevattei keneset velo ba'ir
nor in the synagogues, nor in the city.

גַּם אֵינָם יְכוֹלִים לְהָבִיא לְךָ רְאָיָה לַדְּבָרִים שֶׁהֵם טוֹעֲנִים נֶגְדִּי כָּעֵת
gam einam yecholim lehavi lecha re'ayah laddevarim shehem to'anim negdi ka'et
Neither can they prove to thee the things whereof they now accuse me.

אֲבָל אֶת זֶה אֲנִי מוֹדֶה לְפָנֶיךָ: בַּדֶּרֶךְ הַנִּקְרֵאת בְּפִיהֶם כַּת עוֹבֵד אֲנִי אֶת אֱלֹהֵי אֲבוֹתֵינוּ
aval et zeh ani modeh lefaneicha: badderech hannikret befihem kat oved ani et elohei avoteinu
But this I confess unto thee, that after the Way which they call a sect, so serve I the God of our fathers,

מַעֲשֵׂי הַשְּׁלִיחִים

אֵלֶּה בָּאוּ לְקֵיסַרְיָה, מָסְרוּ אֶת הָאִגֶּרֶת לַנָּצִיב וְהֶעֱמִידוּ אֶת שָׁאוּל לְפָנָיו
elleh ba'u lekeisaryah, maseru et ha'iggeret lannatziv vehe'emidu et sha'ul lefanav
and they, when they came to Cæsarea and delivered the letter to the governor, presented Paul also before him.

הַנָּצִיב קָרָא אֶת הָאִגֶּרֶת וְשָׁאַל מֵאֵיזֶה אֵזוֹר מִמְשָׁל הוּא. כְּשָׁמְעוֹ שֶׁהוּא מִקִּילִיקְיָה אָמַר
hannatziv kara et ha'iggeret vesha'al me'eizeh ezor mimshal hu. keshame'o shehu mikkilikeyah amar
And when he had read it, he asked of what province he was; and when he understood that he was of Cilicia,

אֶשְׁמַע אוֹתְךָ כַּאֲשֶׁר גַּם מַאֲשִׁימֶיךָ יָבוֹאוּ הֵנָּה, וְצִוָּה לְהַחֲזִיקוֹ בְּאַרְמוֹן הוֹרְדוֹס
eshma otecha ka'asher gam ma'ashimeicha yavo'u hennah, vetzivvah lehachaziko be'armon horedos
I will hear thee fully, said he, when thine accusers also are come: and he commanded him to be kept in Herod's palace.

כד

כַּעֲבֹר חֲמִשָּׁה יָמִים יָרַד חֲנַנְיָה הַכֹּהֵן הַגָּדוֹל עִם כַּמָּה זְקֵנִים
ka'avor chamishah yamim yarad chananyah hakkohen haggadol im kammah zkenim
And after five days the high priest Ananias came down with certain elders,

וּבַעַל־דְּבָרִים אֶחָד, טֶרְטוּלוֹס שְׁמוֹ, וְהוֹדִיעוּ לַנָּצִיב אֶת טַעֲנָתָם נֶגֶד שָׁאוּל
uva'al-devarim echad, tertulos shemo, vehodi'u lannatziv et ta'anatam neged sha'ul
and with an orator, one Tertullus; and they informed the governor against Paul.

לְאַחַר שֶׁקָּרְאוּ לְשָׁאוּל הֵחֵל טֶרְטוּלוֹס בַּתְּבִיעָה וְאָמַר
le'achar shekkare'u lesha'ul hechel tertulos battvi'ah ve'amar
And when he was called, Tertullus began to accuse him, saying,

הוֹד מַעֲלָתְךָ, פֶלִיקְס, שָׁלוֹם לְמַכְבִּיר הִשַּׂגְנוּ הוֹדוֹת לְךָ וְתִקּוּנִים נַעֲשׂוּ לְמַעַן הָעָם הַזֶּה בְּהַשְׁגָּחָתְךָ. בְּכָל עֵת וּבְכָל מָקוֹם אֲנַחְנוּ מְקַדְּמִים זֹאת בִּמְלוֹא תּוֹדָה
hod ma'alatecha, felikes, shalom lemachbir hishogenu hodot lecha vetikkunim na'asu lema'an ha'am hazzeh behashgachatecha. bechol et uvechol makom anachnu mekaddemim zot bimlo todah
Seeing that by thee we enjoy much peace, and that by thy providence evils are corrected for this nation, we accept it in all ways and in all places, most excellent Felix, with all thankfulness.

אֲבָל כְּדֵי שֶׁלֹּא אוֹסִיף לִהְיוֹת לְךָ לְטֹרַח, מְבַקֵּשׁ אֲנִי מִמְּךָ לִשְׁמֹעַ אוֹתָנוּ בְּחֶמְלָתְךָ וּנְדַבֵּר בְּקִצְרָה
aval kedei shello osif lihyot lecha letorach, mevakkesh ani mimmcha lishmoa otanu bechemlatecha unedabber biktzarah
But, that I be not further tedious unto thee, I entreat thee to hear us of thy clemency a few words.

מָצָאנוּ אֶת הָאִישׁ הַזֶּה בִּבְחִינַת מַגֵּפָה
matzanu et ha'ish hazzeh bivchinat maggefah
For we have found this man a pestilent fellow,

מְעוֹרֵר מְהוּמוֹת בְּקֶרֶב כָּל הַיְּהוּדִים בְּכָל הָעוֹלָם וּמַנְהִיג שֶׁל כַּת הַנָּצְרִים
me'orer mehumot bekerev kol hayehudim bechol ha'olam umanhig shel kat hannatzerim
and a mover of insurrections among all the Jews throughout the world, and a ringleader of the sect of the Nazarenes:

מַעֲשֵׂי הַשְּׁלִיחִים

וּתְנוּ בְהֵמוֹת לְהַרְכִּיב אֶת שָׁאוּל וְלַהֲבִיאוֹ בְּשָׁלוֹם אֶל פֶּלִיקְס הַנָּצִיב
utenu behemot leharkiv et sha'ul velahavi'o beshalom el feliks hannatziv
and he bade them provide beasts, that they might set Paul thereon, and bring him safe unto Felix the governor.

כְּמוֹ כֵן כָּתַב אִגֶּרֶת בָּזֶה הַלָּשׁוֹן
kemo chen katav iggeret bezeh hallashon
And he wrote a letter after this form:

קְלוֹדְיוֹס לִיסִיאַס אֶל הוֹד מַעֲלָתוֹ הַנָּצִיב פֶּלִיקְס - שָׁלוֹם
kelodeyos lisi'as el hod ma'alato hannatziv feliks - shalom
Claudius Lysias unto the most excellent governor Felix, greeting.

אֶת הָאִישׁ הַזֶּה תָּפַס הֲמוֹן יְהוּדִי וְעָמַד לַהֲרֹג אוֹתוֹ
et ha'ish hazzeh tafas hamon yehudi ve'amad laharog oto
This man was seized by the Jews, and was about to be slain of them,

בָּאתִי עִם הַחַיָּלִים וְחִלַּצְתִּי אוֹתוֹ בְּהִוָּדַע לִי שֶׁהוּא רוֹמִי
bati im hachayalim vechillatzti oto behivvada li shehu romi
when I came upon them with the soldiers and rescued him, having learned that he was a Roman.

הוֹאִיל וְחָפַצְתִּי לָדַעַת מַדּוּעַ הֶאֱשִׁימוּ אוֹתוֹ, הוֹרַדְתִּיו אֶל הַסַּנְהֶדְרִין שֶׁלָּהֶם
ho'il vechafatzti lada'at maddua he'eshimu oto, horadtiv el hassanhedrin shellahem
And desiring to know the cause wherefore they accused him, I brought him down unto their council:

וּמָצָאתִי שֶׁהֶאֱשִׁימוּ אוֹתוֹ בְּעִנְיָנִים הַנּוֹגְעִים לְתוֹרָתָם
umatzati shehe'eshimu oto be'inyanim hannoge'im letoratam
whom I found to be accused about questions of their law,

אַךְ לֹא הָיְתָה שׁוּם אַשְׁמָה שֶׁתְּחַיֵּב מָוֶת אוֹ מַאֲסָר
ach lo hayetah shum ashmah shettechayev mavet o ma'asar
but to have nothing laid to his charge worthy of death or of bonds.

כַּאֲשֶׁר הֻגַּד לִי כִּי נִרְקֶמֶת מְזִמָּה נֶגֶד הָאִישׁ,
ka'asher huggad li ki nirkemet mezzimmah neged ha'ish
And when it was shown to me that there would be a plot against the man,

שְׁלַחְתִּיו אֵלֶיךָ מִיָּד וְגַם צִוִּיתִי עַל מַאֲשִׁימָיו לוֹמַר לְפָנֶיךָ מַה שֶּׁיֵּשׁ לָהֶם לוֹמַר עָלָיו. הֱיֵה שָׁלוֹם
shelachtiv eleicha miyad vegam tzivviti al ma'ashimav lomar lefaneicha mah sheyesh lahem lomar alav
I sent him to thee forthwith, charging his accusers also to speak against him before thee.

עַל־פִּי הַפְּקֻדָּה שֶׁצֻּוּוּ לָקְחוּ הַחַיָּלִים אֶת שָׁאוּל וֶהֱבִיאוּהוּ בַּלַּיְלָה לְאַנְטִיפַּטְרִיס
al-pi happekuddah shetzuvvu lakechu hachayalim et sha'ul vehevi'uhu ballaylah le'antipatris
So the soldiers, as it was commanded them, took Paul and brought him by night to Antipatris.

לְמָחֳרָת הִנִּיחוּ לַפָּרָשִׁים לְהַמְשִׁיךְ אִתּוֹ וְחָזְרוּ לַמְּצוּדָה
lemochorat hinnichu lapparashim lehamshich itto vechazeru lammetzudah
But on the morrow they left the horsemen to go with him, and returned to the castle:

מַעֲשֵׂי הַשְּׁלִיחִים

הָאָסִיר שָׁאוּל קָרָא לִי וּבִקֵּשׁ מִמֶּנִּי לְהָבִיא אֵלֶיךָ אֶת הַבָּחוּר הַזֶּה,
ha'asir sha'ul kara li uvikkesh mimmenni lehavi eleicha et habbachur hazzeh,
Paul the prisoner called me unto him, and asked me to bring this young man unto thee,

כִּי יֵשׁ לוֹ אֵיזֶה דָּבָר לוֹמַר לְךָ
ki yesh lo eizeh davar lomar lecha
who hath something to say to thee.

הֶחֱזִיק שַׂר הָאֶלֶף בְּיָדוֹ, הוֹבִיל אוֹתוֹ הַצִּדָּה וְשָׁאַל: מַה יֵּשׁ לְךָ לְהוֹדִיעַ לִי
hechezik sar ha'elef beyado, hovil oto hatziddah vesha'al: mah yesh lecha lehodia li
And the chief captain took him by the hand, and going aside asked him privately, What is it that thou hast to tell me?

הֵשִׁיב הַבָּחוּר: רָאשֵׁי הַיְּהוּדִים נוֹעֲצוּ יַחְדָּיו לְבַקֵּשׁ מִמְּךָ לְהוֹרִיד מָחָר אֶת שָׁאוּל אֶל הַסַּנְהֶדְרִין
heshiv habbachur: rashei hayehudim no'atzu yachdav levakkesh mimmecha lehorid machar et sha'ul el hassanhedrin
And he said, The Jews have agreed to ask thee to bring down Paul tomorrow unto the council,

כְּאִלּוּ הֵם מִתְכַּוְּנִים לַחֲקֹר אֶת עִנְיָנוֹ בְּיֶתֶר דִּיּוּק
ke'illu hem mitkavvenim lachakor et inyano beyeter diyuk
as though thou wouldest inquire somewhat more exactly concerning him.

לָכֵן אַל נָא תִּשְׁמַע לָהֶם, כִּי יוֹתֵר מֵאַרְבָּעִים אִישׁ מֵהֶם אוֹרְבִים לוֹ
lachen al na tishma lahem, ki yoter me'arba'im ish mehem orevim lo
Do not thou therefore yield unto them: for there lie in wait for him of them more than forty men,

הַלָּלוּ קִבְּלוּ עֲלֵיהֶם בִּשְׁבוּעָה שֶׁלֹּא לֶאֱכֹל וְלֹא לִשְׁתּוֹת עַד שֶׁיַּהַרְגוּ אוֹתוֹ
hallalu kibbelu aleihem bishvu'ah shello le'echol velo lishtot ad sheyahargu oto
who have bound themselves under a curse, neither to eat nor to drink till they have slain him:

וְכָעֵת הֵם מוּכָנִים בְּצִפִּיָּה לְהַבְטָחָה מִמְּךָ
vecha'et hem muchanim betzippiyah lehavtachah mimmcha
and now are they ready, looking for the promise from thee.

שִׁלַּח שַׂר הָאֶלֶף אֶת הַבָּחוּר בְּצַוּוֹתוֹ עָלָיו: אַל תַּגִּיד לְאִישׁ שֶׁהוֹדַעְתָּ לִי אֶת הַדָּבָר הַזֶּה
shillach sar ha'elef et habbachur betzavvoto alav: al taggid le'ish shehoda'ta li et haddavar hazzeh
So the chief captain let the young man go, charging him, Tell no man that thou hast signified these things to me.

הוּא קָרָא לִשְׁנֵי שָׂרֵי מֵאוֹת וְאָמַר
hu kara lishnei sarei me'ot ve'amar
And he called unto him two of the centurions, and said,

הָכִינוּ מָאתַיִם חַיָּלִים כְּדֵי שֶׁיֵּצְאוּ בְּשָׁעָה תֵּשַׁע בַּלַּיְלָה וְיֵלְכוּ לְקֵיסַרְיָה
hachinu matayim chayalim kedei sheyetze'u besha'ah tesha ballaylah veyelechu lekeisaryah
Make ready two hundred soldiers to go as far as Cæsarea,

וְכֵן גַּם שִׁבְעִים פָּרָשִׁים וּמָאתַיִם נוֹשְׂאֵי כִּידוֹן
vechen gam shiv'im parashim umatayim nose'ei kidon
and horsemen threescore and ten, and spearmen two hundred, at the third hour of the night:

מַעֲשֵׂי הַשְּׁלִיחִים

כְּמוֹ שֶׁהֵעִידוֹתָ עָלַי בִּירוּשָׁלַיִם כָּךְ עָלֶיךָ לְהָעִיד גַּם בְּרוֹמָא
kemo sheha'idota alai biyerushalayim kach aleicha leha'id gam beroma
for as thou hast testified concerning me at Jerusalem, so must thou bear witness also at Rome.

בַּבֹּקֶר חָבְרוּ יְהוּדִים יַחַד וְקִבְּלוּ עֲלֵיהֶם בִּשְׁבוּעָה
babboker chavru yehudim yachad vekibblu aleihem bishvu'ah
And when it was day, the Jews banded together, and bound themselves under a curse,

שֶׁלֹּא יֹאכְלוּ וְלֹא יִשְׁתּוּ עַד אֲשֶׁר יַהַרְגוּ אֶת שָׁאוּל
shello yochelu velo yishtu ad asher yahargu et sha'ul
saying that they would neither eat nor drink till they had killed Paul.

מִסְפַּר הַמִּשְׁתַּתְּפִים בַּמְּזִמָּה הַזֹּאת עָלָה עַל אַרְבָּעִים
mispar hammishtattefim bammezimmah hazzot alah al arba'im
And they were more than forty that made this conspiracy.

הֵם בָּאוּ אֶל רָאשֵׁי הַכֹּהֲנִים וְאֶל הַזְּקֵנִים וְאָמְרוּ
hem ba'u el rashei hakkohanim ve'el hazzkenim ve'ameru
And they came to the chief priests and the elders, and said,

קִבַּלְנוּ עָלֵינוּ שְׁבוּעָה שֶׁלֹּא לִטְעֹם מְאוּמָה עַד שֶׁנַּהֲרֹג אֶת שָׁאוּל
kibbalnu aleinu shevu'ah shello lit'om me'umah ad shennaharog et sha'ul
We have bound ourselves under a great curse, to taste nothing until we have killed Paul.

וְעַכְשָׁו אַתֶּם וְהַסַּנְהֶדְרִין הַגִּידוּ לְשַׂר הָאֶלֶף שֶׁיּוֹרִיד אוֹתוֹ אֲלֵיכֶם
ve'achshav attem vehassanhedrin haggidu lesar ha'elef sheyorid oto aleichem
Now therefore do ye with the council signify to the chief captain that he bring him down unto you,

כְּאִלּוּ שֶׁכַּוָּנַתְכֶם לְבָרֵר בְּיֶתֶר דִּיּוּק אֶת עִנְיָנוֹ, וַאֲנַחְנוּ מוּכָנִים לַהֲרֹג אוֹתוֹ לִפְנֵי שֶׁיַּגִּיעַ
ke'illu shekkavvanatchem levarer beyeter diyuk et inyano, va'anachnu muchanim laharog oto lifnei sheyaggia
as though ye would judge of his case more exactly: and we, before he comes near, are ready to slay him.

כַּאֲשֶׁר שָׁמַע בֶּן אֲחוֹתוֹ שֶׁל שָׁאוּל עַל־דְּבַר הַמַּאֲרָב הָלַךְ וְנִכְנַס לַמְּצוּדָה וְהוֹדִיעַ לְשָׁאוּל
ka'asher shama ben achoto shel sha'ul al-devar hamma'arav halach venichnas lammetzudah vehodia lesha'ul
But Paul's sister's son heard of their lying in wait, and he came and entered into the castle and told Paul.

קָרָא שָׁאוּל לְאֶחָד מִשָּׂרֵי הַמֵּאוֹת וְאָמַר
kara sha'ul le'echad missarei hamme'ot ve'amar
And Paul called unto him one of the centurions, and said,

הָבֵא נָא אֶת הַבָּחוּר הַזֶּה אֶל שַׂר הָאֶלֶף, כִּי יֵשׁ לוֹ דָּבָר לְהוֹדִיעוֹ
havei na et habbachur hazzeh el sar ha'elef, ki yesh lo davar lehodi'o
Bring this young man unto the chief captain; for he hath something to tell him.

הוּא הֵבִיא אוֹתוֹ אֶל שַׂר הָאֶלֶף וְאָמַר
hu hevi oto el sar ha'elef ve'amar
So he took him, and brought him to the chief captain, and saith,

מַעֲשֵׂי הַשְּׁלִיחִים

הֵשִׁיב שָׁאוּל: אַחַי, לֹא יָדַעְתִּי שֶׁהוּא הַכֹּהֵן הַגָּדוֹל
heshiv sha'ul: achai, lo yada'ti shehu hakkohen haggadol
And Paul said, I knew not, brethren, that he was high priest:

הֵן כָּתוּב נָשִׂיא בְעַמְּךָ לֹא תָאֹר
hen katuv nasi ve'ammecha lo ta'or
for it is written, Thou shalt not speak evil of a ruler of thy people.

הוֹאִיל וְשָׁאוּל יָדַע כִּי חֵלֶק מֵהֶם צְדוֹקִים וְחֵלֶק פְּרוּשִׁים הִכְרִיז לִפְנֵי הַסַּנְהֶדְרִין
ho'il vesha'ul yada ki chelek mehem tzedokim vechelek perushim hichriz lifnei hassanhedrin
But when Paul perceived that the one part were Sadducees and the other Pharisees, he cried out in the council,

אֲנָשִׁים אַחִים, פָּרוּשׁ בֶּן־פָּרוּשׁ אָנֹכִי וְעַל הַתִּקְוָה לִתְחִיַּת הַמֵּתִים אֲנִי נִשְׁפָּט
anashim achim, parush ben-parush anochi ve'al hattikvah litchiyat hammetim ani nishpat
Brethren, I am a Pharisee, a son of Pharisees: touching the hope and resurrection of the dead I am called in question.

כַּאֲשֶׁר אָמַר זֹאת הֵחֵלָּה הִתְנַצְּחוּת בֵּין הַפְּרוּשִׁים לַצְּדוֹקִים
ka'asher amar zot hechellah hitnatzechut bein happerushim latzedokim
And when he had so said, there arose a dissension between the Pharisees and Sadducees;

וְהַקָּהָל נִתְפַּלֵּג לִשְׁנַיִם
vehakkahal nitpaleg lishnayim
and the assembly was divided.

כִּי הַצְּדוֹקִים אוֹמְרִים שֶׁאֵין תְּחִיָּה וְאֵין מַלְאָךְ וְאֵין רוּחַ, אַךְ הַפְּרוּשִׁים מוֹדִים בְּכָל אֵלֶּה
ki hatzedokim omerim she'ein techiyah ve'ein mal'ach ve'ein ruach, ach happerushim modim vechol elleh
For the Sadducees say that there is no resurrection, neither angel, nor spirit; but the Pharisees confess both.

הָיְתָה הַמֻּלָּה גְדוֹלָה וְאָז קָמוּ סוֹפְרִים אֲחָדִים מִכַּת הַפְּרוּשִׁים וְטָעֲנוּ בְּתֹקֶף
hayetah hamullah gedolah ve'az kamu soferim achadim mikkat happerushim veta'anu betokef
And there arose a great clamor: and some of the scribes of the Pharisees' part stood up, and strove, saying,

אֵין אָנוּ מוֹצְאִים שׁוּם רַע בָּאִישׁ הַזֶּה. וְאִם רוּחַ דִּבְּרָה אֵלָיו אוֹ מַלְאָךְ [אַל נִלָּחֵם בֵּאלֹהִים]
ein anu motze'im shum ra ba'ish hazzeh. ve'im ruach dibberah elav o mal'ach ['al nillachem belohim]
We find no evil in this man: and what if a spirit hath spoken to him, or an angel?

הַהִתְנַצְּחוּת גָּבְרָה מְאֹד וְשַׂר הָאֶלֶף חָשַׁשׁ שֶׁמָּא יְשַׁסְּעוּ אֶת שָׁאוּל
hahitnatzechut gaverah me'od vesar ha'elef chashash shemma yeshasse'u et sha'ul
And when there arose a great dissension, the chief captain, fearing lest Paul should be torn in pieces by them,

לְפִיכָךְ צִוָּה עַל הַחַיָּלִים לָרֶדֶת וְלַחְטֹף אוֹתוֹ מִתּוֹכָם וְלַהֲבִיאוֹ אֶל הַמְּצוּדָה
lefichach tzivvah al hachayalim laredet velachatof oto mittocham velahavi'o el hammetzudah
commanded the soldiers to go down and take him by force from among them, and bring him into the castle.

בַּלַּיְלָה נִצַּב הָאָדוֹן עַל שָׁאוּל וְאָמַר: הִתְחַזֵּק
ballaylah nitzav ha'adon al sha'ul ve'amar: hitchazzek
And the night following the Lord stood by him, and said, Be of good cheer:

מַעֲשֵׂי הַשְּׁלִיחִים

אָמַר שַׂר הָאֶלֶף: אֲנִי בְּכֶסֶף רַב קָנִיתִי אֶת הָאֶזְרָחוּת הַזֹּאת. אֲבָל אֲנִי נוֹלַדְתִּי בָּהּ, אָמַר שָׁאוּל.
amar sar ha'elef: ani bechesef rav kaniti et ha'ezrachut hazzot. aval ani noladti bah, amar sha'ul.
And the chief captain answered, With a great sum obtained I this citizenship. And Paul said, But I am a Roman born.

בְּאוֹתוֹ רֶגַע הִרְפּוּ מִמֶּנּוּ הָאֲנָשִׁים שֶׁעָמְדוּ לַחֲקֹר אוֹתוֹ
be'oto rega hirpu mimmennu ha'anashim she'amedu lachakor oto
They then that were about to examine him straightway departed from him:

אֲפִלּוּ שַׂר הָאֶלֶף פָּחַד כְּשֶׁנּוֹכַח כִּי הוּא רוֹמִי וְכִי כָּבַל אוֹתוֹ
afillu sar ha'elef pachad keshennochach ki hu romi vechi kaval oto
and the chief captain also was afraid when he knew that he was a Roman, and because he had bound him.

לְמָחֳרָת, כֵּיוָן שֶׁרָצָה לָדַעַת נְכוֹנָה מַדּוּעַ הֶאֱשִׁימוּהוּ בְּנֵי עַמּוֹ, הִתִּיר אֶת כְּבָלָיו
lemacharat, keivan sheratzah lada'at nechonah maddua he'eshimuhu benei ammo, hittir et kevalav
But on the morrow, desiring to know the certainty wherefore he was accused of the Jews, he loosed him,

וְצִוָּה עַל רָאשֵׁי הַכֹּהֲנִים וְכָל הַסַּנְהֶדְרִין לְהִתְאַסֵּף. הוּא הֵבִיא אֶת שָׁאוּל וְהֶעֱמִידוֹ לִפְנֵיהֶם
vetzivvah al rashei hakkohanim vechol hassanhedrin lehit'assef. hu hevi et sha'ul vehe'emido lifneihem
and commanded the chief priests and all the council to come together, and brought Paul down and set him before them

כג

הִבִּיט שָׁאוּל בַּסַּנְהֶדְרִין וְאָמַר
hibbit sha'ul bassanhedrin ve'amar
And Paul, looking stedfastly on the council, said,

אֲנָשִׁים אַחִים, אֲנִי בְּמַצְפּוּן נָקִי לְגַמְרֵי הִתְהַלַּכְתִּי לִפְנֵי הָאֱלֹהִים עַד הַיּוֹם הַזֶּה
anashim achim, ani bematzpun naki legamrei hit'hallachti lifnei ha'elohim ad hayom hazzeh
Brethren, I have lived before God in all good conscience until this day.

אָז צִוָּה חֲנַנְיָה הַכֹּהֵן הַגָּדוֹל עַל הָעוֹמְדִים לְיָדוֹ לְהַכּוֹתוֹ עַל פִּיו
az tzivvah chananyah hakkohen haggadol al ha'omedim leyado lehakkoto al piv
And the high priest Ananias commanded them that stood by him to smite him on the mouth.

אָמַר לוֹ שָׁאוּל: עָתִיד אֱלֹהִים לְהַכּוֹת אוֹתְךָ, קִיר מְטֻיָּח שֶׁכְּמוֹתְךָ
amar lo sha'ul: atid elohim lehakkot otcha, kir metuyach shekkemotcha
Then said Paul unto him, God shall smite thee, thou whited wall:

אַתָּה יוֹשֵׁב לִשְׁפֹּט אוֹתִי עַל־פִּי הַתּוֹרָה וּמְצַוֶּה לְהַכּוֹתֵנִי שֶׁלֹּא כַּתּוֹרָה
attah yoshev lishpot oti al-pi hattorah umetzavveh lehakkoteni shello kattorah
and sittest thou to judge me according to the law, and commandest me to be smitten contrary to the law?

אָמְרוּ הָעוֹמְדִים לְיָדוֹ: אֶת הַכֹּהֵן הַגָּדוֹל לֵאלֹהִים אַתָּה מְחָרֵף
ameru ha'omedim leyado: et hakkohen haggadol lelohim attah mecharef
And they that stood by said, Revilest thou God's high priest?

מַעֲשֵׂי הַשְּׁלִיחִים

אַף אֲנִי עָמַדְתִּי שָׁם בְּהַסְכָּמָה לַמַּעֲשֶׂה וְשָׁמַרְתִּי אֶת הַבְּגָדִים שֶׁל הוֹרְגָיו
af ani amadti sham behaskamah lamma'aseh veshamarti et habbegadim shel horgav
I also was standing by, and consenting, and keeping the garments of them that slew him.

אַךְ הוּא אָמַר אֵלַי, לֵךְ, כִּי אֲנִי אֶשְׁלַח אוֹתְךָ הַרְחֵק - אֶל הַגּוֹיִם
ach hu amar elai, lech, ki ani eshlach otecha harchek - el haggoyim
And he said unto me, Depart: for I will send thee forth far hence unto the Gentiles.

עַד לַדָּבָר הַזֶּה הִקְשִׁיבוּ אֵלָיו וְאָז הֵרִימוּ קוֹלָם וְקָרְאוּ:
ad laddavar hazzeh hikshivu elav ve'az herimu kolam vekar'u
And they gave him audience unto this word; and they lifted up their voice, and said,

הָסֵר מֵעַל הָאֲדָמָה אֶחָד שֶׁכָּזֶה! הוּא לֹא רָאוּי לִחְיוֹת
haser me'al ha'adamah echad shekkazeh! hu lo ra'ui lichyot
Away with such a fellow from the earth: for it is not fit that he should live.

הֵם צָעֲקוּ, הִשְׁלִיכוּ אֶת בִּגְדֵיהֶם וְהֵטִילוּ עָפָר בָּאֲוִיר
hem tza'aku, hishlichu et bigdeihem vehetilu afar ba'avir
And as they cried out, and threw off their garments, and cast dust into the air,

בִּתְגוּבָה צִוָּה שַׂר הָאֶלֶף לַהֲבִיאוֹ אֶל תּוֹךְ הַמְּצוּדָה וְהוֹרָה לַחֲקֹר אוֹתוֹ בְּמַלְקוֹת
bitguvah tzivvah sar ha'elef lahavi'o el toch hammetzudah vehorah lachakor oto bemalkot
the chief captain commanded him to be brought into the castle, bidding that he should be examined by scourging,

כְּדֵי לְבָרֵר מַדּוּעַ צָעֲקוּ עָלָיו כָּךְ
kedei levarer maddua tza'aku alav kach
that he might know for what cause they so shouted against him.

אֲבָל בְּעֵת שֶׁקָּשְׁרוּ אוֹתוֹ בִּרְצוּעוֹת אָמַר שָׁאוּל אֶל שַׂר הַמֵּאָה הָעוֹמֵד לְיָדוֹ:
aval be'et shekkasheru oto birtzu'ot amar sha'ul el sar hamme'ah ha'omed leyado
And when they had tied him up with the thongs, Paul said unto the centurion that stood by,

הַאִם מֻתָּר לָכֶם לְהַלְקוֹת אֶזְרָח רוֹמִי בְּלֹא מִשְׁפָּט
ha'im muttar lachem lehalkot ezrach romi belo mishpat
Is it lawful for you to scourge a man that is a Roman, and uncondemned?

שָׁמַע שַׂר הַמֵּאָה, הָלַךְ אֶל שַׂר הָאֶלֶף וְאָמַר לוֹ
shama sar hamme'ah, halach el sar ha'elef ve'amar lo
And when the centurion heard it, he went to the chief captain and told him, saying,

מָה אַתָּה עוֹמֵד לַעֲשׂוֹת? הֲרֵי הָאִישׁ הַזֶּה רוֹמִי
mah attah omed la'asot? harei ha'ish hazzeh romi
What art thou about to do? for this man is a Roman.

בָּא שַׂר הָאֶלֶף וְאָמַר אֵלָיו: הַגֵּד לִי, הַאִם אַתָּה רוֹמִי? הֵשִׁיב שָׁאוּל: כֵּן
ba sar ha'elef ve'amar elav. hagged li, ha'im attah romi? heshiv sha'ul: ken
And the chief captain came and said unto him, Tell me, art thou a Roman? And he said, Yea.

מַעֲשֵׂי הַשְּׁלִיחִים

בְּאוֹתָהּ שָׁעָה רָאִיתִי אוֹתוֹ
be'otah sha'ah ra'iti oto
And in that very hour I looked up on him.

הוֹסִיף וְאָמַר, אֱלֹהֵי אֲבוֹתֵינוּ בָּחַר בְּךָ לָדַעַת אֶת רְצוֹנוֹ
hosif ve'amar, elohei avoteinu bachar becha lada'at et retzono
And he said, The God of our fathers hath appointed thee to know his will,

וְלִרְאוֹת אֶת הַצַּדִּיק וְלִשְׁמֹעַ קוֹל מִפִּיו
velir'ot et hatzadik velishmoa kol mippiv
and to see the Righteous One, and to hear a voice from his mouth.

כִּי תִּהְיֶה לוֹ לְעֵד אֶל כָּל בְּנֵי אָדָם עַל הַדְּבָרִים אֲשֶׁר רָאִיתָ וְשָׁמַעְתָּ
ki tihyeh lo le'ed el kol bnei adam al haddevarim asher ra'ita veshama'ta
For thou shalt be a witness for him unto all men of what thou hast seen and heard.

וְעַכְשָׁו לָמָּה אַתָּה מִתְמַהְמֵהַּ? קוּם, הִטָּבֵל וְהִתְרַחֵץ מֵחֲטָאֶיךָ בְּקָרְאֲךָ בִּשְׁמוֹ
ve'achshav lammah attah mitmahmeah? kum, hittavel vehitrachetz mechata'eicha bekor'acha bishmo
And now why tarriest thou? arise, and be baptized, and wash away thy sins, calling on his name.

כַּאֲשֶׁר חָזַרְתִּי לִירוּשָׁלַיִם וְהִתְפַּלַּלְתִּי בַּמִּקְדָּשׁ הָיְתָה עָלַי יַד־יְהוָה
ka'asher chazarti liyerushalayim vehitpallalti bammikdash hayetah alai yad-hashem
And it came to pass, that, when I had returned to Jerusalem, and while I prayed in the temple, I fell into a trance,

וְרָאִיתִי אוֹתוֹ אוֹמֵר אֵלַי, הִזְדָּרֵז וְצֵא מַהֵר מִירוּשָׁלַיִם
vera'iti oto omer elai, hizdarez vetzei maher miyerushalayim
and saw him saying unto me, Make haste, and get thee quickly out of Jerusalem;

כִּי לֹא יְקַבְּלוּ אֶת עֵדוּתְךָ עָלַי
ki lo yekabbelu et edutecha alai
because they will not receive of thee testimony concerning me.

וַאֲנִי אָמַרְתִּי, אֲדוֹנִי, הֲרֵי הֵם יוֹדְעִים
va'ani amarti, adoni, harei hem yode'im
And I said, Lord, they themselves know

שֶׁאֲנִי הִשְׁלַכְתִּי אֶת הַמַּאֲמִינִים בְּךָ לַכֶּלֶא וְהִלְקֵיתִים בְּבָתֵּי הַכְּנֶסֶת
she'ani hishlachti et hamma'aminim becha lakkelei vehilkeitim bevattei hakkneset
that I imprisoned and beat in every synagogue them that believed on thee:

וְכַאֲשֶׁר נִשְׁפַּךְ דַּם סְטֶפָנוֹס עֵדְךָ
vecha'asher nishpach dam setefanos edcha
and when the blood of Stephen thy witness was shed,

מַעֲשֵׂי הַשְּׁלִיחִים

וְהָלַכְתִּי לְדַמֶּשֶׂק לַעֲצֹר אֶת הַנִּמְצָאִים שָׁם וְלַהֲבִיאָם בִּכְבָלִים לִירוּשָׁלַיִם כְּדֵי שֶׁיֵּעָנְשׁוּ
vehalachti ledammesek la'atzor et hannimtza'im sham velahavi'am bichvalim liyerushalayim kedei sheye'aneshu
and journeyed to Damascus to bring them also that were there unto Jerusalem in bonds to be punished.

וְהִנֵּה כְּשֶׁהָלַכְתִּי וְהִתְקָרַבְתִּי לְדַמֶּשֶׂק, בִּשְׁעַת הַצָּהֳרַיִם בְּעֶרֶךְ
vehinneh keshehalachti vehitkaravti ledammesek, bish'at hatzohorayim be'erech
And it came to pass, that, as I made my journey, and drew nigh unto Damascus, about noon,

לְפֶתַע פִּתְאוֹם נָגַהּ סְבִיבִי אוֹר גָּדוֹל מִן הַשָּׁמַיִם
lefeta pit'om nagah svivi or gadol min hashamayim
suddenly there shone from heaven a great light round about me.

נָפַלְתִּי אַרְצָה וְשָׁמַעְתִּי קוֹל אוֹמֵר אֵלַי, שָׁאוּל, שָׁאוּל, לָמָּה אַתָּה רוֹדֵף אוֹתִי
nafalti artzah veshama'ti kol omer elai, sha'ul, sha'ul, lammah attah rodef oti
And I fell unto the ground, and heard a voice saying unto me, Saul, Saul, why persecutest thou me?

שָׁאַלְתִּי, מִי אַתָּה, אֲדוֹנִי? הֵשִׁיב וְאָמַר אֵלַי, אֲנִי יֵשׁוּעַ מִנָּצְרַת אֲשֶׁר אַתָּה רוֹדֵף
sha'alti, mi attah, adoni? heshiv ve'amar elai, ani yeshua minnatzerat asher attah rodef
And I answered, Who art thou, Lord? And he said unto me, I am Jesus of Nazareth, whom thou persecutest.

הָאֲנָשִׁים שֶׁהָיוּ אִתִּי אָמְנָם רָאוּ אֶת הָאוֹר, אַךְ לֹא שָׁמְעוּ אֶת קוֹלוֹ שֶׁל הַמְדַבֵּר אֵלַי
ha'anashim shehayu itti omnam ra'u et ha'or, ach lo shame'u et kolo shel hamdabber elai
And they that were with me beheld indeed the light, but they heard not the voice of him that spake to me.

אָמַרְתִּי, מֶה עָלַי לַעֲשׂוֹת, אֲדוֹנִי? וְהָאָדוֹן אָמַר אֵלַי, קוּם, לֵךְ אֶל דַּמֶּשֶׂק
amarti, meh alai la'asot, adoni? veha'adon amar elai, kum, lech el dammesek
And I said, What shall I do, Lord? And the Lord said unto me, Arise, and go into Damascus;

וְשָׁם יֵאָמֵר לְךָ כָּל אֲשֶׁר יֻעַד לְךָ לַעֲשׂוֹת
vesham ye'amer lecha kol asher yu'ad lecha la'asot
and there it shall be told thee of all things which are appointed for thee to do.

מֵאַחַר שֶׁלֹּא יָכֹלְתִּי לִרְאוֹת מִפְּנֵי הַזֹּהַר שֶׁל אוֹתוֹ הָאוֹר
me'achar shello yacholeti lir'ot mippenei hazzohar shel oto ha'or,
And when I could not see for the glory of that light,

בָּאתִי לְדַמֶּשֶׂק כְּשֶׁמְּלַוַּי מוֹבִילִים אוֹתִי בַּיָּד
bati ledammesek keshemmelavvai movilim oti bayad
being led by the hand of them that were with me I came into Damascus.

אִישׁ אֶחָד, חֲנַנְיָה שְׁמוֹ, אִישׁ חָסִיד עַל־פִּי הַתּוֹרָה וְשֵׁם טוֹב לוֹ בְּקֶרֶב כָּל הַתּוֹשָׁבִים הַיְּהוּדִים
ish echad, chananyah shemo, ish chasid al-pi hattorah veshem tov lo bekerev kol hattoshavim hayehudim
And one Ananias, a devout man according to the law, well reported of by all the Jews that dwelt there,

בָּא אֵלַי וְעָמַד לְיָדִי. אָמַר אֵלַי, שָׁאוּל אָחִי, רְאֵה שׁוּב
ba elai ve'amad leyadi. amar elai, sha'ul achi, re'eh shuv
came unto me, and standing by me said unto me, Brother Saul, receive thy sight.

מַעֲשֵׂי הַשְּׁלִיחִים

הֵשִׁיב שָׁאוּל וְאָמַר: אִישׁ יְהוּדִי אֲנִי מִטַּרְסוֹס אֲשֶׁר בְּקִילִיקְיָה, אֶזְרָח שֶׁל עִיר לֹא נְחוּתָה
heshiv sha'ul ve'amar: ish yehudi ani mittarsos asher bekilikeyah, ezrach shel ir lo nechutah
But Paul said, I am a Jew, of Tarsus in Cilicia, a citizen of no mean city:

אֲנִי מְבַקֵּשׁ מִמְּךָ, תֶּן לִי לְדַבֵּר אֶל הָעָם
ani mevakkesh mimmecha, ten li ledabber el ha'am
and I beseech thee, give me leave to speak unto the people.

הוּא הִרְשָׁה לוֹ. עָמַד שָׁאוּל עַל הַמַּדְרֵגוֹת וְהֵנִיף אֶת יָדוֹ אֶל הָעָם
hu hirshah lo. amad sha'ul al hammadregot vehenif et yado el ha'am
And when he had given him leave, Paul, standing on the stairs, beckoned with the hand unto the people;

כַּאֲשֶׁר הִשְׂתָּרֵר שֶׁקֶט מֻחְלָט נָשָׂא דְּבָרוֹ בַּשָּׂפָה הָעִבְרִית וְאָמַר
ka'asher histarer sheket muchlat nasa devaro bashofah ha'ivrit ve'amar
and when there was made a great silence, he spake unto them in the Hebrew language, saying,

כב

אֲנָשִׁים אַחִים וְאָבוֹת, שִׁמְעוּ נָא כָּעֵת אֶת דְּבַר הִצְטַדְּקוּתִי לִפְנֵיכֶם
anashim achim ve'avot, shim'u na ka'et et dvar hitztaddekuti lifneichem
Brethren and fathers, hear ye the defence which I now make unto you.

כַּאֲשֶׁר שָׁמְעוּ אוֹתוֹ מְדַבֵּר אֲלֵיהֶם בַּשָּׂפָה הָעִבְרִית הָיְתָה שְׁתִיקָתָם עֲמֻקָּה יוֹתֵר, וְהוּא הִמְשִׁיךְ
ka'asher shame'u oto medabber aleihem bassafah ha'ivrit hayetah shetikatam amukkah yoter, vehu himshich
And when they heard that he spake unto them in the Hebrew language, they were the more quiet: and he saith,

אִישׁ יְהוּדִי אֲנִי, יְלִיד טַרְסוֹס אֲשֶׁר בְּקִילִיקְיָה, אֲבָל גֻּדַּלְתִּי בָּעִיר הַזֹּאת לְרַגְלֵי גַּמְלִיאֵל
ish yehudi ani, yelid tarsos asher bekilikeyah, aval guddalti ba'ir hazzot leraglei gamli'el
I am a Jew, born in Tarsus of Cilicia, but brought up in this city, at the feet of Gamaliel,

חֻנַּכְתִּי עַל־פִּי דִּקְדּוּקֵי תּוֹרַת אֲבוֹתֵינוּ וְהָיִיתִי קַנַּאי לֵאלֹהִים כְּמוֹ כֻּלְּכֶם הַיּוֹם
chunnachti al-pi dikdukei torat avoteinu vehayiti kanna le'elohim kemo kullechem hayom
instructed according to the strict manner of the law of our fathers, being zealous for God, even as ye all are this day:

רָדַפְתִּי אֶת הַדֶּרֶךְ הַזֹּאת עַד מָוֶת. כָּבַלְתִּי אֲנָשִׁים וְנָשִׁים וְהִסְגַּרְתִּי אוֹתָם לְבָתֵּי כֶּלֶא
radafti et hadderech hazzot ad mavet. kavalti anashim venashim vehisgarti otam levattei kele
and I persecuted this Way unto the death, binding and delivering into prisons both men and women.

דָּבָר שֶׁגַּם הַכֹּהֵן הַגָּדוֹל יָעִיד עָלַי וְכָל הַסַּנְהֶדְרִין
davar sheggam hakkohen haggadol ya'id alai vechol hassanhedrin
As also the high priest doth bear me witness, and all the estate of the elders:

מֵהֶם גַּם קִבַּלְתִּי אִגְּרוֹת אֶל אַחֵינוּ
mehem gam kibbalti iggerot el acheinu
from whom also I received letters unto the brethren,

מַעֲשֵׂי הַשְּׁלִיחִים

מִיָּד לָקַח אִתּוֹ חַיָּלִים וְשָׂרֵי מֵאוֹת וְרָץ אֲלֵיהֶם
miyad lakach itto chayalim vesarei me'ot veratz aleihem
And forthwith he took soldiers and centurions, and ran down upon them:

כִּרְאוֹתָם אֶת שַׂר הָאֶלֶף וְאֶת הַחַיָּלִים חָדְלוּ לְהַכּוֹת אֶת שָׁאוּל
kir'otam et sar ha'elef ve'et hachayalim chadlu lehakkot et sha'ul
and they, when they saw the chief captain and the soldiers, left off beating Paul.

נִגַּשׁ שַׂר הָאֶלֶף וְהֶחֱזִיק בּוֹ. הוּא צִוָּה לְכָבֵּל אוֹתוֹ בִּשְׁתֵּי שַׁרְשְׁרוֹת
niggash sar ha'elef vehechezik bo. hu tzivvah lichbol oto bishtei sharsherot
Then the chief captain came near, and laid hold on him, and commanded him to be bound with two chains;

וְשָׁאַל מִיהוּ וּמֶה עָשָׂה
vesha'al mihu umeh asah
and inquired who he was, and what he had done.

כַּמָּה אֲנָשִׁים מִן הֶהָמוֹן צָעֲקוּ דָּבָר אֶחָד וַאֲחֵרִים צָעֲקוּ דָּבָר אַחֵר
kammah anashim min hehamon tza'aku davar echad va'acherim tza'aku davar acher
And some shouted one thing, some another, among the crowd:

בִּגְלַל הַמְּהוּמָה לֹא הָיָה יָכוֹל לְבָרֵר בְּוַדָּאוּת מָה הָעִנְיָן, לָכֵן צִוָּה לַהֲבִיאוֹ אֶל הַמְּצוּדָה
biglal hammehumah lo hayah yachol levarer bevadda'ut mah ha'inyan, lachen tzivvah lahavi'o el hammetzudah
and when he could not know the certainty for the uproar, he commanded him to be brought into the castle.

כַּאֲשֶׁר הִגִּיעַ שָׁאוּל אֶל הַמַּדְרֵגוֹת נָשְׂאוּ אוֹתוֹ הַחַיָּלִים בִּגְלַל לַחַץ הֶהָמוֹן
ka'asher higgia sha'ul el hammadregot nase'u oto hachayalim biglal lachatz hehamon
And when he came upon the stairs, so it was that he was borne of the soldiers for the violence of the crowd;

כִּי הֲמוֹן הָעָם הָלַךְ אַחֲרָיו וְצָעַק: חַסֵּל אוֹתוֹ
ki hamon ha'am halach acharav vetza'ak: chassel oto
for the multitude of the people followed after, crying out, Away with him.

כְּשֶׁעָמְדוּ לְהַכְנִיס אֶת שָׁאוּל לַמְּצוּדָה, אָמַר אֶל שַׂר הָאֶלֶף
keshe'amedu lehachnis et sha'ul lammetzudah, amar el sar ha'elef
And as Paul was about to be brought into the castle, he saith unto the chief captain,

הַאִם מֻתָּר לִי לוֹמַר לְךָ מַשֶּׁהוּ? הֵגִיב הַמְּפַקֵּד: אַתָּה יוֹדֵעַ יְוָנִית?
ha'im muttar li lomar lecha mashehu? hegiv hamfakked: attah yodea yevanit?
May I say something unto thee? And he said, Dost thou know Greek?

הַאִם לֹא אַתָּה הַמִּצְרִי אֲשֶׁר לִפְנֵי זְמַן מָה הֵפִיחַ מֶרֶד
ha'im lo attah hammitzri asher lifnei zeman mah hefiach mered
Art thou not then the Egyptian, who before these days stirred up to sedition

וְהִנְהִיג אֶת אַרְבַּעַת אַלְפֵי הַסִּיקָרִיִּים אֶל הַמִּדְבָּר
vehinhig et arba'at alfei hassikariyim el hammidbar
and led out into the wilderness the four thousand men of the Assassins?

מַעֲשֵׂי הַשְּׁלִיחִים

לְהוֹדִיעַ מָתַי יֻשְׁלְמוּ יְמֵי הַטָּהֳרָה וְיֻקְרַב קָרְבָּן בְּעַד כָּל אֶחָד מֵהֶם
lehodia matai yushlemu yemei hattohorah veyukrav korban be'ad kol echad mehem
declaring the fulfilment of the days of purification, until the offering was offered for every one of them.

סָמוּךְ לִמְלֹאת שִׁבְעַת הַיָּמִים
samuch limlot shiv'at hayamim
And when the seven days were almost completed,

רָאוּהוּ יְהוּדִים מֵאַסְיָה בְּבֵית הַמִּקְדָּשׁ. הֵם הֵסִיתוּ אֶת כָּל הֶהָמוֹן, תָּפְסוּ אוֹתוֹ
ra'uhu yehudim me'asyah beveit hammikdash. hem hesitu et kol hehamon, tafsu oto
the Jews from Asia, when they saw him in the temple, stirred up all the multitude and laid hands on him,

וְצָעֲקוּ: אַנְשֵׁי יִשְׂרָאֵל, עִזְרוּ! זֶהוּ הָאִישׁ הַמְלַמֵּד אֶת כָּל הָאֲנָשִׁים בְּכָל מָקוֹם נֶגֶד הָעָם הַזֶּה
vetza'aku: anshei yisra'el, izru! zehu ha'ish hamlammed et kol ha'anashim bechol makom neged ha'am hazzeh
crying out, Men of Israel, help: This is the man that teacheth all men everywhere against the people,

וְנֶגֶד הַתּוֹרָה וְהַמָּקוֹם הַזֶּה, וַאֲפִלּוּ יְוָנִים הִכְנִיס אֶל הַמִּקְדָּשׁ
veneged hattorah vehammakom hazzeh, va'afillu yevanim hichnis el hammikdash
and the law, and this place; and moreover he brought Greeks also into the temple,

וְחִלֵּל אֶת הַמָּקוֹם הַקָּדוֹשׁ הַזֶּה
vechillel et hammakom hakkadosh hazzeh
and hath defiled this holy place.

זֹאת מִשּׁוּם שֶׁקֹּדֶם לָכֵן רָאוּ אֶת טְרוֹפִימוֹס הָאֶפֶסִי אִתּוֹ בָּעִיר
zot mishum shekkodem lachen ra'u et terofimos ha'efesi itto ba'ir
For they had before seen with him in the city Trophimus the Ephesian,

וְחָשְׁבוּ שֶׁשָּׁאוּל הִכְנִיס אוֹתוֹ אֶל הַמִּקְדָּשׁ
vechashevu shesha'ul hichnis oto el hammikdash
whom they supposed that Paul had brought into the temple.

כָּל הָעִיר רָגְשָׁה. הָאֲנָשִׁים רָצוּ יַחַד, אָחֲזוּ אֶת שָׁאוּל
kol ha'ir ragshah. ha'anashim ratzu yachad, achazu et sha'ul
And all the city was moved, and the people ran together; and they laid hold on Paul,

וְסָחֲבוּ אוֹתוֹ אֶל מִחוּץ לַמִּקְדָּשׁ וּמִיָּד נִסְגְּרוּ הַדְּלָתוֹת
vesachavu oto el michutz lammikdash umiyad nisgeru haddlatot
and dragged him out of the temple: and straightway the doors were shut.

הֵם נִסּוּ לַהֲרֹג אוֹתוֹ, וְהִנֵּה הִגִּיעָה יְדִיעָה אֶל מְפַקֵּד הַגְּדוּד
hem nissu laharog oto, vehinneh higgi'ah yedi'ah el mefakked haggedud
And as they were seeking to kill him, tidings came up to the chief captain of the band,

שֶׁכָּל יְרוּשָׁלַיִם אֲחוּזַת מְהוּמָה
shekkol yerushalayim achuzat mehumah
that all Jerusalem was in confusion.

מַעֲשֵׂי הַשְּׁלִיחִים

וְהֵם שָׁמְעוּ עָלֶיךָ,
vehem shame'u aleicha
and they have been informed concerning thee,

שֶׁאַתָּה מְלַמֵּד אֶת כָּל הַיְהוּדִים אֲשֶׁר בְּקֶרֶב הַגּוֹיִם לַעֲזֹב אֶת מֹשֶׁה
she'attah melammed et kol hayehudim asher bekerev haggoyim la'azov et mosheh
that thou teachest all the Jews who are among the Gentiles to forsake Moses,

בְּאָמְרְךָ לָהֶם שֶׁלֹּא לָמוּל אֶת הַיְלָדִים וְלֹא לִנְהֹג עַל־פִּי הַמִּנְהָגִים
be'omrecha lahem shello lamul et hayladim velo linhog al-pi hamminhagim
telling them not to circumcise their children, neither to walk after the customs.

וּבְכֵן מַה לַעֲשׂוֹת? לְלֹא סָפֵק יִשְׁמְעוּ שֶׁבָּאתָ
uvchen mah la'asot? lelo safek yishme'u shebbata
What is it therefore? they will certainly hear that thou art come.

לָכֵן עֲשֵׂה אֶת מַה שֶׁאֲנַחְנוּ אוֹמְרִים לְךָ: יֵשׁ לָנוּ אַרְבָּעָה אֲנָשִׁים אֲשֶׁר נֶדֶר עֲלֵיהֶם
lachen aseh et mah she'anachnu omerim lecha. yesh lanu arba'ah anashim asher neder aleihem
Do therefore this that we say to thee: We have four men that have a vow on them;

קַח אוֹתָם, הִטַּהֵר אִתָּם וְשַׁלֵּם בַּעֲדָם כְּדֵי שֶׁיְּגַלְּחוּ אֶת רֹאשָׁם
kach otam, hittaher ittam veshallem ba'adam kedei sheyegallechu et rosham
these take, and purify thyself with them, and be at charges for them, that they may shave their heads:

וְהַכֹּל יֵדְעוּ שֶׁהַדְּבָרִים אֲשֶׁר שָׁמְעוּ עָלֶיךָ אֵינָם נְכוֹנִים
vehakkol yede'u shehaddvarim asher shame'u aleicha einam nechonim
and all shall know that there is no truth in the things whereof they have been informed concerning thee;

כִּי גַם אַתָּה בְּעַצְמְךָ שׁוֹמֵר אֶת הַתּוֹרָה
ki gam attah be'atzmecha shomer et hattorah
but that thou thyself also walkest orderly, keeping the law.

וּבְנוֹגֵעַ לַגּוֹיִם אֲשֶׁר נִהְיוּ מַאֲמִינִים כָּתַבְנוּ
uvenogea laggoyim asher nihyu ma'aminim katavnu
But as touching the Gentiles that have believed, we wrote,

וּפָסַקְנוּ שֶׁעֲלֵיהֶם לְהִשָּׁמֵר מִזִּבְחֵי אֱלִילִים
ufasaknu she'aleihem lehishamer mizzivchei elilim
giving judgment that they should keep themselves from things sacrificed to idols,

מִדָּם, מִבְּשַׂר הַנֶּחֱנָק וּמִזְּנוּת
middam, mibbesar hannechenak umizzenut
and from blood, and from what is strangled, and from fornication.

לְמָחֳרָת לָקַח שָׁאוּל אֶת הָאֲנָשִׁים וְנִטְהַר אִתָּם. הוּא נִכְנַס לְבֵית הַמִּקְדָּשׁ
lemacharat lakach sha'ul et ha'anashim venit'har ittam. hu nichnas leveit hammikdash
Then Paul took the men, and the next day purifying himself with them went into the temple,

מַעֲשֵׂי הַשְּׁלִיחִים

הוֹאִיל וְלֹא שָׁמַע לָנוּ חָדַלְנוּ לְהַפְצִיר בּוֹ וְאָמַרְנוּ רְצוֹן אֲדֹנָי יֵעָשֶׂה
ho'il velo shama lanu chadalnu lehaftzir bo ve'amarnu retzon adonai ye'aseh
And when he would not be persuaded, we ceased, saying, The will of the Lord be done.

אַחֲרֵי הַיָּמִים הָהֵם אָרַזְנוּ אֶת חֲפָצֵינוּ וְעָלִינוּ לִירוּשָׁלַיִם
acharei hayamim hahem araznu et chafatzeinu ve'alinu liyerushalayim
And after these days we took up our baggage and went up to Jerusalem.

הָלְכוּ אִתָּנוּ גַּם תַּלְמִידִים אֲחָדִים מִקֵּיסַרְיָה
halechu ittanu gam talmidim achadim mikkeisaryah
And there went with us also certain of the disciples from Cæsarea,

הֵם הֵבִיאוּ אוֹתָנוּ אֶל קַפְרִיסָאִי אֶחָד, תַּלְמִיד וָתִיק וּשְׁמוֹ מְנַסוֹן, כְּדֵי לְהִתְאַכְסֵן אֶצְלוֹ
hem hevi'u otanu el kafrisa'i echad, talmid vatik ushemo menason, kedei lehit'achsen etzlo
bringing with them one Mnason of Cyprus, an early disciple, with whom we should lodge.

כְּשֶׁבָּאנוּ לִירוּשָׁלַיִם קִבְּלוּ אוֹתָנוּ הָאַחִים בְּשִׂמְחָה
kshebbanu liyerushalayim kibbelu otanu ha'achim besimchah
And when we were come to Jerusalem, the brethren received us gladly.

שָׁאוּל נִכְנַס אִתָּנוּ לְמָחֳרָת אֶל יַעֲקֹב, וְכָל הַזְּקֵנִים נָכְחוּ שָׁם
sha'ul nichnas ittanu lemacharat el ya'akov, vechol hazzekenim nachechu sham
And the day following Paul went in with us unto James; and all the elders were present.

הוּא שָׁאַל לִשְׁלוֹמָם
hu sha'al lishlomam
And when he had saluted them,

וְסִפֵּר בְּפֵרוּט מַה שֶּׁעָשָׂה אֱלֹהִים בְּקֶרֶב הַגּוֹיִם דַּרְכּוֹ
vesipper beferut mah she'asah elohim bekerev haggoyim darko
he rehearsed one by one the things which God had wrought among the Gentiles through his ministry.

הֵם שָׁמְעוּ וְשִׁבְּחוּ אֶת אֱלֹהִים. לְאַחַר מִכֵּן אָמְרוּ
hem shame'u veshibbechu et elohim. le'achar mikken ameru
And they, when they heard it, glorified God; and they said unto him,

אַתָּה רוֹאֶה, אָחִינוּ, כַּמָּה רִבְבוֹת יְהוּדִים נִהְיוּ מַאֲמִינִים
attah ro'eh, achinu, kammah rivevot yehudim nihyu ma'aminim
Thou seest, brother, how many thousands there are among the Jews of them that have believed;

וְכֻלָּם קַנָּאִים לַתּוֹרָה
vechullam kanna'im lattorah
and they are all zealous for the law:

מַעֲשֵׂי הַשְּׁלִיחִים

כְּשֶׁסִּיַּמְנוּ אֶת הַמַּסָּע מִצּוֹר הִגַּעְנוּ לְעַכּוֹ
keshessiyamnu et hammassa mitzor higga'nu le'akko
And when we had finished the voyage from Tyre, we arrived at Ptolemais;

שָׁאַלְנוּ אֶת הָאַחִים לִשְׁלוֹמָם וְיָשַׁבְנוּ אֶצְלָם יוֹם אֶחָד
sha'alnu et ha'achim lishlomam veyashavnu etzlam yom echad
and we saluted the brethren, and abode with them one day.

לְמָחֳרָת יָצָאנוּ לַדֶּרֶךְ וּבָאנוּ לְקֵיסַרְיָה
lemacharat yatzanu ladderech uvanu lekeisaryah
And on the morrow we departed, and came unto Cæsarea:

שָׁם נִכְנַסְנוּ לְבֵיתוֹ שֶׁל פִילִיפּוֹס הַמְבַשֵּׂר, שֶׁהָיָה אֶחָד מִן הַשִּׁבְעָה, וְגַרְנוּ אֶצְלוֹ
sham nichnasnu leveito shel filipos hamevasser, shehayah echad min hashiv'ah, vegarnu etzlo
and entering into the house of Philip the evangelist, who was one of the seven, we abode with him.

הָיוּ לוֹ אַרְבַּע בָּנוֹת בְּתוּלוֹת שֶׁהָיוּ מִתְנַבְּאוֹת
hayu lo arba banot betulot shehayu mitnabbe'ot
Now this man had four virgin daughters, who prophesied.

כְּשֶׁהָיִינוּ שָׁם יָמִים רַבִּים יָרַד נָבִיא אֶחָד מִיהוּדָה, אֲגָבוֹס שְׁמוֹ
kshehayinu sham yamim rabbim yarad navi echad mihudah, agavos shemo
And as we tarried there some days, there came down from Judæa a certain prophet, named Agabus.

הוּא נִכְנַס אֵלֵינוּ, לָקַח אֶת חֲגוֹרָתוֹ שֶׁל שָׁאוּל וּלְאַחַר שֶׁקָּשַׁר אֶת רַגְלָיו וְיָדָיו שֶׁלּוֹ אָמַר
hu nichnas eleinu, lakach et chagorato shel sha'ul ule'achar shekkashar et raglav veyadav shello amar
And coming to us, and taking Paul's girdle, he bound his own feet and hands, and said,

כֹּה אוֹמֶרֶת רוּחַ הַקֹּדֶשׁ
koh omeret ruach hakkodesh
Thus saith the Holy Spirit,

הָאִישׁ אֲשֶׁר לוֹ הַחֲגוֹרָה הַזֹּאת, כָּכָה יִקְשְׁרוּ אוֹתוֹ הַיְהוּדִים בִּירוּשָׁלַיִם וְיַסְגִּירוּהוּ בִּידֵי הַגּוֹיִם
ha'ish asher lo hachagorah hazzot, kachah yiksheru oto hayehudim biyerushalayim veyasgiruhu biydei haggoyim
So shall the Jews at Jerusalem bind the man that owneth this girdle, and shall deliver him into the hands of the Gentiles.

כַּאֲשֶׁר שָׁמַעְנוּ זֹאת הִפְצַרְנוּ בּוֹ, אֲנַחְנוּ וְגַם אַנְשֵׁי הַמָּקוֹם, שֶׁלֹּא יַעֲלֶה לִירוּשָׁלַיִם
ka'asher shama'nu zot hiftzarnu bo, anachnu vegam anshei hammakom, shello ya'aleh liyerushalayim
And when we heard these things, both we and they of that place besought him not to go up to Jerusalem.

אַךְ שָׁאוּל הֵשִׁיב: מָה אַתֶּם עוֹשִׂים? לָמָּה אַתֶּם בּוֹכִים וּמְמַסִּים אֶת לִבִּי
ach sha'ul heshiv. mah attem osim? lammah attem bochim umemissim et libbi
Then Paul answered, What do ye, weeping and breaking my heart?

הֲרֵינִי מוּכָן לֹא רַק לְהֵאָסֵר אֶלָּא גַּם לָמוּת בִּירוּשָׁלַיִם עַל שֵׁם הָאָדוֹן יֵשׁוּעַ
hareini muchan lo rak lehe'aser ella gam lamut biyerushalayim al shem ha'adon yeshua
for I am ready not to be bound only, but also to die at Jerusalem for the name of the Lord Jesus.

מַעֲשֵׂי הַשְּׁלִיחִים

כא

לְאַחַר שֶׁנִּפְרַדְנוּ מֵהֶם הִפְלַגְנוּ
le'achar shennifradnu mehem hiflagnu
And when it came to pass that we were parted from them and had set sail,

וּבְנָתִיב יָשָׁר בָּאנוּ אֶל קוֹס. לְמָחֳרַת בָּאנוּ אֶל רוֹדוֹס וּמִשָּׁם אֶל פַּטְרָה
uvenativ yashar banu el kos. lemacharat banu el rodos umisham el patarah
we came with a straight course unto Cos, and the next day unto Rhodes, and from thence unto Patara:

שָׁם מָצָאנוּ אֳנִיָּה שֶׁמְּגַמָּתָהּ פֵּינִיקְיָה. נִכְנַסְנוּ לָאֳנִיָּה וְהִפְלַגְנוּ
sham matzanu oniyah shemmegammatah feinikeyah. nichnasnu lo'oniyah vehiflagnu
and having found a ship crossing over unto Phoenicia, we went aboard, and set sail.

בַּדֶּרֶךְ רָאִינוּ אֶת קַפְרִיסִין וְעָבַרְנוּ עַל פָּנֶיהָ כְּשֶׁהִיא מִשְּׂמֹאלֵנוּ
badderech ra'inu et kafrisin ve'avarnu al paneiha keshehi mishomolenu
And when we had come in sight of Cyprus, leaving it on the left hand,

הִמְשַׁכְנוּ בַּמַּסָּע אֶל סוּרְיָה וְהִגַּעְנוּ אֶל צוֹר, כִּי שָׁם פָּרְקוּ אֶת מִטְעַן הָאֳנִיָּה
himshachnu bammassa el sureyah vehigga'nu el tzor, ki sham pareku et mit'an ho'oniyah
we sailed unto Syria, and landed at Tyre; for there the ship was to unlade her burden.

מָצָאנוּ תַּלְמִידִים וְיָשַׁבְנוּ שָׁם שִׁבְעָה יָמִים.
matzanu talmidim veyashavnu sham shiv'ah yamim
And having found the disciples, we tarried there seven days:

הַלָּלוּ אָמְרוּ לְשָׁאוּל עַל־פִּי הָרוּחַ שֶׁלֹּא יַעֲלֶה לִירוּשָׁלַיִם
hallalu ameru lesha'ul al-pi haruach shello ya'aleh liyerushalayim
and these said to Paul through the Spirit, that he should not set foot in Jerusalem.

כַּאֲשֶׁר תַּמּוּ הַיָּמִים יָצָאנוּ לְדַרְכֵּנוּ
ka'asher tammu hayamim yatzanu ledarkenu
And when it came to pass that we had accomplished the days, we departed and went on our journey;

וְהֵם כֻּלָּם לִוּוּ אוֹתָנוּ עִם נְשֵׁיהֶם וְיַלְדֵיהֶם עַד מִחוּץ לָעִיר
vehem kullam livvu otanu im nesheihem veyaldeihem ad michutz la'ir
and they all, with wives and children, brought us on our way till we were out of the city:

בַּחוֹף כָּרַעְנוּ עַל בִּרְכֵּינוּ וְהִתְפַּלַּלְנוּ
bachof kara'nu al birkeinu vehitpallalnu
and kneeling down on the beach, we prayed, and bade each other farewell;

אַחֲרֵי שֶׁבֵּרַכְנוּ זֶה אֶת זֶה לְשָׁלוֹם וְנִכְנַסְנוּ לָאֳנִיָּה, הֵם שָׁבוּ אִישׁ אִישׁ לְבֵיתוֹ
acharei shebberachnu zeh et zeh leshalom venichnasnu la'oniyah, hem shavu ish ish leveito
and we went on board the ship, but they returned home again.

מַעֲשֵׂי הַשְּׁלִיחִים

לֹא חָדַלְתִּי לְהוֹכִיחַ כָּל אֶחָד וְאֶחָד בִּדְמָעוֹת
lo chadalti lehochiach kol echad ve'echad bidma'ot
I ceased not to admonish every one night and day with tears.

וְעַכְשָׁו אֲנִי מַפְקִיד אֶתְכֶם בִּידֵי אֱלֹהִים וּדְבַר חַסְדּוֹ
ve'achshav ani mafkid etchem biydei elohim udevar chasdo
And now I commend you to God, and to the word of his grace,

לוֹ הַכֹּחַ לִבְנוֹת אֶתְכֶם וְלָתֵת לָכֶם נַחֲלָה בְּקֶרֶב כָּל הַמְקֻדָּשִׁים
lo hakkoach livnot etchem velatet lachem nachalah bekerev kol hamkuddashim
which is able to build you up, and to give you the inheritance among all them that are sanctified.

לֹא חָמַדְתִּי אֶת כַּסְפּוֹ שֶׁל אִישׁ, גַּם לֹא אֶת זְהָבוֹ אוֹ לְבוּשׁוֹ
lo chamadti et kaspo shel ish, gam lo et zehavo o levusho
I coveted no man's silver, or gold, or apparel.

אַתֶּם עַצְמְכֶם יוֹדְעִים שֶׁיָּדַי אֵלֶּה שֵׁרְתוּ בְּעַד צְרָכַי וּבְעַד צָרְכֵי הָאֲנָשִׁים אֲשֶׁר אִתִּי
attem atzmechem yode'im sheyadai elleh sheretu be'ad tzerachai uve'ad tzarechei ha'anashim asher itti
Ye yourselves know that these hands ministered unto my necessities, and to them that were with me.

בַּכֹּל הֶרְאֵיתִי לָכֶם כִּי בִּהְיוֹתֵנוּ עֲמֵלִים כָּךְ יֵשׁ לִתְמֹךְ בַּחַלָּשִׁים
bakkol her'eiti lachem ki bihyotenu amelim kach yesh litmoch bachallashim
In all things I gave you an example, that so laboring ye ought to help the weak,

וְלִזְכֹּר אֶת דִּבְרֵי הָאָדוֹן יֵשׁוּעַ, שֶׁהֲרֵי הוּא אָמַר טוֹב לָתֵת מִלָּקַחַת
velizkor et divrei ha'adon yeshua, sheharei hu amar tov latet millakachat
and to remember the words of the Lord Jesus, that he himself said, It is more blessed to give than to receive.

אַחֲרֵי שֶׁאָמַר אֶת הַדְּבָרִים הָאֵלֶּה כָּרַע עַל בִּרְכָּיו וְהִתְפַּלֵּל עִם כֻּלָּם
acharei she'amar et haddevarim ha'elleh kara al birkav vehitpallel im kullam
And when he had thus spoken, he kneeled down and prayed with them all.

הַכֹּל בָּכוּ בְּכִי רַב, נָפְלוּ עַל צַוְּארֵי שָׁאוּל וְנָשְׁקוּ לוֹ
hakkol bachu bechi rav, nafelu al tzavverei sha'ul venashku lo
And they all wept sore, and fell on Paul's neck and kissed him,

וּבְיוֹתֵר הִתְעַצְּבוּ עַל הַדָּבָר שֶׁאָמַר - שֶׁלֹּא יוֹסִיפוּ עוֹד לִרְאוֹת אֶת פָּנָיו
uveyoter hit'atzevu al haddavar she'amar - shello yosifu od lir'ot et panav
sorrowing most of all for the word which he had spoken, that they should behold his face no more.

אַחֲרֵי כֵן לִוּוּהוּ אֶל הָאֳנִיָּה
acharei chen livvuhu el ho'oniyah
And they brought him on his way unto the ship.

מַעֲשֵׂי הַשְּׁלִיחִים

לְבַד מִזֶּה שֶׁרוּחַ הַקֹּדֶשׁ מַצְהִירָה לִי בְּכָל עִיר וָעִיר וְאוֹמֶרֶת שֶׁכְּבָלִים וְצָרוֹת מְצַפִּים לִי
levad mizzeh sheruach hakkodesh matzhirah li bechol ir va'ir ve'omeret shekkevalim vetzarot metzappim li
save that the Holy Spirit testifieth unto me in every city, saying that bonds and afflictions abide me.

אוּלָם חַיַּי אֵינָם יְקָרִים לִי כָּל עִקָּר וּבִלְבַד שֶׁאַשְׁלִים אֶת מְרוּצָתִי
ulam chayai einam yekarim li kol ikkar uvilvad she'ashlim et merutzati
But I hold not my life of any account as dear unto myself, so that I may accomplish my course,

וְאֶת הַשֵּׁרוּת אֲשֶׁר קִבַּלְתִּי מֵאֵת הָאָדוֹן יֵשׁוּעַ - לְהָעִיד עַל בְּשׂוֹרַת חֶסֶד אֱלֹהִים
ve'et hasherut asher kibbalti me'et ha'adon yeshua - leha'id al besorat chesed elohim
and the ministry which I received from the Lord Jesus, to testify the gospel of the grace of God.

וְכָעֵת אֲנִי יוֹדֵעַ כִּי אַתֶּם כֻּלְּכֶם
vecha'et ani yodea ki attem kullchem
And now, behold, I know that ye all,

אֲשֶׁר בֵּינֵיכֶם הִתְהַלַּכְתִּי וְהִכְרַזְתִּי אֶת הַמַּלְכוּת, לֹא תּוֹסִיפוּ עוֹד לִרְאוֹת אֶת פָּנַי
asher beineichem hit'hallachti vehichrazti et hammalchut, lo tosifu od lir'ot et panai
among whom I went about preaching the kingdom, shall see my face no more.

לָכֵן אֲנִי מֵעִיד בָּכֶם הַיּוֹם הַזֶּה שֶׁנָּקִי אֲנִי מִדַּם כֻּלְּכֶם
lachen ani me'id bachem hayom hazzeh shennaki ani middam kullchem
Wherefore I testify unto you this day, that I am pure from the blood of all men.

כִּי לֹא נִרְתַּעְתִּי מִלְּהוֹדִיעַ לָכֶם אֶת עֲצַת אֱלֹהִים כֻּלָּהּ
ki lo nirta'ti millehodia lachem et atzat elohim kullah
For I shrank not from declaring unto you the whole counsel of God.

הַשְׁגִּיחוּ עַל עַצְמְכֶם וְעַל כָּל הָעֵדֶר
hashgichu al atzmechem ve'al kol ha'eder
Take heed unto yourselves, and to all the flock,

אֲשֶׁר רוּחַ הַקֹּדֶשׁ שָׂמָה אֶתְכֶם לִמְנַהִיגִים בְּתוֹכוֹ, לִרְעוֹת אֶת קְהִלַּת אֱלֹהִים אֲשֶׁר קָנָה בְּדָמוֹ שֶׁלּוֹ
asher ruach hakkodesh samah etchem lemanhigim betocho, lir'ot et kehillat elohim asher kanah bedamo shello
in which the Holy Spirit hath made you bishops, to feed the church of the Lord which he purchased with his own blood.

אֲנִי יוֹדֵעַ שֶׁאַחֲרֵי צֵאתִי יָבוֹאוּ בְּתוֹכְכֶם זְאֵבִים עַזִּים אֲשֶׁר לֹא יָחוּסוּ עַל הָעֵדֶר
ani yodea she'acharei tzeti yavo'u betochechem ze'evim azzim asher lo yachusu al ha'eder
I know that after my departing grievous wolves shall enter in among you, not sparing the flock;

וּמִקִּרְבְּכֶם יָקוּמוּ אֲנָשִׁים דּוֹבְרֵי תַהְפּוּכוֹת לְהַטּוֹת אַחֲרֵיהֶם אֶת הַתַּלְמִידִים
umikirbechem yakumu anashim doverei tahpuchot lehattot achareihem et hattalmidim
and from among your own selves shall men arise, speaking perverse things, to draw away the disciples after them.

עַל כֵּן עִמְדוּ עַל הַמִּשְׁמָר. זִכְרוּ כִּי שָׁלוֹשׁ שָׁנִים, יוֹמָם וָלַיְלָה
al ken imdu al hammishmar. zichru ki shalosh shanim, yomam valaylah
Wherefore watch ye, remembering that by the space of three years

מַעֲשֵׂי הַשְּׁלִיחִים

מִשָּׁם הִפְלַגְנוּ וְהִגַּעְנוּ לְמָחֳרַת אֶל מוּל כִּיּוֹס
misham hiflagnu vehigga'nu lemochorat el mul kiyos
And sailing from thence, we came the following day over against Chios;

יוֹם אַחֲרֵי כֵן עָבַרְנוּ אֶל סָמוֹס וּלְמָחֳרַת בָּאנוּ אֶל מִילֵיטוֹס
yom acharei chen avarnu el samos ulemacharat banu el militos
and the next day we touched at Samos; and the day after we came to Miletus.

כִּי שָׁאוּל הֶחְלִיט לַעֲבֹר בַּיָּם עַל־פְּנֵי אֶפֶסוֹס כְּדֵי שֶׁלֹּא יִצְטָרֵךְ לִשְׁהוֹת בְּאַסְיָה
ki sha'ul hechlit la'avor bayam al-penei efesos kedei shello yitztarech lishhot be'asyah
For Paul had determined to sail past Ephesus, that he might not have to spend time in Asia;

זֹאת מִפְּנֵי שֶׁמִּהֵר בְּדַרְכּוֹ - אוּלַי יוּכַל לִהְיוֹת בִּירוּשָׁלַיִם בְּחַג הַשָּׁבוּעוֹת
zot mippnei shemmiher bedarko - ulai yuchal lihyot biyerushalayim bechag hashavu'ot
for he was hastening, if it were possible for him, to be at Jerusalem the day of Pentecost.

מִמִּילֵיטוֹס שָׁלַח אֶל אֶפֶסוֹס וְקָרָא אֶת זִקְנֵי הַקְּהִלָּה
mimmilitos shalach el efesos vekara et ziknei hakkehillah
And from Miletus he sent to Ephesus, and called to him the elders of the church.

כַּאֲשֶׁר בָּאוּ אֵלָיו אָמַר לָהֶם
ka'asher ba'u elav amar lahem
And when they were come to him, he said unto them,

אַתֶּם יוֹדְעִים כֵּיצַד הָיִיתִי אִתְּכֶם בְּכָל עֵת לְמִן הַיּוֹם הָרִאשׁוֹן שֶׁרַגְלִי דָּרְכָה בְּאַסְיָה
attem yode'im keitzad hayiti ittechem bechol et lemin hayom harishon sheragli darechah be'asyah
Ye yourselves know, from the first day that I set foot in Asia, after what manner I was with you all the time,

עָבַדְתִּי אֶת הָאָדוֹן בְּכָל עֲנָוָה וּבִדְמָעוֹת וּבְמַסּוֹת אֲשֶׁר בָּאוּ עָלַי בִּגְלַל נוֹכְלִים מִבֵּין הַיְּהוּדִים
avadti et ha'adon bechol anavah uvidma'ot uvemassot asher ba'u alai biglal nochelim mibbein hayehudim
serving the Lord with all lowliness of mind, and with tears, and with trials which befell me by the plots of the Jews;

לֹא נִרְתַּעְתִּי מִלְּהוֹדִיעַ לָכֶם כָּל דָּבָר מוֹעִיל
lo nirta'ti millehodia lachem kol davar mo'il
how I shrank not from declaring unto you anything that was profitable,

וּמִלַּמֵּד אֶתְכֶם בָּרַבִּים וּבְכָל בַּיִת וּבַיִת
umillelammed etchem barabbim uvechol bayit uvayit
and teaching you publicly, and from house to house,

בְּהָעִידִי גַּם בַּיְּהוּדִים וְגַם בַּיְּוָנִים לַחֲזֹר בִּתְשׁוּבָה אֶל אֱלֹהִים וּלְהַאֲמִין בַּאֲדוֹנֵנוּ יֵשׁוּעַ
beha'idi gam bayehudim vegam bayevanim lachazor bitshuvah el elohim uleha'amin ba'adonenu yeshua
testifying both to Jews and to Greeks repentance toward God, and faith toward our Lord Jesus Christ.

וְעַכְשָׁו הִנְנִי הוֹלֵךְ לִירוּשָׁלַיִם כָּבוּל בָּרוּחַ וְאֵינִי יוֹדֵעַ מַה יִּקְרֶה לִי שָׁם
ve'achshav hineni holech liyerushalayim kavul baruach ve'eini yodea mah yikreh li sham
And now, behold, I go bound in the spirit unto Jerusalem, not knowing the things that shall befall me there:

מַעֲשֵׂי הַשְּׁלִיחִים

שָׁאוּל, שֶׁעָמַד לָצֵאת לְמׇחֳרָת, דִּבֶּר אֲלֵיהֶם וְהֶאֱרִיךְ אֶת דְּבָרוֹ עַד חֲצוֹת
sha'ul, she'amad latzet lemochorat, dibber aleihem vehe'erich et devaro ad chatzot
Paul discoursed with them, intending to depart on the morrow; and prolonged his speech until midnight.

מְנוֹרוֹת רַבּוֹת הָיוּ בָּעֲלִיָּה שֶׁנֶּאֱסַפְנוּ בָּהּ
menorot rabbot hayu ba'aliyah shenne'esafnu bah
And there were many lights in the upper chamber where we were gathered together.

וּבָחוּר אֶחָד, אֶוטִיכוֹס שְׁמוֹ, יָשַׁב עַל אֶדֶן הַחַלּוֹן כְּשֶׁהוּא שׁוֹקֵעַ בְּתַרְדֵּמָה עֲמֻקָּה.
uvachur echad, evtichos shmo, yashav al eden hachallon keshehu shokea betardemah amukkah
And there sat in the window a certain young man named Eutychus, borne down with deep sleep;

כְּשֶׁהֶאֱרִיךְ שָׁאוּל אֶת דְּבָרוֹ גָּבְרָה עָלָיו הַתַּרְדֵּמָה וְנָפַל מִן הַקּוֹמָה הַשְּׁלִישִׁית לְמַטָּה
keshehe'erich sha'ul et devaro gavrah alav hattardemah venafal min hakkomah hashelishit lemattah
and as Paul discoursed yet longer, being borne down by his sleep he fell down from the third story,

הֵם הֵרִימוּ אוֹתוֹ מֵת
hem herimu oto met
and was taken up dead.

אֲבָל שָׁאוּל יָרַד, גָּהַר עָלָיו וְחִבְּקוֹ בְּיָדָיו. אַל תִּבָּהֲלוּ, אָמַר, נִשְׁמָתוֹ בּוֹ
aval sha'ul yarad, gahar alav vechibbeko beyadav. al tibbahalu, amar, nishmato bo
And Paul went down, and fell on him, and embracing him said, Make ye no ado; for his life is in him.

הוּא עָלָה, בָּצַע אֶת הַלֶּחֶם וְאָכַל
hu alah, batza et hallechem ve'achal
And when he was gone up, and had broken the bread, and eaten,

לְאַחַר שֶׁשּׂוֹחֵחַ אִתָּם שָׁעָה אֲרֻכָּה, עַד אוֹר הַבֹּקֶר, יָצָא לְדַרְכּוֹ
le'achar shessochach ittam sha'ah arukkah, ad or habboker, yatza ledarko
and had talked with them a long while, even till break of day, so he departed.

וְהֵם הֵבִיאוּ אֶת הַצָּעִיר חַי וְהִתְנַחֲמוּ מְאֹד
vehem hevi'u et hatza'ir chai vehitnachamu me'od
And they brought the lad alive, and were not a little comforted.

אֲנַחְנוּ הִקְדַּמְנוּ לַעֲלוֹת לָאֳנִיָּה וְהִפְלַגְנוּ אֶל אַסּוֹס כְּדֵי לָקַחַת שָׁם אֶת שָׁאוּל
anachnu hikdamnu la'alot lo'oniyah vehiflagnu el assos kedei lakachat sham et sha'ul
But we, going before to the ship, set sail for Assos, there intending to take in Paul:

כָּךְ קָבַע, מִשּׁוּם שֶׁהִתְכַּוֵּן לְהַגִּיעַ לְשָׁם בְּדֶרֶךְ הַיַּבָּשָׁה
kach kava', mishum shehitkavven lehaggia lesham bederech hayabbashah
for so had he appointed, intending himself to go by land.

כַּאֲשֶׁר פָּגַשׁ אוֹתָנוּ בְּאַסּוֹס לְקַחְנוּ אוֹתוֹ וּבָאנוּ אֶל מִיטִילִינִי
ka'asher pagash otanu be'assos lakachnu oto uvanu el mitilini
And when he met us at Assos, we took him in, and came to Mitylene.

מַעֲשֵׂי הַשְּׁלִיחִים

קָרָא שָׁאוּל לַתַּלְמִידִים וְעוֹדֵד אוֹתָם. הוּא נִפְרַד מֵהֶם וְיָצָא לְדַרְכּוֹ אֶל מַקְדוֹנְיָה
kara sha'ul lattalmidim ve'oded otam. hu nifrad mehem veyatza ledarko el makedoneyah
Paul having sent for the disciples and exhorted them, took leave of them, and departed to go into Macedonia.

לְאַחַר שֶׁעָבַר בָּאֲזוֹרִים הָהֵם וְעוֹדֵד אֶת הַתַּלְמִידִים בְּדִבְרֵי עִדּוּד רַבִּים, בָּא לְיָוָן
le'achar she'avar ba'azorim hahem ve'oded et hattalmidim bedivrei iddud rabbim, ba leyavan
And when he had gone through those parts, and had given them much exhortation, he came into Greece.

וְיָשַׁב שָׁם שְׁלוֹשָׁה חֳדָשִׁים.
veyashav sham sheloshah chodashim
And when he had spent three months there,

כְּשֶׁעָמַד לְהַפְלִיג לְסוּרְיָה הִתְנַכְּלוּ יְהוּדֵי הַמָּקוֹם לְהָרַע לוֹ,
keshe'amad lehaflig lesureyah hitnakkelu yehudei hammakom leharea lo,
and a plot was laid against him by the Jews as he was about to set sail for Syria,

לְפִיכָךְ הֶחְלִיט לָשׁוּב דֶּרֶךְ מַקְדוֹנְיָה
lefichach hechlit lashuv derech makedoneyah
he determined to return through Macedonia.

נִלְווּ אֵלָיו סוֹפַּטְרוֹס בֶּן־פִּירוֹס אִישׁ בֶּרֵאָה
nilvu elav soppatros ben-piros ish bere'ah
And there accompanied him as far as Asia, Sopater of Beroea, the son of Pyrrhus;

אָרִיסְטַרְכוֹס וּסְקוּנְדוֹס הַתֶּסָּלוֹנִיקִים, גָּיוֹס הַדֶּרְבִּי, טִימוֹתֵיאוֹס,
arisetarchos vesekunedos hattessalonikim, gayos hadderbi, timotei'os,
and of the Thessalonians, Aristarchus and Secundus; and Gaius of Derbe, and Timothy;

וְטִיכִיקוֹס וּטְרוֹפִימוֹס אַנְשֵׁי אַסְיָה
vetichikos uterofimos anshei asyah
and of Asia, Tychicus and Trophimus.

הַלָּלוּ הָלְכוּ לְפָנֵינוּ וְחִכּוּ לָנוּ בִּטְרוֹאַס
hallalu halechu lefaneinu vechikku lanu bitro'as
But these had gone before, and were waiting for us at Troas.

אֲנַחְנוּ הִפְלַגְנוּ מִפִילִיפִּי אַחֲרֵי יְמֵי חַג הַמַּצּוֹת
anachnu hiflagnu mifilipi acharei yemei chag hammatzot
And we sailed away from Philippi after the days of unleavened bread,

וּבָאנוּ אֲלֵיהֶם לִטְרוֹאַס כַּעֲבוֹר חֲמִשָּׁה יָמִים. שָׁם נִשְׁאַרְנוּ שִׁבְעָה יָמִים
uvanu aleihem litro'as ka'avor chamishah yamim. sham nish'arnu shiv'ah yamim
and came unto them to Troas in five days; where we tarried seven days.

בָּרִאשׁוֹן בַּשָּׁבוּעַ נֶאֱסַפְנוּ לִבְצֹעַ לֶחֶם
barishon bashavua ne'esafnu livtzoa lechem
And upon the first day of the week, when we were gathered together to break bread,

מַעֲשֵׂי הַשְּׁלִיחִים

שֶׁהָעִיר אֶפֶסוֹס מֻפְקֶדֶת עַל הֵיכַל אַרְטֵמִיס הַגְּדוֹלָה
sheha'ir efesos mufkedet al heichal artemis haggedolah
that the city of the Ephesians is temple-keeper of the great Diana,

וְעַל צַלְמָהּ שֶׁנָּפַל מִן הַשָּׁמַיִם
ve'al tzalmah shennafal min hashamayim
and of the image which fell down from Jupiter?

מֵאַחַר שֶׁאֵין לְהַכְחִישׁ זֹאת, עֲלֵיכֶם לְהֵרָגַע וְלֹא לַעֲשׂוֹת שׁוּם דָּבָר נִמְהָר
me'achar she'ein lehachchish zot, aleichem leheraga velo la'asot shum davar nimhar
Seeing then that these things cannot be gainsaid, ye ought to be quiet, and to do nothing rash.

הִנֵּה הֲבֵאתֶם אֶת הָאֲנָשִׁים הָאֵלֶּה, שֶׁאֵינָם שׁוֹדְדֵי מִקְדָּשִׁים אַף לֹא מְחַלְּלִים אֶת שֵׁם הָאֵלָה שֶׁלָּכֶם
hinneh havetem et ha'anashim ha'elleh, she'einam shodedei mikdashim af lo mechallelim et shem ha'elah shellachem
For ye have brought hither these men, who are neither robbers of temples nor blasphemers of our goddess.

לָכֵן, אִם יֵשׁ לְדֶמֶטְרִיּוֹס וְלָאֻמָּנִים אֲשֶׁר אִתּוֹ דָּבָר נֶגֶד מִישֶׁהוּ
lachen, im yesh ledemetriyos vela'ummanim asher itto davar neged mishehu
If therefore Demetrius, and the craftsmen that are with him, have a matter against any man,

יֵשׁ בָּתֵּי מִשְׁפָּט וְיֵשׁ שׁוֹפְטִים; שֶׁיִּטְעֲנוּ זֶה נֶגֶד זֶה
yesh battei mishpat veyesh shofetim; sheyit'anu zeh neged zeh
the courts are open, and there are proconsuls: let them accuse one another.

אֲבָל אִם רוֹצִים אַתֶּם מַשֶּׁהוּ נוֹסָף, אֲזַי שֶׁיֵּחָרֵץ בָּאֲסֵפָה חֻקִּית
aval im rotzim attem mashehu nosaf, azai sheyecharetz ba'asefah chukkit
But if ye seek anything about other matters, it shall be settled in the regular assembly.

הֲרֵי עֲלוּלִים אָנוּ לִהְיוֹת מֻאֲשָׁמִים בִּמְהוּמַת הַיּוֹם הַזֶּה, מְהוּמָה לְלֹא שׁוּם סִבָּה,
harei alulim anu lihyot mo'oshamim bimhumat hayom hazzeh, mehumah lelo shum sibbah
For indeed we are in danger to be accused concerning this day's riot, there being no cause for it:

וְלֹא נוּכַל לָתֵת נִמּוּק עַל הַהִתְקַהֲלוּת הַזֹּאת
velo nuchal latet nimmuk al hahitkahalut hazzot
and as touching it we shall not be able to give account of this concourse.

הוּא אָמַר אֶת הַדְּבָרִים הָאֵלֶּה וְשִׁלַּח אֶת הַקָּהָל
hu amar et haddevarim ha'elleh veshillach et hakkahal
And when he had thus spoken, he dismissed the assembly.

כ

אַחֲרֵי שֶׁפָּסְקָה הַמְּהוּמָה
acharei sheppaskah hammehumah
And after the uproar ceased,

מַעֲשֵׂי הַשְּׁלִיחִים

כְּשֶׁהֵם סוֹחֲבִים אֶת גָּיוֹס וְאֶת אֲרִיסְטַרְכוֹס, שְׁנֵי הַמַּקְדוֹנִים חֲבֵרָיו שֶׁל שָׁאוּל לַמַּסָּע
keshehem sochavim et gayos ve'et arisetarchos, shenei hammakedonim chaverav shel sha'ul lammassa
having seized Gaius and Aristarchus, men of Macedonia, Paul's companions in travel.

שָׁאוּל רָצָה לְהִכָּנֵס אֶל תּוֹךְ הֶהָמוֹן, אַךְ הַתַּלְמִידִים לֹא הִנִּיחוּ לוֹ
sha'ul ratzah lehikkanes el toch hehamon, ach hattalmidim lo hinnichu lo
And when Paul was minded to enter in unto the people, the disciples suffered him not.

גַּם כַּמָּה מֵרָאשֵׁי אַסְיָה שֶׁהָיוּ חֲבֵרָיו
gam kammah merashei asyah shehayu chaverav
And certain also of the Asiarchs, being his friends,

שָׁלְחוּ אֵלָיו לְבַקֵּשׁ מִמֶּנּוּ שֶׁלֹּא יִכָּנֵס לָאַמְפִיתֵיאַטְרוֹן
shalechu elav levakkesh mimmennu shello yikkanes la'amfitei'atron
sent unto him and besought him not to adventure himself into the theatre.

בֵּינְתַיִם צָעֲקוּ אֵלֶּה דָּבָר אֶחָד וְאֵלֶּה דָּבָר אַחֵר, כִּי הַקָּהָל הָיָה נָבוֹךְ
beinetayim tza'aku elleh davar echad ve'elleh davar acher, ki hakkahal hayah navoch
Some therefore cried one thing, and some another: for the assembly was in confusion;

וְרֻבָּם לֹא יָדְעוּ לָמָּה הִתְאַסְּפוּ
verubbam lo yade'u lammah hit'assefu
and the more part knew not wherefore they were come together.

אֲנָשִׁים מִן הֶהָמוֹן הִסְבִּירוּ מַשֶּׁהוּ לַאֲלֶכְּסַנְדֶּר לְאַחַר שֶׁבְּנֵי עַמּוֹ הַיְּהוּדִים דְּחָקוּהוּ קָדִימָה
anashim min hehamon hisbiru mashehu la'alekkesander le'achar sebbenei ammo hayehudim dechakuhu kadimah
And they brought Alexander out of the multitude, the Jews putting him forward.

הֵנִיף אֲלֶכְּסַנְדֶּר אֶת יָדוֹ וְרָצָה לְהַשְׁמִיעַ לֶהָמוֹן דְּבַר הֲגַנָּה
henif alekkesander et yado veratzah lehashmia lehamon devar hagannah
And Alexander beckoned with the hand, and would have made a defence unto the people.

אַךְ כְּשֶׁהִבְחִינוּ שֶׁהוּא יְהוּדִי רָעֲמוּ כֻּלָּם בְּקוֹל אֶחָד וּבְמֶשֶׁךְ שְׁעָתַיִם צָעֲקוּ
ach keshehivchinu shehu yehudi ra'amu kullam bekol echad uvemeshech she'atayim tza'aku
But when they perceived that he was a Jew, all with one voice about the space of two hours cried out,

גְּדוֹלָה אַרְטֶמִיס שֶׁל הָאֶפְסִים
gedolah artemis shel ha'efesim
Great is Diana of the Ephesians.

הִשְׁקִיט מַזְכִּיר הָעִיר אֶת הָעָם וְאָמַר
hishkit mazkir ha'ir et ha'am ve'amar
And when the townclerk had quieted the multitude, he saith,

אַנְשֵׁי אֶפְסוֹס, מִי מִבְּנֵי אָדָם אֵינוֹ יוֹדֵעַ
anshei efesos, mi mibbenei adam eino yodea
Ye men of Ephesus, what man is there who knoweth not

מַעֲשֵׂי הַשְּׁלִיחִים

בָּעֵת הַהִיא הָיְתָה מְהוּמָה לֹא קְטַנָּה עַל־אוֹדוֹת דֶּרֶךְ הָאָדוֹן
ba'et hahi hayetah mehumah lo ketannah al-'odot derech ha'adon
And about that time there arose no small stir concerning the Way.

בִּגְלַל צוֹרֵף אֶחָד, דֶּמֶטְרִיּוֹס שְׁמוֹ, שֶׁהָיָה עוֹשֶׂה תַּבְנִיּוֹת כֶּסֶף שֶׁל הֵיכַל אַרְטֶמִיס
biglal tzoref echad, demetriyos shemo, shehayah oseh tavniyot kesef shel heichal artemis
For a certain man named Demetrius, a silversmith, who made silver shrines of Diana,

וּמַמְצִיא רֶוַח לֹא מְבֻטָּל לַפּוֹעֲלִים
umamtzi revach lo mevuttal lappo'alim
brought no little business unto the craftsmen;

הוּא כִּנֵּס אוֹתָם עִם בַּעֲלֵי הַמִּקְצוֹעַ הָעוֹבְדִים בְּאוֹתָהּ מְלָאכָה וְאָמַר
hu kinnes otam im ba'alei hammiktzoa ha'ovedim be'otah melachah ve'amar
whom he gathered together, with the workmen of like occupation, and said,

חֲבֵרִים, אַתֶּם יוֹדְעִים כִּי מֵהַמְּלָאכָה הַזֹּאת יֵשׁ לָנוּ רֶוַח
chaverim, attem yode'im ki mehammelachah hazzot yesh lanu revach
Sirs, ye know that by this business we have our wealth.

וְאַתֶּם רוֹאִים וְשׁוֹמְעִים שֶׁלֹּא רַק בְּאֶפֶסוֹס אֶלָּא כִּמְעַט בְּכָל אַסְיָה
ve'attem ro'im veshome'im shello rak be'efesos ella kim'at bechol asyah
And ye see and hear, that not alone at Ephesus, but almost throughout all Asia,

שָׁאוּל הַזֶּה שִׁכְנֵעַ וְהִדִּיחַ הָמוֹן רַב בְּאָמְרוֹ שֶׁאֵלִים מַעֲשֵׂי יָדַיִם אֵינָם אֵלִים
sha'ul hazzeh shichnea vehiddiach hamon rav be'omro she'elim ma'asei yadayim einam elim
this Paul hath persuaded and turned away much people, saying that they are no gods, that are made with hands:

אֲבָל לֹא רַק מְלַאכְתֵּנוּ זֹאת עֲלוּלָה לִהְיוֹת לְבוּז,
aval lo rak melachtenu zot alulah lihyot levuz
and not only is there danger that this our trade come into disrepute;

אֶלָּא גַּם הַהֵיכָל שֶׁל הָאֵלָה הַגְּדוֹלָה אַרְטֶמִיס עָלוּל לְהֵחָשֵׁב לְאֶפֶס
ella gam haheichal shel ha'elah haggedolah artemis alul lehechashev le'efes
but also that the temple of the great goddess Diana be made of no account,

וְהִיא אֲשֶׁר כָּל אַסְיָה וְכָל הָעוֹלָם עוֹבְדִים אוֹתָהּ גַּם תַּפְסִיד אֶת גְּדֻלָּתָהּ
vehi asher kol asyah vechol ha'olam ovdim otah gam tafsid et gedullatah
and that she should even be deposed from her magnificence whom all Asia and the world worshippeth.

כְּשָׁמְעָם אֶת דְּבָרָיו נִתְמַלְּאוּ זַעַם וְצָעֲקוּ: גְּדוֹלָה אַרְטֶמִיס שֶׁל הָאֶפֶסִים
keshom'am et devarav nitmall'u za'am vetza'aku: gdolah artemis shel ha'efesim
And when they heard this they were filled with wrath, and cried out, saying, Great is Diana of the Ephesians.

מְהוּמָה הִתְפַּשְּׁטָה בְּכָל הָעִיר וְהַתּוֹשָׁבִים רָצוּ כְּאִישׁ אֶחָד אֶל הָאַמְפִיתֵיאַטְרוֹן
mehumah hitpashetah bechol ha'ir vehattoshavim ratzu ke'ish echad el ha'amfitei'atron
And the city was filled with the confusion: and they rushed with one accord into the theatre,

מַעֲשֵׂי הַשְּׁלִיחִים

הִתְנַפֵּל עֲלֵיהֶם הָאִישׁ בַּעַל הָרוּחַ הָרָעָה וּבְחָזְקָה רַבָּה גָּבַר עֲלֵיהֶם
hitnappel aleihem ha'ish ba'al haruach hara'ah uvechozkah rabbah gavar aleihem
And the man in whom the evil spirit was leaped on them, and mastered both of them, and prevailed against them,

עַד כִּי בָּרְחוּ מִן הַבַּיִת הַהוּא עֲרֻמִּים וּפְצוּעִים
ad ki barechu min habbayit hahu arummim ufetzu'im
so that they fled out of that house naked and wounded.

כַּאֲשֶׁר נוֹדַע הַדָּבָר לְכָל הַיְהוּדִים וְהַיְוָנִים תּוֹשָׁבֵי אֶפֶסוֹס
ka'asher noda haddavar lechol hayehudim vehayevanim toshavei efesos
And this became known to all, both Jews and Greeks, that dwelt at Ephesus;

נָפַל פַּחַד עַל כֻּלָּם וְנִתְגַּדֵּל שֵׁם הָאָדוֹן יֵשׁוּעַ
nafal pachad al kulam venitgaddel shem ha'adon yeshua
and fear fell upon them all, and the name of the Lord Jesus was magnified.

רַבִּים מֵאוֹתָם הָאֲנָשִׁים שֶׁקִּבְּלוּ אֶת הָאֱמוּנָה בָּאוּ לְהִתְוַדּוֹת וְסִפְּרוּ אֶת מַעֲשֵׂיהֶם
rabbim me'otam ha'anashim shekkibbelu et ha'emunah ba'u lehitvaddot vesipperu et ma'aseihem
Many also of them that had believed came, confessing, and declaring their deeds.

רַבִּים שֶׁעָסְקוּ בְּכִשּׁוּף אָסְפוּ אֶת סִפְרֵיהֶם וְשָׂרְפוּ אוֹתָם לְעֵינֵי כֹל
rabbim she'aseku bechishuf asefu et sifreihem vesarfu otam le'einei kol
And not a few of them that practised magical arts brought their books together and burned them in the sight of all;

חִשְּׁבוּ וּמָצְאוּ שֶׁמְּחִירָם חֲמִשִּׁים אֶלֶף מַטְבְּעוֹת כֶּסֶף
chishevu umatze'u shemmechiram chamishim elef matbe'ot kesef
and they counted the price of them, and found it fifty thousand pieces of silver.

בִּגְבוּרָה כָּזֹאת שִׂגְשֵׂג וְגָבַר דְּבַר הָאָדוֹן
bigvurah kazot sigseg vegavar dvar ha'adon
So mightily grew the word of the Lord and prevailed.

כַּאֲשֶׁר כָּל זֶה נִגְמַר, עָלָה בְּדַעְתּוֹ שֶׁל שָׁאוּל לַעֲבֹר דֶּרֶךְ מַקֵדוֹנְיָה וְאָכַיָה
ka'asher kol zeh nigmar, alah beda'to shel sha'ul la'avor derech makedoneyah ve'achayah
Now after these things were ended, Paul purposed in the spirit, when he had passed through Macedonia and Achaia,

וּלְהַמְשִׁיךְ בְּדַרְכּוֹ אֶל יְרוּשָׁלַיִם. אָמַר: אַחֲרֵי שֶׁאֶהְיֶה שָׁם עָלַי לִרְאוֹת גַּם אֶת רוֹמָא
ulehamshich bedarko el yerushalayim. amar: acharei she'ehyeh sham alai lir'ot gam et roma
to go to Jerusalem, saying, After I have been there, I must also see Rome.

הוּא שָׁלַח אֶל מַקֵדוֹנְיָה שְׁנַיִם מִן הַמְשָׁרְתִים אוֹתוֹ
hu shalach el makedoneyah shenayim min hamsharetim oto
And having sent into Macedonia two of them that ministered unto him,

אֶת טִימוֹתִיאוֹס וְאֶת אֶרַסְטוֹס, וְהוּא עַצְמוֹ שָׁהָה זְמַן מְסֻיָּם בְּאַסְיָה
et timotei'os ve'et erastos, vehu atzmo shahah zeman mesyam be'asyah
Timothy and Erastus, he himself stayed in Asia for a while.

מַעֲשֵׂי הַשְּׁלִיחִים

יֵשׁ שֶׁהִקְשׁוּ לְבָבָם וְסֵרְבוּ לְהַאֲמִין, וְדִבְּרוּ רָעוֹת עַל הַדֶּרֶךְ הַהִיא בְּאָזְנֵי הַקָּהָל
yesh shehikshu levavam veservu leha'amin, vedibbru ra'ot al hadderech hahi be'azenei hakkahal
But when some were hardened and disobedient, speaking evil of the Way before the multitude,

לָכֵן פָּרַשׁ מֵהֶם בְּהַבְדִּילוֹ מִתּוֹכָם אֶת הַתַּלְמִידִים, וְיוֹם יוֹם דִּבֵּר בְּאוּלָם הַמִּדְרָשׁ שֶׁל טִירָנוֹס
lachen parash mehem behavdilo mittocham et hattalmidim, veyom yom dibber be'ulam hammidrash shel tiranos
he departed from them, and separated the disciples, reasoning daily in the school of Tyrannus.

כָּךְ זֶה הָיָה בְּמֶשֶׁךְ שְׁנָתַיִם
kach zeh hayah bemeshech shnatayim
And this continued for the space of two years;

עַד שֶׁכָּל תּוֹשָׁבֵי אַסְיָה הַיְהוּדִים וְהַיְוָנִים שָׁמְעוּ אֶת דְּבַר הָאָדוֹן
ad shekkol toshavei asyah hayehudim vehayevanim shame'u et devar ha'adon
so that all they that dwelt in Asia heard the word of the Lord, both Jews and Greeks.

וֵאלֹהִים עָשָׂה גְּבוּרוֹת בִּלְתִּי רְגִילוֹת עַל־יְדֵי שָׁאוּל
ve'elohim asah gvurot bilti regilot al-yedei sha'ul
And God wrought special miracles by the hands of Paul:

עַד כְּדֵי כָּךְ שֶׁחוֹלִים נִרְפְּאוּ מִמַּחֲלוֹתֵיהֶם וְהָרוּחוֹת הָרָעוֹת יָצְאוּ מֵהֶם כַּאֲשֶׁר הוּבְאוּ אֲלֵיהֶם מִטְפָּחוֹת אוֹ סִנָּרִים שֶׁנָּגְעוּ בְּעוֹר גּוּפוֹ
ad kedei kach shecholim nirpe'u mimmachaloteihem veharuchot hara'ot yatze'u mehem ka'asher huve'u aleihem mitpachot o sinnarim shennage'u be'or gufo
insomuch that unto the sick were carried away from his body handkerchiefs or aprons, and the diseases departed from them, and the evil spirits went out.

גַּם כַּמָּה יְהוּדִים מְשׁוֹטְטִים שֶׁעָסְקוּ בְּגֵרוּשׁ שֵׁדִים
gam kammah yehudim meshotetim she'aseku begerush shedim
But certain also of the strolling Jews, exorcists,

נִסּוּ לְבַטֵּא אֶת שֵׁם הָאָדוֹן יֵשׁוּעַ עַל אֲחוּזֵי רוּחוֹת רָעוֹת אֲשֶׁר שָׁאוּל מַכְרִיז עָלָיו
nissu levattei et shem ha'adon yeshua al achuzei ruchot ra'ot
took upon them to name over them that had the evil spirits the name of the Lord Jesus,

בְּאָמְרָם: אֲנִי מַשְׁבִּיעַ אֶתְכֶן בְּיֵשׁוּעַ
be'omram: ani mashbia etchen beyeshua asher sha'ul machriz alav
saying, I adjure you by Jesus whom Paul preacheth.

הָעוֹשִׂים זֹאת הָיוּ שִׁבְעַת בָּנָיו שֶׁל סְקֵוָה, כֹּהֵן גָּדוֹל יְהוּדִי
ha'osim zot hayu shiv'at banav shel skevah, kohen gadol yehudi
And there were seven sons of one Sceva, a Jew, a chief priest, who did this.

הֵשִׁיבָה הָרוּחַ הָרָעָה וְאָמְרָה לָהֶם: אֶת יֵשׁוּעַ אֲנִי מַכִּירָה וּמִיהוּ שָׁאוּל אֲנִי יוֹדַעַת, אַךְ מִי אַתֶּם
heshivah haruach hara'ah ve'amerah lahem: et yeshua ani makkirah umihu sha'ul ani yoda'at, ach mi attem
And the evil spirit answered and said unto them, Jesus I know, and Paul I know; but who are ye?

מַעֲשֵׂי הַשְּׁלִיחִים

עָבַר שָׁאוּל בָּאֲזוֹרִים הָעֶלְיוֹנִים וְהִגִּיעַ אֶל אֶפְסוֹס. הוּא מָצָא כַּמָּה תַּלְמִידִים
avar sha'ul ba'azorim ha'elyonim vehiggia el efesos. hu matza kammah talmidim
Paul having passed through the upper country came to Ephesus, and found certain disciples:

וְשָׁאַל אוֹתָם: הַאִם קִבַּלְתֶּם אֶת רוּחַ הַקֹּדֶשׁ כַּאֲשֶׁר הֶאֱמַנְתֶּם
vesha'al otam: ha'im kibbaltem et ruach hakkodesh ka'asher he'emantem
and he said unto them, Did ye receive the Holy Spirit when ye believed?

הֵשִׁיבוּ לוֹ: אַף לֹא שָׁמַעְנוּ שֶׁיֵּשׁ רוּחַ הַקֹּדֶשׁ
heshivu lo: af lo shama'nu sheyesh ruach hakkodesh
And they said unto him, Nay, we did not so much as hear whether the Holy Spirit was given.

שָׁאַל: אִם כֵּן, אֵיזוֹ טְבִילָה נִטְבַּלְתֶּם? אָמְרוּ: טְבִילַת יוֹחָנָן
sha'al: im ken, eizo tevilah nitbaltem? ameru: tevilat yochanan
And he said, Into what then were ye baptized? And they said, Into John's baptism.

אָמַר שָׁאוּל: יוֹחָנָן הִטְבִּיל טְבִילָה שֶׁל תְּשׁוּבָה
amar sha'ul: yochanan hitbil tevilah shel tshuvah
And Paul said, John baptized with the baptism of repentance,

בְּאָמְרוֹ לָעָם שֶׁיַּאֲמִינוּ בְּזֶה שֶׁיָּבוֹא אַחֲרָיו, כְּלוֹמַר, בְּיֵשׁוּעַ
be'amero la'am sheya'aminu bezeh sheyavo acharav, kelomar, beyeshua
saying unto the people that they should believe on him that should come after him, that is, on Jesus.

הֵם שָׁמְעוּ וְנִטְבְּלוּ לְשֵׁם הָאָדוֹן יֵשׁוּעַ
hem sham'u venitbelu leshem ha'adon yeshua
And when they heard this, they were baptized into the name of the Lord Jesus.

כְּשֶׁסָּמַךְ שָׁאוּל אֶת יָדָיו עֲלֵיהֶם, בָּאָה רוּחַ הַקֹּדֶשׁ עֲלֵיהֶם
kshessamach sha'ul et yadav aleihem, ba'ah ruach hakkodesh aleihem
And when Paul had laid his hands upon them, the Holy Spirit came on them;

וְאָז דִּבְּרוּ בִּלְשׁוֹנוֹת וְהִתְנַבְּאוּ
ve'az dibberu bilshonot vehitnabb'u
and they spake with tongues, and prophesied.

כֻּלָּם הָיוּ כִּשְׁנֵים־עָשָׂר אִישׁ
kullam hayu kishneim-'asar ish
And they were in all about twelve men.

הוּא נִכְנַס לְבֵית הַכְּנֶסֶת וְדִבֵּר בְּאֹמֶץ לֵב. בְּמֶשֶׁךְ שְׁלוֹשָׁה חֳדָשִׁים
hu nichnas leveit hakkeneset vedibber be'ometz lev. bemeshech sheloshah chodashim
And he entered into the synagogue, and spake boldly for the space of three months,

טָעַן וְשִׁכְנֵעַ בְּעִנְיַן מַלְכוּת אֱלֹהִים
ta'an veshichnea be'inyan malchut elohim
reasoning and persuading as to the things concerning the kingdom of God.

מַעֲשֵׂי הַשְּׁלִיחִים

אֶל אֶפְסוֹס הִגִּיעַ יְהוּדִי אֶחָד יְלִיד אֲלֶכְּסַנְדְּרִיָּה וּשְׁמוֹ אַשָׁאוּל, אִישׁ־דְּבָרִים
el efesos higgia yehudi echad yelid alekkesanderiyah ushemo asha'ul, ish-devarim
Now a certain Jew named Apollos, an Alexandrian by race, an eloquent man, came to Ephesus;

וְגָדוֹל בַּמִּקְרָא
vegadol bammikra
and he was mighty in the scriptures.

מְלֻמָּד הָיָה בְּדֶרֶךְ הָאָדוֹן, וּבְרוּחַ נִלְהֶבֶת
melummad hayah bederech ha'adon, uveruach nilhevet
This man had been instructed in the way of the Lord; and being fervent in spirit,

דִּבֶּר וְלִמֵּד הֵיטֵב עַל־אֹדוֹת יֵשׁוּעַ, אַךְ יָדַע רַק עַל טְבִילַת יוֹחָנָן
dibber velimmed heitev al-'odot yeshua, ach yada rak al tevilat yochanan
he spake and taught accurately the things concerning Jesus, knowing only the baptism of John:

הוּא הֵחֵל לְדַבֵּר בְּאֹמֶץ לֵב בְּבֵית הַכְּנֶסֶת. כַּאֲשֶׁר שָׁמְעוּ אוֹתוֹ פְּרִיסְקִילָה וַעֲקִילַס
hu hechel ledabber be'ometz lev beveit hakkeneset. ka'asher shame'u oto perisekilah va'akilas
and he began to speak boldly in the synagogue. But when Priscilla and Aquila heard him,

לָקְחוּ אוֹתוֹ אֲלֵיהֶם וְהִסְבִּירוּ לוֹ אֶת דֶּרֶךְ אֱלֹהִים בְּיֶתֶר דִּיּוּק
lakechu oto aleihem vehisbiru lo et derech elohim beyeter diyuk
they took him unto them, and expounded unto him the way of God more accurately.

כַּאֲשֶׁר רָצָה לָלֶכֶת לְאָכַיָה עוֹדְדוּהוּ הָאַחִים
ka'asher ratzah lalechet le'achayah odeduhu ha'achim
And when he was minded to pass over into Achaia, the brethren encouraged him,

וְכָתְבוּ לַתַּלְמִידִים לְקַבֵּל אוֹתוֹ
vechatvu lattalmidim lekabbel oto
and wrote to the disciples to receive him:

הוּא הִגִּיעַ לְשָׁם וְהוֹדוֹת לַחֶסֶד עָזַר הַרְבֵּה לַמַּאֲמִינִים
hu higgia lesham vehodot lachesed azar harbeh lamma'aminim
and when he was come, he helped them much that had believed through grace;

כִּי בְּפֻמְבֵּי וּבְתֹקֶף הוֹכִיחַ לַיְּהוּדִים וְהֶרְאָה עַל־יְדֵי הַכְּתוּבִים שֶׁהַמָּשִׁיחַ הוּא יֵשׁוּעַ
ki befumbei uvetokef hochiach layehudim veher'ah al-yedei hakketuvim shehammashiach hu yeshua
for he powerfully confuted the Jews, and that publicly, showing by the scriptures that Jesus was the Christ.

יט

בְּעֵת שֶׁאַשָׁאוּל הָיָה בְּקוֹרִינְתּוֹס
be'et she'asha'ul hayah bekorinetos
And it came to pass, that, while Apollos was at Corinth,

מַעֲשֵׂי הַשְּׁלִיחִים

אָז שִׁלַּח אוֹתָם מִלִּפְנֵי כֵּס הַמִּשְׁפָּט
az shillach otam millifnei kes hammishpat
And he drove them from the judgment-seat.

תָּפְסוּ כֻלָּם אֶת סוֹסְתֵּנִיס, רֹאשׁ בֵּית הַכְּנֶסֶת, וְהִכּוּהוּ לִפְנֵי כֵּס הַמִּשְׁפָּט
tafsu kullam et sostenis, rosh beit hakkeneset, vehikkuhu lifnei kes hammishpat
And they all laid hold on Sosthenes, the ruler of the synagogue, and beat him before the judgment-seat.

אַךְ לְגַלִּיּוֹן לֹא הָיָה אִכְפַּת
ach legalliyon lo hayah ichpat
And Gallio cared for none of these things.

שָׁאוּל שָׁהָה שָׁם עוֹד יָמִים רַבִּים. אַחֲרֵי כֵן נִפְרַד מֵהָאַחִים וְהִפְלִיג בְּדַרְכּוֹ לְסוּרְיָה
sha'ul shahah sham od yamim rabbim. acharei chen nifrad meha'achim vehiflig bedarko lesureyah
And Paul, having tarried after this yet many days, took his leave of the brethren, and sailed thence for Syria,

יַחַד עִם פְּרִיסְקִילָה וַעֲקִילַס, לְאַחַר שֶׁגָּזַז אֶת שְׂעַר רֹאשׁוֹ בְּקֶנְכְּרֵאָה בִּגְלַל נֶדֶר שֶׁנָּדַר
yachad im prisekilah va'akilas, le'achar sheggazaz et se'ar rosho bekenkere'ah biglal neder shennadar
and with him Priscilla and Aquila: having shorn his head in Cenchreæ; for he had a vow.

הֵם בָּאוּ לְאֶפֶסוֹס וְשָׁם עָזַב אֶת פְּרִיסְקִילָה וַעֲקִילַס
hem ba'u le'efesos vesham azav et perisekilah va'akilas
And they came to Ephesus, and he left them there:

הוּא נִכְנַס לְבֵית הַכְּנֶסֶת וְדִבֵּר עִם הַיְהוּדִים
hu nichnas leveit hakkeneset vedibber im hayehudim
but he himself entered into the synagogue, and reasoned with the Jews.

כְּשֶׁבִּקְשׁוּ מִמֶּנּוּ לְהִשָּׁאֵר זְמַן רַב יוֹתֵר לֹא הִסְכִּים
keshebbikshu mimmennu lehisha'er zman rav yoter lo hiskim
And when they asked him to abide a longer time, he consented not;

אֶלָּא נִפְרַד מֵהֶם וְאָמַר: עוֹד אָשׁוּב אֲלֵיכֶם, אִם יִרְצֶה אֱלֹהִים. הוּא הִפְלִיג מֵאֶפֶסוֹס
ella nifrad mehem ve'amar: od ashuv aleichem, im yirtzeh elohim. hu hiflig me'efesos
but taking his leave of them, and saying, I will return again unto you if God will, he set sail from Ephesus.

וּלְאַחַר שֶׁהִגִּיעַ לְקֵיסַרְיָה עָלָה לִירוּשָׁלַיִם וְשָׁאַל לִשְׁלוֹם הַקְּהִלָּה. אַחֲרֵי כֵן יָרַד לְאַנְטִיוֹכְיָה
ule'achar shehiggia lekeisaryah alah liyerushalayim vesha'al lishlom hakkehillah. acharei chen yarad le'antiyocheyah
And when he had landed at Cæsarea, he went up and saluted the church, and went down to Antioch.

שָׁהָה שָׁם זְמַן מָה וְיָצָא וְעָבַר מִמָּקוֹם לְמָקוֹם בְּאֵזוֹר גָּלַטְיָה
shahah sham zman mah veyatza ve'avar mimmakom lemakom be'ezor galatyah
And having spent some time there, he departed, and went through the region of Galatia,

וּבְאֵזוֹר פְרִיגְיָה כְּשֶׁהוּא מְחַזֵּק אֶת הַתַּלְמִידִים
uve'ezor ferigeyah keshehu mechazzek et hattalmidim
and Phrygia, in order, establishing all the disciples.

מַעֲשֵׂי הַשְּׁלִיחִים

קְרִיסְפּוֹס, רֹאשׁ בֵּית הַכְּנֶסֶת, הֶאֱמִין בָּאָדוֹן הוּא וְכָל בְּנֵי בֵיתוֹ
krisepos, rosh beit hakkeneset, he'emin ba'adon hu vechol benei beito
And Crispus, the ruler of the synagogue, believed in the Lord with all his house;

וְגַם קוֹרִינְתִּים רַבִּים כְּשָׁמְעָם אֶת הַדְּבָרִים הֶאֱמִינוּ וְנִטְבְּלוּ
vegam korinetim rabbim keshom'am et haddevarim he'eminu venitbelu
and many of the Corinthians hearing believed, and were baptized.

בְּלַיְלָה אֶחָד אָמַר הָאָדוֹן אֶל שָׁאוּל בְּחָזוֹן: אַל תִּירָא. דַּבֵּר, אַל תֶּחֱשֶׁה
belaylah echad amar ha'adon el sha'ul bechazon. al tira. dabber, al techesheh
And the Lord said unto Paul in the night by a vision, Be not afraid, but speak and hold not thy peace:

כִּי אִתְּךָ אֲנִי. אִישׁ לֹא יִפְגַּע בְּךָ וְלֹא יָרַע לְךָ, כִּי עַם רַב לִי בָּעִיר הַזֹּאת
ki ittecha ani. ish lo yifga becha velo yarea lecha, ki am rav li ba'ir hazzot
for I am with thee, and no man shall set on thee to harm thee: for I have much people in this city.

וְשָׁאוּל יָשַׁב שָׁם שָׁנָה וְשִׁשָּׁה חֳדָשִׁים וְהָיָה מְלַמֵּד אֶת דְּבַר אֱלֹהִים
vesha'ul yashav sham shanah veshishah chodashim vehayah melammed et dvar elohim
And he dwelt there a year and six months, teaching the word of God among them.

כַּאֲשֶׁר גַּלִּיּוֹן הָיָה נְצִיב מְדִינַת אֲכַיָּה
ka'asher galliyon hayah netziv medinat achayah
But when Gallio was proconsul of Achaia,

חָבְרוּ הַיְּהוּדִים יַחְדָּיו עַל שָׁאוּל וֶהֱבִיאוּהוּ לִפְנֵי כֵּס הַמִּשְׁפָּט
chaveru hayehudim yachdav al sha'ul vehevi'uhu lifnei kes hammishpat
the Jews with one accord rose up against Paul and brought him before the judgment-seat,

אָמְרוּ: הָאִישׁ הַזֶּה מֵסִית בְּנֵי אָדָם לַעֲבֹד אֶת אֱלֹהִים שֶׁלֹּא כַחֹק
ameru: ha'ish hazzeh mesit benei adam la'avod et elohim shello kachok
saying, This man persuadeth men to worship God contrary to the law.

כְּשֶׁהִתְכַּוֵּן שָׁאוּל לְהַתְחִיל לְדַבֵּר אָמַר גַּלִּיּוֹן אֶל הַיְּהוּדִים
keshehitkavven sha'ul lehatchil ledabber amar galliyon el hayehudim
But when Paul was about to open his mouth, Gallio said unto the Jews,

יְהוּדִים, אִלּוּ הָיָה כָּאן אֵיזֶה פֶּשַׁע אוֹ מַעֲשֵׂה נְבָלָה, אֲזַי, לְפִי שׁוּרַת הַהִגָּיוֹן, הָיִיתִי מְקַבֵּל אֶתְכֶם בְּסַבְלָנוּת
yehudim, illu hayah kan eizeh pesha o ma'aseh nevalah, azai, lefi shurat hahiggayon, hayiti mekabbel etchem besavlanut
If indeed it were a matter of wrong or of wicked villany, O ye Jews, reason would that I should bear with you:

אֲבָל אִם אֵלֶּה שְׁאֵלוֹת עַל מִלִּים וְעַל שֵׁמוֹת וְעַל הַתּוֹרָה שֶׁלָּכֶם - זֶה עִנְיַנְכֶם
aval im elleh she'elot al millim ve'al shemot ve'al hattorah shelachem - zeh inyanchem
but if they are questions about words and names and your own law, look to it yourselves;

אֲנִי אֵינֶנִּי רוֹצֶה לִהְיוֹת שׁוֹפֵט בְּעִנְיָנִים כָּאֵלֶּה
ani einneni rotzeh lihyot shofet be'inyanim ka'elleh
I am not minded to be a judge of these matters.

מַעֲשֵׂי הַשְּׁלִיחִים

יח

אַחֲרֵי כֵן יָצָא שָׁאוּל מֵאַתּוּנָה וּבָא אֶל קוֹרִינְתּוֹס
acharei chen yatza sha'ul me'attunah uva el korinetos
After these things he departed from Athens, and came to Corinth.

שָׁם מָצָא יְהוּדִי אֶחָד יְלִיד פּוֹנְטוֹס, עֲקִילַס שְׁמוֹ, שֶׁלֹּא מִכְּבָר בָּא מֵאִיטַלְיָה עִם פְּרִיסְקִילָה אִשְׁתּוֹ
sham matza yehudi echad yelid ponetos, akilas shemo, shello mikkvar ba me'italyah im perisekilah ishto
And he found a certain Jew named Aquila, a man of Pontus by race, lately come from Italy, with his wife Priscilla,

מִשּׁוּם שֶׁקְּלוֹדְיוֹס צִוָּה עַל כָּל הַיְהוּדִים לַעֲזֹב אֶת רוֹמָא
mishum shekklodeyos tzivvah al kol hayehudim la'azov et roma
because Claudius had commanded all the Jews to depart from Rome: and he came unto them;

הוּא בָּא אֲלֵיהֶם וּמֵאַחַר שֶׁהָיָה לוֹ אוֹתוֹ מִקְצוֹעַ, עֲשִׂיַּת אֹהָלִים, הִתְגּוֹרֵר אֶצְלָם וְעָבַד אִתָּם
hu ba aleihem ume'achar shehayah lo oto miktzoa', asiyat ohalim, hitgorer etzlam ve'avad ittam
and because he was of the same trade, he abode with them, and they wrought; for by their trade they were tentmakers.

וּמִדֵּי שַׁבָּת דִּבֵּר בְּבֵית הַכְּנֶסֶת וְשִׁכְנֵעַ הֵן יְהוּדִים וְהֵן יְוָנִים
umiddei shabbat dibber beveit hakkeneset veshichnea hen yehudim vehen yevanim
And he reasoned in the synagogue every sabbath, and persuaded Jews and Greeks.

כְּשֶׁבָּאוּ סִילָא וְטִימוֹתֵיאוֹס מִמַּקֵדוֹנְיָה, שָׁאוּל הִתְמַסֵּר לְגַמְרֵי לִדְבַר הַבְּשׂוֹרָה
keshebba'u sila vetimotei'os mimmakedoneyah, sha'ul hitmasser legamrei lidvar habbesorah
But when Silas and Timothy came down from Macedonia, Paul was constrained by the word,

וְהֵעִיד לַיְהוּדִים שֶׁהַמָּשִׁיחַ הוּא יֵשׁוּעַ
vehe'id layehudim shehammashiach hu yeshua
testifying to the Jews that Jesus was the Christ.

כֵּיוָן שֶׁהִתְנַגְּדוּ וְגִדְּפוּ נִעֵר אֶת בְּגָדָיו וְאָמַר לָהֶם
keivan shehitnaggedu vegiddefu ni'er et begadav ve'amar lahem
And when they opposed themselves and blasphemed, he shook out his raiment and said unto them,

דַּמְכֶם בְּרָאשְׁכֶם. אֲנִי נָקִי. מֵעַתָּה אֵלֵךְ לַגּוֹיִם
damchem beroshechem. ani naki. me'attah elech laggoyim
Your blood be upon your own heads; I am clean: from henceforth I will go unto the Gentiles.

הָלַךְ מִשָּׁם וְנִכְנַס לְבֵיתוֹ שֶׁל אִישׁ יְרֵא אֱלֹהִים, טִיטְיוֹס יוּסְטוֹס שְׁמוֹ
halach misham venichnas leveito shel ish yerei elohim, titeyos yusetos shemo
And he departed thence, and went into the house of a certain man named Titus Justus, one that worshipped God,

וּבֵיתוֹ סָמוּךְ לְבֵית הַכְּנֶסֶת
uveito samuch leveit hakkeneset
whose house joined hard to the synagogue.

מַעֲשֵׂי הַשְּׁלִיחִים

לָכֵן בִּהְיוֹתֵנוּ צֶאֱצָאֵי אֱלֹהִים
lachen bihyotenu tze'etza'ei elohim
Being then the offspring of God,

אֵין אָנוּ צְרִיכִים לַחֲשֹׁב שֶׁהָאֱלֹהוּת דּוֹמָה לְזָהָב אוֹ לְכֶסֶף אוֹ לְאֶבֶן, פְּסִילֵי אֳמָנוּת וּפְרִי מַחֲשֶׁבֶת אָדָם
ein anu tzrichim lachashov sheha'elohut domah lezahav o lechesef o le'even, psilei omanut uferi machashevet adam
we ought not to think that the Godhead is like unto gold, or silver, or stone, graven by art and device of man.

אֱלֹהִים אָמְנָם הִתְעַלֵּם מֵעִתּוֹת הַבַּעֲרוּת
elohim omnam hit'allem me'ittot habba'arut
The times of ignorance therefore God overlooked;

אַךְ כָּעֵת הוּא מְצַוֶּה עַל כָּל בְּנֵי אָדָם בְּכָל מָקוֹם לַחֲזֹר בִּתְשׁוּבָה
ach ka'et hu metzavveh al kol benei adam bechol makom lachazor bitshuvah
but now he commandeth men that they should all everywhere repent:

שֶׁכֵּן יָעַד יוֹם לִשְׁפֹּט תֵּבֵל בְּצֶדֶק,
shekken ya'ad yom lishpot tevel betzedek
inasmuch as he hath appointed a day in which he will judge the world in righteousness

עַל־יְדֵי אִישׁ אֲשֶׁר מִנָּה
al-yedei ish asher minnah
by the man whom he hath ordained;

וְהִמְצִיא הוֹכָחָה לַכֹּל בַּהֲקִימוֹ אוֹתוֹ מִן הַמֵּתִים
vehimtzi hochachah lakkol bahakimo oto min hammetim
whereof he hath given assurance unto all men, in that he hath raised him from the dead.

כַּאֲשֶׁר שָׁמְעוּ עַל תְּחִיַּת מֵתִים, אֲחָדִים לִגְלְגוּ וַאֲחֵרִים אָמְרוּ
ka'asher shame'u al techiyat metim, achadim liglegu va'acherim ameru
Now when they heard of the resurrection of the dead, some mocked; but others said,

נִשְׁמַע אוֹתְךָ בְּעִנְיָן זֶה עוֹד פַּעַם
nishma otcha be'inyan zeh od pa'am
We will hear thee concerning this yet again.

אָז יָצָא שָׁאוּל מִתּוֹכָם
az yatza sha'ul mittocham
Thus Paul went out from among them.

אֲבָל כַּמָּה אֲנָשִׁים הִצְטָרְפוּ אֵלָיו וְהֶאֱמִינוּ
aval kammah anashim hitztarefu elav vehe'eminu
But certain men clave unto him, and believed:

בִּכְלָלָם דִּיּוֹנִיסְיוֹס, מִן הַשּׁוֹפְטִים שֶׁל הָאַרְיוֹפָּגוֹס, וְאִשָּׁה אַחַת, דָּמָרִיס שְׁמָהּ, וַאֲחֵרִים עִמָּהֶם
bichlalam diyoniseyos, min hashofetim shel ha'aryoppagos, ve'ishah achat, damaris shemah, va'acherim immahem
among whom also was Dionysius the Areopagite, and a woman named Damaris, and others with them.

מַעֲשֵׂי הַשְּׁלִיחִים

אַנְשֵׁי אַתּוּנָה, בְּכָל דָּבָר רוֹאֶה אֲנִי שֶׁיִּרְאֵי אֱלֹהוּת אַתֶּם מְאֹד
anshei attunah, bechol davar ro'eh ani sheyir'ei elohut attem me'od
Ye men of Athens, in all things I perceive that ye are very religious.

כִּי כַּאֲשֶׁר עָבַרְתִּי וְהִתְבּוֹנַנְתִּי בְּקָדְשֵׁיכֶם מָצָאתִי גַּם מִזְבֵּחַ שֶׁכָּתוּב עָלָיו
ki ka'asher avarti vehitbonanti bekadesheichem matzati gam mizbeach shekkatuv alav
For as I passed along, and observed the objects of your worship, I found also an altar with this inscription,

לְאֵל בִּלְתִּי נוֹדָע. וּבְכֵן, אֶת זֶה שֶׁאַתֶּם עוֹבְדִים מִבְּלִי לָדַעַת אוֹתוֹ, אוֹתוֹ אֲנִי מַכְרִיז לָכֶם
le'el bilti noda. uvchen, et zeh she'attem ovedim mibbeli lada'at oto, oto ani machriz lachem
TO AN UNKNOWN GOD. What therefore ye worship in ignorance, this I set forth unto you.

הָאֵל אֲשֶׁר עָשָׂה אֶת הָעוֹלָם וְכֹל אֲשֶׁר בּוֹ
ha'el asher asah et ha'olam vechol asher bo
The God that made the world and all things therein,

הוּא אֲדוֹן הַשָּׁמַיִם וְהָאָרֶץ וְאֵין הוּא שׁוֹכֵן בְּהֵיכָלוֹת מַעֲשֵׂה יָדַיִם
hu adon hashamayim veha'aretz ve'ein hu shochen beheichalot ma'aseh yadayim
he, being Lord of heaven and earth, dwelleth not in temples made with hands;

גַּם אֵין יְדֵי אָדָם מְשָׁרְתוֹת אוֹתוֹ כְּאִלּוּ הוּא זָקוּק לְאֵיזֶה דָּבָר
gam ein yedei adam mesharetot oto ke'illu hu zakuk le'eizeh davar
neither is he served by men's hands, as though he needed anything,

שֶׁהֲרֵי לַכֹּל הוּא נוֹתֵן חַיִּים וּנְשָׁמָה וְכָל דָּבָר
sheharei lakkol hu noten chayim uneshamah vechol davar
seeing he himself giveth to all life, and breath, and all things;

מֵאָדָם אֶחָד הוּא יָצַר אֶת כָּל עַמְמֵי בְּנֵי אָדָם לְהוֹשִׁיבָם עַל פְּנֵי כָל הָאָרֶץ
me'adam echad hu yatzar et kol amemei benei adam lehoshivam al pnei kol ha'aretz
and he made of one every nation of men to dwell on all the face of the earth,

וְיָעַד זְמַנִּים קְבוּעִים וְקָבַע אֶת גְּבוּלוֹת מוֹשָׁבָם
veya'ad zemannim kevu'im vekava et gevulot moshavam
having determined their appointed seasons, and the bounds of their habitation;

לְמַעַן יְחַפְּשׂוּ אֶת הָאֱלֹהִים; אוּלַי יְגַשְׁשׁוּ אַחֲרָיו וְיִמְצְאוּ אוֹתוֹ, אַף שֶׁאֵינוֹ רָחוֹק מִכָּל אֶחָד מֵאִתָּנוּ
lema'an yechappesu et ha'elohim; ulai yegasheshu acharav veyimtze'u oto, af she'eino rachok mikkol echad me'ittanu
that they should seek God, if haply they might feel after him and find him, though he is not far from each one of us:

הֵן בּוֹ אֲנַחְנוּ חַיִּים וּמִתְנוֹעֲעִים וְקַיָּמִים, כְּמוֹ שֶׁגַּם אֲחָדִים מִמְּשׁוֹרְרֵיכֶם אָמְרוּ
hen bo anachnu chayim umitno'a'im vekayamim, kemo sheggam achadim mimmeshorereichem amru
for in him we live, and move, and have our being; as certain even of your own poets have said,

שֶׁגַּם אֲנַחְנוּ צֶאֱצָאָיו
sheggam anachnu tze'etza'av
For we are also his offspring.

מַעֲשֵׂי הַשְּׁלִיחִים

כַּאֲשֶׁר שָׁאוּל חִכָּה לָהֶם בְּאַתּוּנָה רָאָה אֶת הָעִיר מְלֵאָה אֱלִילִים וְרוּחוֹ נִסְעֲרָה בְּקִרְבּוֹ
ka'asher sha'ul chikkah lahem be'attunah ra'ah et ha'ir mele'ah elilim verucho nis'arah bekirbo
Now while Paul waited for them at Athens, his spirit was provoked within him as he beheld the city full of idols.

הוּא דִּבֵּר בְּבֵית הַכְּנֶסֶת עִם הַיְהוּדִים וְעִם יִרְאֵי הָאֱלֹהִים,
hu dibber beveit hakkneset im hayehudim ve'im yir'ei ha'elohim
So he reasoned in the synagogue with the Jews and the devout persons,

וּמִדֵּי יוֹם בְּיוֹם דִּבֵּר בְּכִכַּר הָעִיר עִם הַמִּזְדַּמְּנִים לְשָׁם
umiddei yom beyom dibber bechikkar ha'ir im hammizdammenim lesham
and in the marketplace every day with them that met him.

גַּם כַּמָּה פִילוֹסוֹפִים מִן הָאַסְכּוֹלָה הָאֶפִּיקוֹרְסִית וּמִן הָאַסְכּוֹלָה הַסְּטוֹאִית הִתְוַכְּחוּ אִתּוֹ. יֵשׁ שֶׁאָמְרוּ
gam kammah filosofim min ha'askolah ha'eppikoresit umin ha'askolah hasseto'it hitvakkechu itto. yesh she'ameru
And certain also of the Epicurean and Stoic philosophers encountered him. And some said,

מָה רוֹצֶה הַפַּטְפְּטָן הַזֶּה לוֹמַר? וַאֲחֵרִים אָמְרוּ: נִרְאֶה שֶׁהוּא מַכְרִיז עַל אֵלִים זָרִים
mah rotzeh happatpetan hazzeh lomar? va'acherim ameru: nir'eh shehu machriz al elim zarim
What would this babbler say? others, He seemeth to be a setter forth of strange gods:

שֶׁכֵּן בִּשֵּׂר עַל יֵשׁוּעַ וְעַל הַתְּחִיָּה
shekken bisser al yeshua ve'al hattechiyah
because he preached Jesus and the resurrection.

הֵם לָקְחוּ אוֹתוֹ וֶהֱבִיאוּהוּ אֶל גִּבְעַת הַמּוֹעָצָה, הָאַרְיוֹפָּגוֹס, וְאָמְרוּ
hem lakechu oto vehevi'uhu el giv'at hammo'atzah, ha'aryoppagos, ve'amru
And they took hold of him, and brought him unto the Areopagus, saying,

אֶפְשָׁר לָדַעַת מָה הַתּוֹרָה הַחֲדָשָׁה הַזֹּאת שֶׁאַתָּה מַטִּיף
efshar lada'at mah hattorah hachadashah hazzot she'attah mattif
May we know what this new teaching is, which is spoken by thee?

כִּי דְבָרִים מוּזָרִים אַתָּה מַשְׁמִיעַ בְּאָזְנֵינוּ. לָכֵן רְצוֹנֵנוּ לָדַעַת מָה כַּוָּנַת הַדְּבָרִים הָאֵלֶּה
ki devarim muzarim attah mashmia be'ozneinu. lachen retzonenu lada'at mah kavvanat haddevarim ha'elleh
For thou bringest certain strange things to our ears: we would know therefore what these things mean.

בָּעֵת הַהִיא כָּל אַנְשֵׁי אַתּוּנָה וְהַזָּרִים הַגָּרִים בָּהּ לֹא בִלּוּ אֶת זְמַנָּם הַפָּנוּי
ba'et hahi kol anshei attunah vehazzarim haggarim bah lo billu et zmanam happanui
(Now all the Athenians and the strangers sojourning there spent their time in nothing else,

אֶלָּא בְּסִפּוּר דְּבָרִים חֲדָשִׁים אוֹ בִּשְׁמִיעָתָם
ella besippur dvarim chadashim o bishmi'atam
but either to tell or to hear some new thing.)

עָמַד שָׁאוּל בְּאֶמְצַע הָאַרְיוֹפָּגוֹס וְאָמַר
amad sha'ul be'emtza ha'aryoppagos ve'amar
And Paul stood in the midst of the Areopagus, and said,

מַעֲשֵׂי הַשְּׁלִיחִים

כָּךְ הִסְעִירוּ אֶת הָעָם וְאֶת רָאשֵׁי הָעִיר אֲשֶׁר שָׁמְעוּ זֹאת
kach his'iru et ha'am ve'et rashei ha'ir asher sham'u zot
And they troubled the multitude and the rulers of the city, when they heard these things.

וְהַלָּלוּ לָקְחוּ עַרְבוּת מִיָּסוֹן וּמֵהַשְּׁאָר וְשִׁחְרְרוּ אוֹתָם
vehallalu lakechu arvut miyason umehashe'ar veshichreru otam
And when they had taken security from Jason and the rest, they let them go.

בַּלַּיְלָה מִהֲרוּ הָאַחִים לְשַׁלֵּחַ אֶת שָׁאוּל וְאֶת סִילָא לְבֶרֵאָה,
ballaylah miharu ha'achim leshalleach et sha'ul ve'et sila libere'ah
And the brethren immediately sent away Paul and Silas by night unto Beroea:

וּכְשֶׁאֵלֶּה הִגִּיעוּ לְשָׁם נִכְנְסוּ לְבֵית הַכְּנֶסֶת
ucheshe'elleh higgi'u lesham nichnesu leveit hakkeneset
who when they were come thither went into the synagogue of the Jews.

יְהוּדֵי בֶרֵאָה הָיוּ אֲצִילֵי־רוּחַ יוֹתֵר מִן הַיְּהוּדִים שֶׁבְּתֵסָלוֹנִיקִי וְקִבְּלוּ אֶת הַדָּבָר בְּכָל לֵב
yehudei bere'ah hayu atzilei-ruach yoter min hayehudim shebbetessaloniki vekibbelu et haddavar bechol lev
Now these were more noble than those in Thessalonica, in that they received the word with all readiness of mind,

כְּשֶׁהֵם בּוֹדְקִים יוֹם יוֹם בַּכְּתוּבִים אִם הַדְּבָרִים הָאֵלֶּה אָכֵן כָּךְ
keshehem bodkim yom yom bakketuvim im haddevarim ha'elleh achen kach
examining the scriptures daily, whether these things were so.

אָז הֶאֱמִינוּ רַבִּים מֵהֶם וְכֵן גַּם יְוָנִים לֹא מְעַטִּים, הֵן נָשִׁים נִכְבָּדוֹת וְהֵן גְּבָרִים
az he'eminu rabbim mehem vechen gam yevanim lo me'attim, hen nashim nichbadot vehen gevarim
Many of them therefore believed; also of the Greek women of honorable estate, and of men, not a few.

כְּשֶׁנּוֹדַע לְאוֹתָם יְהוּדִים אֲשֶׁר בְּתֵסָלוֹנִיקִי כִּי גַּם בְּבֶרֵאָה מַשְׁמִיעַ שָׁאוּל אֶת דְּבַר אֱלֹהִים
keshennoda le'otam yehudim asher betessaloniki ki gam bebere'ah mashmia sha'ul et devar elohim
But when the Jews of Thessalonica had knowledge that the word of God was proclaimed of Paul at Beroea also,

בָּאוּ גַּם לְשָׁם וְעוֹרְרוּ וְהֵסִיתוּ אֶת הֲמוֹן הָעָם
ba'u gam lesham ve'oreru vehesitu et hamon ha'am
they came thither likewise, stirring up and troubling the multitudes.

מִיָּד שִׁלְּחוּ הָאַחִים אֶת שָׁאוּל כְּדֵי שֶׁיֵּלֵךְ עַד הַיָּם, אַךְ סִילָא וְטִימוֹתִיאוֹס נִשְׁאֲרוּ שָׁם
miyad shillchu ha'achim et sha'ul kedei sheyelech ad hayam, ach sila vetimotei'os nish'aru sham
And then immediately the brethren sent forth Paul to go as far as to the sea: and Silas and Timothy abode there still.

מְלַוָּיו שֶׁל שָׁאוּל הוֹבִילוּ אוֹתוֹ עַד אַתּוּנָה
melavvav shel sha'ul hovilu oto ad attunah
But they that conducted Paul brought him as far as Athens:

וּמִשָּׁם הָלְכוּ לְדַרְכָּם לְאַחַר שֶׁמָּסַר לָהֶם הוֹרָאָה בִּשְׁבִיל סִילָא וְטִימוֹתִיאוֹס - שֶׁיָּבוֹאוּ אֵלָיו בִּמְהֵרָה
umisham halechu ledarkam le'achar shemmasar lahem hora'ah bishvil sila vetimotei'os - sheyavo'u elav bimherah
and receiving a commandment unto Silas and Timothy that they should come to him with all speed, they departed.

מַעֲשֵׂי הַשְּׁלִיחִים

וְהִגִּיעוּ אֶל תֶּסָּלוֹנִיקִי, מָקוֹם שֶׁהָיָה בּוֹ בֵּית כְּנֶסֶת
vehiggi'u el tessaloniki, makom shehayah bo beit keneset
they came to Thessalonica, where was a synagogue of the Jews:

כְּמִנְהָגוֹ נִכְנַס שָׁאוּל אֲלֵיהֶם וְשָׁלוֹשׁ שַׁבָּתוֹת דָּרַשׁ לִפְנֵיהֶם מִתּוֹךְ הַכְּתוּבִים
keminhago nichnas sha'ul aleihem veshalosh shabbatot darash lifneihem mittoch hakketuvim
and Paul, as his custom was, went in unto them, and for three sabbath days reasoned with them from the scriptures,

כְּשֶׁהוּא מַסְבִּיר וּמוֹכִיחַ כִּי הַמָּשִׁיחַ הָיָה צָרִיךְ לִסְבֹּל וְלָקוּם מִן הַמֵּתִים
keshehu masbir umochiach ki hammashiach hayah tzarich lisbol velakum min hammetim
opening and alleging that it behooved the Christ to suffer, and to rise again from the dead;

וְכִי יֵשׁוּעַ זֶה שֶׁאֲנִי מַכְרִיז לָכֶם - הוּא הַמָּשִׁיחַ
vechi yeshua zeh she'ani machriz lachem - hu hammashiach
and that this Jesus, whom, said he, I proclaim unto you, is the Christ.

מִקְצָתָם הֶאֱמִינוּ וְנִסְפְּחוּ אֶל שָׁאוּל וְסִילָא
mikketzatam he'eminu venispechu el sha'ul vesila
And some of them were persuaded, and consorted with Paul and Silas;

וְכֵן גַּם הַרְבֵּה יְוָנִים יִרְאֵי אֱלֹהִים וְנָשִׁים נִכְבָּדוֹת לֹא מְעָט
vechen gam harbeh yevanim yir'ei elohim venashim nichbadot lo me'at
and of the devout Greeks a great multitude, and of the chief women not a few.

אֲבָל הָיוּ יְהוּדִים שֶׁנִּתְמַלְּאוּ קִנְאָה. הֵם לִקְּטוּ כַּמָּה אַנְשֵׁי בְּלִיַּעַל מִן הַשּׁוּק, וּלְאַחַר שֶׁהִקְהִילוּ אֲסַפְסוּף
aval hayu yehudim shennitmalle'u kin'ah. hem likktu kammah anshei beliya'al min hashuk, ule'achar shehik'hilu asafsuf
But the Jews, being moved with jealousy, took unto them certain vile fellows of the rabble, and gathering a crowd,

עוֹרְרוּ מְהוּמָה בָּעִיר וְהִתְקִיפוּ אֶת בֵּיתוֹ שֶׁל יָסוֹן לְחַפֵּשׂ אֶת הַשְּׁנַיִם וְלַהֲבִיאָם לִפְנֵי הָעָם
oreru mehumah ba'ir vehitkifu et beito shel yason lechappes et hashnayim velahavi'am lifnei ha'am
set the city on an uproar; and assaulting the house of Jason, they sought to bring them forth to the people.

כֵּיוָן שֶׁלֹּא מָצְאוּ אוֹתָם סָחֲבוּ אֶת יָסוֹן עִם כַּמָּה אַחִים אֶל רָאשֵׁי הָעִיר וְצָעֲקוּ
keivan shello matze'u otam sachavu et yason im kammah achim el rashei ha'ir vetza'aku
And when they found them not, they dragged Jason and certain brethren before the rulers of the city, crying,

הָאֲנָשִׁים שֶׁהָפְכוּ אֶת כָּל הָעוֹלָם בָּאוּ גַּם לְכָאן
ha'anashim shehafechu et kol ha'olam ba'u gam lechan
These that have turned the world upside down are come hither also;

וְיָסוֹן אֵרַח אוֹתָם בְּבֵיתוֹ. כָּל אֵלֶּה פּוֹעֲלִים נֶגֶד חֻקֵּי הַקֵּיסָר
veyason erach otam beveito. kol elleh po'alim neged chukkei hakkeisar
whom Jason hath received: and these all act contrary to the decrees of Cæsar,

בְּאָמְרָם שֶׁיֵּשׁ מֶלֶךְ אַחֵר - יֵשׁוּעַ
be'ameram sheyesh melech acher - yeshua
saying that there is another king, one Jesus.

מַעֲשֵׂי הַשְּׁלִיחִים

אָמַר הַסּוֹהֵר אֶת הַדְּבָרִים הָאֵלֶּה לְשָׁאוּל

amar hassoher et haddevarim ha'elleh lesha'ul
And the jailor reported the words to Paul, saying,

הַשָּׂרִים שָׁלְחוּ לְשַׁחְרֵר אֶתְכֶם. עַל כֵּן צְאוּ עַכְשָׁו וּלְכוּ לְשָׁלוֹם

hassarim shalchu leshachrer etchem. al ken tze'u achshav ulechu leshalom
The magistrates have sent to let you go: now therefore come forth, and go in peace.

אַךְ שָׁאוּל אָמַר לָהֶם: הִלְקוּ אוֹתָנוּ בְּפֻמְבֵּי בְּלֹא מִשְׁפָּט, אַף כִּי אֶזְרָחִים רוֹמִיִּים אֲנַחְנוּ;

ach sha'ul amar lahem: hilku otanu befumbei belo mishpat, af ki ezrachim romiyiym anachnu
But Paul said unto them, They have beaten us publicly, uncondemned, men that are Romans,

הִשְׁלִיכוּ אוֹתָנוּ לַכֶּלֶא וְעַכְשָׁו הֵם רוֹצִים לְגָרֵשׁ אוֹתָנוּ בַּחֲשַׁאי

hishlichu otanu lakkelei ve'achshav hem rotzim legaresh otanu bachashai
and have cast us into prison; and do they now cast us out privily?

לֹא וָלֹא! שֶׁיָּבוֹאוּ בְּעַצְמָם וְיוֹצִיאוּ אוֹתָנוּ

lo valo! sheyavo'u be'atzmam veyotzi'u otanu
nay verily; but let them come themselves and bring us out.

מָסְרוּ הַשּׁוֹטְרִים אֶת הַדְּבָרִים הָאֵלֶּה לַשָּׂרִים

maseru hashoterim et haddevarim ha'elleh lashorim
And the serjeants reported these words unto the magistrates:

וְכַאֲשֶׁר הַלָּלוּ שָׁמְעוּ שֶׁהֵם אֶזְרָחִים רוֹמִיִּים הֶחֵלּוּ לִפְחֹד

vecha'asher hallalu sham'u shehem ezrachim romiyim hechellu lifchod
and they feared when they heard that they were Romans;

בָּאוּ הַשָּׂרִים וְדִבְּרוּ עַל לִבָּם; אַחֲרֵי כֵן הוֹצִיאוּ אוֹתָם וּבִקְשׁוּ מֵהֶם לָצֵאת מִן הָעִיר

ba'u hashorim vedibberu al libbam; acharei chen hotzi'u otam uvikshu mehem latzet min ha'ir
and they came and besought them; and when they had brought them out, they asked them to go away from the city.

הֵם יָצְאוּ מִן הַכֶּלֶא וּבָאוּ לְבֵיתָהּ שֶׁל לִידְיָה

hem yatze'u min hakkelei uva'u leveitah shel lideyah
And they went out of the prison, and entered into the house of Lydia:

וּלְאַחַר שֶׁרָאוּ אֶת הָאַחִים וְעוֹדְדוּ אוֹתָם הָלְכוּ לְדַרְכָּם

ule'achar shera'u et ha'achim ve'odedu otam halechu ledarkam
and when they had seen the brethren, they comforted them, and departed.

יז

הֵם עָבְרוּ דֶּרֶךְ אַמְפִיפּוֹלִיס וְאַפּוֹלוֹנְיָה

hem averu derech amfipolis ve'appoloneyah
Now when they had passed through Amphipolis and Apollonia,

מַעֲשֵׂי הַשְּׁלִיחִים

וּבְבַת אַחַת נִפְתְּחוּ כָּל הַדְּלָתוֹת וְכָל הַשַּׁרְשְׁרוֹת נִתְּקוּ
uvevat achat niftechu kol haddelatot vechol hasharsherot nitteku
and immediately all the doors were opened; and every one's bands were loosed.

הַסּוֹהֵר הִתְעוֹרֵר מִשְּׁנָתוֹ וּכְשֶׁרָאָה כִּי דַּלְתוֹת הַכֶּלֶא פְּתוּחוֹת
hassoher hit'orer mishnato ucheshera'ah ki daltot hakkelei petuchot
And the jailor, being roused out of sleep and seeing the prison doors open,

שָׁלַף אֶת חַרְבּוֹ וְעָמַד לַהֲרֹג אֶת עַצְמוֹ, בְּחָשְׁבוֹ שֶׁהָאֲסִירִים בָּרְחוּ
shalaf et charbo ve'amad laharog et atzmo, bechoshvo sheha'asirim barchu
drew his sword and was about to kill himself, supposing that the prisoners had escaped.

אַךְ שָׁאוּל קָרָא בְּקוֹל גָּדוֹל וְאָמַר: אַל תַּעֲשֶׂה שׁוּם רַע לְעַצְמְךָ; כֻּלָּנוּ פֹּה
ach sha'ul kara bekol gadol ve'amar: al ta'aseh shum ra le'atzmecha; kullanu poh
But Paul cried with a loud voice, saying, Do thyself no harm: for we are all here.

הַסּוֹהֵר בִּקֵּשׁ שֶׁיַּעֲלוּ אוֹר וּמִהֵר פְּנִימָה, וּבִרְעָדָה נָפַל לְרַגְלֵי שָׁאוּל וְסִילָא.
hassoher bikkesh sheya'alu or umiher pnimah, uvir'adah nafal leraglei sha'ul vesila
And he called for lights and sprang in, and, trembling for fear, fell down before Paul and Silas,

כַּאֲשֶׁר הוֹצִיא אוֹתָם אָמַר: רַבּוֹתַי, מֶה עָלַי לַעֲשׂוֹת כְּדֵי לְהִוָּשַׁע
ka'asher hotzi otam amar: rabbotai, meh alai la'asot kedei lehivvasha
and brought them out and said, Sirs, what must I do to be saved?

הֵשִׁיבוּ וְאָמְרוּ: הַאֲמֵן בָּאָדוֹן יֵשׁוּעַ וְתִוָּשַׁע אַתָּה וּבְנֵי בֵּיתְךָ
heshivu ve'ameru: ha'amen ba'adon yeshua vetivvasha attah uvnei beitcha
And they said, Believe on the Lord Jesus, and thou shalt be saved, thou and thy house.

הֵם הִשְׁמִיעוּ לוֹ אֶת דְּבַר הָאָדוֹן, וּלְכָל אֲשֶׁר הָיוּ אִתּוֹ בְּבֵיתוֹ
hem hishmi'u lo et devar ha'adon, ulechol asher hayu itto beveito
And they spake the word of the Lord unto him, with all that were in his house.

בְּאוֹתָהּ שְׁעַת לַיְלָה לָקַח אוֹתָם וְרָחַץ אֶת חַבּוּרוֹתֵיהֶם, וּמִיָּד נִטְבַּל הוּא וְכָל בְּנֵי בֵּיתוֹ
be'otah she'at laylah lakach otam verachatz et chabburoteihem, umiyad nitbal hu vechol bnei beito
And he took them the same hour of the night, and washed their stripes; and was baptized, he and all his, immediately.

הוּא הֶעֱלָה אוֹתָם אֶל בֵּיתוֹ, עָרַךְ שֻׁלְחָן לִפְנֵיהֶם
hu he'elah otam el beito, arach shulchan lifneihem
And he brought them up into his house, and set food before them,

וְשָׂמַח מְאֹד עִם כָּל בְּנֵי בֵּיתוֹ כִּי שֶׁהֶאֱמִין בֵּאלֹהִים
vesamach me'od im kol benei beito ki shehe'emin be'elohim
and rejoiced greatly, with all his house, having believed in God.

בַּבֹּקֶר שָׁלְחוּ הַשָּׂרִים אֶת הַשּׁוֹטְרִים לוֹמַר לַסּוֹהֵר: שַׁחְרֵר אֶת הָאֲנָשִׁים הָהֵם
babboker shalchu hassarim et hashoterim lomar lassoher: shachrer et ha'anashim hahem
But when it was day, the magistrates sent the serjeants, saying, Let those men go.

מַעֲשֵׂי הַשְּׁלִיחִים

אֲנִי מְצַוֶּה עָלַיִךְ בְּשֵׁם יֵשׁוּעַ הַמָּשִׁיחַ, צְאִי מִמֶּנָּה! בְּאוֹתָהּ שָׁעָה יָצְאָה הָרוּחַ
ani metzavveh alayich beshem yeshua hammashiach, tz'i mimmennah! be'otah sha'ah yatze'ah haruach
I charge thee in the name of Jesus Christ to come out of her. And it came out that very hour.

רָאוּ אֲדוֹנֵי הַנַּעֲרָה כִּי אָבְדָה תִּקְוָתָם לַעֲשׂוֹת רְוָחִים
ra'u adonei hanna'arah ki avedah tikvatam la'asot revachim
But when her masters saw that the hope of their gain was gone,

תָּפְסוּ אֶת שָׁאוּל וְאֶת סִילָא וְסָחֲבוּ אוֹתָם אֶל כִּכַּר הָעִיר לְהַעֲמִידָם לִפְנֵי הַשִּׁלְטוֹנוֹת
tafsu et sha'ul ve'et sila vesachavu otam el kikkar ha'ir leha'amidam lifnei hashiltonot
they laid hold on Paul and Silas, and dragged them into the marketplace before the rulers,

כְּשֶׁהֱבִיאוּ אוֹתָם אֶל הַשָּׂרִים אָמְרוּ
kshehevi'u otam el hassarim ameru
and when they had brought them unto the magistrates, they said,

הָאֲנָשִׁים הָאֵלֶּה מְעוֹרְרִים אַנְדְּרָלָמוּסְיָה בְּעִירֵנוּ. יְהוּדִים הֵם
ha'anashim ha'elleh me'orerim anderalamuseyah be'irenu. yehudim hem
These men, being Jews, do exceedingly trouble our city,

וּמְלַמְּדִים מִנְהָגִים שֶׁאָסוּר לָנוּ לְקַבְּלָם וְאָסוּר לָנוּ לַעֲשׂוֹתָם, שֶׁכֵּן רוֹמִים אֲנַחְנוּ
umelammedim minhagim she'asur lanu lekabbelam ve'asur lanu la'asotam, shekken romim anachnu
and set forth customs which it is not lawful for us to receive, or to observe, being Romans.

אָז קָם עֲלֵיהֶם הֶהָמוֹן כְּאִישׁ אֶחָד
az kam aleihem hehamon ke'ish echad
And the multitude rose up together against them:

וְהַשָּׂרִים קָרְעוּ אֶת בִּגְדֵיהֶם מֵעֲלֵיהֶם וְצִוּוּ לְהַלְקוֹתָם
vehassarim kare'u et bigdeihem me'aleihem vetzivvu lehalkotam
and the magistrates rent their garments off them, and commanded to beat them with rods.

אַחֲרֵי שֶׁהִלְקוּ אוֹתָם מַלְקוֹת רַבּוֹת הִשְׁלִיכוּ אוֹתָם לַכֶּלֶא וְצִוּוּ עַל הַסּוֹהֵר לְשָׁמְרָם הֵיטֵב
acharei shehilku otam malkot rabbot hishlichu otam lakkelei vetzivvu al hassoher leshameram heitev
And when they had laid many stripes upon them, they cast them into prison, charging the jailor to keep them safely:

עִם קַבָּלַת הַפְּקֻדָּה הִשְׁלִיךְ אוֹתָם אֶל הַכֶּלֶא הַפְּנִימִי וְאֶת רַגְלֵיהֶם סָגַר בַּסַּד
im kabbalat happekuddah hishlich otam el hakkelei happnimi ve'et ragleihem sagar bassad
who, having received such a charge, cast them into the inner prison, and made their feet fast in the stocks.

בַּחֲצוֹת הַלַּיְלָה, בְּשָׁעָה שֶׁשָּׁאוּל וְסִילָא הִתְפַּלְּלוּ וְשָׁרוּ שִׁירֵי הַלֵּל לֵאלֹהִים וְהָאֲסִירִים מַקְשִׁיבִים לָהֶם
bachatzot hallaylah, besha'ah shesha'ul vesila hitpallelu vesharu shirei hallel lelohim veha'asirim makshivim lahem
But about midnight Paul and Silas were praying and singing hymns unto God, and the prisoners were listening to them;

הָיְתָה פִּתְאוֹם רְעִידַת אֲדָמָה חֲזָקָה עַד כְּדֵי כָּךְ שֶׁיְּסוֹדוֹת בֵּית הַסֹּהַר הִזְדַּעְזְעוּ,
hayetah pit'om re'idat adamah chazakah ad kedei kach sheyesodot beit hassohar hizda'ze'u
and suddenly there was a great earthquake, so that the foundations of the prison-house were shaken:

מַעֲשֵׂי הַשְּׁלִיחִים

בָּעִיר הַזֹּאת הָיִינוּ כַּמָּה יָמִים
ba'ir hazzot hayinu kammah yamim
and we were in this city tarrying certain days.

בְּיוֹם הַשַּׁבָּת יָצָאנוּ דֶּרֶךְ שַׁעַר הָעִיר אֶל שְׂפַת נָהָר, אֶל מָקוֹם שֶׁחֲשַׁבְנוּהוּ לִמְקוֹם תְּפִלָּה
beyom hashabbat yatzanu derech sha'ar ha'ir el sfat nahar, el makom shechashavnuhu limkom tefillah
And on the sabbath day we went forth without the gate by a river side, where we supposed there was a place of prayer;

וַיֵּשַׁבְנוּ וְדִבַּרְנוּ אֶל הַנָּשִׁים הַנֶּאֱסָפוֹת
veyashavnu vedibbarnu el hannashim hanne'esafot
and we sat down, and spake unto the women that were come together.

הָיְתָה שָׁם אִשָּׁה אַחַת יִרְאַת אֱלֹהִים, לִידְיָה שְׁמָהּ, מוֹכֶרֶת אַרְגָּמָן מִן הָעִיר תִּיאָטִירָה. הִיא שָׁמְעָה
hayetah sham ishah achat yir'at elohim, lideyah shemah, mocheret argaman min ha'ir ti'atirah. hi shame'ah
And a certain woman named Lydia, a seller of purple, of the city of Thyatira, one that worshipped God, heard us:

וְהָאָדוֹן פָּתַח אֶת לִבָּהּ לְהַקְשִׁיב אֶל דִּבְרֵי שָׁאוּל
veha'adon patach et libbah lehakshiv el divrei sha'ul
whose heart the Lord opened to give heed unto the things which were spoken by Paul.

אַחֲרֵי שֶׁנִּטְבְּלָה הִיא וּבְנֵי בֵּיתָהּ, פָּנְתָה בְּבַקָּשָׁה
acharei shennitbelah hi uvenei beitah, pantah bevakkashah
And when she was baptized, and her household, she besought us, saying,

אִם רְאִיתֶם אוֹתִי נֶאֱמָנָה לָאָדוֹן, בּוֹאוּ נָא לְבֵיתִי לְהִתְאַכְסֵן בּוֹ. וְהִיא שִׁכְנְעָה אוֹתָנוּ
im re'item oti ne'emanah la'adon, bo'u na leveiti lehit'achsen bo. vehi shichne'ah otanu
If ye have judged me to be faithful to the Lord, come into my house, and abide there. And she constrained us

כְּשֶׁהָלַכְנוּ פַּעַם לִמְקוֹם הַתְּפִלָּה
keshehalachnu pa'am limkom hattfillah
And it came to pass, as we were going to the place of prayer,

פָּגַשְׁנוּ נַעֲרָה אַחַת אֲחוּזַת רוּחַ נִחוּשׁ, שֶׁעָשְׂתָה הוֹן רַב לַאֲדוֹנֶיהָ בְּנִחוּשׁ הֶעָתִיד
pagashnu na'arah achat achuzat ruach nichush, she'asetah hon rav la'adoneiha benichush he'atid
that a certain maid having a spirit of divination met us, who brought her masters much gain by soothsaying.

אוֹתָהּ נַעֲרָה הָלְכָה אַחֲרֵי שָׁאוּל וְאַחֲרֵינוּ וְקָרְאָה:
otah na'arah halchah acharei sha'ul ve'achareinu vekare'ah
The same following after Paul and us cried out, saying,

הָאֲנָשִׁים הָאֵלֶּה עַבְדֵי אֵל עֶלְיוֹן וְהֵם מַכְרִיזִים לָכֶם דֶּרֶךְ יְשׁוּעָה
ha'anashim ha'elleh avdei el elyon vehem machrizim lachem derech yeshu'ah
These men are servants of the Most High God, who proclaim unto you the way of salvation.

כָּךְ עָשְׂתָה יָמִים רַבִּים. מֵאַחַר שֶׁזֶּה הִטְרִיד מְאֹד אֶת שָׁאוּל, פָּנָה אֶל הָרוּחַ וְאָמַר
kach asetah yamim rabbim. me'achar shezzeh hitrid me'od et sha'ul, panah el haruach ve'amar.
And this she did for many days. But Paul, being sore troubled, turned and said to the spirit,

מַעֲשֵׂי הַשְּׁלִיחִים

אָז הִתְחַזְּקוּ הַקְּהִלּוֹת בָּאֱמוּנָה וּמִסְפַּר הַמַּאֲמִינִים גָּדַל מִיּוֹם לְיוֹם
az hitchazzeku hakkehillot ba'emunah umispar hamma'aminim gadal miyom leyom
So the churches were strengthened in the faith, and increased in number daily.

הֵם עָבְרוּ בְּאֵזוֹר פְרִיגְיָה וְגָלַטְיָה
hem averu be'ezor ferigeyah vegalatyah
And they went through the region of Phrygia and Galatia,

כִּי רוּחַ הַקֹּדֶשׁ מָנְעָה אוֹתָם מִלְהַשְׁמִיעַ אֶת דְּבַר אֱלֹהִים בְּאַסְיָה
ki ruach hakkodesh mane'ah otam millehashmia et devar elohim be'asyah
having been forbidden of the Holy Spirit to speak the word in Asia;

כְּשֶׁבָּאוּ אֶל מִיסְיָה נִסּוּ לָלֶכֶת אֶל בִּיתִינְיָה
kshebba'u el misiyah nissu lalechet el bitineyah,
and when they were come over against Mysia, they assayed to go into Bithynia;

אַךְ רוּחַ יֵשׁוּעַ לֹא הִנִּיחָה לָהֶם
ach ruach yeshua lo hinnichah lahem
and the Spirit of Jesus suffered them not;

לְפִיכָךְ עָבְרוּ לְיַד מִיסְיָה וְיָרְדוּ אֶל טְרוֹאַס
lefichach averu leyad misiyah veyaredu el tro'as
and passing by Mysia, they came down to Troas.

בַּלַּיְלָה נִרְאָה חָזוֹן אֶל שָׁאוּל:
ballaylah nir'ah chazon el sha'ul
And a vision appeared to Paul in the night:

אִישׁ מָקֵדוֹנִי אֶחָד נִרְאָה עוֹמֵד וּמְבַקֵּשׁ מִמֶּנּוּ, עֲבֹר אֶל מָקֵדוֹנְיָה וַעֲזֹר לָנוּ
ish makedoni echad nir'ah omed umevakkesh mimmennu, avor el makedoneyah va'azor lanu
There was a man of Macedonia standing, beseeching him, and saying, Come over into Macedonia, and help us.

מִיָּד לְאַחַר שֶׁרָאָה אֶת הֶחָזוֹן הִשְׁתַּדַּלְנוּ לָצֵאת אֶל מָקֵדוֹנְיָה
miyad le'achar shera'ah et hechazon hishtaddalnu latzet el makedoneyah
And when he had seen the vision, straightway we sought to go forth into Macedonia,

כִּי הֵבַנּוּ שֶׁאֱלֹהִים קוֹרֵא לָנוּ לְבַשֵּׂר לָהֶם אֶת הַבְּשׂוֹרָה
ki hevannu she'elohim korei lanu levasser lahem et habbesorah
concluding that God had called us to preach the gospel unto them.

הִפְלַגְנוּ מִטְּרוֹאַס וְשַׁטְנוּ בְּנָתִיב יָשָׁר אֶל סָמוֹתְרַקְיָה, וּלְמָחֳרָת אֶל נַפּוֹלִיס
hiflagnu mittero'as veshatnu benativ yashar el samoterakyah, ulemochorat el nappolis
Setting sail therefore from Troas, we made a straight course to Samothrace, and the day following to Neapolis;

מִשָּׁם אֶל פִילִיפִּי, עִיר בַּחֶבֶל הָרִאשׁוֹן שֶׁל מָקֵדוֹנְיָה וּמוֹשָׁבָה רוֹמִית
misham el filipi, ir bachevel harishon shel makedoneyah umoshavah romit
and from thence to Philippi, which is a city of Macedonia, the first of the district, a Roman colony:

מַעֲשֵׂי הַשְּׁלִיחִים

לָקַח בַּר־נַבָּא אֶת מַרְקוֹס וְהִפְלִיג לְקַפְרִיסִין
lakach bar-nabba et markos vehiflig lekafrisin
and Barnabas took Mark with him, and sailed away unto Cyprus:

וְשָׁאוּל בָּחַר אֶת סִילָא וְיָצָא לְדַרְכּוֹ לְאַחַר שֶׁהָאַחִים הִפְקִידוּהוּ לְחֶסֶד יהוה
vesha'ul bachar et sila veyatza ledarko le'achar sheha'achim hifkiduhu lechesed hashem
but Paul chose Silas, and went forth, being commended by the brethren to the grace of the Lord.

הוּא עָבַר בְּסוּרְיָה וּבְקִילִיקְיָה וְחִזֵּק אֶת הַקְּהִלּוֹת
hu avar besureyah uvekilikeyah vechizzek et hakkehillot
And he went through Syria and Cilicia, confirming the churches.

טז

הוּא בָּא אֶל דֶּרְבִּי וְאֶל לִיסְטְרָה. הָיָה שָׁם תַּלְמִיד אֶחָד, טִימוֹתִיאוֹס שְׁמוֹ
hu ba el derbi ve'el listerah. hayah sham talmid echad, timotei'os shemo
And he came also to Derbe and to Lystra: and behold, a certain disciple was there, named Timothy,

בֶּן לְאִשָּׁה יְהוּדִיָּה מַאֲמִינָה וּלְאָב יְוָנִי
ben le'ishah yehudiyah ma'aminah ule'av yevani
the son of a Jewess that believed; but his father was a Greek.

וְשֵׁם טוֹב לוֹ בֵּין הָאַחִים אֲשֶׁר בְּלִיסְטְרָה וּבְאִיקוֹנְיוֹן
veshem tov lo bein ha'achim asher beliseterah uve'ikoneyon
The same was well reported of by the brethren that were at Lystra and Iconium.

אִתּוֹ רָצָה שָׁאוּל לָצֵאת לַדֶּרֶךְ
itto ratzah sha'ul latzet ladderech
Him would Paul have to go forth with him;

הוּא לָקַח אוֹתוֹ וּבִגְלַל הַיְּהוּדִים שֶׁהָיוּ בַּמְּקוֹמוֹת הָהֵם מָל אוֹתוֹ
hu lakach oto uviglal hayehudim shehayu bammekomot hahem mal oto
and he took and circumcised him because of the Jews that were in those parts:

שֶׁכֵּן הַכֹּל יָדְעוּ שֶׁאָבִיו יְוָנִי
shekken hakkol yade'u she'aviv yevani
for they all knew that his father was a Greek.

הֵם עָבְרוּ בֶּעָרִים
hem avru be'arim
And as they went on their way through the cities,

וּמָסְרוּ לָהֶם שֶׁיֵּשׁ לִשְׁמֹר אֶת הַהֲלָכוֹת שֶׁפָּסְקוּ הַשְּׁלִיחִים וְהַזְּקֵנִים בִּירוּשָׁלַיִם
umasru lahem sheyesh lishmor et hahalachot sheppaseku hashelichim vehazzekenim biyerushalayim
they delivered them the decrees to keep which had been ordained of the apostles and elders that were at Jerusalem.

מַעֲשֵׂי הַשְּׁלִיחִים

כְּשֶׁקָּרְאוּ הָאַחִים אֶת הָאִגֶּרֶת נִתְמַלְּאוּ שִׂמְחָה עַל הָעִדּוּד
keshekkare'u ha'achim et ha'iggeret nitmalle'u simchah al ha'iddud
And when they had read it, they rejoiced for the consolation.

וִיהוּדָה וְסִילָא, שֶׁהָיוּ גַּם נְבִיאִים, עוֹדְדוּ אוֹתָם בְּמִלִּים רַבּוֹת וְחִזְּקוּ אוֹתָם
viyehudah vesila, shehayu gam nevi'im, odedu otam bemillim rabbot vechizzku otam
And Judas and Silas, being themselves also prophets, exhorted the brethren with many words, and confirmed them.

הֵם שָׁהוּ שָׁם זְמַן מְסֻיָּם וְאַחֲרֵי כֵן
hem shahu sham zeman mesuyam ve'acharei chen
And after they had spent some time there,

שִׁלְּחוּ אוֹתָם הָאַחִים בְּשָׁלוֹם אֶל שׁוֹלְחֵיהֶם
shillchu otam ha'achim beshalom el sholcheihem
they were dismissed in peace from the brethren unto those that had sent them forth.

שָׁאוּל וּבַר-נַבָּא נִשְׁאֲרוּ בְּאַנְטִיּוֹכְיָה, וְיַחַד עִם רַבִּים אֲחֵרִים לִמְּדוּ וּבִשְּׂרוּ אֶת דְּבַר אֱלֹהִים
sha'ul uvar-nabba nish'aru be'antiyocheyah, veyachad im rabbim acherim limmdu uvissru et devar elohim
But Paul and Barnabas tarried in Antioch, teaching and preaching the word of the Lord, with many others also.

לְאַחַר כַּמָּה יָמִים אָמַר שָׁאוּל לְבַר-נַבָּא
le'achar kammah yamim amar sha'ul levar-nabba
And after some days Paul said unto Barnabas,

בּוֹא נַחֲזֹר וּנְבַקֵּר אֶת הָאַחִים בְּכָל עִיר וָעִיר שֶׁהִשְׁמַעְנוּ בָּהּ אֶת דְּבַר אֱלֹהִים,
bo nachzor unevakker et ha'achim bechol ir va'ir shehishma'nu bah et devar elohim,
Let us return now and visit the brethren in every city wherein we proclaimed the word of the Lord,

וְנִרְאֶה מַה מַּצָּבָם
venir'eh mah matzavam
and see how they fare.

בַּר-נַבָּא רָצָה לָקַחַת אִתָּם גַּם אֶת יוֹחָנָן הַמְכֻנֶּה מַרְקוֹס
bar-nabba ratzah lakachat ittam gam et yochanan hamchunneh markos
And Barnabas was minded to take with them John also, who was called Mark.

אַךְ שָׁאוּל חָשַׁב שֶׁלֹּא רָצוּי לָקַחַת אִתָּם אֶת זֶה שֶׁפָּרַשׁ מֵהֶם בְּפַמְפִילְיָה
ach sha'ul chashav shello ratzui lakachat ittam et zeh shepparash mehem bepamfileyah
But Paul thought not good to take with them him who withdrew from them from Pamphylia,

וְלֹא נִתְלַוָּה אֲלֵיהֶם לַעֲבוֹדָה
velo nitlavvah aleihem la'avodah
and went not with them to the work.

הָרִיב הָיָה חָרִיף עַד כְּדֵי כָּךְ שֶׁנִּתְפָּרְדוּ זֶה מִזֶּה
hariv hayah charif ad kedei kach shennitpardu zeh mizzeh
And there arose a sharp contention, so that they parted asunder one from the other,

מַעֲשֵׂי הַשְּׁלִיחִים

הוֹאִיל וְשָׁמַעְנוּ כִּי אֲחָדִים מֵאִתָּנוּ פָּעֲלוּ מִבְּלִי שֶׁצִּוִּינוּ אוֹתָם וּבִלְבְּלוּ אֶתְכֶם בְּדִבְרֵיהֶם וְהֵבִיכוּ אֶת נַפְשׁוֹתֵיכֶם
ho'il veshama'nu ki achadim me'ittanu pa'alu mibbli shetzivvinu otam uvilbelu etchem bedivreihem vehevichu et nafshoteichem
Forasmuch as we have heard that certain who went out from us have troubled you with words, subverting your souls; to whom we gave no commandment;

נִתְקַבֵּל עַל דַּעְתֵּנוּ פֶּה אֶחָד
nitkabbel al da'tenu peh echad
it seemed good unto us, having come to one accord,

לִשְׁלֹחַ אֲלֵיכֶם אֲנָשִׁים נִבְחָרִים יַחַד עִם חֲבִיבֵינוּ בַּר־נַבָּא וְשָׁאוּל
lishloach aleichem anashim nivcharim yachad im chaviveinu bar-nabba vesha'ul
to choose out men and send them unto you with our beloved Barnabas and Paul,

אֲנָשִׁים אֲשֶׁר מָסְרוּ אֶת נַפְשָׁם לְמַעַן שֵׁם אֲדוֹנֵנוּ יֵשׁוּעַ הַמָּשִׁיחַ
anashim asher masru et nafsham lema'an shem adonenu yeshua hammashiach
men that have hazarded their lives for the name of our Lord Jesus Christ.

לָכֵן שָׁלַחְנוּ אֶת יְהוּדָה וְאֶת סִילָא וְהֵם יַגִּידוּ בְּמוֹ פִּיהֶם אֶת אוֹתָם הַדְּבָרִים
lachen shalachnu et yehudah ve'et sila vehem yaggidu bemo fihem et otam haddevarim
We have sent therefore Judas and Silas, who themselves also shall tell you the same things by word of mouth.

נִרְאֶה לְרוּחַ הַקֹּדֶשׁ וְלָנוּ
nir'eh leruach hakkodesh velanu
For it seemed good to the Holy Spirit, and to us,

שֶׁלֹּא לְהַטִּיל עֲלֵיכֶם שׁוּם מַעֲמָסָה נוֹסֶפֶת מִלְּבַד הַדְּבָרִים הַנְּחוּצִים הָאֵלֶּה
shello lehattil aleichem shum ma'amasah nosefet millevad haddevarim hannechutzim ha'elleh
to lay upon you no greater burden than these necessary things:

לְהִמָּנַע מִזִּבְחֵי אֱלִילִים וּמִדָּם, מִבְּשַׂר הַנֶּחֱנָק וּמִן הַזְּנוּת
lehimmana mizzivchei elilim umiddam, mibbsar hannechnak umin hazzeut
that ye abstain from things sacrificed to idols, and from blood, and from things strangled, and from fornication;

אִם תִּשָּׁמְרוּ מֵאֵלֶּה תֵּיטִיבוּ לַעֲשׂוֹת. שָׁלוֹם לָכֶם
im tishameru me'elleh teitivu la'asot. shalom lachem
from which if ye keep yourselves, it shall be well with you. Fare ye well.

הָאֲנָשִׁים שֻׁלְּחוּ לְדַרְכָּם. הֵם יָרְדוּ אֶל אַנְטִיוֹכְיָה
ha'anashim shullchu ledarkam. hem yardu el antiyocheyah
So they, when they were dismissed, came down to Antioch;

כִּנְּסוּ אֶת הָעָם וּמָסְרוּ אֶת הָאִגֶּרֶת
kinnsu et ha'am umaseru et ha'iggeret
and having gathered the multitude together, they delivered the epistle.

מַעֲשֵׂי הַשְּׁלִיחִים

לְמַעַן יִדְרְשׁוּ אֶת יהוה שְׁאֵרִית אָדָם וְכָל הַגּוֹיִם אֲשֶׁר נִקְרָא שְׁמִי עֲלֵיהֶם
lema'an yidreshu et hashem she'erit adam vechol haggoyim asher nikra shmi aleihem
That the residue of men may seek after the Lord, And all the Gentiles, upon whom my name is called,

נְאֻם יהוה עוֹשֶׂה כָל אֵלֶּה הַנּוֹדָעִים מֵעוֹלָם
ne'um hashem oseh chol elleh hannoda'im me'olam
Saith the Lord, who maketh these things known from of old.

עַל כֵּן אֲנִי פּוֹסֵק שֶׁלֹּא לְהַקְשׁוֹת עַל אוֹתָם אֲנָשִׁים מִן הַגּוֹיִם אֲשֶׁר שָׁבִים אֶל אֱלֹהִים
al ken ani posek shello lehakshot al otam anashim min haggoyim asher shavim el elohim
Wherefore my judgment is, that we trouble not them that from among the Gentiles turn to God;

אֶלָּא לִכְתֹּב אֲלֵיהֶם לְהִמָּנַע מִטֻּמְאוֹת אֱלִילִים
ella lichtov aleihem lehimmana mittum'ot elilim
but that we write unto them, that they abstain from the pollutions of idols,

וּמִזְּנוּת, מִבְּשַׂר הַנֶּחֱנָק וּמִן הַדָּם
umizznut, mibbesar hannechenak umin haddam
and from fornication, and from what is strangled, and from blood.

הֲרֵי לְמֹשֶׁה יֵשׁ מִדּוֹרוֹת קְדוּמִים אֲנָשִׁים הַמַּכְרִיזִים אוֹתוֹ בְּכָל עִיר וָעִיר,
harei lemosheh yesh middorot kedumim anashim hammachrizim oto bechol ir va'ir,
For Moses from generations of old hath in every city them that preach him,

וּמִדֵּי שַׁבָּת הוּא נִקְרָא בְּבָתֵּי הַכְּנֶסֶת
umiddei shabbat hu nikra bevattei hakkeneset
being read in the synagogues every sabbath.

נִתְקַבֵּל עַל דַּעַת הַשְּׁלִיחִים וְהַזְּקֵנִים וְכָל הַקְּהִלָּה
nitkabbel al da'at hashelichim vehazzekenim vechol hakkehillah
Then it seemed good to the apostles and the elders, with the whole church,

לִשְׁלֹחַ אֲנָשִׁים שֶׁנִּבְחֲרוּ מִקִּרְבָּם אֶל אַנְטוֹכְיָה, יַחַד עִם שָׁאוּל וּבַר־נַבָּא
lishloach anashim shennivcharu mikkirbam el antivocheyah, yachad im sha'ul uvar-nabba
to choose men out of their company, and send them to Antioch with Paul and Barnabas;

אֶת יְהוּדָה, הַמְכֻנֶּה בַּר־שַׁבָּא, וְאֶת סִילָא אֲשֶׁר הָיוּ מִן הַמַּנְהִיגִים בְּקֶרֶב הָאַחִים
et yehudah, hamchunneh bar-shabba, ve'et sila asher hayu min hammanhigim bekerev ha'achim
namely, Judas called Barsabbas, and Silas, chief men among the brethren:

אֶת הַמִּכְתָּב הַזֶּה מָסְרוּ בְּיָדָם: הַשְּׁלִיחִים וְזִקְנֵי הָאַחִים
et hammichtav hazzeh maseru beyadam: hashelichim veziknei ha'achim
and they wrote thus by them, The apostles and the elders, brethren,

דּוֹרְשִׁים בִּשְׁלוֹם הָאַחִים שֶׁמִּקֶּרֶב הַגּוֹיִם בְּאַנְטִיּוֹכְיָה וּבְסוּרְיָה וּבְקִילִיקְיָה
doreshim bishlom ha'achim shemmikkerev haggoyim be'antiyocheyah uvesureyah uvekilikeyah
unto the brethren who are of the Gentiles in Antioch and Syria and Cilicia, greeting:

מַעֲשֵׂי הַשְּׁלִיחִים

וֵאלֹהִים הַיּוֹדֵעַ אֶת הַלְּבָבוֹת הֵעִיד עֲלֵיהֶם בְּתִתּוֹ לָהֶם אֶת רוּחַ הַקֹּדֶשׁ כְּשֵׁם שֶׁנִּתְּנָה גַּם לָנוּ
ve'elohim hayodea et hallevavot he'id aleihem betitto lahem et ruach hakkodesh keshem shennetanah gam lanu
And God, who knoweth the heart, bare them witness, giving them the Holy Spirit, even as he did unto us;

הוּא לֹא הִבְדִּיל כְּלָל בֵּינֵינוּ לְבֵינָם, כִּי עַל־יְדֵי הָאֱמוּנָה טִהֵר אֶת לְבָבָם
hu lo hivdil kelal beineinu leveinam, ki al-yedei ha'emunah tiher et levavam
and he made no distinction between us and them, cleansing their hearts by faith.

וְעַתָּה מַדּוּעַ תְּנַסּוּ אֶת אֱלֹהִים
ve'attah maddua tenassu et elohim
Now therefore why make ye trial of God,

לָשִׂים עֹל עַל צַוְּארֵי הַתַּלְמִידִים, עֹל אֲשֶׁר גַּם אֲבוֹתֵינוּ וְגַם אֲנַחְנוּ לֹא יָכֹלְנוּ לָשֵׂאת
lasim ol al tzavverei hattalmidim, ol asher gam avoteinu vegam anachnu lo yacholenu laset
that ye should put a yoke upon the neck of the disciples which neither our fathers nor we were able to bear?

אַדְּרַבָּא, אָנוּ מַאֲמִינִים שֶׁבְּחֶסֶד הָאָדוֹן יֵשׁוּעַ הַמָּשִׁיחַ נוֹשַׁעְנוּ, כָּמוֹנוּ כְּמוֹהֶם
addrabba, anu ma'aminim shebbechesed ha'adon yeshua hammashiach nosha'nu, kamonu kemohem
But we believe that we shall be saved through the grace of the Lord Jesus, in like manner as they.

כָּל הַנֶּאֱסָפִים שָׁתְקוּ וְהִטּוּ אֹזֶן לְבַר־נַבָּא וּלְשָׁאוּל
kol hanne'esafim shatku vehittu ozen levar-nabba ulesha'ul
And all the multitude kept silence; and they hearkened unto Barnabas and Paul

אֲשֶׁר סִפְּרוּ אֵלּוּ אוֹתוֹת וּמוֹפְתִים עָשָׂה אֱלֹהִים עַל־יָדָם בְּקֶרֶב הַגּוֹיִם
asher sipperu ellu otot umoftim asah elohim al-yadam bekerev haggoyim
rehearsing what signs and wonders God had wrought among the Gentiles through them.

כְּשֶׁגָּמְרוּ לְסַפֵּר הֵגִיב יַעֲקֹב וְאָמַר: אֲנָשִׁים אַחִים, שִׁמְעוּ אֵלָי
ksheggameru lesapper hegiv ya'akov ve'amar: anashim achim, shim'u elai
And after they had held their peace, James answered, saying, Brethren, hearken unto me:

שִׁמְעוֹן סִפֵּר כֵּיצַד לָרִאשׁוֹנָה פָּקַד אֱלֹהִים אֶת הַגּוֹיִם לָקַחַת מִקִּרְבָּם עַם לִשְׁמוֹ
shim'on sipper keitzad larishonah pakad elohim et haggoyim lakachat mikkirbam am lishmo
Symeon hath rehearsed how first God visited the Gentiles, to take out of them a people for his name.

וְלָזֹאת מַסְכִּימִים דִּבְרֵי הַנְּבִיאִים, כַּכָּתוּב
velazot maskimim divrei hannevi'im, kakkatuv
And to this agree the words of the prophets; as it is written,

אַחֲרֵי כֵן אָשׁוּב וְאָקִים אֶת־סֻכַּת דָּוִיד הַנֹּפֶלֶת
acharei chen ashuv ve'akim et-sukkat david hannofelet
After these things I will return, And I will build again the tabernacle of David, which is fallen;

וַהֲרִיסוֹתָיו אָקִים וּבְנִיתִיהָ
vaharisotav akim uvenitiha
And I will build again the ruins thereof, And I will set it up:

מַעֲשֵׂי הַשְּׁלִיחִים

לָכֵן הֶחְלַט שֶׁשָּׁאוּל וּבַר־נַבָּא וְעוֹד כַּמָּה מֵהֶם
lachen huchlat shesha'ul uvar-nabba ve'od kammah mehem
the brethren appointed that Paul and Barnabas, and certain other of them,

יַעֲלוּ לִירוּשָׁלַיִם אֶל הַשְּׁלִיחִים וְהַזְּקֵנִים בְּנוֹגֵעַ לַשְּׁאֵלָה הַזֹּאת
ya'alu liyerushalayim el hashelichim vehazzekenim benogea lashe'elah hazzot
should go up to Jerusalem unto the apostles and elders about this question.

הֵם שֻׁלְּחוּ לְדַרְכָּם עַל־יְדֵי הַקְּהִלָּה וּכְשֶׁעָבְרוּ בְּפֵינִיקְיָה וּבְשׁוֹמְרוֹן
hem shullchu ledarkam al-yedei hakkehillah uchesche'averu befeinikeyah uveshomron
They therefore, being brought on their way by the church, passed through both Phoenicia and Samaria,

סִפְּרוּ עַל תְּשׁוּבַת הַגּוֹיִם וְגָרְמוּ שִׂמְחָה גְדוֹלָה לְכָל הָאַחִים
sippru al teshuvat haggoyim vegarmu simchah gedolah lechol ha'achim
declaring the conversion of the Gentiles: and they caused great joy unto all the brethren.

בְּהַגִּיעָם לִירוּשָׁלַיִם נִתְקַבְּלוּ עַל־יְדֵי הַקְּהִלָּה וְהַשְּׁלִיחִים וְהַזְּקֵנִים
behaggi'am liyerushalayim nitkabblu al-yedei hakkehillah vehashlichim vehazzekenim
And when they were come to Jerusalem, they were received of the church and the apostles and the elders,

וְסִפְּרוּ אֶת כָּל מַה שֶּׁעָשָׂה אֱלֹהִים עִמָּהֶם
vesippru et kol mah she'asah elohim immahem
and they rehearsed all things that God had done with them.

אַךְ מַאֲמִינִים אֲחָדִים מִכַּת הַפְּרוּשִׁים קָמוּ וְאָמְרוּ
ach ma'aminim achadim mikkat happerushim kamu ve'ameru
But there rose up certain of the sect of the Pharisees who believed, saying,

שֶׁצָּרִיךְ לָמוּל אוֹתָם וּלְצַוּוֹתָם לִשְׁמֹר אֶת תּוֹרַת מֹשֶׁה
shetzarich lamul otam uletzavvotam lishmor et torat mosheh
It is needful to circumcise them, and to charge them to keep the law of Moses.

הִתְכַּנְּסוּ הַשְּׁלִיחִים וְהַזְּקֵנִים לְעַיֵּן בַּדָּבָר הַזֶּה
hitkannsu hashelichim vehazzekenim le'ayen baddavar hazzeh
And the apostles and the elders were gathered together to consider of this matter.

אַחֲרֵי וִכּוּחַ מְמֻשָּׁךְ קָם כֵּיפָא וְאָמַר לָהֶם
acharei vikkuach memushach kam keifa ve'amar lahem
And when there had been much questioning, Peter rose up, and said unto them,

אֲנָשִׁים אַחִים, אַתֶּם יוֹדְעִים כִּי מִיָּמִים רִאשׁוֹנִים בָּחֲרַנִי אֱלֹהִים מִבֵּינֵיכֶם
anashim achim, attem yode'im ki miyamim rishonim becharani elohim mibbeineichem
Brethren, ye know that a good while ago God made choice among you,

כְּדֵי שֶׁמִּפִּי יִשְׁמְעוּ הַגּוֹיִם אֶת דְּבַר הַבְּשׂוֹרָה וְיַאֲמִינוּ
kedei shemmippi yishme'u haggoyim et devar habbesorah veya'aminu
that by my mouth the Gentiles should hear the word of the gospel, and believe.

מַעֲשֵׂי הַשְּׁלִיחִים

הֵם עָבְרוּ דֶּרֶךְ פִּיסִידְיָה וּבָאוּ אֶל פַּמְפִּילְיָה
hem averu derech pisideyah uva'u el pamfileyah
And they passed through Pisidia, and came to Pamphylia.

וְאַחֲרֵי שֶׁהִשְׁמִיעוּ אֶת הַדָּבָר בְּפֶרְגִי יָרְדוּ אֶל אַטַּלְיָה
ve'acharei shehishmi'u et haddavar bepergi yaredu el attalyah
And when they had spoken the word in Perga, they went down to Attalia;

מִשָּׁם הִפְלִיגוּ לְאַנְטִיּוֹכְיָה
misham hifligu le'antiyocheyah
and thence they sailed to Antioch,

אֶל הַמָּקוֹם שֶׁבּוֹ הֻפְקְדוּ בֶּעָבַר לְחֶסֶד אֱלֹהִים לְשֵׁם הָעֲבוֹדָה אֲשֶׁר הִשְׁלִימוּ
el hammakom shebbo hufkedu be'avar lechesed elohim leshem ha'avodah asher hishlimu
from whence they had been committed to the grace of God for the work which they had fulfilled.

כְּשֶׁהִגִּיעוּ כִּנְּסוּ אֶת הַקְּהִלָּה
keshehiggi'u kinnsu et hakkehillah
And when they were come, and had gathered the church together,

וְסִפְּרוּ אֶת כָּל מַה שֶּׁעָשָׂה אֱלֹהִים עִמָּהֶם
vesippru et kol mah she'asah elohim immahem
they rehearsed all things that God had done with them,

וְכִי פָּתַח לַגּוֹיִם אֶת שַׁעַר הָאֱמוּנָה
vechi patach laggoyim et sha'ar ha'emunah
and that he had opened a door of faith unto the Gentiles.

וְשָׁם שָׁהוּ יָמִים לֹא מְעַטִּים עִם הַתַּלְמִידִים
vesham shahu yamim lo me'attim im hattalmidim
And they tarried no little time with the disciples.

טו

כַּמָּה אֲנָשִׁים יָרְדוּ מִיהוּדָה וְלִמְּדוּ אֶת הָאַחִים
kammah anashim yardu miyehudah velimmedu et ha'achim
And certain men came down from Judæa and taught the brethren, saying,

שֶׁאִם לֹא יִמּוֹלוּ כְּדָת מֹשֶׁה לֹא יוּכְלוּ לְהִוָּשַׁע
she'im lo yimmolu kedat mosheh lo yuchelu lehivvasha
Except ye be circumcised after the custom of Moses, ye cannot be saved.

לְשָׁאוּל וּלְבַר-נַבָּא הָיוּ דִין וּדְבָרִים לֹא מְעַטִּים עִמָּהֶם,
lesha'ul ulevar-nabba hayu din udevarim lo me'attim immahem
And when Paul and Barnabas had no small dissension and questioning with them,

מַעֲשֵׂי הַשְּׁלִיחִים

בְּמַעֲשָׂיו הַטּוֹבִים, בְּתִתּוֹ לָנוּ גֶּשֶׁם מִן הַשָּׁמַיִם וְעוֹנוֹת פּוֹרִיּוֹת, וּבְמַלְּאוֹ אֶת לְבּוֹתֵינוּ מָזוֹן וְשִׂמְחָה
bema'asav hattovim, betitto lanu geshem min hashamayim ve'onot poriyot, uvemalle'o et libboteinu mazon vesimchah
in that he did good and gave you from heaven rains and fruitful seasons, filling your hearts with food and gladness.

וְגַם בְּאָמְרָם אֶת הַדְּבָרִים הָאֵלֶּה, בְּקֹשִׁי מָנְעוּ מֵהֲמוֹן הָעָם לְהַקְרִיב לָהֶם קָרְבָּן
vegam be'omram et haddevarim ha'elleh, bekoshi mane'u mehamon ha'am lehakriv lahem korban
And with these sayings scarce restrained they the multitudes from doing sacrifice unto them.

יְהוּדִים מֵאַנְטִיּוֹכְיָה וּמֵאִיקוֹנְיוֹן בָּאוּ לְשָׁם. הֵם הֵסִיתוּ אֶת הֲמוֹן הָעָם
yehudim me'antiyocheyah ume'ikoneyon ba'u lesham. hem hesitu et hamon ha'am
But there came Jews thither from Antioch and Iconium: and having persuaded the multitudes,

וְרָגְמוּ אֶת שָׁאוּל בָּאֲבָנִים. לְאַחַר מִכֵּן גָּרְרוּ אוֹתוֹ אֶל מִחוּץ לָעִיר בְּחָשְׁבָם אוֹתוֹ לְמֵת
veragmu et sha'ul ba'avanim. le'achar mikken gareru oto el michutz la'ir bechoshvam oto lemet
they stoned Paul, and dragged him out of the city, supposing that he was dead.

אֲבָל כַּאֲשֶׁר הִקִּיפוּהוּ הַתַּלְמִידִים קָם וְהָלַךְ הָעִירָה.
aval ka'asher hikkifuhu hattalmidim kam vehalach ha'irah
But as the disciples stood round about him, he rose up, and entered into the city:

לְמָחֳרָת יָצָא עִם בַּר־נַבָּא אֶל דֶּרְבִּי
lemacharat yatza im bar-nabba el derbi
and on the morrow he went forth with Barnabas to Derbe.

הֵם בִּשְּׂרוּ אֶת הַבְּשׂוֹרָה בָּעִיר הַהִיא וְאַחֲרֵי שֶׁהֶעֱמִידוּ תַּלְמִידִים רַבִּים
hem bissru et habbesorah ba'ir hahi ve'acharei shehe'emidu talmidim rabbim
And when they had preached the gospel to that city, and had made many disciples,

חָזְרוּ אֶל לִיסְטְרָה וְאִיקוֹנְיוֹן וְאַנְטִיּוֹכְיָה
chazeru el liseterah ve'ikoneyon ve'antiyocheyah
they returned to Lystra, and to Iconium, and to Antioch,

שָׁם חִזְּקוּ אֶת לֵב הַתַּלְמִידִים וְהֵאִיצוּ בָּהֶם לְהוֹסִיף לַעֲמֹד בָּאֱמוּנָה
sham chizzeku et lev hattalmidim vehe'itzu bahem lehosif la'amod ba'emunah
confirming the souls of the disciples, exhorting them to continue in the faith,

כִּי דֶּרֶךְ צָרוֹת רַבּוֹת עָלֵינוּ לְהִכָּנֵס לְמַלְכוּת אֱלֹהִים
ki derech tzarot rabbot aleinu lehikkanes lemalchut elohim
and that through many tribulations we must enter into the kingdom of God.

בְּכָל קְהִלָּה מִנּוּ לָהֶם זְקֵנִים
bechol kehillah minnu lahem zekenim
And when they had appointed for them elders in every church,

וּלְאַחַר שֶׁהִתְפַּלְּלוּ וְצָמוּ הִפְקִידוּ אוֹתָם בְּיַד הָאָדוֹן אֲשֶׁר הֶאֱמִינוּ בּוֹ
ule'achar shehitpallelu vetzamu hifkidu otam beyad ha'adon asher he'eminu bo
and had prayed with fasting, they commended them to the Lord, on whom they had believed.

מַעֲשֵׂי הַשְּׁלִיחִים

כִּרְאוֹת הֲמוֹן הָעָם אֶת הַמַּעֲשֶׂה שֶׁל שָׁאוּל נָשְׂאוּ קוֹלָם וְאָמְרוּ בַּלָּשׁוֹן הַלִּיקָאוֹנִית
kir'ot hamon ha'am et hamma'aseh shel sha'ul nas'u kolam ve'ameru ballashon hallika'onit
And when the multitude saw what Paul had done, they lifted up their voice, saying in the speech of Lycaonia,

הָאֵלִים יָרְדוּ אֵלֵינוּ בִּדְמוּת אֲנָשִׁים
ha'elim yaredu eleinu bidmut anashim
The gods are come down to us in the likeness of men.

וּלְבַר־נַבָּא קָרְאוּ זֵאוֹס וּלְשָׁאוּל קָרְאוּ הֶרְמֶס, כִּי הָיָה רֹאשׁ הַמְדַבְּרִים
ulevar-nabba kar'u ze'us ulesha'ul kare'u hermes, ki hayah rosh hamdabberim
And they called Barnabas, Jupiter; and Paul, Mercury, because he was the chief speaker.

הַכֹּהֵן שֶׁל זֵאוֹס, שֶׁהֵיכָלוֹ לִפְנֵי הָעִיר, הֵבִיא פָרִים וַעֲטָרוֹת אֶל הַשְּׁעָרִים
hakkohen shel ze'us, sheheichalo lifnei ha'ir, hevi parim va'atarot el hashe'arim
And the priest of Jupiter whose temple was before the city, brought oxen and garlands unto the gates,

וְרָצָה לְהַקְרִיב קָרְבָּנוֹת הוּא וַהֲמוֹן הָעָם
veratzah lehakriv karebanot hu vahamon ha'am
and would have done sacrifice with the multitudes.

כַּאֲשֶׁר שָׁמְעוּ זֹאת שָׁאוּל וּבַר־נַבָּא הַשְּׁלִיחִים, קָרְעוּ אֶת בִּגְדֵיהֶם
ka'asher shame'u zot sha'ul uvar-nabba hashelichim, kar'u et bigdeihem
But when the apostles, Barnabas and Paul, heard of it, they rent their garments,

הֵם רָצוּ אֶל תּוֹךְ הֶהָמוֹן וְצָעֲקוּ
hem ratzu el toch hehamon vetza'aku
and sprang forth among the multitude, crying out

אֲנָשִׁים, לָמָּה אַתֶּם עוֹשִׂים זֹאת? גַּם אֲנַחְנוּ בְּנֵי אֱנוֹשׁ כְּמוֹכֶם, וּמְבַשְּׂרִים לָכֶם אֶת הַבְּשׂוֹרָה
anashim, lammah attem osim zot? gam anachnu bnei enosh kemochem, umevassrim lachem et habbesorah
and saying, Sirs, why do ye these things? We also are men of like passions with you, and bring you good tidings,

כְּדֵי שֶׁתִּפְנוּ מִן הַהֲבָלִים הָאֵלֶּה לֵאלֹהִים חַיִּים
kedei shettifnu min hahavalim ha'elleh lelohim chayim
that ye should turn from these vain things unto a living God,

אֲשֶׁר עָשָׂה אֶת הַשָּׁמַיִם וְאֶת הָאָרֶץ וְאֶת הַיָּם וְאֶת כָּל אֲשֶׁר בָּם
asher asah et hashamayim ve'et ha'aretz ve'et hayam ve'et kol asher bam
who made the heaven and the earth and the sea, and all that in them is:

וַאֲשֶׁר בַּדּוֹרוֹת הַקּוֹדְמִים הִנִּיחַ לְכָל הַגּוֹיִים לָלֶכֶת בְּדַרְכֵיהֶם
va'asher baddorot hakkodemim hinniach lechol haggoyim lalechet bedarcheihem
who in the generations gone by suffered all the nations to walk in their own ways.

וּבְכָל זֹאת לֹא חָדַל לְהָעִיד עַל עַצְמוֹ
uvechol zot lo chadal leha'id al atzmo
And yet he left not himself without witness,

מַעֲשֵׂי הַשְּׁלִיחִים

אֲבָל אֵלֶּה מִן הַיְהוּדִים שֶׁסֵּרְבוּ לְהַאֲמִין
aval elleh min hayehudim shesserevu leha'amin
But the Jews that were disobedient stirred up the souls of the Gentiles,

עוֹרְרוּ שִׂנְאָה בְּלֵב הַגּוֹיִם נֶגֶד הָאַחִים
oreru sin'ah belev haggoyim neged ha'achim
and made them evil affected against the brethren.

הַשְּׁנַיִם יָשְׁבוּ שָׁם זְמַן רַב וְדִבְּרוּ בְּאֹמֶץ לֵב עַל הָאָדוֹן, וְהָאָדוֹן הֵעִיד לְאִשּׁוּר דְּבַר חַסְדּוֹ
hashnayim yashvu sham zman rav vedibbru be'ometz lev al ha'adon, veha'adon he'id le'ishur devar chasdo
Long time therefore they tarried there speaking boldly in the Lord, who bare witness unto the word of his grace,

בַּעֲשׂוֹתוֹ אוֹתוֹת וּמוֹפְתִים דַרְכָּם
ba'asoto otot umoftim darkam
granting signs and wonders to be done by their hands.

אָז הִתְפַּלְּגוּ תּוֹשְׁבֵי הָעִיר; אֵלֶּה אַחֲרֵי קְבוּצַת הַיְהוּדִים וְאֵלֶּה אַחֲרֵי הַשְּׁלִיחִים
az hitpallgu toshavei ha'ir; elleh acharei kevutzat hayehudim ve'elleh acharei hashlichim
But the multitude of the city was divided; and part held with the Jews, and part with the apostles.

גּוֹיִם וִיהוּדִים, יַחַד עִם הָעוֹמְדִים בְּרֹאשָׁם, קָמוּ עֲלֵיהֶם
goyim viyehudim, yachad im ha'omedim berosham, kamu aleihem
And when there was made an onset both of the Gentiles and of the Jews with their rulers,

לְהִתְעַלֵּל בָּהֶם וְלִסְקֹל אוֹתָם
lehit'allel bahem veliskol otam
to treat them shamefully and to stone them,

אַךְ הֵם הִבְחִינוּ בָּזֶה וְנִמְלְטוּ אֶל עָרֵי לִיקָאוֹנְיָה, לִיסְטְרָה וְדֶרְבִּי וְהַסְּבִיבָה
ach hem hivchinu bazeh venimletu el arei lika'oneyah, liseterah vederbi vehassevivah
they became aware of it, and fled unto the cities of Lycaonia, Lystra and Derbe, and the region round about:

וּבִשְּׂרוּ שָׁם אֶת הַבְּשׂוֹרָה
uvissru sham et habbesorah
and there they preached the gospel.

בְּלִיסְטְרָה יָשַׁב אִישׁ אֶחָד רְפֵה רַגְלַיִם, פִּסֵּחַ מִבֶּטֶן אִמּוֹ שֶׁלֹּא הָלַךְ מִיָּמָיו
beliseterah yashav ish echad refeh raglayim, pisseach mibbeten immo shello halach miyamav
And at Lystra there sat a certain man, impotent in his feet, a cripple from his mother's womb, who never had walked.

הוּא שָׁמַע אֶת שָׁאוּל מְדַבֵּר. כְּשֶׁהִבִּיט בּוֹ שָׁאוּל וְרָאָה שֶׁיֵּשׁ לוֹ אֱמוּנָה לְהֵרָפֵא
hu shama et sha'ul medabber. keshehibbit bo sha'ul vera'ah sheyesh lo emunah leherafe
The same heard Paul speaking: who, fastening his eyes upon him, and seeing that he had faith to be made whole,

אָמַר בְּקוֹל גָּדוֹל: קוּם עַל רַגְלֶיךָ וְהִזְדַּקֵּף! הוּא זִנֵּק וְהִתְהַלֵּךְ
amar bekol gadol: kum al ragleicha vehizdakkef! hu zinnek vehit'hallech
said with a loud voice, Stand upright on thy feet. And he leaped up and walked.

מַעֲשֵׂי הַשְּׁלִיחִים

הֵן כֹּה צִוָּנוּ אֲדֹנָי: וּנְתַתִּיךָ לְאוֹר גּוֹיִם

hen koh tzivvanu Adonai: unetatticha le'or goyim
For so hath the Lord commanded us, saying, I have set thee for a light of the Gentiles,

לִהְיוֹת יְשׁוּעָתִי עַד־קְצֵה הָאָרֶץ

lihyot yeshu'ati ad-ktzeh ha'aretz
That thou shouldest be for salvation unto the uttermost part of the earth.

הַגּוֹיִם כְּשָׁמְעָם שָׂמְחוּ וְהִלְלוּ אֶת דְּבַר הָאָדוֹן

haggoyim keshome'am samechu vehilelu et devar ha'adon
And as the Gentiles heard this, they were glad, and glorified the word of God:

וְכָל אֲשֶׁר הָיוּ מְיֻעָדִים לְחַיֵּי עוֹלָם הֶאֱמִינוּ

vechol asher hayu meyu'adim lechayei olam he'eminu
and as many as were ordained to eternal life believed.

דְּבַר הָאָדוֹן הָלַךְ וְנָפוֹץ בְּכָל הָאֵזוֹר

devar ha'adon halach venafotz bechol ha'ezor
And the word of the Lord was spread abroad throughout all the region.

אֲבָל רָאשֵׁי הַיְהוּדִים הֵסִיתוּ אֶת הַנָּשִׁים הַנִּכְבָּדוֹת הַיְרֵאוֹת אֶת אֱלֹהִים וְאֶת נִכְבַּדֵּי הָעִיר

aval rashei hayehudim hesitu et hannashim hannichbadot hayre'ot et elohim ve'et nichbaddei ha'ir
But the Jews urged on the devout women of honorable estate, and the chief men of the city,

וְעוֹרְרוּ רְדִיפָה נֶגֶד שָׁאוּל וּבַר־נַבָּא וְגֵרְשׁוּ אוֹתָם מֵאֵזוֹרָם

ve'oreru redifah neged sha'ul uvar-nabba vegereshu otam me'ezoram
and stirred up a persecution against Paul and Barnabas, and cast them out of their borders.

הַשְּׁנַיִם נִעֲרוּ לְעֶבְרָם אֶת אֲבַק רַגְלֵיהֶם וְהָלְכוּ לְאִיקוֹנְיוֹן

hashenayim ni'aru le'evram et avak ragleihem vehalechu le'ikoneyon
But they shook off the dust of their feet against them, and came unto Iconium.

וְאוּלָם הַתַּלְמִידִים מָלְאוּ שִׂמְחָה וְרוּחַ הַקֹּדֶשׁ

ve'ulam hattalmidim male'u simchah veruach hakkodesh
And the disciples were filled with joy and with the Holy Spirit.

יד

בְּאִיקוֹנְיוֹן נִכְנְסוּ יַחְדָּיו לְבֵית הַכְּנֶסֶת

be'ikoneyon nichnesu yachdav leveit hakkneset
And it came to pass in Iconium that they entered together into the synagogue of the Jews,

וְדִבְּרוּ בְּאֹפֶן כָּזֶה שֶׁעַם רַב מִן הַיְהוּדִים וּמִן הַיְוָנִים הֶאֱמִינוּ

vedibberu be'ofen kazeh she'am rav min hayehudim umin hayevanim he'eminu
and so spake that a great multitude both of Jews and of Greeks believed.

מַעֲשֵׂי הַשְּׁלִיחִים

כִּי־פֹעַל פֹּעֵל בִּימֵיכֶם לֹא תַאֲמִינוּ כִּי יְסֻפָּר
ki-fo'al po'el bimeichem lo ta'aminu ki yesuppar
For I work a work in your days, A work which ye shall in no wise believe, if one declare it unto you.

כְּשֶׁיָּצְאוּ בִּקְשׁוּ מִשָּׁאוּל וּבַר־נַבָּא לְדַבֵּר אֲלֵיהֶם אֶת הַדְּבָרִים הָאֵלֶּה בַּשַּׁבָּת הַבָּאָה
kesheyatze'u biksku misha'ul uvar-nabba ledabber aleihem et haddvarim ha'elleh bashabbat habba'ah
And as they went out, they besought that these words might be spoken to them the next sabbath.

לְאַחַר שֶׁהִתְפַּזְּרוּ בָּאֵי בֵּית הַכְּנֶסֶת
le'achar shehitpazzeru ba'ei beit hakkneset
Now when the synagogue broke up,

הָלְכוּ אַחֲרֵי שָׁאוּל וּבַר־נַבָּא רַבִּים מִן הַיְהוּדִים וּמִן הַגֵּרִים יִרְאֵי הָאֱלֹהִים
halechu acharei sha'ul uvar-nabba rabbim min hayehudim umin haggerim yir'ei ha'elohim
many of the Jews and of the devout proselytes followed Paul and Barnabas;

הַשְּׁנַיִם דִּבְּרוּ אֲלֵיהֶם וְהֵאִיצוּ בָהֶם לְהַמְשִׁיךְ בַּעֲמִידָתָם בְּחֶסֶד הָאֱלֹהִים
hashenayim dibberu aleihem vehe'itzu bahem lehamshich ba'amidatam bechesed ha'elohim
who, speaking to them, urged them to continue in the grace of God.

בַּשַּׁבָּת הַשְּׁנִיָּה הִתְאַסְּפָה כִּמְעַט כָּל הָעִיר לִשְׁמֹעַ אֶת דְּבַר יהוה
bashabbat hashniyah hit'assefah kim'at kol ha'ir lishmoa et devar hashem
And the next sabbath almost the whole city was gathered together to hear the word of God.

אֲבָל כִּרְאוֹת יְהוּדֵי הַמָּקוֹם אֶת הֲמוֹן הָעָם, נִתְמַלְּאוּ קִנְאָה
aval kir'ot yehudei hammakom et hamon ha'am, nitmalle'u kin'ah
But when the Jews saw the multitudes, they were filled with jealousy,

וְהֵחֵלּוּ לְגַדֵּף וּלְדַבֵּר נֶגֶד דִּבְרֵי שָׁאוּל
vehechelu legaddef uledabber neged divrei sha'ul
and contradicted the things which were spoken by Paul, and blasphemed.

הֵשִׁיבוּ שָׁאוּל וּבַר־נַבָּא בְּאֹמֶץ לֵב וְאָמְרוּ
heshivu sha'ul uvar-nabba be'ometz lev ve'ameru
And Paul and Barnabas spake out boldly, and said,

מִן הַהֶכְרֵחַ הָיָה כִּי לָכֶם רִאשׁוֹנָה יַשְׁמִיעוּ אֶת דְּבַר אֱלֹהִים
min hahechreach hayah ki lachem rishonah yashmi'u et dvar elohim
It was necessary that the word of God should first be spoken to you.

אַךְ מִכֵּיוָן שֶׁאַתֶּם דּוֹחִים אוֹתוֹ וְדָנִים אֶת עַצְמְכֶם לְבִלְתִּי רְאוּיִים לְחַיֵּי עוֹלָם
ach mikkeivan she'attem dochim oto vedanim et atzmechem levilti re'uyim lechayei olam
Seeing ye thrust it from you, and judge yourselves unworthy of eternal life,

הִנֵּה אָנוּ פּוֹנִים אֶל הַגּוֹיִם
hinneh anu ponim el haggoyim
lo, we turn to the Gentiles.

מַעֲשֵׂי הַשְּׁלִיחִים

אֱלֹהִים קִיֵּם אוֹתָהּ לָנוּ, הַבָּנִים, בַּהֲקִימוֹ אֶת יֵשׁוּעַ, כְּמוֹ שֶׁכָּתוּב בַּמִּזְמוֹר הַשֵּׁנִי

'elohim kiyem otah lanu, habbanim, bahakimo et yeshua, kemo shekkatuv bammizmor hasheni

that God hath fulfilled the same unto our children, in that he raised up Jesus; as also it is written in the second psalm,

בְּנִי אַתָּה, אֲנִי הַיּוֹם יְלִדְתִּיךָ

bni attah, ani hayom yelidticha

Thou art my Son, this day have I begotten thee.

וְעַל הֲקִימוֹ אוֹתוֹ מִן הַמֵּתִים לְבִלְתִּי שׁוּב עוֹד אֶל שַׁחַת

ve'al hakimo oto min hammetim levilti shuv od el shachat

And as concerning that he raised him up from the dead, now no more to return to corruption,

כֹּה אָמַר: אֶתֵּן לָכֶם חַסְדֵי דָוִד הַנֶּאֱמָנִים

koh amar: etten lachem chasdei david hanne'emanim

he hath spoken on this wise, I will give you the holy and sure blessings of David.

לָכֵן נֶאֱמַר גַּם בְּמָקוֹם אַחֵר: לֹא־תִתֵּן חֲסִידְךָ לִרְאוֹת שַׁחַת

lachen ne'emar gam bemakom acher: lo-titten chasidcha lir'ot shachat

Because he saith also in another psalm, Thou wilt not give thy Holy One to see corruption.

הֵן דָּוִד, לְאַחַר שֶׁשֵּׁרֵת בְּדוֹרוֹ לְפִי תָכְנִית אֱלֹהִים

hen david, le'achar shesheret bedoro lefi tochnit elohim

For David, after he had in his own generation served the counsel of God,

שָׁכַב וְנֶאֱסַף אֶל אֲבוֹתָיו וְרָאָה שַׁחַת

shachav vene'esaf el avotav vera'ah shachat

fell asleep, and was laid unto his fathers, and saw corruption:

אֲבָל זֶה שֶׁאֱלֹהִים הֱקִימוֹ לֹא רָאָה שַׁחַת

aval zeh she'elohim hekimo lo ra'ah shachat

but he whom God raised up saw no corruption.

עַל כֵּן, אֲנָשִׁים אַחִים, שֶׁיְּהֵא יָדוּעַ לָכֶם כִּי הוֹדוֹת לוֹ מֻכְרֶזֶת לָכֶם סְלִיחַת חֲטָאִים

al ken, anashim achim, sheyehei yadua lachem ki hodot lo muchrezet lachem slichat chata'im

Be it known unto you therefore, brethren, that through this man is proclaimed unto you remission of sins:

וּבְכָל הַדְּבָרִים שֶׁלֹּא יְכָלְתֶּם לְהִצָּדֵק בָּהֶם בְּתוֹרַת מֹשֶׁה, הֲרֵי שֶׁבּוֹ נִצְדָּק כָּל מִי שֶׁמַּאֲמִין

uvechol haddevarim shello yechaletem lehitzadek bahem betorat mosheh, harei shebbo nitzdak kol mi shemma'amin

and by him every one that believeth is justified from all things, from which ye could not be justified by the law of Moses.

לָכֵן הִזָּהֲרוּ שֶׁלֹּא יָבוֹא עֲלֵיכֶם הַנֶּאֱמַר בַּנְּבִיאִים

lachen hizzaharu shello yavo aleichem hanne'emar bannevi'im

Beware therefore, lest that come upon you which is spoken in the prophets:

רְאוּ בַגּוֹיִם וְהַבִּיטוּ וְהִתַּמְּהוּ תְּמָהוּ

re'u vaggoyim vehabbitu vehittammehu temahu

Behold, ye despisers, and wonder, and perish;

מַעֲשֵׂי הַשְּׁלִיחִים

אַךְ הִנֵּה הוּא בָּא אַחֲרַי וַאֲנִי אֵינֶנִּי רָאוּי לְהַתִּיר אֶת נְעָלָיו
ach hinneh hu ba acharai va'ani einenni ra'ui lehattir et ne'alav
But behold, there cometh one after me the shoes of whose feet I am not worthy to unloose.

אֲנָשִׁים אַחִים, בְּנֵי מִשְׁפַּחַת אַבְרָהָם, וְיִרְאֵי אֱלֹהִים אֲשֶׁר בְּקִרְבְּכֶם
anashim achim, benei mishpachat avraham, veyir'ei elohim asher bekirbechem;
Brethren, children of the stock of Abraham, and those among you that fear God,

אֵלֵינוּ נִשְׁלַח דְּבַר הַיְשׁוּעָה הַזֹּאת
eleinu nishlach devar hayshu'ah hazzot
to us is the word of this salvation sent forth.

כִּי יוֹשְׁבֵי יְרוּשָׁלַיִם וְהָעוֹמְדִים בְּרֹאשָׁם לֹא הִכִּירוּהוּ
ki yoshevei yerushalayim veha'omedim berosham lo hikkiruhu
For they that dwell in Jerusalem, and their rulers, because they knew him not,

וּבְשָׁפְטָם אוֹתוֹ מִלְאוּ אֶת דִּבְרֵי הַנְּבִיאִים הַנִּקְרָאִים בְּכָל שַׁבָּת
uveshoftam oto mil'u et divrei hannevi'im hannikra'im bechol shabbat
nor the voices of the prophets which are read every sabbath, fulfilled them by condemning him.

וְאַף כִּי לֹא מָצְאוּ שׁוּם עִלָּה לְמִשְׁפַּט מָוֶת בִּקְשׁוּ מִפִּילָטוֹס לַהֲמִיתוֹ
ve'af ki lo matze'u shum illah lemishpat mavet bikshu mippilatos lahamito
And though they found no cause of death in him, yet asked they of Pilate that he should be slain.

כַּאֲשֶׁר הִשְׁלִימוּ אֶת כָּל הַדְּבָרִים הַכְּתוּבִים עָלָיו
ka'asher hishlimu et kol haddevarim hakketuvim alav
And when they had fulfilled all things that were written of him,

הוֹרִידוּהוּ מִן הָעֵץ וְהִנִּיחוּהוּ בַּקֶּבֶר
horiduhu min ha'etz vehinnichuhu bakkever
they took him down from the tree, and laid him in a tomb.

אַךְ אֱלֹהִים הֱקִימוֹ מִן הַמֵּתִים
ach elohim hekimo min hammetim
But God raised him from the dead:

יָמִים רַבִּים נִרְאָה אֶל הָאֲנָשִׁים שֶׁעָלוּ אִתּוֹ מִן הַגָּלִיל לִירוּשָׁלַיִם
yamim rabbim nir'ah el ha'anashim she'alu itto min haggalil liyerushalayim
and he was seen for many days of them that came up with him from Galilee to Jerusalem,

וְעַתָּה הֵם עֵדָיו לִפְנֵי הָעָם
ve'attah hem edav lifnei ha'am
who are now his witnesses unto the people.

וַאֲנַחְנוּ מְבַשְּׂרִים לָכֶם כִּי הַהַבְטָחָה אֲשֶׁר הֻבְטְחָה לַאֲבוֹתֵינוּ
va'anachnu mevashorim lachem ki hahavtachah asher huvtechah la'avoteinu
And we bring you good tidings of the promise made unto the fathers,

מַעֲשֵׂי הַשְּׁלִיחִים

וְרוֹמֵם אֶת הָעָם בִּהְיוֹתָם גֵּרִים בְּאֶרֶץ מִצְרַיִם וּבְיָד רָמָה הוֹצִיאָם מִשָּׁם
veromem et ha'am bihyotam gerim be'eretz mitzrayim uveyad ramah hotzi'am misham
and exalted the people when they sojourned in the land of Egypt, and with a high arm led he them forth out of it.

בְּמֶשֶׁךְ כְּאַרְבָּעִים שָׁנָה נָשָׂא אוֹתָם בַּמִּדְבָּר
bemeshech ke'arba'im shanah nasa otam bammidbar
And for about the time of forty years as a nursing-father bare he them in the wilderness.

וּלְאַחַר שֶׁהִשְׁמִיד שִׁבְעָה גּוֹיִם בְּאֶרֶץ כְּנַעַן
ule'achar shehishmid shiv'ah goyim be'eretz kena'an
And when he had destroyed seven nations in the land of Canaan,

חִלֵּק לָהֶם אֶת אַרְצָם לְנַחֲלָה
chillek lahem et artzam lenachalah
he gave them their land for an inheritance,

כָּל זֶה אָרַךְ כְּאַרְבַּע מֵאוֹת וַחֲמִשִּׁים שָׁנָה וְאַחֲרֵי כֵן נָתַן לָהֶם שׁוֹפְטִים עַד שְׁמוּאֵל הַנָּבִיא
kol zeh arach ke'arba me'ot vachamishim shanah ve'acharei chen natan lahem shoftim ad shemu'el hannavi
for about four hundred and fifty years: and after these things he gave them judges until Samuel the prophet.

לְאַחַר מִכֵּן בִּקְשׁוּ מֶלֶךְ
le'achar mikken bikshu melech
And afterward they asked for a king:

וֵאלֹהִים נָתַן לָהֶם אֶת שָׁאוּל בֶּן-קִישׁ, אִישׁ מִשֵּׁבֶט בִּנְיָמִין, לְמֶשֶׁךְ אַרְבָּעִים שָׁנָה
ve'elohim natan lahem et sha'ul ben-kish, ish mishevet binyamin, lemeshech arba'im shanah
and God gave unto them Saul the son of Kish, a man of the tribe of Benjamin, for the space of forty years.

כַּאֲשֶׁר הֵסִיר אוֹתוֹ הֵקִים לָהֶם אֶת דָּוִד לְמֶלֶךְ וְעָלָיו הֵעִיד בְּאָמְרוֹ
ka'asher hesir oto hekim lahem et david lemelech ve'alav he'id be'omro
And when he had removed him, he raised up David to be their king; to whom also he bare witness and said,

מָצָאתִי דָּוִד בֶּן-יִשַׁי, אִישׁ כִּלְבָבִי, וְהוּא יַעֲשֶׂה אֶת כָּל חֶפְצִי
matzati david ben-yishai, ish kilevavi, vehu ya'aseh et kol cheftzi
I have found David the son of Jesse, a man after my heart, who shall do all my will.

מִזַּרְעוֹ הֵבִיא אֱלֹהִים, כְּפִי הַהַבְטָחָה, מוֹשִׁיעַ לְיִשְׂרָאֵל - אֶת יֵשׁוּעַ
mizzar'o hevi elohim, kefi hahavtachah, moshia leyisra'el - et yeshua
Of this man's seed hath God according to promise brought unto Israel a Saviour, Jesus;

אֲשֶׁר לִפְנֵי בּוֹאוֹ הִכְרִיז יוֹחָנָן אֶת טְבִילַת הַתְּשׁוּבָה אֶל כָּל עַם יִשְׂרָאֵל
asher lifnei bo'o hichriz yochanan et tevilat hattshuvah el kol am yisra'el
when John had first preached before his coming the baptism of repentance to all the people of Israel.

כְּשֶׁהִשְׁלִים יוֹחָנָן אֶת מְרוּצָתוֹ אָמַר, לְמִי אַתֶּם חוֹשְׁבִים אוֹתִי? לֹא אֲנִי הוּא
keshehishlim yochanan et merutzato amar, lemi attem choshevim oti? lo ani hu
And as John was fulfilling his course, he said, What suppose ye that I am? I am not he.

מַעֲשֵׂי הַשְּׁלִיחִים

הַאִם לֹא תֶחְדַּל לְסַלֵּף אֶת דַּרְכֵי אֱלֹהִים הַיְשָׁרִים
ha'im lo techdal lesallef et darchei elohim haysharim
wilt thou not cease to pervert the right ways of the Lord?

וְעַתָּה הִנֵּה יַד־אֱלֹהִים בָּךְ; עִוֵּר תִּהְיֶה וְלֹא תִרְאֶה אֶת אוֹר הַשֶּׁמֶשׁ עַד בּוֹא מוֹעֵד
ve'attah hinneh yad-'elohim becha; ivver tihyeh velo tir'eh et or hashemesh ad bo mo'ed
And now, behold, the hand of the Lord is upon thee, and thou shalt be blind, not seeing the sun for a season.

בּוֹ בַּמָּקוֹם נָפְלָה עָלָיו אֲפֵלָה וַחֲשֵׁכָה. הוּא הָלַךְ הֵנָּה וָהֵנָּה בְּחַפְּשׂוֹ מִישֶׁהוּ שֶׁיּוֹלִיכוֹ בַּיָּד
bo bammakom nafelah alav afelah vachashechah. hu halach hennah vahennah bechappeso mishehu sheyolicho bayad
And immediately there fell on him a mist and a darkness; and he went about seeking some to lead him by the hand.

כְּשֶׁרָאָה הַמּוֹשֵׁל אֶת הַנַּעֲשֶׂה הֶאֱמִין וְהִשְׁתּוֹמֵם עַל תּוֹרַת הָאָדוֹן
keshera'ah hammoshel et hanna'aseh he'emin vehishtomem al torat ha'adon
Then the proconsul, when he saw what was done, believed, being astonished at the teaching of the Lord.

שָׁאוּל וַחֲבֵרָיו הִפְלִיגוּ מִפַּפוֹס וּבָאוּ אֶל פֶּרְגִי שֶׁבְּפַמְפִילְיָה
sha'ul vachaverav hifligu mippafos uva'u el pergi shebbepamfileyah
Now Paul and his company set sail from Paphos, and came to Perga in Pamphylia:

אַךְ יוֹחָנָן עָזַב אוֹתָם וְחָזַר לִירוּשָׁלַיִם
ach yochanan azav otam vechazar liyerushalayim
and John departed from them and returned to Jerusalem.

מִפֶּרְגִי הִמְשִׁיכוּ בְּדַרְכָּם וְהִגִּיעוּ אֶל אַנְטִיוֹכְיָה אֲשֶׁר בְּפִּיסִידְיָה
mippergi himshichu bedarkam vehiggi'u el antiyocheyah asher bepisideyah
But they, passing through from Perga, came to Antioch of Pisidia;

וּבְשַׁבָּת נִכְנְסוּ לְבֵית הַכְּנֶסֶת וְיָשְׁבוּ
uveshabbat nichnesu leveit hakkeneset veyashevu
and they went into the synagogue on the sabbath day, and sat down.

אַחֲרֵי קְרִיאַת הַתּוֹרָה וְהַנְּבִיאִים, שָׁלְחוּ אֲלֵיהֶם רָאשֵׁי בֵּית הַכְּנֶסֶת לֵאמֹר
acharei keri'at hattorah vehannevi'im, shalechu aleihem rashei beit hakkeneset lemor
And after the reading of the law and the prophets the rulers of the synagogue sent unto them, saying,

אֲנָשִׁים אַחִים, אִם יֵשׁ לָכֶם דְּבַר מוּסָר אֶל הָעָם, דַּבְּרוּ
anashim achim, im yesh lachem devar musar el ha'am, dabberu
Brethren, if ye have any word of exhortation for the people, say on.

קָם שָׁאוּל, הֵנִיף אֶת יָדוֹ וְאָמַר: אַנְשֵׁי יִשְׂרָאֵל וְיִרְאֵי הָאֱלֹהִים, שִׁמְעוּ
kam sha'ul, henif et yado ve'amar: anshei yisra'el veyir'ei ha'elohim, shim'u
And Paul stood up, and beckoning with the hand said, Men of Israel, and ye that fear God, hearken:

אֱלֹהֵי הָעָם הַזֶּה, אֱלֹהֵי יִשְׂרָאֵל, בָּחַר בַּאֲבוֹתֵינוּ
elohei ha'am hazzeh, elohei yisra'el, bachar ba'avoteinu
The God of this people Israel chose our fathers,

מַעֲשֵׂי הַשְּׁלִיחִים

לְאַחַר שֶׁצָּמוּ וְהִתְפַּלְלוּ סָמְכוּ אֶת יְדֵיהֶם עֲלֵיהֶם וְשָׁלְחוּ אוֹתָם

le'achar shetzamu vehitpallelu samechu et yedeihem aleihem veshalchu otam
Then, when they had fasted and prayed and laid their hands on them, they sent them away.

הַשְּׁלוּחִים מִטַּעַם רוּחַ הַקֹּדֶשׁ יָרְדוּ אֶל סֶלֶבְקְיָה וּמִשָּׁם הִפְלִיגוּ אֶל קַפְרִיסִין

hasheluchim mitta'am ruach hakkodesh yaredu el selevkiyah umisham hifligu el kafrisin
So they, being sent forth by the Holy Spirit, went down to Seleucia; and from thence they sailed to Cyprus.

הֵם בָּאוּ אֶל סָלָמִיס וְהִשְׁמִיעוּ אֶת דְּבַר אֱלֹהִים בְּבָתֵּי הַכְּנֶסֶת

hem ba'u el salamis vehishmi'u et dvar elohim bevattei hakkeneset
And when they were at Salamis, they proclaimed the word of God in the synagogues of the Jews:

גַּם יוֹחָנָן הָיָה עוֹזֵר עַל יָדָם

gam yochanan hayah ozer al yadam
and they had also John as their attendant.

אַחֲרֵי שֶׁעָבְרוּ בְּכָל הָאִי וְהִגִּיעוּ עַד פָּפוֹס

acharei she'averu bechol ha'i vehiggi'u ad pafos
And when they had gone through the whole island unto Paphos,

מָצְאוּ אִישׁ מְכַשֵּׁף וּנְבִיא שֶׁקֶר, יְהוּדִי אֲשֶׁר שְׁמוֹ בַּר־יֵשׁוּעַ

matze'u ish mechashef unevi sheker, yehudi asher shemo bar-yeshua
they found a certain sorcerer, a false prophet, a Jew, whose name was Bar-Jesus;

וְהוּא מְקֹרָב לַמּוֹשֵׁל סֶרְגְיוֹס פּוֹלוֹס. הַמּוֹשֵׁל, שֶׁהָיָה אָדָם נָבוֹן

vehu mekorav lammoshel sergeyos polos. hammoshel, shehayah adam navon
who was with the proconsul, Sergius Paulus, a man of understanding.

קָרָא לְבַר־נַבָּא וּלְשָׁאוּל וּבִקֵּשׁ לִשְׁמֹעַ אֶת דְּבַר אֱלֹהִים

kara levar-nabba ulesha'ul uvikkesh lishmoa et dvar elohim
The same called unto him Barnabas and Saul, and sought to hear the word of God.

אֶלָּא שֶׁאֱלִימַס הַמְכַשֵּׁף - זֶה תַּרְגוּם שְׁמוֹ - הִתְנַגֵּד לָהֶם

ella she'elimas hamchashef - zeh targum shemo - hitnagged lahem
But Elymas the sorcerer (for so is his name by interpretation) withstood them,

בְּנַסּוֹתוֹ לְהַטּוֹת אֶת הַמּוֹשֵׁל מִן הָאֱמוּנָה

benassoto lehattot et hammoshel min ha'emunah
seeking to turn aside the proconsul from the faith.

שָׁאוּל, הַנִּקְרָא גַּם פּוֹלוֹס, בִּהְיוֹתוֹ מָלֵא רוּחַ הַקֹּדֶשׁ, הִבִּיט בּוֹ וְאָמַר

sha'ul, hannikra gam polos, bihyoto malei ruach hakkodesh, hibbit bo ve'amar
But Saul, who is also called Paul, filled with the Holy Spirit, fastened his eyes on him,

אַתָּה הַמָּלֵא כָּל מִרְמָה וְכָל רֶשַׁע, בֶּן הַשָּׂטָן, שׂוֹנֵא כָּל צֶדֶק

attah hammalei kol mirmah vechol resha, ben hassatan, sonei kol tzedek
and said, O full of all guile and all villany, thou son of the devil, thou enemy of all righteousness,

מַעֲשֵׂי הַשְּׁלִיחִים

בַּיּוֹם הַמְיֻעָד לָבַשׁ הוֹרְדוֹס לְבוּשׁ מַלְכוּת, יָשַׁב עַל כֵּס הַמִּשְׁפָּט וְנָשָׂא לִפְנֵיהֶם נְאוּם
bayom hamyu'ad lavash horedos levush malchut, yashav al kes hammishpat venasa lifneihem ne'um
And upon a set day Herod arrayed himself in royal apparel, and sat on the throne, and made an oration unto them.

זֶה קוֹל אֱלֹהִים וְלֹא קוֹל שֶׁל אָדָם! הֵרִיעַ הַקָּהָל
zeh kol elohim velo kol shel adam! heria hakkahal
And the people shouted, saying, The voice of a god, and not of a man.

מִיָּד הִכָּהוּ מַלְאַךְ יהוה מִשּׁוּם שֶׁלֹּא נָתַן אֶת הַכָּבוֹד לֵאלֹהִים
miyad hikkahu mal'ach hashem mishum shello natan et hakkavod le'elohim
And immediately an angel of the Lord smote him, because he gave not God the glory:

הוּא נָפַח אֶת נַפְשׁוֹ כְּשֶׁהוּא אֲכוּל תּוֹלָעִים
hu nafach et nafsho kshehu achul tola'im
and he was eaten of worms, and gave up the ghost.

דְּבַר אֱלֹהִים שִׂגְשֵׂג וְנָפוֹץ
dvar elohim sigseg venafotz
But the word of God grew and multiplied.

וּבַר־נַבָּא וְשָׁאוּל הִשְׁלִימוּ אֶת שֵׁרוּתָם וְחָזְרוּ מִירוּשָׁלַיִם
uvar-nabba vesha'ul hishlimu et sherutam vechazeru miyerushalayim
And Barnabas and Saul returned from Jerusalem, when they had fulfilled their ministration,

בַּהֲבִיאָם אִתָּם אֶת יוֹחָנָן הַמְכֻנֶּה מַרְקוֹס
bahavi'am ittam et yochanan hamchunneh markos
taking with them John whose surname was Mark.

יג

נְבִיאִים וּמוֹרִים הָיוּ בַּקְּהִלָּה אֲשֶׁר בְּאַנְטִיּוֹכְיָה: בַּר־נַבָּא
nevi'im umorim hayu bakkehillah asher be'antiyocheyah: bar-nabba
Now there were at Antioch, in the church that was there, prophets and teachers, Barnabas,

שִׁמְעוֹן הַנִּקְרָא נִיגֶר, לוּקְיוֹס הַקִּירֵנִי, מְנַחֵם אֲשֶׁר גֻּדַּל עִם הוֹרְדוֹס שַׂר הָרֹבַע, וְשָׁאוּל
shim'on hannikra niger, lukeyos hakkireni, menachem asher guddal im horedos sar harova, vesha'ul
and Symeon that was called Niger, and Lucius of Cyrene, and Manaen the foster-brother of Herod the tetrarch, and Saul.

בְּעֵת שֶׁעָבְדוּ אֶת יהוה וְצָמוּ אָמְרָה רוּחַ הַקֹּדֶשׁ
be'et she'avdu et hashem vetzamu amrah ruach hakkodesh
And as they ministered to the Lord, and fasted, the Holy Spirit said,

הַבְדִּילוּ לִי אֶת בַּר־נַבָּא וְאֶת שָׁאוּל לַעֲבוֹדָה אֲשֶׁר קָרָאתִי אוֹתָם אֵלֶיהָ
havdilu li et bar-nabba ve'et sha'ul la'avodah asher karati otam eleiha
Separate me Barnabas and Saul for the work whereunto I have called them.

מַעֲשֵׂי הַשְּׁלִיחִים

וְרָצָה פְּנִימָה לְהוֹדִיעַ שֶׁכֵּיפָא עוֹמֵד לִפְנֵי הַשַּׁעַר
veratzah penimah lehodia shekkeifa omed lifnei hasha'ar
but ran in, and told that Peter stood before the gate.

אָמְרוּ לָהּ: מְשֻׁגַּעַת, אַךְ הִיא טָעֲנָה בְּתֹקֶף כִּי כֵן הַדָּבָר. אָז אָמְרוּ: זֶה הַמַּלְאָךְ שֶׁלּוֹ
ameru lah. meshugga'at, ach hi ta'anah betokef ki chen haddavar. az ameru. zeh hammal'ach shello
And they said unto her, Thou art mad. But she confidently affirmed that it was even so. And they said, It is his angel.

בֵּינְתַיִם הוֹסִיף כֵּיפָא לִדְפֹּק עַל הַשַּׁעַר, וּכְשֶׁפָּתְחוּ רָאוּ אוֹתוֹ וְהִשְׁתּוֹמְמוּ
beinetayim hosif keifa lidpok al hasha'ar, uchesheppatechu ra'u oto vehishtomemu
But Peter continued knocking: and when they had opened, they saw him, and were amazed.

הוּא רָמַז לָהֶם בְּיָדוֹ לִשְׁתֹּק
hu ramaz lahem beyado lishtok
But he, beckoning unto them with the hand to hold their peace,

וְסִפֵּר לָהֶם כֵּיצַד הוֹצִיאוֹ הָאָדוֹן מִבֵּית הַסֹּהַר
vesipper lahem keitzad hotzi'o ha'adon mibbeit hassohar
declared unto them how the Lord had brought him forth out of the prison.

אָמַר: הַגִּידוּ זֹאת לְיַעֲקֹב וְלָאַחִים. לְאַחַר מִכֵּן יָצָא וְהָלַךְ לְמָקוֹם אַחֵר
amar: haggidu zot leya'akov vela'achim. le'achar mikken yatza vehalach lemakom acher
And he said, Tell these things unto James, and to the brethren. And he departed, and went to another place.

עִם אוֹר הַבֹּקֶר הָיְתָה מְבוּכָה גְּדוֹלָה בֵּין הַחַיָּלִים עַל־אוֹדוֹת כֵּיפָא. תָּמְהוּ: מַה קָּרָה לוֹ
im or habboker haytah mevuchah gedolah bein hachayalim al-'odot keifa. tamehu: mah karah lo
Now as soon as it was day, there was no small stir among the soldiers, what was become of Peter.

כְּשֶׁבִּקֵּשׁ אוֹתוֹ הוֹרְדוֹס וְלֹא מָצָא, חָקַר אֶת הַשּׁוֹמְרִים
keshebbikkesh oto horedos velo matza, chakar et hashomerim
And when Herod had sought for him, and found him not, he examined the guards,

וְצִוָּה לְהוֹצִיאָם לַהוֹרֵג. אַחֲרֵי כֵן יָרַד מִיהוּדָה אֶל קֵיסַרְיָה וְשָׁהָה שָׁם
vetzivvah lehotzi'am lahoreg. acharei chen yarad miyehudah el keisaryah veshahah sham
and commanded that they should be put to death. And he went down from Judæa to Cæsarea, and tarried there.

סִכְסוּךְ חָרִיף הָיָה בֵּין הוֹרְדוֹס לְבֵין אַנְשֵׁי צוֹר וְצִידוֹן
sichsuch charif hayah bein horedos levein anshei tzor vetzidon
Now he was highly displeased with them of Tyre and Sidon:

הֵם בָּאוּ אֵלָיו בְּיַחַד וְאַחֲרֵי שֶׁהִתְרַצּוּ אֶל בְּלַסְטוֹס, הַמְמֻנֶּה עַל חֲצַר הַמֶּלֶךְ
hem ba'u elav beyachad ve'acharei shehitratzu el belastos, hamemunneh al chatzar hammelech
and they came with one accord to him, and, having made Blastus the king's chamberlain their friend,

בִּקְשׁוּ שָׁלוֹם, שֶׁכֵּן פַּרְנָסַת אַרְצָם הָיְתָה תְּלוּיָה בְּאֶרֶץ הַמֶּלֶךְ
bikshu shalom, shekken parnasat artzam hayetah tluyah be'eretz hammelech
they asked for peace, because their country was fed from the king's country.

מַעֲשֵׂי הַשְּׁלִיחִים

אָמַר לוֹ: הִתְעַטֵּף בְּמְעִילְךָ וּבוֹא אַחֲרַי
amar lo: hit'attef bim'ilecha uvo acharai
And he saith unto him, Cast thy garment about thee, and follow me.

יָצָא כֵּיפָא וְהָלַךְ אַחֲרָיו וְלֹא יָדַע כִּי מַה שֶׁנַּעֲשָׂה עַל־יְדֵי הַמַּלְאָךְ הוּא דָּבָר מַמָּשִׁי
yatza keifa vehalach acharav velo yada ki mah shenna'aseh al-yedei hammal'ach hu davar mammashi
And he went out, and followed; and he knew not that it was true which was done by the angel,

אֶלָּא חָשַׁב שֶׁהוּא רוֹאֶה חָזוֹן
ella chashav shehu ro'eh chazon
but thought he saw a vision.

הֵם עָבְרוּ דֶּרֶךְ הַמִּשְׁמֶרֶת הָרִאשׁוֹנָה וְהַשְּׁנִיָּה
hem averu derech hammishmeret harishonah vehasheniyah
And when they were past the first and the second guard,

וּבָאוּ עַד שַׁעַר הַבַּרְזֶל הַפּוֹנֶה אֶל הָעִיר. הַשַּׁעַר נִפְתַּח לִפְנֵיהֶם מֵאֵלָיו
uva'u ad sha'ar habbarzel happoneh el ha'ir. hasha'ar niftach lifneihem me'elav
they came unto the iron gate that leadeth into the city; which opened to them of its own accord:

וְהֵם יָצְאוּ הַחוּצָה וְעָבְרוּ בִּרְחוֹב אֶחָד. פִּתְאוֹם עָזַב אוֹתוֹ הַמַּלְאָךְ
vehem yatze'u hachutzah ve'averu birchov echad. pit'om azav oto hammal'ach
and they went out, and passed on through one street; and straightway the angel departed from him.

כַּאֲשֶׁר שָׁבָה אֵלָיו דַּעְתּוֹ אָמַר כֵּיפָא: עַכְשָׁו אֲנִי יוֹדֵעַ בֶּאֱמֶת כִּי אֲדֹנָי שָׁלַח אֶת מַלְאָכוֹ
ka'asher shavah elav da'to amar keifa. achshav ani yodea be'emet ki adonai shalach et mal'acho
And when Peter was come to himself, he said, Now I know of a truth, that the Lord hath sent forth his angel

וְהִצִּילַנִי מִיַּד הוֹרְדוֹס וּמִכָּל כַּוָּנוֹתֵיהֶם שֶׁל קְהַל הַיְּהוּדִים
vehitzilani miyad horedos umikkol kavvanoteihem shel kehal hayehudim
and delivered me out of the hand of Herod, and from all the expectation of the people of the Jews.

;כְּשֶׁהִכִּיר בַּמְּצִיאוּת הָלַךְ לְבֵית מִרְיָם אֵם יוֹחָנָן הַמְכֻנֶּה מַרְקוֹס
keshehikkir bammetzi'ut halach leveit miryam em yochanan hamchunneh markos
And when he had considered the thing, he came to the house of Mary the mother of John whose surname was Mark;

בְּאוֹתוֹ מָקוֹם נֶאֶסְפוּ רַבִּים וְהִתְפַּלְלוּ
be'oto makom ne'esfu rabbim vehitpallelu
where many were gathered together and were praying.

הוּא דָּפַק עַל דֶּלֶת הַשַּׁעַר וְנַעֲרָה אַחַת, רוֹדָה שְׁמָהּ, נִגְּשָׁה לַעֲנוֹת
hu dafak al delet hasha'ar vena'arah achat, rodah shemah, niggshah la'anot
And when he knocked at the door of the gate, a maid came to answer, named Rhoda.

הִיא הִכִּירָה אֶת קוֹלוֹ שֶׁל כֵּיפָא, אַךְ מִשִּׂמְחָתָהּ לֹא פָּתְחָה אֶת הַשַּׁעַר
hi hikkirah et kolo shel keifa, ach missimchata lo patchah et hasha'ar
And when she knew Peter's voice, she opened not the gate for joy,

מַעֲשֵׂי הַשְּׁלִיחִים

וְהֵמִית בַּחֶרֶב אֶת יַעֲקֹב אֲחִי יוֹחָנָן
vehemit bacherev et ya'akov achi yochanan
And he killed James the brother of John with the sword.

כִּרְאוֹתוֹ שֶׁהָעָם מְרֻצֶּה מִזֶּה הוֹסִיף וְתָפַס גַּם אֶת כֵּיפָא
kir'oto sheha'am merutzeh mizzeh hosif vetafas gam et keifa.
And when he saw that it pleased the Jews, he proceeded to seize Peter also.

אוֹתָם יָמִים הָיוּ יְמֵי חַג הַמַּצּוֹת
otam yamim hayu yemei chag hammatzot
And those were the days of unleavened bread.

לְאַחַר שֶׁעָצַר אֶת כֵּיפָא כָּלָא אוֹתוֹ בְּבֵית הַסֹּהַר
le'achar she'atzar et keifa kala oto beveit hassohar
And when he had taken him, he put him in prison,

וְהִפְקִיד אַרְבַּע מִשְׁמָרוֹת שֶׁל אַרְבָּעָה חַיָּלִים לִשְׁמֹר עָלָיו
vehifkid arba mishmarot shel arba'ah chayalim lishmor alav.
and delivered him to four quaternions of soldiers to guard him;

הוּא הִתְכַּוֵּן לְהַעֲמִיד אוֹתוֹ לִפְנֵי הָעָם אַחֲרֵי הַפֶּסַח
hu hitkavven leha'amid oto lifnei ha'am acharei happesach
intending after the Passover to bring him forth to the people.

וְאוּלָם בְּעֵת שֶׁנִּשְׁמַר כֵּיפָא בְּבֵית הַסֹּהַר הִתְפַּלְלָה הַקְּהִלָּה בַּעֲדוֹ בְּחָזְקָה אֶל הָאֱלֹהִים
ve'ulam be'et shennishmar keifa beveit hassohar hitpallelah hakkehillah ba'ado bechozkah el ha'elohim
Peter therefore was kept in the prison: but prayer was made earnestly of the church unto God for him.

בַּלַּיְלָה, קֹדֶם שֶׁעָמַד הוֹרְדוֹס לַהֲבִיאוֹ לְפָנָיו, יָשַׁן כֵּיפָא בֵּין שְׁנֵי חַיָּלִים
ballaylah, kodem she'amad horedos lahavi'o lefanav, yashan keifa bein shenei chayalim
And when Herod was about to bring him forth, the same night Peter was sleeping between two soldiers,

כְּשֶׁהוּא כָּבוּל בִּשְׁתֵּי שַׁרְשְׁרוֹת, וְהַשּׁוֹמְרִים אֲשֶׁר לִפְנֵי הַדֶּלֶת שָׁמְרוּ עַל בֵּית הַסֹּהַר
kshehu kavul bishtei sharsherot, vehashomerim asher lifnei haddelet shameru al beit hassohar
bound with two chains: and guards before the door kept the prison.

וְהִנֵּה מַלְאַךְ יהוה הוֹפִיעַ וְאוֹר נָגַהּ בַּחֶדֶר
vehinneh mal'ach hashem hofia ve'or nagah bacheder
And behold, an angel of the Lord stood by him, and a light shined in the cell:

הוּא טָפַח עַל צִדּוֹ שֶׁל כֵּיפָא, הֵעִיר אוֹתוֹ וְאָמַר: קוּם מַהֵר! אָז נָפְלוּ הַשַּׁרְשְׁרוֹת מֵעַל יָדָיו
hu tafach al tziddo shel keifa, he'ir oto ve'amar. kum maher! az nafelu hasharsherot me'al yadav
and he smote Peter on the side, and awoke him, saying, Rise up quickly. And his chains fell off from his hands.

אָמַר לוֹ הַמַּלְאָךְ: חֲגֹר מָתְנֶיךָ וּנְעַל נְעָלֶיךָ. כֵּיפָא עָשָׂה כֵן
amar lo hammal'ach: chagor motneicha une'al ne'aleicha. keifa asah chen
And the angel said unto him, Gird thyself, and bind on thy sandals. And he did so.

מַעֲשֵׂי הַשְּׁלִיחִים

אַחֲרֵי כֵן יָצָא אֶל טַרְסוֹס לְחַפֵּשׂ אֶת שָׁאוּל
acharei chen yatza el tarsos lechappes et sha'ul
And he went forth to Tarsus to seek for Saul;

וּכְשֶׁמָּצָא אוֹתוֹ הֱבִיאוֹ לְאַנְטְיוֹכְיָה
ucheshemmatza oto hevi'o le'antiyocheyah
and when he had found him, he brought him unto Antioch.

שָׁנָה תְּמִימָה הִתְאָרְחוּ אֵצֶל הַקְּהִלָּה וְלִמְּדוּ קָהָל רָב
shanah temimah hit'arechu etzel hakkehillah velimmedu kahal rav
And it came to pass, that even for a whole year they were gathered together with the church, and taught much people;

וּבְאַנְטְיוֹכְיָה לָרִאשׁוֹנָה כֻּנּוּ אֶת הַתַּלְמִידִים מְשִׁיחִיִּים
uve'antiyocheyah larishonah kinnu et hattalmidim meshichiyim
and that the disciples were called Christians first in Antioch.

בַּיָּמִים הָהֵם יָרְדוּ נְבִיאִים מִירוּשָׁלַיִם אֶל אַנְטְיוֹכְיָה
bayamim hahem yaredu nevi'im miyerushalayim el antiyocheyah
Now in these days there came down prophets from Jerusalem unto Antioch.

קָם אֶחָד מֵהֶם, אֲגָבוֹס שְׁמוֹ
kam echad mehem, agavos shemo
And there stood up one of them named Agabus,

וְהוֹדִיעַ עַל־פִּי הָרוּחַ כִּי רָעָב גָּדוֹל עָתִיד לָבוֹא עַל כָּל הָעוֹלָם
vehodia al-pi haruach ki ra'av gadol atid lavo al kol ha'olam
and signified by the Spirit that there should be a great famine over all the world:

דָּבָר שֶׁהִתְגַּשֵּׁם בִּזְמַן קְלוֹדְיוֹס
davar shehitgashem bizman klodeyos
which came to pass in the days of Claudius.

הֶחְלִיטוּ הַתַּלְמִידִים לִשְׁלֹחַ, אִישׁ אִישׁ כְּפִי שֶׁיָּדוֹ מַשֶּׂגֶת, לְעֶזְרַת הָאַחִים הַגָּרִים בִּיהוּדָה
hechlitu hattalmidim lishloach, ish ish kefi sheyado masseget, le'ezrat ha'achim haggarim biyehudah
And the disciples, every man according to his ability, determined to send relief unto the brethren that dwelt in Judæa:

הֵם עָשׂוּ כֵן וְשָׁלְחוּ אֶל הַזְּקֵנִים בִּידֵי בַּר־נַבָּא וְשָׁאוּל
hem asu chen veshalechu el hazzekenim biydei bar-nabba vesha'ul
which also they did, sending it to the elders by the hand of Barnabas and Saul.

יב

בָּעֵת הַהִיא שָׁלַח הוֹרְדוֹס הַמֶּלֶךְ אֶת יָדוֹ לִפְגֹעַ בַּאֲנָשִׁים מִן הַקְּהִלָּה
ba'et hahi shalach horedos hammelech et yado lifgoa ba'anashim min hakkehillah
Now about that time Herod the king put forth his hands to afflict certain of the church.

מַעֲשֵׂי הַשְּׁלִיחִים

כְּשָׁמְעָם זֹאת לֹא הֵשִׁיבוּ דָּבָר, אֶלָּא נָתְנוּ כָּבוֹד לֵאלֹהִים בְּאָמְרָם
keshame'am zot lo heshivu davar, ella natenu kavod le'elohim be'omram
And when they heard these things, they held their peace, and glorified God, saying,

אָכֵן גַּם לַגּוֹיִם נָתַן אֱלֹהִים לַחֲזֹר בִּתְשׁוּבָה אֱלֵי חַיִּים
achen gam laggoyim natan elohim lachazor bitshuvah elei chayim
Then to the Gentiles also hath God granted repentance unto life.

הָאֲנָשִׁים שֶׁנָּפוֹצוּ מִפְּנֵי הַצָּרָה אֲשֶׁר נִגְרְמָה עַל־אֹדוֹת סְטֶפָנוֹס הִגִּיעוּ עַד פֵינִיקְיָה
ha'anashim shennafotzu mippenei hatzarah asher nigremah al-'odot setefanos higgi'u ad feinikeyah
They therefore that were scattered abroad upon the tribulation that arose about Stephen travelled as far as Phoenicia,

וְקַפְרִיסִין וְאַנְטִיוֹכְיָה וְלֹא הִשְׁמִיעוּ אֶת דְּבַר אֱלֹהִים אֶלָּא לִיהוּדִים בִּלְבַד
vekafrisin ve'antiyocheyah velo hishmi'u et devar elohim ella liyehudim bilvad
and Cyprus, and Antioch, speaking the word to none save only to Jews.

אֲבָל הָיוּ בֵּינֵיהֶם כַּמָּה אֲנָשִׁים קַפְרִיסָאִים וְקִירֶנִיִּים אֲשֶׁר בְּבוֹאָם לְאַנְטִיוֹכְיָה
aval hayu beineihem kammah anashim kafrisa'im vekireniyim asher bevo'am le'antiyocheyah
But there were some of them, men of Cyprus and Cyrene, who, when they were come to Antioch,

דִּבְּרוּ גַּם אֶל הַיְּוָנִים וּבִשְּׂרוּ עַל הָאָדוֹן יֵשׁוּעַ
dibberu gam el hayevanim uvissru al ha'adon yeshua
spake unto the Greeks also, preaching the Lord Jesus.

יַד־יהוה הָיְתָה עִמָּהֶם וַאֲנָשִׁים רַבִּים הֶאֱמִינוּ וּפָנוּ אֶל הָאָדוֹן
yad-hashem hayetah immahem va'anashim rabbim he'eminu ufanu el ha'adon
And the hand of the Lord was with them: and a great number that believed turned unto the Lord.

נִשְׁמַע הַדָּבָר בְּאָזְנֵי הַקְּהִלָּה אֲשֶׁר בִּירוּשָׁלַיִם
nishma haddavar be'oznei hakkehillah asher biyerushalayim
And the report concerning them came to the ears of the church which was in Jerusalem:

וְשָׁלְחוּ אֶת בַּר־נַבָּא אֶל אַנְטִיוֹכְיָה
veshalechu et bar-nabba el antiyocheyah
and they sent forth Barnabas as far as Antioch:

כַּאֲשֶׁר הִגִּיעַ לְשָׁם וְרָאָה אֶת חֶסֶד אֱלֹהִים, שָׂמַח
ka'asher higgia lesham vera'ah et chesed elohim, samach
who, when he was come, and had seen the grace of God, was glad;

וְהֵאִיץ בְּכֻלָּם לִהְיוֹת דְּבֵקִים בָּאָדוֹן בְּלֵב שָׁלֵם
vehe'itz bechullam lihyot dvekim ba'adon belev shalem
and he exhorted them all, that with purpose of heart they would cleave unto the Lord:

כִּי הָיָה אִישׁ טוֹב, מָלֵא רוּחַ הַקֹּדֶשׁ וֶאֱמוּנָה - וְקָהָל רַב נִסְפַּח אֶל הָאָדוֹן
ki hayah ish tov, malei ruach hakkodesh ve'emunah - vekahal rav nispach el ha'adon
for he was a good man, and full of the Holy Spirit and of faith: and much people was added unto the Lord.

מַעֲשֵׂי הַשְּׁלִיחִים

זֶה הָיָה שָׁלוֹשׁ פְּעָמִים וְהַכֹּל שָׁב וְהֹעֲלָה לַשָּׁמַיִם
zeh hayah shalosh pe'amim vehakkol shav veho'olah lashamayim
And this was done thrice: and all were drawn up again into heaven.

וְהִנֵּה בְּדִיּוּק אָז עָמְדוּ שְׁלוֹשָׁה אֲנָשִׁים לְיַד הַבַּיִת אֲשֶׁר הָיִיתִי בּוֹ וְהֵם נִשְׁלְחוּ אֵלַי מִקֵּיסַרְיָה
vehinneh bediyuk az amedu sheloshah anashim leyad habbayit asher hayiti bo vehem nishlechu elai mikkeisaryah
And behold, forthwith three men stood before the house in which we were, having been sent from Cæsarea unto me.

הָרוּחַ אָמְרָה לִי לָלֶכֶת אִתָּם וְלֹא לְהַסֵּס
haruach amerah li lalechet ittam velo lehasses
And the Spirit bade me go with them, making no distinction.

גַּם שֵׁשֶׁת הָאַחִים הָאֵלֶּה בָּאוּ אִתִּי וְנִכְנַסְנוּ לְבֵיתוֹ שֶׁל הָאִישׁ
gam sheshet ha'achim ha'elleh ba'u itti venichnasnu leveito shel ha'ish
And these six brethren also accompanied me; and we entered into the man's house:

הוּא סִפֵּר לָנוּ שֶׁרָאָה אֶת הַמַּלְאָךְ בְּבֵיתוֹ, עוֹמֵד וְאוֹמֵר
hu sipper lanu shera'ah et hammal'ach beveito, omed ve'omer
and he told us how he had seen the angel standing in his house, and saying,

שְׁלַח אֶל יָפוֹ וּקְרָא לְשִׁמְעוֹן הַמְכֻנֶּה כֵּיפָא
shlach el yafo ukera leshim'on hamchunneh keifa
Send to Joppa, and fetch Simon, whose surname is Peter;

הוּא יְדַבֵּר אֵלֶיךָ דְּבָרִים אֲשֶׁר תִּוָּשַׁע בָּהֶם אַתָּה וְכָל בֵּיתְךָ
hu yedabber eleicha devarim asher tivvasha bahem attah vechol beitcha
who shall speak unto thee words, whereby thou shalt be saved, thou and all thy house.

כַּאֲשֶׁר הִתְחַלְתִּי לְדַבֵּר צָלְחָה עֲלֵיהֶם רוּחַ הַקֹּדֶשׁ כְּמוֹ שֶׁצָּלְחָה עָלֵינוּ בַּתְּחִלָּה
ka'asher hitchalti ledabber tzalechah aleihem ruach hakkodesh kemo shetzalechah aleinu battechillah
And as I began to speak, the Holy Spirit fell on them, even as on us at the beginning.

וְנִזְכַּרְתִּי בַּדָּבָר שֶׁאָמַר הָאָדוֹן, יוֹחָנָן הִטְבִּיל אֶתְכֶם בְּמַיִם
venizkarti baddavar she'amar ha'adon, yochanan hitbil etchem bemayim
And I remembered the word of the Lord, how he said, John indeed baptized with water;

אַךְ אַתֶּם תִּטָּבְלוּ בְּרוּחַ הַקֹּדֶשׁ
ach attem tittavelu beruach hakkodesh
but ye shall be baptized in the Holy Spirit.

וּבְכֵן, אִם אֱלֹהִים נָתַן לָהֶם אֶת אוֹתָהּ הַמַּתָּנָה כְּמוֹ שֶׁנָּתַן לָנוּ
uvechen, im elohim natan lahem et otah hammattanah kemo shennatan lanu
If then God gave unto them the like gift as he did also unto us,

הַמַּאֲמִינִים בָּאָדוֹן יֵשׁוּעַ הַמָּשִׁיחַ, מִי אֲנִי שֶׁאוּכַל לַעֲצֹר בְּעַד אֱלֹהִים
hamma'aminim ba'adon yeshua hammashiach, mi ani she'uchal la'atzor be'ad elohim
when we believed on the Lord Jesus Christ, who was I, that I could withstand God?

מַעֲשֵׂי הַשְּׁלִיחִים

יא

הַשְּׁלִיחִים וְהָאַחִים אֲשֶׁר בִּיהוּדָה שָׁמְעוּ שֶׁגַּם הַגּוֹיִם קִבְּלוּ אֶת דְּבַר אֱלֹהִים
hashelichim veha'achim asher biyehudah shame'u sheggam haggoyim kiblu et devar elohim
Now the apostles and the brethren that were in Judæa heard that the Gentiles also had received the word of God.

אֲבָל כַּאֲשֶׁר עָלָה כֵּיפָא לִירוּשָׁלַיִם הִתְוַכְּחוּ אִתּוֹ בְּנֵי הַמִּילָה בְּאָמְרָם
aval ka'asher alah keifa liyerushalayim hitvakkechu itto benei hammilah be'omram
And when Peter was come up to Jerusalem, they that were of the circumcision contended with him,

נִכְנַסְתָּ אֶל אֲנָשִׁים עֲרֵלִים וְאָכַלְתָּ אִתָּם
nichnasta el anashim arelim ve'achalta ittam
saying, Thou wentest in to men uncircumcised, and didst eat with them.

הִתְחִיל כֵּיפָא לְסַפֵּר לָהֶם אֶת הָעִנְיָן לְפִי הַסֵּדֶר
hitchil keifa lesapper lahem et ha'inyan lefi hasseder
But Peter began, and expounded the matter unto them in order, saying,

מִתְפַּלֵּל הָיִיתִי בָּעִיר יָפוֹ וּבִהְיוֹתִי בְּהִתְעַלּוּת רָאִיתִי מַרְאֶה
mitpallel hayiti ba'ir yafo uvihyoti behit'allut ra'iti mar'eh
I was in the city of Joppa praying: and in a trance I saw a vision,

אֵיזֶה כְּלִי דּוֹמֶה לְמִפְרָשׂ גָּדוֹל מוּרָד בְּאַרְבַּע קְצוֹתָיו מִן הַשָּׁמַיִם וּמַגִּיעַ עַד אֵלָי
eizeh keli domeh lemifras gadol murad be'arba ketzotav min hashamayim umaggia ad elai
a certain vessel descending, as it were a great sheet let down from heaven by four corners; and it came even unto me:

כְּשֶׁהִתְבּוֹנַנְתִּי בּוֹ רָאִיתִי אֶת בֶּהֱמַת הָאָרֶץ
kshehitbonanti bo ra'iti et behemat ha'aretz
upon which when I had fastened mine eyes, I considered, and saw the fourfooted beasts of the earth

אֶת חַיּוֹת הַיַּעַר וְהָרְמָשִׂים וְאֶת עוֹף הַשָּׁמַיִם
et chayot haya'ar veharemasim ve'et of hashamayim
and wild beasts and creeping things and birds of the heaven.

גַּם שָׁמַעְתִּי קוֹל אוֹמֵר אֵלַי, קוּם, כֵּיפָא, שְׁחַט וֶאֱכֹל
gam shama'ti kol omer elai, kum, keifa, shchat ve'echol
And I heard also a voice saying unto me, Rise, Peter; kill and eat.

אֶלָּא שֶׁאָמַרְתִּי, בְּשׁוּם פָּנִים לֹא, אֲדוֹנִי, כִּי מֵעוֹלָם לֹא נִכְנַס לְתוֹךְ פִּי פִּגּוּל אוֹ טָמֵא
ella she'amarti, beshum panim lo, adoni, ki me'olam lo nichnas letoch pi piggul o tamei
But I said, Not so, Lord: for nothing common or unclean hath ever entered into my mouth.

שֵׁנִית הֵשִׁיב קוֹל מִן הַשָּׁמַיִם, לַאֲשֶׁר טִהֵר אֱלֹהִים, אַתָּה אַל תִּקְרָא טָמֵא
shenit heshiv kol min hashamayim, la'asher tiher elohim, attah al tikra tamei
But a voice answered the second time out of heaven, What God hath cleansed, make not thou common.

מַעֲשֵׂי הַשְּׁלִיחִים

הוּא צִוָּה עָלֵינוּ לְהַכְרִיז לָעָם
hu tzivvah aleinu lehachriz la'am
And he charged us to preach unto the people,

וּלְהָעִיד כִּי אוֹתוֹ שָׂם הָאֱלֹהִים לְשׁוֹפֵט הַחַיִּים וְהַמֵּתִים
uleha'id ki oto sam ha'elohim leshofet hachayim vehammetim
and to testify that this is he who is ordained of God to be the Judge of the living and the dead.

עָלָיו כָּל הַנְּבִיאִים מְעִידִים
alav kol hannevi'im me'idim
To him bear all the prophets witness,

כִּי כָּל הַמַּאֲמִין בּוֹ יְקַבֵּל בִּשְׁמוֹ סְלִיחַת חֲטָאִים
ki kol hamma'amin bo yekabbel bishmo slichat chata'im
that through his name every one that believeth on him shall receive remission of sins.

בְּשָׁעָה שֶׁדִּבֵּר כֵּיפָא אֶת הַדְּבָרִים הָאֵלֶּה צָלְחָה רוּחַ הַקֹּדֶשׁ עַל כָּל הַשּׁוֹמְעִים אֶת הַדָּבָר
besha'ah sheddibber keifa et haddevarim ha'elleh tzalchah ruach hakkodesh al kol hashome'im et haddavar
While Peter yet spake these words, the Holy Spirit fell on all them that heard the word.

הַמַּאֲמִינִים בְּנֵי הַמִּילָה אֲשֶׁר נִלְווּ אֶל כֵּיפָא הִשְׁתּוֹמְמוּ
hamma'aminim benei hammilah asher nilvu el keifa hishtomemu
And they of the circumcision that believed were amazed, as many as came with Peter,

עַל שֶׁמַּתְּנַת רוּחַ הַקֹּדֶשׁ נִשְׁפְּכָה גַּם עַל הַגּוֹיִם
al shemmattenat ruach hakkodesh nishpechah gam al haggoyim
because that on the Gentiles also was poured out the gift of the Holy Spirit.

שֶׁכֵּן שָׁמְעוּ אוֹתָם מְדַבְּרִים בִּלְשׁוֹנוֹת וְנוֹתְנִים גְּדֻלָּה לֵאלֹהִים
shekken shame'u otam medabberim bilshonot venotenim gedullah le'elohim
For they heard them speak with tongues, and magnify God. Then answered Peter,

הֵגִיב כֵּיפָא וְאָמַר: הַאִם יָכוֹל מִישֶׁהוּ לִמְנֹעַ אֶת הַטְּבִילָה בַּמַּיִם
hegiv keifa ve'amar: ha'im yachol mishehu limnoa et hattevilah bemayim
Can any man forbid the water, that these should not be baptized,

מֵאֵלֶּה שֶׁקִּבְּלוּ אֶת רוּחַ הַקֹּדֶשׁ כָּמוֹנוּ
me'elleh shekkibbelu et ruach hakkodesh kamonu
who have received the Holy Spirit as well as we?

הוּא צִוָּה עֲלֵיהֶם לְהִטָּבֵל בְּשֵׁם יֵשׁוּעַ הַמָּשִׁיחַ.
hu tzivvah aleihem lehittavel beshem yeshua hammashiach.
And he commanded them to be baptized in the name of Jesus Christ.

אַחֲרֵי כֵן בִּקְשׁוּ מִמֶּנּוּ לְהִשָּׁאֵר אֶצְלָם כַּמָּה יָמִים
acharei chen bikshu mimmennu lehisha'er etzlam kammah yamim
Then prayed they him to tarry certain days.

מַעֲשֵׂי הַשְּׁלִיחִים

פָּתַח כֵּיפָא בִּדְבָרוֹ וְאָמַר: בֶּאֱמֶת רוֹאֶה אֲנִי שֶׁאֱלֹהִים אֵינֶנּוּ נוֹשֵׂא פָנִים
patach keifa bidvaro ve'amar: be'emet ro'eh ani she'elohim einennu nosei panim
And Peter opened his mouth, and said, Of a truth I perceive that God is no respecter of persons:

אֶלָּא בְּכָל עַם וָעַם מִי שֶׁיְּרֵא אוֹתוֹ וְעוֹשֶׂה צֶדֶק רָצוּי לְפָנָיו
ella bechol am ve'am mi sheyarei oto ve'oseh tzedek ratzui lefanav
but in every nation he that feareth him, and worketh righteousness, is acceptable to him.

אַתֶּם יוֹדְעִים אֶת הַדָּבָר שֶׁשָּׁלַח לִבְנֵי יִשְׂרָאֵל, בְּבַשְּׂרוֹ שָׁלוֹם עַל־יְדֵי יֵשׁוּעַ הַמָּשִׁיחַ אֲדוֹן הַכֹּל
attem yode'im et haddavar sheshalach livnei yisra'el, vevassro shalom al-yedei yeshua hammashiach adon hakkol
The word which he sent unto the children of Israel, preaching good tidings of peace by Jesus Christ (he is Lord of all)—

דָּבָר שֶׁהָיָה בְּכָל יְהוּדָה
davar shehayah bechol yehudah
that saying ye yourselves know, which was published throughout all Judæa,

וְהֵחֵל בַּגָּלִיל לְאַחַר הַטְּבִילָה שֶׁהִכְרִיז יוֹחָנָן
vehechel baggalil le'achar hattevilah shehichriz yochanan
beginning from Galilee, after the baptism which John preached;

יֵשׁוּעַ מִנַּצְרַת, אֲשֶׁר אֱלֹהִים מָשַׁח אוֹתוֹ בְּרוּחַ הַקֹּדֶשׁ וּבִגְבוּרָה
yeshua minnatzerat, asher elohim mashach oto beruach hakkodesh uvigvurah
even Jesus of Nazareth, how God anointed him with the Holy Spirit and with power:

הִתְהַלֵּךְ בָּאָרֶץ כְּשֶׁהוּא עוֹשֶׂה חֶסֶד וּמְרַפֵּא אֶת כָּל הַנִּדְכָּאִים תַּחַת יַד הַשָּׂטָן, כִּי אֱלֹהִים הָיָה אִתּוֹ
hit'hallech ba'aretz keshehu oseh chesed umerappei et kol hannidka'im tachat yad hassaan, ki elohim hayah itto
who went about doing good, and healing all that were oppressed of the devil; for God was with him.

וְאָנוּ עֵדִים עַל כָּל מַה שֶּׁעָשָׂה בְּאֶרֶץ הַיְּהוּדִים
ve'anu edim al kol mah she'asah be'eretz hayehudim
And we are witnesses of all things which he did both in the country of the Jews,

וּבִירוּשָׁלַיִם; הוּא אֲשֶׁר גַּם הֲרָגוּהוּ בְּהוֹקָעָה עַל עֵץ
uviyerushalayim; hu asher gam haraguhu behoka'ah al etz
and in Jerusalem; whom also they slew, hanging him on a tree.

אוֹתוֹ הֵקִים הָאֱלֹהִים בַּיּוֹם הַשְּׁלִישִׁי וְנָתַן לוֹ לְהֵרָאוֹת
oto hekim ha'elohim bayom hashelishi venatan lo lehera'ot
Him God raised up the third day, and gave him to be made manifest

,
לֹא לְכָל הָעָם, אֶלָּא לְעֵדִים שֶׁאֱלֹהִים קָבַע אוֹתָם מֵרֹאשׁ
lo lechol ha'am, ella le'edim she'elohim kava otam merosh
not to all the people, but unto witnesses that were chosen before of God,

לָנוּ אֲשֶׁר אָכַלְנוּ וְשָׁתִינוּ אִתּוֹ אַחֲרֵי קוּמוֹ מִן הַמֵּתִים
lanu asher achalnu veshatinu itto acharei kumo min hammetim
even to us, who ate and drank with him after he rose from the dead.

מַעֲשֵׂי הַשְּׁלִיחִים

אַתֶּם יוֹדְעִים שֶׁאָסוּר לְאִישׁ יְהוּדִי
attem yode'im she'asur le'ish yehudi
Ye yourselves know how it is an unlawful thing for a man that is a Jew

לִהְיוֹת חָבֵר לְנָכְרִי אוֹ לָבוֹא אֵלָיו
lihyot chaver lenacheri o lavo elav
to join himself or come unto one of another nation;

אַךְ לִי הֶרְאָה אֱלֹהִים שֶׁלֹּא לִקְרֹא לְשׁוּם אָדָם שִׁקּוּץ אוֹ טָמֵא
ach li her'ah elohim shello likro leshum adam shikkutz o tame
and yet unto me hath God showed that I should not call any man common or unclean:

לָכֵן גַּם בָּאתִי לְלֹא הִתְנַגְּדוּת כְּשֶׁנִּקְרֵאתִי. כָּעֵת אֲנִי שׁוֹאֵל לְשֵׁם מַה קְּרָאתֶם לִי
lachen gam bati lelo hitnaggedut keshennikreti. ka'et ani sho'el leshem mah kratem li
wherefore also I came without gainsaying, when I was sent for. I ask therefore with what intent ye sent for me.

הֵשִׁיב קוֹרְנֵלְיוֹס: לִפְנֵי שְׁלוֹשָׁה יָמִים
heshiv korenelyos: lifnei sheloshah yamim
And Cornelius said, Four days ago, until this hour,

הִתְפַּלַּלְתִּי בְּבֵיתִי בְּדִיּוּק בַּשָּׁעָה הַזֹּאת, בְּשָׁלוֹשׁ אַחֲרֵי הַצָּהֳרַיִם, וְהִנֵּה עָמַד לְפָנַי אִישׁ בִּלְבוּשׁ מַבְהִיק
hitpallalti beveiti bediyuk basha'ah hazzot, beshalosh acharei hatzohorayim, vehinneh amad lefanai ish bilvush mavhik
I was keeping the ninth hour of prayer in my house; and behold, a man stood before me in bright apparel,

וְאָמַר, קוֹרְנֵלְיוֹס, תְּפִלָּתְךָ נִשְׁמְעָה וְצִדְקוֹתֶיךָ עָלוּ לְזִכָּרוֹן לִפְנֵי אֱלֹהִים
ve'amar, korenelyos, tefillatecha nishme'ah vetzidkoteicha alu lezikkaron lifnei elohim
and saith, Cornelius, thy prayer is heard, and thine alms are had in remembrance in the sight of God.

שְׁלַח לְיָפוֹ וּקְרָא לְשִׁמְעוֹן הַמְכֻנֶּה כֵּיפָא
shelach leyafo ukera leshim'on hamchunneh keifa
Send therefore to Joppa, and call unto thee Simon, who is surnamed Peter;

הוּא מִתְאָרֵחַ בְּבֵיתוֹ שֶׁל שִׁמְעוֹן הַבֻּרְסִי עַל־יַד הַיָּם
hu mit'areach beveito shel shim'on habbursi al-yad hayam
he lodgeth in the house of Simon a tanner, by the sea side.

לְפִיכָךְ שָׁלַחְתִּי אֵלֶיךָ מִיָּד וְאָכֵן טוֹב עָשִׂיתָ שֶׁבָּאתָ
lefichach shalachti eleicha miyad ve'achen tov asita shebbata
Forthwith therefore I sent to thee; and thou hast well done that thou art come.

כָּעֵת אֲנַחְנוּ כֻּלָּנוּ נִמְצָאִים לִפְנֵי הָאֱלֹהִים
ka'et anachnu kullanu nimtza'im lifnei ha'elohim
Now therefore we are all here present in the sight of God,

לִשְׁמֹעַ אֶת כָּל מַה שֶׁאֲדֹנָי צִוָּה עָלֶיךָ
lishmoa et kol mah she'adonai tzivvah aleicha
to hear all things that have been commanded thee of the Lord.

מַעֲשֵׂי הַשְּׁלִיחִים

הֵשִׁיבוּ וְאָמְרוּ: שַׂר הַמֵּאָה קוֹרְנֵלְיוֹס, אִישׁ צַדִּיק וִירֵא אֱלֹהִים
heshivu ve'ameru: sar hamme'ah kornelyos, ish tzaddik viyrei elohim
And they said, Cornelius a centurion, a righteous man and one that feareth God,

אֲשֶׁר שֵׁם טוֹב לוֹ בְּקֶרֶב כָּל הָעָם הַיְהוּדִי
asher shem tov lo bekerev kol ha'am hayhudi
and well reported of by all the nation of the Jews,

צֻוָּה עַל־יְדֵי מַלְאָךְ קָדוֹשׁ לִקְרֹא לְךָ אֶל בֵּיתוֹ וְלִשְׁמֹעַ דְּבָרִים מִפִּיךָ
tzuvvah al-yedei mal'ach kadosh likro lecha el beito velishmoa dvarim mippicha
was warned of God by a holy angel to send for thee into his house, and to hear words from thee.

כֵּיפָא הִזְמִינָם לְהִכָּנֵס וְאֵרַח אוֹתָם
keifa hizminam lehikkanes ve'erach otam
So he called them in and lodged them.

לְמָחֳרָת קָם וְיָצָא אִתָּם, וְכַמָּה מִן הָאַחִים שֶׁבְּיָפוֹ נִלְווּ אֵלָיו
lemochorat kam veyatza ittam, vechammah min ha'achim shebbeyafo nilvu elav
And on the morrow he arose and went forth with them, and certain of the brethren from Joppa accompanied him.

יוֹם לְאַחַר מִכֵּן בָּאוּ לְקֵיסַרְיָה
yom le'achar mikken ba'u lekeisaryah
And on the morrow they entered into Cæsarea.

וְקוֹרְנֵלְיוֹס חִכָּה לָהֶם עִם בְּנֵי מִשְׁפַּחְתּוֹ וִידִידָיו הַמְקֹרָבִים שֶׁכִּנֵּס אֶצְלוֹ
vekorenelyos chikkah lahem im benei mishpachto viydidav hamkoravim shekkinnes etzlo
And Cornelius was waiting for them, having called together his kinsmen and his near friends.

כַּאֲשֶׁר הִגִּיעַ כֵּיפָא נִגַּשׁ אֵלָיו קוֹרְנֵלְיוֹס, נָפַל לְרַגְלָיו וְהִשְׁתַּחֲוָה
ka'asher higgia keifa niggash elav korenelyos, nafal leraglav vehishtachavah
And when it came to pass that Peter entered, Cornelius met him, and fell down at his feet, and worshipped him.

הֵקִים אוֹתוֹ כֵּיפָא בְּאָמְרוֹ: קוּם! גַּם אֲנִי עַצְמִי בֶּן אֱנוֹשׁ
hekim oto keifa be'omro. kum! gam ani atzmi ben enosh
But Peter raised him up, saying, Stand up; I myself also am a man.

כְּשֶׁהוּא מְשׂוֹחֵחַ אִתּוֹ נִכְנַס הַבַּיְתָה וּמָצָא נֶאֱסָפִים רַבִּים
keshehu mesocheach itto nichnas habbaytah umatza ne'esafim rabbim
And as he talked with him, he went in, and findeth many come together:

אָמַר לָהֶם
amar lahem
and he said unto them,

מַעֲשֵׂי הַשְּׁלִיחִים

דּוֹמֶה לְמִפְרָשׂ גָּדוֹל, מוּרָד בְּאַרְבַּע קְצוֹתָיו אֶל הָאָרֶץ
domeh lemifras gadol, murad be'arba ketzotav el ha'aretz
as it were a great sheet, let down by four corners upon the earth:

וּבוֹ מִכָּל חַיּוֹת הָאָרֶץ וְהָרְמָשִׂים וּמִכָּל עוֹף הַשָּׁמַיִם
uvo mikkol chayot ha'aretz veharemasim umikkol of hashamayim
wherein were all manner of fourfooted beasts and creeping things of the earth and birds of the heaven.

וְקוֹל הָיָה אֵלָיו: קוּם, כֵּיפָא, שְׁחַט וֶאֱכֹל!
vekol hayah elav: kum, keifa, shechat ve'echol!
And there came a voice to him, Rise, Peter; kill and eat.

אָמַר כֵּיפָא: בְּשׁוּם פָּנִים לֹא, אֲדוֹנִי, כִּי מֵעוֹלָם לֹא אָכַלְתִּי שׁוּם פִּגּוּל וְטָמֵא
amar keifa. beshum panim lo, adoni, ki me'olam lo achalti shum piggul vetame
But Peter said, Not so, Lord; for I have never eaten anything that is common and unclean.

שֵׁנִית הָיָה הַקּוֹל אֵלָיו: לַאֲשֶׁר טִהֵר אֱלֹהִים, אַתָּה אַל תִּקְרָא טָמֵא
shenit hayah hakkol elav: la'asher tiher elohim, attah al tikra tamei
And a voice came unto him again the second time, What God hath cleansed, make not thou common.

כָּךְ הָיָה שָׁלוֹשׁ פְּעָמִים וּמִיָּד נִלְקַח הַכְּלִי הַשָּׁמַיְמָה
kach hayah shalosh pe'amim umiyad nilkach hakkeli hashamaymah
And this was done thrice: and straightway the vessel was received up into heaven.

כֵּיפָא הָיָה עוֹדֶנּוּ חוֹכֵךְ בְּדַעְתּוֹ מַה כַּוָּנַת הַמַּרְאֶה שֶׁרָאָה
keifa hayah odennu chochech beda'to mah kavvanat hammar'eh shera'ah
Now while Peter was much perplexed in himself what the vision which he had seen might mean,

וְהִנֵּה הָאֲנָשִׁים, שֶׁנִּשְׁלְחוּ מֵאֵת קוֹרְנֵלְיוֹס וְחִפְּשׂוּ אֶת בֵּיתוֹ שֶׁל שִׁמְעוֹן, עָמְדוּ בַּשַּׁעַר
vehinneh ha'anashim, shennishlechu me'et korenelyos vechippesu et beito shel shim'on, amdu basha'ar
behold, the men that were sent by Cornelius, having made inquiry for Simon's house, stood before the gate,

הֵם קָרְאוּ וְשָׁאֲלוּ אִם שִׁמְעוֹן הַמְכֻנֶּה כֵּיפָא מִתְאָרֵחַ שָׁם
hem kare'u vesha'alu im shim'on hamchunneh keifa mit'areach sham
and called and asked whether Simon, who was surnamed Peter, were lodging there.

כְּשֶׁהִרְהֵר כֵּיפָא עַל הַמַּרְאֶה אָמְרָה לוֹ הָרוּחַ: הִנֵּה כַּמָּה אֲנָשִׁים מְבַקְשִׁים אוֹתְךָ
keshehirher keifa al hammar'eh amrah lo haruach. hinneh kammah anashim mevakshim otcha
And while Peter thought on the vision, the Spirit said unto him, Behold, three men seek thee.

קוּם, רֵד וְלֵךְ אִתָּם, אַל תְּהַסֵּס, כִּי אֲנִי שְׁלַחְתִּים
kum, red velech ittam, al tehasses, ki ani shelachtim
But arise, and get thee down, and go with them, nothing doubting: for I have sent them.

יָרַד כֵּיפָא אֶל הָאֲנָשִׁים וְאָמַר: הִנֵּה אֲנִי הָאִישׁ שֶׁאַתֶּם מְבַקְשִׁים. לְשֵׁם מַה בָּאתֶם
yarad keifa el ha'anashim ve'amar: hinneh ani ha'ish she'attem mevakshim. leshem mah batem
And Peter went down to the men, and said, Behold, I am he whom ye seek: what is the cause wherefore ye are come?

מַעֲשֵׂי הַשְּׁלִיחִים

מַלְאַךְ אֱלֹהִים בָּא אֵלָיו וְאוֹמֵר לוֹ, קוֹרְנֵלְיוֹס
mal'ach elohim ba elav ve'omer lo, korenelyos
an angel of God coming in unto him, and saying to him, Cornelius.

כְּשֶׁהִבִּיט בּוֹ נִתְמַלֵּא פַּחַד וְאָמַר
keshehibbit bo nitmallei pachad ve'amar
And he, fastening his eyes upon him, and being affrighted, said,

מַה זֶּה, אֲדוֹנִי? הֵשִׁיב לוֹ הַמַּלְאָךְ: תְּפִלּוֹתֶיךָ וְצִדְקוֹתֶיךָ עָלוּ לְזִכָּרוֹן לִפְנֵי הָאֱלֹהִים
mah zeh, adoni? heshiv lo hammal'ach: tefilloteicha vetzidkoteicha alu lezikkaron lifnei ha'elohim
What is it, Lord? And he said unto him, Thy prayers and thine alms are gone up for a memorial before God.

וְעַכְשָׁו שְׁלַח אֲנָשִׁים לְיָפוֹ וּקְרָא לְשִׁמְעוֹן הַמְכֻנֶּה כֵּיפָא
ve'achshav shelach anashim leyafo ukera leshim'on hamchunneh keifa
And now send men to Joppa, and fetch one Simon, who is surnamed Peter:

הוּא מִתְאָרֵחַ אֵצֶל בֻּרְסִי אֶחָד, שִׁמְעוֹן שְׁמוֹ, אֲשֶׁר בֵּיתוֹ עַל־יַד הַיָּם
hu mit'areach etzel bursi echad, shim'on shemo, asher beito al-yad hayam
he lodgeth with one Simon a tanner, whose house is by the sea side.

אַחֲרֵי שֶׁהָלַךְ הַמַּלְאָךְ הַמְדַבֵּר אֵלָיו, קָרָא קוֹרְנֵלְיוֹס לִשְׁנַיִם מֵעֲבָדָיו
acharei shehalach hammal'ach hamdabber elav, kara kornelyos lishnayim me'avadav
And when the angel that spake unto him was departed, he called two of his household-servants,

וּלְחַיָּל יְרֵא שָׁמַיִם שֶׁהָיָה מִמְשָׁרְתָיו הַמְקֹרָבִים
ulechayal yerei shamayim shehayah mimmesharetav hamkoravim
and a devout soldier of them that waited on him continually;

הוּא סִפֵּר לָהֶם אֶת הַכֹּל וְשָׁלַח אוֹתָם לְיָפוֹ
hu sipper lahem et hakkol veshalach otam leyafo
and having rehearsed all things unto them, he sent them to Joppa.

לְמָחֳרָת, כַּאֲשֶׁר נָסְעוּ בַּדֶּרֶךְ וְהִתְקָרְבוּ אֶל הָעִיר
lemochorat, ka'asher nase'u badderech vehitkarevu el ha'ir
Now on the morrow, as they were on their journey, and drew nigh unto the city,

עָלָה כֵּיפָא אֶל הַגַּג לְהִתְפַּלֵּל; זֶה הָיָה בְּעֵרֶךְ בִּשְׁעַת הַצָּהֳרַיִם
alah keifa el haggag lehitpallel; zeh hayah be'erech bish'at hatzohorayim
Peter went up upon the housetop to pray, about the sixth hour:

הוּא הָיָה רָעֵב וְרָצָה לֶאֱכֹל. אֲבָל בְּעֵת שֶׁהֵכִינוּ אֶת הָאֹכֶל הָיְתָה עָלָיו הָרוּחַ
hu hayah ra'ev veratzah le'echol. aval be'et shehechinu et ha'ochel haytah alav haruach
and he became hungry, and desired to eat: but while they made ready, he fell into a trance;

וְהִנֵּה הוּא רוֹאֶה אֶת הַשָּׁמַיִם נִפְתָּחִים וְיוֹרֵד אֵיזֶה כְּלִי
vehinneh hu ro'eh et hashamayim niftachim veyored eizeh keli
and he beholdeth the heaven opened, and a certain vessel descending,

מַעֲשֵׂי הַשְּׁלִיחִים

כְּשֶׁהִגִּיעַ הִכְנִיסוּהוּ אֶל הָעֲלִיָּה, וְכָל הָאַלְמָנוֹת עָמְדוּ לְיָדוֹ בּוֹכִיּוֹת
keshehiggia hichnisuhu el ha'aliyah, vechol ha'almanot amedu leyado bochiyot
And when he was come, they brought him into the upper chamber: and all the widows stood by him weeping,

וְהֶרְאוּ לוֹ כֻּתֳּנוֹת וּבְגָדִים שֶׁעָשְׂתָה צְבִיָּה בְּעוֹדָה עִמָּהֶן
veher'u lo kuttonot uvegadim she'asetah tzeviyah be'odah immahen
and showing the coats and garments which Dorcas made, while she was with them.

הוֹצִיא כֵּיפָא אֶת כֻּלָּם הַחוּצָה, כָּרַע עַל בִּרְכָּיו וְהִתְפַּלֵּל, וּבִפְנוֹתוֹ אֶל הַגּוּפָה אָמַר
hotzi keifa et kulam hachutzah, kara al birkav vehitpallel, uvifnoto el haggufah amar
But Peter put them all forth, and kneeled down, and prayed; and turning to the body, he said,

טָבִיתָא, קוּמִי! הִיא פָּקְחָה אֶת עֵינֶיהָ וּכְשֶׁרָאֲתָה אֶת כֵּיפָא יָשְׁבָה
tavita, kumi! hi pakchah et eineiha ucheshera'atah et keifa yashevah
Tabitha, arise. And she opened her eyes; and when she saw Peter, she sat up.

הוּא הוֹשִׁיט אֵלֶיהָ אֶת יָדוֹ וְהֵקִים אוֹתָהּ. אָז קָרָא לַקְּדוֹשִׁים וְלָאַלְמָנוֹת וְהִצִּיג אוֹתָהּ חַיָּה לִפְנֵיהֶם
hu hoshit eleiha et yado vehekim otah. az kara lakkedoshim vela'almanot vehitzig otah chayah lifneihem
And he gave her his hand, and raised her up; and calling the saints and widows, he presented her alive.

הַדָּבָר נוֹדַע בְּכָל יָפוֹ וְרַבִּים הֶאֱמִינוּ בָּאָדוֹן
haddavar noda bechol yafo verabbim he'eminu ba'adon
And it became known throughout all Joppa: and many believed on the Lord.

אַחֲרֵי כֵן נִשְׁאַר כֵּיפָא בְּיָפוֹ יָמִים רַבִּים אֵצֶל אִישׁ אֶחָד שֶׁהִתְפַּרְנֵס מֵעִבּוּד עוֹרוֹת, שִׁמְעוֹן שְׁמוֹ
acharei chen nish'ar keifa beyafo yamim rabbim etzel ish echad shehitparnes me'ibbud orot, shim'on shemo
And it came to pass, that he abode many days in Joppa with one Simon a tanner.

|

אִישׁ הָיָה בְּקֵיסָרְיָה, קוֹרְנֵלְיוֹס שְׁמוֹ, שַׂר מֵאָה מִן הַגְּדוּד הַנִּקְרָא הָאִיטַלְקִי
ish hayah bekeisaryah, kornelyos shemo, sar me'ah min haggedud hannikra ha'italki
Now there was a certain man in Cæsarea, Cornelius by name, a centurion of the band called the Italian band,

חָסִיד הָיָה וִירֵא אֱלֹהִים הוּא וְכָל בֵּיתוֹ
chasid hayah viyrei elohim hu vechol beito
a devout man, and one that feared God with all his house,

וְגוֹמֵל חֲסָדִים רַבִּים לָעָם וּמִתְפַּלֵּל בְּכָל עֵת
vegomel chasadim rabbim la'am umitpallel bechol et
who gave much alms to the people, and prayed to God always.

בְּאַחַד הַיָּמִים, סָמוּךְ לְשָׁעָה שָׁלוֹשׁ אַחֲרֵי הַצָּהֳרַיִם, רָאָה מַרְאֶה בָּרוּר
be'achad hayamim, samuch lesha'ah shalosh acharei hatzohorayim, ra'ah mar'eh barur
He saw in a vision openly, as it were about the ninth hour of the day,

מַעֲשֵׂי הַשְּׁלִיחִים

וְהִתְהַלְּכָה בְּיִרְאַת יהוה, וְגָדְלָה בְּמִסְפָּר בְּעִדּוּד רוּחַ הַקֹּדֶשׁ

vehit'hallechah beyir'at hashem, vegadelah bemispar be'iddud ruach hakkodesh
and, walking in the fear of the Lord and in the comfort of the Holy Spirit, was multiplied.

כַּאֲשֶׁר סָבַב כֵּיפָא בְּכָל הַמְּקוֹמוֹת יָרַד גַּם אֶל הַקְּדוֹשִׁים שֶׁגָּרוּ בְּלוֹד

ka'asher savav keifa bechol hammekomot yarad gam el hakkedoshim sheggaru belod
And it came to pass, as Peter went throughout all parts, he came down also to the saints that dwelt at Lydda.

שָׁם מָצָא אִישׁ, אֵינְאַס שְׁמוֹ, וְהוּא מְשֻׁתָּק וְשׁוֹכֵב בַּמִּטָּה זֶה שְׁמוֹנֶה שָׁנִים

sham matza ish, ayne'as shemo, vehu meshuttak veshochev bammittah zeh shemoneh shanim
And there he found a certain man named Aeneas, who had kept his bed eight years; for he was palsied.

אָמַר אֵלָיו כֵּיפָא: אֵינְאַס, יֵשׁוּעַ הַמָּשִׁיחַ מְרַפֵּא אוֹתְךָ! קוּם וְסַדֵּר אֶת מִטָּתְךָ! הוּא קָם מִיָּד

amar elav keifa: ayne'as, yeshua hammashiach merappei otecha! kum vesadder et mittatecha! hu kam miyad
And Peter said unto him, Aeneas, Jesus Christ healeth thee: arise, and make thy bed. And straightway he arose.

רָאוּ אוֹתוֹ כָּל תּוֹשָׁבֵי לוֹד וְהַשָּׁרוֹן וּפָנוּ אֶל הָאָדוֹן

ra'u oto kol toshavei lod vehasharon ufanu el ha'adon
And all that dwelt at Lydda and in Sharon saw him, and they turned to the Lord.

בְּיָפוֹ הָיְתָה תַּלְמִידָה וּשְׁמָהּ טָבִיתָא, כְּלוֹמַר צְבִיָּה

beyafo hayetah talmidah ushemah tavita, klomar tzviyah
Now there was at Joppa a certain disciple named Tabitha, which by interpretation is called Dorcas:

וְהִיא רַבַּת מַעֲשִׂים טוֹבִים וּמַרְבָּה בִּגְמִילוּת חֲסָדִים

vehi rabbat ma'asim tovim umarbah bigmilut chasadim
this woman was full of good works and almsdeeds which she did.

בַּיָּמִים הָהֵם חָלְתָה וָמֵתָה

bayamim hahem chaletah vametah
And it came to pass in those days, that she fell sick, and died:

וּלְאַחַר שֶׁרְחָצוּהָ שָׂמוּ אוֹתָהּ בַּחֶדֶר הָעֲלִיָּה

ule'achar sherchatzuha samu otah bachadar ha'aliyah
and when they had washed her, they laid her in an upper chamber.

כֵּיוָן שֶׁלּוֹד קְרוֹבָה לְיָפוֹ וְהַתַּלְמִידִים שָׁמְעוּ כִּי כֵּיפָא שָׁם,

keivan shellod kerovah leyafo vehattalmidim shame'u ki keifa sham
And as Lydda was nigh unto Joppa, the disciples, hearing that Peter was there,

שָׁלְחוּ אֵלָיו שְׁנֵי אֲנָשִׁים לְהַפְצִיר בּוֹ שֶׁיְּמַהֵר לָבוֹא אֲלֵיהֶם

shalchu elav shenei anashim lehaftzir bo sheyemaher lavo aleihem
sent two men unto him, entreating him, Delay not to come on unto us.

כֵּיפָא קָם וְהָלַךְ אִתָּם

keifa kam vehalach ittam
And Peter arose and went with them.

מַעֲשֵׂי הַשְּׁלִיחִים

כַּעֲבֹר זְמַן נִכָּר נוֹעֲצוּ יְהוּדִים אֵלֶּה לַהֲמִיתוֹ
ka'avor zeman nikkar no'atzu yehudim eloh lahamito
And when many days were fulfilled, the Jews took counsel together to kill him:

אַךְ מְזִמָּתָם נוֹדְעָה לְשָׁאוּל. מֵאַחַר שֶׁשָּׁמְרוּ אֶת הַשְּׁעָרִים יוֹמָם וָלַיְלָה כְּדֵי לְהָרְגוֹ
ach mezimmatam node'ah lesha'ul. me'achar sheshameru et hashe'arim yomam valaylah kedei leharego
but their plot became known to Saul. And they watched the gates also day and night that they might kill him:

לָקְחוּ אוֹתוֹ הַתַּלְמִידִים בַּלַּיְלָה וְהוֹרִידוּהוּ בְּסַל מִן הַחוֹמָה
lakechu oto hattalmidim ballaylah vehoriduhu besal min hachomah
but his disciples took him by night, and let him down through the wall, lowering him in a basket.

כַּאֲשֶׁר בָּא שָׁאוּל לִירוּשָׁלַיִם וְנִסָּה לְהִלָּווֹת אֶל הַתַּלְמִידִים
ka'asher ba sha'ul liyerushalayim venissah lehillavot el hattalmidim
And when he was come to Jerusalem, he assayed to join himself to the disciples:

פָּחֲדוּ מִמֶּנּוּ כֻּלָּם, כִּי לֹא הֶאֱמִינוּ שֶׁהוּא תַּלְמִיד
pachadu mimmennu kullam, ki lo he'eminu shehu talmid
and they were all afraid of him, not believing that he was a disciple.

לָקַח אוֹתוֹ בַּר-נַבָּא וֶהֱבִיאוֹ אֶל הַשְּׁלִיחִים. הוּא סִפֵּר לָהֶם כֵּיצַד רָאָה שָׁאוּל בַּדֶּרֶךְ אֶת הָאָדוֹן
lakach oto bar-nabba vehevi'o el hashlichim. hu sipper lahem keitzad ra'ah sha'ul badderech et ha'adon
But Barnabas took him, and brought him to the apostles, and declared unto them how he had seen the Lord in the way,

שֶׁגַּם דִּבֵּר אֵלָיו, וְכֵיצַד בְּדַמֶּשֶׂק דִּבֵּר בְּבִטָּחוֹן בְּשֵׁם יֵשׁוּעַ
sheggam dibber elav, vecheitzad bedammesek dibber bevittachon beshem yeshua
and that he had spoken to him, and how at Damascus he had preached boldly in the name of Jesus.

אַחֲרֵי כֵן הָיָה שָׁאוּל אִתָּם, יוֹצֵא וּבָא בִּירוּשָׁלַיִם וּמְדַבֵּר בְּבִטָּחוֹן בְּשֵׁם הָאָדוֹן יֵשׁוּעַ
acharei chen hayah sha'ul ittam, yotzei uva biyerushalayim umedabber bevittachon beshem ha'adon yeshua
And he was with them going in and going out at Jerusalem, preaching boldly in the name of the Lord:

הוּא דִּבֵּר וְגַם הִתְוַכַּח עִם הַיְהוּדִים הַיְּוָנִים
hu dibber vegam hitvakkeach im hayehudim hayevanim
and he spake and disputed against the Grecian Jews;

וְהֵם נִסּוּ לַהֲמִיתוֹ
vehem nissu lahamito
but they were seeking to kill him.

כְּשֶׁנּוֹדַע הַדָּבָר לָאַחִים הוֹרִידוּהוּ לְקֵיסַרְיָה וְשָׁלְחוּ אוֹתוֹ אֶל טַרְסוֹס
keshennoda haddavar la'achim horiduhu lekeisaryah veshalechu oto el tarsos
And when the brethren knew it, they brought him down to Cæsarea, and sent him forth to Tarsus.

בְּאוֹתָהּ עֵת הָיָה שָׁלוֹם לַקְּהִלָּה בְּכָל יְהוּדָה וְהַגָּלִיל וּבְשׁוֹמְרוֹן; הִיא נִבְנְתָה
be'otah et hayah shalom lakkehillah bechol yehudah vehaggalil uveshomeron; hi nivnetah
So the church throughout all Judæa and Galilee and Samaria had peace, being edified;

מַעֲשֵׂי הַשְּׁלִיחִים

וַאֲנִי אַרְאֶה לוֹ כַּמָּה עָלָיו לִסְבֹּל לְמַעַן שְׁמִי
va'ani ar'eh lo kammah alav lisbol lema'an shemi
for I will show him how many things he must suffer for my name's sake.

הָלַךְ חֲנַנְיָה וְנִכְנַס לַבַּיִת; הוּא סָמַךְ עָלָיו יָדַיִם וְאָמַר:
halach chananyah venichnas labbayit; hu samach alav yadayim ve'amar
And Ananias departed, and entered into the house; and laying his hands on him said,

שָׁאוּל, אָחִי. הָאָדוֹן יֵשׁוּעַ שֶׁנִּרְאָה אֵלֶיךָ בַּדֶּרֶךְ בּוֹאֲךָ שְׁלָחַנִי
sha'ul, achi. ha'adon yeshua shennir'ah eleicha bederech bo'acha shlachani
Brother Saul, the Lord, even Jesus, who appeared unto thee in the way which thou camest, hath sent me,

כְּדֵי שֶׁתִּרְאֶה שׁוּב וְתִמָּלֵא רוּחַ הַקֹּדֶשׁ
kedei shettir'eh shuv vetimmalei ruach hakkodesh
that thou mayest receive thy sight, and be filled with the Holy Spirit.

מִיָּד נָפְלוּ מֵעֵינָיו כְּמוֹ קַשְׂקַשִּׂים וְנִפְקְחוּ עֵינָיו. הוּא קָם וְנִטְבַּל
miyad nafelu me'einav kemo kaskasim venifkechu einav. hu kam venitbal
And straightway there fell from his eyes as it were scales, and he received his sight; and he arose and was baptized;

וּלְאַחַר שֶׁאָכַל הִתְחַזֵּק
ule'achar she'achal hitchazzek
and he took food and was strengthened.

וּבְלִי לְהִתְמַהְמֵהַּ הִכְרִיז עַל יֵשׁוּעַ בְּבָתֵּי הַכְּנֶסֶת, שֶׁהוּא בֶּן־הָאֱלֹהִים
uveli lehitmahmeah hichriz al yeshua vevattei hakkeneset, shehu ben-ha'elohim
And straightway in the synagogues he proclaimed Jesus, that he is the Son of God.

נִדְהֲמוּ כָּל הַשּׁוֹמְעִים וְאָמְרוּ:
nidhamu kol hashome'im ve'ameru
And all that heard him were amazed, and said,

הֲרֵי זֶהוּ הָאִישׁ שֶׁבִּירוּשָׁלַיִם עָשָׂה שַׁמּוֹת בְּקֶרֶב הַקּוֹרְאִים בַּשֵּׁם הַזֶּה
harei zehu ha'ish shebiyerushalayim asah shammot bekerev hakkore'im bashem hazzeh
Is not this he that in Jerusalem made havoc of them that called on this name?

וּלְמַטָּרָה זֹאת בָּא הֵנָּה, לַהֲבִיאָם בִּכְבָלִים אֶל הַכֹּהֲנִים הַגְּדוֹלִים
ulemattarah zot ba hennah, lahavi'am bichvalim el hakkohanim haggedolim
and he had come hither for this intent, that he might bring them bound before the chief priests.

בְּרַם שָׁאוּל נִתְמַלֵּא בְּיֶתֶר כֹּחַ
beram sha'ul nitmallei beyeter koach
But Saul increased the more in strength,

וְהֵבִיךְ אֶת הַיְּהוּדִים הַגָּרִים בְּדַמֶּשֶׂק בְּהוֹכִיחוֹ כִּי זֶהוּ הַמָּשִׁיחַ
vehevich et hayehudim haggarim bedammesek behochicho ki zehu hammashiach
and confounded the Jews that dwelt at Damascus, proving that this is the Christ.

מַעֲשֵׂי הַשְּׁלִיחִים

שָׁאוּל קָם מִן הָאָרֶץ וּכְשֶׁפָּקַח אֶת עֵינָיו לֹא רָאָה דָּבָר
sha'ul kam min ha'aretz uchesheppakach et einav lo ra'ah davar
And Saul arose from the earth; and when his eyes were opened, he saw nothing;

הֶחֱזִיקוּ בְּיָדוֹ וְהוֹלִיכוּהוּ לְדַמֶּשֶׂק
hecheziku beyado veholichuhu ledammesek
and they led him by the hand, and brought him into Damascus.

בְּמֶשֶׁךְ שְׁלוֹשָׁה יָמִים לֹא רָאָה בְּעֵינָיו וְלֹא אָכַל וְלֹא שָׁתָה
bemeshech shloshah yamim lo ra'ah be'einav velo achal velo shatah
And he was three days without sight, and did neither eat nor drink.

בְּדַמֶּשֶׂק הָיָה תַּלְמִיד אֶחָד, חֲנַנְיָה שְׁמוֹ
bedammesek hayah talmid echad, chananyah shemo
Now there was a certain disciple at Damascus, named Ananias;

וְהָאָדוֹן אָמַר אֵלָיו בְּמַרְאֵה חָזוֹן: חֲנַנְיָה! הוּא הֵשִׁיב: הִנֵּנִי, אֲדוֹנִי
veha'adon amar elav bemar'eh chazon. chananyah! hu heshiv: hineni, adoni
and the Lord said unto him in a vision, Ananias. And he said, Behold, I am here, Lord.

אָמַר אֵלָיו הָאָדוֹן: קוּם לֵךְ אֶל הָרְחוֹב הַנִּקְרָא יָשָׁר
amar elav ha'adon: kum lech el harechov hannikra yashar
And the Lord said unto him, Arise, and go to the street which is called Straight,

וּבַקֵּשׁ בְּבֵית יְהוּדָה אִישׁ טַרְסִי, שָׁאוּל שְׁמוֹ. הִנֵּהוּ מִתְפַּלֵּל
uvakkesh beveit yehudah ish tarsi, sha'ul shemo. hinnehu mitpallel
and inquire in the house of Judas for one named Saul, a man of Tarsus: for behold, he prayeth;

וּבְחָזוֹן רָאָה אִישׁ, חֲנַנְיָה שְׁמוֹ, נִכְנָס וְשָׂם עָלָיו אֶת יָדָיו כְּדֵי שֶׁיִּרְאֶה שׁוּב
uvechazon ra'ah ish, chananyah shemo, nichnas vesam alav et yadav kedei sheyir'eh shuv
and he hath seen a man named Ananias coming in, and laying his hands on him, that he might receive his sight.

הֵשִׁיב חֲנַנְיָה: אֲדוֹנִי, שָׁמַעְתִּי מִפִּי רַבִּים עַל הָאִישׁ הַזֶּה, כַּמָּה רָעוֹת עָשָׂה לִקְדוֹשֶׁיךָ בִּירוּשָׁלַיִם
heshiv chananyah: adoni, shamati mippi rabbim al ha'ish hazzeh, kammah ra'ot asah likdosheicha biyerushalayim
But Ananias answered, Lord, I have heard from many of this man, how much evil he did to thy saints at Jerusalem:

וְגַם פֹּה יֵשׁ לוֹ סַמְכוּת מֵאֵת רָאשֵׁי הַכֹּהֲנִים לֶאֱסֹר אֶת כָּל הַקּוֹרְאִים בְּשִׁמְךָ
vegam poh yesh lo samchut me'et rashei hakkohanim le'esor et kol hakkor'im beshimcha
and here he hath authority from the chief priests to bind all that call upon thy name.

אָמַר לוֹ הָאָדוֹן: לֵךְ
amar lo ha'adon: lech
But the Lord said unto him, Go thy way:

כִּי כְּלִי נִבְחָר הוּא לִי לָשֵׂאת אֶת שְׁמִי לִפְנֵי גּוֹיִם וּמְלָכִים וְלִפְנֵי בְּנֵי יִשְׂרָאֵל
ki kli nivchar hu li laset et shemi lifnei goyim umelachim velifnei bnei yisra'el
for he is a chosen vessel unto me, to bear my name before the Gentiles and kings, and the children of Israel:

מַעֲשֵׂי הַשְּׁלִיחִים

וּפִילִיפּוֹס נִרְאָה בְּאַשְׁדּוֹד. הוּא עָבַר וּבִשֵּׂר בְּכָל הֶעָרִים עַד בּוֹאוֹ לְקֵיסַרְיָה
ufilipos nir'ah be'ashdod. hu avar uvisser bechol he'arim ad bo'o lekeisaryah
But Philip was found at Azotus: and passing through he preached the gospel to all the cities, till he came to Cæsarea.

ט

וְשָׁאוּל עוֹדֶנּוּ מֵפִיחַ אִיּוּמִים וָרֶצַח נֶגֶד תַּלְמִידֵי הָאָדוֹן. הוּא בָּא אֶל הַכֹּהֵן הַגָּדוֹל
vesha'ul odennu mefiach iyumim varetzach neged talmidei ha'adon. hu ba el hakkohen haggadol
But Saul, yet breathing threatening and slaughter against the disciples of the Lord, went unto the high priest,

וּבִקֵּשׁ מִמֶּנּוּ אִגְּרוֹת
uvikkesh mimmennu iggrot
and asked of him letters

לְבָתֵּי הַכְּנֶסֶת בְּדַמֶּשֶׂק, כְּדֵי שֶׁיֶּאֱסֹר בִּכְבָלִים אֶת מִי שֶׁיִּמְצָא מִן הַמַּחֲזִיקִים בַּדֶּרֶךְ הַהִיא
levattei hakkeneset bedammesek, kdei sheye'esor bichvalim et mi sheyimtza min hammachazikim badderech hahi
to Damascus unto the synagogues, that if he found any that were of the Way,

הֵן גְּבָרִים וְהֵן נָשִׁים, וְיָבִיא אוֹתָם לִירוּשָׁלַיִם
hen gevarim vehen nashim, veyavi otam liyerushalayim
whether men or women, he might bring them bound to Jerusalem.

בְּעֵת שֶׁהָלַךְ וְהִתְקָרֵב לְדַמֶּשֶׂק
be'et shehalach vehitkarev ledammesek
And as he journeyed, it came to pass that he drew nigh unto Damascus:

פִּתְאוֹם נָגַהּ סְבִיבוֹ אוֹר מִן הַשָּׁמַיִם
pit'om nagah sevivo or min hashamayim
and suddenly there shone round about him a light out of heaven:

הוּא נָפַל אַרְצָה וְשָׁמַע קוֹל אוֹמֵר אֵלָיו: שָׁאוּל, שָׁאוּל, לָמָּה תִּרְדְּפֵנִי
hu nafal artzah veshama kol omer elav: sha'ul, sha'ul, lammah tirdefeni
and he fell upon the earth, and heard a voice saying unto him, Saul, Saul, why persecutest thou me?

שָׁאַל שָׁאוּל: מִי אַתָּה, אֲדוֹנִי? אָנֹכִי יֵשׁוּעַ אֲשֶׁר אַתָּה רוֹדֵף
sha'al sha'ul: mi attah, adoni? anochi yeshua asher attah rodef
And he said, Who art thou, Lord? And he said, I am Jesus whom thou persecutest:

אֲבָל קוּם לֵךְ הָעִירָה וְיֵאָמֵר לְךָ מַה שֶּׁעָלֶיךָ לַעֲשׂוֹת
aval kum lech ha'irah veye'amer lecha mah she'aleicha la'asot
but rise, and enter into the city, and it shall be told thee what thou must do.

הָאֲנָשִׁים הַנּוֹסְעִים אִתּוֹ עָמְדוּ אִלְּמִים. הֵם שָׁמְעוּ אֶת הַקּוֹל, אַךְ לֹא רָאוּ אִישׁ
ha'anashim hannose'im itto amedu illmim. hem shame'u et hakkol, ach lo ra'u ish
And the men that journeyed with him stood speechless, hearing the voice, but beholding no man.

מַעֲשֵׂי הַשְּׁלִיחִים

קֶטַע הַכָּתוּב שֶׁקָּרָא הָיָה
keta hakkatuv shekkara hayah
Now the passage of the scripture which he was reading was this,

כַּשֶּׂה לַטֶּבַח יוּבַל וּכְרָחֵל לִפְנֵי גֹזְזֶיהָ נֶאֱלָמָה, וְלֹא יִפְתַּח פִּיו
kasseh lattevach yuval ucherachel lifnei gozezeiha ne'elamah, velo yiftach piv
He was led as a sheep to the slaughter; And as a lamb before his shearer is dumb, So he openeth not his mouth:

מֵעֹצֶר וּמִמִּשְׁפָּט לֻקָּח וְאֶת-דּוֹרוֹ מִי יְשׂוֹחֵחַ, כִּי נִגְזַר מֵאֶרֶץ חַיִּים
me'otzer umimmishpat lukkach ve'et-doro mi yesocheach, ki nigzar me'eretz chayim
In his humiliation his judgment was taken away: His generation who shall declare? For his life is taken from the earth.

אָמַר הַסָּרִיס אֶל פִילִיפּוֹס: אֶשְׁאַל אוֹתְךָ, עַל מִי הַנָּבִיא אוֹמֵר זֹאת
amar hassaris el filipos: esh'al otecha, al mi hannavi omer zot,
And the eunuch answered Philip, and said, I pray thee, of whom speaketh the prophet this?

עַל עַצְמוֹ אוֹ עַל מִישֶׁהוּ אַחֵר
al atzmo o al mishehu acher
of himself, or of some other?

פָּתַח פִילִיפּוֹס בִּדְבָרוֹ וּבְהַתְחִילוֹ מִן הַכָּתוּב הַזֶּה בִּשֵּׂר לוֹ אֶת יֵשׁוּעַ
patach filipos bidvaro uvehatchilo min hakkatuv hazzeh bisser lo et yeshua
And Philip opened his mouth, and beginning from this scripture, preached unto him Jesus.

כַּאֲשֶׁר נָסְעוּ בַּדֶּרֶךְ בָּאוּ אֶל מְקוֹם מַיִם. אָמַר הַסָּרִיס
ka'asher nase'u badderech ba'u el mekom mayim. amar hassaris
And as they went on the way, they came unto a certain water; and the eunuch saith,

הִנֵּה מַיִם. מַה יִּמְנַע אוֹתִי מֵהִטָּבֵל
hinneh mayim. mah yimna oti mehittavel
Behold, here is water; what doth hinder me to be baptized?

הוּא צִוָּה לַעֲצֹר אֶת הַמֶּרְכָּבָה וּשְׁנֵיהֶם יָרְדוּ אֶל הַמַּיִם
hu tzivvah la'atzor et hammerkavah usheneihem yaredu el hammayim
And he commanded the chariot to stand still: and they both went down into the water,

הֵן פִילִיפּוֹס וְהֵן הַסָּרִיס, וּפִילִיפּוֹס הִטְבִּילוֹ
hen filipos vehen hassaris, ufilipos hitbilo
both Philip and the eunuch; and he baptized him.

כְּשֶׁעָלוּ מִתּוֹךְ הַמַּיִם חָטְפָה רוּחַ יהוה אֶת פִילִיפּוֹס,
keshe'alu mittoch hammayim chatefah ruach hashem et filipos
And when they came up out of the water, the Spirit of the Lord caught away Philip;

וְהַסָּרִיס לֹא רָאָה אוֹתוֹ עוֹד. אָז נָסַע לְדַרְכּוֹ שָׂמֵחַ
vehassaris lo ra'ah oto od. az nasa ledarko sameach
and the eunuch saw him no more, for he went on his way rejoicing.

מַעֲשֵׂי הַשְּׁלִיחִים

הֵשִׁיב שִׁמְעוֹן וְאָמַר: הִתְחַנְנוּ אַתֶּם בַּעֲדִי אֶל הָאָדוֹן שֶׁלֹּא יָבוֹא עָלַי דָּבָר מִמַּה שֶּׁאֲמַרְתֶּם
heshiv shim'on ve'amar: hitchannenu attem ba'adi el ha'adon shello yavo alai davar mimmah she'amartem
And Simon answered and said, Pray ye for me to the Lord, that none of the things which ye have spoken come upon me

לְאַחַר שֶׁהֵעִידוּ אֶת עֵדוּתָם וְדִבְּרוּ אֶת דְּבַר הָאָדוֹן חָזְרוּ לִירוּשָׁלַיִם
le'achar shehe'idu et edutam vedibberu et devar ha'adon chazru liyerushalayim
They therefore, when they had testified and spoken the word of the Lord, returned to Jerusalem,

וּבְדַרְכָּם בִּשְּׂרוּ אֶת הַבְּשׂוֹרָה בִּכְפָרִים רַבִּים שֶׁל שׁוֹמְרוֹנִים
uvedarkam bissru et habbesorah bichfarim rabbim shel shomeronim
and preached the gospel to many villages of the Samaritans.

מַלְאַךְ יְהוָה דִּבֶּר אֶל פִילִיפּוֹס וְאָמַ
mal'ach hashem dibber el filipos ve'amar
But an angel of the Lord spake unto Philip, saying,

קוּם וְלֵךְ דָּרוֹמָה בַּדֶּרֶךְ הַיּוֹרֶדֶת מִירוּשָׁלַיִם לְעַזָּה, בַּדֶּרֶךְ הַמִּדְבָּרִית
kum velech daromah badderech hayoredet miyerushalayim le'azzah, badderech hammidbarit
Arise, and go toward the south unto the way that goeth down from Jerusalem unto Gaza: the same is desert.

הוּא קָם וְהָלַךְ. וְהִנֵּה אִישׁ אֶתְיוֹפִּי
hu kam vehalach. vehinneh ish etyoppi
And he arose and went: and behold, a man of Ethiopia,

סָרִיס וְשַׂר בַּחֲצַר קַנְדָּק מַלְכַּת הָאֶתְיוֹפִּים
saris vesar bachatzar kandak malkat ha'etyoppim
a eunuch of great authority under Candace, queen of the Ethiopians,

וּמְמֻנֶּה עַל כָּל אוֹצְרוֹתֶיהָ, חוֹזֵר לְאַרְצוֹ לְאַחַר שֶׁבָּא לְהִשְׁתַּחֲווֹת בִּירוּשָׁלַיִם
umemunneh al kol otzeroteiha, chozer le'artzo le'achar shebba lehishtachavot biyerushalayim
who was over all her treasure, who had come to Jerusalem to worship;

וְהוּא יוֹשֵׁב בְּמֶרְכַּבְתּוֹ וְקוֹרֵא בְּסֵפֶר יְשַׁעְיָהוּ הַנָּבִיא
vehu yoshev bemerkavto vekorei besefer yesha'yahu hannavi
and he was returning and sitting in his chariot, and was reading the prophet Isaiah.

אָמְרָה הָרוּחַ לְפִילִיפּוֹס: הִתְקָרֵב וְהִלָּוֵה אֶל הַמֶּרְכָּבָה הַזֹּאת
amerah haruach lefilipos: hitkarev vehillaveh el hammerkavah hazzot
And the Spirit said unto Philip, Go near, and join thyself to this chariot.

פִילִיפּוֹס רָץ אֶל הַמֶּרְכָּבָה וְשָׁמַע אוֹתוֹ קוֹרֵא בִּישַׁעְיָהוּ הַנָּבִיא. שָׁאַל אוֹתוֹ: הַאִם אַתָּה מֵבִין מַה שֶּׁאַתָּה קוֹרֵא
filipos ratz el hammerkavah veshama oto korei bisha'yahu hannavi. sha'al oto: ha'im attah mevin mah she'attah korei
And Philip ran to him, and heard him reading Isaiah the prophet, and said, Understandest thou what thou readest?

הֵשִׁיב וְאָמַר: וְאֵיךְ אוּכַל אִם לֹא יַדְרִיךְ אוֹתִי אִישׁ? הוּא בִּקֵּשׁ מִפִילִיפּוֹס שֶׁיַּעֲלֶה וְיֵשֵׁב אִתּוֹ
heshiv ve'amar: ve'eich uchal im lo yadrich oti ish? hu bikkesh mifilipos sheya'aleh veyeshev itto
And he said, How can I, except some one shall guide me? And he besought Philip to come up and sit with him.

מַעֲשֵׂי הַשְּׁלִיחִים

הַשְּׁלִיחִים אֲשֶׁר בִּירוּשָׁלַיִם שָׁמְעוּ שֶׁשּׁוֹמְרוֹן קִבְּלָה אֶת דְּבַר אֱלֹהִים
hashelichim asher biyerushalayim sham'u sheshomeron kibbelah et dvar elohim
Now when the apostles that were at Jerusalem heard that Samaria had received the word of God,

וְשָׁלְחוּ אֲלֵיהֶם אֶת כֵּיפָא וְאֶת יוֹחָנָן
veshalechu aleihem et keifa ve'et yochanan
they sent unto them Peter and John:

הַלָּלוּ יָרְדוּ לְשָׁם וְהִתְפַּלְּלוּ בַּעֲדָם שֶׁיְּקַבְּלוּ אֶת רוּחַ הַקֹּדֶשׁ
hallalu yaredu lesham vehitpallelu ba'adam sheyekabbelu et ruach hakkodesh
who, when they were come down, prayed for them, that they might receive the Holy Spirit:

כִּי עוֹד לֹא צָלְחָה הָרוּחַ עַל אִישׁ מֵהֶם; הֵם רַק נִטְבְּלוּ בְּשֵׁם הָאָדוֹן יֵשׁוּעַ
ki od lo tzalchah haruach al ish mehem; hem rak nitbelu beshem ha'adon yeshua
for as yet it was fallen upon none of them: only they had been baptized into the name of the Lord Jesus.

אָז סָמְכוּ יָדַיִם עֲלֵיהֶם וְהֵם קִבְּלוּ אֶת רוּחַ הַקֹּדֶשׁ
az samchu yadayim aleihem vehem kibblu et ruach hakkodesh
Then laid they their hands on them, and they received the Holy Spirit.

כְּשֶׁרָאָה שִׁמְעוֹן כִּי בִּסְמִיכַת יְדֵי הַשְּׁלִיחִים נִתֶּנֶת רוּחַ הַקֹּדֶשׁ,
keshera'ah shim'on ki bismichat yedei hashelichim nittenet ruach hakkodesh,
Now when Simon saw that through the laying on of the apostles' hands the Holy Spirit was given,

הִגִּישׁ לָהֶם כֶּסֶף בְּאָמְרוֹ
higgish lahem kesef be'omro
he offered them money, saying,

תְּנוּ גַם לִי אֶת הַסַּמְכוּת הַזֹּאת, שֶׁכָּל מִי שֶׁאַנִּיחַ עָלָיו אֶת יָדַי יְקַבֵּל אֶת רוּחַ הַקֹּדֶשׁ
tenu gam li et hassamchut hazzot, shekkol mi she'anniach alav et yadai yekabbel et ruach hakkodesh
Give me also this power, that on whomsoever I lay my hands, he may receive the Holy Spirit.

אָמַר לוֹ כֵּיפָא: כַּסְפְּךָ יְהֵא אִתְּךָ לַאֲבַדּוֹן, מִפְּנֵי שֶׁחָשַׁבְתָּ לִקְנוֹת בְּכֶסֶף אֶת מַתְּנַת אֱלֹהִים
amar lo keifa: kaspecha yehei ittecha la'avaddon, mippnei shechashavta liknot bechesef et mattnat elohim
But Peter said unto him, Thy silver perish with thee, because thou hast thought to obtain the gift of God with money.

אֵין לְךָ חֵלֶק וְנַחֲלָה בַּדָּבָר הַזֶּה, כִּי לְבָבְךָ אֵינֶנּוּ יָשָׁר לִפְנֵי הָאֱלֹהִים
ein lecha chelek venachalah baddavar hazzeh, ki levavecha einennu yashar lifnei ha'elohim
Thou hast neither part nor lot in this matter: for thy heart is not right before God.

עַל כֵּן שׁוּב מֵרִשְׁעָתְךָ זוֹ וְהִתְחַנֵּן אֶל יהוה, אוּלַי תִּסָּלַח לְךָ מְזִמַּת לִבֶּךָ
al ken shuv merish'atecha zo vehitchannen el hashem, ulai tissalach lecha mezimmat libbecha
Repent therefore of this thy wickedness, and pray the Lord, if perhaps the thought of thy heart shall be forgiven thee.

כִּי אֲנִי רוֹאֶה אוֹתְךָ נָתוּן בִּמְרוֹרַת לַעֲנָה וּבְכַבְלֵי רֶשַׁע
ki ani ro'eh otecha natun bimrorat la'anah uvechavlei resha
For I see that thou art in the gall of bitterness and in the bond of iniquity.

מַעֲשֵׂי הַשְּׁלִיחִים

כְּשָׁמְעָם וְכִרְאוֹתָם אֶת הָאוֹתוֹת שֶׁעָשָׂה
keshame'am vechir'otam et ha'otot she'asah
when they heard, and saw the signs which he did.

כִּי רַבִּים אֲשֶׁר הָיוּ אֲחוּזֵי רוּחוֹת טֻמְאָה, הָרוּחוֹת יָצְאוּ מֵהֶם וְהֵן צוֹעֲקוֹת בְּקוֹל גָּדוֹל
ki rabbim asher hayu achuzei ruchot tum'ah, haruchot yatze'u mehem vehen tzo'akot bekol gadol.
For from many of those that had unclean spirits, they came out, crying with a loud voice:

גַּם מְשֻׁתָּקִים וּפִסְחִים רַבִּים נִרְפְּאוּ
gam meshuttakim ufischim rabbim nirpe'u
and many that were palsied, and that were lame, were healed.

וְשִׂמְחָה גְדוֹלָה הָיְתָה בָּעִיר הַהִיא
vesimchah gedolah hayetah ba'ir hahi
And there was much joy in that city.

אִישׁ אֶחָד, שִׁמְעוֹן שְׁמוֹ, הָיָה עוֹסֵק זֶה מִכְּבָר בִּכְשׁוּף בְּשׁוֹמְרוֹן
ish echad, shim'on shmo, hayah osek zeh mikkevar bechishuf beshomeron
But there was a certain man, Simon by name, who beforetime in the city used sorcery,

וּמַדְהִים אֶת תּוֹשָׁבֵי הָעִיר בְּאָמְרוֹ עַל עַצְמוֹ שֶׁהוּא אָדָם גָּדוֹל
umadhim et toshavei ha'ir be'omro al atzmo shehu adam gadol
and amazed the people of Samaria, giving out that himself was some great one:

הַכֹּל הִקְשִׁיבוּ אֵלָיו, מִקָּטָן וְעַד גָּדוֹל. אָמְרוּ: הָאִישׁ הַזֶּה הוּא כֹּחַ הָאֱלֹהִים הַנִּקְרָא הַכֹּחַ הַגָּדוֹל
hakkol hikshivu elav, mikkatan ve'ad gadol. Ameru: ha'ish hazzeh hu koach ha'elohim hannikra hakkoach haggadol
to whom they all gave heed, from the least to the greatest, saying, This man is that power of God which is called Great.

הֵם הִקְשִׁיבוּ אֵלָיו מִפְּנֵי שֶׁזְּמַן רַב הִדְהִים אוֹתָם בִּכְשָׁפָיו
hem hikshivu elav mippenei shezzeman rav hidhim otam bichshafav
And they gave heed to him, because that of long time he had amazed them with his sorceries.

אֲבָל כַּאֲשֶׁר הֶאֱמִינוּ לְפִילִיפּוֹס בְּבַשְּׂרוֹ עַל מַלְכוּת הָאֱלֹהִים וְשֵׁם יֵשׁוּעַ הַמָּשִׁיחַ,
aval ka'asher he'eminu lefilipos bevashoro al malchut ha'elohim veshem yeshua hammashiach
But when they believed Philip preaching good tidings concerning the kingdom of God and the name of Jesus Christ,

נִטְבְּלוּ גְּבָרִים וְנָשִׁים
nitbelu gevarim venashim
they were baptized, both men and women.

וְגַם שִׁמְעוֹן עַצְמוֹ הֶאֱמִין. הוּא נִטְבַּל וְנִסְפַּח אֶל פִילִיפּוֹס
vegam shim'on atzmo he'emin. hu nitbal venispach el filipos
And Simon also himself believed: and being baptized, he continued with Philip;

וְכִרְאוֹתוֹ אֶת הָאוֹתוֹת וְהַמּוֹפְתִים הַגְּדוֹלִים שֶׁנַּעֲשׂוּ, נִתְמַלֵּא תִמָּהוֹן
vechir'oto et ha'otot vehammofetim haggedolim shenna'asu, nitmallei timmahon
and beholding signs and great miracles wrought, he was amazed.

מַעֲשֵׂי הַשְּׁלִיחִים

הֲדָפוּהוּ אֶל מִחוּץ לָעִיר וְסָקְלוּ אוֹתוֹ בָּאֲבָנִים
hadafuhu el michutz la'ir vesakelu oto ba'avanim
and they cast him out of the city, and stoned him:

הָעֵדִים הִנִּיחוּ אֶת בִּגְדֵיהֶם לְרַגְלֵי בָּחוּר אֶחָד, שָׁאוּל שְׁמוֹ
ha'edim hinnichu et bigdeihem leraglei bachur echad, sha'ul shemo
and the witnesses laid down their garments at the feet of a young man named Saul.

וּסְטֶפָנוֹס נִסְקַל כְּשֶׁהוּא זוֹעֵק וְאוֹמֵר: אֲדוֹנִי יֵשׁוּעַ, קַבֵּל אֶת רוּחִי
ustefanos niskal keshehu zo'ek ve'omer: adoni yeshua', kabbel et ruchi
And they stoned Stephen, calling upon the Lord, and saying, Lord Jesus, receive my spirit.

כְּמוֹ כֵן כָּרַע עַל בִּרְכָּיו וְצָעַק בְּקוֹל גָּדוֹל
kemo chen kara al birkav vetza'ak bekol gadol
And he kneeled down, and cried with a loud voice,

אֲדֹנָי, אַל תִּפְקֹד עֲלֵיהֶם אֶת הַחֵטְא הַזֶּה! אָמַר זֹאת וָמֵת
adonai, al tifkod aleihem et hachet hazzeh! amar zot vamet
Lord, lay not this sin to their charge. And when he had said this, he fell asleep.

ח

גַּם שָׁאוּל הִסְכִּים לַהֲרִיגָתוֹ
gam sha'ul hiskim laharigato
And Saul was consenting unto his death.

אָז אָסְפוּ אֲנָשִׁים יִרְאֵי שָׁמַיִם אֶת סְטֶפָנוֹס וְסָפְדוּ עָלָיו מִסְפֵּד גָּדוֹל
az asefu anashim yir'ei shamayim et setefanos vesafedu alav misped gadol
And devout men buried Stephen, and made great lamentation over him.

וְשָׁאוּל עָשָׂה שַׁמּוֹת בַּקְּהִלָּה; הוּא עָבַר מִבַּיִת לְבַיִת וְגָרַר גְּבָרִים וְנָשִׁים וְהִסְגִּירָם לַכֶּלֶא
vesha'ul asah shammot bakkehillah; hu avar mibbayit levayit vegarar gevarim venashim vehisgiram lakkele
But Saul laid waste the church, entering into every house, and dragging men and women committed them to prison.

הָאֲנָשִׁים שֶׁנָּפוֹצוּ עָבְרוּ בָּאָרֶץ וּבִשְּׂרוּ אֶת דְּבַר אֱלֹהִים
ha'anashim shennafotzu averu ba'aretz uvishoru et dvar elohim
They therefore that were scattered abroad went about preaching the word.

אָז יָרַד פִילִיפּוֹס אֶל עִיר בְּשׁוֹמְרוֹן וְהִכְרִיז לָהֶם אֶת הַמָּשִׁיחַ
az yarad filipos el ir beshomeron vehichriz lahem et hammashiach
And Philip went down to the city of Samaria, and proclaimed unto them the Christ.

הֲמוֹן הָעָם הִקְשִׁיב בְּלֵב אֶחָד לְדִבְרֵי פִילִיפּוֹס
hamon ha'am hikshiv belev echad ledivrei filipos
And the multitudes gave heed with one accord unto the things that were spoken by Philip,

מַעֲשֵׂי הַשְּׁלִיחִים

הֲלֹא אֶת־כָּל־אֵלֶּה יָדִי עָשָׂתָה
halo et-kol-'elleh yadi asatah
Did not my hand make all these things?

קְשֵׁי עֹרֶף וְעַרְלֵי לֵב וְאָזְנַיִם, תָּמִיד מִתְנַגְּדִים אַתֶּם לְרוּחַ הַקֹּדֶשׁ, כַּאֲבוֹתֵיכֶם כֵּן גַּם אַתֶּם
kshei oref ve'arlei lev ve'azenayim, tamid mitnaggedim attem leruach hakkodesh, ka'avoteichem ken gam attem
Ye stiffnecked and uncircumcised in heart and ears, ye do always resist the Holy Spirit: as your fathers did, so do ye.

אֶת מִי מֵהַנְּבִיאִים לֹא רָדְפוּ אֲבוֹתֵיכֶם
et mi mehannevi'im lo radfu avoteichem
Which of the prophets did not your fathers persecute?

גַּם הָרְגוּ אֶת אֵלֶּה שֶׁהִגִּידוּ מֵרֹאשׁ אֶת דְּבַר בּוֹא הַצַּדִּיק
gam haregu et elleh shehiggidu merosh et devar bo hatzaddik
and they killed them that showed before of the coming of the Righteous One;

אֲשֶׁר כָּעֵת אַתֶּם הֱיִיתֶם מַסְגִּירָיו וְהוֹרְגָיו
asher ka'et attem heyitem masgirav vehoregav
of whom ye have now become betrayers and murderers;

אַתֶּם שֶׁקִּבַּלְתֶּם אֶת הַתּוֹרָה בְּאֶמְצָעוּת מַלְאָכִים וְלֹא שְׁמַרְתֶּם אוֹתָהּ
attem shekkibbaltem et hattorah be'emtza'ut mal'achim velo shmartem otah
ye who received the law as it was ordained by angels, and kept it not.

כְּשָׁמְעָם אֶת הַדְּבָרִים הָאֵלֶּה כָּעֲסוּ עַד עֹמֶק לִבָּם וְחָרְקוּ עָלָיו שִׁנֵּיהֶם
keshame'am et haddvarim ha'elleh ka'asu ad omek libbam vechareku alav shinneihem
Now when they heard these things, they were cut to the heart, and they gnashed on him with their teeth.

וְהוּא מָלֵא רוּחַ הַקֹּדֶשׁ וּמַבִּיט הַשָּׁמַיְמָה
vehu malei ruach hakkodesh umabbit hashamaymah
But he, being full of the Holy Spirit, looked up stedfastly into heaven,

רָאָה אֶת כְּבוֹד אֱלֹהִים וְאֶת יֵשׁוּעַ עוֹמֵד לִימִין הָאֱלֹהִים
ra'ah et kevod elohim ve'et yeshua omed limin ha'elohim
and saw the glory of God, and Jesus standing on the right hand of God,

וְאָמַר: הִנְנִי רוֹאֶה אֶת הַשָּׁמַיִם פְּתוּחִים וְאֶת בֶּן־הָאָדָם עוֹמֵד לִימִין הָאֱלֹהִים
ve'amar: hineni ro'eh et hashamayim petuchim ve'et ben-ha'adam omed liymin ha'elohim
and said, Behold, I see the heavens opened, and the Son of man standing on the right hand of God.

אַךְ הֵם צָעֲקוּ בְּקוֹל גָּדוֹל, בְּאָטְמָם אֶת אָזְנֵיהֶם, וּכְאִישׁ אֶחָד הִסְתָּעֲרוּ עָלָיו
ach hem tza'aku bekol gadol, be'atemam et azeneihem, uche'ish echad hista'aru alav
But they cried out with a loud voice, and stopped their ears, and rushed upon him with one accord;

מַעֲשֵׂי הַשְּׁלִיחִים

הַזְּבָחִים וּמִנְחָה הִגַּשְׁתֶּם־לִי בַמִּדְבָּר אַרְבָּעִים שָׁנָה, בֵּית יִשְׂרָאֵל

hazzevachim uminchah higgashtem-li vammidbar arba'im shanah, beit yisra'el
Did ye offer unto me slain beasts and sacrifices Forty years in the wilderness, O house of Israel?

וּנְשָׂאתֶם אֶת סֻכַּת מֶלֶךְ וְאֶת כּוֹכַב אֱלֹהֵיכֶם רֵיפָן

unsatem et sukkat molech ve'et kochav eloheichem reifan
And ye took up the tabernacle of Moloch, And the star of the god Rephan,

הַצְּלָמִים אֲשֶׁר עֲשִׂיתֶם לְהִשְׁתַּחֲוֹת לָהֶם. וְהִגְלֵיתִי אֶתְכֶם מֵהָלְאָה לְבָבֶל

hatzelamim asher asitem lehishtachavot lahem. vehigleiti etchem mehale'ah levavel
The figures which ye made to worship them: And I will carry you away beyond Babylon.

מִשְׁכַּן הָעֵדוּת הָיָה לַאֲבוֹתֵינוּ בַּמִּדְבָּר

mishkan ha'edut hayah la'avoteinu bammidbar
Our fathers had the tabernacle of the testimony in the wilderness,

כְּמוֹ שֶׁצִּוָּה הַמְדַבֵּר אֶל מֹשֶׁה לַעֲשׂוֹתוֹ עַל־פִּי הַתַּבְנִית שֶׁרָאָה

kemo shetzivvah hamdabber el mosheh la'asoto al-pi hattavnit shera'ah
even as he appointed who spake unto Moses, that he should make it according to the figure that he had seen.

אֲבוֹתֵינוּ קִבְּלוּ אוֹתוֹ וּבְהַנְהָגַת יְהוֹשֻׁעַ הֱבִיאוּהוּ לַאֲחֻזַּת הַגּוֹיִם

avoteinu kibblu oto uvehanhagat yehoshua hevi'uhu la'achuzzat haggoyim
Which also our fathers, in their turn, brought in with Joshua when they entered on the possession of the nations,

אֲשֶׁר גֵּרְשָׁם אֱלֹהִים מִפְּנֵי אֲבוֹתֵינוּ, עַד שֶׁהִגִּיעוּ יְמֵי דָּוִד

asher geresham elohim mippenei avoteinu, ad shehiggi'u yemei david
that God thrust out before the face of our fathers, unto the days of David;

הוּא מָצָא חֵן בְּעֵינֵי אֱלֹהִים וּבִקֵּשׁ לִמְצֹא מִשְׁכָּן לֵאלֹהֵי יַעֲקֹב

hu matza chen be'einei elohim uvikkesh limtzo mishkan lelohei ya'akov
who found favor in the sight of God, and asked to find a habitation for the God of Jacob.

אָמְנָם שְׁלֹמֹה בָּנָה לוֹ בַּיִת

omnam shelomoh banah lo bayit
But Solomon built him a house.

אַךְ הָעֶלְיוֹן אֵינֶנּוּ שׁוֹכֵן בְּהֵיכָלוֹת מַעֲשֵׂי יָדַיִם, כְּמוֹ שֶׁאוֹמֵר הַנָּבִיא

ach ha'elyon einennu shochen beheichalot ma'asei yadayim, kmo she'omer hannavi
Howbeit the Most High dwelleth not in houses made with hands; as saith the prophet,

הַשָּׁמַיִם כִּסְאִי וְהָאָרֶץ הֲדֹם רַגְלָי

hashamayim kis'i veha'aretz hadom raglai
The heaven is my throne, And the earth the footstool of my feet:

אֵי־זֶה בַיִת אֲשֶׁר תִּבְנוּ־לִי, נְאֻם יהוה, וְאֵי־זֶה מָקוֹם מְנוּחָתִי

ei-zeh vayit asher tivnu-li, ne'um hashem, ve'ei-zeh makom menuchati
What manner of house will ye build me? saith the Lord: Or what is the place of my rest?

מַעֲשֵׂי הַשְּׁלִיחִים

הוּא הוֹצִיאָם בַּעֲשׂוֹתוֹ אוֹתוֹת וּמוֹפְתִים בְּאֶרֶץ מִצְרַיִם
hu hotzi'am ba'asoto otot umoftim be'eretz mitzrayim
This man led them forth, having wrought wonders and signs in Egypt,

וּבְיַם סוּף, וְכֵן גַּם בַּמִּדְבָּר בְּמֶשֶׁךְ אַרְבָּעִים שָׁנָה
uveyam suf, vechen gam bammidbar bemeshech arba'im shanah
and in the Red sea, and in the wilderness forty years.

זֶהוּ אוֹתוֹ מֹשֶׁה אֲשֶׁר אָמַר לִבְנֵי יִשְׂרָאֵל
zehu oto mosheh asher amar livnei yisra'el
This is that Moses, who said unto the children of Israel,

נָבִיא מִקֶּרֶב אֲחֵיכֶם, כָּמוֹנִי, יָקִים לָכֶם יהוה
navi mikkerev acheichem, kamoni, yakim lachem hashem
A prophet shall God raise up unto you from among your brethren, like unto me.

הוּא הָאִישׁ שֶׁהָיָה בַּקָּהָל בַּמִּדְבָּר עִם הַמַּלְאָךְ הַדּוֹבֵר אֵלָיו בְּהַר סִינַי
hu ha'ish shehayah bakkahal bammidbar im hammal'ach haddover elav behar sinai
This is he that was in the church in the wilderness with the angel that spake to him in the mount Sinai,

וְעִם אֲבוֹתֵינוּ
ve'im avoteinu
and with our fathers:

הָאִישׁ שֶׁקִּבֵּל דִּבְרֵי חַיִּים לָתֵת לָנוּ
ha'ish shekkibbel divrei chayim latet lanu
who received living oracles to give unto us:

וַאֲבוֹתֵינוּ לֹא רָצוּ לִשְׁמֹעַ בְּקוֹלוֹ כִּי אִם דָּחוּ אוֹתוֹ וּבִלְבָבָם שָׁבוּ מִצְרַיְמָה
va'avoteinu lo ratzu lishmoa bekolo ki im dachu oto uvilvavam shavu mitzrayemah
to whom our fathers would not be obedient, but thrust him from them, and turned back in their hearts unto Egypt,

בְּאָמְרָם אֶל אַהֲרֹן עֲשֵׂה-לָנוּ אֱלֹהִים אֲשֶׁר יֵלְכוּ לְפָנֵינוּ
be'omram el aharon aseh-lanu elohim asher yelchu lefaneinu
saying unto Aaron, Make us gods that shall go before us:

כִּי-זֶה מֹשֶׁה אֲשֶׁר הֶעֱלָנוּ מֵאֶרֶץ מִצְרַיִם לֹא יָדַעְנוּ מֶה-הָיָה לוֹ
ki-zeh mosheh asher he'elanu me'eretz mitzrayim lo yada'nu meh-hayah lo
for as for this Moses, who led us forth out of the land of Egypt, we know not what is become of him.

וְאָכֵן עָשׂוּ עֵגֶל בְּאוֹתָם יָמִים וְהִקְרִיבוּ זֶבַח לָאֱלִיל, וְשָׂמְחוּ בְּמַעֲשֵׂי יְדֵיהֶם
ve'achen asu egel be'otam yamim vehikrivu zevach la'elil, vesamechu bema'asei yedeihem
And they made a calf in those days, and brought a sacrifice unto the idol, and rejoiced in the works of their hands.

אָז פָּנָה הָאֱלֹהִים וּמָסַר אוֹתָם לְפֻלְחַן צְבָא הַשָּׁמַיִם כַּכָּתוּב בְּסֵפֶר הַנְּבִיאִים,
az panah ha'elohim umasar otam lefulchan tzva hashamayim kakkatuv besefer hannevi'im
But God turned, and gave them up to serve the host of heaven; as it is written in the book of the prophets,

מַעֲשֵׂי הַשְּׁלִיחִים

הַלְהָרְגֵנִי אַתָּה אֹמֵר כַּאֲשֶׁר הָרַגְתָּ אֶתְמוֹל אֶת־הַמִּצְרִי

halharegeni attah omer ka'asher haragta etmol et-hammitzri
Wouldest thou kill me, as thou killedst the Egyptian yesterday?

בִּגְלַל הַדָּבָר הַזֶּה בָּרַח מֹשֶׁה וְהָיָה לְגֵר בְּאֶרֶץ מִדְיָן וְשָׁם הוֹלִיד שְׁנֵי בָנִים

biglal haddavar hazzeh barach mosheh vehayah leger be'eretz midyan vesham holid shenei banim
And Moses fled at this saying, and became a sojourner in the land of Midian, where he begat two sons.

כַּעֲבֹר אַרְבָּעִים שָׁנָה נִרְאָה אֵלָיו מַלְאָךְ בְּמִדְבַּר הַר סִינַי,

ka'avor arba'im shanah nir'ah elav mal'ach bemidbar har sinai,
And when forty years were fulfilled, an angel appeared to him in the wilderness of mount Sinai,

בְּלַבַּת אֵשׁ מִתּוֹךְ הַסְּנֶה

belabbat esh mittoch hassneh
in a flame of fire in a bush.

רָאָה מֹשֶׁה וְתָמַהּ עַל הַמַּרְאֶה, אַךְ כְּשֶׁנִּגַּשׁ לְהַבִּיט הָיָה אֵלָיו קוֹל אֲדֹנָי

ra'ah mosheh vetamah al hammar'eh, ach keshenniggash lehabbit hayah elav kol adonai
And when Moses saw it, he wondered at the sight: and as he drew near to behold, there came a voice of the Lord,

אָנֹכִי אֱלֹהֵי אֲבוֹתֶיךָ, אֱלֹהֵי אַבְרָהָם, יִצְחָק וְיַעֲקֹב

anochi elohei avoteicha, elohei avraham, yitzchak veya'akov
I am the God of thy fathers, the God of Abraham, and of Isaac, and of Jacob.

מֹשֶׁה נֶחֱרַד וְלֹא הֵעֵז לְהַבִּיט

mosheh necherad velo he'ez lehabbit
And Moses trembled, and durst not behold.

אָמַר אֵלָיו אֱלֹהִים, שַׁל־נְעָלֶיךָ מֵעַל רַגְלֶיךָ, כִּי הַמָּקוֹם אֲשֶׁר אַתָּה עוֹמֵד עָלָיו אַדְמַת־קֹדֶשׁ הוּא

amar elav elohim, shal-ne'aleicha me'al ragleicha, ki hammakom asher attah omed alav admat-kodesh hu
And the Lord said unto him, Loose the shoes from thy feet: for the place whereon thou standest is holy ground.

רָאֹה רָאִיתִי אֶת־עֳנִי עַמִּי אֲשֶׁר בְּמִצְרָיִם וְאֶת נַאֲקָתָם שָׁמַעְתִּי

ra'oh ra'iti et-'oni ammi asher bemitzrayim ve'et na'akatam shama'ti
I have surely seen the affliction of my people that is in Egypt, and have heard their groaning,

וָאֵרֵד לְהַצִּילָם; וְעַתָּה לְכָה וְאֶשְׁלָחֲךָ מִצְרָיְמָה

va'ered lehatzilam; ve'attah lechah ve'eshlachacha mitzraymah
and I am come down to deliver them: and now come, I will send thee into Egypt.

מֹשֶׁה זֶה, אֲשֶׁר כָּפְרוּ בוֹ בְּאָמְרָם מִי שָׂמְךָ לְשַׂר וְשֹׁפֵט

mosheh zeh, asher kafru bo be'ameram mi samecha lesar veshofet
This Moses whom they refused, saying, Who made thee a ruler and a judge?

אוֹתוֹ שָׁלַח אֱלֹהִים בְּיַד הַמַּלְאָךְ הַנִּרְאֶה אֵלָיו בַּסְּנֶה, לִהְיוֹת לְשַׂר וְגוֹאֵל

oto shalach elohim beyad hammal'ach hannir'eh elav bassneh, lihyot lesar vego'el
him hath God sent to be both a ruler and a deliverer with the hand of the angel that appeared to him in the bush.

מַעֲשֵׂי הַשְּׁלִיחִים

זֶה הִתְחַכֵּם לְעַמֵּנוּ וְהֵרַע לַאֲבוֹתֵינוּ

zeh hitchakkem le'ammenu vehera la'avoteinu
The same dealt craftily with our race, and ill-treated our fathers,

בְּהַכְרִיחוֹ אוֹתָם לְהַפְקִיר אֶת עוֹלְלֵיהֶם כְּדֵי שֶׁלֹּא יִחְיוּ

behachricho otam lehafkir et oleleihem kedei shello yichyu
that they should cast out their babes to the end they might not live.

בָּעֵת הַהִיא נוֹלַד מֹשֶׁה, שֶׁהָיָה טוֹב בְּעֵינֵי אֱלֹהִים. שְׁלוֹשָׁה חֳדָשִׁים גֻּדַּל בְּבֵית אָבִיו

ba'et hahi nolad mosheh, shehayah tov be'einei elohim. sheloshah chodashim guddal beveit aviv
At which season Moses was born, and was exceeding fair; and he was nourished three months in his father's house:

וְכַאֲשֶׁר הֻפְקַר אֲסָפָה אוֹתוֹ בַּת פַּרְעֹה וְגִדְּלָה אוֹתוֹ לָהּ לְבֵן

vecha'asher hufkar asefah oto bat par'oh vegiddelah oto lah leven
and when he was cast out, Pharaoh's daughter took him up, and nourished him for her own son.

מֹשֶׁה לֻמַּד בְּכָל חָכְמַת הַמִּצְרִים וְהָיָה בֶּן־חַיִל בִּדְבָרָיו וּבְמַעֲשָׂיו

mosheh lummad bechol chachemat hammitzrim vehayah ben-chayil bidvarav uvema'asav
And Moses was instructed in all the wisdom of the Egyptians; and he was mighty in his words and works.

כְּשֶׁמָּלְאוּ לוֹ אַרְבָּעִים שָׁנָה עָלָה עַל לִבּוֹ לִפְקֹד אֶת אֶחָיו בְּנֵי יִשְׂרָאֵל

keshemmale'u lo arba'im shanah alah al libbo lifkod et echav benei yisra'el
But when he was well-nigh forty years old, it came into his heart to visit his brethren the children of Israel.

כִּרְאוֹתוֹ אִישׁ אֶחָד מֻכֶּה הֵגֵן עָלָיו וְנָקַם אֶת נִקְמָתוֹ שֶׁל הַנִּפְגָּע בַּהֲמִיתוֹ אֶת הַמִּצְרִי

kir'oto ish echad mukkeh hegen alav venakam et nikmato shel hannifga bahamito et hammitzri
And seeing one of them suffer wrong, he defended him, and avenged him that was oppressed, smiting the Egyptian:

הוּא חָשַׁב שֶׁאֶחָיו יָבִינוּ כִּי עַל־יָדָיו יִתֵּן לָהֶם אֱלֹהִים תְּשׁוּעָה

hu chashav she'echav yavinu ki al-yadav yitten lahem elohim teshu'ah
and he supposed that his brethren understood that God by his hand was giving them deliverance;

אֶלָּא שֶׁהֵם לֹא הֵבִינוּ

ella shehem lo hevinu
but they understood not.

בַּיּוֹם הַשֵּׁנִי הוֹפִיעַ בֵּינֵיהֶם כַּאֲשֶׁר רָבוּ, וּבִקֵּשׁ לְפַיֵּס אוֹתָם לְשָׁלוֹם בְּאָמְרוֹ,

bayom hasheni hofia beineihem ka'asher ravu, uvikkesh lefayes otam leshalom be'amero
And the day following he appeared unto them as they strove, and would have set them at one again, saying,

אֲנָשִׁים אַחִים אַתֶּם, לָמָּה תָּרֵעוּ זֶה לָזֶה

anashim achim attem, lammah tare'u zeh lazeh
Sirs, ye are brethren; why do ye wrong one to another?

אֲבָל הַפּוֹגֵעַ בְּרֵעֵהוּ הָדַף אוֹתוֹ וְאָמַר, מִי שָׂמְךָ לְשַׂר וְשֹׁפֵט עָלֵינוּ

aval happogea bere'ehu hadaf oto ve'amar, mi samcha lesar veshofet aleinu
But he that did his neighbor wrong thrust him away, saying, Who made thee a ruler and a judge over us?

מַעֲשֵׂי הַשְּׁלִיחִים

וְהִצִּיל אוֹתוֹ מִכָּל צָרוֹתָיו; גַּם נָתַן לוֹ חֵן וְחָכְמָה לִפְנֵי פַּרְעֹה מֶלֶךְ מִצְרַיִם
vehitzil oto mikkol tzarotav; gam natan lo chen vechochmah lifnei par'oh melech mitzrayim
and delivered him out of all his afflictions, and gave him favor and wisdom before Pharaoh king of Egypt;

וְהַלָּה מִנָּה אוֹתוֹ עַל מִצְרַיִם וְעַל כָּל בֵּיתוֹ
vehallah minnah oto al mitzrayim ve'al kol beito
and he made him governor over Egypt and all his house.

אֲבָל רָעָב בָּא עַל כָּל אֶרֶץ מִצְרַיִם וְאֶרֶץ כְּנַעַן וְגַם צָרָה גְּדוֹלָה, וַאֲבוֹתֵינוּ לֹא מָצְאוּ אֹכֶל
aval ra'av ba al kol eretz mitzrayim ve'eretz kena'an vegam tzarah gedolah, va'avoteinu lo matze'u ochel
Now there came a famine over all Egypt and Canaan, and great affliction: and our fathers found no sustenance.

כַּאֲשֶׁר שָׁמַע יַעֲקֹב כִּי יֵשׁ חִטָּה בְּמִצְרַיִם, שָׁלַח אֶת אֲבוֹתֵינוּ בַּפַּעַם הָרִאשׁוֹנָה
ka'asher shama ya'akov ki yesh chittah bemitzrayim, shalach et avoteinu bappa'am harishonah
But when Jacob heard that there was grain in Egypt, he sent forth our fathers the first time.

בַּפַּעַם הַשְּׁנִיָּה הִתְוַדַּע יוֹסֵף אֶל אֶחָיו, וּמוֹצָאוֹ שֶׁל יוֹסֵף נִתְגַּלָּה לְפַרְעֹה
bappa'am hashniyah hitvadda yosef el echav, umotza'o shel yosef nitgallah lefar'oh
And at the second time Joseph was made known to his brethren; and Joseph's race became manifest unto Pharaoh.

שָׁלַח יוֹסֵף וְקָרָא לְיַעֲקֹב אָבִיו וּלְכָל מִשְׁפַּחְתּוֹ, שִׁבְעִים וְחָמֵשׁ נְפָשׁוֹת
shalach yosef vekara leya'akov aviv ulechal mishpachto, shiv'im vechamesh nefashot
And Joseph sent, and called to him Jacob his father, and all his kindred, threescore and fifteen souls.

יַעֲקֹב יָרַד מִצְרַיְמָה וְשָׁם מֵת הוּא וַאֲבוֹתֵינוּ
ya'akov yarad mitzraymah vesham met hu va'avoteinu
And Jacob went down into Egypt; and he died, himself and our fathers;

הֵם הוּבְאוּ לִשְׁכֶם
hem huve'u lishchem
and they were carried over unto Shechem,

וְנִטְמְנוּ בַּקֶּבֶר שֶׁקָּנָה אַבְרָהָם בִּמְחִיר כֶּסֶף מִבְּנֵי חֲמוֹר אֲשֶׁר בִּשְׁכֶם
venitmenu bakkever shekkanah avraham bimchir kesef mibbenei chamor asher bishchem
and laid in the tomb that Abraham bought for a price in silver of the sons of Hamor in Shechem.

כְּשֶׁקָּרַב מוֹעֵד קִיּוּם הַהַבְטָחָה שֶׁנִּשְׁבַּע אֱלֹהִים לְאַבְרָהָם,
keshekkarav mo'ed kiyum hahavtachah shennishba elohim le'avraham,
But as the time of the promise drew nigh which God vouchsafed unto Abraham,

גָּדַל הָעָם וְהִתְרַבָּה בְּמִצְרַיִם
gadal ha'am vehitrabbah bemitzrayim
the people grew and multiplied in Egypt,

עַד שֶׁקָּם מֶלֶךְ־חָדָשׁ אֲשֶׁר לֹא־יָדַע אֶת־יוֹסֵף
ad shekkam melech-chadash asher lo-yada et-yosef
till there arose another king over Egypt, who knew not Joseph.

מַעֲשֵׂי הַשְּׁלִיחִים

וְאָמַר אֵלָיו, לֶךְ־לְךָ מֵאַרְצְךָ וּמִמּוֹלַדְתְּךָ וּבוֹא אֶל־הָאָרֶץ אֲשֶׁר אַרְאֶךָּ

ve'amar elav, lech-lecha me'artzecha umimmoladtecha uvo el-ha'aretz asher areka
and said unto him, Get thee out of thy land, and from thy kindred, and come into the land which I shall show thee.

אָז יָצָא מֵאֶרֶץ כַּשְׂדִּים וְגָר בְּחָרָן

az yatza me'eretz kasdim vegar becharan
Then came he out of the land of the Chaldæans, and dwelt in Haran:

וְאַחֲרֵי מוֹת אָבִיו הֶעֱבִיר אוֹתוֹ אֱלֹהִים מִשָּׁם אֶל הָאָרֶץ הַזֹּאת אֲשֶׁר אַתֶּם גָּרִים בָּהּ כָּעֵת

ve'acharei mot aviv he'evir oto elohim misham el ha'aretz hazzot asher attem garim bah ka'et
and from thence, when his father was dead, God removed him into this land, wherein ye now dwell:

וְלֹא נָתַן לוֹ בָּהּ נַחֲלָה, אַף לֹא מִדְרַךְ כַּף רֶגֶל

velo natan lo bah nachalah, af lo midrach kaf regel
and he gave him none inheritance in it, no, not so much as to set his foot on:

הוּא הִבְטִיחַ לָתֵת אוֹתָהּ לַאֲחֻזָּה לוֹ וּלְזַרְעוֹ אַחֲרָיו בְּטֶרֶם הָיָה לוֹ בֵּן

hu hivtiach latet otah la'achuzzah lo ulezar'o acharav beterem hayah lo ben
and he promised that he would give it to him in possession, and to his seed after him, when as yet he had no child.

כְּמוֹ כֵן אָמַר לוֹ הָאֱלֹהִים כִּי גֵר יִהְיֶה זַרְעוֹ בְּאֶרֶץ נָכְרִיָּה

kmo chen amar lo ha'elohim ki ger yihyeh zar'o be'eretz nochriyah
And God spake on this wise, that his seed should sojourn in a strange land,

וְיַעֲבִידוּ אוֹתוֹ וִיעַנּוּהוּ אַרְבַּע מֵאוֹת שָׁנָה

veya'avidu oto vi'annuhu arba me'ot shanah
and that they should bring them into bondage, and treat them ill, four hundred years.

וְגַם אֶת־הַגּוֹי אֲשֶׁר יַעֲבֹדוּ דָן אָנֹכִי, אָמַר אֱלֹהִים

vegam et-haggoy asher ya'avodu dan anochi, amar elohim
And the nation to which they shall be in bondage will I judge, said God:

וְאַחֲרֵי־כֵן יֵצְאוּ וְיַעַבְדוּנִי בַּמָּקוֹם הַזֶּה

ve'acharei-chen yetze'u veya'avduni bammakom hazzeh
and after that shall they come forth, and serve me in this place.

גַּם נָתַן לוֹ אֶת בְּרִית הַמִּילָה וּכְשֶׁהוֹלִיד אֶת יִצְחָק מָל אוֹתוֹ בַּיּוֹם הַשְּׁמִינִי

gam natan lo et berit hammilah uchesheholid et yitzchak mal oto bayom hashemini
And he gave him the covenant of circumcision: and so Abraham begat Isaac, and circumcised him the eighth day;

וְיִצְחָק אֶת יַעֲקֹב, וְיַעֲקֹב אֶת שְׁנֵים־עָשָׂר הָאָבוֹת

veyitzchak et ya'akov, veya'akov et sheneim-'asar ha'avot
and Isaac begat Jacob, and Jacob the twelve patriarchs.

הָאָבוֹת קִנְּאוּ בְּיוֹסֵף וּמָכְרוּ אוֹתוֹ מִצְרַיְמָה, אַךְ אֱלֹהִים הָיָה אִתּוֹ

ha'avot kinne'u beyosef umacheru oto mitzraymah, ach elohim hayah itto
And the patriarchs, moved with jealousy against Joseph, sold him into Egypt: and God was with him,

מַעֲשֵׂי הַשְּׁלִיחִים

הֵם הִדִּיחוּ אֲנָשִׁים לוֹמַר, שָׁמַעְנוּ אוֹתוֹ מְדַבֵּר דִּבְרֵי נְאָצָה עַל מֹשֶׁה וְעַל אֱלֹהִים

hem hiddichu anashim lomar, shama'nu oto medabber divrei ne'atzah al mosheh ve'al elohim
Then they suborned men, who said, We have heard him speak blasphemous words against Moses, and against God.

וְהֵסִיתוּ אֶת הָעָם וְאֶת הַזְּקֵנִים וְהַסּוֹפְרִים

vehesitu et ha'am ve'et hazzkenim vehassoferim
And they stirred up the people, and the elders, and the scribes,

קָמוּ עָלָיו וְתָפְסוּ אוֹתוֹ וֶהֱבִיאוּהוּ אֶל הַסַּנְהֶדְרִין

kamu alav vetafsu oto vehevi'uhu el hassanhedrin
and came upon him, and seized him, and brought him into the council,

שָׁם הֶעֱמִידוּ עֵדֵי שֶׁקֶר וְהַלָּלוּ אָמְרוּ

sham he'emidu edei sheker vehallalu ameru
and set up false witnesses, who said,

הָאִישׁ הַזֶּה אֵינֶנּוּ חָדֵל לְדַבֵּר דְּבָרִים נֶגֶד הַמָּקוֹם הַקָּדוֹשׁ הַזֶּה וְנֶגֶד הַתּוֹרָה

ha'ish hazzeh einennu chadel ledabber dvarim neged hammakom hakkadosh hazzeh veneged hattorah
This man ceaseth not to speak words against this holy place, and the law:

כִּי שָׁמַעְנוּ אוֹתוֹ אוֹמֵר שֶׁיֵּשׁוּעַ מִנַּצְרַת הַזֶּה יַהֲרֹס אֶת הַמָּקוֹם הַזֶּה

ki shama'nu oto omer sheyeshua minnatzerat hazzeh yaharos et hammakom hazzeh
for we have heard him say, that this Jesus of Nazareth shall destroy this place,

וִישַׁנֶּה אֶת הַחֻקִּים שֶׁמָּסַר לָנוּ מֹשֶׁה

viyshanneh et hachukkim shemmasar lanu mosheh
and shall change the customs which Moses delivered unto us.

הִבִּיטוּ בּוֹ כָּל הַיּוֹשְׁבִים בַּסַּנְהֶדְרִין וְרָאוּ אֶת פָּנָיו כִּפְנֵי מַלְאָךְ

hibbitu bo kol hayoshevim bassanhedrin vera'u et panav kifnei mal'ach
And all that sat in the council, fastening their eyes on him, saw his face as it had been the face of an angel.

ז

שָׁאַל הַכֹּהֵן הַגָּדוֹל: הַאִם נְכוֹנִים הַדְּבָרִים הָאֵלֶּה

sha'al hakkohen haggadol: ha'im nechonim haddevarim ha'elleh
And the high priest said, Are these things so?

הֵשִׁיב סְטֶפָנוֹס וְאָמַר: אֲנָשִׁים, אַחִים וְאָבוֹת, שִׁמְעוּ נָא

heshiv setefanos ve'amar: anashim, achim ve'avot, shim'u na
And he said, Brethren and fathers, hearken:

אֱלֹהֵי הַכָּבוֹד נִרְאָה אֶל אַבְרָהָם אָבִינוּ בִּהְיוֹתוֹ בַּאֲרַם נַהֲרַיִם, לִפְנֵי שֶׁגָּר בְּחָרָן

elohei hakkavod nir'ah el avraham avinu bihyoto ba'aram naharayim, lifnei sheggar becharan
The God of glory appeared unto our father Abraham, when he was in Mesopotamia, before he dwelt in Haran,

מַעֲשֵׂי הַשְּׁלִיחִים

לָכֵן, אַחִים, בַּחֲרוּ מִבֵּינֵיכֶם שִׁבְעָה אֲנָשִׁים בַּעֲלֵי שֵׁם טוֹב
lachen, achim, bacharu mibbeineichem shiv'ah anashim ba'alei shem tov
Look ye out therefore, brethren, from among you seven men of good report,

מְלֵאֵי רוּחַ וְחָכְמָה, וְנַפְקִיד אוֹתָם עַל הָעִנְיָן הַזֶּה
mele'ei ruach vechochmah, venafkid otam al ha'inyan hazzeh
full of the Spirit and of wisdom, whom we may appoint over this business.

וַאֲנַחְנוּ נַתְמִיד בַּתְּפִלָּה וּבְשֵׁרוּת דְּבַר אֱלֹהִים
va'anachnu natmid battefillah uvesherut devar elohim
But we will continue stedfastly in prayer, and in the ministry of the word.

נִתְקַבֵּל הַדָּבָר בְּעֵינֵי כָּל הַקָּהָל וּבָחֲרוּ אֶת סְטֶפָנוֹס, אִישׁ מָלֵא אֱמוּנָה וְרוּחַ הַקֹּדֶשׁ
nitkabbel haddavar be'einei kol hakkahal uvacharu et setefanos, ish malei emunah veruach hakkodesh
And the saying pleased the whole multitude: and they chose Stephen, a man full of faith and of the Holy Spirit,

וְאֶת פִילִיפּוֹס, אֶת פְּרוֹכוֹרוֹס וְאֶת נִיקָנוֹר, אֶת טִימוֹן וְאֶת פַּרְמְנָס וְאֶת נִיקוֹלָאוֹס, שֶׁהָיָה גֵּר מֵאַנְטִיוֹכְיָה
ve'et filipos, et prochoros ve'et nikanor, et timon ve'et parmenas ve'et nikola'os, shehayah ger me'antiyocheyah
and Philip, and Prochorus, and Nicanor, and Timon, and Parmenas, and Nicolaus a proselyte of Antioch;

הֶעֱמִידוּ אוֹתָם לִפְנֵי הַשְּׁלִיחִים, הִתְפַּלְּלוּ וְסָמְכוּ יָדַיִם עֲלֵיהֶם
he'emidu otam lifnei hashlichim, hitpallelu vesamechu yadayim aleihem
whom they set before the apostles: and when they had prayed, they laid their hands upon them.

דְּבַר אֱלֹהִים שִׂגְשֵׂג וּמִסְפַּר הַתַּלְמִידִים בִּירוּשָׁלַיִם גָּדַל מְאֹד
devar elohim sigseg umispar hattalmidim biyerushalayim gadal me'od
And the word of God increased; and the number of the disciples multiplied in Jerusalem exceedingly;

וְגַם הָמוֹן רַב מִן הַכֹּהֲנִים נִשְׁמְעוּ לָאֱמוּנָה
vegam hamon rav min hakkohanim nishme'u la'emunah
and a great company of the priests were obedient to the faith.

סְטֶפָנוֹס, שֶׁהָיָה מָלֵא חֶסֶד וּגְבוּרָה, עָשָׂה אוֹתוֹת וּמוֹפְתִים גְּדוֹלִים בְּקֶרֶב הָעָם
setefanos, shehayah malei chesed ugvurah, asah otot umofetim gedolim bekerev ha'am
And Stephen, full of grace and power, wrought great wonders and signs among the people.

קָמוּ אֲנָשִׁים מִבֵּית הַכְּנֶסֶת שֶׁל הַמְשֻׁחְרָרִים - כָּךְ הָיָה מְכֻנֶּה
kamu anashim mibbeit hakkeneset shel hammeshuchrarim - kach hayah mechunneh
But there arose certain of them that were of the synagogue called the synagogue of the Libertines,

וְגַם אֲנָשִׁים מִקִּירֶנְיָה וַאֲלֶכְּסַנְדְּרִיָּה וּמִקִּלִיקְיָה וְאַסְיָה, וְהִתְוַכְּחוּ עִם סְטֶפָנוֹס
vegam anashim mikkirenyah va'alekkesanderiyah umikkilikeyah ve'asyah, vehitvakkechu im setefanos
and of the Cyrenians, and of the Alexandrians, and of them of Cilicia and Asia, disputing with Stephen.

אַךְ לֹא יָכְלוּ לַעֲמֹד נֶגֶד הַחָכְמָה וְהָרוּחַ אֲשֶׁר בְּעֶזְרָתָן דִּבֵּר
ach lo yachelu la'amod neged hachochmah veharuach asher be'ezratan dibber
And they were not able to withstand the wisdom and the Spirit by which he spake.

מַעֲשֵׂי הַשְּׁלִיחִים

אֲבָל אִם מֵאֵת אֱלֹהִים הִיא, לֹא תוּכְלוּ לְהָפֵר אוֹתָהּ פֶּן תִּמָּצְאוּ נִלְחָמִים בֵּאלֹהִים

aval im me'et elohim hi, lo tochlu lehafer otah pen timmatze'u nilchamim be'elohim
but if it is of God, ye will not be able to overthrow them; lest haply ye be found even to be fighting against God.

הֵם שָׁמְעוּ בְּקוֹלוֹ וְקָרְאוּ לַשְּׁלִיחִים

hem shame'u bekolo vekare'u lashlichim
And to him they agreed: and when they had called the apostles unto them,

לְאַחַר שֶׁהִלְקוּ אוֹתָם וְצִוּוּ עֲלֵיהֶם שֶׁלֹא יְדַבְּרוּ בְּשֵׁם יֵשׁוּעַ, שִׁחְרְרוּ אוֹתָם

le'achar shehilku otam vetzivvu aleihem shello yedabberu beshem yeshua', shichreru otam
they beat them and charged them not to speak in the name of Jesus, and let them go.

יָצְאוּ הַשְּׁלִיחִים מִלִּפְנֵי הַסַּנְהֶדְרִין

yatze'u hashelichim millifnei hassanhedrin
They therefore departed from the presence of the council,

שְׂמֵחִים עַל שֶׁזָּכוּ לִסְבֹּל חֶרְפָּה לְמַעַן הַשֵּׁם

semechim al shezzachu lisbol cherpah lema'an hashem
rejoicing that they were counted worthy to suffer dishonor for the Name.

וְיוֹם יוֹם, בְּבֵית הַמִּקְדָּשׁ וּבַבָּתִּים, לֹא חָדְלוּ לְלַמֵּד וּלְבַשֵּׂר עַל הַמָּשִׁיחַ יֵשׁוּעַ

veyom yom, veveit hammikdash uvabbattim, lo chadelu lelammed ulevasser al hammashiach yeshua'
And every day, in the temple and at home, they ceased not to teach and to preach Jesus as the Christ.

I

בַּיָּמִים הָהֵם, כְּשֶׁגָּדַל מִסְפַּר הַתַּלְמִידִים

bayamim hahem, kesheggadal mispar hattalmidim
Now in these days, when the number of the disciples was multiplying,

הֵחֵלּוּ הַיְּהוּדִים דּוֹבְרֵי הַיְּוָנִית לְהִתְלוֹנֵן עַל דּוֹבְרֵי הָעִבְרִית

hechellu hayehudim doverei hayevanit lehitlonen al doverei ha'ivrit
there arose a murmuring of the Grecian Jews against the Hebrews,

עַל שֶׁהִזְנִיחוּ אֶת אַלְמְנוֹתֵיהֶם בַּחֲלֻקַּת הַסַּעַד הַיּוֹמִית

al shehiznichu et almenoteihem bachalukkat hassa'ad hayomit
because their widows were neglected in the daily ministration.

קָרְאוּ שְׁנֵים־עָשָׂר הַשְּׁלִיחִים אֶת הֲמוֹן הַתַּלְמִידִים וְאָמְרוּ

kare'u sheneim-'asar hashelichim et hamon hattalmidim ve'ameru
And the twelve called the multitude of the disciples unto them, and said,

לֹא רָצוּי שֶׁאֲנַחְנוּ נַעֲזֹב אֶת דְּבַר אֱלֹהִים וּנְשָׁרֵת בַּשֻּׁלְחָנוֹת

lo ratzui she'anachnu na'azov et devar elohim unesharet bashulchanot
It is not fit that we should forsake the word of God, and serve tables.

מַעֲשֵׂי הַשְּׁלִיחִים

אֲנַחְנוּ עֵדֵי הַדְּבָרִים הָאֵלֶּה, וְגַם רוּחַ הַקֹּדֶשׁ אֲשֶׁר נָתַן הָאֱלֹהִים לַשּׁוֹמְעִים בְּקוֹלוֹ
anachnu edei haddevarim ha'elleh, vegam ruach hakkodesh asher natan ha'elohim lashome'im bekolo
And we are witnesses of these things; and so is the Holy Spirit, whom God hath given to them that obey him.

כְּשָׁמְעָם אֶת זֹאת הִתְרַתְּחוּ וְהֶחְלִיטוּ לַהֲרֹג אוֹתָם
keshom'am et zot hitrattchu vehechlitu laharog otam
But they, when they heard this, were cut to the heart, and were minded to slay them.

אֲבָל אֶחָד מִן הַפְּרוּשִׁים בַּסַּנְהֶדְרִין, גַּמְלִיאֵל שְׁמוֹ, מוֹרֵה-תּוֹרָה מְכֻבָּד בְּעֵינֵי כָּל הָעָם,
aval echad min happerushim bassanhedrin, gamli'el shemo, moreh-torah mechubbad be'einei kol ha'am,
But there stood up one in the council, a Pharisee, named Gamaliel, a doctor of the law, had in honor of all the people,

קָם וְצִוָּה לְהוֹצִיא אֶת הַשְּׁלִיחִים הַחוּצָה לִזְמַן-מָה
kam vetzivvah lehotzi et hashelichim hachutzah lizman-mah
and commanded to put the men forth a little while.

אָמַר לָהֶם: אַנְשֵׁי יִשְׂרָאֵל, הִזָּהֲרוּ לָכֶם בַּמֶּה שֶׁאַתֶּם מִתְכַּוְּנִים לַעֲשׂוֹת לָאֲנָשִׁים הָאֵלֶּה
amar lahem: anshei yisra'el, hizzaharu lachem bemah she'attem mitkavvenim la'asot la'anashim ha'elleh
And he said unto them, Ye men of Israel, take heed to yourselves as touching these men, what ye are about to do.

כִּי לִפְנֵי הַיָּמִים הָאֵלֶּה קָם תּוֹדָס, שֶׁהִתְיַמֵּר לִהְיוֹת מִישֶׁהוּ,
ki lifnei hayamim ha'elleh kam todas, shehityammer lihyot mishehu
For before these days rose up Theudas, giving himself out to be somebody;

וְנִסְפְּחוּ אֵלָיו כְּאַרְבַּע מֵאוֹת אִישׁ
venispechu elav ke'arba me'ot ish
to whom a number of men, about four hundred, joined themselves:

הוּא נֶהֱרַג וְכָל אֲשֶׁר שָׁמְעוּ בְּקוֹלוֹ נָפוֹצוּ וְהָיוּ לְאַיִן
hu neherag vechol asher sham'u bekolo nafotzu vehayu le'ayin
who was slain; and all, as many as obeyed him, were dispersed, and came to nought.

אַחֲרָיו קָם יְהוּדָה הַגְּלִילִי בִּימֵי מִפְקַד הַתּוֹשָׁבִים, וּמָשַׁךְ אַחֲרָיו אֲנָשִׁים
acharav kam yehudah haggelili bimei mifkad hattoshavim, umashach acharav anashim
After this man rose up Judas of Galilee in the days of the enrolment, and drew away some of the people after him:

הַלָּה נֶהֱרַג וְכָל הַמְצַיְּתִים לוֹ נִתְפַּזְּרוּ
hallah neherag vechol hamtzayetim lo nitpazzru
he also perished; and all, as many as obeyed him, were scattered abroad.

וְעַתָּה אֲנִי אוֹמֵר לָכֶם, חִדְלוּ מִן הָאֲנָשִׁים הָאֵלֶּה וְהַנִּיחוּ לָהֶם
ve'attah ani omer lachem, chidlu min ha'anashim ha'elleh vehannichu lahem
And now I say unto you, Refrain from these men, and let them alone:

כִּי הָעֵצָה אוֹ הַפְּעֻלָּה הַזֹּאת תּוּפַר -אִם מֵאֵת בְּנֵי אָדָם הִיא
ki ha'etzah o happe'ullah hazzot tufar -'im me'et benei adam hi
for if this counsel or this work be of men, it will be overthrown:

מַעֲשֵׂי הַשְּׁלִיחִים

לִשְׁמֹעַ הַדְּבָרִים הָאֵלֶּה נָבוֹכוּ נְגִיד בֵּית הַמִּקְדָּשׁ וְרָאשֵׁי הַכֹּהֲנִים
leshema haddevarim ha'elleh navochu negid beit hammikdash verashei hakkohanim
Now when the captain of the temple and the chief priests heard these words,

תְּמֵהִים הָיוּ עַל פֵּשֶׁר הַדָּבָר
temehim hayu al pesher haddavar
they were much perplexed concerning them whereunto this would grow.

אָז בָּא מִישֶׁהוּ וְהוֹדִיעַ לָהֶם
az ba mishehu vehodia lahem
And there came one and told them,

הִנֵּה הָאֲנָשִׁים אֲשֶׁר שַׂמְתֶּם בַּמַּאֲסָר עוֹמְדִים בְּבֵית הַמִּקְדָּשׁ וּמְלַמְּדִים אֶת הָעָם
hinneh ha'anashim asher samtem bamma'asar omedim beveit hammikdash umelammedim et ha'am
Behold, the men whom ye put in the prison are in the temple standing and teaching the people.

הָלַךְ הַנָּגִיד עִם הַמְשָׁרְתִים וְהֵבִיאוּ אוֹתָם, אַךְ לֹא בְּכֹחַ
halach hannagid im hamsharetim vehevi'u otam, ach lo bechoach
Then went the captain with the officers, and brought them, but without violence;

כִּי פָחֲדוּ מִן הָעָם פֶּן יִרְגְּמוּ אוֹתָם
ki pachadu min ha'am pen yirgemu otam
for they feared the people, lest they should be stoned.

הֵבִיאוּ אוֹתָם וְהֶעֱמִידוּם לִפְנֵי הַסַּנְהֶדְרִין. שָׁאַל אוֹתָם הַכֹּהֵן הַגָּדוֹל
hevi'u otam vehe'emidum lifnei hassanhedrin. sha'al otam hakkohen haggadol
And when they had brought them, they set them before the council. And the high priest asked them,

הַאִם לֹא צִוִּינוּ עֲלֵיכֶם בְּתֹקֶף שֶׁלֹּא לְלַמֵּד בַּשֵּׁם הַזֶּה
ha'im lo tzivvinu aleichem betokef shello lelammed bashem hazzeh
saying, We strictly charged you not to teach in this name:

וְהִנֵּה מִלֵּאתֶם אֶת יְרוּשָׁלַיִם בְּתוֹרַתְכֶם וְאַתֶּם מִתְכַּוְּנִים לְהָבִיא עָלֵינוּ אֶת דַּם הָאִישׁ הַזֶּה
vehinneh milletem et yerushalayim betoratchem ve'attem mitkavvnim lehavi aleinu et dam ha'ish hazzeh
and behold, ye have filled Jerusalem with your teaching, and intend to bring this man's blood upon us.

הֵשִׁיב כֵּיפָא עִם הַשְּׁלִיחִים וְאָמַר: לֵאלֹהִים צָרִיךְ לְהִשָּׁמַע יוֹתֵר מֵאֲשֶׁר לִבְנֵי אָדָם
heshiv keifa im hashelichim ve'amar: le'elohim tzarich lehishama yoter me'asher livnei adam
But Peter and the apostles answered and said, We must obey God rather than men.

אֱלֹהֵי אֲבוֹתֵינוּ הֵקִים אֶת יֵשׁוּעַ אֲשֶׁר הֲרַגְתֶּם בְּהוֹקָעָה עַל עֵץ
elohei avoteinu hekim et yeshua asher haragtem behoka'ah al etz
The God of our fathers raised up Jesus, whom ye slew, hanging him on a tree.

אֶת זֶה הֵרִים אֱלֹהִים בִּימִינוֹ לִהְיוֹת שַׂר וּמוֹשִׁיעַ, לָתֵת לְיִשְׂרָאֵל תְּשׁוּבָה וּסְלִיחַת חֲטָאִים
et zeh herim elohim biymino lihyot sar umoshia', latet leyisra'el tshuvah uslichat chata'im
Him did God exalt with his right hand to be a Prince and a Saviour, to give repentance to Israel, and remission of sins.

מַעֲשֵׂי הַשְּׁלִיחִים

הַכֹּהֵן הַגָּדוֹל וְכָל אֲנָשָׁיו, אַנְשֵׁי כַּת הַצְּדוֹקִים
hakkohen haggadol vechol anashav, anshei kat hatzedokim
But the high priest rose up, and all they that were with him (which is the sect of the Sadducees),

נִתְמַלְאוּ קִנְאָה
nitmalle'u kin'ah
and they were filled with jealousy,

הֵם קָמוּ תָּפְסוּ אֶת הַשְּׁלִיחִים וְשָׂמוּ אוֹתָם בַּכֶּלֶא הָעִירוֹנִי
hem kamu, tafsu et hashelichim vesamu otam bakkelei ha'ironi
and laid hands on the apostles, and put them in public ward.

אֶלָּא שֶׁמַּלְאַךְ יהוה פָּתַח בַּלַּיְלָה אֶת דַּלְתוֹת בֵּית הַכֶּלֶא וְהוֹצִיאָם בְּאָמְרוֹ
ella shemmal'ach hashem patach ballaylah et daltot beit hakkelei vehotzi'am be'omro
But an angel of the Lord by night opened the prison doors, and brought them out, and said,

לְכוּ וְהִתְיַצְּבוּ בַּמִּקְדָּשׁ וְדַבְּרוּ אֶל הָעָם אֶת כָּל דִּבְרֵי הַחַיִּים הָאֵלֶּה
lechu vehityatzevu bammikdash vedabberu el ha'am et kol divrei hachayim ha'elleh
Go ye, and stand and speak in the temple to the people all the words of this Life.

הֵם שָׁמְעוּ וְעִם שַׁחַר נִכְנְסוּ לְבֵית הַמִּקְדָּשׁ וְהֵחֵלּוּ לְלַמֵּד.
hem shame'u ve'im shachar nichnesu leveit hammikdash vehechellu lelammed
And when they heard this, they entered into the temple about daybreak, and taught.

בָּא הַכֹּהֵן הַגָּדוֹל וַאֲנָשָׁיו וְכִנְּסוּ אֶת הַסַּנְהֶדְרִין
ba hakkohen haggadol va'anashav vechinnsu et hassanhedrin
But the high priest came, and they that were with him, and called the council together,

וְכָל מוֹעֶצֶת זִקְנֵי בְּנֵי יִשְׂרָאֵל
vechol mo'etzet ziknei benei yisra'el
and all the senate of the children of Israel,

הֵם שָׁלְחוּ אֶל הַכֶּלֶא לְהָבִיא אוֹתָם
hem shalechu el hakkelei lehavi otam
and sent to the prison-house to have them brought.

אַךְ כְּשֶׁבָּאוּ הַמְשָׁרְתִים לֹא מָצְאוּ אוֹתָם בַּכֶּלֶא. חָזְרוּ וְהוֹדִיעוּ
ach keshebba'u hamsharetim lo matze'u otam bakkele. chazeru vehodi'u
But the officers that came found them not in the prison; and they returned, and told,

מָצָאנוּ אֶת בֵּית הַסֹּהַר סָגוּר בְּאֹפֶן בָּטוּחַ לַחֲלוּטִין וְהַשּׁוֹמְרִים נִצָּבִים לְיַד הַדְּלָתוֹת
matzanu et beit hassohar sagur be'ofen batuach lachalutin vehashomerim nitzavim leyad haddelatot
saying, The prison-house we found shut in all safety, and the keepers standing at the doors:

אֲבָל כְּשֶׁפָּתַחְנוּ לֹא מָצָאנוּ אִישׁ בִּפְנִים
aval kesheppatachnu lo matzanu ish bifnim
but when we had opened, we found no man within.

מַעֲשֵׂי הַשְּׁלִיחִים

הִנֵּה בַּפֶּתַח רַגְלֵי הַקּוֹבְרִים אֶת בַּעֲלֵךְ וְהֵם יִשְׂאוּ אוֹתָךְ הַחוּצָה

hinneh bappetach raglei hakkoverim et ba'alech vehem yisseu otach hachutzah
behold, the feet of them that have buried thy husband are at the door, and they shall carry thee out.

מִיָּד נָפְלָה לְרַגְלָיו וְנָפְחָה אֶת רוּחָהּ

miyad nafelah leraglav venafechah et ruchah
And she fell down immediately at his feet, and gave up the ghost:

כְּשֶׁנִּכְנְסוּ הַבַּחוּרִים מְצָאוּהָ מֵתָה. הֵם נָשְׂאוּ אוֹתָהּ הַחוּצָה וְקָבְרוּ אוֹתָהּ עַל־יַד בַּעֲלָהּ

kshennichnesu habbachurim metza'uha metah. hem nase'u otah hachutzah vekavru otah al-yad ba'alah
and the young men came in and found her dead, and they carried her out and buried her by her husband.

פַּחַד גָּדוֹל נָפַל עַל כָּל הַקְּהִלָּה וְעַל כָּל הַשּׁוֹמְעִים אֶת הַדְּבָרִים הָאֵלֶּה

pachad gadol nafal al kol hakkehillah ve'al kol hashome'im et haddevarim ha'elleh
And great fear came upon the whole church, and upon all that heard these things.

אוֹתוֹת וּמוֹפְתִים רַבִּים עָשׂוּ הַשְּׁלִיחִים בְּקֶרֶב הָעָם

otot umofetim rabbim asu hashelichim bekerev ha'am
And by the hands of the apostles were many signs and wonders wrought among the people:

וְהַכֹּל נֶאֶסְפוּ לֵב אֶחָד בְּאוּלָם שְׁלֹמֹה

vehakkol ne'esfu lev echad be'ulam shlomoh
and they were all with one accord in Solomon's porch.

מִן הָאֲחֵרִים לֹא הֵעֵז אִישׁ לְהִצְטָרֵף אֲלֵיהֶם, אַךְ הָעָם הוֹקִיר אוֹתָם

min ha'acherim lo he'ez ish lehitztaref aleihem, ach ha'am hokir otam
But of the rest durst no man join himself to them: howbeit the people magnified them;

וְאָמְנָם נִסְפְּחוּ אֶל הָאָדוֹן עוֹד מַאֲמִינִים, גְּבָרִים וְנָשִׁים רַבִּים מְאֹד

ve'omnam nispechu el ha'adon od ma'aminim, gvarim venashim rabbim me'od
and believers were the more added to the Lord, multitudes both of men and women:

עַד כִּי נָשְׂאוּ אֶת הַחוֹלִים אֶל הָרְחוֹבוֹת וְשָׂמוּ אוֹתָם עַל מִטּוֹת וּמַצָּעִים

ad ki nase'u et hacholim el harechovot vesamu otam al mittot umatza'im
insomuch that they even carried out the sick into the streets, and laid them on beds and couches,

כְּדֵי שֶׁבְּבוֹא כֵּיפָא אֲפִלּוּ רַק צִלּוֹ יָצֵל עַל כַּמָּה מֵהֶם

kedei shebbevo keifa afillu rak tzillo yatzel al kammah mehem
that, as Peter came by, at the least his shadow might overshadow some one of them.

גַּם הֲמוֹן הָעָם מִן הֶעָרִים הַסְּמוּכוֹת לִירוּשָׁלַיִם נִקְבְּצוּ

gam hamon ha'am min he'arim hassmuchot liyerushalayim nikbetzu
And there also came together the multitude from the cities round about Jerusalem,

כְּשֶׁהֵם נוֹשְׂאִים חוֹלִים וּמְעֻנִּים עַל־יְדֵי רוּחוֹת טְמֵאוֹת, וְכֻלָּם נִרְפְּאוּ

kshehem nose'im cholim ume'unnim al-yedei ruchot teme'ot, vechullam nirpe'u
bringing sick folk, and them that were vexed with unclean spirits: and they were healed every one.

מַעֲשֵׂי הַשְּׁלִיחִים

בִּידִיעַת אִשְׁתּוֹ הוּא נָטַל לְעַצְמוֹ חֵלֶק מִן הַכֶּסֶף
biydi'at ishto hu natal le'atzmo chelek min hakkesef
and kept back part of the price, his wife also being privy to it,

וְאַחֲרֵי כֵן הֵבִיא חֵלֶק מְסֻיָּם וְהִנִּיחוֹ לְרַגְלֵי הַשְּׁלִיחִים
ve'acharei chen hevi chelek mesuyam vehinnicho leraglei hashelichim
and brought a certain part, and laid it at the apostles' feet.

אָמַר לוֹ כֵּיפָא
amar lo keifa
But Peter said,

חֲנַנְיָה, לָמָּה זֶה מִלֵּא הַשָּׂטָן אֶת לִבְּךָ לְשַׁקֵּר לְרוּחַ הַקֹּדֶשׁ וְלִטֹּל לְעַצְמְךָ מִמְּחִיר הַשָּׂדֶה
chananyah, lammah zeh millei hashotan et libbcha leshakker leruach hakkodesh velittol le'atzmecha mimmchir hassade
Ananias, why hath Satan filled thy heart to lie to the Holy Spirit, and to keep back part of the price of the land?

הֲרֵי כְּשֶׁעָמַד בִּרְשׁוּתְךָ - שֶׁלְּךָ הָיָה, וְאַחֲרֵי שֶׁנִּמְכַּר עָמְדָה תְּמוּרָתוֹ בִּרְשׁוּתְךָ
harei keshe'amad birshutecha - shellcha hayah, ve'acharei shennimkar amedah temurato birshutecha
While it remained, did it not remain thine own? and after it was sold, was it not in thy power?

לָמָּה עָלָה עַל לִבְּךָ מַעֲשֶׂה זֶה? לֹא לִבְנֵי אָדָם שִׁקַּרְתָּ כִּי אִם לֵאלֹהִים
lammah alah al libbecha ma'aseh zeh? lo livnei adam shikkarta ki im lelohim
How is it that thou hast conceived this thing in thy heart? thou hast not lied unto men, but unto God.

כְּשֶׁשָּׁמַע חֲנַנְיָה אֶת הַדְּבָרִים הָאֵלֶּה נָפַל וְנָפַח אֶת רוּחוֹ, וּפַחַד גָּדוֹל נָפַל עַל כָּל הַשּׁוֹמְעִים
kesheshama chananyah et haddevarim ha'elleh nafal venafach et rucho, ufachad gadol nafal al kol hashome'im
And Ananias hearing these words fell down and gave up the ghost: and great fear came upon all that heard it.

קָמוּ הַצְּעִירִים, עָטְפוּ אוֹתוֹ, נְשָׂאוּהוּ הַחוּצָה וְקָבְרוּ אוֹתוֹ
kamu hatze'irim, atefu oto, nesa'uhu hachutzah vekaveru oto
And the young men arose and wrapped him round, and they carried him out and buried him.

כְּשָׁלוֹשׁ שָׁעוֹת לְאַחַר מִכֵּן נִכְנְסָה אִשְׁתּוֹ וְהִיא אֵינֶנָּה יוֹדַעַת מַה שֶּׁאֵרַע
keshalosh sha'ot le'achar mikken nichnesah ishto vehi einennah yoda'at mah she'era
And it was about the space of three hours after, when his wife, not knowing what was done, came in.

פָּנָה אֵלֶיהָ כֵּיפָא וְאָמַר: הַגִּידִי לִי, הַאִם בַּמְּחִיר הַזֶּה מְכַרְתֶּם אֶת הַשָּׂדֶה
panah eleiha keifa ve'amar: haggidi li, ha'im bammechir hazzeh mechartem et hassadeh
And Peter answered unto her, Tell me whether ye sold the land for so much.

אָמְרָה: כֵּן, בַּמְּחִיר הַזֶּה
amerah: ken, bammechir hazzeh
And she said, Yea, for so much.

אָמַר לָהּ כֵּיפָא: לָמָּה הִתְאַחַדְתֶּם שְׁנֵיכֶם לְנַסּוֹת אֶת רוּחַ אֱלֹהִים
amar lah keifa: lammah hit'achadtem sheneichem lenassot et ruach elohim
But Peter said unto her, How is it that ye have agreed together to try the Spirit of the Lord?

מַעֲשֵׂי הַשְּׁלִיחִים

קְהַל הַמַּאֲמִינִים הָיָה לֵב אֶחָד וְנֶפֶשׁ אַחַת

kehal hamma'aminim hayah lev echad venefesh achat

And the multitude of them that believed were of one heart and soul:

אִישׁ מֵהֶם לֹא אָמַר עַל דָּבָר מִקִּנְיָנָיו כִּי שֶׁלּוֹ הוּא, אֶלָּא שֻׁתָּפִים הָיוּ בַּכֹּל

ish mehem lo amar al davar mikkinyanav ki shello hu, ella shuttafim hayu bakkol

and not one of them said that aught of the things which he possessed was his own; but they had all things common.

הַשְּׁלִיחִים הֵעִידוּ בְּכֹחַ רַב עַל תְּחִיַּת הָאָדוֹן יֵשׁוּעַ

hashelichim he'idu bechoach rav al techiyat ha'adon yeshua

And with great power gave the apostles their witness of the resurrection of the Lord Jesus:

וְחֶסֶד רַב הָיָה עַל כֻּלָּם

vechesed rav hayah al kullam

and great grace was upon them all.

גַּם לֹא הָיָה בָּהֶם אִישׁ שָׁרוּי בְּמַחְסוֹר

gam lo hayah bahem ish sharui bemachsor

For neither was there among them any that lacked:

כִּי כָּל בַּעֲלֵי הַשָּׂדוֹת וּבַעֲלֵי הַבָּתִּים מָכְרוּ אֶת נִכְסֵיהֶם וְהֵבִיאוּ אֶת כֶּסֶף מְחִירָם

ki kol ba'alei hashodot uva'alei habbattim macheru et nichseihem vehevi'u et kesef mechiram

for as many as were possessors of lands or houses sold them, and brought the prices of the things that were sold,

הֵם הִנִּיחוּהוּ לְרַגְלֵי הַשְּׁלִיחִים וּלְכָל אִישׁ נִתַּן כְּפִי צָרְכּוֹ

hem hinnichuhu leraglei hashelichim ulechal ish nittan kefi tzorko

and laid them at the apostles' feet: and distribution was made unto each, according as any one had need.

וְיוֹסֵף, אֲשֶׁר הַשְּׁלִיחִים כִּנּוּהוּ בַּר-נַבָּא

veyosef, asher hashelichim kinnuhu bar-nabba

And Joseph, who by the apostles was surnamed Barnabas

כְּלוֹמַר בֶּן הַנֶּחָמָה, אִישׁ לֵוִי יְלִיד קַפְרִיסִין

kelomar ben hannechamah, ish levi yelid kafrisin

(which is, being interpreted, Son of exhortation), a Levite, a man of Cyprus by race,

מָכַר אֶת שָׂדֵהוּ וְגַם הוּא הֵבִיא אֶת הַכֶּסֶף וְהִנִּיחוֹ לְרַגְלֵי הַשְּׁלִיחִים

machar et sadehu vegam hu hevi et hakkesef vehinnicho leraglei hashelichim

having a field, sold it, and brought the money and laid it at the apostles' feet.

ה

אִישׁ אֶחָד, חֲנַנְיָה שְׁמוֹ, וְאִשְׁתּוֹ שַׁפִּירָה מָכְרוּ שָׂדֶה

ish echad, chananyah shemo, ve'ishto shappirah machru sadeh

But a certain man named Ananias, with Sapphira his wife, sold a possession,

מַעֲשֵׂי הַשְּׁלִיחִים

בְּפִי עַבְדְּךָ דָּוִד אָבִינוּ אָמַרְתָּ בְּרוּחַ הַקֹּדֶשׁ
befi avdecha david avinu amarta beruach hakkodesh
who by the Holy Spirit, by the mouth of our father David thy servant, didst say,

לָמָּה רָגְשׁוּ גוֹיִם וּלְאֻמִּים יֶהְגּוּ־רִיק
lammah ragshu goyim ule'ummim yehgu-rik
Why did the Gentiles rage, And the peoples imagine vain things?

יִתְיַצְּבוּ מַלְכֵי־אֶרֶץ וְרוֹזְנִים נוֹסְדוּ־יָחַד
yityatzvu malchei-'eretz veroznim nosdu-yachad
The kings of the earth set themselves in array, And the rulers were gathered together,

עַל־יהוה וְעַל־מְשִׁיחוֹ
al-hashem ve'al-meshicho
Against the Lord, and against his Anointed:

כִּי אָמְנָם נֶאֶסְפוּ בָּעִיר הַזֹּאת הוֹרְדוֹס וּפוֹנְטִיּוֹס פִּילָטוֹס עִם גּוֹיִם וּלְאֻמֵּי יִשְׂרָאֵל עַל עַבְדְּךָ הַקָּדוֹשׁ יֵשׁוּעַ אֲשֶׁר מָשַׁחְתָּ
ki omnam ne'esfu ba'ir hazzot horedos veponeteyos pilatos im goyim ule'ummei yisra'el al avdecha hakkadosh yeshua asher mashachta
for of a truth in this city against thy holy Servant Jesus, whom thou didst anoint, both Herod and Pontius Pilate, with the Gentiles and the peoples of Israel, were gathered together,

לַעֲשׂוֹת אֵת מַה שֶּׁבְּיָדְךָ וַעֲצָתְךָ כְּבָר מִקֶּדֶם גָּזַרְתָּ שֶׁיִּהְיֶה
la'asot et mah shebeyadecha va'atzatecha kevar mikkedem gazarta sheyihyeh
to do whatsoever thy hand and thy council foreordained to come to pass.

וְכָעֵת, אֲדֹנָי, רְאֵה אֶת אִיּוּמֵיהֶם וְתֵן לַעֲבָדֶיךָ לוֹמַר אֶת דְּבָרֶךָ בְּכָל אֹמֶץ הַלֵּב
vecha'et, adonai, re'eh et iyumeihem veten la'avadeicha lomar et dvarecha bechol ometz hallev
And now, Lord, look upon their threatenings: and grant unto thy servants to speak thy word with all boldness,

בִּנְטוֹתְךָ אֶת יָדְךָ לְמַרְפֵּא
bintotecha et yadecha lemarpei
while thou stretchest forth thy hand to heal;

וְלַעֲשִׂיַּת אוֹתוֹת וּמוֹפְתִים עַל־יְדֵי שֵׁם יֵשׁוּעַ עַבְדְּךָ הַקָּדוֹשׁ
vela'asiyat otot umofetim al-yedei shem yeshua avdecha hakkadosh
and that signs and wonders may be done through the name of thy holy Servant Jesus.

כְּשֶׁסִּיְּמוּ אֶת תְּפִלָּתָם הִזְדַּעְזַע הַמָּקוֹם שֶׁהִתְאַסְּפוּ בּוֹ
keshessiyemu et tefillatam hizda'za hammakom shehit'assefu bo
And when they had prayed, the place was shaken wherein they were gathered together;

וְכֻלָּם נִתְמַלְּאוּ רוּחַ הַקֹּדֶשׁ וְדִבְּרוּ אֶת דְּבַר אֱלֹהִים בְּאֹמֶץ לֵב
vechullam nitmalle'u ruach hakkodesh vedibberu et devar elohim be'ometz lev
and they were all filled with the Holy Spirit, and they spake the word of God with boldness.

מַעֲשֵׂי הַשְּׁלִיחִים

נָאֵיֶם עֲלֵיהֶם שֶׁלֹּא יְדַבְּרוּ עוֹד בַּשֵׁם הַזֶּה אֶל שׁוּם אָדָם

ne'ayem aleihem shelo yedabberu od bashem hazzeh el shum adam
let us threaten them, that they speak henceforth to no man in this name.

הֵם קָרְאוּ לָהֶם וְצִוּוּ אוֹתָם שֶׁלֹּא לְדַבֵּר וְלֹא לְלַמֵּד דָּבָר בְּשֵׁם יֵשׁוּעַ

hem kare'u lahem vetzivvu otam shello ledabber velo lelammed davar beshem yeshua
And they called them, and charged them not to speak at all nor teach in the name of Jesus.

הֵשִׁיבוּ כֵּיפָא וְיוֹחָנָן וְאָמְרוּ לָהֶם

heshivu keifa veyochanan ve'amru lahem
But Peter and John answered and said unto them,

הַאִם מֻצְדָּק לִפְנֵי אֱלֹהִים לִשְׁמֹעַ לָכֶם יוֹתֵר מֵאֲשֶׁר לֵאלֹהִים? שִׁפְטוּ אַתֶּם

ha'im mutzdak lifnei elohim lishmoa lachem yoter me'asher le'elohim? shiftu attem
Whether it is right in the sight of God to hearken unto you rather than unto God, judge ye:

הֲרֵי אֵינֶנּוּ יְכוֹלִים שֶׁלֹּא לְהַגִּיד אֶת אֲשֶׁר רָאִינוּ וְשָׁמַעְנוּ

harei einennu yecholim shello lehaggid et asher ra'inu veshama'nu
for we cannot but speak the things which we saw and heard.

אַחֲרֵי אִיּוּמִים נוֹסָפִים שִׁחְרְרוּ אוֹתָם, כִּי לֹא מָצְאוּ דֶּרֶךְ לְהַעֲנִישׁ אוֹתָם

acharei iyumim nosafim shichreru otam, ki lo matze'u derech leha'anish otam
And they, when they had further threatened them, let them go, finding nothing how they might punish them,

בִּגְלַל הָעָם, שֶׁכֵּן הַכֹּל שִׁבְּחוּ אֶת אֱלֹהִים עַל מַה שֶׁנַּעֲשָׂה

biglal ha'am, shekken hakkol shibbchu et elohim al mah shenna'asah
because of the people; for all men glorified God for that which was done.

כִּי בֶּן אַרְבָּעִים שָׁנָה וָמַעְלָה הָיָה הָאִישׁ אֲשֶׁר נַעֲשָׂה בּוֹ נֵס הָרִפּוּי הַזֶּה

ki ben arba'im shanah vama'lah hayah ha'ish asher na'asah bo nes harippui hazzeh
For the man was more than forty years old, on whom this miracle of healing was wrought.

לְאַחַר שֶׁשִּׁחְרְרוּ הָלְכוּ אֶל חַבְרֵיהֶם

le'achar sheshuchreru halchu el chavreihem
And being let go, they came to their own company,

וְסִפְּרוּ מַה שֶּׁאָמְרוּ לָהֶם רָאשֵׁי הַכֹּהֲנִים וְהַזְּקֵנִים

vesipperu mah she'ameru lahem rashei hakkohanim vehazzekenim
and reported all that the chief priests and the elders had said unto them.

הֵם שָׁמְעוּ זֹאת וּבְלֵב אֶחָד נָשְׂאוּ קוֹלָם לֵאלֹהִים וְאָמְרוּ: אֲדֹנָי

hem shame'u zot uvelev echad nase'u kolam lelohim ve'ameru: adonai
And they, when they heard it, lifted up their voice to God with one accord, and said, O Lord,

אַתָּה אֲשֶׁר עָשִׂיתָ אֶת־הַשָּׁמַיִם וְאֶת־הָאָרֶץ אֶת־הַיָּם וְאֶת־כָּל־אֲשֶׁר־בָּם

attah asher asita et-hashamayim ve'et-ha'aretz et-hayam ve'et-kol-'asher-bam
thou that didst make the heaven and the earth and the sea, and all that in them is:

מַעֲשֵׂי הַשְּׁלִיחִים

שֶׁיְהֵא יָדוּעַ לְכֻלְּכֶם וּלְכָל עַם יִשְׂרָאֵל כִּי בְּשֵׁם יֵשׁוּעַ הַמָּשִׁיחַ מִנָּצְרַת, אֲשֶׁר אַתֶּם צְלַבְתֶּם
sheyehei yadua lechullchem ulechol am yisra'el ki beshem yeshua hammashiach minnatzerat
be it known unto you all, and to all the people of Israel, that in the name of Jesus Christ of Nazareth,

וַאֲשֶׁר אֱלֹהִים הֱקִימוֹ מִן הַמֵּתִים, בַּשֵּׁם הַזֶּה הוּא עוֹמֵד בָּרִיא לִפְנֵיכֶם
asher attem tzlavtem va'asher elohim hekimo min hammetim, bashem hazzeh hu omed bari lifneichem
whom ye crucified, whom God raised from the dead, even in him doth this man stand here before you whole.

הוּא הָאֶבֶן שֶׁמְּאַסְתֶּם, אַתֶּם הַבּוֹנִים, אֲשֶׁר הָיְתָה לְרֹאשׁ פִּנָּה
hu ha'even shemme'astem, attem habbonim, asher hayetah lerosh pinnah
He is the stone which was set at nought of you the builders, which was made the head of the corner.

וְאֵין רְפוּאָה בְּאַחֵר
ve'ein refu'ah be'acher
And in none other is there salvation:

כִּי אֵין שֵׁם אַחֵר נָתוּן לִבְנֵי אָדָם תַּחַת הַשָּׁמַיִם, וּבוֹ עָלֵינוּ לְהֵרָפֵא
ki ein shem acher natun livnei adam tachat hashamayim, uvo aleinu leherafe
for neither is there any other name under heaven, that is given among men, wherein we must be saved.

כְּשֶׁרָאוּ אֶת בִּטְחוֹנָם שֶׁל כֵּיפָא וְיוֹחָנָן וְהִבְחִינוּ שֶׁהֵם אֲנָשִׁים פְּשׁוּטִים וּבִלְתִּי מְלֻמָּדִים
kshera'u et bitchonam shel keifa veyochanan vehivchinu shehem anashim pshutim uvilti melummadim
Now when they beheld the boldness of Peter and John, and had perceived that they were unlearned and ignorant men,

תָּמְהוּ. הֵם זִהוּ אוֹתָם, שֶׁבֶּעָבָר הָיוּ יַחַד עִם יֵשׁוּעַ
tamhu. hem zihu otam, shebbe'avar hayu yachad im yeshua
they marvelled; and they took knowledge of them, that they had been with Jesus.

אַךְ בִּרְאוֹתָם אֶת הָאִישׁ שֶׁנִּרְפָּא עוֹמֵד עִמָּהֶם, לֹא הָיָה לָהֶם מַה לִּטְעֹן
ach bir'otam et ha'ish shennirpa omed immahem, lo hayah lahem mah lit'on
And seeing the man that was healed standing with them, they could say nothing against it.

לְאַחַר שֶׁצִּוּוּ עֲלֵיהֶם לָצֵאת מִן הַסַּנְהֶדְרִין הִתְיָעֲצוּ יַחְדָּיו
le'achar shetzivvu aleihem latzet min hassanhedrin hitya'atzu yachdav
But when they had commanded them to go aside out of the council, they conferred among themselves,

אָמְרוּ: מַה נַּעֲשֶׂה לָאֲנָשִׁים הָאֵלֶּה? הֲרֵי אוֹת בָּרוּר נַעֲשָׂה עַל-יָדָם
Ameru: mah na'aseh la'anashim ha'elleh? harei ot barur na'asah al-yadam
saying, What shall we do to these men? for that indeed a notable miracle hath been wrought through them,

גָּלוּי הוּא לְכָל יוֹשְׁבֵי יְרוּשָׁלַיִם וְאֵין אָנוּ יְכוֹלִים לְהַכְחִישׁ אוֹתוֹ
galui hu lechol yoshevei yerushalayim ve'ein anu yecholim lehachchish oto
is manifest to all that dwell in Jerusalem; and we cannot deny it.

אֲבָל כְּדֵי שֶׁלֹּא יוֹסִיף הַדָּבָר לְהִתְפַּרְסֵם בָּעָם
aval kedei shello yosif haddavar lehitparsem ba'am
But that it spread no further among the people,

מַעֲשֵׂי הַשְּׁלִיחִים

ד

כַּאֲשֶׁר דִּבְּרוּ אֶל הָעָם בָּאוּ אֲלֵיהֶם הַכֹּהֲנִים וּנְגִיד בֵּית הַמִּקְדָּשׁ וְהַצְּדוֹקִים
ka'asher dibberu el ha'am ba'u aleihem hakkohanim unegid beit hammikdash vehatzedokim
And as they spake unto the people, the priests and the captain of the temple and the Sadducees came upon them,

כּוֹעֲסִים הָיוּ עַל שֶׁלִּמְּדוּ אֶת הָעָם וּבִשְּׂרוּ בְּיֵשׁוּעַ אֶת הַתְּחִיָּה מִן הַמֵּתִים
ko'asim hayu al shellimmdu et ha'am uvissru beyeshua et hattechiyah min hammetim
being sore troubled because they taught the people, and proclaimed in Jesus the resurrection from the dead.

הֵם תָּפְסוּ אוֹתָם וְכֵיוָן שֶׁהָיָה כְּבָר עֶרֶב כָּלְאוּ אוֹתָם עַד לְמָחֳרָת
hem tafesu otam vecheivan shehayah kevar erev kale'u otam ad lemochorat
And they laid hands on them, and put them in ward unto the morrow: for it was now eventide.

אוּלָם רַבִּים מֵהַשּׁוֹמְעִים אֶת הַדָּבָר הֶאֱמִינוּ, וּמִסְפָּרָם הָיָה כַּחֲמֵשֶׁת אֲלָפִים אִישׁ
ulam rabbim mehashome'im et haddavar he'eminu, umisparam hayah kachameshet alafim ish
But many of them that heard the word believed; and the number of the men came to be about five thousand.

לְמָחֳרָת נֶאֶסְפוּ שָׂרֵיהֶם וְזִקְנֵיהֶם וְסוֹפְרֵיהֶם בִּירוּשָׁלַיִם
lemacharat ne'esfu sareihem vezikneihem vesofereihem biyerushalayim
And it came to pass on the morrow, that their rulers and elders and scribes were gathered together in Jerusalem;

גַּם חָנָן הַכֹּהֵן הַגָּדוֹל וְקַיָּפָא וְיוֹחָנָן וַאֲלֶכְּסַנְדֶּר
gam chanan hakkohen haggadol vekayafa veyochanan va'alekkesander
and Annas the high priest was there, and Caiaphas, and John, and Alexander,

וּבְנֵי מִשְׁפְּחוֹת הַכֹּהֲנִים הַגְּדוֹלִים
uvnei mishpechot hakkohanim haggedolim
and as many as were of the kindred of the high priest.

הֵם הֶעֱמִידוּ אוֹתָם בַּתָּוֶךְ וְשָׁאֲלוּ: בְּאֵיזֶה כֹּחַ אוֹ בְּאֵיזֶה שֵׁם עֲשִׂיתֶם אֶת זֹאת
hem he'emidu otam battavech vesha'alu: be'eizeh koach o be'eizeh shem asitem et zot
And when they had set them in the midst, they inquired, By what power, or in what name, have ye done this?

כֵּיפָא נִתְמַלֵּא רוּחַ הַקֹּדֶשׁ וְאָמַר לָהֶם: שָׂרֵי הָעָם וְזִקְנֵי יִשְׂרָאֵל
keifa nitmallei ruach hakkodesh ve'amar lahem. sarei ha'am vezihnei yisra'el
Then Peter, filled with the Holy Spirit, said unto them, Ye rulers of the people, and elders,

אִם אֲנַחְנוּ נֶחְקָרִים הַיּוֹם עַל מַעֲשֶׂה טוֹב שֶׁנַּעֲשָׂה לְאִישׁ חוֹלֶה
im anachnu nechkarim hayom al ma'aseh tov shenna'asah le'ish choleh
if we this day are examined concerning a good deed done to an impotent man,

כֵּיצַד נִרְפָּא הָאִישׁ הַזֶּה
keitzad nirpa ha'ish hazzeh
by what means this man is made whole;

מַעֲשֵׂי הַשְּׁלִיחִים

וְהוּא יִשְׁלַח אֶת אֲשֶׁר יֻעַד לָכֶם מִקֶּדֶם, אֶת הַמָּשִׁיחַ יֵשׁוּעַ
vehu yishlach et asher yu'ad lachem mikkedem, et hammashiach yeshua
and that he may send the Christ who hath been appointed for you, even Jesus:

אֲשֶׁר צָרִיךְ שֶׁיְּקַבְּלוּ אוֹתוֹ הַשָּׁמַיִם עַד עֵת הָשָׁבַת הַכֹּל לְתִקּוּנוֹ
asher tzarich sheyekabbelu oto hashamayim ad et hashavat hakkol letikkuno
whom the heaven must receive until the times of restoration of all things,

דָּבָר שֶׁאֱלֹהִים דִּבֶּר מֵעוֹלָם בְּפִי נְבִיאָיו הַקְּדוֹשִׁים
davar she'elohim dibber me'olam befi nevi'av hakkedoshim
whereof God spake by the mouth of his holy prophets that have been from of old.

הֵן מֹשֶׁה אָמַר אֶל אֲבוֹתֵינוּ: נָבִיא יָקִים לָכֶם יהוה אֱלֹהֵיכֶם מִקֶּרֶב אֲחֵיכֶם, כָּמוֹנִי
hen mosheh amar el avoteinu: navi yakim lachem hashem eloheichem mikkerev acheichem, kamoni
Moses indeed said, A prophet shall the Lord God raise up unto you from among your brethren, like unto me;

אֵלָיו תִּשְׁמָעוּן כְּכֹל אֲשֶׁר יְדַבֵּר אֲלֵיכֶם
elav tishma'un kechol asher yedabber aleichem
to him shall ye hearken in all things whatsoever he shall speak unto you.

וְהָיָה כָּל הַנֶּפֶשׁ אֲשֶׁר לֹא תִשְׁמַע אֶל הַנָּבִיא הַהוּא וְנִכְרְתָה מֵעַמֶּיהָ
vehayah kol hannefesh asher lo tishma el hannavi hahu venichretah me'ammeiha
And it shall be, that every soul that shall not hearken to that prophet, shall be utterly destroyed from among the people

וְכָל הַנְּבִיאִים מִשְּׁמוּאֵל וָאֵילָךְ
vechol hannevi'im mishemu'el va'eilach,
Yea and all the prophets from Samuel and them that followed after,

כֻּלָּם דִּבְּרוּ וְהוֹדִיעוּ עַל־אֹדוֹת הַיָּמִים הָאֵלֶּה
kullam dibberu vehodi'u al-'odot hayamim ha'elleh
as many as have spoken, they also told of these days.

אַתֶּם בְּנֵי הַנְּבִיאִים וּבְנֵי הַבְּרִית אֲשֶׁר כָּרַת אֱלֹהִים עִם אֲבוֹתֵינוּ בְּאָמְרוֹ אֶל אַבְרָהָם
attem bnei hannevi'im uvnei habberit asher karat elohim im avoteinu be'amero el avraham
Ye are the sons of the prophets, and of the covenant which God made with your fathers, saying unto Abraham,

וְנִבְרְכוּ בְזַרְעֲךָ כֹּל מִשְׁפְּחוֹת הָאֲדָמָה
venivrechu bezar'acha kol mishpechot ha'adamah
And in thy seed shall all the families of the earth be blessed.

לָכֶם רִאשׁוֹנָה הֵקִים אֱלֹהִים אֶת עַבְדּוֹ וְשָׁלַח אוֹתוֹ לְבָרֵךְ אֶתְכֶם
lachem rishonah hekim elohim et avdo veshalach oto levarech etchem
Unto you first God, having raised up his Servant, sent him to bless you,

בְּשׁוּבְכֶם אִישׁ אִישׁ מִדַּרְכּוֹ הָרָעָה
beshuvechem ish ish middarko hara'ah
in turning away every one of you from your iniquities.

מַעֲשֵׂי הַשְּׁלִיחִים

רָאָה זֹאת כֵּיפָא וְאָמַר אֶל הָעָם: אַנְשֵׁי יִשְׂרָאֵל, לָמָּה אַתֶּם תְּמֵהִים עַל הַדָּבָר הַזֶּה?
ra'ah zot keifa ve'amar el ha'am: anshei yisra'el, lammah attem temehim al haddavar hazzeh
And when Peter saw it, he answered unto the people, Ye men of Israel, why marvel ye at this man?

וּמַדּוּעַ אַתֶּם מִסְתַּכְּלִים בָּנוּ כְּאִלּוּ בְּכֹחֵנוּ אוֹ בַּחֲסִידוּתֵנוּ עָשִׂינוּ שֶׁהוּא יִתְהַלֵּךְ
umaddua attem mistakkelim banu ke'illu bechochenu o bachasidutenu asinu shehu yit'halech
or why fasten ye your eyes on us, as though by our own power or godliness we had made him to walk?

אֱלֹהֵי אַבְרָהָם וְיִצְחָק וְיַעֲקֹב, אֱלֹהֵי אֲבוֹתֵינוּ, פֵּאֵר בְּכָבוֹד אֶת עַבְדּוֹ יֵשׁוּעַ
elohei avraham veyitzchak veya'akov, elohei avoteinu, pe'er bechavod et avdo yeshua
The God of Abraham, and of Isaac, and of Jacob, the God of our fathers, hath glorified his Servant Jesus;

אֲשֶׁר מְסַרְתֶּם אוֹתוֹ וּכְפַרְתֶּם בּוֹ לִפְנֵי פִּילָטוֹס כַּאֲשֶׁר הֶחְלִיט לְשַׁלְּחוֹ לַחָפְשִׁי
asher mesartem oto uchfartem bo lifnei pilatos ka'asher hechlit leshallecho lachofshi
whom ye delivered up, and denied before the face of Pilate, when he had determined to release him.

אַתֶּם כְּפַרְתֶּם בַּקָּדוֹשׁ וּבַצַּדִּיק וּבִקַּשְׁתֶּם שֶׁיְּשַׁחְרֵר לָכֶם אִישׁ רוֹצֵחַ
attem kfartem bakkadosh uvatzaddik uvikkashtem sheyeshachrer lachem ish rotzeach
But ye denied the Holy and Righteous One, and asked for a murderer to be granted unto you,

וְאֶת שַׂר הַחַיִּים הֲרַגְתֶּם - הוּא אֲשֶׁר אֱלֹהִים הֱקִימוֹ מִן הַמֵּתִים וְעַל זֹאת אֲנַחְנוּ עֵדִים
ve'et sar hachayim haragtem - hu asher elohim hekimo min hammetim ve'al zot anachnu edim
and killed the Prince of life; whom God raised from the dead; whereof we are witnesses.

עַל-סֶמַךְ הָאֱמוּנָה בִּשְׁמוֹ חִזֵּק שְׁמוֹ אֶת הָאִישׁ הַזֶּה אֲשֶׁר אַתֶּם רוֹאִים וּמַכִּירִים
al-semach ha'emunah bishmo chizzek shemo et ha'ish hazzeh asher attem ro'im umakkirim
And by faith in his name hath his name made this man strong, whom ye behold and know:

וְהָאֱמוּנָה בּוֹ נָתְנָה לָאִישׁ אֶת הָרְפוּאָה הַשְּׁלֵמָה הַזֹּאת לְעֵינֵי כֻּלְּכֶם
veha'emunah bo natenah la'ish et harefu'ah hashelemah hazzot le'einei kullchem
yea, the faith which is through him hath given him this perfect soundness in the presence of you all.

וְעַתָּה, אַחַי, אֲנִי יוֹדֵעַ שֶׁבִּבְלִי דַעַת פְּעַלְתֶּם, כְּמוֹ שֶׁפָּעֲלוּ מַנְהִיגֵיכֶם
ve'attah, achai, ani yodea shebbivli da'at pe'altem, kemo sheppa'alu manhigeichem
And now, brethren, I know that in ignorance ye did it, as did also your rulers.

אַךְ אֱלֹהִים קִיֵּם בְּדֶרֶךְ זֹאת אֶת אֲשֶׁר הוֹדִיעַ מִקֶּדֶם בְּפִי כָּל הַנְּבִיאִים - שֶׁמְּשִׁיחוֹ יִסְבֹּל
ach elohim kiyem bederech zot et asher hodia mikkedem befi kol hannevi'im - shemmeshicho yisbol
But the things which God foreshowed by the mouth of all the prophets, that his Christ should suffer, he thus fulfilled.

לָכֵן הִתְחָרְטוּ וְשׁוּבוּ בִּתְשׁוּבָה כְּדֵי שֶׁיִּמָּחוּ חֲטָאֵיכֶם
lachen hitchartu veshuvu bitshuvah kedei sheyimmachu chata'eichem
Repent ye therefore, and turn again, that your sins may be blotted out,

לְמַעַן יָבוֹאוּ יְמֵי רְוָחָה מִלִּפְנֵי אֲדֹנָי
lema'an yavo'u yemei revachah millifnei adonai
that so there may come seasons of refreshing from the presence of the Lord;

מַעֲשֵׂי הַשְּׁלִיחִים

נָעַץ בּוֹ כֵּיפָא אֶת עֵינָיו, וְכֵן עָשָׂה גַם יוֹחָנָן, וְאָמַר: הַבֵּט אֵלֵינוּ
na'atz bo keifa et einav, vechen asah gam yochanan, ve'amar: habbet eleinu
And Peter, fastening his eyes upon him, with John, said, Look on us.

הוּא הִסְתַּכֵּל אֲלֵיהֶם בְּקַוֺּתוֹ לְקַבֵּל מֵהֶם מַשֶּׁהוּ
hu histakkel aleihem bekavvoto lekabbel mehem mashehu
And he gave heed unto them, expecting to receive something from them.

אֶלָּא שֶׁכֵּיפָא אָמַר: כֶּסֶף וְזָהָב אֵין לִי, אֲבָל אֶת מַה שֶּׁיֶּשׁ לִי, אֶת זֶה אֶתֵּן לְךָ
ella shekkeifa amar: kesef vezahav ein li, aval et mah sheyesh li, et zeh etten lecha
But Peter said, Silver and gold have I none; but what I have, that give I thee.

בְּשֵׁם יֵשׁוּעַ הַמָּשִׁיחַ מִנַּצְרַת - הִתְהַלֵּךְ
beshem yeshua hammashiach minnatzerat - hit'hallech
In the name of Jesus Christ of Nazareth, walk.

הוּא הֶחֱזִיק בְּיָדוֹ הַיְמָנִית וְהֵקִים אוֹתוֹ, וּפִתְאוֹם הִתְחַזְּקוּ רַגְלָיו וְקַרְסֻלָּיו
hu hechezik beyado hayemanit vehekim oto, ufit'om hitchazzku raglav vekarsullav
And he took him by the right hand, and raised him up: and immediately his feet and his ankle-bones received strength.

קָפַץ הָאִישׁ וְעָמַד עַל רַגְלָיו. מִיָּד הָלַךְ וְנִכְנַס אִתָּם לְבֵית הַמִּקְדָּשׁ
kafatz ha'ish ve'amad al raglav. miyad halach venichnas ittam leveit hammikdash
And leaping up, he stood, and began to walk; and he entered with them into the temple,

כְּשֶׁהוּא מְהַלֵּךְ וּמְקַפֵּץ וּמְהַלֵּל אֶת אֱלֹהִים
kshehu mehallech umekappetz umehallel et elohim
walking, and leaping, and praising God.

רָאוּהוּ כָּל הָאֲנָשִׁים מִתְהַלֵּךְ וּמְשַׁבֵּחַ אֶת אֱלֹהִים
ra'uhu kol ha'anashim mit'hallech umeshabbeach et elohim
And all the people saw him walking and praising God:

וְהִכִּירוּ שֶׁזֶּה הוּא אֲשֶׁר הָיָה יוֹשֵׁב לְבַקֵּשׁ נְדָבוֹת בַּשַּׁעַר הַמְהֻדָּר שֶׁל בֵּית הַמִּקְדָּשׁ
vehikkiru shezzeh hu asher hayah yoshev levakkesh nedavot basha'ar hamhuddar shel beit hammikdash
and they took knowledge of him, that it was he that sat for alms at the Beautiful Gate of the temple;

נִתְמַלְּאוּ תִּמָּהוֹן וְתַדְהֵמָה עַל מַה שֶּׁקָּרָה לוֹ
nitmalle'u timmahon vetadhemah al mah shekkarah lo
and they were filled with wonder and amazement at that which had happened unto him.

הָאִישׁ לֹא הִרְפָּה מִכֵּיפָא וְיוֹחָנָן
ha'ish lo hirpah mikkeifa veyochanan
And as he held Peter and John,

וְאָז רָצוּ אֲלֵיהֶם כָּל הָאֲנָשִׁים, מְלֵאֵי הִשְׁתּוֹמְמוּת, בָּאוּלָם הַנִּקְרָא אוּלָם שְׁלֹמֹה
ve'az ratzu aleihem kol ha'anashim, mele'ei hishtomemut, ba'ulam hannikra ulam shelomoh
all the people ran together unto them in the porch that is called Solomon's, greatly wondering.

מַעֲשֵׂי הַשְּׁלִיחִים

כָּל נֶפֶשׁ נִתְמַלְאָה יִרְאָה וּמוֹפְתִים וְאוֹתוֹת רַבִּים עָשׂוּ הַשְּׁלִיחִים
kol nefesh nitmalle'ah yir'ah umofetim ve'otot rabbim asu hashlichim
And fear came upon every soul: and many wonders and signs were done through the apostles.

כָּל הַמַּאֲמִינִים הָיוּ יַחְדָּיו וּבְכָל אֲשֶׁר הָיָה לָהֶם הָיוּ שֻׁתָּפִים
kol hamma'aminim hayu yachdav uvechol asher hayah lahem hayu shuttafim
And all that believed were together, and had all things common;

הֵם מָכְרוּ אֶת אֲחֻזּוֹתֵיהֶם וְאֶת רְכוּשָׁם וְחִלְּקוּ אוֹתָם לַכֹּל, לְכָל אִישׁ כְּפִי צָרְכּוֹ
hem macheru et achuzzoteihem ve'et rechusham vechilleku otam lakkol, lechol ish kefi tzarko
and they sold their possessions and goods, and parted them to all, according as any man had need.

יוֹם יוֹם הִתְמִידוּ לִהְיוֹת לֵב אֶחָד בְּבֵית הַמִּקְדָּשׁ וְהָיוּ בּוֹצְעִים אֶת הַלֶּחֶם בְּבָתֵּיהֶם
yom yom hitmidu lihyot lev echad beveit hammikdash vehayu botze'im et hallechem bevatteihem
And day by day, continuing stedfastly with one accord in the temple, and breaking bread at home,

אוֹכְלִים אֶת מְזוֹנָם בְּשִׂמְחָה וּבְתֹם לֵב
ochelim et mezonam besimchah uvetom lev
they took their food with gladness and singleness of heart,

וּמְשַׁבְּחִים אֶת אֱלֹהִים. הֵם מָצְאוּ חֵן בְּעֵינֵי כָּל הָעָם, וְהָאָדוֹן הוֹסִיף עֲלֵיהֶם יוֹם יוֹם אֶת הַנּוֹשָׁעִים
umeshabbechim et elohim. hem matze'u chen be'einei kol ha'am, veha'adon hosif aleihem yom yom et hannosha'im
praising God, and having favor with all the people. And the Lord added to them day by day those that were saved.

ג

כֵּיפָא וְיוֹחָנָן הָיוּ בְּדַרְכָּם אֶל בֵּית הַמִּקְדָּשׁ בְּעֵת תְּפִלַּת מִנְחָה, בְּשָׁעָה שָׁלוֹשׁ אַחֲרֵי הַצָּהֳרַיִם
keifa veyochanan hayu bedarkam el beit hammikdash be'et tefillat minchah, besha'ah shalosh acharei hatzohorayim
Now Peter and John were going up into the temple at the hour of prayer, being the ninth hour.

וְאִישׁ אֶחָד, פִּסֵּחַ מִבֶּטֶן אִמּוֹ, נִשָּׂא לְשָׁם
ve'ish echad, pisseach mibbeten immo, nissa lesham
And a certain man that was lame from his mother's womb was carried,

מִדֵּי יוֹם בְּיוֹמוֹ הָיוּ מַנִּיחִים אוֹתוֹ לְיַד שַׁעַר בֵּית הַמִּקְדָּשׁ, הַשַּׁעַר הַמְכֻנֶּה מְהֻדָּר
middei yom beyomo hayu mannichim oto leyad sha'ar beit hammikdash, hasha'ar hamchunneh mehuddar
whom they laid daily at the door of the temple which is called Beautiful,

לְבַקֵּשׁ נְדָבוֹת מִן הַבָּאִים אֶל בֵּית הַמִּקְדָּשׁ
levakkesh nedavot min habba'im el beit hammikdash
to ask alms of them that entered into the temple;

כִּרְאוֹתוֹ אֶת כֵּיפָא וְאֶת יוֹחָנָן עוֹמְדִים לְהִכָּנֵס לְבֵית הַמִּקְדָּשׁ, בִּקֵּשׁ מֵהֶם נְדָבָה
kir'oto et keifa ve'et yochanan omedim lehikkanes leveit hammikdash, bikkesh mehem nedavah
who seeing Peter and John about to go into the temple, asked to receive an alms.

מַעֲשֵׂי הַשְּׁלִיחִים

אֶת יֵשׁוּעַ זֶה אֲשֶׁר אַתֶּם צְלַבְתֶּם
et yeshua zeh asher attem tzelavtem
this Jesus whom ye crucified.

כְּשָׁמְעָם הִתְעַצְּבוּ מְאֹד בְּלִבָּם
keshome'am hit'atzevu me'od belibbam
Now when they heard this, they were pricked in their heart,

וְאָמְרוּ לְכֵיפָא וְלִשְׁאָר הַשְּׁלִיחִים: אֲנָשִׁים אַחִים, מֶה עָלֵינוּ לַעֲשׂוֹת
ve'ameru lecheifa velish'ar hashelichim: anashim achim, meh aleinu la'asot
and said unto Peter and the rest of the apostles, Brethren, what shall we do?

אָמַר לָהֶם כֵּיפָא:
amar lahem keifa
And Peter said unto them,

שׁוּבוּ בִּתְשׁוּבָה וְהִטָּבְלוּ אִישׁ אִישׁ מִכֶּם בְּשֵׁם יֵשׁוּעַ הַמָּשִׁיחַ לִסְלִיחַת חֲטָאֵיכֶם
shuvu bitshuvah vehittavelu ish ish mikkem beshem yeshua hammashiach lislichat chata'eichem
Repent ye, and be baptized every one of you in the name of Jesus Christ unto the remission of your sins;

וּתְקַבְּלוּ אֶת מַתְּנַת רוּחַ הַקֹּדֶשׁ
utkabbelu et mattenat ruach hakkodesh
and ye shall receive the gift of the Holy Spirit.

כִּי לָכֶם הַהַבְטָחָה וְלִבְנֵיכֶם וּלְכָל הָרְחוֹקִים
ki lachem hahavtachah velivneichem ulechal harechokim
For to you is the promise, and to your children, and to all that are afar off,

לְכָל אֲשֶׁר יִקְרָא לָהֶם אֲדֹנָי אֱלֹהֵינוּ
lechol asher yikra lahem adonai eloheinu
even as many as the Lord our God shall call unto him.

גַּם בְּמִלִּים רַבּוֹת אֲחֵרוֹת הֵעִיד בָּהֶם וְהֵאִיץ בָּהֶם בְּאָמְרוֹ: הִמָּלְטוּ מִן הַדּוֹר הַסּוֹרֵר הַזֶּה
gam bemillim rabbot acherot he'id bahem vehe'itz bahem be'omeo: himmaletu min haddor hassorer hazzeh
And with many other words he testified, and exhorted them, saying, Save yourselves from this crooked generation.

אֵלֶּה שֶׁקִּבְּלוּ בְּרָצוֹן אֶת דְּבָרוֹ נִטְבְּלוּ
elleh shekkibbelu beratzon et dvaro nitbelu,
They then that received his word were baptized:

וּבְאוֹתוֹ יוֹם נוֹסְפוּ כִּשְׁלֹשֶׁת אֲלָפִים נְפָשׁוֹת
uve'oto yom nosefu kishloshet alafim nefashot
and there were added unto them in that day about three thousand souls.

הֵם הָיוּ שׁוֹקְדִים עַל תּוֹרַת הַשְּׁלִיחִים, עַל הַהִתְחַבְּרוּת, עַל בְּצִיעַת הַלֶּחֶם וְעַל הַתְּפִלּוֹת
hem hayu shokdim al torat hashelichim, al hahitchabberut, al betzi'at hallechem ve'al hattfillot
And they continued stedfastly in the apostles' teaching and fellowship, in the breaking of bread and the prayers.

מַעֲשֵׂי הַשְּׁלִיחִים

אֲנָשִׁים אַחִים, אֶפְשָׁר לוֹמַר לָכֶם בְּבִטָּחוֹן עַל דָּוִד אָבִינוּ
anashim achim, efshar lomar lachem bevittachon al david avinu
Brethren, I may say unto you freely of the patriarch David,

שֶׁהוּא מֵת וְגַם נִקְבַּר וְקִבְרוֹ נִמְצָא עִמָּנוּ עַד הַיּוֹם הַזֶּה
shehu met vegam nikbar vekivro nimtza immanu ad hayom hazzeh
that he both died and was buried, and his tomb is with us unto this day.

מִכֵּיוָן שֶׁהָיָה נָבִיא וְיָדַע כִּי אֱלֹהִים נִשְׁבַּע לוֹ שְׁבוּעָה
mikkeivan shehayah navi veyada ki elohim nishba lo shevu'ah
Being therefore a prophet, and knowing that God had sworn with an oath to him,

לְהוֹשִׁיב מִפְּרִי חֲלָצָיו עַל כִּסְאוֹ
lehoshiv mipperi chalatzav al kis'o
that of the fruit of his loins he would set one upon his throne;

בַּחֲזוֹתוֹ מֵרֹאשׁ דִּבֶּר עַל תְּחִיַּת הַמָּשִׁיחַ
bachazoto merosh dibber al techiyat hammashiach
he foreseeing this spake of the resurrection of the Christ,

שֶׁלֹּא נֶעֶזְבָה לִשְׁאוֹל נַפְשׁוֹ וּבְשָׂרוֹ לֹא רָאָה שַׁחַת
shello ne'ezvah lish'ol nafsho uvesaro lo ra'ah shachat
that neither was he left unto Hades, nor did his flesh see corruption.

אֶת יֵשׁוּעַ זֶה הֵקִים אֱלֹהִים לִתְחִיָּה וְעַל זֹאת אֲנַחְנוּ כֻּלָּנוּ עֵדִים
et yeshua zeh hekim elohim litchiyah ve'al zot anachnu kullanu edim
This Jesus did God raise up, whereof we all are witnesses.

וּלְאַחַר שֶׁנִּשָּׂא אֶל יְמִין הָאֱלֹהִים וְקִבֵּל מֵאֵת הָאָב אֶת רוּחַ הַקֹּדֶשׁ הַמֻּבְטַחַת,
ule'achar shennisho el yemin ha'elohim vekibbel me'et ha'av et ruach hakkodesh hammuvtachat
Being therefore by the right hand of God exalted, and having received of the Father the promise of the Holy Spirit,

שָׁפַךְ אוֹתָהּ כְּפִי שֶׁאַתֶּם רוֹאִים וְגַם שׁוֹמְעִים
shafach otah kefi she'attem ro'im vegam shome'im
he hath poured forth this, which ye see and hear.

הֲרֵי דָּוִד לֹא עָלָה הַשָּׁמַיְמָה, אֶלָּא שֶׁהוּא אוֹמֵר נְאֻם יְהוָה לַאדֹנִי, שֵׁב לִימִינִי
harei david lo alah hashamaymah, ella shehu omer ne'um hashem la'adoni, shev liymini
For David ascended not into the heavens: but he saith himself, The Lord said unto my Lord, Sit thou on my right hand,

עַד אָשִׁית אוֹיְבֶיךָ הֲדֹם לְרַגְלֶיךָ
ad ashit oyveicha hadom leragleicha
Till I make thine enemies the footstool of thy feet.

לָכֵן יֵדַע נָא כָּל בֵּית יִשְׂרָאֵל בְּבֵרוּר, שֶׁאֱלֹהִים שָׂם לְאָדוֹן וּלְמָשִׁיחַ.
lachen yeda na kol beit yisra'el beverur, she'elohim sam le'adon ulemashiach
Let all the house of Israel therefore know assuredly, that God hath made him both Lord and Christ,

מַעֲשֵׂי הַשְּׁלִיחִים

וְהָיָה כֹּל אֲשֶׁר־יִקְרָא בְּשֵׁם יהוה יִמָּלֵט
vehayah kol asher-yikra beshem hashem yimmalet
And it shall be, that whosoever shall call on the name of the Lord shall be saved.

אַנְשֵׁי יִשְׂרָאֵל, שִׁמְעוּ אֶת הַדְּבָרִים הָאֵלֶּה
anshei yisra'el, shim'u et haddevarim ha'elleh
Ye men of Israel, hear these words:

יֵשׁוּעַ מִנָּצְרַת, אִישׁ שֶׁנִּתְאַשֵּׁר לָכֶם מִטַּעַם אֱלֹהִים בִּגְבוּרוֹת וּבְנִסִּים וּבְאוֹתוֹת
yeshua minnatzrat, ish shennit'asher lachem mitta'am elohim bigvurot uvenissim uve'otot
Jesus of Nazareth, a man approved of God unto you by mighty works and wonders and signs

אֲשֶׁר הָאֱלֹהִים עָשָׂה עַל־יָדָיו בְּתוֹכְכֶם, כְּפִי שֶׁאַתֶּם עַצְמְכֶם יוֹדְעִים
asher ha'elohim asah al-yadav betochechem, kefi she'attem atzmechem yode'im
which God did by him in the midst of you, even as ye yourselves know;

הוּא שֶׁהֻסְגַּר עַל־פִּי עֲצַת אֱלֹהִים הַנֶּחֱרָצָה וִידִיעָתוֹ־מֵרֹאשׁ
hu shehusgar al-pi atzat elohim hannecheratzah vidi'ato-merosh
him, being delivered up by the determinate counsel and foreknowledge of God,

אוֹתוֹ לְקַחְתֶּם וּבִידֵי רְשָׁעִים צְלַבְתֶּם וַהֲרַגְתֶּם
oto lekachtem uvidei resha'im tzelavtem vaharagtem
ye by the hand of lawless men did crucify and slay:

וֵאלֹהִים הֱקִימוֹ לִתְחִיָּה בְּהַתִּירוֹ אֶת חֶבְלֵי הַמָּוֶת, שֶׁכֵּן הַמָּוֶת לֹא הָיָה יָכוֹל לַעֲצֹר אוֹתוֹ
v'elohim hekimo litchiyah behattiro et chevlei hammavet, shekken hammavet lo hayah yachol la'atzor oto
whom God raised up, having loosed the pangs of death: because it was not possible that he should be holden of it.

הֵן דָּוִד אוֹמֵר עָלָיו
hen david omer alav ki
For David saith concerning him,

שִׁוִּיתִי יהוה לְנֶגְדִּי תָמִיד כִּי מִימִינִי בַּל־אֶמּוֹט
shivviti hashem lenegdi tamid, miymini bal-'emmot
I beheld the Lord always before my face; For he is on my right hand, that I should not be moved:

לָכֵן שָׂמַח לִבִּי וַיָּגֶל כְּבוֹדִי אַף־בְּשָׂרִי יִשְׁכֹּן לָבֶטַח
lachen samach libbi vayagel kevodi af-besari yishkon lavetach
Therefore my heart was glad, and my tongue rejoiced; Moreover my flesh also shall dwell in hope:

כִּי לֹא־תַעֲזֹב נַפְשִׁי לִשְׁאוֹל. לֹא־תִתֵּן חֲסִידְךָ לִרְאוֹת שָׁחַת
ki lo-ta'azov nafshi lish'ol, lo-titten chasidcha lir'ot shachat
Because thou wilt not leave my soul unto Hades, Neither wilt thou give thy Holy One to see corruption.

תּוֹדִיעֵנִי אֹרַח חַיִּים, שֹׂבַע שְׂמָחוֹת אֶת־פָּנֶיךָ
todi'eni orach chayim, sova smachot et-paneicha
Thou madest known unto me the ways of life; Thou shalt make me full of gladness with thy countenance.

מַעֲשֵׂי הַשְּׁלִיחִים

אֲבָל אֲחֵרִים לַעֲגוּ וְאָמְרוּ: מְלֵאֵי יַיִן הֵם
aval acherim la'agu ve'ameru: mele'ei yayin hem
But others mocking said, They are filled with new wine.

עָמַד כֵּיפָא עִם הָאַחַד־עָשָׂר, נָשָׂא קוֹלוֹ וְדִבֶּר אֲלֵיהֶם
amad keifa im ha'achad-'asar, nasa kolo vedibber aleihem
But Peter, standing up with the eleven, lifted up his voice, and spake forth unto them, saying,

אֲנָשִׁים יְהוּדִים, וְכָל יוֹשְׁבֵי יְרוּשָׁלַיִם. זֹאת דְּעוּ לָכֶם וְהַקְשִׁיבוּ לִדְבָרַי
anashim yehudim, vechol yoshevei yerushalayim. zot de'u lachem vehakshivu lidvarai
Ye men of Judæa, and all ye that dwell at Jerusalem, be this known unto you, and give ear unto my words.

הָאֲנָשִׁים הָאֵלֶּה אֵינָם שִׁכּוֹרִים, כְּמוֹ שֶׁאַתֶּם סְבוּרִים, שֶׁכֵּן הַשָּׁעָה תֵּשַׁע בַּבֹּקֶר
ha'anashim ha'elleh einam shikkorim, kemo she'attem sevurim, shekken hasha'ah tesha babboker
For these are not drunken, as ye suppose; seeing it is but the third hour of the day;

אֶלָּא שֶׁזֶּה הַדָּבָר שֶׁנֶּאֱמַר עַל־יְדֵי יוֹאֵל הַנָּבִיא
ella shezzeh haddavar shenne'emar al-yedei yo'el hannavi
but this is that which hath been spoken through the prophet Joel:

וְהָיָה בְּאַחֲרִית הַיָּמִים, נְאֻם אֱלֹהִים, אֶשְׁפּוֹךְ אֶת־רוּחִי עַל־כָּל־בָּשָׂר
vehayah be'acharit hayamim, ne'um elohim, 'eshpoch et-ruchi al-kol-basar
And it shall be in the last days, saith God, I will pour forth of my Spirit upon all flesh:

וְנִבְּאוּ בְּנֵיכֶם וּבְנוֹתֵיכֶם בַּחוּרֵיכֶם חֶזְיוֹנוֹת יִרְאוּ
venibbe'u bneichem uvnoteichem bachureichem chezyonot yir'u
And your sons and your daughters shall prophesy, And your young men shall see visions,

וְזִקְנֵיכֶם חֲלֹמוֹת יַחֲלֹמוּן
vezikneichem chalomot yachlomun
And your old men shall dream dreams:

וְגַם עַל עֲבָדַי וְעַל שִׁפְחוֹתַי בַּיָּמִים הָהֵמָּה אֶשְׁפֹּךְ אֶת־רוּחִי וְנִבְּאוּ
vegam al avadai ve'al shifchotai bayamim hahemmah eshpoch et-ruchi venibbe'u
Yea and on my servants and on my handmaidens in those days Will I pour forth of my Spirit; and they shall prophesy.

וְנָתַתִּי מוֹפְתִים בַּשָּׁמַיִם מִמַּעַל וְאוֹתוֹת בָּאָרֶץ מִתָּחַת, דָּם וָאֵשׁ וְתִימְרוֹת עָשָׁן
venatatti mofetim bashamayim mimma'al, ve'otot ba'aretz mittachat, dam va'esh vetimrot ashan
And I will show wonders in the heaven above, And signs on the earth beneath; Blood, and fire, and vapor of smoke:

הַשֶּׁמֶשׁ יֵהָפֵךְ לְחֹשֶׁךְ וְהַיָּרֵחַ לְדָם
hashemesh yehafech lechoshech vehayareach ledam
The sun shall be turned into darkness, And the moon into blood,

לִפְנֵי בּוֹא יוֹם יהוה הַגָּדוֹל וְהַנּוֹרָא
lifnei bo yom hashem haggadol vehannora
Before the day of the Lord come, That great and notable day:

מַעֲשֵׂי הַשְּׁלִיחִים

וְכֻלָּם נִמְלְאוּ רוּחַ הַקֹּדֶשׁ וְהֵחֵלּוּ לְדַבֵּר בִּלְשׁוֹנוֹת אֲחֵרוֹת כְּפִי שֶׁנָּתְנָה לָהֶם הָרוּחַ לְדַבֵּר
vechullam nimle'u ruach hakkodesh vehechellu ledabber bilshonot acherot kefi shennatenah lahem haruach ledabber
And they were all filled with the Holy Spirit, and began to speak with other tongues, as the Spirit gave them utterance.

בִּירוּשָׁלַיִם הִתְגּוֹרְרוּ יְהוּדִים יִרְאֵי אֱלֹהִים מִכָּל עַם וָעָם אֲשֶׁר תַּחַת הַשָּׁמַיִם
biyerushalayim hitgoreru yehudim yir'ei elohim mikkol am ve'am asher tachat hashamayim
Now there were dwelling at Jerusalem Jews, devout men, from every nation under heaven.

כַּאֲשֶׁר נִשְׁמַע הַקּוֹל הַזֶּה הִתְקַהֲלוּ עַם רָב וְכֻלָּם נָבוֹכוּ
ka'asher nishma hakkol hazzeh hitkahalu am rav vechullam navochu
And when this sound was heard, the multitude came together, and were confounded,

שֶׁכֵּן כָּל אִישׁ שָׁמַע אוֹתָם מְדַבְּרִים בִּשְׂפָתוֹ שֶׁלּוֹ
shekken kol ish shama otam medabbrim bisfato shello
because that every man heard them speaking in his own language.

הֵם נִתְמַלְּאוּ תִּמָּהוֹן וּפְלִיאָה וְאָמְרוּ: הֲרֵי כָּל הַמְדַבְּרִים הָאֵלֶּה גְּלִילִיִּים
hem nitmalle'u timmahon ufeli'ah ve'ameru: harei kol hamdabberim ha'elleh geliliyim
And they were all amazed and marvelled, saying, Behold, are not all these that speak Galilæans?

וְאֵיךְ כָּל אֶחָד מֵאִתָּנוּ שׁוֹמֵעַ בִּשְׂפַת מוֹלַדְתּוֹ
ve'eich kol echad me'ittanu shomea bisfat moladto
And how hear we, every man in our own language wherein we were born?

פַּרְתִּים אֲנַחְנוּ וּמָדִים, עֵילָמִים וְתוֹשָׁבֵי אֲרַם נַהֲרַיִם, תּוֹשְׁבֵי יְהוּדָה וְקַפַּדוֹקְיָה וּפוֹנְטוֹס וְאַסְיָה
partim anachnu umadim, eilamim vetoshavei aram naharayim, toshvei yehudah vekappadokeyah ufontos ve'asyah
Parthians and Medes and Elamites, and the dwellers in Mesopotamia, in Judæa and Cappadocia, in Pontus and Asia,

פְרִיגְיָה וּפַמְפִילְיָה, מִצְרַיִם וּמְחוֹזוֹת לוּב הַסְּמוּכִים לְקִירֶנְיָה,
ferigeyah vepamfileyah, mitzrayim umechozot luv hassemuchim lekirenyah,
in Phrygia and Pamphylia, in Egypt and the parts of Libya about Cyrene,

תּוֹשְׁבֵי רוֹמָא הַמִּתְגּוֹרְרִים כָּאן
toshavei roma hammitgorerim kan
and sojourners from Rome, both Jews and proselytes,

יְהוּדִים וְגֵרִים, כְּרֵתִיִּים וְעַרְבִים -
yehudim vegerim, keretiyim ve'arvim -
Cretans and Arabians,

וְהִנֵּה אֲנַחְנוּ שׁוֹמְעִים אוֹתָם מְסַפְּרִים בִּלְשׁוֹנוֹתֵינוּ אֶת גְּדֻלּוֹת הָאֱלֹהִים
vehinneh anachnu shome'im otam mesapperim bilshonoteinu et gdullot ha'elohim
we hear them speaking in our tongues the mighty works of God.

הַכֹּל הִשְׁתּוֹמְמוּ וְנָבוֹכוּ. אָמְרוּ זֶה אֶל זֶה: מַה זֶּה צָרִיךְ לִהְיוֹת
hakkol hishtomemu venavochu. ameru zeh el zeh: mah zeh tzarich lihyot
And they were all amazed, and were perplexed, saying one to another, What meaneth this?

מַעֲשֵׂי הַשְּׁלִיחִים

הָחֵל מִטְּבִילַת יוֹחָנָן עַד יוֹם הִנָּשְׂאוֹ מֵאִתָּנוּ
hachel mittevilat yochanan ad yom hinnase'o me'ittanu
beginning from the baptism of John, unto the day that he was received up from us,

יִהְיֶה עֵד אִתָּנוּ עַל תְּחִיָּתוֹ
yihyeh ed ittanu al tchiyato
of these must one become a witness with us of his resurrection.

הֵם הֶעֱמִידוּ שְׁנַיִם, אֶת יוֹסֵף הַנִּקְרָא בַּר־שַׁבָּא וְהַמְכֻנֶּה גַּם יוּסְטוֹס, וְאֶת מַתִּתְיָה
hem he'emidu shenayim, et yosef hannikra bar-shabba vehamchunneh gam yustos, ve'et mattityah
And they put forward two, Joseph called Barsabbas, who was surnamed Justus, and Matthias.

הִתְפַּלְלוּ וְאָמְרוּ
hitpallelu ve'ameru
And they prayed, and said,

אַתָּה אֲדֹנָי הַיּוֹדֵעַ כָּל הַלְּבָבוֹת, הַרְאֵה נָא מִי הוּא הָאֶחָד מִן הַשְּׁנַיִם שֶׁבָּחַרְתָּ בּוֹ
attah adonai hayodea kol hallevavot, har'eh na mi hu ha'echad min hashnayim shebbacharta bo
Thou, Lord, who knowest the hearts of all men, show of these two the one whom thou hast chosen,

לָקַחַת אֶת מְקוֹם הַשֵּׁרוּת הַזֶּה וְהַשְּׁלִיחוּת אֲשֶׁר סָטָה מִמֶּנָּה יְהוּדָה בְּלֶכְתּוֹ אֶל מְקוֹמוֹ שֶׁלּוֹ
lakachat et mekom hasherut hazzeh vehashlichut asher satah mimmennah yehudah belechto el mekomo shello
to take the place in this ministry and apostleship from which Judas fell away, that he might go to his own place.

נָתְנוּ לָהֶם גּוֹרָלוֹת; הַגּוֹרָל נָפַל עַל מַתִּתְיָה וְהוּא נִסְפַּח אֶל אַחַד־עָשָׂר הַשְּׁלִיחִים
natnu lahem goralot; haggoral nafal al mattityah vehu nispach el achad-'asar hashelichim
And they gave lots for them; and the lot fell upon Matthias; and he was numbered with the eleven apostles.

ב

בְּיוֹם מְלֹאת שִׁבְעַת הַשָּׁבוּעוֹת הָיוּ כֻלָּם יַחְדָּו
beyom mlot shiv'at hashavu'ot hayu kullam yachdav
And when the day of Pentecost was now come, they were all together in one place.

פִּתְאֹם הָיָה קוֹל מִן הַשָּׁמַיִם, כְּקוֹל מַשַּׁב רוּחַ עַזָּה
pit'om hayah kol min hashamayim, kekol mashav ruach azzah
And suddenly there came from heaven a sound as of the rushing of a mighty wind,

וְהוּא מִלֵּא אֶת כָּל הַבַּיִת אֲשֶׁר יָשְׁבוּ בּוֹ
vehu millei et kol habbayit asher yashvu bo
and it filled all the house where they were sitting.

אָז הוֹפִיעוּ לְנֶגֶד עֵינֵיהֶם לְשׁוֹנוֹת כְּלַהֲבוֹת אֵשׁ, שֶׁהִתְפַּזְּרוּ וְנָחוּ אַחַת אַחַת עַל כָּל אֶחָד מֵהֶם
az hofi'u leneged eineihem leshonot kelahavot esh, shehitpazzru venachu achat achat al kol echad mehem
And there appeared unto them tongues parting asunder, like as of fire; and it sat upon each one of them.

מַעֲשֵׂי הַשְּׁלִיחִים

בָּאוֹתָם יָמִים קָם כֵּיפָא בֵּין הָאַחִים
be'otam yamim kam keifa bein ha'achim
And in these days Peter stood up in the midst of the brethren,

מִסְפַּר הָאֲנָשִׁים שֶׁנִּקְהֲלוּ יַחַד הָיָה כְּמֵאָה וְעֶשְׂרִים - וְאָמַר
mispar ha'anashim shennik'halu yachad hayah keme'ah ve'esrim - ve'amar
and said (and there was a multitude of persons gathered together, about a hundred and twenty),

אֲנָשִׁים אַחִים, צָרִיךְ הָיָה שֶׁיִּתְקַיֵּם הַכָּתוּב
anashim achim, tzarich hayah sheyitkayem hakkatuv
Brethren, it was needful that the scripture should be fulfilled,

אֲשֶׁר רוּחַ הַקֹּדֶשׁ דִּבְּרָה מִקֶּדֶם בְּפִי דָוִד עַל יְהוּדָה, זֶה שֶׁנִּהְיָה הַמּוֹבִיל שֶׁל תּוֹפְסֵי יֵשׁוּעַ
asher ruach hakkodesh dibbrah mikkedem befi david al yehudah, zeh shennihyah hammovil shel tofsei yeshua
which the Holy Spirit spake before by the mouth of David concerning Judas, who was guide to them that took Jesus.

הוּא נִמְנָה אִתָּנוּ וְקִבֵּל חֵלֶק בַּשֵּׁרוּת הַזֶּה
hu nimnah ittanu vekibbel chelek basherut hazzeh
For he was numbered among us, and received his portion in this ministry.

וְהִנֵּה קָנָה לוֹ שָׂדֶה בִּשְׂכַר הָרֶשַׁע
vehinneh kanah lo sadeh bischar haresha
(Now this man obtained a field with the reward of his iniquity;

וּבְנָפְלוֹ נִבְקְעָה בִּטְנוֹ וְכָל מֵעָיו נִשְׁפְּכוּ הַחוּצָה
uvenafelo nivke'ah bitno vechol me'av nishpechu hachutzah
and falling headlong, he burst asunder in the midst, and all his bowels gushed out.

הַדָּבָר הַזֶּה נוֹדַע לְכָל יוֹשְׁבֵי יְרוּשָׁלַיִם
haddavar hazzeh noda lechol yoshevei yerushalayim
And it became known to all the dwellers at Jerusalem;

וּלְפִיכָךְ נִקְרָא אוֹתוֹ שָׂדֶה בִּלְשׁוֹנָם חֲקַל דְּמָא, שֶׁפֵּרוּשׁוֹ שְׂדֵה הַדָּם
ulefichach nikra oto sadeh bilshonam chakal dema, shepperusho sdeh haddam
insomuch that in their language that field was called Akeldama, that is, The field of blood.)

שֶׁהֲרֵי כָּתוּב בְּסֵפֶר תְּהִלִּים
sheharei katuv besefer tehillim
For it is written in the book of Psalms,

תְּהִי־טִירָתוֹ נְשַׁמָּה וְאַל־יְהִי בָהּ יוֹשֵׁב, וְגַם פְּקֻדָּתוֹ יִקַּח אַחֵר
tehi-tirato neshammah ve'al-yehi vah yoshev, vegam pekuddato yikkach acher
Let his habitation be made desolate, And let no man dwell therein: and, His office let another take.

עַל כֵּן צָרִיךְ שֶׁאֶחָד מִן הָאֲנָשִׁים אֲשֶׁר נִלְווּ אֵלֵינוּ בְּכָל הָעֵת אֲשֶׁר הָאָדוֹן יֵשׁוּעַ בָּא וְיָצָא בְּתוֹכֵנוּ
al ken tzarich she'echad min ha'anashim asher nilvu eleinu bechol ha'et asher ha'adon yeshua ba veyatza betochenu
Of the men therefore that have companied with us all the time that the Lord Jesus went in and went out among us,

מַעֲשֵׂי הַשְּׁלִיחִים

אֲבָל בְּבוֹא עֲלֵיכֶם רוּחַ הַקֹּדֶשׁ תְּקַבְּלוּ כֹּחַ וְתִהְיוּ עֵדַי
aval bevo aleichem ruach hakkodesh tekabbelu koach vetihyu edai
But ye shall receive power, when the Holy Spirit is come upon you: and ye shall be my witnesses

הֵן בִּירוּשָׁלַיִם וְהֵן בְּכָל יְהוּדָה וְשֹׁמְרוֹן, עַד קְצֵה הָאָרֶץ
hen biyerushalayim vehen bechol yehudah veshomeron, ad ktzeh ha'aretz
both in Jerusalem, and in all Judæa and Samaria, and unto the uttermost part of the earth.

אַחֲרֵי שֶׁאָמַר אֶת הַדְּבָרִים הָאֵלֶּה נִשָּׂא מֵעֲלֵיהֶם בְּעוֹדָם מִסְתַּכְּלִים, וְעָנָן נָטַל אוֹתוֹ מִנֶּגֶד עֵינֵיהֶם
charei she'amar et haddevarim ha'elleh nissa me'aleihem be'odam mistakkelim, ve'anan natal oto minneged eineihem
And when he had said these things, as they were looking, he was taken up; and a cloud received him out of their sight.

עוֹדָם מַבִּיטִים הַשָּׁמַיְמָה בַּעֲלִיָּתוֹ, וְהִנֵּה שְׁנֵי אֲנָשִׁים לְבוּשֵׁי לָבָן נִצְּבוּ לְיָדָם
odam mabbitim hashamaymah ba'aliyato, vehinneh shnei anashim levushei lavan nitzevu leyadam
And while they were looking stedfastly into heaven as he went, behold two men stood by them in white apparel;

וְאָמְרוּ: אַנְשֵׁי הַגָּלִיל, לָמָּה אַתֶּם עוֹמְדִים וּמִסְתַּכְּלִים אֶל הַשָּׁמַיִם
ve'ameru: anshei haggalil, lammah attem omedim umistakkelim el hashamayim
who also said, Ye men of Galilee, why stand ye looking into heaven?

יֵשׁוּעַ זֶה אֲשֶׁר נִשָּׂא מֵעֲלֵיכֶם הַשָּׁמַיְמָה - בֹּא יָבוֹא בְּאוֹתוֹ אֹפֶן שֶׁרְאִיתֶם אוֹתוֹ עוֹלֶה לַשָּׁמַיִם
yeshua zeh asher nisho me'aleichem hashamaymah - bo yavo be'oto ofen sher'item oto oleh lashamayim
This Jesus, who was received up from you into heaven, shall so come in like manner as ye beheld him going into heaven.

אַחֲרֵי כֵן שָׁבוּ לִירוּשָׁלַיִם מֵהַר הַזֵּיתִים
acharei chen shavu liyerushalayim mehar hazzeitim,
Then returned they unto Jerusalem from the mount called Olivet,

הַקָּרוֹב לִירוּשָׁלַיִם כְּדֶרֶךְ תְּחוּם שַׁבָּת
hakkarov liyerushalayim kederech tchum shabbat
which is nigh unto Jerusalem, a sabbath day's journey off.

בָּאוּ כֵּיפָא וְיוֹחָנָן וְיַעֲקֹב, אַנְדְּרֵי וּפִילִיפּוֹס וְתֹאמָא, בַּר-תַּלְמַי וּמַתַּי וְיַעֲקֹב בֶּן-חַלְפַי, שִׁמְעוֹן הַקַּנַּאי וִיהוּדָה בֶּן-יַעֲקֹב, וְעָלוּ אֶל הָעֲלִיָּה - הַמָּקוֹם שֶׁנָּהֲגוּ לִשְׁהוֹת בּוֹ
ba'u keifa veyochanan veya'akov, anderei ufilipos vetoma, bar-talmai umattai veya'akov ben-chalfai, shim'on hakkanna viyehudah ben-ya'akov, ve'alu el ha'aliyah - hammakom shennahagu lishhot bo
And when they were come in, they went up into the upper chamber, where they were abiding; both Peter and John and James and Andrew, Philip and Thomas, Bartholomew and Matthew, James the son of Alphæus, and Simon the Zealot, and Judas the son of James.

כָּל אֵלֶּה הִתְמִידוּ בְּלֵב אֶחָד בַּתְּפִלָּה, הֵם וְהַנָּשִׁים
kol elleh hitmidu belev echad bitfillah, hem vehannashim
These all with one accord continued stedfastly in prayer, with the women,

וּמִרְיָם אֵם יֵשׁוּעַ וְאֶחָיו
umiryam em yeshua ve'echav
and Mary the mother of Jesus, and with his brethren.

מַעֲשֵׂי הַשְּׁלִיחִים

*Remember: Hebrew is Read from Right to Left
מַעֲשֵׂי הַשְּׁלִיחִים

תֵּיאוֹפִילוֹס, בַּחִבּוּר הָרִאשׁוֹן כָּתַבְתִּי עַל כָּל מַה שֶׁיֵּשׁוּעַ עָשָׂה וְלִמֵּד מִתְּחִלָּה
tei'ofilos, bachibbur harishon katavti al kol mah sheyeshua asah velimmed mittchillah
The former treatise I made, O Theophilus, concerning all that Jesus began both to do and to teach,

וְעַד יוֹם הִלָּקְחוֹ לַמָּרוֹם
ve'ad yom hillakcho lammarom
until the day in which he was received up,

לְאַחַר שֶׁמָּסַר הוֹרָאוֹת, לְפִי רוּחַ הַקֹּדֶשׁ, לַשְּׁלִיחִים אֲשֶׁר בָּחַר בָּהֶם
le'achar shemmasar hora'ot, lefi ruach hakkodesh, lashelichim asher bachar bahem
after that he had given commandment through the Holy Spirit unto the apostles whom he had chosen:

לִפְנֵיהֶם הוּא הוֹפִיעַ חַי בְּהוֹכָחוֹת רַבּוֹת, אַחֲרֵי עִנּוּתוֹ, וּבְמֶשֶׁךְ אַרְבָּעִים יוֹם נִרְאָה אֲלֵיהֶם
lifneihem hu hofia chai behochachot rabbot, acharei enuto, uvemeshech arba'im yom nir'ah aleihem
to whom he also showed himself alive after his passion by many proofs, appearing unto them by the space of forty days

וְדִבֶּר אִתָּם עַל מַלְכוּת הָאֱלֹהִים
vedibber ittam al malchut ha'elohim
and speaking the things concerning the kingdom of God:

כַּאֲשֶׁר הָיָה בְּחֶבְרָתָם צִוָּה עֲלֵיהֶם: אַל תַּעַזְבוּ אֶת יְרוּשָׁלַיִם
ka'asher hayah bechevratam tzivvah aleihem: al ta'azvu et yerushalayim
and, being assembled together with them, he charged them not to depart from Jerusalem,

כִּי אִם חַכּוּ לְקִיּוּם הַבְטָחַת הָאָב אֲשֶׁר שְׁמַעְתֶּם אוֹתָהּ מִפִּי
ki im chakku lekiyum havtachat ha'av asher shema'tem otah mippi
but to wait for the promise of the Father, which, said he, ye heard from me:

כִּי יוֹחָנָן הִטְבִּיל בְּמַיִם, אֲבָל אַתֶּם תִּטָּבְלוּ בְּרוּחַ הַקֹּדֶשׁ בְּעוֹד יָמִים לֹא רַבִּים
ki yochanan hitbil bemayim, aval attem tittavelu beruach hakkodesh be'od yamim lo rabbim
For John indeed baptized with water; but ye shall be baptized in the Holy Spirit not many days hence.

שָׁאֲלוּ אוֹתוֹ הַנֶּאֱסָפִים
sha'alu oto hanne'esafim
They therefore, when they were come together, asked him, saying,

אֲדוֹנֵנוּ, הַאִם בַּזְּמַן הַזֶּה תָּשִׁיב אֶת הַמַּלְכוּת לְיִשְׂרָאֵל
adonenu, ha'im bazzeman hazzeh tashiv et hammalchut leyisra'el
Lord, dost thou at this time restore the kingdom to Israel?

עָנָה לָהֶם: לֹא לָכֶם לָדַעַת עִתִּים וּזְמַנִּים שֶׁקָּבַע הָאָב בְּסַמְכוּתוֹ שֶׁלּוֹ
anah lahem: lo lachem lada'at ittim uzemannim shekkava ha'av besamchuto shello
And he said unto them, It is not for you to know times or seasons, which the Father hath set within his own authority.

Philemon - Filimon - פִּילִימוֹן

Hebrews - Ha'ivrim - הָעִבְרִים

James - Ya'akov - יַעֲקֹב

1 Peter - Petros Harishona - פֶּטְרוֹס הָרִאשׁוֹנָה

2 Peter - Petros Hashniya - פֶּטְרוֹס הַשְּׁנִיָּה

1 John - Yochanan Harishona - יוֹחָנָן הָרִאשׁוֹנָה

2 John - Yochanan Hashniya - יוֹחָנָן הַשְּׁנִיָּה

3 John - Yochanan Hashlishit - יוֹחָנָן הַשְּׁלִישִׁית

Jude - Yehuda - יְהוּדָה

Revelation – Hahitgalut - הַהִתְגַּלּוּת

TO FOLLOW ALONG WITH THE HEBREW AUDIO, VISIT:

hebrewaudiobible.com

Acts - Ma'asei Hashlichim - מַעֲשֵׂי הַשְּׁלִיחִים

Romans - Haromim - הָרוֹמִים

1 Corinthians - El Hakorintim Alef - אֶל הַקּוֹרִינְתִים א

2 Corinthians - El Hakorintim Bet - אֶל הַקּוֹרִינְתִים ב

Galatians - Hagalatim - הַגָּלָטִים

Ephesians - Ha'efesim - הָאֶפֶסִים

Philippians - Hafilipim - הַפִילִיפִּים

Colossians - Hakolosim - הַקּוֹלוֹסִים

1 Thessalonians - Hatesalonikim Alef - הַתֶּסָלוֹנִיקִים א

2 Thessalonians - Hatesalonikim Bet - הַתֶּסָלוֹנִיקִים ב

1 Timothy - Timoteus Alef - טִימוֹתֵיאוֹס א

2 Timothy - Timoteus Bet - טִימוֹתֵיאוֹס ב

Titus - Titos - טִיטוֹס

א	A			א	1
ב	V			ב	2
ב	B			ג	3
ג	G	אָ	ah	ד	4
ד	D	אַ	ah	ה	5
ה	H	אֲ	ah	ו	6
ו	V	אָה	ah	ז	7
ז	Z	אֶ	ei	ח	8
ח	KH	אֱ	e	ט	9
ט	T	אֵ	e	י	10
י	Y	אֵי	ei	יא	11
כ	KH	אִ	ee	יב	12
כ	K	אִי	ee	יג	13
ל	L	אֹ	oh	יד	14
מ	M	אֳ	oh	טו	15
ם	M	אָ	oh	טז	16
נ	N	אוֹ	oh	יז	17
ן	N	אֻ	oo	יח	18
ס	S	אוּ	oo	יט	19
ע	A	אְ	e	כ	20
פ	F				
פ	P				
צ	TS				
ק	K				
ר	R				
ש	SH				
ש	S				
ת	T				

**הַבְּרִית הַחֲדָשָׁה
Habrit Hachadashah
The New Testament**

Made in the USA
Las Vegas, NV
12 May 2022